UNIVERSITY CASEBOOK SERIES®

# FUNDAMENTALS OF FEDERAL INCOME TAXATION

## CASES AND MATERIALS

### NINETEENTH EDITION

JAMES J. FREELAND
Late Professor of Law
University of Florida

DANIEL J. LATHROPE
Distinguished E. L. Wiegand Professor of Law
University of San Francisco School of Law

STEPHEN A. LIND
Albert R. Abramson Distinguished Professor of Law, Emeritus
Hastings College of the Law

RICHARD B. STEPHENS
Late Professor of Law
University of Florida

FOUNDATION
PRESS

*University Casebook Series* is a trademark registered in the U.S. Patent and Trademark Office.

© 1972, 1977, 1981, 1982, 1985, 1987, 1991, 1994, 1996, 1998, 2000, 2002, 2004 FOUNDATION PRESS
© 2006, 2009, 2011 THOMSON REUTERS/FOUNDATION PRESS
© 2013, 2016 LEG, Inc. d/b/a West Academic
© 2018 LEG, Inc. d/b/a West Academic
  444 Cedar Street, Suite 700
  St. Paul, MN 55101
  1-877-888-1330

Printed in the United States of America

**ISBN:** 978-1-64020-852-0

*This book is dedicated to our co-author*
*RICHARD B. STEPHENS*
*in appreciation for all that he taught us about taxation,*
*about writing and about life itself.*

# PREFACE

During the lifespan of the Sixth Edition of this book, our co-author, RICHARD B. STEPHENS, died. This book is dedicated to him. Dick's gift with words is demonstrated by the Preface that he wrote to the Sixth Edition which is substantially republished as the Preface to this Edition. Dick's words, cogent and timely then, remain so today:

Tar, pitch, and turpentine, all begins with a. Look again. Tricky, isn't it? The federal income tax law is tricky, too. Confronted by protesting students, a colleague used to say, "It's the law that's tricky, not I." You are about to begin to enjoy learning some of the tricks.

The Internal Revenue Code, the glue that holds together the pages of this book, is complex. Perhaps it is the Rubik's Cube of legislation. But even the marvels of the prestidigitator lose their mystery when some of his methods are disclosed.

Tax books are perishable—not much affected by freeze but fragile when it comes to political heat. The law has been called evanescent, fleeting. And in some respects the description is apt when Congress changes its mind as often as it has in the past decade or so. If we could we would call: "Time out!" But that is why we are here soon after an earlier edition, at the beginning of the Sixth Edition of this book, which is responsive to very comprehensive legislation that makes it no longer possible to "Take the Fifth."

If tax law is tricky, complex, and perishable, do we suggest despair? By no means! For one thing, our national fiscal system, at least until such time as we can adopt a better one, has a very great need for lawyers who are competent in the area of taxation. A plug here for "the arts:" We think the best professional is one who has had a broad education, followed by comprehensive legal study, capped by technical tax training. But whatever! The object of this book is to aid in your technical tax training.

Moreover, the fundamentals of federal taxation have a very long shelf life: One could profitably study now the First Edition of this book. Basic concepts of income, deduction, rates, and credits appear there in some cases with astonishing similarity and in all cases in a manner that would aid in the understanding of today's concepts. Although we watch frequent additions, corrections, and amendments, they are rather like hanging meat on the skeleton of the Brontosaurus; underneath the structure remains much the same.

As its title indicates, the purpose of this book is to aid in the teaching of the fundamentals of the federal income tax. The accomplishment of such a purpose involves, first, a selective determination of basic principles and concepts and, second, a decision of the manner and depth of treatment of the matters that are deemed fundamental. There is wide room for disagreement on both points. Nevertheless, the authors are confident that a thoughtful study of the materials presented in this book will afford the student a good income tax foundation. Those who do not proceed beyond the fundamentals may not be "tax experts," but at least they will have a useful awareness of how the federal income tax impinges on practically everything that goes on in our society and economy. Others will have a good basis for enlarging their tax knowledge through advanced law school courses, or graduate study, or practice, or some combination of all three.

Although the major tax legislation of 1986 is called "reform," it [and we would add, subsequent legislation] moves us further away from the dream of simplicity, even fails to effect any simplification. The demands made of the tax lawyer are heavy; but legal educators need to keep in mind that a practitioner must be a lawyer first and a tax lawyer only second. The tax lawyer should receive the bulk of his specialized training either through graduate study or, in the time-honored tradition of the legal profession, through his own scholarly efforts in practice. In law school some tax study may be essential for all, but not to the point that law school becomes trade school at the expense of the study of jurisprudence, comparative law and other courses needed to develop perspective.

The approach taken in this book to various aspects of the income tax varies from one of great attention to detail to one of very general descriptive notes. These differences are not haphazard. For one thing, the authors, although aware of time limitations, are certain that to present a uniformly general survey approach to income taxation would be a meaningless exercise, a serious disservice to students and a waste of faculty energy and time. A substantial amount of detailed study and analysis, selectively presented, is the only way to achieve a basic understanding of what federal taxation is all about.

What we have done is attempt to make the detailed study portions of the book serve a second purpose of giving the student a tight grasp of tax concepts and principles that are of wide application and importance. For example, the "gotcha" (I.R.C. Section 1245, the first broad recapture provision which makes its appearance in Chapter 22) is examined closely both as to purpose and effect, because both it and other related recapture provisions crop up repeatedly, and they frequently affect all types of taxpayers, individuals, trusts, partnerships, corporations, and so forth. Section 1245 is primarily a characterization provision and although the concept of characterization is not as significant as in the past, it still retains some vitality. On the other hand, with regard to restrictions on deductions (considered in Chapter 17) the effect of illegality or impropriety on the deductibility of an expenditure, although it has been the subject of several interesting and highly "teachable" Supreme Court decisions, is largely relegated to an explanatory note that discusses the cases, because the problem is of far less frequent occurrence. We are content to present the constitutional status of the income tax by way of a note. When the modern income tax was first enacted in 1913, almost every conceivable constitutional objection was raised against it; and various objections dealt with in the note should be known to the student, even though they do not have much current importance. There is a current need to guard against constitutional tax principles falling into a state of innocuous desuetude.

Students should also have some understanding of tax procedure, which they can get from [Chapter 28], presented as text, even if busy instructors find no class time for this material.

There are some matters that must be classified as important which are not dealt with in detail. For example, deferred compensation arrangements, touched on in Chapter 20, affect the lives of millions of taxpaying employers and employees. And the tax rules applicable to trusts, partnerships, and corporations accorded only sparing recognition in Chapter 13 with regard to problems of assignment of income, also must be classified as important on the basis of any similar numerical test. Nevertheless, it simply cannot all be done in a basic course. And so, of necessity, some important matters are alluded to in notes but not considered in detail and are left for development in additional income tax courses at the J.D. or LL.M. level. The first edition of this book anticipated this trend which continues. A study of the taxation of individuals is the beginning, and it will serve as the cornerstone on which additional income tax courses can rest.

Brief note treatment of some matters not presented in detail reflects an effort to resist the academic compulsion to appear erudite. The purpose of such notes is only to create a general awareness. We know more about some of these matters, but it is more than we choose to tell. In this spirit we have resisted the inclination to let the book "grow." Nevertheless, references are often included to more nourishing books and articles that may be of assistance if, at another time, the student would undertake his own detailed exploration of an area.

The authors have attempted to take account of the fact that students arrive at their first law school tax course with a wide variety of educational and other experiences. Those who have little accounting background are apprehensive and likely to feel they "will not like tax." This attitude, as we know, is not fully justified, and experience has shown that many of these people will find a new dimension in tax law. Nevertheless, in many instances in which instruction is bound to encroach on the domain of the accountant, an effort is made, sometimes through informative comment such as the note on depreciation in Chapter 14 and on inventories in Chapter 19, to render the material manageable regardless of the student's background knowledge. Sometimes we are sneaky too, for example, by using the caption "Timing," rather than the intimidating term "Accounting." Moreover if, partly due to past lack of experience, the present study seems to get off to a slow beginning, the student may anticipate a quickening pace as later chapters unfold. In fact, most students will discern a mounting crescendo with something in the nature of fireworks at the end of the show.

Many of the judicial opinions and other documents quoted in this work have fallen prey to our editorial license. Deletions are indicated conventionally by the use of ellipses and asterisks, and editorial additions are bracketed. Where necessary, footnotes are renumbered to take account of omissions. In general, the materials included are based on the status of the law [as of May, 2018.]

The authors acknowledge an indebtedness to the hundreds of law students who have passed through their classes over a combined teaching period approaching 100 years. Not only have these young men and women served as guinea pigs for various experiments; their perception and insight have been a part of the continuing education of their instructors, making former students substantial contributors to the form and substance of this book.

RICHARD B. STEPHENS

June, 1987

During the lifespan of the Eighth Edition of this book, JAMES J. FREELAND ended his long and distinguished teaching career along with his participation in co-authoring this book, and during the lifespan of the Eleventh Edition of this book, Jack died. Both his humorous and clever classroom teaching and his humorous input and substantial contributions to this text will be sorely missed. Happily, however, because this book involves Fundamentals much of both Dick and Jack's insight and humor remain in this Nineteenth Edition.

Professor Patricia Dilley at the University of Florida (in the area of Deferred Compensation) and late Professor Patricia Morgan at Georgia State University (in the area of Tax Procedure) have provided valuable assistance on prior editions of the book. Adjunct Professor Davis Yee at the University of San Francisco (in the areas of Tax Procedure and Professional Responsibility) provided valuable assistance on this edition of the book.

In addition, over the years, numerous intelligent and industrious students at law schools where the authors were teaching have served as assistants in the preparation of the several prior editions of this book. It may not be sufficient but we seek to preserve a sign of our gratitude to them by listing their names in this preface.

Students to whom our thanks are due for assistance on prior editions are: Jeff Anthony, Brad Arnold, Steven Arsenault, Bernie Barton, Bart Bassett, Craig Bornell, David Bowen, Mike Brittingham, Darrin Brown, David Brownhill, David Clark, Andrew Coblentz, Scott Collins, Brian Coughlan, Walt Davis, Chris Detzel, Nat Doliner, Mary Sue Donsky, Clint Eddy, Bruce Ellisen, Susan Elsey, Alan Friedman, Mari Gaines, John Griffin, Adam Halperin, John Huntington, Robert Jackson, Paul Johnson, Garo Kalfayan, David Kastanis, Jay Katz, Robin Kaufman, Kevin Keenan, Peter Kirkwood, Mel Knotts, Jack Levine, Mike Little, Steve Looney, Paul Lundberg, Lorne Maltenfort, Todd Mayo, Tom McLendon, Richard Moore, Michael O'Leary, Tim Patterson, Kendall Patton, William Poovey, Stan Riddell, Greg Rovenger, John Scheuring, Amy Shelf, Sharon Selk, Chuck Tallant, Lisa Thomas, Phil Tingle, Steve Uejio, Steve Voglesang, Kenneth Wheeler and Susan York Janin.

STEPHEN A. LIND

DANIEL J. LATHROPE

May, 2018

# SUMMARY OF CONTENTS

## PART 1. INTRODUCTION

## PART 2. IDENTIFICATION OF INCOME
## SUBJECT TO TAXATION

## PART 9. FEDERAL TAX PROCEDURE, PROFESSIONAL RESPONSIBILITY, AND TAX POLICY

# TABLE OF CONTENTS

## PART 8. CONVERTING TAXABLE INCOME INTO TAX LIABILITY

## PART 9. FEDERAL TAX PROCEDURE, PROFESSIONAL RESPONSIBILITY, AND TAX POLICY

# TABLE OF CASES

The principal cases are in bold type.

# TABLE OF INTERNAL REVENUE CODE SECTIONS

# TABLE OF TREASURY REGULATIONS

# TABLE OF INTERNAL REVENUE RULINGS

The principal rulings are in bold type.

# TABLE OF MISCELLANEOUS RULINGS

The principal rulings are in bold type.

# TABLE OF AUTHORITIES

# FUNDAMENTALS OF FEDERAL INCOME TAXATION

## CASES AND MATERIALS

### NINETEENTH EDITION

# PART 1

# INTRODUCTION

# CHAPTER 1

# ORIENTATION

## A. A LOOK FORWARD

The question is: What can you tell a law student that will help to make one a good tax student? We have no universal wisdom. Nevertheless, having watched hundreds of law students in the beginning, middle, and never-ending process of learning about the federal income tax, the authors offer a few remarks that may be helpful.

A student may find unexpected excitement in the study of the income tax. The uninitiated are likely to think of taxes as a kind of sterile game of questions and answers, largely involving only arithmetic and little philosophy. Forget it! Nice reasoning and a careful consideration of underlying (often non-tax) policy considerations lurk behind every legislative tax effort, every administrative determination of the Treasury Department, every judicial decision in cases of tax controversy, and all but routine struggles of taxpayers, their counsel, and students to arrive at proper tax conclusions.

You are undertaking a study in communication. English majors take heart; the use of the language is as important here as it is in any area of the law. But of course other prior training and experience are likewise helpful. There is no such thing as pure tax law. Instead, tax principles relate to events and transactions that would go on even if there were no federal income tax, although many events and transactions are shaped by an awareness of relevant tax principles. There is a clue here to the nature of your study. You must be sure you understand what it is that is happening which gives rise to the tax question. You may have to learn a little (or a little more) about the respective rights and obligations of a mortgagor and mortgagee before you can properly appraise the tax consequences of their transactions; you may have to ponder the nature of an interest free loan before you can determine how it should be taxed; and you must learn about annuity and endowment contracts if you would like to discover how Congress taxes (or relieves from tax) amounts that are received under such agreements. In the pages that follow, a case or a note will often be of assistance in this subordinate but important endeavor. As you know, taxes are so pervasive that the above examples could be extended indefinitely. But, while these remarks are intended as a word of caution to the neophyte, an encouraging note should also be detected. It is the very diversity of circumstances giving rise to tax questions that makes tax study appealing to many. It is difficult to imagine any more broadening endeavor, for tax questions lead one into all segments of law and society often raising, at least indirectly, broad social, economic, and political considerations. Every substantive course in any law school's curriculum has an outer ripple of tax ramifications.

The communications study being undertaken is learning to decipher the messages of the Internal Revenue Code. This is not quite akin to foreign language study for, after all, the Code is written in English, and it is quite correct in matters of grammar and syntax. If it falters occasionally rhetorically, this is not the usual rule. The messages are there, in general written with about as much clarity as is possible, allowing for the complexity of the thoughts expressed. The origin of the present statute, indicated briefly in the next part of this chapter, may increase your respect for the document with which you are dealing. Our suggestion here, then, is not to throw down the statute in exasperation when an initial look at a provision does not provide much nourishment. Struggle with the language, rejecting the notion that it is not understandable and with confidence that persistence will pay off. This is an essential part of your training. The cryptic language of the Code has a key, a style which you, as have others before you, can learn to decipher.

We wrote the foregoing paragraph nearly fifty years ago in the first edition of this book. It is essentially still true; but successive legislative events in recent years have strained our patience and somewhat dampened our conviction. The Code, formerly a carefully crafted document has succumbed to an assembly-line type of product of political and economic expediency. As one might expect, quality control in drafting and substantive content have suffered. Your persistence, but lots of it, will pay off, because the messages are still there and are understandable.

Just reading the Internal Revenue Code in cold blood is neither very much fun nor very productive. It must be read with an eye toward the circumstances to which its messages are directed. As you move into this course you will quickly see how hopeless it would be to try to teach the fundamentals of federal income taxation with the Code as the only material to be studied by students. Among other things, this explains repeated references in the pages that follow to selected provisions in the regulations. For there, sometimes by way of narrative and often by way of illustration, you will gain an understanding of what the cryptic statutory rules are all about. We venture this prediction concerning the progress of students who go about their study in the right way: (1) They will read the assigned provision in the statute without very much comprehension. (2) They will study the assigned material in the regulations with growing awareness. (3) They will return to what seems almost new statutory language, even discovering words in the statute which initially they did not realize were there. This third phrase involves what German psychologists call a "gestalt." A student once more quaintly characterized the third stage as "hitting the Ah hah! button."

The process just described suggests growth but not maturity and admittedly the "gestalt" does not always arrive on schedule. Moreover, even as general awareness grows, different people will derive somewhat different meanings from the same language, much as two cooks following the same recipe will bake rather different cakes. And so there is need for further effort toward understanding. The materials that appear in the following pages of this book: cases, rulings, committee reports, notes, problems, etc., are presented as an aid to that effort.

Tax practice is of two main types: (1) an application of tax principles to past events or transactions, and (2) advice as to how tax principles will apply to proposed events or transactions. The more interesting and rewarding activity is of the latter, planning type. But in either case, a prediction is called for. The tax practitioner must attempt to say how the administration and the courts will deal with the circumstances with which the practitioner is presented; indeed, one must often also attempt to foresee possible *legislative* change. We now begin to see the need for a kind of two-phase approach to tax study—what may be called a Why? Why? approach.[1]

*Why* do we postulate a particular answer to a tax problem? The bible tells us so. That is, the Code provides, or seems to provide, this answer. But then *why* did Congress write this provision into the Code? Here we are in the realm of policy; why are we concerned with this second "why?" To be sure, a great many tax questions can be answered routinely without major struggle. But in law school, a law student is aware of the frailties of the language, of the necessarily short-hand nature of statutory language, of substantial uncertainties as to meaning in varying circumstances. The second "why?" calls for knowledge that may bear heavily on meaning in cases of obscurity; and it also has a direct bearing on the matter of predicting possible legislative change. For example: Why did Congress enact the first "minimum tax" in 1969? Why did Congress abandon the 1969 tax and create a new "alternative" minimum tax in the Tax Reform Act of 1986? Why does Congress revisit the alternative minimum tax practically every year, most recently in 2017, to insure that it does not extend to too many taxpayers?

There are several by-products to seeking an understanding of the reasons behind tax legislation. For one thing, it makes the study far more interesting; a comparison might be the appeal of Euclidian geometry over elementary arithmetic. Secondly, the knowledge acquired has much longer life and usefulness. Finally, this is the *only* way to develop any comfortable feel for prediction in areas that cannot properly be regarded as settled. Of course, the policy reasons behind a statutory provision are not always discernible; one recalls the tradesman's classic reply: "There's no reason for it; it's just our policy!" But if there really is no reason (or perhaps no longer is any reason) for a legislative rule, is this in itself a basis for predicting legislative change, or at least narrow judicial interpretation?

It is also a truism that "the life of the law is not logic but experience." Judicial notions of what is sound policy often affect the way in which

---

[1] Since the first edition of this book was published, the authors have learned that, while the normal owl says " 'Who? Who?', the psychotic owl says 'Why? Why?' " but we persist.

statutory language is read and not infrequently present the student with surprise interpretations quite at variance with the student's own possibly reasonable, literal reading of the statute. Thus, experience is essential to tax practice but, on any given matter, some experience can be gained quite quickly vicariously. As a student you begin the process of gaining experience by reliving the tax controversies of others, which are presented in numerous cases and rulings that appear in the pages that follow. The controversies of others serve as a catalyst to your analysis of the Code.

In most parts of this book problems appear, which the student is expected to work out. Usually, one can arrive at supportable answers on the basis of the related assigned materials. Proper effort in this regard teaches the required close reading of the statute and, gradually, yields a more comfortable feeling about wading into fresh thickets of Code verbiage. But enough difficult questions and questions to which authoritative answers seem surprising are included to create also a healthy skepticism. In many instances in which answers are elusive or unexpected a case or ruling is cited, which may be considered when the student has attempted his own analysis. The discovery, appraisal, and persuasive use of precedent are as important in tax cases as in others.

Now it must be admitted that tax study presents the student with a mass of material, statutory and otherwise. Practice is of course no different in this respect. It is equally obvious that not everything can be learned at the same time, and the authors feel that initial study must be episodic rather than comprehensive. As in other law school courses, you must constantly ask yourself where you are. And you may not always be quite sure, just as the blind man's initial impression of an elephant depends upon whether he first grasps the trunk or the tail. We venture three suggestions here. After examining the brief historical, constitutional and resources discussions that follow in the next three segments of this chapter, study the last portion entitled "The Road Ahead". An effort is made there to give you an overview of the areas covered by this book. It would then be wise to take a careful look at the table of contents. While it will not now be perfectly meaningful, it will give you a start toward orientation. And, as you proceed with your study, pay attention to chapter headings and subheadings. This is obviously good practice in any course as an aid to directing pre-class efforts. Finally, as you go along consciously prepare your own notes for subsequent review. Again this is not a novel thought. But it can well be said that in the course of tax study knowledge grows with geometric rather than arithmetic progression; and the more you learn the greater your learning capacity. That which is obscure and difficult at the beginning of the course will become relatively clear and easy toward the end, as broader comprehension aids perception. Hours spent in review at the end may provide a greater yield than hours spent at the beginning, but only if the requisite hours *were* spent at the beginning.

## B. A GLIMPSE BACKWARD

Historians often give too little recognition to the federal income tax despite its profound impact on political, economic, and social developments in the United States.[1] We do not attempt in any comprehensive way to fill that gap. Works looking back more comprehensively at income taxation in the United States are Paul, Taxation in the United States (1954), and Blakey, The Federal Income Tax (1940). Probing the legislative history of specific statutory provisions is facilitated by Seidman, Legislative History of Federal Income Tax Laws, 1953–1939 (1954); Seidman, Legislative History of Federal Income Tax Laws, 1938–1861 (1938); and Goldstein, Barton's Federal Tax Laws Correlated (1968). There are numerous historical references in subsequent chapters of this book, which are an aid to understanding specific provisions in the income tax laws. Some further comments are in order here regarding the origin of the present income tax statute.

The Congressional Joint Committee on Internal Revenue Taxation has summarized the first one hundred and fifty years of internal revenue taxation as follows:[2]

### LAWS PRIOR TO 1939

The first internal-revenue tax law was enacted on March 3, 1791, and imposed a tax on distilled spirits and stills. This was followed by legislation imposing taxes upon carriages, retail dealers in wines and foreign spirituous liquors, snuff, refined sugar, property sold at auction, legal instruments, real estate and slaves. All of these taxes and the offices created for their enforcement were abolished in 1802. During this first era of taxation the internal-revenue receipts amounted to only $6,758,764.26. Comparing this with the receipts for the fiscal year 1938, amounting to $5,658,765,314, it will be noted that the Internal Revenue Service collects at the present time more than twice as much from internal-revenue taxes in one day as the original organization collected in 10 years. [The "present time" was 1939. Collections now exceed a trillion dollars annually. Ed.]

Due to the necessities occasioned by the War of 1812, internal-revenue taxes were again imposed in 1813. These taxes were levied on refined sugar, carriages, distillers, sales at auction, distilled spirits, manufactured articles, household furniture, watches, gold, silver, plated ware, jewelry, real estate, and slaves. An officer known as the Commissioner of Revenues was in charge of the administration of such taxes. All these

---

[1]   See, e.g., Samuel Eliot Morison's otherwise excellent History of the American People (1965).

[2]   "Codification of Internal Revenue Law," p. IX (1939), reproduced at 26 U.S.C.A. XIX–XX.

taxes were repealed by the act of December 23, 1817, and the office of Commissioner of Revenues was discontinued, effective upon the completion of the collection of the outstanding taxes. The collections during the 5-year period from 1813 to 1818 amounted to $25,833,449.43.

For a period of 43 years, namely, 1818 to 1861, no internal-revenue taxes were imposed. On July 6, 1861, an act was passed imposing a tax on incomes and real property. No income tax was ever collected under this act, and all of the tax collected on real property was returned to the States under authority of the act of March 2, 1891.

The act of July 1, 1862, is largely the basis of our present system of taxation. It contained the first law under which any income tax was collected, and it created the office of Commissioner of Internal Revenue. It taxed practically everything which Congress thought was susceptible of yielding revenue. The three sources of revenue which remained for a long time the backbone of the internal revenue system, namely, spirits, tobacco, and beer, received particular attention from the lawmakers.

The internal-revenue laws were first codified in the Revised Statutes of 1873, Title XXXV, which was made absolute law. A perfected edition of the Revised Statutes was prepared in 1878, but was only prima facie, not absolute law. The internal-revenue laws were again codified in Title 26 of the United States Code, which was enacted as prima facie law in 1924. Scrutiny of the Code was invited in its preface for the purpose of correcting errors, eliminating obsolete matter, and restatement.

In 1930, the Joint Committee on Internal Revenue Taxation published a complete substitute for Title 26 of the United States Code, containing all the law of a permanent character, relating exclusively to internal revenue, in force on December 1, 1930. This was not a mere duplication of the old Title, for in addition to correcting errors and eliminating obsolete matter, certain omitted provisions were added and the Title completely rearranged in a manner considered logical and useful.

In 1933, a new edition was published containing the internal-revenue laws in force on July 16, 1932. This edition was substituted for Title 26 of the United States Code, and was prima facie law. A third edition was published in 1938, containing the internal-revenue laws in force at the beginning of that year.

Prior to 1939, the mere ascertainment of statutory provisions that might affect the determination of a tax question threw the tax practitioner into the hodge-podge of the Statutes at Large. Happily, a

1939 development relieved the practitioner (but not necessarily the scholar) from this awkwardness, except as regards transitional problems that reached back to earlier years. The Report of the Ways and Means Committee on the Bill that became the Internal Revenue Code of 1939[3] included the following statement:

### THE NEED OF AN INTERNAL REVENUE CODE

The need for enactment into absolute law of a codification of internal revenue laws has long been recognized. The last such enactment was in 1874, when the Revised Statutes were adopted. If the need for enactment into law of a codification was recognized in 1874, when only 17 volumes of the Statutes at Large had been published and our internal revenue was derived almost entirely from taxes on liquor and tobacco, that need must be much greater today, when 34 additional volumes have been published and our internal revenue is derived from more than a hundred separate sources.

The United States Code is itself the culmination of more than 30 years' effort. Due to the mass of legislation contained in that Code, it was thought best by the Congress to put it through a testing period before its enactment into law. It was, therefore, made only prima facie evidence of the law, and scrutiny of it was invited for the purpose of correcting errors, eliminating obsolete matter, and restatement.

* * *

This Code contains all the law of a general and permanent character relating exclusively to internal revenue in force on January 2, 1939. In addition, it contains the internal revenue law relating to temporary taxes, the occasion for which arises after the enactment of the Code. The following should be noted in connection with the general character of the Code:

First. It makes no changes in existing law.

Second. It makes liberal use of catchwords, headlines, different types, indentations, and other typographical improvements.

Third. By a system of cross-references, it correlates not only its own provisions but also provisions of the United States Code not relating exclusively to internal revenue.

Fourth. To obviate confusion with the law itself, the cross-references are in type different from that containing the law.

Fifth. It is arranged with a view of giving prominence to matters which concern the ordinary transactions of the ordinary classes of taxpayers.

---

[3]   H.Rep. No. 6, 76th Cong., 1st Sess. (1939) 1939–2 C.B. 532–533.

* * *

The 1939 effort was largely a matter of sorting and putting together currently operative internal revenue statutes—*codification*. Even so, the result was the tax practitioner's "bible," the Internal Revenue Code of 1939. Wholesale *revision* of the internal revenue laws was first accomplished in 1954, yielding a new (King James Version?) "bible" for the practitioner. When the 1954 legislation was presented to the Senate, Senator Millikin, Chairman of the Senate Finance Committee said:[4]

### INTERNAL REVENUE CODE OF 1954

Mr. President, the Senate has before it H.R. 8300, a bill to revise the internal revenue laws of the United States. The bill contains over 820 pages.

The need for revenue revision is evident from the fact that many of our revenue statutes are antiquated and ill-adapted to present-day conditions. Some have not been changed since the days of the Civil War. We have not had a complete revision of the internal revenue laws since 1875, more than 79 years ago.

In 1939, Congress enacted a codification of existing internal revenue laws. The 1939 code collected all the internal revenue laws in one document, eliminated obsolete matter and made typographical improvements in titles and cross-references. That code did not change the existing law, so that many of the complications and inequities of existing law were continued. It has been over 15 years since the 1939 code was enacted.

Since 1939, over 200 internal revenue statutes have been enacted, including 14 major revenue acts. I cannot too strongly emphasize the value of the 1939 code, which was enacted with the unanimous support of both parties. Without the basic work undertaken in the 1939 code, it would not have been possible to have H.R. 8300 ready for enactment at this time.

H.R. 8300 is the culmination of studies on tax revision extending over a period of nearly 2½ years. The Joint Committee on Taxation instructed its staff to make a study of tax revision in the spring of 1952. In July of that year, the staff prepared a questionnaire seeking suggestions from farm, labor and business groups, and from individual taxpayers, on how to improve the internal revenue laws. Over 17,000 replies were received from this questionnaire, coming from every State in the country.

* * *

As in the case of its predecessor, the 1954 Code was amended many times. A major revision occurred in 1969. Since the 1972 publication of

---

[4]    100 Cong.Rec. 8536 (1954), reproduced at 26 U.S.C.A. XXI.

the first edition of this book there were eight significant revisions of the 1954 Code. Several were undertaken in an effort to stimulate the economy.[5] Other changes to the 1954 Code were designed to raise revenues, reduce federal budget deficits, and reform the tax system.[6]

The Internal Revenue Code of 1954 was replaced by the Internal Revenue Code of 1986. The 1986 legislation, it was said, was to be *broad-based, simple, fair, and revenue neutral* (not productive of greater or less amounts of revenue). Toward that end the 1986 Act reallocated the tax burden, subjected more items to taxation and, at the same time, reduced tax rates, essentially from a maximum rate of 50 percent to a maximum rate of 28 percent. The goals of the 1986 legislation (we sometimes refer to it as the Tax Obfuscation Act of 1986) have not been achieved. Today, the 1986 Code is much more complex not more simple than its predecessor. A failure to achieve simplification dooms efforts toward fairness. It may be true that the elimination of some escape hatches has subjected more transactions to tax and some transactions to more tax accomplishing a base-broadening effect. But even so, a broader tax base does not necessarily translate to *simple* or *fair* for either Bart Simpson or high income taxpayers. The 1986 legislation has been followed by further tinkering of the 1986 Code in almost every year, often by several acts in a single year. But recent legislation, including the massive 1986 legislation, has not been accompanied with the type of careful, extensive studies that preceded the 1939 and 1954 legislation. This is certainly so in the case of the 2017 "Tax Cuts and Jobs Act."[7] That Act was initially aimed at simplification, but while it eliminated the need for many individual taxpayers to make complex computations, it also retains, and even adds, substantial complexity to the Code.

*Haste* has been the hallmark of recent tax legislation. There must be some way to link that up with *waste*. In any event, as these remarks indicate, "What's past is prologue," and our income tax provisions should be expected to undergo further and perhaps constant and very likely extensive change. Nevertheless, students should not feel that their learning in this area is evanescent. The fundamentals of federal income taxation remain remarkably constant. And that is what this book is

---

[5]   See, for example, The Revenue Act of 1971, Pub. Law No. 92–178, 92d Cong., 1st Sess. (1971), provided tax reductions for individuals and tax incentives for business to give a shot in the arm to the then sagging economy. The largest tax reduction in history was provided by the Economic Recovery Tax Act of 1981, Pub. Law No. 97–34, 97th Cong., 1st Sess. (1981), in a further effort to encourage economic growth by increasing savings and spurring investment. The Recovery Act included rate reductions for all individuals, marriage penalty relief for working couples, accelerated depreciation schedules for businesses, and a liberalization of estate and gift tax provisions.

[6]   See, for example, The Tax Equity and Fiscal Responsibility Act of 1982, Pub. Law No. 97–248, 97th Cong., 2d Sess. (1982), was an effort to increase revenues in a fashion to insure that all individuals and businesses would pay a fair share of the tax burden. It was followed by the Tax Reform Act of 1984, Pub. Law No. 98–369, 98th Cong., 2d Sess. (1984), which had four objectives: to reduce budget deficits; to prevent erosion of the tax base by tax sheltering activities; to insure all taxpayers pay a fair share of the tax burden; and to improve administration and efficiency of the tax system.

[7]   Pub. Law No. 115–97, 115th Cong., 1st Sess. (2017).

about. Certainly many of the details presented will be altered and some soon. But the student should join the authors in a search for basic concepts and policy considerations supporting basic principles. Such an approach is not only an aid in predicting change but also in understanding changes as they occur. This nineteenth edition of The Fundamentals is not published to present *new* fundamentals but, instead, to facilitate the study of long-standing fundamentals realistically in a setting that involves many new details.

## C. THE INCOME TAX AND THE UNITED STATES CONSTITUTION

The very limited purpose of this note is to present what every good Scout should know about the constitutional aspects of the federal income tax. The treatment of the subject is neither comprehensive nor detailed and, indeed, may reasonably be termed superficial. Nevertheless, these matters are relatively quiescent these days and for most purposes the elementary thoughts presented may be sufficient. The investigation and prosecution of tax fraud are not given detailed consideration in this book; but of course they are areas in which constitutional issues are constantly at the forefront.[1]

*The Power to Tax.* The federal government's power to tax is derived from Article 1, Section 8, clause 1 of the Constitution of the United States, which confers on Congress the "power to lay and collect taxes, duties, imposts and excises * * *." If no other constitutional provision affected the taxing power, this would clearly be enough to authorize the imposition of an income tax. However, Section 2, clause 3 and Section 9, clause 4 of Article 1 require that "direct" taxes be apportioned among the several states in accordance with their respective populations. Further, Article 1, Section 8, clause 1 reads: "all duties, imposts, and excises shall be uniform throughout the United States." These provisions provide the substance for Mr. Justice Chase's famous quote: "[T]he power of Congress to tax is a very extensive power. It is given in the Constitution, with only * * * two qualifications. Congress * * * must impose direct taxes by the rule of apportionment, and indirect taxes by the rule of uniformity."[2]

What is the difference between a "direct" tax and an "indirect" tax? A direct tax is a tax demanded from the very person who is intended to pay it. An indirect tax is a tax paid primarily by a person who can shift the burden of the tax to someone else or who at least is under no legal compulsion to pay the tax.[3] By way of example, a tax at a flat rate on all

---

[1]    See Crowley and Manning, *Criminal Tax Fraud—Representing the Taxpayer before Trial* (P.L.I.1976); Balter, *Tax Fraud and Evasion,* (Warren, Gorham and Lamont 5th Ed.1983); Lipton, "Constitutional Protection for Books and Records in Tax Fraud Investigations," *Tax Fraud,* p. 75 (I.C.L.E.1973). A brief note on procedure in tax fraud cases appears in Chapter 28A3.

[2]    License Tax Cases, 72 U.S. (5 Wall.) 462, 471 (1866).

[3]    Pollock v. Farmers' Loan & Trust Co., 157 U.S. 429, 558, 15 S.Ct. 673, 680–681 (1895).

persons is a direct tax. In contrast, a sales tax is an indirect tax, because it is imposed on the seller who may shift it to the purchaser. A person may avoid an indirect tax by not buying the article subject to the tax.

*Apportionment Among the States.* The rule of apportionment to which direct taxes must conform requires that, after Congress has established a sum to be raised by direct taxation, the sum must be divided among the states in proportion to their respective populations. This determines the share that must be collected within each particular state. There would be no inequality (but query as to unfairness) *among the states* in a tax at a flat rate on all persons, because a capitation tax is self-apportioning. But inequality of a sort would result if an unapportioned direct tax were levied on all carriages within the United States and a particular state had only 5% of the population but 10% of the carriages. Of course one might wonder today whether it was bad for a small state with many carriages to bear more of the federal tax burden than a more populous state with few.

Congress once did enact an unapportioned tax on carriages—hence this seemingly quaint example—which appeared to be a direct tax. However, it was held not to be direct but rather an excise tax on the *use* of carriages and therefore valid.[4] The court was influenced by dicta in prior opinions indicating direct taxes are only capitation taxes or taxes on land.

As one ponders the possible use of direct taxes as federal revenue raising measures, one is likely to come to the conclusion that (1) a failure to provide an apportionment rule might make it possible for a central taxing authority improperly to burden some states to the great advantage of others, but (2) application of an apportionment rule might create interpersonal inequities at least as bad as the interstate inequities sought to be avoided. Perhaps, it is for these reasons that Congress does not enact direct taxes, unless the income tax is still properly so classified.

What is the proper classification of the income tax? Prior to the enactment of the Income Tax Act of 1894 the United States Supreme Court had found that a tax on the premiums received by an insurance company[5] and a tax on income which an individual derived in part from professional earnings and in part from the interest on bonds[6] were not direct taxes. In the landmark case of Pollock v. Farmers' Loan & Trust Co.,[7] the Court was asked to decide the constitutionality of an income tax statute that included as income rents from real estate. On the principle that substance must prevail over form, the Court held that a tax on the income from property so burdened the property as to be the equivalent of a tax on the property. The Court held the intention of the drafters of the

---

[4] Hylton v. United States, 3 U.S. (3 Dall.) 171 (1796).

[5] Pacific Ins. Co. v. Soule, 74 U.S. (7 Wall.) 433 (1868).

[6] Springer v. United States, 102 U.S. (12 Otto) 586 (1880).

[7] Note 3, supra.

Constitution was to prevent the imposition of tax burdens on accumulations of property, except in accordance with the rule of apportionment,[8] and for this reason invalidated the tax. This decision was met with great criticism. At the time individual incomes varied sharply from state to state and it was observed that the effect of the decision, if income taxes had to be subject to the rule of apportionment, might be to cause a citizen in Massachusetts to pay only 2.8% of his income while a citizen in Minnesota had to pay 32.9% of his income.[9] There is also language in later Supreme Court opinions criticizing the *Pollock* case as an erroneous application of a principle of constitutional law.[10]

*The 16th Amendment.* The foregoing capsule tax history may help in understanding the 16th Amendment. In the Amendment, emphasis is to be placed on the phrase "from whatever source derived," not on the "power" language. The power was already reposed in Congress by Article I. What the 16th Amendment provides is that income taxes shall not be subject to the rule of apportionment regardless of the *sources* from which the taxed income is derived.[11] With appropriate emphasis the Amendment reads:

AMENDMENT XVI

The Congress shall have power to lay and collect taxes on incomes, *from whatever source derived,* without apportionment among the several States, and without regard to any census or enumeration.

It matters not that a tax on salary income may be an excise and a tax on rental income a direct tax; Congress may enact a statute that taxes both without concern for the apportionment requirement.

Another reason it is important not to look at the 16th Amendment as an isolated power-granting provision is that, if it were so read, it might appear to authorize an unapportioned tax on incomes only if Congress taxed *all* incomes regardless of source. This would invalidate a provision granting an exemption of some income, such as municipal bond interest, or perhaps invalidate an entire taxing act making such an exemption, an argument which the Supreme Court has rejected.[12] The primary message of the 16th Amendment is that, for future income taxes, the principle (apportionment) upon which the *Pollock* case invalidated the 1894 income tax statute shall be laid aside.

Despite the relatively minor role that constitutional issues such as apportionment now play in federal tax practice, reference may be made

---

[8] Note 3, supra at 583.

[9] Seligman, *The Income Tax,* p. 587 (MacMillan Company 1914).

[10] E.g., Graves v. People of New York ex rel. O'Keefe, 306 U.S. 466, 480, 59 S.Ct. 595, 598 (1939), citing People of New York ex rel. Cohn v. Graves, 300 U.S. 308, 313, 57 S.Ct. 466, 467 (1937).

[11] Brushaber v. Union Pac. R. Co., 240 U.S. 1, 36 S.Ct. 236 (1916).

[12] Id. at 21, 36 S.Ct. at 243.

here to one interesting issue that seems to loom on the horizon. In 1974 Congress added Section 84 to the Internal Revenue Code, which treats as income subject to tax appreciation inherent in property, if a taxpayer gives the property to a political organization. A related development has been proposals to tax pre-death appreciation in a decedent's property upon its transmission at the time of the owner's death.[13] It can be argued that provisions of this type attempt to tax property rather than income, because under traditional notions the gain, which could become income, has not been "realized" by the taxpayer. The conclusion could be that the attempted tax is direct and therefore invalid because not apportioned.

At an early date the concept of realization entered the federal tax picture when the Supreme Court stressed that the 16th Amendment applied to gains *derived* from capital or labor and that, with respect to gains on property, income included profit gained through a sale or conversion of the property.[14] A later opinion added:[15]

> While it is true that economic gain is not always taxable as income, * * * [g]ain may occur as a result of exchange of property, payment of taxpayer's indebtedness, relief from a liability, or other profit realized from the completion of a transaction.

It has never been determined, however, that mere appreciation in property that continues to be held by the taxpayer is within the "incomes" concept of the 16th Amendment and, indeed, to this time it has been generally supposed that appreciation or gain is not "realized" and thus not brought within the "incomes" concept by a mere gift of appreciated property.[16] If Section 84 is to be sustained, it will be under judicial tax doctrine newly announced, because Section 84 pretty much requires that we treat any *disposition* of appreciated property,[17] not just its "sale or conversion", as giving rise to realized gain within the "incomes" concept of the 16th Amendment.[18] Old constitutional lawyers never die; they just

---

[13] See such proposals and the discussion of the unlikely repeal of the estate tax and the enactment of I.R.C. § 1022 considered in Chapter 6B4, infra.

[14] Eisner v. Macomber, 252 U.S. 189, 207, 40 S.Ct. 189, 193 (1920).

[15] Helvering v. Bruun, 309 U.S. 461, 469, 60 S.Ct. 631, 634 (1940).

[16] Compare Helvering v. Horst, 311 U.S. 112, 61 S.Ct. 144 (1940), with Campbell v. Prothro, 209 F.2d 331 (5th Cir.1954). Dicta in *Horst* seems to imply that the concept of "realization" may be a matter of administrative convenience only supporting a postponement of tax to the final event of enjoyment of the income by the taxpayer. Helvering v. Horst, supra at 116. One commentator, embracing the *Horst* dicta, suggested some years ago that therefore the doctrine of realization is not a constitutional mandate at all, but only one of expedience, inviting administrative discretion. Surrey, "The Supreme Court and the Federal Income Tax: Some Implications of the Recent Decisions," 35 Ill.L.Rev. 779, 791 (1941).

[17] The question here must not be confused with the assignment of income issue principally involved in Helvering v. Horst, note 16, supra. Mere appreciation in property is certainly not ripe "fruit" which when later plucked by another to whom it has been given may be attributed to the transferor. See Helvering v. Horst and other materials at Chapter 12C, infra. When the transferee disposes of the property the gain may indeed have vanished. Helvering v. Bruun, note 15 supra, may be similarly differentiated.

[18] The somewhat parallel treatment under I.R.C. § 170(e), reducing the deduction allowed for charitable contributions of appreciated property, avoids the realization issue.

flail away. Do we flail a dead horse in persisting upon the importance of "realization" to the concept of income. To be impartial we must say here that some young Turks think so. Will that change as the Supreme Court continues to edge to starboard? Academicians don't always answer all the questions they raise.

Perhaps we have waded in a little too deep here for this introductory discussion; a briefer look now at the uniformity requirement.

*Uniformity Among the States.* The other qualification imposed by the Constitution on the federal taxing power is the rule of uniformity. Article 1, Section 8, clause 1 states:

> * * * but all duties, imposts, and excises shall be uniform throughout the United States.

This provision does not expressly mention "taxes"; can it successfully be argued that a direct "tax" is to be differentiated from "Duties, Imposts, and Excises" and is therefore free from the uniformity requirement? No. An income tax is in the nature of an excise, the government literally "excising" and taking for its use a portion of the taxpayer's gain. If as when it taxes rental income from property the present income tax may be termed direct, it does not escape the uniformity requirement. Of course, a direct tax that had to be apportioned could not be imposed uniformly, a temporary effect of *Pollock,* criticized at the time. But when the 16th Amendment removed the income tax from the apportionment requirement, it clearly left it fully subject to the constitutional requirement of uniformity.[19]

If it follows that all federal income taxation must be uniform throughout the United States, what then is the meaning of the constitutional term "uniform?" It might appear that if both A and B have $10,000 of income but A is taxed on her *salary* income and B is not taxed on his municipal bond *interest,*[20] the income tax is not being imposed in a uniform manner. However, it is well settled that the Constitution requires only geographic uniformity.[21] Although under principles dating back at least to *Brushaber*[22] certain exemptions may be constitutional, this does not mean that Congress may exempt the state bond interest of New Yorkers while taxing that kind of income of California residents. Similarly, the incomes of A and B may be subjected to different rates of tax; if A is taxed on part of her income at a higher rate than B pays, the constitutional uniformity requirement is not offended if it is because of different income levels and a graduated rate table and not because A and B are merely in different places.[23] Whenever some manner or mode of

---

[19]  See Seligman, note 9 supra, at 622.

[20]  Compare I.R.C. § 61 with § 103.

[21]  Knowlton v. Moore, 178 U.S. 41, 20 S.Ct. 747 (1900).

[22]  Note 11, supra.

[23]  Cf. Knowlton v. Moore, supra note 21 at 84, 20 S.Ct. at 764.

taxation is used somewhere in the United States, the same manner or mode must be used everywhere throughout the United States.[24]

Notwithstanding the constitutional fiat of uniformity, in the practical application of the income tax laws some lack of uniformity creeps in, even in the geographical sense. There are always uncertainties in the interpretation of statutes, tax or otherwise, but perhaps more in the tax area than in others. Crystallized differences in meaning develop in various parts of the country. A New York district judge may hold a person taxable on an alleged item of income which is held *not* taxable by a district judge in California. On appeal, the Second and Ninth Circuits may similarly differ. Unless the matter goes to the Supreme Court, in a practical sense the law is different on the east and west coasts and possibly different in one trial forum from another.

Prior to 1970, the Tax Court said it was never bound to follow decisions of the Courts of Appeal as to issues of law when the same issue appeared before the Tax Court for later decision.[25] This was the Court's settled view even when the appeal in the later case would be to an appellate court that had previously expressly overruled the Tax Court.[26] The Tax Court advanced an important argument that a part of its mission as a court not subject to geographic division was to work towards a uniform interpretation of the tax laws throughout the nation, a mission best accomplished by adhering to its own views until the Supreme Court took a hand in the matter. However, the Tax Court has changed its position and now decides cases on the basis of the law in the circuit to which an appeal will lie.[27]

In recent years even the Treasury has indicated it will sometimes apply different tax principles in different circuits depending on the law as determined by the controlling Court of Appeals.[28] These disparities are hardly more palatable than direct geographic discrimination by Congress, which the Constitution expressly condemns. Can it be said that, even if a taxing *statute* is seemingly untainted, an unconstitutional lack of uniformity may arise by virtue of inconsistent *judicial* and *administrative* action?

*Due Process.* Congress sometimes makes use of its taxing power in a retrospective manner, but this generally does not offend any constitutional proscription. It has long been settled that Congress may impose an income tax measured by the income of a prior year or by income of the year of the enactment earned before the enactment date.[29]

---

[24]   Ibid.

[25]   Lawrence v. Commissioner, 27 T.C. 713 (1957).

[26]   Holt v. Commissioner, 23 T.C. 469, 473 (1954).

[27]   Golsen v. Commissioner, 54 T.C. 742 (1970), affirmed 445 F.2d 985 (10th Cir.1971), cert. denied 404 U.S. 940, 92 S.Ct. 284 (1971). See Patterson and Hughes, "The Golsen Rule 18 Years Later," 20 Tax Adv. 123 (1989).

[28]   E.g., Rev.Rul. 72–583, 1972–2 C.B. 534, no longer of substantive significance because of the addition of I.R.C. § 2501(a)(4).

[29]   Stockdale v. Atlantic Ins. Companies, 87 U.S. (20 Wall.) 323, 331 (1873).

In fact, the 16th Amendment became operative March 1, 1913, and the imposition of a tax on income earned after that date was upheld even though the taxing *statute* was not enacted until October 3, 1913.[30] If questions can be raised about retrospective taxation, the Fifth Amendment seems the likely weapon. But in *Brushaber*[31] the Court expressly held that the due process clause of the Fifth Amendment "is not a limitation upon the taxing power conferred upon Congress by the Constitution * * * ,". Although the Fifth Amendment may not limit the taxing power, it can vitiate a statute which, while masquerading as a tax, in reality amounts to confiscation. If a supposed taxing statute is so arbitrary or capricious as to amount to spoliation or confiscation it may be held invalid as a denial of due process. Dicta in *Brushaber*[32] supports this proposition.[33]

The principal message here is that most taxing statutes are not vulnerable to constitutional attack. The Supreme Court will clearly not attempt to determine in the countless circumstances that arise whether Congress has nicely balanced the tax burden or is instead depriving some taxpayers of property in such a discriminatory manner that it might be considered denial of due process. But there is always the chance that Congress may go too far.[34]

*Self-Incrimination.* One of the vexatious problems in current tax litigation arises out of the Fifth Amendment provision that "[n]o person * * * shall be compelled in any criminal case to be a witness against himself." It is of course well settled that requiring a taxpayer to file an income tax return does not violate that Fifth Amendment privilege; rather, the proper place to raise the objection is in the return itself.[35] But to what extent, if at all, does the Fifth Amendment privilege apply in tax investigations?[36]

## D. THE TAX PRACTITIONER'S TOOLS

In any matter governed by statutory law, as are all federal tax questions, the approach to an answer is two-fold. (1) The statutory law, all such law that bears on the problem must first be found. (2) The proper meaning must be ascribed to such law.[1] The first step *can* always be accomplished and very well better be. The second step involves opinion,

---

[30] Note 11, supra.

[31] Id. at 24, 36 S.Ct. at 237.

[32] Ibid.

[33] Ibid.; and see Heiner v. Donnan, 285 U.S. 312, 52 S.Ct. 358 (1932); Nichols v. Coolidge, 274 U.S. 531, 542, 47 S.Ct. 710, 713–714 (1927).

[34] A Pennsylvania income tax statute was surprisingly held to offend the state constitution and therefore to be invalid in Amidon v. Kane, 444 Pa. 38, 279 A.2d 53 (1971).

[35] United States v. Sullivan, 274 U.S. 259, 47 S.Ct. 607 (1927); Garner v. United States, 424 U.S. 648, 96 S.Ct. 1178 (1976).

[36] See Chapter 28A3, infra.

[1] There is a third facet to which most students receive a jolting introduction when they enter practice; all the relevant facts must be *ascertained*.

judgment, and often controversy, but there are guides, sometimes controlling, that must be discovered and appraised.

To some extent this course emphasizes well-settled tax principles of wide application, basic statutory concepts that have a well-burnished gloss. But an effort is made as well to help the student develop a technique for proceeding with some assurance when, as is so often the case, answers are elusive or obscure. A feel for a tax solution is not an innate gift so much as it is a result of a broad understanding of the phenomena of our federal taxing system. A beginning toward such understanding can be made by attaining an awareness of legislative, administrative, and judicial procedures that affect federal taxes, identifying the products of such procedures, and pondering the effect such products have on the solution of a tax problem. When we speak of such "products" we are referring to the *primary* materials of federal taxation, which are discussed immediately below. Secondary (unofficial) materials, often indispensible in the proper use of the primary materials, are discussed more briefly at the end of this chapter.

**Legislative Materials**

*The Code.* The taxing power of the federal government is vested in Congress. Congress exercises its power by enacting legislation. Therefore, the exercise of the federal taxing power is by *statute* and, as far as internal taxes are concerned, the current statutory document is the Internal Revenue Code of 1986. It is fair to say in this area that the Code is *the* law; other materials to which the researcher resorts are only aids to establishing the meaning of the Code, sometimes challenging, at times persuasive, and occasionally controlling. All tax decisions and controversies center around the meaning of provisions of the Code.[2]

Of course the plenary taxing power of Congress is subject to some restraints; federal taxing statutes must square with the requirements of the Constitution much the same as any other federal statute. However, beyond the brief comments in the prior section, discussion of the point will not be extended here because only infrequently in recent years has a civil tax case turned on a constitutional issue.

Not all the statutory law of federal income taxation can be found in the Internal Revenue Code. Some provisions affecting tax liability appear in other federal statutes.[3] But this is highly unusual, and the Code is the

---

[2]  The improvement in tax teaching in the law schools has been dramatic in the past seventy-five years. Much credit for this goes to Erwin Griswold, one time professor and long time dean of the Harvard Law School, and more recently Solicitor General of the United States. And one of the world's few possessors of a solid gold golf putter. In broadest outline, the organization of this book is similar to his innovative casebook, Cases on Federal Taxation, first published by Foundation Press in 1940. Moreover, present day stress on THE STATUTE (and the regulations) also largely originated with him. Whether known or acknowledged, many tax practitioners trained in the past four decades, and most tax instructors who have come along in that period, all are to some extent indebted to Erwin Griswold.

[3]  Pub. Law No. 93–490, 1974–2 C.B. 451, without amending the Code fixed some special rules for the deductibility of moving expenses of armed forces personnel. Rev.Rul. 76–2, 1976–1 C.B. 82. Section 506(c) of the Tax Reform Act of 1976 added subsection 217(g) which deals with

basic, and often the only relevant statutory document. By-products of the legislative process should now be briefly noted.

*Bills.* The formal beginning of the tax legislative process is the introduction of a bill in the House of Representatives where, under the Constitution, bills for raising revenue are supposed to originate.[4] As a matter of fact, most bills involving comprehensive tax legislation have had their origin in the Treasury Department, but they enter the legislative branch when they are introduced by a member of the House. The introduction of a tax bill, which is given publicity by the press and tax informational services, alerts the public to proposed changes in the law. But post-enactment examination of the bills introduced and the changes made in them as they passed through Congress rarely sheds much light on the final statutory product.

*Hearings.* Upon submission, in both the Senate and the House, tax bills are usually referred to committees. In the House, the Ways and Means Committee to which a tax bill is referred may hold quite extensive hearings on the proposed legislation. Important officials of the Treasury Department appear with a prepared statement and are questioned by committee members. But many others may also appear, some merely representing themselves and others representing various trade associations, industry groups, professional societies, etc. Similar proceedings may take place in the Finance Committee in the Senate. Transcripts of these hearings are published and can be the source of much interesting material reflecting both private and governmental policy views on tax matters. But the hearings are only rarely useful in attempting to give meaning to the statutes ultimately enacted.

*Committee Reports.* When the Ways and Means Committee brings a bill back to the floor of the House, a report accompanies the bill. Basically, the report seeks to explain to the other House members just what the bill is designed to do, usually with illustrations. Later, when the Finance Committee reports its bill to the Senate another committee report emerges. These reports are the most important part of the so-called "legislative history" of a statute and, in this country, practitioners, the Treasury, and the courts often resort to them as guides to the meaning of the legislation. As a matter of fact, a good bit of approved literary piracy goes on here. The House committee report may borrow heavily from statements before the committee by Treasury officials. When the Senate committee prepares its report with respect to parts of the bill that have not been altered, the Senate report comments are likely

---

moving expenses of the armed forces. Section 2117 of the same act, however, limits tax liability potentially arising out of cancellation of certain student loans, without amending the Code. The 1984 Act subsequently added I.R.C. § 108(f) to incorporate this rule.

[4] A sophisticated analysis of the tax legislative process appears in Surrey, "The Congress and the Tax Lobbyist—How Special Tax Provisions Get Enacted," 70 Harv.L.Rev. 1145 (1957), reprinted in Sander and Westfall, Readings in Federal Taxation, 3 (1970) and in Graetz, "Reflections on the Tax Legislative Process: Prelude to Reform," 58 Virg.L.Rev. 1389 (1972). See also Shaviro, "Beyond Public Choice and Public Interest: A Study of the Legislative Process as Illustrated by Tax Legislation in the 1980s," 139 U.Penn.L.R. 1 (1990).

to be identical to the comments in the House report. This custom-sanctioned plagiarism is usually carried one step further when the Treasury issues new regulations under the statute as enacted, echoing the language of the committee reports.

Usually a tax bill emerges from the Senate in a form somewhat different from the form in which it was passed by the House. Before such a bill can go to the President, the disagreeing votes of the two houses must be reconciled. This task is undertaken by a conference committee, made up of Senate and House members. When agreement is reached in the committee, the managers report the bill back to their respective houses, generally resulting in passage in the newly agreed form. The conference committee report is often a rather brief and cryptic document, mainly identifying the areas of disagreement on which each house receded. But it may be accompanied by a statement on the part of the managers of the bill which is informative as to the reasons for action taken in conference. And the conference committee may also issue an explanation of the bill as it has been developed by the committee members. There is always the possibility that such reports and explanations will afford some insight into the meaning of new legislation, which would be missed upon a reading of the bare words of the statute.

Distinct from *ad hoc* conference committees is the permanent Joint Committee on Taxation, made up of five members of the Finance Committee and five members of the Ways and Means Committee. Its role in Congress is collateral to the formal legislative process.[5] Nevertheless, it has a staff of experts and authority, among other things, to investigate the tax laws and their administration, and some of its publications are enlightening as to the likelihood of changes in the law or as to the meaning of recent statutory changes.

*Debates.* Our legislative process contemplates parliamentary debate of proposed legislation. A tax bill is no exception. Congressional proceedings, including such debates, are published in the Congressional Record. This product of the legislative process may also have a bearing on the meaning ultimately accorded a new statute. But, of all the subordinate legislative materials mentioned, the committee reports are clearly the most significant.

*Prior Laws.* The modern income tax dates from 1913, the year in which the Sixteenth Amendment was ratified. From then until 1939, Congress enacted numerous internal revenue acts among which the controlling statutory law was scattered. In 1939, the internal revenue laws were codified, first as the Internal Revenue Code of 1939. Thereafter, for fifteen years, internal revenue legislation took the form of additions to or other changes in that Code. Wholesale revision in 1954 produced the Internal Revenue Code of 1954 which was the subject of many additions, deletions, and other changes over a thirty-two year span

---

[5]   See I.R.C. §§ 8001–8023.

until the 1986 Act replaced it with the Internal Revenue Code of 1986. Shop talk about this or that section was greatly hampered by enactment of the 1954 Code as all but one of the 1939 Code section numbers were changed. Although the most recent changes are both broad and deep, most friendly old sections of the 1954 Code retain numerical identity in the 1986 version.

Statutory changes present two special problems for the student and practitioner. First, if we are not talking about tax liability for the current year (questions controlled by the Code most recently enacted or as most recently amended), what was the status of the statutory law as of the year with which we are concerned? Second, if we find a case bearing on a tax problem, a current problem, did the decision in that case rest on provisions of statutory law that are the same as or at least similar to the current provisions? If not, the case is obviously irrelevant. Generally, the opinion will set out the pertinent statute, either in the text or in the margin, so that it can be compared with the current provisions. Where the problem arises otherwise, web-based research services, such as Westlaw or LexisNexis, or tax-specific research services like Thomson Reuters Checkpoint or Wolters Kluwer IntelliConnect may save time in searching for effective date provisions of numerous amendatory acts.

*Treaties.* In the hierarchy of laws in the United States, a federal statute and a treaty enjoy equal status. Treaties made under the authority of the United States are the supreme law of the land, along with laws made in pursuance of the Constitution and the Constitution itself. Consequently, a tax treaty, of which we now have many can supersede a provision of the Internal Revenue Code. The point is made as a precautionary gesture but will not be further explored here.

Generally it is the practice in this casebook to delete from a judicial opinion or its footnotes the quotation of statutory language that is essentially the same as that appearing in the Code in its present form. When that is done a reference to the current Code provision replaces the footnote, as it is assumed that students will have the Code available. Opinions quoting language no longer in the Code or substantially different from the Code's present language are not changed in this respect. A comparative analysis may have to be undertaken by the student to see what current relevance the case may have despite the statutory changes, an effort that has educational value in and of itself. Statutory assignments throughout the book will usually quickly bring the student to the current provisions with which the old should be compared. The matter discussed here is illustrated in *Glenshaw Glass* set out in Chapter 2, where the Court quotes I.R.C. (1939) Section 22(a) in the text and then in footnote 11 discusses a minor change of language in the parallel I.R.C. (1954) Section 61(a).

## Administrative Materials

The administrative branch of tax governance, the Treasury, issues a wide range of documents providing its interpretation of the Internal

Revenue Code. The administrative documents have different weights of authority. Some have substantial weight while others have little or no weight as they are merely for the Service's internal use; however, pursuant to the Freedom of Information Act,[6] they must be released to the public.

*Regulations.* The Secretary of the Treasury is given general authority to "prescribe all needful rules and regulations for the enforcement" of the Internal Revenue Code.[7] This is a lawful congressional delegation of subordinate legislative authority. The final regulations promulgated under this authority become a kind of proliferation of the statute.

In the process of enacting final regulations, the Treasury enacts proposed or temporary regulations raising a trial balloon offering guidance as to its intention with respect to a Code section in subsequent final regulations. Regulations which are issued as temporary regulations are also issued as proposed regulations to ensure that they are the subject of public comment.[8] Proposed regulations are useful in tax planning and, although they have limited precedential value, they can frequently be relied on prior to the enactment of contrary finalized regulations.

In this course, principal emphasis is placed on the Code and the regulations. And students should learn at once to think of the initial approach to a tax question as follows: (1) What Code provisions bear on the problem? (2) Do the regs shed any light on their meaning in the setting at hand? This is not the end, but it is the right beginning for the solution of a tax problem.

The regulations are especially valuable to the student, often enabling one to move from the general and abstract language of the statute to a specific, concrete example of its application. The practitioner, as a student, is of course accorded the same opportunity. Nevertheless, in using the regulations it is important to remember that they are generally subordinate to the statute and, in any instance in which an exact answer must be achieved, it is entirely improper to rely on the regulations (or on instructions on a tax form, which generally have about the same status) as a substitute for the statute. Indeed, it may well be necessary to go beyond both, as further comments below will indicate.

Regulations, of course, may be challenged and are subject to judicial review. In the final analysis, the *judiciary* has the right to say whether the regulations promulgated by the *executive* conform to the statute enacted by the *legislature*. However, a student should not lightly assume that a regulation is invalid. Although the Internal Revenue Code is

---

[6]   5 U.S.C.A. § 552 (1967). See infra Text at page 25 note 18.

[7]   I.R.C. § 7805. In general, the Treasury may not issue retroactive regulations. I.R.C. § 7805(b)(1). But see I.R.C. § 7805(b)(2)–(8).

[8]   I.R.C. § 7805(e)(1). Temporary regulations expire three years after their issuance date (I.R.C. § 7805(e)(2)), but no such limitation applies to proposed regulations.

detailed and comprehensive, ambiguities in the statute do arise and it is the Service's role in administering the tax laws to resolve those ambiguities. In the *Mayo Foundation* case, at the end of this subpart, the Supreme Court sets out the standards a taxpayer must satisfy to successfully challenge a regulation.

*Rulings and Other Treasury Documents.* The regulations are not the only income tax documents emanating from the Treasury Department. For example there are Revenue Rulings that are issued under the same statutory authority as the regulations. They are generally the Treasury's answer to a specific question raised by a taxpayer concerning the taxpayer's tax liability.[9] In the interest of a uniform application of the tax laws, they are published to provide precedents for use in the disposition of like cases. While they do not have the force and effect of regulations, they do at least reflect the current policies of the Internal Revenue Service and they may be cited and relied on.[10] The Service will not invariably respond to a request for a ruling. See Rev.Proc. 2018–1, 2018–1 I.R.B. 1 (procedure for rulings, determination letters, and closing agreements),[11] and Rev. Proc. 2018–3, 2018–1 I.R.B. 130 ("no ruling" areas). Published Revenue Rulings appear in the weekly Internal Revenue Bulletin. Until 2008, the I.R.S. would collect the weekly bulletins and publish them in more permanent form, in the semi-annual Cumulative Bulletin (cited as "C.B."). After 2007, the Service stopped its practice of publishing cumulative bulletins. The Internal Revenue Bulletins and the earlier Cumulative Bulletins are also generally a source for the tax legislation committee reports, otherwise rather elusive documents.

A Revenue Procedure is a statement of the Treasury's practice and procedures. It generally deals with a broad subject.[12] The Treasury also publicizes its views in Announcements or Notices, which address timely topics of wide interest and Information Releases, which are press releases that provide public notice of general interest items. All of these publications have the same precedential value as Revenue Rulings and are published in the Internal Revenue Bulletin.[13]

---

[9] See Rev. Proc. 89–14, 1989–1 C.B. 814, stating the objectives of, and standards for, the publication of both revenue rulings and revenue procedures.

[10] See Galler, "Emerging Standards for Judicial Review of I.R.S. Revenue Rulings," 72 B.U.L. Rev. 841 (1992).

Most revenue rulings apply retroactively unless otherwise stated. I.R.C. § 7805(b)(8).

[11] See § 7.02[4] of the ruling for expedited handling of ruling requests.

[12] See, e.g., Rev. Proc. 87–56, 1987–2 C.B. 674, providing classification of property for purposes of I.R.C. § 168 depreciation allowances; Rev. Proc. 87–57, 1987–2 C.B. 687, providing assistance with respect to depreciation deduction computations.

[13] Prior to 1996, the Service also issued General Counsel Memorandums ("GCM"s) which were legal memorandums issued by the Chief Counsel's Office in response to requests from within the Service for legal advice.

What is the status of the taxpayer who has requested and received an administrative ruling on a question of federal income tax liability?[14] In very brief summary, there is no statutory obstacle to the Service's reneging on a ruling if the matter has not been handled so as to conform with the requirements for a closing or compromise agreement.[15] However, if the facts have not materially changed, the Treasury generally will not retroactively revoke a ruling so as to upset the expectations of the one to whom the ruling was issued.[16] For this reason, taxpayers feel they can rely on rulings issued to them and, even though procedures have been streamlined, rather rarely seek closing agreements.

The great majority of rulings are not officially published and thus remain "private" in the sense that they are issued in response to the request of a taxpayer and are officially kept confidential. However, as part of the Tax Reform Act of 1976, Congress added Section 6110 to the Code generally to require that many such private "letter rulings" be open to public inspection. This provision is intended to assure that all taxpayers have access to the rulings positions of the Service as well as to increase the public's confidence that the tax system operates in a fair and even-handed manner.[17] Congress was also motivated by judicial decisions that private letter rulings were subject to disclosure under the Freedom of Information Act,[18] and hence Congress chose to establish some legislative guidelines to the disclosures. The relevant regulations explain that copies of the text of the rulings to which this disclosure provision applies will be furnished to any person requesting them.[19] Private rulings take the form of Private Letter Rulings ("PLR"s), which are similar to revenue rulings as they are a response to a taxpayer's request to the Treasury to issue its response to the tax consequences of a particular transaction. Private rulings also include Technical Advice Memorandums ("TAM"s) which are similar to revenue procedures as they are the Service's response to a request for advice on a technical or procedural question. Although such rulings may not be relied upon as authority by anyone other than the taxpayer to whom the ruling was issued, they serve a useful function as planning tools especially in light of the announced policy of the Service that only rulings that involve important substantive tax questions and issues of widespread interest will be officially published as Revenue Rulings in the future.[20]

---

[14]  See Rugovin, "Four R's: Regulations, Rulings, Reliance and Retroactivity," 43 Taxes 756, 763 et seq. (1965).

[15]  Cf. Dixon v. United States, 381 U.S. 68, 85 S.Ct. 1301 (1965). See Chapter 28A3, infra.

[16]  Rev. Proc. 2018–1, 2018–1 I.R.B. 1 at § 11.06.

[17]  House Rep. No. 94–658, 94th Cong., 1st Sess. (1975), 1976–3 (vol. 2) C.B. 1006.

[18]  5 U.S.C.A. § 552 (1967). See, e.g., Fruehauf Corp. v. Internal Revenue Serv., 566 F.2d 574 (6th Cir.1977).

[19]  Reg. § 301.6110–1(c).

[20]  This change in policy was announced during "The Federal Tax Process" conference (May 18–19, 1980), presented jointly by the Tax Section of the ABA and The Tax Division of the American Institute of Certified Public Accountants.

The Service also issues Announcements ("Ann"s) and Notices ("Not"s) which address topics of wide interest and can be cited as precedent by taxpayers.[21] Information Releases ("IR"s) are also issued by the Service to the press to bring items of general interest (rather than technical issues) to public attention.

*Action on Decisions.* The Internal Revenue Service also issues Action on Decisions ("AOD"s) in which it states its position when it has lost an issue in a Tax Court case. An AOD provides guidance to taxpayers as to whether the Service agrees (acquiesces, "acq.") or disagrees (nonacquiesces, "nonacq.") in the Tax Court's determination of issues adverse to the government. Such actions do not affect the taxpayer who has just won the case but, in essence, the Service is saying either we will or we will not continue to contest the point as it arises in other cases. Less methodically, notice is given from time to time whether the Treasury will follow a decision of the Court of Federal Claims, a district court, or court of appeals; obviously, Supreme Court decisions are controlling. These indications of adherence to or shifts in Treasury views, first published in the Internal Revenue Bulletin and eventually appearing in the Cumulative Bulletin, are of course of great importance in tax planning.

In addition to its essentially legislative and administrative activities, the Treasury performs a quasi-judicial function as well. If a deficiency in tax is asserted by the Treasury, or if the taxpayer claims a refund on the grounds of an overpayment of tax, the initial decision of any ensuing controversy must be made by the Treasury. But such determinations give rise to no published opinions or reports, and procedures for judicial review always take the form of trials *de novo*. It will be important in Chapter 28A to consider intra-agency procedures but, as we are here mainly concerned with the *materials* of Federal taxation and no such materials are generated by such procedures, we turn now to the judicial process.

## Judicial Materials

The decisional process serves to put the meat on the skeletal law of the statute.[22] In broad perspective the Code lays down bare legal norms and cursory fact norms, sometimes clearly and separately identifiable and sometimes coalescing and indistinguishable. When a tax controversy gets into court, the court's function, at least at the trial level, is to identify the problem, determine the relevant facts (findings of fact), and interpret and apply the Code provisions. In essence the tribunal must draw a line in each case; that is the primary job of the courts. The growing body of decisions in many areas of the tax law takes on a meaningful profile which can have significant value as an aid in predicting the outcome of

---

[21] Announcements and Notices have the same precedential value as Revenue Rulings and Revenue Procedures.

[22] See Ginsberg, "Making Tax Law Through the Judicial Process," 70 A.B.A.J. (No. 3) 74 (1984).

future controversies involving similar issues. Thus lines drawn by the courts in prior decisions can be plotted and are useful tools to the tax practitioner planning prospective transactions and are essential to the practitioner in deciding whether to litigate an issue that is the subject of current administrative controversy.

An appellate tribunal can of course review the findings of fact as determined by the trial court, but in general it cannot reject such findings unless they are virtually entirely unsupported by evidence. Hence the function of the appellate process is not so much fact line drawing as it is interpretation. You will discover that appellate courts are rather adept at enunciating legal norms or rules or tests, which are then applied by trial courts in specific factual settings. Generally speaking, the appellate tribunal is at its best when the issue before it is a question of law. Thus, for example in Williams v. McGowan[23] the only issue the Court of Appeals had to decide was whether the sale of a proprietorship business was a sale of an entity or whether such a sale was a sale of each constituent asset separately. The facts were clear and undisputed. The Code did not provide a ready answer. The Court held as a matter of law that a proprietorship is simply an aggregate of many things, not an entity.

The cases presented in this casebook are representative, not only of the substantive areas of tax law, but also of what courts do. In your study of other law school courses you have become generally aware of the federal court structure—district courts, courts of appeals, and the Supreme Court. You now meet two new federal trial courts, perhaps for the first time: The United States Tax Court and the United States Court of Federal Claims.

*Tax Court Decisions.* If the Commissioner of Internal Revenue asserts a deficiency in income tax (charges in effect that the taxpayer has paid less than he owed) for any year, one thing the taxpayer can do is petition the Tax Court for a redetermination of the deficiency (or hopefully, a decision that no additional tax is due). As such suits are always between the taxpayer and the Commissioner (who is represented by attorneys in the office of the Chief Counsel of the Treasury Department), prior to 1977 such cases were often referred to only by the taxpayer's name, e.g., Nora Payne Hill, 13 T.C. 291 (1949). The adversarial nature of Tax Court cases is now clearly indicated by the inclusion of "Commissioner" in the style of the cases, e.g., Diedrich v. Commissioner, 39 T.C.M. 433 (1979). The Tax Court, created as the Board of Tax Appeals in 1924 and changed in name only in 1942 was, until 1970, an independent administrative agency in the executive branch of the government. The Tax Reform Act of 1969 established the Tax Court as an Article I Court to be known as the United States Tax Court.[24] Though

---

[23]   152 F.2d 570 (2d Cir.1945), set out infra at page 758.

[24]   Cf. I.R.C. § 7441 stating that the Tax Court is not an agency of, and shall be independent of, the executive branch of the government.

not an Article III Court (the judiciary article of the Constitution) the United States Tax Court is now a de jure court albeit under the Legislative Article of the Constitution.[25]

It may be well to recognize three categories of Tax Court decisions. (1) The Court sits in divisions so that only one of the nineteen regular judges hears and decides a case. A Tax Court case is always tried without a jury before one of the judges. Such cases *may* be officially reported in the Tax Court (formerly B.T.A.) Reports, after required review by the Chief Judge. (2) The decision may not be officially reported if it involves primarily factual determinations and the application only of settled legal principles. Commerce Clearing House and the Research Institute of America, however, do publish such so-called "Memorandum Decisions." (3) Some officially reported decisions are, upon determination of the Chief Judge prior to publication, reviewed by the entire court. In such instances, the Court can reject the decision of the judge who heard the case. Constitutional challenge to this procedure has been rejected.[26] In any event, a decision that has the concurrence of all the judges of the Tax Court (or which has at least been considered by all) may have somewhat greater weight than the decision of a single judge. Still in the final analysis, it will usually be the judge's insight and the persuasiveness of his opinion, whether the case is reported, reviewed by the Court, or merely a memorandum decision, which will determine whether it will be followed administratively and by other courts.

*District Court Decisions.* When a tax deficiency is asserted the taxpayer's judicial remedy is not limited to suit in the Tax Court. One can pay the deficiency, file an administrative claim for refund and, upon its denial or prolonged administrative inaction, file suit in the district court for a refund. Fact issues may be determined by a jury if the plaintiff demands a jury trial. The same procedure is open to a taxpayer who merely asserts an initial overpayment of tax.[27] The tax decisions in the district courts emerge in the Federal Supplement.

*Court of Federal Claims Decisions.* An alternative forum for refund suits is the United States Court of Federal Claims an Article I trial forum replacing the Court of Claims.[28] The court is composed of sixteen judges who are authorized to sit nationwide. It resembles the Tax Court in organization and procedure. It is similar to the District Court in that it is a forum for refund claims, but no jury trial is available in the Court of Federal Claims. Decisions of the Court of Federal Claims appear in the

---

[25] This action was held constitutional in Burns, Stix Friedman & Co., Inc. v. Commissioner, 57 T.C. 392 (1971); and it is fairly clear the Tax Court now has power to punish for contempt and to enforce its orders. See Dubroff, "The United States Tax Court: An Historical Analysis," 40 Albany L.Rev. 7 (1975).

[26] Estate of Varian v. Commissioner, 396 F.2d 753 (9th Cir.1968).

[27] See Chapter 28A3, infra.

[28] Pub.Law No. 97–164, 97th Cong., 2d Sess. (1982). See Sen.Rep. No. 97–275, 97th Cong., 2d Sess. (1982). The court was previously known as the United States Claims Court.

Federal Supplement and in a separate claims court reporter published by West Publishing Co.

*Court of Appeals Decisions.* Tax decisions of the district courts and of the Tax Court can be appealed (as of right) by either party to the courts of appeal, and tax decisions of the Court of Federal Claims are appealable to the Court of Appeals for the Federal Circuit. Decisions on such appeals are reported in the Federal Reporter. It is not uncommon, as such appeals fan out to the various circuits, to find divergent views expressed on like questions in the several courts of appeal. This is often unsettling in matters of tax planning and often a factor taken into account in the forum-shopping stage of tax litigation.[29]

*Supreme Court Decisions.* Many tax decisions in the Supreme Court represent that Court's determination (upon petition for certiorari) to settle a point on which the courts of appeal have taken divergent positions. Even so, the activities of the Tax Court, although its decisions are sometimes upset on judicial review, are so much more extensive that they clearly have more positive effect on the development of the tax law and on a uniform administration of the tax laws than the occasional forays of the Supreme Court.

Judicial decisions in federal tax cases (*except* those of the Tax Court) are collected in two important series of reports: (1) *United States Tax Cases* (cited, e.g., 2016–2 U.S.T.C. ¶ __) published by Commerce Clearing House, Inc., and (2) *American Federal Tax Reports* (cited __ A.F.T.R. __) published by Research Institute of America. Thus, in contrast to the space now occupied by complete sets of the Federal Supplement, the Federal Reporter, and the United States Reports, a complete set of federal tax (other than Tax Court) cases is compressed into significantly less bookshelf space.

## Unofficial Tax Materials

Federal tax practice would be almost impossible without the help of the major tax services. This is partly because of the bulk of material and partly because in detail tax principles are constantly changing. Both the Standard Federal Tax Reporter of Commerce Clearing House, Inc., and The United States Tax Reporter published by the Research Institute of America do an elaborate job of indexing and digesting tax materials and keep their subscribers current by way of weekly advance sheet reports. The Research Institute of America publishes separately a Federal Tax Citator, which is the most comprehensive tool for "Shepardizing" tax cases. A more modest, selective citator volume is included in the C.C.H. service. *Tax Notes* published by Tax Analysts provides a weekly update of tax matters. Somewhat similar research assistance may be found in the *Federal Tax Coordinator,* published by the Research Institute of America, *Bender's Federal Tax Service* published by Matthew Bender &

---

[29] Consider again the Constitutional requirement that federal taxes be uniform throughout the United States discussed in Chapter 1C, supra.

Co., and Mertens, *Law of Federal Income Taxation,* all published in loose-leaf form and kept current by fairly frequent supplements. The Bureau of National Affairs, Inc. publishes an extensive series of Tax Management portfolios, which are frequently revised. A tax research tool that has recently emerged, which can be of valuable assistance to beginning students as well as seasoned tax attorneys, is Bittker and Lokken's *Federal Taxation of Income, Estates and Gifts* published by Warren, Gorham & Lamont. A helpful guide to fundamental income tax concepts is Chirelstein's *Federal Income Tax* published by Foundation Press.

There is a great deal of excellent literature available on federal income tax problems. As would be expected, all the major law reviews publish tax articles from time to time. The Florida Tax Review contains articles of a detailed and scholarly nature with each article separately published to provide a forum for rapid publication. Detailed and scholarly articles are also published in the Tax Law Review (a New York University Law School publication) made up exclusively of tax writing. Other tax periodicals more practitioner oriented are The Journal of Taxation and Taxes. Commerce Clearing House publishes, and keeps up to date, a publication entitled Federal Tax Articles. The indexing—by subject, Code section, and author—is good, and a brief description of the subject matter of each listed article is presented. A similar Index to Federal Tax Articles is published by Warren, Gorham & Lamont. For tax articles, all that these volumes purport to cover, these services are somewhat superior to the better-known Index to Legal Periodicals. The various online research services also provide access to academic and professional tax journals.

Annual Institutes, such as the New York University Institute on Federal Taxation, the Southern Federal Tax Institute, the Florida Tax Institute, and the Tax Institute of the University of Southern California yield volumes of papers usually addressed to current tax problems. And there are numerous useful treatises on special areas of tax law.

Further specific reference is made in the chapters that follow to helpful unofficial materials. The literature cited is of varying quality and depth and, as to some that may be classified as superficial, the editors' objective is to identify materials that may be helpful to the beginning student.

## Mayo Foundation for Medical Education and Research v. United States

Supreme Court of the United States, 2011.
562 U.S. 44, 131 S.Ct. 704.

■ CHIEF JUSTICE ROBERTS delivered the opinion of the Court.

[The *Mayo Foundation* case involves the obligation to collect Social Security taxes. The case is important in a class on the federal *income tax* because the principles set out by the Supreme Court apply to a challenge of any administrative regulation.

Under Social Security, both employers and employees are generally required to pay taxes on the "wages" employees earn. Wages are defined broadly and generally encompass "all remuneration for employment." However, there are exemptions for different types of services and taxpayers. An exemption from taxation exists for "service performed in the employ of . . . a school, college, or university . . . if such service is performed by a student who is enrolled and regularly attending classes at such school, college, or university." Until 2005, the Treasury interpreted this exemption as applying to students who worked for their schools "as an incident to" their course of study. Determinations under this standard were made on a case-by-case basis, with the number of hours the student worked and the student's course load being the primary considerations.

Mayo Foundation and the other parties to the litigation offer medical residency programs designed to assist medical school graduates obtain education in various medical specialties. Medical residency programs typically last from three to five years and residents often spend between 50 and 80 hours a week caring for patients. In this work, residents are supervised by more senior residents and faculty members. Residents are paid annual "stipends" ranging between $41,000 and $56,000, plus benefits.

The Social Security Administration (SSA) took the same case-by-case approach to the corresponding student exemption in the Social Security Act. The SSA, however, always held that resident physicians were not students. In 1998, the Court of Appeals for the Eight Circuit held that SSA could not categorically exclude medical residents from student status since its regulations provided for a case-by-case approach. After that decision, the Internal Revenue Service received over 7000 claims for a refund of Social Security tax liability based on the ground that medical residents qualified as "students" under Section 3121(b)(10) of the Internal Revenue Code.

In 2004, the Treasury adopted a new regulation stating that an employee's service is "incident" to his studies only when "[t]he educational aspect of the relationship between the employer and the employee, as compared to the service aspect of the relationship, [is] predominant." The regulation also provided that "[t]he services of a full-time employee" (including any employee normally scheduled to work 40 hours or more per week) "are not incident to and for the purpose of pursuing a course of study." The amended regulation also made it clear that the analysis of whether an individual is a student is not affected by the fact that the services that are performed may have "an educational, instructional, or training aspect." An example dealing specifically with medical residents provides that because a resident's normal work schedule is greater than 40 or more hours per week, the work is not incident to, and for the purposes of, pursuing a course of study and therefore the resident is not an exempt "student."

After the Treasury issued its new full-time employee regulation, Mayo filed suit seeking a refund of the money it had withheld and paid on residents' stipends. Mayo asserted that its residents were exempt under Section 3121(b)(10) and that the new regulation was invalid. Mayo was granted summary judgment in the District Court. The court held that the new regulation was inconsistent with the unambiguous text of Section 3121, which the court thought dictated that "an employee is a 'student' so long as the educational aspect of his service predominates over the service aspect of the relationship with his employer." The District Court also held that the Supreme Court's analysis in National Muffler Dealers Assn., Inc. v. United States, 440 U.S. 472 (1979), indicated that the regulation was invalid.

The government appealed the District Court's decision and the Court of Appeals reversed. 568 F.3d 675. Based upon Chevron U.S.A. Inc. v. Natural Resources Defense Council, Inc., 467 U.S. 837 (1984), the court held that "the statute is silent or ambiguous on the question whether a medical resident working for the school full-time is a 'student'" for purposes of section 3121(b)(10), and the Treasury's amended regulation "is a permissible interpretation of the statut[e]." 568 F.3d, at 679–680, 683.

The Supreme Court granted Mayo's petition for certiorari. Ed.]

\* \* \*

## II

### A

We begin our analysis with the first step of the two-part framework announced in *Chevron*, \* \* \* , and ask whether Congress has "directly addressed the precise question at issue." We agree with the Court of Appeals that Congress has not done so. The statute does not define the term "student," and does not otherwise attend to the precise question whether medical residents are subject to FICA. See 26 U.S.C. § 3121(b)(10).

Mayo nonetheless contends that the Treasury Department's full-time employee rule must be rejected under *Chevron* step one. Mayo argues that the dictionary definition of "student"—one "who engages in 'study' by applying the mind 'to the acquisition of learning, whether by means of books, observation, or experiment'"—plainly encompasses residents. \* \* \* (quoting Oxford Universal Dictionary 2049–2050 (3d ed.1955)). And, Mayo adds, residents are not excluded from that category by the only limitation on students Congress has imposed under the statute—that they "be 'enrolled and regularly attending classes at [a] school.'" \* \* \* (quoting 26 U.S.C. § 3121(b)(10)).

Mayo's reading does not eliminate the statute's ambiguity as applied to working professionals. In its reply brief, Mayo acknowledges that a full-time professor taking evening classes—a person who presumably would satisfy the statute's class-enrollment requirement and apply his mind to learning—could be excluded from the exemption and taxed because he is not " 'predominant[ly]' " a student. * * *. Medical residents might likewise be excluded on the same basis; the statute itself does not resolve the ambiguity.

The District Court interpreted § 3121(b)(10) as unambiguously foreclosing the Department's rule by mandating that an employee be deemed "a 'student' so long as the educational aspect of his service predominates over the service aspect of the relationship with his employer." * * * We do not think it possible to glean so much from the little that § 3121 provides. In any event, the statutory text still would offer no insight into how Congress intended predominance to be determined or whether Congress thought that medical residents would satisfy the requirement.

To the extent Congress has specifically addressed medical residents in § 3121, moreover, it has expressly excluded these doctors from exemptions they might otherwise invoke. * * * That choice casts doubt on any claim that Congress specifically intended to insulate medical residents from FICA's reach in the first place.

In sum, neither the plain text of the statute nor the District Court's interpretation of the exemption "speak[s] with the precision necessary to say definitively whether [the statute] applies to" medical residents. * * *

**B**

In the typical case, such an ambiguity would lead us inexorably to *Chevron* step two, under which we may not disturb an agency rule unless it is " 'arbitrary or capricious in substance, or manifestly contrary to the statute.' " * * * In this case, however, the parties disagree over the proper framework for evaluating an ambiguous provision of the Internal Revenue Code.

Mayo asks us to apply the multi-factor analysis we used to review a tax regulation in *National Muffler,* 440 U.S. 472, 99 S.Ct. 1304, 59 L.Ed.2d 519. There we explained:

> "A regulation may have particular force if it is a substantially contemporaneous construction of the statute by those presumed to have been aware of congressional intent. If the regulation dates from a later period, the manner in which it evolved merits inquiry. Other relevant considerations are the length of time the regulation has been in effect, the reliance placed on it, the consistency of the Commissioner's interpretation, and the degree of scrutiny Congress has devoted to the regulation during subsequent re-enactments of the statute." *Id.,* at 477, 99 S.Ct. 1304.

The Government, on the other hand, contends that the *National Muffler* standard has been superseded by *Chevron.* The sole question for the Court at step two under the *Chevron* analysis is "whether the agency's answer is based on a permissible construction of the statute." 467 U.S., at 843, 104 S.Ct. 2778.

Since deciding *Chevron,* we have cited both *National Muffler* and *Chevron* in our review of Treasury Department regulations. * * *

Although we have not thus far distinguished between *National Muffler* and *Chevron,* they call for different analyses of an ambiguous statute. Under *National Muffler,* for example, a court might view an agency's interpretation of a statute with heightened skepticism when it has not been consistent over time, when it was promulgated years after the relevant statute was enacted, or because of the way in which the regulation evolved. * * * The District Court in this case cited each of these factors in rejecting the Treasury Department's rule, noting in particular that the regulation had been promulgated after an adverse judicial decision. * * *.

Under *Chevron,* in contrast, deference to an agency's interpretation of an ambiguous statute does not turn on such considerations. We have repeatedly held that "[a]gency inconsistency is not a basis for declining to analyze the agency's interpretation under the *Chevron* framework." * * *. We have instructed that "neither antiquity nor contemporaneity with [a] statute is a condition of [a regulation's] validity." * * *. And we have found it immaterial to our analysis that a "regulation was prompted by litigation." * * *. Indeed, in *United Dominion Industries, Inc. v. United States,* 532 U.S. 822, 838, 121 S.Ct. 1934, 150 L.Ed.2d 45 (2001), we expressly invited the Treasury Department to "amend its regulations" if troubled by the consequences of our resolution of the case.

Aside from our past citation of *National Muffler,* Mayo has not advanced any justification for applying a less deferential standard of review to Treasury Department regulations than we apply to the rules of any other agency. In the absence of such justification, we are not inclined to carve out an approach to administrative review good for tax law only. To the contrary, we have expressly "[r]ecogniz[ed] the importance of maintaining a uniform approach to judicial review of administrative action." * * *. See, *e.g., Skinner v. Mid-America Pipeline Co.,* 490 U.S. 212, 222–223, 109 S.Ct. 1726, 104 L.Ed.2d 250 (1989) (declining to apply "a different and stricter nondelegation doctrine in cases where Congress delegates discretionary authority to the Executive under its taxing power").

The principles underlying our decision in *Chevron* apply with full force in the tax context. *Chevron* recognized that "[t]he power of an administrative agency to administer a congressionally created . . . program necessarily requires the formulation of policy and the making of rules to fill any gap left, implicitly or explicitly, by Congress." * * * It acknowledged that the formulation of that policy might require "more than ordinary knowledge respecting the matters subjected to agency regulations." * * *. Filling gaps in the Internal Revenue Code plainly requires the Treasury Department to make interpretive choices for statutory implementation at least as complex as the ones other agencies must make in administering their statutes. Cf. *Bob Jones Univ. v. United States,* 461 U.S. 574, 596, 103 S.Ct. 2017, 76 L.Ed.2d 157 (1983) ("[I]n an area as complex as the tax system, the agency Congress vests with administrative responsibility must be able to exercise its authority to meet changing conditions and new problems"). We see no reason why our review of tax regulations should not be guided by agency expertise pursuant to *Chevron* to the same extent as our review of other regulations.

As one of Mayo's *amici* points out, however, both the full-time employee rule and the rule at issue in *National Muffler* were promulgated pursuant to the Treasury Department's general authority under 26 U.S.C. § 7805(a) to "prescribe all needful rules and regulations for the enforcement" of the Internal Revenue Code. * * * In two decisions predating *Chevron,* this Court stated that "we owe the [Treasury Department's] interpretation less deference" when it is contained in a rule adopted under that "general authority" than when it is "issued under a specific grant of authority to define a statutory term or prescribe a method of executing a statutory provision." *Rowan Cos. v. United States,* 452 U.S. 247, 253, 101 S.Ct. 2288, 68 L.Ed.2d 814 (1981); *United States v. Vogel Fertilizer Co.,* 455 U.S. 16, 24, 102 S.Ct. 821, 70 L.Ed.2d 792 (1982) (quoting *Rowan*).

Since *Rowan* and *Vogel* were decided, however, the administrative landscape has changed significantly. We have held that *Chevron* deference is appropriate "when it appears that Congress delegated authority to the agency generally to make rules carrying the force of law, and that the agency interpretation claiming deference was promulgated in the exercise of that authority." [citing United States v. Mead Corp., 533 U.S. 218, 226–227, 121 S.Ct. 2164 (2001). Ed.]. Our inquiry in that regard does not turn on whether Congress's delegation of authority was general or specific. For example, in *National Cable & Telecommunications Assn.,* [545 U.S. 967, 125 S.Ct. 2688 (2005). Ed.], we held that the Federal Communications Commission was delegated "the authority to promulgate binding legal rules" entitled to *Chevron* deference under statutes that gave the Commission "the authority to 'execute and enforce,'" and "to 'prescribe such rules and regulations as may be necessary in the public interest to carry out the provisions' of," the Communications Act of 1934. 545 U.S., at 980–981, 125 S.Ct. 2688 (quoting 47 U.S.C. §§ 151, 201(b)). See also *Sullivan v. Everhart,* 494 U.S. 83, 87, 88–89, 110 S.Ct. 960, 108 L.Ed.2d 72 (1990) (applying *Chevron* deference to rule promulgated pursuant to delegation of "general authority to 'make rules and regulations and to establish procedures, not inconsistent with the provisions of this subchapter, which are necessary or appropriate to carry out such provisions'" (quoting 42 U.S.C. § 405(a) (1982 ed.))).

We believe *Chevron* and *Mead,* rather than *National Muffler* and *Rowan,* provide the appropriate framework for evaluating the full-time employee rule. The Department issued the full-time employee rule pursuant to the explicit authorization to "prescribe all needful rules and regulations for the enforcement" of the Internal Revenue Code. 26 U.S.C. § 7805(a). We have found such "express congressional authorizations to engage in the process of rulemaking" to be "a very good indicator of delegation meriting *Chevron* treatment." *Mead, supra,* at 229, 121 S.Ct. 2164. The Department issued the full-time employee rule only after notice-and-comment procedures, 69 Fed.Reg. 76405, again a consideration identified in our precedents as a "significant" sign that a rule merits *Chevron* deference. * * *.

We have explained that "the ultimate question is whether Congress would have intended, and expected, courts to treat [the regulation] as within, or outside, its delegation to the agency of 'gap-filling' authority." * * *. In the Long Island Care case, we found that Chevron provided the appropriate standard of review "[w]here an agency rule sets forth important individual rights and duties, where the agency focuses fully and directly upon the issue, where the agency uses full notice-and-comment procedures to promulgate a rule, [and] where the resulting rule falls within the statutory grant of authority." * * *. These same considerations point to the same result here. This case falls squarely within the bounds of, and is properly analyzed under, *Chevron* and *Mead.*

C

The full-time employee rule easily satisfies the second step of Chevron, which asks whether the Department's rule is a "reasonable interpretation" of the enacted text. * * *. To begin, Mayo accepts that "the 'educational aspect of the relationship between the employer and the employee, as compared to the service aspect of the relationship, [must] be predominant'" in order for an individual to qualify for the exemption. * * *. Mayo objects, however, to the Department's conclusion that residents who work more than 40 hours per week categorically cannot satisfy that requirement. Because residents' employment is itself educational, Mayo argues, the hours a resident spends working make him "more of a student, not less of one." * * *. Mayo contends that the Treasury Department should be required to engage in a case-by-case inquiry into "what [each] employee does [in his service] and why" he does it. * * *. Mayo also objects that the Department has drawn an arbitrary distinction between "hands-on training" and "classroom instruction." * * *.

We disagree. Regulation, like legislation, often requires drawing lines. Mayo does not dispute that the Treasury Department reasonably sought a way to distinguish between workers who study and students who work, see IRS Letter Ruling 9332005 (May 3, 1993). Focusing on the hours an individual works and the hours he spends in studies is a perfectly sensible way of accomplishing that goal. The Department explained that an individual's service and his "course of study are separate and distinct activities" in "the vast majority of cases," and reasoned that "[e]mployees who are working enough hours to be considered full-time employees . . . have filled the conventional measure of available time with work, and not study." 69 Fed.Reg. 8607. The Department thus did not distinguish classroom education from clinical training but rather education from service. The Department reasonably concluded that its full-time employee rule would "improve administrability," id., at 76405, and it thereby "has avoided the wasteful litigation and continuing uncertainty that would inevitably accompany any purely case-by-case approach" like the one Mayo advocates, *United States v. Correll*, 389 U.S. 299, 302, 88 S.Ct. 445, 19 L.Ed.2d 537 (1967).

As the Treasury Department has explained, moreover, the full-time employee rule has more to recommend it than administrative convenience. The Department reasonably determined that taxing residents under FICA would further the purpose of the Social Security Act and comport with this Court's precedent. As the Treasury Department appreciated, this Court has understood the terms of the Social Security Act to " 'import a breadth of coverage,' " * * * and we have instructed that "exemptions from taxation are to be construed narrowly," *Bingler v. Johnson,* 394 U.S. 741, 752, 89 S.Ct. 1439, 22 L.Ed.2d 695 (1969). Although Mayo contends that medical residents have not yet begun their "working lives" because they are not "fully trained," * * * , the Department certainly did not act irrationally in concluding that these doctors—"who work long hours, serve as highly skilled professionals, and typically share some or all of the terms of employment of career employees"—are the kind of workers that Congress intended to both contribute to and benefit from the Social Security system. * * *.

The Department's rule takes into account the SSA's concern that exempting residents from FICA would deprive residents and their families of vital disability and survivorship benefits that Social Security provides. * * * Mayo wonders whether the full-time employee rule will result in residents being taxed under FICA but denied coverage by the SSA. The Government informs us, however, that the SSA continues to adhere to its longstanding position that medical residents are not students and thus remain eligible for coverage. * * *.

We do not doubt that Mayo's residents are engaged in a valuable educational pursuit or that they are students of their craft. The question whether they are "students" for purposes of § 3121, however, is a different matter. Because it is one to which Congress has not directly spoken, and because the Treasury Department's rule is a reasonable construction of what Congress has said, the judgment of the Court of Appeals must be affirmed.

*It is so ordered.*

■ JUSTICE KAGAN took no part in the consideration or decision of this case.

## E. THE ROAD AHEAD

Although Wordsworth's ambling dreamer happily happened upon a host of golden daffodils, one better embarks on a journey or project with a destination or goal clearly in mind. The goal in this course is to expose the fundamentals of income taxation by exploring the manner in which many basic transactions and events bear upon an individual's liability for income tax. This note summarizes the steps by which this book works toward that goal; a course has been set for which this note is a skeletal road map to the destination.

You have survived the scattered but important introductory material in most of Part One, although there may be some things to return to there. Part Two of this book seeks to corral all items required to be included in a taxpayer's gross income. Listing of course is impossible. Instead, an examination is made of judicial and administrative interpretation of the broad congressional language "income from whatever source derived" and its constitutional counterpart. This is followed by a detailed study of the Code sections by which Congress specifically excludes from or includes in gross income all or parts of specified items. The purpose here is not to memorize a laundry list, but much more to learn to manage the language of the Code, really a new language or at least *patois*.

After learning to identify gross income, a question may be: Who is to pay tax on it? Part Three of the book examines the so-called assignment of income doctrine which is aimed at preventing the artificial shifting of tax liability among individuals and other taxable entities. All right! Macy's won't pay Nordstrom's tax. But there are challenging problems here which will unfold in due time.

Once one has gathered all items of income and assigned them to the proper taxpayer (in tax parlance, has determined gross income for the year), various deductions are allowed to reach the net figure "taxable income", the base to which the tax rates are applied. Congress might have imposed a tax on gross income but, after all, fair is fair and almost as a required matter of legislative grace it determined instead to allow numerous statutory deductions. Part Four of this book considers these deductions.

Individuals are not the only taxpayers under our federal taxing system. Corporations, trusts, and estates pay income taxes as well and, while not actually taxed as entities, a partnership, a limited liability company, and an S corporation also must determine their "taxable income". While this book emphasizes individual income tax liability, nevertheless, principles and concepts involved in determining tax liability (gross income, taxpayer identification, taxable income, rates, credits, etc.) are often similar or the same for all affected entities. Some of this spill-over is especially apparent in Part Four which treats deductions in five chapters dealing respectively with: business deductions; deductions for profit-making, non-business activities; deductions not limited to business or profit-making activities; limitations on deductions; and deductions for individuals only. The material includes cases and rulings relevant to but not specifically directed to individual taxpayers.

In determining taxable income for the year, three additional questions must be considered with respect to each item of income or deduction. They are: (1) For what taxable year is an item income or deductible? This will soon be seen to be quite important when rate tables and statutes limiting the period of liability or of refund recovery are considered. (2) What is the character (capital gain or loss, or ordinary income or loss) of various items? Tax advantages and limitations too attend such determinations. (3) Is gain or loss immediately to be recognized? Some items seemingly taxable or deductible get a deferment, sometimes essential or at least helpful and at others disadvantageous or even disastrous.

The timing matters identified in number (1), above, are considered in Part Five of the book. Conventional usage might cause the first chapter there to be entitled Tax Accounting, which normally puts the fear of God into political science majors who conjure up thoughts of balance sheets, debits and credits, and electronic calculators. The concepts involved will prove much less frightening when actually encountered. Our income taxing system is based on annual reporting (tax liability is determined and paid on a twelve month basis), and principles of tax accounting seek to say into what annual period an income or deduction item is properly included. These matters can be wonderfully complex; but the fundamental rules, the things with which we are concerned here, are really pretty simple.

The second question mentioned above is known as characterization of income and deductions. Congress has determined that income from some sources is to be given preferential treatment (taxed at lower rates). It has put a rate ceiling of between zero percent and 28 percent on net capital gains while subjecting other ordinary income to a maximum rate of 37 percent, and it has continued to mandate that deductions of losses from such sources are to be subject to limitations. Part Six of the book illustrates that one must characterize each item of income or deduction and see whether the items when combined are to be given preferential treatment or subjected to limitations. Some deductions are not considered until Part Six because they cannot be intelligently considered separately from the characterization concept. Also, beware! Part Six is the den of the "Gotcha!" Enter with care, at your own risk. The "Gotcha!" is a sneaky kind of character assassin.

In some situations, even though one has income or loss, even *realized* income or loss, nevertheless Congress has seen fit not immediately to accord it tax consequences. Part Seven examines the nonrecognition or deferral of some gains and the nonrecognition or sometimes outright disallowance of some losses.

Consideration of all of the above leads to the determination of taxable income, next to be converted into tax liability. Part Eight of the book explains that conversion. Different rates of tax are applied to various classifications of taxpayers. Corporations are taxed at a flat rate found in Section 11, while estates and trusts are taxed at the essentially flat rates in Section 1(j)(2)(E). Individuals are further classified into various categories: married taxpayers filing joint returns and surviving spouses in Section 1(j)(2)(A), heads of households in Section 1(j)(2)(B), unmarried individuals in Section 1(j)(2)(C), and married individuals filing separately in Section 1(j)(2)(D), for which more progressive tax rate tables are provided. Part Eight studies the development of these individual classifications and the tax rates applicable to them.

Part Eight also considers tax credits. Tax credits are subtracted from the amount of tax otherwise actually to be paid. They are therefore preferred by the taxpayer over deductions used to determine taxable income. Credits reduce tax dollar for dollar and may even produce a tax refund, while deductions are effective in reducing tax only to the extent of one's marginal tax rates.

Finally, Part Eight also introduces the Alternative Minimum Tax, an essentially separate and complicated taxing scheme. Under this tax, taxpayers compute their taxable income in a manner different from the regular tax system (generally with a broader tax base as a result of the disallowance of exclusions and deductions) and pay tax at generally flatter rates than the regular rates. This tax applies in any year only to the extent that it generates greater revenue from the taxpayer than the regular tax.

We have reached the Moon but not the Millennium. Nobody is perfect, and mistakes are made in federal taxes as much as or more than anywhere. Tax procedures are available for correcting mistakes and by administrative and judicial proceedings for settling inevitable controversies. Still in a fundamental way Part Nine, the last section of this book, deals with these phenomena. It also considers professional responsibility in the tax profession and tax policy issues which are postponed until one has a fundamental understanding of the current tax system.

From here, in the words of your favorite Baedeker, as the sun settles softly behind the blue mountains that reach down to the shimmering sea, it's off to Part Two and Gross Income!

Bon voyage!

# PART 2

# IDENTIFICATION OF INCOME SUBJECT TO TAXATION

# CHAPTER 2

# GROSS INCOME: THE SCOPE OF SECTION 61

## A. INTRODUCTION TO INCOME

Internal Revenue Code: Section 61.

---

The Federal income tax is imposed annually on a net figure known as "taxable income." Taxable income is "gross income" less certain authorized deductions. The scope of the gross income concept is taken as the starting point for this course, just as gross income is the starting point in the computation of tax liability.

Code Section 61 defines gross income as "all *income* from whatever source derived." It may appear that Congress has violated a cardinal principle against defining a word in terms of the very word being defined—"water" means "water". But this of course is not the case. "Gross income" is a distinct statutory concept which could as well have been called "gross take" or something of the sort. If it wished to, which of course it does not, Congress could define gross income to include only amounts received as salary or wages or as dividends or in some other very restricted manner. Under the statutory definition, the meaning of the term "gross income" depends initially upon the meaning accorded "income." According to the legislative history of Section 61, the term "income" is used in its constitutional sense.[1] A long standing question has therefore been: What is "income"?

The term "income" in the Code, "incomes" in the Sixteenth Amendment, has a tax meaning that may vary from the meaning accorded the term in other contexts. A finder's treasure trove may not be "income" to the economist because it is not a recurring kind of receipt; but is it "income" in the tax sense? It may be that for some purposes one has income if one's wealth increases by way of an appreciation in one's investments; but does such appreciation constitute income for tax purposes? Still it should not be understood that the question is always broad and elusive. The statute itself offers some illustrations in Section 61; and there are two important series of statutory rules of inclusion and exclusion which are taken up beginning with Chapter 3. Moreover, in recent years important court decisions have greatly narrowed the area of

---

[1]   S.Rep. No. 1622, 83rd Cong., 2d Sess. 168 (1954).

uncertainty, and long-standing administrative practice has added some clarification.[2]

# B. EQUIVOCAL RECEIPT OF FINANCIAL BENEFIT

Internal Revenue Code: Section 61.

Regulations: Sections 1.61–1, –2(a)(1), –2(d)(1), –14(a).

---

## Cesarini v. United States

United States District Court, Northern District of Ohio, 1969.
296 F.Supp. 3, affirmed per curiam 428 F.2d 812 (6th Cir.1970).

■ YOUNG, DISTRICT JUDGE.

This is an action by the plaintiffs as taxpayers for the recovery of income tax payments made in the calendar year 1964. Plaintiffs contend that the amount of $836.51 was erroneously overpaid by them in 1964, and that they are entitled to a refund in that amount, together with the statutory interest from October 13, 1965, the date which they made their claim upon the Internal Revenue Service for the refund.

Plaintiffs and the United States have stipulated to the material facts in the case, and the matter is before the Court for final decision. The facts necessary for a resolution of the issues raised should perhaps be briefly stated before the Court proceeds to a determination of the matter. Plaintiffs are husband and wife, and live within the jurisdiction of the United States District Court for the Northern District of Ohio. In 1957, the plaintiffs purchased a used piano at an auction sale for approximately $15.00, and the piano was used by their daughter for piano lessons. In 1964, while cleaning the piano, plaintiffs discovered the sum of $4,467.00 in old currency, and since have retained the piano instead of discarding it as previously planned. Being unable to ascertain who put the money there, plaintiffs exchanged the old currency for new at a bank, and reported the sum of $4,467.00 on their 1964 joint income tax return as ordinary income from other sources. On October 18, 1965, plaintiffs filed an amended return with the District Director of Internal Revenue in Cleveland, Ohio, this second return eliminating the sum of $4,467.00 from the gross income computation, and requesting a refund in the amount of $836.51, the amount allegedly overpaid as a result of the former inclusion of $4,467.00 in the original return for the calendar year of 1964. On January 18, 1966, the Commissioner of Internal Revenue rejected taxpayers' refund claim in its entirety, and plaintiffs filed the instant action in March of 1967.

---

[2]    There is a comprehensive analysis of the concept of gross income in Magill, Taxable Income (1945); see also Sneed, "The Configurations of Gross Income" (1967) and Lowndes, "Current Conceptions of Taxable Income," 25 Ohio St.L.J. 151 (1964).

Plaintiffs make three alternative contentions in support of their claim that the sum of $836.51 should be refunded to them. First, that the $4,467.00 found in the piano is not includable in gross income under Section 61 of the Internal Revenue Code. (26 U.S.C.A. § 61) Secondly, even if the retention of the cash constitutes a realization of ordinary income under Section 61, it was due and owing in the year the piano was purchased, 1957, and by 1964, the statute of limitations provided by 26 U.S.C.A. § 6501 had elapsed. And thirdly, that if the treasure trove money is gross income for the year 1964, it was entitled to capital gains treatment under Section 1221 of Title 26. The Government, by its answer and its trial brief, asserts that the amount found in the piano is includable in gross income under Section 61(a) of Title 26, U.S.C.A., that the money is taxable in the year it was actually found, 1964, and that the sum is properly taxable at ordinary income rates, not being entitled to capital gains treatment under 26 U.S.C.A. §§ 1201 et seq.

After a consideration of the pertinent provisions of the Internal Revenue Code, Treasury Regulations, Revenue Rulings, and decisional law in the area, this Court has concluded that the taxpayers are not entitled to a refund of the amount requested, nor are they entitled to capital gains treatment on the income item at issue.

The starting point in determining whether an item is to be included in gross income is, of course, Section 61(a) of Title 26 U.S.C.A., and that section provides in part:

> "Except as otherwise provided in this subtitle, *gross income means all income from whatever source derived,* including (but not limited to) the following items: * * *" (Emphasis added.)

Subsections (1) through (15) of Section 61(a) then go on to list fifteen items specifically included in the computation of the taxpayer's gross income, and Part II of Subchapter B of the 1954 Code (Sections 71 et seq.) deals with other items expressly included in gross income. While neither of these listings expressly includes the type of income which is at issue in the case at bar, Part III of Subchapter B (Sections 101 et seq.) deals with items specifically *excluded* from gross income, and found money is not listed in those sections either. This absence of express mention in any of the code sections necessitates a return to the "all income from whatever source" language of Section 61(a) of the code, and the express statement there that gross income is "not limited to" the following fifteen examples. Section 1.61–1(a) of the Treasury Regulations, the corresponding section to Section 61(a) in the 1954 Code, reiterates this broad construction of gross income, providing in part:

> "Gross income means all income from whatever source derived, unless excluded by law. *Gross income includes income realized in any form,* whether in money, property, or services. * * *" (Emphasis added.)

The decisions of the United States Supreme Court have frequently stated that this broad all-inclusive language was used by Congress to exert the full measure of its taxing power under the Sixteenth Amendment to the United States Constitution. * * *

In addition, the Government in the instant case cites and relies upon an I.R.S. Revenue Ruling which is undeniably on point:

> "The finder of treasure-trove is in receipt of taxable income, for Federal income tax purposes, to the extent of its value in United States currency, for the taxable year in which it is reduced to undisputed possession." Rev.Rul. 61, 1953–1, Cum.Bull. 17.

The plaintiffs argue that the above ruling does not control this case for two reasons. The first is that subsequent to the Ruling's pronouncement in 1953, Congress enacted Sections 74 and 102 of the 1954 Code, § 74, expressly *including* the value of prizes and awards in gross income in most cases, and § 102 specifically *exempting* the value of gifts received from gross income. From this, it is argued that Section 74 was added because prizes might otherwise be construed as non-taxable gifts, and since no such section was passed expressly taxing treasure-trove, it is therefore a gift which is non-taxable under Section 102. This line of reasoning overlooks the statutory scheme previously alluded to, whereby income from all sources is taxed unless the taxpayer can point to an express exemption. Not only have the taxpayers failed to list a specific exclusion in the instant case, but also the Government *has* pointed to express language covering the found money, even though it would not be required to do so under the broad language of Section 61(a) and the foregoing Supreme Court decisions interpreting it.

The second argument of the taxpayers in support of their contention that Rev.Rul. 61, 1953–1 should not be applied in this case is based upon the decision of Dougherty v. Commissioner, 10 T.C.M. 320, P-H Memo. T.C. ¶ 51,093 (1951). In that case the petitioner was an individual who had never filed an income tax return, and the Commissioner was attempting to determine his gross income by the so-called "net worth" method. Dougherty had a substantial increase in his net worth, and attempted to partially explain away his lack of reporting it by claiming that he had found $31,000.00 in cash inside a used chair he had purchased in 1947. The Tax Court's opinion deals primarily with the factual question of whether or not Dougherty actually *did* find this money in a chair, finally concluding that he did not and from this petitioners in the instant case argue that if such found money is clearly gross income, the Tax Court would not have reached the fact question, but merely included the $31,000.00 as a matter of law. Petitioners argue that since the Tax Court did not include the sum in Dougherty's gross income until they had found as a fact that it *was not* treasure trove, then by implication such discovered money is not taxable. This argument must fail for two reasons. First, the *Dougherty* decision precedes Rev.Rul. 61, 1953–1 by two years, and thus was dealing with what then was an uncharted area of the gross income provisions of the Code. Secondly, the case cannot be read as authority for the proposition that treasure trove is not includable in gross income, even if the revenue ruling had not been issued two years later.[1]

In partial summary, then, the arguments of the taxpayers which attempt to avoid the application of Rev.Rul. 61, 1953–1 are not well taken. The *Dougherty* case simply does not hold one way or another on the problem before this Court, and therefore petitioners' reliance upon it is misplaced. The other branch of their argument, that found money must be construed to be a gift under Section 102 of the 1954 Code since it is not expressly included as are prizes in Section 74 of the Code, would not even be effective were it being urged at a time prior to 1953, when the ruling had not yet been promulgated. In addition to the numerous cases in the Supreme Court which uphold the broad sweeping construction of Section 61(a) found in Treas.Reg. § 1.61–1(a), other courts and commentators writing at a point in time before the ruling came down took the position that windfalls, including found monies, were properly includable in gross income under Section 22(a) of the 1939 Code, the predecessor of Section 61(a) in the 1954 Code. See, for example, the decision in Park & Tilford Distillers Corp. v. United States, 107 F.Supp. 941, 123 Ct.Cl. 509 (1952);[2] and Comment, "Taxation of Found Property and Other Windfalls," 20 U.Chi.L.Rev. 748, 752 (1953).[3] While it is generally true that revenue rulings may be disregarded by the courts if in conflict with the code and the regulations, or with other judicial decisions, plaintiffs in the instant case have been unable to point to any inconsistency between the gross income sections of the code, the interpretation of them by the regulations and the courts, and the revenue

---

[1]   The Dougherty Court, after carefully considering the evidence before it on the factual question of whether or not the taxpayer actually found the $31,000.00 as claimed, stated:

"In short, we do not believe the money was in the chair when the chair was acquired by the petitioner.

"Where the petitioner got the money which he later took from the chair and in what manner it was obtained by him, we do not know. It is accordingly impossible for us to conclude and hold the $31,000 here in question was not acquired by him in a manner such as would make it income to him within the meaning of the statute. Such being the case, *we do not reach the question whether money, if acquired in the manner claimed by the petitioner, is income under the statute.*" (Emphasis added.) 10 T.C.M. 320 at 323 (1951).

[2]   In this taxpayer's suit for a refund of corporation taxes, Judge Madden of the Court of Claims stated at pages 943–944: " * * * It is not, and we think could not rationally be, suggested that Congress lacks the power to tax windfalls as income. * * * A windfall may, of course, be a gift, and thus expressly exempt from income tax. But if, as in the instant case, the windfall is clearly not a gift, but a payment required by a statute * * * we do not see how its exemption could be reconciled with the reiterated statements that Congress intended, by Section 22(a), to tax income to the extent of its constitutional power." 107 F.Supp. at 943, 944.

[3]   This article, after stating arguments both ways on the question, and thus suggesting by implication that the area was not clearly defined at that time, went on to state at page 752: "Perhaps a more appropriate interpretation of Section 22(a) would be to hold that all windfalls * * * are taxable income under its sweeping language. * * * Insofar as the policy of Section 22(a) is to impose similar tax burdens on persons in similar circumstances, there is no basis for distinguishing value received as windfall and * * * value received as salary." Footnote 50 of the Comment indicates that the article was in printing when Rev.Rul. 61–53–1 came out.

ruling which they herein attack as inapplicable. On the other hand, the United States *has* shown a consistency in letter and spirit between the ruling and the code, regulations, and court decisions.

Although not cited by either party, and noticeably absent from the Government's brief, the following Treasury Regulation appears in the 1964 Regulations, the year of the return in dispute:

"§ 1.61–14 Miscellaneous items of gross income.

"(a) In general. In addition to the items enumerated in section 61(a), there are many other kinds of gross income * * * *Treasure trove, to the extent of its value in United States currency, constitutes gross income for the taxable year in which it is reduced to undisputed possession.*" (Emphasis added.)

Identical language appears in the 1968 Treasury Regulations, and is found in all previous years back to 1958. This language is the same in all material respects as that found in Rev.Rul. 61–53–1, Cum.Bull. 17, and is undoubtedly an attempt to codify that ruling into the Regulations which apply to the 1954 Code. This Court is of the opinion that Treas.Reg. § 1.61–14(a) is dispositive of the major issue in this case if the $4,467.00 found in the piano was "reduced to undisputed possession" in the year petitioners reported it, for this Regulation was applicable to returns filed in the calendar year of 1964.

This brings the Court to the second contention of the plaintiffs: that if any tax was due, it was in 1957 when the piano was purchased, and by 1964 the Government was blocked from collecting it by reason of the statute of limitations. Without reaching the question of whether the voluntary payment in 1964 constituted a *waiver* on the part of the taxpayers, this Court finds that the $4,467.00 sum was properly included in gross income for the calendar year of 1964. Problems of when title vests, or when possession is complete in the field of federal taxation, in the absence of definitive federal legislation on the subject, are ordinarily determined by reference to the law of the state in which the taxpayer resides, or where the property around which the dispute centers is located. Since both the taxpayers and the property in question are found within the State of Ohio, Ohio law must govern as to when the found money was "reduced to undisputed possession" within the meaning of Treas.Reg. § 1.61–14 and Rev.Rul. 61–53–1, Cum.Bull. 17.

In Ohio, there is no statute specifically dealing with the rights of owners and finders of treasure trove, and in the absence of such a statute the common-law rule of England applies, so that "title belongs to the finder as against all the world except the true owner." Niederlehner v. Weatherly, 78 Ohio App. 263, 69 N.E.2d 787 (1946), appeal dismissed, 146 Ohio St. 697, 67 N.E.2d 713 (1946). The *Niederlehner* case held, *inter alia,* that the owner of real estate upon which money is found does not have title as against the finder. Therefore, in the instant case if plaintiffs had resold the piano in 1958, not knowing of the money within it, they later would not be able to succeed in an action against the purchaser who *did* discover it. Under Ohio law, the plaintiffs must have actually *found* the money to have superior title over all but the true owner, and they did not discover the old currency until 1964. Unless there is present a specific state statute to the contrary,[4] the majority of jurisdictions are in accord with the Ohio rule.[5] Therefore, this Court finds that the $4,467.00 in old currency was not "reduced to undisputed possession" until its actual discovery in 1964, and thus the United States was not barred by the statute of limitations from collecting the $836.51 in tax during that year.

Finally, plaintiffs' contention that they are entitled to capital gains treatment upon the discovered money must be rejected. * * *

[This portion of the opinion is omitted. The characterization of income and its tax significance are considered in Chapter 21, infra. Ed.]

## Old Colony Trust Co. v. Commissioner

Supreme Court of the United States, 1929.
279 U.S. 716, 49 S.Ct. 499.

■ MR. CHIEF JUSTICE TAFT delivered the opinion of the Court.

William M. Wood was president of the American Woolen Company during the years 1918, 1919 and 1920. In 1918 he received as salary and commissions from the company $978,725, which he included in his federal income tax return for 1918. In 1919 he received as salary and commissions from the company $548,132.27, which he included in his return for 1919.

August 3, 1916, the American Woolen Company had adopted the following resolution, which was in effect in 1919 and 1920:

> "Voted: That this company pay any and all income taxes, State and Federal, that may hereafter become due and payable upon the salaries of all the officers of the company, including the president, William M. Wood; the comptroller, Parry C. Wiggin; the auditor, George R. Lawton; and the following members of the staff, to wit: Frank H. Carpenter, Edwin L. Heath, Samuel R. Haines, and William M. Lasbury, to the end that said persons and officers shall receive their salaries or other compensation in full without deduction on account of income taxes, State or Federal, which taxes are to be paid out of the treasury of this corporation."

This resolution was amended on March 25, 1918, as follows:

---

[4]   See, for example, United States v. Peter, 178 F.Supp. 854 (E.D.La.1959) where it is held that under the Louisiana Civil Code and the Code D'Napolean the finder of treasure does not own it, and can only become the owner if no one else can prove that the treasure is his property.

[5]   See Weeks v. Hackett, 104 Me. 264, 71 A. 858, 860 (1908) for a review of the authorities in jurisdictions where the finder is the owner as against all but the true owner. Also, see Finding Lost Goods 36A C.J.S. § 5, p. 422 (1961).

"Voted: That, in referring to the vote passed by this board on August 3, 1916, in reference to income taxes, State and Federal, payable upon the salaries or compensation of the officers and certain employees of this company, the method of computing said taxes shall be as follows, viz:

"The difference between what the total amount of his tax would be, including his income from all sources, and the amount of his tax when computed upon his income excluding such compensation or salaries paid by this company."

Pursuant to these resolutions, the American Woolen Company paid to the collector of internal revenue Mr. Wood's federal income and surtaxes due to salary and commissions paid him by the company, as follows:

Taxes for 1918 paid in 1919          $681,169.88

Taxes for 1919 paid in 1920          $351,179.27

The decision of the Board of Tax Appeals here sought to be reviewed was that the income taxes of $681,169.88 and $351,179.27 paid by the American Woolen Company for Mr. Wood were additional income to him for the years 1919 and 1920.

The question certified by the Circuit Court of Appeals for answer by this Court is:

"Did the payment by the employer of the income taxes assessable against the employee constitute additional taxable income to such employee?"

* * *

Coming now to the merits of this case, we think the question presented is whether a taxpayer, having induced a third person to pay his income tax or having acquiesced in such payment as made in discharge of an obligation to him, may avoid the making of a return thereof and the payment of a corresponding tax. We think he may not do so. The payment of the tax by the employers was in consideration of the services rendered by the employee and was a gain derived by the employee from his labor. The form of the payment is expressly declared to make no difference. Section 213, Revenue Act of 1918, c. 18, 40 Stat. 1065.[1] It is therefore immaterial that the taxes were directly paid over to the Government. The discharge by a third person of an obligation to him is equivalent to receipt by the person taxed. The certificate shows that the taxes were imposed upon the employee, that the taxes were actually paid by the employer and that the employee entered upon his duties in the years in question under the express agreement that his income taxes would be paid by his employer. This is evidenced by the terms of the

---

[1]   The legislative history of the 1954 Code makes it clear that, while § 61 omits the phrase "in whatever form paid," the definition of gross income still includes "income realized in any form." Sen.Rep. No. 1622, 83d Cong., 2d Sess. 168 (1954). Ed.

resolution passed August 3, 1916, more than one year prior to the year in which the taxes were imposed. The taxes were paid upon a valuable consideration, namely, the services rendered by the employee and as part of the compensation therefor. We think therefore that the payment constituted income to the employee.

This result is sustained by many decisions. * * *

Nor can it be argued that the payment of the tax * * * was a gift. The payment for services, even though entirely voluntary, was nevertheless compensation within the statute. This is shown by the case of Noel v. Parrott, 15 F.2d 669. There it was resolved that a gratuitous appropriation equal in amount to $3 per share on the outstanding stock of the company be set aside out of the assets for distribution to certain officers and employees of the company and that the executive committee be authorized to make such distribution as they deemed wise and proper. The executive committee gave $35,000 to be paid to the plaintiff taxpayer. The court said, p. 672:

> "In no view of the evidence, therefore, can the $35,000 be regarded as a gift. It was either compensation for services rendered, or a gain or profit derived from the sale of the stock of the corporation, or both; and, in any view, it was taxable as income."

It is next argued against the payment of this tax that if these payments by the employer constitute income to the employee, the employer will be called upon to pay the tax imposed upon this additional income, and that the payment of the additional tax will create further income which will in turn be subject to tax, with the result that there would be a tax upon a tax. This it is urged is the result of the Government's theory when carried to its logical conclusion and results in an absurdity which Congress could not have contemplated.

In the first place, no attempt has been made by the Treasury to collect further taxes, upon the theory that the payment of the additional taxes creates further income, and the question of a tax upon a tax was not before the Circuit Court of Appeals and has not been certified to this Court. We can settle questions of that sort when an attempt to impose a tax upon a tax is undertaken, but not now. * * * It is not, therefore, necessary to answer the argument based upon an algebraic formula to reach the amount of taxes due. The question in this case is, "Did the payment by the employer of the income taxes assessable against the employee constitute additional taxable income to such employee?" The answer must be "Yes."

■ [The separate opinion of MR. JUSTICE MCREYNOLDS has been omitted. Ed.]

# Commissioner v. Glenshaw Glass Co.*

Supreme Court of the United States, 1955.**
348 U.S. 426, 75 S.Ct. 473, rehearing denied, 349 U.S. 925, 75 S.Ct. 657 (1955).

■ MR. CHIEF JUSTICE WARREN delivered the opinion of the Court.

This litigation involves two cases with independent factual backgrounds yet presenting the identical issue. The two cases were consolidated for argument before the Court of Appeals for the Third Circuit and were heard *en banc*. The common question is whether money received as exemplary damages for fraud or as the punitive two-thirds portion of a treble-damage antitrust recovery must be reported by a taxpayer as gross income under § 22(a) of the Internal Revenue Code of 1939.[1] In a single opinion, 211 F.2d 928, the Court of Appeals affirmed the Tax Court's separate rulings in favor of the taxpayers. 18 T.C. 860; 19 T.C. 637. Because of the frequent recurrence of the question and differing interpretations by the lower courts of this Court's decisions bearing upon the problem, we granted the Commissioner of Internal Revenue's ensuing petition for certiorari. 348 U.S. 813, 75 S.Ct. 50.

The facts of the cases were largely stipulated and are not in dispute. So far as pertinent they are as follows:

> Commissioner v. Glenshaw Glass Co.—The Glenshaw Glass Company, a Pennsylvania corporation, manufactures glass bottles and containers. It was engaged in protracted litigation with the Hartford-Empire Company, which manufacturers machinery of a character used by Glenshaw. Among the claims advanced by Glenshaw were demands for exemplary damages for fraud[2] and treble damages for injury to its business by reason of Hartford's violation of the federal antitrust laws.[3] In December, 1947, the parties concluded a settlement of all pending litigation, by which Hartford paid Glenshaw approximately $800,000. Through a method of allocation which was approved by the Tax Court, 18 T.C. 860, 870–872, and which is no longer in issue, it was ultimately determined that, of the total settlement, $324,529.94 represented payment of punitive damages for fraud and antitrust violations. Glenshaw did not report this portion of the settlement as income for the tax year involved. The Commissioner determined a deficiency claiming as taxable the entire sum less only deductible legal

---

    *   See Wright, "The Effect of the Source of Realized Benefits upon the Supreme Court's Concept of Taxable Receipts," 8 Stan.L.Rev. 164 (1956). Ed.

    **   Some footnotes omitted.

    [1]   53 Stat. 9, 53 Stat. 574, 26 U.S.C.A. § 22(a). [See note 11, infra. Ed.]

    [2]   For the bases of Glenshaw's claim for damages from fraud, see Shawkee Manufacturing Co. v. Hartford-Empire Co., 322 U.S. 271, 64 S.Ct. 1014, Hazel-Atlas Glass Co. v. Hartford-Empire Co., 322 U.S. 238, 64 S.Ct. 997.

    [3]   See Hartford-Empire Co. v. United States, 323 U.S. 386, 65 S.Ct. 373.

fees. As previously noted, the Tax Court and the Court of Appeals upheld the taxpayer.

Commissioner v. William Goldman Theatres, Inc.—William Goldman Theatres, Inc., a Delaware corporation operating motion picture houses in Pennsylvania, sued Loew's, Inc., alleging a violation of the federal antitrust laws and seeking treble damages. After a holding that a violation had occurred, William Goldman Theatres v. Loew's, Inc., 150 F.2d 738, the case was remanded to the trial court for a determination of damages. It was found that Goldman had suffered a loss of profits equal to $125,000 and was entitled to treble damages in the sum of $375,000. William Goldman Theatres v. Loew's, Inc., 69 F.Supp. 103, aff'd, 164 F.2d 1021, cert. denied, 334 U.S. 811. Goldman reported only $125,000 of the recovery as gross income and claimed that the $250,000 balance constituted punitive damages and as such was not taxable. The Tax Court agreed, 19 T.C. 637, and the Court of Appeals, hearing this with the *Glenshaw* case, affirmed. 211 F.2d 928.

It is conceded by the respondents that there is no constitutional barrier to the imposition of a tax on punitive damages. Our question is one of statutory construction: are these payments comprehended by § 22(a)?

The sweeping scope of the controverted statute is readily apparent:

"SEC. 22. GROSS INCOME.

"(a) GENERAL DEFINITION.—'Gross income' includes gains, profits, and income derived from salaries, wages, or compensation for personal service * * * of whatever kind and in whatever form paid, or from professions, vocations, trades, businesses, commerce, or sales, or dealings in property, whether real or personal, growing out of the ownership or use of or interest in such property; also from interest, rent, dividends, securities, or the transaction of any business carried on for gain or profit, *or gains or profits and income derived from any source whatever.* * * * " (Emphasis added.)[4]

This Court has frequently stated that this language was used by Congress to exert in this field "the full measure of its taxing power." * * * Respondents contend that punitive damages, characterized as "windfalls" flowing from the culpable conduct of third parties, are not within the scope of the section. But Congress applied no limitations as to the source of taxable receipts, nor restrictive labels as to their nature. And the Court has given a liberal construction to this broad phraseology in recognition of the intention of Congress to tax all gains except those specifically exempted. * * * Thus, the fortuitous gain accruing to a lessor by reason of the forfeiture of a lessee's improvements on the rented

---

4   See note 1, supra.

property was taxed in Helvering v. Bruun, 309 U.S. 461, 60 S.Ct. 631. * * * Such decisions demonstrate that we cannot but ascribe content to the catchall provision of § 22(a), "gains or profits and income derived from any source whatever." The importance of that phrase has been too frequently recognized since its first appearance in the Revenue Act of 1913[5] to say now that it adds nothing to the meaning of "gross income."

Nor can we accept respondents' contention that a narrower reading of § 22(a) is required by the Court's characterization of income in Eisner v. Macomber, 252 U.S. 189, 207, 40 S.Ct. 189, as "the gain derived from capital, from labor, or from both combined."[6] The Court was there endeavoring to determine whether the distribution of a corporate stock dividend constituted a realized gain to the shareholder, or changed "only the form, not the essence," of his capital investment. Id., at 210. It was held that the taxpayer had "received nothing out of the company's assets for his separate use and benefit." Id., at 211. The distribution, therefore, was held not a taxable event. In that context—distinguishing gain from capital—the definition served a useful purpose. But it was not meant to provide a touchstone to all future gross income questions. * * *

Here we have instances of undeniable accessions to wealth, clearly realized, and over which the taxpayers have complete dominion. The mere fact that the payments were extracted from the wrongdoers as punishment for unlawful conduct cannot detract from their character as taxable income to the recipients. Respondents concede, as they must, that the recoveries are taxable to the extent that they compensate for damages actually incurred. It would be an anomaly that could not be justified in the absence of clear congressional intent to say that a recovery for actual damages is taxable but not the additional amount extracted as punishment for the same conduct which caused the injury. And we find no such evidence of intent to exempt these payments.

It is urged that re-enactment of § 22(a) without change since the Board of Tax Appeals held punitive damages nontaxable in Highland Farms Corp., 42 B.T.A. 1314, indicates congressional satisfaction with that holding. Re-enactment—particularly without the slightest affirmative indication that Congress ever had the Highland Farms decision before it—is an unreliable indicium at best. * * * Moreover, the Commissioner promptly published his nonacquiescence in this portion of the Highland Farms holding[7] and has, before and since, consistently

---

[5]   38 Stat. 114, 167.

[6]   The phrase was derived from Stratton's Independence, Ltd. v. Howbert, 231 U.S. 399, 415, 34 S.Ct. 136, 140, and Doyle v. Mitchell Bros. Co., 247 U.S. 179, 185, 38 S.Ct. 467, 469, two cases construing the Revenue Act of 1909, 36 Stat. 11, 112. Both taxpayers were "wasting asset" corporations, one being engaged in mining, the other in lumbering operations. The definition was applied by the Court to demonstrate a distinction between a return on capital and "a mere conversion of capital assets." Doyle v. Mitchell Bros. Co., supra, at 184. The question raised by the instant case is clearly distinguishable.

[7]   1941–1 Cum.Bull. 16.

maintained the position that these receipts are taxable.[8] It therefore cannot be said with certitude that Congress intended to carve an exception out of § 22(a)'s pervasive coverage. Nor does the 1954 Code's[9] legislative history, with its reiteration of the proposition that statutory gross income is "all-inclusive,"[10] give support to respondents' position. The definition of gross income has been simplified, but no effect upon its present broad scope was intended.[11] Certainly punitive damages cannot reasonably be classified as gifts, * * * nor do they come under any other exemption provision in the Code. We would do violence to the plain meaning of the statute and restrict a clear legislative attempt to bring the taxing power to bear upon all receipts constitutionally taxable were we to say that the payments in question here are not gross income. * * *

Reversed.

■ MR. JUSTICE DOUGLAS dissents.

■ MR. JUSTICE HARLAN took no part in the consideration or decision of this case.

## Charley v. Commissioner*
United States Court of Appeals, Ninth Circuit, 1996.
91 F.3d 72.

■ Before: FARRIS, O'SCANNLAIN, and TASHIMA.

### OPINION

■ O'SCANNLAIN, CIRCUIT JUDGE:

Do travel credits converted to cash in a personal travel account established by an employer constitute gross income to the employee for federal income tax purposes?

### I

Dr. Philip Charley and his wife Katherine Charley appeal the tax court's determination of an income tax deficiency for tax year 1988 in the

---

[8]  The long history of departmental rulings holding personal injury recoveries nontaxable on the theory that they roughly correspond to a return of capital cannot support exemption of punitive damages following injury to property. See 2 Cum.Bull. 71; I–1 Cum.Bull. 92, 93; VII–2 Cum.Bull. 123; 1954–1 Cum.Bull. 179, 180. Damages for personal injury are by definition compensatory only. Punitive damages, on the other hand, cannot be considered a restoration of capital for taxation purposes.

[9]  68A Stat. 3 et seq. Section 61(a) of the Internal Revenue Code of 1954, 68A Stat. 17, is the successor to § 22(a) of the 1939 Code.

[10]  H.R.Rep. No. 1337, 83d Cong., 2d Sess. A18; S.Rep. No. 1622, 83d Cong., 2d Sess. 168.

[11]  In discussing § 61(a) of the 1954 Code, the House Report states:

"This section corresponds to section 22(a) of the 1939 Code. While the language in existing section 22(a) has been simplified, the all-inclusive nature of statutory gross income has not been affected thereby. Section 61(a) is as broad in scope as section 22(a).

"Section 61(a) provides that gross income includes 'all income from whatever source derived.' This definition is based upon the 16th Amendment and the word 'income' is used in its constitutional sense." H.R.Rep. No. 1337, supra, note 10, at A18.

A virtually identical statement appears in S.Rep. No. 1622, supra, note 10, at 168.

*  Footnotes omitted.

amount of $882 and an addition to tax of $44 pursuant to Internal Revenue code ("IRC") § 6653. We affirm on the merits and reverse the penalty.

During 1988, Truesdail Laboratories ("Truesdail") engaged in the testing business, including testing urine for horse racing activities and investigating the causes of industrial accidents. Philip was the President of Truesdail and, together with Katherine, owned 50.255% of its shares. Philip performed various services for Truesdail including inspecting mechanical devices suspected of failure.

Philip, in his capacity as an employee of Truesdail, traveled to various accident sites to inspect machinery. Truesdail had an "unwritten policy" that the frequent flyer miles that were earned during an employee's travel for Truesdail became the sole property of the employee.

During the year at issue, the following procedures were followed by Truesdail with respect to Philip's travel:

(1) A client would engage the services of Truesdail and would direct that Philip travel to a particular accident site;

(2) If Philip chose to travel to the site by air, Truesdail would bill the client for round-trip, first class air travel;

(3) Philip would instruct a travel agent, Archer Travel Services ("Archer"), to arrange for coach service to and from the site, but to charge Truesdail for first class travel;

(4) Philip then would use his frequent flyer miles (largely earned in connection with his business travel for Truesdail) to upgrade the coach ticket to first class; and

(5) Philip would instruct Archer to transfer funds to his personal travel account amounting to the difference in price between the first class ticket for which Truesdail was charged and the coach ticket, albeit upgraded, which Philip actually used.

Over the course of 1988, Archer maintained separate travel accounts for Philip and Truesdail. Philip took four business trips that year, and using the procedures outlined above, received $3,149.93 in his personal travel account from his "sale" of the frequent flyer miles.

The parties stipulated that Philip and Katherine did not know that the receipt of the travel credits was taxable income, and that they did not intend to conceal the process utilized to obtain the travel credits.

The tax court held that the travel credits constituted taxable income.

* * *

## II

The statute at issue, I.R.C. § 61, provides that gross income "means all income from whatever source derived." Gross income has been defined as an "undeniable accession[ ] to wealth, clearly realized and over which

*Constitutional decision* [handwritten annotation]

the taxpayer[ ] [has] complete dominion." *Commissioner v. Glenshaw*, 348 U.S. 426, 431 (1955). The tax court noted that there was no indication Philip could not use the travel credits for personal travel or redeem them for cash. Consequently, the tax court upheld the IRS' determination of deficiency on the ground that:

> Whether we regard this fact situation as a straight "rip-off" by petitioner of his employer or a highly technical "sale" of his frequent flyer miles (which have zero basis) for the credits, the fact remains that petitioner was wealthier after the transaction than before. In such circumstances, the accretion of wealth is the receipt of income.

The Charleys do not dispute the tax court's finding that travel credits were Philip's to use for personal travel. Nor do they dispute the tax court's conclusion that Philip had sole control over the credits in his account. Rather, the Charleys argue that no taxable event occurred. We find this argument unpersuasive.

The Charleys argue that this case raises the question of whether, in the abstract, frequent flyer miles constitute gross income. We disagree and do not reach that issue.

As the tax court noted, the case can be analyzed in one of two ways. First, the travel credits which were converted to cash can be characterized as additional compensation. On this view, Philip received property from his employer in the form of an account upon which he could draw up to $3,149.93, which he did. This is so because Truesdail paid for first-class airfare and allowed Archer to credit Philip's account with the difference between the first-class price and the coach price. The funds constituting the difference came from Truesdail; Philip consequently received compensation in the amount of $3,149.93 from his employer. The fact that the travel credits were exchanged for frequent flyer miles simply is not relevant to the analysis.

In the alternative, if it is assumed that the frequent flyer miles were not given to Philip by Truesdail, but belonged to him all along, then the transaction can be viewed as a disposition of his own property. Gross income includes "[g]ains derived from dealings in property." I.R.C. § 61(a)(3). A gain from the disposition of property is equal to the "amount realized" from the disposition minus the property's adjusted basis. I.R.C. § 1001(a). The amount realized from a disposition of property is the sum of any money received plus the fair market value of the property (other than money) received. I.R.C. § 1001(b). The adjusted basis is generally determined by reference to cost. I.R.C. § 1012.

Because Philip received the frequent flyer miles at no cost, he had a basis of zero. He then exchanged his frequent flyer miles for cash, resulting in a gain of $3,149.93 (the fair market value of the property received minus the adjusted basis of zero).

* * *

In sum, we hold that the tax court was correct in concluding that the travel credits under the fact of this case constituted taxable income.

\* \* \*

## NOTE

The Supreme Court in *Glenshaw Glass* attempts to define gross income or at least to indicate some criteria for gross income[1] when it refers to "undeniable accessions to wealth, clearly realized, and over which the taxpayers have complete dominion." Within these requirements, do borrowers have income on the receipt of loans? Clearly not; loans are based on concurrently acknowledged obligations to repay which, offsetting the receipt, negate any accession to wealth.[2] A security deposit may be likened to a loan for tax purposes. In Commissioner v. Indianapolis Power & Light Company,[3] the Supreme Court concluded that the contractual arrangement between the customers and the power company cast the deposit as a loan to the company. Of course if the borrower has no intent to repay a "loan" and the lender is unaware of that fact, the "loan" is not a loan but an illegal appropriation of the would-be creditor's property, which is income to the so-called borrower under Section 61.[4]

At one time the line between loans and illegal income was difficult to draw. Initially, in Commissioner v. Wilcox[5] the Supreme Court did not tax embezzlers, because they could be compelled by victims to return the property involved. It analogized embezzlers to borrowers who, as suggested above, achieved no accession to wealth. Would a burglar's status be the same? Later in Rutkin v. U.S.,[6] the Court distinguished the receipts of an extortionist from those of an embezzler on the ground that an extortionist is less likely to be asked for repayment, taxing that kind of illegal loot. Still later, however, in James v. U.S.[7] the Court overruled *Wilcox* outright, deciding that illegal gain is income despite a legal obligation to make restitution.[8]

Beginning students in income taxation, or anyone else for that matter, may reasonably question whether gross income includes wealth acquired by illegal means, but the Supreme Court has left little doubt. Supplying an

---

[1]   In other opinions the Supreme Court has not attempted an all-encompassing definition of gross income. See, for example, Commissioner v. Wilcox, 327 U.S. 404, 407, 66 S.Ct. 546, 548–549 (1946).

[2]   Lorenzo C. Dilks, 15 B.T.A. 1294 (1929); William H. Stayton, Jr., 32 B.T.A. 940 (1935).

[3]   493 U.S. 203, 110 S.Ct. 589 (1990).

[4]   United States v. Rochelle, 384 F.2d 748 (5th Cir.1967), cert. denied 390 U.S. 946, 88 S.Ct. 1032 (1968).

[5]   Note 1, supra.

[6]   343 U.S. 130, 72 S.Ct. 571 (1952).

[7]   366 U.S. 213, 81 S.Ct. 1052 (1961).

[8]   The series of cases is discussed in Libin and Haydon, "Embezzled Funds as Taxable Income: A Study in Judicial Footwork," 61 Mich.L.Rev. 425 (1963) and Bittker, "Taxing Income from Unlawful Activities," 25 Case West.L.Rev. 130 (1974).

affirmative answer in *James,* the Court provided the following convenient summary of the area:[9]

> It had been a well-established principle * * * that unlawful, as well as lawful gains are comprehended within the term "gross income". Section 11B of the Income Tax Act of 1913 provided that "the net income of a taxable person shall include gains, profits, and income * * * from * * * the transaction of any *lawful* business carried on for gain or profit, or gains or profits and income derived from any source whatever. * * *" (Emphasis supplied.) 38 Stat. 167. When the statute was amended in 1916, the one word "lawful" was omitted. This revealed, we think, the obvious intent of that Congress to tax income derived from both legal and illegal sources, to remove the incongruity of having the gains of the honest laborer taxed and the gains of the dishonest immune. * * * Thereafter, the Court held that gains from illicit traffic in liquor are includible within "gross income". Ibid. * * * And, the Court has pointed out, with approval, that there "has been a widespread and settled administrative and judicial recognition of the taxability of unlawful gains of many kinds" * * * These include protection payments made to racketeers, ransom payments paid to kidnappers, bribes, money derived from the sale of unlawful insurance policies, graft, black market gains, funds obtained from the operation of lotteries, income from race track bookmaking and illegal prize fight pictures. Ibid.[10]

The taxation of illegal gains has caused some interesting results. It was the evasion of income tax laws and not a conviction of murder, robbery, or some similar crime that led to the conviction and imprisonment of gangster Al Capone in 1931.[11] A taxpayer's attempt to create some black letter law (bathed perhaps in red light) failed when the Tax Court said, in effect: Madame, the wages of sin are not exempt from taxation![12] One judge who disagreed with treating illegal pilfering the same as legal profiting was Judge Martin Manton of the Second Circuit Court of Appeals who felt such action was degrading to the government.[13] Ironically, the same Judge Manton was later held liable for tax on bribes accepted to influence his decisions,[14] after having been convicted,[15] imprisoned and disbarred for accepting the bribes. The Commissioner has been successful in taxing some scurrilous swindlers. In Akers v. Scofield[16] an ingenious scheme involving

---

[9]   Note 7, supra at 218, 81 S.Ct. at 1054. See also Reg. § 1.61–14.

[10]   Reporting of such gains can raise important 5th Amendment self-incrimination questions. See United States v. Sullivan, 274 U.S. 259, 47 S.Ct. 607 (1927), and Chapter 28A3.

[11]   See Bittker, note 8, supra.

[12]   Blanche E. Lane, 15 T.C.M. 1088 (1956).

[13]   The argument was offered in his concurring opinion in Steinberg v. United States, 14 F.2d 564, 569 (2d Cir.1926).

[14]   Martin T. Manton, T.C.M. 48262 (1948). Judge Manton's philosophy is considered in greater detail in the Bittker article cited note 8, supra.

[15]   United States v. Manton, 107 F.2d 834 (2d Cir.1939), cert. denied 309 U.S. 664, 60 S.Ct. 590 (1940).

[16]   167 F.2d 718 (5th Cir.1948), cert. denied 335 U.S. 823, 69 S.Ct. 47 (1948).

maps, hidden "gold" bars, and an intrigued and probably greedy widow was successful up to a point but hit the fiscal fan when the Commissioner successfully taxed the swindler's proceeds. In a more timely vein, the Commissioner has been successful in taxing gains on the illegal sale of narcotics.[17]

Although the judicial opinions speak in terms of the question whether an illegal receipt is gross income and, if so, when, a third dimension of this problem is less often expressed. If a pickpocket's daily take is gross income, his failure to report it ultimately on his Form 1040 is itself a crime.[18] And it is of course a federal crime. One wonders therefore how much a desire to add a federal sanction to existing state sanctions for various offenses may affect the seeming effort to define and time the receipt of gross income.

## PROBLEMS

1.  Would the results to the taxpayers in the *Cesarini* case be different if, instead of discovering $4,467 in old currency in the piano, they discovered that the piano, a Steinway, was the first Steinway piano ever built and it is worth $500,000?

2.  Winner attends the opening of a new department store. All persons attending are given free raffle tickets for a watch worth $200. Disregarding any possible application of I.R.C. § 74, must Winner include anything within gross income when she wins the watch in the raffle?

3.  Employee has worked for Employer's incorporated business for several years at a salary of $80,000 per year. Another company is attempting to hire Employee but Employer persuades Employee to agree to stay for at least two more years by giving Employee 2% of the company's stock, which is worth $100,000, and by buying Employee's spouse a new car worth $30,000. How much income does Employee realize from these transactions?

4.  Insurance Adjuster refers clients to an auto repair firm that gives Adjuster a kickback of 10% of billings on all referrals.

    (a)  Does Adjuster have gross income?

    (b)  Even if the arrangement violates local law?

5.  Owner agrees to rent Tenant her lake house for the summer for $4,000.

    (a)  How much income does Owner realize if she agrees to charge only $1,000 if Tenant makes $3,000 worth of improvements to the house?

    (b)  Is there a difference in result to Owner in (a), above, if Tenant effects exactly the same improvements but does all the labor himself and incurs a total cost of only $500?

    (c)  Are there any tax consequences to Tenant in part (b), above?

6.  Flyer receives frequent flyer mileage credits in the following situations. Should Flyer have gross income?

---

17  Farina v. McMahon, 58–2 U.S.T.C. ¶ 9938 (1958).

18  See, e.g., I.R.C. §§ 7201 and 7206.

(a)     Flyer receives the mileage credits as a part of a purchase of ticket for a personal trip. The credits are assignable.

(b)     Flyer receives credits from the airline for business flights paid for by Employer. The credits are assignable.

(c)     Flyer receives the credits under the circumstances of (b), above, but they are nonassignable.

(d)     Same as (c), above, except Flyer uses the nonassignable credits to take a trip.

(e)     Flyer opens a bank account, receives 50,000 "thank you points" from Bank, and redeems the points for a flight valued at $650.

## C. INCOME WITHOUT RECEIPT OF CASH OR PROPERTY

Internal Revenue Code: Section 61.

Regulations: Sections 1.61–2(a)(1), –2(d)(1).

---

## Helvering v. Independent Life Ins. Co.*

Supreme Court of the United States, 1934.
292 U.S. 371, 54 S.Ct. 758.

[This case raised the question whether a taxpayer must include in gross income the rental value of a building owned and occupied by the taxpayer. Whether or not the statute purported to subject that value to the income tax, it was the taxpayer's position that such a tax was foreclosed by Article I, § 9, cl. 4 of the Constitution, which requires the apportionment of direct taxes. See the discussion of basic constitutional principles in Chapter 1C. The Court sustained this position, saying in part:]

If the statute lays taxes on the part of the building occupied by the owner or upon the rental value of that space, it cannot be sustained, for that would be to lay a direct tax requiring apportionment. * * * The rental value of the building used by the owner does not constitute income within the meaning of the Sixteenth Amendment.

## Revenue Ruling 79–24

1979–1 Cum.Bull. 60.

FACTS

*Situation 1.* In return for personal legal services performed by a lawyer for a housepainter, the housepainter painted the lawyer's personal residence. Both the lawyer and the housepainter are members of a barter club, an organization that annually furnishes its members a

---

    *    See Bittker & Lokken, Federal Taxation of Income, Estates and Gifts ¶ 5.3 (Warren, Gorham & Lamont), for a discussion of imputed income. Ed.

directory of members and the services they provide. All the members of the club are professional or trades persons. Members contact other members directly and negotiate the value of the services to be performed.

*Situation 2.* An individual who owned an apartment building received a work of art created by a professional artist in return for the rent-free use of an apartment for six months by the artist.

LAW

The applicable sections of the Internal Revenue Code of 1954 and the Income Tax Regulations thereunder are 61(a) and 1.61–2, relating to compensation for services.

Section 1.61–2(d)(1) of the regulations provides that if services are paid for other than in money the fair market value of the property or services taken in payment must be included in income. If the services were rendered at a stipulated price, such price will be presumed to be the fair market value of the compensation received in the absence of evidence to the contrary.

HOLDINGS

*Situation 1.* The fair market value of the services received by the lawyer and the housepainter are includible in their gross incomes under section 61 of the Code.

*Situation 2.* The fair market value of the work of art and the six months fair rental value of the apartment are includible in the gross incomes of the apartment-owner and the artist under section 61 of the Code.

# Dean v. Commissioner

United States Court of Appeals, Third Circuit, 1951.
187 F.2d 1019.

■ GOODRICH, CIRCUIT JUDGE.

This appeal from the Tax Court raises the question of the correctness of a claim for income tax against the taxpayer based on the rental value of property held in the name of a corporation of which the taxpayer and his wife are the sole shareholders. The facts are simple and undisputed.

The taxpayer and his wife are the sole shareholders in a personal holding company called the Nemours Corporation. The wife owns 80% of the stock. The real estate which is the subject matter of this controversy was owned by the taxpayer's wife prior to her marriage. She and the taxpayer continued to occupy it after their marriage and the taxpayer's wife expended and has continued to expend appreciable sums in keeping up and beautifying the property. In 1931 the Nemours Corporation was indebted to a bank for a large sum. The bank insisted that the residence property above mentioned be transferred to the corporation. This was done. The parties continued to occupy the place as a home following the transfer. The taxpayer was in military service during the late war, but received from the corporation the difference between his military pay and the salary he had previously received. He also shared in the occupancy of the home at such times as he was free to do so.

The Commissioner takes the position that the fair rental value of the residence property is to be included in the taxpayer's gross income under the general provisions of Section 22 of the Internal Revenue Code, 26 U.S.C.A. § 22. The Tax Court agreed with the Commissioner. We do likewise. Although the taxpayer endeavors to distinguish it, we think our decision in Chandler v. Commissioner, 3 Cir., 1941, 119 F.2d 623, governs this case and the discussion therein is, for the most part, applicable here. It was the taxpayer's legal obligation to provide a family home and if he did it by the occupancy of a property which was held in the name of a corporation of which he was president, we think the fair value of that occupancy was income to him.

The fact that the corporation was simply a means by which the taxpayer and his wife carried on certain business activities does not change the case. We have no reason for thinking that the corporate existence was anything but bona fide. And we think that the real estate deeded to the corporation would clearly have been held to belong to it had the bank had occasion, which it did not, to take advantage of the corporation's title to the property. Our position is not based upon any thought that there is in this case any suggestion of tax evasion or avoidance. It is instead based upon taxpayer's valuable occupation of the corporation real estate.

The decision of the Tax Court will be affirmed.

## PROBLEMS

1. Vegy grows vegetables in her garden. Does Vegy have gross income when:

    (a) Vegy harvests her crop?

    (b) Vegy and her family consume $100 worth of vegetables?

    (c) Vegy sells vegetables for $100?

    (d) Vegy exchanges $100 worth of vegetables with Charlie for $100 worth of tuna which Charlie caught?

2. Doctor needs to have his income tax return prepared. Lawyer would like a general physical check up. Doctor would normally charge $200 for the physical and Lawyer would normally charge $200 for the income tax return preparation.

    (a) What tax consequences to each if they simply swap services without any money changing hands?

    (b) Does Lawyer realize any income when she fills out her own tax return?

# CHAPTER 3

# THE EXCLUSION OF GIFTS AND INHERITANCES

## A. RULES OF INCLUSION AND EXCLUSION

Internal Revenue Code: Section 102(a) and (b) first sentence.

Regulations: Sections 1.102–1(a), (b).

---

As Chapter 2 illustrates, gross income is a very broad concept. Over the years, numerous administrative and judicial decisions have gone a long way toward delineating its scope. Nevertheless, partly because of past uncertainties and partly because of a desire to accord special treatment for some types of receipts or benefits, Congress has been unwilling to rely on gross income, unexplained or only generally defined, as the starting point in the computation of federal income tax liability. Instead, two series of sections have undertaken to say that certain items are specifically includable in gross income, or partially includable, Sections 71–91, and other items are specifically excludable from gross income, or partially excludable, Sections 101–139G. As cases such as *Cesarini* and *Glenshaw Glass* set out in Chapter 2 indicate, these special statutory rules do not purport to be exhaustive; some questions remain to be answered without special statutory help under the general definition of gross income in Section 61. But of course when an explicit statutory provision is applicable it takes precedence over the general definition. For example, interest is an illustration of an item of gross income specified in Section 61(a)(4), but according to Section 103(a) gross income does not include interest on some State and local bonds. In the materials that follow, be sure to differentiate exclusions from gross income from deductions which are considered later in the Text and are available in determining taxable income and which have a similar, but not identical, effect.

It is not possible to present a definition of gross income that will answer all questions which may arise. But here is a kind of checklist that may be helpful and which will be more meaningful as the study of gross income progresses:

Gross income includes the receipt of any financial benefit which is:

1.  Not a mere return of capital, and

2.  Not accompanied by a contemporaneously acknowledged obligation to repay, and

3.  Not excluded by a specific statutory provision.

A comparatively simple, long-standing exclusionary rule is found in Section 102. We begin with it. It often comes as a surprise to a taxpayer who has grown accustomed to the income tax bite to learn that when Uncle Harry died and left her securities worth $10,000 the amount will not appear at all on her Form 1040. The section may safely be read fairly literally and is as generous as it sounds. Could and should Congress tax such receipts as income?[1]

Of course if the securities received subsequently produce dividends for the taxpayer, the dividends must be treated as income. Perhaps redundantly, the statute makes this clear in Section 102(b)(1).

Somewhat less certain at an earlier time was the taxpayer's status if Uncle Harry left her the right only to the income from securities, perhaps by way of a trust under which the securities themselves were to be retained for a remainderperson who would get them upon the taxpayer's death. In the famous case of Irwin v. Gavit,[2] the Supreme Court held, in effect, that language such as now appears in Section 102(a), excluding from gross income property acquired by bequest, did not exclude a gift *of the income* from property. A codification of that principle now appears in Section 102(b)(2).

Some other questions that arise in the application of Section 102 are considered in the materials that follow in this chapter.

## B. GIFTS

### 1. THE INCOME TAX MEANING OF GIFT

Internal Revenue Code: Section 102(a).

---

## Commissioner v. Duberstein*

Supreme Court of the United States, 1960.
363 U.S. 278, 80 S.Ct. 1190.

■ MR. JUSTICE BRENNAN delivered the opinion of the Court.

These two cases concern the provision of the Internal Revenue Code which excludes from the gross income of an income taxpayer "the value of property acquired by gift."[1] They pose the frequently recurrent question whether a specific transfer to a taxpayer in fact amounted to a

---

[1]   See Oliver and Peel, Tax Policy Readings and Materials, Ch. 9, Income Tax Treatment of Property Transferred at Death or by Gift (Found.Press 1996); Hudson, "Tax Policy and the Federal Taxation of Transfer of Wealth," 19 Willamette L.Rev. 1 (1983); Dodge, "Beyond Estate and Gift Tax Reform: Including Gifts and Bequests in Income," 91 Harv.L.Rev. 1177 (1978).

[2]   268 U.S. 161, 45 S.Ct. 475 (1925).

*   See Klein, "An Enigma in the Federal Income Tax: The Meaning of the Word 'Gift'," 48 Minn.L.Rev. 215 (1963). Ed.

[1]   The operative provision in the cases at bar is § 22(b)(3) of the 1939 Internal Revenue Code. The corresponding provision of the present Code is § 102(a).

"gift" to him within the meaning of the statute. The importance to decision of the facts of the cases requires that we state them in some detail.

No. 376, Commissioner v. Duberstein. The taxpayer, Duberstein,[2] was president of the Duberstein Iron & Metal Company, a corporation with headquarters in Dayton, Ohio. For some years the taxpayer's company had done business with Mohawk Metal Corporation, whose headquarters were in New York City. The president of Mohawk was one Berman. The taxpayer and Berman had generally used the telephone to transact their companies' business with each other, which consisted of buying and selling metals. The taxpayer testified, without elaboration, that he knew Berman "personally" and had known him for about seven years. From time to time in their telephone conversations, Berman would ask Duberstein whether the latter knew of potential customers for some of Mohawk's products in which Duberstein's company itself was not interested. Duberstein provided the names of potential customers for these items.

One day in 1951 Berman telephoned Duberstein and said that the information Duberstein had given him had proved so helpful that he wanted to give the latter a present. Duberstein stated that Berman owed him nothing. Berman said that he had a Cadillac as a gift for Duberstein, and that the latter should send to New York for it; Berman insisted that Duberstein accept the car, and the latter finally did so, protesting however that he had not intended to be compensated for the information. At the time Duberstein already had a Cadillac and an Oldsmobile, and felt that he did not need another car. Duberstein testified that he did not think Berman would have sent him the Cadillac if he had not furnished him with information about the customers. It appeared that Mohawk later deducted the value of the Cadillac as a business expense on its corporate income tax return.

Duberstein did not include the value of the Cadillac in gross income for 1951, deeming it a gift. The Commissioner asserted a deficiency for the car's value against him, and in proceedings to review the deficiency the Tax Court affirmed the Commissioner's determination. It said that "The record is significantly barren of evidence revealing any intention on the part of the payor to make a gift. * * * The only justifiable inference is that the automobile was intended by the payor to be remuneration for services rendered to it by Duberstein." The Court of Appeals for the Sixth Circuit reversed. 265 F.2d 28.

No. 546, Stanton v. United States. The taxpayer, Stanton, had been for approximately 10 years in the employ of Trinity Church in New York City. He was comptroller of the Church corporation, and president of a corporation, Trinity Operating Company, the church set up as a fully

---

[2] In both cases the husband will be referred to as the taxpayer, although his wife joined with him in joint tax returns.

owned subsidiary to manage its real estate holdings, which were more extensive than simply the church property. His salary by the end of his employment there in 1942 amounted to $22,500 a year. Effective November 30, 1942, he resigned from both positions to go into business for himself. The Operating Company's directors, who seem to have included the rector and vestrymen of the church, passed the following resolution upon his resignation: "Be it Resolved that in appreciation of the services rendered by Mr. Stanton * * * a gratuity is hereby awarded to him of Twenty Thousand Dollars, payable to him in equal instalments of Two Thousand Dollars at the end of each and every month commencing with the month of December, 1942; provided that, with the discontinuance of his services, the Corporation of Trinity Church is released from all rights and claims to pension and retirement benefits not already accrued up to November 30, 1942."

The Operating Company's action was later explained by one of its directors as based on the fact that, "Mr. Stanton was liked by all of the Vestry personally. He had a pleasing personality. He had come in when Trinity's affairs were in a difficult situation. He did a splendid piece of work, we felt. Besides that * * * he was liked by all of the members of the Vestry personally." And by another: "[W]e were all unanimous in wishing to make Mr. Stanton a gift. Mr. Stanton had loyally and faithfully served Trinity in a very difficult time. We thought of him in the highest regard. We understood that he was going in business for himself. We felt that he was entitled to that evidence of good will."

On the other hand, there was a suggestion of some ill-feeling between Stanton and the directors, arising out of the recent termination of the services of one Watkins, the Operating Company's treasurer, whose departure was evidently attended by some acrimony. At a special board meeting on October 28, 1942, Stanton had intervened on Watkins' side and asked reconsideration of the matter. The minutes reflect that "resentment was expressed as to the 'presumptuous' suggestion that the action of the Board, taken after long deliberation, should be changed." The Board adhered to its determination that Watkins be separated from employment, giving him an opportunity to resign rather than be discharged. At another special meeting two days later it was revealed that Watkins had not resigned; the previous resolution terminating his services was then viewed as effective; and the Board voted the payment of six months' salary to Watkins in a resolution similar to that quoted in regard to Stanton, but which did not use the term "gratuity." At the meeting, Stanton announced that in order to avoid any such embarrassment or question at any time as to his willingness to resign if the Board desired, he was tendering his resignation. It was tabled, though not without dissent. The next week, on November 5, at another special meeting, Stanton again tendered his resignation which this time was accepted.

The "gratuity" was duly paid. So was a smaller one to Stanton's (and the Operating Company's) secretary, under a similar resolution, upon her resignation at the same time. The two corporations shared the expense of the payments. There was undisputed testimony that there were in fact no enforceable rights or claims to pension and retirement benefits which had not accrued at the time of the taxpayer's resignation, and that the last proviso of the resolution was inserted simply out of an abundance of caution. The taxpayer received in cash a refund of his contributions to the retirement plans, and there is no suggestion that he was entitled to more. He was required to perform no further services for Trinity after his resignation.

The Commissioner asserted a deficiency against the taxpayer after the latter had failed to include the payments in question in gross income. After payment of the deficiency and administrative rejection of a refund claim, the taxpayer sued the United States for a refund in the District Court for the Eastern District of New York. The trial judge, sitting without a jury, made the simple finding that the payments were a "gift,"[3] and judgment was entered for the taxpayer. The Court of Appeals for the Second Circuit reversed. 268 F.2d 727.

The Government, urging that clarification of the problem typified by these two cases was necessary, and that the approaches taken by the Court of Appeals for the Second and Sixth Circuits were in conflict, petitioned for certiorari in No. 376, and acquiesced in the taxpayer's petition in No. 546. On this basis, and because of the importance of the question in the administration of the income tax laws, we granted certiorari in both cases. 361 U.S. 923, 80 S.Ct. 291.

The exclusion of property acquired by gift from gross income under the federal income tax laws was made in the first income tax statute[4] passed under the authority of the Sixteenth Amendment, and has been a feature of the income tax statutes ever since. The meaning of the term "gift" as applied to particular transfers has always been a matter of contention.[5] Specific and illuminating legislative history on the point does not appear to exist. Analogies and inferences drawn from other revenue provisions, such as the estate and gift taxes, are dubious. * * * The meaning of the statutory term has been shaped largely by the decisional law. With this, we turn to the contentions made by the Government in these cases.

*First.* The Government suggests that we promulgate a new "test" in this area to serve as a standard to be applied by the lower courts and by the Tax Court in dealing with the numerous cases that arise.[6] We reject

---

[3]   See note 14, infra.

[4]   II.B., c.16, 38 Stat. 167.

[5]   The first case of the Board of Tax Appeals officially reported in fact deals with the problem. Parrott v. Commissioner, 1 B.T.A. 1.

[6]   The Government's proposed test is stated: "Gifts should be defined as transfers of property made for personal as distinguished from business reasons."

this invitation. We are of opinion that the governing principles are necessarily general and have already been spelled out in the opinions of this Court, and that the problem is one which, under the present statutory framework, does not lend itself to any more definitive statement that would produce a talisman for the solution of concrete cases. The cases at bar are fair examples of the settings in which the problem usually arises. They present situations in which payments have been made in a context with business overtones—an employer making a payment to a retiring employee; a businessman giving something of value to another businessman who has been of advantage to him in his business. In this context, we review the law as established by the prior cases here.

The course of decision here makes it plain that the statute does not use the term "gift" in the common-law sense but in a more colloquial sense. This Court has indicated that a voluntary executed transfer of his property by one to another, without any consideration or compensation therefor, though a common-law gift, is not necessarily a "gift" within the meaning of the statute. For the Court has shown that the mere absence of a legal or moral obligation to make such a payment does not establish that it is a gift. Old Colony Trust Co. v. Commissioner, 279 U.S. 716, 730, 49 S.Ct. 499, 504. And, importantly, if the payment proceeds primarily from "the constraining force of any moral or legal duty," or from "the incentive of anticipated benefit" of an economic nature, * * * it is not a gift. And, conversely, "[w]here the payment is in return for services rendered, it is irrelevant that the donor derives no economic benefit from it." Robertson v. United States, 343 U.S. 711, 714, 72 S.Ct. 994, 996.[7] A gift in the statutory sense, on the other hand, proceeds from a "detached and disinterested generosity," * * * "out of affection, respect, admiration, charity or like impulses." * * * And in this regard, the most critical consideration, as the Court was agreed in the leading case here, is the transferor's "intention." Bogardus v. Commissioner, 302 U.S. 34, 43, 58 S.Ct. 61, 65. "What controls is the intention with which payment, however voluntary, has been made." Id., 302 U.S. at 45, 58 S.Ct. at 66 (dissenting opinion).[8]

The Government says that this "intention" of the transferor cannot mean what the cases on the common-law concept of gift call "donative intent." With that we are in agreement, for our decisions fully support

---

[7] The cases including "tips" in gross income are classic examples of this. See, e.g., Roberts v. Commissioner, 176 F.2d 221.

[8] The parts of the *Bogardus* opinion which we touch on here are the ones we take to be basic to its holding, and the ones that we read as stating those governing principles which it establishes. As to them we see little distinction between the views of the Court and those taken in dissent in *Bogardus*. The fear expressed by the dissent at 302 U.S., at 44, 58 S.Ct., at 66, that the prevailing opinion "seems" to hold "that every payment which in any aspect is a gift is * * * relieved of any tax" strikes us now as going beyond what the opinion of the Court held in fact. In any event, the Court's opinion in *Bogardus* does not seem to have been so interpreted afterwards. The principal difference, as we see it, between the Court's opinion and the dissent lies in the weight to be given the findings of the trier of fact.

this. Moreover, the *Bogardus* case itself makes it plain that the donor's characterization of his action is not determinative—that there must be an objective inquiry as to whether what is called a gift amounts to it in reality. * * * It scarcely needs adding that the parties' expectations or hopes as to the tax treatment of their conduct in themselves have nothing to do with the matter.

It is suggested that the *Bogardus* criterion would be more apt if rephrased in terms of "motive" rather than "intention." We must confess to some skepticism as to whether such a verbal mutation would be of any practical consequence. We take it that the proper criterion, established by decision here, is one that inquires what the basic reason for his conduct was in fact—the dominant reason that explains his action in making the transfer. Further than that we do not think it profitable to go.

*Second.* The Government's proposed "test," while apparently simple and precise in its formulation, depends frankly on a set of "principles" or "presumptions" derived from the decided cases, and concededly subject to various exceptions; and it involves various corollaries, which add to its detail. Were we to promulgate this test as a matter of law, and accept with it various presuppositions and stated consequences, we would be passing far beyond the requirements of the cases before us, and would be painting on a large canvas with indeed a broad brush. The Government derives its test from such propositions as the following: That payments by an employer to an employee, even though voluntary, ought, by and large, to be taxable; that the concept of a gift is inconsistent with a payment's being a deductible business expense; that a gift involves "personal" elements; that a business corporation cannot properly make a gift of its assets. The Government admits that there are exceptions and qualifications to these propositions. We think, to the extent they are correct, that these propositions are not principles of law but rather maxims of experience that the tribunals which have tried the facts of cases in this area have enunciated in explaining their factual determinations. Some of them simply represent truisms: it doubtless is, statistically speaking, the exceptional payment by an employer to an employee that amounts to a gift. Others are over-statements of possible evidentiary inferences relevant to a factual determination on the totality of circumstances in the case: it is doubtless relevant to the over-all inference that the transferor treats a payment as a business deduction, or that the transferor is a corporate entity. But these inferences cannot be stated in absolute terms. Neither factor is a shibboleth. The taxing statute does not make nondeductibility by the transferor a condition on the "gift" exclusion; nor does it draw any distinction, in terms, between transfers by corporations and individuals, as to the availability of the "gift" exclusion to the transferee. The conclusion whether a transfer amounts to a "gift" is one that must be reached on consideration of all the factors.

Specifically, the trier of fact must be careful not to allow trial of the issue whether the receipt of a specific payment is a gift to turn into a trial of the tax liability, or of the propriety, as a matter of fiduciary or corporate law, attaching to the conduct of someone else. The major corollary to the Government's suggested "test" is that, as an ordinary matter, a payment by a corporation cannot be a gift, and, more specifically, there can be no such thing as a "gift" made by a corporation which would allow it to take a deduction for an ordinary and necessary business expense. As we have said, we find no basis for such a conclusion in the statute; and if it were applied as a determinative rule of "law," it would force the tribunals trying tax cases involving the donee's liability into elaborate inquiries into the local law of corporations or into the peripheral deductibility of payments as business expenses. The former issue might make the tax tribunals the most frequent investigators of an important and difficult issue of the laws of the several States, and the latter inquiry would summon one difficult and delicate problem of federal tax law as an aid to the solution of another.[9] Or perhaps there would be required a trial of the vexed issue whether there was a "constructive" distribution of corporate property, for income tax purposes, to the corporate agents who had sponsored the transfer.[10] These considerations, also, reinforce us in our conclusion that while the principles urged by the Government may, in non-absolute form as crystallizations of experience, prove persuasive to the trier of facts in a particular case, neither they, nor any more detailed statement than has been made, can be laid down as a matter of law.

*Third.* Decision of the issue presented in these cases must be based ultimately on the application of the fact-finding tribunal's experience with the mainsprings of human conduct to the totality of the facts of each case. The nontechnical nature of the statutory standard, the close relationship of it to the data of practical human experience, and the multiplicity of relevant factual elements, with their various combinations, creating the necessity of ascribing the proper force to each, confirm us in our conclusion that primary weight in this area must be given to the conclusions of the trier of fact.[11] * * *

---

[9] Justice Cardozo once described in memorable language the inquiry into whether an expense was an "ordinary and necessary" one of a business:

"One struggles in vain for any verbal formula that will supply a ready touchstone. The standard set up by the statute is not a rule of law; it is rather a way of life. Life in all its fullness must supply the answer to the riddle." Welch v. Helvering, 290 U.S. 111, 115, 54 S.Ct. 8, 9.

The same comment well fits the issue in the cases at bar.

[10] Cf., e.g., Nelson v. Commissioner, 203 F.2d 1.

[11] In *Bogardus,* the Court was divided 5 to 4 to the scope of review to be extended the fact-finder's determination as to a specific receipt, in a context like that of the instant cases. The majority held that such a determination was "a conclusion of law or at least a determination of a mixed question of law and fact." 302 U.S., at 39, 58 S.Ct. at 64. This formulation it took as justifying it in assuming a fairly broad standard of review. The dissent took a contrary view. The approach of this part of the Court's ruling in *Bogardus,* which we think was the only part on which there was real division among the Court, see note 8, supra, has not been afforded

This conclusion may not satisfy an academic desire for tidiness, symmetry and precision in this area, any more than a system based on the determinations of various fact-finders ordinarily does. But we see it as implicit in the present statutory treatment of the exclusion for gifts, and in the variety of forums in which federal income tax cases can be tried. If there is fear of undue uncertainty or overmuch litigation, Congress may make more precise its treatment of the matter by singling out certain factors and making them determinative of the matter, as it has done in one field of the "gift" exclusion's former application, that of prizes and awards.[12] Doubtless diversity of result will tend to be lessened somewhat since federal income tax decisions, even those in tribunals of first instance turning on issues of fact, tend to be reported, and since there may be a natural tendency of professional triers of fact to follow one another's determinations, even as to factual matters. But the question here remains basically one of fact, for determination on a case-by-case basis.

One consequence of this is that appellate review of determinations in this field must be quite restricted. Where a jury has tried the matter upon correct instructions, the only inquiry is whether it cannot be said that reasonable men could reach differing conclusions on the issue. * * * Where the trial has been by a judge without a jury, the judge's findings must stand unless "clearly erroneous." Fed.Rules Civ.Proc., 52(a). "A finding is 'clearly erroneous' when although there is evidence to support it, the reviewing court on the entire evidence is left with the definite and firm conviction that a mistake has been committed." * * * The rule itself applies also to factual inferences from undisputed basic facts, * * * as will on many occasions be presented in this area. * * * And Congress has in the most explicit terms attached the identical weight to the findings of the Tax Court. I.R.C. § 7482(a).[13]

subsequent respect here. In *Heininger,* a question presenting at the most elements no more factual and untechnical than those here—that of the "ordinary and necessary" nature of a business expense—was treated as one of fact. Cf. note 9, supra. And in Dobson v. Commissioner, 320 U.S. 489, 498, n. 22, 64 S.Ct. 239, 245, *Bogardus* was adversely criticized, insofar as it treated the matter as reviewable as one of law. While *Dobson* is, of course, no longer the law insofar as it ordains a greater weight to be attached to the findings of the Tax Court than to those of any other fact-finder in a tax litigation, see note 13, infra, we think its criticism of this point in the *Bogardus* opinion is sound in view of the dominant importance of factual inquiry to decision of these cases.

[12] I.R.C. § 74, which is a provision new with the 1954 Code. Previously, there had been holdings that such receipts as the "Pot O' Gold" radio giveaway, Washburn v. Commissioner, 5 T.C. 1333, and the Ross Essay Prize, McDermott v. Commissioner, 80 U.S.App.D.C. 176, 150 F.2d 585, were "gifts." Congress intended to obviate such rulings. S.Rep. No. 1622, 83d Cong., 2d Sess., p. 178. We imply no approval of those holdings under the general standard of the "gift" exclusion. Cf. Robertson v. United States, supra.

[13] "The United States Courts of Appeals shall have exclusive jurisdiction to review the decisions of the Tax Court * * * in the same manner and to the same extent as decisions of the district courts in civil actions tried without a jury. * * *" The last words first came into the statute through an amendment to § 1141(a) of the 1939 Code in 1948 (§ 36 of the Judicial Code Act, 62 Stat. 991). The purpose of the 1948 legislation was to remove from the law the favored position (in comparison with District Court and Court of Claims rulings in tax matters) enjoyed by the Tax Court under this Court's ruling in Dobson v. Commissioner, 320 U.S. 489, 64 S.Ct. 239. Cf. note 11, supra. See Grace Bros., Inc. v. Commissioner, 173 F.2d 170, 173.

*Fourth.* A majority of the Court is in accord with the principles just outlined. And, applying them to the *Duberstein* case, we are in agreement, on the evidence we have set forth, that it cannot be said that the conclusion of the Tax Court was "clearly erroneous." It seems to us plain that as trier of the facts it was warranted in concluding that despite the characterization of the transfer of the Cadillac by the parties and the absence of any obligation, even of a moral nature, to make it, it was at bottom a recompense for Duberstein's past services, or an inducement for him to be of further service in the future. We cannot say with the Court of Appeals that such a conclusion was "mere suspicion" on the Tax Court's part. To us it appears based in the sort of informed experience with human affairs that fact-finding tribunals should bring to this task.

As to *Stanton,* we are in disagreement. To four of us, it is critical here that the District Court as trier of fact made only the simple and unelaborated finding that the transfer in question was a "gift."[14] To be sure, conciseness is to be strived for, and prolixity avoided, in findings; but, to the four of us, there comes a point where findings become so sparse and conclusory as to give no revelation of what the District Court's concept of the determining facts and legal standard may be. * * * Such conclusory, general findings do not constitute compliance with Rule 52's direction to "find the facts specially and state separately * * * conclusions of law thereon." While the standard of law in this area is not a complex one, we four think the unelaborated finding of ultimate fact here cannot stand as a fulfillment of these requirements. It affords the reviewing court not the semblance of an indication of the legal standard with which the trier of fact has approached his task. For all that appears, the District Court may have viewed the form of the resolution or the simple absence of legal consideration as conclusive. While the judgment of the Court of Appeals cannot stand, the four of us think there must be further proceedings in the District Court looking toward new and adequate findings of fact. In this, we are joined by Mr. Justice Whittaker, who agrees that the findings were inadequate, although he does not concur generally in this opinion.

Accordingly, in No. 376, the judgment of this Court is that the judgment of the Court of Appeals is reversed, and in No. 546, that the judgment of the Court of Appeals is vacated, and the case is remanded to the District Court for further proceedings not inconsistent with this opinion.

It is so ordered.

---

[14] The "Findings of Fact and Conclusions of Law" were made orally, and were simply: "The resolution of the Board of Directors of the Trinity Operating Company, Incorporated, held November 19, 1942, after the resignations had been accepted of the plaintiff from his positions as controller of the corporation of the Trinity Church, and the president of the Trinity Operating Company, Incorporated, whereby a gratuity was voted to the plaintiff, Allen [*sic*] D. Stanton, in the amount of $20,000 payable to him in monthly installments of $2,000 each, commencing with the month of December, 1942, constituted a gift to the taxpayer, and therefore need not have been reported by him as income for the taxable years 1942, or 1943."

■ [Concurring and dissenting opinions of MESSRS. JUSTICE HARLAN, WHITTAKER, DOUGLAS and BLACK have been omitted. Ed.]

■ MR. JUSTICE FRANKFURTER, concurring in the judgment in No. 376 and dissenting in No. 546, [said in part:]

\* \* \*

The Court has made only one authoritative addition to the previous course of our decisions. Recognizing Bogardus v. Commissioner, 302 U.S. 34, 58 S.Ct. 61, as "the leading case here" and finding essential accord between the Court's opinion and the dissent in that case, the Court has drawn from the dissent in *Bogardus* for infusion into what will now be a controlling qualification, recognition that it is "for the triers of the facts to seek among competing aims or motives the ones that dominated conduct." 302 U.S. 34, 45, 58 S.Ct. 61, 66 (dissenting opinion). All this being so in view of the Court, it seems to me desirable not to try to improve what has "already been spelled out" in the opinions of this Court but to leave to the lower courts the application of old phrases rather than to float new ones and thereby inevitably produce a new volume of exegesis on the new phrases.

Especially do I believe this when fact-finding tribunals are directed by the Court to rely upon their "experience with the mainsprings of human conduct" and on their "informed experience with human affairs" in appraising the totality of the facts of each case. Varying conceptions regarding the "mainsprings of human conduct" are derived from a variety of experiences or assumptions about the nature of man, and "experience with human affairs," is not only diverse but also often drastically conflicting. What the Court now does sets fact-finding bodies to sail on an illimitable ocean of individual beliefs and experiences. This can hardly fail to invite, if indeed not encourage, too individualized diversities in the administration of the income tax law. I am afraid that by these new phrasings the practicalities of tax administration, which should be as uniform as is possible in so vast a country as ours, will be embarrassed. By applying what has already been spelled out in the opinions of this Court, I agree with the Court in reversing the judgment in Commissioner v. Duberstein.

But I would affirm the decision of the Court of Appeals for the Second Circuit in Stanton v. United States.

\* \* \*

## NOTE

The Supreme Court's decision in *Duberstein* agrees with the trial court's (Tax Court's) decision in the case. The Court holds that the question whether a transfer of money or property constitutes a gift within the exclusion of Section 102(a) is an issue of fact to be determined by the trial court trier of fact. In Stanton v. U.S., the Supreme Court considered the findings of fact, as determined by the district court sitting without a jury, to be inadequate.

The case was therefore remanded. The district court, on remand with more detailed findings of facts, held that Stanton had received a gift,[1] and the court of appeals affirmed.[2]

Recall that in the *Duberstein* opinion, the Supreme Court expressly refused to lay down a test for determining whether a payment or transfer of property constitutes a gift, aware that its "conclusion may not satisfy an academic desire for tidiness, symmetry and precision in this area * * *".[3] However, earlier in its opinion, the Court, quoting language from some of its own decisions handed down many years ago involving this same issue, gratuitously said: "A gift in the statutory sense * * * proceeds from a 'detached and disinterested generosity,' * * * 'out of affection, respect, admiration, charity or like impulses' * * *, the most critical consideration * * * is the transferor's 'intention'."[4] Perhaps the message was not intended as the formulation of criteria. But even so, it is a test of sorts, and the lower courts use those criteria in resolving the factual controversy of gift or no gift in cases decided subsequent to *Duberstein*.[5]

## PROBLEMS

**1.** Our system of self-assessment requires the taxpayer to make the initial determination of gift or income, and tax administration procedures give the Commissioner the power to challenge that decision. If a judicial controversy develops, why is the decision of the trial court so important, and what role may an appellate court play?

**2.** At the Heads Eye Casino in Vegas, Lucky Louie gives the maître d' a $50 tip to assure a good table, and gives the croupier a $50 "toke" after a good night with the cubes. Does either the maître d' or the croupier have gross income?

## 2. EMPLOYEE GIFTS

Internal Revenue Code: Sections 102(c); 274(b). See Sections 74(c); 132(e); 274(j).

Proposed Regulations: Section 1.102–1(f).

---

At one time, many cases turned on the possible application of the "gift" exclusion to transfers between persons in employer-employee relationships. Such cases typically arose on a payment or property transfer by an employer in one of three general contexts: to an employee

---

[1]   186 F.Supp. 393 (E.D.N.Y.1960).
[2]   United States v. Stanton, 287 F.2d 876 (2d Cir.1961).
[3]   Commissioner v. Duberstein, 363 U.S. 278, 290, 80 S.Ct. 1190, 1199 (1960); see page 66, supra.
[4]   Id. at 285, 80 S.Ct. at 1197; see page 70, supra.
[5]   E.g. Max Kralstein, 38 T.C. 810 (1962); acq., 1963–2 C.B. 3.

during an ongoing employment relationship;[1] to an employee upon or after retirement;[2] and to survivors upon the death of an employee.[3]

The issue in these cases was whether the recipient had gross income as a result of the purported "gift".[4] In the years involved, Section 102 did not address specifically whether a transfer by an employer to an employee could be a gift.[5] Section 102(c) was later added to the Code as an exception to the broad exclusionary rule of Section 102(a).[6] The message of Section 102(c)(1) is fairly straight forward. An employee "shall not exclude from gross income any amount transferred by or for an employer to, or for the benefit of, an employee."[7] The legislative history makes no specific mention of Section 102(c) and it mentions Section 102 only in passing, as follows:[8]

> Except to the extent that the new section 74(c) exclusion or section 132(e) applies, the fair market value of an employee award (whether or not satisfying the definition of an employee achievement award) is includible in the employee's gross income under section 61, and is not excludible under section 74 (as amended by the bill) or section 102 (gifts).

While legislative history is lacking, the statute seems to indicate a broad congressional intent to deny "gift" classification to all transfers by employers to employees. The regulations recognize that to tax "all" transfers from an employer to an employee would be unfair, and they carve out an exception for "extraordinary transfers to the natural objects of an employer's bounty * * * if the employee can show that the transfer was not made in recognition of the employee's employment."[9]

As the legislative history quoted above reports, there are two additional limited exceptions to the Section 102(c) inclusion rule. First, under Section 132(e) certain traditional retirement gifts are treated as de minimis fringe benefits; and second, under Section 74(c) certain employee achievement awards are freed from tax. Both exceptions are examples of a specific statutory rule of exclusion overriding a broader

---

[1]    See Fisher v. Commissioner, 59 F.2d 192 (2d Cir.1932); Painter v. Campbell, 110 F.Supp. 503 (N.D.Tex.1953).

[2]    See Hubert v. Commissioner, 212 F.2d 516 (5th Cir.1954); Commissioner v. Duberstein, 363 U.S. 278, 80 S.Ct. 1190 (1960).

[3]    See Bausch's Estate v. Commissioner, 186 F.2d 313 (2d Cir.1951); Bounds v. United States, 262 F.2d 876 (4th Cir.1958), and United States v. Allinger, 275 F.2d 421 (6th Cir.1960).

[4]    For example, see Fisher, supra note 1, in which the United States Court of Appeals, Second Circuit, rejected contentions that a $6,000 payment by an employer to the taxpayer, made because "it would do something for" the employee, actually was a gift and not compensation for services.

[5]    See I.R.C. § 102.

[6]    Pub.Law. No. 99–514, 99th Cong., 2d Sess. § 112(b) (1986).

[7]    I.R.C. § 102(c)(1).

[8]    Sen.Rep. No. 99–313, 99th Cong., 2d Sess. 53 (1986).

[9]    Prop. Reg. § 1.102–1(f)(2).

statutory rule of inclusion and both are considered in upcoming chapters.[10]

Section 274(b)(1) generally limits the deductible amount of business gifts to $25 per donee per year,[11] but it defines the term "gift", with minor exceptions, as items excludable from the recipient's gross income under Section 102. As employee "gifts" now are includible in gross income under Section 102(c),[12] they are not subject to the Section 274(b)(1) ceiling. That ceiling is applicable only to non-employee business gifts.

## PROBLEMS

1.    Employer gives all of her employees, except her son, a case of wine at Christmas, worth $120. She gives Son, who also is an employee, a case of wine, worth $700. Does Son have gross income?

2.    The congregation for whom Reverend serves as a minister gives her a check for $5,000 on her retirement. Does Reverend have gross income?

3.    Employee receives a $5,000 trip on Employee's 50th birthday. To pay for the cost of the trip, Employer contributed $2,000, and fellow employees of Employee contributed $3,000. Does Employee have gross income?

## C.  BEQUESTS, DEVISES, AND INHERITANCES

Internal Revenue Code: Section 102(a), (b) first sentence, (c).

Regulations: Section 1.102–1(a), (b).

---

## Lyeth v. Hoey

Supreme Court of the United States, 1938.
305 U.S. 188, 59 S.Ct. 155.

■ MR. CHIEF JUSTICE HUGHES delivered the opinion of the Court.

The question presented is whether property received by petitioner from the estate of a decedent in compromise of his claim as an heir is taxable as income under the Revenue Act of 1932.

Petitioner is a grandson of Mary B. Longyear who died in 1931, a resident of Massachusetts, leaving as her heirs four surviving children and the petitioner and his brother, who were sons of a deceased daughter. By her will, the decedent gave to her heirs certain small legacies and the entire residuary estate, amounting to more than $3,000,000, was bequeathed to trustees of a so-called Endowment Trust, created April 5, 1926, the income from which was payable to another set of trustees under another trust described as the Longyear Foundation. The main purpose

---

[10]   See respectively Chapters 4 and 5, infra.

[11]   Although discussion of deductions generally comes later in the Text in Chapters 14 through 18, infra, consideration of the deductibility of business gifts is relevant here.

[12]   I.R.C. § 102(c).

of the latter trust was to preserve "the records of the earthly life of Mary Baker Eddy," the founder of the Christian Science religion.

When the will was offered for probate in Massachusetts there was objection by the heirs upon the grounds, among others, of lack of testamentary capacity and undue influence. After hearing, at which a statement was made by the respective parties of their proposed evidence, the probate court granted a motion for the framing of issues for trial before a jury. In that situation a compromise agreement was entered into between the heirs, the legatees, the devisees and the executors under the will, and the Attorney General of Massachusetts. This agreement provided that the will should be admitted to probate and letters testamentary issued; that the specific and pecuniary bequests to individuals should be enforced; that the bequest of the residuary estate to the Endowment Trust should be disregarded; that $200,000 should be paid to the heirs and a like amount to the Endowment Trust, and that the net residue of the estate, as defined, should be equally divided between the trustees of the Endowment Trust and the heirs. The net residue to which the heirs were thus entitled was to be payable in units of stock owned by the decedent in certain corporations, Longyear Estate, Inc., Longyear Corporation and Longyear Realty Corporation, and for that purpose a unit was to consist of three shares, one share of each corporation.

The compromise was approved by the probate court pursuant to a statute of Massachusetts * * * and a decree was entered on April 26, 1932, admitting the will to probate, issuing letters testamentary to the executors and directing them "to administer the estate of said deceased in accordance with the terms of said will and said agreement of compromise." Owing to the Depression and the necessity of discharging pecuniary legacies amounting to about $300,000, which were entitled to priority in payment before distribution of the residue, the heirs undertook to finance one-half of these legacies and the residuary legatees the other one-half. For this purpose the heirs formed a corporation known as Longyear Heirs, Inc., to which they assigned their interests in the estate in exchange for common stock. Preferred stock was issued to the pecuniary legatees.

In July, 1933, the executors distributed to Longyear Heirs, Inc., as assignee of the petitioner, his distributable share of the estate, consisting of $80.17 in cash and a certificate of deposit for 358 units, each unit representing one share of each of the three corporations mentioned in the compromise agreement. The Commissioner of Internal Revenue valued this distributable share at $141,484.03 and treated the whole amount as income for the year 1933 in which it was received. An additional tax of $56,389.65 was assessed, which petitioner paid in October, 1936, with interest. Claim for refund was then filed and on its rejection this suit was brought against the collector.

On motion of petitioner the District Court entered a summary judgment in his favor, 20 F.Supp. 619, which the Circuit Court of Appeals reversed. 96 F.2d 141. Because of a conflict with the decision of the Circuit Court of Appeals of the Fourth Circuit in Magruder v. Segebade, 94 F.2d 177, certiorari was granted.

The Court of Appeals overruled the contentions of petitioner that the property he received was within the statutory exemption (§ 22(b)(3) of the Revenue Act of 1932) and, further, that the property was not income either under the statute or under the Sixteenth Amendment of the Federal Constitution. As the view of the Court of Appeals upon these questions determined the rights of the parties, it was found unnecessary to discuss certain affirmative defenses set up by the answer of the respondent and these defenses are not pressed in this court.

*First.* By § 22(b)(3) of the Revenue Act of 1932, there is exempted from the income tax—

"The value of property acquired by gift, bequest, devise, or inheritance. * * *"

Whether property received by an heir from the estate of his ancestor is acquired by inheritance, when it is distributed under an agreement settling a contest by the heir of the validity of the decedent's will, is a question upon which state courts have differed. The question has arisen in the application of state laws of taxation. In Massachusetts, the rule is that when a will is admitted to probate under a compromise agreement, the state succession tax is applied to the property "that passes by the terms of the will as written and not as changed by any agreement for compromise." * * * Although under the Massachusetts statute relating to compromise[1] it is the practice to insert a clause in the court's decree that the estate is to be administered in accordance with the agreement, "yet the rights of the parties so far as they rest upon the agreement are contractual and not testamentary." * * * Thus, when a contest was withdrawn under a compromise and the residuary estate was divided equally between the legatee and the heirs, it was held that the tax was properly levied upon the entire residuary legacy and that the administrators with the will annexed had no right to pay out of the share transferred to the heirs one-half of the tax thus collectible from the legatee unless the compromise agreement expressly or impliedly so provided. * * * Several States have a similar rule.[2] In other States the amount received by an heir under an agreement compromising a contest of his ancestor's will is considered to be received by virtue of his heirship and is subject to an inheritance tax unless the statute exempts him.[3]

In the instant case, the Court of Appeals applied the Massachusetts rule, holding that whether the property was received by way of

---

[1]   Massachusetts General Laws 1932, Chap. 204, §§ 13–18.

[2]   [Citations omitted. Ed.]

[3]   [Citations omitted. Ed.]

inheritance depended "upon the law of the jurisdiction under which this taxpayer received it." We think that this ruling was erroneous. The question as to the construction of the exemption in the federal statute is not determined by local law. We are not concerned with the peculiarities and special incidences of state taxes or with the policies they reflect. Undoubtedly the state law determines what persons are qualified to inherit property within the jurisdiction. * * * The local law determines the right to make a testamentary disposition of such property and the conditions essential to the validity of wills, and the state courts settle their construction. * * * The State establishes the procedure governing the probate of wills and the processes of administration. Petitioner's status as heir was thus determined by the law of Massachusetts. That law also regulated the procedure by which his rights as an heir could be vindicated. The state law authorized its courts to supervise the making of agreements compromising contests by heirs of the validity of an alleged will of their ancestor, in order that such compromises shall be just and reasonable with respect to all persons in interest.[4] But when the contestant is an heir and a valid compromise agreement has been made and there is a distribution to the heir from the decedent's estate accordingly, the question whether what the heir has thus received has been "acquired by inheritance" within the meaning of the federal statute necessarily is a federal question. It is not determined by local characterization.

In dealing with the meaning and application of an act of Congress enacted in the exercise of its plenary power under the Constitution to tax income and to grant exemptions from that tax, it is the will of Congress which controls, and the expression of its will, in the absence of language evidencing a different purpose, should be interpreted "so as to give a uniform application to a nationwide scheme of taxation." * * * Congress establishes its own criteria and the state law may control only when the federal taxing act by express language or necessary implication makes its operation dependent upon state law. * * * There is no such expression or necessary implication in this instance. Whether what an heir receives from the estate of his ancestor through the compromise of his contest of his ancestor's will should be regarded as within the exemption from the federal tax should not be decided in one way in the case of an heir in Pennsylvania or Minnesota and in another way in the case of an heir in Massachusetts or New York,[5] according to the differing views of the state courts. We think that it was the intention of Congress in establishing this exemption to provide a uniform rule.

*Second.* In exempting from the income tax the value of property acquired by "bequest, devise, or inheritance," Congress used comprehensive terms embracing all acquisitions in the devolution of a

---

4   See Note 1. Such agreements are "entirely valid outside of the statute." Ellis v. Hunt, 228 Mass. 39, 44, 116 N.E. 956.

5   See Notes 2 and 3.

decedent's estate. For the word "descent," as used in the earlier acts,[6] Congress substituted the word "inheritance" in the 1926 Act and the subsequent revenue acts as "more appropriately including both real and personal property."[7] Thus the acquisition by succession to a decedent's estate whether real or personal was embraced in the exemption. Further, by the "estate tax," Congress has imposed a tax upon the transfer of the entire net estate of every person dying after September 8, 1916,[8] allowing such exemptions as it sees fit in arriving at the net estate. Congress has not indicated any intention to tax again the value of the property which legatees, devisees or heirs receive from the decedent's estate.

Petitioner was concededly an heir of his grandmother under the Massachusetts statute. It was by virtue of that heirship that he opposed probate of her alleged will which constituted an obstacle to the enforcement of his right. Save as heir he had no standing. Seeking to remove that obstacle, he asserted that the will was invalid because of want of testamentary capacity and undue influence. In accordance with local practice, he asked the probate court to frame these issues for a jury trial. It then became necessary for him to satisfy the court that the issues were substantial. Issues are not to be framed unless it appears from statements by counsel of expected evidence or otherwise that there is a "genuine question of fact supported by evidence of such a substantial nature as to afford ground for reasonable expectation of a result favorable to the party requesting the framing of issues." * * * Petitioner satisfied that condition and the probate court directed the framing of jury issues. It was in that situation, facing a trial of the issue of the validity of the will, that the compromise was made by which the heirs, including the petitioner, were to receive certain portions of the decedent's estate.

There is no question that petitioner obtained that portion, upon the value of which he is sought to be taxed, because of his standing as an heir and of his claim in that capacity. It does not seem to be questioned that if the contest had been fought to a finish and petitioner had succeeded, the property which he would have received would have been exempt under the federal act. Nor is it questioned that if in any appropriate proceeding, instituted by him as heir, he had recovered judgment for a part of the estate, that part would have been acquired by inheritance within the meaning of the act. We think that the distinction sought to be made between acquisition through such a judgment and acquisition by a compromise agreement in lieu of such a judgment is too formal to be sound, as it disregards the substance of the statutory exemption. It does so, because it disregards the heirship which underlay the compromise, the status which commanded that agreement and was recognized by it. While the will was admitted to probate, the decree also required the

---

[6]   See Act of October 3, 1913, c. 16, § II, 38 Stat. 167; Revenue Acts of 1918, 1921 and 1924, § 213(b)(3).

[7]   Revenue Act of 1926, § 213(b)(3); Acts of 1928 and 1932, § 22(b)(3). Sen.Rep. No. 52, 69th Cong., 1st Sess., p. 20.

[8]   Act of September 8, 1916, c. 463, Title II, 39 Stat. 777.

distribution of the estate in accordance with the compromise and, so far as the latter provided for distribution to the heirs, it overrode the will. So far as the will became effective under the agreement it was because of the heirs' consent and release and in consideration of the distribution they received by reason of their being heirs. Respondent agrees that the word "inheritance" as used in the federal statute is not solely applicable to cases of complete intestacy. The portion of the decedent's property which petitioner obtained under the compromise did not come to him through the testator's will. That portion he obtained because of his heirship and to that extent he took in spite of the will and as in case of intestacy. The fact that petitioner received less than the amount of his claim did not alter its nature or the quality of its recognition through the distribution which he did receive.

We are not convinced by the argument that petitioner had but "the expectations" of an heir and realized on a "bargaining position." He was heir in fact. Whether he would receive any property in that capacity depended upon the validity of his ancestor's will and the extent to which it would dispose of his ancestor's estate. When, by compromise and the decree enforcing it, that disposition was limited, what he got from the estate came to him because he was heir, the compromise serving to remove *pro tanto* the impediment to his inheritance. We are of the opinion that the exemption applies.

In this view we find it unnecessary to consider the other questions that have been discussed at the bar.

The judgment of the Circuit Court of Appeals is reversed and that of the District Court is affirmed.

Reversed.

## Wolder v. Commissioner[*]

United States Court of Appeals, Second Circuit, 1974.
493 F.2d 608.

■ OAKES, CIRCUIT JUDGE:

These two cases, involving an appeal and cross-appeal in the individual taxpayers' case and an appeal by the Commissioner in the estate taxpayer's case, essentially turn on one question: whether an attorney contracting to and performing lifetime legal services for a client receives income when the client, pursuant to the contract, bequeaths a substantial sum to the attorney in lieu of the payment of fees during the client's lifetime. In the individual taxpayer's case, the Tax Court held that the fair market value of the stock and cash received under the client's will constituted taxable income under § 61, Int.Rev.Code of 1954, and was not exempt from taxation as a bequest under § 102 of the Code.

* See Kemp, "Federal Tax Aspects of Will Contests," 23 U.Miami L.Rev. 72 (1968); Schenk, "Tax Effects of Will Contests and Compromises," 10 Tulane Tax Inst. 214 (1961). Ed.

From this ruling the individual taxpayers, Victor R. Wolder, the attorney, and his wife, who signed joint returns, appeal.

\* \* \*

There is no basic disagreement as to the facts. On or about October 3, 1947, Victor R. Wolder, as attorney, and Marguerite K. Boyce, as client, entered into a written agreement which, after reciting Mr. Wolder's past services on her behalf in an action against her ex-husband for which he had made no charge, consisted of mutual promises, first on the part of Wolder to render to Mrs. Boyce "such legal services as she shall in her opinion personally require from time to time as long as both \* \* \* shall live and not to bill her for such services," and second on the part of Mrs. Boyce to make a codicil to her last will and testament giving and bequeathing to Mr. Wolder or to his estate "my 500 shares of Class B common stock of White Laboratories, Inc." or "such other \* \* \* securities" as might go to her in the event of a merger or consolidation of White Laboratories. Subsequently, in 1957, White Laboratories did merge into Schering Corp. and Mrs. Boyce received 750 shares of Schering common and 500 shares of Schering convertible preferred. In 1964 the convertible preferred was redeemed for $15,845. In a revised will dated April 23, 1965, Mrs. Boyce, true to the agreement with Mr. Wolder, bequeathed to him or his estate the sum of $15,845 and the 750 shares of common stock of Schering Corp. There is no dispute but that Victor R. Wolder had rendered legal services to Mrs. Boyce over her lifetime (though apparently these consisted largely of revising her will) and had not billed her therefor so that he was entitled to performance by her under the agreement, on which she had had a measure of independent legal advice. At least the New York Surrogate's Court (DiFalco, J.) ultimately so found in contested proceedings in which Mrs. Boyce's residuary legatees contended that the will merely provided for payment of a debt and took the position that Wolder was not entitled to payment until he proved the debt in accordance with § 212, New York Surrogate's Court Act.[1]

\* \* \*

Wolder argues that the legacy he received under Mrs. Boyce's will is specifically excluded from income by virtue of § 102(a), Int.Rev.Code of 1954, which provides that "Gross Income does not include the value of property acquired by gift, bequest, devise or inheritance \* \* \*" See also Treas.Reg. 1.102–1(a). The individual taxpayer, as did dissenting Judge Quealy below, relies upon United States v. Merriam, 263 U.S. 179, 44 S.Ct. 69 (1923), and its progeny for the proposition that the term "bequest" in § 102(a) has not been restricted so as to exclude bequests made on account of some consideration flowing from the beneficiary to the decedent. In *Merriam* the testator made cash bequests to certain

---

[1] Subsequently another surrogate held that the estate would not be obligated under the so-called tax clause in Mrs. Boyce's will to reimburse Mr. Wolder for any income tax payable by him by reason of the bequest made to him in accordance with the 1947 contract.

persons who were named executors of the estate, and these bequests were "in lieu of all compensation or commissions to which they would otherwise be entitled as executors or trustees." 263 U.S. at 184, 44 S.Ct. at 70. The Court held nevertheless that the legacies were exempt from taxation, drawing a distinction—which in a day and age when we look to substance and not to form strikes us as of doubtful utility—between cases where "compensation [is] fixed by will for services to be rendered by the executor and [where] a legacy [is paid] to one upon the implied condition that he shall clothe himself with the character of executor." 263 U.S. at 187, 44 S.Ct. at 71. In the former case, Mr. Justice Sutherland said, the executor "must perform the services to earn the compensation" while in the latter case "he need do no more than in good faith comply with the condition [that he be executor] in order to receive the bequest." The Court went on to take the view that the provision in the will that the bequest was in lieu of commissions was simply "an expression of the testator's will that the executor shall not receive statutory allowances for the services he may render." While the distinction drawn in the Merriam case hardly stands economic analysis, Bank of New York v. Helvering, 132 F.2d 773 (2d Cir.1943), follows it on the basis that it is controlling law.[2]

* * *

But we think that Merriam is inapplicable to the facts of this case, for here there is no dispute but that the parties did contract for services and—while the services were limited in nature—there was also no question but that they were actually rendered. Thus the provisions of Mrs. Boyce's will, at least for federal tax purposes, went to satisfy her obligation under the contract. The contract in effect was one for the postponed payment of legal services, i.e., by a legacy under the will for services rendered during the decedent's life.

Moreover, the Supreme Court itself has taken an entirely different viewpoint from Merriam when it comes to interpreting § 102(a), or its predecessor, § 22(b)(3), Int.Rev.Code of 1939, in reference to what are gifts. In Commissioner v. Duberstein, 363 U.S. 278, 80 S.Ct. 1190 (1960), the Court held that the true test is whether in actuality the gift is a bona fide gift or simply a method for paying compensation. This question is resolved by an examination of the intent of the parties, the reasons for the transfer, and the parties' performance in accordance with their intentions—"what the basic reason for [the donor's] conduct was in fact—the dominant reason that explains his action in making the transfer." * * * There are other cases holding testamentary transfers to be taxable

___

[2] One also doubts the present day validity of the underlying philosophical premise of Merriam, that "If the words are doubtful, the doubt must be resolved against the government and in favor of the taxpayer." 263 U.S. at 188, 44 S.Ct. at 71. In White v. United States, 305 U.S. 281, 292, 59 S.Ct. 179, 184 (1938), after noting for the majority that it was not "impressed" by this very argument, Mr. Justice Stone said, "It is the function and duty of courts to resolve doubts. We know of no reason why that function should be abdicated in a tax case more than in any other where the rights of suitors turn on the construction of a statute and it is our duty to decide what that construction fairly should be."

compensation for services as opposed to tax-free bequests. * * * True, in each of these cases the testator did not fulfill his contractual obligation to provide in his will for payment of services rendered by the taxpayer, forcing the taxpayers to litigate the merits of their claims against the estates, whereas in the case at bar the terms of the contract were carried out. This is a distinction without a difference, and while we could decline to follow them in the case at bar, we see no reason to do so.

Indeed, it is to be recollected that § 102 is, after all, an exception to the basic provision in § 61(a) that "Except as otherwise provided in this subtitle, gross income means all income from whatever source derived, including * * * (1) Compensation for services, including fees, commissions and similar items * * *." The congressional purpose is to tax income comprehensively. * * * A transfer in the form of a bequest was the method that the parties chose to compensate Mr. Wolder for his legal services, and that transfer is therefore subject to taxation, whatever its label whether by federal or by local law may be. * * *

Taxpayer's argument that he received the stock and cash as a "bequest" under New York law and the decisions of the surrogates is thus beside the point. New York law does, of course, control as to the extent of the taxpayer's legal rights to the property in question, but it does not control as to the characterization of the property for federal income tax purposes. * * * New York law cannot be decisive on the question whether any given transfer is income under § 61(a) or is exempt under § 102(a) of the Code. We repeat, we see no difference between the transfer here made in the form of a bequest and the transfer under Commissioner v. Duberstein, supra, which was made without consideration, with no legal or moral obligation, and which was indeed a "common-law gift," but which was nevertheless held not to be a gift excludable under § 102(a).

## PROBLEMS

1.    Consider whether it is likely that § 102 applies in the following circumstances:

(a)    Father leaves Daughter $20,000 in his will.

(b)    Father dies intestate and Daughter receives $20,000 worth of real estate as his heir.

(c)    Father leaves several family members out of his will and Daughter and others attack the will. As a result of a settlement of the controversy Daughter receives $20,000.

(d)    Father leaves Daughter $20,000 in his will stating that the amount is in appreciation of Daughter's long and devoted service to him.

(e)    Father leaves Daughter $20,000 pursuant to a written agreement under which Daughter agreed to care for Father in his declining years.

(f) Same agreement as in (e), above, except that Father died intestate and Daughter successfully enforced her $20,000 claim under the agreement against the estate. *No*

(g) Same as (f), above, except that Daughter settles her $20,000 claim for a $10,000 payment. *No? Leverage as her*

(h) Father appointed Daughter executrix of his estate and Father's will provided Daughter was to receive $20,000 for services as executrix. *—102 but not apply — Yes?*

(i) Father appointed Daughter executrix of his estate and made a $20,000 bequest to her in lieu of all compensation or commissions to which she would otherwise be entitled as executrix. *— No — but only bc of fact Merman case not being overturned*

**2.** Boyfriend who has a "mental problem" with marriage agrees with Taxpayer that he will leave her "everything" at his death in return for her staying with him without marriage. She does, he doesn't, she sues his estate on a theory of quantum meruit and settles her claim. Is her settlement excludable under § 102? *No*

**3.** If the *Wolder* case arose today, would § 102(c) apply to resolve the issue?

*Probably — it's probably an employee/employer relationship for tax purposes*

# CHAPTER 4

# EMPLOYEE BENEFITS

## A. EXCLUSIONS FOR FRINGE BENEFITS*

Internal Revenue Code: Section 132 (omit (j)(2) and (5), (m), and (n)). See Sections 61(a)(1); 79; 83; 112; 125.

Regulations: Sections 1.61–1(a), –21(a)(1) and (2), (b)(1) and (2).

---

Chapter 2 of this book presents the standard broad definition of gross income under Section 61. Section 61(a)(1) specifically includes in gross income "compensation for services". Such compensation may take the form of property as well as cash,[1] and it can be indirectly as well as directly paid.[2] The Supreme Court has stated that Section 61(a)(1) "is broad enough to include in taxable income any economic or financial benefit conferred on the employee as compensation, whatever the form or mode by which it is effected."[3]

Technically, then, whether an employee is paid in dollars, property or use of property, any form of compensation is gross income. But comes now the fringe benefit which seems to challenge this broad, established concept. For example, employer has an office coffee maker and employees are allowed to consume all the free coffee they want. Technically, each cup is income. Realistically, reporting and enforcing the reporting of such income is impossible. Similar conclusions can be reached with respect to a secretary's typing of a personal letter for the boss or either's occasional personal use of the company copying machine. Such items are de minimis anyway and no big deal; but what happens when a so-called fringe becomes more substantial, such as travel passes to airline stewards or courtesy discounts to department store clerks?

All the above items are commonly known as fringe benefits. Although their value is conceptually gross income, nevertheless to some extent over the years the Service, even without statutory authorization, has allowed taxpayers not to report them. The exact scope of such administratively created exclusions has been vague. Occasionally Congress has enacted a statute specifically to exclude a fringe benefit

---

* See Simon, "Fringe Benefits and Tax Reform Historical Blunders and a Proposal for Structural Change," 36 U.Fla.L.Rev. 871 (1984); Halperin, "Broadening the Base—The Case of Fringe Benefits," 37 Nat'l Tax J. 271 (1984).

[1] Reg. § 1.61–1(a).

[2] E.g., A may have income if B discharges a debt of A to C. Old Colony Trust Co. v. Commissioner, 279 U.S. 716, 49 S.Ct. 499 (1929).

[3] Commissioner v. Smith, 324 U.S. 177, 181, 65 S.Ct. 591, 593 (1945).

from gross income[4] or to include or partly include a fringe within gross income.[5] In other areas, vagueness as to the inclusion of fringes in gross income has led to inconsistency in the administration of the tax laws and perhaps sometimes to taxpayer misconception that any non-cash fringe benefit may be excluded.

Congress eventually decided to bring certainty to this area by enacting specific legislation to deal with fringes. The House Committee Report,[6] below, provides the reasons for the legislation:

> In providing statutory rules for exclusion of certain fringe benefits for income and payroll tax purposes, the committee has attempted to strike a balance between two competing objectives.
>
> First, the committee is aware that in many industries, employees may receive, either free or at a discount, goods and services which the employer sells to the general public. In many cases, these practices are long established, and have been treated by employers, employees, and the IRS as not giving rise to taxable income. Although employees may receive an economic benefit from the availability of these free or discounted goods or services, employers often have valid business reasons, other than simply providing compensation, for encouraging employees to avail themselves of the products which they sell to the public. For example, a retail clothing business will want its salespersons to wear, when they deal with customers, the clothing which it seeks to sell to the public. In addition, the fact that the selection of goods and services usually available from a particular employer usually is restricted makes it appropriate to provide a limited exclusion, when such discounts are generally made available to employees, for the income employees realize from obtaining free or reduced-cost goods or services. The committee believes, therefore, that many present practices under which employers may provide to a broad group of employees, either free or at a discount, the products and services which the employer sells or provides to the public do not serve merely to replace cash compensation. These reasons support the committee's decision to codify the ability of employers to continue these practices without imposition of income or payroll taxes.
>
> The second objective of the committee's bill is to set forth clear boundaries for the provision of tax-free benefits. Because of the moratorium on the issuance of fringe benefit regulations, the Treasury Department has been precluded from clarifying the tax treatment of many of the forms of noncash compensation

---

[4]   See I.R.C. § 106, excluding employer contributions to employee accident and health plans.

[5]   See I.R.C. § 79, classifying employer payment for group term life insurance.

[6]   H. Rep. No. 98–432, 98th Cong., 2d Sess. 1591–2 (1984).

commonly in use. As a result, the administrators of the tax law have not had clear guidelines in this area, and hence taxpayers in identical situations have been treated differently. The inequities, confusion, and administrative difficulties for business, employees, and the IRS resulting from this situation have increased substantially in recent years. The committee believes that it is unacceptable to allow these conditions * * * to continue any longer.

In addition, the committee is concerned that without any well-defined limits on the ability of employers to compensate their employees tax-free by using a medium other than cash, new practices will emerge that could shrink the income tax base significantly, and further shift a disproportionate tax burden to those individuals whose compensation is in the form of cash. [Students may wish to let their imaginations run with this. Ed.] A shrinkage of the base of the social security payroll tax could also pose a threat to the viability of the social security system * * *. Finally, an unrestrained expansion of noncash compensation would increase inequities among employees in different types of business, and among employers as well.

The nondiscrimination rule is an important common thread among the types of fringe benefits which are excluded under the bill from income and employment taxes. Under the bill, most fringe benefits may be made available tax-free to officers, owners, or highly compensated employees only if the benefits are also provided on substantially equal terms to other employees. The committee believes that it would be fundamentally unfair to provide tax-free treatment for economic benefits that are furnished only to highly paid executives. Further, where benefits are limited to the highly paid, it is more likely that the benefit is being provided so that those who control the business can receive compensation in a nontaxable form; in that situation, the reasons stated above for allowing tax-free treatment would not be applicable. Also, if highly paid executives could receive free from taxation economic benefits that are denied to lower-paid employees, while the latter are compensated only in fully taxable cash, the committee is concerned that this situation would exacerbate problems of noncompliance among taxpayers. In this regard, some commentators argue that the current situation—in which the lack of clear rules for the tax treatment of nonstatutory fringe benefits encourages the nonreporting of many types of compensatory benefits—has led to nonreporting of types of cash income which are clearly taxable under present-law rules, such as interest and dividends.

In summary, the committee believes that by providing rules which essentially codify many present practices under which employers provide their own products and services tax-free to a broad group of employees, and by ending the uncertainties arising from a moratorium on the Treasury Department's ability to clarify the tax treatment of these benefits, the bill substantially improves the equity and administration of the tax system.

The tax law on fringe benefits is now completely statutory and, while subject of course to customary administrative and judicial interpretative refinements, it is not to be *created* administratively.[7] If an employee benefit is not specifically excluded from gross income, its value must be included within gross income[8] under Section 61.[9]

Congress had previously enacted other Code sections that expressly include or exclude some equivocal benefits from gross income.[10] Most of the exclusionary rules now appear in Code Section 132. But that section is not exclusive; and other sections may overlap to exclude a particular benefit from gross income.[11] Section 132 excludes from gross income a large variety of categories of fringes. A brief examination of some of the excludable fringe benefits follows.

Section 132 may be a student's first foray into an intricate statutory section that is difficult to read. One of the objectives of a course in federal income taxation is for students to develop their skills in dealing with complex statutory material. We suggest that you initially read the note that follows and then read the assigned Code provisions to see if you can extract the explanations in the note from the statutory language.

In all cases, Section 132 excludes fringes provided to "employees". In the first two classifications of fringe benefits (no-additional-cost services and qualified employee discounts[12]) the definition of an employee is expanded to include not only persons currently employed but also retired and disabled ex-employees and the surviving spouses of employees or retired or disabled ex-employees[13] as well as spouses and dependent children of employees.[14]

---

[7]  Reg. § 1.61–21(a)(2). See I.R.C. § 132(*l*).

[8]  Reg. § 1.61–21(b)(1) and (2). As income, it is also subject to withholding tax and social security and unemployment insurance payroll taxes (FICA and FUTA) to be paid by the employer.

[9]  See also I.R.C. § 83, which establishes the amount and timing of such income. See Chapter 24D, infra.

[10]  Some of those sections are discussed below.

[11]  I.R.C. § 132(*l*). See Text at notes 67–71, infra.

[12]  I.R.C. § 132(a)(1) and (2). See infra pages 93 and 94.

[13]  I.R.C. § 132(h)(1).

[14]  I.R.C. § 132(h)(2). See also I.R.C. § 132(h)(3) treating a parent of an employee as an employee with respect to the use of air transportation. The regulations pertaining to no additional cost services, qualified employee discounts, working condition fringes, de minimis fringes, and on premises athletic facilities provide that the term employee includes a partner rendering services to a partnership. Reg. § 1.132–1(b)(1)–(4). But see § 132(f)(5)(E) which for

Section 132 excludes the first two classifications of fringes,[15] employee eating facilities,[16] and qualified retirement and planning services[17] provided to highly compensated employees only if those fringes also are offered on a nondiscriminatory basis.[18] The nondiscrimination requirement denies highly compensated employees an exclusion for those fringes unless the fringes are provided on substantially the same terms to a broad group of employees.[19] If a classification of fringes is discriminatory, highly compensated employees have gross income, but the exclusion still applies to those employees (if any) who receive the benefit and who are not members of the highly compensated group.[20]

*Section 132(a)(1): No-Additional-Cost Services.* The first type of fringe benefit excluded from an employee's gross income under Section 132 is services provided to an employee by an employer. Their value escapes gross income if the services are offered for sale to customers in the same line of business as that in which the employee is performing services,[21] the employer incurs no substantial additional cost in providing the service to the employee[22] and, in the case of highly compensated employees, the services are provided on a nondiscriminatory basis.[23] The amount of revenue an employer loses because of providing the service to the employee rather than to a paying customer and the amount of time spent by the other employees in providing a service for the employer are factors taken into consideration to determine whether there is substantial additional cost.[24] Examples of no-additional-cost services that are given in the legislative history of the section include airline, railroad, or subway seats and hotel rooms furnished to employees, if they are working in those respective businesses, in a way that does not displace non-employee customers, and free telephone service to telephone employees within existing capacity of the employer company.[25] The exclusion is allowed whether the services are provided free of charge, at cost or some partial charge, or under a cash rebate program.[26]

As previously stated, the services must be provided in the same line of business as that in which the employee is employed. Thus, if an

---

purposes of qualified transportation fringes excludes from the definition of "employee" any individual who is an employee within the meaning of § 401(c) (dealing with self-employed individuals).

[15] See note 12, supra.

[16] I.R.C. § 132(e)(2).

[17] I.R.C. § 132(a)(7).

[18] I.R.C. § 132(j)(1) and (6), (e)(2), (m)(2). See also I.R.C. § 414(q).

[19] Id. See Reg. § 1.132–8(a)(2).

[20] Id.

[21] I.R.C. § 132(b)(1). Cf. I.R.C. § 132(k).

[22] I.R.C. § 132(b)(2).

[23] I.R.C. § 132(j)(1).

[24] Reg. § 1.132–2(a)(5)(i).

[25] H.Rep. No. 98–432, supra note 6 at 1594. See also Reg. § 1.132–2(a)(2).

[26] Cf. I.R.C. § 132(b)(2). Reg. § 1.132–2(a)(3).

employee is a steward for an airline owned by a company that also owns a cruise ship, free standby airline flights for the employee, his spouse and his dependents are excludable but a free cruise is not. This restriction is framed carefully to preclude an unfair advantage for employees of conglomerates.[27] On the other hand, if two companies have a written reciprocal agreement that makes the services of one available to the employees of the other, employees of one company may exclude, as no-additional-cost services, services provided by the other, if the services in question are in the employee's line of business.[28] Thus a steward could exclude the value of standby flights on another airline, if there is the requisite written agreement between the airlines and neither airline incurs any substantial additional cost in providing standby flights pursuant to the agreement.

*Section 132(a)(2): Qualified Employee Discounts.* Historically, an employee has been allowed to exclude from gross income the value of "courtesy discounts" on items purchased from his employer for use by the employee.[29] Subject to some restrictions, this exclusion continues under Section 132. As in the case of the no-additional-cost services exclusion, both the nondiscrimination[30] and the same-line-of business[31] limitations apply.[32] The exclusion applies to purchases of both property (other than real property and personal property held for investment)[33] and purchases of services which includes, the legislative history indicates,[34] purchases of insurance policies,[35] but it does not apply to loans to employees of financial institutions. The discount may take the form of either a price reduction or a rebate.[36]

The Code imposes a ceiling on the amount of the exclusion. In the case of services the exclusion may not exceed 20% of the price at which the services are offered by the employer to customers.[37] The maximum discount for property is essentially the employer's profit on the goods in

---

[27] If an employee were employed by the conglomerate in a position related to both businesses, perhaps as an accountant for both businesses, he would qualify for exclusions in each line of business if he performed substantial services in each line of business. Reg. § 1.132–4(a)(1)(iv)(A).

[28] I.R.C. § 132(i)(2). See I.R.C. § 132(b)(1), Reg. § 1.132–2(b).

[29] Cf. Reg. § 31.3401(a)–1(b)(10).

[30] I.R.C. § 132(j)(1).

[31] I.R.C. § 132(c)(4). See also I.R.C. § 132(j)(2) which under some circumstances allows employees of lessees of department store space (concessions) to be treated as employees of the department store itself, if the store allows discounts to their employees.

[32] The reciprocal agreement allowance is inapplicable to employee discounts. I.R.C. § 132(i) applies only to § 132(a)(1) fringes. See Reg. § 1.132–3(a)(3).

[33] I.R.C. § 132(c)(4). Such property may be either tangible or intangible property. Reg. § 1.132–3(a)(2)(ii).

[34] H.Rep. No. 98–432, supra note 6 at 1600, n. 12.

[35] Cf. Commissioner v. Minzer, 279 F.2d 338 (5th Cir.1960).

[36] Reg. § 1.132–3(a)(4).

[37] I.R.C. § 132(c)(1)(B).

the employee's line of business. That profit, statutorily labelled the "gross profit percentage,"[38] is computed as follows:

$$\frac{\text{aggregate sales price reduced by cost}}{\text{aggregate sales price}}$$

The fraction is based on sales of all property in the employee's line of business (not just the discounted item) taking into account the employer's experience during a representative period.[39] Thus, if an employee works for a home appliance store and her employer has total sales for the entire year of $800,000 and paid $600,000 for the goods sold, the gross profit percentage is 25% determined as follows:

$$\frac{\$800{,}000 \text{ less } \$600{,}000}{\$800{,}000} \quad = \quad \frac{\$200{,}000}{\$800{,}000} \quad = 25\%$$

Thus, if an employer allows an employee to buy an appliance regularly selling for $1,000 for a price of $750 or more, the full discount is subject to the exclusion. If the price is below $750 the exclusion is limited to $250, and the employee must report some income from the transaction (the excess over the permitted exclusion).[40]

*Section 132(a)(3): Working Condition Fringe.* Congress allows an exclusion for any property or services provided to an employee the cost of which, if the employee had paid for the property or services, would have qualified for a deduction by the employee as a business expense or by way of depreciation deductions.[41] At this point, it is premature to consider either Section 162 business expenses or Section 167 depreciation deductions, both of which are discussed in Chapter 14. A rationale for the exclusion is that there would likely be a "wash" (inclusion with matching deduction) on the employee's tax return if the exclusion were not allowed.[42] There is no discrimination limitation on this exclusion[43] and probably none is needed.

Examples of items that qualify under the working condition exclusion, as recounted in the legislative history,[44] are: use of a company car or airplane for business purposes; an employer's subscription to a business periodical for the employee; a bodyguard provided to an employee for security reasons; and on-the-job training provided by an employer.

Section 132(j)(3) adds as a working condition fringe a full time auto salesperson's use value of an employer-provided demonstration car if the

---

[38] I.R.C. § 132(c)(1)(A).

[39] I.R.C. § 132(c)(2)(B).

[40] Reg. § 1.132–3(e).

[41] I.R.C. § 132(d).

[42] A wash would occur as a result of I.R.C. § 62(a)(2)(A).

[43] Reg. § 1.132–5(q).

[44] H.Rep. No. 98–432, supra note 6 at 1601–1602. See also Reg. § 1.132–6(e)(1). No dollar limitations are imposed on these exclusions.

car is used primarily to facilitate the salesperson's performance of services for the employer and there are substantial restrictions on the personal use of the car by the salesperson.[45] The value is excluded even though it would not be fully deductible as a business expense if the cost were incurred by an employee.

*Section 132(a)(4): De Minimis Fringes.* This exclusion is very much in keeping with the original administrative allowance of fringe benefits. Any property or service whose value is so small as to make required accounting for it unreasonable or administratively impracticable is excluded as a de minimis fringe benefit.[46] In determining whether an item is within the de minimis concept, the frequency with which similar fringes are provided by an employer to employees must be taken into account.[47]

Again the legislative history assists with examples of benefits that may be excluded.[48] Included are: typing of personal letters by a company secretary; occasional personal use of the company copying machine; occasional cocktail parties or picnics for employees; occasional supper money or taxi fare advanced because of overtime work; coffee and doughnuts furnished to employees; occasional theater or sporting event tickets; and low value holiday gifts. The legislative history states that also excluded are "traditional retirement gifts presented to an employee on his or her retirement after completing lengthy service."[49]

In addition the statute provides that bargains at employer-operated eating facilities will be treated as de minimis fringes if they are located on or near the employer's business premises and the revenue generated from their operation *normally* equals or exceeds their operating costs.[50] The exclusion dealing with eating facilities is restricted in the case of upper echelon employees by certain non-discrimination requirements.[51] And it does not apply to food and other items furnished to spouses and dependent children.[52]

*Section 132(a)(5): Qualified Transportation Fringe.* Congress also permits an exclusion for a qualified transportation fringe.[53] A qualified transportation fringe includes the value of benefits provided to an employee by an employer in the form of: transportation in a "commuter highway vehicle" between an employee's residence and place of

---

[45]  I.R.C. § 132(j)(3)(B).

[46]  I.R.C. § 132(e)(1).

[47]  Id. Reg. § 1.132–6(b).

[48]  H.Rep. No. 98–432, supra note 6 at 1603.

[49]  Sen.Rep. No. 99–313, 99th Cong., 2d Sess. 53 (1986).

[50]  I.R.C. § 132(e)(2)(A) and (B).

[51]  I.R.C. § 132(e)(2) last sentence. See note 18, supra.

[52]  See I.R.C. § 132(h) whose rules apply only to § 132(a)(1) and (2) fringes.

[53]  I.R.C. § 132(a)(5). Congress has frequently tinkered with the I.R.C. § 132(a)(5) rules. See I.R.C. § 132(f)(2) and (4).

These types of fringes may be less frequently provided by employers after 2017 as they are no longer deductible by employers. I.R.C. § 274(a)(4).

employment;[54] a transit pass, token, fare card, voucher, or similar item for mass transit facilities or for a commercial transportation service;[55] and qualified parking[56] provided on or near the business premises or on or near the location from which employee is picked up by a commuter vehicle.[57] Employers may offer an employee a choice between a cash option (which if chosen is included in gross income) or one or more of the qualified transportation benefits (which if chosen does not cause the employee to lose the exclusion).[58] The exclusion generally applies to cash reimbursements for qualifying items.[59] The exclusion is limited to $175 per month (adjusted for inflation)[60] either for benefits in the form of commuter highway vehicle transportation and transit passes, etc. or for qualified parking.[61]

If a fringe is within the definition of a qualified transportation fringe (before consideration of the maximum dollar limitations), it may not also qualify as a working condition fringe or a de minimis fringe.[62] For example, any amounts paid for qualified transportation which exceed the limits provided may not be excluded by any other subsection of Section 132.

*Section 132(j)(4): Athletic Facilities.* Tucked away in the depths of Section 132 is an additional classification of an excludable fringe benefit allowed under the section. Employees may exclude from gross income the value of the use of any on-premises athletic facility.[63] The exclusion applies to a gym, pool, golf course, tennis courts or other athletic facility[64] located on the employer's premises and operated by the employer, if substantially all the facility's use is by employees, their spouses, and their dependent children.[65]

After many years of stumbling inaction, one may applaud the enactment of Section 132 in an effort to bring some order to the tax

---

[54]   I.R.C. § 132(f)(1)(A). A "commuter highway vehicle" must have a seating capacity for at least 6 adults in addition to the driver and must be reasonably expected to be used 80 percent of the time for such commuting or business trips. I.R.C. § 132(f)(5)(B). The vehicle may be operated by or for the employer. I.R.C. § 132(f)(5)(D).

[55]   I.R.C. §§ 132(f)(1)(B) and (5)(A). The commercial transportation must be in a vehicle which has a seating capacity for at least 6 adults in addition to the driver. I.R.C. § 132(f)(5)(A)(ii) & (B)(i).

[56]   I.R.C. § 132(f)(1)(C).

[57]   I.R.C. § 132(f)(5)(C). It does not include parking on or near one's residence. Id.

[58]   I.R.C. § 132(f)(4).

[59]   I.R.C. § 132(f)(3). A cash reimbursement for a transit pass qualifies only if a voucher or similar item which may be exchanged only for a transit pass is not readily available for direct distribution by the employer to the employee. Id.

[60]   I.R.C. § 132(f)(6).

[61]   I.R.C. § 132(f)(2).

[62]   I.R.C. § 132(f)(7).

[63]   I.R.C. § 132(j)(4).

[64]   Reg. § 1.132–1(e)(1).

[65]   I.R.C. § 132(j)(4)(B). There is no nondiscriminatory restriction imposed because, under a related self-policing provision, if the facility is used discriminatorily the employer receives no deduction. See I.R.C. § 274(e)(4).

treatment of employees' fringe benefits.[66] Especially is this so when chaos gives way to principles and policies that are to be commended as they seek a nice balance of fairness and practicability. But statutory change is almost always high caloric and, here again, the Code has gained quite a few clauses. If the statute also seems complex, perhaps the answer to that is that Section 132 is supplying answers to complicated questions that previously had been swept under the rug.

*The Statutory Exclusion of Other Fringe Benefits.* As stated above, Section 132 is not the only section that provides for the exclusion of fringe benefits from gross income.[67] Some employee exclusions are the subject of other chapters of this book.[68] Others are considered more generally below. An important point to recall is that generally only fringes that are expressly excluded by statute are tax-free fringes.[69] Section 132 indicates that if another Code section provides an exclusion for a type of benefit, Section 132 is generally inapplicable to that type of benefit; an ad hoc provision prevails over the general rules of Section 132.[70] Some other sections excluding fringe benefits from gross income that are not discussed elsewhere in the book include: Section 79 which excludes group term life insurance premiums for up to a maximum of $50,000 of coverage from an employee's gross income; Section 112 which excludes compensation received by military personnel for service in a combat zone and compensation for periods during which the person is hospitalized as a result of wounds, disease or injury incurred while serving in a combat zone; Section 129 which excludes amounts paid by an employer for "dependent care assistance" up to a maximum annual amount of $5,000. ($2,500 for a married individual filing separately); Section 137 which excludes employer payments of qualified adoption expenses under an adoption assistance program;[71] and Section 134 which excludes some additional military benefits. Finally Section 125 provides for the establishment of "cafeteria plans," which allow employees to choose the fringe benefits they would like to have from a number of available fringe benefits. Within the cafeteria plan, the employee has flexibility to choose the benefits without the loss of any exclusion from gross income.

---

[66] I.R.C. § 132 provides a continuing and ever expanding list of excludable fringes: § 132(a)(7) qualified retirement planning services, see § 132(m) and Chapter 20C3, infra; § 132(a)(8) a qualified military base realignment and closure fringe, see § 132(n).

[67] See I.R.C. § 132(*l*).

[68] See I.R.C. § 117(d) excluding qualified tuition reductions and § 127 dealing with employer funded educational assistance programs, both considered in Chapter 5, infra, and see § 106, excluding employer contributions to employee accident and health plans, considered in Chapter 9, infra.

[69] Reg. § 1.61–21(a)(2).

[70] I.R.C. § 132(*l*). See I.R.C. § 132(e) and see H.Rep. No. 98–432, supra note 6 at 1608.

[71] The rules applicable to this exclusion closely parallel the rules applicable to the credit for qualified adoption expenses under I.R.C. § 23. See Chapter 27B2, infra.

## PROBLEM

**1.** Consider whether or to what extent the fringe benefits listed below may be excluded from gross income and, where possible, support your conclusions with statutory authority:

(a) Employee of a national hotel chain stays in one of the chain's hotels in another town rent-free while on vacation. The hotel has several empty rooms. *excludable 132 (a)(1)*

*don't forget "same line or business" + discriminatory*

(b) Same as (a), above, except that the desk clerk bounces a paying guest so Employee can stay rent-free. See Reg. §§ 1.132–2(a)(2) and (5). *— no — "foregone revenue" in 5*

*can't my to avarge ephe value*

(c) Same as (a), above, except that Employee pays the bill and receives a cash rebate from the chain. See Reg. § 1.132–2(a)(3). *— Not excluded — cash rebate still not same rule*

(d) Same as (a), above, except that Employee's spouse and dependent children travelling without Employee use the room on their vacation.

(e) Same as (a), above, except that Employee stays in the hotel of a rival chain under a written reciprocal agreement under which employees pay 50% of the normal rent. *— Fine 1.132–2(b) 132(i)*

(f) Same as (a), above, except that Employee is an officer in the hotel chain and rent-free use is provided only to officers of the chain and all other employees pay 60% of the normal rent. See Reg. § 1.132–8(a)(2)(i). *— discriminatory*

(g) Hotel chain is owned by a conglomerate which also owns a shipping line. The facts are the same as in (a), above, except that Employee works for the shipping line. *→ ne benefit hotel? 1.132-4 (a)*

(h) Same as (g), above, except that Employee is comptroller of the conglomerate. See Reg. § 1.132–4(a)(1)(iv).

(i) Employee sells insurance and employer Insurance Company allows Employee 20% off the $1,000 cost of the policy. *— if property, yes (1.132-3(a)(ii) 132(c)(1)(B)*

(j) Employee is a salesman in a home furnishings store. The prior year the store had $1,000,000 in sales and a $600,000 cost of goods sold. Employee buys a $2,000 sofa from Employer for $1,000. *— No - 132(c)(1)(A)*

(k) Employee attends a business convention in another town. Employer picks up Employee's costs. *→ 132(d) (working condition)* *— Not a fringe benefit*

(l) Employer has a bar and provides the Employees with happy hour cocktails at the end of each week's work. *— regular, not de minimis — Not excludable 132(e)(1)*

(m) Employer gives Employee a case of scotch each Christmas. See Reg. § 1.132–6(e)(1). *→ low market value holiday gift, not cash*

(n) Employee is an officer of corporation which pays Employee's parking fees at a lot one block from the corporate headquarters. Non-officers pay their own parking fees. Assume there is no post-2001 inflation. *discrimination? — Not discriminatory 1.132(a)(1) — excludable → 132(a)(5)*

(o)   Employer provides Employee with $185 worth of vouchers each month for commuting on a public mass transit system. Assume there is no post-2001 inflation.

(p)   Employer puts in a gym at the business facilities for the use of the employees and their families.

## B. EXCLUSIONS FOR MEALS AND LODGING

Internal Revenue Code: Sections 107; 119(a). See Section 119(d).

Regulations: Section 1.119–1.

---

# Hatt v. Commissioner*

Tax Court of the United States, 1969.
28 T.C.M. 1194, affirmed per curiam 457 F.2d 499 (7th Cir.1972).

■ FEATHERSTON, JUDGE:

Findings of Fact

Hatt was a legal resident of Evansville, Indiana, at the time his petition was filed. He did not file income tax returns for 1957, 1958, 1959, and 1960. He filed timely income tax returns for 1961 and 1962.

Johann is a corporation organized under the laws of the State of Indiana. At the time its petition was filed its principal place of business was Evansville, Indiana. Johann filed corporation income tax returns for the calendar years 1955 and 1957 through 1961 with the district director of internal revenue, Indianapolis, Indiana. During the years in issue Johann operated a funeral home and embalming business.

Hatt was born July 9, 1932. He finished grade school, attended high school for four or five months, and then entered the Army in 1952, being discharged therefrom in August or September 1954. Prior to his military service he had held numerous jobs, such as delivering newspapers, picking up and delivering laundry and dry cleaning, and working as a helper for a lathe operator. Upon his discharge from the Army he worked in California for a short time as a taxicab driver and as a salesman in a jewelry store. Thereafter, in late 1954, he returned to Indianapolis, Indiana, where he had resided as a child, and started working for Household Sewing Machine Company as a salesman.

In the fall of 1955 Hatt opened a place of business known as the "Select Sewing Center," an individual proprietorship located in Evansville, Indiana, which engaged in the business of selling sewing machines. The business consisted primarily of contacting customers in their homes after they had answered advertisements.

---

\*   Footnotes omitted.

Prior to 1957 Hatt became acquainted with Dorothy Echols (hereinafter Dorothy), the president and majority stockholder of Johann. They were married on March 2, 1957, at which time Hatt was approximately 25 years of age and she was about 43. Pursuant to an antenuptial agreement she then transferred to him 130 shares, a majority, of the stock of Johann, and he became the president and general manager of the corporation.

\* \* \*

*Issue 4.  The Apartment*

Immediately after his marriage to Dorothy, Hatt moved into an apartment located in the building used by Johann for its funeral home business, and he resided there during the years 1957 through 1962. Dorothy had resided in the same apartment prior to her marriage to Hatt. In addition to this apartment the building contained another apartment, which was rented, and a dormitory to house the ambulance crew. The telephone used by Johann rang in Hatt's apartment as well as in the business office. He answered the telephone in the apartment when the office was closed, and met there with customers who came to the home to discuss service after regular business hours. It is customary in the Evansville area for the manager or another employee authorized to deal with customers to live on the premises of a funeral home.

\* \* \*

*Issue 4.  The Apartment*

Section 119 grants an exclusion from gross income of the value of lodging furnished to an employee if three conditions are met: (1) The lodging is on the business premises of the employer; (2) the employee is "required to accept such lodging \* \* \* as a condition of his employment"; and (3) the lodging is furnished for the convenience of the employer. Respondent does not question petitioner's compliance with the first condition, but contends that neither of the last two conditions has been met and that, therefore, Johann is not entitled to deductions for maintenance of Hatt's apartment and that Hatt is taxable on its fair rental value as a constructive dividend. The issue is primarily factual, and petitioners, of course, have the burden of proof. \* \* \*.

The "condition of his employment" requirement of section 119 means that the employee must "be required to accept the lodging in order to enable him properly to perform the duties of his employment. Lodging will be regarded as furnished to enable the employee properly to perform the duties of his employment when, for example, the lodging is furnished because the employee is required to be available for duty at all times \* \* \*." Sec. 1.119–1(b), Income Tax Regs.

The "convenience of the employer" test and the "condition of his employment" test prescribed by section 119 are basically similar, \* \* \* as are the arguments made by respondent under those tests—that Hatt was president and majority stockholder of Johann, thus enabling him to determine the "convenience" of Johann and the "conditions" of his own employment, and that one or more members of the ambulance crew was available at all times to take calls or answer the telephone, thus eliminating the necessity of Hatt's presence on the premises of Johann.

The facts that Hatt was the president and majority stockholder of Johann necessitate careful scrutiny of the arrangement but, in our view, do not alone disqualify Hatt for the exclusion or Johann for the claimed deductions. * * * Hatt also is not disqualified for the exclusion merely because the apartment was a convenience for him. * * *

The funeral business is of such character that it requires someone to be in attendance 24 hours a day to answer telephone calls, to meet the family members of decedents, and to make financial arrangements, as well as to arrange to pick up the bodies of decedents. Family members of decedents in the Evansville area expect someone to be in the funeral home at all times. The undisputed testimony is that the manager or some other designated employee lived on the premises of every other funeral home in Evansville. In addition, supervision of the 24-hour ambulance service maintained by Johann during this period, a source of funeral business, was also required. The telephone in Johann's business office rang in Hatt's apartment, and, as manager of the funeral home, he took calls and handled business with customers. While the ambulance crew could have received the calls, they were not authorized to handle funeral business, particularly its financial aspects. Finally, we note that Dorothy, the president of Johann before Hatt, had lived in the same apartment for several years without paying rent to the corporation, and the corporation had deducted depreciation on the apartment's furnishings and related utility costs.

We think that petitioners have made the requisite showings for the claimed exclusion under section 119 and the deductions for utilities expense claimed by Johann under section 162(a).

## NOTE

The "on the business premises" requirement of Section 119(a)(1) and (2) was not at issue in the *Hatt* case. But it has been stage center in litigation in other cases. In Commissioner v. Anderson[1] a motel manager was always "on call" at a residence owned by the motel owner two blocks from the motel. The court concluded that ownership was not the test of business premises and that the term means "either at a place where the employee performs a significant portion of his duties or where the employer conducts a significant portion of his business."[2] Section 119 was held inapplicable because the "on call" status did not constitute a significant portion of the taxpayer employee's duties. Compare Jack B. Lindeman[3] which held that a residence adjacent to

---

[1]   371 F.2d 59 (6th Cir.1966), cert. denied 387 U.S. 906, 87 S.Ct. 1687 (1967).

[2]   Id. at 67.

[3]   60 T.C. 609 (1973), acq. 1973–2 C.B. 1.

the motel (across the street) was not geographically separated from the motel and was therefore "on the business premises."

Section 119(d) allows an employee of an educational institution[4] to exclude from gross income the value of lodging, not otherwise excluded under Section 119(a), if the lodging is located on or in the proximity of the campus of the educational institution.[5] The lodging may be used as a residence by the employee and the employee's spouse and dependents.[6] There is a ceiling on the amount of the exclusion.[7]

Housing benefits provided to a "minister of the gospel"[8] are excluded from the minister's gross income by Section 107 but, somewhat anomalously, they must be furnished to the minister "as compensation." The exclusion applies not only to the fair rental value of a home actually provided for the minister's use, similar to Section 119, but also to a rental allowance.[9] In order to qualify, an allowance must be specifically earmarked in the minister's employment contract, the church minutes, or some similar documents,[10] and then it is excluded only to the extent that it is actually used to rent or provide a home that is the minister's principal residence.[11] Congress may have made Section 107[12] more liberal than Section 119, because ministers are more likely to use their homes in conjunction with church activities than are other employees in their business activities.

## PROBLEMS

1.   Employer provides Employee and Spouse and Child a residence on Employer's business premises, having a rental value of $15,000 per year, but charging Employee only $6,000.

    (a)   What result if the nature of Employee's work does not require Employee to live on the premises as a condition of employment?

                                          L— *Fails to meet 1.119-1(b)*

---

    [4]   I.R.C. § 119(d)(4)(A). See I.R.C. §§ 119(d)(4)(B) and 170(b)(1)(A)(ii).

    [5]   I.R.C. § 119(d)(3)(A).

    [6]   I.R.C. § 119(d)(3)(B).

    [7]   I.R.C. § 119(d)(2).

    [8]   Reg. § 1.107–1(a). Compare Silverman v. Commissioner, 73–2 USTC ¶ 9546 (8th Cir.1973), § 107 applied to a cantor in the Jewish faith who, although unordained, had duties essentially the same as a minister in non-Jewish faith, with Marc H. Tanenbaum, 58 T.C. 1 (1972), ordained rabbi employed as the National Director of Interreligious Affairs by the American Jewish Committee who did not have sacerdotal duties and was not a minister. See Block, "Who is a 'Minister of the Gospel' for Purposes of the Parsonage Exclusion?" 51 Taxes 47 (1973).

    [9]   The allowance may include the fair rental value of the home, including furnishings and appurtenances such as a garage, plus the cost of utilities. I.R.C. § 107(2).

    [10]   Reg. § 1.107–1(a). See Rev.Rul. 72–462, 1972–2 C.B. 76.

    [11]   Driscoll v. Comm'r, 669 F.3d 1309 (11th Cir. 2012) cert. den. 133 S. Ct. 358 (2012). Cf. I.R.C. § 121(a).

    [12]   Cf. I.R.C. § 265(a)(6), which provides that ministers receiving excludible parsonage allowances, as well as military personnel receiving excludible military housing allowances, are not precluded by § 265(a)(1) from deducting mortgage interest or real property taxes on their residences.

(b) What result if Employer and Employee simply agreed to a clause in the employment contract requiring Employee to live in the residence?

(c) What result if Employee's work and contract require Employee to live on the premises and Employer furnishes Employee and family $6,000 worth of groceries during the year?

(d) What result if Employer transferred the residence to Employee in fee simple in the year that Employee accepted the position and commenced work? Does the value of the residence constitute excluded lodging?

2.     Planner incorporated her motel business and the corporation purchased a piece of residential property adjacent to the motel. The corporation by contract "required" Planner to use the residence and also furnished her meals. Planner worked at the motel and was on call 24 hours a day. May Planner exclude the value of the residence or the meals or both from her gross income?

3.     State highway patrolman is required to be on duty from 8 a.m. to 5 p.m. At noon he eats lunch at various privately owned restaurants which are adjacent to the state highway. At the end of each month the state reimburses him for his luncheon expenses. Are such cash reimbursements included in his gross income? See Commissioner v. Kowalski, 434 U.S. 77, 98 S.Ct. 315 (1977).

4.     Doodle, a high-tech firm in Silicon Valley, hires Jacques and his staff from an exclusive restaurant to provide gourmet meals at its offices around the clock to its employees. Doodle believes the meals will incentivize employees to work longer hours, shorten the time taken for meal breaks, attract new employees, and help it remain competitive with other Silicon Valley high-tech firms. Are the employees' meals excluded under § 119?

# CHAPTER 5

# AWARDS

## A. PRIZES

Internal Revenue Code: Section 74. See Sections 102(c); 132(a)(4), (e); 274(j).

Regulations: Section 1.74–1. Proposed Regulations: Section 1.74–1(b).

---

### McDonell v. Commissioner
Tax Court of the United States, 1967.
26 T.C.M. 115.

### Memorandum Findings of Fact and Opinion

■ TANNENWALD, JUDGE:

Respondent determined a deficiency in income tax and an addition to tax under section 6653(a)[1] for 1960 in the amounts of $246.83 and $12.34, respectively.

Because of concessions by respondent, the only issue remaining for decision is whether all or any portion of expenses of a trip taken by petitioners and paid for by petitioner Allen's employer are includable in petitioners' income or, if so, are deductible in arriving at adjusted gross income.

### Findings of Fact

Some of the facts are stipulated and are found accordingly.

Allen J. and Jeanne M. McDonell, husband and wife, residing at 5505 Russett Road, Madison, Wisconsin, filed their joint tax return for 1960 with the district director of internal revenue, Milwaukee, Wisconsin.

Allen was employed by Dairy Equipment Co. (hereinafter referred to as DECO) in 1956 as assistant sales manager and he continued in that position through the taxable year in question. At the time of hiring Allen DECO pursuant to established policy, interviewed Jeanne. The purpose of interviewing the wife of a potential home office salesman was to be sure the wife understood that her husband would be required to do considerable traveling for the company and to evaluate her capacity to discharge social responsibilities required in connection with the company's business activities.

At no time did either of the petitioners own any stock in DECO.

---

[1]  All references are to the Internal Revenue Code of 1954.

DECO is a sales company, distributing bulk milk coolers manufactured for it on a subcontract basis. During the period in question, DECO coolers were sold through territorial salesmen and independent distributors. They handled other products dissimilar to those of DECO but competitive in terms of demand upon their time and effort.

Sales supervision was provided by home office salesmen. Allen, as assistant sales manager, was one of eight home office salesmen. None of the home office salesmen was assigned to a specific territory; each would be sent into the field when and where needed.

Beginning in 1959, DECO initiated an incentive sales contest for its 31 distributors and 9 territorial salesmen. The prize in 1959 for achieving an established sales quota was a trip to Hawaii for each winner and his wife. Home office salesmen did not participate.

There were 11 winners. They had produced $3,929,690.62 in gross sales, representing 56 percent of the total sales volume generated by the company during the period of the contest. Of the 11 winners in 1959, 10 decided to take the trip.

At the time of initiating the contest, DECO management decided to send one home office salesman and his wife for each of three contest winners. This decision was based upon the company's past experience that unguided gatherings of salesmen and distributors often turned into complaint sessions and were otherwise damaging to the company's business interests. DECO assigned four home office salesmen and their wives to the trip. They were selected by placing the names of all the home office salesmen in a hat and drawing out four names. This random method was used to avoid discontent and dissatisfaction. The same random method was used for selecting home office personnel to represent the company on subsequent similar trips. A home office salesman chosen one year was eligible the next year. Those selected to go on a particular trip received no cut in pay and did not lose vacation time. Those not chosen received no substitute benefit.

Allen was one of the four chosen. At the time of drawing the names, the home office salesmen were told that those selected and their wives were expected to go, although they would have been excused for good reasons. They were instructed that they should consider the trip as an assignment and not as a vacation and that their job was to stay constantly with the contest winners, to participate in all the scheduled activities, and not to go off alone. Their objective was not only to make sure that every winner enjoyed himself but to guide anticipated informal discussion relating to DECO's business in order to protect and enhance DECO's image with its distributors and territorial salesmen. The wives were considered essential participants in the achievement of this objective. DECO felt it would be impossible for stag salesmen to host a trip for couples.

The contest winners and the home office personnel departed from Madison, Wisconsin, on February 4, 1960, arriving in Honolulu on February 5. They left Hawaii on February 14, returning to Madison on February 15. Aside from one day which was devoted to a sales meeting, there were no direct business activities on the trip.

Petitioners performed their assigned duties, which consumed substantially all of the trip time. Neither had any spare time, as they had hoped to have, to go swimming or shopping.

The portion of the trip costs paid by DECO and attributable to petitioners was $1,121.96.

Petitioners reported $600 as miscellaneous commissions in their tax return for 1960 as the estimated cost to DECO attributable to Jeanne's presence on the trip.

Respondent determined a deficiency based on the entire cost of the trip.[2] Petitioners now claim that they erroneously reported the $600 and seek a refund in addition to the determination that respondent's deficiency was in error.

## Opinion

The battle lines in this case are clearly drawn. Petitioners assert that they took the trip in order to carry out duties required of them by virtue of Allen's employment by DECO. Respondent counters that the trip represented an award, taxable to petitioners under section 74, or additional compensation, taxable under section 61. We agree with petitioners.

The mere fact that petitioners were selected by a random drawing does not make the trip a taxable prize or award under section 74. Surely there would have been no question if the drawing had been designed to choose a home office salesman to take a trip without his wife to handle a disgruntled customer. The method of selection was founded on a sound business reason, namely, to choose those who were to serve DECO's business objectives on a basis which would obviate any feeling of discrimination. The situation of petitioners is to be distinguished from that of the contest winners, whose tax liability is not before us and for whom the trip was both a reward and an incentive.

Similarly, the fact that the trip was a vacation for the contest winners does not necessarily make it a vacation for petitioners. Unlike the contest winners, petitioners were expected to go as an essential part of Allen's employment. The right to go carried with it the duty to go. The trip was not a vacation for the petitioners. It was realistically a command performance to work. What was a social benefit to the contest winners was a work obligation to these petitioners. More importantly, petitioners herein were expected to devote substantially all of their time on the trip

---

[2]   Respondent concedes that the deficiency is partially in error because of the amount reported by petitioners.

to the performance of duties on behalf of DECO in order to achieve, albeit subtly, DECO's well-defined business objectives. In this respect, the situation is unlike that in Patterson v. Thomas, 289 F.2d 108 (C.A.5, 1961), certiorari denied 368 U.S. 837, 82 S.Ct. 35 (1961); where the Court found that, although the taxpayer had an obligation to attend the convention, his work responsibility was minimal.

Nor do we consider it material that petitioners enjoyed the trip. Pleasure and business, unlike oil and water, can sometimes be mixed. * * * Similarly, although the fact that the trip involved a resort area is an element to be taken into account, cf. Patterson v. Thomas, supra, it is not conclusive. A resort may be heaven to certain people but something less than that to others, depending on the circumstances. See Mr. Justice Douglas dissenting in Rudolph v. United States, 370 U.S. 269, 280, 82 S.Ct. 1277, 1283 (1962). It is noteworthy that neither of petitioners went swimming or shopping during their entire stay, two activities for which Hawaii is famous.

Again, unlike the taxpayer in Patterson v. Thomas, supra, petitioners' right to go on the trip was not determined by any standard of work performance. In addition, home office salesmen who did not go on the trip received no substitute compensation and those who did go were not eliminated from consideration for trips in subsequent years. There is not the slightest suggestion that the trip which the petitioners took was conceived of as disguised remuneration to them. On the contrary, DECO had sound business reasons for them to go. We recognize that the presence of an employer business purpose does not thereby preclude a finding of compensation to the employee. Patterson v. Thomas, supra. But such business reasons, when coupled with the equally compelling business circumstances involving these petitioners' participation, made the trip no different from any other business trip requiring their services—including Jeanne, whose duties were substantial and could not have been performed by stag men. * * *

We hold that, under all the facts and circumstances herein, the expenses of the trip are not includable in the gross income of petitioners. In view of this holding, we need not consider an alternative argument of petitioners that the trip had no fair market value to them. See, e.g., Lawrence W. McCoy, 38 T.C. 841 (1962).

Decision will be entered under Rule 50.

## NOTE

Two major congressional goals in enacting the *revenue-neutral* Tax Reform Act of 1986[1] were to broaden the tax base (increase the amount of taxable income subject to the income tax) and to lower the income tax rates. There are two principal ways to broaden the tax base: one is to increase items included in gross income, and the other is to decrease items allowed as

---

[1]  See Chapter 1B, supra.

deductions. Gross income is of course increased by the reduction of items that are excluded from gross income. This chapter examines two exclusionary areas that were substantially reduced by the 1986 legislation in order to broaden the tax base, i.e., prizes and awards, and scholarships and fellowships.

Prizes and awards are considered first. The Section 74 income tax rules on prizes and awards relate to such things as receipts for winning a company's sales or other contest,[2] the Nobel Peace Prize, the Pulitzer Prize, the Hickok belt, a contest to guess the most jelly beans in a jar, to mention just a few of the many items covered. Awards of a different nature such as scholarships and fellowships are subject to separate legislation in Section 117.

Prior to the enactment of the 1954 Code, there were no statutory provisions that dealt expressly with prizes and awards. Controversy arose whether prizes and awards were excluded from gross income as gifts under the 1939 Code predecessor to Section 102.[3] In 1954, Congress enacted Section 74(a) expressly including prizes and awards in gross income but, in Section 74(b), carved out an exception for a prize or award made primarily to recognize achievement in one of several specified fields (religious, charitable, scientific, educational, artistic, literary, or civic) if the recipient was selected without any action on the recipient's part to enter the contest or proceeding and was not required to render substantial future services as a condition to receiving the prize or award. As a part of its 1986 base-broadening action, Congress substantially curtailed the exclusion.

The statute now excludes prizes and awards from gross income only in very limited circumstances. First, under current Section 74(b) prizes and awards that satisfy the requirements of old Section 74(b) are excluded from gross income only if, in addition to the prior requirements, the taxpayer winner designates a governmental unit or a charity[4] to receive the award and if the award is transferred directly to the designee without any use or enjoyment of it by the taxpayer.[5] Thus the only way the winner can escape an inclusion in gross income is never to receive the award.[6] However, the designation of the recipient can be made before or after the taxpayer is aware of being the recipient of the award.[7]

Second, Section 74(c) creates an exclusion for "employee achievement awards".[8] The amount of employee exclusion[9] is geared to the extent to which

---

[2]   Cf. McDonell v. Commissioner at page 105, supra.

[3]   Pauline C. Washburn, 5 T.C. 1333 (1945); McDermott v. Commissioner, 150 F.2d 585 (D.C.Cir.1945). See also Sen.Rep.No. 1622, 83rd Cong., 2d Sess. 178–179 (1954).

[4]   Only charities listed in I.R.C. § 170(c)(1) or (2) qualify. I.R.C. § 74(b)(3). See Chapter 23B, infra, which discusses charitable contributions.

[5]   I.R.C. § 74(b)(3). See Prop. Reg. § 1.74–1(c)–(f).

[6]   See Prop.Reg. § 1.74–1(d).

[7]   The recipient of the award must designate a charitable or governmental recipient within 45 days of the date the prize or award is granted. Prop.Reg. § 1.74–1(c)(1).

[8]   See I.R.C. § 274(j)(3)(A), Prop. Reg. § 1.74–2.

[9]   I.R.C. § 74(c).

the employer qualifies for a deduction for the awards under Section 274(j),[10] a section full of ifs, ands, and buts that are not "fundamental."

Congress has added an exception to the prizes and awards rules which provides an exclusion from gross income for the value of any medal or prize money received from the United States Olympic Committee as a result of competition in the Olympic or Paralympic Games.[11] The exclusion is inapplicable if, including the value of the medal and prize money, the recipient has a high amount of income.[12]

A final thought: Do you think Nobel (Pulitzer, etc.) would have set up such handsomely remunerative devices if told that the sums involved were to be divided by the winners and the United States government on an essentially 60 to 40 ratio?[13]

## PROBLEM

1.     Each year national sportswriters get together and select the single most outstanding amateur athlete in the country and award that person a check for $5,000. Michael, a talented swimmer, has been selected for this year's award. The award is given with the stipulation that the winner deliver a 15 minute "acceptance speech" at an awards banquet. Michael, essentially delivering an acceptable rejection "acceptance speech," designates the Paralympic Games, a charity under § 170, to receive the $5,000 award. The sportswriters send the check to the Paralympic Games.

(a)   Will Michael be able to exclude the $5,000 from his gross income?

(b)   What result if Michael receives the $5,000 check from the United States Olympic Committee for his performance at the Olympics and deposits the check in his personal account?

## B. SCHOLARSHIPS AND FELLOWSHIPS

Internal Revenue Code: Sections 117; 127(a), (b)(1), (c)(1).

Proposed Regulations: Section 1.117–6(b), (c)(1)–(4), (d)(1)–(3).

——————

Prior to the enactment of the 1954 Internal Revenue Code there was no statutory provision that dealt expressly with the income tax aspects of scholarship or fellowship grants. Such grants were occasionally excluded from gross income based on the overworked, generic exclusion for gifts during the years affected by the 1939 Code. Outside of routine matters, factual variations in the "gift" area required that the tax status

---

[10]   See I.R.C. § 274(j)(1), (2) and (3)(B).

[11]   I.R.C. § 74(d)(1).

[12]   I.R.C. § 74(d)(2)(A). In general, if the recipient has adjusted gross income (see Chapter 18C, infra) in excess of $1 million (including the value of the medal and prize money) the exclusion is not applicable. In computing adjusted gross income under several other Code sections, the § 74(d)(1) exclusion is excluded from consideration. I.R.C. § 74(d)(2)(B).

[13]   See I.R.C. § 1(j)(2)(A)–(E).

of scholarships and fellowships be determined largely on a case by case approach. In 1954, Congress enacted Section 117 with the express purpose of providing a clear-cut method for distinguishing between taxable and nontaxable educational grants.[1] As in the case of the exclusion for prizes and awards, the exclusion for scholarships and fellowships was substantially narrowed by the Tax Reform Act of 1986.[2]

Section 117(a) excludes from gross income amounts received as a "qualified scholarship"[3] by a degree candidate[4] at an educational organization.[5] The principal requirements of the exclusion are found in the definition of a qualified scholarship, which is defined as any amount received as a scholarship or fellowship[6] grant that in accordance with the grant is used for "qualified tuition and related expenses."[7] Those expenses encompass tuition and enrollment fees at the educational organization[8] as well as fees, books, supplies and equipment required for courses of instruction.[9] There is no exclusion for amounts which cover personal living expenses, such as meals and lodging, or for travel and research.[10]

Under Section 117(c), a portion of an otherwise excluded scholarship or fellowship is generally required to be included in the recipient's gross income to the extent that the portion represents a payment for teaching, research or other services by the student required as a condition for receiving the otherwise excludable amount.[11] The problem of distinguishing nontaxable scholarships from taxable compensation has been rife in several circumstances. Educational grants made by an employer to a current or former employee have generally been held taxable because they represent compensation for past, present or future

---

    1    Sen.Rep. No. 1622, 83rd Cong., 2d Sess. 17 (1954).

    2    H.Rep. No. 3838, 99th Cong., 2d Sess. 101 (1985). One rationale for the reduction of the exclusion under the 1986 legislation was that many scholarship and fellowship recipients would not be taxed anyway as a result of the increase in the threshold of income level at which individuals became subject to tax.

    3    I.R.C. § 117(b). See Prop.Reg. § 1.117–6(c)(1).

    4    Prop.Reg. § 1.117–6(c)(4). The definition is broad enough to include a degree at various educational levels including primary and secondary schools and undergraduate and graduate colleges and universities.

    5    I.R.C. § 117(a) adopts the definition of "educational organization" contained in § 170(b)(1)(A)(ii), which provides that an "educational organization" is an institution which maintains a regular faculty and curriculum and has a regularly enrolled body of students in attendance at a place where the educational activities are regularly carried on.

    6    I.R.C. § 117 fails to define the terms "scholarship" and "fellowship". The regulations attempt to fill the statutory gap. Prop.Reg. § 1.117–6(c)(3)(i). They define a scholarship or fellowship generally as an amount paid for the benefit of student to aid him in the pursuit of study or research. Id. However the terms do not include amounts provided by an individual to aid a relative, friend, or other individual in pursuit of study or research if the grantor is motivated by family or philanthropic considerations. Id.

    7    I.R.C. § 117(b)(1). The terms of the grant need not expressly require that the awards received be used for tuition and related expenses. Prop.Reg. § 1.117–6(c)(1) (2d sentence).

    8    I.R.C. § 117(b)(2)(A).

    9    I.R.C. § 117(b)(2)(B).

    10    Prop.Reg. § 1.117–6(c)(2).

    11    Prop.Reg. § 1.117–6(d). But see I.R.C. § 117(c)(2).

services.[12] This result has been reached even in cases in which the employee has no contractual obligation to render future services if there is a "clear expectation" that the employment relationship will continue.[13] Services rendered to the education institution which is awarding the scholarship or fellowship will also result in taxable compensation even though such services are required of all persons (regardless of whether they are receiving a scholarship or fellowship) qualifying for the degree.[14] However, the Service has allowed an exclusion for a university athletic scholarship if the university expects but does not require the student to participate in a particular sport, requires no particular activity in lieu of participation, and cannot terminate the scholarship if the student cannot participate.[15] Thus, to qualify for the exclusion, there must still be a gratuitous or non-contractual flavor to the grant, similar to the gift concept as ultimately developed out of the well-known *Duberstein* opinion.[16]

The Code contains two additional employment-related exclusions of educational benefits.[17] First, Section 117(d) allows a "qualified tuition reduction"[18] to be excluded from gross income in the case of education below the graduate level[19] or at the graduate level if the graduate student is engaged in teaching or research activities.[20] The reduction may be available to the employees of the educational organization granting the reduction or to employees of some other educational organization as well.[21] The term "employee" is defined by reference to the broad definition of employee in Section 132(h), which includes the employee, the employee's spouse and dependent children, and the surviving spouse of a deceased employee.[22] The exclusion invokes the Section 132 concept of nondiscrimination: Section 117(d) is applicable to highly compensated employees only on a nondiscriminatory basis.[23] Although a qualified tuition reduction is eligible for an exclusion from gross income, to the extent that the reduction represents payment for research, teaching, or other services required of the student to receive the reduction, the qualified tuition reduction is required to be included in gross income.[24]

---

[12] Prop.Reg. §§ 1.117–6(d)(2) and –6(d)(5) Examples (1) and (2). See, e.g., Bingler v. Johnson, 394 U.S. 741, 89 S.Ct. 1439 (1969); Leonard T. Fielding, 57 T.C. 761 (1972).

[13] John E. MacDonald, Jr., 52 T.C. 386 (1969); see also Ehrhart v. Commissioner, 470 F.2d 940 (1st Cir.1973).

[14] I.R.C. § 117(c). See Prop.Reg. § 1.117–6(d)(1) and (2) and –6(d)(5) Examples (3)–(5).

[15] Rev.Rul. 77–263, 1977–2 C.B. 47.

[16] Commissioner v. Duberstein, 363 U.S. 278, 80 S.Ct. 1190 (1960).

[17] See Chapter 11C, infra, for other exclusions related to educational costs.

[18] I.R.C. § 117(d)(2) defines this term.

[19] See I.R.C. § 117(d)(2) (1st parenthetical).

[20] I.R.C. § 117(d)(5).

[21] I.R.C. § 117(d)(2) (2nd parenthetical).

[22] I.R.C. § 117(d)(2)(B). See page 92, supra.

[23] I.R.C. § 117(d)(3). See page 93, supra.

[24] I.R.C. § 117(c). For an illustration of this rule, see Prop.Reg. § 1.117–6(d)(5) Example (6).

Section 127 permits an employee to exclude up to $5,250 from gross income for amounts paid by the employer for educational assistance at the undergraduate and graduate levels of education,[25] provided the educational assistance program meets certain requirements[26] related primarily to nondiscrimination in favor of highly compensated employees. Educational assistance under Section 127 includes tuition, books, supplies and an employer provided educational course, but it does not include assistance for courses involving sports, games, or hobbies.[27] By its very nature the educational assistance is compensation; thus, as compared to the Section 117(a) and Section 117(d) exclusions, one is not required to jump the compensation (payment for services) hurdle for an exclusion under Section 127.

## PROBLEMS

1.   Student working toward an A.B. degree is awarded a scholarship of $15,000 for full tuition and for room and board during the academic year. The tuition, including the cost of books, is $10,000, and the room and board costs $5,000. As a scholarship recipient, Student is required to do about 300 hours of research for the professor to whom he is assigned. Nonscholarship students, if hired, receive $10.00 per hour for such work.

   (a)   What tax consequences to Student?

   (b)   What tax consequences to Student if all students are required to do 300 hours of research for faculty?

   (c)   What result if Student is not required to do any research but receives the $15,000 as an athletic scholarship?

   (d)   What tax consequences to Student if Student receives only a tuition scholarship worth $9,000 (no books) because Student's spouse is an employee at a neighboring educational institution and the tuition scholarship is part of a nondiscriminatory plan between several institutions applicable to all employees of such institutions?

2.   Secretary, in a large tax law firm, receives a $10,000 stipend from her firm to assist her while on a leave of absence to obtain a college degree. The stipend is part of a firm plan under which all recipients are required to return to the firm following their educational leave.

   (a)   What tax consequences to Secretary?

   (b)   What tax consequences to Secretary if she is not required to return to the firm after completing her degree?

---

[25]   I.R.C. § 127(c)(1). See I.R.S. Service Advice Review 2010–3901 F. Amounts in excess of the maximum or which are disqualified by the last sentence of I.R.C. § 127(c)(1) may qualify for an exclusion as a working condition fringe under § 132(d). I.R.C. § 132(j)(8).

[26]   I.R.C. § 127(b)(2)–(6).

[27]   I.R.C. § 127(c)(1).

(c)  What are the tax consequences to Secretary if she is not an employee, but instead receives the stipend as a prize in an essay contest?

*Gross income to she*

# CHAPTER 6

# GAIN FROM DEALINGS IN PROPERTY

## A. FACTORS IN THE DETERMINATION OF GAIN

Internal Revenue Code: Sections 1001(a), (b) first sentence, (c); 1011(a); 1012(a).

Regulations: Section 1.1001–1(a).

---

If T lends B money and later B pays it back no one would suppose that T has gross income upon the mere repayment of the principal amount of the loan. In tax parlance, the reason for this conclusion is that the repayment constitutes a mere *return of capital* to T. There is no element of gain in such a transaction and, consequently, this exclusionary rule has always been recognized just as if the principle were spelled out in the statutory provisions.

But the return-of-capital concept is by no means restricted to the loan repayment area. It arises in many more sophisticated ways, both as a kind of common law rule and as a statutory principle. In other circumstances, it may be more difficult to say to what extent the taxpayer's capital is merely being returned. In general the device adopted for aid in measuring this is "basis." Basis, unadjusted, essentially answers the question: How much have I got in it? Thus, if T buys property for $10,000, T has that amount in it, and T's basis is $10,000. Basis and value must be carefully differentiated. If the property so acquired is securities that increase in *value* to $15,000, *basis* is still only $10,000. Avoid the student inclination to use these terms indiscriminately.

If the value of the property increases to $15,000 and T sells the property for $15,000, T has made $5,000 on the investment because the property has appreciated in value to that extent and because T has liquidated the investment. This rather obvious result is translated into tax terminology by Section 1001(a), which identifies gain on the disposition of property as the excess of the "amount realized" over the "adjusted basis". The "amount realized" is defined in Section 1001(b) as the amount of money received and the fair market value of property (other than money) received on the disposition. Here the amount realized by T is $15,000 (only money was received) and, if T's basis is $10,000, T's § 1001(a) realized gain is $5,000. Section 1001(c) requires gain realized to be recognized unless otherwise provided by another Code section. Current attention is directed only to the "amount" of gain; Part Six of this book is addressed to the "character" of gain and the tax consequences of such characterization and Part Seven is addressed to possible "nonrecognition" of gain. What would be the result to T under Section 1001(a) if, instead of appreciating, the property had declined in value and T had sold it for $8,000 cash? Again, characterization and final tax consequences are intended to be deferred.

Determination of the "amount realized" on a disposition of property and of the property's "adjusted basis" are not always as simple as in the hypothetical posed above. The materials that follow suggest ways, other than by purchase, in which basis is established and circumstances calling for adjustment in basis, both upward and downward. They also present some less obvious circumstances in which the "amount realized" must be determined as a factor in the measurement of gain on a sale or other disposition of property.

## B. DETERMINATION OF BASIS

### 1. COST AS BASIS*

Internal Revenue Code: Sections 109; 1011(a); 1012(a); 1016(a)(1); 1019.
Regulations: Sections 1.61–2(d)(2)(i); 1.1012–1(a).

---

### Philadelphia Park Amusement Co. v. United States**

Court of Claims of the United States, 1954.
126 F.Supp. 184.

[In 1889, the taxpayer had been granted a 50-year franchise to operate a passenger railway in Fairmount Park, Philadelphia. At a cost of $381,000, it built the Strawberry Bridge over the Schuylkill River, which was used by its streetcars. In 1934, it deeded the bridge to the city in exchange for a ten-year extension of its franchise. In 1946, when the extended franchise still had three years to run, it was abandoned, and the taxpayer arranged bus transportation for visitors to its amusement park. The taxpayer's basis for the ten-year extension of its franchise became important when the taxpayer asserted depreciation deductions based on the cost of the extension and a loss upon abandonment of the franchise. Basis questions for these purposes are essentially the same as those that arise in the determination of gain or loss on the disposition of an asset. Ed.]

---

\* There is an early but comprehensive discussion of cost as basis in Greenbaum, "The Basis of Property Shall Be the Cost of Such Property: How is Cost Defined?" 3 Tax.L.Rev. 351 (1948); See also Kohl, "The Identification Theory of Basis," 40 Tax L.Rev. 623 (1985).

\*\* Some footnotes omitted.

■ LARAMORE, JUDGE.

\* \* \*

This brings us to the question of what is the cost basis of the 10-year extension of taxpayer's franchise. Although defendant contends that Strawberry Bridge was either worthless or not "exchanged" for the 10-year extension of the franchise, we believe that the bridge had some value, and that the contract under which the bridge was transferred to the City clearly indicates that the one was given in consideration of the other. \* \* \*.

The gain or loss, whichever the case may have been, should have been recognized, and the cost basis under section 113(a)[4] of the Code, of the 10-year extension of the franchise was the cost to the taxpayer. The succinct statement in section 113(a) that "the basis of property shall be the cost of such property" although clear in principle, is frequently difficult in application. One view is that the cost basis of property received in a taxable exchange is the fair market value of the property *given* in the exchange. The other view is that the cost basis of property received in a taxable exchange is the fair market value of the property *received* in the exchange. As will be seen from the cases and some of the Commissioner's rulings[7] the Commissioner's position has not been altogether consistent on this question. The view that "cost" is the fair market value of the property given is predicated on the theory that the cost to the taxpayer is the economic value relinquished. The view that "cost" is the fair market value of the property received is based upon the theory that the term "cost" is a tax concept and must be considered in the light of the \* \* \* prime role that the basis of property plays in determining tax liability. We believe that when the question is considered in the latter context that the cost basis of the property received in a taxable exchange is the fair market value of the property *received* in the exchange.

When property is exchanged for property in a taxable exchange the taxpayer is taxed on the difference between the adjusted basis of the property given in exchange and the fair market value of the property received in exchange. For purposes of determining gain or loss the fair market value of the property received is treated as cash and taxed accordingly. To maintain harmony with the fundamental purpose of these sections, it is necessary to consider the fair market value of the property received as the cost basis to the taxpayer. The failure to do so would result in allowing the taxpayer a stepped-up basis, without paying a tax therefor, if the fair market value of the property received is less than the fair market value of the property given, and the taxpayer would

---

[4] Section 113(a) provides: "Basis, (unadjusted) of property. The basis of property shall be the cost of such property; except that \* \* \*." 26 U.S.C.A. § 113. [See I.R.C. § 1012. Ed.]

[7] Compare I.T. 2212, IV–2 C.B. 118 with I.T. 3523, 1941–2 C.B. 124 and the Commissioner's equivocal acquiescence in Estate of Isadore L. Myers case, supra, 1943–1 C.B. 17.

be subjected to a double tax if the fair market value of the property received is more than the fair market value of the property given. By holding that the fair market value of the property received in a taxable exchange is the cost basis, the above discrepancy is avoided and the basis of the property received will equal the adjusted basis of the property given plus any gain recognized, or that should have been recognized, or minus any loss recognized, or that should have been recognized.

Therefore, the cost basis of the 10-year extension of the franchise was its fair market value on August 3, 1934, the date of the exchange. The determination of whether the cost basis of the property received is its fair market value or the fair market value of the property given in exchange therefor, although necessary to the decision of the case, is generally not of great practical significance because the value of the two properties exchanged in an arms-length transaction are either equal in fact, or are presumed to be equal. The record in this case indicates that the 1934 exchange was an arms-length transaction and, therefore, if the value of the extended franchise cannot be determined with reasonable accuracy, it would be reasonable and fair to assume that the value of Strawberry Bridge was equal to the 10-year extension of the franchise. The fair market value of the 10-year extension of the franchise should be established but, if that value cannot be determined with reasonable certainty, the fair market value of Strawberry Bridge should be established and that will be presumed to be the value of the extended franchise. This value cannot be determined from the facts now before us since the case was prosecuted on a different theory.

The taxpayer contends that the market value of the extended franchise or Strawberry Bridge could not be ascertained and, therefore, it should be entitled to carry over the undepreciated cost basis of the bridge as the cost of the extended franchise under section 113(b)(2).[9] If the value of the extended franchise or bridge cannot be ascertained with a reasonable degree of accuracy, the taxpayer is entitled to carry over the undepreciated cost of the bridge as the cost basis of the extended franchise. * * *. However, it is only in rare and extraordinary cases that the value of the property exchanged cannot be ascertained with reasonable accuracy. We are presently of the opinion that either the value of the extended franchise or the bridge can be determined with a reasonable degree of accuracy. Although the value of the extended franchise may be difficult or impossible to ascertain because of the nebulous and intangible characteristics inherent in such property, the value of the bridge is subject to more exact measurement. Consideration may be given to expert testimony on the value of comparable bridges,

---

[9] Section 113(b)(2) provides: "Substituted basis. The term 'substituted basis' as used in this subsection means a basis determined under any provision of subsection (a) of this section or under any corresponding provision of a prior income tax law, providing that the basis shall be determined—(A) by reference to the basis in the hands of a transferor, donor, or grantor, or (B) by reference to other property held at any time by the person for whom the basis is to be determined." [See I.R.C. § 7701(a)(42)–(44). Ed.]

Strawberry Bridge's reproduction cost and its undepreciated cost, as well as other relevant factors.

Therefore, because we deem it equitable, judgment should be suspended and the question of the value of the extended franchise on August 3, 1934, should be remanded to the Commissioner of this court for the taking of evidence and the filing of a report thereon.

The failure of taxpayer to properly record the transaction in 1934 and thereafter does not prevent the correction of the error, especially under the circumstances of this case.

\* \* \*

We, therefore, conclude that the 1934 exchange was a taxable exchange and that the taxpayer is entitled to use as the cost basis of the 10-year extension of its franchise its fair market value on August 3, 1934, for purposes of determining depreciation and loss due to abandonment, as indicated in this opinion.

Accordingly, judgment will be suspended and the question of the value of the extended franchise on August 3, 1934, is remanded to the Commissioner of this court for the taking of evidence and the filing of a report thereon.

■ JONES, CHIEF JUDGE, and MADDEN, WHITAKER, and LITTLETON, JUDGES, concur.

## NOTE

In the vast majority of "real world" situations, a taxpayer's acquisition basis in property is the cost basis determined when the property is purchased. While the principles of the *Philadelphia Park Amusement Co.* case are important in illustrating the cost basis of property received in an exchange, who ever heard of an exchange of a bridge for a ten-year franchise to operate a railroad?! Most acquisitions of both tangible and intangible property are by purchase and the purchase price simply establishes the cost basis. So if a taxpayer buys equipment, land, corporate stock, or some other asset, the purchase price for the asset is its cost basis.[1] In a purchase of an asset, it is also established that the concept of "cost" generally includes amounts paid as transactional costs to facilitate the acquisition. So, for example, if taxpayer purchases land and in connection with the purchase must pay a lawyer's fees to negotiate the deal and a commission to a broker, the attorney's fees and the broker's commission are included in the cost basis of the land.[2]

---

[1]   Reg. § 1.1012–1(a); see also Reg. §§ 1.263(a)–2(a), –4(a). The Code is designed to ensure that while the property gets a cost basis the taxpayer is not simultaneously allowed to deduct (i.e., subtract) the cost of the property in computing tax liability. To prevent this type of "double dipping," the regulations which deny a deduction are consistent with I.R.C. § 1012 and require the cost to be "capitalized," i.e., added to the property's basis. Thus, those regulations confirm and reinforce the rules in § 1012 regarding cost basis. Principles of capitalization are generally discussed in connection with the rules for deductions in Chapter 14B2.

[2]   Reg. § 1.263(a)–2(f)(1), (2)(ii)(C) & (I); –2(g).

But, as the problems below illustrate, the concept of "cost" has some additional wrinkles. To preview some of the issues, consider the following questions. What does an asset "cost" if the taxpayer first pays for an option to purchase the asset at a set price and, later, exercises the option? Should the amount paid for the option be included as part of the asset's cost basis? Or suppose a taxpayer constructs a building and pays for architectural fees, permits, and other incidental costs. Should the taxpayer's construction costs be the property's basis and what do those costs include?[3] Finally, to preview a topic encountered in connection with deductions, suppose a taxpayer owns property and decides to improve it by paying for an addition to the property. Should the addition be treated essentially like the acquisition of additional property and added to the basis of the property? Or does the addition fall into the category of a "repair" which can be deducted immediately (a write off!) and not added to basis.[4] The basic point is the while the Section 1012 basis rules are studied in this Chapter, the principles underlying cost basis arise in other areas that will be explored later in the Text. So the topics previewed here will be revisited.

## PROBLEMS

1. Owner purchases some land for $10,000 and later sells it for $16,000.

   (a) Determine the amount of Owner's gain on the sale. *6n*

   (b) What difference in result in (a), above, if Owner purchased the land by paying $1,000 for an option to purchase the land for an additional $9,000 and subsequently exercised the option? *6n*

   (c) What result to Owner in (b), above, if rather than ever actually acquiring the land Owner sold the option to Investor for $1,500? *5n*

   (d) What difference in result in (a), above, if Owner purchased the land by making a $2,000 cash payment from Owner's funds and an $8,000 payment by borrowing $8,000 from the bank in a recourse mortgage (on which Owner is personally liable)? Would it make any difference if the mortgage was a nonrecourse liability (on which only the land was security for the obligation)? *6n - 10*

   (e) What result in (a), above, if Owner purchased the land for $10,000, spent $2,000 in clearing the land prior to its sale, and sold it for $18,000? *6n*

   (f) What difference in result in (e), above, if Owner had previously rented the land to Lessee for five years for $1,000 per year cash rental and permitted Lessee to expend $2,000 clearing the property? Assume that, although Owner properly reported the cash rental payments as gross income, the $2,000 expenditures were properly excluded under § 109. See § 1019.

---

[3] See Chapter 14B2 and problem 1 at page 417, infra.

[4] See Chapter 14B2.

(g)   What difference in result in (a), above, if when the land had a value of $10,000, Owner, a real estate salesperson, received it from Employer as a bonus for putting together a major real estate development? Owner paid $3,000 of income tax on the $10,000 fair market value receipt of the land.

(h)   What difference if Owner is a salesperson in an art gallery and Owner purchases a $10,000 painting from the art gallery, but is required to pay only $9,000 for it (instead of $10,000 because Owner is allowed a 10% employee discount which is excluded from gross income under § 132(a)(2)), and Owner later sells the painting for $16,000?

2.   In an arm's-length exchange, Sharp exchanges some land with a cost basis of $6,000 and a value of $9,000 with Dull for some non-publicly traded stock which Dull owns and in which Dull has a basis of $8,000 and is worth $10,000 at the time of the exchange.

(a)   Consider Sharp and Dull's gains on the exchange and their respective cost bases in the assets they receive.

(b)   What results in (a), above, if the value of Dull's stock cannot be determined with any reasonable certainty?

## 2.  PROPERTY ACQUIRED BY GIFT

Internal Revenue Code: Section 1015(a). See Sections 1015(d)(1)(A), (4) and (6).

Regulations: Section 1.1015–1(a).

---

## Taft v. Bowers

Supreme Court of the United States, 1929.
278 U.S. 470, 49 S.Ct. 199.

■ MR. JUSTICE MCREYNOLDS delivered the opinion of the Court.

Petitioners, who are donees of stocks, seek to recover income taxes exacted because of advancement in the market value of those stocks while owned by the donors. The facts are not in dispute. Both causes must turn upon the effect of [Section 1015(a). Ed.] which prescribes the basis for estimating taxable gain when one disposes of property which came to him by gift. The records do not differ essentially and a statement of the material circumstances disclosed by No. 16 will suffice.

During the calendar years 1921 and 1922, the father of petitioner Elizabeth C. Taft, gave her certain shares of Nash Motors Company stock then more valuable than when acquired by him. She sold them during 1923 for more than their market value when the gift was made.

The United States demanded an income tax reckoned upon the difference between cost to the donor and price received by the donee. She paid accordingly and sued to recover the portion imposed because of the advance in value while the donor owned the stock. The right to tax the increase in value after the gift is not denied.

Abstractly stated, this is the problem—

In 1916 A purchased 100 shares of stock for $1,000 which he held until 1923 when their fair market value had become $2,000. He then gave them to B who sold them during the year 1923 for $5,000. The United States claim that, under the Revenue Act of 1921, B must pay income tax upon $4,000, as realized profits. B maintains that only $3,000—the appreciation during her ownership—can be regarded as income; that the increase during the donor's ownership is not income assessable against her within intendment of the Sixteenth Amendment.

The District Court ruled against the United States; the Circuit Court of Appeals held with them.

\* \* \*

We think the manifest purpose of Congress expressed in [Section 102(a) and 1015(a). Ed.] was to require the petitioner to pay the exacted tax.

The only question subject to serious controversy is whether Congress had power to authorize the exaction.

It is said that the gift became a capital asset of the donee to the extent of its value when received and, therefore, when disposed of by her no part of that value could be treated as taxable income in her hands.

The Sixteenth Amendment provides—

"The Congress shall have power to lay and collect taxes on incomes from whatever source derived, without apportionment among the several States, and without regard to any census or enumeration."

Income is the thing which may be taxed—income from any source. The Amendment does not attempt to define income or to designate how taxes may be laid thereon, or how they may be enforced.

Under former decisions here the settled doctrine is that the Sixteenth Amendment confers no power upon Congress to define and tax as income without apportionment something which theretofore could not have been properly regarded as income.

Also, this Court has declared—"Income may be defined as the gain derived from capital, from labor, or from both combined, provided it be understood to include profit gained through a sale or conversion of capital assets." Eisner v. Macomber, 252 U.S. 189, 207, 40 S.Ct. 189, 193. The "gain derived from capital," within the definition, is "not a gain accruing to capital, nor a growth or increment of value in the investment, but a gain, a profit, something of exchangeable value proceeding from the property, severed from the capital however invested, and coming in, that is, received or drawn by the claimant for his separate use, benefit and disposal." United States v. Phellis, 257 U.S. 156, 169, 42 S.Ct. 63, 65.

If, instead of giving the stock to petitioner, the donor had sold it at market value, the excess over the capital he invested (cost) would have been income therefrom and subject to taxation under the Sixteenth Amendment. He would have been obliged to share the realized gain with the United States. He held the stock—the investment—subject to the right of the sovereign to take part of any increase in its value when separated through sale or conversion and reduced to his possession. Could he, contrary to the express will of Congress, by mere gift enable another to hold this stock free from such right, deprive the sovereign of the possibility of taxing the appreciation when actually severed, and convert the entire property into a capital asset of the donee, who invested nothing, as though the latter had purchased at the market price? And after a still further enhancement of the property, could the donee make a second gift with like effect, etc.? We think not.

In truth the stock represented only a single investment of capital—that made by the donor. And when through sale or conversion the increase was separated therefrom, it became income from that investment in the hands of the recipient subject to taxation according to the very words of the Sixteenth Amendment. By requiring the recipient of the entire increase to pay a part into the public treasury, Congress deprived her of no right and subjected her to no hardship. She accepted the gift with knowledge of the statute and, as to the property received, voluntarily assumed the position of her donor. When she sold the stock she actually got the original sum invested, plus the entire appreciation; and out of the latter only was she called on to pay the tax demanded.

The provision of the statute under consideration seems entirely appropriate for enforcing a general scheme of lawful taxation. To accept the view urged in behalf of petitioner undoubtedly would defeat, to some extent, the purpose of Congress to take part of all gain derived from capital investments. To prevent that result and insure enforcement of its proper policy, Congress had power to require that for purposes of taxation the donee should accept the position of the donor in respect of the thing received. And in so doing, it acted neither unreasonably nor arbitrarily.

\* \* \*

There is nothing in the Constitution which lends support to the theory that gain actually resulting from the increased value of capital can be treated as taxable income in the hands of the recipient only so far as the increase occurred while he owned the property. And Irwin v. Gavit, 268 U.S. 161, 167, 45 S.Ct. 475, 476, is to the contrary.

The judgments below are

Affirmed.

■ THE CHIEF JUSTICE took no part in the consideration or decision of these causes.

# Farid-Es-Sultaneh v. Commissioner

United States Court of Appeals, Second Circuit, 1947.
160 F.2d 812.

■ CHASE, CIRCUIT JUDGE.

The problem presented by this petition is to fix the cost basis to be used by the petitioner in determining the taxable gain on a sale she made in 1938 of shares of corporate stock. She contends that it is the adjusted value of the shares at the date she acquired them because her acquisition was by purchase. The Commissioner's position is that she must use the adjusted cost basis of her transferor because her acquisition was by gift. The Tax Court agreed with the Commissioner and redetermined the deficiency accordingly.

The pertinent facts are not in dispute and were found by the Tax Court as they were disclosed in the stipulation of the parties substantially as follows:

The petitioner is an American citizen who filed her income tax return for the calendar year 1938 with the Collector of Internal Revenue for the Third District of New York and in it reported sales during that year of 12,000 shares of the common stock of the S.S. Kresge Company at varying prices per share, for the total sum of $230,802.36 which admittedly was in excess of their cost to her. How much this excess amounted to for tax purposes depends upon the legal significance of the facts now to be stated.

In December 1923 when the petitioner, then unmarried, and S.S. Kresge, then married, were contemplating their future marriage, he delivered to her 700 shares of the common stock of the S.S. Kresge Company which then had a fair market value of $290 per share. The shares were all in street form and were to be held by the petitioner "for her benefit and protection in the event that the said Kresge should die prior to the contemplated marriage between the petitioner and said Kresge." The latter was divorced from his wife on January 9, 1924, and on or about January 23, 1924 he delivered to the petitioner 1800 additional common shares of S.S. Kresge Company which were also in street form and were to be held by the petitioner for the same purposes as were the first 700 shares he had delivered to her. On April 24, 1924, and when the petitioner still retained the possession of the stock so delivered to her, she and Mr. Kresge executed a written ante-nuptial agreement wherein she acknowledged the receipt of the shares "as a gift made by the said Sebastian S. Kresge, pursuant to this indenture, and as an ante-nuptial settlement, and in consideration of said gift and said ante-nuptial settlement, in consideration of the promise of said Sebastian S. Kresge to marry her, and in further consideration of the consummation of said promised marriage" she released all dower and other marital rights, including the right to her support to which she otherwise would have been entitled as a matter of law when she became his wife. They were married in New York immediately after the ante-nuptial agreement was executed and continued to be husband and wife until the petitioner obtained a final decree of absolute divorce from him on, or about, May 18, 1928. No alimony was claimed by, or awarded to, her.

The stock so obtained by the petitioner from Mr. Kresge had a fair market value of $315 per share on April 24, 1924, and of $330 per share on, or about May 6, 1924, when it was transferred to her on the books of the corporation. She held all of it for about three years, but how much she continued to hold thereafter is not disclosed except as that may be shown by her sales in 1938. Meanwhile her holdings had been increased by a stock dividend of 50 per cent, declared on April 1, 1925; one of 10 to 1 declared on January 19, 1926; and one of 50 per cent, declared on March 1, 1929. Her adjusted basis for the stock she sold in 1938 was $10.66⅔ per share computed on the basis of the fair market value of the shares which she obtained from Mr. Kresge at the time of her acquisition. His adjusted basis for the shares she sold in 1938 would have been $0.159091.[1]

When the petitioner and Mr. Kresge were married he was 57 years old with a life expectancy of 16½ years. She was then 32 years of age with a life expectancy of 33¾ years. He was then worth approximately $375,000,000 and owned real estate of the approximate value of $100,000,000.

The Commissioner determined the deficiency on the ground that the petitioner's stock obtained as above stated was acquired by gift within the meaning of that word as used in § 113(a)(2) of the Revenue Act of 1938, * * * and * * * used as the basis for determining the gain on her sale of it the basis it would have had in the hands of the donor.[2] This was correct if the just mentioned statute is applicable, and the Tax Court held it was on the authority of Commissioner v. Wemyss, 324 U.S. 303, 65 S.Ct. 652, 156 A.L.R. 1022, and Merrill v. Fahs, 324 U.S. 308, 65 S.Ct. 655.

The issue here presented cannot, however, be adequately dealt with quite so summarily. The Wemyss case determined the taxability to the transferor as a gift, under §§ 501 and 503 of the Revenue Act of 1932, * * * and the applicable regulations, of property transferred in trust for the benefit of the prospective wife of the transferor pursuant to the terms of an ante-nuptial agreement. It was held that the transfer, being solely in consideration of her promise of marriage, and to compensate her for loss of trust income which would cease upon her marriage, was not for an adequate and full consideration in money or money's worth within the meaning of § 503 of the statute, the Tax Court having found that the

[1] [Current rules for allocation of basis in the case of stock dividends appear in I.R.C. § 307. Ed.]

[2] [See I.R.C. (1986) § 1015(a). Ed.]

transfer was not one at arm's length made in the ordinary course of business. But we find nothing in this decision to show that a transfer, taxable as a gift under the gift tax, is ipso facto to be treated as a gift in construing the income tax law.

In Merrill v. Fahs, supra, it was pointed out that the estate and gift tax statutes are in pari materia and are to be so construed. * * *. The estate tax provisions in the Revenue Act of 1916 required the inclusion in a decedent's gross estate of transfers made in contemplation of death, or intended to take effect in possession and enjoyment at or after death except when a transfer was the result of "a bona fide sale for a fair consideration in money or money's worth." * * *. The first gift tax became effective in 1924, and provided inter alia, that where an exchange or sale of property was for less than a fair consideration in money or money's worth the excess should be taxed as a gift. * * *. While both taxing statutes thus provided, it was held that a release of dower rights was a fair consideration in money or money's worth. * * *. Following that, Congress in 1926 replaced the words "fair consideration" in the 1924 Act limiting the deductibility of claims against an estate with the words "adequate and full consideration in money or money's worth" and in 1932 the gift tax statute as enacted limited consideration in the same way. * * *. Although Congress in 1932 also expressly provided that the release of marital rights should not be treated as a consideration in money or money's worth in administering the estate tax law, * * * and failed to include such a provision in the gift tax statute, it was held that the gift tax law should be construed to the same effect.[3] Merrill v. Fahs, supra.

We find in this decision no indication, however, that the term "gift" as used in the income tax statute should be construed to include a transfer which, if made when the gift tax were effective, would be taxable to the transferor as a gift merely because of the special provisions in the gift tax statute defining and restricting consideration for gift tax purposes. A fortiori, it would seem that limitations found in the estate tax law upon according the usual legal effect to proof that a transfer was made for a fair consideration should not be imported into the income tax law except by action of Congress. In our opinion the income tax provisions are not to be construed as though they were in pari materia with either the estate tax law or the gift tax statutes. They are aimed at the gathering of revenue by taking for public use given percentages of what the statute fixes as net taxable income. Capital gains and losses are, to the required or permitted extent, factors in determining net taxable income. What is known as the basis for computing gain or loss on transfers of property is established by statute in those instances when the resulting gain or loss is recognized for income tax purposes and the basis for succeeding sales or exchanges will, theoretically at least, level off tax-wise any hills and valleys in the consideration passing either way on previous sales or exchanges. When Congress provided that gifts

---

[3]    [See I.R.C. (1986) §§ 2043(b) and 2512(b). Ed.]

should not be treated as taxable income to the donee there was, without any correlative provisions fixing the basis of the gift to the donee, a loophole which enabled the donee to make a subsequent transfer of the property and take as the basis for computing gain or loss its value when the gift was made. Thus it was possible to exclude from taxation any increment in value during the donor's holding and the donee might take advantage of any shrinkage in such increment after the acquisition by gift in computing gain or loss upon a subsequent sale or exchange. It was to close this loophole that Congress provided that the donee should take the donor's basis when property was transferred by gift. * * *. This change in the statute affected only the statutory net taxable income. The altered statute prevented a transfer by gift from creating any change in the basis of the property in computing gain or loss on any future transfer. In any individual instance the change in the statute would but postpone taxation and presumably would have little effect on the total volume of income tax revenue derived over a long period of time and from many taxpayers. Because of this we think that a transfer which should be classed as a gift under the gift tax law is not necessarily to be treated as a gift income-tax-wise. Though such a consideration as this petitioner gave for the shares of stock she acquired from Mr. Kresge might not have relieved him from liability for a gift tax, had the present gift tax then been in effect, it was nevertheless a fair consideration which prevented her taking the shares as a gift under the income tax law since it precluded the existence of a donative intent.

Although the transfers of the stock made both in December 1923, and in the following January by Mr. Kresge to this taxpayer are called a gift in the ante-nuptial agreement later executed and were to be for the protection of his prospective bride if he died before the marriage was consummated, the "gift" was contingent upon his death before such marriage, an event that did not occur. Consequently, it would appear that no absolute gift was made before the ante-nuptial contract was executed and that she took title to the stock under its terms, viz: in consideration for her promise to marry him coupled with her promise to relinquish all rights in and to his property which she would otherwise acquire by the marriage. Her inchoate interest in the property of her affianced husband greatly exceeded the value of the stock transferred to her. It was a fair consideration under ordinary legal concepts of that term for the transfers of the stock by him. * * *. She performed the contract under the terms of which the stock was transferred to her and held the shares not as a donee but as a purchaser for a fair consideration.

As the decisive issue is one of law only, the decision of the Tax Court interpreting the applicable statutory provisions has no peculiar finality and is reviewable. * * *.

Decision reversed.

■ [The dissenting opinion of CIRCUIT JUDGE CLARK has been omitted. Ed.]

## PROBLEMS

**1.** Donor gave Donee property under circumstances that required no payment of gift tax. What gain or loss to Donee on the subsequent sale of the property if:

    (a) The property had cost Donor $20,000, had a $30,000 fair market value at the time of the gift, and Donee sold it for:

        (1) $35,000?

        (2) $15,000?

        (3) $25,000?

    (b) The property had cost Donor $30,000, had a $20,000 fair market value at the time of the gift, and Donee sold it for:

        (1) $35,000?

        (2) $15,000?

        (3) $24,000?

**2.** Father had some land that he had purchased for $100,000 but which had increased in value to $200,000. He transferred it to Daughter for $100,000 in cash in a transaction properly identified as in part a gift and in part a sale.* Assume no gift tax was paid on the transfer.

    (a) What gain to Father and what basis to Daughter under Reg. §§ 1.1001–1(e) and 1.1015–4(a)(1)?

    (b) Suppose the transaction were viewed as a sale of one-half of the land for full consideration and an outright gift of the other one half. How would this affect Father's gain and Daughter's basis? Is it a more realistic view than that of the Regulations? Cf. §§ 170(e)(2) and 1011(b), relating to bargain sales to charities.

## 3. PROPERTY ACQUIRED BETWEEN SPOUSES OR INCIDENT TO DIVORCE

Internal Revenue Code: Section 1041(a) and (b).

Regulations: Section 1.1041–1T(a) and (d).

---

    Property acquired by purchase has a cost basis to the buyer in the amount of what the buyer paid for it.[1] Depending on the nature of the property, the seller's gain or loss is determined by whether the amount realized[2] by the seller exceeds or is less than the seller's adjusted basis

---

    * See Freeland, Maxfield and Sawyer, "Part Gift-Part Sale: An Income Tax Analysis with Policy Considerations," 47 Tax.L.Rev. 407 (1992); Wurzel, "The Tax Basis for Assorted Bargain Purchases, or: The Inordinate Cost of 'Ersatz' Legislation," 20 Tax L.Rev. 165 (1964).

    [1] I.R.C. § 1012.

    [2] I.R.C. § 1001(b).

in the property.[3] In general and in contrast to the gift of property, the sale or exchange of property is not a tax neutral transaction.

Property that is acquired by gift costs the donee nothing; it is not even includable in the donee's gross income.[4] Therefore, the donee's basis in property acquired solely by gift is never a cost or quasi-cost basis.[5] A special provision generally accords the donee a transferred basis in such property.[6] Except for purposes of determining a loss on the sale of property whose value was less than the donor's basis at the time of the gift, the basis of property in the hands of a donee is the same basis the property had in the hands of the donor.[7] A consequence of this transferred basis rule is that pre-gift appreciation remains taxable in the event of a subsequent sale or exchange of the property by the donee. For purposes of determining gain (and sometimes loss), the donee steps into the basis shoes of the donor. The transfer of property by gift between the donor and the donee can properly be said to have neutral income tax consequences.

Before Congress enacted Section 1041, the transfer of appreciated property to a spouse in a sale or exchange for full value resulted in a gain to the transferor[8] and the transferee spouse was accorded a "cost" basis equal to the fair market value of the property received. The above gain recognition rules also applied if the transfer of appreciated property to a spouse (or former spouse) was in exchange for the release of marital claims,[9] and the transferee spouse again was accorded a "cost" basis of full fair market value in the property but with no income tax price to pay for such basis.[10] The results, however, were not uniform as the various states have differing types of property ownership within a marriage.[11] For these and other reasons, Congress considered it inappropriate to tax transfers of property between spouses or former spouses. The policy implemented here reflects the attitude that a husband and wife are a single economic unit, and the tax laws governing transfers of property between spouses and sometimes between former spouses should be as unintrusive as possible.[12]

Section 1041 accords almost complete tax neutrality to transfers of property between spouses and between former spouses if, in the latter

---

[3]  I.R.C. § 1001(a).

[4]  I.R.C. § 102(a).

[5]  Cf. Reg. § 1.1015–4.

[6]  I.R.C. § 1015(a).

[7]  Id. See also I.R.C. § 1015(d).

[8]  I.R.C. § 267 disallowed losses on sales or exchanges between spouses. I.R.C. § 267(a)(1), (b)(1), (c)(4). See Chapter 25A, infra and see I.R.C. § 267(g) making § 267 inapplicable to transfers within § 1041.

[9]  See, e.g., United States v. Davis, 370 U.S. 65, 82 S.Ct. 1190 (1962); cf. note 8, supra.

[10]  Rev.Rul. 67–221, 1967–2 C.B. 63.

[11]  See page 203, infra.

[12]  H.Rep. No. 98–432, Part 2, 98th Cong., 2d Sess. 1491–1492 (1984).

instance, the transfer is incident to divorce.[13] No gain or loss is recognized.[14] This rule applies whether the transfer of property is for cash or other property, for the relinquishment of marital rights or for any other consideration[15] or for the assumption of liabilities in excess of basis (unless the transfer is to a trust).[16] So now we are finally able to answer the Trivial Pursuit game question: When is a sale-purchase not a sale-purchase? Answer: When Section 1041 applies. We do not mean to imply that this is trivial, for Section 1041 is amazingly generous in most circumstances.

It is premature at this point, but a student should be warned of circumstances in which a taxpayer is adversely affected by the rules of Section 1041. The key is the attending basis provision. In the case of any transfer of property between spouses or former spouses, the transferee is treated as if the property were acquired by gift,[17] and the basis of the property in the hands of the transferee is the same as the basis of the property in the hands of the transferor.[18] Unlike the gift basis rule,[19] the Section 1041 transferee spouse or former spouse *always* takes a transferred basis,[20] even for computing loss.

Query: Do the rules of Section 1041 apply to transfers of property after marriage which are incident to an antenuptial agreement executed by an engaged couple? And what if they do? Look again at *Farid-Es-Sultaneh*. Would Section 1041 apply to both Farid and Kresge?

## PROBLEM

1. Andre purchased some land ten years ago for $40,000 cash. The property appreciated to $70,000 at which time Andre sold it to his wife Steffi for $70,000 cash, its fair market value.

    (a)   What are the income tax consequences to Andre?

    (b)   What is Steffi's basis in the property?

    (c)   What gain to Steffi if she immediately resells the property?

    (d)   What results in (a)–(c), above, if the property had declined in value to $30,000 and Andre sold it to Steffi for $30,000?

    (e)   What results (gains, losses, and bases) to Andre and Steffi if Steffi transfers other property with a basis of $50,000 and

---

[13] This aspect of I.R.C. § 1041 is considered in more detail in Chapter 10. See page 203, infra.

[14] I.R.C. § 1041(a). This is an example of a non-recognition provision. Other such provisions are considered in Chapter 26, infra. Cf. I.R.C. § 1001(c) under which generally a realized gain is required to be recognized.

[15] Note 12, supra.

[16] I.R.C. § 1041(e). Cf. Diedrich v. Commissioner, 457 U.S. 191, 102 S.Ct. 2414 (1982), discussed at page 153, infra.

[17] I.R.C. § 1041(b)(1); see also I.R.C. § 1015(e).

[18] I.R.C. § 1041(b)(2).

[19] I.R.C. § 1015(a).

[20] I.R.C. § 1015(e).

value of $70,000 (rather than cash) to Andre in return for his property?

*A     S*
*G  30k  -30k*
*B  50k  40k*

## 4. PROPERTY ACQUIRED FROM A DECEDENT

Internal Revenue Code: Sections 1014(a), (b)(1) and (6), (e), (f).

Regulations: Sections 1.1014–3(a); 20.2031–1(b).

---

While property that is the subject of a gift receives what is commonly referred to as a carryover or transferred basis, the same is not true of property acquired by bequest, devise, or inheritance. Under Section 1014(a) property acquired from a decedent generally receives a basis equal to its fair market value on the date on which it was valued for federal estate tax purposes.[1] The effect of this basis rule is to give property that appreciated during the decedent's ownership a "stepped-up" basis with no income tax cost to anyone. Of course a "stepped-down" basis results without deductible loss if property declined in value during decedent's ownership.

Section 1014 applies not only to property held by the decedent at death, but also to some property that decedent transferred during life if the value of the property is nevertheless required to be included in decedent's gross estate for federal estate tax purposes.[2]

To prevent inconsistent valuations of property to the disadvantage of the government, Section 1014 has rules that generally provide that the basis of property under Section 1014 cannot exceed the value of the property used for estate tax purposes.[3] These rules require information reporting by the executor of the estate to the beneficiaries[4] and the IRS,

---

[1] Fair market value is defined as "the price at which the property would change hands between a willing buyer and a willing seller, neither being under any compulsion to buy or to sell and both having reasonable knowledge of relevant facts." Reg. § 20.2031–1(b).

The estate tax is usually based on date of death value, but the executor may sometimes use an alternate valuation date, usually the date six months after decedent's death but sometimes a date within that six months period. I.R.C. §§ 2031 and 2032. See also I.R.C. § 2032A for situations in which a value other than fair market value may be used.

The date-of-death value basis rule was often criticized. See "Taxation of Appreciation of Assets Transferred at Death or by Gift," United States Treasury Dept., Tax Reform Studies and Proposals, 91st Cong., 1st Sess., Pt. 3, at 331–340 (1969); see also Waterbury, "A Case for Realizing Gains at Death in Terms of Family Interests," 52 Minn.L.Rev. 1 (1967); Zelenak, "Taxing Gains at Death," 46 Vand.L.Rev. 361 (1993); Subotnick, "On constructively Realizing Constructive Realization: Building the Case for Death and Taxes," 38 Kans.L.Rev. 1 (1989); Smith, "Burying the Estate Tax Without Resurrecting Its Problems," 55 Tax Notes 1799 (1992); Kwall, "When Should Asset Appreciation Be Taxed?: The Case for a Disposition Standard of Realization," 86 Ind.L.J. 77 (2011); Cunningham & Cunningham, "Realization of Gains Under the Comprehensive Inheritance Tax," 63 Tax L.Rev. 271 (2009).

[2] See I.R.C. § 1014(b)(2)–(10). See Stephens, Maxfield, Lind & Calfee, *Federal Estate and Gift Taxation,* ¶ 4.07 through ¶ 4.16 (Warren, Gorham & Lamont, 9th Ed. 2013), which criticizes different treatment of direct transfers from transfers in trust in this respect.

[3] I.R.C. § 1014(f)(1). See I.R.C. § 1014(f)(2).

[4] See I.R.C. § 6035.

and they are buttressed by penalties for claiming a basis greater than the basis reported by the executor.[5]

In the late 1940s, Congress brought into the Code a number of provisions designed, at least roughly, to equalize the tax status of persons in noncommunity property and community property states.[6] As a part of that enactment, Section 1014(b)(6) was added which gives a Section 1014 basis to a surviving spouse's one-half share of community property, if at least one-half of the whole of the community interest in such property was included in the decedent spouse's estate (whether or not the estate was of sufficient size to require an estate tax return or payment of tax).[7] This is a somewhat perplexing provision, because the surviving spouse's share is not subjected to estate tax on the decedent's death. However, an examination of Section 2056 will reveal that in a common law state a decedent's property that passes to his spouse, which automatically gets a Section 1014 basis, also may escape tax by way of the estate tax marital deduction.

The Section 1014 basis rule is an important element in estate planning. It means that, although appreciated property is potentially subjected to the estate tax,[8] the appreciation itself entirely escapes the income tax. Thus, elderly people with substantially appreciated property often choose not to sell such property in order to avoid income taxation and are said to be "locked-in" to their positions.

At one time, the Section 1014 basis rule was potentially subject to abuse. If a younger person who owned appreciated property gave it to an elderly or ill relative or friend and then, at death, the property passed from the elderly or ill person back to the younger person, she received it with a Section 1014 stepped-up basis.[9] Quite possibly the Commissioner could have successfully attacked this gambit upon a showing of collusion. Section 1014(e) now prevents this abuse mechanically without the need to show culpability. If "appreciated property"[10] is acquired by a decedent within the one-year period ending on the decedent's death and if the property (or property acquired with the proceeds from its sale by the estate) passes from the decedent back to the donor or the donor's spouse, the basis in the property is the adjusted basis of the property in the hands of the decedent immediately before death.[11] Thus if Son owns some land that he purchased for $20,000 which is worth $100,000 and he gives it to his ill Mother who dies within a year devising the property back to Son,

---

[5]   I.R.C. § 6662(b)(8), (k). Penalties also potentially apply if the executor fails to properly provide information statements.

[6]   See Chapter 27A2, infra at page 930.

[7]   Reg. § 1.1014–2(a)(5).

[8]   See I.R.C. § 2010, which generally excludes $10 million (adjusted for inflation to $11.2 million in 2018) of a decedent's property from estate taxation.

[9]   The decedent may have had to pay an estate tax on the property. See I.R.C. § 2001(c). But see I.R.C. § 2010.

[10]   I.R.C. § 1014(e)(2)(A).

[11]   I.R.C. § 1014(e)(1) and (2)(B).

under Section 1014(e) upon reacquisition Son's basis in the land is still $20,000, rather than $100,000.

The step-up in basis provided by Section 1014 has been attacked both on economic and social policy grounds,[12] and there have been proposals for legislation either to provide a transferred basis at death, to subject the appreciation to income tax at death, or to provide an estate tax surcharge measured by the amount of untaxed appreciation.[13] The Section 1014 basis rule, however, generally has been retained.[14]

## PROBLEM

1.   In the current year, Giver holds two blocks of identical stock, both worth $1,000,000. Giver purchased the first block years ago for $50,000 and the second block more recently for $950,000. Giver plans to make an inter vivos gift of one block and retain the second until death. Which block of stock should Giver transfer inter vivos and why?

## C.  THE AMOUNT REALIZED

Internal Revenue Code: Section 1001(b).

Regulations: Section 1.1001–1(a), –2(a), (b), (c) Examples (1) and (2).

---

# International Freighting Corporation, Inc. v. Commissioner

United States Court of Appeals, Second Circuit, 1943.
135 F.2d 310.

■ Before L. HAND, CHASE and FRANK, CIRCUIT JUDGES.

During the years 1933 to 1935, inclusive, E.I. duPont deNemours and Company, Inc., owned all of taxpayer's stock and during the year 1936 it owned two-thirds of taxpayer's stock, the balance being owned by the General Motors Corporation. During the years 1933 to 1936, inclusive, taxpayer informally adopted the bonus plan of the duPont Company as its own bonus plan. Class A or class B bonus awards, or both,

---

12  See references cited at note 1, supra.

13  See Graetz, "Taxation of Unrealized Gains at Death—An Evaluation of the Current Proposals," 59 Virg.L.R. 830 (1973); but see G. Break and J. Pechman, Tax Reform: The Impossible Dream, pp. 13–18 (1975).

14  There was a brief hiatus in the year 2010 when a decedent's estate was allowed to elect out of the estate tax at a cost of essentially losing a Section 1014 basis adjustment. See the "Tax Relief, Unemployment Insurance Reauthorization and Job Creation Act of 2010," Pub.L.No 111–312, 111th Cong., 2d Sess. § 301(c)(2010). See also I.R.C. § 1022(a).

In 1976, Congress had retained the estate tax but had also enacted a similar carryover basis provision for property acquired from a decedent. Tax Reform Act of 1976, Pub. Law No. 99–514, § 2005(a) (1976). Reacting to a public outcry that the provision imposed an onerous burden on executors and attorneys to ascertain a decedent's basis, Congress retroactively repealed the provision in 1980. Windfall Profit Tax Act of 1980, Pub. Law No. 96–223, § 401 (1980). See Blum, "Carryover Basis: The Case for Repeal," 57 Texas L. Rev. 204 (1979).

might be made to employees under that plan. Class B bonus awards (the only ones here involved) might be granted to those employees who, by their ability, efficiency and loyalty, had contributed most in a general way to the taxpayer's success, and were to be made from the portion of taxpayer's profits which its finance committee had set aside in the class B bonus fund. Only those employees were eligible for class B awards who on January first of the year in which the awards were made had been in the continuous employ of taxpayer at least two years. Recommendations for bonuses were to be made by the president or the heads of departments and were to be acted on by the executive committee or the board of directors. It was not incumbent on the executive committee or the board of directors to distribute the entire amount available in the fund. The taxpayer reserved the right at any time to discontinue the awarding of any bonuses.

Bonuses were in the form of common stock of the duPont Company or in the form of cash to be invested in such stock.

\* \* \*

During the calendar year 1936 taxpayer paid over and distributed to the beneficiaries of its class B bonus award, certificates representing 150 shares of the common stock of the duPont Company, whose cost to taxpayer at the date of delivery was $16,153.36 and whose market value was then $24,858.75. Each of the employees receiving those shares in 1936 paid a tax thereon, computing the market value at the time of delivery as taxable income.

Taxpayer took a deduction of $24,858.75 in its income tax return for 1936 on account of the 150 shares of stock distributed in that year to its employees. In a notice of deficiency the Commissioner reduced the deduction from $24,858.75 to $16,153.35, a difference of $8,705.39, determining that, as the bonus was paid in property, "the basis for calculation of the amount thereof is the cost of such property and not its market value as claimed on the return." This was the only adjustment which the Commissioner made to taxpayer's return and, as a result, the Commissioner determined a deficiency in the amount of $2,156.76, in taxpayer's tax liability for the year. Taxpayer filed a petition with the Tax Court for a redetermination of the deficiency thus determined. By an amended answer, the Commissioner, in the alternative, alleged that if it were held that taxpayer was entitled to a deduction in the amount of $24,858.75 on account of the payment of bonus in stock, then taxpayer realized a taxable profit of $8,705.39 on the disposition of the shares, and taxpayer's net taxable income otherwise determined should be increased accordingly.

The Tax Court held that taxpayer was entitled to a deduction for compensation paid in the year 1936 in the amount of $24,858.75. The Tax Court decided for the Commissioner, however, on the defense set forth in the Commissioner's amended answer, holding that taxpayer realized a gain of $8,705.39 in 1936 by paying the class B bonus in stock which had cost taxpayer $8,705.39 less than its market value when taxpayer transferred the stock to its employees. The deficiency resulting from this decision was $2,156.76. From that decision taxpayer seeks review.

■ FRANK, CIRCUIT JUDGE.

1. Up to the time in 1936 when the shares were delivered to the employees, the taxpayer retained such control of the shares that title had not passed to the employees.[1] We think the Tax Court correctly held that the market value at the time of delivery was properly deducted by the taxpayer as an ordinary expense of the business under [Section 162(a). Ed.] because that delivery was an additional reasonable compensation for past services actually rendered. Cf. Lucas v. Ox Fibre Brush Co., 281 U.S. 115, 50 S.Ct. 273.[2] The payment depleted the taxpayer's assets in an amount equal to that market value fully as much as if taxpayer had, at the time of delivery, first purchased those shares.

2. We turn to the question whether the transaction resulted in taxable gain to taxpayer. We think that the Tax Court correctly held that it did. The delivery of those shares was not a gift, else (1) it would have been wrongful as against taxpayer's stockholders, (2) the value of the shares could not have been deducted as an expense under [Section 162(a). Ed.], and (3) the employees as donees would not be obliged to pay, as they must,[3] an income tax on what they received. It was not a gift precisely because it was "compensation for services actually rendered," i.e., because the taxpayer received a full quid pro quo. Accordingly, cases holding that one is not liable for an income tax when he makes a gift of shares are not in point.

But, as the delivery of the shares here constituted a disposition for a valid consideration, it resulted in a closed transaction with a consequent realized gain. It is of no relevance that here the taxpayer had not been legally obligated to award any shares or pay any additional compensation to the employees; bonus payments by corporations are recognized as proper even if there was no previous obligation to make them; although then not obligatory, they are regarded as made for a sufficient consideration.[4] Since the bonuses would be invalid to the extent that what was delivered to the employees exceeded what the services of the employees were worth, it follows that the consideration received by the taxpayer from the employees must be deemed to be equal at least to the value of the shares in 1936. Here then, as there was no gift but a disposition of shares for a valid consideration equal at least to the market

---

[1]   Cf. Olson v. Commissioner, 7 Cir., 67 F.2d 726, 729.

[2]   [§ 162(a). Ed.] permits deduction of "all the ordinary and necessary expenses paid or incurred during the taxable year in carrying on any trade or business, including a reasonable allowance for salaries or other compensation for personal services actually rendered."

[3]   Old Colony Trust Co. v. Commissioner, 279 U.S. 716, 49 S.Ct. 499; Fisher v. Commissioner, 2 Cir., 59 F.2d 192; Olson v. Commissioner, supra.

[4]   Cf. The cases cited in the preceding footnote.

value of the shares when delivered, there was a taxable gain equal to the difference between the cost of the shares and that market value.

For [Section 1001(a). Ed.] provides that the gain from "the sale or other disposition of property" shall be the excess of "the amount realized therefrom" over "the adjusted basis" provided in [Section 1016. Ed.] in the light of [Section 1012. Ed.]—makes the "basis" the cost of such property. True, [Section 1001(b). Ed.] provides that "the amount realized" is the sum of "any money received plus the fair market value of the property (other than money) received." Literally, where there is a disposition of stock for services, no "property" or "money" is received by the person who thus disposes of the stock. But, in similar circumstances, it has been held that "money's worth" is received and that such a receipt comes within [Section 1001(b). Ed.]. * * *.[5]

The taxpayer properly asks us to treat this case "as if there had been no formal bonus plan" and as if taxpayer "had simply paid outright 150 shares of duPont stock to selected employees as additional compensation." On that basis, surely there was a taxable gain. For to shift the equation once more, the case supposed is the equivalent of one in which the taxpayer in the year 1936, without entering into a previous contract fixing the amount of compensation, had employed a transposition expert for one day and, when he completed his work, had paid him 5 shares of duPont stock having market value at that time of $500 but which it had bought in a previous year for $100. There can be no doubt that, from such a transaction, taxpayer would have a taxable gain. And so here.

The order of the Tax Court is affirmed.

## Crane v. Commissioner[*]

Supreme Court of the United States, 1947.
331 U.S. 1, 67 S.Ct. 1047.

[The Crane case, which follows, is hard going at best. One key to understanding the concepts that are developed in the opinion is some understanding of the income tax aspects of depreciation and consequent

---

[5]   In these cases the taxpayer paid a money claim by delivering stock. What the taxpayer received was literally neither property nor money, yet it was held that there was a taxable transaction under § [1001(b). Ed.].

[*]   See Bittker, "Tax Shelters, Nonrecourse Debt, and the *Crane* Case," 33 Tax L.Rev. 277 (1978); Simmons, "Nonrecourse Debt and Basis: Mrs. Crane Where Are You Now?" 53 So.Cal.Rev. 1 (1979); Del Cotto, "Basis and Amount Realized Under Crane: A Current View of Some Tax Effects in Mortgage Financing," 118 U. of Pa.L.Rev. 69 (1969); Adams, "Exploring the Outer Boundaries of the Crane Doctrine; An Imaginary Supreme Court Opinion," 21 Tax L.Rev. 159 (1966), reprinted in Sander and Westfall, Readings in Federal Taxation at page 325 (Foundation Press 1970); Cooper, "Negative Basis," 75 Harv.L.Rev. 1352 (1962); White, "Realization, Recognition, Reconciliation, Rationality and the Structure of the Federal Income Tax System," 88 Mich.L.Rev. 2034 (1990); Robinson, "Nonrecourse Indebtedness," 11 Virg.Tax.Rev. 1 (1991). Ed.

basis adjustments. If this is a new problem for you, as a student, you may benefit from a reading of the note on depreciation in Chapter 14E. Ed.]

■ MR. CHIEF JUSTICE VINSON delivered the opinion of the Court.

The question here is how a taxpayer who acquires depreciable property subject to an unassumed mortgage, holds it for a period, and finally sells it still so encumbered, must compute her taxable gain.

Petitioner was the sole beneficiary and the executrix of the will of her husband, who died January 11, 1932. He then owned an apartment building and lot subject to a mortgage,[1] which secured a principal debt of $255,000.00 and interest in default of $7,042.50. As of that date, the property was appraised for federal estate tax purposes at a value exactly equal to the total amount of this encumbrance. Shortly after her husband's death, petitioner entered into an agreement with the mortgagee whereby she was to continue to operate the property— collecting the rents, paying for necessary repairs, labor, and other operating expenses, and reserving $200.00 monthly for taxes—and was to remit the net rentals to the mortgagee. This plan was followed for nearly seven years, during which period petitioner reported the gross rentals as income, and claimed and was allowed deductions for taxes and operating expenses paid on the property, for interest paid on the mortgage, and for the physical exhaustion of the building. Meanwhile, the arrearage of interest increased to $15,857.71. On November 29, 1938, with the mortgagee threatening foreclosure, petitioner sold to a third party for $3,000.00 cash, subject to the mortgage, and paid $500.00 expenses of sale.

Petitioner reported a taxable gain of $1,250.00. Her theory was that the "property" which she had acquired in 1932 and sold in 1938 was only the equity, or the excess in the value of the apartment building and lot over the amount of the mortgage. This equity was of zero value when she acquired it. No depreciation could be taken on a zero value.[2] Neither she nor her vendee ever assumed the mortgage, so, when she sold the equity, the amount she realized on the sale was the net cash received, or $2,500.00. This sum less the zero basis constituted her gain, of which she reported half as taxable on the assumption that the entire property was a "capital asset."[3]

The Commissioner, however, determined that petitioner realized a net taxable gain of $23,767.03. His theory was that the "property" acquired and sold was not the equity, as petitioner claimed, but rather the physical property itself, or the owner's rights to possess, use, and

---

[1] The record does not show whether he was personally liable for the debt.

[2] This position is, of course, inconsistent with her practice in claiming such deductions in each of the years the property was held. The deductions so claimed and allowed by the Commissioner were in the total amount of $25,500.00.

[3] See § 117(a), (b), Revenue Act of 1938, c. 289, 52 Stat. 447. Under this provision only 50% of the gain realized on the sale of a "capital asset" need be taken into account, if the property had been held more than two years.

dispose of it, undiminished by the mortgage. The original basis thereof was $262,042.50, its appraised value in 1932. Of this value $55,000.00 was allocable to land and $207,042.50 to building.[4] During the period that petitioner held the property, there was an allowable depreciation of $28,045.10 on the building,[5] so that the adjusted basis of the building at the time of sale was $178,997.40. The amount realized on the sale was said to include not only the $2,500.00 net cash receipts, but also the principal amount[6] of the mortgage subject to which the property was sold, both totaling $257,500.00. * * *.

The Tax Court * * * [essentially] adopted petitioner's contentions, and expunged the deficiency.[9] * * *. [T]he Circuit Court of Appeals reversed, one judge dissenting.[10] We granted certiorari because of the importance of the questions raised as to the proper construction of the gain and loss provisions of the Internal Revenue Code.[11]

The 1938 Act,[12] § 111(a), defines the gain from "the sale or other disposition of property" as "the excess of the amount realized therefrom over the adjusted basis provided in section 113(b) * * *." It proceeds, § 111(b), to define "the amount realized from the sale or other disposition of property" as "the sum of any money received plus the fair market value of the property (other than money) received." [See Sections 1001(a) and (b). Ed.] Further, in § 113(b), the "adjusted basis for determining the gain or loss from the sale or other disposition of property" is declared to be "the basis determined under subsection (a), adjusted * * * [(1)(B)] * * * for exhaustion, wear and tear, obsolescence, amortization * * * to the extent allowed (but not less than the amount allowable) * * *." [See Section 1016(a)(2). Ed.] The basis under subsection (a) "if the property was acquired by * * * devise * * * or by the decedent's estate from the decedent," § 113(a)(5), is "the fair market value of such property at the time of such acquisition." [See Section 1014(a)(1). Ed.]

---

[4] The parties stipulated as to the relative parts of the 1932 appraised value and of the 1938 sales price which were allocable to land and building.

[5] The parties stipulated that the rate of depreciation applicable to the building was 2% per annum.

[6] The Commissioner explains that only the principal amount, rather than the total present debt secured by the mortgage, was deemed to be a measure of the amount realized, because the difference was attributable to interest due, a deductible item.

[9] 3 T.C. 585. The Court held that the building was not a "capital asset" within the meaning of § 117(a) and that the entire gain on the building had to be taken into account under § 117(b), because it found that the building was of a character subject to physical exhaustion and that petitioner had used it in her trade or business.

But because the Court accepted petitioner's theory that the entire property had a zero basis, it held that she was not entitled to the 1938 depreciation deduction on the building which she had inconsistently claimed.

For these reasons, it did not expunge the deficiency in its entirety.

[10] 153 F.2d 504.

[11] 328 U.S. 826, 66 S.Ct. 980.

[12] All subsequent references to a revenue act are to this Act unless otherwise indicated. The relevant parts of the gain and loss provisions of the Act and Code are identical.

Logically, the first step under this scheme is to determine the unadjusted basis of the property, under § 113(a)(5), and the dispute in this case is as to the construction to be given the term "property." If "property," as used in that provision, means the same thing as "equity," it would necessarily follow that the basis of petitioner's property was zero, as she contends. If, on the contrary, it means the land and building themselves, or the owner's legal rights in them, undiminished by the mortgage, the basis was $262,042.50.

We think that the reasons for favoring one of the latter constructions are of overwhelming weight. In the first place, the words of statutes— including revenue acts—should be interpreted where possible in their ordinary, everyday senses.[13] The only relevant definitions of "property" to be found in the principal standard dictionaries[14] are the two favored by the Commissioner, i.e., either that "property" is the physical thing which is a subject of ownership, or that it is the aggregate of the owner's rights to control and dispose of that thing. "Equity" is not given as a synonym, nor do either of the foregoing definitions suggest that it could be correctly so used. Indeed, "equity" is defined as "the value of a property * * * above the total of the liens. * * *."[15] The contradistinction could hardly be more pointed. Strong countervailing considerations would be required to support a contention that Congress, in using the word "property," meant "equity," or that we should impute to it the intent to convey that meaning.[16]

In the second place, the Commissioner's position has the approval of the administrative construction of § 113(a)(5). With respect to the valuation of property under that section, Reg. 101, Art. 113(a)(5)–1, promulgated under the 1938 Act, provided that "the value of property as of the date of the death of the decedent as appraised for the purpose of the Federal estate tax * * * shall be deemed to be its fair market value * * *." The land and building here involved were so appraised in 1932, and their appraised value—$262,042.50—was reported by petitioner as part of the gross estate. This was in accordance with the estate tax law[17] and regulations,[18] which had always required that the value of decedent's property, undiminished by liens, be so appraised and returned, and that mortgages be separately deducted in computing the net estate.[19] As the quoted provision of the Regulations has been in effect since 1918,[20] and

---

[13] Old Colony R. Co. v. Commissioner, 284 U.S. 552, 560, 52 S.Ct. 211, 213.

[14] See Webster's New International Dictionary, Unabridged, 2d Ed.; Funk & Wagnalls' New Standard Dictionary; Oxford English Dictionary.

[15] See Webster's New International Dictionary, supra.

[16] Crooks v. Harrelson, 282 U.S. 55, 59, 51 S.Ct. 49, 50.

[17] See §§ 202 and 203(a)(1) Revenue Act of 1916; §§ 402 and 403(a)(1), Revenue Acts of 1918 and 1921; §§ 302, 303(a)(1), Revenue Acts of 1924 and 1926; § 805, Revenue Act of 1932.

[18] See Reg. 37, Arts. 13, 14, and 47; Reg. 63, Arts. 12, 13, and 41; Reg. 68, Arts. 11, 13, and 38; Reg. 70, Arts. 11, 13, and 38; Reg. 80, Arts. 11, 13, and 38.

[19] See City Bank Farmers' Trust Co. v. Bowers, 68 F.2d 909, cert. denied, 292 U.S. 644, 54 S.Ct. 778; Rodiek v. Helvering, 87 F.2d 328; Adriance v. Higgins, 113 F.2d 1013.

[20] [Citations omitted. Ed.]

as the relevant statutory provision has been repeatedly reenacted since then in substantially the same form,[21] the former may itself now be considered to have the force of law.[22]

Moreover, in the many instances in other parts of the Act in which Congress has used the word "property," or expressed the idea of "property" or "equity," we find no instances of a misuse of either word or of a confusion of the ideas.[23] In some parts of the Act other than the gain and loss sections, we find "property" where it is unmistakably used in its ordinary sense.[24] On the other hand, where either Congress or the Treasury intended to convey the meaning of "equity," it did so by the use of appropriate language.[25]

A further reason why the word "property" in § 113(a) should not be construed to mean "equity" is the bearing such construction would have on the allowance of deductions for depreciation and on the collateral adjustments of basis.

Section 23(*l*) permits deduction from gross income of "a reasonable allowance for the exhaustion, wear and tear of property. * * *." Sections 23(n) and 114(a) declare that the "basis upon which exhaustion, wear and tear * * * are to be allowed" is the basis "provided in section 113(b) for the purpose of determining the gain upon the sale" of the property, which is the § 113(a) basis "adjusted * * * for exhaustion, wear and tear * * * to the extent allowed (but not less than the amount allowable). * * *."* [See Section 167. Ed.]

Under these provisions, if the mortgagor's equity were the § 113(a) basis, it would also be the original basis from which depreciation allowances are deducted. If it is, and if the amount of the annual allowances were to be computed on that value, as would then seem to be required,[26] they will represent only a fraction of the cost of the

---

[21]  [Citations omitted. Ed.]

[22]  Helvering v. Reynolds Co., 306 U.S. 110, 114, 59 S.Ct. 423.

[23]  Cf. Helvering v. Stockholms Bank, 293 U.S. 84, 87, 55 S.Ct. 50, 51.

[24]  Sec. 23(a)(1) permits the deduction from gross income of "rentals * * * required to be made as a condition to the continued use * * * for purposes of the trade or business, of *property* * * * in which he [the taxpayer] has no *equity*." (Italics supplied.)

Sec. 23(*l*) permits the deduction from gross income of "a reasonable allowance for the exhaustion, wear and tear of *property* used in the trade or business * * *." (Italics supplied.) See also § 303(a)(1), Revenue Act of 1926, c. 27, 44 Stat. 9; § 805, Revenue Act of 1932, c. 209, 47 Stat. 280.

[25]  See § 23(a)(1), *supra*, note 24; § 805, Revenue Act of 1932, supra, note 24; § 3482, I.R.C.; Reg. 105, § 81.38. This provision of the Regulations, first appearing in 1937, T.D. 4729, 1937–1 Cum.Bull. 284, 289, permitted estates which were not liable on mortgages applicable to certain of decedent's property to return "only the value of the equity of redemption (or value of the property, less the indebtedness) * * *."

*  In the Internal Revenue Code of 1986, as compared with earlier Acts cited here, the depreciation deduction is authorized by § 167(a); § 167(g) makes reference to § 1011 for a determination of the basis upon which deductions are to be claimed. Detailed differences are not of significance here. Ed.

[26]  Secs. 23(n) and 114(a), in defining the "basis upon which" depreciation is "to be allowed," do not distinguish between basis as the minuend from which the allowances are to be deducted,

corresponding physical exhaustion, and any recoupment by the mortgagor of the remainder of that cost can be effected only by the reduction of his taxable gain in the year of sale.[27] If, however, the amount of the annual allowances were to be computed on the value of the property, and then deducted from an equity basis, we would in some instances have to accept deductions from a minus basis or deny deductions altogether.[28] The Commissioner also argues that taking the mortgagor's equity as the § 113(a) basis would require the basis to be changed with each payment on the mortgage,[29] and that the attendant problem of repeatedly recomputing basis and annual allowances would be a tremendous accounting burden on both the Commissioner and the taxpayer. Moreover, the mortgagor would acquire control over the timing of his depreciation allowances.

Thus it appears that the applicable provisions of the Act expressly preclude an equity basis, and the use of it is contrary to certain implicit principles of income tax depreciation, and entails very great administrative difficulties.[30] It may be added that the Treasury has never furnished a guide through the maze of problems that arise in connection with depreciating an equity basis, but, on the contrary, has consistently permitted the amount of depreciation allowances to be computed on the full value of the property, and subtracted from it as a basis. Surely, Congress' long-continued acceptance of this situation gives it full legislative endorsement.[31]

We conclude that the proper basis under § 113(a)(5) is the value of the property, undiminished by mortgages thereon, and that the correct basis here was $262,042.50. The next step is to ascertain what adjustments are required under § 113(b). As the depreciation rate was stipulated, the only question at this point is whether the Commissioner was warranted in making any depreciation adjustments whatsoever.

---

and as the dividend from which the amount of the allowance is to be computed. The Regulations indicate that the basis of property is the same for both purposes. Reg. 101, Art. 23(*l*)–4, 5.

[27]  This is contrary to Treasury practice, and to Reg. 101, Art. 23(*l*)–5, which provides in part:

> "The capital sum to be recovered shall be charged off over the useful life of the property, either in equal annual installments or in accordance with any other recognized trade practice, such as an apportionment of the capital sum over units of production."

See Detroit Edison Co. v. Commissioner, 319 U.S. 98, 101, 63 S.Ct. 902, 903.

[28]  So long as the mortgagor remains in possession, the mortgagee can not take depreciation deductions, even if he is the one who actually sustains the capital loss, as § 23(*l*) allows them only on property "used in the trade or business."

[29]  Sec. 113(b)(1)(A) requires adjustment of basis "for expenditures * * * properly chargeable to capital account * * *."

[30]  Obviously we are not considering a situation in which a taxpayer has acquired and sold an equity of redemption only, i.e., a right to redeem the property without a right to present possession. In that situation, the right to redeem would itself be the aggregate of the taxpayer's rights and would undoubtedly constitute "property" within the meaning of § 113(a). No depreciation problems would arise. See note 28.

[31]  See note 22.

Section 113(b)(1)(B) provides that "proper adjustment in respect of the property *shall in all cases be made* * * * for exhaustion, wear and tear * * * to the extent allowed (but not less than the amount allowable)." * * *. (Italics supplied.)* The Tax Court found on adequate evidence that the apartment house was property of a kind subject to physical exhaustion, that it was used in taxpayer's trade or business, and consequently that the taxpayer would have been entitled to a depreciation allowance under § 23(l), except that, in the opinion of that Court, the basis of the property was zero, and it was thought that depreciation could not be taken on a zero basis. As we have just decided that the correct basis of the property was not zero, but $262,042.50, we avoid this difficulty, and conclude that an adjustment should be made as the Commissioner determined.

Petitioner urges to the contrary that she was not entitled to depreciation deductions, whatever the basis of the property, because the law allows them only to one who actually bears the capital loss,[32] and here the loss was not hers but the mortgagee's. We do not see, however, that she has established her factual premise. There was no finding of the Tax Court to that effect, nor to the effect that the value of the property was ever less than the amount of the lien. Nor was there evidence in the record, or any indication that petitioner could produce evidence, that this was so. The facts that the value of the property was only equal to the lien in 1932 and that during the next six and one-half years the physical condition of the building deteriorated and the amount of the lien increased, are entirely inconclusive, particularly in the light of the buyer's willingness in 1938 to take subject to the increased lien and pay a substantial amount of cash to boot. Whatever may be the rule as to allowing depreciation to a mortgagor on property in his possession which is subject to an unassumed mortgage and clearly worth less than the lien, we are not faced with that problem and see no reason to decide it now.

At last we come to the problem of determining the "amount realized" on the 1938 sale. Section 111(b), it will be recalled, defines the "amount realized" from "the sale * * * of property" as "the sum of any money received plus the fair market value of the property (other than money) received," and § 111(a) defines the gain on "the sale * * * of property" as the excess of the amount realized over the basis. Quite obviously, the word "property" used here with reference to a sale, must mean "property" in the same ordinary sense intended by the use of the word with reference to acquisition and depreciation in § 113, both for certain of the reasons stated heretofore in discussing its meaning in § 113, and also because the functional relation of the two sections requires that the word mean the same in one section that it does in the other. If the "property" to be valued

---

\*   See I.R.C. (1986) § 1016(a)(2); refinements in the amounts of the adjustments in basis required do not affect the principles for which the case is studied here. Ed.

[32]  See Helvering v. Lazarus & Co., 308 U.S. 252, 60 S.Ct. 209; Duffy v. Central R. Co., 268 U.S. 55, 64, 45 S.Ct. 429.

on the date of acquisition is the property free of liens, the "property" to be priced on a subsequent sale must be the same thing.[33]

Starting from this point, we could not accept petitioner's contention that the $2,500.00 net cash was all she realized on the sale except on the absurdity that she sold a quarter-of-a-million dollar property for roughly one per cent of its value, and took a 99 per cent loss. Actually, petitioner does not urge this. She argues, conversely, that because only $2,500.00 was realized on the sale, the "property" sold must have been the equity only, and that consequently we are forced to accept her contention as to the meaning of "property" in § 113. We adhere, however, to what we have already said on the meaning of "property," and we find that the absurdity is avoided by our conclusion that the amount of the mortgage is properly included in the "amount realized" on the sale.

Petitioner concedes that if she had been personally liable on the mortgage and the purchaser had either paid or assumed it, the amount so paid or assumed would be considered a part of the "amount realized" within the meaning of § 111(b).[34] The cases so deciding have already repudiated the notion that there must be an actual receipt by the seller himself of "money" or "other property," in their narrowest senses. It was thought to be decisive that one section of the Act must be construed so as not to defeat the intention of another or to frustrate the Act as a whole,[35] and that the taxpayer was the "beneficiary" of the payment in "as real and substantial [a sense] as if the money had been paid it and then paid over by it to its creditors."[36]

Both these points apply to this case. The first has been mentioned already. As for the second, we think that a mortgagor, not personally liable on the debt, who sells the property subject to the mortgage and for additional consideration, realizes a benefit in the amount of the mortgage as well as the boot.[37] If a purchaser pays boot, it is immaterial as to our problem whether the mortgagor is also to receive money from the purchaser to discharge the mortgage prior to sale, or whether he is merely to transfer subject to the mortgage—it may make a difference to the purchaser and to the mortgagee, but not to the mortgagor. Or put in another way, we are no more concerned with whether the mortgagor is,

---

[33]  See Maguire v. Commissioner, 313 U.S. 1, 8, 61 S.Ct. 789, 794.

We are not troubled by petitioner's argument that her contract of sale expressly provided for the conveyance of the equity only. She actually conveyed title to the property, and the buyer took the same property that petitioner had acquired in 1932 and used in her trade or business until its sale.

[34]  United States v. Hendler, 303 U.S. 564, 58 S.Ct. 655; Brons Hotels, Inc., 34 B.T.A. 376; Walter F. Haass, 37 B.T.A. 948. See Douglas v. Willcuts, 296 U.S. 1, 8, 56 S.Ct. 59, 62.

[35]  See Brons Hotels, Inc., supra, 34 B.T.A. at 381.

[36]  See United States v. Hendler, supra, 303 U.S. at 566, 58 S.Ct. at 656.

[37]  Obviously, if the value of the property is less than the amount of the mortgage, a mortgagor who is not personally liable cannot realize a benefit equal to the mortgage. Consequently, a different problem might be encountered where a mortgagor abandoned the property or transferred it subject to the mortgage without receiving boot. That is not this case. [But see the *Tufts* case at page 145, infra and problem 1(i) at page 154, infra. Ed.]

strictly speaking, a debtor on the mortgage, than we are with whether the benefit to him is, strictly speaking, a receipt of money or property. We are rather concerned with the reality that an owner of property, mortgaged at a figure less than that at which the property will sell, must and will treat the conditions of the mortgage exactly as if they were his personal obligations.[38] If he transfers subject to the mortgage, the benefit to him is as real and substantial as if the mortgage were discharged, or as if a personal debt in an equal amount had been assumed by another.

Therefore we conclude that the Commissioner was right in determining that petitioner realized $257,500.00 on the sale of this property.

The Tax Court's contrary determinations, that "property," as used in § 113(a) and related sections, means "equity," and that the amount of a mortgage subject to which property is sold is not the measure of a benefit realized, within the meaning of § 111(b), announced rules of general applicability on clear-cut questions of law.[39] The Circuit Court of Appeals therefore had jurisdiction to review them.[40]

Petitioner contends that the result we have reached taxes her on what is not income within the meaning of the Sixteenth Amendment. If this is because only the direct receipt of cash is thought to be income in the constitutional sense, her contention is wholly without merit.[41] If it is because the entire transaction is thought to have been "by all dictates of common sense * * * a ruinous disaster," as it was termed in her brief, we disagree with her premise. She was entitled to depreciation deductions for a period of nearly seven years, and she actually took them in almost the allowable amount. The crux of this case, really, is whether the law permits her to exclude allowable deductions from consideration in computing gain.[42] We have already showed that, if it does, the taxpayer can enjoy a double deduction, in effect, on the same loss of assets. The Sixteenth Amendment does not require that result any more than does the Act itself.

Affirmed.

---

[38] For instance, this petitioner returned the gross rentals as her own income, and out of them paid interest on the mortgage, on which she claimed and was allowed deductions. See Reg. 77, Art. 141; Reg. 86, Art. 23(b)–1; Reg. 94, Art. 23(b)–1 Reg. 101, Art. 23(b)–1.

[39] See Commissioner v. Wilcox, 327 U.S. 404, 410, 66 S.Ct. 546, 550; Trust of Bingham v. Commissioner, 325 U.S. 365, 369–372, 65 S.Ct. 1232, 1234–1236. Cf. John Kelley Co. v. Commissioner, 326 U.S. 521, 527, 698, 66 S.Ct. 299, 302; Dobson v. Commissioner, 320 U.S. 489, 64 S.Ct. 239.

[40] Ibid; see also § 1141(a) and (c), I.R.C.

[41] Douglas v. Willcuts, supra, 296 U.S. 1, 56 S.Ct. 59; Burnet v. Wells, 289 U.S. 670, 677, 53 S.Ct. 761, 763.

[42] In the course of the argument some reference was made, as by analogy, to a situation in which a taxpayer acquired by devise property subject to a mortgage in an amount greater than the then value of the property, and later transferred it to a third person, still subject to the mortgage, and for a cash boot. Whether or not the difference between the value of the property on acquisition and the amount of the mortgage would in that situation constitute either statutory or constitutional income is a question which is different from the one before us, and which we need not presently answer.

■ MR. JUSTICE JACKSON, dissenting.

The Tax Court concluded that this taxpayer acquired only an equity worth nothing. The mortgage was in default, the mortgage debt was equal to the value of the property, any possession by the taxpayer was forfeited and terminable immediately by foreclosure, and perhaps by a receiver *pendente lite.* Arguments can be advanced to support the theory that the taxpayer received the whole property and thereupon came to owe the whole debt. Likewise it is argued that when she sold she transferred the entire value of the property and received release from the whole debt. But we think these arguments are not so conclusive that it was not within the province of the Tax Court to find that she received an equity which at that time had a zero value. * * *. The taxpayer never became personally liable for the debt, and hence when she sold she was released from no debt. The mortgage debt was simply a subtraction from the value of what she did receive, and from what she sold. The subtraction left her nothing when she acquired it and a small margin when she sold it. She acquired a property right equivalent to an equity of redemption and sold the same thing. It was the "property" bought and sold as the Tax Court considered it to be under the Revenue Laws. We are not required in this case to decide whether depreciation was properly taken, for there is no issue about it here.

We would reverse the Court of Appeals and sustain the decision of the Tax Court.

■ MR. JUSTICE FRANKFURTER and MR. JUSTICE DOUGLAS join in this opinion.

## Commissioner v. Tufts[*]

Supreme Court of the United States, 1983.[**]
461 U.S. 300, 103 S.Ct. 1826.

■ JUSTICE BLACKMUN delivered the opinion of the Court.

Over 35 years ago, in Crane v. Commissioner, 331 U.S. 1, 67 S.Ct. 1047 (1947), this Court ruled that a taxpayer, who sold property encumbered by a nonrecourse mortgage (the amount of the mortgage being less than the property's value), must include the unpaid balance of the mortgage in the computation of the amount the taxpayer realized on the sale. The case now before us presents the question whether the same rule applies when the unpaid amount of the nonrecourse mortgage exceeds the fair market value of the property sold.

---

[*]   See Turner, "Nonrecourse Liabilities as Tax Shelter Devices After *Tufts*: Elimination of Fair Market Value and Contingent Liability Defenses," 35 U.Fla.L.Rev. 904 (1983); Blackburn, "Important Common Law Developments for Nonrecourse Notes: Tufting It Out," 18 Geo.L.Rev. 1 (1983); Narciso, "Some Reflections on Commissioner v. Tufts: Mrs. Crane Shops at Kirby Lumber," 35 Rutgers L.Rev. 929 (1983); and Simmons, "Tufts v. Commissioner: Amount Realized Limited to Fair Market Value," 15 U.C. Davis L.Rev. 577 (1982) (discussing the Fifth Circuit opinion).

[**]   Some footnotes omitted.

I

On August 1, 1970, respondent Clark Pelt, a builder, and his wholly owned corporation, respondent Clark, Inc., formed a general partnership. The purpose of the partnership was to construct a 120-unit apartment complex in Duncanville, Tex., a Dallas suburb. Neither Pelt nor Clark, Inc., made any capital contribution to the partnership. Six days later, the partnership entered into a mortgage loan agreement with the Farm & Home Savings Association (F & H). Under the agreement, F & H was committed for a $1,851,500 loan for the complex. In return, the partnership executed a note and a deed of trust in favor of F & H. The partnership obtained the loan on a nonrecourse basis: neither the partnership nor its partners assumed any personal liability for repayment of the loan. Pelt later admitted four friends and relatives, respondents Tufts, Steger, Stephens, and Austin, as general partners. None of them contributed capital upon entering the partnership.

The construction of the complex was completed in August 1971. During 1971, each partner made small capital contributions to the partnership; in 1972, however, only Pelt made a contribution. The total of the partners' capital contributions was $44,212. In each tax year, all partners claimed as income tax deductions their allocable shares of ordinary losses and depreciation. The deductions taken by the partners in 1971 and 1972 totalled $439,972. Due to these contributions and deductions, the partnership's adjusted basis in the property in August 1972 was $1,455,740.

In 1971 and 1972, major employers in the Duncanville area laid off significant numbers of workers. As a result, the partnership's rental income was less than expected, and it was unable to make the payments due on the mortgage. Each partner, on August 28, 1972, sold his partnership interest to an unrelated third party, Fred Bayles. As consideration, Bayles agreed to reimburse each partner's sale expenses up to $250; he also assumed the nonrecourse mortgage.

On the date of transfer, the fair market value of the property did not exceed $1,400,000. Each partner reported the sale on his federal income tax return and indicated that a partnership loss of $55,740 had been sustained.[1] The Commissioner of Internal Revenue, on audit, determined that the sale resulted in a partnership capital gain of approximately $400,000. His theory was that the partnership had realized the full amount of the nonrecourse obligation.[2]

Relying on Millar v. Commissioner, 577 F.2d 212, 215 (CA3), cert. denied, 439 U.S. 1046, 99 S.Ct. 721 (1978), the United States Tax Court,

---

[1]   The loss was the difference between the adjusted basis, $1,455,740, and the fair market value of the property, $1,400,000. On their individual tax returns, the partners did not claim deductions for their respective shares of this loss. In their petitions to the Tax Court, however, the partners did claim the loss.

[2]   The Commissioner determined the partnership's gain on the sale by subtracting the adjusted basis, $1,455,740, from the liability assumed by Bayles, $1,851,500. * * *.

in an unreviewed decision, upheld the asserted deficiencies. 70 T.C. 756 (1978). The United States Court of Appeals for the Fifth Circuit reversed. 651 F.2d 1058 (1981). That court expressly disagreed with the *Millar* analysis, and, in limiting Crane v. Commissioner, supra, to its facts, questioned the theoretical underpinnings of the *Crane* decision. We granted certiorari to resolve the conflict. 456 U.S. 960, 102 S.Ct. 2034 (1982).

II

* * *. Section 1001 governs the determination of gains and losses on the disposition of property. Under § 1001(a), the gain or loss from a sale or other disposition of property is defined as the difference between "the amount realized" on the disposition and the property's adjusted basis. Subsection (b) of § 1001 defines "amount realized": "The amount realized from the sale or other disposition of property shall be the sum of any money received plus the fair market value of the property (other than money) received." At issue is the application of the latter provision to the disposition of property encumbered by a nonrecourse mortgage of an amount in excess of the property's fair market value.

A

In Crane v. Commissioner, supra, this Court took the first and controlling step toward the resolution of this issue. * * *.

* * *

In a footnote, pertinent to the present case, the Court observed:

"Obviously, if the value of the property is less than the amount of the mortgage, a mortgagor who is not personally liable cannot realize a benefit equal to the mortgage. Consequently, a different problem might be encountered where a mortgagor abandoned the property or transferred it subject to the mortgage without receiving boot. That is not this case." Id., at 14, n. 37, 67 S.Ct., at 1054–55, n. 37.

B

This case presents that unresolved issue. We are disinclined to overrule *Crane*, and we conclude that the same rule applies when the unpaid amount of the nonrecourse mortgage exceeds the value of the property transferred. *Crane* ultimately does not rest on its limited theory of economic benefit; instead, we read *Crane* to have approved the Commissioner's decision to treat a nonrecourse mortgage in this context as a true loan. This approval underlies *Crane's* holdings that the amount of the nonrecourse liability is to be included in calculating both the basis and the amount realized on disposition. That the amount of the loan exceeds the fair market value of the property thus becomes irrelevant.

When a taxpayer receives a loan, he incurs an obligation to repay that loan at some future date. Because of this obligation, the loan proceeds do not qualify as income to the taxpayer. When he fulfills the obligation, the repayment of the loan likewise has no effect on his tax liability.

Another consequence to the taxpayer from this obligation occurs when the taxpayer applies the loan proceeds to the purchase price of property used to secure the loan. Because of the obligation to repay, the taxpayer is entitled to include the amount of the loan in computing his basis in the property; the loan, under § 1012, is part of the taxpayer's cost of the property. Although a different approach might have been taken with respect to a nonrecourse mortgage loan,[5] the Commissioner has chosen to accord it the same treatment he gives to a recourse mortgage loan. The Court approved that choice in *Crane,* and the respondents do not challenge it here. The choice and its resultant benefits to the taxpayer are predicated on the assumption that the mortgage will be repaid in full.

When encumbered property is sold or otherwise disposed of and the purchaser assumes the mortgage, the associated extinguishment of the mortgagor's obligation to repay is accounted for in the computation of the amount realized. * * *. Because no difference between recourse and nonrecourse obligations is recognized in calculating basis,[7] *Crane* teaches that the Commissioner may ignore the nonrecourse nature of the obligation in determining the amount realized upon disposition of the encumbered property. He thus may include in the amount realized the amount of the nonrecourse mortgage assumed by the purchaser. The rationale for this treatment is that the original inclusion of the amount of the mortgage in basis rested on the assumption that the mortgagor incurred an obligation to repay. Moreover, this treatment balances the fact that the mortgagor originally received the proceeds of the

---

[5] The Commissioner might have adopted the theory, implicit in Crane's contentions, that a nonrecourse mortgage is not true debt, but, instead, is a form of joint investment by the mortgagor and the mortgagee. On this approach, nonrecourse debt would be considered a contingent liability, under which the mortgagor's payments on the debt gradually increase his interest in the property while decreasing that of the mortgagee. [Citations omitted. Ed.] Because the taxpayer's investment in the property would not include the nonrecourse debt, the taxpayer would not be permitted to include that debt in basis. [Citations omitted. Ed.]

We express no view as to whether such an approach would be consistent with the statutory structure and, if so, and *Crane* were not on the books, whether that approach would be preferred over *Crane's* analysis. We note only that the *Crane* Court's resolution of the basis issue presumed that when property is purchased with proceeds from a nonrecourse mortgage, the purchaser becomes the sole owner of the property. 331 U.S., at 6, 67 S.Ct., at 1050. Under the *Crane* approach, the mortgagee is entitled to no portion of the basis. Id., at 10, n. 28, 67 S.Ct., at 1052, n. 28. The nonrecourse mortgage is part of the mortgagor's investment in the property, and does not constitute a coinvestment by the mortgagee. * * *.

[7] The Commissioner's choice in *Crane* "laid the foundation stone of most tax shelters," Bittker, Tax Shelters, Nonrecourse Debt, and the *Crane* Case, 33 Tax.L.Rev. 277, 283 (1978), by permitting taxpayers who bear no risk to take deductions on depreciable property. Congress recently has acted to curb this avoidance device by forbidding a taxpayer to take depreciation deductions in excess of amounts he has at risk in the investment. Pub.L. 94–455, § 204(a), 90 Stat. 1531 (1976), 26 U.S.C. § 465; Pub.L. 95–600, §§ 201–204, 92 Stat. 2814–2817 (1978), 26 U.S.C. § 465(a) (1976 ed., Supp. V). Real estate investments, however, are exempt from this prohibition. § 465(c)(3)(D) (1976 ed., Supp. V). Although this congressional action may foreshadow a day when nonrecourse and recourse debts will be treated differently, neither Congress nor the Commissioner has sought to alter *Crane's* rule of including nonrecourse liability in both basis and the amount realized.

nonrecourse loan tax-free on the same assumption. Unless the outstanding amount of the mortgage is deemed to be realized, the mortgagor effectively will have received untaxed income at the time the loan was extended and will have received an unwarranted increase in the basis of his property.[8] The Commissioner's interpretation of § 1001(b) in this fashion cannot be said to be unreasonable.

C

The Commissioner in fact has applied this rule even when the fair market value of the property falls below the amount of the nonrecourse obligation. Treas.Reg. § 1.1001–2(b), 26 CFR § 1.1001–2(b) (1982);[9] Rev.Rul. 76–111, 1976–1 Cum.Bull. 214. Because the theory on which the rule is based applies equally in this situation, see Millar v. Commissioner, 67 T.C. 656, 660 (1977), aff'd on this issue, 577 F.2d 212, 215–216 (CA3), cert. denied, 439 U.S. 1046, 99 S.Ct. 721 (1978);[10] * * * we have no reason, after *Crane,* to question this treatment.

Respondents received a mortgage loan with the concomitant obligation to repay by the year 2012. The only difference between that mortgage and one on which the borrower is personally liable is that the mortgagee's remedy is limited to foreclosing on the securing property. This difference does not alter the nature of the obligation; its only effect is to shift from the borrower to the lender any potential loss caused by devaluation of the property.[12] If the fair market value of the property falls below the amount of the outstanding obligation, the mortgagee's ability to protect its interests is impaired, for the mortgagor is free to abandon the property to the mortgagee and be relieved of his obligation.

This, however, does not erase the fact that the mortgagor received the loan proceeds tax-free and included them in his basis on the understanding that he had an obligation to repay the full amount. See

---

[8] Although the *Crane* rule has some affinity with the tax benefit rule, see Bittker, supra, at 282; Del Cotto, Sales and Other Dispositions of Property Under Section 1001: The Taxable Event, Amount Realized and Related Problems of Basis, 26 Buffalo L.Rev. 219, 323–324 (1977), the analysis we adopt is different. Our analysis applies even in the situation in which no deductions are taken. It focuses on the obligation to repay and its subsequent extinguishment, not on the taking and recovery of deductions. See generally Note, 82 Colum.L.Rev., at 1526–1529.

[9] The regulation was promulgated while this case was pending before the Court of Appeals for the Fifth Circuit. T.D. 7741, 45 Fed.Reg. 81743, 1981–1 Cum.Bull. 430 (1980). It merely formalized the Commissioner's prior interpretation, however.

[10] The Court of Appeals for the Third Circuit in *Millar* affirmed the Tax Court on the theory that inclusion of nonrecourse liability in the amount realized was necessary to prevent the taxpayer from enjoying a double deduction. 577 F.2d, at 215; cf. n. 4, supra. Because we resolve the question on another ground, we do not address the validity of the double deduction rationale.

[12] In his opinion for the Court of Appeals in *Crane,* Judge Learned Hand observed:

"[The mortgagor] has all the income from the property; he manages it; he may sell it; any increase in its value goes to him; any decrease falls on him, until the value goes below the amount of the lien. * * *. When therefore upon a sale the mortgagor makes an allowance to the vendee of the amount of the lien, he secures a release from a charge upon his property quite as though the vendee had paid him the full price on condition that before he took title the lien should be cleared. * * *." 153 F.2d 504, 506 (C.A.2 1945).

Woodsam Associates, Inc. v. Commissioner, 198 F.2d 357, 359 (C.A.2 1952); Bittker, 33 Tax.L.Rev., at 284. When the obligation is canceled, the mortgagor is relieved of his responsibility to repay the sum he originally received and thus realizes value to that extent within the meaning of § 1001(b). From the mortgagor's point of view, when his obligation is assumed by a third party who purchases the encumbered property, it is as if the mortgagor first had been paid with cash borrowed by the third party from the mortgagee on a nonrecourse basis, and then had used the cash to satisfy his obligation to the mortgagee.

Moreover, this approach avoids the absurdity the Court recognized in *Crane.* Because of the remedy accompanying the mortgage in the nonrecourse situation, the depreciation in the fair market value of the property is relevant economically only to the mortgagee, who by lending on a nonrecourse basis remains at risk. To permit the taxpayer to limit his realization to the fair market value of the property would be to recognize a tax loss for which he has suffered no corresponding economic loss.[13] Such a result would be to construe "one section of the Act * * * so as * * * to defeat the intention of another or to frustrate the Act as a whole." * * *.

In the specific circumstances of *Crane,* the economic benefit theory did support the Commissioner's treatment of the nonrecourse mortgage as a personal obligation. The footnote in *Crane* acknowledged the limitations of that theory when applied to a different set of facts. *Crane* also stands for the broader proposition, however, that a nonrecourse loan should be treated as a true loan. We therefore hold that a taxpayer must account for the proceeds of obligations he has received tax-free and included in basis. Nothing in either § 1001(b) or in the Court's prior decisions requires the Commissioner to permit a taxpayer to treat a sale of encumbered property asymmetrically, by including the proceeds of the nonrecourse obligation in basis but not accounting for the proceeds upon transfer of the encumbered property. * * *.

IV

When a taxpayer sells or disposes of property encumbered by a nonrecourse obligation, the Commissioner properly requires him to include among the assets realized the outstanding amount of the obligation. The fair market value of the property is irrelevant to this calculation. We find this interpretation to be consistent with Crane v.

---

[13]  In the present case, the Government bore the ultimate loss. The nonrecourse mortgage was extended to respondents only after the planned complex was endorsed for mortgage insurance under §§ 221(b) and (d)(4) of the National Housing Act, 12 U.S.C. § 1715(b) and (d)(4) (1976 ed. and Supp. V). After acquiring the complex from respondents, Bayles operated it for a few years, but was unable to make it profitable. In 1974, F & H foreclosed, and the Department of Housing and Urban Development paid off the lender to obtain title. In 1976, the Department sold the complex to another developer for $1,502,000. The sale was financed by the Department's taking back a note for $1,314,800 and a nonrecourse mortgage. To fail to recognize the value of the nonrecourse loan in the amount realized, therefore, would permit respondents to compound the Government's loss by claiming the tax benefits of that loss for themselves.

Commissioner, 331 U.S. 1, 67 S.Ct. 1047 (1947), and to implement the statutory mandate in a reasonable manner. * * *.

The judgment of the Court of Appeals is therefore reversed.

It is so ordered.

■ JUSTICE O'CONNOR, concurring.

I concur in the opinion of the Court, accepting the view of the Commissioner. I do not, however, endorse the Commissioner's view. Indeed, were we writing on a slate clean except for the *Crane* decision, I would take quite a different approach—that urged upon us by Professor Barnett as *amicus.*

*Crane* established that a taxpayer could treat property as entirely his own, in spite of the "coinvestment" provided by his mortgagee in the form of a nonrecourse loan. That is, the full basis of the property, with all its tax consequences, belongs to the mortgagor. That rule alone, though, does not in any way tie nonrecourse debt to the cost of property or to the proceeds upon disposition. I see no reason to treat the purchase, ownership, and eventual disposition of property differently because the taxpayer also takes out a mortgage, an independent transaction. In this case, the taxpayer purchased property, using nonrecourse financing, and sold it after it declined in value to a buyer who assumed the mortgage. There is no economic difference between the events in this case and a case in which the taxpayer buys property with cash; later obtains a nonrecourse loan by pledging the property as security; still later, using cash on hand, buys off the mortgage for the market value of the devalued property; and finally sells the property to a third party for its market value.

The logical way to treat both this case and the hypothesized case is to separate the two aspects of these events and to consider, first, the ownership and sale of the property, and, second, the arrangement and retirement of the loan. Under *Crane,* the fair market value of the property on the date of acquisition—the purchase price—represents the taxpayer's basis in the property, and the fair market value on the date of disposition represents the proceeds on sale. The benefit received by the taxpayer in return for the property is the cancellation of a mortgage that is worth no more than the fair market value of the property, for that is all the mortgagee can expect to collect on the mortgage. His gain or loss on the disposition of the property equals the difference between the proceeds and the cost of acquisition. Thus, the taxation of the transaction *in property* reflects the economic fate of the *property.* If the property has declined in value, as was the case here, the taxpayer recognizes a loss on the disposition of the property. The new purchaser then takes as his basis the fair market value as of the date of the sale. * * *.

In the separate borrowing transaction, the taxpayer acquires cash from the mortgagee. He need not recognize income at that time, of course, because he also incurs an obligation to repay the money. Later, though, when he is able to satisfy the debt by surrendering property that is worth less than the face amount of the debt, we have a classic situation of cancellation of indebtedness, requiring the taxpayer to recognize income in the amount of the difference between the proceeds of the loan and the amount for which he is able to satisfy his creditor. 26 U.S.C. § 61(a)(12). The taxation of the financing transaction then reflects the economic fate of the loan.

The reason that separation of the two aspects of the events in this case is important is, of course, that the Code treats different sorts of income differently. A gain on the sale of the property may qualify for capital gains treatment, §§ 1202, 1221 (1976 ed. and Supp. V), while the cancellation of indebtedness is ordinary income, but income that the taxpayer may be able to defer. §§ 108, 1017 (1976 ed. Supp. V). Not only does Professor Barnett's theory permit us to accord appropriate treatment to each of the two types of income or loss present in these sorts of transactions, it also restores continuity to the system by making the taxpayer-seller's proceeds on the disposition of property equal to the purchaser's basis in the property. Further, and most important, it allows us to tax the events in this case in the same way that we tax the economically identical hypothesized transaction.

Persuaded though I am by the logical coherence and internal consistency of this approach, I agree with the Court's decision not to adopt it judicially. We do not write on a slate marked only by *Crane*. The Commissioner's longstanding position, Rev.Rul. 76–111, 1976–1 C.B. 214, is now reflected in the regulations. Treas.Reg. § 1.1001–2, 26 CFR § 1.1001–2 (1982). In the light of the numerous cases in the lower courts including the amount of the unrepaid proceeds of the mortgage in the proceeds on sale or disposition, * * * it is difficult to conclude that the Commissioner's interpretation of the statute exceeds the bounds of his discretion. As the Court's opinion demonstrates, his interpretation is defensible. One can reasonably read § 1001(b)'s reference to "the amount realized *from* the sale or other disposition of property" (emphasis added) to permit the Commissioner to collapse the two aspects of the transaction. As long as his view is a reasonable reading of § 1001(b), we should defer to the regulations promulgated by the agency charged with interpretation of the statute. * * *. Accordingly, I concur.

## NOTE

The *Crane* and *Tufts* cases arose in the context of *sales* of property subject to liabilities. Do the same realization rules apply if a donor gives away property subject to either a recourse or nonrecourse liability? The answer is "yes" and if the liability exceeds the donor's adjusted basis in the property, the donor has a gain equal to the excess.[1] Such a transfer is treated

---

[1] Malone v. United States, 326 F. Supp. 106 (N.D. Miss. 1972), aff'd per curiam, 455 F. 2d 502 (5th Cir. 1972) (personal liability); Johnson v. Commissioner, 495 F. 2d. 1079 (6th Cir. 1974) (nonrecourse liability).

as a part-gift and part-sale transaction,[2] with basis consequences to the donee as well.

The same tax consequences occur if the liability the donor is relieved of is created in the transfer itself.[3] This can happen in what is known as a "net gift." A net gift occurs when a donor transfers property to a donee on the condition that the donee pay the amount of the gift tax arising from the transfer. Since, in essence, the donee agrees to pay something (the gift tax) for the transferred property, the amount paid by the donee reduces the amount of the donor's gift. Of course a reduction in the amount of the donor's gift reduces the gift tax on the transfer which, in turn, increases the amount of the gift and the gift tax. If you are getting dizzy don't be surprised or upset. The Service has advanced an algebraic formula for the solution of this cyclical problem.[4] For example, assume that there is a flat 50 percent gift tax rate and that Donor transfers property worth $150,000 to Donee in a net gift transfer. Under the algebraic formula, Donor ends up with a $100,000 gift (Donor's gift of $150,000 less the gift tax of $50,000), and Donee pays a $50,000 gift tax.

So, you are probably asking yourself, "What's all this gift tax information doing in a basic income tax course?" Well, let's assume the property transferred that is worth $150,000 is highly appreciated stock with an adjusted basis to the donor of only $10,000 and Donee pays the $50,000 of gift tax. The Supreme Court, citing *Crane*, appropriately held that Donor has a gain of $40,000,[5] the excess of the Donor's $50,000 amount realized (the amount of gift tax liability which Donor is relieved from paying) less the Donor's $10,000 adjusted basis. It does not matter that the liability arose out of the transfer of the property and was not, as in *Crane*, a pre-existing liability.

There is one additional scenario to consider where a taxpayer transfers property and is relieved of a liability that is greater than the property's basis. Suppose taxpayer owns property worth $100,000 with an adjusted basis of $30,000, and a $50,000 mortgage encumbers the property. What should happen if the taxpayer *dies*? It is true that the property's basis will jump up to $100,000 under Section 1014, but that is the basis taken by the one who receives the property from the decedent and the question here is whether the decedent should be taxed on a $20,000 gain under the principles of the *Crane* case. Despite the apparent similarity of the situation, the I.R.S. has never asserted that a decedent is making a taxable sale in this situation.[6] Thus, death appears to be the only avenue for escaping the tax burden from relief of liabilities in excess of basis.

---

[2]   See problem 2 on page 128 of the Text.

[3]   Diedrich v. Commissioner, 497 U.S. 191, 102 S. Ct. 2414 (1982).

[4]   Rev. Rul. 75–72, 1975–1 CB 310 at 311. See Stephens, Maxfield, Lind & Calfee, Federal Estate and Gift Taxation ¶ 10.02[6][d] (Warren Gorham & Lamont 9th ed. 2013).

[5]   Diedrich v. Commissioner, 457 U.S. 191, 102 S.Ct. 2414 (1982).

[6]   Bittker & Lokken, Federal Taxation of Income, Estates and Gifts ¶ 44.4.3 (Warren, Gorham & Lamont).

## PROBLEMS

**1.** Mortgagor purchases a parcel of land from Seller for $100,000. Mortgagor borrows $80,000 from Bank and pays that amount and an additional $20,000 of cash to Seller giving Bank a nonrecourse mortgage on the land. The land is the security for the mortgage which bears an adequate interest rate.

(a)   What is Mortgagor's cost basis in the land?

(b)   Two years later when the land has appreciated in value to $300,000 and Mortgagor has paid only interest on the $80,000 mortgage, Mortgagor takes out a second nonrecourse mortgage of $100,000 with adequate rates of interest from Bank again using the land as security. Does Mortgagor have income when she borrows the $100,000? See Woodsam Associates, Inc. v. Commissioner, 198 F.2d 357 (2d Cir.1952).

(c)   What is Mortgagor's basis in the land if the $100,000 of mortgage proceeds are used to improve the land?

(d)   What is Mortgagor's basis in the land if the $100,000 of mortgage proceeds are used to purchase stocks and bonds worth $100,000?

(e)   What result under the facts of (d), above, if when the principal amount of the two mortgages is still $180,000 and the land is still worth $300,000, Mortgagor sells the property subject to both mortgages to Purchaser for $120,000 of cash? What is Purchaser's cost basis in the land?

(f)   What result under the facts of (d), above, if instead Mortgagor gives the land subject to the mortgages and still worth $300,000 to her Son? What is Son's basis in the land?

(g)   What results under the facts of (f), above, if Mortgagor gives the land to her Spouse rather than to her Son? What is Spouse's basis in the land? What is Spouse's basis in the land after Spouse pays off the $180,000 of mortgages?

(h)   What results to Mortgagor under the facts of (d), above, if the land declines in value from $300,000 to $180,000 and Mortgagor transfers the land by means of a quitclaim deed to Bank? See Parker v. Delaney, 186 F.2d 455 (1st Cir.1950).

(i)   What results to Mortgagor under the facts of (h), above, if the land declines in value from $300,000 to $170,000 at the time of the quitclaim deed?

**2.** Investor purchased three acres of land, each acre worth $100,000 for $300,000. Investor sold one of the acres in year one for $140,000 and a second in year two for $160,000. The total amount realized by Investor was $300,000 which is not in excess of her total purchase price. Does Investor have any gain or loss on the sales? See Reg. § 1.61–6(a).

**3.**   Gainer acquired an apartment in a condominium complex by inter vivos gift from Relative. Both used it only as a residence. It had been purchased by Relative for $200,000 cash and was given to Gainer when it was worth $300,000. Relative paid a $60,000 gift tax on the transfer. Gainer later sells the apartment to Shelterer.

(a) What gain or loss to Gainer on his sale to Shelterer for $320,000?

(b) What is Shelterer's basis in the apartment?

(c) Same questions now assuming that Relative acquired the property for $80,000 cash, but subject to a $120,000 mortgage on which neither she nor Gainer was ever personally liable or ever paid any amount of principal, and that Relative paid $30,000 tax on the gift. See § 1015(d)(6). Upon purchase, Shelterer merely took the property subject to the mortgage, paying $200,000 cash for it.

# CHAPTER 7

# LIFE INSURANCE PROCEEDS AND ANNUITIES

## A. LIFE INSURANCE PROCEEDS

Internal Revenue Code: Sections 101(a), (c), (d), and (g).

Regulations: Sections 1.101–1(a)(1), (b)(1), –4(a)(1)(i), (b)(1), (c).

---

It should be acknowledged at the beginning that the tax picture presented here of life insurance and annuities is no more than a long-range photograph taken without the benefit of a telephoto lens. This is for two reasons: (1) the presentation is in only one dimension ignoring, as it does, related estate and gift tax considerations that are likely to be of even more importance here than in other portions of this book; and (2) many details are set aside as out of keeping with the objective of this book to try to establish a good grounding in income tax fundamentals. Students should, nevertheless, emerge with an understanding of basic congressional policy in the area, an ability to apply the statute in routine circumstances, and a foundation for grappling with complexities that arise in other situations.

A common element of all life insurance policies is the agreement by the insurer to make payments upon the insured's death to the insured's estate or to others who are designated as beneficiaries. The plain thrust of Section 101(a)(1) is to exclude the proceeds of such policies from the gross income of the recipients. Usually an insurance policy will identify a fixed sum to be paid at death (the "face amount" of the policy). Essentially, it is this amount that is to be received tax-free. We might pause to wonder why this amount should not be taxed to the recipient. Consider the possibility that Young Married took out a $100,000 term policy on his life paying only the initial premium of $100. A week later he was killed in an automobile accident, and the insurer paid Mrs. Married $100,000. Neither of the Marrieds will ever be taxed on a clear gain (crass thought) of $99,900. Consider whether this a reflection of a "suffered enough" notion?[1] Consider also the relationship of the philosophy behind Sections 102 and 1014.[2]

---

[1] See I.R.C. § 104 considered at Chapter 9C, infra; see also Swihart, "Federal Taxation of Life Insurance Wealth," 37 Ind.L.J. 167 (1962).

[2] The exclusion seems justified when one analogizes a life insurance policy to other types of appreciated property acquired at the insured's death which are accorded an I.R.C. § 1014 stepped-up basis. The analogy loses some of its appeal when one recognizes that if the life insurance policy was the subject of an inter vivos gift, it would initially be accorded a § 1015 carryover basis to the donee, but its proceeds would still be allowed a § 101(a)(1) exclusion on

Justifiably, various restrictions and conditions cloud the apparent simplicity of the Section 101(a)(1) exclusion. For instance, the exclusion applies only to amounts "paid by reason of the death of the insured." It is possible, for example, that after a policy has been in effect for some time, the cash surrender value of the policy (the amount the insurer will pay the policy owner *during* the insured's life in discharge of all rights under the policy) will exceed the net premiums paid. If so and if the insured elects to take the cash surrender value, the insured will realize an amount in excess of basis, which is a taxable gain unprotected by the exclusionary rules of Section 101(a)(1), because it is an amount *not* paid by reason of the insured's death. Perhaps more important, an insurance policy that guarantees payments on the insured's death often contains alternative lifetime benefits that may be elected. For example, the insured may be able to demand the payment of fixed annual sums for life in lieu of and upon cancellation of any right to death benefits. If such a demand is made, the receipts are obviously not paid by reason of the insured's death and they are not excluded under Section 101(a)(1).[3]

Congress has provided an exception where even though a policy is cashed out during the insured's lifetime, the gain on the policy is excluded from gross income. Under Section 101(g), accelerated death benefits received from a life insurance policy on the life of a "terminally ill" or "chronically ill" insured person are treated as paid "by reason of the death of the insured" and are, therefore, excluded from gross income under Section 101(a)(1).[4] A "terminally ill" individual is one whom a physician certifies as having an illness or physical condition that can reasonably be expected to result in death within 24 months of the certification.[5] A "chronically ill" individual is a person who is certified within the preceding 12-month period by a licensed health care practitioner either as being unable to perform at least 2 activities of daily living for a period of at least 90 days due to a loss of functional capacity or as having severe cognitive impairment requiring substantial supervision to protect the individual from threats to health and safety.[6] The accelerated death benefits may be received from the insurer or received as a result of a sale of the policy to a "viatical settlement provider," one who is engaged in the trade or business of purchasing or taking assignments of life insurance policies on the lives of the individuals described above.[7] There is no ceiling on amounts paid with

---

payment at the insured's death, whereas other types of property would retain a § 1015 basis at death and would result in a gain if liquidated.

[3]     But see the comments below on the exclusionary rules of I.R.C. § 72.

[4]     I.R.C. § 101(g)(1). Seemingly this exclusion applies even though the policy is held by and the proceeds are paid to one other than the terminally ill or chronically ill insured person. However, the exclusion is inapplicable to payments on business-related policies on the life of a terminally ill or chronically ill person. I.R.C. § 101(g)(5).

[5]     I.R.C. § 101(g)(4)(A). See I.R.C. § 101(g)(4)(D).

[6]     I.R.C. §§ 101(g)(4)(B), 7702B(c)(2). A chronically ill person would include a person with Alzheimer's or Parkinson's disease.

[7]     I.R.C. § 101(g)(1)(A) and (g)(2).

respect to policies on the lives of terminally ill insureds. Amounts paid with respect to chronically ill insureds are limited to costs of qualified long-term care[8] or to payments of $175 per day ($63,875 per year),[9] both reduced by any reimbursements from medical insurance proceeds.[10]

Even though the proceeds of a policy are paid by reason of the death of the insured, the Section 101(a)(1) exclusion generally does not apply to the proceeds of a policy if the policy has been transferred for valuable consideration *during* the insured's life.[11] This rule was enacted to discourage the trafficking of life insurance policies.[12] The rule does not apply if the transfer of the policy for consideration was to a transferee who acquired the policy with a transferred basis,[13] or the transfer was to the insured, a partner of the insured, or a partnership or corporation in which the insured has an interest.[14]

Although it might appear Section 101(a)(1) excludes from gross income *whatever* amount is paid by reason of the insured's death, the section's introductory reference to subsection (d) calls attention to an important limitation. Under most life insurance policies Mrs. Married from the example above would have an option to accept something different from the $100,000 face amount of the policy. She might, instead, be entitled to elect fixed monthly payments of amounts, determined with reference to her age and life expectancy, for the rest of her life. Without close regard to mortality tables and actuarial principles, let us assume that she can and does elect to be paid $250 each month ($3,000 per year) for life and that her life expectancy is 50 years. If she should live just that long, she will receive, overall, $150,000 (50 × $3,000).[15] What, now, should be excluded? At one time, the entire $150,000 was excluded on these facts. But is this consistent with the basic policy behind the exclusion? Congress has decided that it is not, and that is what Section 101(d) is all about. If there are reasons for allowing an exclusion of $100,000 on the above facts, is it not just as clear that amounts that may be paid in excess of that sum represent amounts earned after the death

---

[8]   I.R.C. § 101(g)(3)(A)(i). Such amounts must meet requirements applicable to long-term care services. I.R.C. § 101(g)(3)(A)(ii), (B). See I.R.C. § 7702B.

[9]   I.R.C. §§ 101(g)(3)(D), 7702B(d)(2)–(6). A person who is both terminally ill and chronically ill is treated as terminally ill and is not subject to any limitations on the amount of recovery. I.R.C. § 101(g)(4)(B).

[10]   I.R.C. §§ 101(g)(3)(A)(i), 7702B(d)(2)(B).

[11]   I.R.C. § 101(a)(2). The excess of the policy proceeds over the transferee's costs incurred (amounts paid including consideration and premiums) are included in the recipient's gross income. For example, a viatical settlement provider (see note 7 supra) who purchases a policy must include in its gross income the amount of its gain on the receipt of the proceeds at the insured's death. See Lawthers, "Income Tax Aspects of Transfers of Life Insurance Policies and of Various Forms of Settlement Options," 22 N.Y.U. Inst. on Fed. Tax'n. 1299 (1964).

[12]   S. Rep. No. 1622, 83rd Cong., 2d Sess. 14 (1954).

[13]   I.R.C. § 101(a)(2)(A).

[14]   I.R.C. § 101(a)(2)(B). However, these exceptions do not apply if the acquirer of the policy has no substantial family, business, or financial relationship with the insured. I.R.C. § 101(a)(3).

[15]   Obviously, an insurer will agree to pay a larger sum over a long time than the amount to be paid as a lump sum immediately, because the insurer has the use of much of the money over the long period.

of the insured on property of the beneficiary, much the same as on any other investment? With this much background, attack Section 101(d) to determine the congressional answer to this problem. You should conclude that Mrs. Married would in each of the 50 years of her remaining life exclude $2,000 from and include $1,000 in gross income. Logical?[16] If she lived years beyond her life expectancy, the same exclusionary rule continues to apply in subsequent years.[17]

An insurance beneficiary may have the right to leave the entire $100,000 of proceeds with the insurer, drawing only interest on the amount that otherwise would be paid as a lump sum. Section 101(c) specifies that such interest payments are fully taxable like the interest earned on a bank account, but any subsequent receipt of the $100,000 proceeds is not taxable. In general, Sections 101(c) and (d) are mutually exclusive; whenever any recurring payments substantially eat into the principal amount of the insurance, (d), not (c), applies.[18]

## PROBLEMS

1.    Insured died in the current year owning a policy of insurance that would pay Beneficiary $100,000 but under which several alternatives were available to Beneficiary.

(a)    What result if Beneficiary simply accepts the $100,000 in cash? *Not GI — 101(a)(1)*

(b)    What result in (a), above, if Beneficiary instead leaves all the proceeds with the company and they pay her $6,000 interest in the current year? *101(c) → 6k is gross income*

(c)    What result if Insured's Daughter is Beneficiary of the policy and, in accordance with an option that she elects, the company pays her $12,000 in the current year? Assume that such payments will be made annually for her life and that she has a 25-year life expectancy.

(d)    What result in (c), above, if Insured's Daughter lives beyond her 25-year life expectancy and receives $12,000 in the twenty-sixth year?

2.    Jock agreed to play football for Pro Corporation. Pro, fearful that Jock might not survive, acquired a $1 million insurance policy on Jock's life. If Jock dies during the term of the policy and the proceeds of the policy are paid to Pro, what different consequences will Pro incur under the following alternatives?

---

[16]   Cf. I.R.C. § 102(b)(1).

[17]   Reg. § 1.101–4(c); and see Sen.Rep.No. 1622, note 12 supra, at 181. However, if she died prior to her life expectancy, there would be no deduction of the amount of the unrecovered proceeds.

[18]   Reg. § 1.101–3(a); but see Reg. § 1.101–4(h).

See Irenas, "Life Insurance Interest Income Under the Federal Income Tax," 21 Tax.L.Rev. 297 (1966).

    (a)    With Jock's consent Pro took out and paid $20,000 for a two year term policy on Jock's life.

    (b)    Jock owned a paid-up two-year term $1 million policy on his life which he sold to Pro for $20,000, Pro being named beneficiary of the policy.

    (c)    Same as (b), above, except that Jock was a shareholder of Pro Corporation.

**3.**    Insured purchases a single premium $100,000 life insurance policy on her life for a cost of $40,000. Consider the income tax consequences to Insured and the purchaser of the policy in each of the following alternative situations:

    (a)    Insured sells the policy to her Child for its $60,000 fair market value and, on Insured's death, the $100,000 of proceeds are paid to Child.

    (b)    Insured sells the policy to her Spouse for its $60,000 fair market value and, on Insured's death, the $100,000 of proceeds are paid to Spouse.

    (c)    Insured is certified by her physician as terminally ill and she sells the policy for its $80,000 fair market value to Viatical Settlement Provider who collects the $100,000 of proceeds on Insured's death.

## B. ANNUITY PAYMENTS

Internal Revenue Code: Sections 72(a)(1), (b), (c).

Regulations: Section 1.72–4(a), –9 (Table V).

———————

    Broadly speaking, an annuity is an arrangement under which one buys a right to future money payments. Being a mere matter of contract, the variety of such arrangements is limited only by the scope of human ingenuity. But there are some common classes: (1) A single-life annuity calls for fixed money payments to the annuitant for her life after which all rights under the contract cease. (2) Under a self-and-survivor annuity, fixed payments are made to an annuitant during her life and are then continued to another (in the same or a different amount) after her death. (3) The joint-and-survivor type annuity pays amounts jointly to two annuitants while both are living, and then payments are continued (in the same or a different amount) to the survivor. It is also common for the agreement to contain a refund feature; the contract may guarantee the payment of a sum certain to assure against severe loss through the premature death of the annuitants. Moreover the payments may be for a term certain, rather than for the life or lives of individuals. That is, the purchaser may buy the right to receive $1,000 per month for twenty years, in which case payments would continue to her designee in the event of her death before expiration of the term. Such arrangements are sometimes called endowment contracts, and at an earlier time they were differentiated from annuities for tax purposes,[1] but both types of arrangements are now treated alike under Section 72.

In recent years the practice has developed of combining the annuity with the mutual fund concept to produce what is called the variable annuity.[2] Under one form of variable annuity, the annuitant in effect acquires an interest (generally described as a certain number of "units") in a diversified investment portfolio. When she starts receiving payments her rights are defined in terms of the number of units credited to her which are to be distributed to her or her survivors over the pay-out period. But the amount she receives each time varies with the investment experience of the fund, hence the term "variable". The use of variable annuities is becoming fairly common under qualified employee's pension plans[3] in an effort to provide against the ravages of inflation.[4] Variable annuities outside the qualified plan area present some tax difficulties not expressly answered in Section 72 and are the subject of special rules in the regulations[5] which, however, are not discussed here.

Most annuity arrangements are made with insurance companies, although the rules of Section 72 are equally applicable to contracts between individuals.[6]

Even these brief remarks on annuities suggest the complexity of the area. Any attempt to explore the tax aspects of all the variations would of course be out of keeping with the objectives of this book. Accordingly, we turn now in as simple a setting as possible to the fundamental questions: How are annuities taxed and why? The keys to basic understanding are that (1) Income connotes gain and (2) A mere return of capital is not income. These are concepts that are familiar from the preceding chapter.

Assume now that Abouto Retire pays an insurance company $60,000 for their agreement to pay her $5,000 each year for the rest of her life. Payments begin and Retire receives $5,000 in the current year. Does this, or some part of it, represent income? If there were no special statutory rule applicable, we might say that Retire has just received a partial

---

[1] See I.R.C. (1939) § 22(b)(2) and Reg. § 39.22(b)(2)–2.

[2] Cf. I.R.C. § 817(d). Earlier, some employees' annuities were made variable in accordance with the Cost of Living Index. See Kern, "The Income Taxation of Variable Annuities," 55 A.B.A.J. 369 (1969); and see, generally, Bartlett, "Variable Annuities: Evolution and Analysis," 19 Stan.L.Rev. 150 (1966), a non-tax treatment.

[3] See Goodman, "Planning for Maximum Tax Benefits with Variable Annuities in Qualified Pension Plans," 30 J.Tax'n. 300 (1969).

[4] Employees' annuities are not further discussed here, but it might be noted that, except where an employee has contributed his own taxed dollars to the purchase of an annuity under a qualified plan, his receipts under the annuity whether variable or fixed will generally be fully taxable to him as ordinary income. I.R.C. §§ 72(d) and 402(a)(1); but see § 402(a)(2).

[5] Reg. § 1.72–2(b)(3) and see Reg. § 1.72–4(d)(3) Example.

[6] So-called "private" annuities present some special tax considerations, which are explored in Wojnaroski, "Private Annuities and Self-Canceling Notes," Tax Mgmt. Portfolio (BNA) No. 805–3rd (2011); see also Vernava, "Tax Planning for the Not-so-Rich: Variable and Private Annuities," 11 Wm. and Mary L.Rev. 1 (1969). See note 13, infra.

return of her capital which should go untaxed. Indeed, that was the law in the early years of the income tax. Of course its corollary was that after 12 years when Retire had fully recovered her capital (12 × $5,000 = $60,000), any further payments she received would be fully taxable and, under facts such as these, Retire might have a life expectancy of twenty years when the annuity payments began.

Congress eventually[7] took account of a deficiency in this taxing plan. It was recognized that there was really an income element in *each* annuity payment from the outset. Somewhat arbitrarily, that element was identified as an amount equal to 3% of the cost of the contract. Congress decided to tax that amount and to exclude from gross income the balance of each year's receipts. Thus, one in Retire's circumstances became taxable, as to each $5,000 payment, on $1,800 (3% of $60,000) and could exclude from gross income $3,200 ($5,000–$1,800). Under this statutory approach the exclusions continued until the tax-free portions of her receipts equalled the cost of the contract. In Retire's case this might work out pretty well. That is, it would take about 19 years (19 × $3200 = $60,800) for her to recover her investment tax free, and we have assumed Retire might have a life expectancy of twenty years. But the 3% rule was subject to criticism in that it did not purport to fix the amount of the tax-free receipt with respect to the relationship of the cost of the annuity and the life expectancy and probable return to the annuitant. In some circumstances it was quite possible that one who had little or no chance for a full tax-free recovery of her investment was, nevertheless, taxed on portions of her annual receipts.[8]

The philosophy of present Section 72 is not sharply different from the 3% rule it replaced. Congress still attempts properly to accord tax neutrality to the taxpayer's return of capital. Examine the statute. It allows a recovery of capital over the expected life of the contract by excluding the portion of each payment which is in the ratio of the "investment in the contract"[9] to the "expected return under the contract."[10] The excess receipt is taxed as the income element in each payment.[11] Assuming Abouto Retire, under the facts above, under tables provided in the regulations[12] has a 20-year life expectancy,[13] she would

---

[7] § 22(b)(2), 48 Stat. 680, 686 (1934).

[8] See Vernava, supra note 6, at 10.

[9] I.R.C. § 72(c)(1) defines this term as cost less recoveries of such cost under the pre-1954 code.

[10] I.R.C. § 72(c)(3).

[11] I.R.C. § 72(a)(1); see I.R.C. § 72(a)(2) which in essence allows only a portion of the annuity payment to be annualized where only a portion of the contract price is used to purchase current annuity payments.

[12] See Reg. § 1.72–9 Table V.

[13] These tables (V–VIII) are applicable to post-June 1986 investment in the contract and are not based on the sex of the taxpayer. The Supreme Court has held that retirement benefits based on the recipient's sex violate Title VII. Arizona Governing Committee, etc. v. Norris, 463 U.S. 1073, 103 S.Ct. 3492 (1983). The Service has also issued unisex tables under Reg. §§ 20.2031–7 and 25.2512–5 for valuing income interests and remainders. Rev.Rul. 84–162, 1984–2 C.B. 200, makes those valuations applicable to I.R.C. § 72. Reg. § 1.72–9 Tables I–IV

include $2,000 of each $5,000 payment in income, excluding $3,000, 60,000/100,000 of each $5,000 payment.

What if Abouto Retire lives beyond her life expectancy and receives a $5,000 payment in year 21? What if, in the alternative, she lives less than 20 years? At one time, a taxpayer merely was subject to the luck of the draw and the rules were like the life insurance rules, allowing the exclusion to continue even though the taxpayer lived beyond her life expectancy, denying a deduction if she died prior to her life expectancy.[14] Congress decided to change this result and added two special rules to Section 72(b). If an annuitant lives beyond her life expectancy and fully recovers her investment in the contract, the *full* amount of any subsequent annuity payment is included in her gross income.[15] In the alternative, if she dies without fully recovering her investment, i.e., with an unrecovered investment in the contract, the amount of the unrecovered investment is allowed as a deduction on her last income tax return.[16]

One must question the policy of these changes. If one lives beyond her life expectancy and is accustomed to receiving an annuity only *part* of which is taxed, is it appropriate when the annuitant has reached an elderly age to begin then to tax the *full* amount of the annuity payment? Admittedly, an income tax deduction on one's final return is beneficial; but to whom? Certainly not the annuitant. On the law of averages the Treasury should reap the same amount of revenue under either approach, but isn't the prior law fairer and more appropriate?

Annuities are not all as simple as those above. For example, if Abouto purchased again for $60,000 a self-and-survivor annuity that paid $5,000 per year until the survivor of Abouto and her spouse died and we assume this creates a payment expectancy of 30 years,[17] then each $5,000 payment would include $3,000 of taxable income, after excluding $2,000, 60,000/150,000 of each $5,000 payment.[18] Some annuities contain what are known as "refund features." One example of a refund occurs if any annuity is paid to an annuitant for her life, but if the annuity payments made prior to the annuitant's death do not equal the premiums

---

are based on the sex of the taxpayer and are applicable to a pre-July 1986 investment in the contract. See Reg. § 1.72–6(d)(3).

[14] See Chapter 7A at note 17, supra. Recall that life benefits under a life insurance policy are subject to tax under I.R.C. § 72, rather than § 101, because they are not received by reason of the death of the insured. But when § 101 applies, § 72 is inapplicable. Reg. § 1.72–2(b)(1).

[15] I.R.C. § 72(b)(2) and (4).

[16] I.R.C. § 72(b)(3). The deduction qualifies for an I.R.C. § 172 net operating loss carryover. See I.R.C. § 72(b)(3)(C) and Chapter 20D, infra.

[17] See Reg. § 1.72–9 Tables II and VI. See note 13, supra.

[18] Another alternative here is an annuity in which the survivorship annuity payments are only one-half the regular payments ($2500). If such an assumption were cranked into our text hypothetical, obviously the "investment in the contract" and the "expected return" would be less. However, whatever exclusion ratio is established by those factors remains constant over the life of the contract, whether the full or reduced payments are being received.

paid for the contract, the excess is refunded.[19] In such a situation Section 72(c)(2) requires that the value of the potential refund (based on the annuitant's life expectancy) be subtracted from the "investment in the contract," which has of course the intended effect of increasing the income portion of each annuity payment.[20] The legislative history indicates that, as the refund itself is exempt from tax,[21] the purpose of Section 72(c)(2) is to avoid a double exclusion from tax.[22]

That is not to imply that all refunds are exempt from tax. Refunds may be totally or partially included in income under Section 72(e). For example, Les Abouto Retire at age 55 pays $60,000 for an annuity which is to begin payment of $6,000 per year to him at age 65 but, after a time, he may cancel the contract prior to age 65 and receive back amounts in excess of $60,000, more the longer he waits. Les has purchased a single premium deferred life annuity with a refund feature and if he cancels at age 62 receiving $66,000 he has $6,000 of gross income.[23] There are numerous other possible types of refunds.[24]

If a beneficiary who has a right to a lump sum refund not fully tax exempt, instead exercises an option to receive a second annuity in lieu of such refund and does so within 60 days of the lump sum refund becoming payable, then no part of the lump sum refund is included in income.[25] The annuity payments are then included in income to the extent they constitute Section 72 income.

Now, after a careful examination of the statute, test your grasp of the basic working of these principles by way of the problems below.

## PROBLEM

1.   In the current year, T purchases a single life annuity with no refund feature for $48,000. Under the contract T is to receive $3,000 per year for life. T has a 24-year life expectancy.

    (a)   To what extent, if at all, is T taxable on the $3,000 received in the first year?

---

[19]  Reg. § 1.72–7(a).

[20]  See Reg. § 1.72–7(b). A taxpayer, age 57 with a 20-year life expectancy might be entitled to receive $5,000 per year under a single life annuity but, if she died prior to recovering the $60,000 premium paid, her estate would receive a payment equal to the excess of the premium over prior annuity payments received. As computed under Reg. §§ 1.72–7(b) and 1.72–9 Table VII, the refund feature would amount to $2400. The "investment in the contract" would be reduced to $57,600 and her exclusion ratio would be $57,600/$100,000. She would include 42.4% of each $5,000 payment in income or $2120 (as compared with $2,000 above). See note 13, supra.

[21]  It would be excluded from gross income under I.R.C. § 72(e) or as an insurance payment under § 101(a).

[22]  S.Rep. No. 1622, 83rd Cong., 2d Sess. 11 (1954).

[23]  I.R.C. § 72(e).

[24]  See Reg. § 1.72–11(c)(2).

[25]  I.R.C. § 72(h).

(b) If the law remains the same and T is still alive, how will T be taxed on the $3,000 received in the thirtieth year of the annuity payments?

(c) If T dies after nine years of payments will T or T's estate be allowed an income tax deduction? How much?

(d) To what extent are T and T's spouse taxable on the $3,000 received in the current year if at a cost of $76,500 they purchase a joint and survivorship annuity to pay $3,000 per year as long as either lives and they have a joint life expectancy of 34 years?

# CHAPTER 8

# DISCHARGE OF INDEBTEDNESS

Internal Revenue Code: Sections 61(a)(12); 102(a); 108(a), (b)(1), (d)(1)–(3), (e)(1) and (5); 1017(a).

Regulations: Sections 1.61–12(a); 1.1001–2(a), 2(c) Ex. (8).

## United States v. Kirby Lumber Co.[*]

Supreme Court of the United States, 1931.
284 U.S. 1, 52 S.Ct. 4.

■ MR. JUSTICE HOLMES delivered the opinion of the Court.

In July, 1923, the plaintiff, the Kirby Lumber Company, issued its own bonds for $12,126,800 for which it received their par value. Later in the same year it purchased in the open market some of the same bonds at less than par, the difference of price being $137,521.30. The question is whether this difference is a taxable gain or income of the plaintiff for the year 1923. By the Revenue Act of (November 23,) 1921, c. 136, § 213(a) gross income includes "gains or profits and income derived from any source whatever," and by the Treasury Regulations authorized by § 1303, that have been in force through repeated reenactments, "If the corporation purchases and retires any of such bonds at a price less than the issuing price or face value, the excess of the issuing price or face value over the purchase price is gain or income for the taxable year." * * *. We see no reason why the Regulations should not be accepted as a correct statement of the law.

In Bowers v. Kerbaugh-Empire Co., 271 U.S. 170, 46 S.Ct. 449, the defendant in error owned the stock of another company that had borrowed money repayable in marks or their equivalent for an enterprise that failed. At the time of payment the marks had fallen in value, which so far as it went was a gain for the defendant in error, and it was contended by the plaintiff in error that the gain was taxable income. But the transaction as a whole was a loss, and the contention was denied. Here there was no shrinkage of assets and the taxpayer made a clear gain. As a result of its dealings it made available $137,521.30 assets previously offset by the obligation of bonds now extinct. We see nothing to be gained by the discussion of judicial definitions. The defendant in error has realized within the year an accession to income, if we take words in their plain popular meaning, as they should be taken here. * * *.

---

[*]   See Bittker and Thompson, "Income From the Discharge of Indebtedness: The Progeny of United States v. Kirby Lumber Co.," 66 Calif.L.Rev. 1159 (1978).

Judgment reversed.

# Zarin v. Commissioner*

United States Court of Appeals, Third Circuit, 1990.**
916 F.2d 110.

■ COWEN, CIRCUIT JUDGE:

David Zarin ("Zarin") appeals from a decision of the Tax Court holding that he recognized $2,935,000 of income from discharge of indebtedness resulting from his gambling activities, and that he should be taxed on the income. This Court has jurisdiction to review the Tax Court's decision under section 7482 of the Internal Revenue Code (1954) (the "Code"). After considering the issues raised by this appeal, we will reverse.

I.

Zarin was a professional engineer who participated in the development, construction, and management of various housing projects. A resident of Atlantic City, New Jersey, Zarin occasionally gambled, both in his hometown and in other places where gambling was legalized. To facilitate his gaming activities in Atlantic City, Zarin applied to Resorts International Hotel ("Resorts") for a credit line in June, 1978. Following a credit check, Resorts granted Zarin $10,000 of credit. Pursuant to this credit arrangement with Resorts, Zarin could write a check, called a marker,[2] and in return receive chips, which could then be used to gamble at the casino's tables.

Before long, Zarin developed a reputation as an extravagant "high roller" who routinely bet the house maximum while playing craps, his game of choice. Considered a "valued gaming patron" by Resorts, Zarin had his credit limit increased at regular intervals without any further credit checks, and was provided a number of complimentary services and privileges. By November, 1979, Zarin's permanent line of credit had been raised to $200,000. Between June, 1978, and December, 1979, Zarin lost $2,500,000 at the craps table, losses he paid in full.

Responding to allegations of credit abuses, the New Jersey Division of Gaming Enforcement filed with the New Jersey Casino Control Commission a complaint against Resorts. Among the 809 violations of casino regulations alleged in the complaint of October, 1979, were 100 pertaining to Zarin. Subsequently, a Casino Control Commissioner issued an Emergency Order, the effect of which was to make further extensions of credit to Zarin illegal.

---

* See Shaviro, "The Man Who Lost Too Much: *Zarin v. Commissioner* and the Measurement of Taxable Consumption," 45 Tax.L.Rev. 215 (1990).

** Some footnotes omitted.

2 A "marker" is a negotiable draft payable to Resorts and drawn on the marker's bank.

Nevertheless, Resorts continued to extend Zarin's credit limit through the use of two different practices: "considered cleared" credit and "this trip only" credit.[3] Both methods effectively ignored the Emergency Order and were later found to be illegal.

By January, 1980, Zarin was gambling compulsively and uncontrollably at Resorts, spending as many as sixteen hours a day at the craps table.[5] During April, 1980, Resorts again increased Zarin's credit line without further inquiries. That same month, Zarin delivered personal checks and counterchecks to Resorts which were returned as having been drawn against insufficient funds. Those dishonored checks totaled $3,435,000. In late April, Resorts cut off Zarin's credit.

Although Zarin indicated that he would repay those obligations, Resorts filed a New Jersey state court action against Zarin in November, 1980, to collect the $3,435,000. Zarin denied liability on grounds that Resort's claim was unenforceable under New Jersey regulations intended to protect compulsive gamblers. Ten months later, in September, 1981, Resorts and Zarin settled their dispute for a total of $500,000.

The Commissioner of Internal Revenue ("Commissioner") subsequently determined deficiencies in Zarin's federal income taxes for 1980 and 1981, arguing that Zarin recognized $3,435,000 of income in 1980 from larceny by trick and deception. After Zarin challenged that claim by filing a Tax Court petition, the Commissioner abandoned his 1980 claim, and argued instead that Zarin had recognized $2,935,000 of income in 1981 from the cancellation of indebtedness which resulted from the settlement with Resorts.

Agreeing with the Commissioner, the Tax Court decided, eleven judges to eight, that Zarin had indeed recognized $2,935,000 of income from the discharge of indebtedness, namely the difference between the original $3,435,000 "debt" and the $500,000 settlement. *Zarin v. Commissioner,* 92 T.C. 1084 (1989). Since he was in the seventy percent tax bracket, Zarin's deficiency for 1981 was calculated to be $2,047,245. With interest to April 5, 1990, Zarin allegedly owes the Internal Revenue Service $5,209,033.96 in additional taxes. Zarin appeals the order of the Tax Court.

II.

The sole issue before this Court is whether the Tax Court correctly held that Zarin had income from discharge of indebtedness. Section 108 and section 61(a)(12) of the Code set forth "the general rule that gross income includes income from the discharge of indebtedness." I.R.C. § 108(e)(1). The Commissioner argues, and the Tax Court agreed, that

---

[3] Under the "considered cleared" method, Resorts would treat a personal check as a cash transaction, and would therefore not apply the amount of the check in calculating the amount of credit extended Zarin. "This trip only" credit allowed Resorts to grant temporary increases of credit for a given visit, so long as the credit limit was lowered by the next visit.

[5] Zarin claims that at the time he was suffering from a recognized emotional disorder that caused him to gamble compulsively.

pursuant to the Code, Zarin did indeed recognize income from discharge of gambling indebtedness.

Under the Commissioner's logic, Resorts advanced Zarin $3,435,000 worth of chips, chips being the functional equivalent of cash. At that time, the chips were not treated as income, since Zarin recognized an obligation of repayment. In other words, Resorts made Zarin a tax-free loan. However, a taxpayer does recognize income if a loan owed to another party is cancelled, in whole or in part. I.R.C. §§ 61(a)(12), 108(e). The settlement between Zarin and Resorts, claims the Commissioner, fits neatly into the cancellation of indebtedness provisions in the Code. Zarin owed $3,435,000, paid $500,000, with the difference constituting income. Although initially persuasive, the Commissioner's position is nonetheless flawed for two reasons.

III.

Initially, we find that sections 108 and 61(a)(12) are inapplicable to the Zarin/Resorts transaction. Section 61 does not define indebtedness. On the other hand, section 108(d)(1), which repeats and further elaborates on the rule in section 61(a)(12), defines the term as any indebtedness "(A) for which the taxpayer is liable, or (B) subject to which the taxpayer holds property." I.R.C. § 108(d)(1). In order to come within the sweep of the discharge of indebtedness rules, then, the taxpayer must satisfy one of the two prongs in the section 108(d)(1) test. Zarin satisfies neither.

Because the debt Zarin owed to Resorts was unenforceable as a matter of New Jersey state law, it is clearly not a debt "for which the taxpayer is liable." I.R.C. § 108(d)(1)(A). Liability implies a legally enforceable obligation to repay, and under New Jersey law, Zarin would have no such obligation.

Moreover, Zarin did not have a debt subject to which he held property as required by section 108(d)(1)(B). Zarin's indebtedness arose out of his acquisition of gambling chips. The Tax Court held that

---

[7]     The Tax Court held that the Commissioner had not met its burden of proving that the debt owed Resorts was enforceable as a matter of state law. *Zarin*, 92 T.C. at 1090. There was ample evidence to support that finding. In New Jersey, the extension of credit by casinos "to enable [any] person to take part in gaming activity as a player" is limited. N.J.Stat.Ann. § 5:12–101(b) (1988). Under N.J.Stat.Ann. § 5:12–101(f), any credit violation is "invalid and unenforceable for the purposes of collection . . ." In Resorts Int'l Hotel, Inc. v. Salomone, 178 N.J.Super. 598, 429 A.2d 1078 (App.Div.1981), the court held that "casinos must comply with the Legislature's strict control of credit for gambling purposes. Unless they do, the debts reflected by players' checks will not be enforced . . ." Id. at 607, 429 A.2d at 1082.

With regards to the extension of credit to Zarin after the Emergency Order of October, 1979, was issued, Resorts did not comply with New Jersey regulations. The Casino Control Commission specifically stated in 1983 "that Resorts was guilty of infractions, violations, improprieties, with the net effect that [Zarin] was encouraged to continue gambling long after, one, his credit line was reached, and exceeded; two, long after it became apparent that the gambler was an addicted gambler; three, long after the gambler had difficulty in paying his debts; and four, Resorts knew the individual was gambling when he should not have been gambling." Appendix at 325–326. It follows, therefore, that under New Jersey law, the $3,435,000 debt Zarin owed Resorts was totally unenforceable.

gambling chips were not property, but rather, "a medium of exchange within the Resorts casino" and a "substitute for cash." Alternatively, the Tax Court viewed the chips as nothing more than "the opportunity to gamble and incidental services . . ." *Zarin,* 92 T.C. at 1099. We agree with the gist of these characterizations, and hold that gambling chips are merely an accounting mechanism to evidence debt.

Gaming chips in New Jersey during 1980 were regarded "solely as evidence of a debt owed to their custodian by the casino licensee and shall be considered at no time the property of anyone other than the casino licensee issuing them." N.J.Admin.Code tit. 19k, § 19:46–1.5(d) (1990). Thus, under New Jersey state law, gambling chips were Resorts' property until transferred to Zarin in exchange for the markers, at which point the chips became "evidence" of indebtedness (and not the property of Zarin).

Even were there no relevant legislative pronouncement on which to rely, simple common sense would lead to the conclusion that chips were not property in Zarin's hands. Zarin could not do with the chips as he pleased, nor did the chips have any independent economic value beyond the casino. The chips themselves were of little use to Zarin, other than as a means of facilitating gambling. They could not have been used outside the casino. They could have been used to purchase services and privileges within the casino, including food, drink, entertainment, and lodging, but Zarin would not have utilized them as such, since he received those services from Resorts on a complimentary basis. In short, the chips had no economic substance.

Although the Tax Court found that theoretically, Zarin could have redeemed the chips he received on credit for cash and walked out of the casino, *Zarin,* 92 T.C. at 1092, the reality of the situation was quite different. Realistically, before cashing in his chips, Zarin would have been required to pay his outstanding IOUs. New Jersey state law requires casinos to "request patrons to apply any chips or plaques in their possession in reduction of personal checks or Counter Checks exchanged for purposes of gaming prior to exchanging such chips or plaques for cash or prior to departing from the casino area." * * *. Since his debt at all times equalled or exceeded the number of chips he possessed, redemption would have left Zarin with no chips, no cash, and certainly nothing which could have been characterized as property.

Not only were the chips non-property in Zarin's hands, but upon transfer to Zarin, the chips also ceased to be the property of Resorts. Since the chips were in the possession of another party, Resorts could no longer do with the chips as it pleased, and could no longer control the chips' use. Generally, at the time of a transfer, the party in possession of the chips can gamble with them, use them for services, cash them in, or walk out of the casino with them as an Atlantic City souvenir. The chips therefore become nothing more than an accounting mechanism, or evidence of a debt, designed to facilitate gambling in casinos where the use of actual money was forbidden.[8] Thus, the chips which Zarin held were not property within the meaning of I.R.C. § 108(d)(1)(B).[9]

In short, because Zarin was not liable on the debt he allegedly owed Resorts, and because Zarin did not hold "property" subject to that debt, the cancellation of indebtedness provisions of the Code do not apply to the settlement between Resorts and Zarin. As such, Zarin cannot have income from the discharge of his debt.

IV.

Instead of analyzing the transaction at issue as cancelled debt, we believe the proper approach is to view it as disputed debt or contested liability. Under the contested liability doctrine, if a taxpayer, in good faith, disputed the amount of a debt, a subsequent settlement of the dispute would be treated as the amount of debt cognizable for tax purposes. The excess of the original debt over the amount determined to have been due is disregarded for both loss and debt and accounting purposes. Thus, if a taxpayer took out a loan for $10,000, refused in good faith to pay the full $10,000 back, and then reached an agreement with the lendor that he would pay back only $7,000 in full satisfaction of the debt, the transaction would be treated as if the initial loan was $7,000. When the taxpayer tenders the $7,000 payment, he will have been deemed to have paid the full amount of the initially disputed debt. Accordingly, there is no tax consequence to the taxpayer upon payment.

The seminal "contested liability" case is N. Sobel, Inc. v. Commissioner, 40 B.T.A. 1263 (1939). In *Sobel*, the taxpayer exchanged a $21,700 note for 100 shares of stock from a bank. In the following year, the taxpayer sued the bank for recision, arguing that the bank loan was violative of state law, and moreover, that the bank had failed to perform certain promises. The parties eventually settled the case in 1935, with the taxpayer agreeing to pay half of the face amount of the note. In the year of the settlement, the taxpayer claimed the amount paid as a loss. The Commissioner denied the loss because it had been sustained five years earlier, and further asserted that the taxpayer recognized income from the discharge of half of his indebtedness.

---

[8]  Although, as noted above, Zarin would not have been able to leave the casino with cash or chips, and probably would not have used the chips for services, these facts do not change the character of the chips. Despite the aforementioned limitations upon Zarin's use of the chips, they remain an accounting mechanism or evidence of a debt. Resorts' increased interest in Zarin's chips does not rise to the level of a property interest, since Zarin still has dominion over the chips within the casino.

[9]  The parties stipulated before the Tax Court that New Jersey casino "chips are property which are not negotiable and may not be used to gamble or for any other purpose outside the casino where they were issued." It could be argued that we are bound by this stipulation to accept the proposition that chips are property. We do not dispute the notion that chips are property, but as discussed above, they are only property in the hands of the casino. The stipulation is consistent with this idea. In fact, both parties agreed in their briefs that chips are property of the casino. Moreover, during oral arguments, both parties agreed that chips were not property when held by the gambler.

The Board of Tax Appeals held that since the loss was not fixed until the dispute was settled, the loss was recognized in 1935, the year of the settlement, and the deduction was appropriately taken in that year. Additionally, the Board held that the portion of the note forgiven by the bank "was not the occasion for a freeing of assets and that there was no gain . . ." Id. at 1265. Therefore, the taxpayer did not have any income from cancellation of indebtedness.

There is little difference between the present case and *Sobel*. Zarin incurred a $3,435,000 debt while gambling at Resorts, but in court, disputed liability on the basis of unenforceability. A settlement of $500,000 was eventually agreed upon. It follows from *Sobel* that the settlement served only to fix the amount of debt. No income was realized or recognized. When Zarin paid the $500,000, any tax consequence dissolved.[10]

Only one other court has addressed a case factually similar to the one before us. In United States v. Hall, 307 F.2d 238 (10th Cir.1962), the taxpayer owed an unenforceable gambling debt alleged to be $225,000. Subsequently, the taxpayer and the creditor settled for $150,000. The taxpayer then transferred cattle valued at $148,110 to his creditor in satisfaction of the settlement agreement. A jury held that the parties fixed the debt at $150,000, and that the taxpayer recognized income from cancellation of indebtedness equal to the difference between the $150,000 and the $148,110 value affixed to the cattle. Arguing that the taxpayer recognized income equal to the difference between $225,000 and $148,000, the Commissioner appealed.

The Tenth Circuit rejected the idea that the taxpayer had any income from cancellation of indebtedness. Noting that the gambling debt was unenforceable, the Tenth Circuit said, "The cold fact is that taxpayer suffered a substantial loss from gambling, the amount of which was determined by the transfer." Id. at 241. In effect, the Court held that because the debt was unenforceable, the amount of the loss and resulting debt cognizable for tax purposes were fixed by the settlement at $148,110. Thus, the Tenth Circuit lent its endorsement to the contested liability doctrine in a factual situation strikingly similar to the one at issue.[11]

---

[10]   Had Zarin not paid the $500,000 dollar settlement, it would be likely that he would have had income from cancellation of indebtedness. The debt at that point would have been fixed, and Zarin would have been legally obligated to pay it.

[11]   The Commissioner argues that the decision in *Hall* was based on United States Supreme Court precedent since overruled, and therefore *Hall* should be disregarded. Indeed, the *Hall* court devoted a considerable amount of time to Bowers v. Kerbaugh-Empire Co., 271 U.S. 170, 46 S.Ct. 449 (1926), a case whose validity is in question. We do not pass on the question of whether or not *Bowers* is good law. We do note that *Hall* relied on *Bowers* only for the proposition that "a court need not in every case be oblivious to the net effect of the entire transaction." United States v. Hall, 307 F.2d at 242, quoting Bradford v. Commissioner, 233 F.2d 935, 939 (6th Cir.1956). *Hall*'s reliance on *Bowers* did not extend to the issue of contested liability, and even if it did, the idea that "Courts need not apply mechanical standards which smother the reality of a particular transaction," Id. at 241, is hardly an exceptional concept in the tax realm.

The Commissioner argues that *Sobel* and the contested liability doctrine only apply when there is an unliquidated debt; that is, a debt for which the amount cannot be determined. See Colonial Sav. Ass'n v. Commissioner, 85 T.C. 855, 862–863 (1985) (*Sobel* stands for the proposition that "there must be a liquidated debt"), aff'd, 854 F.2d 1001 (7th Cir.1988). See also N. Sobel, Inc. v. Commissioner, 40 B.T.A. at 1265 (there was a dispute as to "liability and the amount" of the debt). Since Zarin contested his liability based on the unenforceability of the entire debt, and did not dispute the amount of the debt, the Commissioner would have us adopt the reasoning of the Tax Court, which found that Zarin's debt was liquidated, therefore barring the application of *Sobel* and the contested liability doctrine. *Zarin,* 92 T.C. at 1095 (Zarin's debt "was a liquidated amount" and "[t]here is no dispute about the amount [received].").

We reject the Tax Court's rationale. When a debt is unenforceable, it follows that the amount of the debt, and not just the liability thereon, is in dispute. Although a debt may be unenforceable, there still could be some value attached to its worth. This is especially so with regards to gambling debts. In most states, gambling debts are unenforceable, and have "but slight potential . . . " United States v. Hall, 307 F.2d 238, 241 (10th Cir.1962). Nevertheless, they are often collected, at least in part. For example, Resorts is not a charity; it would not have extended illegal credit to Zarin and others if it did not have some hope of collecting debts incurred pursuant to the grant of credit.

Moreover, the debt is frequently incurred to acquire gambling chips, and not money. Although casinos attach a dollar value to each chip, that value, unlike money's, is not beyond dispute, particularly given the illegality of gambling debts in the first place. This proposition is supported by the facts of the present case. Resorts gave Zarin $3.4 million dollars of chips in exchange for markers evidencing Zarin's debt. If indeed the only issue was the enforceability of the entire debt, there would have been no settlement. Zarin would have owed all or nothing. Instead, the parties attached a value to the debt considerably lower than its face value. In other words, the parties agreed that given the circumstances surrounding Zarin's gambling spree, the chips he acquired might not have been worth $3.4 million dollars, but were worth something. Such a debt cannot be called liquidated, since its exact amount was not fixed until settlement.

To summarize, the transaction between Zarin and Resorts can best be characterized as a disputed debt, or contested liability. Zarin owed an unenforceable debt of $3,435,000 to Resorts. After Zarin in good faith disputed his obligation to repay the debt, the parties settled for $500,000, which Zarin paid. That $500,000 settlement fixed the amount of loss and the amount of debt cognizable for tax purposes. Since Zarin was deemed

---

See Commissioner v. Tufts, 461 U.S. 300, 103 S.Ct. 1826 (1983); Hillsboro Nat'l Bank v. Commissioner, 460 U.S. 370, 103 S.Ct. 1134 (1983).

to have owed $500,000, and since he paid Resorts $500,000, no adverse tax consequences attached to Zarin as a result.[12]

V.

In conclusion, we hold that Zarin did not have any income from cancellation of indebtedness for two reasons. First, the Code provisions covering discharge of debt are inapplicable since the definitional requirement in I.R.C. section 108(d)(1) was not met. Second, the settlement of Zarin's gambling debts was a contested liability. We reverse the decision of the Tax Court and remand with instructions to enter judgment that Zarin realized no income by reason of his settlement with Resorts.

**Dissenting Opinion**

■ STAPLETON, CIRCUIT JUDGE, dissenting:

I respectfully dissent because I agree with the Commissioner's appraisal of the economic realities of this matter.

Resorts sells for cash the exhilaration and the potential for profit inherent in games of chance. It does so by selling for cash chips that entitle the holder to gamble at its casino. Zarin, like thousands of others, wished to purchase what Resorts was offering in the marketplace. He chose to make this purchase on credit and executed notes evidencing his obligation to repay the funds that were advanced to him by Resorts. As in most purchase money transactions, Resorts skipped the step of giving Zarin cash that he would only return to it in order to pay for the opportunity to gamble. Resorts provided him instead with chips that entitled him to participate in Resorts' games of chance on the same basis as others who had paid cash for that privilege.[1] Whether viewed as a one or two-step transaction, however, Zarin received either $3.4 million in cash or an entitlement for which others would have had to pay $3.4 million.

Despite the fact that Zarin received in 1980 cash or an entitlement worth $3.4 million, he correctly reported in that year no income from his dealings with Resorts. He did so *solely* because he recognized, as evidenced by his notes, an offsetting obligation to repay Resorts $3.4 million in cash. * * *. In 1981, with the delivery of Zarin's promise to pay Resorts $500,000 and the execution of a release by Resorts, Resorts surrendered its claim to repayment of the remaining $2.9 million of the

[12] The Commissioner argues in the alternative that Zarin recognized $3,435,000 of income in 1980. This claim has no merit. Recognition of income would depend upon a finding that Zarin did not have cancellation of indebtedness income solely because his debt was unenforceable. We do not so hold. Although unenforceability is a factor in our analysis, our decision ultimately hinges upon the determination that the "disputed debt" rule applied, or alternatively, that chips are not property within the meaning of I.R.C. section 108.

[1] I view as irrelevant the facts that Resorts advanced credit to Zarin solely to enable him to patronize its casino and that the chips could not be used elsewhere or for other purposes. When one buys a sofa from the furniture store on credit, the fact that the proprietor would not have advanced the credit for a different purpose does not entitle one to a tax-free gain in the event the debt to the store is extinguished for some reason.

money Zarin had borrowed. As of that time, Zarin's assets were freed of his potential liability for that amount and he recognized gross income in that amount. Commissioner v. Tufts, 461 U.S. 300 (1983); United States v. Kirby Lumber Company, 284 U.S. 1 (1931); Vukasovich, Inc. v. Commissioner, 790 F.2d 1409 (9th Cir.1986). But see United States v. Hall, 307 F.2d 238 (10th Cir.1962).[2]

*Because the debt would be unenforceable from the asset*

The only alternatives I see to this conclusion are to hold either (1) that Zarin realized $3.4 million in income in 1980 at a time when both parties to the transaction thought there was an offsetting obligation to repay or (2) that the $3.4 million benefit sought and received by Zarin is not taxable at all. I find the latter alternative unacceptable as inconsistent with the fundamental principle of the Code that anything of commercial value received by a taxpayer is taxable unless expressly excluded from gross income.[3] Commissioner v. Glenshaw Glass Co., 348 U.S. 426 (1955); *United States v. Kirby Lumber Co.*, supra. I find the former alternative unacceptable as impracticable. In 1980, neither party was maintaining that the debt was unenforceable and, because of the settlement, its unenforceability was not even established in the litigation over the debt in 1981. It was not until 1989 in this litigation over the tax consequences of the transaction that the unenforceability was first judicially declared. Rather than require such tax litigation to resolve the correct treatment of a debt transaction, I regard it as far preferable to have the tax consequences turn on the manner in which the debt is treated by the parties. For present purposes, it will suffice to say that where something that would otherwise be includable in gross income is received on credit in a purchase money transaction, there should be no recognition of income so long as the debtor continues to recognize an obligation to repay the debt. On the other hand, income, if not earlier recognized, should be recognized when the debtor no longer recognizes an obligation to repay and the creditor has released the debt or acknowledged its unenforceability.

---

[2]   This is not a case in which parties agree subsequent to a purchase money transaction that the property purchased has a value less than thought at the time of the transaction. In such cases, the purchase price adjustment rule is applied and the agreed-upon value is accepted as the value of the benefit received by the purchaser; see e.g., Commissioner v. Sherman, 135 F.2d 68 (6th Cir.1943); N. Sobel, Inc. v. Commissioner, 40 B.T.A. 1263 (1939). Nor is this a case in which the taxpayer is entitled to rescind an entire purchase money transaction, thereby to restore itself to the position it occupied before receiving anything of commercial value. In this case, the illegality was in the extension of credit by Resorts and whether one views the benefit received by Zarin as cash or the opportunity to gamble, he is no longer in a position to return that benefit.

[3]   As the court's opinion correctly points out, this record will not support an exclusion under § 108(a) which relates to discharge of debt in an insolvency or bankruptcy context. Section 108(e)(5) of the Code, which excludes discharged indebtedness arising from a "purchase price adjustment" is not applicable here. Among other things, § 108(e)(5) necessarily applies only to a situation in which the debtor still holds the property acquired in the purchase money transaction. Equally irrelevant is § 108(d)'s definition of "indebtedness" relied upon heavily by the court. Section 108(d) expressly defines that term solely for the purposes of § 108 and not for the purposes of § 61(a)(12).

In this view, it makes no difference whether the extinguishment of the creditor's claim comes as a part of a compromise. Resorts settled for 14 cents on the dollar presumably because it viewed such a settlement as reflective of the odds that the debt would be held to be enforceable. While Zarin should be given credit for the fact that he had to pay 14 cents for a release, I see no reason why he should not realize gain in the same manner as he would have if Resorts had concluded on its own that the debt was legally unenforceable and had written it off as uncollectible.[5]

I would affirm the judgment of the Tax Court.

## NOTE

If Holmes, J., can be characteristically succinct, perhaps so can we. We seek to emulate him with some *brief* comments on the *Kirby* area.

The *Kirby Lumber* case accords some meaning to the cryptic language of Section 61(a)(12), requiring that income from the discharge of indebtedness be included within gross income. The simplest view of *Kirby* is that it reflects the corollary of the 34th Street lullaby, "buy low-sell high;" with respect to one's obligations, if one sells high and then buys back low, one can profit equally. The receipt of money in the form of a loan has, by itself, no income tax consequences. To be sure, the taxpayer derives an economic benefit from the funds obtained through a loan; however, the obligation to repay, whether in the form of a note, account payable or a simple "I.O.U.", offsets the receipt of the loan proceeds, effecting a "wash" for tax purposes. No income is realized. But if a taxpayer pays off a debt for less than the amount owing, the difference constitutes income to him, because he realizes an economic benefit by way of an increase in his net worth much as if he had sold property at a profit. The taxable event is the freeing of assets that previously were held subject to the obligation. However, the *Kirby Lumber* doctrine is subject to exceptions most of which were judicially developed.[1] Many of the exceptions have been codified by Congress.[2] The following excerpt of legislative history[3] explains the background of the judicial exceptions and includes editorially bracketed comments for subsequent changes. Much of the legislation is too detailed for consideration here. Nevertheless the assigned portion of the statutes (Sections 108 and 1017), a glimpse into the Congressional mind through the window of a

---

[5]   A different situation exists where there is a bona fide dispute over the amount of a debt and the dispute is compromised. Rather than require tax litigation to determine the amount of income received, the Commission treats the compromise figure as representing the amount of the obligation. I find this sensible and consistent with the pragmatic approach I would take.

[1]   See Eustice, "Cancellation of Indebtedness and the Federal Income Tax: A Problem of Creeping Confusion," 14 Tax L.Rev. 225 (1959) and Stone, "Cancellation of Indebtedness," 34 N.Y.U.Inst. on Fed. Tax. 555 (1976).

[2]   Pub.Law No. 96–589, 96th Cong., 2d Sess. (1980). A statutory exception in a solvency situation was repealed in the 1986 legislation. Pub.Law No. 99–514, 99th Cong., 2d Sess. § 822 (1986). But see I.R.C. § 108(g). See Heinlen, "The ABCs of Cancellation of Indebtedness Income and Attribute Reduction," 40 N.Y.U.Inst. on Fed. Tax'n Ch. 42 (1982); Asofsky and Tatlock, "Bankruptcy Tax Act Radically Alters Treatment of Bankruptcy and Discharging Debts," 54 J.Tax. 106 (1981).

[3]   Sen.Rep.No. 96–1035, 96th Cong., 2d Sess. 8 (1980), 1980–2 C.B. 620 at 623.

Committee Report, and problems three and four (at the end of the Chapter) should provide a feel for the fundamental aspects of the *Kirby Lumber* exceptions.

## SENATE FINANCE COMMITTEE REPORT

### A.  Tax Treatment of Discharge of Indebtedness

#### *Present Law*

*In General.*—Under present law, income is realized when indebtedness is forgiven or in other ways cancelled (sec. 61(a)(12) of the Internal Revenue Code). For example, if a corporation has issued a $1,000 bond at par which it later repurchases for only $900, thereby increasing its net worth by $100, the corporation realizes $100 of income in the year of repurchase (United States v. Kirby Lumber Co., 284 U.S. 1, 52 S.Ct. 4 (1931)).

There are several exceptions to the general rule of income realization. Under a judicially developed "insolvency exception," no income arises from discharge of indebtedness if the debtor is insolvent both before and after the transaction;[1] and if the transaction leaves the debtor with assets whose value exceeds remaining liabilities, income is realized only to the extent of the excess.[2]

\* \* \*

A debt cancellation which constitutes a gift or bequest is not treated as income to the donee debtor (Code sec. 102).[6]

\* \* \*

#### *Reasons for Change*

**Overview.**—\* \* \*. The committee's bill provides tax rules in the Internal Revenue Code applicable to debt discharge in the case of bankrupt or insolvent debtors, and makes related changes to existing Code provisions applicable to debt discharge in the case of solvent debtors outside bankruptcy.

\* \* \*

#### *Explanation of Provisions*

**Debt Discharge in Bankruptcy.**—*In General.*—Under the bill, no amount is to be included in income for Federal income tax purposes by reason of a discharge of indebtedness in a bankruptcy case.[11] Instead, the amount of discharged debt which is excluded

---

[1]  Treas.Reg. § 1.61–12(b)(1); Dallas Transfer & Terminal Warehouse Co. v. Commissioner, 70 F.2d 95 (5th Cir.1934).

[2]  Lakeland Grocery Co., 36 B.T.A. 289 (1937).

[6]  Debt discharge that is only a medium for some other form of payment, such as a gift or salary, is treated as that form of payment rather than under the debt discharge rules. Treas.Regs. § 1.61–12(a). [This continues to be so even after the 1980 changes. Ed.]

[11]  For purposes of these rules, the term "bankruptcy case" (referred to in the bill as a "title 11 case") means a case under new title 11 of the U.S. Code, but only if the taxpayer is under the

from gross income by virtue of the bill's provisions (the "debt discharge amount") is to be applied to reduce certain tax attributes.

[The bill then provides technical rules related to certain tax attributes requiring them to be reduced (in a set order) to "pay" for the exclusion of the *Kirby Lumber* income in a bankruptcy situation. See Section 108(b)(2)(A)–(F). In the alternative, a bankrupt taxpayer may elect to disregard the order of tax attributes reduced by the Code and *first* reduce the basis of certain depreciable assets. See Section 108(b)(5). When a taxpayer reduces the basis of depreciable property to pay for the exclusion (either by election under Section 105(b)(5) or by Section 108(b)(2)(E)), the basis of the property is reduced (see Section 1017) but not below the amount of the taxpayer's remaining undischarged liabilities. Section 1017(b)(2). In order to make these complicated rules comprehensible at this point in your introduction to income tax fundamentals, *assume* that Section 108(b)(2) simply provides for a reduction in the adjusted basis of the taxpayer's assets (to the extent of such basis) to pay for the amounts of excluded *Kirby Lumber* income. Ed.]

Any amount of debt discharge which is left after attribute reduction under these rules is disregarded, i.e., does not result in income or have other tax consequences.

\* \* \*

**Debt Discharge Outside Bankruptcy—Insolvent Debtors.**—The bill provides that if a discharge of indebtedness occurs when the taxpayer is insolvent (but is not in a bankruptcy case), the amount of debt discharge is excluded from gross income up to the amount by which the taxpayer is insolvent.[16] The excluded amount is applied to reduce tax attributes in the same manner as if the discharge had occurred in a bankruptcy case. Any balance of the debt discharged which is not excluded from gross income (because it exceeds the insolvency amount) is treated in the same manner as debt cancellation in the case of a wholly solvent taxpayer.

\* \* \*

**Certain Reductions as Purchase Price Adjustments.**—The bill provides that if the seller of specific property reduces the debt of the purchaser which arose out of the purchase, and the reduction to the purchaser does not occur in a bankruptcy case or when the purchaser is insolvent, then the reduction to the

---

jurisdiction of the court in the case and the discharge of indebtedness is granted by the court or is pursuant to a plan approved by the court. [See I.R.C. § 108(d)(2). Ed.]

[16]  The bill defines "insolvent" as the excess of liabilities over the fair market value of assets, determined with respect to the taxpayer's assets and liabilities immediately before the debt discharge. [See I.R.C. § 108(d)(3). Ed.] The bill provides that except pursuant to section 108(a)(1)(B) of the Code (as added by the bill), there is to be no insolvency exception from the general rule that gross income includes income from discharge of indebtedness.

purchaser of the purchase money is to be treated (for both the seller and the buyer) as a purchase price adjustment on that property. This rule applies only if but for this provision the amount of the reduction would be treated as income from discharge of indebtedness.

This provision [see Section 108(e)(5). Ed.] is intended to eliminate disagreements between the Internal Revenue Service and the debtor as to whether, in a particular case to which the provision applies, the debt reduction should be treated as discharge income or a true price adjustment. If the debt has been transferred by the seller to a third party (whether or not related to the seller), or if the property has been transferred by the buyer to a third party (whether or not related to the buyer), this provision does not apply to determine whether a reduction in the amount of purchase-money debt should be treated as discharge income or a true price adjustment. Also, this provision does not apply where the debt is reduced because of factors not involving direct agreements between the buyer and the seller, such as the running of the statute of limitations on enforcement of the obligation.

Congress has also enacted an array of other specialized exceptions to the *Kirby Lumber* rule. One of those exceptions[4] allows some solvent farmers[5] essentially to use the insolvency exception to the *Kirby Lumber* doctrine to exclude income from the relief from debts incurred in their farming businesses.[6] Attribute adjustments must be made under Section 108(b) to pay for the amount of the exclusion.[7]

Because of a decline in real estate values in the early 1990s, Congress added a further exception to the *Kirby Lumber* rule to exclude income generated by the discharge of "qualified real property business indebtedness."[8] The exclusion is elective[9] and it applies only after the bankruptcy, insolvency or qualified farm indebtedness exceptions apply.[10] The exception applies to the discharge of indebtedness secured by real property used in a trade or business.[11] The amount of exclusion is limited in several ways.[12] Once the exclusion amount is determined, the taxpayer must reduce the adjusted basis of taxpayer's depreciable real property by the amount excluded from gross income.[13]

---

[4]  I.R.C. § 108(a)(1)(C) and (g).

[5]  The taxpayer must be a "qualified person" as defined in I.R.C. § 49(a)(1)(D)(iv), and at least 50 percent of his average gross receipts for the prior three years must have been attributable to farming operations. I.R.C. § 108(g)(1)(B) and (2). See also I.R.C. § 1017(b)(4).

[6]  I.R.C. § 108(g)(2)(A).

[7]  I.R.C. § 108(b)(1).

[8]  I.R.C. § 108(a)(1)(D) and (c). For a definition of "qualified real property business indebtedness," see I.R.C. § 108(c)(3).

[9]  I.R.C. § 108(c)(3)(C).

[10]  I.R.C. § 108(c)(2)(B). The exception is inapplicable to C corporations. I.R.C. § 108(a)(1)(D).

[11]  I.R.C. § 108(c)(3)(A).

[12]  See I.R.C. § 108(c)(2) and (3).

[13]  I.R.C. § 108(c)(1)(A). See I.R.C. § 1017(b)(3)(A) and (F).

In a move to address the mortgage foreclosure crisis in the late 2000s, Congress created an exception to the *Kirby Lumber* rule to allow taxpayers to exclude up to $2 million of gross income[14] from the discharge of mortgage acquisition indebtedness[15] on the taxpayer's principal residence.[16] The provision applies if the taxpayer restructures the debt or loses the residence in a foreclosure.[17] The basis of the principal residence must be reduced by the excluded amount, but not below zero.[18] This exception is effective for indebtedness discharged through the year 2017.[19] However, in the past the provision has been extended.

Another *Kirby Lumber* exception appears in Section 108(f). It relates to the relief from obligations to repay student loans. It differs from the exceptions above, because it does not require the usual reduction of attribute adjustments. If pursuant to the terms of a student loan[20] a person, such as a doctor, nurse, lawyer, or teacher is relieved of the obligation to repay a student loan upon fulfillment of the person's agreement to work in a rural or low-income area, Section 108(f) applies.[21] In addition, it applies when a student loan is forgiven because of the death or total disability of the student.[22] Although the amount of the obligation discharged constitutes gross income under *Kirby Lumber,* Section 108(f) excludes it from gross income without any basis or other attribute adjustment. Subsidy is the word here, not mere postponement. This exception is illustrated in Revenue Ruling 2008–34.

## Revenue Ruling 2008–34

2008–28 I.R.B. 76.

### ISSUE

Do the terms of a loan made under the Loan Repayment Assistance Program (LRAP) described below satisfy the requirements of § 108(f)(1)

---

[14] The $2 million limit is reduced to $1 million for married taxpayers filing separately. I.R.C. § 108(h)(2). See I.R.C. § 163(h)(3)(B)(ii).

[15] Acquisition indebtedness is defined in I.R.C. § 163(h)(3)(B) as indebtedness incurred in the acquisition, construction, or substantial improvement of the taxpayer's residence that is secured by the residence. I.R.C. § 108(h)(2). See page 488, infra.

[16] I.R.C. § 108(a)(1)(E), (h). The term "principal residence" is determined in the same manner as under I.R.C. § 121. I.R.C. § 108(h)(5). See Reg. § 1.121–1(b) and page 217, infra. The $2 million exclusion does not apply if the discharge is on account of services performed for the lender or other factor not related to the decline in value of the residence or financial condition of the taxpayer. I.R.C. § 108(h)(3). The exclusion also does not apply to a taxpayer in a Title 11 bankruptcy case or to an insolvent taxpayer who elects not to apply this exception. I.R.C. § 108(a)(2)(A) and (C).

[17] H. Rep. No. 110–356, 110th Cong., 2d Sess. (2007).

[18] I.R.C. § 108(h)(1).

[19] I.R.C. § 108(a)(1)(E).

[20] I.R.C. § 108(f)(2). In order to qualify for the exclusion, the loan must have been made by one of the lenders described in I.R.C. § 108(f)(2)(A) through (D).

[21] The exclusion does not apply to the discharge of a loan made by a tax exempt educational institution if the discharge is made on account of services performed for such organization. I.R.C. § 108(f)(3).

[22] I.R.C. § 108(f)(5).

of the Internal Revenue Code, and is the LRAP loan a "student loan" within the meaning of § 108(f)(2)?

## FACTS

A, an individual, attended law school and has student loan debt. Neither the loans nor the underlying loan documents addressed whether any of the indebtedness would be forgiven if A worked in a particular profession for a specified period of time.

A's law school offers a Loan Repayment Assistance Program (LRAP) to help reduce the student loan debt of graduates who engage in public service. The LRAP is designed to encourage graduates to enter into public service in occupations or areas with unmet needs. Under the LRAP, the law school makes loans that refinance the graduates' original student loan(s). To qualify for an LRAP loan, a graduate must work in a law-related public service position for, or under the direction of, a tax-exempt charitable organization or a governmental unit, including a position in (1) a public interest or community service organization, (2) a legal aid office or clinic, (3) a prosecutor's office, (4) a public defender's office, or (5) a state, local, or federal government office. The amount of the LRAP loan is based on the graduate's outstanding student loan debt and annual income. After the graduate works for the required period in a qualifying position, the law school will forgive all or part of the graduate's LRAP loan.

After A graduates from law school, A signs an LRAP promissory note and accepts the terms and conditions of the law school's LRAP loan. The LRAP loan provides that the indebtedness will be forgiven if A works for a certain minimum period of time in a qualifying law-related public service position.

## LAW

Section 61(a) provides that gross income means all income from whatever source derived. Section 61(a)(12) provides that gross income includes income from the discharge of indebtedness.

Section 108(f)(1) provides that in the case of an individual, gross income does not include any amount which (but for § 108(f)) would be includible in gross income by reason of the discharge (in whole or in part) of any student loan if such discharge was pursuant to a provision of such loan under which all or part of the indebtedness of the individual would be discharged if the individual worked for a certain period of time in certain professions for any of a broad class of employers.

Section 108(f)(2) defines "student loan" for purposes of § 108(f) to include any loan to an individual to assist the individual in attending an educational organization described in § 170(b)(1)(A)(ii) made by (A) the United States, or an instrumentality or agency thereof, (B) a State, territory, or possession of the United States, or the District of Columbia, or any political subdivision thereof, or (C) certain tax-exempt public benefit corporations. The Taxpayer Relief Act of 1997 (1997 Act), Pub. L.

105–34, added § 108(f)(2)(D), which amended and expanded the definition of "student loan" to include loans made by the educational organizations themselves if the loans were made either:

(i)  pursuant to an agreement with any entity described in subparagraph (A), (B), or (C) under which the funds from which the loan was made were provided to such educational organization, or

(ii)  pursuant to a program of such educational organization which is designed to encourage its students to serve in occupations with unmet needs or in areas with unmet needs and under which the services provided by the students (or former students) are for or under the direction of a governmental unit or an organization described in section 501(c)(3) and exempt from tax under section 501(a).

The 1997 Act further amended § 108(f)(2) to provide that the term "student loan" includes any loan made by an educational organization described in section 170(b)(1)(A)(ii) or by an organization exempt from tax under section 501(a) "to refinance a loan to an individual to assist the individual in attending any such educational organization but only if the refinancing loan is pursuant to a program of the refinancing organization which is designed as described in subparagraph (D)(ii)."* The legislative history to the 1997 Act explains that, in the case of loans made or refinanced by educational organizations (and loans refinanced by certain tax-exempt organizations), the student's work must fulfill a "public service requirement." See H.R. Conf. Rep. No. 105–220, at 375–76 (1997).

## ANALYSIS

The terms of A's LRAP loan provide for loan forgiveness only if A works for a certain minimum period of time in a qualifying law-related public service position. This requirement is consistent with the requirement in § 108(f)(1) to work in certain professions for a certain period of time.

Additionally, the law school's LRAP is designed to encourage its students to engage in public service in occupations or areas with unmet needs. All of the positions listed in the LRAP are for, or under the direction of, a governmental unit or a tax-exempt charitable organization. Further, the LRAP loan was made to refinance A's original student loans. Therefore, the LRAP loan meets the definition of a "student loan" in § 108(f)(2).

---

*  A technical correction clarified that gross income does not include amounts from the forgiveness of loans made by educational organizations and certain tax-exempt organizations to refinance any existing student loan (and not just loans made by educational organizations). See Pub. L. 105–206, § 6004(f)(1), and H. R. Rep. No. 356, 105th Cong., 1st Sess. 10 (1997).

## HOLDING

The terms of the loan made under the LRAP satisfy the requirements of § 108(f)(1), and the LRAP loan is a "student loan" within the meaning of § 108(f)(2).

## PROBLEMS

1.   Poor borrowed $10,000 from Rich several years ago. What tax consequences to Poor if Poor pays off the so far undiminished debt with:

(a)   A settlement of $7,000 of cash?

(b)   A painting with a basis and fair market value of $8,000?

(c)   A painting with a value of $8,000 and a basis of $5,000?

(d)   Services, in the form of remodeling Rich's office, which are worth $10,000?

(e)   Services that are worth $8,000?

(f)   Same as (a), above, except that Poor's Employer makes the $7,000 payment to Rich, renouncing any claim to repayment by Poor.

2.   Mortgagor purchases a parcel of land held for investment from Seller for $100,000 with $20,000 of cash paid directly by Mortgagor and $80,000 paid from the proceeds of a recourse mortgage incurred from Bank. Mortgagor is personally liable for the loan and the land is security for the loan. When the land increases in value to $300,000, Mortgagor borrows another $100,000 from Bank again incurring personal liability and again with the land as security. Mortgagor uses the $100,000 of loan proceeds to purchase stocks and bonds. Several years later when the principal amount of the mortgages is still $180,000, the land declines in value to $170,000, Mortgagor transfers the land to the Bank, and the Bank discharges all of Mortgagor's indebtedness.

(a)   What are the tax consequences to Mortgagor? See Reg. §§ 1.1001–2(a) and 2(c) Example (8).

(b)   What are the tax consequences to Mortgagor if the liabilities had been nonrecourse liabilities. See problem 1(i) at page 154 of the Text.

3.   Businessperson borrows $100,000 from Creditor to start an ambulance service and then purchases ambulances for use in the business at a cost of $100,000. Assume the ambulances are Businessperson's only depreciable property and, unrealistically, that after some time their adjusted basis and value are still $100,000. What consequences in the following circumstances:

(a)   Businessperson is solvent but is having financial difficulties and Creditor compromises the debt for $60,000.

(b)   Same as (a), above, except that Creditor is also the ambulance dealer who sold the ambulances to Businessperson.

(c)   Assume that Businessperson declares bankruptcy and the $100,000 liability is discharged at the time that

Businessperson's adjusted basis in the ambulances (as a result of depreciation) is $75,000.

  (d) Assume that Businessperson is insolvent because Businessperson's liabilities of $100,000 exceed the $90,000 value of the ambulances (whose adjusted basis is $75,000). Creditor discharges $40,000 of the $100,000 liability without any payment.

4. Decedent owed Friend $5,000 and Nephew owed Decedent $10,000.

  (a) At Decedent's death Friend neglected to file a claim against Decedent's estate in the time allowed by state law and Friend's claim was barred by the statute of limitations. (Let's defer our concern for Nephew.) What result to Decedent's estate?

*D—no income neutral*

  (b) What result to the estate in (a), above, (with Decedent still in cold storage) if instead Friend simply permitted the statute to run stating that she felt sorry for Decedent's widow, the residuary beneficiary of his estate?

*D— No income?*

  (c) Now, what result to Nephew if Decedent's will provided that his estate not collect Nephew's debt to the estate?

*income*

*N → 10K → D → 5K → f*

# CHAPTER 9

# Damages and Related Receipts

## A. Introduction

An ongoing effort to enable students to determine what is and what is not gross income has indicated by this time that the identification of basic principles in tax law is much the same as in other fields of law. A tax *common law* rule may develop: Is there any element of gain in a receipt? If not, the receipt falls outside the income concept, as in the case of the payment of principal on a loan. There may be a controlling *statutory* rule: How sweet it is to receive a gift, bequest, devise, or inheritance, the essence of gain! And yet by statutory proscription, Section 102, property received by gift, bequest, devise, or inheritance is excluded from gross income.

Amounts received as damages or reimbursements for damages are governed *in part* by statute. Code Sections 104–106, considered in Part C of this chapter contain most of the tax rules on compensation for injuries and sickness.[1] But some other similar receipts are not accorded express congressional recognition and so their treatment must be worked out under more general tax principles. It is these general principles that, for example, add gloss to the phrase "income from whatever source derived" in Section 61, which are referred to as the common law of federal taxation.[2] Of course, federal taxation is not a common law subject and the statute is "the thing." But when a statutory term is general a body of case law soon grows around it which is not unlike the growth of the common law and so it is with the kinds of receipts that are the subject of discussion in this chapter.

A detailed study of the area covered by this chapter could well be justified. But by now an inescapable fact of life must be plain to the student: It is impossible in any course or even a series of courses to cover in detail *all* facets of federal taxation. Federal taxation is the life-size shadow of "life in all its fullness"; and who can ever know *all* about life, much less its tax shadow? These comments of course again explain why there are scattered notes throughout this book which are intended to be

---

[1] A number of other Code sections deal with the includibility as gross income of damages or settled recoveries of other types or with other special rules regarding such recoveries. Not discussed in this Note but considered elsewhere in the Text are: § 111, Recovery of tax benefit items; § 1341, Computation of tax where taxpayer recovers substantial amount held by another under a claim of right.

[2] See Ericksen, "The Common Law of Federal Taxation," 7 U. of Fla.L.Rev. 178 (1954); see also Frolik, "Personal Injury Compensation as a Tax Preference," 37 Maine L.Rev. 1 (1985).

read and to be informative without making the related statute the subject of detailed examination.

## B.  DAMAGES IN GENERAL

### Raytheon Production Corporation v. Commissioner*

United States Court of Appeals, First Circuit, 1944.
144 F.2d 110, cert. denied 323 U.S. 779, 65 S.Ct. 192 (1944).

[Taxpayer settled a lawsuit under the federal anti-trust laws against R.C.A. The issue was whether the settlement was required to be included in the taxpayer's gross income. Ed.]

■ MAHONEY, CIRCUIT JUDGE.

\* \* \*

Damages recovered in an antitrust action are not necessarily nontaxable as a return of capital. As in other types of tort damage suits, recoveries which represent a reimbursement for lost profits are income. . . . The reasoning is that since the profits would be taxable income, the proceeds of litigation which are their substitute are taxable in like manner.

Damages for violation of the anti-trust acts are treated as . . . income where they represent compensation for loss of profits. . . .

The test is not whether the action was one in tort or contract but rather the question to be asked is "In lieu of what were the damages awarded?" . . . Where the suit is not to recover lost profits but is for injury to good will, the recovery represents a return of capital and, with certain limitations to be set forth below, is not taxable. . . . "Care must certainly be taken in such cases to avoid taxing recoveries for injuries to good will or loss of capital." 1 Paul and Mertens Law of Federal Income Taxation § 6.48.

Upon examination of Raytheon's declaration in its anti-trust suit we find nothing to indicate that the suit was for the recovery of lost profits. The allegations were that the illegal conduct of R.C.A. "completely destroyed the profitable interstate and foreign commerce of the plaintiff and thereby, by the early part of 1928, the said tube business of the plaintiff and the property good will of the plaintiff therein had been totally destroyed at a time when it then had a present value in excess of three million dollars and thereby the plaintiff was then injured in its business and property in a sum in excess of three million dollars." This was not the sort of antitrust suit where the plaintiff's business still exists and where the injury was merely for loss of profits. The allegations and evidence as to the amount of profits were necessary in order to establish

---

\*    Footnotes omitted.

the value of the good will and business since that is derived by a capitalization of profits. A somewhat similar idea was expressed in Farmers' & Merchants' Bank v. Commissioner, . . . , 59 F.2d at page 913. "Profits were one of the chief indications of the worth of the business; but the usual earnings before the injury, as compared with those afterward, were only an evidential factor in determining actual loss and not an independent basis for recovery." Since the suit was to recover damages for the destruction of the business and good will, the recovery represents a return of capital. Nor does the fact that the suit ended in a compromise settlement change the nature of the recovery; "the determining factor is the nature of the basic claim from which the compromised amount was realized." . . .

But, to say that the recovery represents a return of capital in that it takes the place of the business good will is not to conclude that it may not contain a taxable benefit. Although the injured party may not be deriving a profit as a result of the damage suit itself, the conversion thereby of his property into cash is a realization of any gain made over the cost or other basis of the good will prior to the illegal interference. Thus A buys Blackacre for $5,000. It appreciates in value to $50,000. B tortiously destroys it by fire. A sues and recovers $50,000 tort damages from B. Although no gain was derived by A from the suit, his prior gain due to the appreciation in value of Blackacre is realized when it is turned into cash by the money damages.

Compensation for the loss of Raytheon's good will in excess of its cost is gross income. * * *.

\* \* \*

## NOTE

As a general proposition, taxability of a recovery of damages can be determined, in part, by identifying the nature of the injury.[1] As the First Circuit properly stated the issue in the *Raytheon Production Corporation* case above, "In lieu of what were the damages awarded?"[2]

If a taxpayer recovers damages for loss of profits incurred on account of an injury to the taxpayer's business, the damages as a substitute for lost profits are easily identified as gross income.[3] And as one learned in the *Glenshaw Glass* case, punitive or exemplary damages recovered in a recovery arising in a business context are taxable even if they are properly characterized as a windfall.[4] Of course this basic principle may be altered by statute. In instances such as a recovery for patent infringement, antitrust violations, breach of contract, or breach of a fiduciary duty, a compensating

---

[1]   United States v. Burke, 504 U.S. 229, 112 S.Ct. 1867 (1992).

[2]   Raytheon Production Corp. v. Commissioner, 144 F.2d 110, 113 (1st Cir.1944), cert. denied 323 U.S. 779, 65 S.Ct. 192 (1944).

[3]   Id.; H. Liebes & Co. v. Commissioner, 90 F.2d 932 (9th Cir.1937).

[4]   Commissioner v. Glenshaw Glass Co., 348 U.S. 426, 75 S.Ct. 473 (1955), rehearing denied, 349 U.S. 925, 75 S.Ct. 657 (1955).

deduction may nullify the inclusion in gross income.[5] Suppose a contract for the sale of property classifies damages for an anticipatory breach as liquidated damages rather than penalties. While arguably the transaction represents a mere recovery of capital with a concurrent basis reduction, the recoveries are nevertheless treated as income.[6] And properly so, as the seller is left in exactly the same position where the seller began, having given up no property or property interests. Generally, damages or other recoveries for the improper taking of or injury to physical property operate simply to reduce the loss deduction otherwise potentially available,[7] but they may become taxable income where the recovered amounts exceed the property's basis. Tax analysis requires allocation of the award in such circumstances.[8]

The above commentary highlights the need for one to look at a transaction's *substance*, rather than its form, in determining the appropriate tax treatment of a damage recovery.

## PROBLEM

1.   Plaintiff brought suit and unless otherwise indicated successfully recovered. Discuss the tax consequences in the following alternative situations:

(a)   Plaintiff's suit was based on a recovery of an $8,000 loan made to Debtor. Plaintiff recovered $8,500 cash, $8,000 for the loan plus $500 of interest.

(b)   What result to Debtor under the facts of (a), above, if instead Debtor transferred some land worth $8,500 with a basis of $2,000 to Plaintiff to satisfy the obligation? What is Plaintiff's basis in the land?

(c)   Plaintiff's suit was based on a breach of a business contract and Plaintiff recovered $8,000 for lost profits and also recovered $16,000 of punitive damages.

(d)   Plaintiff's suit was based on a claim of injury to the goodwill of Plaintiff's business arising from a breach of a business contract. Plaintiff had a $4,000 basis for the goodwill. The goodwill was worth $10,000 at the time of the breach of contract.

     (1)   What result to Plaintiff if the suit is settled for $10,000 in a situation where the goodwill was totally destroyed?

---

[5]  I.R.C. § 186.

[6]  Harold S. Smith v. Commissioner, 50 T.C. 273 (1968), affirmed per curiam 418 F.2d 573 (9th Cir.1969); Meyer Mittleman v. Commissioner, 56 T.C. 171 (1971).

[7]  See Chapter 14D2, infra. Cf. I.R.C. § 123, considered at page 831, infra.

[8]  Compare State Fish Corp. v. Commissioner, 48 T.C. 465 (1967) acq. 1968–2 C.B. 1 (amounts received for damages to goodwill escaped tax as not in excess of taxpayer's basis for goodwill) with Raytheon Production Corp. v. Commissioner, note 2, supra (recovery for the destruction of business and goodwill were fully taxable for failure to establish a basis for the business and the goodwill of the company).

(2)   What result if Plaintiff recovers $4,000 of cash because the goodwill was partially destroyed and worth only $6,000 after the breach of contract?

(3)   What result if Plaintiff recovers only $3,000 of cash because the goodwill was worth $7,000 after the breach of contract?

## C.   DAMAGES AND OTHER RECOVERIES FOR PERSONAL INJURIES

Internal Revenue Code: Sections 104(a); 105(a)–(c) and (e); 106(a).

Regulations: Sections 1.104–1(a), (c), (d); 1.105–1(a); 1.106–1.

---

Some benevolent provisions of the Internal Revenue Code rest simply on the compassionate thought that the taxpayer has suffered enough. Sections 104–106 are of this order. In broad outline they say that one who has incurred some types of personal injury should not additionally suffer injury to one's purse in the form of tax liability on the receipt of some financial recompense.

*Section 104(a)(2).* After years of controversy, Section 104(a)(2) was dramatically limited by legislation enacted in 1996. Prior to 1997, Section 104(a)(2) excluded "any amounts recovered for personal injuries or sickness," a phrase that generated substantial litigation. A series of lower court cases excluded recoveries for such *nonphysical* personal injuries as defamation,[1] First Amendment rights,[2] and sex and age discrimination[3] from gross income, even though the recoveries were based at least in part on lost business profits or underpaid wages that would have been included in income if received in due course. The Supreme Court finally stepped in and issued two opinions substantially restricting the apparently broad exclusion provided by Section 104(a)(2). In the first decision, the Court refused to exclude an award for backpay arising from a sex discrimination claim by limiting the Section 104(a)(2) exclusion to damages received on account of a claim that redresses a tort-like personal injury.[4] The Court subsequently further tightened the reins in a second case denying a plaintiff recovery in an age discrimination case by formulating a two-prong test which a taxpayer had to satisfy to qualify for the Section 104(a)(2) exclusion.[5] The Court repeated its requirement

---

[1]   See Roemer v. Commissioner, 716 F.2d 693 (9th Cir.1983); Threlkeld v. Commissioner, 848 F.2d 81 (6th Cir.1988).

[2]   Bent v. Commissioner, 835 F.2d 67 (3d Cir.1987).

[3]   See Byrne v. Commissioner, 883 F.2d 211 (3d Cir.1989) (sex discrimination); Rickel v. Commissioner, 900 F.2d 655 (3d Cir.1990) (age discrimination); Pistillo v. Commissioner, 912 F.2d 145 (6th Cir.1990) (age discrimination). Cf. Thompson v. Commissioner, 866 F.2d 709 (4th Cir.1989) (sex discrimination).

[4]   United States v. Burke, 504 U.S. 229, 112 S.Ct. 1867 (1992).

[5]   Commissioner v. Schleier, 515 U.S. 323, 115 S.Ct. 2159 (1995).

that the underlying action must be based upon tort or tort-type rights and it added that the damages must be incurred on account of personal injuries or sickness.

A second controversial issue under pre-1997 Section 104(a)(2) was whether the exclusion of "any" damages under the language of that provision included an exclusion for punitive damages. While punitive damages arising from a nonphysical personal injury suit were statutorily required to be included in gross income,[6] the issue whether punitive damages arising from physical personal injuries were excluded was unclear. The lower courts were divided,[7] until the Supreme Court sided with the Commissioner's no exclusion position in a decision rendered subsequent to the enactment of the 1996 legislation.[8]

Congress acted in 1996 amending Section 104(a)(2) to narrow its scope and to resolve much of the surrounding uncertainty.[9] The Section 104(a)(2) exclusion is now limited to damages incurred on account of personal *physical* injuries or *physical* sickness. Damages received for *nonphysical* personal injuries, such as defamation, First Amendment rights, and sex and age discrimination are no longer excludable. Recoveries for emotional distress depend on the nature of the underlying action. Damages recovered for emotional distress incurred on account of physical injury are excludable. However, emotional distress itself is not a physical injury, despite the manifestation of physical symptoms, and recoveries arising out of emotional distress are included in gross income except to the extent that damages are received for amounts paid for medical care which is attributable to the emotional distress.[10]

The Congressional action also resolved the controversy surrounding the inclusion of punitive damages under Section 104(a)(2). Punitive damages recovered even in a physical personal injury suit are now specifically included within gross income.[11] However, there is an exception (in tax law, it seems that there's always an exception!) for punitive damages awarded in a wrongful death action under state law in effect on September 12, 1995 if the punitive damages are the only wrongful death recovery.[12]

---

[6]   I.R.C. § 104(a)(2) last sentence prior to the 1996 legislation.

[7]   *Compare* Horton v. Commissioner, 33 F.3d 625 (6th Cir.1994) (punitive damages recovery for a physical personal injury claim excluded from gross income) *with* Commissioner v. Miller, 914 F.2d 586 (4th Cir.1990), Wesson v. United States, 48 F.3d 894 (5th Cir.1995), Hawkins v. United States, 30 F.3d 1077 (9th Cir.1994), cert. den. 515 U.S. 1141, 115 S.Ct. 2576 (1995), Reese v. United States, 24 F.3d 228 (Fed.Cir.1994), and Rev. Rul. 84–108, 1984–2 C.B. 32 (punitive damages included in gross income).

[8]   O'Gilvie v. United States, 519 U.S. 79, 117 S.Ct. 452 (1996).

[9]   See Burke and Friel, "Getting Physical: Excluding Personal Injury Awards Under the New Section 104(a)(2)," 58 Mont.L.Rev. 167 (1997).

[10]   I.R.C. § 104(a) flush language. See Rev. Rul. 96–65, 1996–2 C.B. 6. "Medical care" for purposes of this rule is defined in I.R.C. § 213(d)(1)(A) and (B).

[11]   I.R.C. § 104(a)(2) (first parenthetical).

[12]   I.R.C. § 104(c).

Section 104(a)(2) creates several knotty allocation issues when there is a settlement of a personal injury case. The most obvious are allocating a recovery (1) between excludable claims for physical personal injuries and claims for other injuries, and (2) between excludable claims for compensatory damages and claims for punitive damages. The Internal Revenue Service ordinarily will not issue a ruling or determination letter regarding whether an allocation of the amount of a settlement award (including a lump sum award) between back pay, compensatory damages, punitive damages, etc. is a proper allocation for federal tax purposes.[13] However, in a revenue ruling[14] the Service concluded that the taxpayer's complaint was the best evidence for determining a proper allocation of a settlement. In the ruling, the taxpayer requested 15x dollars for compensatory damages and 45x dollars of punitive damages. The taxpayer received 24x dollars in full settlement of all claims and the ruling concludes that the settlement should be characterized in proportion to the request in the complaint (25 percent for compensatory damages and 75 percent for punitive damages).

A number of the Tax Court decisions have explored the taxation of settlement payments under Section 104(a)(2).[15] According to the Tax Court, the critical question in determining the taxation of the settlement payments is, in lieu of what was the settlement amount paid. The Tax Court has stated that an express allocation in the settlement agreement generally will be followed for the tax purposes if the agreement is entered in an adversarial context at arm's length and in good faith. But an express allocation in the settlement is not necessarily determinative if other facts indicate that the payment was intended by the parties to be for a different purpose.[16] The determination of whether the parties are adversarial with regards to the allocation is a factual inquiry with the Tax Court closely examining many factors, including the various claims initially brought by the plaintiff and the strength of each of those claims, which party drafted the allocation language, and whether the allocation was tax motivated.[17] The normal course of negotiating a settlement agreement seems to work to the taxpayer's disadvantage in these cases. Typically, settlement negotiations revolve around one critical issue—the total amount that the defendant will pay the plaintiff. Once that central question is resolved, the parties turn their attention to the settlement agreement and, frequently, it is at this point when tax considerations become significant. Often the plaintiff and defendant have some common goals in the settlement. For example, typically neither party will favor

---

[13]  Rev. Proc. 2002–3, § 4.01(7), 2002–1 C.B. 117, 121.

[14]  Rev. Rul. 85–98, 1985–2 C.B. 51.

[15]  See Bagley v. Commissioner, 105 T.C. 396 (1995); Robinson v. Commissioner, 102 T.C. 116 (1994), affd. in part, revd. in part and remanded 70 F.3d 34 (5th Cir.1995); McKay v. Commissioner, 102 T.C. 465 (1994); Burditt v. Commissioner, 77 T.C.M. 37 (1997); Lefleur v. Commissioner, 74 T.C.M. 37 (1997).

[16]  Robinson v. Commissioner, supra note 15; Bagley v. Commissioner, note 15, supra.

[17]  See Burditt v. Commissioner, note 15, supra; Lefleur v. Commissioner, note 15, supra.

labeling part of the settlement as punitive damages, since punitive damages (even for physical personal injuries) are taxable to the plaintiff and the defendant generally will not want to admit fault in the settlement agreement.[18] The simple point is that the parties may be quite adversarial in negotiating the amount of the settlement, but not adversarial in drafting the terms of the settlement agreement. The Tax Court has recognized this reality when it has determined the tax consequences of settlement agreements.[19] Thus, the normal process of negotiating the settlement agreement and concern about tax issues in drafting it may undermine the respect given to the allocation in determining the tax consequences of the settlement.[20]

*Section 106(a).* While Section 104(a)(2) is related to recoveries of *damages* for personal injuries, several other Code sections are related to the tax aspects of *other recoveries* related to personal injuries. Section 106(a) excludes from an employee's gross income an employer's contributions to accident and health plans set up to pay compensation to employees for injuries or sickness. The exclusion under Section 106(a) relates, not to amounts paid to employees who are sick or injured, but to amounts paid by employers for insurance premiums or into funded plans to set up benefits for employees in case of future sickness or injury. The function of Section 106(a) is to equalize the tax status of (1) employees whose employers "self-insure," by undertaking to pay health or accident benefits to employees directly, and (2) employees whose employers cannot self-insure, but who accomplish the same results through the purchase of insurance or the funding of benefit plans. The latter amounts are excluded from the employee's gross income.[21]

*Section 104(a)(1).* In most states, statutes assure employees compensation for injuries and illnesses arising out of and in the course of their employment. These are the classic "worker's compensation acts" contemplated by Section 104(a)(1). Section 104(a)(1) is interpreted literally to exclude benefits paid to an employee's survivors under worker's compensation acts and similar statutes in the case of job-related death, not mere injury.[22] However, to be excluded under Section 104(a)(1) the amount in question must be paid for death or injury that is job-related, not merely under a statute entitled "worker's compensation law." Nonoccupational benefits, such as amounts paid for disability during

---

[18] The defendant's insurance coverage also typically will not cover punitive damages.

[19] See Burditt v. Commissioner, note 15, supra: Lefleur v. Commissioner, note 15, supra.

[20] Cf. McKay v. Commissioner, note 15, supra; (parties were adversarial; taxpayer never had freedom to structure settlement on his own); McShane v. Commissioner, 53 T.C.M. 409 (1987) (settlement agreement respected where the tax consequences were never considered).

[21] I.R.C. § 106(b) and (d) also exclude an employer's contribution to an Archer medical savings account trust or to a health savings account. See I.R.C. §§ 220, 223.

[22] Reg. § 1.104–1(b).

employment but not caused by injury or sickness related to the employment, are not covered by Section 104(a)(1).[23]

*Section 104(a)(3).* Section 104(a)(3) excludes from gross income amounts received under accident and health insurance policies (or through a self-insurance arrangement[24]) for personal injuries or sickness.[25] However, as a result of the second parenthetical clause of Section 104(a)(3), this rule is limited to the proceeds of policies paid for by the individual and should be compared with the treatment of certain employee health and accident benefits under Section 105, described below. Since Section 104(a)(3) applies to *all* amounts received from non-employer funded policies, it appears that the subsection holds out an opportunity for a tax-free profit in health and accident insurance. If such policies pay a stated number of dollars per day for hospitalized illness and will pay even if other policies in effect have already defrayed the charges, any excess receipts are excluded from gross income. Insurance companies in their never-ending goal of limiting recoveries rarely allow this to occur.

*Sections 104(a)(4) and 104(a)(5).* Section 104(a)(4) excludes disability pensions of members of the armed forces and certain other governmental units.[26] Section 104(a)(5) excludes disability income attributable to injuries incurred as a result of a terrorist or military activity.

*Section 105(a).* Section 105(a) addresses taxpayers who *as employees* receive some financial benefit arising out of their employer's concern for their health. Some comments above, explaining the limited scope of Section 104(a)(3) which generally excludes amounts received through accident and health plans, serve as an introduction to this provision. Its first thrust is generally to label *includible* gross income amounts that an employee receives through accident or health insurance. These amounts are expressly includible if (1) attributable to an employer's contributions to a plan which were not taxed to the employee under Section 106(a) or (2) simply paid directly by the employer. It will be recalled that these are the very amounts that failed to be excluded under Section 104(a)(3). Is all lost? No. The main messages of Section 105 are in subsections (b) and (c), which back off from the general rule of inclusion provided in subsection (a).

---

[23] See Rev. Rul. 85–104, 1985–2 C.B. 52; Rev. Rul. 83–77, 1983–1 C.B. 37. These amounts may however qualify fully or partially for exclusion under I.R.C. § 105, discussed below.

[24] The amounts received under a self-insurance arrangement must involve a risk-shifting plan and they must not constitute mere reimbursement arrangements. Conf. Rep. No. 104–736, 104 Cong. 2d Sess. 14 (1996). Cf. I.R.C. § 162(*l*).

[25] This has been held to include "no fault" insurance disability benefits received for loss of income or earning capacity. Rev. Rul. 73–155, 1973–1 C.B. 50.

[26] Subsection (b) of I.R.C. § 104 limits the application of § 104(a)(4). In general, it "grandfathers" in persons who were receiving benefits excluded under § 104(a)(4) in 1975 and continues its application to persons receiving compensation for combat-related injuries or who would, upon application, be entitled to disability compensation from the Veterans' Administration.

*Section 105(b).* If an employer directly or indirectly *reimburses* an employee for expenses of medical care[27] for the employee or the employee's spouse or dependents,[28] the amount received is excluded from gross income under Section 105(b). Note that here it is the amount of medical care actually paid for which measures the exclusion, in contrast to the possibility under Section 104(a)(3) that the amounts received under a health or accident policy, which measure the exclusions, may exceed the medical expenses incurred.[29]

*Section 105(c).* This subsection provides that, if an employee receives payments through health or accident insurance[30] provided by an employer without tax cost to the employee for loss of a member or function of the body or for disfigurement of the employee or the employee's spouse or dependent,[31] and if the amount is computed only with regard to the nature of the injury and not to the period the employee is absent from work,[32] the amount is excluded from gross income.[33] As a rule the employee will receive payment for casualties of this type under worker's compensation legislation and can exclude the receipts under Section 104(a)(1). When this is so Section 104(a)(1) preempts Section 105(c).[34] This seems to make little difference, however, because amounts that are of the type received under worker's compensation acts but are outside Section 104 because they exceed what is provided for *are* permitted to be excluded under Section 105(c).[35] However,

---

[27] The I.R.C. § 213(d) definition is expressly adopted.

[28] The I.R.C. § 152 definition of dependent is generally adopted, although for purposes of this section any child to whom § 152(e) (concerning children of divorced parents) applies is treated as a dependent.

[29] The term "reimburse" limits the I.R.C. § 105(b) exclusion. The interrelationship of § 105(b) and § 104(a)(3) can be complicated. Assume an individual has two accident and health insurance policies, the premiums of one being paid by the individual and the other by employer, and both compensate individual for the same illness. Under § 104(a)(3), all proceeds from the individual's own policy are excluded from income, but § 105(b) limits the exclusion for the employer-provided policy to amounts which "reimburse" the individual for medical care. Assume, for example, that an employee had $900 of medical expenses related to an illness and that employee received $800 from an employer funded policy and $400 from employee's own policy. Thus, the question arises as to what amount of the $800 received from the employer funded policy may be excluded. Revenue Ruling 69–154, 1969–1 C.B. 46, Situation 3, indicates that the amount of medical expense to be considered paid by each policy is proportionate to the benefits received from each policy. Under this approach, if the employee received $800 from the employer's policy and $400 from the employee's own policy (a total of $1,200), $800/$1,200 or two-thirds of the medical expense is deemed paid by the employer's policy. Therefore, two-thirds of the $900 of medical expenses, or $600, will be considered as paid for out of the proceeds of the employer policy. It follows that of the $800 received from the employer funded policy only $600 is excluded by § 105(b), because the exclusion under § 105(b) is limited to the amount of reimbursement for actual expenses. $200 of the $800 received is included in the employee's gross income. Of course, the full $400 received from the employee's policy is excluded under § 104(a)(3) which has no such limitation.

[30] Recall the broad definition in I.R.C. § 105(e).

[31] The I.R.C. § 152 definition of dependent is expressly adopted.

[32] See Rev. Rul. 74–603, 1974–2 C.B. 35.

[33] Receipts of this kind do not affect the amount of a taxpayer's medical expense deduction. See I.R.C. § 105(f).

[34] Reg. § 1.105–3 last sentence.

[35] Reg. § 1.104–1(b).

nonoccupational injuries and disfigurement and also injuries and disfigurement of an employee's spouse and dependents may produce financial compensation outside Section 104 which is excluded from gross income by Section 105(c).[36]

All exclusions under Section 104 and Section 105(b) are restricted by an "except" clause. It reads:

> Except in the case of amounts attributable to (and not in excess of) deductions allowed under Section 213 (relating to medical, etc., expenses) for any prior taxable year, * * *.

The general effect of this exception is to *include* in gross income any amount, otherwise excluded, which constitutes reimbursement of a medical expense that served as the basis of a Section 213 deduction in a prior year. The obvious objective is to dovetail the exclusionary rule with the medical expense deduction. Assume in year one $T$ incurred $500 of *deductible* medical expenses that were reimbursed in year two. If $T$ were allowed to claim the deduction in year one and exclude the reimbursement in year two, $T$ would have a *double* tax benefit, a $500 deduction with no out-of-pocket expense.[37]

If reimbursement is received in the same year the expense is incurred, the exclusion applies, as there has been no deduction with respect to that amount in any "prior taxable year." This fits well, however, with Section 213(a) which denies the deduction for expenses of medical care which are "compensated for by insurance or otherwise." That is, the medical expense deduction will not have been allowed for such reimbursed amounts.[38]

## Revenue Ruling 79–313
1979–2 Cum. Bull. 75.

### ISSUE

Are payments received by the taxpayer, under the circumstances described below, excludable from the gross income of the taxpayer under section 104(a)(2) of the Internal Revenue Code?

### FACTS

In 1977, the taxpayer sustained severe and permanent personal injuries as the result of being struck by an automobile. Thereafter, the taxpayer brought an action against $X$, the owner-operator of the

---

[36] Ibid.

[37] This disregards, as it seems we should, the 7½% floor under the medical expense deduction. I.R.C. § 213(a). See Chapter 18A, infra.

[38] The I.R.C. §§ 104 and 105 exceptions are statutory expressions of the tax benefit doctrine, partially codified more broadly in § 111. See Chapter 20B, infra. The related principles of §§ 104 and 105 and § 213 are rather well illustrated in the regulations. See, e.g., Reg. § 1.213–1(g)(1)–(3)(iii).

automobile. *X* carried automobile liability insurance with *M*, an insurance company.

In 1979, *M* proposed a settlement of taxpayer's suit against *X*, which the taxpayer accepted. Pursuant to the settlement agreement, *M* agreed to make fifty consecutive annual payments to the taxpayer, the first payment to be made one year after the date of settlement. These payments are for "personal injury, pain and suffering, disability, and loss of bodily function." The amount of each annual payment will be increased by five percent over the amount of the preceding annual payment.

The settlement also provides that the taxpayer does not have the right to accelerate any payment or increase or decrease the amount of the annual payments specified.

Under the agreement, *M* is not required to set aside specific assets to secure any part of its obligation to the taxpayer. The taxpayer's rights against *M* are no greater than those of *M's* general creditors. *M's* obligations to the taxpayer result solely from the settlement out of court of the legal action that the taxpayer instituted against *X* who was insured by *M*.

## LAW AND ANALYSIS

Section 104(a)(2) of the Code provides that except in the case of amounts attributable to (and not in excess of) deductions allowed under section 213 for any prior taxable year, gross income does not include the amount of any damages received (whether by suit or agreement) on account of personal injuries or sickness.

Section 1.104–1(c) of the Income Tax Regulations provides that the term "damages received (whether by suit or agreement)" means an amount received (other than workmen's compensation) through prosecution of a legal suit or action based upon tort or tort type rights, or through a settlement agreement entered into in lieu of such prosecution.

The annual payments to be received by the taxpayer are amounts received through a settlement agreement entered into in lieu of the prosecution of a legal suit based upon tort or tort rights within the meaning of section 1.104–1(c) of the regulations.

Rev. Rul. 65–29, 1965–1 C.B. 59, holds that, when the taxpayer actually received the present value of an award for personal injury in a lump sum and invested it, any interest earned on the amount invested was taxable. However, in the instant case, even though the settlement agreement provides for increasing payments to be made annually the taxpayer has neither actual nor constructive receipt, nor the economic benefit of the present value of the damages.

## HOLDING

All payments received by the taxpayer in this case, pursuant to the settlement agreement, are excludable from the gross income of the taxpayer under section 104(a)(2) of the Code.

## PROBLEMS

1.    Plaintiff brought suit and successfully recovered in the following situations. Discuss the tax consequences to Plaintiff.

   (a)   Plaintiff, a professional gymnast, lost the use of her leg after a psychotic fan assaulted her with a tire iron. Plaintiff was awarded damages of $100,000.

   (b)   $50,000 of the recovery in (a), above, is specifically allocated as compensation for scheduled performances Plaintiff failed to make as a result of the injured leg.

   (c)   The jury also awards Plaintiff $200,000 in punitive damages.

   (d)   The jury also awards Plaintiff damages of $200,000 to compensate for Plaintiff's suicidal tendencies resulting from the loss of the use of her leg.

   (e)   Plaintiff in a separate suit recovered $100,000 of damages from a fan who mercilessly taunted Plaintiff about her unnaturally high, squeaky voice, causing Plaintiff extreme anxiety and stress.

   (f)   Plaintiff recovered $200,000 in a suit of sexual harassment against her former coach.

   (g)   Plaintiff dies as a result of the leg injury, and Plaintiff's parents recover $1,000,000 of punitive damages awarded in a wrongful death action under long-standing State statute?

2.    Injured and Spouse were injured in an automobile accident. Their total medical expenses incurred were $2,500.

   (a)   In the year of the accident they properly deducted $1,500 of the expenses under § 213 on their joint income tax return and filed suit against Wrongdoer. In the succeeding year they settled their claim against Wrongdoer for $2,500. What income tax consequences on receipt of the $2,500 settlement?

   (b)   In the succeeding year Spouse was ill but, fortunately, they carried medical insurance and additionally Spouse had insurance benefits under a policy provided by Employer. Spouse's medical expenses totalled $4,000 and they received $3,000 of benefits under their policy and $2,000 of benefits under Employer's policy. To what extent are the benefits included in their gross income? (See footnote 29 on page 196, supra.)

   (c)   Under the facts of (b), above, may Injured and Spouse deduct the medical expenses? (See § 213(a).)

3.    Injured, who has a 20-year life expectancy, recovers $1 million in a personal injury suit arising out of a boating accident.

   (a)   What are the tax consequences to Injured if the $1 million is deposited in a money market account paying 5% interest?

(b)   What are the tax consequences to Injured if the $1 million is used by Injured to purchase an annuity to pay Injured $100,000 a year for Injured's life?

(c)   What are the tax consequences to Injured if the case was settled, and in the settlement, Injured received payments from Defendant of $100,000 a year for life?

(d)   What are the tax consequences to Injured if the case was settled, and in the settlement, Defendant purchased an annuity with the payments paid directly to Injured who had rights to the payments but no other rights in the annuity including no right to receive the fund paying the annuity?

# CHAPTER 10

# SEPARATION AND DIVORCE

## A. ALIMONY AND SEPARATE MAINTENANCE PAYMENTS

Internal Revenue Code: Sections 71(a), (b)(1); 215(a) and (b).

---

Prior to 1942 in the absence of explicit statutory provisions, alimony payments were looked upon as nondeductible personal expenses of the payor spouse,[1] like family expenses in an unbroken home. Similarly, alimony was not required to be included in a divorced payee spouse's gross income, because it was considered merely an interest in the payor's property to which the payee was equitably entitled.[2] When World War II required a substantial escalation of income tax rates, it became possible for alimony and income taxes to exceed the entire net income of divorced payors. Even in less extreme circumstances, nondeductible alimony payments were very burdensome. Consequently, it was not surprising that in the 1942 Revenue Act Congress effected a statutory reversal of previously established principles; alimony would be included within the payee's gross income and, to the extent so included, would be deductible by the payor.[3]

Until 2019, under Section 71, alimony or separate maintenance payments generally are included in the gross income of a payee spouse if the following series of statutory requirements are met:

(1) The payment is received by, or on behalf of, a spouse under a divorce or separation instrument;[4]

(2) The divorce or separation instrument does not designate the payment as a non-alimony payment;[5]

(3) In the case of a decree of legal separation or of divorce, the parties are not members of the same household at the time the payment is made;[6]

---

[1]  See I.R.C. § 262.

[2]  Gould v. Gould, 245 U.S. 151, 38 S.Ct. 53 (1917).

[3]  The constitutional validity of the 1942 provision was sustained in Mahana v. United States, 115 Ct.Cl. 716, 88 F.Supp. 285 (1950), which held that *Gould,* supra note 2, was not based on a decision that alimony was not income within the Sixteenth Amendment, but instead on a determination that the Income Tax Act of 1913 did not purport to tax it.

[4]  I.R.C. § 71(a)(1)(A). See I.R.C. § 71(b)(2) for the definition of a divorce or separation agreement. I.R.C. § 71 also applies a special timing rule when payments are "front loaded" into the first two years that payments are made. See I.R.C. § 71(f).

[5]  I.R.C. § 71(a)(1)(B).

[6]  I.R.C. § 71(a)(1)(C).

  (4) There is no liability to make any payment in cash or property, after the death of the payee spouse;[7] and

  (5) The payment is not for child support.[8]

Section 215 allows a payor spouse a deduction for alimony or separate maintenance payments to the extent the payments are includible in the gross income of the payee spouse under Section 71.[9]

The statutory requirements of Section 71 for classifying payments as alimony or separate maintenance payments offer a myriad of choices to separating or divorcing spouses. A favorable tax result can be obtained to the mutual satisfaction of each party by an awareness of the criteria and careful drafting of the divorce or separation agreement. If the payments qualify as alimony or separate maintenance payments, the statute permits allocation (income-deduction treatment) of the tax in accordance with the wishes of the parties; if not, there is no tax (neutral) splitting. It is as simple as that.

It came as something of a surprise when the 2017 Tax Cuts and Jobs Act reversed course and repealed Sections 71 and 215, generally effective after December 31, 2018, making alimony or separate maintenance payments a tax-neutral event.[10] Thus, in the case of payment made under divorce instruments executed before 2019, Sections 71 and 215 still apply. However, if an instrument executed before 2019 is modified after 2018, and the modification expressly provides that Sections 71 and 215 are inapplicable to the payments, those sections do not apply to the subsequent payments.[11]

The legislative history of the 2017 Act implies that Congress assumed that a payor spouse usually is subject to higher tax rates than the payee spouse, so that deductible alimony or separate maintenance payments were saving payor spouses more total tax that the government was collecting from payee spouses. Thus, the switch in course regarding the long-term tax treatment of alimony and separate maintenance payments was likely intended as a revenue-generating device. Query whether Congress will again reverse course and reinstate the pre-2019 Sections 71 and 215 rules? The Text does not burden you with all of the complexity of those rules (you're welcome!) but you are on notice that they may reappear.

## PROBLEM

**1.** Payor Spouse, who pays tax at a flat 30 percent rate, is required to pay Payee Spouse $100,000 per year as alimony or separate maintenance under

---

 [7] I.R.C. § 71(a)(1)(D).

 [8] I.R.C. § 71(c).

 [9] I.R.C. § 215(a), (b). The I.R.C. § 215 deduction is an "above-the-line" deduction allowed in arriving at adjusted gross income. I.R.C. § 62(a)(10). See Chapter 18C.

 [10] Pub. L. No. 115–97, 115th Cong., 1st Sess., § 11051(b)(1)(B) (2017).

 [11] Pub. L. No. 115–97, 115th Cong., 1st Sess., § 11051(c) (2017).

a pre-2019 divorce instrument. Assume Payee Spouse pays tax at a flat 15 percent rate. Payor Spouse wants to amend the divorce instrument to have the post-2018 law apply (i.e. Sections 71 and 215 would no longer apply to the payments). You represent Payee Spouse.

   (a) If Payor Spouse requests a reduction in the payments under the agreement to $70,000, what is your reaction? *[handwritten: is k too suut]*

   (b) What result in (a), above, both spouses pay a flat 30 percent rate? *[handwritten: fine]*

   (c) What result in (a), above, if Payor Spouse pays tax at a flat 30 percent rate and Payee Spouse, who inherited money, pays a flat 35 percent rate? *[handwritten: No!. Hurts me more]*

*[handwritten marginal notes: 100 ↓, 100 ↓, 65]*

# B. PROPERTY SETTLEMENTS

Internal Revenue Code: Section 1041. See Section 1015(e).

Regulations: Section 1.1041–1T(b).

-------

Before the enactment of Section 1041, the tax treatment of transfers of noncash property between spouses in the case of divorce was a complex area that largely depended on the spouses' property rights under state law. In United States v. Davis,[1] the Supreme Court held that a husband was taxable on the gain in his separate property, measured by the difference between the property's fair market value and its adjusted basis, when the property was transferred to his wife in satisfaction of her dower rights. Later the Service ruled that a spouse in Mrs. Davis' position, who received her spouse's property in exchange for relinquishing her marital rights, has no gain or loss and takes a fair market value basis in property that she received.[2] In contrast to the *Davis* result, a husband and wife who divided their community property in a divorce were deemed not to engage in a taxable event; they were viewed as simply retaining their preexisting property interests, even where each individual community asset was not divided equally.[3] Because a division of community property by divorcing spouses was nontaxable, the basis of the property carried over to the transferee; i.e. stayed with the property.[4]

The enactment of Section 1041 quiets this controversial area and rescues all noncommunity property taxpayers by reversing the holding in *Davis*.[5] We have previously seen that Section 1041 actually reaches

---

[1]   370 U.S. 65, 82 S.Ct. 1190 (1962), rehearing denied 371 U.S. 854, 83 S.Ct. 14 (1962).

[2]   Rev.Rul. 67–221, 1967–2 C.B. 63.

[3]   E.g., Jean C. Carrieres, 64 T.C. 959 (1975), acq. 1976–2 C.B. 1, affirmed per curiam 552 F.2d 1350 (9th Cir.1977); Rev.Rul. 76–83, 1976–1 C.B. 213.

[4]   Rev.Rul. 76–83, 1976–1 C.B. 213.

[5]   Pub.Law No. 98–369, § 421 98th Cong., 2d Sess. (1984). See Gabinet, "Section 1041: The High Price of Quick Fix Reform in Taxation of Interspousal Transfers," 5 Amer.J. of Tax Pol. 13 (1986); Lepow, "Tax Policy for Lovers and Cynics: How Divorce Settlement Became the Last Tax

beyond the *Davis* facts,[6] providing a clear nonrecognition rule for gains and losses with respect to *any* transfer of property between married persons[7] and also between formerly married persons.[8] In the latter instance, however, the nonrecognition rule applies only if the transfer is "incident to divorce."[9] Further, consistent with the nonrecognition result, the transferee spouse or former spouse takes the property with a transferred basis.[10]

The reasons for the change in the law and a brief explanation of Section 1041 are succinctly expressed in the House Report, as follows:[11]

### Reasons for Change

The committee believes that, in general, it is inappropriate to tax transfers between spouses. This policy is already reflected in the Code rule that exempts marital gifts from the gift tax, and reflects the fact that a husband and wife are a single economic unit.

The current rules governing transfers of property between spouses or former spouses incident to divorce have not worked well and have led to much controversy and litigation. Often the rules have proved a trap for the unwary as, for example, where the parties view property acquired during marriage (even though held in one spouse's name) as jointly owned, only to find that the equal division of the property upon divorce triggers recognition of gain.

Furthermore, in divorce cases, the government often gets whipsawed. The transferor will not report any gain on the transfer, while the recipient spouse, when he or she sells, is entitled under the *Davis* rule to compute his or her gain or loss by reference to a basis equal to the fair market value of the property at the time received.

The committee believes that to correct these problems, and make the tax laws as unintrusive as possible with respect to relations between spouses, the tax laws governing transfers between spouses and former spouses should be changed.

---

Shelter in America," 62 Notre Dame L.Rev. 32 (1986); Asimow, "The Assault on Tax-Free Divorce: Carryover Basis and the Assignment of Income," 44 Tax.L.Rev. 65 (1989); Nunnallee, "The Assignment of Income Doctrine as Applied to Section 1041 Divorce Transfers: How the Service Got it Wrong," 68 Ore.L.Rev. 615 (1989).

   [6]  See Chapter 6B3, supra.

   [7]  I.R.C. § 1041(a)(1).

   [8]  I.R.C. § 1041(a)(2).

   [9]  See I.R.C. § 1041(c). The term incident to divorce is considered in more detail in the Text at note 13, infra.

   [10]  I.R.C. § 1041(b). Cf. I.R.C. § 1015(a) and (e).

   [11]  H.Rep. No. 98–432, 98th Cong., 2d Sess., 1491 (1984).

*Explanation of Provision*

The bill provides that the transfer of property to a spouse incident to a divorce[12] will be treated, for income tax purposes, in the same manner as a gift. Gain (including recapture income) or loss will not be recognized to the transferor, and the transferee will receive the property at the transferor's basis (whether the property has appreciated or depreciated in value). A transfer will be treated as incident to a divorce if the transfer occurs within one year after the parties cease to be married or is related to the divorce. [A transfer of property is treated as related to the cessation of the marriage if the transfer is pursuant to a divorce or separation instrument, as defined in section 71(b)(2), and the transfer occurs not more than 6 years after the date on which the marriage ceases. A divorce or separation instrument includes a modification or amendment to such decree or instrument. Any transfer not pursuant to a divorce or separation instrument and any transfer occurring more than 6 years after the cessation of the marriage is presumed to be not related to the cessation of the marriage. The temporary regulations provide that this presumption may be rebutted only by showing that the transfer was made to effect the division of property owned by the former spouses at the time of the cessation of the marriage. For example, the presumption may be rebutted by showing that (a) the transfer was not made within the one- and six-year periods described above because of factors which hampered an earlier transfer of the property, such as legal or business impediments to transfer or disputes concerning the value of the property owned at the time of the cessation of the marriage, and (b) the transfer is effected promptly after the impediment to transfer is removed. Ed.][13] This nonrecognition rule applies whether the transfer is for the relinquishment of marital rights, for cash or other property, for the assumption of liabilities in excess of basis, or for other consideration and is intended to apply to any indebtedness which is discharged. Thus, uniform Federal income tax consequences will apply to these transfers notwithstanding that the property may be subject to differing state property laws.

In addition, this nonrecognition rule applies in the case of transfers of property between spouses during marriage.

Where an annuity is transferred, or a beneficial interest in a trust is transferred or created, incident to divorce or separation, the transferee will be entitled to the usual annuity treatment, including recovery of the transferor's investment in the contract (under sec. 72), or the usual treatment as the

---

[12]  For purposes of this provision, an annulment is treated as a divorce.

[13]  [Temp.Regs. 1.1041–1T(b) at A–7.]

beneficiary of a trust (by reason of sec. 682), notwithstanding that the annuity payments or payments by the trust qualify as alimony or otherwise discharge a support obligation.[14] The transfer of a life insurance contract to a spouse incident to a divorce or separation generally will no longer result in the proceeds of the policy later being includible in income, since the policy will have a carryover basis and therefore the transfer for value rules (sec. 101(a)(2)) will not apply. * * *.

The student is cautioned that the holding of *Davis* extends well beyond the context of a divorce property settlement situation. Although Section 1041 reverses the holding of *Davis* for a narrow situation including all interspousal transfers of property and transfers between nonspouses which are incident to divorce, the holding has continued vitality in all other situations involving the transfer of property in discharge of obligations. In these other circumstances whenever appreciated or loss property is transferred to satisfy an obligation, a gain subject to tax or possibly a deductible loss occurs.[15]

## Young v. Commissioner[*]
United States Court of Appeals, Fourth Circuit, 2001.
240 F.3d 369.

### OPINION

■ DIANA GRIBBON MOTZ, CIRCUIT JUDGE:

This case presents two tax questions arising from the settlement of a property dispute between former spouses. The first is whether a 1992 transfer of land from a husband to his former wife constitutes a transfer "incident to" their 1988 divorce for purposes of the nonrecognition of rules. * * * [The second issue is omitted. Ed.] We agree with the Tax Court's holding that both questions must be answered in the affirmative.

I.

Louise Young and John Young married in 1969 and divorced in 1988. The following year they entered into a Mutual Release and Acknowledgment of Settlement Agreement ("1989 Settlement Agreement") to resolve "their Equitable Distribution [of] Property claim and all other claims arising out of the marital relationship." Pursuant to this agreement, Mr. Young delivered to Mrs. Young a promissory note for $1.5 million, payable in five annual installments plus interest, which was secured by a deed of trust on 71 acres of property that Mr. Young received as part of the same 1989 Settlement Agreement.

---

[14]  This rule relates, in part, to amendments made to Code section 71 by section 423 of the bill.

[15]  See, e.g., International Freighting Corporation, Inc. v. Commissioner, 135 F.2d 310 (2d Cir.1943) at page 133, supra and Kenan v. Commissioner, 114 F.2d 217 (2d Cir.1940) at page 709, infra.

[*]  Some footnotes omitted.

In October 1990, Mr. Young defaulted on his obligations under the 1989 Settlement Agreement; the next month Mrs. Young brought a collection action in state court in North Carolina. On May 1, 1991, that court entered judgment for Mrs. Young, awarding her principal, interest, and reasonable attorneys' fees. Mr. Young paid only $160,000 toward satisfaction of that judgment, thus prompting Mrs. Young to initiate steps to execute the judgment. Before execution, however, Mr. and Mrs. Young entered into a Settlement Agreement and Release ("1992 Agreement"), which provided that Mr. Young would transfer to Mrs. Young, in full settlement of his obligations, a 59-acre tract of land (42.3 of the 71 acres that had collaterized his $1.5 million note and 16.7 acres adjoining that tract). Pursuant to the 1992 Agreement, Mr. Young retained an option to repurchase the land for $2.2 million before December 1992. Mr. Young assigned the option to a third party, who exercised the option and bought the land from Mrs. Young for $2.2 million.

On her 1992 and 1993 federal income tax returns, Mrs. Young reported no capital gain from the sale of the property nor the $300,606 portion of the $2.2 million that went directly to pay her attorneys' fees. At the same time, Mr. Young did not report any gain from his transfer of property, in which he had a $130,794 basis, to satisfy his then almost $2.2 million obligation to Mrs. Young. Thus, the appreciation of this property went untaxed despite the occurrence of a taxable event, i.e., the transfer or the sale.

The Commissioner asserted deficiencies against both Mr. Young and Mrs. Young. Each then petitioned the Tax Court, which consolidated the two cases. After trial, the Tax Court ruled that the capital gain was properly taxable to Mrs. Young under 26 U.S.C. section 1041(a)(2) (1994), which provides that "[n]o gain or loss shall be recognized on a transfer of property . . . to . . . a former spouse, . . . if the transfer is incident to the divorce." See Young v. Commissioner, 113 T.C. 152, 156 (1999). Because the Tax Court held that the 1992 property transfer was "incident to the divorce," it concluded that Mr. Young realized no gain through his transfer of this property to his former spouse. Id. Rather, according to the Tax Court, Mrs. Young took Mr. Young's adjusted basis in the land and should have recognized a taxable gain upon the subsequent sale of that property. In addition, the Tax Court held that the portion of the proceeds from the sale, which was paid directly to her attorneys, must be included in Mrs. Young's gross income. As a result of these holdings, the Tax Court ruled that Louise Young and her then husband, James Ausman, owed $206,323 in additional income tax in 1992, and Louise alone owed $262,657 in additional income tax in 1993.

Mrs. Young and James Ausman appeal both rulings. The Commissioner files a protective cross-appeal on the section 1041 issue, urging that if we do not agree with the Tax Court's conclusion that Mrs. Young (and Mr. Ausman) realized taxable capital gains, we also reverse its holding with respect to Mr. Young so that he is required to recognize the gain.

II.

We first consider the Tax Court's ruling involving section 1041, which provides that no taxable gain or loss results from a transfer of property to a former spouse if the transfer is "incident to the divorce." 26 U.S.C. section 1041(a)(2). Section 1041 further provides that "a transfer of property is incident to the divorce" if it is "related to the cessation of the marriage." 26 U.S.C. section 1041(c)(2). The statute does not further define the term "related to the cessation of the marriage," but temporary Treasury regulations provide some guidance. Those regulations extend a safe harbor to transfers made within six years of divorce if also "pursuant to a divorce or separation instrument, as defined in section 71(b)(2)." Temp. Treas. Reg. section 1.1041–1T(b) (2000). Section 71(b)(2) defines a "divorce or separation instrument" as a "decree of divorce or separate maintenance or a written instrument incident to such a decree." 26 U.S.C. section 71(b)(2) (1994). A property transfer not made pursuant to a divorce instrument "is presumed to be not related to the cessation of the marriage." Temp. Treas. Reg. section 1.1041–1T(b).

This presumption may be rebutted "by showing that the transfer was made to effect the division of property owned by the former spouses at the time of the cessation of the marriage." Id.

The Tax Court held that the 1992 transfer from Mr. Young to Mrs. Young was "related to the cessation of the marriage," thus neither party recognized a gain or loss on the transfer, and Mrs. Young took the same basis in the land that the couple had when they were married. Young, 113 T.C. at 156. The court applied the regulatory safe harbor provision, but also found that the transfer "completed the division of marital property" and, regardless of the safe harbor provision, it "satisfied the statutory requirement that the transfer be 'related to the marriage.' " Id. We agree with the Tax Court that the 1992 land transfer was "related to the cessation of the marriage," finding that it "effect[ed] the division of [marital] property." Temp. Treas. Reg. section 1.1041–1T(b).

\* \* \*

\* \* \* Mrs. Young challenges the Tax Court's finding and argues that the 1992 transfer did not "effect the division of [marital] property." In support of her contention, Mrs. Young notes that she was a judgment creditor when she entered into the 1992 Agreement. But the only status relevant for section 1041 purposes is "spouse" or "former spouse." Beyond her position as a former spouse, Mrs. Young's status makes no difference when determining whether the transfer is taxable; section 1041 looks to the character of and reason for the transfer, not to the status of the transferee as a creditor, lien-holder, devisee, trust beneficiary, or otherwise. Indeed, in Barnum v. Commissioner, 19 T.C. 401, 407–08 (1952), although the former wife had obtained a judgment against her husband for alimony arrearage, the Tax Court found the resulting settlement to be "incident to a divorce" because, like the 1992 Agreement in this case, it settled the "dispute over obligations arising from a divorce decree." Id.

Additionally, Mrs. Young's reliance on a private letter ruling issued to another taxpayer is misplaced. P.L.R. 9306015 (Feb. 12, 1993).[4] In that case, the divorce decree contemplated a sale of the former marital house, in which each spouse owned a one-half interest, to a third party. The IRS ruled that the husband's subsequent sale of his one-half interest in the house to his former wife instead of a third party was an "arm's-length transaction between two parties that *happen to be former spouses*," and thus did not "effect the division" of marital property pursuant to section 1041 and its regulations. Id. (emphasis added.) Because the husband in the private letter ruling had no obligation stemming from the divorce decree to sell his half interest in the home to his wife, the fact that the parties were former spouses truly had no bearing on the sale except as the means of their association. In contrast, Mr. Young transferred the 59 acres to satisfy an obligation that originated from the dissolution of the Youngs' marriage. Mr. Young's transfer of this land was not an independent decision "[un]related to the cessation of the marriage." And Mrs. Young did not just "happen" to be Mr. Young's "former spouse." Instead, the transaction occurred only BECAUSE she was his former spouse enforcing her rights growing out of the dissolution of their marriage.

Mrs. Young's argument based on state court jurisdiction is no more persuasive. She asserts that the 1992 Agreement could not have effectuated the division of marital property, because the judgment that precipitated the 1992 Agreement was rendered by a North Carolina Superior Court, and not a North Carolina District Court, which "is the proper division . . . for . . . the enforcement of separation or property settlement agreements between spouses, or recovery for the breach thereof." N.C. Gen. Stat. section 7A–244. Whatever the merits of this argument as to the jurisdiction of North Carolina courts, it cannot be the basis for a decision as to the federal tax consequences of a transfer of property. The Commissioner does not contend that the suit upon which the 1992 Agreement was based was for "recovery for the breach" of a property settlement agreement under North Carolina law, but only that the 1992 Agreement completed "the division" of marital property under section 1041 of the Internal Revenue Code.

Nor do we find Mrs. Young's "fairness" argument compelling. She points out that under the 1989 Settlement Agreement she was to receive $1.5 million plus interest, but if forced to pay the capital gains tax she will receive a lesser amount. For this reason, she argues that application

---

[4]   We note that Congress has mandated that a private letter ruling, which by its terms is directed only to the taxpayer who requested it, has no precedential value. See 26 U.S.C. section 6110(j)(3) (1994).

of section 1041 to the 59-acre transfer would "result in a radical and unfair re-division of the Young's [sic] marital property." Brief of Appellant at 29. But this argument overlooks the fact that Mrs. Young agreed to accept the 59 acres in lieu of enforcing her judgment against Mr. Young and receiving a cash payment. For whatever reason—and the record is silent as to Mrs. Young's motivations—she chose not to follow the latter route. In addition, if Mrs. Young had agreed to accept land in 1989, as she ultimately did in 1992, the resulting transfer would unquestionably have "effect[ed] the division of [marital] property" and been within section 1041. That the transfer occurred three years later does not alter its "effect," or its treatment under section 1041.

The sole reason for the 1992 Agreement was to resolve the disputes that arose from the Youngs' divorce and subsequent property settlement. Had the Youngs reached this settlement at the time of their divorce, there is no question that this transaction would have fallen under section 1041. There is no reason for the holding to differ here where the same result occurred through two transactions instead of one.

The policy animating section 1041 is clear. Congress has chosen to "treat a husband and wife [and former husband and wife acting incident to divorce] as one economic unit, and to defer, but not eliminate, the recognition of any gain or loss on interspousal property transfers *until the property is conveyed to a third party outside the economic unit.*" Blatt v. Commissioner, 102 T.C. 77, 80 (1994) (emphasis added). See also H.R. Rep. No. 98–432, at 1491 (1984), reprinted in 1984 U.S.C.C.A.N. 1134. Thus, no taxable event occurred and no gain was realized by either Mr. or Mrs. Young until Mrs. Young sold the 59 acres to a third party.

Indeed, holding otherwise would contradict the very purpose of section 1041. Congress enacted that statute to "correct the[ ] problems" caused by United States v. Davis, 370 U.S. 65 (1962), in which "[t]he Supreme Court ha[d] ruled that a transfer of appreciated property to a spouse (or former spouse) in exchange for the release of marital claims results in the recognition of gain to the transferor." H.R. Rep. No. 98–432, at 1491–92 (1984), reprinted in 1984 U.S.C.C.A.N. 113435. Congress found this result "inappropriate," id., and thus amended the tax code in 1984 to add section 1041. Given this history, to impute a gain to Mr. Young on his transfer of "appreciated property . . . in exchange for the release of [Mrs. Young's] marital claims" would abrogate clear congressional policy. Id.

The dissent's contention that the result we reach here is not supported by equitable considerations misses the point. Congress has already weighed the equities and established a policy that no gain or loss will be recognized on a transfer between former spouses incident to their divorce. Thus anytime former spouses transfer appreciated property incident to their divorce, the transferee spouse will bear the tax burden of the property's appreciated value after selling it and receiving the proceeds. Although this rule will undoubtedly work a hardship in some cases, the legislature has clearly set and codified this policy. We cannot disregard that choice to satisfy our own notions of equity.

In so concluding, we do not suggest that the boundaries defining when a transfer is "related to the cessation of the marriage" or made "to effect the division of [marital] property" are always clear. We cannot, however, on the facts of this case hold that Mr. Young's "interspousal property transfer" was a taxable event, when the purpose behind Mr. Young's transfer was to satisfy his obligations arising from the "cessation of the marriage." To do so would, we believe, contravene the language, purpose, and policy of 1041 and the regulations promulgated pursuant thereto.

* * *

IV.

Therefore, the Tax Court's judgment is in all respects

AFFIRMED.

■ [The dissenting opinion of CIRCUIT JUDGE WILKINS on the first issue is omitted. Ed.]

## PROBLEMS

1. Brad and Jen's divorce decree becomes final on January 1 of year one. Discuss the tax consequences of the following transactions to both Brad and Jen:

   (a) Pursuant to their divorce decree, Brad transfers to Jen in March of year one a parcel of unimproved land he purchased 10 years ago. The land has a basis of $100,000 and a fair market value of $500,000. Jen sells the land in April of year one for $600,000.

   (b) Same as (a), above, except that the land is transferred to satisfy a debt that Brad owes Jen. The land has a basis of $500,000 and a fair market value of $400,000 at the time of the transfer. Jen sells the land for $350,000.

   (c) What result if pursuant to the divorce decree, Brad transfers the land in (a), above, to Jen in March of year four.

   (d) Same as (c), above, except that the transfer is required by a written instrument incident to the divorce decree.

   (e) Same as (c), above, except the transfer is made in March of year seven.

2. Brad and Angelina divorce in 2019 and Brad makes the following alimony payments to Angelina pursuant to their divorce instrument. Consider the tax consequences of the payments.

   (a) Brad transfers $200,000 of cash to Angelina in 2019.

(b)   Brad is short of cash and to satisfy his obligation to pay $200,000 of cash, he transfers property worth $200,000 with an adjusted basis of $50,000 to Angelina in 2019.

(c)   Brad transfers the property in (b), above, to Angelina in 2029.

# CHAPTER 11

# OTHER EXCLUSIONS FROM GROSS INCOME

Several statutory exclusions from gross income not identified elsewhere in the book are of sufficient significance to warrant brief discussion. Of course, not all exclusions from gross income occur as a result of a specific statutory provision. Most benefits received under federal Social Security legislation are administratively excluded from gross income by way of lenient interpretation of less than specific statutory language.[1] However, Section 86 expressly requires *inclusion* of an increasing amount of such benefits.[2] Items may also be excluded from gross income by federal legislation not within the Internal Revenue Code. For example, payments of benefits under any law administered by the Veteran's Administration are excluded from gross income by Title 38 of the United States Code.[3] This chapter considers statutory exclusions under: Section 121, excluding some gain on the sale of a principal residence; Section 911, excluding some income earned abroad; under a series of provisions related to exclusions of income related to higher education expenses; and Section 103, excluding interest paid on some governmental obligations which also has constitutional overtones. The latter is taken up along with other constitutional concepts.

## A. GAIN FROM THE SALE OF A PRINCIPAL RESIDENCE

Internal Revenue Code: Section 121 (omit (d)(4) and (5), (e)).

Regulations: Section 1.121–1(a), (b)(1), (2) and (4) Example 1, (c)(1), (d), –2(a)(1)–(4) Example 2, –3(b), (c)(1)–(4) Example 1, (d)(1)–(3) Example 1, (e)(1) and (2), (f), (g)(1)–(2) Example 1.

---

[1] Old age and survivors insurance benefit payments are excluded by Rev.Rul. 70–217, 1970–1 C.B. 12, and Medicare benefits by Rev.Rul. 70–341, 1970–2 C.B. 31. See Reg. § 1.61–11(b). This includes educational assistance allowances. See Rev.Rul. 71–536, 1971–2 C.B. 78. Compare Rev.Rul. 76–121, 1976–1 C.B. 24, holding social security benefits paid by the United Kingdom to a resident of the United States includible in gross income and Rev.Rul. 66–34, 1966–1 C.B. 22, involving a similar payment by Germany to a United States resident.

[2] See Chapter 18C, infra.

[3] 38 U.S.C.A. § 3101(a). Cf. Strickland v. Commissioner, 540 F.2d 1196 (4th Cir.1976).

# Senate Report No. 105–33 and Conference Report No. 105–220

105th Cong., 1st Sess. 35–37, 387 (1997).

*[Senate Report]*

## Present Law

### Rollover of gain

No gain is recognized on the sale of a principal residence if a new residence at least equal in cost to the sales price of the old residence is purchased and used by the taxpayer as his or her principal residence within a specified period of time (sec. 1034). This replacement period generally begins two years before and ends two years after the date of sale of the old residence. The basis of the replacement residence is reduced by the amount of any gain not recognized on the sale of the old residence by reason of this gain rollover rule.

### One-time exclusion

In general, an individual, on a one-time basis, may exclude from gross income up to $125,000 of gain from the sale or exchange of a principal residence if the taxpayer (1) has attained age 55 before the sale, and (2) has owned the property and used it as a principal residence for three or more of the five years preceding the sale (sec. 121).

## Reasons for Change

Calculating capital gain from the sale of a principal residence is among the most complex tasks faced by a typical taxpayer. Many taxpayers buy and sell a number of homes over the course of a lifetime, and are generally not certain of how much housing appreciation they can expect. Thus, even though most homeowners never pay any income tax on the capital gain on their principal residences, as a result of the rollover provisions and the $125,000 one-time exclusion, detailed records of transactions and expenditures on home improvements must be kept, in most cases, for many decades. To claim the exclusion, many taxpayers must determine the basis of each home they have owned, and appropriately adjust the basis of their current home to reflect any untaxed gains from previous housing transactions. This determination may involve augmenting the original cost basis of each home by expenditures on improvements. In addition to the record-keeping burden this creates, taxpayers face the difficult task of drawing a distinction between improvements that add to basis, and repairs that do not. The failure to account accurately for all improvements leads to errors in the calculation of capital gains, and hence to an under- or over-payment of the capital gains on principal residences. By excluding from taxation capital gains on principal residences below a relatively high threshold, few taxpayers would have to refer to records in determining income tax consequences of transactions related to their house.

To postpone the entire capital gain from the sale of a principal residence, the purchase price of a new home must be greater than the sales price of the old home. This provision of present law encourages some taxpayers to purchase larger and more expensive houses than they otherwise would in order to avoid a tax liability, particularly those who move from areas where housing costs are high to lower-cost areas. This promotes an inefficient use of taxpayer's financial resources.

Present law also may discourage some older taxpayers from selling their homes. Taxpayers who would realize a capital gain in excess of $125,000 if they sold their home and taxpayers who have already used the exclusion may choose to stay in their homes even though the home no longer suits their needs. By raising the $125,000 limit and by allowing multiple exclusions, this constraint to the mobility of the elderly would be removed.

While most homeowners do not pay capital gains tax when selling their homes, current law creates certain tax traps for the unwary that can result in significant capital gains taxes or loss of the benefits of the current exclusion. For example, an individual is not eligible for the one-time capital gains exclusion if the exclusion was previously utilized by the individual's spouse. This restriction has the unintended effect of penalizing individuals who marry someone who has already taken the exclusion. Households that move from a high housing-cost area to a low housing-cost area may incur an unexpected capital gains tax liability. Divorcing couples may incur substantial capital gains taxes if they do not carefully plan their house ownership and sale decisions.

## Explanation of Provision

Under the bill a taxpayer generally is able to exclude up to $250,000 ($500,000 if married filing a joint return) of gain realized on the sale or exchange of a principal residence. The exclusion is allowed each time a taxpayer selling or exchanging a principal residence meets the eligibility requirements, but generally no more frequently than once every two years. The bill provides that gain would be recognized to the extent of any depreciation allowable with respect to the rental or business use of such principal residence for periods after May 6, 1997.

To be eligible for the exclusion, a taxpayer must have owned the residence and occupied it as a principal residence for at least two of the five years prior to the sale or exchange. A taxpayer who fails to meet these requirements by reason of a change of place of employment, health, or unforeseen circumstances is able to exclude the fraction of the $250,000 ($500,000 if married filing a joint return) equal to the fraction of two years that these requirements are met.

In the case of joint filers not sharing a principal residence, an exclusion of $250,000 is available on a qualifying sale or exchange of the principal residence of one of the spouses. Similarly, if a single taxpayer who is otherwise eligible for an exclusion marries someone who has used the exclusion within the two years prior to the marriage, the bill would allow the newly married taxpayer a maximum exclusion of $250,000. Once both spouses satisfy the eligibility rules and two years have passed since the last exclusion was allowed to either of them, the taxpayers may exclude $500,000 of gain on their joint return.

Under the bill, the gain from the sale or exchange of the remainder interest in the taxpayer's principal residence may qualify for the otherwise allowable exclusion.

## Effective Date

The provision is available for all sales or exchanges of a principal residence occurring on or after May 7, 1997, and replaces the present-law rollover and one-time exclusion provisions applicable to principal residences.

\* \* \*

If a taxpayer acquired his or her current residence in a rollover transaction, periods of ownership and use of the prior residence would be taken into account in determining ownership and use of the current residence.

*[Conference Report]*

## Conference Agreement

The conference agreement generally follows the House bill and the Senate amendment.

The conferees wish to clarify that the provision limiting the exclusion to only one sale every two years by the taxpayer does not prevent a husband and wife filing a joint return from each excluding up to $250,000 of gain from the sale or exchange of each spouse's principal residence provided that each spouse would be permitted to exclude up to $250,000 of gain if they filed separate returns.

## NOTE

As the legislative history indicates, the current exclusion under Section 121 replaces the old Section 121 "once in a lifetime" $125,000 exclusion provision and the old Section 1034 nonrecognition provision[1] for the "rollover" of principal residences without recognition of gain. As a practical matter, most taxpayers who satisfy the ownership and use requirements will be able to simply avoid the inclusion of *any* gain in gross income on their sale of a principal residence and this is what Congress had in mind. Furthermore the exclusion applies to the subsequent sales of principal residences so long as the ownership and use requirements are met.[2] However, some taxpayers will not be so fortunate as to exclude all of their gain, especially some who

---

[1]  For an example of a nonrecognition provision, see I.R.C. § 1041 considered in Chapters 6B3 and 10B. See also Chapter 26, infra.

[2]  I.R.C. § 121(a). For a detailed discussion of I.R.C. § 121, see McMahon, "Taxation of Sales of Principal Residences After the Taxpayer Relief Act of 1997," 75 Taxes 610 (1997).

previously used Section 1034 on prior residences and have gains in excess of the exclusion, some who depreciated their principal residences,[3] and some who live in areas where there is substantial appreciation in the housing market beyond the exclusion amount.

The term residence is defined broadly to include not only a house, but a house trailer, a house boat, stock in a cooperative housing unit,[4] and any other dwelling place.[5] Quantitatively, a residence can include surrounding vast acreage, so long as it is not used for business or profit.[6] The statute expressly requires that the residence qualify as the taxpayer's *principal* residence. Thus, if a taxpayer resides in a New York City apartment during the week, using a country house only on weekends, the sale of the country house will not meet the test of the statute. This is so because the apartment is considered the principal residence.[7] In other circumstances, if the residence otherwise qualifies as the principal residence and the two out of five-year ownership and use requirements are met,[8] the statute sanctions temporary rental of the dwelling.[9]

If a taxpayer sells principal residences too frequently, not all the residential sales qualify for an exclusion. In general, if a taxpayer sells a principal residence at a gain to which Section 121(a) applies, a subsequent sale of a principal residence within a two-year period does not qualify for a Section 121 exclusion.[10] However, a taxpayer may elect to have Section 121 not apply to a sale[11] and if such an election has been made with respect to the prior sale, Section 121 may be used on the subsequent sale. Generally, the multiple-sale rule will not apply and is unnecessary because the two-year ownership and use requirements would not be satisfied in such circumstances.[12] However, if the two-year ownership and use tests or the multiple-sales-within-two-years rule are not met because the subsequent sale is job related, health related, or due to other "unforeseen circumstances"

---

[3]   See I.R.C. § 121(d)(6), Chapters 14E and 15B, infra.

[4]   See I.R.C. § 121(d)(4).

[5]   Reg. § 1.121–1(b)(1).

[6]   See e.g., Clayburn M. Bennett v. United States, 61–2 U.S.T.C. ¶ 9697 (1961); Lokan v. Commissioner, 39 T.C.M. 168 (1979). See also Reg. § 1.121–1(b)(3), –1(b)(4) Examples 3 and 4.

[7]   William C. Stolk, 40 T.C. 345 (1963), affirmed per curiam 326 F.2d 760 (2d Cir.1964); Reg. § 1.121–1(b)(2), –1(b)(4) Examples 1 and 2.

[8]   I.R.C. § 121(a)(1). See Chapter 15B, infra. The two year period does not require two consecutive years. Reg. § 1.121–1(c)(1).

[9]   See I.R.C. § 121(d)(6), Reg. § 1.121–1(c)(4) Example 1. But see also I.R.C. § 121(b)(5) discussed in the Text at notes 17–21, infra.

[10]   I.R.C. § 121(b)(3).

[11]   I.R.C. § 121(f). This election would rarely be made. However, it would be useful if, say, single taxpayer lived in a residence for several years, then married and the spouses lived in a principal residence where they met the two-year requirements. If taxpayer sold the first residence (at a small gain) and they then sold the second residence (at a large gain) within a two-year period, the taxpayer would want to make an I.R.C. § 121(f) election on the sale of the first residence so that the large gain in the second residence would qualify for the exclusion.

[12]   But see I.R.C. § 121(g) allowing a tacking of ownership and use from a § 1034 sale and reinvestment. Note, as well, that I.R.C. § 121(b)(3) applies to the time frame between the sales of the principal residences. Cf. Text at notes 8 and 9, supra.

as provided in regulations,[13] there is an exception and a portion of the normal $250,000 or $500,000 exclusion amount applies.[14] The portion is the ratio of the *shorter* of the actual ownership and use during the prior five years or the time between the prior and current sale *to* two years.[15] A special rule also applies if a taxpayer satisfies the ownership and use requirements for one year in the five-year period prior to sale and then becomes physically or mentally incapable of self-care and moves to a care facility. Under the rule, the taxpayer is treated as using the principal residence during the time actually spent in the facility.[16]

Another Section 121 rule prevents a taxpayer from excluding gain allocated to periods of "nonqualified use."[17] The portion of gain attributable to periods of nonqualified use is equal to the amount of gain multiplied by a ratio which is the aggregate periods of nonqualified use divided by the period the property was owned by the taxpayer.[18] A residence is held for a nonqualified use during any period after 2008 when it is not being used as a principal residence of the taxpayer, the taxpayer's spouse, or a former spouse.[19] Thus, the rule reduces the benefits of Section 121 for periods after 2008 when the property might be held as a rental property or otherwise is not used as a principal residence (e.g., a vacation home.) Periods of nonqualified use do not include (1) any period that is part of Section 121's five-year testing period after the last date the property is used as a principal residence, and (2) any period (up to two years) where the taxpayer is absent due to change of employment, health condition, or unforeseen circumstances (as defined by the IRS).[20] A special rule also applies to taxpayers who are members of the uniformed services, foreign service or intelligence community.[21]

Finally, the statute also contains a variety of rules that apply to (1) deceased[22] and divorced spouses[23] attributing ownership and use from one to the other in a variety of circumstances and (2) certain military personnel and government workers.[24]

## PROBLEMS

1.    Determine the amount of gain that Taxpayers (a married couple filing a joint return) must include in gross income in the following situations:

---

[13]  I.R.C. § 121(c)(2). See Reg. § 1.121–3, especially Reg. § 1.121–3(e) discussing unforeseen circumstances.

[14]  I.R.C. § 121(c)(1).

[15]  Id. See Reg. § 1.121–3(g)(1), 3(g)(2) Examples.

[16]  I.R.C. § 121(d)(7).

[17]  I.R.C. § 121(b)(5).

[18]  I.R.C. § 121(b)(5)(B).

[19]  I.R.C. § 121(b)(5)(C)(i).

[20]  I.R.C. § 121(b)(5)(C)(ii)(I) & (III).

[21]  I.R.C. § 121(b)(5)(C)(ii)(II), (d)(9).

[22]  I.R.C. § 121(d)(2).

[23]  I.R.C. § 121(d)(3).

[24]  I.R.C. § 121(d)(9).

(a)    Taxpayers sold their principal residence for $600,000. They had purchased the residence several years ago for $200,000 and lived in it over those years.

(b)    Taxpayers in (a), above, purchased another principal residence for $600,000 and sold it 2½ years later for $1 million.

(c)    What result in (b), above, if the second sale occurred 1½ years later?

(d)    What result in (b), above, if Taxpayers had sold their first residence and were granted nonrecognition under former Section 1034 (the rollover provision) and, as a result, their basis in the second residence was $200,000?

(e)    What result in (a), above, if the residence was Taxpayers' summer home which they used 3 months of the year?

(f)    What result if Taxpayer who met the ownership and use requirements is a single taxpayer who sold a principal residence for $400,000 and it had an adjusted basis of $190,000 after Taxpayer validly took $10,000 of post-1997 depreciation deductions on the residence which served as an office in Taxpayer's home?

**2.**    Single Taxpayer purchased a principal residence for $500,000 and after using it for one year, Single sold the residence for $600,000 because Single's employer transferred Single to a new job location.

(a)    How much gain must Single include in gross income?

(b)    What result in (a), above, if Single sold the residence for $700,000?

**3.**    Single Taxpayer buys a mountain cabin on January 1, 2013 for $200,000 which Single used as a vacation home through December 31, 2015. In 2015, Single sells her principal residence at a gain which is excluded under § 121. On January 1, 2016, Single moves into the mountain cabin and uses it as her principal residence.

(a)    If Single sells the mountain cabin for $350,000 on January 1, 2018, how much of the gain is included in her gross income?

(b)    What result in (a), above, if Single sells the mountain cabin for $900,000?

(c)    What result in (a), above, if Single purchased the mountain cabin and began using it as a vacation home on January 1, 2004?

(d)    Do the nonqualified use rules apply to Single if Single purchases and uses a principal residence for two years, then rents it out for two years prior to selling it?

**4.**    Taxpayer has owned and lived in Taxpayer's principal residence for 10 years, the last year with Taxpayer's Spouse after they married. Spouses decide to sell the residence which has a $100,000 basis for $500,000.

    (a)   If the Spouses file a joint return do they have any gross income?

    (b)   What result if the Spouses had lived together for two years in Taxpayer's residence prior to their marriage and sold the residence after one year of marriage for $500,000?

    (c)   What result in (a), above, if after one year of marriage Taxpayer pursuant to their divorce decree deeded one-half of the residence to Spouse and Spouse lived in the residence while Taxpayer moved out and, one year later, they sold the residence for $500,000?

    (d)   What result in (a), above, if after one year of marriage Taxpayer pursuant to their divorce decree deeded one-half of the residence to Spouse and Taxpayer continued to occupy the residence while Spouse moved out, and, one year later, they sold the residence for $500,000?

## B. INCOME EARNED ABROAD

Internal Revenue Code: See Section 911.

---

Income earned abroad is allowed special income tax treatment. This area is especially typical of the current congressional practice of continually changing the rules, which requires tax attorneys constantly to analyze and apply new statutes. Although the United States taxes both its citizens and mere residents on their worldwide income, historically there has been a limited exclusion from gross income for income earned abroad. Obviously, this is in anticipation of a tax on the income at its source as well.

The current exclusion from gross income under Section 911[1] may be substantial. To qualify for the exclusion an American citizen must be a bona fide resident of a foreign country or countries for an uninterrupted period that includes an entire taxable year, or an American citizen or resident must be present in a foreign country or countries for at least 330 days during any period of twelve consecutive months.[2] The exclusion applies only to foreign earned income which is defined as income from a foreign source which is attributable to the taxpayer's performance of services.[3] The maximum exclusion is $80,000, and it is indexed for inflation beginning in 2006.[4]

---

[1]   Pub.Law No. 97–314, §§ 111, 112, 97th Cong., 1st Sess. (1981).

[2]   I.R.C. § 911(d)(1).

[3]   I.R.C. § 911(b)(1)(A). Foreign earned income does not include amounts received as a pension or annuity, amounts paid by the United States or its agencies to their employees, amounts received from certain trusts, or amounts received after the close of the taxable year in which the services to which the amounts are attributable are performed. I.R.C. § 911(b)(1)(B).

[4]   I.R.C. § 911(b)(2)(D). Specific dollar limitations on the exclusion have varied over time. They were provided to prevent abuses by highly paid persons (particularly entertainers and

Section 911 also provides an exclusion for amounts paid as reimbursement of foreign "housing expenses" in excess of a statutorily provided base housing amount,[5] if the housing expenses are paid for by the taxpayer's employer. Qualified taxpayers whose housing costs are not paid for by employers may elect to deduct a limited amount of housing costs in computing adjusted gross income.[6] Housing expenses include reasonable amounts paid for housing[7] (including utility bills and insurance) in a foreign country for the taxpayer and family members if they live together.[8]

Both the earned income and foreign housing cost exclusions are elective.[9] Elections for each are made separately[10] and, once made, remain in effect in future years unless revoked.[11] The exclusions are denied to a taxpayer for earned income and housing expenses in a foreign country in which travel by United States citizens and residents is restricted.[12]

## C. EXCLUSIONS AND OTHER TAX BENEFITS RELATED TO THE COSTS OF HIGHER EDUCATION

Internal Revenue Code: Sections 25A; 135; 529; 530. See Sections 72(e)(2)(B), (8)(B), (9); 108(f); 117; 127; 132(c)(3); 221; 222.

---

Until the late 1980s, Congress seemed relatively oblivious to the cost to taxpayers of higher education, providing few direct tax benefits for persons incurring such costs. In the late 1990s, Congress finally became aware of the burden that such costs impose on taxpayers, especially those in the lower and middle income ranges. As a result, there are a variety of tax benefits which Congress continues to expand that are available to such taxpayers. Because the benefits take several different forms, they are considered at several different places in the text, although most of

---

athletes) who might otherwise be tempted to move abroad to escape U.S. income tax. See Sen.Rep. No. 97–144, 97th Cong., 1st Sess. 36 (1981).

[5] The base housing amount equals 16% of the I.R.C. § 911(b)(2)(D) amount (see note 4, supra) times the applicable period during the year. I.R.C. § 911(c)(1)(B).

[6] I.R.C. § 911(c)(4).

[7] Housing expenses do not include amounts paid as interest or taxes which are independently deductible. I.R.C. § 911(c)(3)(A)(ii). See I.R.C. §§ 163, 164. The housing exclusion amount is further limited to 30% of the I.R.C. § 911(c)(1)(B) amount. I.R.C. § 911(c)(2).

[8] I.R.C. § 911(c)(3)(A). If dangerous or other adverse conditions require the taxpayer to maintain a separate residence for his family overseas, the excess housing costs of both households are eligible for the exclusion. See also I.R.C. § 119(c) which provides an exclusion from gross income for employer-provided meals and lodging in remote "camps" in foreign countries.

[9] I.R.C. § 911(a).

[10] Id.

[11] I.R.C. § 911(e).

[12] I.R.C. § 911(d)(8).

them are listed here simply to acquaint one with the smorgasbord of possibilities that are available.

We've already seen exclusions for scholarships under Section 117,[1] for employer educational assistance programs under Section 127[2] and for student loan forgiveness under Section 108(f).[3] We will see that some educational expenses (admittedly a small percentage) are deductible under Section 162[4] and to the extent that an employer funds such costs, such funding is a working condition fringe benefit excluded by Section 132(a)(3).[5] There are also other forms of tax benefits provided for higher education. For example, Section 221 allows an interest deduction for some interest payments on "qualified education loans"[6] and § 222 allows a deduction for "qualified tuition and related expenses."[7] Some of the other benefits are considered below.

*Section 25A. The American Opportunity and Lifetime Learning Credits.* In order to assist taxpayers in meeting the costs of higher education, Section 25A provides for two credits that have a substantial degree of overlap. This is your first introduction to *credits* which are considered in detail in a later Chapter.[8] Credits directly reduce tax liability; thus, the amount of a credit reduces one's tax liability dollar for dollar. If one owed $10,000 in taxes, but was allowed a $1,500 credit, the tax bill would be reduced to $8,500. Section 25A is generally a *nonrefundable* credit; it generally cannot generate a tax refund.[9] For example, if a taxpayer was allowed a $1,500 credit but had a tax liability of only $1,000, the taxpayer would not be given a $500 refund. $500 of the benefit of the credit would be lost.[10] However, the amount of a nonrefundable Section 25A credit reduces tax liability and that can increase the size of a refundable credit.[11]

The Section 25A credits are allowed for a taxpayer's payment of qualified tuition and related expenses[12] at an eligible institution of

---

[1] See Chapter 5B, supra.

[2] Id.

[3] See Chapter 8, supra.

[4] See Chapter 14C4, infra.

[5] See Chapter 4A, supra.

[6] See Chapter 16B, infra.

[7] See Chapter 18B, infra.

[8] See Chapter 27B, infra. See also Chapter 16A, infra.

[9] But see I.R.C. § 25A(i) and the Text at note 36, infra.

[10] See I.R.C. § 26(a). Some excess credits are permitted to be carried over for use in future years. There is no carryover of an unused I.R.C. § 25A credit. See Chapter 27B, infra.

[11] For example, if law student and spouse who file a joint return have gross income from spouse's services, an I.R.C. § 31 credit for withholding on wages (which is refundable), a $1,000 nonrefundable credit under § 25A and tax liability in excess of $1,000, the § 25A credit will reduce the tax liability and if the § 31 credit exceeds the remaining tax liability, it will increase the amount of the taxpayer's refund.

[12] I.R.C. § 25A(f)(1).

higher education[13] for a student[14] who is the taxpayer or the taxpayer's spouse or dependent.[15] Qualified tuition and related expenses include tuition and fees for the cost of enrollment or attendance at the eligible educational institution.[16] In the case of the American Opportunity Credit (but not the Lfetime Learning Credit), they include the costs of course materials.[17] They generally do not include costs for housing, for student and sports activities which are unrelated to academic instruction,[18] or for courses related to sports or hobbies, unless such courses are part of the student's degree program.[19] Under Section 25A, any tuition or related fee that is funded with an amount that is excluded from gross income (i.e., by Section 117 or Section 127) does not qualify for the Section 25A credit.[20] However, tuition and related fees that are funded by gifts that are excluded from gross income under Section 102(a)[21] or by loans[22] do qualify for the credit.

The first Section 25A credit is the "American Opportunity Tax Credit."[23] It is a *per student* credit generally of (1) 100 percent of the first $2000 of qualified tuition, related fees, and course materials,[24] and (2) 25 percent of the amount between $2000 and $4000 of such expenses, or a maximum $2,500 credit.[25] This credit generally is allowed only for the *first four years* of the student's post-secondary education.[26] The second credit is the Lifetime Learning Credit which is a *per taxpayer* credit computed on a family-wide basis of 20 percent of qualified tuition and

---

[13] I.R.C. § 25A(f)(2). The definition includes some vocational schools.

[14] A credit is allowed only if the name and TIN of the student is included on the taxpayer's return. I.R.C. § 25A(g)(1)(A). See also I.R.C. § 25A(g)(1)(B) imposing further identification restrictions on the American Opportunity Credit.

[15] I.R.C. § 25A(f)(1)(A). The term "dependent" is defined in I.R.C. § 152 and is considered in Chapter 18E, infra. Costs actually paid by a dependent are deemed to be paid by the taxpayer. I.R.C. § 25A(g)(3). Thus, if a dependent pays $1,000 of the cost of higher education, the payment is deemed to be made by the taxpayer.

[16] I.R.C. § 25A(f)(1)(A). To the extent that a deduction is allowed for qualified tuition and related expenses, for example under I.R.C. § 162 or under § 222, no § 25A credit is allowed for such tuition and expenses. I.R.C. § 25A(g)(5). See I.R.C. § 222(c)(2)(A).

[17] I.R.C. § 25A(f)(1)(D). Cf. I.R.C. § 25A(c)(2)(B).

[18] I.R.C. § 25A(f)(1)(C). See Reg. § 1.25A–2(d). See the Text at note 24, infra.

[19] I.R.C. § 25A(f)(1)(B).

[20] I.R.C. § 25A(g)(2) . If the proceeds of an I.R.C. § 135 bond are used to fund tuition and related expenses, the interest element on the bond which is excluded by § 135 and is used to fund tuition and related fees would not qualify for the credit. See the Text at notes 40–54, infra. Similarly, amounts excluded by I.R.C. §§ 529 and 530 would not qualify for the credit. See the Text at notes 55–89, infra.

[21] I.R.C. § 25A(g)(2)(C).

[22] Cf. I.R.C. § 25A(g)(2)(C).

[23] The "American Opportunity Tax Credit" replaces the Hope Scholarship Credit.

[24] I.R.C. § 25A(f)(1)(D).

[25] I.R.C. § 25A(b)(1).

[26] I.R.C. § 25A(b)(2)(C). The student must have been at least a one-half time student during the year. I.R.C. § 25A(b)(2)(B). See also I.R.C. § 25A(b)(2)(A).

related expenses[27] of up to $10,000 of expenses (a maximum credit of $2000) *for any year* of the student's post-secondary education.[28]

The amount of the American Opportunity Credit is reduced (starts to phase out) as the taxpayer's modified adjusted gross income[29] exceeds $80,000 for a single taxpayer and $160,000 for a married couple filing a joint return,[30] and the credit is fully phased out as the modified adjusted gross income reaches $90,000 and $180,000, respectively.[31] The Lifelong Learning Credit generally is reduced (starts to phase out) as the taxpayer's modified adjusted gross income[32] exceeds $40,000 for a single taxpayer and $80,000 for a married couple filing a joint return[33] and the credit is fully phased out as modified adjusted gross income reaches $50,000 and $100,000,[34] respectively. Both credits are elective.[35] In addition, 40 percent of the American Opportunity Credit generally is a refundable credit.[36]

With respect to any year, only one of the credits is allowed with respect to any student;[37] thus the Lifetime Learning Credit may not be elected for a student in a year if the American Opportunity Credit is allowed for the year.[38] Further, in a fairly complicated mechanism, the statutes preclude any expenses from being allowed a double advantage of both a credit and an exclusion or a deduction under some other provisions, although taxpayers are allowed flexibility in determining which benefit to employ.[39]

*Section 135. Savings Bond Income Used to Pay Higher Education Tuition and Fees.* In an effort to help low and medium income taxpayers fund the cost of their or their dependents' higher education tuition payments, Congress provides an exclusion from gross income of interest on certain discounted federal bonds whose proceeds are used directly or

---

[27] See Text at notes 16–22, supra. Note that course materials are not a related expense. Cf. I.R.C. § 25A(f)(1)(D).

[28] I.R.C. § 25A(c)(1). The credit does not require one-half time student status. See note 26, supra.

[29] I.R.C. § 25A(d)(3).

[30] Married couples filing separately are allowed no credit. I.R.C. § 25A(g)(6).

[31] I.R.C. § 25A(d)(1).

[32] I.R.C. § 25A(d)(3).

[33] Married couples filing separately are allowed no credit. I.R.C. § 25A(g)(6). The phase-out amounts are adjusted for inflation post-2001. I.R.C. § 25A(h).

[34] I.R.C. § 25A(d)(2).

[35] I.R.C. § 25A(e).

[36] I.R.C. § 25A(i).

[37] I.R.C. § 25A(c)(2)(A).

[38] If one of the credits is used for a student in a year, the other credit may be used for other students in the same year, and the other credit may be used for the same student in a subsequent year. Reg. § 1.25A–1(b). Conf.Rep. No. 101–220, 101st Cong., 1st Sess. 346 (1997).

[39] I.R.C. § 25A(g)(2). See I.R.C. § 25A(e) which makes § 25A an elective provision. See also the Text at notes 20–22, supra, I.R.C. § 222(c)(2)(A), and note 63, infra.

indirectly to finance such educational costs.[40] Section 135(a) allows an exclusion from gross income for the gain[41] on the redemption of "qualified United States savings bonds"[42] to the extent that a taxpayer pays "qualified higher education expenses"[43] during the year. A United States savings bond is qualified if it is issued at a discount after 1989 to an individual who has attained age 24 before the date of the bond's issuance.[44] The exclusion is not available to a parent if the bonds are purchased by the parent but put in the name of a person under age 24 or are purchased by a person under age 24.[45]

Qualified higher education expenses include tuition and fees[46] at an eligible educational institution for the taxpayer and the taxpayer's spouse and dependents[47] during the year of the bond redemption.[48] In computing qualified higher education expenses, the amount of tuition and fees is reduced by scholarships, fellowships, employer-funded educational assistance, other tuition reductions, and any expenses to the extent that they were used in computing a Section 25A higher education cost credit and any expenses taken into account in determining the exclusion for distributions from a Qualified Tuition Program or an Educational Savings Account.[49]

There are two special limitations on the exclusion. If the bond redemption proceeds in a year exceed the qualified higher education expenses for the year, only a portion of the interest income from bonds is excluded equal to the ratio of the expenses to the proceeds.[50] The second limitation limits the exclusion to low and medium-income taxpayers. Under the limitation there is a phase-out of the amount of the amount of exclusion if the taxpayer's "modified adjusted gross income"[51] exceeds $40,000. in the case of a single taxpayer or $60,000 in the case of a joint

---

[40] I.R.C. § 135. See Williams, "Financing a College Education: A Taxing Dilemma," 50 Ohio State L.J. 561 (1989); Sumutka, "Qualified U.S. Saving Bonds are a Viable Education Savings Alternative," 43 Tax'n for Accts. 370 (1989).

[41] The bonds are issued at a discount with the result that the gain is attributable to interest earned on the bonds over the life of the bond. See I.R.C. § 135(c)(1)(C).

[42] I.R.C. § 135(c)(1).

[43] I.R.C. § 135(c)(2).

[44] I.R.C. § 135(c)(1). The exclusion applies to series EE and series I bonds. I.R.C. § 135(c)(1)(C).

[45] Conf.Rep. No. 100–1104, 100th Cong., 2d Sess. 141 (1988), reprinted in 1988–3 C.B. 631. A child may not use the exclusion if the bond is purchased by or for a child prior to reaching age 24. I.R.C. § 135(c)(1)(B).

[46] I.R.C. § 135(c)(2)(A). Such amounts also include contributions to an I.R.C. § 529 Qualified Tuition Program and a § 530 Educational Savings Account. I.R.C. § 135(c)(2)(C).

[47] I.R.C. § 135(c)(2)(A)(i)–(iii). The taxpayer must be allowed an I.R.C. § 151 deduction for the year with respect to a dependent. I.R.C. § 135(c)(2)(A)(iii). See Chapter 18E, infra.

[48] I.R.C. § 135(c)(2)(A), (c)(3). The term "eligible education institution" is defined identically for purposes of I.R.C. §§ 135, 529, and 530. See I.R.C. §§ 135(c)(3), 529(e)(5), 530(b)(3).

[49] I.R.C. § 135(d)(1), (2). See the Text generally at notes 12–39, supra and 55–89, infra.

[50] I.R.C. § 135(b)(1). The term proceeds includes the original cost of the bond as well as any income interest generated by the bond. Id.

[51] I.R.C. § 135(c)(4).

return[52] with the dollar amounts adjusted for inflation for the years after 1990.[53] The exclusion is fully phased out as the taxpayer's modified adjusted gross income exceeds $55,000 (or $90,000 in the case of a joint return), with those dollar amounts adjusted for inflation for years after 1990.[54]

*Section 529. Qualified Tuition Programs.* Many states have established state tuition programs allowing taxpayers to prepay higher education costs by purchasing tuition credits or certificates or by establishing saving account plans for the qualified higher education expenses of a designated beneficiary at an eligible educational institution.[55] The tax consequences of such programs were originally unclear, but Congress enacted Section 529 to clarify the picture for "qualified state tuition programs."[56] The benefits of qualified state tuition programs are extended to apply to *private* institutions which have programs for purchasing tuition credits or certificates,[57] but not for private institutions which establish saving account plans.[58]

The plans must provide funds for qualified higher education expenses which are defined broadly to include tuition, fees, books, supplies, equipment (including computer equipment and technology), expenses of a special needs beneficiary in connection with enrollment or attendance at the educational institution, and, generally, room and board expenses.[59] Only cash contributions may be made to such plans[60], and there is no immediate tax benefit on the contribution. However, generally, the earnings of the plan are not taxed as they are earned,[61] but they may be taxed on their distribution.[62] In general, distributions for such plans are not taxable to the extent that they are used to fund (1) qualified higher educational expenses of the beneficiary or (2) subject to

---

[52]  I.R.C. § 135(b)(2)(A). No exclusion is allowed if the taxpayer is married and files a separate return. I.R.C. § 135(d)(3).

[53]  I.R.C. § 135(b)(2)(B). The amount of the phase-out is determined by multiplying the exclusion times a fraction the numerator of which is the excess of the taxpayer's modified adjusted gross income over the $40,000 or $60,000 amount and the denominator is $15,000 in the case of a single taxpayer or $30,000 in the case of a taxpayer filing a joint return. I.R.C. § 135(b)(2)(A).

[54]  I.R.C. § 135(b)(2)(B).

[55]  Cf. I.R.C. § 529(b)(1), (e)(5).

[56]  Cf. I.R.C. § 529(b)(1). For a state tuition program to be qualified it must meet the requirement of I.R.C. § 529(b)(2)–(6).

[57]  The assets of such programs must be held in a qualified trust. I.R.C. § 529(b)(1) (flush language). See I.R.C. § 408(a)(2), (5). Distributions from such plans after the year 2003 qualify for § 529 treatment. For a program of a private institution to be qualified, it must also meet the requirements of I.R.C. § 529(b)(2)–(6).

[58]  See I.R.C. § 529(b)(1)(A)(ii).

[59]  I.R.C. § 529(e)(3). This is broader than the mere tuition and related expenses which qualify for the I.R.C. § 25A credit. See notes 12–19, and 24, supra. Cf. note 63, infra.

[60]  I.R.C. § 529(b)(2). However, such contributions may result in gift tax consequences to the contributor (I.R.C. § 529(c)(2)), but such contributions are not immediate income to the designated beneficiary of the plan. I.R.C. § 529(c)(1)(A).

[61]  I.R.C. § 529(a), (c)(3).

[62]  I.R.C. § 529(c)(3).

a $10,000 per student limitation, amounts paid for tuition in connection with enrollment or attendance at an elementary or secondary public, private, or religious school.[63] Any excess distributions are generally[64] taxable to the distributee beneficiary using Section 72 annuity principles, thus excluding prior contributions but taxing the income element.[65] For example, if $40,000 were contributed to a plan, and in the four years of college the designated beneficiary receives payments or in kind distributions of $30,000 per year, $20,000 of which is used for qualified higher education expenses[66] only $10,000 per year would be treated as an annuity payment and the ratio of the investment in the contract to the expected return ($40,000/$120,000) to each $10,000 payment, here $3,333, would be excluded from gross income and $6,667 would be included and taxed in the *beneficiary's* gross income in each year.[67] Taxation of distributions may be avoided, subject to several limitations, by a rollover within 60 days of distribution from such plans to other plans or to other family members.[68] However, if a distribution is taxed, there is a 10 percent penalty tax on the amount taxed, i.e. $667 each year in the example above.[69] There is no phase-out of such plan for higher income contributors or for benefits paid to high income beneficiaries.

*Section 530. Coverdell Educational Savings Accounts.* The taxation of Education Savings Accounts[70] bears a strong resemblance to the taxation of Qualified Tuition Plans, although there are some significant as well as subtle differences between the two.[71] Educational Savings Accounts must be established exclusively for the purpose of paying qualified education expenses, either qualified higher education

---

[63]　I.R.C. § 529(c)(3)(B), (c)(7), (e)(3)(A). The amount of expenses which qualify as qualified higher education expenses (see note 59, supra) is reduced by amounts excluded from gross income for expenses such as under I.R.C. § 117 (I.R.C. § 25A(g)(2)) and expenses for which a credit is claimed under § 25A. I.R.C. § 529(c)(3)(B)(v). If such expenses are funded by both a Qualified Tuition Program and an Educational Savings Account (see I.R.C. § 530) and the distributions exceed the reduced qualified expenses, the expenses are allocated among the distributions. I.R.C. § 529(c)(3)(B)(vi). Thus, a taxpayer has flexibility in allocating proceeds and in using a § 25A credit or a § 222 deduction so long as the distribution does not produce a double exclusion under §§ 529 and 530 and is not used for the same education expenses for which a credit or deduction is claimed. See also I.R.C. § 222(c)(2)(B).

[64]　See note 68, infra.

[65]　I.R.C. § 529(c)(3)(A).

[66]　See note 59, supra.

[67]　See I.R.C. § 72(e)(2)(B), (8)(B), (9). The same result would occur, for example, if the qualified tuition program made a matching grant which was excluded as an I.R.C. § 117 scholarship. See Chapter 7B, supra. For example, if the payment was $30,000 a year of which $20,000 was a § 117 matching grant, only the $10,000 distribution would be included in the computation and only $6,667 would be included in gross income.

[68]　I.R.C. §§ 529(c)(3)(C), 529(e)(2).

[69]　I.R.C. §§ 529(c)(6), 530(d)(4).

[70]　I.R.C. § 530 was originally captioned Education IRAs. It was subsequently renamed Coverdell Education Savings Accounts which we have shortened to mere Education Savings Accounts. If § 530 accounts are *similar* to any IRAs, they most resemble Roth IRAs. See Chapter 20C3, infra.

[71]　The most significant difference is the ceiling on contributions and the phase-out for high income taxpayers. See the Text at notes 78 and 80–81, infra.

expenses,[72] qualified elementary or secondary education expenses,[73] or subject to special rules, contributions to qualified tuition programs,[74] of a named individual.[75] The nondeductible contributions must be made in cash,[76] and in the case of an individual contributor,[77] they may not exceed $2,000 per year.[78] Contributions must be made prior to the individual beneficiary's 18th birthday.[79] The $2,000 contribution ceiling is phased out for high income taxpayers with modified adjusted gross income[80] between $95,000 and $110,000 (the amounts are $190,000 and $220,000 for married contributors filing a joint return).[81] No contribution may be made in a year to the extent that anyone makes a contribution to a Section 529 Qualified Tuition Plan for the beneficiary of the plan.[82]

The other rules with respect to Education Savings Accounts are very similar to the rules applicable to Qualified Tuition Programs. Income earned by the Educational Saving Account is generally exempt from tax.[83] Taxation of distributions from an Educational Savings Account is similar to the taxation of distributions from Qualified Tuition Programs.[84] Distributions are excluded from gross income to the extent that they do not exceed the qualified education expenses[85] incurred by the beneficiary in the year the distribution is made.[86] If there is an excess distribution to the beneficiary, it is taxed using Section 72 rules[87] and it is subject to a 10 percent penalty.[88] The income inclusion and penalty are again avoided if the excess amount is contributed (rolled-over) to an

---

[72] Qualified higher education expenses are defined in the same manner as under I.R.C. § 529. I.R.C. §§ 530(b)(2)(A)(i), 529(e)(3). See note 59, supra.

[73] I.R.C. § 530(b)(2)(A)(ii), (b)(3).

[74] I.R.C. § 530(b)(2)(B).

[75] I.R.C. § 530(b)(1). Thus, the individual must be a life in being.

[76] I.R.C. § 530(b)(1)(A)(i). See I.R.C. § 530(b)(4). Such contributions may result in gift tax consequences to the contributor (I.R.C. § 530(d)(3)), but such contributions are not immediate income to the designated beneficiary of the plan. See I.R.C. § 530(d).

[77] Contributions may be made by a corporation or other entity, and there are no ceiling limitations on the amount of such contributions. Cf. I.R.C. § 530(c)(1).

[78] I.R.C. § 530(b)(1)(A)(iii).

[79] I.R.C. § 530(b)(1)(A)(ii). The age limitations are inapplicable to any designated beneficiary with special needs. I.R.C. § 530(b)(1) (flush language).

[80] I.R.C. § 530(c)(2).

[81] I.R.C. § 530(c)(1). The statute is silent whether the lower limit applies to married taxpayers filing separate returns.

[82] Conf.Rep. No. 105–220, 105th Cong., 1st Sess. 363 (1997). See the Text at notes 55–69, supra. Cf. I.R.C. § 530(b)(2)(B) involving using proceeds from an Education Savings Account to fund a Qualified Tuition Plan.

[83] I.R.C. § 530(a).

[84] See the Text at notes 62–69, supra.

[85] See notes 72–75, supra. Such expenses may be reduced under rules identical to those applied to Qualified Tuition Programs. I.R.C. § 530(d)(2)(C). See note 63, supra.

[86] I.R.C. § 530(d)(2)(A).

[87] I.R.C. §§ 530(d)(2)(B), 72(e)(2)(B), (8)(B), (9). For example assume $10,000 is distributed from an Educational IRA, there are $8,000 of qualified expenses, and $3,000 of the $10,000 represents the income element in the fund. As a result, the distribution exceeds qualified expenses by $2,000 ($10,000 less $8,000) and 30 percent, or $3,000/$10,000 of the $2,000 or $600 is included in the beneficiary's gross income.

[88] I.R.C. § 530(d)(4)(A). See I.R.C. § 530(d)(4)(B).

Educational Savings Account benefitting the same beneficiary or another family member beneficiary if the beneficiary is under age 30 and the rollover occurs within 60 days of the distribution.[89]

## PROBLEMS

1. Law Student and Spouse are self-supporting and Spouse works while Student attends Law School. Consider the amount of any Section 25A credit they may elect in the following circumstances assuming they file a joint return:

    (a) Student pays $10,000 in tuition for the current year. Spouse works and Spouses have a modified adjusted gross income of $30,000 for the year.

    (b) Same as (a), above, except the tuition is paid from a student loan.

    (c) Same as (a), above, except that Student is granted a $7,000 scholarship excluded by § 117 that reduces the tuition to $3,000.

    (d) Same as (a), above, except that Student's Parents pay $8,000 of the tuition and Student pays $2,000, although Student is not a dependent of Parents.

    (e) Same as (a), above, except that Spouses have a modified adjusted gross income of $100,000 for the year.

    (f) What result in (a), above, if, before credits, the Spouses had $3,000 of tax liability and $3,000 of withholding from wages which qualifies for a potentially refundable credit under § 31? (See footnote 11 on page 222, supra.)

    (g) Same as (a), above, except that Spouse is also in college. Spouse is in the third year of college and pays $5,000 in tuition.

    (h) Same as (a), above, except that after Law Student graduates, Spouse, who has not previously attended college, quits work and enters a vocational school as defined in § 25A(f)(2). Spouse pays $10,000 in tuition and Lawyer earns $75,000.

2. Young Professional Couple are concerned as to the funding of their children's higher educations. Their alma mater has a Qualified Tuition Program and they have also heard about savings bonds and Educational Savings Accounts. What is your advice to them?

## D. FEDERAL TAXES AND STATE ACTIVITIES

Internal Revenue Code: Sections 103; 115; 141(a) and (e). See Sections 141; 142; 148; 149.

_____

[89] I.R.C. § 530(d)(5).

"The power to tax involves the power to destroy." So wrote Chief Justice Marshall in 1819 in M'Culloch v. Maryland.[1] This classic dictum is the foundation of a doctrine of intergovernmental immunity. That doctrine imposes some restraints upon federal and local government undertakings to impose taxes impinging upon each other.[2]

The doctrine finds no express support in the Constitution. It rests instead upon an implied guarantee of governmental self-preservation, and over the years, the courts have limited the scope of the doctrine. Even when the doctrine of intergovernmental immunity imposes no obstacles, important policy questions exist. The questions center on the extent to which the federal government should exercise restraint in imposing taxes that have an impact on state activities.

The Court applied the philosophy of M'Culloch in reverse (applied it to a federal tax) in The Collector v. Day.[3] The Court in Day held invalid the imposition of a federal tax (the Civil War Income Tax) on the salary of a state judge. The Court reasoned that the tax threatened an essential function of the state. Later, the Court expressed the reciprocal nature of the intergovernmental immunity doctrine as follows:[4]

> As the States cannot tax the powers, the operations, or the property of the United States, nor the means which they employ to carry their powers into execution, so it has been held that the United States have no power under the Constitution to tax either the instrumentalities or the property of a State.

Intergovernmental immunity had bold beginnings and a vigorous early life but has suffered a marked decline over the past half century. Much of its attrition occurred around World War II. By 1939, Mr. Justice Frankfurter referred to Chief Justice Marshall's dictum, quoted above, as a mere "seductive cliche."[5] The Court rejected the reciprocal nature of the doctrine about this time:[6]

> [I]n laying a federal tax on state instrumentalities the people of the states, acting through their representatives, are laying a tax on their own institutions and consequently are subject to political restraints which can be counted on to prevent abuse. State taxation of national instrumentalities is subject to no such restraint, for the people outside the state have no

---

[1] 17 U.S. (4 Wheat.) 316, 431 (1819).

[2] The actual holding of M'Culloch repudiated a state tax imposed on the privilege of issuing bank notes, but applicable in fact only to national banks. The Court held the tax invalid as an improper interference with powers expressly granted to the federal government.

[3] 78 U.S. (11 Wall.) 113 (1870).

[4] Pollock v. Farmers' Loan & Trust Co., 157 U.S. 429, 584, 15 S.Ct. 673, 690 (1895).

[5] Graves v. People of State of New York ex rel. O'Keefe, 306 U.S. 466, 489, 59 S.Ct. 595, 602 (1939). Earlier, Mr. Justice Holmes had delivered the classic comment: "The power to tax is not the power to destroy while this Court sits." Panhandle Oil Co. v. Mississippi ex rel. Knox, 277 U.S. 218, 223, 48 S.Ct. 451, 453 (1928).

[6] Helvering v. Gerhardt, 304 U.S. 405, 412, 58 S.Ct. 969, 971–972 (1938).

representatives who participate in the legislation; and in a real sense, as to them, the taxation is without representation.

Shortly thereafter, the Court nailed the coffin shut on reciprocity with the following:[7]

> The considerations bearing upon taxation by the states of activities or agencies of the Federal Government are not correlative with the considerations bearing upon federal taxation of state agencies or activities.

The question whether a tax has an adverse impact on an essential governmental function[8] has shifted to a consideration whether the tax applies even-handedly in a non-discriminatory fashion. The Court first differentiated *Day* in a decision involving a federal tax on a less-than-essential state employee.[9] Then, the Court overruled *Day*, holding:[10]

> So much of the burden of a non-discriminatory general tax upon the incomes of employees of a government, state or national, as may be passed on economically to that government, through the effect of the tax on the price level of labor or materials, is but the normal incident of the organization within the same territory of two governments, each possessing the taxing power.

Intergovernmental immunity still may generate nostalgic feelings in law professors at state universities. In the final analysis, however, neither state nor federal employees enjoy immunity from state or federal income taxes.[11]

The tattered doctrine of intergovernmental immunity long hovered over the taxation of interest paid on state and local obligations. There was little reason for this. In Pollock v. Farmers Loan & Trust, in which the Supreme Court nullified the 1894 federal income tax statute, there is dictum that Congress could not validly tax the interest on state bonds.[12] However, since 1894 the Court has condoned a federal tax on salaries of state employees which, by analogy, goes a long way to undermine the *Pollock* dictum. Arguably a state's activities are affected no differently if it must pay higher (taxable) interest on its bonds than if it must pay higher (taxable) salaries to its employees. The issue was put to rest by the holding of the Supreme Court in South Carolina v. Baker[13] that taxation of interest on state bonds did not violate the doctrine of intergovernmental tax immunity.[14]

---

7   New York v. United States, 326 U.S. 572, 577, 66 S.Ct. 310, 312 (1946).

8   See The Collector v. Day, note 3, supra.

9   Helvering v. Gerhardt, note 6, supra.

10  Graves, note 5, supra.

11  See the Public Salary Tax Act of 1939, 53 Stat. 574.

12  Pollock v. Farmers' Loan & Trust Co., note 4, supra.

13  485 U.S. 505, 108 S.Ct. 1355 (1988).

14  The Court also held that such taxation did not violate the Tenth Amendment limitation on the authority of Congress to regulate state activities.

The bond interest question is becoming less academic. States, of course, do not tax interest paid on federal bonds. But the federal income tax, has begun to recognize that some state bonds support private functions. Section 103(a) contains a deceptively broad statement that excludes interest on *any* state or local bond from gross income.[15] But, the exclusion, historically intended to apply to interest on bonds the proceeds of which are used to finance operations of state and local governmental units, does not extend to interest paid on a "private activity bond", unless it is a "qualified bond", an "arbitrage bond", or a bond which is not in "registered form".[16]

Private activity bonds are obligations of state or local governments issued to finance nongovernmental undertakings. Thus a bond to raise money to build public buildings such as a courthouse, a library or a school is a public bond; but a bond to build a building for a private company to use tax-free, to encourage it to locate within a state or community, is a private activity bond. A private activity bond is any bond that is part of a bond issue where, in general, more than 10 percent of the proceeds are to be used for a private use,[17] and the payment of the principal or of interest on more than 10 percent of the proceeds of the issue is secured by an interest on private use property.[18] In the alternative, a bond is treated as a private activity bond if it is part of an issue of which more than 5 percent or $5 million of the proceeds, whichever is less, is used to finance direct or indirect loans to borrowers other than "governmental units" or to acquire "nongovernmental output property."[19]

Certain bonds, despite being classified as private activity bonds, may nevertheless receive the interest exclusion benefits of Section 103(a).[20] Such private activity bonds, known as "qualified bonds", are: exempt facility bonds, qualified mortgage bonds, qualified veteran's mortgage bonds, qualified small issue bonds, qualified student loan bonds, qualified redevelopment bonds, and bonds the proceeds of which are to

---

[15] I.R.C. § 103(a), stating "gross income does not include interest on any State or local bond."

[16] I.R.C. § 103(b).

[17] I.R.C. § 141(a)(1)(A). This is known as the "private business use" test. See I.R.C. § 141(b)(1).

[18] I.R.C. § 141(a)(1)(B). This is known as the "private security or payment" test. See I.R.C. § 141(b)(2).

This 10% ceiling under both I.R.C. § 141(a)(1)(A) and (B) becomes 5% where the private use being financed is unrelated to the governmental use being financed. I.R.C. § 141(b)(3). For example, a privately operated newsstand located in a courthouse is related to the courthouse, and a privately operated school cafeteria is related to the school in which it is located. Conf.Rep. No. 99–841, 99th Cong., 2d Sess. II–691 (1986). If, however, 6% of the proceeds of a school construction bond issue is used to build a privately operated cafeteria in the county's administrative office building the related use restriction is violated. Id. at Example 1.

[19] I.R.C. § 141(c), (d). A governmental unit is defined to exclude any agency or instrumentality of the United States. I.R.C. § 150(a)(2). Nongovernmental output property is essentially property which before its acquisition was used by a nongovernmental unit in connection with an output facility. I.R.C. § 141(d)(2).

[20] I.R.C. § 103(b)(1).

benefit certain charitable organizations.[21] The restrictions applicable to each type of qualified bond are extremely intricate; and there are also volume limitations on the amount of such bonds an issuer may offer without loss of preferred status.[22]

The exclusion of interest paid on state or local bonds under Section 103(a) does not extend to any "arbitrage bond".[23] Arbitrage occurs when any portion of the proceeds of a bond issue is used to acquire investment property which produces a yield that is "materially higher" than the return paid on the bond issue itself.[24] Prior to enactment of arbitrage restrictions, state and local governments issued tax exempt bonds, on which they paid low interest rates because of their tax exempt status, and invested the proceeds in other securities (generally taxable bonds) with a higher yield, thereby producing tax free income at the expense of the federal coffers. There are several exceptions to the current arbitrage rules.[25]

Finally, the Section 103 exclusion is not applicable to interest paid on state and local bonds that do not meet the registration requirements of Section 149.[26] Congress was concerned that the use of bearer (nonregistered) tax exempt bonds facilitated abuses within the tax system. Without registration of the bonds taxpayers could easily conceal from the Internal Revenue Service income tax gains on bearer bonds (which gains are taxable even if the interest they pay is not) and, for estate and gift tax purposes, could conceal the bonds themselves (or their transfer). Congress, generally, requires tax exempt bonds to be in registered form in order to qualify for the Section 103(a) interest exclusion.[27] In addition, unregistered bonds are subject to various punitive provisions.[28]

*Should* Congress continue a provision that generates huge sources of untaxed income? Note that taxpayers in a 30 percent bracket receive a yield on a 7 percent tax-exempt bond worth the same as the yield on a 10

---

[21]  I.R.C. § 141(e)(1). Nevertheless the Tax Reform Act of 1986 broke historic ground by indirectly subjecting some interest exempted from regular income tax by I.R.C. § 103(a) to taxation under the alternative minimum tax. I.R.C. § 57(a)(5). See page 962, infra. See generally I.R.C. §§ 55–59 and Chapter 27C, infra.

[22]  See I.R.C. §§ 141–147, especially § 141(e)(2) and § 146.

[23]  I.R.C. § 103(b)(2).

[24]  I.R.C. § 148(a) and (b).

[25]  See I.R.C. § 148(c) through (g). For instance, a state or local government may save the tax exempt status of a bond issue by refunding to the federal government any arbitrage profits. I.R.C. § 148(f)(2). In addition, a small portion of the proceeds (5% or $100,000 whichever is lesser) may be invested in higher yielding investments (I.R.C. § 148(e)), a temporary investment may be made until the proceeds are needed for their specified purposes (I.R.C. § 148(c)) or 10% of the proceeds may be placed in a reserve fund (I.R.C. § 148(d)).

[26]  I.R.C. § 103(b)(3). The constitutionality of such taxation was upheld in South Carolina v. Baker, supra note 13.

[27]  Pub.Law No. 97–448, 97th Cong., 2d Sess. § 306(b)(2) (1982). Cf. I.R.C. § 149(c)(2)(A).

[28]  See, for example, I.R.C. §§ 163(f) and 165(j).

percent taxable bond.[29] Historically, Congressional efforts to eliminate the perceived inequity have been rebuffed.[30] One problem is the extent to which any such change might be accorded retroactive effect to tax the interest on outstanding state bonds. And of course a constant problem is the extent to which the fiscal situations could stand further complication by the increased costs of state borrowing, which would follow if the interest on state bonds were subject to the income tax. There is the possibility that state losses could be made up by the *states* extending their income taxes to interest on Federal obligations.[31]

---

[29] If a taxpayer receives 10% interest on a $10,000 taxable bond and pays tax at a 30% rate on that amount, the taxpayer will receive $1,000 of interest, pay $300 of tax, and net $700 after taxes, the same after-tax return as the taxpayer would receive on a 7% $10,000 tax-exempt bond. For a discussion written when tax rates were higher than after enactment of the Tax Reform Act of 1986, see generally, Surrey, "Federal Income Taxation of State and Local Government Obligation," 36 Tax Policy 3 (1969), reprinted in Sander and Westfall, Readings in Federal Taxation, page 277 (1970) and Morris, "Tax Exemption for State and Local Bonds," 42 Geo.Wash.L.Rev. 483 (1974).

[30] See Yamamoto, "A Proposal for the Elimination of the Exclusion for State Bond Interest," 50 Fla.L.Rev. 145 (1998); Maxwell, "Exclusion from Income of Interest on State and Local Government Obligations," House Comm. on Ways and Means, 86th Cong., 2d Sess., 1 Tax Revision Compendium 701, 702–703 (1959). In 1969, an unsuccessful effort was made to bring such interest at least within the reach of the Minimum Tax for Tax Preferences, I.R.C. (1954) §§ 56–58. H.Rep. No. 91–413 (Part 1), 91st Cong., 1st Sess. (1969), 1969–2 C.B. 249.

[31] This is one to conjure with. It is likely Congress could by legislation prohibit the imposition of state income taxes on the interest paid on Federal obligations. Congressional power to protect its agencies and activities clearly extends beyond any automatic immunities inferred from the Constitution. See Graves v. New York ex rel. O'Keefe, note 5, supra at 478, 59 S.Ct. at 597, and cases there cited. However, to do so would seem to lend support to the argument of the states that the imposition of federal income tax on interest paid on state obligations should be precluded under remnants of the constitutional doctrine of intergovernmental immunity on a kind of fair's fair principle.

# PART 3

# IDENTIFICATION OF THE PROPER TAXPAYER

# CHAPTER 12

# ASSIGNMENT OF INCOME

## A. INTRODUCTION

Internal Revenue Code: Sections 1(a) through (e), (h); 6013(a). See Sections 1(g); 63; 66; 73.

---

A principal feature of the federal income tax has been that the tax is imposed on "taxable income"[1] at "progressive" rates under which increasing rates are applicable to additional increments of taxable income.[2] The degree of progressivity under the income tax has varied through the years as Congress has needed more or less revenue or has decided that the tax burden or individuals should be adjusted. For example, at one time individual tax rates were spread among fifteen separate tax brackets and, for a long period prior to the 1980s, the highest tax rate for individuals was 70 percent.

Progressive income tax rates provide a strong incentive for an individual taxpayer to try to fragment income.[3] Thus, if a taxpayer in the highest tax rate bracket can transfer some income to another individual or entity in the lowest bracket, the taxpayer will reduce the total amount of tax owed to the government. In many instances it is a matter of indifference to a taxpayer whether the taxpayer actually receives an item of income or whether it goes instead to a related individual or an economically related entity such as a trust, a partnership, or a corporation. In a sense, the game is to have-your-cake and eat-it too, and the temptation is great to spread income among family members or entities or both in an effort to reduce total tax liability.

The Tax Reform Act of 1986 generally reduced the highest tax rate imposed on an individual's income and, as a consequence, Congress took much of the sport out of the "assignment of income" game. Following the 1986 Act, the top rate for individuals was a mere 28 percent! Since then, Congress has continued to tinker with the tax rate tables and, currently, an individual's taxable income is subject to a seven-bracket rate structure, with a top rate of 37 and a bottom rate of 10 percent. The different rates are phased in at various income levels depending upon

---

[1] Taxable income, defined in I.R.C. § 63, is essentially the taxpayer's gross income reduced by all allowable deductions. Credits are ignored here.

[2] See Blum and Kalven, "The Uneasy Case for Progressive Taxation," 19 U. of Chi.L.Rev. 417 (1952); Smith, "High Progressive Tax Rates: Inequity and Immorality?" 20 U. of Fla. L.Rev. 451 (1968); Bankman & Griffith, "Social Welfare and the Rate Structure: A New Look at Progressive Taxation," 75 Cal. L.Rev. 1905 (1987); Zolt, "The Uneasy Case for Uniform Taxation" 16 Virg. Tax Rev. 39 (1996).

[3] Often *estate tax* planning is a motivation for transactions that raise *income tax* assignment or shifting of income questions.

classification of the taxpayer.[4] Thus, today if one is successful in shifting income say from the 37 percent to the 10 percent bracket, there is an over 70 percent saving in the amount of taxes paid.[5]

Successfully achieving such a saving is often easier said than done. Congress has added some "rules" to the game which affect the degree of success one can achieve by assignments of income. For example, a child generally under the age of 18 years (24 if a student) is generally taxed on almost all of her *unearned* income at the trust and estate tax rate, nullifying the tax advantage in assignment of income to such minors.[6] This is commonly referred to as "the kiddie tax." Similarly Congress has sharply curtailed the incentives to assign income to trust entities (see Chapter 13) by phasing in the top 37 percent tax rate on trusts at a low level of taxable income.[7]

Although the spoils of victory are not as great as they may have once been, nevertheless some will persist in playing the game. In the income tax area there are both statutory and judge-made restraints on the efficacy of "assignment of income," the subject of this and the next Chapter. This Chapter deals with assignments of income to other individuals; Chapter 13 concerns assignments of income when artificial entities, like trusts and corporations, as well as other individuals, enter the picture.

In one instance the Code itself provides a mandatory rule that has the computational consequence of an effective assignment of income. The rule is Section 73. Under some state laws income arising out of the *services* of a minor child is deemed to be the property of the parents. Such income probably could be taxed to the parents as *theirs*.[8] However, Section 73 provides that "amounts received in respect of the services of a child shall be included in his gross income * * *." Thus, a uniform rule is provided for federal tax purposes, which operates independently of the vagaries of state property laws. Obviously, the rule is generally favorable to taxpayers.[9] The tax rule of course does not bear on who ultimately gets to keep the income but, instead, only on how the tax on it is to be determined.[10]

---

[4]    See Chapter 27A2, infra.

[5]    A reduction from 35% to 10% would constitute an almost 71½% savings; a reduction from 32% to 10% would constitute an almost 70% savings; a reduction from 24% to 10% would constitute an almost 60% savings; and a reduction from 22% to 10% would constitute a roughly 55% savings.

[6]    I.R.C. § 1(g) and (j)(2)(E). This provision is considered in more detail in Chapters 13 and 27A5, infra.

[7]    I.R.C. § 1(j)(2)(E). Cf. I.R.C. § 1(f).

[8]    But compare Lucas v. Earl with Commissioner v. Giannini, both infra, this Chapter.

[9]    But see I.R.C. § 6201(c), sometimes making a parent liable for the child's tax on income included in gross income by § 73.

[10]   See I.R.C. § 66 which applies a similar type rule to some community property and treats the entire amount (not merely one half) of community property income earned by a taxpayer as that taxpayer's income for federal income tax purposes. § 66 applies only if: the spouses file separate returns; the spouses live apart at all times during the year; there is community property earned income (see § 911(b)) in the year; and subject to a de minimis exception, no

So-called "income-splitting" provisions available on an elective basis to married taxpayers are of greater significance. If they elect to file a joint return,[11] their combined taxable income is taxed at rates provided in Section 1(a). If they file separately, each is taxed at rates provided in Section 1(d). A comparison of the two rate tables will show that, the tax on the combined taxable income of husband and wife under Section 1(a) is twice the tax on one-half their combined taxable income using 1(d) rates. Consequently, the filing of a joint return, even where one spouse has all the income, produces the same tax as if the income were equally divided and each half were taxed under the Section 1(d) rates.[12]

We retain historical coverage of the concepts of assignment of income in this edition of the book fully recognizing that for various reasons the game will not be played as it was in years past. Lucas v. Earl, which follows immediately, is a landmark case. It involved a husband and wife but a tax year before 1948 when income splitting was enacted. What is the present importance of the case? Was the assignment in Lucas v. Earl effected for tax reasons? Note the date of the contract in the case.

## B. INCOME FROM SERVICES

### Lucas v. Earl

Supreme Court of the United States, 1930.
281 U.S. 111, 50 S.Ct. 241.

■ MR. JUSTICE HOLMES delivered the opinion of the Court.

This case presents the question whether the respondent, Earl, could be taxed for the whole of the salary and attorney's fees earned by him in the years 1920 and 1921, or should be taxed for only a half of them in view of a contract with his wife which we shall mention. The Commissioner of Internal Revenue and the Board of Tax Appeals imposed a tax upon the whole, but their decision was reversed by the Circuit Court of Appeals, 30 F.2d 898. A writ of certiorari was granted by this Court.

By the contract, made in 1901, Earl and his wife agreed "that any property either of us now has or may hereafter acquire * * * in any way, either by earnings (including salaries, fees, etc.), or any rights by contract

---

portion of the earned income is transferred between spouses. Thus, if in a community property state, spouses are living apart for the year and file separate returns and one earns $50,000 and the other $20,000, § 66 requires them to report $50,000 and $20,000, respectively, rather than each reporting $35,000.

11  I.R.C. § 6013 permits this, even if one of the spouses has no gross income.

12  This is an artificial splitting only for tax purposes. Before 1971, the statutory splitting device was more apparent in the statute. Pre-1971, I.R.C. § 2(a) provided that, if a joint return was filed, "the tax imposed by section 1 shall be twice the tax which would be imposed if the taxable income were cut in half." The change was required by a reduction in tax rates applicable to unmarried taxpayers. See I.R.C. § 1(j)(2)(C). The origin of this statutory income-splitting device and computation questions concerning the several § 1 rate tables are further explored in Chapter 27A2, infra.

or otherwise, during the existence of our marriage, or which we or either of us may receive by gift, bequest, devise, or inheritance, and all the proceeds, issues, and profits of any and all such property shall be treated and considered and hereby is declared to be received, held, taken, and owned by us as joint tenants, and not otherwise, with the right of survivorship." The validity of the contract is not questioned, and we assume it to be unquestionable under the law of the State of California, in which the parties lived. Nevertheless we are of opinion that the Commissioner and Board of Tax Appeals were right.

The Revenue Act of 1918 * * * , imposes a tax upon the net income of every individual including "income derived from salaries, wages, or compensation for personal service * * * of whatever kind and in whatever form paid," § 213(a). The provisions of the Revenue Act of 1921, * * * , are similar to those of the above. A very forcible argument is presented to the effect that the statute seeks to tax only income beneficially received, and that taking the question more technically the salary and fees became the joint property of Earl and his wife on the very first instant on which they were received. We well might hesitate upon the latter proposition, because however the matter might stand between husband and wife he was the only party to the contracts by which the salary and fees were earned, and it is somewhat hard to say that the last step in the performance of those contracts could be taken by anyone but himself alone. But this case is not to be decided by attenuated subtleties. It turns on the import and reasonable construction of the taxing act. There is no doubt that the statute could tax salaries to those who earned them and provide that the tax could not be escaped by anticipatory arrangements and contracts however skilfully devised to prevent the salary when paid from vesting even for a second in the man who earned it. That seems to us the import of the statute before us and we think that no distinction can be taken according to the motives leading to the arrangement by which the fruits are attributed to a different tree from that on which they grew.

Judgment reversed.

■ The CHIEF JUSTICE took no part in this case.

## Commissioner v. Giannini

United States Court of Appeals, Ninth Circuit, 1942.
129 F.2d 638.

■ STEPHENS, CIRCUIT JUDGE.

Petition by the Commissioner of Internal Revenue for a review of a decision of the Board of Tax Appeals * * * to the effect that there is no deficiency in taxpayer's federal income tax for the year 1928.

The facts upon which the Commissioner relies in claiming a deficiency are as follows:

The taxpayer and his wife at all relevant times were husband and wife and were residents of California. The taxpayer was a Director and President of Bancitaly Corporation from 1919 until its dissolution after the tax year in question. From 1919 to 1925 he performed the services of these offices without compensation, and on January 22, 1925, the Board of Directors authorized a committee of three to devise a plan to compensate him, he in the meantime to have the privilege of drawing upon the corporation for his current expenditures.

On April 19th, 1927, the committee reported and on June 27th, 1927, the Directors unanimously approved the report. It was: "The committee as above met on Wednesday, April 13, 1927, at 2:00 o'clock, in Mr. Fagan's office, in the Crocker First National Bank, San Francisco, and unanimously agreed to, and hereby do, recommend to the directors of the Bancitaly Corporation that Mr. A.P. Giannini, for his services as President of your Corporation, be given 5% of the net profits each year, with a guaranteed minimum of $100,000 per year, commencing January 1, 1927, in lieu of salary."*

On November 20, 1927, the withdrawal account of taxpayer showed an indebtedness to the corporation of $215,603.76, and on that date his account was credited and the salary account on the books of the corporation was debited with the amount of $445,704.20, being the equivalent of 5% of the corporation net profits from January 1, 1927, to July 22, 1927.

In 1927 after the taxpayer learned the amount of the profits from January to July of that year and that he would receive $445,704.20 as his 5% thereof, the taxpayer informed members of the Board of Directors of the corporation that he would not accept any further compensation for the year 1927, and suggested that the corporation do something worthwhile with the money. The finding of the Board in this respect is that the refusal was "definite" and "absolute", and there is ample evidence in the record to support such finding.

The corporation never credited to the taxpayer or his wife any portion of the 5% of the net profits for the year 1927, other than the $445,704.20 above referred to, nor did it set any part of the same aside for the use of the taxpayer or his wife. The only action of the corporation in this respect is as follows:

On January 20, 1928, the Board of Directors of Bancitaly Corporation adopted a resolution reading in part as follows:

> "Whereas, this Corporation is prepared now to pay to Mr. A.P. Giannini for his services as its President and General Manager five per cent (5%) of the net profits of this Corporation computed from July 23, 1927 to the close of business January

---

\* About twenty years earlier the directors had voted Mr. Giannini, as founder and vice-president, a salary of $200 a month. Thomas and Witts, The San Francisco Earthquake, 41 (1971). Ed.

20, 1928, which five percent (5%) amounts to the sum of One Million Five Hundred Thousand Dollars ($1,500,000.00); and

"Whereas, Mr. A.P. Giannini refuses to accept any part of said sum but has indicated that if the Corporation is so minded he would find keen satisfaction in seeing it devote such a sum or any lesser adequate sum to the objects below enumerated or kindred purposes; and

"Whereas, we believe that this Corporation would do a great good and derive a great benefit from the establishment of a Foundation of Agricultural Economics at the University of California, and we believe that something should be done by this Corporation to evidence its appreciation of the fact that without the general confidence and hearty cooperation of the people of the State of California the great success of this Corporation would not have been possible * * * ;

* * *

"Now, Therefore, Be it Resolved, by the Board of Directors of this Corporation, that the aforesaid sum of One Million Five Hundred Thousand Dollars ($1,500,000.00) be set apart from the undivided profits of this Corporation in a Special Reserve Account for the purpose hereinafter described, and the whole of said sum be donated to the Regents of the University of California for the purpose of establishing a Foundation of Agricultural Economics; and

"Be it Further Resolved, that said donation be made in honor of Mr. A.P. Giannini, and that said Foundation shall be named after him; and

"Be it Further Resolved, that a Committee consisting of James A. Bacigalupi, P.C. Hale and A. Pedrini be appointed to confer with the President of the University of California, for the purpose of discussing and determining upon the general scope of said Foundation, and with full power of settling all details in connection therewith; * * *."

In accordance with said resolution the Corporation in February, 1928, submitted a written offer of contribution to the Regents of the University of California, and the offer was accepted. One deviation occurred in carrying out the plan, however, in that 5% of the profits of the Bancitaly Corporation for the period January 1, 1927, to January 20, 1928, less the sum of $445,704.20 credited to taxpayer amounted to $1,357,607.40 instead of the estimated $1,500,000.00, and the difference of $142,392.60 was paid by the taxpayer personally. There is no question in this appeal concerning this $142,392.60.

The taxpayer and his wife in reporting their income for taxation purposes in 1928 did not report any portion of the $1,357,607.40 paid to the Regents of the University of California by the Bancitaly Corporation as aforesaid, and it is the Commissioner's contention that one-half of said sum should be reported by each.* Based upon this theory the Commissioner assessed a deficiency of $137,343.50 in the case of the taxpayer in this appeal and a deficiency of $123,402.71 in the case of his wife. Separate appeals have been taken by each party, but it is stipulated by the parties that the decision in the wife's case is to abide the final decision in the case now before this court.

The Commissioner's argument in support of the claimed deficiency may be summarized as follows: That actual receipt of money or property is not always necessary to constitute taxable income; that it is the "realization" of taxable income rather than actual receipt which gives rise to the tax; that a taxpayer "realizes" income when he directs the disposition thereof in a manner so that it reaches the object of his bounty; that in the instant case the taxpayer had a right to claim and receive the whole 5% of the corporation profit as compensation for his services; and that his waiver of that right with the suggestion that it be applied to some useful purpose was such a disposition thereof as to render the taxpayer taxable for income "realized" in the tax year in which the suggestion is carried out. In connection with this latter argument the Commissioner states in his opening brief that "For the purposes of income tax it would seem immaterial whether the taxpayer waived his compensation, thus in effect giving it to Bancitaly Corporation, with the suggestion that it be applied to some useful purpose, or whether he failed to waive the right to receive the compensation and directed that it be paid to a donee of his choice." Again it is stated by the Commissioner, "Insofar as the question of taxation is concerned it would not seem to make much difference whether he directed Bancitaly Corporation to pay his compensation to the University of California or whether he merely told his employer to keep it."

Supplemental to the argument as above summarized, the Commissioner urges that the Board's finding that the money paid to the Foundation of Agricultural Economics as above set forth "was the property of Bancitaly and the petitioner [taxpayer] had no right, title or interest therein" is unsupported by the evidence; and that in any event such finding is an "ultimate finding" and therefore reviewable by this court under the rule announced in Commissioner v. Boeing, 9 Cir., 106 F.2d 305 and cases therein cited. We agree that the question of the effect of the taxpayer's unqualified refusal to take the compensation for his services is a question of law subject to review by this court. That question is the sole question presented by this appeal.

The taxpayer, on the other hand, urges that "A person has the right to refuse property proffered to him, and if he does so, absolutely and

---

\* Between the tax year involved in *Earl*, a principal case above, and this case, California became a community property state. The effect, reflected here, was actual income-splitting between husband and wife. Ed.

unconditionally, his refusal amounts to a renunciation of the proffered property, which, legally, is an abandonment of right to the property without a transfer of such right to another. Property which is renounced (i.e. abandoned) cannot be 'diverted' or 'assigned' by the renouncer, and cannot be taxed upon the theory that it was received."

The Commissioner takes issue with the argument of the taxpayer as above quoted by arguing that the amount involved was more than "property proffered to" the taxpayer, but was instead compensation which the taxpayer had a contractual right to receive. The point is that any disposition of this contractual right, whether it be by waiver, transfer, assignment or any other means, and whether it be before or after the rendition of the services involved, results in taxable income under the rules announced in the cases of Lucas v. Earl, 281 U.S. 111, 50 S.Ct. 241; Helvering v. Horst, 311 U.S. 112, 61 S.Ct. 144, 131 A.L.R. 655; Helvering v. Eubank, 311 U.S. 122, 61 S.Ct. 149; and Harrison v. Schaffner, 312 U.S. 579, 61 S.Ct. 759.

The *Earl* case arises out of an assignment of salary and attorneys fees by a husband to his wife in advance of the rendition of the services. It was claimed that the husband never beneficially received them, but the Court refused to follow this reasoning and held that "the tax could not be escaped by anticipatory arrangements and contracts however skillfully devised to prevent the salary when paid from vesting even for a second in the man who earned it". The gist of the decision appears to be that the salary was accepted, and the employee's dominance over it amounted to his receipt of it.

In the *Horst* case the taxpayer gave away interest bearing coupons, and the donee collected the interest during the taxpayer's taxable year. A conflict was asserted between the Circuit Court decision and the case of Lucas v. Earl, supra. In commenting upon the rule that income is not taxable until "realized", the Court * * * asserted that such rule is a rule of postponement of the tax to the final event of enjoyment, saying "income is 'realized' by the assignor * * * who owns or controls the source * * * controls the disposition * * * and diverts. * * * The donor [taxpayer] here, * * * has * * * by his act, procured payment of the interest, as a valuable gift * * *. Such a use * * * would seem to be the enjoyment of the income * * *."

In the *Eubank* case a life insurance agent, after terminating agency contracts, made assignments of renewal commissions payable to him for services rendered in procuring policies. The Court held the renewal commissions taxable to the assignor. Here again [in *Eubank*], the dominance over the fund by the assignor was shown.

In the *Schaffner* case the life beneficiary of a trust assigned to children income from the trust for the year following the assignment. In holding that the income was taxable to the assignor the Court analyzes and compares these three cited cases. The Court said * * * ,

"Since granting certiorari we have held, following the reasoning of Lucas v. Earl, supra, that one who is entitled to receive, at a future date, interest or compensation for services and who makes a gift of it by an anticipatory assignment, realizes taxable income quite as much as if he had collected the income and paid it over to the object of his bounty. Helvering v. Horst, 311 U.S. 112, 61 S.Ct. 144, 131 A.L.R. 655; Helvering v. Eubank, 311 U.S. 122, 61 S.Ct. 149."

Here again [in *Schaffner*] the dominance over the fund and taxpayer's direction show that he beneficially received the money by exercising his right to divert it to a use.

Now, turning again to the instant case. The findings of the Board, supported by the evidence, are to the effect that the taxpayer did not receive the money, and that he did not direct its disposition. All that he did was to unqualifiedly refuse to accept any further compensation for his services with the suggestion that the money be used for some worthwhile purpose. So far as the taxpayer was concerned, the corporation could have kept the money. All arrangements with the University of California regarding the donation to the Foundation were made by the corporation, the taxpayer participating therein only as an officer of the corporation.

In this circumstance we cannot say as a matter of law that the money was beneficially received by the taxpayer and therefore subject to the income tax provisions of the statute. It should be kept in mind that there is no charge of fraud in this case. It would be impossible to support the Commissioner in his contention that the money was received by the taxpayer without arriving at the conclusion that the taxpayer was acting in less than full and open frankness.[1] The Board rejects this suggestion and we see no occasion for drawing inferences from the evidence contrary to the plain intent of the testimony which is not disputed. To support the Commissioner's argument we should have to hold that only one reasonable inference could be drawn from the evidence, which is that the donation is but a donation of the taxpayer masquerading as a creature of the corporation to save the true donors [taxpayer and his wife] some tax money. The circumstances do not support this contention. In our opinion the inferences drawn by the Board are more reasonable and comport with that presumption of verity that every act of a citizen of good repute should be able to claim and receive.

Affirmed.

---

[1]  We say that the Commissioner's argument compels this conclusion for the reason that the claimed deficiency is for the tax year in which the donation was actually made to the Foundation. It should be recalled that the taxpayer's unqualified refusal to take any further compensation for his services in 1927 was made prior to December 31, 1927. If the Commissioner were earnestly taking the position that a waiver of compensation, with nothing more, is such an exercise of dominion over the moneys to be received as to render it taxable, it seems apparent that the deficiency if any would be in the year of the waiver, rather than some subsequent year in which the corporation disposes of the fund in some other manner.

■ [The concurring opinion of CIRCUIT JUDGE HEALY is omitted. Ed.]

# Revenue Ruling 66–167

1966–1 Cum.Bull. 20.

In the instant case, the taxpayer served as the sole executor of his deceased wife's estate pursuant to the terms of a will under which he and his adult son were each given a half interest in the net proceeds thereof. The laws of the state in which the will was executed and probated impose no limitation on the use of either principal or income for the payment of compensation to an executor and do not purport to deal with whether a failure to withdraw any particular fee or commission may properly be considered as a waiver thereof.

The taxpayer's administration of his wife's estate continued for a period of approximately three full years during which time he filed two annual accountings as well as the usual final accounting with the probate court, all of which reported the collection and disposition of a substantial amount of estate assets.

At some point within a reasonable time after first entering upon the performance of his duties as executor, the taxpayer decided to make no charge for serving in such capacity, and each of the aforesaid accountings accordingly omitted any claim for statutory commissions and was so filed with the intention to waive the same. The taxpayer-executor likewise took no other action which was inconsistent with a fixed and continuing intention to serve on a gratuitous basis.

The specific questions presented are whether the amounts which the taxpayer-executor could have received as fees or commissions are includible in his gross income for Federal income tax purposes and whether his waiver of the right to receive these amounts results in a gift for Federal gift tax purposes.

In Revenue Ruling 56–472, the executor of an estate entered into an agreement to serve in such capacity for substantially less than all of the statutory commissions otherwise allowable to him and also formally waived his right to receive the remaining portion thereof. The basic agreement with respect to his acceptance of a reduced amount of compensation antedated the performance of any services and the related waiver of the disclaimed commissions was signed before he would otherwise have become entitled to receive them. Under these circumstances, the ruling held that the difference between the commissions which such executor could have otherwise acquired an unrestricted right to obtain and the lesser amount which he actually received was not includible in his income and that his disclaimer did not effect any gift thereof.

In Revenue Ruling 64–225, the trustees of a testamentary trust in the State of New York waived their rights to receive one particular class of statutory commissions. This waiver was effected by means of certain formal instruments that were not executed until long after the close of most of the years to which such commissions related. This circumstance, along with all the other facts described therein, indicated that such trustees had not intended to render their services on a gratuitous basis. The Revenue Ruling accordingly held that such commissions were includible in the trustees' gross income for the taxable year when so waived and that their execution of the waivers also effected a taxable gift of these commissions.

The crucial test of whether the executor of an estate or any other fiduciary in a similar situation may waive his right to receive statutory commissions without thereby incurring any income or gift tax liability is whether the waiver involved will at least primarily constitute evidence of an intent to render a gratuitous service. If the timing, purpose, and effect of the waiver make it serve any other important objective, it may then be proper to conclude that the fiduciary has thereby enjoyed a realization of income by means of controlling the disposition thereof, and at the same time, has also effected a taxable gift by means of any resulting transfer to a third party of his contingent beneficial interest in a part of the assets under his fiduciary control * * *.

The requisite intention to serve on a gratuitous basis will ordinarily be deemed to have been adequately manifested if the executor or administrator of an estate supplies one or more of the decedent's principal legatees or devisees, or of those principally entitled to distribution of decedent's intestate estate, within six months after his initial appointment as such fiduciary, with a formal waiver of any right to compensation for his services. Such an intention to serve on a gratuitous basis may also be adequately manifested through an implied waiver, if the fiduciary fails to claim fees or commissions at the time of filing the usual accountings and if all the other attendant facts and circumstances are consistent with a fixed and continuing intention to serve gratuitously. If the executor or administrator of an estate claims his statutory fees or commissions as a deduction on one or more of the estate, inheritance, or income tax returns which are filed on behalf of the estate, such action will ordinarily be considered inconsistent with any fixed or definite intention to serve on a gratuitous basis. No such claim was made in the instant case.

Accordingly, the amounts which the present taxpayer-executor would have otherwise become entitled to receive as fees or commissions are not includible in his gross income for Federal income tax purposes, and are not gifts for Federal gift tax purposes.

Revenue Ruling 56–472 is clarified to remove any implication that, although an executor effectively waives his right to receive commissions, such commissions are includible in his gross income unless the waiver is executed prior to performance of any service.

Revenue Ruling 64–225 is distinguished.

## Revenue Ruling 74–581

1974–2 Cum.Bull. 25.

Advice has been requested concerning the Federal income tax treatment of payments received for services performed by a faculty member or a student of a university's school of law under the circumstances described below.

The university's school of law has as part of its regular teaching curriculum several clinical programs. The clinics include programs in Constitutional Litigation, Urban Legal Problems, Women's Rights, Prisoner's Rights and Corrections, and from time to time other clinical programs as well. Each program is supervised and conducted by full-time faculty members of the school of law's teaching staff.

At times, various clinics in the law school program handle criminal matters wherein faculty members are assigned as counsel. On occasion, the faculty member is appointed by a Federal District Court, * * * pursuant to the provisions of the Criminal Justice Act of 1964, as amended, 18 U.S.C.A. 3006A ("Criminal Justice Act"), which authorizes the payment of compensation of attorneys appointed to represent indigent defendants. In the cases for which an appointment under the Criminal Justice Act is made, the students in the clinical programs assist the attorney-faculty member in investigation of the case, research of the case, and preparation of the litigation papers as the case may require. In other circumstances, the individual student may be able to participate directly in the legal representation of the client pursuant to the newly promulgated rule of the United States Court of Appeals for the Third Circuit (Local Rule 9(2), Entry of Appearance by Eligible Law Students), or under similar rules in other jurisdictions.

When an attorney-faculty member is appointed in a criminal case by the Federal Courts pursuant to the Criminal Justice Act, the attorney is entitled to submit a voucher for the expenditure of time and for disbursements incident to the representation. With regard to the clinical programs of the law school, each faculty member has agreed, as a condition of participation in the program, that since the time spent in supervising work of students on these cases and in the representation of the client is part of the faculty member's teaching duties for which the faculty member is compensated by a total annual salary, all amounts received under the Criminal Justice Act will be endorsed over to the law school. The attorney-faculty members involved are working solely as agents of the law school, while supervising the law students within the scope of the clinical programs, and realize no personal gain from payments for their services in representing the indigent defendants.

Although the Criminal Justice Act itself does not specify that the monies may not be paid directly to the law school, the Clerk of the District Court has taken the generally acknowledged position that under the Criminal Justice Act payment cannot be arranged through the law school or its clinical programs. Therefore, as a matter of practice, the vouchers would be submitted by the attorney-faculty member to the appropriate Federal court in the name of the faculty member, and upon receipt of the check, he would endorse it over to the university's law school accounts.

Section 61(a) of the Internal Revenue Code of 1954 provides that, unless excluded by law, gross income means all income from whatever source derived including (but not limited to) compensation for services, including fees and similar items.

The Supreme Court of the United States has stated that the dominant purpose of the revenue laws is the taxation of income to those who earn or otherwise create the right to receive it and enjoy the benefit of it when paid. Helvering v. Horst, 311 U.S. 112 (1940), 1940–2 C.B. 296. Consistent with this, it is well established that a taxpayer's anticipatory assignment of a right to income derived from the ownership of property will not be effective to redirect that income to the assignee for tax purposes. See the *Horst* case and Lucas v. Earl, 281 U.S. 111 (1930).

However, the Internal Revenue Service has recognized that amounts that would otherwise be deemed income are not, in certain unique factual situations, subject to the broad rule of inclusion provided by section 61(a) of the Code.

For example, Rev.Rul. 65–282, 1965–2 C.B. 21, holds that statutory legal fees received by attorneys for representing indigent defendants are not includible in gross income where the attorneys, pursuant to their employment contracts, immediately turn the fees over to their employer, a legal aid society.

Rev.Rul. 58–220, 1958–1 C.B. 26, holds that the amount of the checks received by a physician from patients he has treated in the hospital by which he is employed full-time, which checks he is required to endorse over to the hospital, is not includible in his gross income.

Similarly, Rev.Rul. 58–515, 1958–2 C.B. 28, considers a situation where a police officer, in the performance of duties as an employee of the police department, entered into private employment for the purpose of obtaining certain information for the department. Pursuant to the rules and procedures of the department, the officer remitted to the police pension fund the compensation he received from the private employer. That Revenue Ruling holds that the officer was acting as an agent of the department while privately employed and that the compensation remitted to the pension fund is not includible in his gross income.

In similar circumstances, Rev.Rul. 69–274, 1969–1 C.B. 36, holds that faculty physicians of a medical school who provide medical services to indigent patients at a hospital are not required to include in their income fees collected and remitted to the university in accordance with the university policy and agreement.

Accordingly, in the instant case, amounts received for services performed by a faculty member or a student of the university's school of law under the clinical programs and turned over to the university are not includible in the recipient's income.

## PROBLEM

1.   Executive has a salaried position with Hi Rolling Corporation under which she earns $80,000 each calendar year.

(a)   Who is taxed if Executive, at the beginning of the year, directs that $20,000 of her salary be paid to her aged parents?

(b)   Who is taxed if Executive at the beginning of the year directs that $20,000 of her salary be paid to any charity the Board of Directors of Hi Rolling selects? (Executive is not a member of the Board.)

(c)   Same as (b), above, except that Executive makes the same request with respect to a $10,000 year-end bonus which Corporation has announced toward the end of the year, based on services rendered during the year?

(d)   Who is taxed if Executive, in her corporate role, gives a series of lectures on corporate finance at a local business school and, pursuant to her contract with Hi Rolling, turns her $1,000 honorarium over to Corporation?

## C.   INCOME FROM PROPERTY

### Helvering v. Horst

Supreme Court of the United States, 1940.
311 U.S. 112, 61 S.Ct. 144.

■ MR. JUSTICE STONE delivered the opinion of the Court.

The sole question for decision is whether the gift, during the donor's taxable year, of interest coupons detached from the bonds, delivered to the donee and later in the year paid at maturity, is the realization of income taxable to the donor.

In 1934 and 1935 respondent, the owner of negotiable bonds, detached from them negotiable interest coupons shortly before their due date and delivered them as a gift to his son who in the same year collected them at maturity. The Commissioner ruled that under the applicable § 22 of the Revenue Act of 1934, * * *, the interest payments were taxable, in the years when paid, to the respondent donor who reported his income on the cash receipts basis. The Circuit Court of Appeals reversed the order of the Board of Tax Appeals sustaining the tax. * * *. We granted certiorari, * * *, because of the importance of the question in the administration of the revenue laws and because of an asserted conflict in principle of the decision below with that of Lucas v. Earl, 281 U.S. 111, 50 S.Ct. 241, and with that of decisions by other circuit courts of appeals. * * *.

The court below thought that as the consideration for the coupons had passed to the obligor, the donor had, by the gift, parted with all control over them and their payment, and for that reason the case was distinguishable from *Lucas v. Earl, supra,* and *Burnet v. Leininger,* * * *, where the assignment of compensation for services had preceded the rendition of the services, and where the income was held taxable to the donor.

The holder of a coupon bond is the owner of two independent and separable kinds of right. One is the right to demand and receive at maturity the principal amount of the bond representing capital investment. The other is the right to demand and receive interim payments of interest on the investment in the amounts and on the dates specified by the coupons. Together they are an obligation to pay principal and interest given in exchange for money or property which was presumably the consideration for the obligation of the bond. Here respondent, as owner of the bonds, had acquired the legal right to demand payment at maturity of the interest specified by the coupons and the power to command its payment to others, which constituted an economic gain to him.

Admittedly not all economic gain of the taxpayer is taxable income. From the beginning the revenue laws have been interpreted as defining "realization" of income as the taxable event, rather than the acquisition of the right to receive it. And "realization" is not deemed to occur until the income is paid. But the decisions and regulations have consistently recognized that receipt in cash or property is not the only characteristic of realization of income to a taxpayer on the cash receipts basis. Where the taxpayer does not receive payment of income in money or property realization may occur when the last step is taken by which he obtains the fruition of the economic gain which has already accrued to him. *Old Colony Trust Co. v. Commissioner,* 279 U.S. 716, 49 S.Ct. 499; *Corliss v. Bowers,* 281 U.S. 376, 378, 50 S.Ct. 336. Cf. *Burnet v. Wells,* 289 U.S. 670, 53 S.Ct. 761.

In the ordinary case the taxpayer who acquires the right to receive income is taxed when he receives it, regardless of the time when his right to receive payment accrued. But the rule that income is not taxable until realized has never been taken to mean that the taxpayer, even on the cash receipts basis, who has fully enjoyed the benefit of the economic gain represented by his right to receive income, can escape taxation because he has not himself received payment of it from his obligor. The rule, founded on administrative convenience, is only one of postponement of the tax to the final event of enjoyment of the income, usually the receipt of it by the taxpayer, and not one of exemption from taxation where the enjoyment is consummated by some event other than the taxpayer's personal receipt of money or property. * * *. This may occur when he has made such use or disposition of his power to receive or control the income as to procure in its place other satisfactions which are of economic worth.

The question here is, whether because one who in fact receives payment for services or interest payments is taxable only on his receipt of the payments, he can escape all tax by giving away his right to income in advance of payment. If the taxpayer procures payment directly to his creditors of the items of interest or earnings due him, * * *, or if he sets up a revocable trust with income payable to the objects of his bounty, * * *, he does not escape taxation because he did not actually receive the money. * * *.

Underlying the reasoning in these cases is the thought that income is "realized" by the assignor because he, who owns or controls the source of the income, also controls the disposition of that which he could have received himself and diverts the payment from himself to others as the means of procuring the satisfaction of his wants. The taxpayer has equally enjoyed the fruits of his labor or investment and obtained the satisfaction of his desires whether he collects and uses the income to procure those satisfactions, or whether he disposes of his right to collect it as the means of procuring them. * * *.

Although the donor here, by the transfer of the coupons, has precluded any possibility of his collecting them himself, he has nevertheless, by his act, procured payment of the interest as a valuable gift to a member of his family. Such a use of his economic gain, the right to receive income, to procure a satisfaction which can be obtained only by the expenditure of money or property, would seem to be the enjoyment of the income whether the satisfaction is the purchase of goods at the corner grocery, the payment of his debt there, or such nonmaterial satisfactions as may result from the payment of a campaign or community chest contribution, or a gift to his favorite son. Even though he never receives the money, he derives money's worth from the disposition of the coupons which he has used as money or money's worth in the procuring of a satisfaction which is procurable only by the expenditure of money or money's worth. The enjoyment of the economic benefit accruing to him by virtue of his acquisition of the coupons is realized as completely as it would have been if he had collected the interest in dollars and expended them for any of the purposes named. * * *.

In a real sense he has enjoyed compensation for money loaned or services rendered, and not any the less so because it is his only reward for them. To say that one who has made a gift thus derived from interest or earnings paid to his donee has never enjoyed or realized the fruits of his investment or labor, because he has assigned them instead of collecting them himself and then paying them over to the donee, is to affront common understanding and to deny the facts of common experience. Common understanding and experience are the touchstones for the interpretation of the revenue laws.

The power to dispose of income is the equivalent of ownership of it. The exercise of that power to procure the payment of income to another is the enjoyment, and hence the realization, of the income by him who exercises it. We have had no difficulty in applying that proposition where the assignment preceded the rendition of the services, Lucas v. Earl, supra; Burnet v. Leininger, supra, for it was recognized in the Leininger case that in such a case the rendition of the service by the assignor was the means by which the income was controlled by the donor and of making his assignment effective. But it is the assignment by which the disposition of income is controlled when the service precedes the assignment, and in both cases it is the exercise of the power of disposition of the interest or compensation, with the resulting payment to the donee, which is the enjoyment by the donor of income derived from them.

This was emphasized in Blair v. Commissioner, 300 U.S. 5, 57 S.Ct. 330, on which respondent relies, where the distinction was taken between a gift of income derived from an obligation to pay compensation and a gift of income-producing property. In the circumstances of that case, the right to income from the trust property was thought to be so identified with the equitable ownership of the property, from which alone the beneficiary derived his right to receive the income and his power to command disposition of it, that a gift of the income by the beneficiary became effective only as a gift of his ownership of the property producing it. Since the gift was deemed to be a gift of the property, the income from it was held to be the income of the owner of the property, who was the donee, not the donor—a refinement which was unnecessary if respondent's contention here is right, but one clearly inapplicable to gifts of interest or wages. Unlike income thus derived from an obligation to pay interest or compensation, the income of the trust was regarded as no more the income of the donor than would be the rent from a lease or a crop raised on a farm after the leasehold or the farm had been given away. Blair v. Commissioner, supra, 12, 13 and cases cited. * * *. We have held without deviation that where the donor retains control of the trust property the income is taxable to him although paid to the donee. Corliss v. Bowers, supra. Cf. Helvering v. Clifford, supra.

The dominant purpose of the revenue laws is the taxation of income to those who earn or otherwise create the right to receive it and enjoy the benefit of it when paid. * * *. The tax laid by the 1934 Revenue Act upon income "derived from * * * wages, or compensation for personal service, of whatever kind and in whatever form paid, * * * ; also from interest * * * " therefore cannot fairly be interpreted as not applying to income derived from interest or compensation when he who is entitled to receive it makes use of his power to dispose of it in procuring satisfactions which he would otherwise procure only by the use of the money when received.

It is the statute which taxes the income to the donor although paid to his donee. Lucas v. Earl, supra; Burnet v. Leininger, supra. True, in those cases the service which created the right to income followed the assignment, and it was arguable that in point of legal theory the right to the compensation vested instantaneously in the assignor when paid, although he never received it; while here the right of the assignor to receive the income antedated the assignment which transferred the right and thus precluded such an instantaneous vesting. But the statute affords no basis for such "attenuated subtleties." The distinction was explicitly rejected as the basis of decision in Lucas v. Earl. It should be rejected here; for no more than in the Earl case can the purpose of the statute to tax the income to him who earns, or creates and enjoys it be escaped by "anticipatory arrangements however skillfully devised" to prevent the income from vesting even for a second in the donor.

Nor is it perceived that there is any adequate basis for distinguishing between the gift of interest coupons here and a gift of salary or commissions. The owner of a negotiable bond and of the investment which it represents, if not the lender, stands in the place of the lender. When, by the gift of the coupons, he has separated his right to interest payments from his investment and procured the payment of the interest to his donee, he has enjoyed the economic benefits of the income in the same manner and to the same extent as though the transfer were of earnings, and in both cases the import of the statute is that the fruit is not to be attributed to a different tree from that on which it grew. See Lucas v. Earl, supra, 115.

Reversed.

■ [The dissenting opinion of MR. JUSTICE MCREYNOLDS, in which the CHIEF JUSTICE and MR. JUSTICE ROBERTS concurred, has been omitted. Ed.]

## Blair v. Commissioner

Supreme Court of the United States, 1937.
300 U.S. 5, 57 S.Ct. 330.

■ MR. CHIEF JUSTICE HUGHES delivered the opinion of the Court.

[The taxpayer-petitioner owned an income interest in a trust for life. He assigned a portion of all of his future unearned income from the trust to his children. The Supreme Court concluded that under state law the taxpayer-petitioner had made a valid assignment of his interest in the trust. Ed.]

* * *

*Third.* The question remains whether, treating the assignments as valid, the assignor was still taxable upon the income under the federal income tax act. That is a federal question.

Our decisions in Lucas v. Earl, . . . , and Burnet v. Leininger, . . . , are cited. In the Lucas case the question was whether an attorney was taxable for the whole of his salary and fees earned by him in the tax years or only upon one-half by reason of an agreement with his wife by which his earnings were to be received and owned by them jointly. We were of the opinion that the case turned upon the construction of the taxing act. We said that "the statute could tax salaries to those who earned them and provide that the tax could not be escaped by anticipatory arrangements and contracts however skillfully devised to prevent the same when paid from vesting even for a second in the man who earned it." That was deemed to be the meaning of the statute as to compensation for personal service, and the one who earned the income was held to be subject to the tax. In Burnet v. Leininger, supra, a husband, a member of a firm, assigned future partnership income to his wife. We found that the revenue act dealt explicitly with the liability of partners as such. The wife did not become a member of the firm; the act specifically taxed the distributive share of each partner in the net income of the firm; and the husband by the fair import of the act remained taxable upon his distributive share. These cases are not in point. The tax here is not upon earnings which are taxed to the one who earns them. Nor is it a case of income attributable to a taxpayer by reason of the application of the income to the discharge of his obligation. * * * There is here no question of evasion or of giving effect to statutory provisions designed to forestall evasion; or of the taxpayer's retention of control. * * *

In the instant case, the tax is upon income as to which, in the general application of the revenue acts, the tax liability attaches to ownership. * * *.

The Government points to the provisions of the revenue acts imposing upon the beneficiary of a trust the liability for the tax upon the income distributable to the beneficiary.[1] But the term is merely descriptive of the one entitled to the beneficial interest. These provisions cannot be taken to preclude valid assignments of the beneficial interest, or to affect the duty of the trustee to distribute income to the owner of the beneficial interest, whether he was such initially or becomes such by valid assignment. The one who is to receive the income as the owner of the beneficial interest is to pay the tax. If under the law governing the trust the beneficial interest is assignable, and if it has been assigned without reservation, the assignee thus becomes the beneficiary and is entitled to rights and remedies accordingly. We find nothing in the revenue acts which denies him that status.

The decision of the Circuit Court of Appeals turned upon the effect to be ascribed to the assignments. The court held that the petitioner had no interest in the corpus of the estate and could not dispose of the income until he received it. Hence it was said that "the income was *his*" and his assignment was merely a direction to pay over to others what was due to himself. The question was considered to involve "the date when the income became transferable." * * *. The Government refers to the terms of the assignment,—that it was of the interest in the income "which the said party of the first part now is, or may hereafter be, entitled to receive during his life from the trustees." From this it is urged that the assignments "dealt only with a right to receive the income" and that "no

---

[1]  Revenue Acts of 1921, § 219(a)(d); 1924 and 1926, § 219(a)(b); 1928, § 162(a)(b). [See I.R.C. (1986) §§ 652(a) and 662(a)(1). Ed.]

attempt was made to assign any equitable right, title or interest in the trust itself." This construction seems to us to be a strained one. We think it apparent that the conveyancer was not seeking to limit the assignment so as to make it anything less than a complete transfer of the specified interest of the petitioner as the life beneficiary of the trust, but that with ample caution he was using words to effect such a transfer. That the state court so construed the assignments appears from the final decree which described them as voluntary assignments of interests of the petitioner "in said trust estate," and it was that aspect that petitioner's right to make the assignments was sustained.

The will creating the trust entitled the petitioner during his life to the net income of the property held in trust. He thus became the owner of an equitable interest in the corpus of the property. * * * By virtue of that interest he was entitled to enforce the trust, to have a breach of trust enjoined and to obtain redress in case of breach. The interest was present property alienable like any other, in the absence of a valid restraint upon alienation. * * * The beneficiary may thus transfer a part of his interest as well as the whole. See Restatement of the Law of Trusts, §§ 130, 132 et seq. The assignment of the beneficial interest is not the assignment of a chose in action but of the "right, title and estate in and to property." * * *

We conclude that the assignments were valid, that the assignees thereby became the owners of the specified beneficial interests in the income, and that as to these interests they and not the petitioner were taxable for the tax years in question. The judgment of the Circuit Court of Appeals is reversed and the cause is remanded with direction to affirm the decision of the Board of Tax Appeals.

Reversed.

## Estate of Stranahan v. Commissioner*

United States Court of Appeals, Sixth Circuit, 1973.
472 F.2d 867.

■ PECK, CIRCUIT JUDGE:

This appeal comes from the United States Tax Court, which partially denied appellant estate's petition for a redetermination of a deficiency in the decedent's income tax for the taxable period January 1, 1965 through November 10, 1965, the date of decedent's death.

The facts before us are briefly recounted as follows: On March 11, 1964, the decedent, Frank D. Stranahan, entered into a closing agreement with the Commissioner of Internal Revenue Service (IRS) under which it was agreed that decedent owed the IRS $754,815.72 for interest due to deficiencies in federal income, estate and gift taxes regarding several trusts created in 1932. Decedent, a cash-basis

---

* Some footnotes omitted.

taxpayer, paid the amount during his 1964 tax year. Because his personal income for the 1964 tax year would not normally have been high enough to fully absorb the large interest deduction, decedent accelerated his future income to avoid losing the tax benefit of the interest deduction. To accelerate the income, decedent executed an agreement dated December 22, 1964, under which he assigned to his son, Duane Stranahan, $122,820 in anticipated stock dividends from decedent's Champion Spark Plug Company common stock (12,500 shares). At the time both decedent and his son were employees and shareholders of Champion. As consideration for this assignment of future stock dividends, decedent's son paid the decedent $115,000 by check dated December 22, 1964. The decedent thereafter directed the transfer agent for Champion to issue all future dividend checks to his son, Duane, until the aggregate amount of $122,820 had been paid to him. Decedent reported this $115,000 payment as ordinary income for the 1964 tax year and thus was able to deduct the full interest payment from the sum of this payment and his other income. During decedent's taxable year in question, dividends in the total amount of $40,050 were paid to and received by decedent's son. No part of the $40,050 was reported as income in the return filed by decedent's estate for this period. Decedent's son reported this dividend income on his own return as ordinary income subject to the offset of his basis of $115,000, resulting in a net amount of $7,282 of taxable income.

Subsequently, the Commissioner sent appellant (decedent's estate) a notice of deficiency claiming that the $40,050 received by the decedent's son was actually income attributable to the decedent. After making an adjustment which is not relevant here, the Tax Court upheld the deficiency in the amount of $50,916.78. The Tax Court concluded that decedent's assignment of future dividends in exchange for the present discounted cash value of those dividends "though conducted in the form of an assignment of a property right, was in reality a loan to [decedent] masquerading as a sale and so disguised lacked any business purpose; and, therefore, decedent realized taxable income in the year 1965 when the dividend was declared paid."

As pointed out by the Tax Court, several long-standing principles must be recognized. First, under Section 451(a) of the Internal Revenue Code of 1954, a cash basis taxpayer ordinarily realizes income in the year of receipt rather than the year when earned. Second, a taxpayer who assigns future income for consideration in a bona fide commercial transaction will ordinarily realize ordinary income in the year of receipt. Commissioner v. P.G. Lake, Inc., 356 U.S. 260, 78 S.Ct. 691 (1958); Hort v. Commissioner, 313 U.S. 28, 61 S.Ct. 757 (1941). Third, a taxpayer is free to arrange his financial affairs to minimize his tax liability;[1] thus, the presence of tax avoidance motives will not nullify an otherwise bona

---

[1]  "Any one may so arrange his affairs that his taxes shall be as low as possible; he is not bound to choose that pattern which will best pay the Treasury; there is not even a patriotic duty to increase one's taxes." Helvering v. Gregory, 69 F.2d 809, 810 (2d Cir.1934) (Hand, J. Learned), aff'd 293 U.S. 465, 55 S.Ct. 266.

fide transaction.[2] We also note there are no claims that the transaction was a sham, the purchase price was inadequate or that decedent did not actually receive the full payment of $115,000 in tax year 1964. And it is agreed decedent had the right to enter into a binding contract to sell his right to future dividends. 12 Ohio Jur.2d, Corporations, Sec. 604.

The Commissioner's view regards the transaction as merely a temporary shift of funds, with an appropriate interest factor, within the family unit. He argues that no change in the beneficial ownership of the stock was effected and no real risks of ownership were assumed by the son. Therefore, the Commissioner concludes, taxable income was realized not on the formal assignment but rather on the actual payment of the dividends.

It is conceded by taxpayer that the sole aim of the assignment was the acceleration of income so as to fully utilize the interest deduction. Gregory v. Helvering, 293 U.S. 465, 55 S.Ct. 266 (1935), established the landmark principle that the substance of a transaction, and not the form, determines the taxable consequences of that transaction. * * *. In the present transaction, however, it appears that both the form and the substance of the agreement assigned the right to receive future income. What was received by the decedent was the present value of that income the son could expect in the future. On the basis of the stock's past performance, the future income could have been (and was) estimated with reasonable accuracy. Essentially, decedent's son paid consideration to receive future income. Of course, the fact of a family transaction does not vitiate the transaction but merely subjects it to special scrutiny. Helvering v. Clifford, 309 U.S. 331, 60 S.Ct. 554 (1940).

We recognize the oft-stated principle that a taxpayer cannot escape taxation by legally assigning or giving away a portion of the income derived from income producing property retained by the taxpayer. Lucas v. Earl, 281 U.S. 111, 50 S.Ct. 241 (1930); Helvering v. Horst, 311 U.S. 112, 61 S.Ct. 144 (1940); Commissioner v. P.G. Lake, Inc., supra. Here, however, the acceleration of income was not designed to avoid or escape recognition of the dividends but rather to reduce taxation by fully utilizing a substantial interest deduction which was available. As stated previously, tax avoidance motives alone will not serve to obviate the tax benefits of a transaction. Further, the fact that this was a transaction for good and sufficient consideration, and not merely gratuitous, distinguishes the instant case from the line of authority beginning with Helvering v. Horst, supra.

The Tax Court in its opinion relied on three cases. In Fred W. Warner, 5 B.T.A. 963 (1926), which involved an assignment by taxpayer

---

[2] "As to the astuteness of taxpayers in ordering their affairs so as to minimize taxes, we have said that 'the very meaning of a line in the law is that you intentionally may go as close to it as you can if you do not pass it.' Superior Oil Co. v. Mississippi, 280 U.S. 390, 395–396, [50 S.Ct. 169]. This is so because 'nobody owes any public duty to pay more than the law demands; taxes are enforced exactions, not voluntary contributions.'" Atlantic Coast Line v. Phillips, 332 U.S. 168, 172–173, 67 S.Ct. 1584, 1587 (1947) (Frankfurter, J.).

to his wife of all dividend income respecting his 12,500 shares of General Motors Corporation stock, it was held the dividends were income to the taxpayer and were not diverted to the wife through the purported assignment. However, this was a mere gratuitous assignment of income since apparently the only consideration for the assignment was ten dollars. Alfred Le Blanc, 7 B.T.A. 256 (1927), involved a shareholder-father assigning dividends to his son for as long as the son remained with the father's corporation. The Court held that in effect the father postdated his assignment to the dates when he was to receive dividends and hence the dividends were income to the father. However, here again it is apparent that at the time of the assignment there was no consideration.

* * *

[The third case is omitted. Ed.]

Hence the fact that valuable consideration was an integral part of the transaction distinguishes this case from those where the simple expedient of drawing up legal papers and assigning income to others is used. The Tax Court uses the celebrated metaphor of Justice Holmes regarding the "fruit" and the "tree", and concludes there has been no effective separation of the fruit from the tree. Judge Cardozo's comment that "[m]etaphors in law are to be narrowly watched, for starting as devices to liberate thought, they end often by enslaving it" (Berkey v. Third Avenue Railway Co., 244 N.Y. 84, 94, 155 N.E. 58, 61 (1926)) is appropriate here, as the genesis of the metaphor lies in a gratuitous transaction, while the instant situation concerns a transaction for a valuable consideration.

The Commissioner also argues that the possibility of not receiving the dividends was remote, and that since this was particularly known to the parties as shareholders and employees of the corporation, no risks inured to the son. The Commissioner attempts to bolster this argument by pointing out that consideration was computed merely as a discount based on a prevailing interest rate and that the dividends were in fact paid at a rate faster than anticipated. However, it seems clear that risks, however remote, did in fact exist. The fact that the risks did not materialize is irrelevant. Assessment of the risks is a matter of negotiation between the parties and is usually reflected in the terms of the agreement. Since we are not in a position to evaluate those terms, and since we are not aware of any terms which dilute the son's dependence on the dividends alone to return his investment, we cannot say he does not bear the risks of ownership.

Accordingly, we conclude the transaction to be economically realistic, with substance, and therefore should be recognized for tax purposes even though the consequences may be unfavorable to the Commissioner. The facts established decedent did in fact receive payment. Decedent deposited his son's check for $115,000 to his personal account on

December 23, 1964, the day after the agreement was signed. The agreement is unquestionably a complete and valid assignment to decedent's son of all dividends up to $122,820. The son acquired an independent right against the corporation since the latter was notified of the private agreement. Decedent completely divested himself of any interest in the dividends and vested the interest on the day of execution of the agreement with his son.

The Commissioner cites J.A. Martin, 56 T.C. 1255 (1971), aff'd No. 72–1416 (5th Cir., August 18, 1972), to show how similar attempts to accelerate income have been rejected by the courts. There taxpayer assigned future rents in return for a stated cash advance. Taxpayer agreed to repay the principal advanced plus a 7% per annum interest. These facts distinguish this situation from the instant case as there the premises were required to remain open for two years' full rental operation, suggesting a guarantee toward repayment. No such commitment is apparent here.

The judgment is reversed and the cause remanded for further proceedings consistent with this opinion.

## Salvatore v. Commissioner

Tax Court of the United States, 1970.
29 T.C.M. 89.

■ FEATHERSTON, JUDGE:

Respondent determined a deficiency in petitioner's income tax for 1963 in the amount of $31,016.60. The only issue presented for decision is whether petitioner is taxable on all or only one-half of the gain realized on the sale of certain real property in 1963.

Findings of Fact

Petitioner was a legal resident of Greenwich, Connecticut, at the time her petition was filed. She filed an individual Federal income tax return for 1963 with the district director of internal revenue, Hartford, Connecticut.

Petitioner's husband operated an oil and gas service station in Greenwich, Connecticut, for a number of years prior to his death on October 7, 1948. His will, dated December 6, 1941, contained the following pertinent provisions:

> SECOND: I give devise and bequeath all of my estate both real and personal of whatsoever the same may consist and wheresoever the same may be situated of which I may die possessed or be entitled to at the time of my decease, to my beloved wife, SUSIE SALVATORE, to be hers absolutely and forever.

> I make no provision herein for my beloved children because I am confident that their needs and support will be provided for by my beloved wife.

* * *

> FOURTH: I hereby give my Executors full power to sell any and all of my property in their discretion and to execute any and all necessary deed or deeds of conveyance of my said property or any part or parts thereof, and which said deed or deeds, conveyance or assignment so executed by my Executors shall be as good and effectual to pass the title to the property therein described and conveyed as if the same had been executed by me in my lifetime.

For several years after her husband's death petitioner's three sons, Amedeo, Eugene, and Michael, continued operating the service station with the help of her daughter Irene, who kept the books of the business. Sometime prior to 1958, however, Michael left the service station to undertake other business endeavors; and in 1958 Eugene left to enter the real estate business, leaving Amedeo alone to manage and operate the service station.

During this period and until 1963, petitioner received $100 per week from the income of the service station. This sum was not based on the fair rental of the property, but was geared to petitioner's needs for her support. The remaining income was divided among the family members who worked in the business.

The land on which the service station was located became increasingly valuable. Several major oil companies from time to time made purchase proposals, which were considered by members of the family. Finally, in the early summer of 1963 representatives of Texaco, Inc. (hereinafter Texaco), approached Amedeo regarding the purchase of the service station property. Petitioner called a family conference and asked for advice on whether the property should be sold. Realizing that Amedeo alone could not operate the station at peak efficiency, petitioner and her children decided to sell the property if a reasonable offer could be obtained.

Amedeo continued his negotiations with Texaco and ultimately received an offer of $295,000. During the course of the negotiations Eugene discovered that tax liens in the amount of $8,000 were outstanding against the property. In addition, there was an outstanding mortgage, securing a note held by Texaco, on which approximately $50,000 remained unpaid. The family met again to consider Texaco's offer.

As a result of the family meeting (including consultation with petitioner's daughter Geraldine, who lived in Florida), it was decided that the proposal should be accepted and that the proceeds should be used, first, to satisfy the tax liens and any other outstanding liabilities. Second, petitioner was to receive $100,000, the estimated amount needed to generate income for her life of about $5,000 per year—the approximate equivalent of the $100 per week she previously received out of the service station income. Third, the balance was to be divided equally among the five children. To effectuate this family understanding, it was agreed that petitioner would first convey a one-half interest in the property to the children and that deeds would then be executed by petitioner and the children conveying the property to Texaco.

On July 24, 1963, petitioner formally accepted Texaco's offer by executing an agreement to sell the property to Texaco for $295,000, the latter making a down payment of $29,500. Subsequently, on August 28, 1963, petitioner executed a warranty deed conveying an undivided one-half interest in the property to her five children. This deed was received for record on September 6, 1963. By warranty deeds dated August 28 and 30, 1963, and received for record on September 6, 1963, petitioner and her five children conveyed their interest in the property to Texaco; Texaco thereupon tendered $215,582.12, the remainder of the purchase price less the amount due on the outstanding mortgage.

Petitioner filed a Federal gift tax return for 1963, reporting gifts made to each of her five children on August 1, 1963, of a $1/10$ interest in the property and disclosing a gift tax due in the amount of $10,744.35.

After discharge of the mortgage and the tax liens the remaining proceeds of the sale (including the down payment) amounted to $237,082, of which one-half, $118,541, was paid to petitioner. From the other half of the proceeds the gift tax of $10,744.35 was paid and the balance was distributed to the children.

In her income tax return for 1963 petitioner reported as her share of the gain from the sale of the service station property a long-term capital gain of $115,063 plus an ordinary gain of $665. Each of the children reported in his 1963 return a proportionate share of the balance of the gain.

In the notice of deficiency respondent determined that petitioner's gain on the sale of the service station property was $238,856, all of which was taxable as long-term capital gain. Thereafter each of petitioner's children filed protective claims for refund of the taxes which they had paid on their gains from the sale of the service station property.

Opinion

The only question is whether petitioner is taxable on all or only one-half of the gain realized from the sale of the service station property. This issue must be resolved in accordance with the following principle stated by the Supreme Court in Commissioner v. Court Holding Co., 324 U.S. 331, 334, 65 S.Ct. 707 (1945):

"The incidence of taxation depends upon the substance of a transaction. The tax consequences which arise from gains from a sale of property are not finally to be determined solely by the means employed to transfer legal title. Rather, the transaction must be viewed as a whole, and each step, from the commencement of negotiations to the consummation of the sale, is relevant. *A sale by one person cannot be transformed for tax purposes into a sale by another by using the latter as a conduit through which to pass title.* To permit the true nature of a transaction to be disguised by mere formalisms, which exist solely to alter tax liabilities, would seriously impair the effective administration of the tax policies of Congress." [Footnote omitted. Emphasis added.]

\* \* \*

The evidence is unmistakably clear that petitioner owned the service station property prior to July 24, 1963, when she contracted to sell it to Texaco. Her children doubtless expected ultimately to receive the property or its proceeds, either through gifts or inheritance, and petitioner may have felt morally obligated to pass it on to them. But at that time the children "held" no property interest therein.[1] Petitioner's subsequent conveyance, unsupported by consideration, of an undivided one-half interest in the property to her children—all of whom were fully aware of her prior agreement to sell the property—was merely an intermediate step in the transfer of legal title from petitioner to Texaco; petitioner's children were only "conduit[s] through which to pass title." That petitioner's conveyance to the children may have been a bona fide completed gift prior to the transfer of title to Texaco, as she contends, is immaterial in determining the income tax consequences of the sale, for the form of a transaction cannot be permitted to prevail over its substance. In substance, petitioner made an anticipatory assignment to her children of one-half of the income from the sale of the property.

The artificiality of treating the transaction as a sale in part by the children is confirmed by the testimony by petitioner's witnesses that the sum retained by her from the sale was a computed amount—an amount sufficient to assure that she would receive income in the amount of approximately $5,000 annually. If the sales price had been less, petitioner would have retained a larger percentage of the proceeds; if more, we infer, she would have received a smaller percentage.[2] While the

---

[1]   Sec. 1221, I.R.C.1954, defines the term "capital asset" to mean "property held by the taxpayer."

[2]   Eugene Salvatore testified as follows:

Q. You stated that you wanted one hundred thousand dollars for your mother. That is, this was to be her share, more or less?

A. Yes.

Q. If the property was sold for one hundred thousand dollars would your mother have kept all the money?

A. She had to.

Q. She would have?

A. She would have kept all the money.

Q. Because she needed the money to live on the interest?

children's desire to provide for their mother's care and petitioner's willingness to share the proceeds of her property with her children during her lifetime may be laudable, her tax liabilities cannot be altered by a rearrangement of the legal title after she had already contracted to sell the property to Texaco.

All the gain from sale of the service station property was taxable to petitioner. We find nothing in Oscar Deinert, 11 B.T.A. 651 (1928), or Charles W. Walworth, 6 B.T.A. 788 (1927), cited by petitioner, which requires an opposite conclusion.

Decision will be entered for the respondent.

## Revenue Ruling 69–102
### 1969–1 Cum.Bull. 32.

Advice has been requested by an individual with respect to the Federal income tax consequences to him upon the maturity and surrender for their cash surrender values of an endowment life insurance contract and an annuity contract under the circumstances described below.

In the instant case, the taxpayer sold an unencumbered endowment life insurance contract to a charitable organization described in section 170(c) of the Internal Revenue Code of 1954 for an amount equal to his basis therein, net aggregate of premiums or other consideration paid less dividends received, donating his remaining interest to the charity. [Since 1969 such a transaction would require an allocation of taxpayer's basis between the portion sold to a charity and the portion given so that there would be a taxable gain on these facts at the time of the transfer. Section 1011(b). See Section 1011(b) and Chapter 23B, infra at page 808. Ed.] At the same time he made a gift of an unencumbered annuity contract to his son. In the donor's succeeding taxable year both contracts matured and were surrendered by the donees to the insurance company for their then cash surrender values. The cash surrender value of each contract at the time of the transfers to the donees exceeded the amount of the donor's basis. In accordance with the terms of the policy, the insurance company was notified of its assignment and provided with the name and address of the new owners.

Section 1.61–1 of the Income Tax Regulations provides, in part, that gross income includes income realized in any form. It is well established that income is taxable to the person who realizes it, the incidence of the tax not being shifted by a gift thereof to another. Lucas v. Guy C. Earl, 281 U.S. 111 (1930). Also, it has been pointed out that "one who is entitled to receive at a future date, interest or compensation for services and who

---

A. Because we felt she needed it to live on.

Q. The children would have got nothing?

A. If she got $90 a week the five children would have made up the difference. We felt she needed the money to live on.

makes a gift of it by an anticipatory assignment, realizes taxable income quite as much as if he had collected the income and paid it over to the object of his bounty" and "the power to dispose of income is the equivalent of ownership of it and * * * the exercise of the power to procure its payment to another, whether to pay a debt or to make a gift, is within the reach of the statute taxing income 'derived from any source whatever.' " Harrison v. Sarah H. Schaffner, 312 U.S. 579 (1941), Ct.D. 1503, C.B. 1941–1, 321, 322. The Tax Court of the United States has held that "The theory of the cases dealing with anticipatory assignment of income by gift has not been concerned with when the income was accrued in a legal sense of accrual but rather with whether the income has been earned so that the right to the payment at a future date existed when the gift was made. * * *. It is the giving away of this right to income in advance of payments which has been held not to change the *incidence* of the tax." (Emphasis added.) S.M. Friedman v. Commissioner, 41 T.C. 428, 435, affirmed 346 F.2d 506 (1965).

As to the time of realization, the Supreme Court of the United States has said, "Where the taxpayer does not receive payment of income in money or property realization may occur when the last step is taken by which he obtains the fruition of the economic gain *which has already accrued to him.*" (Emphasis added.) Helvering v. Paul R.G. Horst, 311 U.S. 112, 115 (1940), Ct.D. 1472, C.B. 1940–2, 206, 207. It follows that the time of the gift is not determinative of the time when income is realized. It has been consistently held that a gift of income does not operate to accelerate the year of taxability. See the *Friedman* case, above, wherein the following was said (p. 436):

> "A cash basis taxpayer is not taxable on income until he receives it actually or constructively. The making of a gift of his right to receive income does not cause such income to be received until the donor derives the economic benefit of having the income received by his donee. * * *."

* * *

In the instant case, it is held that the taxpayer is in receipt of taxable income for the taxable year in which the endowment and annuity contracts were surrendered for their cash surrender values by the recipients, the amount of such income being the excess of the cash surrender value of each contract at the time of gift over the taxpayer's basis in that contract. The gain realized through the transfer of the contracts is ordinary income. Commissioner v. Percy W. Phillips, et al., 275 F.2d 33 (1960).

The excess of the fair market value of the endowment contract sold to the charitable organization over the amount received therefor is the measure of the charitable contribution for the taxable year in which the contract was transferred.

## NOTE

The "fruit-tree" tax area is a very large orchard indeed, stretching out over many acres not visible from the vantage point of materials included in this Chapter.[1]

At this point of time the *Horst* case seems easy. The owner of the tree picks some fruit and gives it to another who converts it to cash. As the owner has kept the tree that produces the fruit, the tree's produce (interest later paid) remains his for tax purposes, even though economically it has become the property of another. Rev.Rul. 69–102, set out above, is illuminating as to the period for which the owner must report the income thus attributed to him. In both the *Blair* and the *Stranahan* cases, the fruit that was transferred to other persons was taxed to those other persons. Why? How do you distinguish *Blair* from *Horst*? And how do you distinguish *Stranahan* from *Horst*?

If the owner gives away the tree (the bond itself in the *Horst* setting), the donee in general is taxable on fruit subsequently produced (later interest payments), because he has become the owner of the income-producing property itself. But what if there is ripe fruit hanging on the tree at the time of the gift? Rev.Rul. 69–102, set out above, has a message here, also, and see Austin v. Commissioner.[2] In many instances, however, it is difficult to say what should be regarded as fruit. Mere appreciation in the value of the property (the tree) is not fruit until it is realized. What further concept was applied, then, to tax Susie Salvatore on the gain on the sale of the property? Can appreciation ripen into fruit?

In Campbell v. Prothro[3] the taxpayer raised calves. On May 7 he transferred 100 head of calves by written instrument to a charitable donee.[4] The donated calves were never physically separated from the rest of the calves. On June 8 taxpayer and the charitable donee entered into a contract to sell the entire calf crop to a third party. The court held that gain on the sale of the calves given to the charity could not be attributed to the donor. Rejecting the Commissioner's argument that no gift in fact occurred prior to the sale, the court went on to say:[5]

> We find ourselves in agreement with appellees' views. In the Horst case, the father, when the coupons on the bonds involved had become, or were about to become due, gave them to his son who collected them, and the court there properly held that the gift constituted an anticipatory assignment of the interest as income, within the Lucas-Earl rule (Lucas v. Earl, 281 U.S. 111, 50 S.Ct.

---

[1]    The classic work in the orchard is Lyon and Eustice, "Assignment of Income: Fruit and Tree as Irrigated by the P.G. Lake Case," 17 Tax L.Rev. 293 (1962); supplemented in Eustice, "Contract Rights, Capital Gain, and Assignment of Income—The Ferrer Case," 20 Tax L.Rev. 1 (1964).

[2]    161 F.2d 666 (6th Cir.1947), cert. denied 332 U.S. 767, 68 S.Ct. 75 (1947).

[3]    209 F.2d 331 (5th Cir.1954).

[4]    The fact that the donee was a charity makes no difference with respect to the ripeness of income issue raised by the case. However, since 1969 the charitable deduction question in cases of this sort is sharply affected by I.R.C. § 170(e)(1)(A). See Chapter 23B, infra.

[5]    Campbell v. Prothro, supra note 3 at 335–336.

241). It was not there held, nor has any case cited to or found by us held that if both principal and interest are given, and the principal matures in the year of the assignment, there would be an anticipatory assignment of income as to the principal, so as to make the giver taxable on unrealized appreciation in its value, or on interest accruing in successive years. Indeed, the contrary has been held in Austin v. Commissioner of Internal Revenue, 6 Cir., 161 F.2d 666.

Here the facts are entirely different from those of any of the cited cases. Here not interest due on choses in action in the year in which the assignment is made, but calves, chattels, whose value would be realized only by a sale, were given. We have found no case, we have been referred to none holding that unrealized appreciation in the value of cattle given away would be regarded as ordinary income merely because they had no base, were kept for sale in the ordinary course of business, and when sold by the taxpayer would have been ordinary income. * * *.

\* \* \*

Were the calves when transferred by gift to the Y.M.C.A. realized income to the appellees in the taxable sense? We think it clear that they were not. If they were, then every appreciation in value of property passing by gift is realized income. We know that this is not so, and that, though it is and has been the contention of the Bureau that it ought to be, Congress has never enacted legislation so providing.

If appellant's position is sustained here, it must be because the calves were already income to the taxpayers. If in their hands the calves were then their income, of course the making of the gift did not change this status. If they were not income in taxpayers' hands, their gift of them could not, in the present state of the law, result in the receipt of income by them. It is true that efforts have been made to procure the enactment of statutes to change the rule that a gift does not make the donor taxable on unrealized appreciation in the value of the property given. Congress has so far not adopted, indeed has declined to adopt that view. Under the statutes as they exist, the court may not do so. The judgment is right. It is affirmed.

The opposite result was reached in the distinguishable case of Tatum v. Commissioner.[6] In *Tatum* taxpayers owned land which they leased to sharecroppers who paid their rent in the form of a portion of the crops produced. Had the rent been payable in cash or in any form other than crop shares, the landlord would have had to report the rent as gross income for the year of receipt. However, Reg. § 1.61–4(a), a reporting regulation, permits a landlord to defer reporting crop share rent until the year in which such crops are reduced to money or the equivalent of money. Taxpayer landlords upon receiving the crops immediately transferred them to a

---

[6]    400 F.2d 242 (5th Cir.1968).

charitable donee, which sold them in the same year. The court agreed with the Commissioner that the value of the crops was required to be included in taxpayers' income and differentiated Campbell v. Prothro, saying:[7]

> Turning to the question of law we conclude that crop shares in the hands of the landlord essentially are income assets, taxable when reduced to money or the equivalent of money, rather than, like crops in the hands of a farmer, appreciated property items not taxable if assigned to a third party prior to the realization of any income.
>
> An operating farmer who donates crops to a third party prior to a taxable event, and prior to the point at which he must recognize income, is not required to include the value of the crops in gross income. Rev.Rul. 55–138, supra; Rev.Rul. 55–531, supra. The farmer has done nothing more than assign to another a property asset which has appreciated in value. There has been no taxable event. Neither the harvesting of the crop nor the donative transfer is a taxable event. E.g., Campbell v. Prothro, supra. Thus far Congress has not seen fit to tax unrealized appreciation in property value.
>
> The share-crop landlord, on the other hand, enters an agreement with his tenant whereby the tenant is given the use of the land in return for a share of the crops produced. When the crops are harvested and delivered the landlord has been paid in kind for the use of his land. Crop shares representing payment by the tenant for the use of the land are rental income assets no less than money paid for the same purpose.

\* \* \*

> For present purposes it is enough to say that crop shares are potential income assets, not property, and that a landlord may not avoid taxation by assigning his rights to the income prior to the reduction of the crop shares to money or its equivalent. The assignment of income principles of Helvering v. Horst, supra, and the rule of Treas.Reg. § 1.61(a) are applicable to this case and dispositive of the issues it presents.

The *Tatum* case was followed in Parmer v. Commissioner;[8] and now the Treasury also accepts the timing principles expressed in *Tatum*.[9] Usually, of course, realization of income by the donee fixes the donor's time of reporting in assignment of income cases. The *Tatum* case and its followers differentiate *Horst* on this issue, which at least subsumed that the donor of income (ripe fruit) property should take it into income just as and when he would if he had made no gift and had in fact received the income. The difference lies in the peculiar nature of crop shares which *are* realized income but which, as a

---

[7]  Id. at 246–248.

[8]  468 F.2d 705 (10th Cir.1972); cf. Harold N. Sheldon, 62 T.C. 96 (1974).

[9]  Rev.Rul. 75–11, 1975–1 C.B. 27, partially repudiating Rev.Rul. 63–66, 1963–1 C.B. 13.

matter of administrative convenience, are not required to be reported until converted into money or its equivalent.

Under an extension of the fruit-tree metaphor, it is not just fruit but *ripe* fruit that may leave a donor taxable on post-transfer income. Generally a determination of ripeness is simple, at least once we get the hang of it. Thus in *Tatum,* crop shares in hand represent realized income just waiting around to be taxed. If the income generated by property accrues ratably over time, that portion accrued at the time of the gift is likewise ripe. For example, if interest on a coupon bond is payable semi-annually on January 1 and July 1 and a donor transfers the bond (not just the coupon) on April 1 midway between payment dates, one-half of the current interest coupon is "ripe" as of the time of the transfer and one-half the amount of the coupon is taxed to the donor and the other one-half is taxed to the donee, generally upon payment.[10] This same principle applies to rents, interest on bank accounts and other items that accrue or are generated merely by the passage of time. Dividends on stock create a more difficult problem. They do not automatically accrue with time but are dependent on a decision by the Board of Directors to issue dividends. Consequently, for business purposes a relevant date must be determined on which ownership of the stock fixes the right to the dividend, the so-called "record" date. There are normally four important dates with respect to the issuance of dividends: the declaration date, the record date, the payment date and the date of actual receipt. Sometimes, especially in a closely held corporation,[11] two dates, possibly the record and payment dates, coincide. In one such case[12] the court held that the fruit ripened on the declaration date, taxing the dividend to a donor who made a gift of the stock the day before the record date. But the case involved a small, closely held corporation. In contrast, in Bishop v. Shaughnessy,[13] involving a minority shareholder of a more widely held corporation, the court reached the conclusion that the fruit ripened on the record date because no enforceable right accrued to any shareholder at the time of the dividend declaration. Is this distinction between closely held and more widely held corporations justified? Are we confronted with conflicting doctrines on assignment of dividend income or merely with divergent tax results sometimes called for, especially in close family circumstances, under the broad rubric of sham transactions?

## PROBLEMS

1.   Father owns land which he purchased several years ago for $80,000. It has a current fair market value of $90,000. Father leases the land on a ten-year lease and is paid $6,000 of rent each year, semi-annually April 1st and October 1st (i.e., $3,000 each payment), for the prior six months use of the land. What tax consequences to Father and Daughter in the following alternative situations?

---

[10]  The timing depends upon the donor's and donee's accounting methods. See Chapter 19, infra.

[11]  E.g. Smith's Estate v. Commissioner, 292 F.2d 478 (3d Cir.1961).

[12]  Ibid.

[13]  195 F.2d 683 (2d Cir.1952).

(a)  On April 2 of the current year, Father assigns Daughter all the future rental payments.

(b)  On April 2, Father gives Daughter the land with the right to all the future rental payments.

(c)  On April 2, Father gives Daughter a one-half interest in the land and the right to all the future rental payments.

(d)  Father owns an income interest in a trust which owns the land and on April 2, Father gives his income interest (the right to the succeeding rental payments) to Daughter.

(e)  On December 31, Father gives Daughter the land with the right to all the future rental payments.

(f)  On April 2, Father sells Daughter the right to the two succeeding rental payments for $5,000, their fair market value as of the time of sale.

(g)  On April 2, Father sells the land and directs that the $90,000 sale price be paid to Daughter.

(h)  Prior to April 2, Father negotiates the above sale and on April 2 he transfers the land to Daughter who transfers the land to Buyer who pays Daughter the $90,000.

2.  Determine who is taxed on the lottery winnings below if:

(a)  Lucky purchases a lottery ticket and gives it to Child prior to the lottery winner being announced. The ticket is the winning lottery ticket.

(b)  Same as (a), above, except that Lucky's gift occurs after the lottery winner is announced.

(c)  Lucky wins the lottery, but properly elects (see § 451(h)) to be taxed on the lottery winnings in the form of an annuity each year for 20 years. After 2 years of annuity payments, Lucky gives the remaining 18 years of payments to Child.

3.  Inventor develops a new electric switch which she patents. Who is taxed on the proceeds of its subsequent sale if:

(a)  The patent is transferred gratuitously to Son who sells it to Buyer?

(b)  Inventor transfers all her interest in the patent to Buyer for a royalty contract and then transfers the contract gratuitously to Son prior to receiving any royalties? See Heim v. Fitzpatrick, 262 F.2d 887 (2d Cir.1959).

# CHAPTER 13

# INCOME PRODUCING ENTITIES

## A. INTRODUCTION

The Internal Revenue Code recognizes three principal types of income producing entities: partnerships, corporations and trusts. To what extent do they lend themselves to income fragmentation with an eye toward tax savings? As seen in Chapter 12, individual taxpayers historically have encountered a progressive tax rate structure under which higher rates are applicable to additional amounts of taxable income.[1] Graduated rates provide an incentive to shift income producing assets to family members subject to lower rates and to utilize partnerships, corporations and trusts as vehicles to fragment income so as to sidestep the higher rates.[2]

Since the Tax Reform Act of 1986, the top tax rate for individuals has always remained below 40 percent. As seen in Chapter 12, lower and flatter individual rates reduce some of the tax incentive for fragmenting income directly. An entity, such as a partnership, a limited liability company, an S corporation, a corporation, or a trust, potentially is a vehicle for fragmenting income in order to achieve tax savings. The ability to successfully achieve tax savings using an entity depends upon several factors. An initial question is whether the entity will have to pay a tax on its income or whether it is viewed as a conduit with the investors bearing the total tax burden at their tax rates? If the entity is taxable, the next question is how high are the entity's tax rates and how do those rates compare to the individual rates. And if the entity is taxed, an additional consideration is whether the investors must bear a second tax, and at what rates, when they receive distributions of profits from the entity? The answers to these questions require an examination of the current rates and the basic tax characteristics of each entity.

The current rate structures[3] are compressed into seven rates (10, 12, 22, 24, 32, 35, and 37 percent) with respect to individuals,[4] into four rates (10, 24, 35, and 37 percent) for trusts and estates,[5] and a single flat 21 percent rate in the case of corporations. The reduced flattened rates for individuals plus "the kiddie tax," a special provision for taxing the

---

[1]  See Chapter 12A, supra.

[2]  For illustrative purposes, if a taxpayer in a 37% tax rate bracket could transfer some of the taxpayer's income to another individual or entity in a 10% bracket, the taxpayer would reduce the amount of tax on the income by over 70%.

[3]  I.R.C. §§ 1(j)(2)(A)–(E), 11.

[4]  I.R.C. § 1(j)(2)(A)–(D).

[5]  I.R.C. § 1(j)(2)(E). Trusts pay a maximum 37 percent rate when their taxable income exceeds $12,500, adjusted for inflation after 2018. See I.R.C. § 1(j)(3).

unearned income of a child generally under age 18 (24 if a student),[6] at trust rates, serve to reduce, if not eliminate, much of the tax benefit of fragmenting income among individuals. However, the low 21 percent corporate tax rate, which became effective in 2018, has made a corporation a tax-preferred entity and will likely spark interest in using a corporation as a vehicle to operate a business. Congress, however, enacted a new 20 percent deduction for business income earned in pass-through entities (e.g., a partnership, a limited liability company, or an S corporation) to help offset the attractiveness of the low corporate rate.[7]

The tax rate structures, the double tax on corporations and their shareholders, the special 20 percent deduction for business earned by pass-through entities,[8] and the special rates that you will learn about for net capital gains and qualified dividends,[9] all play a part in the broader "choice-of-entity" question. That is, the decision about which type of entity to employ when involved in a venture. In addition to tax, state law distinctions among the various entities, such as protection from personal liability, centralization of management, transferability of interests, and access to capital markets also must be considered in selecting the best entity for operating an enterprise. The routine tax treatment of and detailed measures designed to prevent the tax abuse of each entity, as well as choice-of-entity considerations, are large areas of study usually relegated to separate courses. This part of this Chapter describes the basic tax characteristics of each entity, and the parts that follow explore some income assignment questions with respect to each.

*Partnerships.* The Internal Revenue Code provisions that present special rules for income earned by partnerships appear in Subchapter K, Sections 701 through 761. A partnership is essentially a conduit for income tax purposes, because it is required to file only an information return reporting its annual income or loss,[10] and the income is taxed to, or the loss deducted by the various partners, individually even if there is no actual distribution of income to any partner.[11] A partnership's "taxable income" is computed under Section 703, but this is for the purpose of allocating taxable amounts among the members, as "[p]ersons carrying on business as partners shall be liable for income tax only in their separate or individual capacities."[12] The amount of any partnership income that a partner is required to include in gross income produces an

---

[6]   I.R.C. § 1(g), (j)(4). See Chapter 27A5, infra.

[7]   I.R.C. § 199A. See Chapter 27A3, infra.

[8]   Id.

[9]   See Chapter 21B and 27A4, infra.

[10]   Form 1065 required by I.R.C. § 6031. See I.R.C. § 6698 imposing a penalty for failure to file a timely partnership tax return even though the return is only informational.

A partnership may be treated as an entity for procedural purposes. See I.R.C. §§ 6221–6241. These rules are designed to assure uniformity of treatment of items by all members of a single partnership. Certain partnerships with 100 or fewer partners may elect to be excluded from these rules. I.R.C. § 6221(a)(1).

[11]   I.R.C. § 702.

[12]   I.R.C. § 701.

increase in the basis of the partner's interest in the partnership.[13] And when there is a distribution to a partner, the symmetry is complete as the distribution, to the extent of the partner's basis in the partnership interest, generally is not included in income but serves only to reduce that basis.[14]

In general, the tax impact of partnership transactions on each individual partner is determined by the partnership agreement. With some exceptions, such private agreements fix a "partner's distributive share of income, gain, loss, deduction, or credit * * *."[15]

Certain "publicly traded partnerships" are not treated as partnerships. They are instead classified as corporations for tax purposes with the same tax consequences as are applicable to corporations.[16]

The partnership form of doing business is of course very flexible; almost everything depends upon what is agreed to by the members. The tax laws take account of such flexibility and, to a great extent, give effect to the private agreements made. When transactions are at arm's length, this works rather well. But the obvious question here is to what extent family members may make agreements at variance with economic reality and then seek to insist that such agreements be accorded tax recognition. Is there, at least at first blush, an invitation to income assignment?

*Limited Liability Companies.* A more recent statutorily concocted business entity is a limited liability company which has been created by statutes in every state. It is essentially a partnership with limited liability, and it is generally treated as a partnership for federal tax purposes.[17]

*Corporations.* The Internal Revenue Code provisions that provide special rules for the income taxation of corporations and shareholders

---

[13] I.R.C. § 705(a)(1).

[14] I.R.C. §§ 705(a)(2), 731(a)(1), 733.

[15] I.R.C. § 704(a).

[16] I.R.C. § 7704. A publicly traded partnership is any partnership whose interests are traded on an established securities market or are readily tradeable on a secondary market (or its substantial equivalent). I.R.C. § 7704(b). There is an important exception to such reclassification if 90 percent or more of the partnership's gross income for all years after 1987 consists of various types of passive income items (interest, dividends, rent from real property, gains from the sale of real property, and income and gains from certain natural resource activities). I.R.C. § 7704(c). Publicly traded partnerships in existence as of December 17, 1987 are allowed to elect noncorporate treatment by paying a 3.5 percent tax on gross income from the active conduct of a trade or business. I.R.C. § 7704(g).

[17] Historically the question of partnership vs. corporate classification for federal tax purposes depended upon a number of factors spelled out in what were commonly known as the *Kintner* regulations. As of January 1, 1997, the Treasury adopted Reg. § 301.7701–1–3 which now allows any unincorporated entity other than a publicly traded partnership to elect to be treated as either a partnership or a corporation for federal taxation purposes. The regulations are commonly referred to as the "check-the-box" regulations. See generally, Field, "Checking in on 'Check-the-Box'", 42 Loy. L.A. L.Rev. 451 (2009). The validity of the check-the-box regulations has been upheld in Littriello v. United States, 484 F.3d 372 (6th Cir. 2007), cert. denied 552 U.S. 1186, 128 S.Ct. 1290 (2008); McNamee v. Treasury, 488 F.3d 100 (2d Cir. 2007); and Medical Practice Solutions v. Commissioner, 132 T.C. 125 (2009); aff'd in unpublished decision 2010–2 U.S.T.C. ¶ 50,584 (1st Cir. 2010); cert. denied, Britton v. Comm'r, 563 U.S. 1034 (2011).

appear in Subchapter C, Sections 301 through 385. A corporation is at the opposite end of the tax spectrum from a partnership. A corporation is an entity that is taxed under Section 11 at a 21 percent rate applicable only to corporations. When corporate after-tax income is distributed as dividends to shareholders, it is taxed (again?) to the shareholders in their individual capacities.[18] A corporate distribution is a dividend only to the extent of the corporation's "earnings and profits," earnings of the current year or accumulated from prior years.[19] A preferential 15 or 20 percent rate generally applies to "qualified dividend income," which is defined as including most dividend distributions.[20] These lower rates are designed to alleviate the total tax burden on distributions of profits taxed at the corporate and then the shareholder levels.

While a partner is not insulated from partnership income for tax purposes, a shareholder usually is insulated from the income of a corporation. In general, a corporation is an entity separate and apart from its shareholders.[21] Therefore, the incorporation of a partnership or sole proprietorship is itself a fragmentation device, because a new taxpayer has come upon the scene. But is this invariably a tax advantage? Recall the tax treatment of corporate distributions in combination with the taxation of the corporate entity. Are there double fragmentation possibilities with respect to income earned by corporations?[22]

*S Corporations.* A corporation that qualifies as a "small business corporation", one with not more than 100 shareholders, can elect, with unanimous shareholder consent, to be an S corporation,[23] rather than a C corporation, which is discussed above.[24] The provisions of Subchapter S, while quite complex in detail, can be summarized in a simple fashion. In general, with two exceptions,[25] an S corporation is not subject to

---

[18] I.R.C. §§ 61(a)(7), 301.

[19] I.R.C. § 316.

[20] I.R.C. § 1(h)(1)(C) and (D), (3)(B), (11). See Chapter 27A4.

[21] The exceptions are a corporation that is treated as a mere sham and ignored, United States v. McGuire, 249 F.Supp. 43 (S.D.N.Y.1965), and an "S Corporation." An S Corporation is a corporation that elects under Subchapter S of the Code generally to be taxed as a conduit. I.R.C. §§ 1361–1379.

[22] The student should be fully aware that many assignment of income problems in the business area are largely ignored here. See, e.g., I.R.C. § 482, authorizing the commissioner to reallocate income, deductions, etc., among related taxpayers; § 269, disallowing some expected tax benefits questionably sought by way of corporate acquisitions and transfers; § 1561, denying various tax benefits to some multiple incorporations.

[23] See I.R.C. § 1361, especially § 1361(b)(1)(A). See Coven and Hess, "The Subchapter S Revision Act: An Analysis and Appraisal," 50 Tenn.L.Rev. 569 (1983); Grant, "Subchapter S Corporation vs. Partnerships as Investment Vehicles," 36 U.S.C. Inst. on Fed. Tax'n 13 (1984); Maine, "Evaluating Subchapter S in a 'Check-the-Box' World," 51 Tax Law. 717 (1998); August, "Benefits and Burdens of Subchapter S in a Check-the-Box World," 4 Fla. Tax Rev. 287 (1999).

[24] Subchapter S, I.R.C. §§ 1361–1379, govern the tax treatment of S corporations. See I.R.C. § 1362(a).

[25] I.R.C. §§ 1374 and 1375.

income tax;[26] it simply pays no tax on its income.[27] In this respect it is much like a partnership. Each shareholder must take into account the shareholder's pro rata share of the S corporation's income for the shareholder's taxable year in which the taxable year of the S corporation ends.[28] Since there is in general no corporate tax on such income, what we have here then is a quantitative and qualitative[29] conduit whereby the income constructively passes through the S corporation to be taxed to the shareholders ratably for each taxable year. There need not be any actual distribution of any amount of income to any shareholder. The amount of S corporation income that the shareholder is required to include in gross income effects an increase in the basis of the shareholder's stock.[30] And the symmetry is complete when we consider an actual S corporation distribution of money to its respective shareholders. In that circumstance, its distribution to the extent of the shareholder's basis in the shareholder's stock[31] is not included in income but serves only to reduce that basis.

The point can now be made that with respect to S corporations and their shareholders there is no double taxation. There generally is only one tax and that is at the shareholder level.[32]

*Trusts.* For tax purposes a trust falls between a partnership and a corporation. Depending upon the circumstances, the income from a trust may be taxed to the beneficiaries, to the trust, or in part to each. The Internal Revenue Code provisions that present special rules for the determination of tax liability on income earned by trusts (and decedents' estates) appear in Subchapter J, Sections 641 through 692. While quite successful in fitting trusts and estates into a comprehensive scheme of federal taxation, the provisions are highly complex. But this is not to say the area should be completely ignored in a course on tax fundamentals. The objectives here are two-fold: first, to describe very generally the way in which trust and estate income is taxed and second, as in the partnership and corporate area, to look in just a little more detail at specified circumstances in which Congress prescribes a departure from the usual trust rules in order to prevent tax abuses that could arise out of questionable income assignment devices.

Congress has identified a trust as a tax-paying entity whose tax liability is generally determined in a manner similar to that of

---

[26] I.R.C. § 1363(a).

[27] See I.R.C. § 1363(b).

[28] I.R.C. § 1366(a). Similarly if an S corporation has a loss, it passes through to the shareholders. Id.

[29] Id.; see I.R.C. § 1366(b).

[30] I.R.C. § 1367(a).

[31] I.R.C. § 1368(b)(1). Since it is regarded as a tax-free recovery of tax-paid dollars with respect to the shareholder, only to the extent that a distribution by an S corporation exceeds stock basis is the shareholder subjected to income tax with respect to distributions. I.R.C. § 1368(b)(2).

[32] I.R.C. § 1366(a).

individuals.[33] On the other hand, a basic aspect of congressional policy is that trust income is to be taxed only once on its way into the hands of its beneficial owners. A further aspect of the plan, seemingly inconsistent with the objective of taxing trust income but once, is to tax trust beneficiaries on amounts of trust income to which they are entitled or which are in fact properly distributed to them.[34] If income may be taxed to the beneficiaries *and* to the trust, how is the one tax objective to be accomplished? The answer is a distribution deduction for the trust, commensurate with the amount of its income which is distributed and taxed to the beneficiaries.[35] In determining the *taxable* income of the trust, a deduction is allowed generally for amounts required to be, or otherwise properly paid to beneficiaries. In effect, *such* income escapes tax at the trust level but is taxed to the beneficiaries.[36]

It will be observed that in the case of what is called a "simple" trust (essentially one required to distribute all its income currently) the trust, while a *potential* taxable entity, serves as little more than a conduit for both tax and non-tax purposes, simply funneling income to the trust beneficiaries. In other trusts, known as "complex" trusts, where all or a part of the trust income may be accumulated, all or a part of the income may be taxed to the trust and none or only a part of the income to beneficiaries. Consider, then, how a trust appears to present a double fragmentation opportunity somewhat similar to that noted with respect to corporations.

This general description can be extended without getting into too much detail. The statute operates with regard to trust income for the taxable year of the trust.[37] The objective is a division of the tax on such *annual* income between the trust and its beneficiaries. Some students will see a difference from the corporate approach in which previously accumulated (not just current) earnings and profits affect the taxability of corporate distributions.

In another respect, however, the trust provisions resemble the corporate rules. For trust purposes a "distributable net income" of the trust is determined annually,[38] which is somewhat similar to *current* corporate earnings and profits in its regulation of the *amount* on which distributees may be subject to tax.[39] In effect D.N.I., as it is often called, identifies a kind of net income for the year, which could be taxed entirely to the trust or partly or entirely to beneficiaries. However, in the trust (and estate) area, this quantitative objective is not the sole function of

---

[33] I.R.C. § 641.

[34] I.R.C. §§ 652, 662.

[35] I.R.C. §§ 651, 661.

[36] These broad comments apply equally to the income of estates and their beneficiaries. See I.R.C. § 641.

[37] There are possible abusive uses of the trust not discussed here. See I.R.C. §§ 665–668.

[38] I.R.C. § 643(a).

[39] I.R.C. §§ 651(b), 652(a), 661(a), 662(a).

D.N.I. In keeping with an essentially conduit approach to the taxation of trust income, D.N.I. is seen as made up of the various *kinds* of income received by the trust, and distributions are considered to consist of ratable portions of each *kind* of income.[40] In this respect, D.N.I. serves a characterization or *qualitative* function in addition to its quantitative function. Thus, if a trust properly distributes half its income to a beneficiary and if half of the trust's income is tax-exempt interest, one half of what the beneficiary receives retains its tax-exempt character in the beneficiary's hands.[41]

One should note the compressed tax rate schedule applicable to trusts (and estates) in Section 1(j)(2)(E) and compare that with the rate schedule applicable to individuals generally in Section 1(j)(2)(A) through (D). In this respect, the 1986 legislative history stated:[42]

> The committee believes that the tax benefits which result from the ability to split income between a trust or estate and its beneficiaries should be eliminated or significantly reduced. On the other hand, the committee believes that significant changes in the taxation of trusts and estates are unnecessary to accomplish this result. Accordingly, the bill attempts to reduce the benefits arising from the use of trusts and estates by revising the rate schedule applicable to trusts and estates so that retained income of the trust or estate will not benefit significantly from a progressive tax rate schedule that might otherwise apply. This is accomplished by reducing the amount of income that must be accumulated by a trust or estate before that income is taxed at the top marginal rate. The committee believes that these changes will significantly reduce the tax benefits inherent in the present law rules of taxing trusts and estates while still retaining the existing structure of taxing these entities.[43]

A detailed description of the federal income tax characteristics of each of these three types of entities is beyond the scope of this book. Such details, however, are well supplied in McKee, Nelson and Whitmire, *Federal Taxation of Partnerships and Partners* (Warren, Gorham and Lamont); Willis, Pennell and Postlewaite, *Partnership Taxation* (Warren, Gorham and Lamont); Bittker and Eustice, *Federal Income Taxation of Corporations and Shareholders* (Warren, Gorham and Lamont); and Ferguson, Freeland, and Ascher, *Federal Income Taxation of Estates, Trusts, and Beneficiaries* (Aspen), in large part as applicable to trusts as to estates.

---

[40] I.R.C. §§ 652(b), 662(b); see also § 661(b) and Reg. § 1.651(b)–1.

[41] Recall, e.g., the tax-exempt nature of some bond interest under I.R.C. § 103. See Chapter 11D, supra.

[42] Sen.Rep.No. 99–313, 99th Cong., 2d Sess. 868 (1986).

[43] The current trust and estate tax rate schedule is discussed in note 5, supra. Ed.

# B. PARTNERSHIPS*

Internal Revenue Code: Sections 701; 704(e); 761(b). See Sections 1(g); 707(c).

Regulations: Sections 1.704–1(e)(1)(i), (2)(i).

---

## Commissioner v. Culbertson

Supreme Court of the United States, 1949.
337 U.S. 733, 69 S.Ct. 1210.

■ MR. CHIEF JUSTICE VINSON delivered the opinion of the Court.

This case requires our further consideration of the family partnership problem. The Commissioner of Internal Revenue ruled that the entire income from a partnership allegedly entered into by respondent and his four sons must be taxed to respondent,[1] and the Tax Court sustained that determination. The Court of Appeals for the Fifth Circuit reversed. 168 F.2d 979. We granted certiorari, 335 U.S. 883, to consider the Commissioner's claim that the principles of Commissioner v. Tower, 327 U.S. 280, 66 S.Ct. 532 (1946), and Lusthaus v. Commissioner, 327 U.S. 293, 66 S.Ct. 539 (1946), have been departed from in this and other courts of appeals decisions.

Respondent taxpayer is a rancher. From 1915 until October 1939, he had operated a cattle business in partnership with R.S. Coon. Coon, who had numerous business interests in the Southwest and had largely financed the partnership, was 79 years old in 1939 and desired to dissolve the partnership because of ill health. To that end, the bulk of the partnership herd was sold until, in October of that year, only about 1,500 head remained. These cattle were all registered Herefords, the brood or foundation herd. Culbertson wished to keep these cattle and approached Coon with an offer of $65 a head. Coon agreed to sell at that price, but only upon condition that Culbertson would sell an undivided one-half interest in the herd to his four sons at the same price. His reasons for imposing this condition were his intense interest in maintaining the Hereford strain which he and Culbertson had developed, his conviction that Culbertson was too old to carry on the work alone, and his personal interest in the Culbertson boys. Culbertson's sons were enthusiastic about the proposition, so respondent thereupon bought the remaining cattle from the Coon and Culbertson partnership for $99,440. Two days later Culbertson sold an undivided one-half interest to the four boys, and the following day they gave their father a note for $49,720 at 4 per cent interest due one year from date. Several months later a new note for

---

*   See Note, "Family Partnerships and the Federal Income Tax," 41 Ind.L.J. 684 (1966); Lifton, "The Family Partnership: Here We Go Again," 7 Tax L.Rev. 461 (1952).

[1]   Gladys Culbertson, the wife of W.O. Culbertson, Sr., is joined as a party because of her community of interest in the property and income of her husband under Texas law.

$57,674 was executed by the boys to replace the earlier note. The increase in amount covered the purchase by Culbertson and his sons of other properties formerly owned by Coon and Culbertson. This note was paid by the boys in the following manner:

Credit for overcharge ................................................... $ 5,930

Gifts from respondent ..................................................... 21,744

One-half of a loan procured by Culbertson & Sons
   partnership.................................................................... 30,000

The loan was repaid from the proceeds from operation of the ranch.

The partnership agreement between taxpayer and his sons was oral. The local paper announced the dissolution of the Coon and Culbertson partnership and the continuation of the business by respondent and his boys under the name of Culbertson & Sons. A bank account was opened in this name, upon which taxpayer, his four sons and a bookkeeper could check. At the time of formation of the new partnership, Culbertson's oldest son was 24 years old, married, and living on the ranch, of which he had for two years been foreman under the Coon and Culbertson partnership. He was a college graduate and received $100 a month plus board and lodging for himself and his wife both before and after formation of Culbertson & Sons and until entering the Army. The second son was 22 years old, was married and finished college in 1940, the first year during which the new partnership operated. He went directly into the Army following graduation and rendered no services to the partnership. The two younger sons, who were 18 and 16 years old respectively in 1940, went to school during the winter and worked on the ranch during the summer.[2]

The tax years here involved are 1940 and 1941. A partnership return was filed for both years indicating a division of income approximating the capital attributed to each partner. It is the disallowance of this division of the income from the ranch that brings this case into the courts.

*First.* The Tax Court read our decisions in Commissioner v. Tower, supra, and Lusthaus v. Commissioner, supra, as setting out two essential tests of partnership for income-tax purposes: that each partner contribute to the partnership either vital services or capital originating with him. Its decision was based upon a finding that none of respondent's sons had satisfied those requirements during the tax years in question. Sanction for the use of these "tests" of partnership is sought in this paragraph from our opinion in the *Tower* case:

"There can be no question that a wife and a husband may, under certain circumstances, become partners for tax, as for other,

---

[2]   A daughter was also made a member of the partnership some time after its formation upon the gift by respondent of one-quarter of his one-half interest in the partnership. Respondent did not contend before the Tax Court that she was a partner for tax purposes.

purposes. If she either invests capital originating with her or substantially contributes to the control and management of the business, or otherwise performs vital additional services, or does all of these things she may be a partner as contemplated by 26 U.S.C. §§ 181, 182. The Tax Court has recognized that under such circumstances the income belongs to the wife. A wife may become a general or a limited partner with her husband. But when she does not share in the management and control of the business, contributes no vital additional service, and where the husband purports in some way to have given her a partnership interest, the Tax Court may properly take these circumstances into consideration in determining whether the partnership is real within the meaning of the federal revenue laws." 327 U.S. at 290, 66 S.Ct. at 537.

It is the Commissioner's contention that the Tax Court's decision can and should be reinstated upon the mere reaffirmation of the quoted paragraph.

The Court of Appeals, on the other hand, was of the opinion that a family partnership entered into without thought of tax avoidance should be given recognition tax-wise whether or not it was intended that some of the partners contribute either capital or services during the tax year and whether or not they actually made such contributions, since it was formed "with the full expectation and purpose that the boys would, in the future, contribute their time and services to the partnership."[3] We must consider, therefore, whether an intention to contribute capital or services sometime in the future is sufficient to satisfy ordinary concepts of partnership, as required by the *Tower* case. The sections of the Internal Revenue Code involved are §§ 181 and 182,[4] which set out the method of taxing partnership income, and §§ 11 and 22(a),[5] which relate to the taxation of individual incomes.

In the *Tower* case we held that, despite the claimed partnership, the evidence fully justified the Tax Court's holding that the husband, through his ownership of the capital and his management of the business, actually created the right to receive and enjoy the benefit of the income and was thus taxable upon that entire income under §§ 11 and 22(a). In such case, other members of the partnership cannot be considered "Individuals carrying on business in partnership" and thus "liable for income tax * * * in their individual capacity" within the meaning of § 181. If it is conceded that some of the partners contributed neither capital nor services to the partnership during the tax years in

---

[3]  168 F.2d 979 at 982. The court further said: "Neither statute, common sense, nor impelling precedent requires the holding that a partner must contribute capital or render services to the partnership prior to the time that he is taken into it. These tests are equally effective whether the capital and the services are presently contributed and rendered or are later to be contributed or to be rendered." Id. at 983. See Note, 47 Mich.L.Rev. 595.

[4]  26 U.S.C.A. §§ 181, 182.

[5]  26 U.S.C.A. §§ 11, 22(a).

question, as the Court of Appeals was apparently willing to do in the present case, it can hardly be contended that they are in any way responsible for the production of income during those years.[6] The partnership sections of the Code are, of course, geared to the sections relating to taxation of individual income, since no tax is imposed upon partnership income as such. To hold that "Individuals carrying on business in partnership" includes persons who contribute nothing during the tax period would violate the first principle of income taxation: that income must be taxed to him who earns it. * * *.

Furthermore, our decision in Commissioner v. Tower, supra, clearly indicates the importance of participation in the business by the partners during the tax year. We there said that a partnership is created "when persons join together their money, goods, labor, or skill for the purpose of carrying on a trade, profession, or business and when there is community of interest in the profits and losses." Id. at 286. This is, after all, but the application of an often iterated definition of income—the gain derived from capital, from labor, or from both combined[7]—to a particular form of business organization. A partnership is, in other words, an organization for the production of income to which each partner contributes one or both of the ingredients of income—capital or services. * * *. The intent to provide money, goods, labor or skill sometime in the future cannot meet the demands of §§ 11 and 22(a) of the Code that he who presently earns the income through his own labor and skill and the utilization of his own capital be taxed therefor. The vagaries of human experience preclude reliance upon even good faith intent as to future conduct as a basis for the present taxation of income.[8]

*Second.* We turn next to a consideration of the Tax Court's approach to the family partnership problem. It treated as essential to membership in a family partnership for tax purposes the contribution of either "vital services" or "original capital."[9] Use of these "tests" of partnership

---

[6]  Of course one who has been a bona fide partner does not lose that status when he is called into military or government service, and the Commissioner has not so contended. On the other hand, one hardly becomes a partner in the conventional sense merely because he might have done so had he not been called.

[7]  Eisner v. Macomber, 252 U.S. 189, 207, 40 S.Ct. 189 (1920); Merchants' Loan & Trust Co. v. Smietanka, 255 U.S. 509, 519, 41 S.Ct. 386 (1921). See Treas.Reg. 101, Art. 2(a)–1. See 1 Mertens, Law of Federal Income Taxation, 159 et seq.

[8]  The *reductio ad absurdum* of the theory that children may be partners with their parents before they are capable of being entrusted with the disposition of partnership funds or of contributing substantial services occurred in Tinkoff v. Commissioner, 120 F.2d 564, where a taxpayer made his son a partner in his accounting firm the day the son was born.

[9]  While the Tax Court went on to consider other factors, it is clear from its opinion that a contribution of either "vital services" or "original capital" was considered essential to membership in the partnership. After finding that none of respondent's sons had, in the court's opinion, contributed either, the court continued: "In addition to the above inquiry as to the presence of those elements deemed by the *Tower* case essential to partnerships recognizable for Federal tax purposes, * * *." 6 CCH TCM 692, 699. Again, the court commented:

"Though, the petitioner urges that many cattle businesses are composed of fathers and sons, and that the nature of the industry so requires, we think the same is probably equally true of other industries where men wish to take children into business with them. Nevertheless, we think that fact does not override the many decisions to the

indicates, at best, an error in emphasis. It ignores what we said is the ultimate question for decision, namely, "whether the partnership is real within the meaning of the federal revenue laws" and makes decisive what we described as "circumstances [to be taken] into consideration" in making that determination.[10]

The *Tower* case thus provides no support for such an approach. We there said that the question whether the family partnership is real for income-tax purposes depends upon

> "whether the partners really and truly intended to join together for the purpose of carrying on business and sharing in the profits or losses or both. And their intention in this respect is a question of fact, to be determined from testimony disclosed by their 'agreement, considered as a whole, and by their conduct in execution of its provisions.' Drennen v. London Assurance Corp., 113 U.S. 51, 56, 5 S.Ct. 341; Cox v. Hickman, 8 H.L.Cas. 268. We see no reason why this general rule should not apply in tax cases where the Government challenges the existence of a partnership for tax purposes." 327 U.S. at 287, 66 S.Ct. at page 536.

The question is not whether the services or capital contributed by a partner are of sufficient importance to meet some objective standard supposedly established by the *Tower* case, but whether, considering all the facts—the agreement, the conduct of the parties in execution of its provisions, their statements, the testimony of disinterested persons, the relationship of the parties, their respective abilities and capital contributions, the actual control of income and the purposes for which it is used, and any other facts throwing light on their true intent—the parties in good faith and acting with a business purpose intended to join together in the present conduct of the enterprise.[11] There is nothing new

---

general effect that partners must contribute capital originating with them, or vital services." Id. at 700.

[10] See Mannheimer and Mook, A Taxwise Evaluation of Family Partnerships, 32 Iowa L.Rev. 436, 447–48.

[11] This is not, as we understand it, contrary to the approach taken by the Bureau of Internal Revenue in its most recent statement of policy. I.T. 3845, 1947 Cum.Bull. 66, states at p. 67:

> "Where persons who are closely related by blood or marriage enter into an agreement purporting to create a so-called family partnership or other arrangement with respect to the operation of a business or income-producing venture, under which agreement all of the parties are accorded substantially the same treatment and consideration with respect to their designated interests and prescribed responsibilities in the business as if they were strangers dealing at arm's length; where the actions of the parties as legally responsible persons evidence an intent to carry on a business in a partnership relation; and where the terms of such agreement are substantially followed in the operation of the business or venture, as well as in the dealings of the partners or members with each other, it is the policy of the Bureau to disregard the close family relationship existing between the parties and to recognize, for Federal income tax purposes, the division of profits as prescribed by such agreement. However, where the instrument purporting to create the family partnership expressly provides that the wife or child or other member of the family shall not be required to participate in the management of the business, or is merely silent on that point, the extent and nature

or particularly difficult about such a test. Triers of fact are constantly called upon to determine the intent with which a person acted.[12] The Tax Court, for example, must make such a determination in every estate tax case in which it is contended that a transfer was made in contemplation of death, for "The question, necessarily, is as to the state of mind of the donor." United States v. Wells, 283 U.S. 102, 117, 51 S.Ct. 446 (1931). See Allen v. Trust Co. of Georgia, 326 U.S. 630, 66 S.Ct. 389 (1946). Whether the parties really intended to carry on business as partners is not, we think, any more difficult of determination or the manifestations of such intent any less perceptible than is ordinarily true of inquiries into the subjective.

But the Tax Court did not view the question as one concerning the bona fide intent of the parties to join together as partners. Not once in its opinion is there even an oblique reference to any lack of intent on the part of respondent and his sons to combine their capital and services "for the purpose of carrying on the business." Instead, the court, focusing entirely upon concepts of "vital services" and "original capital," simply decided that the alleged partners had not satisfied those tests when the facts were compared with those in the *Tower* case. The court's opinion is replete with such statements as "we discern nothing constituting what we think is a requisite contribution to a real partnership," "we find no son adding 'vital additional service' which would take the place of capital contributed because of formation of a partnership," and "the sons made no capital contribution, within the sense of the *Tower* case."[13] 6 CCH TCM 698, 699.

Unquestionably a court's determination that the services contributed by a partner are not "vital" and that he has not participated in "management and control of the business"[14] or contributed "original capital" has the effect of placing a heavy burden on the taxpayer to show the bona fide intent of the parties to join together as partners. But such a determination is not conclusive, and that is the vice in the "tests"

---

of the services of such individual in the actual conduct of the business will be given appropriate evidentiary weight as to the question of intent to carry on the business as partners."

[12] Nearly three-quarters of a century ago, Bowen, L.J., made the classic statement that "the state of a man's mind is as much a fact as the state of his digestion." Edgington v. Fitzmaurice, 29 L.R.Ch.Div. 459, 483. State of mind has always been determinative of the question whether a partnership has been formed as between the parties. See, e.g., Drennen v. London Assurance Corp., 113 U.S. 51, 56, 5 S.Ct. 341 (1885); Meehan v. Valentine, 145 U.S. 611, 621, 12 S.Ct. 972 (1892); Barker v. Kraft, 259 Mich. 70, 242 N.W. 841 (1932); Zuback v. Bakmaz, 346 Pa. 279, 29 A.2d 473 (1943); Kennedy v. Mullins, 155 Va. 166, 154 S.E. 568 (1930).

[13] In the *Tower* case the taxpayer argued that he had a right to reduce his taxes by any legal means, to which this Court agreed. We said, however, that existence of a tax avoidance motive gives some indication that there was no bona fide intent to carry on business as a partnership. If *Tower* had set up objective requirements of membership in a family partnership, such as "vital services" and "original capital," the motives behind adoption of the partnership form would have been irrelevant.

[14] Although "management and control of the business" was one of the circumstances emphasized by the *Tower* case, along with "vital services" and "original capital," the Tax Court did not consider it an alternative "test" of partnership. . . .

adopted by the Tax Court. It assumes that there is no room for an honest difference of opinion as to whether the services or capital furnished by the alleged partner are of sufficient importance to justify his inclusion in the partnership. If, upon a consideration of all the facts, it is found that the partners joined together in good faith to conduct a business, having agreed that the services or capital to be contributed presently by each is of such value to the partnership that the contributor should participate in the distribution of profits, that is sufficient. The *Tower* case did not purport to authorize the Tax Court to substitute its judgment for that of the parties; it simply furnished some guides to the determination of their true intent. Even though it was admitted in the *Tower* case that the wife contributed no original capital, management of the business, or other vital services, this Court did not say as a matter of law that there was no valid partnership. We said, instead, that "There was, thus, more than ample evidence to support the Tax Court's finding that no genuine union for partnership business purposes *was ever intended* and that the husband earned the income." 327 U.S. at 292, 66 S.Ct. at page 538. (Italics added.)

\* \* \*

The cause must therefore be remanded to the Tax Court for a decision as to which, if any, of respondent's sons were partners with him in the operation of the ranch during 1940 and 1941. As to which of them, in other words, was there a bona fide intent that they be partners in the conduct of the cattle business, either because of services to be performed during those years, or because of contributions of capital of which they were the true owners, as we have defined that term in the *Clifford, Horst,* and *Tower* cases? No question as to the allocation of income between capital and services is presented in this case, and we intimate no opinion on that subject.

The decision of the Court of Appeals is reversed with directions to remand the cause to the Tax Court for further proceedings in conformity with this opinion.

Reversed and remanded.

■ [The separate concurring opinions of JUSTICES BLACK and RUTLEDGE, BURTON, JACKSON, and FRANKFURTER have been omitted. Ed.]

## PROBLEMS

1.  Consider the likelihood that the partnership formed in the following situations will be respected for federal tax purposes:

(a)  Father is a doctor who makes his Son (a law student) a partner in his practice, assuming applicable state law does not prohibit such associations.

(b)  Father is a doctor who makes his Daughter (a recent medical school graduate) a partner in his practice.

(c)  Father owns a shopping center and he transfers the shopping center to a partnership with Son and Daughter.

**2.**  Mother owns a group of apartments which she transfers to a partnership with Son and two Daughters who provide no consideration for their ¼ interests in the partnership. The income from the partnership is $100,000. Assume the partnership is respected for federal income tax purposes under the *Culbertson* case.

(a)  What result if Mother renders services worth $20,000 to the partnership, but the partnership agreement merely calls for splitting the income ¼ each and each partner actually receives $25,000?

(b)  What result if Mother renders no services but the agreement provides the income is to be divided 10% to Mother and 30% each to Son and each of her Daughters?

(c)  What result if Mother and Son both render services worth $20,000 and the agreement is the same as in part (b), above. See Reg. § 1.704–1(e)(3)(i)(b).

## C. CORPORATIONS

Internal Revenue Code: Sections 11(a) and (b); 482. See Section 269A.

------

### Overton v. Commissioner

United States Court of Appeals, Second Circuit, 1947.
162 F.2d 155.

■ SWAN, CIRCUIT JUDGE.

These appeals involve gift tax liability of petitioner Overton for the years 1936 and 1937 and income tax liability of petitioner Oliphant for the year 1941. Each petitioner was held liable on the theory that dividends received by his wife in the year in question on stock registered in her name on the books of Castle & Overton, Inc., a New York corporation, were income of the husband for tax purposes. No gift tax return with respect to such dividends was filed by Mr. Overton in 1936 or 1937, and the dividends received by Mrs. Oliphant in 1941 were not included in her husband's return for that year.

There is no dispute as to the evidentiary facts. They are stated in detail in the opinion of the Tax Court, 6 T.C. 304, and will be here repeated only so far as may be necessary to render intelligible the discussion which follows. On May 26, 1936 the corporation had outstanding 1,000 shares of common stock without par value but having a liquidating value of at least $120 per share. On that date, pursuant to a plan devised to lessen taxes, the certificate of incorporation was amended to provide for changing the outstanding common stock into 2,000 shares without par value, of which 1,000 were denominated Class

A and 1,000 Class B. The old stock was exchanged for the new, the shareholders then gave the B stock to their respective wives, and new certificates therefor were issued to the wives. The B stock had a liquidating value of one dollar per share; everything else on liquidation was to belong to the holders of the A stock, who had also the sole voting rights for directors and on all ordinary matters.[1] By virtue of an agreement made in April 1937 restricting alienation of their stock, the wives were precluded from realizing more than one dollar a share by selling their shares. The A stock was to receive noncumulative dividends at the rate of $10 a share per year before payment of any dividend on the B stock; if dividends in excess of $10 per share were paid on the A stock in any year, such excess dividends were to be shared by both classes of stock in the ratio of one-fifth thereof for the A stock and four-fifths for the B stock. During the six year period ending in December 1941, the dividends paid on B stock totaled $150.40 a share as against $77.60 a share paid on A stock. In 1941 the A stock had a book value of $155 per share.

The Tax Court was of opinion that the 1936 arrangement, though made in the form of a gift of stock, was in reality an assignment of part of the taxpayers' future dividends. Unless form is to be exalted above substance this conclusion is inescapable. Since the total issue of B stock represented only $1,000 of the corporate assets, it is plain that the property which earned the large dividends received by the B shareholders was the property represented by the A stock held by the husbands. In transferring the B shares to their wives they parted with no substantial part of their interest in the corporate property. Had they been content to transfer some of the original common stock, they could have accomplished their purpose of lessening taxes on the family group,[2] but they would then have made substantial gifts of capital. The arrangement they put into effect gave the wives nothing, or substantially nothing, but the right to future earnings flowing from property retained by the husbands. That anticipatory assignments of income, whatever their formal cloak, are ineffective taxwise is a principle too firmly established to be subject to question. See Lucas v. Earl, 281 U.S. 111, 50 S.Ct. 241; Helvering v. Horst, 311 U.S. 112, 61 S.Ct. 144; * * *. We think the Tax Court correctly applied this principle to the facts of the case at bar.

Orders affirmed.

---

[1]   Whether the amendment of the certificate of incorporation excluded B shareholders from voting on extraordinary matters specified in section 51 of the Stock Corporation Law of New York, McK.Consol.Laws, c. 59, in effect on May 26, 1937, the Tax Court did not find it necessary to determine; nor do we.

[2]   See Blair v. Commissioner, 300 U.S. 5, 57 S.Ct. 330.

## NOTE

The *Overton* case involves a situation where the court looked through the formal steps that the parties had taken to determine the economic substance of the transaction; i.e., an attempted assignment of income to the spouses of the taxpayers from stock that the taxpayers owned. Over the years, the "economic substance" doctrine has been employed by the courts to identify the true nature of a transaction in order to arrive at the proper tax result. However, among different courts there has been a lack of uniformity as to how to apply the doctrine.[1]

In the Health Care and Education Reconciliation Act of 2010[2] (where you would least expect Congress to address the economic substance conflict!), Congress enacted legislation to resolve the lack of judicial uniformity regarding how to apply the doctrine.[3] Under Section 7701(*o*), a transaction must satisfy two requirements to have economic substance: (1) an objective test under which the transaction must change in a meaningful way (apart from Federal income tax effects) the taxpayer's economic position; and (2) a subjective test that the taxpayer must have a substantial non-Federal-income-tax purpose for entering the transaction.[4] A taxpayer may rely on factors other than a profit potential to satisfy the two tests.[5]

The economic substance doctrine has been employed most often by the Internal Revenue Service in a corporate context, so it is not covered in detail in this Text. In fact, the rules described above apply to individuals only in the case of transactions entered into in connection with a trade or business or an activity engaged in for profit.[6]

---

[1] Some courts have applied a conjunctive test that requires a taxpayer to establish both economic substance and a business purpose for a transaction to survive judicial scrutiny. Rice's Toyota World, Inc. v. Commissioner, 752 F.2d 89 (4th Cir. 1985). Other courts have concluded that either economic substance or business purpose is sufficient for the form of a transaction to be respected. Klamath Strategic Investment Fund v. United States, 568 F.3d 537 (5th Cir. 2009). Still other courts have used economic substance and business purpose as mere factors in determining whether a transaction is valid. James v. Commissioner, 899 F.2d 905 (10th Cir. 1990).

[2] Pub. L. No. 111–152, 111th Cong, 2d Sess. (2010). See Lipton, " 'Codification' of Economic Substance Doctrine—Much Ado About Nothing?," 112 J.Tax'n 325 (2010); Lipton, "IRS Provides Helpful Guidance to Agents as to the Application of the Economic Substance Doctrine," 115 J.Tax'n 166 (2011).

[3] I.R.C. § 7701(*o*). See I.R.C. § 7701(*o*)(5)(A) defining the term "economic substance doctrine" and limiting application of the doctrine to Subtitle A (the income tax).

Penalties are imposed on any transaction that lacks economic substance. I.R.C. § 6662, especially § 6662(b)(6). See Notice 2014–58, 2014–44 I.R.B. 746.

[4] Any state or local income tax effect which is related to a Federal income tax effect is treated in the same manner as a Federal income tax effect. I.R.C. § 7701(*o*)(3). See also I.R.C. § 7701(*o*)(4), which disregards a financial accounting benefit as a valid purpose if the origin of the financial accounting benefit is a reduction of Federal income tax.

[5] However, if a taxpayer relies on the potential for profit to satisfy the tests, the present value of reasonably expected pre-tax profits must be substantial in relation to the present value of the expected net tax benefits that would be allowed if the transaction were respected. I.R.C. § 7701(*o*)(2)(A).

[6] I.R.C. § 7701(*o*)(5)(B). Cf. Chapters 14 and 15, infra. Thus, in the case of an individual, economic substance analysis potentially would apply if the "hobby loss" rules in I.R.C. § 183 were not applicable. See Chapter 17C, infra.

# Johnson v. Commissioner*

Tax Court of the United States, 1982.
78 T.C. 882, affirmed in an unpublished opinion, 734 F.2d 20 (9th Cir.1984), cert.
denied, 469 U.S. 857, 105 S.Ct. 185 (1984).

■ FAY, JUDGE:

[Taxpayer, a professional basketball player, executed a contract with PMSA granting it the right to his services in professional sports for a limited time with PMSA obligated to pay Taxpayer a monthly salary. PMSA licensed its rights to EST who made the payments to Taxpayer and remitted 95 percent of its net revenue to PMSA. Taxpayer signed a professional basketball contract with the Warriors and assigned all his rights to EST and the Warriors made their compensation payments to EST.]

OPINION

At issue is whether amounts paid by the Warriors with respect to petitioner's services as a basketball player are income to petitioner or to the corporation to which the amounts were remitted. Respondent, relying on the rule of *Lucas v. Earl,* 281 U.S. 111 (1930), that income must be taxed to its earner, contends petitioner was the true earner. Petitioner maintains this is a "loan-out" case like *Fox v. Commissioner,* 37 B.T.A. 271 (1938), and that *Lucas v. Earl* is inapplicable. We find *Lucas v. Earl* indistinguishable in any meaningful sense and hold for respondent.

In *Lucas v. Earl,* the taxpayer executed an agreement with his wife that any property acquired by either of them, including wages and salary, would be considered joint property. The U.S. Supreme Court accepted the validity of that contract, but held the taxpayer earned the salary in issue therein and must be taxed on it. In so holding, the Court noted:

> It [the case] turns on the import and reasonable construction of the taxing act. There is no doubt that the statute could tax salaries to those who earned them and provide that the tax could not be escaped by anticipatory arrangements and contracts however skillfully devised to prevent the salary when paid from vesting even for a second in the man who earned it. That seems to us the import of the statute [sec. 61] before us. * * *. [281 U.S. at 114–115.]

From that quote is derived the oft-cited "first principle of income taxation: That income must be taxed to him who earns it." *Commissioner v. Culbertson,* 337 U.S. 733, 739–740 (1949). See also *United States v. Basye,* 410 U.S. 441, 449 (1973).

However, the realities of the business world prevent an overly simplistic application of the *Lucas v. Earl* rule whereby the true earner may be identified by merely pointing to the one actually turning the spade or dribbling the ball. Recognition must be given to corporations as

---

\*    Some footnotes omitted.

taxable entities which, to a great extent, rely upon the personal services of their employees to produce corporate income. When a corporate employee performs labors which give rise to income, it solves little merely to identify the actual laborer. Thus, a tension has evolved between the basic tenets of *Lucas v. Earl* and recognition of the nature of the corporate business form.[13]

While the generally accepted test for resolving the "who is taxed" tension is who actually earns the income, that test may easily become sheer sophistry when the "who" choices are a corporation or its employee. Whether a one-person professional service corporation or a multi-faceted corporation is presented, there are many cases in which, in a practical sense, the key employee is responsible for the influx of moneys. Nor may a workable test be couched in terms of for whose services the payor of the income intends to pay. In numerous instances, a corporation is hired solely in order to obtain the services of a specific corporate employee.[14]

Given the inherent impossibility of logical application of a per se actual earner test, a more refined inquiry has arisen in the form of who controls the earning of the income. * * *. An examination of the case law from *Lucas v. Earl* hence reveals two necessary elements before the corporation, rather than its service-performer employee, may be considered the controller of the income.[15] First, the service-performer employee must be just that—an employee of the corporation whom the corporation has the right to direct or control in some meaningful sense. * * *. Second, there must exist between the corporation and the person or entity using the services a contract or similar indicium recognizing the corporation's controlling position. * * *.

In the case before us, we accept arguendo that the PMSA-petitioner agreement was a valid contract which required the payments with respect to petitioner's performance as a basketball player ultimately to be made to PMSA or EST. * * *. We also accept arguendo that the PMSA-petitioner agreement gave PMSA a right of control over petitioner's services, although respondent maintains the agreement's control provisions systematically were ignored. * * * Thus, the first element is satisfied. However, the second element is lacking, and that is what brings

---

[13] That tension is most acute when a corporation operates a personal service business and has as its sole or principal employee its sole or principal shareholder. In those cases where sec. 482 applies, resort to general sec. 61 principles usually is not necessary since sec. 482 provides a smoother route to the same "who is taxed" result. See *Pacella v. Commissioner,* 78 T.C. 604 (1982); *Keller v. Commissioner,* 77 T.C. 1014 (1981), appeal filed (10th Cir. Apr. 2, 1982). However, see *Rubin v. Commissioner,* 51 T.C. 251 (1968), revd. and remanded 429 F.2d 650 (2d Cir.1970), decided on remand 56 T.C. 1155 (1971), aff'd. per curiam 460 F.2d 1216 (2d Cir.1972), wherein application of secs. 61 and 482 led to different results. Unless otherwise provided, all section references are to the Internal Revenue Code of 1954 as amended.

[14] Such instances are commonplace in personal service businesses such as law, medicine, accounting, and entertainment. * * *.

[15] Although some of the cited cases deal with trusts rather than with corporations, their discussions of general sec. 61 principles apply to both entities. See sec. 1.671–1(c), Income Tax Regs. We couch our discussion herein in terms of corporations simply because it comports with the facts before us.

this case within *Lucas v. Earl* rather than the cases relied on by petitioner.

In *Fox v. Commissioner,* 37 B.T.A. 271 (1938), the taxpayer, was a cartoonist who formed a corporation. He transferred to the corporation cash and property and assigned to the corporation copyrights and his exclusive services for a number of years. The corporation executed a contract with a syndicate giving the syndicate the right to use the taxpayer's cartoons in return for a percentage of gross sales. The amount the corporation thus received greatly exceeded the amount the corporation paid the taxpayer for his services. The Court held the excess amounts were not the taxpayer's income. *Lucas v. Earl* was inapplicable because the employment relationships existed between the corporation and the syndicate and between the corporation and the taxpayer and not between the taxpayer and the syndicate.[17]

In *Laughton v. Commissioner,* 40 B.T.A. 101 (1939), the taxpayer, an actor, formed a corporation. He contracted with the corporation to receive a weekly payment and certain expense payments in return for his exclusive services. The corporation executed contracts with two film studios whereby the taxpayer's services were loaned to the film studios. The Court held the taxpayer was not taxable on the amounts paid to the corporation by the studios because those amounts were paid "under contracts between it [the corporation] and the studios" and there simply was no assignment of income by the taxpayer. See *Laughton v. Commissioner, supra* at 106–107.

Petitioner herein stands upon vastly different ground than did the taxpayers in *Fox* and *Laughton.* While petitioner had a contract with PMSA, and by assignment, EST, he also had an employment contract with the Warriors. Crucial is the fact that there was no contract or agreement between the Warriors and PMSA or EST. Nor can any oral contract between those entities be implied. * * *. The Warriors adamantly refused to sign any contract or agreement with any person or entity other than petitioner.[20] Thus, the existing employment relationships were between petitioner and PMSA/EST and between petitioner and the Warriors. The relationship between PMSA/EST and the Warriors necessary for PMSA/EST to be considered actually in control of the earnings was not present. As with Mr. Earl, petitioner "was

---

[17] Petitioner also relies on the Second Circuit Court of Appeals reversal in *Rubin v. Commissioner,* note 13 *supra.* However, as we understand the Court of Appeals' opinion, it merely mandated preferential application of sec. 482. Nevertheless, in *Rubin,* there existed a contract between the taxpayer's corporation and the entity benefiting from the taxpayer's services.

[20] The reasons for the Warriors's refusal to so contract is not particularly relevant. However, many of the Warriors's concerns may perhaps be unique to professional sports. But, petitioner was not in a position where his goal of assured future income was unobtainable solely due to his choice of professions. Deferred compensation arrangements are common in professional sports, and many are accepted for tax purposes. See J. Weistart & C. Lowell, The Law of Sports sec. 7.06(1979).

the only party to the contracts by which the salary * * * [was] earned." See *Lucas v. Earl,* 281 U.S. 111, 114 (1930).[21]

Nor may the assignments of earnings executed by petitioner suffice to make PMSA/EST the taxable party. Such assignments merely demonstrate petitioner's control over the earnings such as would an ordinary assignment of wages to a bank. Nor is it important that petitioner contractually was obligated to pay his earnings to PMSA/EST. The U.S. Supreme Court in *Lucas v. Earl* accepted the validity of the contract involved therein requiring transmission of one-half to Mrs. Earl, but nevertheless held Mr. Earl taxable as the true earner.

In summary, we find petitioner, rather than PMSA or EST, actually controlled the earning of the amounts paid by the Warriors with respect to petitioner's services. Thus, those amounts were income to petitioner under section 61(a)(1).

To reflect the foregoing,

*Decisions will be entered for the respondent.*

# Borge v. Commissioner[*]

United States Court of Appeals, Second Circuit, 1968.
405 F.2d 673, cert. denied 395 U.S. 933, 89 S.Ct. 1994 (1969).

■ HAYS, CIRCUIT JUDGE:

Petitioners seek review of a decision of the Tax Court sustaining the Commissioner's determination of deficiencies in their income tax payments for the years 1958 through 1962, inclusive. The Tax Court upheld * * * the Commissioner's allocation to Borge[1] under Section 482 of the Internal Revenue Code of 1954, 26 U.S.C.A. § 482 (1964), of a portion of the compensation received by Danica Enterprises, Inc., Borge's wholly owned corporation, for services performed by Borge as an entertainer. * * *. We affirm.

[From 1952 to 1958 Borge, as an individual, operated ViBo Farms where he developed, produced, processed and sold quality chickens known as rock cornish hens. He had substantial losses each year which he deducted against the substantial income he earned as an entertainer. Ed.]

* * *

---

[21] We do not mean to imply this case necessarily would have been decided in petitioner's favor had a contract been executed between the Warriors and PMSA or EST. * * *.

[*] See Katz, "Can Section 482 Be Used to Negate the Tax Effect of a Bona Fide Corporation?" 28 J.Tax. 2 (1968). Ed.

[1] "Borge" refers herein to Victor Borge. His wife has been included as a party to the action solely because of the filing of joint returns. [Discussion in the opinion of an alternative issue of tax liability under I.R.C. § 269 has been deleted. Ed.]

* * *. Borge organized Danica, and, on March 1, 1958, transferred to the corporation, in exchange for all of its stock and a loan payable, the assets of the poultry business (except the farm real property).

Borge is a well-known professional entertainer. During the years preceding the organization of Danica he made large sums from television, stage and motion picture engagements.

Since Danica had no means of meeting the expected losses from the poultry business, Borge and Danica entered into a contract at the time of the organization of the corporation under which Borge agreed to perform entertainment and promotional services for the corporation for a 5-year period for compensation from Danica of $50,000 per year. Danica offset the poultry losses[3] against the entertainment profits, which far exceeded the $50,000 per year it had contracted to pay Borge.[4] Borge obviously would not have entered into such a contract with an unrelated party.

Danica did nothing to aid Borge in his entertainment business. Those who contracted with Danica for Borge's entertainment services required Borge personally to guarantee the contracts. Danica's entertainment earnings were attributable solely to the services of Borge, and Danica's only profits were from the entertainment business.

The only year during the period in dispute in which Danica actually paid Borge anything for his services was 1962, when Borge was paid the full $50,000.

The issues in controversy are (1) whether the Commissioner, acting under Section 482 of the Internal Revenue Code of 1954, 26 U.S.C.A. § 482 (1964), properly allocated to Borge from Danica $75,000 per year from 1958 through 1961 and $25,000 for 1962, * * *.

I.

When two or more organizations, trades or businesses, whether or not incorporated, are owned or controlled by the same interests, Section 482 of the Internal Revenue Code of 1954, 26 U.S.C.A. § 482 (1964), authorizes the Commissioner to apportion gross income between or among such organizations, trades or businesses if he deems that apportionment is necessary clearly to reflect income or to prevent evasion of tax.[5] We conclude that the Commissioner could properly have found that for purposes of Section 482 Borge owned or controlled two businesses, an entertainment business and a poultry business, and that the allocation to Borge of part of the entertainment compensation paid to the corporation was not error.[6]

---

[3]   [Details of the poultry losses are omitted. Ed.]

[4]   [Details of Danica's net entertainment income are omitted. Ed.]

[5]   [I.R.C. § 482 is omitted. Ed.]

[6]   We agree with petitioners' contention that since Borge's employment contract with Danica went into effect on March 1, 1958, the 1958 allocation should have been only $62,500 ($5/6 of $75,000). A recomputation of Borge's deficiency to this extent should be made.

We accept, as supported by the record, the Tax Court's finding: that Borge operated an entertainment business and merely assigned to Danica a portion of his income from that business; that Danica did nothing to earn or to assist in the earning of the entertainment income; that Borge would not have contracted for $50,000 per year with an unrelated party to perform the services referred to in his contract with Danica. Thus Borge was correctly held to be in the entertainment business.

At the same time Danica, Borge's wholly owned corporation, was in the poultry business.

Petitioners, relying primarily on Whipple v. Commissioner, 373 U.S. 193, 83 S.Ct. 1168 (1963), argue that Borge is not an "organization, trade or business" and that Section 482 is therefore inapposite.

In *Whipple* the Supreme Court held only that where one renders services to a corporation as an investment, he is not engaging in a trade or business:

> "Devoting one's time and energies to the affairs of a corporation is not of itself, and without more, a trade or business of the person so engaged. Though such activities may produce income, profit or gain in the form of dividends or enhancement in the value of an investment, this return is distinctive to the process of investing and is generated by the successful operation of the corporation's business as distinguished from the trade or business of the taxpayer himself. When the only return is that of an investor, the taxpayer has not satisfied his burden of demonstrating that he is engaged in a trade or business since investing is not a trade or business and the return to the taxpayer, though substantially the product of his services, legally arises not from his own trade or business but from that of the corporation." 373 U.S. at 202, 83 S.Ct. at 1174.

Here, however, Borge was in the business of entertaining. He was not devoting his time and energies to the corporation; he was carrying on his career as an entertainer, and merely channeling a part of his entertainment income through the corporation.

Moreover, in *Whipple* petitioner was devoting his time and energies to a corporation in the hope of realizing capital gains treatment from the sale of appreciated stock. When the hoped-for appreciation did not materialize he attempted to deduct his losses as ordinary losses. The Court decided that where one stands to achieve capital gains through an investment, any losses incurred in connection with the investment are capital losses. Borge is clearly earning ordinary income; the only question is who should pay the taxes on it. Thus, *Whipple* is not apposite.

For somewhat similar reasons we find Commissioner v. Gross, 236 F.2d 612 (2d Cir.1956), on which petitioner also seeks to rely, also inapposite.

Nor do we consider the other cases cited by petitioners persuasive. The Commissioner is not arguing here, as he did, for example, in Charles Laughton, 40 B.T.A. 101 (1939), remanded, 113 F.2d 103 (9th Cir.1940), that the taxpayer should be taxed on the entire amount paid into the wholly owned corporation, i.e. that the corporation should be ignored. See also Pat O'Brien, 25 T.C. 376 (1955); Fontaine Fox, 37 B.T.A. 271 (1938). Instead he recognizes the existence of the corporation, but under Section 482 allocates a portion of its income to its sole shareholder who alone was responsible for the production of such income.

Petitioner contends that the Congress, in enacting the personal holding company and collapsible corporation provisions of the Code, precluded the Commissioner's action in this case under Section 482. We do not read those provisions, however, as the only available methods for dealing with the situations there involved. As the Third Circuit said in National Sec. Corp. v. Commissioner, 137 F.2d 600, 602 (3d Cir.), cert. denied, 320 U.S. 794, 64 S.Ct. 262:

> "In every case in which [Section 482] is applied its application will necessarily result in an apparent conflict with the literal requirements of some other provision of the [Internal Revenue Code]. If this were not so Section [482] would be wholly superfluous."

The fact that similar, but not identical, factual situations have been dealt with by legislation does not mean that this situation, because it was not also specifically dealt with by legislation, cannot be reached even by a general code provision.

We thus conclude that the Tax Court was correct in upholding the Commissioner's ruling that Borge controlled two separate businesses. * * *.

The Commissioner's action in allocating a part of Danica's income to Borge was based upon his conclusion that such allocation was necessary in order clearly to reflect the income of the two businesses under Borge's common control. The Commissioner's allocation has received the approval of the Tax Court. As this Court held in dealing with the predecessor of Section 482, "Whether the Tax Court was correct in allocating income to the petitioner under § 45 [of the Internal Revenue Code of 1939] is essentially one of fact and the decision below must be affirmed if supported by substantial evidence." * * *. Here the determination of the Commissioner and the decision of the Tax Court are supported by substantial evidence that the income of Borge's two businesses has been distorted through Borge's having arranged for Danica to receive a large part of his entertainment income although Danica did nothing to earn that income, and the sole purpose of the arrangement was to permit Danica to offset losses from the poultry business with income from the entertainment business. The amount allocated by the Commissioner ($75,000 per year) was entirely reasonable—indeed, generous—in view of the fact that Danica's annual net income from Borge's entertainment services averaged $166,465 during the years in question.

\* \* \*

## PROBLEM

1.   Father runs his own hardware store and has income far in excess of his needs. Several years ago he started a small manufacturing company that produces high-tech products. For the first few years of operation, the business operated at a loss, but the company recently produced a "hot product" and business is booming. Father has no need for all of this income and in fact has considered transferring the business to Son and Daughter. Father ultimately decides that by incorporating the business, electing S Corporation status, and retaining 51% of the stock, he can maintain control of the business and still transfer part of the business (and hence the income) to Son and Daughter. Will Father's plan successfully rid him of the surplus income? See § 1366(e).

## D.  TRUSTS AND ESTATES

Internal Revenue Code: Sections 671; 672(a), (b), (e); 673; 676; 677. See Sections 1(g); 672(c), (d); 674; 675; 678.

Regulations: Sections 1.671–1(a)–(c); 1.676(a)–1.

---

### Corliss v. Bowers

Supreme Court of the United States, 1930.
281 U.S. 376, 50 S.Ct. 336.

■ MR. JUSTICE HOLMES delivered the opinion of the Court.

This is a suit to recover the amount of an income tax paid by the plaintiff, the petitioner, under the Revenue Act of 1924, \* \* \*. The complaint was dismissed by the District Court, 30 F.2d 135, and the judgment was affirmed by the Circuit Court of Appeals, 34 F.2d 656. A writ of certiorari was granted by this Court.

The question raised by the petitioner is whether the above section of the Revenue Act can be applied constitutionally to him upon the following facts. In 1922 he transferred the fund from which arose the income in respect of which the petitioner was taxed, to trustees, in trust to pay the income to his wife for life with remainder over to their children. By the instrument creating the trust the petitioner reserved power "to modify or alter in any manner, or revoke in whole or in part, this indenture and the trusts then existing, and the estates and interests in property hereby created" etc. It is not necessary to quote more words because there can be no doubt that the petitioner fully reserved the power at any moment to abolish or change the trust at his will. The statute referred to provides that "when the grantor of a trust has, at any time during the taxable year, * * * the power to revest in himself title to any part of the corpus of the trust then the income of such part of the trust for such taxable year shall be included in computing the net income of the grantor." § 219(g) with other similar provisions as to income in § 219(h). [See Sections 676 and 677. Ed.] There can be no doubt either that the statute purports to tax the plaintiff in this case. But the net income for 1924 was paid over to the petitioner's wife and the petitioner's argument is that however it might have been in different circumstances the income never was his and he cannot be taxed for it. The legal estate was in the trustee and the equitable interest in the wife.

But taxation is not so much concerned with the refinements of title as it is with actual command over the property taxed—the actual benefit for which the tax is paid. If a man directed his bank to pay over income as received to a servant or friend, until further orders, no one would doubt that he could be taxed upon the amounts so paid. It is answered that in that case he would have a title, whereas here he did not. But from the point of view of taxation there would be no difference. The title would merely mean a right to stop the payment before it took place. The same right existed here although it is not called a title but is called a power. The acquisition by the wife of the income became complete only when the plaintiff failed to exercise the power that he reserved. * * *. Still speaking with reference to taxation, if a man disposes of a fund in such a way that another is allowed to enjoy the income which it is in the power of the first to appropriate it does not matter whether the permission is given by assent or by failure to express dissent. The income that is subject to a man's unfettered command and that he is free to enjoy at his own option may be taxed to him as his income whether he sees fit to enjoy it or not. We consider the case too clear to need help from the local law of New York or from arguments based on the power of Congress to prevent escape from taxes or surtaxes by devices that easily might be applied to that end.

Judgment affirmed.

■ THE CHIEF JUSTICE took no part in this case.

# Helvering v. Clifford

Supreme Court of the United States, 1940.
309 U.S. 331, 60 S.Ct. 554.

■ MR. JUSTICE DOUGLAS delivered the opinion of the Court.

In 1934, respondent declared himself trustee of certain securities which he owned. All net income from the trust was to be held for the "exclusive benefit" of respondent's wife. The trust was for a term of five years, except that it would terminate earlier on the death of either respondent or his wife. On termination of the trust the entire corpus was to go to respondent, while all "accrued or undistributed net income" and "any proceeds from the investment of such net income" was to be treated as property owned absolutely by the wife. During the continuance of the trust respondent was to pay over to his wife the whole or such part of the net income as he in his "absolute discretion" might determine. And during that period he had full power (a) to exercise all voting powers incident to the trusteed shares of stock; (b) to "sell, exchange, mortgage, or pledge" any of the securities under the declaration of trust "whether as part of the corpus or principal thereof or as investments or proceeds and any income therefrom, upon such terms and for such consideration" as respondent in his "absolute discretion may deem fitting"; (c) to invest "any cash or money in the trust estate or any income therefrom" by loans, secured or unsecured, by deposits in banks, or by purchase of securities or other personal property "without restriction" because of their "speculative character" or "rate of return" or any "laws pertaining to the investment of trust funds"; (d) to collect all income; (e) to compromise, etc., any claims held by him as trustee; (f) to hold any property in the trust estate in the names of "other persons or in my own name as an individual" except as otherwise provided. Extraordinary cash dividends, stock dividends, proceeds from the sale of unexercised subscription rights, or any enhancement, realized or not, in the value of the securities were to be treated as principal, not income. An exculpatory clause purported to protect him from all losses except those occasioned by his "own wilful and deliberate" breach of duties as trustee. And finally it was provided that neither the principal nor any future or accrued income should be liable for the debts of the wife; and that the wife could not transfer, encumber, or anticipate any interest in the trust or any income therefrom prior to actual payment thereof to her.

It was stipulated that while the "tax effects" of this trust were considered by respondent they were not the "sole consideration" involved in his decision to set it up, as by this and other gifts he intended to give "security and economic independence" to his wife and children. It was also stipulated that respondent's wife had substantial income of her own from other sources; that there was no restriction on her use of the trust income, all of which income was placed in her personal checking account, intermingled with her other funds, and expended by her on herself, her children and relatives; that the trust was not designed to relieve respondent from liability for family or household expenses and that after execution of the trust he paid large sums from his personal funds for such purposes.

Respondent paid a federal gift tax on this transfer. During the year 1934 all income from the trust was distributed to the wife who included it in her individual return for that year. The Commissioner, however, determined a deficiency in respondent's return for that year on the theory that income from the trust was taxable to him. The Board of Tax Appeals sustained that redetermination. 38 B.T.A. 1532. The Circuit Court of Appeals reversed. 105 F.2d 586. We granted certiorari because of the importance to the revenue of the use of such short term trusts in the reduction of surtaxes.

Sec. 22(a) of the Revenue Act of 1934, 48 Stat. 680, includes among "gross income" all "gains, profits, and income derived * * * from professions, vocations, trades, businesses, commerce, or sales, or dealings in property, whether real or personal, growing out of the ownership or use of or interest in such property; also from interest, rent, dividends, securities, or the transaction of any business carried on for gain or profit, or gains or profits and income derived from any source whatever." The broad sweep of this language indicates the purpose of Congress to use the full measure of its taxing power within those definable categories. Cf. Helvering v. Midland Mutual Life Insurance Co., 300 U.S. 216, 57 S.Ct. 423. Hence our construction of the statute should be consonant with that purpose. Technical considerations, niceties of the law of trusts or conveyances, or the legal paraphernalia which inventive genius may construct as a refuge from surtaxes should not obscure the basic issue. That issue is whether the grantor after the trust has been established may still be treated, under this statutory scheme, as the owner of the corpus. See Blair v. Commissioner, 300 U.S. 5, 12, 57 S.Ct. 330, 333. In absence of more precise standards or guides supplied by statute or appropriate regulations,[1] the answer to that question must depend on an analysis of the terms of the trust and all the circumstances attendant on its creation and operation. And where the grantor is the trustee and the beneficiaries are members of his family group, special scrutiny of the arrangement is necessary lest what is in reality but one economic unit be multiplied into two or more[2] by devices which, though valid under state law, are not conclusive so far as § 22(a) is concerned.

In this case we cannot conclude, as a matter of law that respondent ceased to be the owner of the corpus after the trust was created. Rather, the short duration of the trust, the fact that the wife was the beneficiary, and the retention of control over the corpus by respondent all lead irresistibly to the conclusion that respondent continued to be the owner for purposes of § 22(a).

So far as his dominion and control were concerned it seems clear that the trust did not effect any substantial change. In substance his control over the corpus was in all essential respects the same after the trust was created, as before. The wide powers which he retained included for all practical purposes most of the control which he as an individual would have. There were, we may assume, exceptions, such as his disability to make a gift of the corpus to others during the term of the trust and to make loans to himself. But this dilution in his control would seem to be insignificant and immaterial, since control over investment remained. If

---

[1] We have not considered here Art. 166–1 of Treasury Regulations 86 promulgated under § 166 of the 1934 Act and in 1936 amended (T.D. 4629) so as to rest on § 22(a) also, since the tax in question arose prior to that amendment.

[2] See Paul, "The Background of the Revenue Act of 1937," 5 Univ.Chic.L.Rev. 41.

it be said that such control is the type of dominion exercised by any trustee, the answer is simple. We have at best a temporary reallocation of income within an intimate family group. Since the income remains in the family and since the husband retains control over the investment, he has rather complete assurance that the trust will not effect any substantial change in his economic position. It is hard to imagine that respondent felt himself the poorer after this trust had been executed or, if he did, that it had any rational foundation in fact. For as a result of the terms of the trust and the intimacy of the familial relationship respondent retained the substance of full enjoyment of all the rights which previously he had in the property. That might not be true if only strictly legal rights were considered. But when the benefits flowing to him indirectly through the wife are added to the legal rights he retained, the aggregate may be said to be a fair equivalent of what he previously had. To exclude from the aggregate those indirect benefits would be to deprive § 22(a) of considerable vitality and to treat as immaterial what may be highly relevant considerations in the creation of such family trusts. For where the head of the household has income in excess of normal needs, it may well make but little difference to him (except income-tax-wise) where portions of that income are routed—so long as it stays in the family group. In those circumstances the all-important factor might be retention by him of control over the principal. With that control in his hands he would keep direct command over all that he needed to remain in substantially the same financial situation as before. Our point here is that no one fact is normally decisive but that all considerations and circumstances of the kind we have mentioned are relevant to the question of ownership and are appropriate foundations for findings on that issue. Thus, where, as in this case, the benefits directly or indirectly retained blend so imperceptibly with the normal concepts of full ownership, we cannot say that the triers of fact committed reversible error when they found that the husband was the owner of the corpus for the purposes of § 22(a). To hold otherwise would be to treat the wife as a complete stranger; to let mere formalism obscure the normal consequences of family solidarity; and to force concepts of ownership to be fashioned out of legal niceties which may have little or no significance in such household arrangements.

The bundle of rights which he retained was so substantial that respondent cannot be heard to complain that he is the "victim of despotic power when for the purpose of taxation he is treated as owner altogether." See Du Pont v. Commissioner, 289 U.S. 685, 689, 53 S.Ct. 766, 767.

We should add that liability under § 22(a) is not foreclosed by reason of the fact that Congress made specific provision in § 166 for revocable trusts [Section 676. Ed.], but failed to adopt the Treasury recommendation in 1934, Helvering v. Wood, post, p. 344, that similar specific treatment should be accorded income from short term trusts. [See

Section 673, not added until 1954. Ed.] Such choice, while relevant to the scope of § 166, Helvering v. Wood, supra, cannot be said to have subtracted from § 22(a) what was already there. Rather, on this evidence it must be assumed that the choice was between a generalized treatment under § 22(a) or specific treatment under a separate provision[3] (such as was accorded revocable trusts under § 166); not between taxing or not taxing grantors of short term trusts. In view of the broad and sweeping language of § 22(a), a specific provision covering short term trusts might well do no more than to carve out of § 22(a) a defined group of cases to which a rule of thumb would be applied. The failure of Congress to adopt any such rule of thumb for that type of trust must be taken to do no more than to leave to the triers of fact the initial determination of whether or not on the facts of each case the grantor remains the owner for purposes of § 22(a).

In view of this result we need not examine the contention that the trust device falls within the rule of Lucas v. Earl, 281 U.S. 111, 50 S.Ct. 241 and Burnet v. Leininger, 285 U.S. 136, 52 S.Ct. 345, relating to the assignment of future income; or that respondent is liable under § 166, taxing grantors on the income of revocable trusts.

The judgment of the Circuit Court of Appeals is reversed and that of the Board of Tax Appeals is affirmed.

Reversed.

■ MR. JUSTICE ROBERTS, dissenting:

I think the judgment should be affirmed.

The decision of the court disregards the fundamental principle that legislation is not the function of the judiciary but of Congress. * * *.

■ MR. JUSTICE MCREYNOLDS joins in this opinion.

## NOTE

One should note that in *Clifford* the settlor assigned *property* to the trust, not mere naked rights to income as was the case involving an outright assignment in Helvering v. Horst.[1] The trust was irrevocable; otherwise Section 676 would have been enough to tax the settlor on the trust income.[2] Also, in *Clifford* the government stipulated that the income of the trust was not used for the support of the settlor's wife; for, if the income were so used,

---

[3] As to the disadvantage of a specific statutory formula over more generalized treatment see Vol. I, Report, Income Tax Codification Committee (1936), a committee appointed by the Chancellor of the Exchequer in 1927. In discussing revocable settlements the Committee stated, p. 298:

 "This and the three following clauses reproduce section 20 of the Finance Act, 1922, an enactment which has been the subject of much litigation, is unsatisfactory in many respects, and is plainly inadequate to fulfill the apparent intention to prevent avoidance of liability to tax by revocable dispositions of income or other devices. We think the matter one which is worthy of the attention of Parliament."

[1] 311 U.S. 112, 61 S.Ct. 144 (1940), supra at page 250.

[2] Cf., Corliss v. Bowers, 281 U.S. 376, 50 S.Ct. 336 (1930), supra at page 295.

it would have been taxable to Clifford under Section 677, and it is doubtful the case would have reached the Supreme Court.[3] Thus one can surmise that, in frustration resulting from the failure of Congress to enact specific Code provisions dealing with short-term, family control trusts, the government, in a calculated risk, sought to combat such devices in a maneuver relying solely on the vagueness of Section 61; and it paid off. It is clear that the settlor's retention of control over the property was the basis for the court's decision. The short duration of the trust is properly regarded as one of the settlor's retained strings of control. Following *Clifford,* the question became how many and what strings of control could a settlor of a trust retain without incurring tax liability on income that is payable to others. The answers were forthcoming, but over a period of more than forty years in several separate stages.

The immediate impact of *Clifford* was confusion because, while Clifford himself may have retained enough of the bundle of rights to be held to "own" the trust property, the outer limits of the *Clifford* doctrine were very obscure. In 1945, the Treasury sought to accord some definition to the doctrine by elaborate and expansive regulations, promulgated under the generic provision of what is now Section 61.[4] In the enactment of the Internal Revenue Code of 1954, Congress undertook to give the grantor trust area a more substantial statutory underpinning by the enactment of Sections 671–675 and 678. The Tax Reform Act of 1976 added Section 679 to deal with problems arising under some foreign trusts. As indicated in *Clifford,* Sections 676 and 677 had a much earlier origin.[5] What is the scope and effect of the restrictive language in the last sentence of Section 671?

Some feel for the grantor trust area can be attained by a look at Sections 673 through 677. A general feel for the area is all that is intended to be gleaned from an examination of the problems in this book. However, here are a few comments on the so-called "grantor trust" provisions, which may help to round out the broad picture.

*Section 673.* The grantor trust rules were tightened up considerably by the Tax Reform Act of 1986. The significant changes here affect the reversionary interest rule of Section 673. Prior to 1986, the grantor of a trust was taxed on the income from the trust (see Section 671) if the grantor retained a reversionary interest in corpus or income which might reasonably be expected to revert to the grantor within ten years.[6] Thus the law provided a safe and easily determinable harbor for a temporary transfer of income-producing property where certain powers and interests retained by the

---

   [3]   See Morrill v. United States, 228 F.Supp. 734 (D.C.Me.1964).

   [4]   Treas.Reg. § 29.22(a)–21 (1943); see Alexandre, "Case Method Restatement of The New Clifford Regulations," 3 Tax L.Rev. 189 (1947).

   [5]   See Revenue Act of 1924, §§ 219(g) and (h), 43 Stat. 253, 277 (1942); and see Corliss v. Bowers set out at page 295, supra. An early basic discussion of the 1954 legislative changes appears in Greenberger, "Changes in the Income Taxation of Clifford Type Trust," 13 N.Y.U.Inst. on Fed.Tax. 165 (1955), and see Yohlin, "The Short-Term Trust—A Respectable Tax-Saving Device," 14 Tax L.Rev. 109 (1958).

   [6]   I.R.C. § 673(a). Prior to the enactment of I.R.C. § 7872 under the 1984 Act, old § 673 was easily circumvented by interest-free loans whose use was judicially approved by J. Simpson Dean, 35 T.C. 1083 (1961), and other cases. Interest-free loans are considered in Chapter 16B, infra.

grantor did not become operative for a period of ten years.[7] Moreover, the 1954 version of Section 673 contained an exception to the ten-year reversionary interest rule if the expectation of reversion depended only on the life expectancy of the income beneficiary.[8] And the former statute did virtually nothing with respect to the avoidance possibilities of a spousal remainder trust, pursuant to which the grantor retained no reversionary interest but on termination of the trust, the remainder would pass to the grantor's spouse.[9]

Today, a grantor is treated as holding any power or interest that is held by an individual who was the spouse of the grantor at the creation of the power or interest or who became the spouse of the grantor after the creation of the power or interest, but only for periods after the individual became the grantor's spouse.[10] Note that this provision appears in Section 672, which means that it applies to each of the substantive provisions found in Sections 673 through 678.

Under current Section 673, the grantor is treated as the owner of any portion of a trust (possibly all) in which the grantor has a reversionary interest in either the corpus or the income, if the value of the reversionary interest exceeds 5 percent of the value of that portion of the trust.[11] This provision replaces the "ten year" reversionary interest rule of prior law.[12] The value of the reversionary interest is measured as of the inception of that portion of the trust in which the grantor has an interest. The application of the 5 percent rule which is imported from the estate tax area[13] may require an actuarial determination of the grantor's chances of surviving others who have beneficial interests in the trust and a valuation of those chances in relation to the value of the property in the trust.[14] In very general terms, if the amount a third party would pay the grantor for a reversionary interest that *might* vest in the grantor a portion of the trust property is more than 5 percent of the value of that portion of the trust, then the grantor is treated as the owner of such portion and must pay the tax on the income generated by that portion of the trust. The value of the grantor's reversionary interest is determined by assuming the maximum exercise of discretion in favor of the grantor.[15] A very limited exception to the reversionary interest rule applies if the reversionary interest will take effect only by reason of the death

---

[7]   See I.R.C. §§ 674(b)(2); 676(b); 677(a), last flush sentence.

[8]   I.R.C. § 673(c).

[9]   See e.g. Sen.Rep. No. 99–313, 99th Cong., 2d Sess. 871 (1986).

[10]   I.R.C. § 672(e)(1). Individuals are not considered married if they are legally separated under a decree of divorce or separate maintenance. I.R.C. § 672(e)(2).

[11]   I.R.C. § 673(a). Any postponement of the date for the reversionary interest is treated as a new transfer in trust commencing with the date the postponement is effective. I.R.C. § 673(d).

[12]   I.R.C. § 673(a).

[13]   See I.R.C. § 2037. Under I.R.C. § 2037(b), "reversionary interest" includes a possibility that the property transferred may return to the decedent transferor or to his estate, or a possibility that it may become subject to a power of disposition by him.

[14]   See Stephens, Maxfield, Lind, & Calfee, *Federal Estate and Gift Taxation*, ¶ 4.09[4][d] (Warren, Gorham & Lamont 9th Ed. 2013).

[15]   I.R.C. § 673(c). Seemingly, this subsection is applicable regardless of whether the power holder is adverse to the exercise of the power.

of a minor lineal descendant of the grantor[16] before reaching age 21.[17] But this is so only if the descendant is a beneficiary who has all of the present interest in the portion of the trust in question.[18]

*Section 674.* Under Section 674(a), the grantor of a trust is taxed on the income from the trust if the grantor or a nonadverse party[19] holds a power, without the approval of an adverse party, to determine who, other than the grantor,[20] will receive the income or the corpus of the trust. Subsections (b), (c) and (d) provide exceptions to the general rule of Section 674(a) identifying groups of situations in which the grantor is not taxed even though such powers are held. The exceptions look to two factors, the nature of the power held and the person holding the power. Generally very indirect or weak powers to alter the beneficial enjoyment may be held by anyone, including the grantor, without invoking Section 674(a).[21] As the scope of the power increases, it will render the grantor taxable unless it is held by someone not closely associated with the grantor.[22]

*Section 675.* This section may apply if a grantor or a nonadverse party holds merely administrative powers over the trust corpus. For example, a power to dispose of trust property for less than full consideration is proscribed;[23] and so is a power to borrow trust corpus or income without payment of adequate interest or the posting of adequate security.[24] Generally, Section 675 may apply in situations in which normal stringent fiduciary standards are waived by the trust instrument.[25]

*Section 676.* This section appropriately treats the grantor as the owner of any portion of a trust if the grantor or a non-adverse party has the power to revest title to the trust in the grantor.[26] Such a power may arise by operation of local law.[27] A very limited exception applies if the power to revoke or revest title arises only after the circumstances creating an exception under Section 673(b).[28]

*Section 677.* The income from a trust need not be actually paid to the grantor to provide benefits to the grantor. If the income from a trust may

---

[16]  I.R.C. § 673(b)(1).

[17]  I.R.C. § 673(b).

[18]  I.R.C. § 673(b)(2). The "present interest" concept, borrowed from the federal gift tax, in general requires that the beneficiary have an immediate, in contrast to a future interest, in the trust or a portion of the trust. See Stephens, Maxfield, Lind, & Calfee, supra note 14 at § 9.04[1][c].

[19]  See I.R.C. § 672(a) and (b).

[20]  I.R.C. § 677(a) controls if the income may be used for the grantor's benefit.

[21]  I.R.C. § 674(b).

[22]  I.R.C. § 674(c) and (d). See Westfall, "Trust Grantors and Section 674: Adventures in Income Tax Avoidance," 60 Colum.L.Rev. 326 (1960), reprinted in Sander and Westfall, Readings in Federal Taxation 471 (Foundation Press 1970).

[23]  I.R.C. § 675(1).

[24]  I.R.C. § 675(2). The grantor of the trust is sometimes taxed if the grantor borrows from the trust even where adequate interest and security is provided. I.R.C. § 675(3).

[25]  I.R.C. § 675(4).

[26]  I.R.C. § 676(a).

[27]  See, e.g., California Probate Code § 15,400 which provides that a trust is revocable unless it is specifically made irrevocable.

[28]  I.R.C. § 676(b). See Text supra at notes 17–18.

benefit the grantor, directly or indirectly, Congress has provided in Section 677 that the grantor may be taxed on the income. Also, Congress decided that the same result should follow if the income may be used directly or indirectly for the grantor's spouse.[29] In general, the provisions of Section 677 apply if the income "may be" used for the proscribed purposes, regardless of how it is in fact used.[30]

*Section 678.* This section presents a new twist to the so-called grantor provisions. Under this section a third person (not the grantor), not necessarily a beneficiary, may be taxed on the income of a trust, if the grantor escapes the other grantor trust provisions[31] and the third person has a power to obtain the income or corpus for the third person's own benefit[32] or has previously released or modified such a power but has retained grantor trust type dominion or control.[33]

## PROBLEMS

1.     Grantor who is a lawyer creates a trust for the benefit of her adult Son with income to Son for life, remainder to Son's children. Who is taxed on the income paid to Son in the following circumstances:

    (a)     Grantor transfers to the trust accounts receivable for services which have never been included in her gross income. The clients pay the fees represented by the receivables in the succeeding year.

    (b)     Grantor owns a building subject to a long term lease. She transfers the right to future rentals under the lease to the trust.

    (c)     Same as (b), above, except that she transfers the building along with the right to the rentals at a time when no rent has accrued.

    (d)     Same as (c), above, except that six months' rent has accrued on the lease at the time of Grantor's transfer.

    (e)     Same as (c), above, except that Grantor retains the right to revoke the trust at any time.

    (f)     Same as (c), above, except that Grantor holds liberal powers to change the income beneficiary of the trust from Son to anyone other than Grantor.

---

[29] Tax Reform Act of 1969, § 332. See I.R.C. § 672(e) which now makes the provision superfluous.

[30] But see I.R.C. § 677(b), relieving the grantor of tax on income that may be used to support a dependent (other than his spouse) except to the extent it is so used.

[31] See I.R.C. § 678(b).

[32] I.R.C. § 678(a)(1). A person's possession of a power, as a fiduciary, merely to have trust income used for the support of his dependents does not invite tax, except to the extent the income is so used. I.R.C. § 678(c); and cf. § 677(b). One might escape I.R.C. § 678 by reason of a trust requirement that *another* person join in the exercise of his power. Reg. § 1.678(c)–1(b). However, the Treasury holds that one whose obligations are discharged by trust distributions is taxable as a beneficiary under §§ 652 or 662. See Reg. § 1.662(a)–4.

[33] I.R.C. § 678(a)(2).

(g)   Same as (c), above, except that at Son's death the property reverts to Grantor if Grantor is then living. The value of the reversionary interest exceeds 5% of the value of the trust corpus.

(h)   Same as (g), above, except that Son is a 19 year old minor.

(i)   Same as (h), above, except that the trust instrument provides that the corpus shall revert to Grantor only if Son dies prior to reaching 21 years of age.

(j)   Same as (c), above, except that Grantor may direct the sale of the trust corpus to any person including herself for any price she wishes.

(k)   Same as (c), above, except that Son is a minor and the income from the trust while Son is a student is used to pay Son's tuition at a private high school which Son attends.

(l)   Same as (c), above, except that under the terms of the trust, Husband may require the trustee to pay the income from the trust to him in any year.

2.    Do you see a relationship between the results in problem one and the messages of the *Earl, Horst,* and other cases of Chapter 12? What additional concept does the grantor trust provisions add?

# PART 4

# DEDUCTIONS IN COMPUTING TAXABLE INCOME

# CHAPTER 14

# BUSINESS DEDUCTIONS

## A. INTRODUCTION

Internal Revenue Code: See Sections 1; 63.

---

There is no constitutional obstacle to a tax on *gross* income. This is not to say the 16th Amendment would support an unapportioned tax on gross receipts, for the term "incomes" as used there connotes *gain* at least to the extent that a mere return of capital is not "income." But expenses incurred earning income might constitutionally be disregarded in the computation of the tax. For this reason, deductions are spoken of as a matter of "legislative grace;" and it is at least true that, as a taxpayer has no constitutional right to a deduction,[1] a taxpayer must find a statutory provision that specifically allows the deduction claimed.

Is the "grace" aspect of deduction provisions of importance in their interpretation? There may be some notion that by allowing a deduction Congress bestows a *special* benefit that should be narrowly construed. Consider whether this is a proper view of any or all the deduction provisions presented in this Part. At least where it is not, should not the courts seek to give meaning to a deduction provision in the same manner as they approach any other congressional product?[2]

Since the statute is all-important in the deduction area, its basic design should be noted. The individual income tax rates[3] are applied to "taxable income."[4] In general, under Section 63 taxable income is gross income minus the deductions provided in the statute.[5]

This Part of the book divides deductions allowed in computing taxable income into four groups. Chapter 14 is concerned with trade and business deductions; and these provisions apply alike to individuals and corporations, although sometimes with variations. For individuals only, Congress identifies a kind of sub-business category in which some expenditures that are not incurred in "business" are considered sufficiently connected with income or profit-seeking activities to warrant their deduction. Chapter 15 is addressed to the deductibility of these expenditures.

---

[1] First Nat. Bank & Trust Co. v. United States, 115 F.2d 194 (5th Cir. 1940).

[2] See Griswold, "An Argument Against the Doctrine that Deductions Should Be Narrowly Construed as a Matter of Legislative Grace," 56 Harv.L.Rev. 1142 (1943).

[3] I.R.C. § 1.

[4] See I.R.C. § 63. Consideration must be given later to (1) computation of tax in the case of joint returns, I.R.C. § 1(j)(2)(A), and certain other special circumstances, and (2) to the tax tables for low-income taxpayers, I.R.C. § 3.

[5] See Chapter 18D, infra.

A general appreciation of the dichotomy recognized in Chapters 14 and 15 can be gleaned from an examination of some of the Code sections making use of the differing concepts. For example, Sections 162 (expenses), 165(c)(1) (losses), and 167(a)(1) (depreciation) all relate specifically to "trade or business" activities. In contrast Sections 165(c)(2) (losses), 167(a)(2) (depreciation), and 212(1) and (2) are all concerned with activities directed toward the "production of income," the "collection of income" or "transactions entered into for profit" without regard to whether the activity involved can be classified as a trade or business.

A third group of deductions available alike to individuals and corporations are allowed without regard to whether they have a business, or income, or profit connection. These are presented in Chapter 16. Finally, Chapter 18 identifies a group of deductions, also outside the business, or income, or profit area which, however, are available only to individuals.

In the deduction area, there are some negative provisions that sometimes countermand what seems to be clear statutory allowance. Thus a practitioner (and of course a student) must be on the alert for congressional finger-crossing. Throughout these Chapters, references are made to these negative provisions, many of which (but not all, see, e.g., Sections 183, 274, 465 and 469) are grouped in the Code at Sections 261–280H. A glance at the headings of those sections might be in order at this point. Chapters 17 and 18C consider some of the negative statutory limitations imposed on the deductions examined in Chapters 14, 15 and 16.

This Chapter begins with Section 162 which is the most comprehensive of the sections concerning business deductions. By this stage a student knows that one does not read the Code the way one does a novel and will appreciate therefore a kind of pondering analysis of the opening clause of Section 162(a). Significant words and phrases will light up as if electrified by the push of a button. For example, it will appear that it is "expenses" that are allowed as deductions by the section. What kinds of expenditures are properly classified as expenses? It will appear further that it is only "ordinary and necessary" expenses that are to be deducted. Does "ordinary" have its ordinary meaning here? And does "necessary" mean absolutely necessary? Further, the expenses that are deductible are only those that relate to "carrying on" a trade or business. Are we "carrying on" when we are getting ready to do business?

The next three segments of this Chapter are addressed directly to the questions just raised. Of course, that does not exhaust the interesting words and phrases of the introductory clause of Section 162(a). For example, it is expenses "paid or incurred" that may be deducted and of course the question further arises whether an expense was paid or incurred "during the taxable year." These are timing questions and, while they necessarily arise here in some circumstances, their development is reserved for later treatment in Chapter 19.

Obviously, deduction under Section 162 also hinges on the expenses involved being related to a "trade or business." This Chapter devotes no separate treatment to that concept because, as indicated above, it arises in numerous contexts throughout the tax areas to which this book is addressed. Accordingly, Part B of this Chapter develops three crucial factors in the application of Section 162 ("ordinary and necessary," "expenses," and "carrying on") and then examines specific expenditures that the statute (which is similar to Section 61 in that it provides a nonexclusive list) identifies as deductible business expenses when all requirements of Section 162 are met.

## B. THE ANATOMY OF THE BUSINESS DEDUCTION WORKHORSE: SECTION 162

### 1. "ORDINARY AND NECESSARY"

Internal Revenue Code: Section 162(a).

Regulations: Section 1.162–1(a).

---

### Welch v. Helvering

Supreme Court of the United States, 1933.
290 U.S. 111, 54 S.Ct. 8.

■ MR. JUSTICE CARDOZO delivered the opinion of the Court.

The question to be determined is whether payments by a taxpayer, who is in business as a commission agent, are allowable deductions in the computation of his income if made to the creditors of a bankrupt corporation in an endeavor to strengthen his own standing and credit.

In 1922 petitioner was the secretary of the E.L. Welch Company, a Minnesota corporation, engaged in the grain business. The company was adjudged an involuntary bankrupt, and had a discharge from its debts. Thereafter the petitioner made a contract with the Kellogg Company to purchase grain for it on a commission. In order to reestablish his relations with customers whom he had known when acting for the Welch Company and to solidify his credit and standing, he decided to pay the debts of the Welch business so far as he was able. In fulfillment of that resolve, he made payments of substantial amounts during five successive years. In 1924, the commissions were $18,028.20; the payments $3,975.97; in 1923, the commissions $31,377.07; the payments $11,968.20; in 1926, the commissions $20,925.25; the payments $12,815.72; in 1927, the commissions $22,119.61; the payments $7,379.72; and in 1928, the commissions $26,177.56, the payments $11,068.25. The Commissioner ruled that these payments were not deductible from income as ordinary and necessary expenses, but were rather in the nature of capital expenditures, an outlay for the development of reputation and good will. The Board of Tax Appeals sustained the action of the Commissioner (25 B.T.A. 117), and the Court of Appeals for the Eighth Circuit affirmed. 63 F.2d 976. The case is here on certiorari.

"In computing net income there shall be allowed as deductions * * * all the ordinary and necessary expenses paid or incurred during the taxable year in carrying on any trade or business." [The Court cites revenue acts and regulations applicable to the different taxable years. Ed.]

We may assume that the payments to creditors of the Welch Company were necessary for the development of the petitioner's business, at least in the sense that they were appropriate and helpful. McCulloch v. Maryland, 17 U.S. (4 Wheat.) 316. He certainly thought they were, and we should be slow to override his judgment. But the problem is not solved when the payments are characterized as necessary. Many necessary payments are charges upon capital. There is need to determine whether they are both necessary and ordinary. Now, what is ordinary, though there must always be a strain of constancy within it, is none the less a variable affected by time and place and circumstance. Ordinary in this context does not mean that the payments must be habitual or normal in the sense that the same taxpayer will have to make them often. A lawsuit affecting the safety of a business may happen once in a lifetime. The counsel fees may be so heavy that repetition is unlikely. None the less, the expense is an ordinary one because we know from experience that payments for such a purpose, whether the amount is large or small, are the common and accepted means of defense against attack. Cf. Kornhauser v. United States, 276 U.S. 145, 48 S.Ct. 219. The situation is unique in the life of the individual affected, but not in the life of the group, the community, of which he is a part. At such times there are norms of conduct that help to stabilize our judgment, and make it certain and objective. The instance is not erratic, but is brought within a known type.

The line of demarcation is now visible between the case that is here and the one supposed for illustration. We try to classify this act as ordinary or the opposite, and the norms of conduct fail us. No longer can we have recourse to any fund of business experience, to any known business practice. Men do at times pay the debts of others without legal obligation or the lighter obligation imposed by the usages of trade or by neighborly amenities, but they do not do so ordinarily, not even though the result might be to heighten their reputation for generosity and opulence. Indeed, if language is to be read in its natural and common meaning * * *, we should have to say that payment in such circumstances, instead of being ordinary is in a high degree extraordinary. There is nothing ordinary in the stimulus evoking it, and none in the response. Here, indeed, as so often in other branches of the law, the decisive distinctions are those of degree and not of kind. One struggles in vain for any verbal formula that will supply a ready touchstone. The standard set up by the statute is not a rule of law; it is rather a way of life. Life in all its fullness must supply the answer to the riddle.

The Commissioner of Internal Revenue resorted to that standard in assessing the petitioner's income, and found that the payments in controversy came closer to capital outlays than to ordinary and necessary expenses in the operation of a business. His ruling has the support of a presumption of correctness, and the petitioner has the burden of proving it to be wrong. * * *. Unless we can say from facts within our knowledge that these are ordinary and necessary expenses according to the ways of conduct and the forms of speech prevailing in the business world, the tax must be confirmed. But nothing told us by this record or within the sphere of our judicial notice permits us to give that extension to what is ordinary and necessary. Indeed, to do so would open the door to many bizarre analogies. One man has a family name that is clouded by thefts committed by an ancestor. To add to his own standing he repays the stolen money, wiping off, it may be, his income for the year. The payments figure in his tax return as ordinary expenses. Another man conceives the notion that he will be able to practice his vocation with greater ease and profit if he has an opportunity to enrich his culture. Forthwith the price of his education becomes an expense of the business, reducing the income subject to taxation. There is little difference between these expenses and those in controversy here. Reputation and learning are akin to capital assets, like the good will of an old partnership. Cf. Colony Coal & Coke Corp. v. Commissioner, 52 F.2d 923. For many, they are the only tools with which to hew a pathway to success. The money spent in acquiring them is well and wisely spent. It is not an ordinary expense of the operation of a business.

Many cases in the federal courts deal with phases of the problem presented in the case at bar. To attempt to harmonize them would be a futile task. They involve the appreciation of particular situations, at times with borderline conclusions. Typical illustrations are cited in the margin.[1]

---

[1] Ordinary expenses: Commissioner v. People's-Pittsburgh Trust Co., 60 F.2d 187, expenses incurred in the defense of a criminal charge growing out of the business of the taxpayer; American Rolling Mill Co. v. Commissioner, 41 F.2d 314, contributions to a civic improvement fund by a corporation employing half of the wage earning population of the city, the payments being made, not for charity, but to add to the skill and productivity of the workmen (cf. the decisions collated in 30 Columbia Law Review 1211, 1212, and the distinctions there drawn); Corning Glass Works v. Lucas, 59 App.D.C. 168; 37 F.2d 798, donations to a hospital by a corporation whose employees with their dependents made up two thirds of the population of the city; Harris v. Lucas, 48 F.2d 187, payments of debts discharged in bankruptcy, but subject to be revived by force of a new promise. Cf. Lucas v. Ox Fibre Brush Co., 281 U.S. 115, 50 S.Ct. 273, where additional compensation, reasonable in amount, was allowed to the officers of a corporation for services previously rendered.

Not ordinary expenses: Hubinger v. Commissioner, 36 F.2d 724, payments by the taxpayer for the repair of fire damage, such payments being distinguished from those for wear and tear; Lloyd v. Commissioner, 55 F.2d 842, counsel fees incurred by the taxpayer, the president of a corporation, in prosecuting a slander suit to protect his reputation and that of his business; 105

The decree should be

Affirmed.

## PROBLEMS

**1.** Taxpayer is a businessman, local politician who is also an officer-director of a savings and loan association of which he was a founder. When, partially due to his mismanagement, the savings and loan began to go under, he voluntarily donated nearly one half a million dollars to help bail it out. Is the payment deductible under § 162? See Elmer W. Conti, 31 T.C.M. 348 (1972).

**2.** Consultant incurred ordinary and necessary expenses on a business trip for which she was entitled to reimbursement from Client upon filing an expense report. However, Consultant did not file an expense report and was not reimbursed but, instead, deducted her costs on her income tax return. Is Consultant entitled to a § 162 deduction? See Heidt v. Commissioner, 274 F.2d 25 (7th Cir.1959).

## 2. "EXPENSES"

Internal Revenue Code: Sections 162(a); 263(a).

Regulations: Sections 1.162–4(a); 1.263(a)–1(b), (d); 1.263(a)–2(d)(1), (d)(2) Examples 1, 5, 6, & 8, (f)(1), (f)(2)(i) & (ii); 1.263(a)–3(d), (e)(2)(i), (e)(3)(i), (i)(1), (j)(1), (j)(3) Examples 1, 2, 5, 12 & 13, (k)(1), (k)(7) Examples 14 and 15, (*l*)(1), (*l*)(3) Examples 1 & 2; 1.263(a)–4(a), (b)(1), (c)(1), (d)(1), (e)(1)(i), (e)(4)(i); 1.263(a)–5(a)(1), (b)(1).

———————

Section 162(a) allows a taxpayer to deduct *"expenses"* paid or incurred during the taxable year. On the other hand, Section 263(a) states that no deduction shall be allowed for "any amount paid out for new buildings or for permanent improvements or betterments made to increase the value of any property. . . ." In tax jargon, Section 263(a) denies a current deduction for *"capital expenditures."* Thus, the Code requires taxpayers to distinguish expenses, that are currently deductible, from capital expenditures that cannot be deducted when they are made. Drawing the line between expenses and capital expenditures is not always easy and any attempt to harmonize all of the cases and authorities dealing with that distinction would, in the words of Mr. Justice Cardozo in the *Welch* case, be "a futile task."

The question is really only one of timing because, as a general rule, in a business the cost incurred will either be (1) deducted immediately,

———————

West 55th Street v. Commissioner, 42 F.2d 849, and Blackwell Oil & Gas Co. v. Commissioner, 60 F.2d 257, gratuitous payments to stockholders in settlement of disputes between them, or to assume the expense of a lawsuit in which they had been made defendants; White v. Commissioner, 61 F.2d 726, payments in settlement of a lawsuit against a member of a partnership, the effect being to enable him to devote his undivided efforts to the partnership business and also to protect its credit.

"expensed" as the accountants say, (2) capitalized and written off over a period of time by way of depreciation or amortization deductions, or (3) taken into account on a realization of gain or loss from the property. But, of course, timing is important as it relates to the concept of the *time value of money*. Thus, the issue is whether the taxpayer will continue to have the use of the dollars at least momentarily saved by way of a deduction for an expense or whether one must let the government have the use of the money paid as tax when the expense deduction is disallowed and get back one's costs piecemeal by way of deductions or reduction in gain in future years. It is therefore not surprising, although it is unfortunate, to discover much controversy and expensive litigation in this area and too little light for always sound prediction.

*Regulations.* The Treasury has provided regulations with guidance on capitalization rules for over fifty years. But in the last decade, the Treasury has substantially expanded the regulations, most recently by issuing regulations in the year 2013,[1] demonstrating that capitalization issues remain high on the Treasury's agenda. A brief examination of Regulation § 1.263(a)–1 provides the general rules and an outline of the more detailed rules in other regulations. The other regulations include rules on:

(1)  Amounts paid to acquire or produce tangible property, both real and personal;[2]

(2)  Amounts paid to improve tangible property, both real and personal;[3]

(3)  Amounts paid to acquire or create intangible property;[4]

(4)  Amounts paid or incurred to facilitate an acquisition of a trade or business and similar business transactions;[5]

## Amounts Paid to Acquire or Produce Tangible Property

Questions of capitalization and the timing of the deductibility of expenditures are not unique to Section 162. We will encounter similar timing issues elsewhere throughout these materials. Here we deal with three specific areas where the capitalization rules apply. The first is when a taxpayer acquires or produces tangible property. You have already been exposed to the concept of a capital expenditure. In Chapter 6 you saw that when a taxpayer purchases tangible property, such as land or a building, the expenditure has to be capitalized and the taxpayer obtains a cost basis in the property.[6] Similarly, if a taxpayer purchases

---

[1]  The regulations generally apply to taxable years beginning on or after January 1, 2014. Reg. § 1.263(a)–1(h), –2(j)(1), –3(r)(1).

[2]  Reg. § 1.263(a)–2.

[3]  Reg. § 1.263(a)–3.

[4]  Reg. § 1.263(a)–4.

[5]  Reg. § 1.263(a)–5.

[6]  Reg. § 1.263(a)–2(d)(1), (d)(2) Examples 5 and 6. See I.R.C. § 1012.

intangible property, like stocks or bonds, the same principle applies.[7] Additionally, the cost of real estate, including brokerage costs and amounts paid to facilitate the acquisition, must also be capitalized as part of a property's basis.[8] The general rules also provide that commissions and transaction costs paid in the purchase or sale of property generally must be capitalized (added to the cost basis) or be a reduction in the amount realized.[9]

If a taxpayer constructs a building rather than purchasing one, the costs of construction must be capitalized.[10] The amount capitalized as part of the constructed building's basis would include various items such as architect fees, permits, and other incidental costs.[11] Suppose that a taxpayer uses equipment in the construction process and the equipment normally would qualify for depreciation deductions in the taxpayer's business. In *Commissioner v. Idaho Power Co.*,[12] the Supreme Court held that the amount of depreciation deductions on the equipment must be capitalized (rather than deducted) as part of the basis of the constructed property, stating:[13]

> Accepted accounting practice and established tax principles require the capitalization of the cost of acquiring a capital asset. In *Woodward v. Commissioner*, 397 U.S. 572, 575, 90 S.Ct. 1302 (1970), the Court observed: "It has long been recognized, as a general matter, that costs incurred in the acquisition . . . of a capital asset are to be treated as capital expenditures." This principle has obvious application to the acquisition of a capital asset by purchase, but it has been applied, as well, to the costs incurred in a taxpayer's construction of capital facilities. * * *

> There can be little question that other construction-related expense items, such as tools, materials, and wages paid construction workers, are to be treated as part of the cost of acquisition of a capital asset. The taxpayer does not dispute this. Of course, reasonable wages paid in the carrying on of a trade or business qualify as a deduction from gross income. * * * But when wages are paid in connection with the construction or acquisition of a capital asset, they must be capitalized and then are entitled to be amortized over the life of the capital asset so acquired. * * *

> Construction-related depreciation is not unlike expenditures for wages for construction workers. The significant

---

[7]  See Reg. § 1.263(a)–4(c)(1).

[8]  Reg. § 1.263(a)–2(d) and (f).

[9]  Reg. § 1.263(a)–1(b)–(e).

[10]  Reg. § 1.263(a)–2(d)(2) Example 8.

[11]  Reg. § 1.263(a)–2(f)(2)(ii).

[12]  418 U.S. 1, 94 S.Ct. 2757 (1974).

[13]  Commissioner v. Idaho Power Co., 418 U.S. 1, 12–14, 94 S.Ct. 2757, 2764–2765 (1974) (footnotes omitted).

fact is that the exhaustion of construction equipment does not represent the final disposition of the taxpayer's investment in that equipment; rather, the investment in the equipment is assimilated into the cost of the capital asset constructed. Construction-related depreciation on the equipment is not an expense to the taxpayer of its day-to-day business. It is, however, appropriately recognized as a part of the taxpayer's cost or investment in the capital asset. The taxpayer's own accounting procedure reflects this treatment, for on its books the construction-related depreciation was capitalized by a credit to the equipment account and a debit to the capital facility account. By the same token, this capitalization prevents the distortion of income that would otherwise occur if depreciation property allocable to asset acquisition were deducted from gross income currently realized. * * *

An additional pertinent factor is that capitalization of construction-related depreciation by the taxpayer who does its own construction work maintains tax parity with the taxpayer who has its construction work done by an independent contractor. The depreciation on the contractor's equipment incurred during the performance of the job will be an element of cost charged by the contractor for his construction services, and the entire cost, of course, must be capitalized by the taxpayer having the construction work performed. * * *

The principle of the *Idaho Power Co.* case has been generally codified in Section 263A, a section that deals with capitalization of costs to construct tangible personal property and real property.[14] A glance at that section and its regulations makes clear how complex these rules have become.

**Repairs Versus Improvements**

A second area where capitalization issues arise is drawing the line between costs related to tangible property that are incurred as repairs (currently deductible expenses) and expenditures that are improvements to the property (amounts required to be capitalized).[15] As the *Midland Empire Packing Co.* case illustrates, that distinction is frequently blurred.

---

[14]  See Reg. § 1.263(a)–1(b) for the interrelationship of I.R.C. §§ 263 and 263A.
[15]  See Reg. § 1.263(a)–3.

# Midland Empire Packing Co. v. Commissioner

Tax Court of the United States, 1950.
14 T.C. 635.

■ ARUNDELL, JUDGE:

The issue in this case is whether an expenditure for a concrete lining in petitioner's basement to oilproof it against an oil nuisance created by a neighboring refinery is deductible as an ordinary and necessary expense under section [162(a)] of the Internal Revenue Code, on the theory it was an expenditure for a repair, or, in the alternative, whether the expenditure may be treated as the measure of the loss sustained during the taxable year and not compensated for by insurance or otherwise within the meaning of section [165] of the Internal Revenue Code.

The respondent has contended, in part, that the expenditure is for a capital improvement and should be recovered through depreciation charges and is, therefore, not deductible as an ordinary and necessary business expense or as a loss.

It is none too easy to determine on which side of the line certain expenditures fall so that they may be accorded their proper treatment for tax purposes. Treasury Regulations 111,[1] from which we quote in the margin, is helpful in distinguishing between an expenditure to be classed as a repair and one to be treated as a capital outlay. In Illinois Merchants Trust Co., Executor, 4 B.T.A. 103, at page 106, we discussed this subject in some detail and in our opinion said:

"It will be noted that the first sentence of the article * * * relates to repairs, while the second sentence deals in effect with replacements. In determining whether an expenditure is a capital one or is chargeable against operating income, it is necessary to bear in mind the purpose for which the expenditure was made. To repair is to restore to a sound state or to mend, while a replacement connotes a substitution. A repair is an expenditure for the purpose of keeping the property in an ordinarily efficient operating condition. It does not add to the value of the property, nor does it appreciably prolong its life. It merely keeps the property in an operating condition over its probable useful life for the uses for which it was acquired. Expenditures for that purpose are distinguishable from those for replacements, alterations, improvements, or additions which prolong the life of the property, increase its value, or make it adaptable to a different use. The one is a maintenance charge,

---

[1] [Reg. § 1.162–4. Ed.] Repairs.—The cost of incidental repairs which neither materially add to the value of the property nor appreciably prolong its life, but keep it in an ordinarily efficient operating condition, may be deducted as expense, provided the plant or property account is not increased by the amount of such expenditures. Repairs in the nature of replacements, to the extent that they arrest deterioration and appreciably prolong the life of the property, should be charged against the depreciation reserve if such account is kept. * * *

while the others are additions to capital investment which should not be applied against current earnings."

It will be seen from our findings of fact that for some 25 years prior to the taxable year petitioner had used the basement rooms of its plant as a place for the curing of hams and bacon and for the storage of meat and hides. The basement had been entirely satisfactory for this purpose over the entire period in spite of the fact that there was some seepage of water into the rooms from time to time. In the taxable year it was found that not only water, but oil, was seeping through the concrete walls of the basement of the packing plant and, while the water would soon drain out, the oil would not, and there was left on the basement floor a thick scum of oil which gave off a strong odor that permeated the air of the entire plant, and the fumes from the oil created a fire hazard. It appears that the oil which came from a nearby refinery had also gotten into the water wells which served to furnish water for petitioner's plant, and as a result of this whole condition the Federal meat inspectors advised petitioner that it must discontinue the use of the water from the wells and oilproof the basement, or else shut down its plant.

To meet this situation, petitioner during the taxable year undertook steps to oilproof the basement by adding a concrete lining to the walls from the floor to a height of about four feet and also added concrete to the floor of the basement. It is the cost of this work which it seeks to deduct as a repair. The basement was not enlarged by this work nor did the oilproofing serve to make it more desirable for the purpose for which it had been used through the years prior to the time that the oil nuisance had occurred. The evidence is that the expenditure did not add to the value or prolong the expected life of the property over what they were before the event occurred which made the repairs necessary. It is true that after the work was done the seepage of water, as well as oil, was stopped, but, as already stated, the presence of the water had never been found objectionable. The repairs merely served to keep the property in an operating condition over its probable useful life for the purpose for which it was used.

While it is conceded on brief that the expenditure was "necessary," respondent contends that the encroachment of the oil nuisance on petitioner's property was not an "ordinary" expense in petitioner's particular business. But the fact that petitioner had not theretofore been called upon to make a similar expenditure to prevent damage and disaster to its property does not remove that expense from the classification of "ordinary" for, as stated in Welch v. Helvering, 290 U.S. 111, "ordinary in this context does not mean that the payments must be habitual or normal in the sense that the same taxpayer will have to make them often. * * * the expense is an ordinary one because we know from experience that payments for such a purpose, whether the amount is large or small, are the common and accepted means of defense against attack. Cf. Kornhauser v. United States, 276 U.S. 145, 48 S.Ct. 219. The situation is unique in the life of the individual affected, but not in the life of the group, the community, of which he is a part." Steps to protect a business building from the seepage of oil from a nearby refinery, which had been erected long subsequent to the time petitioner started to operate its plant, would seem to us to be a normal thing to do, and in certain sections of the country it must be a common experience to protect one's property from the seepage of oil. Expenditures to accomplish this result are likewise normal.

In American Bemberg Corporation, 10 T.C. 361, we allowed as deductions, on the ground that they were ordinary and necessary expenses, extensive expenditures made to prevent disaster, although the repairs were of a type which had never been needed before and were unlikely to recur. In that case the taxpayer, to stop cave-ins of soil which were threatening destruction of its manufacturing plant, hired an engineering firm which drilled to the bedrock and injected grout to fill the cavities where practicable, and made incidental replacements and repairs, including tightening of the fluid carriers. In two successive years the taxpayer expended $734,316.76 and $199,154.33, respectively, for such drilling and grouting and $153,474.20 and $79,687.29, respectively, for capital replacements. We found that the cost (other than replacement) of this program did not make good the depreciation previously allowed, and stated in our opinion:

> "In connection with the purpose of the work, the Proctor program was intended to avert a plant-wide disaster and avoid forced abandonment of the plant. The purpose was not to improve, better, extend, or increase the original plant, nor to prolong its original useful life. Its continued operation was endangered; the purpose of the expenditures was to enable petitioner to continue the plant in operation not on any new or better scale, but on the same scale and, so far as possible, as efficiently as it had operated before. The purpose was not to rebuild or replace the plant in whole or in part, but to keep the same plant as it was and where it was."

The petitioner here made the repairs in question in order that it might continue to operate its plant. Not only was there danger of fire from the oil and fumes, but the presence of the oil led the Federal meat inspectors to declare the basement an unsuitable place for the purpose for which it had been used for a quarter of a century. After the expenditures were made, the plant did not operate on a changed or larger scale, nor was it thereafter suitable for new or additional uses. The expenditure served only to permit petitioner to continue the use of the plant, and particularly the basement for its normal operations.

In our opinion, the expenditure of $4,868.81 for lining the basement walls and floor was essentially a repair and, as such, it is deductible as an ordinary and necessary business expense. This holding makes unnecessary a consideration of petitioner's alternative contention that the expenditure is deductible as a business loss, nor need we heed the respondent's argument that any loss suffered was compensated for by "insurance or otherwise."

Decision will be entered under Rule 50.

## NOTE

Tax Lawyer (T.L.) kept at the side of her bed a collection of cases carefully selected for her by her law clerk to be used by her as a substitute for Nytol when sleep was elusive. She had just finished reading *Midland Empire Packing Co.* and was comfortably close to dozing when her eye caught *Mt. Morris Drive-In Theatre Co.*[1] Hastily scanning the one-page Tax Court opinion, she discovered that when the Theatre Company was required by threat of a lawsuit by adjacent property owners to expend money for a drainage system that would protect the Company's neighbors from the flow of water from its land, it had made a nondeductible capital expenditure. She noticed also that when the Tax Court opinion was reviewed, one judge concurred in two sentences, to which when read by another he said, "uh huh." On the other hand, another judge spent four sentences dissenting and picked up four of his brethren as followers. But T.L. was not sure she could see a difference in the expenditures to prevent liquid incursion by an offended flowee from those of an offending flower.

T.L. had a bad night. She *could* see, as did the concurring Tax Court judge, that if the drainage expenditure had been undertaken initially when the drive-in theatre had been first built, it certainly would have been a capital cost of construction, not an expense. However, she felt most frustrated by not being able to ask the concurring Tax Court judge how the *Midland Empire* expenditure would have been treated if it, too, had been made at the time the packing plant was being built. She found very little tranquility in the comment in the Tax Court opinion that in the business expense, capital expenditure area, "The decisive test is * * * the character of the transaction which gives rise to the payment."

After a wholly sleepless night, T.L.'s first action at the office in the morning was to dictate a memorandum to her law clerk directing him to select no more cases for her dealing with the question whether an expenditure is an expense or one to be capitalized.[2]

---

[1] Mt. Morris Drive-In Theatre Co. v. Commissioner, 25 T.C. 272 (1955), affirmed 238 F.2d 85 (6th Cir.1956).

[2] The dilemma reflected in *Midland Empire* and *Mt. Morris Drive-In* can be elaborated to present a possible *three-way* tax view of a single expenditure. In Hochschild v. Commissioner, 161 F.2d 817 (2d Cir.1947), a taxpayer had paid attorneys' fees defending a stockholders' derivative suit. The Tax Court in the later income tax case treated the fees in part as capital expenditures, a cost of defending title to the taxpayer's stock and in part as deductible expense incurred for the collection of income (see I.R.C. § 212(1)). Could at least a part, as the taxpayer argued, have been treated as an I.R.C. § 162 business expense, sufficiently related to the taxpayer's business as a corporate employee? Indeed, it does not upset the purpose of this example to state that in reversing the Tax Court the Second Circuit, noting the taxpayer was defending a charge of malfeasance in his position as a director and officer, treated the *entire* fee as a § 162 expense.

And so it is with equivocal expenditures such as those in *Midland Empire* and *Mt. Morris*. The Section 162 regulation on "repairs" attempts to differentiate deductible expenses from capital expenditures somewhat enigmatically. The Section 162 regulation defers to the Section 263 capitalization regulations by stating that a taxpayer is allowed to deduct amounts paid for repairs and maintenance of tangible property if those amounts are not otherwise required to be capitalized.[3]

Under the capitalization regulations, a taxpayer generally must capitalize amounts paid to improve a unit of property.[4] A unit of property is considered "improved" if amounts are paid after the property is placed in service that (1) result in the betterment of the property,[5] (2) restore the property,[6] or (3) adapt the property to a new or different use.[7] In the case of personal property, all components that are functionally interdependent generally are considered a unit of property.[8] For buildings, each building system (e.g., plumbing, electrical, fire and alarm, security, and all elevators), including the structural components thereof, generally is considered a unit of property for applying the rules on improvements.[9]

The capitalization regulations provide that a "betterment" results only if an amount paid (1) ameliorates a material condition or defect in property that either existed at acquisition or arose during production of the property, whether or not the taxpayer was aware of the condition or defect, (2) results in a material addition to the property, or (3) is reasonably expected to result in a material increase in capacity, productivity, efficiency, strength, or quality of the property.[10] For example, if a taxpayer buys a store located on a parcel of land that contained gasoline storage tanks that leaked causing soil contamination, the remediation costs to the soil are a betterment to the land because the costs ameliorate a material preexisting condition or defect.[11] But if a taxpayer owns a building that was constructed with insulation containing asbestos and decides to remove the insulation to reduce potential health risks, the costs of removal are not a betterment because the insulation was not a preexisting or material defect of the building because asbestos was widely used before the health dangers were recognized. The removal and replacement of the asbestos insulation is not a material addition to the building and does not materially increase the capacity, productivity, efficiency, strength, or quality of the building.[12]

A "restoration" of property includes situations where the amount paid (1) returns the property to its ordinarily efficient operating condition after it deteriorated to a state of disrepair where it was no longer functional for its

---

[3]   Reg. § 1.162–4(a).

[4]   Reg. § 1.263(a)–3(d).

[5]   Reg. § 1.263(a)–3(j).

[6]   Reg. § 1.263(a)–3(k).

[7]   Reg. § 1.263(a)–3(*l*).

[8]   See Reg. § 1.263(a)–3(e)(3).

[9]   See Reg. § 1.263(a)–3(e)(2).

[10]   Reg. § 1.263(a)–3(j)(1).

[11]   Reg. § 1.263(a)–3(j)(3) Example 1.

[12]   Reg. § 1.263(a)–3(j)(3) Example 2.

intended use, or (2) is a replacement of a part or a combination of parts that comprise a major component or structural part of the property.[13] For example, assume a taxpayer owns a store and discovers a leak in the roof and hires a contractor to inspect and fix the leak. The contractor determines that a major portion of the roof has rotted and recommends replacement of the entire roof. In that case, the roof is a major component of the building and its replacement will be a restoration that is an improvement which must be capitalized.[14] However, if the contractor had recommended replacement of a waterproof rubber membrane connected to the roof decking, the replacement does not constitute a substantial structural part of the building and the cost would not have to be capitalized.[15]

An amount that is paid to adapt a property to a new or different use must also be capitalized if the adaptation is not consistent with the taxpayer's intended ordinary use of the property at the time it was originally placed in service by the taxpayer.[16] For example, if a manufacturer owns a manufacturing building and pays amounts to convert the building into a showroom for its business, the costs of the conversion adapt the building to a new use and are an improvement which must be capitalized.[17] But if a taxpayer owns a building consisting of multiple retail rental spaces and incurs costs to reconfigure three such spaces into one larger space for a new tenant, those costs are not an improvement because the combination of retail rental spaces is consistent with the intended ordinary use of the building.[18]

The regulations on improvements to tangible property also contain safe harbors for routine maintenance performed on a unit of property.[19] Such routine maintenance is deemed not to be an improvement. Routine maintenance is defined as recurring activities that a taxpayer expects to perform as a result of the use of the property to keep it in its ordinarily efficient operating condition. Examples of routine maintenance include inspection, cleaning, testing, and certain replacement of parts (not amounting to a restoration).[20] To be routine the activity generally must be done more than once over the property's life and factors such as industry practice, the manufacture's recommendations, and the taxpayer's experience are considered in determining whether the taxpayer is performing routine maintenance.[21]

While the regulations are extensive and detailed we are still at times dealing with concepts that have edges no more sharp than those of "fraud",

---

[13] Reg. § 1.263(a)–3(k)(1)(iv), (vi). A restoration also occurs when the amount paid (1) is a replacement for a component or a repair of damage that was previously deducted as a loss, or (2) rebuilds the property to a like-new condition after the end of its class life under the alternate depreciation system under I.R.C. § 168(g). See Reg. § 1.263(a)–3(k)(1).

[14] Reg. § 1.263(a)–3(k)(7) Example 14.

[15] Reg. § 1.263(a)–3(k)(7) Example 15. See also Reg. § 1.263(a)–3(j)(3) Example 13.

[16] Reg. § 1.263(a)–3(*l*)(1).

[17] Reg. § 1.263(a)–3(*l*)(3) Example 1.

[18] Reg. § 1.263(a)–3(*l*)(3) Example 2.

[19] Reg. § 1.263(a)–3(i)(1). See also Reg. § 1.263(a)–3(h) for a safe harbor for "small" taxpayers.

[20] Reg. § 1.263(a)–3(i)(1)(i).

[21] Id.

"proximate cause" or "reasonably prudent person". Past decisions in the area often defy reconciliation. Nevertheless, it is helpful in understanding the approach of the regulations to refocus on the basic policy or theory underlying the inquiry. The general idea is that the cost of property acquired for business use is a charge against income that it helps to earn, ratably over the expected useful life of the property.[22] Expenditures made to enable the taxpayer to use the property for *that* expected period and for the planned purpose generally should be deductible expenses. Thus a taxpayer can paint and patch and repaper and add some new shingles to the roof and charge the costs against income;[23] but if one undertakes the same activities as a part of the overall restoration of a building or adapt it to some new use, one must capitalize these and related expenditures.[24]

Nor is it material that the work is done under compulsion, as pursuant to the order of the city building commissioner,[25] or under threat of an injunction.[26]

The challenge in the repair-versus-capitalization area is in applying general principles to specific fact situations. Thus, it is instructive to consider how the *Midland Empire Packing Co.* and *Mt. Morris Drive-In Theatre* cases would likely be decided under the current regulations. The issue in each case would be whether there was a "betterment" to the property that was an improvement which must be capitalized.[27] In considering *Midland Empire Packing*, was the oil nuisance a defect that existed prior to acquisition of the property? Recall that the basement had been satisfactorily used for 25 years with just some slight seepage of water during that time. Did the lining of the basement constitute a major addition to the property or materially increase its capacity, productivity, strength, or quality? Certainly not in comparison to its condition prior to the oilproofing of the basement. Seemingly, the work in *Midland Empire* would be a repair.[28] Regarding the *Mt. Morris* case, the construction of a drainage system would likely constitute the production of tangible property or be a betterment to the building because it ameliorates a preexisting material condition or defect. Thus, the costs would likely be treated as a capital expenditure.[29]

Much more could be said here about the repair/capital expenditure dichotomy. But it would probably not be profitable. Many matters are crisp and clean, as just a little research will show. The gray areas are best approached by a wide reading of the cases and regulations; it may be more a

---

[22]  See I.R.C. § 168(a)(2), (c).

[23]  Chesapeake Corp. of Virginia v. Commissioner, 17 T.C. 668 (1951), acq. Rev.Rul. 65–13, 1965–1 C.B. 87. See Reg. § 1.263(a)–3(i).

[24]  Regenstein v. Edwards, 121 F.Supp. 952 (M.D.Ga.1954). See Reg. § 1.263(a)–3(k) and (*l*).

[25]  Ibid. See Reg. § 1.263(a)–3(g)(4).

[26]  See Woolrich Woolen Mills v. United States, 289 F.2d 444 (3d Cir.1961), addition of filtration plant required by state antipollution law.

[27]  Reg. § 1.263(a)–3(j).

[28]  See Reg. § 1.263(a)–3(j)(3) Example 12.

[29]  See Reg. § 1.263(a)–3(j)(2) and cf. Reg. § 1.263(a)–3(j)(3) Example 5.

matter of developing a "feel" for the problems than just acquiring some knowledge.[30]

### Amounts Paid to Acquire or Create Intangible Property

A third area where the issue of capitalization has achieved notoriety is the question of capitalization of costs related to the acquisition or creation of various types of intangible assets. The Supreme Court announced a broad and expansive standard for capitalization of such costs in INDOPCO, Inc. v. Commissioner, portions of which appear below in the text, but the Treasury has issued regulations that retreat somewhat from that position. The regulations are discussed in the note following the *INDOPCO* case.

## INDOPCO, Inc. v. Commissioner[*]

Supreme Court of the United States, 1992.
503 U.S. 79, 112 S.Ct. 1039.

■ JUSTICE BLACKMUN delivered the opinion of the Court.

In this case we must decide whether certain professional expenses incurred by a target corporation in the course of a friendly takeover are deductible by that corporation as "ordinary and necessary" business expenses under § 162(a) of the Internal Revenue Code.

[The *INDOPCO* case can be challenging for a student in an introductory federal income tax course since it involves a sophisticated corporate transaction. The case is included in a text on the federal income tax despite its corporate setting because it addresses principles of capitalization that apply to all taxpayers.

The taxpayer in the case is the National Starch and Chemical Corporation, a Delaware corporation that changed its name to INDOPCO. Another Delaware corporation, Unilever United States, Inc., expressed an interest in acquiring National Starch, which was one of its suppliers, through a friendly takeover transaction. In November, 1997, National Starch's directors were formally advised of Unilever's interest in acquiring the corporation and the proposed transaction. To accomplish the transaction, National Starch hired both investment bankers and legal counsel. National Starch eventually paid its investment banker a fee of $2,225,586. National Starch's legal counsel charged it $505,069. National Starch also incurred expenses aggregating $150,962 for miscellaneous items—such as accounting, printing, proxy solicitation, and Securities and Exchange Commission fees—in connection with the transaction. The amount of all these fees was reasonable.

On its federal tax return, National Starch claimed a deduction for $2,225,586 paid to the investment banker, but did not deduct the $505,069 paid to its legal counsel or the other expenses. The

---

[30] This note deals with the expense/capital expenditure dichotomy largely on the basis of whether something is a repair or an improvement. The problem is of course very much broader as the *Welch* case, supra page 311 indicates.

[*] Some footnotes omitted.

Commissioner of Internal Revenue disallowed the claimed deduction and issued a notice of deficiency. National Starch then went to Tax Court and asserted not only the right to deduct the investment banking fees and expenses but, as well, the legal and miscellaneous expenses it incurred. Ed.]

\* \* \*

The Tax Court, in an unreviewed decision, ruled that the expenditures were capital in nature and therefore not deductible under § 162(a) in the 1978 return as "ordinary and necessary expenses." *National Starch and Chemical Corp. v. Commissioner*, 93 T.C. 67 (1989). The court based its holding primarily on the long-term benefits that accrued to National Starch from the Unilever acquisition. *Id.*, at 75. The United States Court of Appeals for the Third Circuit affirmed, upholding the Tax Court's findings that "both Unilever's enormous resources and the possibility of synergy arising from the transaction served the long-term betterment of National Starch." *National Starch & Chemical Corp. v. Commissioner*, 918 F.2d 426, 432–433 (1990). In so doing, the Court of Appeals rejected National Starch's contention that, because the disputed expenses did not "create or enhance . . . a separate and distinct additional asset," see *Commissioner v. Lincoln Savings & Loan Assn.*, 403 U.S. 345, 354 (1971), they could not be capitalized and therefore were deductible under § 162(a). 918 F.2d, at 428–431. We granted certiorari to resolve a perceived conflict on the issue among the Courts of Appeals. 500 U.S. 914 (1991).

II

Section 162(a) of the Internal Revenue Code allows the deduction of "all the ordinary and necessary expenses paid or incurred during the taxable year in carrying on any trade or business." 26 U.S.C. § 162(a). In contrast, § 263 of the Code allows no deduction for a capital expenditure—an "amount paid out for new buildings or for permanent improvements or betterments made to increase the value of any property or estate." § 263(a)(1). The primary effect of characterizing a payment as either a business expense or a capital expenditure concerns the timing of the taxpayer's cost recovery: While business expenses are currently deductible, a capital expenditure usually is amortized and depreciated over the life of the relevant asset, or, where no specific asset or useful life can be ascertained, is deducted upon dissolution of the enterprise. \* \* \*. Through provisions such as these, the Code endeavors to match expenses with the revenues of the taxable period to which they are properly attributable, thereby resulting in a more accurate calculation of net income for tax purposes. . . .

In exploring the relationship between deductions and capital expenditures, this court has noted the "familiar rule" that "an income tax deduction is a matter of legislative grace and that the burden of clearly showing the right to the claimed deduction is on the taxpayer." \* \* \*. The notion that deductions are exceptions to the norm of capitalization finds support in various aspects of the code. Deductions are specifically enumerated and thus are subject to disallowance in favor of capitalization. See §§ 161 and 261. Nondeductible capital expenditures, by contrast, are not exhaustively enumerated in the Code; rather than providing a "complete list of nondeductible expenditures," *Lincoln Savings*, 403 U.S., at 358, § 263 serves as a general means of distinguishing capital expenditures from current expenses. See *Commissioner v. Idaho Power Co.*, 418 U.S., at 16. For these reasons, deductions are strictly construed and allowed only "as there is a clear provision therefor." * * *.

The Court also has examined the interrelationship between the Code's business expense and capital expenditure provisions.[5] In so doing, it has had occasion to parse § 162(a) and explore certain of its requirements. For example, in *Lincoln Savings*, we determined that, to qualify for deduction under § 162(a), "an item must (1) be 'paid or incurred during the taxable year,' (2) be for 'carrying on any trade or business,' (3) be an 'expense,' (4) be a 'necessary' expense, and (5) be an 'ordinary' expense." 403 U.S., at 352. See also *Commissioner v. Tellier*, 383 U.S. 687, 689 (1966) (the term "necessary" imposes "only the minimal requirement that the expense be 'appropriate and helpful' for 'the development of the [taxpayer's] business,' ") quoting *Welch v. Helvering*, 290 U.S. 111, 113 (1933); *Deputy v. Du Pont*, 308 U.S., at 495 (to qualify as "ordinary," the expense must relate to a transaction "of common or frequent occurrence in the type of business involved"). The Court has recognized, however, that the "decisive distinctions" between current expenses and capital expenditures "are those of degree and not of kind," *Welch v. Helvering*, 290 U.S., at 114, and that because each case "turns on its special facts," *Deputy v. Du Pont*, 308 U.S., at 496, the cases sometimes appear difficult to harmonize. See *Welch v. Helvering*, 290 U.S., at 116.

---

[5] See, *e.g.*, *Commissioner v. Idaho Power Co.*, 418 U.S. 1 (1974) (equipment depreciation allocable to construction of capital facilities is to be capitalized); *United States v. Mississippi Chemical Corp.*, 405 U.S. 298 (1972) (cooperatives' required purchases of stock in Bank for Cooperatives are not currently deductible); *Commissioner v. Lincoln Savings & Loan Assn.*, 403 U.S. 345 (1971) (additional premiums paid by bank to federal insurers are capital expenditures); *Woodward v. Commissioner*, 397 U.S. 572 (1970) (legal, accounting, and appraisal expenses incurred in purchasing minority stock interest are capital expenditures); *United States v. Hilton Hotels Corp.*, 397 U.S. 580 (1970) (consulting, legal, and other professional fees incurred by acquiring firm in minority stock appraisal proceeding are capital expenditures); *Commissioner v. Tellier*, 383 U.S. 687 (1966) (legal expenses incurred in defending against securities fraud charges are deductible under § 162(a)); *Commissioner v. Heininger*, 320 U.S. 467 (1943) (legal expenses incurred in disputing adverse postal designation are deductible as ordinary and necessary expenses); *Interstate Transit Lines v. Commissioner*, 319 U.S. 590 (1943) (payment by parent company to cover subsidiary's operating deficit is not deductible as a business expense); *Deputy v. Du Pont*, 308 U.S. 488 (1940) (expenses incurred by shareholder in helping executives of company acquire stock are not deductible); *Helvering v. Winmill*, 305 U.S. 79 (1938) (brokerage commissions are capital expenditures); *Welch v. Helvering*, 290 U.S. 111 (1933) (payments of former employer's debts are capital expenditures).

National Starch contends that the decision in *Lincoln Savings* changed these familiar backdrops and announced an exclusive test for identifying capital expenditures, a test in which "creation or enhancement of an asset" is a prerequisite to capitalization, and deductibility under § 162(a) is the rule rather than the exception. Brief for Petitioner 16. We do not agree, for we conclude that National Starch has overread *Lincoln Savings*.

In *Lincoln Savings*, we were asked to decide whether certain premiums, required by federal statute to be paid by a savings and loan association to the Federal Savings and Loan Insurance Corporation (FSLIC), were ordinary and necessary expenses under § 162(a), as Lincoln Savings argued and the Court of Appeals had held, or capital expenditures under § 263, as the Commissioner contended. We found that the "additional" premiums, the purpose of which was to provide FSLIC with a secondary reserve fund in which each insured institution retained a pro rata interest recoverable in certain situations, "serv[e] to create or enhance for Lincoln what is essentially a separate and distinct additional asset." 403 U.S., at 354. "[A]s an inevitable consequence," we concluded, "the payment is capital in nature and not an expense, let alone an ordinary expense, deductible under § 162(a)." *Ibid.*

*Lincoln Savings* stands for the simple proposition that a taxpayer's expenditure that "serves to create or enhance . . . a separate and distinct" asset should be capitalized under § 263. It by no means follows, however, that *only* expenditures that create or enhance separate and distinct assets are to be capitalized under § 263. We had no occasion in *Lincoln Savings* to consider the tax treatment of expenditures that, unlike the additional premiums at issue there, did not create or enhance a specific asset, and thus the case cannot be read to preclude capitalization in other circumstances. In short, *Lincoln Savings* holds that the creation of a separate and distinct asset well may be a sufficient, but not a necessary, condition to classification as a capital expenditure. See *General Bancshares Corp. v. Commissioner*, 326 F.2d 712, 716 (CA8) (although expenditures may not "resul[t] in the acquisition or increase of a corporate asset, . . . these expenditures are not, because of that fact, deductible as ordinary and necessary business expenses"), cert. denied, 379 U.S. 832 (1964).

Nor does our statement in *Lincoln Savings*, 403 U.S., at 354, that "the presence of an ensuing benefit that may have some future aspect is not controlling" prohibit reliance on future benefit as a means of distinguishing an ordinary business expense from a capital expenditure.[6] Although the mere presence of an incidental future benefit—"*some* future aspect"—may not warrant capitalization, a taxpayer's realization of

---

[6] Petitioner contends that, absent a separate-and-distinct-asset requirement for capitalization, a taxpayer will have no "principled basis" upon which to differentiate business expenses from capital expenditures. . . . We note, however, that grounding tax status on the existence of an asset would be unlikely to produce the bright-line rule that petitioner desires, given that the notion of an "asset" is itself flexible and amorphous. . . .

benefits beyond the year in which the expenditure is incurred is undeniably important in determining whether the appropriate tax treatment is immediate deduction or capitalization. See *United States v. Mississippi Chemical Corp.*, 405 U.S. 298, 310 (1972) (expense that "is of value in more than one taxable year" is a nondeductible capital expenditure); *Central Texas Savings & Loan Assn. v. United States*, 731 F.2d 1181, 1183 (C.A.5 1984) ("While the period of the benefits may not be controlling in all cases, it nonetheless remains a prominent, if not predominant, characteristic of a capital item"). Indeed, the text of the Code's capitalization provision, § 263(a)(1), which refers to "permanent improvements or betterments," itself envisions an inquiry into the duration and extent of the benefits realized by the taxpayer.

## III

In applying the foregoing principles to the specific expenditures at issue in this case, we conclude that National Starch has not demonstrated that the investment banking, legal, and other costs it incurred in connection with Unilever's acquisition of its shares are deductible as ordinary and necessary business expenses under § 162(a).

Although petitioner attempts to dismiss the benefits that accrued to National Starch from the Unilever acquisition as "entirely speculative" or "merely incidental," Brief for Petitioner 39–40, the Tax Court's and the Court of Appeals' findings that the transaction produced significant benefits to National Starch that extended beyond the tax year in question are amply supported by the record. For example, in commenting on the merger with Unilever, National Starch's 1978 "Progress Report" observed that the company would "benefit greatly from the availability of Unilever's enormous resources, especially in the area of basic technology." App. 43. See also *id.*, at 46 (Unilever "provides new opportunities and resources"). Morgan Stanley's report to the National Starch board concerning the fairness to shareholders of a possible business combination with Unilever noted that National Starch management "feels that some synergy may exist with the Unilever organization given a) the nature of the Unilever chemical, paper, plastics and packaging operations . . . and b) the strong consumer products orientation of Unilever United States, Inc." *Id.*, at 77–78.

In addition to these anticipated resource-related benefits, National Starch obtained benefits through its transformation from a publicly held, freestanding corporation into a wholly owned subsidiary of Unilever. The Court of Appeals noted that National Starch management viewed the transaction as " 'swapping approximately 3500 shareholders for one.' " 918 F.2d, at 427; see also App. 223. Following Unilever's acquisition of National Starch's outstanding shares, National Starch was no longer subject to what even it terms the "substantial" shareholder-relations expenses a publicly traded corporation incurs, including reporting and disclosure obligations, proxy battles, and derivative suits. Brief for Petitioner 24. The acquisition also allowed National Starch, in the interests of administrative convenience and simplicity, to eliminate previously authorized but unissued shares of preferred and to reduce the total number of authorized shares of common from 8,000,000 to 1,000. See 93 T.C., at 74.

Courts long have recognized that expenses such as these, " 'incurred for the purpose of changing the corporate structure for the benefit of future operations are not ordinary and necessary business expenses.' " *General Bancshares Corp. v. Commissioner,* 326 F.2d, at 715 (quoting *Farmers Union Corp. v. Commissioner,* 300 F.2d 197, 200 (CA9), cert. denied, 371 U.S. 861 (1962)). See also B. Bittker & J. Eustice, Federal Income Taxation of Corporations and Shareholders 5–33 to 5–36 (5th ed. 1987) (describing "well-established rule" that expenses incurred in reorganizing or restructuring corporate entity are not deductible under § 162(a)). Deductions for professional expenses thus have been disallowed in a wide variety of cases concerning changes in corporate structure.[7] Although support for these decisions can be found in specific terms of § 162(a), which require that deductible expenses be "ordinary and necessary" and incurred "in carrying on any trade or business," courts more frequently have characterized an expenditure as capital in nature because "the purpose for which the expenditure is made has to do with the corporation's operations and betterment, sometimes with a continuing capital asset, for the duration of its existence or for the indefinite future or for a time somewhat longer than the current taxable year." *General Bancshares Corp. v. Commissioner,* 326 F.2d, at 715. See also *Mills Estate, Inc. v. Commissioner,* 206 F.2d 244 (C.A.2 1953). The rationale behind these decisions applies equally to the professional charges at issue in this case.

IV

The expenses that National Starch incurred in Unilever's friendly takeover do not qualify for deduction as "ordinary and necessary" business expenses under § 162(a). The fact that the expenditures do not create or enhance a separate and distinct additional asset is not controlling; the acquisition-related expenses bear the indicia of capital expenditures and are to be treated as such.

The judgment of the Court of Appeals is affirmed.

*It is so ordered.*

---

[7]  See, *e.g., McCrory Corp. v. United States,* 651 F.2d 828 (C.A.2 1981) (statutory merger under 26 U.S.C. § 368(a)(1)(A)); *Bilar Tool & Die Corp. v. Commissioner,* 530 F.2d 708 (C.A.6 1976) (division of corporation into two parts); *E. I. du Pont de Nemours & Co. v. United States,* 432 F.2d 1052 (C.A.3 1970) (creation of new subsidiary to hold assets of prior joint venture); *General Bancshares Corp. v. Commissioner,* 326 F.2d 712, 715 (CA8) (stock dividends), cert. denied, 379 U.S. 832 (1964); *Mills Estate, Inc. v. Commissioner,* 206 F.2d 244 (C.A.2 1953) (recapitalization).

## NOTE

The taxpayer's and the Treasury's positions in the *INDOPCO* case could be easily anticipated. The taxpayer wanted to expense its costs while the government argued that the taxpayer's outlays were nondeductible capital expenditures. In *INDOPCO*, the Supreme Court rejected the taxpayer's argument that its expenditures were not a capital expenditure because they did not create a separate and distinct asset. Instead, the Court held that while the creation of a separate asset may be sufficient to require capitalization of an expenditure, it is not a necessary condition. The Court stated that a realization of benefits beyond the year of the expenditure is also an important factor in deciding whether the taxpayer has incurred a business expense or made a capital expenditure. Because the takeover transaction "produced significant benefits . . . that extended beyond the tax year in question,"[1] the costs of the transaction were required to be capitalized.

The Supreme Court's "significant future benefits" standard in *INDOPCO* initially caused consternation among taxpayers and their advisors because many routine business expenditures that had traditionally been expensed can be viewed as producing future benefits. The Treasury responded to the unease following *INDOPCO* by issuing a series of revenue rulings to reassure taxpayers that the case had not put the deductibility of various traditional business expenses at risk. For example, the Service issued rulings in the wake of *INDOPCO* allowing deductions for advertising expenses,[2] incidental building repairs,[3] and employer-incurred training costs of an ongoing business.[4] But, because capitalization issues abound and those issues are uniquely factual in nature, it was inevitable that it would be left to the lower federal courts to interpret and apply the *INDOPCO* standard.

The case-by-case examination of the *INDOPCO* standard was well under way[5] when the Treasury issued regulations explaining how Section

---

[1]   INDOPCO, Inc. v. Commissioner, 503 U.S. 79, 88, 112 S.Ct. 1039, 1045 (1992).

[2]   Rev. Rul. 92–80, 1992–2 C.B. 57.

[3]   Rev. Rul. 94–12, 1994–1 C.B. 36.

[4]   Rev. Rul. 96–62, 1996–2 C. B. 9.

[5]   Not surprisingly, the results in the courts on *INDOPCO* questions were mixed. See, e.g., United Dairy Farmers, Inc. v. United States, 267 F.3d 510 (6th Cir.2001) (taxpayer could not currently deduct (1) soil remediation expenses related to purchased properties; (2) accounting fees related to corporate reorganization, and (3) engineering studies); Wells Fargo & Co. v. Commissioner, 224 F.3d 874 (8th Cir.2000) (salaries paid to corporate officers related to corporate acquisition could be currently deducted; legal fees related to the investigatory stage of the transaction could be currently deducted; expenses after "final decision" was made had to be capitalized); PNC Bancorp, Inc. v. Commissioner, 212 F.3d 822 (3d Cir.2000) (bank could deduct as ordinary and necessary expenses its costs for marketing, researching, and originating loans); A.E. Staley Manufacturing Co. v. Commissioner, 119 F.3d 482 (7th Cir.1997) (target corporation could deduct expenses on resisting hostile takeover; expenses to defend a business preserve the status quo and do not produce future benefit); Lychuk v. Commissioner, 116 T.C. 374 (2001) (costs related to making auto loans must be capitalized rejecting the reasoning in *PNC Bancorp*); Ingram Industries v. Commissioner, 80 T.C.M. 532 (2000) (taxpayer allowed to currently deduct extensive maintenance on towboats as "repairs;" the court stated that *INDOPCO* did not change the long-established standards dealing with repairs and maintenance expenses).

263(a) applies to amounts paid to acquire, create, or enhance intangible assets.[6] The Treasury signaled its concerns prior to issuing the regulations:[7]

> The difficulty of translating general capitalization principles into clear, consistent, and administrable standards has been recognized for decades. . . . Because courts focus on particular facts before them, the results reached by courts are often difficult to reconcile and, particularly in recent years, have contributed to substantial uncertainty and controversy. The IRS and Treasury Department are concerned that the current level of uncertainty and controversy is neither fair to taxpayers nor consistent with sound and efficient tax administration.

The regulations generally require capitalization of (1) an amount paid to acquire, create, or enhance an intangible asset, (2) an amount paid to facilitate an acquisition or creation of an intangible, and (3) an amount paid to facilitate a restructuring or reorganization of a business entity or a transaction involving the acquisition of capital, including a stock issuance, borrowing, or recapitalization.[8]

Much of the regulations should be familiar after your study of the principles that generally apply to capital expenditures. For example, if a taxpayer acquires an intangible asset, including (but not limited to) stock in a corporation, a partnership interest, a bond or other debt instrument, an option, a patent or copyright, a franchise, goodwill or going concern value, computer software, or any separate and distinct intangible asset,[9] the cost of the asset must be capitalized.[10] Likewise, if a taxpayer creates specific types of intangible assets, the costs generally also must be capitalized.[11] For example, the amount a taxpayer pays to a governmental agency to obtain a trademark is an amount paid to create an intangible that must be

---

[6]  Reg. § 1.263(a)–4. See generally, Bambino & Nugent, "The Proposed INDOPCO Regulations: A Primer," 99 Tax Notes 259 (April 14, 2003); Hardesty, "The New Proposed Regulations Under Section 263 on Capitalization of Intangibles," 98 J. Tax'n 86 (2003). While the regulations generally apply only to intangible property, they also apply to amounts paid in connection with real property relinquished to another or owned by another if the real property can reasonably be expected to produce significant economic benefits for the taxpayer. See Reg. § 1.263(a)–4(d)(8).

[7]  Announcement 2002–9, 2002–1 C.B. 536. See, Evans, "*INDOPCO*—The Treasury Finally Acts," 80 Taxes 47 (2002).

[8]  Reg. § 1.263(a)–4(b)(1), –5(a).

[9]  An asset is separate and distinct if it is a property interest of ascertainable and measurable value in money's worth that is subject to protection under law and the possession and control of which can be sold, transferred, or pledged. Reg. § 1.263(a)–4(b)(3)(i).

[10]  Reg. § 1.263(a)–4(c)(1), (2).

[11]  Reg. § 1.263(a)–4(d)(1). The amounts that the regulations generally require a taxpayer to capitalize include: (1) amounts paid to create various financial interests (e.g., stock in a corporation, a debt instrument, or an option), (2) amounts paid as prepaid expenses, (3) amounts paid to obtain or renew a membership or privilege (e.g., a fee paid by a doctor to obtain staff privileges at a hospital), (4) amounts paid to obtain a right granted by a governmental agency (e.g., a fee paid by an attorney to obtain a license to practice law), (5) amounts paid to enter into, renew, or renegotiate certain contract rights (e.g., a fee paid to extend the term of a lease or an amount paid for a covenant not to compete), (6) amounts paid to terminate certain contracts (e.g., an amount paid to terminate a covenant not to compete), and (7) amounts paid to another party defend or perfect title to intangible property where the other party challenges the taxpayer's title to the property. See Reg. § 1.263(a)–4(d)(2)–(7), (9).

capitalized.[12] In addition, the Treasury may in published guidance identify a future benefit that is an intangible asset for which capitalization is required.[13]

The regulations also require a taxpayer to capitalize an amount paid to "facilitate" (1) an acquisition, creation, or enhancement of an intangible asset[14] or (2) a restructuring or reorganization of a business entity or a transaction involving the acquisition of capital.[15] An amount is paid to facilitate such a transaction if it is paid in the process of pursuing the transaction.[16] For example, the cost of outside legal counsel to negotiate a commercial lease has to be capitalized under this rule.[17] However, compensation paid to employees (including bonuses and commissions),[18] overhead, and de minimis costs (generally, amounts less than $5,000)[19] do not have to be capitalized as amounts that facilitate a transaction.[20]

Some criticized the regulations for abandoning the *INDOPCO* "significant future benefits" standard.[21] However, the Preamble to the proposed version of the regulations explained the approach of those regulations and the Treasury's dissatisfaction with that standard:[22]

> A fundamental purpose of section 263(a) is to prevent the distortion of taxable income through current deduction of expenditures relating to the production of income in future years. Thus, in determining whether an expenditure should be capitalized, the Supreme Court has considered whether the expenditure produces a significant future benefit. INDOPCO, Inc. v. Commissioner, 503 U.S. 79, 112 S.Ct. 1039 (1992). A "significant future benefit" standard, however, does not provide the certainty and clarity necessary for compliance with, and sound administration of, the law. Consequently the IRS and Treasury Department believe that simply restating the significant future benefit test, without more, would lead to continued uncertainty on the part of taxpayers and continued controversy between taxpayers and the IRS. Accordingly, the IRS and Treasury Department have initially defined the exclusive scope of the significant future benefit test through the specific categories of intangible assets for which

---

[12]  Reg. § 1.263(a)–4(d)(5).

[13]  Reg. § 1.263(a)–4(b)(2).

[14]  Reg. § 1.263(a)–4(b)(1)(v), (e).

[15]  Reg. § 1.263(a)–5(a).

[16]  Reg. § 1.263(a)–4(e)(1)(i), –5(b). Whether the amount is paid in the process of pursuing a transaction is determined based on all facts and circumstances. The fact that an amount would (or would not) have been paid but for the transaction is relevant, but is not determinative. Id.

[17]  Reg. § 1.263(a)–4(e)(5) Example 1.

[18]  In addition, amounts paid to an employee to acquire an intangible from the employee are not required to be capitalized if the amounts are treated as compensation for personal services includible in the employee's gross income. Reg. § 1.263(a)–4(c)(3).

[19]  Reg. § 1.263(a)–4(e)(4)(iii), –5(d)(3).

[20]  Reg. § 1.263(a)–4(e)(4)(i), –5(d)(1).

[21]  See, Johnson, "Destroying the Tax Base: The Proposed INDOPCO Capitalization Regulations," 99 Tax Notes 1381 (2003); Sheppard, "Bringing Back the Separate-Asset Test From the Dead," 97 Tax Notes 1655 (2002).

[22]  Preamble to Proposed Regulations, 67 Fed. Reg. 77701, 77702 (Dec. 19, 2002).

capitalization is required in the proposed regulations. The future benefit standard underlies many of these categories.

The exceptions in the regulations for employee compensation and de minimis costs were also criticized as not merited and overly generous.[23]

## PROBLEMS

1.   Landlord incurs the following expenses during the current year on a ten-unit apartment complex. Is each expenditure a currently deductible repair or a capital expenditure?

  (a)   $500 for painting three rooms of one of the apartments.

  (b)   $4,000 for replacing the roof over one of the apartments. The roof had suffered termite damage.

  (c)   $1,000 for patching the entire asphalt parking lot area.

  (d)   $3,000 for adding a carport to an apartment.

  (e)   $100 for advertising for a tenant to occupy an empty apartment.

2.   Are the regulations on capitalization of amounts paid to acquire, create, or enhance intangible assets consistent with the Supreme Court's decision in *INDOPCO*?

3.   Suppose the taxpayer in *INDOPCO* had performed some of the services in connection with the takeover transaction itself "in house." Would the regulations require those expenses to be capitalized? See Reg. § 1.263(a)–5(d)(1) and (2). Compare that situation with the taxpayer who pays an employee in connection with the construction of a new building. Is the difference in the results justified?

## 3.   "CARRYING ON" BUSINESS

Internal Revenue Code: Sections 162(a); 195; 262.

Regulations: Section 1.195–1(b).

---

# Frank v. Commissioner
### Tax Court of the United States, 1953.
### 20 T.C. 511.

The respondent determined an income tax deficiency against the petitioners for the year 1946 in the amount of $2,914.92. The only issue presented is whether the petitioners are entitled to deduct traveling expenses and legal fees in the amount of $5,965 in the taxable year.

---

[23]   See, Johnson, supra note 21 at 1390; Sheppard, supra note 21 at 1661–63.

Findings of Fact

Morton Frank and Agnes Dodds Frank, the petitioners, are husband and wife who filed a joint income tax return for 1946 with the collector of internal revenue for the eighteenth district of Ohio. In November 1945, Morton Frank was released from the Navy. His place of residence during the period of his service was Pittsburgh, Pennsylvania. Prior to the war, he had been employed by such newspapers as The Pittsburgh Press, The Braddock Free Press, The Braddock Daily News Herald, and The Michigan Daily. His wife, an attorney, had no experience in the newspaper business and during the war had been employed by several government agencies. During and prior to his service in the Navy, Morton Frank was interested in purchasing and operating a newspaper or radio station. Near the end of November 1945, the petitioners began a trip to examine newspapers and radio properties throughout the country. The purpose of the trip was to investigate, and, if possible, acquire a newspaper or radio enterprise to operate.

The trip took both petitioners westward from Pittsburgh through Ohio, Indiana, Michigan, Minnesota, Wisconsin, Oklahoma, and New Mexico. They interviewed persons in these states with respect to local newspapers and radio stations. On January 1, 1946, the petitioners were in San Diego, California. They then traveled through California, New Mexico, Texas, and Arizona. They arrived in Phoenix, Arizona, on February 12, 1946. The taxpayers estimated that their travel and communication expenses from January 1 to February 12, 1946, aggregated $1,596.44.

The petitioners took employment in Phoenix with The Arizona Times and remained in that city from February to Mid-July 1946. While working in Phoenix, the petitioners made several trips to various cities throughout the country in search of a newspaper plant to purchase. They traveled to Los Angeles and Santa Barbara, California, Yuma, Arizona, Pittsburgh, Pennsylvania, and Wilmington, Delaware. Offers of purchase were made to the owners of several newspapers. While in Phoenix, the petitioners lived first in a hotel and later in a house which they acquired. The petitioners estimated their traveling, telephone, and telegraph expenses from March through December 1946, at $5,027.94. Included within this total was a legal fee of $1,000 paid to an attorney for services rendered in connection with unsuccessful negotiations to purchase a newspaper in Wilmington, Delaware. None of these claimed expenses were incurred in connection with the petitioners' employment in Phoenix, Arizona. A portion of it was based on estimated allowances of mileage at 6 cents per mile, lodging at $5 per day per person, and other costs at comparable rates, the whole expenditures reasonably aggregating $5,027.94. In November 1946, the petitioners purchased a newspaper in Canton, Ohio, and commenced publication of the Canton Economist in that month.

Opinion

■ VAN FOSSAN, JUDGE:

The only question presented is whether the petitioners may deduct $5,965 in the determination of their net income for the year 1946 as ordinary and necessary business expenses or as losses. The petitioners base their claim for deductions upon section 23(a)(1) and (2) and (e)(2) of the Internal Revenue Code.[1] The evidence reasonably establishes that the petitioners expended the amount of expenses stated in our Findings of Fact during the taxable year in traveling, telephone, telegraph, and legal expenses in the search for and investigation of newspaper and radio properties. This total amount was spent by the petitioners in their travels through various states in an endeavor to find a business which they could purchase and operate. These expenses do not include amounts spent while living in Phoenix, Arizona.

The travel expenses and legal fees spent in searching for a newspaper business with a view to purchasing the same cannot be deducted under the provisions of section 23(a)(1), Internal Revenue Code. The petitioners were not engaged in any trade or business at the time the expenses were incurred. The trips made by the taxpayers from Phoenix, Arizona, were not related to the conduct of the business that they were then engaged in but were preparatory to locating a business venture of their own. The expenses of investigating and looking for a new business and trips preparatory to entering a business are not deductible as an ordinary and necessary business expense incurred in carrying on a trade or business. George C. Westervelt, 8 T.C. 1248. The word "pursuit" in the statutory phrase "in pursuit of a trade or business" is not used in the sense of "searching for" or "following after," but in the sense of "in connection with" or "in the course of" a trade or business. It presupposes an existing business with which petitioner is connected. The fact that petitioners had no established home during the period of their travels further complicates the question and alone may be fatal to petitioners' case. If they had no home, how could they have expenses "away from home"? The issue whether all or part of the expenses so incurred were capital expenditures is not raised or argued and we do not pass judgment on such question.

\* \* \*

We conclude that the petitioners may not deduct the expenses claimed for 1946 under the applicable provisions of the Internal Revenue Code.

Decision will be entered for the respondent.

---

[1]   [The 1939 Code section cited is omitted. See I.R.C. (1986) §§ 162(a), 165(a) and (c)(2), 212. The portion of the opinion dealing with I.R.C. §§ 165 and 212 has been deleted. Ed.]

## NOTE

Section 162(a) provides: "There shall be allowed as a deduction all the ordinary and necessary expenses paid or incurred during the taxable year in carrying on any trade or business * * * " The corresponding clause in Section 23(a)(1) of the Internal Revenue Code of 1939, which controlled in *Morton Frank*, supra, was identical. Reference in the opinion to the phrase "in pursuit of a trade or business" may be confusing. It appears in Section 162(a)(2) and its predecessor, Section 23(a)(1)(A) of the 1939 Code, in connection with the specific provision on business travel. Even so, the "pursuit" phrase takes color from the more general "carrying on" expression and, as the opinion in *Frank* suggests, both phrases have about the same meaning.

It seems almost axiomatic that one cannot be "carrying on" a business unless one *has* a business, a frailty in the *Frank* circumstances which, among other factors,[1] foreclosed any Section 162 deduction. Nevertheless, the opinion should not be read so broadly as to suggest all costs incurred in seeking employment can never give rise to a Section 162 deduction. If *Frank* had been in a trade or business and was seeking to expand that business or some branch of it, his position would have been stronger.[2]

The *Frank* situation also should be distinguished from the situation where the taxpayer has proceeded beyond an initial investigation stage and has entered a transactional stage. When the taxpayer reaches the transactional stage,[3] amounts paid to complete the transaction generally must be capitalized.[4] If subsequent developments compel the taxpayer to abandon the venture prior to engaging in it, this is not necessarily a bar to a deduction of such transactional stage expenses, but the deduction claimed should be for a loss on a transaction entered into for profit allowed by Section 165(c)(2), not a business expense under Section 162.[5]

---

[1] See the discussion of the meaning of "away from home", infra page 357.

[2] Colorado Springs Nat. Bank v. United States, 505 F.2d 1185 (10th Cir.1974); First Nat. Bank of South Carolina v. United States, 558 F.2d 721 (4th Cir.1977); but see Central Texas Savings & Loan Ass'n v. United States, 731 F.2d 1181 (5th Cir.1984).

[3] The courts have generally held that the transactional stage is reached at the point where the preliminary investigation had led to the decision to purchase a specific business, but further investigation of the business continues. Domenie v. Commissioner, 34 T.C.M. 469, 472 (1975); Seed v. Commissioner, 52 T.C. 880 (1969). In Rev. Rul. 99–23, 1999–1 C.B. 998, The Service described the transactional stage as beginning when the taxpayer has focused on the acquisition of a specific business. In the case of intangibles, regulations now draw a bright line requiring capitalization of amounts that are (1) "inherently facilitative" (e.g., amounts paid to prepare and review transactional documents), or (2) related to activities performed after the earlier of the date of a letter of intent to acquire (or similar document) or the date the acquisition is approved by the taxpayer (e.g., approval by a corporation's board of directors). Reg. § 1.263(a)–5(e). The Service recognizes that the rule in the regulations departs from Revenue Ruling 99–23, and has indicated that it is considering the same bright line standard for acquisition of tangible assets. Preamble to Proposed Regulations, 67 Fed. Reg. 77701, 77706 (Dec. 19, 2002).

[4] For example, the capitalized costs would include expenditures for appraisals, transactional documents, regulatory approvals, advice on the tax consequences of the transaction. See, e.g. Reg. § 1.263(a)–5(e)(2). The regulations on acquisitions of intangibles exclude compensation to employees (including bonuses and commissions), overhead, and de minimis costs (generally, not in excess of $5,000) from the category of transactional costs that have to be capitalized. Reg. § 1.263(a)–5(d).

[5] See Chapter 15B, infra, and see note 13, infra.

*Section 195 Start-up Expenditures.* Congress enacted Section 195 in order to clarify the treatment of "start-up expenditures," expenses incurred in establishing a trade or business that are not part of the transactional stage. Section 195 permits a taxpayer to elect to deduct up to $5,000 of start-up expenditures in the year in which the business "begins," reduced by the amount of start-up expenditures that exceed $50,000 (thus phased out at $55,000).[6] The remaining start-up expenditures are amortized over a period of not less than 180 months from the month in which the business "begins".[7] Consequently, the taxpayer must actually enter a trade or business successfully to elect Section 195.[8]

Start-up expenditures are defined in Section 195(c)(1)(A) as amounts incurred with respect to:

> (i) investigating the creation or acquisition of an active trade or business;
>
> (ii) creating an active trade or business; or
>
> (iii) activities engaged in for profit * * * before the day on which the active trade or business begins, in anticipation of such activity becoming an active trade or business.

Additionally, the expenditures must be of the type that would be allowable as a deduction if paid or incurred by an existing trade or business.[9] Eligible expenditures thus include both "investigatory costs" incurred before reaching the transactional stage (e.g., costs for market studies, evaluation of products and labor supplies) and "start-up" costs incurred after the transactional stage but before the business begins operation (e.g., costs for advertising, training employees, lining up distributors or potential customers and fees for professional services in setting up books).[10] However, the statute specifically provides that amounts deductible under Sections 163 (interest), 164 (taxes), and 174 (research expenses) do not constitute start-up expenditures. As such, these expenses need not be amortized but instead may be deducted currently to the extent allowable under the respective sections.[11]

All start-up expenditures must be either deducted and amortized over the requisite period or capitalized and treated as nondeductible

---

[6] I.R.C. § 195(b)(1)(A).

[7] I.R.C. § 195(b)(1)(B).

[8] Expenditures attributable to the acquisition of an investment are not eligible for I.R.C. § 195. See also §§ 248 and 709 which provide for a similar deduction and amortization of corporate and partnership "organizational expenditures".

[9] Ordinary and necessary expenditures incurred in the expansion of an existing business are currently deductible under I.R.C. § 162. Expenditures that are not deductible by an existing trade or business under § 162 are ineligible for amortization under § 195. See note 2, supra. Ineligible expenditures include amounts paid for the acquisition of property held for sale or depreciable property, amounts paid as part of the acquisition cost of a trade or business and amounts paid in connection with the sale of stock, securities or partnership interests (e.g., securities registration expenses, underwriters commissions). See Sen. Rep. No. 96–1036, 96th Cong., 2d Sess. (1980).

[10] Id.

[11] I.R.C. § 195(c)(1). Cf. I.R.C. § 263A.

expenditures.[12] Section 195 also sets forth the manner in which start-up expenditures are to be treated in cases where the business is terminated before the close of the amortization period. Section 195(b)(2) provides that where a business is completely disposed of prior to the completion of the amortization period, any start-up expenditures not previously deducted may be deducted to the extent provided in Section 165.[13]

*Employment-Seeking Expenses.* Though Section 195 clarifies the extent to which start-up expenses may be deducted, it has no application to an individual having employee status with respect to the deduction of expenses incurred in seeking new employment. Instead, the general provisions of Sections 162 and 212 must be relied on in order to determine whether, and to what extent, such expenses are deductible. It is well settled that being an employee constitutes carrying on a trade or business,[14] but questions have arisen whether a prospective employee is in a trade or business[15] and whether new employment, perhaps of short duration, prevents one from continuing to be considered as carrying on one's former trade, and whether lack of employment ends a trade altogether. As the Section 162 statutory language is the same for an employee as for a self-employed person, the deductibility of expenses ought to be the same.

Now a person who has never before "carried on" a particular trade or business as an employee or a self-employed person may be permitted a deduction for expenses incurred in entering that trade or business. Although it might seem that pre-employment expenses could never be deductible under Section 162 because not incurred in carrying on a trade or business, the Tax Court earlier sensibly made an exception in a situation where services were rendered to one who was to become the employee of a third party prior to the commencement of his employment, but payment for those services was contingent upon his becoming employed[16] as he later did. In *Hundley,* the petitioner who later became employed as a major league baseball player, was earlier taught the tools of his trade by his father, a former semi-professional baseball player. As compensation for those services, it had been agreed that the petitioner (son) would pay his father fifty percent of any bonus that might be paid to the petitioner under the terms of a professional baseball contract if one should later be signed.[17] The petitioner eventually signed a bonus contract with a professional baseball club and paid one half of the bonus to his father. The Tax Court found that this expense was not paid or incurred prior to petitioner's entering into the business of baseball, because the payment of compensation to the father was

---

[12] I.R.C. § 195(a), (b)(1). Cf. Hoopengarner v. Commissioner, 80 T.C. 538 (1983).

[13] Seemingly, all start-up expenses would be deductible under I.R.C. § 165(c)(1).

[14] David J. Primuth v. Commissioner, 54 T.C. 374 (1970); United States v. Generes, 405 U.S. 93, 92 S.Ct. 827 (1972).

[15] Rev.Rul. 75–120, 1975–1 C.B. 55, 56. Cf. Reg. § 1.162–5(b)(2)(i) and (3)(i). The Service had previously ruled that fees paid to employment agencies for actually securing an initial employment (as distinguished from merely seeking employment) were deductible. Rev.Rul. 60–223, 1960–1 C.B. 57. The Ruling, conditioning deductibility on success, not properly a condition to the deduction, was revoked in Rev.Rul. 75–120, supra.

[16] C.R. Hundley, Jr. v. Commissioner, 48 T.C. 339 (1967).

[17] Id. at 340.

not due or incurred or payable until the petitioner was engaged in the business of baseball.[18] The court concluded that the payments made under the terms of the agreement were paid for services actually rendered in carrying on a trade or business and thus were deductible,[19] and the Commissioner has acquiesced.[20] The rationale of the *Hundley* decision could extend to any situation in which payment for trade or business seeking services is contingent upon employment and does not become due until trade or business status is secured.

Once a person has entered a trade or business one issue is: How long does one remain in that trade or business during periods of unemployment or diversification into other businesses? It is becoming clear that, once having entered a trade or business, not currently engaging in it does not prevent one from still being considered in a trade or business,[21] but there are qualifications. A prolonged length of time away from one's usual trade or business is a factor that may be considered in determining one is no longer carrying on that trade or business. In one case, the Tax Court held that the petitioner was not entitled to deduct the cost of newspaper advertisements that were unsuccessful in locating him a new teaching position.[22] He had previously held a teaching position for several years, but not during the year of the advertisements, and the court found that he was not in that trade or business at any time during the year at issue. The Tax Court also denied a taxpayer a deduction for education expenses where over a four year period up to the time of litigation, the taxpayer did no teaching while obtaining a graduate degree.[23]

The Treasury states the position in Revenue Ruling 75–120[24] that it will not allow deductions under Section 162 for expenses incurred by individuals who have been unemployed for such a period of time that there is a substantial lack of continuity between their past employments and their endeavors to find new employments, but the length of time necessary to establish this substantial lack of continuity remains uncertain.

Another factor bearing on whether an unemployed person is in a trade or business is the length of time one has been employed before becoming unemployed. However, in one case, a law student who had passed his state's bar examination and had worked as an attorney for only three months with a law firm was (surprisingly?) held to be carrying on a trade or business when he went back to graduate school.[25] In contrast, an engineering student who worked for a year after graduation prior to doing graduate work in

---

[18]  Id. at 348.

[19]  Id. at 349. With Hundley, id., compare Richard A. Allen v. Commissioner, 50 T.C. 466 (1968).

[20]  1967–2 C.B. 2.

[21]  Furner v. Commissioner, 393 F.2d 292 (7th Cir.1968); Harold Haft v. Commissioner, 40 T.C. 2 (1963); Rev.Rul. 75–120, supra note 15.

[22]  Protiva v. Commissioner, 29 T.C.M. 1318 (1970).

[23]  Corbett v. Commissioner, 55 T.C. 884 (1971).

[24]  Supra note 15 at 56. See Rev.Rul. 77–32, 1977–1 C.B. 38.

[25]  Ruehmann v. Commissioner, 30 T.C.M. 675 (1971).

engineering was found not to have entered a trade or business that he could be carrying on to make his education expenses deductible.[26]

Even if it is clear an individual is engaged in a trade or business, question may be raised under Section 162 whether one's expenses were incurred in carrying on *that* trade or business, which of course they must be to be deductible.

After some extensive judicial battering,[27] the Treasury conceded[28] that a taxpayer's expenses in seeking employment elsewhere but in the same trade are deductible whether or not successful. This determination does not of course extend to first jobs, lengthy unemployment, or new trades or businesses.[29] This concession by the Treasury followed on the heels of several cases holding that success is not an element in the deductibility of employment-seeking expenses.[30]

*Limitations on the Deductibility of Employee Business Expenses.* You have completed an examination of the critical factors in application of Section 162 ("ordinary and necessary," "expenses," and "carrying on"). It is now time to mention an additional problem faced by an employee in deducting business expenses. This is a brief preview of a topic covered in Chapter 18C.

Recall that the end goal of the Code is to determine a taxpayer's taxable income and tax liability. The journey to reach taxable income might be analogized to an obstacle course. A taxpayer must satisfy various standards or tests, like the requirements in Section 162, before moving on to the additional obstacles and challenges that lay ahead. There is a great deal of congressional finger-crossing on the road to taxable income. Congress, at times, allows a deduction in a particular Code section, only to later snatch it away when the taxpayer confronts some new limitation or restriction on its deductibility.[31] So it goes with employee business expenses.

As previously noted, an employee in his or her work status is involved in a trade or business. And an employee is capable of satisfying all of the requirements in Section 162 for a business expense deduction. Thus, Section 162 will *allow* an employee a deduction for qualifying business expenses. But that is just the first step of the analysis. As you will later discover in Chapter 18C, unless an employee's business expense deduction is also described in Section 62(a) (see especially the last clause in Section 62(a)(1) and Section 62(a)(2)) *or* unless it is specifically listed in Section 67(b), it will not be allowed to be deducted in computing the employee's taxable income. As a result, only a very few employee business expenses are actually deductible

---

[26]  Reisine v. Commissioner, 29 T.C.M. 1429 (1970). Business deductions for education expenses are considered further, at page 381, infra.

[27]  David J. Primuth, 54 T.C. 374 (1970); Kenneth R. Kenfield, 54 T.C. 1197 (1970); Roy E. Blewitt, Jr. v. Commissioner, 31 T.C.M. 1225 (1972); Leonard F. Cremona v. Commissioner, 58 T.C. 219 (1972).

[28]  Leonard F. Cremona, supra note 27, acq., 1975–1 C.B. 1. See Rev.Rul. 75–120, supra note 15.

[29]  Ibid.

[30]  Ibid. See note 15, supra.

[31]  See, e.g., I.R.C. § 274 discussed in Chapter 17B.

in determining taxable income and result in a tax savings. Compare the treatment of a self-employed taxpayer. A self-employed individual's Section 162 deductions generally are described in Section 62(a)(1), so they will end up reducing taxable income. Again, the key point being made here is that meeting the requirements of Section 162 is just the first step for determining whether a business expense actually reduces taxable income and tax liability.

## PROBLEMS

1.  Determine the deductibility under §§ 162 and 195 of expenses incurred in the following situations.

(a)  Tycoon, a doctor, unexpectedly inherited a sizeable amount of money from an eccentric millionaire. Tycoon decided to invest a part of her fortune in the development of industrial properties and she incurred expenses in making a preliminary investigation.

(b)  The facts are the same as in (a), above, except that Tycoon, rather than having been a doctor, was a successful developer of residential and shopping center properties.

(c)  The facts are the same as in (b), above, except that Tycoon, desiring to diversify her investments, incurs expenses in investigating the possibility of purchasing a professional sports team.

(d)  The facts are the same as in (c), above, and Tycoon purchases a sports team. However, after two years Tycoon's fortunes turn sour and she sells the team at a loss. What happens to the deferred investigation expenses?

2.  Law student's Spouse completed computer programming school just prior to student entering law school. Spouse contacts a talent search firm to help find a position as a part-time computer programmer (i.e., an independent contractor). Consider whether Spouse's search fees are deductible in the following circumstances:

(a)  The firm is unsuccessful in finding Spouse a position.

(b)  The firm is successful in finding Spouse a position.

(c)  Same as (b), above, except that the firm's fee was contingent upon its securing a position for Spouse and the payments will not become due until Spouse has begun working.

(d)  Same as (a) and (b), above, except that Spouse previously worked as a computer programmer in Old Town and seeks a position in New Town where student attends law school.

(e)  Same as (d), above, except that the firm is successful in finding Spouse a position in New Town as a sales representative.

## C.  SPECIFIC BUSINESS DEDUCTIONS

## 1.  "REASONABLE" SALARIES

Internal Revenue Code: Section 162(a)(1). See Sections 162(m); 280G.

Regulations: Section 1.162–7, –8, –9.

---

## Exacto Spring Corporation v. Commissioner

United States Court of Appeals, Seventh Circuit, 1999.
196 F.3d 833.

■ POSNER, CHIEF JUDGE.

This appeal from a judgment by the Tax Court, T.C. Memo 1998–220, 75 T.C.M. (CCH) 2522 (1998), requires us to interpret and apply 26 U.S.C. § 162(a)(1), which allows a business to deduct from its income its "ordinary and necessary" business expenses, including a "reasonable allowance for salaries or other compensation for personal services actually rendered." In 1993 and 1994, Exacto Spring Corporation, a closely held corporation engaged in the manufacture of precision springs, paid its cofounder, chief executive, and principal owner, William Heitz, $1.3 and $1.0 million, respectively, in salary. The Internal Revenue Service thought this amount excessive, that Heitz should not have been paid more than $381,000 in 1993 or $400,000 in 1994, with the difference added to the corporation's income, and it assessed a deficiency accordingly, which Exacto challenged in the Tax Court. That court found that the maximum reasonable compensation for Heitz would have been $900,000 in the earlier year and $700,000 in the later one—figures roughly midway between his actual compensation and the IRS's determination—and Heitz has appealed.

In reaching its conclusion, the Tax Court applied a test that requires the consideration of seven factors, none entitled to any specified weight relative to another. The factors are, in the court's words, "(1) the type and extent of the services rendered; (2) the scarcity of qualified employees; (3) the qualifications and prior earning capacity of the employee; (4) the contributions of the employee to the business venture; (5) the net earnings of the employer; (6) the prevailing compensation paid to employees with comparable jobs; and (7) the peculiar characteristics of the employer's business." 75 T.C.M. at 2525. It is apparent that this test, though it or variants of it (one of which has the astonishing total of 21 factors, Foos v. Commissioner, 1981 T.C. Memo 61, 41 T.C.M. (CCH) 863, 878–79 (1981)), are encountered in many cases, see, e.g., Edwin's Inc. v. United States, 501 F.2d 675, 677 (7th Cir.1974); Owensby & Kritikos, Inc. v. Commissioner, 819 F.2d 1315, 1323 (5th Cir.1987); Mayson Mfg. Co. v. Commissioner, 178 F.2d 115, 119 (6th Cir.1949); 1 Boris I. Bittker & Lawrence Lokken, Federal Taxation of Income, Estates, and Gifts

¶ 22.2.2, p. 22–21 (3d ed. 1999), leaves much to be desired—being, like many other multi-factor tests, "redundant, incomplete, and unclear." Palmer v. City of Chicago, 806 F.2d 1316, 1318 (7th Cir.1986).

To begin with, it is nondirective. No indication is given of how the factors are to be weighed in the event they don't all line up on one side. And many of the factors, such as the type and extent of services rendered, the scarcity of qualified employees, and the peculiar characteristics of the employer's business, are vague.

Second, the factors do not bear a clear relation either to each other or to the primary purpose of section 162(a)(1), which is to prevent dividends (or in some cases gifts), which are not deductible from corporate income, from being disguised as salary, which is. E.g., Rapco, Inc. v. Commissioner, 85 F.3d 950, 954 n. 2 (2d Cir.1996). Suppose that an employee who let us say was, like Heitz, a founder and the chief executive officer and principal owner of the taxpayer rendered no services at all but received a huge salary. It would be absurd to allow the whole or for that matter any part of his salary to be deducted as an ordinary and necessary business expense even if he were well qualified to be CEO of the company, the company had substantial net earnings, CEOs of similar companies were paid a lot, and it was a business in which high salaries are common. The multifactor test would not prevent the Tax Court from allowing a deduction in such a case even though the corporation obviously was seeking to reduce its taxable income by disguising earnings as salary. The court would not allow the deduction, but not because of anything in the multi-factor test; rather because it would be apparent that the payment to the employee was not in fact for his services to the company. Treas. Reg. § 1.162–7(a); 1 Bittker & Lokken, supra, ¶ 22.2.1, p. 22–19.

Third, the seven-factor test invites the Tax Court to set itself up as a superpersonnel department for closely held corporations, a role unsuitable for courts, as we have repeatedly noted in the Title VII context, e.g., Jackson v. E.J. Brach Corp., 176 F.3d 971, 984 (7th Cir.1999), and as the Delaware Chancery Court has noted in the more germane context of derivative suits alleging excessive compensation of corporate employees. Gagliardi v. TriFoods Int'l, Inc., 683 A.2d 1049, 1051 (Del.Ch.1996). The test—the irruption of "comparable worth" thinking (see, e.g., American Nurses' Ass'n v. Illinois, 783 F.2d 716 (7th Cir.1986)) in a new context—invites the court to decide what the taxpayer's employees *should* be paid on the basis of the judges' own ideas of what jobs are comparable, what relation an employee's salary should bear to the corporation's net earnings, what types of business should pay abnormally high (or low) salaries, and so forth. The judges of the Tax Court are not equipped by training or experience to determine the salaries of corporate officers; no judges are.

Fourth, since the test cannot itself determine the outcome of a dispute because of its nondirective character, it invites the making of arbitrary decisions based on uncanalized discretion or unprincipled rules of thumb. The Tax Court in this case essentially added the IRS's determination of the maximum that Mr. Heitz should have been paid in 1993 and 1994 to what he was in fact paid, and divided the sum by two. It cut the baby in half. One would have to be awfully naive to believe that the seven-factor test generated this pleasing symmetry.

Fifth, because the reaction of the Tax Court to a challenge to the deduction of executive compensation is unpredictable, corporations run unavoidable legal risks in determining a level of compensation that may be indispensable to the success of their business.

The drawbacks of the multi-factor test are well illustrated by its purported application by the Tax Court in this case. With regard to factor (1), the court found that Heitz was "indispensable to Exacto's business" and "essential to Exacto's success." 75 T.C.M. at 2525. Heitz is not only Exacto's CEO; he is also the company's chief salesman and marketing man plus the head of its research and development efforts and its principal inventor. The company's entire success appears to be due on the one hand to the research and development conducted by him and on the other hand to his marketing of these innovations (though he receives some additional compensation for his marketing efforts from a subsidiary of Exacto). The court decided that factor (1) favored Exacto.

Likewise factor (2), for, as the court pointed out, the design of precision springs, which is Heitz's specialty, is "an extremely specialized branch of mechanical engineering, and there are very few engineers who have made careers specializing in this area," let alone engineers like Heitz who have "the ability to identify and attract clients and to develop springs to perform a specific function for that client. . . . It would have been very difficult to replace Mr. Heitz." Id. Notice how factors (1) and (2) turn out to be nearly identical.

Factors (3) and (4) also supported Exacto, the court found. "Mr. Heitz is highly qualified to run Exacto as a result of his education, training, experience, and motivation. Mr. Heitz has over 40 years of highly successful experience in the field of spring design." Id. And his "efforts were of great value to the corporation." Id. at 2526. So factor (4) duplicated (2), and so the first four factors turn out to be really only two.

With regard to the fifth factor—the employer's (Exacto's) net earnings—the Tax Court was noncommittal. Exacto had reported a loss in 1993 and very little taxable income in 1994. But it conceded having taken some improper deductions in those years unrelated to Heitz's salary. After adjusting Exacto's income to remove these deductions, the court found that Exacto had earned more than $1 million in each of the years at issue net of Heitz's supposedly inflated salary.

The court was noncommital with regard to the sixth factor— earnings of comparable employees—as well. The evidence bearing on this factor had been presented by expert witnesses, one on each side, and the court was critical of both. The taxpayer's witness had arrived at his estimate of Heitz's maximum reasonable compensation in part by aggregating the salaries that Exacto would have had to pay to hire four people each to wear one of Heitz's "hats," as chief executive officer, chief manufacturing executive, chief research and development officer, and chief sales and marketing executive. Although the more roles or functions an employee performs the more valuable his services are likely to be, Dexsil Corp. v. Commissioner, 147 F.3d 96, 102–03 (2d Cir.1998); Elliotts, Inc. v. Commissioner, 716 F.2d 1241, 1245–46 (9th Cir.1983), an employee who performs four jobs, each on a part-time basis, is not necessarily worth as much to a company as four employees each working full time at one of those jobs. It is therefore arbitrary to multiply the normal full-time salary for one of the jobs by four to compute the reasonable compensation of the employee who fills all four of them. Anyway salaries are determined not by the method of comparable worth but, like other prices, by the market, which is to say by conditions of demand and supply. Especially in the short run, salaries may vary by more than any difference in the "objective" characteristics of jobs. An individual who has valuable skills that are in particularly short supply at the moment may command a higher salary than a more versatile, better-trained, and more loyal employee whose skills are, however, less scarce.

The Internal Revenue Service's expert witness sensibly considered whether Heitz's compensation was consistent with Exacto's investors' earning a reasonable return (adjusted for the risk of Exacto's business), which he calculated to be 13 percent. But in concluding that Heitz's compensation had pushed the return below that level, he neglected to consider the concessions of improper deductions, which led to adjustments to Exacto's taxable income. The Tax Court determined that with those adjustments the investors' annual return was more than 20 percent despite Heitz's large salary. The government argues that the court should not have calculated the investors' return on the basis of the concessions of improper deductions, because when Heitz's compensation was determined the corporation was unaware that the deductions would be disallowed. In other words, the corporation thought that its after-tax income was larger than it turned out to be. But if the ex ante perspective is the proper one, as the government contends, it favors the corporation if when it fixed Heitz's salary it thought there was more money in the till for the investors than has turned out to be the case.

What is puzzling is how disallowing deductions and thus increasing the taxpayer's tax bill could increase the investors' return. What investors care about is the corporate income available to pay dividends or be reinvested; obviously money paid in taxes to the Internal Revenue Service is not available for either purpose. The reasonableness of Heitz's compensation thus depends not on Exacto's taxable income but on the corporation's profitability to the investors, which is reduced by the disallowance of deductions—if a corporation succeeds in taking phantom deductions, shareholders are better off because the corporation's tax bill is lower. But the government makes nothing of this. Its only objection is to the Tax Court's having taken account of adjustments made after Heitz's salary was fixed. Both parties, plus the Tax Court, based their estimates of investors' returns on the after-tax income shown on Exacto's tax returns, which jumped after the deductions were disallowed, rather than on Exacto's real profits, which declined. The approach is inconsistent with a realistic assessment of the investors' rate of return, but as no one in the case questions it we shall not make an issue of it.

Finally, under factor (7) ("peculiar characteristics"), the court first and rightly brushed aside the IRS's argument that the low level of dividends paid by Exacto (zero in the two years at issue, but never very high) was evidence that the corporation was paying Heitz dividends in the form of salary. The court pointed out that shareholders may not want dividends. They may prefer the corporation to retain its earnings, causing the value of the corporation to rise and thus enabling the shareholders to obtain corporate earnings in the form of capital gains taxed at a lower rate than ordinary income. The court also noted that while Heitz, as the owner of 55 percent of Exacto's common stock, obviously was in a position to influence his salary, the corporation's two other major shareholders, each with 20 percent of the stock, had approved it. They had not themselves been paid a salary or other compensation, and are not relatives of Heitz; they had no financial or other incentive to allow Heitz to siphon off dividends in the form of salary.

Having run through the seven factors, all of which either favored the taxpayer or were neutral, the court reached a stunning conclusion: "We have considered the factors relevant in deciding reasonable compensation for Mr. Heitz. On the basis of all the evidence, we hold that reasonable compensation for Mr. Heitz" was much less than Exacto paid him. 75 T.C.M. at 2528. The court's only effort at explaining this result when Heitz had passed the seven-factor test with flying colors was that "we have balanced Mr. Heitz' unique selling and technical ability, his years of experience, and the difficulty of replacing Mr. Heitz with the fact that the corporate entity would have shown a reasonable return for the equity holders, after considering petitioners' concessions." Id. But "the fact that the corporate entity would have shown a reasonable return for the equity holders" after the concessions is on the *same side* of the balance as the other factors; it does not favor the Internal Revenue Service's position. The government's lawyer was forced to concede at the argument of the appeal that she could not deny the possibility that the Tax Court had pulled its figures for Heitz's allowable compensation out of a hat.

The failure of the Tax Court's reasoning to support its result would alone require a remand. But the problem with the court's opinion goes deeper. The test it applied does not provide adequate guidance to a rational decision. We owe no deference to the Tax Court's statutory interpretations, its relation to us being that of a district court to a court of appeals, not that of an administrative agency to a court of appeals. * * * The federal courts of appeals, whose decisions do of course have weight as authority with us even when they are not our own decisions, have been moving toward a much simpler and more purposive test, the "independent investor" test. Dexsil Corp. v. Commissioner, supra; Elliotts, Inc. v. Commissioner, supra, 716 F.2d at 1245–48; Rapco, Inc. v. Commissioner, supra, 85 F.3d at 954–55. We applaud the trend and join it.

Because judges tend to downplay the element of judicial creativity in adapting law to fresh insights and changed circumstances, the cases we have just cited prefer to say (as in *Dexsil* and *Rapco*) that the "independent investor" test is the "lens" through which they view the seven (or however many) factors of the orthodox test. But that is a formality. The new test dissolves the old and returns the inquiry to basics. The Internal Revenue Code limits the amount of salary that a corporation can deduct from its income primarily in order to prevent the corporation from eluding the corporate income tax by paying dividends but calling them salary because salary is deductible and dividends are not. (Perhaps they should be, to avoid double taxation of corporate earnings, but that is not the law.) In the case of a publicly held company, where the salaries of the highest executives are fixed by a board of directors that those executives do not control, the danger of siphoning corporate earnings to executives in the form of salary is not acute. The danger is much greater in the case of a closely held corporation, in which ownership and management tend to coincide; unfortunately, as the opinion of the Tax Court in this case illustrates, judges are not competent to decide what business executives are worth.

There is, fortunately, an indirect market test, as recognized by the Internal Revenue Service's expert witness. A corporation can be conceptualized as a contract in which the owner of assets hires a person to manage them. The owner pays the manager a salary and in exchange the manager works to increase the value of the assets that have been entrusted to his management; that increase can be expressed as a rate of return to the owner's investment. The higher the rate of return (adjusted for risk) that a manager can generate, the greater the salary he can command. If the rate of return is extremely high, it will be difficult to prove that the manager is being overpaid, for it will be implausible that if he quit if his salary was cut, and he was replaced by a lower-paid manager, the owner would be better off; it would be killing the goose that lays the golden egg. The Service's expert believed that investors in a firm like Exacto would expect a 13 percent return on their investment. Presumably they would be delighted with more. They would be *overjoyed* to receive a return more than 50 percent greater than they expected— and 20 percent, the return that the Tax Court found that investors in

Exacto had obtained, is more than 50 percent greater than the benchmark return of 13 percent.

When, notwithstanding the CEO's "exorbitant" salary (as it might appear to a judge or other modestly paid official), the investors in his company are obtaining a far higher return than they had any reason to expect, his salary is presumptively reasonable. We say "presumptively" because we can imagine cases in which the return, though very high, is not due to the CEO's exertions. Suppose Exacto had been an unprofitable company that suddenly learned that its factory was sitting on an oil field, and when oil revenues started to pour in its owner raised his salary from $50,000 a year to $1.3 million. The presumption of reasonableness would be rebutted. There is no suggestion of anything of that sort here and likewise no suggestion that Mr. Heitz was merely the titular chief executive and the company was actually run by someone else, which would be another basis for rebuttal.

The government could still have prevailed by showing that while Heitz's salary may have been no greater than would be reasonable in the circumstances, the company did not in fact intend to pay him that amount as salary, that his salary really did include a concealed dividend though it need not have. This is material (and the "independent investor" test, like the multifactor test that it replaces, thus incomplete, though invaluable) because any business expense to be deductible must be, as we noted earlier, a bona fide expense as well as reasonable in amount. The fact that Heitz's salary was approved by the other owners of the corporation, who had no incentive to disguise a dividend as salary, goes far to rebut any inference of bad faith here, which in any event the Tax Court did not draw and the government does not ask us to draw.

The judgment is reversed with directions to enter judgment for the taxpayer.

REVERSED.

## NOTE

In the *Exacto Spring Corporation* case, the Seventh Circuit became the first Court of Appeals to abandon a multi-factor approach and adopt the "independent investor" test as the exclusive method for determining whether a business may deduct compensation under Section 162. The Courts of Appeal that have considered the issue since *Exacto Spring*, have either retained the multi-factor standard,[1] or used the independent investor test in conjunction with the multi-factor approach.[2] Thus, it remains to be seen

---

[1] See Metro Leasing and Development Corp. v. Commissioner, 376 F.3d 1015 (9th Cir. 2004) (the court retained the multi-factor approach); Eberl's Claim Service, Inc. v. Commissioner, 249 F.3d 994 (10th Cir.2001) (the court stated that it was bound by prior decisions to use the multi-factor approach).

[2] See e.g., Haffner's Service Stations, Inc. v. Commissioner, 326 F.3d 1 (1st Cir. 2003) (retaining multi-factor test and looking at return on equity); Dexsil Corp. v. Commissioner, 147 F.3d 96 (2d Cir. 1998); Alpha Medical Inc. v. Commissioner, 172 F.3d 942 (6th Cir. 1999); LabelGraphics, Inc. v. Commissioner, 221 F.3d 1091 (9th Cir.2000). See also, McClung & Weld,

whether the analysis in *Exacto Spring* will spread beyond the Seventh Circuit.

## Harolds Club v. Commissioner*

United States Court of Appeals, Ninth Circuit, 1965.
340 F.2d 861.

■ HAMLEY, CIRCUIT JUDGE.

[In the years 1952 to 1956 Harolds Club, an incorporated gaming establishment in Nevada, paid Raymond I. Smith salary in annual amounts ranging from about $350,000 to $560,000. The Commissioner disallowed in part the corporation's deductions based on these payments. Smith was not a shareholder in the corporation all the stock of which was owned by his two sons. However, the business was essentially a continuation of one that Smith had earlier operated illegally in California but which, upon the move to Nevada, became at first that of son Harold, as a proprietorship, and later in 1938 a partnership owned by Harold and another son of Smith. The partnership was incorporated in 1946. The scope of the business is suggested by the fact that by 1952 there were seven bars in the Club. Harolds Club did not prosper initially but in 1935 Smith, while not an owner as indicated, agreed to take over management of the Club. Ed.]

\* \* \*

At the outset, Smith was paid a salary, plus a bonus which was determined at the end of each year. In the early part of January, 1941, Smith and his sons decided upon a fixed percentage arrangement, Smith suggesting that he be paid twenty percent of the profits. Since Smith was running the club at this time and was the "brains" of the organization, his sons had no objection. Percentage employment contracts were not uncommon in the gaming business. On January 15, 1941, Smith and his sons entered into a formal written contract, under which Smith would receive an annual salary of ten thousand dollars plus twenty percent of the yearly net profits accruing from the operation of the club.

\* \* \*

By 1952, Harolds Club was employing approximately eight hundred people. Harold was then an assistant manager and Raymond was in the bookkeeping department. The club also employed a business manager and a casino manager, both of whom reported directly to Smith. On several occasions between 1941 and 1956, one or the other of the three

---

"Unreasonable Compensation and the Independent Investor Test," 79 Taxes 35 (2001), for a chart describing the tests used by the different Courts of Appeals.

\* See Sugarman, "Contingent Compensation Agreement Leads to Disallowance of Corporate Deduction," 53 Calif.L.Rev. 1544 (1965); Ford and Page, "Reasonable Compensation: Continuous Controversy," 5 J.Corp.Tax 307 (1979); Footer and Sczepanski, "Current Factors Being Used to Determine When Compensation is Deductible as Reasonable," 32 Tax'n for Acct's 226 (1984). Ed.

Smiths proposed to expand gaming activities into other areas. A majority vote decided against each of the proposals, Smith sometimes thereby getting his way, and sometimes not.

* * *

For the tax years 1952 through 1956 the annual net income of Harolds Club ranged from $1,367,029.88 to $2,098,906.01. The amounts paid to Smith for those years have already been indicated. Harold and Raymond each received salaries of from sixty thousand to seventy-five thousand dollars a year during this period.

Competitors testified that, in their opinion, the salary contract between Smith and Harolds Club was reasonable, and that he was worth all that was paid to him. As before noted however, Harolds Club does not here challenge the Tax Court's implicit finding that annual amounts paid to Smith in excess of ten thousand dollars plus fifteen percent of yearly net profits constituted unreasonable compensation for the years 1952 to 1956.

Petitioner predicates its claimed business expense deductions for the entire amounts paid to Smith during these years upon section 162(a) of the 1954 Code and section 23(a)(1)(A) of the 1939 Code.[1] Since the amount of compensation was contingent upon the amount of net profits of the business, petitioner also relied on Treasury Regulations 111, § 29.23(a)(6) and Treasury Regulations 118, § 39.23(a)(6) for the years 1952 and 1953, and Treasury Regulations § 1.162–7(b) for the remaining years.[2]

Under the quoted regulations contingent compensation, generally speaking, should be allowed as a deduction even though it may prove to be greater than the amount which would ordinarily be paid, if paid pursuant to a "free bargain" between the employer and the individual, and if the contract for compensation was reasonable under the circumstances "existing at the date when the contract for services was made."

The Tax Court determined that the amount paid to Smith as compensation in the years 1952 to 1956, under the contract for contingent compensation, was greater than the amount which would ordinarily be paid in those years, a conclusion which is not here disputed. The Court then proceeded to determine whether the deduction was nevertheless allowable under Regulation § 1.162–7(b), because such compensation resulted from a "free bargain" which, when entered into, was reasonable. It concluded that the 1941 salary agreement was not the result of a "free bargain" within the meaning of the quoted regulation, and that therefore reasonableness must be judged as of the time the compensation was paid. In reaching this conclusion the Court placed primary reliance upon the

---

1   [I.R.C. § 162(a)(1) is omitted. Ed.]
2   [Reg. § 1.162–7(b)(2) and (3) are omitted. Ed.]

family relationship between Smith and his employers in 1941, and circumstances indicating that he dominated them at that time.[3]

In contesting this conclusion petitioner first points out that the Commissioner, after audit, agreed that the salaries paid to Smith under the 1941 formula in the years 1941 through 1949 were reasonable. Petitioner reasons from this that if the contract was reasonable and entitled to recognition when the owners-sons were younger and more likely to be dominated by their father than when they themselves were over forty, " * * * it would seem that logically the contract would not become unreasonable as the domination abated."

The precise question before us, however, is not as to the Tax Court determination concerning the reasonableness of the contract at any particular time, but as to its determination that the contract was not the result of a "free bargain" in 1941. The Internal Revenue Service had no occasion to look into the latter question until it first determined that the compensation was unreasonable for a particular tax year. Since the agency determined that the compensation was in fact reasonable for the years 1941 through 1949, it made no determination for those years as to whether the 1941 contract resulted from a "free bargain."[4]

Petitioner next contends that the Tax Court erred in attributing adverse significance to the family relationship between Smith and the 1941 owners of the business, in view of the fact that the owners-sons were adults and legally competent.

The question of whether the 1941 compensation agreement resulted from a "free bargain," is one of fact. In determining that question all circumstances bearing upon the ability of the employer to exercise a free and independent judgment are relevant.

One such circumstance is family relationship. The fact that Harold and Raymond were competent adults at the time they entered into the 1941 contract tends to minimize the significance which should be attached to the fact, standing alone, that they were the sons of Smith. But that fact did not stand alone. The record fully supports the Tax Court's finding that Smith dominated the sons, notwithstanding their adulthood and competency. Indeed, the latter finding is not challenged

---

[3] The Tax Court said, in part:

"In view of the family relationship existing between Harold and Raymond, the employers, and Smith, the employee; the ages and experience of the employers; Smith's domination over his sons in the past; the respective roles and duties of the sons and Smith in Harolds Club's creation and organization; and the reasons offered by Harold and Raymond for agreeing to Smith's 'suggested' compensation, we cannot say that petitioner has established that the original employment contract (1941) between Harolds Club and Smith was the product of a free bargain or arm's-length transaction."

[4] Even if the reasonableness of Smith's compensation were here in question we fail to see how its solution is promoted by considering the likelihood that Smith's domination decreased as the years went by. Reasonableness of compensation for services depends upon the value of the services rendered. Under that test, compensation could be reasonable or unreasonable wholly apart from any factor of domination.

on this review. Where there is such domination, lack of ability to bargain freely may exist even as between competent adults.

Petitioner asserts that in concluding that the 1941 agreement did not result from a free bargain, the Tax Court applied a standard which is the exact and precise opposite of the correct standard. Petitioner asserts that the statute permitting business expense deductions is designed to prevent deduction for salaries in excess of the employee's true worth. The Tax Court therefore erred, petitioner urges, in accepting the Commissioner's argument that Smith's services were so essential to the success of his sons' business that the sons could not bargain with him on equal terms, hence the "bargain" was not "free." Under this reasoning, petitioner argues, only drones can bargain freely for their compensation.

Whatever the Commissioner may have argued in the Tax Court, we find no indication that the Court predicated its resolution of the "free bargain" question upon the theory that the sons felt obliged to enter into the 1941 agreement because of their belief that Smith's services were indispensable. The only court finding which might imply such a view is the statement that since Smith was running the club in 1941 and was the "brains" of the organization, his sons had no objection to the percentage arrangement. In our opinion this finding tends more to show that the sons surrendered their judgments to that of their father's because he exerted control rather than because he was indispensable.[5]

The Tax Court did consider the value of Smith's services in deciding what compensation for the years in question was reasonable. But the question now under discussion is the entirely different one of whether the 1941 contract resulted from a free bargain.

Petitioner argues, additionally, that apart from the above-discussed regulation pertaining to contingent compensation, the statute does not authorize the "double taxation" of payments made solely as compensation for personal services and not as disguised dividends or as the purchase price of property. By "double taxation" petitioner refers to the fact that Smith has paid personal income taxes on the full amount paid to him and, to the extent that such compensation is not allowed as a business expense deduction, petitioner must also pay a corporate income tax thereon.

Petitioner acknowledges that there is good reason to set reasonable bounds upon ostensible salaries paid to employees who are also shareholders or who are selling property to the corporation. Regulation § 1.162–7(b)(1), quoted in the margin, gives recognition to this need.[6] But

---

[5]   As indicated in the Tax Court findings quoted in note 3, one of the factors which the Court took into account in determining that the 1941 bargain was not "free," was " * * * the reasons offered by Harold and Raymond for agreeing to Smith's 'suggested' compensation, * * *." We have examined that part of Harold's and Raymond's testimony contained in the excerpted record before us and find nothing therein to indicate that they agreed to the 1941 arrangement because of Smith's indispensability.

[6]   [Reg. § 1.162–7(b)(1) is omitted. Ed.]

petitioner argues that Congress did not intend to authorize the Commissioner to sit in judgment on salaries paid to nonshareholders. This is true, petitioner reasons, because such salaries are, unless the disguised purchase price of property, paid solely to obtain personal services. No revenue purpose is served, petitioner urges, because the progressive tax structure on individuals goes higher than the corporate tax rate, consequently what is gained in corporate income taxes will be more than lost in reduced personal income taxes.

Whatever practical effect the disallowance of salary as a corporate business expense deduction may have upon the tax revenue,[7] the statute in question admits of no such qualification. Under section 162(a)(1) of the 1954 Code, only "reasonable" compensation is made deductible. Petitioner's thesis would read "reasonable" out of the statute, for it would sanction disallowance only where the payment was not compensation at all, but was really disguised dividends, property payments or gifts. The Tax Court, however, has been sustained in disallowing what was held to be unreasonable compensation which could not have been a dividend or purchase price of property. See Patton v. Commissioner, 6 Cir., 168 F.2d 28.

The fact that the regulation quoted in note 6 singles out cases where a salary is disallowed in part because it is a disguised dividend or payment for property does not alter the requirement that the salary must be reasonable to be deductible. The regulation purports only to give illustrative examples of the practical application of the Code and not to define the limits of its application.

Petitioner contends that to interpret and apply the Code section as is here done makes it a regulatory provision to control salary and wage scales. Congress, petitioner argues, intended no such regulation.

Section 162(a)(1) is designed to define which expenses are deductible. To the extent that a salary is unreasonable it is not deductible. The disallowance of a deduction for an unreasonable salary with resulting adverse tax effects to the business has a regulatory effect to the extent that it discourages the employer from disbursing, as salaries to employees what, if disbursed at all, should be distributed to such employees or others as dividends or gifts. But this regulatory effect is unavoidably incident to the tax scheme whereby only necessary business expenses may be deducted in calculating the employer's income tax.

Other arguments advanced by petitioner have been examined but are without merit.

---

[7]   Petitioner's argument as to the practical effect of the Tax Court ruling is open to question. Corporate net income withheld from disbursement as compensation for services, because in excess of reasonable compensation, would ordinarily be distributed, to a large extent, as dividends. To this extent it would be subject to both corporate and personal income taxes, whereas if disbursed as compensation for services, with an offsetting business expense deduction, it would be subject only to personal income taxes.

The Tax Court's construction of the Code provisions and regulations is correct and its determination based thereon is affirmed.

## NOTE

*$1 Million Ceiling.* The amount of compensation received by highly paid corporate executives has been the subject of Congressional scrutiny and criticism. As a result, seemingly in an attempt to deter such payments, Congress has imposed a $1 million ceiling[1] on the amount of compensation (either cash or other remuneration) that a publicly held corporation[2] may deduct in any year[3] as remuneration for services performed by a covered employee.[4] A covered employee generally includes the principal executive officer, the principal financial officer, and the three other highest paid employees.[5] Amounts that are excluded from the recipient's gross income (including amounts paid to a qualified retirement plan) are not taken into account in computing the $1 million ceiling.[6] The $1 million ceiling does not modify the Section 162(a)(1) requirement that compensation must be reasonable in order to be deductible; thus compensation of less than $1 million may not be deductible.[7]

*Golden Parachutes.* Oftentimes when ownership of a corporation changes hands through a takeover, merger, or otherwise, a key executive may "bail out," either voluntarily or involuntarily. The executive's landing back into the job market may be cushioned by a stack of dollar bills, required by an employment contract granting considerable severance pay under such circumstances, a "parachute payment." When generous, these severance packages are known as golden parachutes.[8] Section 280G[9] lets the air out of golden parachutes by prohibiting a Section 162 deduction to the payor corporation for excess parachute payments[10] and by tagging the recipient of

---

[1]   The $1 million cap is reduced by excess parachute payments (see I.R.C. § 280G) that are not deductible by the corporation. I.R.C. § 162(m)(4)(D).

[2]   A corporation is publicly held if it has securities that are required to be registered under § 12 of the Securities Exchange Act of 1934 or it is required to file reports under § 15(d) of that Act. I.R.C. § 162(m)(2). Generally, this includes a corporation whose securities are listed on a national securities exchange or a corporation with $10 million or more of assets and 2,000 or more holders of securities.

[3]   The services do not have to be performed in the same year that the deduction is taken. I.R.C. § 162(m)(4)(A).

[4]   I.R.C. § 162(m)(1). The ceiling is reduced to $500,000 for a covered executive of an "applicable employer," an employer from which one or more troubled assets are acquired in a purchase by the Treasury Department of total assets in excess of $300 million. I.R.C. § 162(m)(5).

[5]   I.R.C. § 162(m)(3). The three other highest paid employees are covered employees only if the employees' compensation is required to be reported for the taxable year under the Securities Exchange Act of 1934. I.R.C. § 162(m)(3)(B).

[6]   I.R.C. § 162(m)(4).

[7]   H.R. 2264, the Conference Bill for the Revenue Reconciliation Bill of 1993 at page 93 (1993).

[8]   Advisory Comm. on Tender Offers, U.S. Sec. and Exchange Comm., Report of Recommendations (July 8, 1983).

[9]   See Hood and Benge, "Golden Parachute Agreements: Reasonable Compensation or Disguised Bribery?" 53 U.M.K.C.L.Rev. 199 (1985).

[10]   I.R.C. § 280G(a). See Text at notes 18 and 19, infra.

such payments with a 20 percent excise tax[11] in addition to income and social security taxes.

A parachute payment[12] is any payment in the nature of compensation made to a "disqualified" individual.[13] The payment must be contingent[14] on a change in the ownership or effective control of a corporation, and the aggregate present value[15] of all such payments[16] must equal or exceed three times the disqualified individual's base amount.[17] If a parachute payment meets the threshold requirements above, then to the extent that the payment in any year exceeds the individual's base amount[18] (not three times that amount) the excess is presumed to be an unreasonable amount of compensation.[19] The payor can rebut, through clear and convincing evidence, the presumption of unreasonableness.[20] To the extent that the taxpayer fails to rebut the presumption that the payment is unreasonable compensation, the Section 162 deduction is disallowed.[21] The statute also provides some detailed exemptions from the golden parachute rules.[22]

## PROBLEM

1. Employee is the majority shareholder (248 of 250 outstanding shares) and president of Corporation. Shortly after Corporation was incorporated, its Directors adopted a resolution establishing a contingent compensation contract for Employee. The plan provided for Corporation to pay Employee a nominal salary plus an annual bonus based on a percentage of Corporation's net income. In the early years of the plan, payments to Employee averaged $50,000 annually. In recent years, Corporation's profits have increased

---

[11] I.R.C. § 4999.

[12] I.R.C. § 280G(b)(2)(A). A compensation payment to a disqualified individual automatically qualifies as a parachute payment if it violates any general enforced securities laws or regulations. I.R.C. § 280G(b)(2)(B).

[13] A disqualified individual is an employee, independent contractor or other person specified in regulations who performs personal services for the corporation *and* who is an officer, shareholder, or highly compensated individual of such corporation. I.R.C. § 280G(c). A highly compensated individual is an individual who is a member of the group consisting of the highest paid 1 percent of the employees of the corporation or, if less, the highest paid 250 employees of the corporation. Id.

[14] I.R.C. § 280G(b)(2)(A)(i). If payments are made pursuant to a contract formed or amended within one year of a change of ownership they are presumed to be contingent upon the change. I.R.C. § 280G(b)(2)(C). The amendment must be significant. H.Rep. No. 98–861, 98th Cong., 2d Sess. 851 (1984).

[15] Present value is determined by using a discount rate equal to 120% of the § 1274(d) applicable Federal rate, compounded semiannually. I.R.C. § 280G(d)(4).

[16] Transfers of property are treated as payments and are taken into account at fair market value. I.R.C. § 280G(d)(3).

[17] I.R.C. § 280G(b)(2)(A)(ii). A disqualified individual's base amount is essentially the average annual income received from the corporation for the five years preceding the taxable year in which the contingency occurs. I.R.C. § 280G(b)(3)(A), (d)(1) and (2).

[18] I.R.C. § 280G(b)(1).

[19] I.R.C. § 280G(b)(4).

[20] Id.

[21] I.R.C. § 280G(b)(4). Cf. I.R.C. § 4999(b) and (c)(2).

[22] I.R.C. § 280G(b)(5) and (6).

substantially and, as a consequence, Employee has received payments averaging more than $200,000 per year.

(a) What are Corporation's possible alternative tax treatments for the payments?

(b) What factors should be considered in determining the proper tax treatment for the payments?

(c) The problem assumes Employee *always* owned 248 of the Corporation's 250 shares. Might it be important to learn that the compensation contract was made at a time when Employee held only 10 out of the 250 outstanding shares?

## 2. TRAVEL "AWAY FROM HOME"*

Internal Revenue Code: Sections 162(a)(2), 162(a) second to last sentence; 274(n)(1). See Sections 162(h); 274(c), (h) and (m)(1) and (3).

Regulations: Section 1.162–2 (omit –2(c)).

---

### Rosenspan v. United States**
United States Court of Appeals, Second Circuit, 1971.
438 F.2d 905, cert. denied 404 U.S. 864, 92 S.Ct. 54 (1971).

■ FRIENDLY, CIRCUIT JUDGE:

This appeal is from the dismissal on the merits of an action for refund of income taxes, brought in the District Court for the Eastern District of New York. The taxes were paid as a result of the Commissioner's disallowance of deductions for unreimbursed expenses for meals and lodging allegedly incurred "while away from home in the pursuit of a trade or business," I.R.C. § 162(a)(2), in 1962 and 1964.

Plaintiff, Robert Rosenspan, was a jewelry salesman who worked on a commission basis, paying his own traveling expenses without reimbursement. In 1962 he was employed by one and in 1964 by two New York City jewelry manufacturers. For some 300 days a year he traveled by automobile through an extensive sales territory in the Middle West, where he would stay at hotels and motels and eat at restaurants. Five or six times a year he would return to New York and spend several days at his employers' offices. There he would perform a variety of services essential to his work—cleaning up his sample case, checking orders,

---

\*   See Tallant, Logan and Milton, "The Travelling Taxpayer: A Rational Framework for His Deductions," 29 U.Fla.L.R. 119 (1976); Klein, "Income Taxation and Commuting Expenses: Tax Policy and the Need for Nonsimplistic Analysis of 'Simple' Problems," 54 Cornell L.Rev. 871 (1969); Klein, "The Deductibility of Transportation Expenses of a Combination Business and Pleasure Trip—A Conceptual Analysis," 18 Stan.L.Rev. 1099 (1966); Rose, "The Deductibility of Daily Transportation Expenses To and From Distant Temporary Worksites," 36 Vanderbilt L.Rev. 541 (1983).

\*\*   Note, "Section 162(a)(2): Resolving the Tax Home Dispute," 2 Va.Tax.Rev. 153 (1982).

discussing customers' credit problems, recommending changes in stock, attending annual staff meetings, and the like.

Rosenspan had grown [up] in Brooklyn and during his marriage, had maintained a family home there. After his wife's death in 1948, he abandoned this. From that time through the tax years in question he used his brother's Brooklyn home as a personal residential address, keeping some clothing and other belongings there, and registering, voting, and filing his income tax returns from that address. The stipulation of facts states that, on his trips to New York City, "out of a desire not to abuse his welcome at his brother's home, he stayed more often" at an inn near the John F. Kennedy Airport. It recites also that "he generally spent his annual vacations in Brooklyn, where his children resided, and made an effort to return to Brooklyn whenever possible," but affords no further indication where he stayed on such visits. In 1961 he changed the registration of his automobile from New York to Ohio, giving as his address the address of a cousin in Cincinnati, where he also received mail, in order to obtain cheaper automobile insurance. Rosenspan does not contend that he had a permanent abode or residence in Brooklyn or anywhere else.

The basis for the Commissioner's disallowance of a deduction for Rosenspan's meals and lodging while in his sales territory was that he had no "home" to be "away from" while traveling. Not denying that this would be true if the language of § 162(a)(2) were given its ordinary meaning, Rosenspan claimed that for tax purposes his home was his "business headquarters," to wit, New York City where his employers maintained their offices, and relied upon the Commissioner's long advocacy of this concept of a "tax home," see e.g., G.C.M. 23672, 1943 Cum.Bull. 66–67. The Commissioner responded that although in most circumstances "home" means "business headquarters," it should be given its natural meaning of a permanent abode or residence for purposes of the problem here presented. Rosenspan says the Commissioner is thus trying to have it both ways.

The provision of the Internal Revenue Code applicable for 1962 read:

"SEC. 162. TRADE OR BUSINESS EXPENSES.

   (a)  In general.—There shall be allowed as a deduction all the ordinary and necessary expenses paid or incurred during the taxable year in carrying on any trade or business, including—

* * *

   (2)  traveling expenses (including the entire amount expended for meals and lodging) while away from home in the pursuit of a trade or business; * * * "

For 1964 the statute remained the same except for the interpolation in the parenthesis after "lodging" of the words "other than amounts which are lavish or extravagant under the circumstances"—a change not relevant in this case.

What is now § 162(a)(2) was brought into the tax structure by § 214 of the Revenue Act of 1921, 42 Stat. 239. Prior to that date, § 214 had permitted the deduction of "ordinary and necessary expenses paid or incurred * * * in carrying on any trade or business," Revenue Act of 1918, 40 Stat. 1066 (1918), without further specification. In a regulation, the Treasury interpreted the statute to allow deduction of "traveling expenses, including railroad fares, and meals and lodging *in an amount in excess of any expenditures ordinarily required for such purposes when at home*," T.D. 3101, amending Article 292 of Regulations 45, 3 Cum.Bull. 191 (1920) (emphasis supplied). A formula was provided for determining what expenditures were thus "ordinarily required"; the taxpayer was to compute such items as rent, grocery bills, light, etc. and servant hire for the periods when he was away from home, and divide this by the number of members of his family. Mim. 2688, 4 Cum.Bull. 209–11 (1921). The puzzlement of the man without a home was dealt with in a cryptic pronouncement, O.D. 905, 4 Cum.Bull. 212 (1921):

> Living expenses paid by a single taxpayer who has no home and is continuously employed on the road may not be deducted in computing net income.

The 1921 amendment, inserting what is now § 162(a)(2)'s allowance of a deduction for the entire amount of qualified meals and lodging, stemmed from a request of the Treasury based on the difficulty of administering the "excess" provision of its regulation. See United States v. Correll, 389 U.S. 299, 301 n. 6, 88 S.Ct. 445 (1967). While the taxpayer cites statements of legislators in the 1921 Congress that the amendment would provide "a measure of justice" to commercial travelers,[1] there is nothing to indicate that the members making or hearing these remarks were thinking of the unusual situation of the traveler without a home. There is likewise nothing to indicate that the Treasury sought, or that Congress meant to require, any change in the ruling that disallowed deductions for living expenses in such a case. The objective was to eliminate the need for computing the expenses "ordinarily required" at home by a taxpayer who had one, and the words used were appropriate to that end. If we were to make the unlikely assumption that the problem of the homeless commercial traveler ever entered the legislators' minds, the language they adopted was singularly inept to resolve it in the way for which plaintiff contends. Thus, if the literal words of the statute were decisive, the Government would clearly prevail on the simple ground that a taxpayer cannot be "away from home" unless he has a home from which to be away, cf. Haddleton, Traveling Expenses "Away from Home," 17 Tax.L.Rev. 261, 263, 286 (1962); 49 Va.L.Rev. 125, 126–28 (1963).

---

[1]  Representative Hawley, a member of the Committee on Ways and Means, 61 Cong.Rec. 5201 (1921); see also the remarks of Senator Walsh, a member of the Committee on Finance, 61 Cong.Rec. 6673 (1921).

Although that is our ultimate conclusion, the Supreme Court has wisely admonished that "More than a dictionary is thus required to understand the provision here involved, and no appeal to the 'plain language' of the section can obviate the need for further statutory construction," United States v. Correll, supra, 389 U.S. at 304 n. 16, 88 S.Ct. at 448. We turn, therefore, in the first instance to the Court's decisions.

The initial Supreme Court decision bearing on our problem is C.I.R. v. Flowers, 326 U.S. 465, 66 S.Ct. 250 (1946). Flowers, a lawyer, had a "home" in the conventional sense in Jackson, Mississippi, but his principal post of business was at the main office of his employer, the Gulf, Mobile & Ohio Railroad in Mobile, Alabama. Flowers sought to deduct the cost of transportation for his trips to Mobile and the meal and lodging expenses which he incurred in that city. In upholding the Commissioner's disallowance of these deductions, the Court said that "three conditions must thus be satisfied before a traveling expense deduction may be made" under what was substantially the present statute, 326 U.S. at 470, 66 S.Ct. at 252. These were:

> (1) The expense must be a reasonable and necessary traveling expense, as that term is generally understood. This includes such items as transportation fares and food and lodging expenses incurred while traveling.

> (2) The expense must be incurred "while away from home."

> (3) The expense must be incurred in pursuit of business. This means that there must be a direct connection between the expenditure and the carrying on of the trade or business of the taxpayer or of his employer. Moreover, such an expenditure must be necessary or appropriate to the development and pursuit of the business or trade.

It noted that "The meaning of the word 'home' * * * with reference to a taxpayer residing in one city and working in another has engendered much difficulty and litigation," with the Tax Court and the administrative officials having "consistently defined it as the equivalent of the taxpayer's place of business" and two courts of appeals having rejected that view and "confined the term to the taxpayer's actual residence," 326 U.S. at 471–72, 66 S.Ct. at 253. The Court found it "unnecessary here to enter into or to decide this conflict," 326 U.S. at 472. This was because the Tax Court had properly concluded "that the necessary relationship between the expenditures and the railroad's business was lacking." The railroad's interest was in having Mr. Flowers at its headquarters in Mobile; it "gained nothing" from his decision to continue living in Jackson, 326 U.S. at 472–74, 66 S.Ct. at 253–254; hence, the third condition the *Flowers* Court had enunciated as a prerequisite to deductibility was absent. Mr. Justice Rutledge dissented. He did not believe that when Congress used the word "home," it meant "business headquarters," and thought the case presented no other question, 326 U.S. at 474, 66 S.Ct. 250. The most that Rosenspan can extract from *Flowers* is that it did not decide *against* his contention that the employer's business headquarters is the employee's tax home.

The Court's next venture into this area was in Peurifoy v. C.I.R., 358 U.S. 59, 79 S.Ct. 104 (1958). That case dealt with three construction workers employed at a site in Kinston, North Carolina, for periods of 20½, 12½, and 8½ months respectively, who maintained permanent residences elsewhere in the state. The Tax Court had allowed them deductions for board and lodging during the employment at Kinston and expenses in regaining their residences when they left, apparently of their own volition and before completion of the project.[2] The Fourth Circuit had reversed, C.I.R. v. Peurifoy, 254 F.2d 483 (1957). After having granted certiorari "to consider certain questions as to the application of § 23(a)(1)(A) of the Internal Revenue Code of 1939 raised by the course of decisions in the lower courts since our decision in Commissioner v. Flowers," 358 U.S. at 59–60, 79 S.Ct. at 105, the Court announced in a *per curiam* opinion that it had "found it inappropriate to consider such questions." It read *Flowers* as establishing that "a taxpayer is entitled to deduct unreimbursed travel expenses * * * only when they are required by 'the exigencies of business,'" a "general rule" which the majority seemed to feel would mandate disallowance of the deductions under consideration. However, the Court went on to acknowledge an exception to this rule engrafted by the Tax Court, which would have allowed the claimed deductions if the taxpayer's employment were shown to be "temporary" rather than "indefinite" or "indeterminate." Nevertheless, even within this framework, the majority thought that the Court of Appeals had been justified in holding the Tax Court's finding of temporary employment to be clearly erroneous. Mr. Justice Douglas, joined by Justices Black and Whittaker, dissented. Adopting Mr. Justice Rutledge's position in *Flowers,* they disagreed "with the Commissioner's contention that 'home' is synonymous with the situs of the employer's business." While adhering to "the exigencies of business" test announced in *Flowers* they thought this requirement was satisfied by the fact that, in view of the impracticability of construction workers' moving their homes from job to job, "the expenses incurred were necessary, not to the business of the contractor for whom the taxpayers worked, but for the taxpayers themselves in order to carry on their chosen trade," 358 U.S. at 62–63 n. 6, 79 S.Ct. at 107. While the three dissenting Justices thus rejected the Commissioner's identification of "home" with "the situs of the employer's business," the majority did not adopt it and, so far as our problem is concerned, that matter remained in the state of indecision where *Flowers* had left it.

We come finally to C.I.R. v. Stidger, 386 U.S. 287, 87 S.Ct. 1065 (1967), where the Court sustained the disallowance of the expense for meals incurred by a Marine Corps captain who had been assigned to a

---

[2]   The Court of Appeals explicitly so found with respect to two of the three. 254 F.2d 483, 485 (4 Cir.1957).

base in Japan, while his wife and children—prohibited from accompanying him to that post—remained near his previous duty station in California. After noting that in this case there could be no question of the "direct connection between the expenditure and the carrying on of the trade or business of the taxpayer or of his employer," 386 U.S. at 289–90, 87 S.Ct. at 1067, the Court reviewed the continuing disagreement among the circuits over the Commissioner's view "that 'home' meant the taxpayer's principal place of business or employment whether or not it coincided with his place of residence,"[3] * * *. However, the Court again found it unnecessary either to approve or to disapprove the Commissioner's interpretation of "home," since it found that "in the context of the military taxpayer, the Commissioner's position has a firmer foundation." 386 U.S. at 292, 87 S.Ct. at 1069. This built "on the terminology employed by the military services to categorize various assignments and tours of duty, and also on the language and policy of the statutory provisions prescribing travel and transportation allowance for military personnel," id. The Court particularly stressed "the fact that Congress traditionally has provided a special system of tax-free allowances for military personnel," 386 U.S. at 294, 87 S.Ct. at 1070. Mr. Justice Douglas, who had written the dissent in *Peurifoy,* again joined by Justice Black and now by Justice Fortas, dissented. He thought it was "clear that home means residence, with the qualification that a taxpayer should establish his residence as near to his place of employment as is reasonable," 386 U.S. at 297, 87 S.Ct. at 1071.[5] The fact that Congress provides special allowances for military personnel did not, in Justice Douglas' view, call for what he deemed an unnatural reading of § 162(a)(2) even in that context.

Proper analysis of the problem has been beclouded, and the Government's position in this case has been made more difficult than it need be, by the Commissioner's insistence that "home" means "business headquarters," despite the Supreme Court's having thrice declined to endorse this, and its rejection by several courts of appeals, * * *. When Congress uses such a non-technical word in a tax statute, presumably it wants administrators and courts to read it in the way that ordinary people would understand, and not "to draw on some unexpressed spirit outside the bounds of the normal meaning of words," Addison v. Holly Hill Fruit Prods., Inc., 322 U.S. 607, 617, 64 S.Ct. 1215 (1944). The construction which the Commissioner has long advocated not only violates this principle but is unnecessary for the protection of the revenue that he seeks. That purpose is served, without any such distortion of language, by the third condition laid down in *Flowers,* supra, 326 U.S. at

---

[3]  Although the opinion lists this circuit as having subscribed to the Commissioner's definition of "home," citing O'Toole v. C.I.R., 243 F.2d 302 (2 Cir.1957), and a sentence in our per curiam opinion does read that way, the facts of O'Toole presented a typical Flowers situation and the ratio decidendi was the same as in that case, namely, that "The job, not the taxpayer's pattern of living, must require the traveling expenses," 243 F.2d at 303.

[5]  Perhaps more accurately, he should be treated as if he had done so.

470, 66 S.Ct. at 252, namely, "that there must be a direct connection between the expenditure and the carrying on of the trade or business of the taxpayer or of his employer" and that "such an expenditure must be necessary or appropriate to the development and pursuit of the business or trade." These requirements were enough to rule out a deduction for Flowers' lodging and meals while in Mobile even if he was "away from home" while there. The deduction would not have been available to his fellow workers living in that city who obtained similar amenities in their homes or even in the very restaurants that Flowers patronized, and Flowers was no more compelled by business to be away from his home while in Mobile than were other employees of the railroad who lived there.

Since the Commissioner's definition of "home" as "business headquarters" will produce the same result as the third *Flowers* condition in the overwhelming bulk of cases arising under § 162(a)(2), courts have often fallen into the habit of referring to it as a ground or an alternate ground of decision, as this court did in O'Toole v. C.I.R., 243 F.2d 302 (1957), see fn. 3. But examination of the string of cases cited by plaintiff as endorsing the "business headquarters" test has revealed almost none, aside from the unique situations involving military personnel considered above, which cannot be explained on the basis that the taxpayer had no permanent residence, or was not away from it, or maintained it in a locale apart from where he regularly worked as a matter of personal choice rather than business necessity.[6] This principle likewise affords a satisfactory rationale for the "temporary" employment cases, see 49 Va.L.Rev., supra, at 162–63. When an assignment is truly temporary, it would be unreasonable to expect the taxpayer to move his home, and the expenses are thus compelled by the "exigencies of business"; when the assignment is "indefinite" or "indeterminate," the situation is different and, if the taxpayer decides to leave his home where it was, disallowance is appropriate, not because he has acquired a "tax home" in some lodging house or hotel at the worksite but because his failure to move his home was for his personal convenience and not compelled by business necessity. Under the facts here presented, we need not decide whether in the case of a taxpayer who is not self-employed the

---

[6] Whether the "personal choice" principle has not sometimes been pressed too far is another matter. * * * It is also hard to be completely satisfied with the distinction between Barnhill v. C.I.R., 148 F.2d 913 (4 Cir.1945), disallowing meals and lodging deductions while in the state capital to justices of the Supreme Court of North Carolina who spent approximately 7 months a year there, but maintained their residences elsewhere, in deference to a custom that, at the time of selection, the justices should be fairly distributed throughout the state and a decision allowing such a deduction in the case of a justice of the Supreme Court of Louisiana who spent 9 months at the Court's headquarters in New Orleans but who, in contrast to the unwritten North Carolina practice, was required by the state constitution to maintain his residence in his own parish. United States v. LeBlanc, 278 F.2d 571 (5 Cir.1960). England v. United States, 345 F.2d 414 (7 Cir.1965), cert. denied, 382 U.S. 986, 86 S.Ct. 537 (1966), is another case in which the "personal choice" principle scarcely provides a satisfactory basis of decision if it suffices that the expenses be necessary to the taxpayer-employee's "trade or business" as distinguished from his employer's. [As to this, see the discussion in the Text, infra. Ed.]

"exigencies of business" which compel the traveling expenses away from home refer solely to the business of his employer or to the business of the taxpayer as well. We note only that the latter contention is surely not foreclosed by decisions to date. See Peurifoy v. C.I.R., 358 U.S., supra, at 62–63, 79 S.Ct. at 107, n. 6 (Douglas, J., dissenting); Rev.Rul. 60–189, 1960–1 Cum.Bull. 60; see generally 49 Va.L.Rev., supra, at 136–45; and Trent v. C.I.R., 291 F.2d 669, and cases cited, especially at 674 (2 Cir.1961).

Shifting the thrust of analysis from the search for a fictional "tax home" to a questioning of the business necessity for incurring the expense away from the taxpayer's permanent residence thus does not upset the basic structure of the decisions which have dealt with this problem. Compare 49 Va.L.Rev., supra, at 162–63, with Haddleton, supra, at 286. It merely adopts an approach that better effectuates the congressional intent in establishing the deduction and thus provides a sounder conceptual framework for analysis while following the ordinary meaning of language. Cf. 19 U.Chi.L.Rev. 534, 545 (1952); 49 Va.L.Rev., supra, at 163. We see no basis whatever for believing that when the 1921 Congress eliminated the requirement for determining the excess of the costs of meals and lodging while on the road over what they would have been at home, it meant to disallow a deduction to someone who had the expense of maintaining a home from which business took him away but possessed no business headquarters. By the same token we find it impossible to read the words "away from home" out of the statute, as Rosenspan, in effect, would have us do and allow a deduction to a taxpayer who had no "home" in the ordinary sense. The limitation reflects congressional recognition of the rational distinction between the taxpayer with a permanent residence—whose travel costs represent a duplication of expense or at least an incidence of expense which the existence of his permanent residence demonstrates he would not incur absent business compulsion—and the taxpayer without such a residence. Cf. James v. United States, supra, 308 F.2d at 207. We fail to see how Rosenspan's occasional trips to New York City, assuming for the sake of argument that his "business headquarters" was in New York rather than in his sales territory, differentiate him economically from the homeless traveling salesman without even the modicum of a business headquarters Rosenspan is claimed to have possessed. Yet we approved disallowance of the deduction in such a case many years ago. Duncan v. C.I.R., 17 B.T.A. 1088 (1929), aff'd per curiam, 47 F.2d 1082 (2 Cir.1931), as the Ninth Circuit has done more recently, James v. United States, supra, 308 F.2d 204.

It is enough to decide this case that "home" means "home" and Rosenspan had none. He satisfied the first and third conditions of Flowers, supra, 326 U.S. at 470, 66 S.Ct. 250, but not, on our reading of the statute, the second. The judgment dismissing the complaint must therefore be affirmed.

## Andrews v. Commissioner*
United States Court of Appeals, First Circuit, 1991.
931 F.2d 132.

■ LEVIN H. CAMPBELL, CIRCUIT JUDGE.

Edward W. Andrews and his wife, Leona J. Andrews, brought this action in the Tax Court for a redetermination of an income tax deficiency that the Commissioner had assessed for the tax year 1984. At issue is Andrews' deduction of travel expenses, including meals and costs associated with maintaining a second home at Lighthouse Point, Florida, as "traveling expenses . . . while away from home in the pursuit of a trade or business." Internal Revenue Code of 1954, 26 U.S.C. § 162(a)(2). Personal living expenses are generally not deductible. 26 U.S.C. § 262. The Tax Court sustained the Commissioner's disallowance of the deduction on the grounds that Andrews was not "away from home" when these expenses were incurred. *Andrews v. Commissioner,* 60 T.C.M. (CCH) 277, T.C.Memo 1990–391. Andrews appeals to this court pursuant to 26 U.S.C. § 7482.

*Background*

We summarize the Tax Court's findings only to the extent helpful in understanding this decision. Andrews was president and chief executive officer of Andrews Gunite Co., Inc. ("Andrews Gunite"), which is engaged in the swimming pool construction business in New England, a seasonal business. His salary in 1984 was $108,000. Beginning in 1964, during the off-season, Andrews, establishing a sole proprietorship known as Andrews Farms, began to race and breed horses in New England, and in 1972 moved his horse business to Pompano, Florida. Andrews' horse business proliferated and prospered.

In 1974, Andrews Gunite diversified by establishing a Florida-based division, known as Pilgrim Farms, to acquire horses to breed with two of Andrews Farms' most successful horses and to develop a racing stable similar to Andrews Farms. By 1975, Andrews Farms had 130 horses, and by 1984 Pilgrim Farms had twenty to thirty horses. Andrews was responsible, in 1984, for managing and training Pilgrim Farms horses and Andrews Farms horses, though he was compensated for his services to Pilgrim Farms only by payment of his airfare to Florida. While in Florida during racing season, Andrews worked at the racetrack from seven in the morning until noon, and he returned to the track to solicit sales of his horses and watch the races on four nights per week.

Also, in 1983, Andrews' son, who had worked for Andrews Gunite, sought to establish a pool construction business in Florida. Andrews, along with his brother and son, formed a corporation, originally known as East Coast Pools by Andrews, Inc. and renamed Pools by Andrews, Inc., to purchase the assets of a troubled pool business in Florida.

---

\*   Some footnotes omitted.

Andrews owned one-third of Pools by Andrews, Inc. in 1984. Andrews assisted his son in the Florida pool business, but drew no salary for his services. By the time of trial, this pool business was one of the biggest, if not the biggest builder of pools in Florida, with offices in West Palm Beach and Orlando and plans for a third office in Tampa.

Andrews resided in Lynnfield, Massachusetts with his wife prior to and during 1984. During this period, the expansion of the horse business required Andrews to make an increasing number of trips to Florida. In order to reduce travel costs and facilitate lodging arrangements, Andrews purchased a condominium in Pompano Beach, Florida in 1976, which he used as a residence when in Florida during the racing season. The neighborhood around the condominium became unsafe, and Andrews decided to move, purchasing a single family home with a swimming pool in Lighthouse Point, Florida in 1983. The home was closer than the condominium to the Pompano Beach Raceway, where Andrews maintained, trained, and raced many of the Andrews Farms and Pilgrim Farms horses. Andrews used the Florida house as his personal residence during the racing season.

The Tax Court concluded that in 1984 Andrews worked in Florida primarily in his horse business for six months, from January through April and during November and December, and that Andrews worked primarily in his pool construction business in Massachusetts for six months, from May to October. On his 1984 amended return, Andrews claimed one hundred percent business usage on his Florida house, and claimed depreciation deductions on the furniture and house in connection with his horse racing business. He also characterized tax, mortgage interest, utilities, insurance, and other miscellaneous expenses as "lodging expenses," which he deducted in connection with the Florida pools and horse racing businesses, along with expenses for meals while he was in Florida.[5]

---

[5] Andrews has no records to substantiate the claimed meals expenses, which he calculated by multiplying $28.40 a day by the 140 days he claimed he was in Florida on business. The Tax Court found that, even if it had concluded that Andrews was away from home during his six months in Florida, it would still sustain the Commissioner's disallowance of the meals deduction because Andrews failed to comply with the substantiation requirements of 26 U.S.C. § 274(d).

Andrews does not contest the Tax Court's finding that the meals expenses were unsubstantiated and therefore non-deductible at the claimed $28.40/day rate. Nevertheless, he contends that he is entitled to a deduction for unsubstantiated meals expenses in the amount of $9.00 per day pursuant to Rev.Proc. 83–71, 1983–2 C.B. 590, for what he now contends totalled two hundred days away from Massachusetts conducting business in 1984. The Commissioner agrees that Andrews would be entitled to deduction of $9.00 per day for meals expenses if he was "away from home" while in Florida in pursuit of business, though the Commissioner contends Andrews was not "away from home" while in Florida.

We need not address this issue on appeal. As discussed below, the Tax Court determined that Andrews was not entitled to business travel deductions under section 162(a)(2) for living expenses incurred in Florida, and did not reach the question of what unsubstantiated meals expenses may be deducted had it found Andrews was entitled to any section 162(a)(2) deductions.

*Discussion*

The Tax Court correctly stated: "The purpose of the section 162(a)(2) deduction is to mitigate the burden upon a taxpayer who, because of the exigencies of his trade or business, must maintain two places of abode and thereby incur additional living expenses." *See Hantzis v. Commissioner,* 638 F.2d 248, 256 (1st Cir.), *cert. denied,* 452 U.S. 962, 101 S.Ct. 3112, 69 L.Ed.2d 973 (1981); *Dilley v. Commissioner,* 58 T.C. 276 (1972); *Kroll v. Commissioner,* 49 T.C. 557, 562 (1968). The Tax Court then stated its general rule that "a taxpayer's home for purposes of section 162(a) is the area or vicinity of his principal place of business." Responding thereafter to the Commissioner's contention that during the horse racing season Florida was Andrews' "tax home," rendering Andrews' Florida meals and lodging expenses personal and nondeductible living expenses under sections 262 and 162(a)(2), the Tax Court concluded that Andrews had two "tax homes" in 1984. The Tax Court, without further elaboration, based its decision on an observation that Andrews' business in Florida between January and mid-April and during November and December of each year was recurrent with each season, rather than temporary.

On appeal, the Commissioner who, while maintaining its ongoing position that the taxpayer's home for purposes of section 162(a)(2) is his principal place of business and that Andrews' principal place of business was in Florida, agrees with Andrews that the Tax Court erred in finding that he had more than one tax home and urges that we remand for the Tax Court to determine the location of Andrews' principal place of business. For the reasons that follow, we hold that the Tax Court erred in determining that Andrews had two "tax homes" in this case.[6]

As we have previously stated, section 162 provides a category of deductible business expenses which reflects "a fundamental principle of taxation: that a person's taxable income should not include the cost of producing that income." *Hantzis,* 638 F.2d at 249. A specific example of a deductible cost of producing income is section 162(a)(2) travel expenses. *Id.* The Supreme Court first construed the meaning of the travel expense

---

[6]   The Tax Court also determined that 26 U.S.C. § 280A(a) (which provides that no deduction is generally allowable "with respect to the use of a dwelling unit used by the taxpayer during the taxable year as his residence"), would prohibit allowance of Andrews' deduction for his Florida home lodging expenses. We agree, however, with both Andrews and the Commissioner that the Tax Court erred by ignoring the effect of section 280A(f)(4), which states:

> **(4)   Coordination with section 162(a)(2).**—Nothing in this section shall be construed to disallow any deduction allowable under section 162(a)(2) (or any deduction which meets the tests of section 162(a)(2) but is allowable under another provision of this title) by reason of the taxpayer's being away from home in the pursuit of a trade or business (other than the trade or business of renting dwelling units).

Also, as the Commissioner correctly points out in his brief, the Congressional floor debates pertaining to the enactment of section 280A(f)(4) indicate that, in appropriate circumstances, expenses incurred in connection with ownership of a home could qualify as deductible business lodging expenses. *See* 127 Cong.Rec. 31968 (Dec. 16, 1981) ("Finally, this provision will clarify that the personal use rules of section 280A will not be construed to deny otherwise allowable business expenses for travel away from home.") (statement of Sen. Dole); *see also* 127 Cong.Rec. 3159, 31971–31973 (1981).

deduction provision[7] in *Commissioner v. Flowers,* 326 U.S. 465, 66 S.Ct. 250, 90 L.Ed. 203 (1946). In *Flowers,* the Court construed this provision to mean that travel expenses are deductible only if: (1) "reasonable and necessary"; (2) "incurred 'while away from home' "; and (3) incurred "in pursuit of business." *Id.* at 470, 66 S.Ct. at 252.

The issue of the reasonableness or necessity of Andrews' Florida expenses is not presented in this appeal. Rather, the Tax Court based its decision on a holding that Andrews did not satisfy the second *Flowers* requirement for deduction of his Florida expenses; as the Tax Court determined Andrews' home in 1984 was in both Massachusetts and Florida, he was not away from home when these expenses were incurred. We turn, then, to interpret the meaning of the "away from home" language of section 162(a)(2). The question here is whether, within the meaning of "home" in section 162(a)(2), Andrews could have had two homes in 1984.

The Supreme Court, in *Flowers,* noted: "The meaning of the word 'home' in [the travel expense deduction provision] with reference to a taxpayer residing in one city and working in another has engendered much difficulty and litigation." *Id.* at 471, 66 S.Ct. at 253; *see also Commissioner v. Stidger,* 386 U.S. 287, 292, 87 S.Ct. 1065, 1068, 18 L.Ed.2d 53 (1967). The Internal Revenue Service has consistently taken the position that a taxpayer's home for purposes of section 162(a) is the area or vicinity of his principal place of employment. Rev.Rul. 75–432, 1975–2 C.B. 60; Rev.Rul. 63–82, 1963–1 C.B. 33; Rev.Rul. 61–67, 1961–1 C.B. 25. The Tax Court in this case acknowledged the general validity of that rule, as have a number of courts of appeals. *See, e.g., Coombs v. Commissioner,* 608 F.2d 1269, 1275 (9th Cir.1979); *Markey v. Commissioner,* 490 F.2d 1249, 1255 (6th Cir.1974). Judge Friendly, writing for the Second Circuit, however, reasoned that Congress intended that "home" should be accorded its natural non-technical ordinary meaning of primary residence in a tax statute. *Rosenspan v. United States,* 438 F.2d 905, 911 (2d Cir.), *cert. denied,* 404 U.S. 864, 92 S.Ct. 54, 30 L.Ed.2d 108 (1971).

This court, in *Hantzis,* after reviewing cases addressing this issue, declined in that case to focus upon the "principal place of business" or "primary residence" definitions of "home," and suggested a "functional definition of the term," 638 F.2d at 253. Effectuation of the travel expense provision must be guided by the policy underlying the provision that costs necessary to producing income may be deducted from taxable income. *Id.* at 251. Where business necessity requires that a taxpayer maintain two places of abode, and thereby incur additional and duplicate living expenses, such duplicate expenses are a cost of producing income and should ordinarily be deductible. We believe it continues to be the case

---

[7]    The travel expense provision at issue in *Flowers* was substantially the same as the provision at issue here, and was then-codified at 26 U.S.C. § 23(a)(1)(A), as amended, 56 Stat. 819.

that, "[w]hether it is held in a particular decision that a taxpayer's home is his residence or his principal place of business, the ultimate allowance or disallowance of a deduction is a function of the court's assessment of the reason for a taxpayer's maintenance of two homes." *Id.* "The exigencies of business rather than the personal conveniences and necessities of the traveler must be the motivating factors." *Flowers,* 326 U.S. at 474, 66 S.Ct. at 254. The Commissioner and courts have adhered consistently to this policy that living expenses duplicated as a result of business necessity are deductible, whereas those duplicated as a result of personal choice are not.

The principle—that living expenses are deductible to the extent business necessity requires that they be duplicated—is also reflected in cases concerning temporary and itinerant workers. The courts and the Commissioner have agreed that a taxpayer cannot be expected to relocate her primary residence to a place of temporary employment. Hence, duplicate living expenses incurred at the place of temporary employment (if different from the place of usual abode), result from business exigency in satisfaction of the third prong of the *Flowers* test. An exception to the "principal place of business" definition of "tax home" is made where the business assignment is only temporary. *See Peurifoy v. Commissioner,* 358 U.S. 59, 79 S.Ct. 104, 3 L.Ed.2d 30 (1958) (*per curiam*); *Yeates v. Commissioner,* 873 F.2d 1159, 1160 (8th Cir.1989) (*per curiam*); *Hantzis,* 638 F.2d at 254–55; *Six v. United States,* 450 F.2d 66 (2d Cir.1971); *Harvey v. Commissioner,* 283 F.2d 491 (9th Cir.1960). Moreover, an "itinerant" worker who has no principal place of business and has no permanent place of abode ordinarily does not bear duplicate living expenses at all, and no deduction is generally allowable. *See Deamer v. Commissioner,* 752 F.2d 337, 339 (8th Cir.1985) (*per curiam*); *Rosenspan,* 438 F.2d at 912;[8] *Duncan v. Commissioner,* 47 F.2d 1082 (2d Cir.1931); Rev.Rul. 60–189, 1960–1, C.B. 60.

Here, we face a situation where the Tax Court found that the taxpayer, Andrews, had two businesses which apparently required that he spend a substantial amount of time in each of two widely separate places in 1984. However, the Tax Court's conclusion—that Andrews had two "tax homes"—is inconsistent with the well-settled policy underlying section 162(a)(2): that duplicated living expenses necessitated by business are deductible. We have previously said that "a taxpayer who is required to travel to get to a place of secondary employment which is sufficiently removed from his place of primary employment is just as

---

8   In *Rosenspan,* Judge Friendly explained the limitation that deductions are not allowable for a travelling salesman taxpayer who has no "home," notwithstanding the existence of a "business headquarters" or "principal place of business," as follows:

> The limitation reflects congressional recognition of the rational distinction between the taxpayer with a permanent residence—whose travel costs represent a duplication of expense or at least an incidence of expense which the existence of his permanent residence demonstrates he would not incur absent business compulsion—and the taxpayer without such a residence.

*Rosenspan,* 438 F.2d at 912.

much within the [travel expense deduction] provision as an employee who must travel at the behest of his employer." *Chandler v. Commissioner,* 226 F.2d 467, 469 (1st Cir.1955), *disapproved on other grounds, Commissioner v. Bagley,* 374 F.2d 204, 208 n. 11 (1st Cir.1967), *cert. denied,* 389 U.S. 1046, 88 S.Ct. 761, 19 L.Ed.2d 838 (1968). On the facts the Tax Court has found, it appears that Andrews, due to his geographically disparate horse and pool construction businesses, was required to incur duplicate living expenses. The Tax Court found that Andrews maintained at least the Massachusetts house throughout the year, and duplicate expenses were seemingly incurred by maintaining the Florida house, at least in part attributable to business exigency. If so, Andrews could have had only one "home" for purposes of section 162(a)(2) in 1984; duplicate living expenses while on business at the other house were a cost of producing income.[9]

We do not seek to instruct the Tax Court how to determine which house in 1984, in Florida or in Massachusetts, was Andrews' "tax home," and which house gave rise to deductible duplicate living expenses while "away from home in pursuit of a trade or business," for purposes of section 162(a)(2). The guiding policy must be that the taxpayer is reasonably expected to locate his "home," for tax purposes, at his "major post of duty" so as to minimize the amount of business travel away from home that is required; a decision to do otherwise is motivated not by business necessity but by personal considerations, and should not give rise to greater business travel deductions. The length of time spent engaged in business at each location should ordinarily be determinative of which is the taxpayer's "principal place of business" or "major post of duty."[10] Defining that location as the taxpayer's "tax home" should result

---

[9]  In support of its decision that Andrews had two "tax homes" in 1984, the Tax Court cited *Regan v. Commissioner,* 54 T.C.M. (CCH) 846, T.C.Memo 1987–512. In *Regan,* the taxpayer was employed near Tampa, Florida from January through June, and in the vicinity of Gainesville, Florida from July through December. The taxpayer argued that his home was in Tampa, and he continued to pay rent on his Tampa apartment when he was in Gainesville. Unpersuaded, the Tax Court found that the taxpayer spent an equal amount of time, engaged in an equal amount of business, derived an equal amount of income from his activities, and "merely rented an apartment" in both places. The Tax Court concluded from these facts that the taxpayer's principal place of business, and hence "tax home," was in Tampa from January to June, and in Gainesville from July through December. On this basis, the Tax Court sustained the disallowance of the taxpayer's deduction of travel expenses for his time in Gainesville. We doubt this decision was correct, as the taxpayer appears to have incurred duplicate lodging expenses, including at least rent, as a result of business exigency. We note that prior memorandum decisions of the Tax Court are not treated by that court as binding precedent. *Newman v. Commissioner,* 68 T.C. 494, 502 n. 4 (1977).

This is not to say we could not imagine a rare case where a finding of "two tax homes" would be appropriate and would fit within the policies underlying section 162(a)(2). A taxpayer, spending six months of the year engaged in business in each of two different places, and maintaining a permanent home in neither place (for example, living in hotels at both places), might not incur duplicate expenses. Such a taxpayer, whether viewed in the nature of an "itinerant," *see supra,* or as having two "tax homes," should not generally be allowed to deduct meals and lodging as business travel deductions under section 162(a)(2). This, however, is not the case here.

[10]  The Sixth Circuit has established an "objective test" to determine the situs of a taxpayer's "major post of duty," including three factors: (1) the length of time spent at the location; (2) the degree of activity in each place; and (3) the relative portion of taxpayer's income

in allowance of deductions for duplicate living expenses incurred at the other "minor post of duty." Business necessity requires that living expenses be duplicated only for the time spent engaged in business at the "minor post of duty," whether that is the "primary residence" or not. *See Montgomery v. Commissioner,* 532 F.2d 1088 (6th Cir.1976); *Markey, supra,* 490 F.2d at 1252; *Sherman v. Commissioner,* 16 T.C. 332 (1951).

*Vacated and remanded for further proceedings consistent with this opinion.*

## Revenue Ruling 99–7
1999–1 C.B. 361.

ISSUE

Under what circumstances are daily transportation expenses incurred by a taxpayer in going between the taxpayer's residence and a work location deductible under § 162(a) of the Internal Revenue Code?

LAW AND ANALYSIS

Section 162(a) allows a deduction for all the ordinary and necessary expenses paid or incurred during the taxable year in carrying on any trade or business. Section 262, however, provides that no deduction is allowed for personal, living, or family expenses.

A taxpayer's costs of commuting between the taxpayer's residence and the taxpayer's place of business or employment generally are nondeductible personal expenses under §§ 1.162–2(e) and 1.262–1(b)(5) of the Income Tax Regulations. However, the costs of going between one business location and another business location generally are deductible under § 162(a). Rev.Rul. 55–109, 1955–1 C.B. 261.

Section 280A(c)(1)(A) * * * provides, in part, that a taxpayer may deduct expenses for the business use of the portion of the taxpayer's personal residence that is exclusively used on a regular basis as the principal place of business for any trade or business of the taxpayer. (In the case of an employee, however, such expenses are deductible only if the exclusive and regular use of the portion of the residence is for the convenience of the employer.) [See Chapter 17D, infra. Ed.] In *Curphey v. Commissioner,* 73 T.C. 766 (1980), the Tax Court held that daily transportation expenses incurred in going between an office in a taxpayer's residence and other work locations were deductible where the home office was the taxpayer's principal place of business within the meaning of § 280A(c)(1)(A) for the trade or business conducted by the

---

derived from each place. *Markey,* 490 F.2d at 1255. The first factor would ordinarily be the most important, since the time spent as a business necessity at the location is a reasonable proxy for the amount of living expenses that business requires be incurred in each place. *See Markey,* 490 F.2d at 1252; *Sherman v. Commissioner,* 16 T.C. 332 (1951) (amount of income derived from activity at each location not controlling); Rev.Rul. 82, 1963–1 C.B. 33; Rev.Rul. 67, 1961–1, C.B. 25. We recognize, however, that other factors might be considered or even found determinative under appropriate circumstances.

taxpayer at those other work locations. The court stated that "[w]e see no reason why the rule that local transportation expenses incurred in travel between one business location and another are deductible should not be equally applicable *where the taxpayer's principal place of business with respect to the activities involved in his residence.*" 73 T.C. at 777–778 (emphasis in original). Implicit in the court's analysis in *Curphey* is that the deductibility of daily transportation expenses is determined on a business-by-business basis.

Rev.Rul. 190, 1953–2 C.B. 303, provides a limited exception to the general rule that the expenses of going between a taxpayer's residence and a work location are nondeductible commuting expenses. Rev.Rul. 190 deals with a taxpayer who lives and ordinarily works in a particular metropolitan area but who is not regularly employed at any specific work location. In such a case, the general rule is that daily transportation expenses are not deductible when paid or incurred by the taxpayer in going between the taxpayer's residence and a *temporary* work site *inside* that metropolitan area because that area is considered the taxpayer's regular place of business. However, Rev.Rul. 190 holds that daily transportation expenses are deductible business expenses when paid or incurred in going between the taxpayer's residence and a *temporary* work site *outside* that metropolitan area.

Rev.Rul. 90–23, 1990–1 C.B. 28, distinguishes Rev.Rul. 190 and holds, in part, that, for a taxpayer who has one or more regular places of business, daily transportation expenses paid or incurred in going between the taxpayer's residence and *temporary* work locations are deductible business expenses under § 162(a), regardless of the distance.

Rev.Rul. 94–47, 1994–2 C.B. 18, amplifies and clarifies Rev.Rul. 190 and Rev.Rul. 90–23, and provides several rules for determining whether daily transportation expenses are deductible business expenses under § 162(a). Under Rev.Rul. 94–47, a taxpayer generally may not deduct daily transportation expenses incurred in going between the taxpayer's residence and a work location. A taxpayer, however, may deduct daily transportation expenses incurred in going between the taxpayer's residence and a *temporary* work location *outside* the metropolitan area where the taxpayer lives and normally works. In addition, Rev.Rul. 94–47 clarifies Rev.Rul. 90–23 to provide that a taxpayer must have at least one regular place of business located "away from the taxpayer's residence" in order to deduct daily transportation expenses incurred in going between the taxpayer's residence and a *temporary* work location in the same trade or business regardless of the distance. In this regard, Rev.Rul. 94–47 also states that the Service will not follow the decision in *Walker v. Commissioner*, 101 T.C. 537 (1993). Finally, Rev.Rul. 94–47 amplifies Rev.Rul. 190 and Rev.Rul. 90–23 to provide that, if the taxpayer's residence is the taxpayer's principal place of business within the meaning of § 280A(c)(1)(A), the taxpayer may deduct daily transportation expenses incurred in going between the taxpayer's residence and another work location in the same trade or business regardless of whether the other work location is regular or *temporary* and regardless of the distance.

For purposes of both Rev.Rul. 90–23 and Rev.Rul. 94–47, a *temporary* work location is defined as any location at which the taxpayer performs services on an irregular or short-term (*i.e.,* generally a matter of days or weeks) basis. However, for purposes of determining whether daily transportation expense allowances and per diem travel allowances for meal and lodging expenses are subject to income tax withholding under § 3402, Rev.Rul. 59–371, 1959–2 C.B. 236, provides a 1-year standard to determine whether a work location is *temporary*. Similarly, for purposes of determining the deductibility of travel away-from-home expenses under § 162(a)(2), Rev.Rul. 93–86, 1993–2 C.B. 71, generally provides a 1-year standard to determine whether a work location will be treated as *temporary*.

The Service has reconsidered the definition of a *temporary* work location in Rev.Rul. 90–23 and Rev.Rul. 94–47, and will replace the "irregular or short-term (*i.e.,* generally a matter of days or weeks) basis" standard in those rulings with a 1-year standard similar to the rules set forth in Rev.Rul. 59–371 and Rev.Rul. 93–86.

If an office in the taxpayer's residence satisfies the principal place of business requirements of § 280A(c)(1)(A), then the residence is considered a business location for purposes of Rev.Rul. 90–23 or Rev.Rul. 94–47. In these circumstances, the daily transportation expenses incurred in going between the residence and other work locations in the same trade or business are ordinary and necessary business expenses (deductible under § 162(a)). *See Curphey; see also Wisconsin Psychiatric Services v. Commissioner,* 76 T.C. 839 (1981). In contrast, if an office in the taxpayer's residence does not satisfy the principal place of business requirements of § 280A(c)(1)(A), then the business activity there (if any) is not sufficient to overcome the inherently personal nature of the residence and the daily transportation expenses incurred in going between the residence and regular work locations. In these circumstances, the residence is not considered a business location for purposes of Rev.Rul. 90–23 or Rev.Rul. 94–47, and the daily transportation expenses incurred in going between the residence and regular work locations are personal expenses (nondeductible under §§ 1.162–2(e) and 1.262–1(b)(5)). *See Green v. Commissioner;* 59 T.C. 456 (1972); *Fryer v. Commissioner,* T.C. Memo 1974–77.

For purposes of determining the deductibility of travel-away-from-home expenses under § 162(a)(2), Rev.Rul. 93–86 defines "home" as the "taxpayer's regular or principal (if more than one regular) place of business." *See Daly v. Commissioner,* 72 T.C. 190 (1979), aff'd, 662 F.2d 253 (4th Cir.1981); *Flowers v. Commissioner,* 326 U.S. 465 (1946), 1946–1 C.B. 57.

HOLDING

In general, daily transportation expenses incurred in going between a taxpayer's residence and a work location are nondeductible commuting expenses. However, such expenses are deductible under the circumstances described in paragraph (1), (2), or (3) below.

(1) A taxpayer may deduct daily transportation expenses incurred in going between the taxpayer's residence and *temporary* work location *outside* the metropolitan area where the taxpayer lives and normally works. However, unless paragraph (2) or (3) below applies, daily transportation expenses incurred in going between the taxpayer's residence and a *temporary* work location *within* that metropolitan area are nondeductible commuting expenses.

(2) If a taxpayer has one or more regular work locations away from the taxpayer's residence, the taxpayer may deduct daily transportation expenses incurred in going between the taxpayer's residence and a *temporary* work location in the same trade or business, regardless of the distance. (The Service will continue not to follow the *Walker* decision.)

(3) If a taxpayer's residence is the taxpayer's principal place of business within the meaning of § 280A(c)(1)(A), the taxpayer may deduct daily transportation expenses incurred in going between the residence and another work location in the same trade or business, regardless of whether the other work location is *regular* or *temporary* and regardless of the distance.

For purposes of paragraphs (1), (2), and (3), the following rules apply in determining whether a work location is *temporary*. If employment at a work location is realistically expected to last (and does in fact last) for 1 year or less, the employment is *temporary* in the absence of facts and circumstances indicating otherwise. If employment at a work location is realistically expected to last for more than 1 year or there is no realistic expectation that the employment will last for 1 year or less, the employment is *not temporary*, regardless of whether it actually exceeds 1 year. If employment at a work location initially is realistically expected to last for 1 year or less, but at some later date the employment is realistically expected to exceed 1 year, that employment will be treated as temporary (in the absence of facts and circumstances indicating otherwise) until the date that the taxpayer's realistic expectation changes, and will be treated as *not temporary* after that date.

The determination that a taxpayer's residence is the taxpayer's principal place of business within the meaning of § 280A(c)(1)(A) is not necessarily determinative of whether the residence is the taxpayer's tax home for other purposes, including the travel-away-from-home deduction under § 162(a)(2).

\* \* \*

## PROBLEMS

1. Commuter owns a home in Suburb of City and drives to work in City each day. He eats lunch in various restaurants in City.

   (a) May Commuter deduct his costs of transportation and/or meals? See Reg. § 1.162–2(e). *[handwritten: – no, holding (1)]*

   (b) Same as (a), above, but Commuter is a self-employed attorney and often must travel between his office and the City Court House to file papers, try cases, etc. May Commuter deduct all or any of his costs of transportation and meals? *[handwritten: yes Not meals]*

   (c) Commuter resides and works in City, but occasionally must fly to Other City on business. He eats lunch in Other City and returns home in the late afternoon or early evening. May he deduct all or a part of his costs? *[handwritten: yes NO – not overnight]*

2. Taxpayer lives with her husband and children in City and works there.

   (a) If she works in Metro on business for two days and one night each week, what may she deduct? See § 274(n)(1). *[handwritten: I don't think any (not temporary)]*

   (b) Same as (a), above, except that she works three days and spends two nights each week in Metro and maintains an apartment there. *[handwritten: None still]*

   (c) Taxpayer and Husband own a home in City and Husband works there. Taxpayer works in Metro, maintaining an apartment there, and travels to City each weekend to visit her husband and family. What may she deduct? See Robert A. Coerver, 36 T.C. 252 (1961), affirmed per curiam 297 F.2d 837 (3d Cir.1962), and Virginia Foote, 67 T.C. 1 (1976). *[handwritten: Nothing]*

3. Burly is a professional football player for the City Stompers. He and his wife own a home in Metro where they reside during the 7-month "off season."

   (a) If Burly's only source of income is his salary from the Stompers, may Burly deduct any of his City living expenses which he incurs during the football season? See Ronald L. Gardin, 64 T.C. 1079 (1975). *[handwritten: – not exigencies of business]*

   (b) Would there be any difference in result in (a), above, if during the 7-month "off season" Burly owned an insurance agency in Metro and worked there? *[handwritten: Some in some instances]*

4. Consultant operates a management consulting business in City where Consultant and his family live.

   (a) Consultant has a client with troubles in Other City in another state. The client asks Consultant to perform services in Other City for nine months. Consultant's family stays in City and he rents an apartment in Other City. Are Consultant's expenses in Other City deductible? *[handwritten: assuming they only last 9 months]*

   (b) What result in (a), above, if the time period Consultant is expected to be in Other City is nine months, but after eight months it is extended to fifteen months? See Rev. Rul. 93–86, *No* 1993–2 C.B. 71.

(c)   What result in (a), above, if Consultant and his family had lived in a furnished apartment in City and he and family gave the apartment up and moved to Other City where they lived in a furnished apartment for the nine months? Compare J.B. Stewart, 30 T.C.M. 1316 (1971), with Alvin L. Goldman, 32 T.C.M. 574 (1973).

*Not necessary — not worth it — just resold*

## 3. NECESSARY RENTAL AND SIMILAR PAYMENTS

Internal Revenue Code: Section 162(a)(3).

Regulations: Section 1.162–11(a).

---

## Starr's Estate v. Commissioner

United States Court of Appeals, Ninth Circuit, 1959.
274 F.2d 294.

■ CHAMBERS, CIRCUIT JUDGE.

Yesterday's equities in personal property seem to have become today's leases. This has been generated not a little by the circumstance that one who leases as a lessee usually has less trouble with the federal tax collector. At least taxpayers think so.

But the lease still can go too far and get one into tax trouble. While according to state law the instrument will probably be taken (with the consequent legal incidents) by the name the parties give it, the internal revenue service is not always bound and can often recast it according to what the service may consider the practical realities.[1] We have so held in Oesterreich v. Commissioner, 9 Cir., 226 F.2d 798, and Commissioner of Internal Revenue v. Wilshire Holding Corporation, 9 Cir., 244 F.2d 904, certiorari denied 355 U.S. 815, 78 S.Ct. 16. The principal case concerns a fire sprinkler system installed at the taxpayer's plant at Monrovia, California, where Delano T. Starr,[2] now deceased, did business as the Gross Manufacturing Company. The "lessor" was "Automatic" Sprinklers of the Pacific, Inc., a California corporation. The instrument entitled "Lease Form of Contract" (hereafter "contract") is just about perfectly couched in terms of a lease for five years with annual rentals of $1,240. But it is the last paragraph thereof, providing for nominal rental for five years, that has caused the trouble. It reads as follows:

---

[1]   Thus it shifts rental payments of a business (fully deductible) to a capital purchase for the business. If the nature of the property is wasting, then depreciation may be taken, but usually not all in one year.

[2]   Presumably the plant and the business were California community property of Starr and his wife, Mary W. Starr. For each of the calendar years 1951 and 1952, they filed joint tax returns.

"28. At the termination of the period of this lease, if Lessee has faithfully performed all of the terms and conditions required of it under this lease, it shall have the privilege of renewing this lease for an additional period of five years at a rental of $32.00 per year. If Lessee does not elect to renew this lease, then the Lessor is hereby granted the period of six months in which to remove the system from the premises of the Lessee."

Obviously, one renewal for a period of five years is provided at $32.00 per year, if Starr so desired. Note, though, that the paragraph is silent as to status of the system beginning with the eleventh year. Likewise the whole contract is similarly silent.

The tax court sustained the commissioner of internal revenue, holding that the five payments of $1,240, or the total of $6,200, were capital expenditures and not pure deductible rental.[3] Depreciation of $269.60 was allowed for each year. Generally, we agree.

Taxpayers took the deduction as a rental expense under trade or business pursuant to Section 23(a) of the Internal Revenue Code, as amended by Section 121(a) of the Revenue Act of 1942.[4]

The law in this field for this circuit is established in Oesterreich v. Commissioner, supra, and Robinson v. Elliot, 9 Cir., 262 F.2d 383. There we held that for tax purposes form can be disregarded for substance and, where the foreordained practical effect of the rent is to produce title eventually, the rental agreement can be treated as a sale.

In this, Starr's case, we do have the troublesome circumstance that the contract does not by its terms ever pass title to the system to the "lessee." Most sprinkler systems have to be tailor-made for a specific piece of property and, if removal is required, the salvageable value is negligible. Also, it stretches credulity to believe that the "lessor" ever intended to or would "come after" the system. And the "lessee" would be an exceedingly careless businessman who would enter into such contract with the practical possibility that the "lessor" would reclaim the installation. He could have believed only that he was getting the system for the rental money. And we think the commissioner was entitled to take into consideration the practical effect rather than the legal, especially when there was a record that on other such installations the "lessor", after the term of the lease was over, had not reclaimed from those who had met their agreed payments. It is obvious that the nominal rental payments after five years of $32.00 per year were just a service charge for inspection.[5]

---

3   Starr, Estate of v. Commissioner, 30 T.C. 856.

4   [I.R.C. (1939) § 23(a) is omitted. See I.R.C. (1986) § 162(a). Ed.]

5   It is true that the normal inspection fee would be $64.00. However, the difference between $32.00 and $64.00 would not seem to ruin the tax court's determination for income tax purposes that there was a sale.

Recently the Court of Appeals for the Eighth Circuit has decided Western Contracting Corporation v. Commissioner, 1959, 271 F.2d 694, reversing the tax court in its determination that the commissioner could convert leases of contractor's equipment into installment purchases of heavy equipment. The taxpayer believes that case strongly supports him here. We think not.[6]

There are a number of facts there which make a difference. For example, in the contracts of Western there is no evidence that the payments on the substituted basis of rent would produce for the "lessor" the equivalent of his normal sales price plus interest. There was no right to acquire for a nominal amount at the end of the term as in Oesterreich and the value to the "lessor" in the personalty had not been exhausted as in Starr's case. And there was no basis for inferring that Western would just keep the equipment for what it had paid. It appears that Western paid substantial amounts to acquire the equipment at the end of the term. There was just one compelling circumstance against Western in its case: What it had paid as "rent" was apparently always taken into full account in computing the end purchase price. But on the other hand, there was almost a certainty that the "lessor" would come after his property if the purchase was not eventually made for a substantial amount. This was not even much of a possibility in Oesterreich and not a probability in Starr's case.

In Wilshire Holding Corporation v. Commissioner, 9 Cir., 262 F.2d 51, we referred the case back to the tax court to consider interest as a deductible item for the lessee. We think it is clearly called for here. Two yardsticks are present. The first is found in that the normal selling price of the system was $4,960 while the total rental payments for five years were $6,200. The difference could be regarded as interest for the five years on an amortized basis. The second measure is in clause 16 (loss by fire), where the figure of six per cent per annum discount is used. An allowance might be made on either basis, division of the difference (for the five years) between "rental payments" and "normal purchase price" of $1,240, or six per cent per annum on the normal purchase price of $4,960, converting the annual payments into amortization. We do not believe that the "lessee" should suffer the pains of a loss for what really was paid for the use of another's money, even though for tax purposes his lease collapses.

We do not criticize the commissioner. It is his duty to collect the revenue and it is a tough one. If he resolves all questions in favor of the taxpayers, we soon would have little revenue. However, we do suggest that after he has made allowance for depreciation, which he concedes,

6   It is unnecessary to determine here whether the Ninth Circuit would follow the decision of the Eighth Circuit or the decision of the tax court. (Western Contracting Corp. v. Commissioner, 17 TCM 371, T.C.Memo. 1958–77, CCH Dec. 22, 1960 [M]). It is enough here to say that the Ninth Circuit regards the Eighth Circuit's opinion distinguishable from Starr's case and not inconsistent with the holding herein.

and an allowance for interest, the attack on many of the "leases" may not be worth while in terms of revenue.

Decision reversed for proceedings consistent herewith.

## NOTE

If one makes a transfer of business property (either by a sale or more likely by a gift) to say a family member and then leases the property back at a fair rental value, are the rental payments deductible under Section 162? A thoughtful student will see, not an isolated business deduction issue, but a new facet of the assignment of income problem to which attention is directed principally in Chapters 12 and 13. Income may be fragmented among an intimate group as much by way of deductible payments that are taxable to the recipients as by more direct devices suggested by the familiar *Earl, Horst,* and *Clifford* cases. The analogy is so pat that one might confidently expect like administrative, judicial, and legislative attacks on the problem. In contrast, however,[1] Congress has been relatively inactive in the deduction sector, which has encouraged an aggressive posture by the Commissioner. In the typical or at least *early* typical case,[2] where a plan was prepared to yield maximum tax benefits, a doctor, say, would transfer her office and equipment to her Child who would then lease the property to Doctor for its fair rental value. As rent was paid it would be paid and taxed to Child and Doctor would claim a Section 162(a)(3) deduction. Abstractly, the matter would look like this:

## BEFORE

*Doctor:* Income, $100,000 (Ignoring Depreciation Deductions).

## AFTER

| Doctor | | *Child* | |
|---|---|---|---|
| Income | $100,000 | | |
| Rent | −20,000 | Rent | $20,000 |
| Income taxed | $80,000 | Income Taxed | $20,000 |

With $20,000 peeled off the top of Doctor's income and subjected to possibly lower rates as income of Child, the scene would be:

*Doctor*: Taxable Income, $80,000.

*Child*: Taxable Income, $20,000.[3]

Use of these arrangements was substantially curtailed by the Tax Reform Act of 1986. As seen in the Introduction to Chapter 12, lower top tax

---

[1]  Compare, e.g., I.R.C. §§ 671–678 and 704(e), dealing with income assignment, with § 267(a)(2), mildly restraining deduction for some intrafamily payments.

[2]  See Van Zandt v. Commissioner, 341 F.2d 440 (5th Cir.1965), cert. denied 382 U.S. 814, 86 S.Ct. 32 (1965).

[3]  In the typical case, Child's taxable income will be reduced by depreciation deductions on the property which would have been available to Doctor if the transfer had not occurred. I.R.C. §§ 167(a) and (d), 168(a).

rates and the enactment of "the kiddie tax" (generally taxing unearned income of minors under age 19 (or students under age 24) at their parents' rates) should result in fewer attempted direct assignments of income and, as here, the somewhat similar contrived generation of deductions. In addition, most assignments of income attempted by means of deductions were carried out through *Clifford* trusts in which the grantor retained a reversion at the end of a ten plus year period, at times successfully and at other times unsuccessfully.[4] With the 1986 amendment substantially extending the reversionary period of Section 673,[5] the successful use of reversionary *Clifford* trusts was also essentially eliminated. Thus we see substantially fewer transfer and leasebacks by means of the use of trusts.

The viability of the transfer and leaseback arrangement should be tested against the rules for more direct income assignment under the *Horst* doctrine which addresses directly the taxation of income from property.[6] Of course, taxation is properly interested in things only as they *are*, not as they *seem*. Consequently, an alleged transfer and leaseback that lacked reality, possibly shown to be a sham by the donor retaining control of the property or by unrealistic rental payments, could properly be disregarded merely by refusing to exalt form over substance.[7] But assuming that all *t*'s are crossed and all *i*'s dotted, it is difficult to see from a policy point of view why the asserted rental deduction is vulnerable. Assuming that a *real* ownership interest is created in another person of property that a taxpayer uses in business, payment of fair rental for use of the property should accord the taxpayer a business deduction under Section 162. Only one respectable question can be raised about this conclusion. Section 162 permits the deduction of "necessary" expenses: Is an expense unnecessary if it arises only because the taxpayer gives away (directly or to a trust) or sells[8] the property to one to whom it must *then* pay rent for its use?

These are mixed feelings on the issue amongst the circuit courts. Fusing the gift and the lease agreement, two circuits found a lack of necessity for the rental payments in the absence of any "business purpose" for the arrangement.[9] The majority of the circuits, viewing the gift and the rental agreement as separate transactions have been willing to find the requisite necessity for the rental payment after the property in question has been placed in the hands of a trustee for the benefit of others.[10] Whether the

---

[4]   See Peroni, "Untangling the Web of Gift-Leaseback Jurisprudence," 68 Minn. L.R. 735 (1984); Eller, "The Second Circuit Approves Intrafamily Gift-Leaseback, But Fails to Scrutinize Strictly the Underlying Clifford Trust," 50 Brooklyn L. Rev. 839 (1984).

[5]   See Chapter 13D, supra.

[6]   Cf. I.R.C. §§ 671–678, 704(e).

[7]   White v. Fitzpatrick, 193 F.2d 398 (2d Cir. 1951), cert. denied, 343 U.S. 928, 72 S.Ct. 762 (1952); Kirschenmann v. Westover, 225 F.2d 69 (9th Cir.1955), cert. denied 350 U.S. 834, 76 S.Ct. 70 (1955); and cf. W.H. Armston Co. v. Commissioner, 188 F.2d 531 (5th Cir.1951).

[8]   See Sun Oil Co. v. Commissioner, 35 T.C.M. 173 (1976).

[9]   Mathews v. Commissioner, 520 F.2d 323 (5th Cir. 1975), cert. denied 424 U.S. 967, 96 S.Ct. 1463 (1976); Perry v. United States, 520 F.2d 235 (4th Cir.1975), cert. denied 423 U.S. 1052, 96 S.Ct. 782 (1976); Frank L. Butler v. Commissioner, 65 T.C. 327 (1975), denying the rental deduction, but under the *Golsen* principle requiring the court merely to analyze and apply the teachings of the Fifth Circuit.

[10]   Rosenfeld v. Commissioner, 706 F.2d 1277 (2d Cir.1983); Brown v. Commissioner, 180 F.2d 926 (3d Cir.1950), cert. denied 340 U.S. 814, 71 S.Ct. 42 (1950); Skemp v. Commissioner,

unified or separate view is more appropriate seems a better question for Congress than for the courts. Nevertheless, as there are several clear ways to skin this very cat and apt analogies regarding the treatment of *income* from property that has been the subject of a gift, it seems that the minority circuits have been led far afield by a spurious but aromatic red herring and the deduction should be more freely allowed. It would be well for Congress to so specify along the lines of the language in Section 704(e).

## D. OTHER BUSINESS DEDUCTIONS

The three business expense deductions listed in paragraphs (1) through (3) of Section 162(a) are illustrative only and by no means exclusive. The statute specifically states that *all* ordinary and necessary business expenses are deductible *including* those specifically listed, and it is similar in that regard to Section 61.[1] It would be impossible to list every conceivable type of deduction within the section, especially since the test varies among different businesses. This section will, however, attempt to highlight some of the more important business expense deductions.

### 1. EXPENSES FOR EDUCATION[*]

Internal Revenue Code: Sections 162(a); 262; 274(m)(2).

Regulations: Section 1.162–5(a), (b)(1), (2)(i), (3)(i), (c), (e)(1).

————————

There are two cases presented in this segment, *Hill* and *Coughlin*. They were decided by the Fourth Circuit and the Second Circuit in 1950 and 1953, respectively. Each seems to clash with a dictum in Justice Cardozo's 1933 opinion in Welch v. Helvering:[1]

> [A] man conceives the notion that he will be able to practice his vocation with greater ease and profit if he has an opportunity to enrich his culture. Forthwith the price of his education becomes [the Justice is being facetious] an expense of the business, reducing the income subject to taxation.

The clash is apparent only, and *Hill* and *Coughlin* can now be found in distilled form as paragraphs (1) and (2) (but in reverse order) of Reg. § 1.162–5(a), an affirmative general rule on the deductibility of expenses for education.

————————

168 F.2d 598 (7th Cir.1948); Quinlivan v. Commissioner, 599 F.2d 269 (8th Cir.1979), cert. denied 444 U.S. 996, 100 S.Ct. 531 (1979); May v. Commissioner, 723 F.2d 1434 (9th Cir.1984).

   1   On the Code meaning of "including," see I.R.C. § 7701(b).

   *   See McNulty, "Tax Policy and Tuition Credit Legislation: Federal Income Tax Allowances for Personal Costs of Higher Education," 61 Calif.L.Rev. 1 (1973); Schoenfeld, "The Educational Expense Deduction: The Need for a Rational Approach," 27 Villanova L.Rev. 237 (1982).

   1   See page 311, supra.

The two basic concepts expressed in the general rule of the regulations are fairly simple and forthright and answer a great many questions. Even so, nice distinctions have been drawn in numerous circumstances: How do we decide whether an Internal Revenue Agent should be allowed to deduct the expenses he incurs in obtaining a law degree?[2]

Recent developments have made the area one of greater concern to lawyers with respect to their own personal tax liability not just that of their clients. Some states are now requiring continuing education for the bar. Others are permitting specialty designation or certification by lawyers who can establish expertise in various areas of the law, either by way of experience or education.[3] As more lawyers will be getting more formal education and spending more for it, and as similar developments are taking place in other disciplines, the importance of studying the tax aspects of education expenses is obvious.

The topic of education business expenses comes with a reminder regarding a point made earlier in the Text.[4] Employee business expenses will not reduce taxable income and save taxes.[5] Thus, education expenses paid for by an employee will be disallowed when determining taxable income. However, the education expenses of a self-employed taxpayer will be deductible and generate tax savings.[6]

## Hill v. Commissioner

United States Court of Appeals, Fourth Circuit, 1950.
181 F.2d 906.

■ DOBIE, CIRCUIT JUDGE.

This is an appeal by Nora Payne Hill (hereinafter called taxpayer) from a decision of the Tax Court of the United States entered on September 7, 1949, affirming a determination of the Commissioner of Internal Revenue that there is a deficiency in the income tax due by taxpayer in the amount of $57.52 for the calendar year 1945.

During the taxable year and for twenty-seven years prior thereto, taxpayer was engaged in the business of teaching school in the State of Virginia. During the taxable year in question, she attended summer school at Columbia University in New York City, for which she incurred expenses in an amount of $239.50, which she deducted in computing her net income on her federal income tax return for the year 1945. These

---

[2]   See Melnik v. United States, 521 F.2d 1065 (9th Cir.1975), cert. denied 425 U.S. 911, 96 S.Ct. 1506 (1976).

[3]   See Kalb and Roberts, "The Deductibility of Post-graduate Legal Education Expenses," 27 U.Fla.L.Rev. 995 (1975), written in partial satisfaction of requirements for the LL.M. degree at the University of Florida and Mock, "Deductibility of Educational Expenses for Full Time Graduate Study," 25 Okla.L.R. 582 (1972).

[4]   See page 341, supra.

[5]   See I.R.C. § 67(a) and (g) and Chapter 18C, infra.

[6]   See I.R.C. § 62(a)(1) and Chapter 18C, infra.

expenses were disallowed upon the grounds that they were personal expenses and were not deductible for federal income tax purposes. The only question for decision by us is: Was the taxpayer correct in deducting those expenses as ordinary and necessary expenses incurred in carrying on her trade or business? We think this question must be answered in the affirmative. The reasonableness of the amount of these expenses is not disputed.

[The Court quotes here I.R.C. (1939) Sections 23(a)(1)(A), 23(a)(2) and 24(a)(1) which for purposes of this case are essentially the same as I.R.C. (1986) Section 162(a), concerning trade or business expenses, Section 212, concurring expenses for the production of income and Section 262, disallowing any deduction for personal expenses. Ed.]

The pertinent provisions of the Virginia Code Annotated, 1942, applicable to the issues before us, are as follows:

Title 11, Chapter 33, Section 660

* * *. No teacher shall be employed or paid from the public funds unless such teacher holds a certificate in full force in accordance with the rules of certification laid down by the State Board of Education, provided, that, where a teacher holding a certificate in force is not available, a former teacher holding an expired certificate may be employed temporarily as a substitute teacher to meet an emergency * * *.

Title 11, Chapter 35, Section 786(b)(3)

* * * provided, that no school board shall employ or pay any teacher from the public funds unless the teacher shall hold a certificate in full force, according to the provisions of section six hundred and sixty of the laws relating to the public free schools in counties; * * *.

The Regulations Governing the Certification of Teachers and the Qualifications of Administrators and Supervisors in Virginia required for the renewal of a teacher's certificate that taxpayer present evidence that she had been a successful teacher, had read at least five books on the Teachers' Reading Course during the life of her certificate and also must either (a) present evidence of college credits in professional or academic subjects earned during the life of the certificate or (b) pass an examination on five books selected by the State Department of Education from the Teachers' Reading Course for the year in which her license expired.

In 1945, taxpayer was head of the Department of English and a teacher of English and Journalism at the George Washington High School in Danville, Virginia. A Master of Arts of Columbia University, she held the Collegiate Professional Certificate, the highest certificate issued to public school teachers by the Virginia State Board of Education. She was notified of the expiration of her certificate and that the certificate could not be renewed unless she complied with the Regulations set out above.

The alternatives required for the renewal of taxpayer's certificate were: (a) acquiring college credits or (b) passing an examination on five selected books. She elected (a) and attended the Summer School of Columbia University. We hardly think it open to question that she chose the alternative which would most effectively add to her efficiency as a teacher. At Columbia she took two courses: one on the technique of short story writing, which was right in her alley; another in abnormal psychology, which would be most useful to a teacher whose pupils were adolescents.

It is clear that to be deductible as a business expense the item must be—(a) "paid or incurred" within the taxable year; (b) incurred in carrying on a "trade or business"; and (c) both "ordinary and necessary." As a corollary, the expenses must not be personal in their nature. We think taxpayer has completely satisfied all these requisites, so that the decision of the Tax Court must be reversed.

In its opinion, the Tax Court stated:

We cannot assume that public school teachers *ordinarily* attend summer school to renew their certificates when alternative methods are available. The record does not show that the course pursued by petitioner was the usual method followed by teachers in obtaining renewals of their certificates or that it was necessary so to do. * * *.

The record is devoid of any showing that petitioner was employed to continue in her position as teacher at the time she attended summer school in 1945 and made the expenditures in connection therewith for which she seeks a deduction. The inference may well be that she took the summer course to obtain a renewal of her certificate that would qualify her for reemployment. The expense incurred was more in the nature of a preparation to qualify her for teaching in the High School in Danville, Virginia.

Also, in support of its decision, the Tax Court quoted O.D. 892, 4 C.B. 209 (1921): "The expenses incurred by school-teachers in attending summer school are in the nature of personal expenses incurred in advancing their education and are not deductible in computing net income."

As to the first of these statements, we think it is quite unreasonable to require a statistical showing by taxpayer of the comparative number of Virginia teachers who elect, for a renewal of their certificates, the acquisition of college credits rather than the much less desirable alternative of standing an examination on the five selected books. The existence of two methods for the renewal of these certificates, one or the other of which is compulsory, is not in itself vital in this connection. If the particular course adopted by the taxpayer is a response that a reasonable person would normally and naturally make under the specific circumstances, that would suffice. Even if a statistical study actually revealed that a majority of Virginia teachers adopted the examination on the selected books, in order to renew their certificates, rather than the method of acquiring college credits, our conclusion here would be the same. Manifestly, the added expense of attending a summer school, in the light of the slender salaries paid to teachers, would deter many teachers from such a course, however strong might be their predilections in favor of such a procedure. We note that the statistical requirement does not seem to have been enforced in the cases subsequently cited in this opinion—cases, we think, far less meritorious than the one before us.

Nor do we approve the reasoning of the Tax Court that the taxpayer's failure to show by positive evidence that she was employed to continue in her position as teacher when she incurred the summer school expenses should negative the deduction of these expenses. She did prove to the Tax Court that she had been continuously so engaged for consecutive decades. She had not resigned her position and no practical advantage would accrue to her upon a renewal of her certificate other than the privilege and power to continue as a teacher. Clearly, the very logic of the situation here shows that she went to Columbia to maintain her present position, not to attain a new position; to preserve, not to expand or increase; to carry on, not to commence. Any other view seems to us unreal and hypercritical. And taxpayer, in her petition to the Tax Court for a review of its decision, showed conclusively that when she went to Columbia University in the summer of 1945, she was then under contract with the Danville School Board to teach for the ensuing session of 1945–1946 and that to carry out this existing contract, she was obligated to renew her certificate by complying with the pertinent regulations.

\* \* \*

Dictionary definitions of the words "ordinary," "necessary," and "personal" afford scant assistance in the solution of our problem. Quite helpful, though, are the opinions in the decided cases. Frequently quoted is the observation of Mr. Justice Cardozo, in Welch v. Helvering, 290 U.S. 111, 113, 54 S.Ct. 8, 9: "Now, what is ordinary, though there must always be a strain of constancy within it, is none the less a variable affected by time and place and circumstance. Ordinary in this context does not mean that the payments must be habitual or normal in the sense that the same taxpayer will have to make them often. A lawsuit affecting the safety of a business may happen once in a lifetime. The counsel fees may be so heavy that repetition is unlikely. None the less, the expense is an ordinary one because we know from experience that payments for such a purpose, whether the amount is large or small, are the common and accepted means of defense against attack. Cf. Kornhauser v. United States, 276 U.S. 145, 48 S.Ct. 219. The situation is unique in the life of the individual affected, but not in the life of the group, the community, of which he is a part. At such times there are norms of conduct that help to stabilize our judgment, and make it certain and objective. The instance is not erratic, but is brought within a known type."

\* \* \*

Said Mr. Justice Douglas, in Deputy v. du Pont, 308 U.S. 488, 496, 60 S.Ct. 363: "One of the extremely relevant circumstances is the nature and scope of the particular business out of which the expense in question accrued. The fact that an obligation to pay has arisen is not sufficient. It is the kind of transaction out of which the obligation arose and its *normalcy in the particular business* which are crucial and controlling." (Italics ours.)

\* \* \*

We quote a trenchant critique on the decision of the Tax Court from Maguire, Individual Federal Income Tax in 1950, 35 American Association of University Professors Bulletin, 748, 762: "As to the matters just discussed, Nora P. Hill, 13 T.C. [291] No. 41 (1949), is an interesting decision, if scarcely an encouragement. The taxpayer, a Virginia public school teacher, sought to deduct as an ordinary and necessary business expense for 1945 the cost of attending summer courses in Columbia University. Her teaching certificate, the highest granted by the State Board of Education, came up for renewal in 1945. Virginia law required for renewal of teaching certificates either the taking of professional or academic courses for credit or the passing of examinations on prescribed reading. The Tax Court denied the claim of deduction. Part of its reasoning was that because the Virginia legal requirements might be satisfied by pursuing either of the two alternatives, the showing was insufficient that what the taxpayer had done was the ordinary method of satisfaction. Another part of the reasoning was that the taxpayer had not explicitly shown she was employed to continue as a teacher at the time she took the summer school courses. Hence, said the Court, it might be inferred that the taxpayer was seeking to qualify for reemployment as distinguished from merely maintaining an employed status. While these views seem hypercritical and are an invitation to the same teacher or another teacher to try again with more carefully detailed proof, the tone of the opinion hints at strong distaste for this sort of deduction."

Our conclusion is that the expenses incurred by the taxpayer here were incurred in carrying on a trade or business, were ordinary and necessary, and were not personal in nature. She has, we think, showed that she has complied with both the letter and the spirit of the law which permits such expenses to be deducted for federal income tax purposes. We do not hold (and it is not necessary for us to hold) that all expenses incurred by teachers in attending summer schools are deductible. Our decision is limited to the facts of the case before us. The decision of the Tax Court of the United States is, accordingly, reversed and the case is remanded to that Court with instructions to allow taxpayer as a deduction the expenses which she claims.

Reversed.

## Coughlin v. Commissioner*

United States Court of Appeals, Second Circuit, 1953.
203 F.2d 307.

■ CHASE, CIRCUIT JUDGE.

The petitioner has been a member of the bar for many years and in 1944 was admitted to practice before the Treasury Department. In 1946 he was in active practice in Binghamton, N.Y., as a member of a firm of lawyers there. The firm engaged in general practice but did considerable work which required at least one member to be skilled in matters pertaining to Federal taxation and to maintain such skill by keeping informed as to changes in the tax laws and the significance of pertinent court decisions when made. His partners relied on him to keep advised on that subject and he accepted that responsibility. One of the various ways in which he discharged it was by attending, in the above mentioned year, the Fifth Annual Institute on Federal Taxation which was conducted in New York City under the sponsorship of the Division of General Education of New York University. In so doing he incurred expenses for tuition, travel, board and lodging of $305, which he claimed as an allowable deduction under section 23(a)(1)(A) I.R.C., as ordinary and necessary expenses incurred in carrying on a trade or business and no question is raised as to their reasonableness in amount. The Commission[er] disallowed the deduction and the Tax Court, four judges dissenting, upheld the disallowance on the ground that the expenses were non-business ones "because of the educational and personal nature of the object pursued by the petitioner."

The Tax Court found that the Institute on Federal Taxation was not conducted for the benefit of those unversed in the subject of Federal taxation and students were warned away. In 1946, it was attended by 408 attorneys, accountants, trust officers, executives of corporations and the like. In 1947, over 1500 of such people from many states were in attendance. It was "designed by its sponsors to provide a place and atmosphere where practitioners could gather trends, thinking and developments in the field of Federal taxation from experts accomplished in that field."

Thus there is posed for solution a problem which involves no dispute as to the basic facts but is, indeed, baffling because, as is so often true of legal problems, the correct result depends upon how to give the facts the right order of importance.

---

* See Niswander, "Tax Aspects of Education: When Ordinary and Necessary; When Personal," 26 N.Y.U.Inst. on Fed. Tax. 27 (1968). Ed.

We may start by noticing that the petitioner does not rely upon section 23(a)(2) which permits the deduction of certain non-trade or non-business expenses, but rests entirely upon his contention that the deduction he took was allowable as an ordinary and necessary expense incurred in the practice of his profession. The expenses were deductible under section 23(a)(1)(A) if they were "directly connected with" or "proximately resulted from" the practice of his profession. Kornhauser v. United States, 276 U.S. 145, 153, 48 S.Ct. 219, 220. And if it were usual for lawyers in practice similar to his to incur such expenses they were "ordinary." Deputy v. du Pont, 308 U.S. 488, 495, 60 S.Ct. 363. They were also "necessary" if appropriate and helpful. Welch v. Helvering, 290 U.S. 111, 54 S.Ct. 8. But this is an instance emphasizing how dim a line is drawn between expenses which are deductible because incurred in trade or business, i.e., because professional, and those which are nondeductible because personal. Section 24(a)(1) of Title 26.

The respondent relies upon T.R. 111, § 29.23(a)–15, which provides that "expenses of taking special courses or training" are not allowable as deductions under section 23(a)(2). But section 23(a)(2) concerns non-trade or non-business expenses. It is not necessary to decide whether, in the light of the regulation, an expense of the nature here involved would be deductible if incurred in connection with a profit-making venture that is not a trade or business. It will suffice to say that, since the expense was incurred in a trade or business within the meaning of section 23(a)(1)(A), the regulation interpreting section 23(a)(2) is not a bar to allowance here.

In Welch v. Helvering, supra, 290 U.S. at page 115, 54 S.Ct. at page 9, there is a dictum that the cost of acquiring learning is a personal expense. But the issue decided in that case is far removed from the one involved here. There the taxpayer paid debts for which he was not legally liable whose payment enhanced his reputation for personal integrity and consequently the value of the good will of his business, and it was held that these payments were personal expenses. The general reference to the cost of education as a personal expense was made by way of illustrating the point then under decision, and it related to that knowledge which is obtained for its own sake as an addition to one's cultural background or for possible use in some work which might be started in the future. There was no indication that an exception is not to be made where the information acquired was needed for use in a lawyer's established practice.

T.R. 111, § 29.23(a)–5, makes clear that among the expenses which a professional man may deduct under Section 23(a)(1)(A) are dues to professional societies, subscriptions to professional journals, and amounts currently expended for books whose useful life is short. Such expenses as are here in question are not expressly included or excluded, but they are analogous to those above stated which are expressly characterized as allowable deductions.

This situation is closely akin to that in Hill v. Commissioner, 4 Cir., 181 F.2d 906, where the expenses incurred by a teacher in attending a summer school were held deductible. The only difference is in the degree of necessity which prompted the incurrence of the expenses. The teacher couldn't retain her position unless she complied with the requirements for the renewal of her teaching certificate; and an optional way to do that, and the one she chose, was to take courses in education at a recognized institution of learning. Here the petitioner did not need a renewal of his license to practice and it may be assumed that he could have continued as a member of his firm whether or not he kept currently informed as to the law of Federal taxation. But he was morally bound to keep so informed and did so in part by means of his attendance at this session of the Institute. It was a way well adapted to fulfill his professional duty to keep sharp the tools he actually used in his going trade or business. It may be that the knowledge he thus gained incidentally increased his fund of learning in general and, in that sense, the cost of acquiring it may have been a personal expense; but we think that the immediate, over-all professional need to incur the expenses in order to perform his work with due regard to the current status of the law so overshadows the personal aspect that it is the decisive feature.

It serves also to distinguish these expenditures from those made to acquire a capital asset. Even if in its cultural aspect knowledge should for tax purposes be considered in the nature of a capital asset as was suggested in Welch v. Helvering, supra, the rather evanescent character of that for which the petitioner spent his money deprives it of the sort of permanency such a concept embraces.

Decision reversed and cause remanded for the allowance of the deduction.

## PROBLEMS

1. Alice, Barbara, Cathy, and Denise were college roommates who after graduating went on to become a self-employed doctor, dentist, accountant (C.P.A.), and lawyer, respectively. In the current year, after some time in practice as an orthopedic surgeon, Alice, who was often called upon to give medical testimony in malpractice suits, decided to go to law school so as to better understand this aspect of her medical practice. Barbara enrolled in a course of postgraduate study in orthodontics, intending to restrict her dental practice to that specialty in the future. Cathy enrolled part time in law school (with eventual prospects of attaining a degree) so as better to perform her accounting duties in areas in which law and accounting tend to overlap. And Denise took a leave of absence from her firm to enroll in an LL.M. course in taxation, intending to practice exclusively in the tax area. Which, if any, is incurring deductible expenses of education?

2. Assume Denise's expenses in problem 1, above, are deductible. If she is a practitioner in Seattle, Washington, who travels to Gainesville, Florida for

a year to participate in their LL.M. program, what expenses, in addition to tuition and books, may she deduct? See Reg. § 1.162–5(e) and I.R.C. § 274(n).

**3.** Carl earned a bachelor's degree in education and he teaches world history in a junior high school. In the current year he contemplates a summer European tour doing things that will be beneficial to his teaching efforts. He wishes to know if he may deduct his expenses. What do you advise? See I.R.C. § 274(m)(2).   No

**4.** Self-employed Dentist attends a five day dental seminar at a ski resort. All of the seminar proceedings are taped and Dentist skis on clear days and watches all of the tapes on snowy days or in other off-the-slopes time prior to his return home. Are Dentist's travel, meals and lodging deductible?

## 2. BUSINESS LOSSES

Internal Revenue Code: Sections 165(a), (b), and (c)(1); 280B.

___

If a transaction or event produces a "loss", the threshold question *whether* the loss may be deductible must always be answered on the basis of the rules in Section 165. It is the Code's central switchboard for *all* losses. But statutory restrictions may be encountered elsewhere, and the *manner* in which the taxpayer may make use of loss deductions is the subject of a number of special provisions. The most recent restrictive developments are the subject of comment at the end of this brief note.

Although Section 165(a) seems to make all losses deductible,[1] attention is directed to Section 165(c). An individual taxpayer can deduct only such losses as are identified there. Section 165(c)(1) permits the deduction by an individual of any loss "incurred in a trade or business." As this Chapter is addressed to business deductions, we defer for later consideration other individual losses that may be deducted under Section 165(c)(2) or (3), and focus on business losses.[2]

What is a business "loss"?[3] At the outset, it must be stated that only "realized" losses are taken into account. The concept of realization is essentially the same here as in the income area. Just as mere appreciation in the value of property is not income subject to tax, so a mere decline in the value of the property is not a loss that can be deducted. To be deductible, a loss must be evidenced by a closed and completed transaction, such as a sale, or fixed by an identifiable event, such as a fire.[4]

Here are a few examples of deductible business losses. A buys a delivery truck for use in her business and sells it a year later for less than

___

[1]  In general, they are for corporate taxpayers.

[2]  I.R.C. § 165(c)(2) and (3) losses are considered in Chapters 15B and 23C, respectively.

[3]  The question whether the taxpayer is engaged in a "trade or business" is the same here as in I.R.C. § 162(a) and § 167(a)(1) and is not further explored at this point.

[4]  Reg. § 1.165–1(b).

its adjusted basis. B buys a tractor for use on his farm and, when he determines it is completely worn out, abandons it—gives it to the junk man for no consideration. C pays $1,000 for an option on a plant to be used in her business, but forfeits the $1,000 when she decides not to exercise the option. D buys a Chris Craft which he operates for hire at a resort, but the boat, which is not insured, is demolished in a storm. The measurement of the loss deduction depends in part on the adjusted basis of the property.[5] Thus, A's loss will be the familiar difference between the amount realized and adjusted basis. In B's and C's cases the loss deduction will probably be the adjusted basis of the tractor or the option.[6] D's loss is a casualty loss and, since his boat is totally destroyed, his loss is the amount of his basis in the boat.[7] If the boat were only damaged, D's casualty loss would be measured by the difference between its fair market value before and after the storm, limited, however, by the adjusted basis of the property.[8] To the extent that D's loss (or for that matter, any loss) is compensated by insurance D's deductible loss is reduced;[9] if the insurance recovery exceeds D's adjusted basis in the boat he has a casualty gain.[10] To illustrate, if D had a $6,000 adjusted basis for his boat and it had a $10,000 value before the storm and its value after the storm (uncompensated by insurance) is $7,000 D has a $3,000 loss. If the uninsured boat is totally destroyed D would have a $6,000 loss. In the latter case, if D recovered $4,000 of insurance for the boat his loss would be limited to $2,000. Finally if the boat were fully insured, D's recovery of $10,000 of insurance would result in a $4,000 casualty gain.[11]

Each of the losses suggested above will ultimately have a direct impact on the taxable income reported by the individual. If the Section 165(c)(1) losses incurred in a business during the year, along with its other expenses, exceed its income, the business will be unprofitable and the owner will have an overall business loss for the year.[12] The business loss can be deducted against other types of income such as income from investments, other businesses, or salaries. If one has a business loss and no other income (or if the business loss exceeds one's other income) so that the loss cannot be fully utilized to reduce taxable income, the person will get the benefit of a net operating loss carryback or carryover to another taxable year.[13]

---

[5] I.R.C. § 165(b).

[6] Id. See, e.g., Reg. § 1.165–7(b)(1), last sentence.

[7] I.R.C. § 165(b).

[8] Reg. § 1.165–7(b)(1).

[9] I.R.C. § 165(a).

[10] I.R.C. § 1001(a).

[11] For characterization of business casualty gains and losses see I.R.C. § 1231(a), especially (a)(4)(C) and page 752, infra.

[12] Some gains and losses, even if incurred in a separate identifiable business, must be aggregated with the results of other transactions outside the business. See especially Chapter 21B, C and H2, infra.

[13] See Chapter 20D, infra.

Not every closed transaction that involves financial disadvantages supports a deductible tax loss. If Simple Simon were around these days, he would probably claim Section 280B as a "kissin' cousin", for simple it appears to be. *Prior* to Section 280B, the question whether a demolition loss deduction was allowed rested upon a subjective analysis of the taxpayer's motivation.[14] If there was an intent at the time of purchase of improved property immediately to demolish the building, no basis was allocated to the building and no loss deduction was allowed on its demolition.[15] Instead, the entire purchase price for the property was allocated to the land.[16] If no such intent existed or if there was an intent to demolish at a subsequent time, some basis was allocated to the building.[17] Thus, upon a later demolition of the building, a loss deduction would be allowed in the amount of the building's unamortized basis.[18]

Except for special equities involved in the cases, it was difficult to see any support for these decisions. Furthermore, inquiry into why one acquired real property and removed an existing structure on it was much more difficult than the mere objective question *whether* one had done so. Now under Section 280B, whether the property was newly acquired or held for some time even for varying purposes, the taxpayer is denied a loss deduction for the structure and denied any deduction for expenses incurred in the demolition. Instead of a deduction, any basis the taxpayer had in the removed structure and any cost incurred in its removal are simply added to the basis for the *land* on which the structure stood. When Section 280B was added, the change from the past was that sometimes these costs were allowed as deductions, instead of having to be capitalized and that sometimes the taxpayer's basis for the removed structure became a part of the basis for the replacement structure rather than merely having to be added to the land. As land is not depreciable, the effect of Section 280B is to place unamortized cost of razed buildings and of expenses of demolition as far as possible away from affording any benefit to the taxpayer as a charge in computing taxable income.

## PROBLEM

1.  Taxpayer has an automobile used exclusively in Taxpayer's business which was purchased for $40,000 and, as a result of depreciation deductions, has an adjusted basis of $22,000. When the automobile was worth $30,000,

---

[14]   Reg. § 1.165–3.

[15]   Reg. § 1.165–3(a)(1). Time of purchase means the time equitable title passes (signing of a contract) not the later date of transfer of the deed. If an intent to demolish arises between such dates, a demolition loss is allowed. The First Nat. Bank & Trust Co. of Chickasha v. United States, 462 F.2d 908 (10th Cir.1972).

[16]   Reg. § 1.165–3(a)(1).

[17]   Reg. § 1.165–3(a)(2); McBride v. Commissioner, 50 T.C. 1 (1968), acq., 1969–1 C.B. 21; Commissioner v. Appleby's Estate, 123 F.2d 700 (2d Cir.1941), affirming 41 B.T.A. 18, non acq., 1940–2 C.B. 9.

[18]   See, e.g., A.F. McBride, Jr., note 17, supra; J.A. Rider v. Commissioner, 30 T.C.M. 188 (1971).

it was totally destroyed in an accident and Taxpayer received $15,000 of insurance proceeds.

(a) What is Taxpayer's deductible loss under Section 165?

(b) What result in (a), above, if the automobile had not been totally destroyed but was worth $10,000 after the accident? See Reg. § 1.165–7(b)(1).

(c) What is Taxpayer's adjusted basis in the automobile in (b), above, if Taxpayer incurs $17,000 fixing the automobile?

## 3. QUALIFIED BUSINESS INCOME DEDUCTION

Internal Revenue Code: Section 199A(a)(1), (b)(1) and (2).

---

The 2017 Tax Cuts and Jobs Act[1] reduced the top tax rate paid by a corporation on its taxable income from 35 percent to 21 percent. In addition, shareholders pay tax on dividends that are distributed by the corporation generally at a 15 or 20 percent rate.[2] In comparison, a business operated in a sole proprietorship, a partnership, a limited liability company, or an S corporation has its income taxed as high as 37 percent under the individual income tax rates. To create greater parity between corporations and so-called "pass-through entities," the 2017 Act created a new deduction in Section 199A, which generally permits a taxpayer a deduction for up to 20 percent of domestic "qualified business income."[3] Qualified business income generally is the net income from a qualified business, but it does not include compensation for services as an employee or specified investment-related income.[4] The effect of the Section 199A deduction, if fully available (it is subject to numerous special definitions, restrictions, and limitations), is to reduce the top rate that an individual will have to pay on qualified business income to 29.6 percent (80 percent of 37 percent).[5] Because the principal effect of Section 199A is to reduce the tax rates on business income, a detailed examination of Section 199A is deferred until Chapter 27A3. However, Section 199A is a critically important *business deduction* for noncorporate taxpayers[6] and, therefore, it is previewed at this point in the Text.

---

[1] Pub. L. No. 115–97, 115th Cong., 1st Sess. (2017).

[2] I.R.C. § 1(h)(11). The dividends may also be subject to the 3.8 percent tax on net investment income. I.R.C. § 1411.

[3] I.R.C. § 199A(a)(1), (b)(1)(A), (2)(A).

[4] I.R.C. § 199A(c)(1), (3)(B), (d)(1)(B).

[5] The income may also be subject to the 3.8 percent tax on net investment income. I.R.C. § 1411.

[6] Noncorporate taxpayers include the shareholders of an S corporation.

## E. DEPRECIATION

## 1. INTRODUCTION

Internal Revenue Code: Sections 167(a), (c)(1); 168(a)–(c), (e)(1), (f)(1), (g)(1)(E), (2), and (7); 1016(a)(2). See Section 62(a)(1) and (4); 168(d); 263(a); 263A(a), (b)(1), (c)(1).

Regulations: Sections 1.162–4; 1.167(a)–1(a), –10; 1.167(b)–0(a), –1(a), –2(a).

---

### Depreciation: Concepts and Principles

     T leaves his position with a shoe manufacturing company to go into business by himself, making and selling shoes. He sets up shop in a garage on the back of his property and purchases an electric stitching machine for $80,000, his only significant piece of equipment. For eight years T purchases each year $100,000 worth of leather and other supplies and electricity that cost him $20,000. Each year he makes 2000 pairs of shoes and sells them at $100.00 each.

     T sees the following results each year:

| | |
|---|---:|
| Receipts | $200,000 |
| Less materials and supplies | 120,000 |
| Profit for the year | $80,000 |

And over the eight year period he considers he has made a profit of $640,000 (8 × $80,000).

     But now he learns that his stitching machine is worn out and must be replaced. Looking back he wonders about his profit. While it appears he made $640,000, he now sees that he has incurred another $80,000 cost and has made only $560,000. But did he make nothing in the first year (when he bought the machine) and $80,000 each year for the next seven years? Or maybe $80,000 for each of the first seven years and nothing in the eighth year when the machine finally wore out? Neither possibility makes good sense, if he wishes to think (or must for tax purposes) in terms of annual profit. The sensible thing is to allocate cost for something like the stitcher over the period it is useful to him. And this is what depreciation is all about. Under the simplest approach to the problem, T can quickly be made to see that if he used up his $80,000 stitcher over eight years of work it has been an added manufacturing cost to him of $10,000 each year. He now sees each year's results as:

| | | |
|---|---|---|
| Receipts | | $200,000 |
| Less: | | |
| Materials & supplies | 120,000 | |
| Depreciation | 10,000 | |
| | | 130,000 |
| Profit for year | | $ 70,000 |

And his profit for eight years is $560,000 (8 × $70,000), as before, but more appropriately determined on the basis of a like amount of profit each year. Should he worry, too, that his garage is eight years older?

For Federal income tax purposes, Sections 167 and 168 treat depreciation as if it were an operating expense by allowing deductions for exhaustion and wear and tear (including predictable obsolescence) of property. The business community utilized the concept in the determination of annual profits even before there was a Federal income tax.[1] Section 167 technically allows the deduction for depreciation and has requirements and special rules relating to depreciation. At one time, Section 167 also contained the rules for calculating the deduction ("historical depreciation") and those rules generally were relatively subjective tests particular to the individual taxpayer.[2] Today, depreciation is generally calculated under the rules in Section 168, which is referred to as the Modified Accelerated Cost Recovery System (MACRS), and which uses more objective rules for computing depreciation.[3]

*Prerequisites for Deduction.* Sections 167(a) and 168(a) restrict the depreciation deduction to either (1) property used in a trade or business or (2) property held for the production of income. Thus inventory and property held for sale to customers are placed outside the scope of the section. And so is property that is held for merely personal use, even though it too declines in value over a period of time. Why?

Generally, only property that will be consumed, wear out, become obsolete, or otherwise becomes useless to the taxpayer can qualify for the deduction. Thus, unimproved realty is said to be non-depreciable, meaning, in the tax sense, that it cannot be the subject of a depreciation

---

[1]   Knoxville v. Knoxville Water Co., 212 U.S. 1, 29 S.Ct. 148 (1909).

[2]   See the Text at notes 4–21, infra.

[3]   See the Text at notes 26–58, infra.

deduction.[4] And if realty is improved, it is only the improvements that can qualify.[5]

*The Useful Life Concept.* As is apparent in the shoemaker illustration above, depreciation is a cost spreading device, and the concept historically anticipated that cost would be spread over the period the property is to be used.[6] Years ago, the Supreme Court stated:[7]

> The amount of the allowance for depreciation is the sum which should be set aside for the taxable year, in order that, at the end of the useful life of the [asset] in the business, the aggregate of the sums set aside will (with the salvage value) suffice to provide an amount equal to the original cost.

More recently, Congress simply creates or assumes a useful life for property.[8]

The useful life employed for depreciation also pegs the so-called depreciation rate. For example, if an asset is to be depreciated for 5 years and the deductions are to be spread equally over that period, the rate must be 20 percent (100 percent/5 years) in order for the entire cost to be taken into account over the life of the asset.

It is obvious that the period of useful life with respect to any particular property is speculative and a likely subject for disagreement between the Treasury and the taxpayer. Long ago, the burden of proving useful life was on the taxpayer,[9] and Treasury personnel took a restrictive approach to depreciation.[10] In an effort to alleviate such disagreements, both the Treasury and Congress have provided various guidelines or requirements for the determination of normal useful lives which taxpayers may use as a shield against attack on audit. Over the years, the general trend has been to shorten and clarify the recognized lives of assets. In 1971 Congress enacted the asset depreciation range (A.D.R.) system[11] which set various class lives for property which were shorter lives than under prior depreciation rules. MACRS, discussed in

---

[4] Reg. § 1.167(a)–2; but see comments on depletion under "Related Concepts," below and see Henderson, "Land Cost Expenditures: Recent Trend Shows Many Such Costs Are Now Depreciable," 38 J.Tax. 78 (1973). However, property need not be tangible to be allowed cost recovery. See I.R.C. § 197, discussed at page 425, infra, which assigns a 15-year useful life to goodwill and many other intangibles acquired by the taxpayer.

[5] See, for example, Rev.Rul. 74–265, 1974–1 C.B. 56, allowing depreciation of the cost of landscaping an apartment complex over the life of the apartment buildings if replacement of the buildings will destroy the landscaping. If not, landscaping is not depreciable.

[6] Under the rules prior to enactment of I.R.C. § 168, property was depreciable to a taxpayer only for the number of years the taxpayer intended to use the property not for the number of years of the property's life. Massey Motors, Inc. v. United States, 364 U.S. 92, 80 S.Ct. 1411 (1960). But see Simon v. Commissioner, 68 F.3d 41 (2d Cir. 1995) at page 409, infra.

[7] United States v. Ludey, 274 U.S. 295, 300, 47 S.Ct. 608, 610 (1927).

[8] See MACRS Recovery Period at page 401, infra and I.R.C. § 197 at note 4, supra.

[9] T.D. 4422, XIII–1 C.B. 58 (1934).

[10] Stephens, "Tax Amortization is the Key to the Stable Door," 5 U. of Fla.L.Rev. 261, 266–271 (1952).

[11] See note 26, infra.

detail later,[12] generally continues the trend of shortening the useful lives of assets.[13]

*Depreciable Amount.* The word "cost" is used loosely in the above discussion. One may have a machine that "cost" her nothing but which is subject to depreciation. If, for example, she acquired the machine by gift, Section 1015 accords her a basis for the property. And she is entitled to write off *that* basis by way of depreciation deductions.[14] Thus, it is cost or other basis which is deductible by way of depreciation. Because cost or other basis fixes the overall limits of the depreciation deductions for any asset, an acquisition of a depreciable asset has the same ultimate impact on taxable income as any deductible expense; only the amount of the expenditure is deductible. When the depreciable cost of an asset is "recovered" (charged off by way of depreciation deductions) depreciation deductions stop.

Historically under Section 167, the cost of an asset took into account not only acquisition cost but also the amount that would be recovered on disposition of the asset, commonly referred to as its *salvage value.* Thus, the deductions taken over the useful life should equal only net cost, i.e., cost less salvage value. Over the years the determination of salvage value, like the useful life concept, led to substantial controversy; the MACRS rules now simply disregard salvage value in the computation of the deduction.[15]

*Depreciation Methods.* With respect to property used in one's business or held for the production of income, once the property's depreciable amount and useful life are known, several different methods of depreciation may be available to the taxpayer. These methods regulate the timing of depreciation deductions within the cost limitations indicated above. One can spread the depreciation deduction evenly over the life of the property, the so-called *"straight-line"* method. There are also several expressly authorized *"accelerated"* methods of depreciation which increase depreciation deductions in the early years of the asset's useful life and decrease them in later years. However, the depreciable amount (i.e., the total amount of depreciation) that can ultimately be claimed is generally the same under each of the methods.[16]

In 1954 when statutory accelerated depreciation methods were first proposed under the Section 167 historic depreciation rules, the Senate

---

[12]  See page 400, infra.

[13]  See page 401, infra

[14]  See I.R.C. § 167(c).

[15]  I.R.C. § 168(b)(4) and (g)(2)(A).

[16]  However, since salvage is disregarded under MACRS, total depreciation on property under that system may exceed the total depreciation when salvage value reduced the depreciable amount.

Report explained some of the authorized depreciation methods as follows:[17]

(1)  The straight-line method—

Under this method, the cost or other basis of the property . . . is deducted in equal annual installments over the period of its estimated useful life. The depreciation deduction is obtained by dividing the amount to be depreciated by the estimated useful life. This may be expressed as a rate of depreciation computed by dividing the estimated life into 1. The deduction per taxable year may be arrived at by multiplying the cost or other basis . . . by the resulting rate.

(2)  Declining balance method—

Under this method a uniform rate is applied to the unrecovered basis of the asset. Since the basis is always reduced by prior depreciation, the rate is applied to a constantly declining basis. . . . The rate to be used under this paragraph may never exceed twice the rate which would have been used had the deduction been computed under the method described in paragraph (1).[18]

In all instances, it is important to bear in mind, as explained above,[19] that the depreciation deduction is merely a method of cost allocation which recognizes that to the extent buildings, equipment, and other items are consumed in profit-making activities, the value consumed represents a cost to be spread over the item's life and taken into account in determining a net income or loss for each year in the life of the item. Neither for business nor for tax accounting is any effort made to determine the exact value shrinkage in each accounting period as a means of determining an asset's cost for the period. Nor is it intended that cost less depreciation reflect *value* at any given point of time; "adjusted basis" and "value" are not synonymous. The cost-spreading methods described above are conventions, which operate mechanically and quite differently, depending upon the method selected.

The principal methods which are illustrated are not applicable to all types of property[20] and are not exclusive. Other methods of depreciation may be used. They include methods which make depreciation dependent upon the percentage of total income flow with respect to the property in any year, upon the percentage of production which occurs in a year as compared to expected production over the asset's life, or upon the

---

[17]  Sen.Rep. No. 1622, 83rd Cong., 3rd Sess. pp. 201–202 (1954). The report stated that more than one method could be used on various property or classes of property of the taxpayer. Id.

[18]  This is the 200 percent declining balance method. Ed.

[19]  See page 394, supra.

[20]  I.R.C. § 168(f).

percentage of hours a machine is used in relation to the number of hours it will be used, and on the income forecast method.[21]

## The Relationship of Depreciation to Basis

When a taxpayer claims depreciation on property, the deduction is attended by a commensurate reduction in the basis for the property.[22] Thus, the cost or other basis for depreciable property may be likened to a limited supply of deductions from which the taxpayer may draw in accordance with various methods until the supply is used up. If the supply is to be tapped over a period of several years, there must be a device for keeping track of the supply. Basis is the device, although of course it serves other purposes as well. As deductions are claimed, downward basis adjustments effect a shrinkage of the supply, and "adjusted" basis reflects the remaining amount that can be claimed as deductions. In a tax sense, the taxpayer thus achieves a "return" of capital as the taxpayer "expenses" the capital expenditure piecemeal over the period during which depreciation deductions are claimed.

Basis adjustments arising out of depreciation are governed by Section 1016(a)(2). The downward adjustment required is at least the amount of depreciation deduction permitted ("*allowable*") under the depreciation method employed by the taxpayer.[23] This is because depreciation is in the nature of a continuing expense, unaffected by the success or failure of the taxpayer's business, and Congress does not permit a taxpayer to time depreciation deductions for one's own convenience any more than one can time deductions for rent or salary. Thus, while depreciation does not involve a current pay-out, as salary expense may, it is properly viewed as a continuing expense each year, just as if it were salary expense paid or accrued. Consequently, basis is reduced even if the taxpayer claims no depreciation deduction. The amount of depreciation allowable is determined in accordance with the depreciation method that has been adopted by the taxpayer. If one has claimed no depreciation and has therefore adopted no method, the statute specifies that allowable depreciation is to be determined under the straight-line method.[24]

It may be that a taxpayer will claim depreciation deductions in excess of those permitted. This could come about, for example, by an erroneous use of too high a basis for an asset or by an assumption of an improperly short useful life. What should be the effect on basis of claiming excessive deductions? If the amount claimed is not challenged (and is therefore "*allowed*"), should the full amount claimed work to reduce basis, even though it exceeds the amount permitted by the statute (the amount "allowable")? Congress has said that it should, the sensible

---

[21]  I.R.C. §§ 167(g), 168(f)(1).

[22]  I.R.C. § 1016(a)(2).

[23]  I.R.C. § 1016(a)(2) flush language.

[24]  I.R.C. § 1016(a)(2) flush language 1st complete sentence.

notion being that if the taxpayer's taxable income has been reduced by the deduction, even improperly, the taxpayer has had the use of the capital expenditure to that extent. Thus, in general, the plan has been to call for downward basis adjustment for depreciation "allowed" but not less than the amount "allowable".[25]

## The Modified Accelerated Cost Recovery System (MACRS)

Congress seems to be constantly tinkering with the depreciation system. The basic underlying concepts of the system which are discussed above (useful life, depreciable amount, depreciation methods, and basis adjustments) are applicable to all types of tangible depreciable property—real and personal, and new and used. Yet different detailed rules apply to the different types of property. The current depreciation system applicable to tangible property, in effect since 1987, is the Modified Accelerated Cost Recovery System (MACRS), found in Section 168.[26]

MACRS is mandatory,[27] not elective, although some elections may be made *within* the system.[28] MACRS applies to most tangible depreciable property.[29] Intangible property does not qualify for MACRS treatment; however, under Section 197 certain acquired intangibles may be "amortized" over 15 years.[30] The statute also excludes from MACRS property depreciated under a method not expressed in terms of time of utility, such as property depreciated under the unit-of-production method.[31] If for any reason MACRS does not apply, Section 167 may apply and a separate set of rules comes into play.[32] Thus, MACRS is not the exclusive depreciation deduction section; it is mandatory when it

---

[25] I.R.C. § 1016(a)(2). Depreciation allowed in excess of the amount allowable effects a basis reduction only to the extent that the excess resulted in a reduction of the taxpayer's taxes. I.R.C. § 1016(a)(2)(B).

[26] Pub. Law No. 99–514, 99th Cong., 2d Sess. § 201 (1986). The depreciation mechanism was overhauled in the Economic Recovery Tax Act of 1981 and those provisions were referred to as the Accelerated Cost Recovery System (ACRS). ACRS was generally applicable to property placed in service after December 31, 1980 and before January 1, 1987. The ACRS rules are not considered here. Congress tinkered with the ACRS system several times and substantially revised it in the Tax Reform Act of 1986. Because the 1986 changes were so substantial the depreciation rules are now referred to as "Modified" ACRS. We generally will refer to the current rules as "MACRS." Property placed in service by the taxpayer after December 31, 1986 generally is subject to MACRS. Pub. Law No. 99–514, § 203(a)(1)(A), supra.

[27] I.R.C. § 168(a).

[28] See, e.g., the Text at note 51, infra.

[29] I.R.C. § 168(a).

[30] See I.R.C. § 197 discussed at page 425, infra. "Amortization" is essentially the same as depreciation, but it relates to intangible property. It requires an equal amount of annual writeoff, the same as straight-line depreciation.

[31] I.R.C. § 168(f)(1). See also I.R.C. § 168(f)(2)–(4) listing some other property that does not qualify for MACRS.

[32] Some of those rules are considered in the historic rules discussed supra at pages 394 through 399, and some rules specifically related to personal property are discussed at Chapter 14E2, infra.

applies, but if it is inapplicable, generally Section 167 or Section 197 is used.[33]

*Recovery Periods.* MACRS varies from the previously considered Section 167 rules in several respects. Under MACRS taxpayers recover the entire cost of tangible depreciable property over lives known as "recovery periods" that are, for the most part, shorter[34] than the useful lives previously employed.[35] This is accomplished by assigning all such property to one of several classes with predetermined useful lives or recovery periods. A happy consequence is elimination of controversy between government and taxpayer over the useful life of the property.[36] MACRS also varies from historic depreciation by providing for the use of the same schedules whether the property is new or used property.[37]

Under MACRS each item of property is assigned to one of several classifications which is generally dependent upon the property's class life under the A.D.R. system.[38] Under each *classification* items of property are assigned to an applicable *recovery period* which becomes the period of time over which that property is depreciated.[39] Most personal property is classified as either "3-year", "5-year" or "7-year" property which has respective recovery periods of 3, 5, or 7 years.[40] Some property specifically listed in Section 168(e)(3) is subject to special classification. For example, automobiles are specifically placed within the 5-year class with a 5 year recovery period.[41] Almost all depreciable real property is assigned either a 27.5 year or a 39 year recovery period.[42]

*Disregard of Salvage Value.* As previously discussed, MACRS completely disregards salvage value in the computation of depreciation,

---

[33] In addition, the "anti-churning" rules, considered below, may make the current MACRS rules inapplicable bringing either a prior MACRS rule, ACRS (see note 26, supra), or I.R.C. § 167 into play. See the Text at note 55, infra.

[34] However, see the MACRS recovery periods assigned to real property. I.R.C. § 168(c). See Chapter 14E3, infra.

[35] The recovery periods assigned to property under MACRS are generally shorter than the lives under the A.D.R. system. See note 26, supra. For example, office furniture now depreciable over 7 years was depreciable over 10 years under the A.D.R. system. See Rev.Proc. 83–35, 1983–1 C.B. 745 at 746.

[36] The system also eliminates any controversy over the requirement that the property be depreciated over its useful life *to the taxpayer.* See Massey Motors, Inc., note 6, supra.

[37] Under I.R.C. § 167 historic depreciation used property could be subject to less rapid depreciation method than new property. See Rev.Rul. 57–352, 1957–2 C.B. 150.

[38] I.R.C. § 168(e)(1) and (i)(1). But see I.R.C. § 168(e)(2) and (3) establishing separate classifications of most real property and special classifications for some other types of property. See the Text at note 11 and see note 26, supra, introducing the A.D.R. system.

[39] I.R.C. § 168(c).

[40] 3-year property includes property with a class life under the A.D.R. system of 4 years; 5-year property is property with an A.D.R. class life of 5 through 9 years; and 7-year property is property with an A.D.R. class life of 10 through 15 years. I.R.C. § 168(e)(1).

[41] I.R.C. § 168(c) and (e)(3)(B)(i).

[42] I.R.C. § 168(c)(1). See I.R.C. § 168(e)(2).

both simplifying the computation and alleviating controversy over the amount of salvage value.[43]

*Depreciation Methods.* MACRS provides that the depreciation methods available with respect to property also depend upon the classification of property.[44] Depending on the classification of property,[45] MACRS employs the 200% declining balance method,[46] the 150% declining balance method,[47] and the straight-line method.[48] If one of the accelerated depreciation methods is employed, there is a switch within the system to the straight-line method in the year when the straight-line method yields a greater depreciation allowance.[49] Under Section 168(g), MACRS also provides an alternative depreciation system that is required for some properties[50] and may be elected for any other MACRS property.[51] Generally, the alternative system uses straight-line depreciation with longer lives than the MACRS rules above causing, of course, a slower depreciation of assets. Why, you may ask, would a taxpayer elect to use slower depreciation? In the formative years of a business or, indeed, in any period of losses, one considers the deferral of deductions to a period for which they will save taxes. Otherwise, although one would rarely elect to use the alternative system, it is required in some cases.[52]

*Conventions.* The MACRS system also adopts certain "conventions," administrative rules of convenience which, for depreciation purposes, treat property as if it were placed in service at a set point in time during a year or month, rather than on the specific date its use commences. The convention rules also apply on the disposition of depreciable property.[53] There are separate conventions for personal and real property.[54]

---

[43]  See Text at note 15, supra. In our example above, if the shoemaker acquires a stitcher, it has an 11 year class life under the A.D.R. system. Rev. Proc. 83–35, supra note 35 at 752. It is classified as 7-year property under MACRS and has a 7 year recovery period. I.R.C. § 168(c) and (e)(1). If the shoemaker buys it for $80,000 and places it in service, he uses the 7-year recovery period even though he actually plans to use the stitcher for a shorter or longer period. Also, since MACRS disregards salvage value, the shoemaker is permitted to recover the entire cost of the stitcher over 7 years, even if he hopes to sell it for a salvage value of $4,000 after 10 years. I.R.C. § 168(b)(4) and (g)(2)(A).

[44]  See I.R.C. § 168(b) and (e).

[45]  Id.

[46]  I.R.C. § 168(b)(1).

[47]  I.R.C. § 168(b)(2).

[48]  I.R.C. § 168(b)(3).

[49]  I.R.C. § 168(b)(1)(B) and (2). See I.R.C. § 168(b)(4).

[50]  I.R.C. §§ 168(g)(1)(A)–(D) and 280F(b)(1). See page 424, infra.

[51]  I.R.C. § 168(g)(1)(E).

[52]  Note 50, supra. Moreover, the alternative system is sometimes used in the computation of the alternative minimum tax which is considered later in this course. See Chapter 27C, infra.

[53]  I.R.C. § 168(d)(4) parentheticals.

[54]  I.R.C. § 168(d).

*Anti-Churning Rules.* MACRS also provides a series of "anti-churning" rules[55] that are designed to prevent taxpayers from bringing within the MACRS rules property that "related persons"[56] used before the MACRS rules applied. MACRS is intended to encourage new capital investment, and Congress does not want taxpayers merely to churn their old investments to take advantage of the more rapid MACRS writeoffs. Therefore the anti-churning rules apply if, *and only if,* the MACRS rules allow the taxpayer a more rapid writeoff (more depreciation) in the first year the property is placed in service than depreciation allowed for that year by the rules under which the property was being depreciated by the related person or entity.[57] If they apply, the taxpayer must use the depreciation method used by the related taxpayer.[58]

## Collateral Effects

Congressional adjustments in the depreciation deduction are by no means based solely on a search for the best way to determine a net income for the taxable year. Over the years, Congress made liberalizing changes in the rules in an effort to stimulate the economy. Congress has also made adjustments in the depreciation deduction in the hope of inducing sociological improvements and ecological advances. For example, at times special rules have applied to encourage investments in low-income housing and facilities for pollution control, on the job training, and child care.

## The Related Concept of Depletion

Those who drill oil, mine natural resources, or cut timber may encounter a phenomenon somewhat like the shoemaker's exhaustion of his stitcher. Or perhaps their situation should be likened to a merchant who gradually sells off stock in trade. In either event, it is clear that in a business operation they are using up or otherwise parting with something for which they probably have a tax basis. Question arises how the "depletion" of their resource should affect their tax liability.

Congress legislated specifically on the problem in the enactment of the first modern income tax statute. The Revenue Act of 1913 permitted "cost" depletion.[59] The effect of this provision was very much like the current depreciation deduction, allowing a recovery of cost or other basis as the wasting asset was consumed by its exploitation. The deduction was

---

[55] I.R.C. § 168(f)(5). Actually most of the anti-churning rules are found in I.R.C. § 168(e)(4) of the 1954 Code and § 168(f)(5)(A) merely incorporates them by reference.

[56] For purposes of the anti-churning rules, "related persons" include family members of the taxpayer including spouses, brothers, sisters, ancestors and descendants and entities such as corporations, partnerships and trusts in which the taxpayer has an interest. See I.R.C. § 168(e)(4)(D) of the 1954 Code.

[57] I.R.C. § 168(f)(5)(B). The half-year convention is used in making all the calculations. I.R.C. § 168(f)(5)(B)(ii)(II).

[58] I.R.C. § 168(f)(5)(A). Conf.Rep. No. 99–841, 99th Cong., 2d Sess. II–54 (1986). The anti-churning rules are inherently inapplicable to most real property and are also inapplicable to some other property. I.R.C. § 168(f)(5)(B)(i) and (ii), respectively.

[59] Revenue Act of 1913, § 11B, 38 Stat. 166, 167 (1913).

limited, however, to an amount not in excess of 5 percent of the value of the product mined.[60]

A more controversial depletion provision appeared in 1924, when Congress invented "percentage depletion." The concept gets its name from the fact that the amount of the deduction, annually, is determined by a stated percentage of the "gross income from the property" subject to the allowance.[61] There is no ceiling on the amount of the deductions that can be claimed over the years—no limitation to cost or other basis or even to discovery value. Section 613(b) presents a long list of the types of property that are subject to percentage depletion.[62] For each a percentage of gross income ranging from 5 percent to 22 percent is stated, which measures the amount of the deduction.[63] However, major oil companies are not permitted to use percentage depletion.[64]

# Sharp v. United States

United States District Court, District of Delaware, 1961.
199 F.Supp. 743, affirmed 303 F.2d 783 (3d Cir.1962).

■ LAYTON, DISTRICT JUDGE.

This is a ruling on cross motions for summary judgment under Rule 56[1] by taxpayers and defendant in these two actions brought by taxpayers to recover alleged overpayments of federal income taxes for the calendar year 1954. The two actions were consolidated previously on stipulation of counsel.

Plaintiffs, Hugh R. Sharp, Jr., and Bayard Sharp, were equal partners in a partnership which on December 17, 1946, purchased a Beechcraft airplane at a cost of $45,875. From 1948 to 1953, additional capital expenditures were made with respect to the airplane in the amount of $8,398.50. Thus, the total cost of the airplane, including capital expenditures, was $54,273.50. Title was held by the partnership. During the period of ownership, the airplane was used by the partnership 73.654% for the personal use of the partners and 26.346% for business purposes.[2] Therefore, the partnership was allowed depreciation on the

---

[60] Ibid.

[61] I.R.C. § 613.

[62] In Heisler v. United States, 463 F.2d 375 (9th Cir.1972), cert. denied 410 U.S. 927, 93 S.Ct. 1358 (1973) the court denied percentage depletion on taxpayers bodies because they did not constitute "other natural deposits" within I.R.C. § 613(b).

[63] A discussion of depletion, touching on problems not alluded to above, appears in Bittker and Lokken, Federal Taxation of Income, Estates and Gifts, Ch. 24 (Warren, Gorham & Lamont).

[64] I.R.C. § 613(d).

[1] 28 U.S.C.A. F.R.Civ.P. 56.

[2] The stipulation is not precise as to the exact nature of the division into percentages of personal and business use. It was assumed in the briefs and at oral argument, and therefore it is assumed in this opinion, that the parties are agreed, for purposes of ruling on these motions, that the airplane was used from the beginning, and throughout its ownership by taxpayers, approximately ¼ for business and ¾ for pleasure, without variations. Other considerations might apply if the nature of the ¼–¾ division of use had been different. Suppose, for example,

basis of only $14,298.90, or 26.346% of the airplane's total cost. Depreciation taken by the partnership and allowed on this basis during the period totaled $13,777.92. During 1954, the airplane was sold by the partnership for $35,380. At issue here is the amount of gain or loss realized by the partnership on the sale of the airplane.

The taxpayers earnestly contend that, if anything, they suffered a loss on the sale, but certainly that they realized no gain. They contend that the relevant statutes permit no other conclusion. Taxpayers point out that the basis of property is its cost.[3] The total cost of the airplane was $54,273.50. For determining gain or loss, numerous adjustments in this basis are permissible, including subtracting from the cost basis the amount of depreciation allowed.[4] Since the depreciation allowed on the airplane was $13,777.92, taxpayers have subtracted this amount from $54,273.50, giving an adjusted basis of $40,495.58. The Code explicitly states that the loss recognized on the sale of property is the excess of the adjusted basis over the amount realized from the sale of the property.[5] The selling price of the airplane was $35,380. Accordingly, taxpayers subtracted this amount from the adjusted basis of $40,495.58 and compute their loss on the sale of the airplane as being $5,115.58. The taxpayers, as the Court understands their argument, do not seek to deduct any part of this loss. Their only claim is that no gain was realized on the sale.

The government theory is grounded in the fact that the airplane was used by the partnership 73.654% for pleasure and 26.346% for business purposes. Both the adjusted basis and the proceeds of sale of the plane are allocated in these proportions, giving in effect two sales. A gain on the business part of the sale is balanced against a non-deductible loss on the personal part, producing a net gain. More detail will clarify the government theory. It will be recalled that in computing depreciation, the cost basis was allocated so that depreciation was allowed on only 26.346% of the cost basis, i.e., $14,298.90.[6] The remainder of the cost basis, i.e., $39,974.60, was allocated to the personal use of the airplane and no depreciation was allowed. The government has adjusted only the business basis, by subtracting from $14,298.90 the depreciation allowed, i.e., $13,777.92, producing an adjusted business basis of $520.98. Now that the airplane is being sold, the government takes the view that this same allocation should be continued for purposes of gain or loss computation on the sale. Accordingly, the proceeds from the sale of the

---

during the total 8 years of ownership, that for the first 6 years the plane had been used exclusively for pleasure, and that for the last 2 years it had been used exclusively for business. Under such circumstances, gain or loss might depend not only on the original cost and the depreciation taken but also on the value of the plane when it was converted to a business use. See Treasury Regulations § 1.165–9(b).

[3]   26 U.S.C.A. § 1012.

[4]   26 U.S.C.A. § 1016(a)(2)(A).

[5]   26 U.S.C.A. § 1001(a).

[6]   See 26 U.S.C.A. § 167(a).

airplane, i.e., $35,380, have been allocated in accordance with the percentages of past business and personal use into portions of $9,321.21 and $26,058.79, respectively. The government then subtracts the adjusted business basis of $520.98 from the proceeds of the sale which were allocated to the business use of the airplane, $9,321.21, and concludes that the taxpayers realized a gain of $8,800.23 on the sale. Any loss on the personal use of the airplane is not deductible because of its personal nature and is disregarded. The taxpayers, being equal partners, have each been assessed with a taxable gain on one-half of $8,800.23, or $4,400.11.

Counsel for the government have said this is the first challenge by a taxpayer to Rev.Rul. 286, 1953–2 Cum.Bull. 20,[7] and that if the position argued for by the taxpayers be sustained, it would "produce serious and far reaching inequities in the administration of the internal revenue laws."

While research has disclosed no decided case in which an allocation has been made in accordance with percentages of past business and personal use of property, taxpayers are clearly in error if it is their contention that courts will not regard a thing, normally accepted as an entity, as divisible for tax purposes. There are numerous decisions in which the sale proceeds from an orange grove, for instance, have been allocated between the trees (capital gain) and the unharvested crop (income),[8] or where the proceeds from the sale of an interest in a partnership have been allocated between the earned but uncollected fees,[9] or income producing property[10] (income), and the other assets of the business (capital gain). A different sort of allocation was ordered in a leading Third Circuit case, Paul v. Commissioner.[11] In Paul, taxpayer, who was in the business of holding rental property for investment purposes, bought a partially completed apartment building in May, which he sold more than six months later, in November. The issue was whether the taxpayer could treat the entire gain or any part thereof as long term capital gain, under Section 117(j) of the Internal Revenue Code of 1939.[12] The Court held that a portion of the gain must be allocated to

---

[7]   The relevant portion of the Rev.Rul. 286, 1953–2 Cum.Bull. 20, reads as follows: "Only that part of a loss resulting from the sale of property used for both personal and income-producing purposes that can be allocated to the income-producing portion of the property constitutes a loss within the meaning of § 23(e) of the Internal Revenue Code [26 U.S.C.A. (I.R.C.1939), § 23(e)]. In determining the gain or loss on the sale, there must be an actual allocation of the amounts which represent cost, selling price, depreciation allowed or allowable, and selling expenses to the respective portions of property in the same manner as if there were two separate transactions."

[8]   See e.g., Watson v. Commissioner, 345 U.S. 544, 73 S.Ct. 848 (1953); Smyth v. Cole, 218 F.2d 667 (9th Cir.1955).

[9]   Tunnell v. United States, 259 F.2d 916 (3d Cir.1958); United States v. Snow, 223 F.2d 103 (9th Cir.1955).

[10]   Williams v. McGowan, 152 F.2d 570 (2d Cir.1945).

[11]   206 F.2d 763 (3d Cir.1953); see also Commissioner v. Williams, 256 F.2d 152 (5th Cir.1958).

[12]   26 U.S.C.A. (1939) § 117(j).

the part of the building erected more than six months before the sale and given long term treatment.[13] The remainder of the proceeds allocable to the construction between May and November was taxed as short term gain.

The closest analogy to the case at bar is the sale of depreciable and non-depreciable property as a unit—the sale of a building and land together, for instance. In United States v. Koshland,[14] a hotel caught fire and was destroyed. At issue in the case was the amount of the casualty loss deduction permissible under the circumstances. However, in the course of its opinion, the Court discussed the allocation problem directly, noting that the hotel was depreciable whereas the land on which it stood was not.

> " * * *. The result is that there is no single 'adjusted basis' for the land and building as a unit. The depreciation allowed or allowable on the building reduces the basis of the building only. No depreciation is allowed on the land, and the original basis of the land therefore remains unaffected. The adjusted basis of the building and the basis of the land cannot be combined into a single 'adjusted basis' for the property as a whole, for to do so would in effect be reducing the basis of the whole, by depreciation allowed or allowable only as against the building, a part.

> "Thus, for tax purposes, upon a sale of the property as a whole the selling price must be allocated between the land and building and the gain or loss separately determined upon each, by reference to the adjusted basis of each."[15]

This principle has been recognized in other cases without discussion.[16] The taxpayers point out that an airplane is not capable of separation into business and personal uses in the same way that a hotel is separable from the land on which it stands, or in the same way that the unharvested crop may be separated from the trees of the grove, or the accounts receivable from the other partnership assets. There were not two airplanes, say the taxpayers—a business airplane and a personal airplane—there was one airplane. There were not two sales; there was but one sale, one adjusted basis and one selling price. Any division or allocation, therefore, involves resorting to fiction, which is anathema to the tax law.

The taxpayers' argument against allocation in this case has superficial appeal. The whole idea of allocation is lacking in explicit

---

[13]  206 F.2d at 766.

[14]  208 F.2d 636 (9th Cir.1953).

[15]  208 F.2d at 640.

[16]  See, e.g., Crane v. Commissioner, 331 U.S. 1, 4–5, 67 S.Ct. 1047 (1947); Tracy v. Commissioner, 53 F.2d 575, 577 (6th Cir.1931); Belle Isle Creamery Co. v. Commissioner, 14 B.T.A. 737, 738 (1928); C.D. Johnson Lumber Corp. v. Commissioner, 12 T.C. 348, 356, 365 (1949).

authority from the literal words of the relevant sections in the Code. Since the situation here is not covered literally by the Statute, perhaps any interstices in statutory coverage should be filled by Congress not the Court. But this argument ignores the basic fact that no tax statute can encompass every situation which may arise. The Statute is phrased in general terms leaving it to the Commissioner by regulation or ruling and the Courts by interpretation to solve problems arising under unusual and novel facts. Merely because Congress did not specifically provide for the facts presented here does not mean it intended to exempt profits arising from the sale of property used both for business and pleasure. The taxpayers' argument also overlooks the fact that allocation has long been accepted by the courts in other cases. In dealing with another allocation problem, the Third Circuit Court of Appeals has said:

> "The federal revenue laws are to be construed in the light of their general purpose 'so as to give a uniform application to a nation-wide scheme of taxation.' * * *."[17]

But if taxpayers' theory prevails, there will be lack of uniformity in tax treatment between those who use property partially for business and pleasure on the one hand, and those who use property exclusively for business on the other. To use round figures, if property used exclusively for business has an adjusted basis of $500 ($14,000 cost less $13,500 depreciation) and it is sold for $9,000, nobody will deny that a taxable gain of $8,500 has been realized. Now, suppose that a larger piece of property is used only ¼ for business purposes and ¾ for pleasure, but that the adjusted basis of the business part is the same as in the first example, namely $500, and that depreciation figures and cost of the business part are also the same. Taxes levied on the business segment of the larger property should not be different from taxes levied on the other property used exclusively for business. To put it another way, taxpayers having two business properties with the same cost and depreciation should pay the same taxes, if the properties are sold for the same price. The fact that one of the properties was also used for pleasure should make no difference.

Under the government's allocation theory, uniformity is achieved; under the taxpayers', it is not. If the government's theory involves, as the taxpayers suggest, "dividing" the plane up, it can only be replied that this is precisely what was done in calculating the depreciation deduction to which the taxpayers acquiesced. There is no greater peculiarity in doing the same thing when computing gain or loss on a sale. The depreciable business use and non-depreciable personal use of the airplane are not essentially different from the depreciable hotel and non-depreciable land discussed in the Koshland case, supra.

The fairness of the government's theory can be seen more easily using a different analysis. This different analysis involves allocation of

---

[17] Paul v. Commissioner, 206 F.2d 763, 765–766 (3d Cir.1953).

loss instead of sale proceeds and cost basis. Continuing the use of round numbers, the $20,000 loss on the sale of the airplane (cost of $55,000 less sale proceeds of $35,000) can be allocated ¾ to the personal use and ¼ to the business use. If the property had not been depreciable, but used in the same fashion, it would seem proper that the taxpayer should be allowed to deduct $5,000 as a business loss—no more, no less. Since depreciation deductions were taken in our case with respect to the business use of the airplane of about $13,500, and whereas the actual loss on this part of the plane's use was only $5,000, it would appear that taxpayer has received fortuitously the benefit of depreciation deductions equal to the difference between $13,500 and $5,000, or $8,500. Even though all depreciation was allowed or allowable, it is the government's position that the "excessive" depreciation should be taxed.[18] This Court agrees.

Application of the rationale and certain of the language of Paul v. Commissioner[19] to the instant case compels the following conclusion. Allocation of the proceeds from the sale of this plan in accordance with its percentages of business and personal use is "practical and fair." This Court believes that Rev.Rule 286, 1953–2 Cum.Bull. 20, as applied here, represents a reasonable exercise by the Commissioner of his rule making power. There is no reason to make this an "all or nothing proposition." It is realistic to recognize that there are "gradations" between the percentage of business and personal use of a piece of property. It is concluded here that it is "proper that those gradations have tax significance."

The taxpayers' motion for summary judgment is denied and the government's is granted. Let an order be submitted in conformity herewith.

## Simon v. Commissioner[*]

United States Court of Appeals, Second Circuit, 1995.[**]
68 F.3d 41.

■ Before: OAKES, WINTER and MAHONEY, CIRCUIT JUDGES.

■ WINTER, CIRCUIT JUDGE:

This appeal from the Tax Court raises the question whether professional musicians may take a depreciation deduction for wear and tear on antique violin bows under the Accelerated Cost Recovery System ("ACRS") of the Economic Recovery Tax Act of 1981 ("ERTA"), Pub.L. No.

---

[18] Assuming that taxpayers are in a high tax bracket, it may be noted that complete equalization of tax benefits is not accomplished in the government's theory. Taxpayer took the $8,500 "excess" depreciation as ordinary deductions. Taxpayers are now being taxed on this amount at only capital gain rates. It would seem that taxpayers are still ahead.

[19] 206 F.2d 763, 766 (3d Cir.1953).

[*] Some footnotes omitted.

[**] Nonacq. 1996–2 C.B. 2.

97–34, 95 Stat. 172, although the taxpayers cannot demonstrate that the bows have a "determinable useful life."

The parties agree that under the pre-ERTA Internal Revenue Code of 1954 and the Treasury Department regulations interpreting that Code, the bows would be considered depreciable property only if the taxpayers could demonstrate a determinable useful life. The issue here is to what extent, if any, the ACRS modified the determinable useful life requirement.

BACKGROUND

\* \* \*

The business property at issue consists of two violin bows ("the Tourte bows") made in the nineteenth century by Francois Tourte, a bowmaker renowned for technical improvements in bow design. These bows were purchased by the Simons in 1985 and were in a largely unused condition at the time. The Tax Court found that "[o]ld violins played with old bows produce exceptional sounds that are superior to sounds produced by newer violins played with newer bows." *Simon v. Commissioner*, 103 T.C. 247, 250 (1994). The Tax Court also found that violin bows suffer wear and tear when used regularly by performing musicians. With use, a violin bow will eventually become "played out," producing an inferior sound. *Id.* at 252, 253. However, a "played out" Tourte bow retains value as a collector's item notwithstanding its diminished utility. The Simons' Tourte bows, for example, were appraised in 1990 at $45,000 and $35,000, even though they had physically deteriorated since their purchase by the Simons in 1985 for $30,000 and $21,500, respectively.

The Simons use the Tourte bows regularly in their trade. In 1989, the tax year in question, the Simons performed in four concerts per week as well as numerous rehearsals with the Philharmonic. *Id.* at 249. Their use of the Tourte bows during the tax year at issue subjected the bows to substantial wear and tear. *Id.* at 252. Believing that they were entitled to depreciate the bows under the ACRS, the Simons claimed depreciation deductions for the two bows on their 1989 Form 1040 in the amount of $6,300 and $4,515. The parties stipulated that these amounts represent the appropriate ACRS deductions if deductions are allowable.

The Tax Court agreed with the Simons and allowed the depreciation deductions. The Commissioner brought the present appeal.[1]

DISCUSSION

This appeal turns on the interpretation of the ACRS provisions of I.R.C. § 168, which provide a depreciation deduction for "recovery property" placed into service after 1980. Recovery property is defined by

---

[1]    The Third Circuit has recently held for the taxpayers in a companion case raising the same issues presented here. *See Liddle v. Commissioner*, 65 F.3d 329 (3d Cir.1995), *aff'g* 103 T.C. 285 (1994).

that section as "tangible property of a character subject to the allowance for depreciation" when "used in a trade or business, or . . . held for the production of income." I.R.C. § 168(c)(1). The record establishes that the Simons' Tourte bows were tangible property placed in service after 1980 and used in the taxpayers' trade or business. The Commissioner contends, however, that the bows are not "property of a character subject to the allowance for depreciation."

The parties agree that Section 168's phrase "of a character subject to depreciation" must be interpreted in light of the I.R.C. § 167(a) allowances for "exhaustion, wear and tear, and . . . obsolescence." The Simons and the Tax Court maintain that, when read in conjunction with the plain language of Section 167, Section 168 requires only that the Tourte bows suffer wear and tear in the Simons' trade to qualify as "recovery property." *See* 103 T.C. at 260. The Commissioner, on the other hand, argues that because all property used in a trade or business is necessarily subject to wear and tear, the Simons' construction of Section 168 would effectively render Section 168's phrase "of a character subject to the allowance for depreciation" superfluous, a result that Congress presumably could not have intended. *See United States v. Nordic Village, Inc.*, 503 U.S. 30, 35, 112 S.Ct. 1011, 1015, 117 L.Ed.2d 181 (1992) (It is a "settled rule that a statute must, if possible, be construed in such a fashion that every word has some operative effect."). Therefore, Section 168's requirement that the property be "of a character subject to the allowance for depreciation" must include an element beyond wear and tear, namely the "determinable useful life" requirement embodied in 26 C.F.R. § 1.167(a)–1, a Treasury regulation of pre-ERTA vintage.

We do not agree with the Commissioner's premise because some tangible assets used in business are not exhausted, do not suffer wear and tear, or become obsolete. For example, paintings that hang on the wall of a law firm merely to be looked at—to please connoisseur clients or to give the appearance of dignity to combative professionals—do not generally suffer wear or tear. More to the point, the Simon's Tourte bows were playable for a time precisely because they had been kept in a private collection and were relatively unused since their manufacture. Indeed, it appears that one had never been played at all. Had that collection been displayed at a for-profit museum, the museum could not have depreciated the bows under ERTA because, although the bows were being used in a trade or business, they were not subject to wear and tear. The Tourte bows are not unlike numerous kinds of museum pieces or collectors' items. The Commissioner's textual argument thus fails because there are tangible items not subject to wear and tear.

The Commissioner next argues that Congressional intent and the notion of depreciation itself require that Section 168's statutory language be supplemented by reading into the word "character" a requirement that tangible property have a demonstrable useful life. To address that issue, we must briefly examine the history of the depreciation allowance.

The tax laws have long permitted deductions for depreciation on certain income-producing assets used in a trade or business. * * *. The original rationale for the depreciation deduction was to allow taxpayers to match accurately, for tax accounting purposes, the cost of an asset to the income stream that the asset produced. *See Massey Motors, Inc. v. United States*, 364 U.S. 92, 104, 80 S.Ct. 1411, 1418, 4 L.Ed.2d 1592 (1960) ("it is the primary purpose of depreciation accounting to further the integrity of periodic income statements by making a meaningful allocation of the cost entailed in the use . . . of the asset to the periods to which it contributes"). In its traditional incarnation, therefore, the pace of depreciation deductions was determined by the period of time that the asset would produce income in the taxpayer's business. As the Supreme Court noted in *Massey,* "Congress intended by the depreciation allowance not to make taxpayers a profit thereby, but merely to protect them from a loss. . . . Accuracy in accounting requires that correct tabulations, not artificial ones, be used." *Id.* at 101, 80 S.Ct. at 1416.

To implement this accurate tax accounting, the concept of a determinable useful life was necessary because, without such a determination, one could not calculate the proper annual allowance—"the sum which should be set aside for the taxable year, in order that, at the end of the useful life of the plant in the business, the aggregate of the sums set aside will (with the salvage value) suffice to provide an amount equal to the original cost." *United States v. Ludey*, 274 U.S. 295, 300–01, 47 S.Ct. 608, 610, 71 L.Ed. 1054 (1927). The regulation that the Commissioner now relies upon was promulgated under the 1954 Internal Revenue Code and reflects the rationale underlying the accounting scheme in effect just prior to ERTA. . . .

ERTA, however, altered the depreciation scheme for two reasons other than sound accounting practice that are not consistent with the Commissioner's argument. First, the ACRS introduced accelerated depreciation periods as a stimulus for economic growth. . . . Under ACRS, the cost of an asset is recovered over a predetermined period unrelated to—and usually shorter than—the useful life of the asset. Moreover, the depreciation deductions do not assume consistent use throughout the asset's life, instead assigning inflated deductions to the earlier years of use. *See* I.R.C. § 168(b). Therefore, the purpose served by the determinable useful life requirement of the pre-ERTA scheme—allowing taxpayers to depreciate property over its actual use in the business—no longer exists under the ACRS.[4] *See generally Massey*, 364 U.S. 92, 80 S.Ct. 1411. Because the ACRS is different by design, there is no logic in the Commissioner's suggestion that depreciation practice under the old

---

[4] We do acknowledge, as the Tax Court did, that the concept of useful life retains some utility under the ACRS for determining whether recovery property is 3-year or 5-year class property. 103 T.C. at 264. *See Clinger v. Commissioner*, 60 T.C.M. (CCH) 598 (1990). Insofar as the memorandum opinion in *Clinger* also embraces a threshold determinable useful life requirement, we decline to follow it.

Section 167 calls for the imposition of a determinable useful life requirement after ERTA.

A second congressional purpose embodied in ERTA also militates against reading a determinable useful life prerequisite into Section 168. In addition to stimulating investment, Congress sought to simplify the depreciation rules by eliminating the need to adjudicate matters such as useful life and salvage value, which are inherently uncertain and result in unproductive disagreements between taxpayers and the Internal Revenue Service. S.Rep. No. 144 at 47. Indeed, the legislation specifically sought to "de-emphasize" the concept of useful life. *Id.* On this point, we agree with the Tax Court that:

> [The Commissioner's] argument that a taxpayer must first prove the useful life of personal property before he or she may depreciate it over the 3-year or 5-year period would bring the Court back to pre-ERTA law and reintroduce the disagreements that the Congress intended to eliminate by its enactment of ERTA.

103 T.C. at 263. *See also Liddle*, 65 F.3d at 333–34.

We also cannot accept the Commissioner's suggestion that her proposed interpretation deemphasizes useful life by requiring establishment of a demonstrable useful life for only a "narrow category" of property. Insofar as the Commissioner seeks to do this by singling out usable antiques and other business property likely to appreciate in real economic value, she relies on a concept that has nothing whatsoever to do with the useful life of the asset in the business. As the Supreme Court noted in *Massey*, "useful life is measured by the use in a taxpayer's business, not by the full abstract economic life of the asset in any business." *Massey*, 364 U.S. at 97, 80 S.Ct. at 1414. Nor, *a fortiori*, does the concept of useful life bear on the asset's eligibility under the ACRS. Indeed, the Commissioner's position that deductions for depreciation may not be taken for property that retains value after use in a business seems designed to avoid the consequences of ERTA's explicit rejection of "salvage value." *See Clinger v. Commissioner*, 60 T.C.M. (CCH) 598 (1990) (concept of salvage value has been eliminated under ERTA).[5]

---

[5]   We accept the Tax Court's finding that the bows have no "determinable useful life." That finding is based on the assumption that there is no distinction between the value of the bows to professional violinists and their value as antiques after they are no longer functional.

ERTA's abandonment of the concept of salvage value may be the rub that causes the Commissioner to take the position that the Tourte bows have no determinable useful life and are not depreciable. If salvage value could be used to offset depreciation, the Commissioner could, without loss to the Treasury, concede that the bows could be used to play the violin for only so long and simply offset the depreciation deduction by their continued value as antiques. The bows had been sparingly used, or not used at all, before they were purchased by the Simons and, having been used extensively, now have much less value as business property while retaining substantial value as antiques. The Commissioner may thus lean upon the thin reed of a supposed continuing determinable useful life requirement because Congress's intent to do away with the concept of salvage values is indisputable. In doing so, however, she fails to distinguish between a useful life as property used in a particular business—playing the violin as a professional—and value as non-functioning antiques.

The Commissioner's strongest support for her claim that Congress intended to maintain Section 1.167(a)–1's determinable useful life requirement comes from the House Conference Report, which noted that

> Under present law, assets used in a trade or business or for the production of income are depreciable if they are subject to wear and tear, decay or decline from natural causes or obsolescence. Assets that do not decline in value on a predictable basis or that do not have a determinable useful life, such as land, goodwill, and stock, are not depreciable.

H.R.Conf.Rep. No. 215 at 206, U.S.C.C.A.N. 1981, p. 296. The Simons unsuccessfully attempt to recharacterize this statement as an inartful catalogue of assets that are not subject to exhaustion, wear and tear, or obsolescence. The House report means what it says but gives us slight pause. In light of the overriding legislative intent to abandon the unnecessarily complicated rules on useful life, we cannot employ two sentences in a legislative report to trump statutory language and a clearly stated legislative purpose. Continued reliance on 26 C.F.R. § 1.167(a)–1 is in sharp conflict with the overall legislative history of ERTA, which definitively repudiates the scheme of complex depreciation rules, including "current regulations." S.Rep. No. 144 at 47. We are thus not persuaded by the Commissioner's call for us to interpret a statute that abrogates a current regulatory regime as in fact incorporating the details of that scheme. In particular, we reject the argument that we should retain regulatory provisions now divorced from their functional purpose.

When a coherent regulatory system has been repudiated by statute—as this one has—it is inappropriate to use a judicial shoehorn to retain an isolated element of the non-dismembered regulation. We thus hold that, for the purposes of the "recovery property" provisions of Section 168, "property subject to the allowance for depreciation" means property that is subject to exhaustion, wear and tear, or obsolescence.

* * *

We acknowledge that the result of our holding may give favorable treatment to past investment decisions that some regard as wasteful, such as a law firm's purchase of expensive antique desks, the cost of which could have been quickly depreciated under our current ruling. However, Congress wanted to stimulate investment in business property generally, and it is not our function to draw subjective lines between the wasteful and the productive. Moreover, courts should take care that the Commissioner's role as revenue maximizer does not vitiate Congress's intent to sacrifice revenue to generate economic activity. *See LeCroy Research Sys. Corp. v. Commissioner*, 751 F.2d 123, 128 (2d Cir.1984). If taxpayers cannot trust that such tax measures will be fully honored, some or all of the hoped-for activity will not occur. *Id.*

One should not exaggerate the extent to which our holding is a license to hoard and depreciate valuable property that a taxpayer expects to appreciate in real economic value.[7] The test is whether property will suffer exhaustion, wear and tear, or obsolescence in its use by a business. Even without a determinable useful life requirement, a business that displayed antique automobiles, for example, and kept them under near-ideal, humidity-controlled conditions, would still have difficulty demonstrating the requisite exhaustion, wear and tear, or obsolescence necessary to depreciate the automobiles as recovery property. *Cf. Harrah's Club v. United States*, 661 F.2d 203 (Ct.Cl.1981). Nor is valuable artwork purchased as office ornamentation apt to suffer anything more damaging than occasional criticism from the tutored or untutored, *cf. Associated Obstetricians & Gynecologists, P.C. v. Commissioner*, 762 F.2d 38 (6th Cir.1985), and it too would probably fail to qualify as recovery property. Indeed, even a noted artwork that serves as a day-to-day model for another artist's work cannot be depreciated as recovery property if it does not face exhaustion, wear and tear, or obsolescence in the pertinent business. *Cf. Clinger*, 60 T.C.M. (CCH) 598.

For the foregoing reasons, we affirm.

■ OAKES, SENIOR CIRCUIT JUDGE, dissenting:

I cannot believe that Congress, in changing the depreciation deduction from the Asset Depreciation Range System ("ADRS") for recovery of assets placed in service after December 31, 1980, to the Accelerated Cost Recovery System ("ACRS") whereby the cost of an asset is recovered over a predetermined period shorter than the useful life of the asset or the period the asset is used to produce income, intended to abandon the concept underlying depreciation, namely, that to permit the deduction the property must have a useful life capable of being estimated. *See Harrah's Club v. U.S.*, 661 F.2d 203, 207 (Ct. of Cl. 1981). I find no indication in either the changes of statutory language or the well-documented legislative history that Congress intended such a radical change as the majority of this panel, the Tax Court majority, and the Third Circuit in *Liddle v. C.I.R.*, 65 F.3d 329 (3d Cir.1995), have held it did. Indeed, it seems to me that the statutory language and the legislative history—consistent with the dual congressional purpose of simplification and stimulating economic growth by permitting accelerated depreciation periods—retained the fundamental principle that, in order to depreciate, the asset involved must have a determinable useful life.

---

[7] We note that our decision today is limited to "recovery property," a concept that was deleted from the statute in the Tax Reform Act of 1986, Pub.L. No. 99–514, 100 Stat. 2085. Moreover, ACRS' depreciation deductions first became available in 1981. Therefore, this opinion applies only to property placed in service between January 1, 1981 and January 1, 1987. [See Selig v. Commissioner, 70 T.C.M. 1125 (1995) in which the Court concludes that Congress did not intend to reimpose the useful life requirement in the post-1986 amendment to I.R.C. § 168. Id. at 1128. Ed.]

First, with respect to the statutory language, the question before us is whether antique violin bows constitute depreciable "recovery property" under section 168(c)(1) of the Internal Revenue Code effective during 1989, the year in issue. I.R.C. § 168(c)(1) defined "recovery property" by saying:

> except as provided in subsection (e) the term "recovery property" means *tangible property of a character subject to the allowance for depreciation*—(A) used in a trade or business, or (B) held for the production of income.

*Id.* (emphasis added). Moreover, section 168(c)(2) assigned "recovery property" into four classes or tiers, and defined "recovery property" (other than real property) as "section 1245 property." Section 1245(a)(3) defined "section 1245 property" as "any property which is or has been property of a character subject to the allowance for depreciation provided in section 167. . . ." How section 168(c)(2), section 1245(a)(3), and section 167 could all be read out of the statute as they have been by the majority of this panel, the Tax Court majority, and the Third Circuit, seems to me incomprehensible. Needless to say, the cases are legion that under section 167, taxpayers must establish that the property being depreciated has a determinable useful life. *See Browning v. C.I.R.*, 890 F.2d 1084, 1086–87 (9th Cir.1989) (disallowing depreciation deductions for antique violins); *Associated Obstetricians and Gynecologists, P.C. v. C.I.R.*, 762 F.2d 38, 39–40 (6th Cir.1985) (disallowing depreciation deductions for art works on medical office walls); and *Hawkins v. C.I.R.*, 713 F.2d 347, 353–54 (8th Cir.1983) (disallowing investment tax credit for law office art works). *See generally* Jacob Mertens, Jr., *Mertens Law of Federal Income Taxation* § 23 A.01 (Clark Boardman Callaghan ed. 1995) (1942).

Under the majority's interpretation, however, the only criterion necessary to obtain a deduction under section 168(c) is that the property be subject to wear and tear. Thus, a car buff in the trade or business of buying, collecting, and selling antique automobiles, who drives his autos to auto shows may obtain a depreciation deduction, or the law office that buys fine Sheraton or Chippendale desks or chairs for office use can take a deduction, though in each case the auto or furniture is actually appreciating in value and has no determinable useful life.

As for legislative history, the majority candidly admits that House Conference Report 97–215, which states that "assets that do not decline in value on a predictable basis or that do not have a determinable useful life, such as land, goodwill, and stock, are not depreciable," "means what it says,". . . . The majority then adds that the Report "gives us slight pause."

The majority of this court joins the Tax Court majority and the Third Circuit in holding that section 168(c)(1) applies to all tangible property that is subject to "wear and tear." I agree with the Commissioner that such an interpretation renders meaningless the phrase in section

168(c)(1) "of a character subject to the allowance for depreciation," since all tangible property used in a trade of business is necessarily subject to wear and tear. *See* Commissioner's Rep.Br. at 3–4 (citing to *U.S. v. Nordic Village Inc.*, 503 U.S. 30, 35, 112 S.Ct. 1011, 1015, 117 L.Ed.2d 181 (1992) ("a statute must, if possible, be construed in such fashion that every word has some operative effect")). This point is confirmed by the General Explanation of the Economic Recovery Tax Act of 1981 which states that section 168 "does not change the determination under prior law as to whether property is depreciable or non-depreciable." Staff of Joint Comm. on Taxation, 97th Cong., 1st Sess. 77 (Comm.Print 1981).

Nor can reliance be placed, as it is by the majority, upon the fact that section 168(f)(9) changed prior law by removing "salvage value" from the depreciation calculus. The fact that Congress eliminated salvage value while simultaneously defining the term "recovery property" as "tangible property of a character subject to the allowance for depreciation," cannot support the conclusion that section 168 eliminated the threshold requirement that taxpayers establish a determinable useful life for their property. Had Congress intended otherwise, the statute simply would have defined "recovery property" as "tangible property used in a trade or business" rather than as "tangible property of a character subject to the allowance for depreciation," and not specified that the recovery property be "section 1245 property," which, as stated, refers us back to section 167.

Since, concededly, taxpayers Richard and Fiona Simon have not established that the bows in question have determinable useful lives, the bows do not qualify for the depreciation deduction. It is a long way from the dual purpose of section 168 (to shorten the depreciation periods for property that would have been depreciable under section 167 in order to stimulate investment and to simplify the complex series of rules and regulations pertaining to useful lives by substituting a four-tier system of three-year, five-year, ten-year, and fifteen-year property), to abandonment of the underlying concept of depreciable property altogether. In my view, the decision of the Tax Court should be reversed and accordingly I hereby dissent.

## PROBLEM

1.   Section 263(a) provides "no deduction shall be allowed for any amount paid out for new buildings. . . ." Thus if one pays for salaries or for painting etc. in construction of a building, the expenses are capitalized and the total cost of the building is then depreciated assuming the § 167 or § 168 requirements are met.

   (a)   If Company owns trucks that are used during the year exclusively in constructing a new storage plant for the Company, is Company allowed a depreciation deduction for the trucks during the year? Consider what tax alternative there might be and then see Commissioner v. Idaho Power Co., 418 U.S. 1, 94 S.Ct. 2757 (1974).

    (b)    Are interest on loans connected with property and taxes on the property which are paid during the construction period currently deductible? See § 263A.

## 2. DEPRECIATION AND AMORTIZATION RULES FOR PERSONAL PROPERTY

Internal Revenue Code: Sections 167(a), (c)(1); 168(a)–(c), (d)(1), (4)(A), (e)(1), (g)(1)(E), (2), (3)(D), and (7), (k)(1), (2)(A), (E)(ii), and (F)(i), (6)(A), and (7); 179 (omit (b)(5), (d)(4)–(10), (e), (f)); 280F(a), (b), (d) (omit (d)(6)(C) and (D) and (9) and (10)). See Sections 168(e)(3), (i)(1); 197; 1016(a)(2).

---

### Depreciation of Tangible Personal Property

The income tax deduction for depreciation of *tangible* personal property is claimed under a variety of methods which are examined below. Temporarily disregarding special provisions or limitations, there are essentially two sets of general rules. Most tangible personal property acquired after 1986 is subject to the Section 168 MACRS rules, the Modified Accelerated Cost Recovery System. If post-1986 personal property does not qualify for MACRS treatment because it is excluded under those rules,[1] the long-standing rules in Section 167 come into play. We begin our consideration of this area with a discussion of MACRS, including Section 168(k). We then examine so-called first-year bonus depreciation under Section 179 and the Section 280F limitations on these allowances.

Thus far, the Text has focused on depreciation's role in measuring a taxpayer's income from a business or income-producing activity. Recall the shoe manufacturer who purchased an electric stitching machine for $80,000 and planned to use the machine for eight years. The depreciation of the stitching machine makes one focus on the proper measurement of the taxpayer's annual income from the shoe manufacturing enterprise. How should the cost of the stitching machine be matched to the income produced by its consumption? At times, Congress has modified the depreciation rules in order to provide a stimulus to the economy. Speeding up the rate at which property is depreciable may act as economic incentive for taxpayers to invest in new equipment, and thereby produce a stimulus for the economy as a whole. Imagine if the tax law suddenly changed and stitching machines were depreciable over just one year. The shortening of the depreciation period would provide an incentive for those considering a purchase to acquire a machine. The ability to deduct the cost of the machine over a shortened period generates tax savings in the early years of using the machine and puts cash in the pocket of the taxpayer which may be invested elsewhere.

---

[1]   I.R.C. § 168(f)(1)–(4).

In the 2017 Tax Cuts and Jobs Act[2] Congress moved taxpayers into an era where the "economic incentive" rationale for rapid depreciation of property is paramount. Generally, beginning in 2018 and currently extending through 2022, Section 168(k) allows a taxpayer to fully expense the cost of tangible personal property in the year it is placed in service (a 100 percent deduction!), unless a taxpayer elects not to use the provision.[3] The ability to immediately expense such property makes many of the other rules regarding depreciation largely irrelevant. We nevertheless examine those other rules because they apply to property previously placed in service and are scheduled to once again apply when the special allowance in Section 168(k) begins to phase-out.

*Section 168 MACRS.* As previously indicated, MACRS applies to most tangible personal property placed in service after 1986. Under MACRS, one must first determine the *recovery period* for the property.[4] The recovery period determines both the number of years of depreciation and the depreciation methods allowed for the property.[5] Salvage value is disregarded under each method.[6] If the applicable recovery period is not in excess of ten years, the system employs the 200% (double) declining balance method of depreciation; and if it is more than ten years, the system employs the 150% declining balance method.[7] Elective alternatives are available to a taxpayer who qualifies for MACRS to switch to any less accelerated depreciation method.[8] If any of the alternatives is elected, the election is applied to *all* MACRS property within the same *class* which is placed in service during the year of election.[9]

MACRS generally uses the "half-year convention" for the depreciation of tangible personal property. The "half-year convention" is an administrative rule of convenience which, for depreciation purposes, treats property as if it were placed in service at the midpoint of the year no matter when during the year it is actually placed in service. Thus, one-half of a year's depreciation is allowed for the year the property is acquired regardless of whether the property is placed in service on January 1 or December 31 of the year. The half-year convention is

---

[2]  Pub. L. No. 115–97, 115th Cong., 1st Sess. (2017).

[3]  I.R.C. § 168(k)(7).

[4]  I.R.C. § 168(c) and (e).

[5]  See I.R.C. § 168(b).

[6]  I.R.C. § 168(b)(4).

[7]  I.R.C. § 168(b)(1), (2), and (4). Under both methods, MACRS calls for a switch to the straight-line method in the first year in which the straight-line method based on the adjusted basis of the property *at that time* results in a greater amount of depreciation than the continued use of the applicable declining balance method. I.R.C. § 168(b)(1)(B) and (b)(2). When this occurs, the one-half year convention continues to extend the life of the property an additional one half of a year. See the Text at note 11, infra.

[8]  I.R.C. § 168(b)(2)(C), (3)(D), (5), (c), and (g)(2).

[9]  I.R.C. § 168(b)(5) and (g)(7). This rule is inapplicable to nonresidential real property and residential rental property. Id.

applicable to all the methods of depreciation under consideration.[10] In determining the deduction under the straight-line method (or in a switch from an accelerated method to the straight-line method), a half-year deduction is necessitated for the year following the end of the normal recovery period.[11] That is to say that if we think of an asset with a normal recovery period of five years, the allowance of a half-year for the second half of year one and a half-year for the first half of year six and a full allowance for each of the four other years results in a full five years of depreciation.[12]

The comparative results under MACRS can be seen by a reconsideration of a hypothetical situation using numbers similar to the ones used with respect to the shoemaker and his stitching machine. Assume that a taxpayer on January 1 purchases new manufacturing equipment with a $80,000 cost, that the taxpayer intends to use it for an 8-year period, and that the equipment will have salvage value at the end of the 8 years. The equipment also has an A.D.R. class life of 8 years and is therefore classified as 5-year property with a 5-year recovery period under MACRS.[13] The comparative depreciation results are illustrated in the following chart:

| | 200% D.B. | | Straight-Line | | Alternative Depreciation | |
|---|---|---|---|---|---|---|
| Year | Annual | Adjusted Basis | Annual | Adjusted Basis | Annual | Adjusted Basis |
| 1 | 16,000 | 64,000 | 8,000 | 72,000 | 5,000 | 75,000 |
| 2 | 25,600 | 38,400 | 16,000 | 56,000 | 10,000 | 65,000 |
| 3 | 15,360 | 23,040 | 16,000 | 40,000 | 10,000 | 55,000 |
| 4 | 9,220 | 13,820 | 16,000 | 24,000 | 10,000 | 45,000 |
| 5 | 9,210[14] | 4,610 | 16,000 | 8,000 | 10,000 | 35,000 |
| 6 | 4,610 | 0 | 8,000 | 0 | 10,000 | 25,000 |
| 7 | 0 | 0 | 0 | 0 | 10,000 | 15,000 |
| 8 | 0 | 0 | 0 | 0 | 10,000 | 5,000 |
| 9 | | | | | 5,000 | 0 |

---

[10]  I.R.C. § 168(a)(3), (d)(1), (g)(2)(B).

[11]  See the chart below in the Text.

[12]  To forestall abuse by a taxpayer who tries to take advantage of the half-year convention rule by loading up on personal property late in the year, the statute substitutes a special "mid-quarter" convention. I.R.C. § 168(d)(4)(C). If more than 40 percent of the cost of all MACRS personal property acquired during a year is placed in service in the fourth quarter of the year, the mid-quarter rule is invoked. I.R.C. § 168(d)(3)(A). Note that nonresidential real estate and residential rental property are disregarded in making the 40% determination. I.R.C. § 168(d)(3)(B).

[13]  I.R.C. § 168(c), (e)(1). Assistance in making the computations below is provided by the Service in Rev.Proc. 87–57, 1987–2 C.B. 687. See especially Tables 1 and 8 of the Rev. Proc. at pages 696 and 703, respectively.

[14]  A switch to straight line depreciation occurs here where that method results in a greater allowance than the double declining balance method.

If MACRS personal property is disposed of prior to completion of the recovery period, the half-year convention applies in computing the depreciation for the year of disposition.[15] Thus, if half-year convention personal property with a 5-year recovery period is disposed of on the last day of the fourth year of its recovery period, a depreciation deduction is allowed for only one-half of year four.

However, MACRS is not always applicable. If MACRS is inapplicable to property[16] or a taxpayer elects out of Section 168 to use the unit-of-production or some comparable method,[17] Section 167 controls. And, as previously stated, the anti-churning rules aimed at preventing taxpayers from churning their old investments between related individuals or economic entities to take advantage of more rapid MACRS write-offs can take personal property out of the current MACRS rules and toss it into a prior system.[18]

*Section 168(k) Additional Depreciation.* In an effort to stimulate a sagging economy, Congress has added an extra depreciation deduction[19] on most types of new and used[20] depreciable personal property[21] acquired by a taxpayer. In the case of depreciable personal property acquired and placed in service after September 27, 2017 and before 2023, the Section 168(k) additional allowance for depreciation is 100 percent of the adjusted basis of the property. You read that right! In those years, a taxpayer may simply "expense" the cost of depreciable tangible personal property.[22] Thus, the taxpayer generally simply writes off the entire capital expenditure and need not be concerned with the other MACRS rules because the property then has a zero adjusted basis.[23] A taxpayer may elect out of the Section 168(k) additional allowance for depreciation, but rarely would do so.[24]

*Section 179 Bonus Depreciation.* Section 168(k) is not the end of the story. If a taxpayer elects out of that provision, other MACRS rules apply.

---

[15] I.R.C. § 168(d)(4)(A) parenthetical. While this result appears harsh, allowing the deduction would generally only result in a wash. See I.R.C. §§ 1001(b), 1016(a)(2), and 1245(a). If the mid-quarter convention applied on acquisition, it also applies on disposition. I.R.C. § 168(d)(4)(C) parenthetical.

[16] See I.R.C. § 168(f)(2)–(4).

[17] I.R.C. § 168(f)(1).

[18] I.R.C. § 168(f)(5).

[19] I.R.C. § 168(k)(1).

[20] I.R.C. § 168(k)(2)(A)(ii), (E)(ii).

[21] The deduction applies to "qualified property" (I.R.C. § 168(k)(1)) which is defined in I.R.C. § 168(k)(2)(A)(i) to include property to which § 168 applies which has a recovery period of 20 years or less and certain other specialized categories of property.

[22] I.R.C. § 168(k)(1)(A), (2)(A)(iii), and (6)(A)(i). If the property is placed in service in years 2023 through 2026, the 100 percent amount is reduced by 20 percent per year to 80 percent in 2023, 60 percent in 2024, 40 percent in 2025, and 20 percent in 2026. I.R.C. § 168(k)(6)(A).

[23] I.R.C. § 168(k)(1)(B). The basis reduction prevents a double depreciation deduction. Thus, I.R.C. § 168(k) generally accelerates the recovery of the cost, but does not alter the total depreciation that would have been allowed if the taxpayer had elected out of the provision and held the property for its full recovery period.

[24] I.R.C. § 168(k)(7). The election applies to all property in a class to which an election is made during the year. Id.

Under those other MACRS rules, personal property may also qualify for bonus depreciation under Section 179.[25] Section 179 allows a taxpayer to elect to write off a part of the cost of some depreciable personal property as an ordinary expense deduction in the year in which the property is placed in service.

However, taxpayers are limited to $1 million of such bonus depreciation they may deduct in a year.[26] The limit applies, not to each piece of property, but to all qualifying property a taxpayer places in service during the year;[27] and the limitation is reduced by one dollar for each one dollar of total cost of Section 179 property placed in service during the year in excess of $2.5 million.[28] Thus, if the total of such property placed in service for the year were $3.5 million, there could be no § 179 deduction for the year. These amounts are adjusted for inflation beginning after 2018.[29] In addition, the Section 179 deduction may not exceed the amount of taxable income derived from the taxpayer's active conduct of trades or businesses during the year.[30] If a taxpayer elects out of Section 168(k), the effect of Section 179 is to allow additional depreciation in the year property[31] is placed in service. Just as the basis of property must be reduced by Section 167 or Section 168 depreciation deductions,[32] the basis must also reflect a Section 179 deduction which is, in essence, a depreciation deduction. The basis of the Section 179 property must be reduced before the property is depreciated under the

---

[25] Technically, the statute treats the I.R.C. § 179 amount as an expense, thus allowing a current deduction and not allowing the amount to be treated as a capital expenditure added to the property's basis. Thus, the § 179 deduction is taken prior to the § 168 deduction.

[26] I.R.C. § 179(b)(1). The limits are in general cut in half if spouses file separate returns. I.R.C. § 179(b)(4).

[27] I.R.C. § 179(b)(1).

[28] I.R.C. § 179(b)(2).

[29] I.R.C. § 179(b)(6).

[30] I.R.C. § 179(b)(3)(A). Taxable income is computed without regard to the I.R.C. § 179 deduction. I.R.C. § 179(b)(3)(C). Any amount allowed by § 179(b)(1) and (2) but disallowed by § 179(b)(3)(A) is carried over to subsequent years. I.R.C. § 179(b)(3)(B).

[31] Not all depreciable personal property qualifies for the I.R.C § 179 election. The section generally is applicable only to property qualifying under MACRS or to off-the-shelf computer software. I.R.C. § 179(d)(1)(A). See § 197(e)(3)(A)(i), (B). The property must be "section 1245 property" and must be acquired by *purchase* for use in the active conduct of the taxpayer's trade or business. I.R.C. § 179(d)(1)(B) and (C). This is property which is defined in I.R.C. § 1245(a)(3). See page 776, infra. Property merely held for the production of income does not qualify for I.R.C. § 179 expensing. I.R.C. § 179(d)(1)(C). The term "purchase" is defined by I.R.C. § 179(d)(2) to include acquisitions of property other than acquisitions from certain related persons and acquisitions in certain nonrecognition transactions, by gift, or from a decedent (if the basis is determined under I.R.C. § 1014). I.R.C. § 179(d)(2)(A)–(C).

Some real property also qualifies as "Section 179 property." The definition is not limited to personal property but applies to "section 1245 property" which includes some real property (see I.R.C. § 1245(a)(3)). In addition, "qualified real property" and certain property defined in I.R.C. 50(b)(2) related to property used to provide lodging, are both § 179 property.

[32] I.R.C. § 1016(a)(2). See page 399, supra.

provisions in Section 168.[33] The reduction precludes a double depreciation deduction.[34]

The benefits of any deduction allowed under Section 179 with respect to a property must be recaptured if such property is no longer used predominantly in the taxpayer's trade or business.[35]

*Section 280F Limitations on "Luxury" Automobiles.* The *current* MACRS system fixes a five-year recovery period for automobiles;[36] but Congress has decided that depreciating expensive, "luxury" cars over such a short period is too much of a good thing. Congress has also decided that the Section 168(k) 100-percent depreciation allowance should not be fully available for luxury cars.[37] So under Section 280F(a), the life of such cars is in effect extended by allowing a maximum of $52,880 ($60,880 if the Section 168(k) allowance is claimed) of cost recovery over the usual six-year period, adjusted for inflation for years after 2018.[38] Disregarding inflation adjustments, this may be claimed $10,000 in year one ($18,000 if the Section 168(k) allowance is claimed), $16,000 in year two, $9,600 in year three, and $5,760 in years four, five and six.[39] To the extent that a car is luxurious (costs more than the $52,880 or $60,880 figures), disregarding inflation, a maximum amount of $5,760 can be written off in each year following the first six years during which the taxpayer continues to use the car in a depreciable capacity,[40] until of course the acquisition basis is exhausted. If in any year of its depreciable life the car

---

[33]  See I.R.C. § 179(a) and note 23, supra. Cf. I.R.C. § 1016(a)(2).

[34]  If the property is held for its full recovery period, I.R.C. § 179 does not change the total amount of deductions a taxpayer may take with respect to a particular piece of property; it simply changes the timing of the taxpayer's cost recovery. Thus, if property is held for its full recovery period, a taxpayer will recover its entire cost, and no more, whether or not § 179 is elected. For example, assume that in 2018 a taxpayer places a machine in service which costs $1 million and is eligible for the § 179 deduction and the taxpayer purchases no other eligible property during the year. The taxpayer may deduct the full $1 million under I.R.C. § 168(k) or may elect to treat the entire $1 million cost of the machine as a § 179 deduction. However, because the "adjusted basis" of the machine will be zero, the taxpayer has no further basis to depreciate and can take no further § 168 deductions. If the machine costs $1.5 million, the taxpayer can deduct the full $1.5 million under § 168(k) or can elect to "expense" $1 million under § 179, and compute the other § 168 deductions using an "adjusted basis" of $500,000.

[35]  I.R.C. § 179(d)(10). See Reg. § 1.179–1(e).

[36]  I.R.C. § 168(e)(3)(B)(i).

[37]  See I.R.C. § 168(k)(2)(F) which increases the first-year allowance under I.R.C. § 280F(a)(1)(A) by $8,000.

[38]  The $52,880 amount (but not the $8,000 amount) is adjusted by an "automobile price inflation adjustment" rounded to the nearest $100 for years after 2018. I.R.C. § 280F(d)(7).

The dollar limitations are also essentially applicable to automobiles that are leased as well as to automobiles that are purchased. See I.R.C. § 280F(c).

[39]  I.R.C. § 280F(a)(2)(A).

[40]  I.R.C. § 280F(a)(2)(A)(iv).

is used only a portion of the time for business,[41] only that portion of the potential deduction is allowed.[42]

*Section 280F Limitations on "Listed Property".* Section 280F also limits MACRS deductions allowed on certain other "listed property" that has a business use of 50 percent or less[43] (i.e., is not used predominantly for business purposes in the taxable year). "Listed property" includes: passenger automobiles and other property used as a means of transportation as well as property generally used for entertainment, recreation, or amusement purposes.[44] Listed property with a business use of 50 percent or less, can be depreciated using only the alternative depreciation system of Section 168(g).[45] For example, five-year property used less than 50 percent in business must be depreciated using the straight-line method over a recovery period generally equal to its A.D.R. class life of between five and nine years.[46] There are several special rules here.[47] For example, automobiles continue to be specifically assigned a 5-year recovery period for the alternative depreciation system.[48]

To add to the pain, if the *more-than-50-percent* test is met for the year that a listed property is placed in service, but is not met in a subsequent year, all excess depreciation claimed in the first and subsequent years over the depreciation that would have been allowed using the alternative depreciation system is recaptured as gross income in the subsequent year.[49]

The Service appropriately requires that taxpayers substantiate the use of listed property by adequate, contemporaneous records. If a taxpayer does not keep such records the taxpayer loses the benefits of the depreciation deduction and may be vulnerable to added liability for negligence or possibly even fraud.[50] The records must reflect with substantial accuracy the business use of the property and indicate its business purposes, unless the purpose is clear from the surrounding circumstances. For example, in regard to automobiles, logs must be kept which show the date and mileage of trips for business purposes.

---

[41] If the portion is 50% or less, the listed property limitations come into play. See the discussion below.

[42] Cf. Sharp v. United States, 199 F.Supp. 743 (D.Del.1961), affirmed 303 F.2d 783 (3d Cir.1962) at page 404, supra. Any nondepreciable portion related to nonbusiness use may not be written off as a deduction in a succeeding year. Cf. I.R.C. § 262(a).

[43] I.R.C. § 280F(b)(1).

[44] I.R.C. § 280F(d)(4). The regulations may add similar types of property to the list. I.R.C. § 280F(d)(4)(A)(vi). In general, any use of listed property in connection with the performance of services by an employee is not considered business use, unless the use is for the convenience of the employer and is required as a condition of employment. I.R.C. § 280F(d)(3).

[45] I.R.C. § 280F(b)(1).

[46] I.R.C. § 168(g)(2)(C). See I.R.C. § 168(e)(1).

[47] I.R.C. § 168(g)(3).

[48] I.R.C. § 168(g)(3)(D).

[49] I.R.C. § 280F(b)(2).

[50] I.R.C. §§ 274(d)(3); 6662; 6663.

*Additional Thoughts.* We have explored numerous intricate rules with respect to depreciation of tangible personal property. The problems below test your ability to apply those rules. But first, take a moment to reflect both on Congressional policy in this area and on the interrelationship of the relevant sections. Under the 2017 Tax Cuts and Jobs Act, Congress generally allows most tangible personal property to be expensed in the year in which it is placed in service. As a practical matter, Section 168(k) alleviates the need to deal with the other intricate MACRS rules. If a taxpayer either elects out of Section 168(k) (or cannot use it), then the appropriate order to apply the other provisions is first Section 179, then the rules in Section 168 (other than (k)), and, finally, the limitations in Section 280F.

## Amortization of Intangible Personal Property

Amortization permits a ratable write-off of the basis of an intangible asset over the useful life of the asset. The deduction is similar to straight-line depreciation.[51] Historically, there has been considerable controversy with respect to the useful lives of many types of intangible assets. In the case of a subscribers' list in a newspaper merger, the Supreme Court held that the acquisition cost of the list is amortizable if the taxpayer could prove that the asset can be valued and that the asset has a limited useful life which can be ascertained with reasonable accuracy.[52] But the Court acknowledged that the taxpayer's burden of proof is significant and that it "often will prove too great to bear."[53] Congress, recognizing that the Supreme Court test would lead not only to a substantial amount of controversy, but seemingly also to extremely speculative costs to the fisc,[54] enacted Section 197 to simplify the law and to specify a single method and period for recovering the cost of most acquired intangible assets.

Under the provision, the adjusted basis of any "Section 197 intangible" which is "acquired" by a taxpayer in connection with the conduct of a trade or business or an activity engaged in for the production of income may be amortized over a 15-year period beginning with the month in which the asset is acquired.[55] The asset must be "acquired" by the taxpayer; thus Section 197 is generally inapplicable to an asset that is self-created by the taxpayer.[56]

The term "Section 197 intangible" to which the 15-year amortization rule applies includes a broad range of intangible assets some of which were previously not amortizable. It includes goodwill (value attributable

---

[51] See Reg. § 1.167(a)–3 and note 30, at page 400, supra.

[52] Newark Morning Ledger Co. v. United States, 507 U.S. 546, 113 S.Ct. 1670 (1993).

[53] Id. at 566, 113 S.Ct. at 1681.

[54] H.R. 2141, 103rd Cong., 1st Sess. 322 (1993).

[55] I.R.C. § 197(a), (c)(1). No other depreciation or amortization deduction is allowed with respect to such assets. I.R.C. § 197(b). Cf. I.R.C. § 195(b)(1)(B) considered in Chapter 14B3, supra.

[56] I.R.C. § 197(c)(2). But see I.R.C. § 197(d)(1)(D)–(F).

to expectation of continued customer patronage); going concern value (value attributable to the fact that the property involves a going concern); certain specified types of intangible property that generally relate to workforce (composition of the workforce), information base (customer or subscription lists, etc.), know-how (patents, copyrights, etc.); any license, permit, or other right granted by the governmental unit or agency or instrumentality thereof; any covenant not to compete or similar arrangement;[57] and any franchise, trademark, or trade name.[58] The term does not include a variety of items, including a financial interest in a corporation, a partnership, or a trust or estate.[59] Section 197 also contains a variety of specialized rules that are not detailed here.[60]

The 15-year amortization period is employed elsewhere in the Code. Recall that Section 195 provides that nondeductible start-up expenditures are amortized over a 15-year period.[61] The regulations on capitalization of amounts to create or enhance intangible assets[62] also provide a 15-year safe harbor amortization period[63] for certain created or enhanced intangible assets that do not have readily ascertainable useful lives.[64] For example, this rule would apply to a payment for a membership or privilege of an unlimited duration.[65] Amortization under the 15-year safe harbor rule uses the straight line method with no salvage value.[66] These rules apply in the absence of some other rule that specifically prescribes the amortization period for the asset.[67]

## PROBLEMS

1. On January 2 of the current year for $300,000 Depreciator purchases new equipment for use in her business. The purchase is made from an unrelated person. The equipment has a 6-year class life and is 5-year property under § 168(c). Depreciator plans to use the equipment for seven years, and expects it to have a salvage value of $30,000 at the end of that time. Depreciator is a single, calendar year taxpayer, and she uses the equipment *only* in her business.

In the following problems, compute the depreciation deductions with respect to the equipment in each of the first two years of its use and

---

[57] Thus even if the time period involved is less than 15 years, the covenant must be written off over 15 years. See Reg. § 1.197–2(k) Example 6.

[58] I.R.C. § 197(d)(1)(A)–(F). See H.R. 2141, note 54 supra at 324–328, for detailed examples of I.R.C. § 197 intangibles. See also I.R.C. § 197(d)(2) and (3).

[59] I.R.C. § 197(e). See I.R.C. § 167(f) and (g) which may be applicable when § 197 is inapplicable.

[60] I.R.C. § 197(f).

[61] I.R.C. § 195(b)(1)(B). See Chapter 14B3, supra.

[62] See page 331, supra.

[63] Reg. § 1.167(a)–3(b).

[64] Reg. § 1.167(a)–3(b)(1)(iii).

[65] Preamble to Proposed Regulations, 67 Fed. Reg. 77701, 77709 (Dec. 19, 2002).

[66] Reg. § 1.167(a)–3(b)(3).

[67] Reg. § 1.167(a)–3(b)(1)(i).

determine Depreciator's adjusted basis for the equipment at the end of each of those years.

(a)　Depreciator does not elect out of § 168(k).

(b)　Depreciator elects out of § 168(k), but also elects to use § 179. Assume Depreciator satisfies the § 179 requirements and has no other § 179 property in the year.

(c)　Depreciator elects out of § 168(k) and does not elect § 179.

(d)　Same as (c), above, except that Depreciator elects under § 168(b)(5) to use the straight-line method for the equipment and all other property in its class placed in service during the year.

(e)　Same as (c), above, except that the equipment has a 6-year class life and Depreciator elects to use the § 168(g) alternative depreciation system for the equipment and all other property in its class placed in service during the year.

(f)　Depreciator purchases the equipment, which is used property, from an unrelated party and does not elect out of § 168(k).

(g)　Same as (f), above, except that Depreciator purchases the equipment from Depreciator's sister. In general, what result?

**2.**　Hi Roller buys a "luxury" automobile for business and personal use at a cost of $65,000 in the current year. Assume there is no inflation after 2018. (see § 280F(d)(7)).

(a)　Compute the maximum depreciation deductions available to Hi assuming § 168(k) applies and there is no personal use of the car.

(b)　What results to Hi under the facts of (a), above, if the car is used for business purposes the following percentages of the time in the following years: year one 70%; year two 80%; year three 70%; year four and later 60% each year.

(c)　What general result (no computations) to Hi in (b), above, if in years four and following the automobile is used only 50% for business use?

**3.**　Vic purchased a restaurant from Owner and made the following payments as part of that purchase or in starting the restaurant. Determine the deductibility of Vic's payments:

(a)　A payment to Owner for goodwill.

(b)　A payment to Owner for a covenant not to compete lasting for a five-year period.

(c)　A payment to the media to advertise the restaurant.

(d)　A payment to Owner to buy Owner's restaurant franchise.

(e)　A payment to the state to acquire a liquor license that has a five-year life. See Reg. § 1.197–2(c)(13). What if (perhaps unrealistically) the liquor license is extended indefinitely?

**4.** Law Student incurs $3,000 in expenses to take a Bar Review course and $500 in Bar Admission fees. Discuss the deductibility of the expenses. See Reg. §§ 1.162–5(b)(2)(iii) Example 3, 1.263(a)–4(d)(5)(ii) Example 2.

## 3. DEPRECIATION RULES FOR REALTY

Internal Revenue Code: Sections 168(a), (b)(3)(A), (B), and (G), (4), (c), (d)(2) and (4)(B), (e)(2) and (6), (g)(1)(E), (2), and (7); 179(f). See Sections 42; 46(1); 47(a) and (c).

———————

*General Rules.* Under MACRS, real estate is classified as either "residential rental property"[1] or "nonresidential real property."[2] Both types of real property must be depreciated using only the straight-line method[3] and in making the straight-line computation, residential rental property is assigned a 27.5-year life, while nonresidential real property is assigned a 39-year life.[4] The alternative depreciation system may be elected with respect to both types of property. Under that system, residential rental property is assigned a 30-year life and nonresidential real property is assigned a 40-year life.[5] As always under MACRS, salvage value is disregarded.[6]

Rental property is classified as "residential" only if 80 percent or more of the gross rental income from a building is from dwelling units.[7] The Code further provides that "dwelling units" do not include units in a building, such as a hotel, in which more than one-half of the units are used on a transient basis.[8] Generally, all other depreciable real estate falls into the nonresidential real property classification.[9]

The depreciation of these two classifications of real property under MACRS varies in several ways from the depreciation of tangible personal property. As seen above, only the straight-line depreciation method is available to real estate.[10] An election to use the alternative depreciation system is made on a property by property, not a class by class basis.[11] In addition, for the year such real property is placed in service, rather than applying the half-year convention, which generally applies to tangible

———————

[1] See I.R.C. § 168(e)(2)(A).

[2] See I.R.C. § 168(e)(2)(B). Real property with a class life of less than 27.5 years is not nonresidential real property.

[3] I.R.C. § 168(b)(3)(A) and (B).

[4] I.R.C. § 168(c).

[5] I.R.C. § 168(g)(2)(C). Recall that only straight-line depreciation is available under the alternative depreciation system.

[6] I.R.C. § 168(b)(4) and (g)(2)(A).

[7] I.R.C. § 168(e)(2)(A)(i).

[8] I.R.C. § 168(e)(2)(A)(ii)(I).

[9] I.R.C. § 168(e)(2)(B). Some real property used in business may be assigned a class life of less than 27.5 years; it is not subjected to the above rules. I.R.C. § 168(e)(2)(B)(ii). See Rev.Rul. 83–35, 1983–1 C.B. 745.

[10] I.R.C. § 168(b)(3)(A) and (B).

[11] I.R.C. § 168(g)(7)(A). Cf. I.R.C. § 168(b)(5).

personal property, depreciation deductions are allowed for the property according to a "mid-month convention" allowing depreciation beginning in the middle of the month for the month that the property is first placed in service.[12] Similarly, such real property is depreciable in the year of disposition only for the months during which the property was held by the taxpayer (again using a mid-month convention).[13] Finally, the longer lives and the mandatory straight-line depreciation method applicable to these two classifications of real estate provide no incentive to churn such property. Accordingly, the MACRS anti-churning rules are inapplicable to such real property.[14]

*Qualified Improvement Property.* If a taxpayer already owns depreciable real property and wants to remodel or improve it, is the improvement recovered using straight-line depreciation over the normal 27.5 or 39 year recovery periods? In some situations the answer is "yes," but if the property is qualified improvement property, special rules potentially (we will get to the "potentially" soon) apply. Qualified improvement property is defined as any improvement to the interior portion of a building which is *nonresidential* real property if such improvement is placed in service after the date the building was first placed in service.[15] But a qualified improvement does not include any improvement for which the expenditure is attributable to enlargement of the building, any elevator or escalator, or the structural framework of the building.[16]

It appears from the legislative history to 2017 Tax Cuts and Jobs Act,[17] that Congress intended for qualified improvement property to have a 15-year recovery period under MACRS. The problem is that the Code was not amended to make that change. Thus, as the Code reads today, qualified improvement property is recovered over 39 years. One expects (hopes?) for a technical correction to remedy the problem. Assuming that occurs, qualified improvement property may be written off over a 15-year period using the straight-line method.[18] If qualified improvement property is assigned a 15-year recovery period, it would be eligible for the Section 168(k) 100-percent special allowance.[19] Since property under Section 168(k) generally must have a recovery period of 20 years or less and until Section 168 is amended to give qualified improvement property a 15-year recovery period, it does not satisfy that requirement and does not qualify for Section 168(k).

---

[12] I.R.C. § 168(d)(2) and (4)(B).

[13] I.R.C. § 168(d)(4)(B) parentheticals.

[14] I.R.C. § 168(f)(5)(B)(i).

[15] I.R.C. § 168(e)(6)(A).

[16] I.R.C. § 168(e)(6)(B).

[17] H. Rep. No. 115–466, Joint Explanatory Statement, 115–97, 115th Cong., 1st Sess. 205 (2017).

[18] I.R.C. § 168(b)(3)(G).

[19] Cf. I.R.C. § 168(k)(2)(A)(i)(I).

*Qualified Real Property.* Certain real property ("Qualified Real Property") may be expensed under the rules in Section 179.[20] Qualified real property includes qualified improvement property.[21] In addition, qualified real property includes expenditures to nonresidential real property for roofs, heating, ventilation, air-conditioning property, and fire protection and alarms.[22]

*Rehabilitation Credit.* Congress has traditionally provided two additional sets of rules to encourage investment in special types of real estate to achieve two quite different goals. The first goal is to encourage investment in the rehabilitation of historically significant real estate. Costs incurred in the restoration of older depreciable real property qualify for an investment credit[23] if various requirements are met.[24] Congress allows a credit equal to 20 percent[25] of the "qualified rehabilitation expenditures"[26] of restoration of a "certified historic structure."[27] Section 47(c)(1) imposes various requirements related to the type and the cost of rehabilitation of the property to qualify for the credit, including a requirement that the rehabilitation costs must exceed the greater of the adjusted basis of the building or $5,000. If a rehabilitation credit is allowed, it is claimed ratably over five years, although the basis of the property is reduced by the full amount of the credit prior to its depreciation under MACRS.[28]

*Low-Income Housing Credit.* The second set of rules is aimed at encouraging investment in low income housing. The rules allow credits for costs incurred by owners of residential rental property which qualifies as "low income housing." The low income housing credit is subject to myriad rules[29] but, if both the property and the expenditure qualify, the owner of the property qualifies for a substantial tax benefit. For construction costs of new property or rehabilitation costs of used property placed in service, a total credit equivalent to 70 percent of the present value of the qualified basis of the property is allowed over a 10-year period if the low income units are conventionally financed;[30] if the costs are financed with tax exempt bonds or some other similar type of federal subsidiaries, a credit equivalent to 30 percent of the present value is

---

[20]  I.R.C. § 179(d)(1)(B)(ii), (f).

[21]  I.R.C. § 179(f)(1).

[22]  I.R.C. § 179(f)(2).

[23]  I.R.C. § 46(1). The investment credit is subject to a number of special rules and is itself a part of the general business credit. I.R.C. § 38. See page 952, infra.

[24]  I.R.C. § 47(c) and (d).

[25]  I.R.C. § 47(a)(2).

[26]  I.R.C. § 47(c)(2).

[27]  I.R.C. § 47(c)(3).

[28]  I.R.C. §§ 47(a), 50(c)(1).

[29]  See generally I.R.C. § 42. See Callison, "New Tax Credit for Low-Income Housing Provides Investment Incentive," 66 J.Tax'n 100 (1987); Racaniello, "Extending the Low-Income Housing Tax Credit: An Empirical Analysis," 22 Rutgers L.J. 753 (1991).

[30]  I.R.C. § 42(a), (b)(1)(A), (b)(2)(B)(i), and (f)(1).

allowed over a 10-year period.[31] The actual annual percentages to achieve these results are determined by the Service.[32] In qualified census tracts and difficult development areas,[33] 70-percent and 30-percent amounts may be increased to 91-percent and 39-percent.[34] An indirect benefit here is that the property's basis for depreciation purposes is not reduced by the credits claimed.[35] Thus the full cost qualifies for depreciation deductions as well. Pay dirt?! The credit would be no more than a fitting reward for mastering the reams of statute involved! Not quite. Certainly the credit is a good deal, *but* not quite so good as it looks. As stated above, there are lots of technical requirements which must be satisfied.[36] Among them, stringent limits are imposed on the rents one can charge for the use of such property.[37] Thus, the tax advantages, which are tremendous, may be balanced by reduced revenues from the investment. Nevertheless, if we are to depart from purely revenue objectives for the tax laws, we have here a commendable Congressional goal for which investors still may be well rewarded.

Both of the above credits are part of the general business credit which is considered in Chapter 27B, infra and which imposes further possible limits upon their utility. Additionally, both are potentially subject to the passive investment activities credit limitation, considered in Chapter 17D, infra.

## PROBLEM

1. During the current year, Depreciator purchases a piece of new improved real property at a cost of $130,000 of which $100,000 is attributable to the building and $30,000 to the land. Depreciator immediately rents the property to others. Compute Depreciator's depreciation in the subsequent year in the following situations:

(a) The building is an apartment building.

(b) The building is an office building.

(c) The buildings in (a) and (b), above, are used, not new, property and were purchased from Depreciator's sister who originally purchased them in 1982.

---

[31] I.R.C. § 42(a), (b)(1)(B)(ii), and (f)(1).

[32] I.R.C. § 42(b)(1)(B). A special rule provides that in the case of conventionally financed low-income housing the annual percentage allowed shall not be less than 9 percent. I.R.C. § 42(b)(2).

[33] I.R.C. § 42(d)(5)(B)(ii) and (iii).

[34] I.R.C. § 42(d)(5)(B)(i). This result occurs because taxpayers are allowed a 70 or 30 percent credit of 130 percent of their basis. Id. A "qualified census tract" is an area in which 50 percent or more of the households have an income which is less than 60 percent of the area median gross income. I.R.C. § 42(d)(5)(B)(ii). A "difficult development area" is an area which has high construction, land or utility costs relative to area median gross income. I.R.C. § 42(d)(5)(B)(iii).

[35] Conf.Rep. No. 99–841, 99th Cong., 2d Sess. II–103 (1986), reprinted in 1986–3 C.B. Vol. 4 at 103. Cf. I.R.C. § 50(c)(1) and (3).

[36] See generally I.R.C. § 42(c)(2), (g), (h), (i), (k) and (*l*).

[37] I.R.C. § 42(g)(1).

(d)  Depreciator elects the alternative depreciation system with respect to the buildings in (a) and (b), above.

(e)  Some years later, $150,000 is spent to make "qualified improvements" to the buildings in (a) and (b), above.

(f)  Some years later, $100,000 is spent to rehabilitate the internal structural framework of the buildings in (a) and (b), above, which are certified historic structures built in 1940.

# CHAPTER 15

# DEDUCTIONS FOR PROFIT-MAKING, NONBUSINESS ACTIVITIES

## A. SECTION 212 EXPENSES

Internal Revenue Code: Section 212; 274(h)(7). See Sections 62(a), 67(b) and (g).

Regulations: Sections 1.212–1(g), (k), (*l*), (m); 1.262–1(b)(7).

---

### Higgins v. Commissioner

Supreme Court of the United States, 1941.
312 U.S. 212, 61 S.Ct. 475.

■ MR. JUSTICE REED delivered the opinion of the Court.

Petitioner, the taxpayer, with extensive investments in real estate, bonds and stocks, devoted a considerable portion of his time to the oversight of his interests and hired others to assist him in offices rented for that purpose. For the tax years in question, 1932 and 1933, he claimed the salaries and expenses incident to looking after his properties were deductible under § 23(a) of the Revenue Act of 1932.[1] The Commissioner refused the deductions. The applicable phrases are: "In computing net income there shall be allowed as deductions: (a) *Expenses.*—All the ordinary and necessary expenses paid or incurred during the taxable year in carrying on any trade or business * * *." There is no dispute over whether the claimed deductions are ordinary and necessary expenses. As the Commissioner also conceded before the Board of Tax Appeals that the real estate activities of the petitioner in renting buildings[2] constituted a business, the Board allowed such portions of the claimed deductions as were fairly allocable to the handling of the real estate. The same offices and staffs handled both real estate and security matters. After this adjustment there remained for the year 1932 over twenty and for the year 1933 over sixteen thousand dollars expended for managing the stocks and bonds.

Petitioner's financial affairs were conducted through his New York office pursuant to his personal detailed instructions. His residence was

---

[1]  47 Stat. 169, c. 209 [The parallel language in the 1986 Internal Revenue Code is of course found in § 162(a). Ed.]

[2]  Cf. Pinchot v. Commissioner, 113 F.2d 718.

in Paris, France, where he had a second office. By cable, telephone and mail, petitioner kept a watchful eye over his securities. While he sought permanent investments, changes, redemptions, maturities and accumulations caused limited shiftings in his portfolio. These were made under his own orders. The offices kept records, received securities, interest and dividend checks, made deposits, forwarded weekly and annual reports and undertook generally the care of the investments as instructed by the owner. Purchases were made by a financial institution. Petitioner did not participate directly or indirectly in the management of the corporations in which he held stock or bonds. The method of handling his affairs under examination had been employed by petitioner for more than thirty years. No objection to the deductions had previously been made by the Government.

The Board of Tax Appeals[3] held that these activities did not constitute carrying on a business and that the expenses were capable of apportionment between the real estate and the investments. The Circuit Court of Appeals affirmed,[4] and we granted certiorari because of conflict.[5]

Petitioner urges that the "elements of continuity, constant repetition, regularity and extent" differentiate his activities from the occasional like actions of the small investor. His activity is and the occasional action is not "carrying on business." On the other hand, the respondent urges that "mere personal investment activities never constitute carrying on a trade or business, no matter how much of one's time or of one's employees' time they may occupy."

Since the first income tax act, the provisions authorizing business deductions have varied only slightly. The Revenue Act of 1913[6] allowed as a deduction "the necessary expenses actually paid in carrying on any business." By 1918 the present form was fixed and has so continued.[7] No regulation has ever been promulgated which interprets the meaning of "carrying on a business," nor any rulings approved by the Secretary of the Treasury, i.e., Treasury Decisions.[8] Certain rulings of less dignity, favorable to petitioner,[9] appeared in individual cases but they are not determinative.[10] Even acquiescence[11] in some Board rulings after defeat does not amount to settled administrative practice.[12] Unless the

---

[3]   39 B.T.A. 1005.

[4]   111 F.2d 795.

[5]   Kales v. Commissioner, 101 F.2d 35; du Pont v. Deputy, 103 F.2d 257.

[6]   38 Stat. 167, § IIB.

[7]   40 Stat. 1066, § 214(a)(1).

[8]   Cf. Helvering v. New York Trust Co., 292 U.S. 455, 467–468, 54 S.Ct. 806, 809–810.

[9]   O.D. 537, 2 C.B. 175 (1920); O.D. 877, 4 C.B. 123 (1921); I.T. 2751, XIII–1 C.B. 43 (1934). See also 1934 C.C.H. Federal Tax Service, Vol. 3, ¶ 6035, p. 8027.

[10]   Biddle v. Commissioner, 302 U.S. 573, 582, 58 S.Ct. 379, 383. Cf. Estate of Sanford v. Commissioner, 308 U.S. 39, 52, 60 S.Ct. 51, 59. But see Helvering v. Bliss, 293 U.S. 144, 151, 55 S.Ct. 17, 20, and McFeely v. Commissioner, 296 U.S. 102, 108, 56 S.Ct. 54, 57.

[11]   Kissel v. Commissioner, 15 B.T.A. 1270, acquiesced in VIII–2 C.B. 28 (1929); Croker v. Commissioner, 27 B.T.A. 588, acquiesced in XII–1 C.B. 4 (1933).

[12]   Higgins v. Smith, 308 U.S. 473, 478–479, 60 S.Ct. 355, 358.

administrative practice is long continued and substantially uniform in the Bureau and without challenge by the Government in the Board and courts, it should not be assumed, from rulings of this class, that Congressional reenactment of the language which they construed was an adoption of their interpretation.

While the Commissioner has combated views similar to petitioner's in the courts, sometimes successfully[13] and sometimes unsuccessfully,[14] the petitioner urges that the Bureau accepted for years the doctrine that the management of one's own securities might be a business where there was sufficient extent, continuity, variety and regularity. We fail to find such a fixed administrative construction in the examples cited. It is true that the decisions are frequently put on the ground that the taxpayer's activities were sporadic but it does not follow that had those activities been continuous the Commissioner would not have used the argument advanced here, i.e., that no amount of personal investment management would turn those activities into a business. Evidently such was the Government's contention in the *Kales,* cases,[15] where the things the taxpayer did met petitioner's tests, and in Foss v. Commissioner[16] and Washburn v. Commissioner[17] where the opinions turned on the extent of the taxpayer's participation in the management of the corporations in which investments were held.[18]

Petitioner relies strongly on the definition of business in Flint v. Stone Tracy Company:[19] " 'Business' is a very comprehensive term and embraces everything about which a person can be employed." This definition was given in considering whether certain corporations came under the Corporation Tax law which levies a tax on corporations engaged in business. The immediate issue was whether corporations engaged principally in the "holding and management of real estate"[20] were subject to the act. A definition given for such an issue is not controlling in this dissimilar inquiry.[21]

To determine whether the activities of a taxpayer are "carrying on a business" requires an examination of the facts in each case. As the Circuit Court of Appeals observed, all expenses of every business transaction are not deductible. Only those are deductible which relate to carrying on a business. The Bureau of Internal Revenue has this duty of determining

---

[13] Bedell v. Commissioner, 30 F.2d 622, 624; Monell v. Helvering, 70 F.2d 631; Kane v. Commissioner, 100 F.2d 382.

[14] Kales v. Commissioner, 101 F.2d 35; du Pont v. Deputy, 103 F.2d 257, 259, reversed on other grounds, 308 U.S. 488, 60 S.Ct. 363.

[15] Kales v. Commissioner, 34 B.T.A. 1046, 101 F.2d 35.

[16] 75 F.2d 326.

[17] 51 F.2d 949, 953.

[18] Cf. Roebling v. Commissioner, 37 B.T.A. 82; Heilbroner v. Commissioner, 34 B.T.A. 1200.

[19] 220 U.S. 107, 171, 31 S.Ct. 342, 357.

[20] Id. 169.

[21] Cohens v. Virginia, 6 Wheat. 264, 399; Puerto Rico v. Shell Co., 302 U.S. 253, 269, 58 S.Ct. 167, 174.

what is carrying on a business, subject to reexamination of the facts by the Board of Tax Appeals[22] and ultimately to review on the law by the courts on which jurisdiction is conferred.[23] The Commissioner and the Board appraised the evidence here as insufficient to establish petitioner's activities as those of carrying on a business. The petitioner merely kept records and collected interest and dividends from his securities, through managerial attention for his investments. No matter how large the estate or how continuous or extended the work required may be, such facts are not sufficient as a matter of law to permit the courts to reverse the decision of the Board. Its conclusion is adequately supported by this record, and rests upon a conception of carrying on business similar to that expressed by this Court for an antecedent section.[24]

The petitioner makes the point that his activities in managing his estate, both realty and personalty, were a unified business. Since it was admittedly a business in so far as the realty is concerned, he urges, there is no statutory authority to sever expenses allocable to the securities. But we see no reason why expenses not attributable, as we have just held these are not, to carrying on business cannot be apportioned. It is not unusual to allocate expenses paid for services partly personal and partly business.[25]

Affirmed.

## NOTE

The congressional reaction to the *Higgins* decision was negative. But, instead of attempting to mitigate the problem by defining a trade or business as including income-producing activity, Congress enacted what is now Section 212(1) and (2) as part of the Revenue Act of 1942.[1] Subparagraph (3) of Section 212 first appeared with the enactment of the Internal Revenue Code of 1954.[2]

If a bridge is needed here from a preoccupation with trade or business problems in Chapter 14, it is the question: All right, we do not fit the trade or business requirements of Section 162; so what? Is there, nevertheless a proper basis for asserting deductibility? Our inquiry here carries us primarily into Section 212[3] where "the production [or collection] of income" test replaces that of the "trade or business" concept of Section 162. The *Higgins* background of Section 212 supports the other similarities of Sections 162 and 212; note especially that in either case it is only "expenses" that are "ordinary and necessary" which are deductible.

---

[22]   Revenue Act of 1932, 47 Stat. 169, § 272; Internal Revenue Code, § 272.

[23]   Internal Revenue Code, § 1141.

[24]   Van Wart v. Commissioner, 295 U.S. 112, 115, 55 S.Ct. 660.

[25]   3 Paul & Mertens, Law of Federal Income Taxation § 23.65; cf. National Outdoor Advertising Bureau v. Helvering, 89 F.2d 878, 881.

[1]   § 121, 55 Stat. 798, 819 (1942).

[2]   Paragraph (3) was prompted by the decision in Lykes v. United States, 343 U.S. 118, 72 S.Ct. 585 (1952) which, essentially, it overruled.

[3]   Further possibilities are explored in Chapters 16, 18, and 23, infra.

What Congress grants, it also can take away! The congressional finger-crossing that occurs with respect to an employee's Section 162 trade or business expenses[4] is also true with respect to many of an investor's Section 212 expenses. Today, Mr. Higgins' expenses in connection with his bonds and stocks would qualify for a deduction under Section 212, but that does not mean that those expenses would also reduce his taxable income and tax liability. As with employee business expenses, unless Mr. Higgin's Section 212 expenses are described in Section 62(a), or are specifically listed in Section 67(b), they will not be allowed in computing his taxable income.[5] Similarly, the Section 212(3) deduction is disallowed in computing taxable income.[6] The question of whether Section 212 deductions actually reduce taxable income is considered in Chapter 18C. The preliminary question, considered here, is whether a Section 212 deduction is initially allowed.

Other quasi-business deductions crop up in this chapter as well. A question may be whether a loss is one that, if not in business, arises out of a "transaction entered into for profit" as that phrase is used in Section 165(c)(2). If one is seeking income (Section 212), is one engaged in a transaction entered into for profit (Section 165(c)(2)), and vice versa? It is worth noting here that in other respects Section 165 clearly differs from Section 212 (and Section 162), not being concerned with "expenses" or the question whether what occurred was "ordinary" or "necessary." A related problem is whether property is "held for the production of income" so as to be subject to depreciation under Section 167(a)(2),[7] even if not used in a trade or business.[8]

Problems of the kind dealt with here cover a wide range of human activity and, thinking in terms of two of the cases that follow, it may be difficult to see that Mr. Surasky's proxy expenses (he won) have very much in common with those involved in Mr. Fleischman's divorce (he lost). However, if the following materials are approached with the underlying statutory concepts in mind they will not only appear less fragmentary, but they will also supply a basis for dealing with many other problems not specifically presented here.

## Bowers v. Lumpkin

United States Court of Appeals, Fourth Circuit, 1944.
140 F.2d 927, cert. denied 322 U.S. 755, 64 S.Ct. 1266 (1944).

■ SOPER, CIRCUIT JUDGE.

This suit was brought by Mrs. Lumpkin to recover individual federal income taxes alleged to have been overpaid for the years 1936 and 1937.

---

[4]   See page 341, supra.

[5]   I.R.C. § 67(g).

[6]   Id.

[7]   See Chapter 14E, supra.

[8]   These related concepts are ably discussed by Kilbourn, "Deductible Expenses: Transactions Entered into for Profit: Income-Producing Property," 21 N.Y.U. Inst. on Fed.Tax. 193 (1963). See also Lang, "The Scope of Deductions Under Section 212," 7 Rev. of Tax. of Inds. 291 (1983).

It was tried before the District Judge without a jury and resulted in a judgment for the plaintiff in the sum of $22,680.10. The taxpayer had a life interest under a trust created for her benefit by the will of her former husband in one-half of the stock of a corporation which owned valuable rights in the sale and distribution of coca cola syrup in South Carolina. She purchased the remaining stock of the corporation for $255,885 from trustees to whom it had been bequeathed to establish and maintain an orphanage. The Attorney General of South Carolina instituted an action to invalidate the sale and require the taxpayer to account for profits and the taxpayer was obliged to defend the suit in the courts of South Carolina where she finally won a decision upholding the sale. In connection with this litigation she incurred expenses of $250 in 1936 and $26,798.22 in 1937 which she deducted from gross income in preparing her income tax returns for these years. The Commissioner of Internal Revenue disallowed the deductions and assessed additional taxes and interest of $155 for 1936 and $19,187.72 for 1937, which were paid under protest and form the basis of the instant suit.

The taxpayer relies upon § 121(a) of the Revenue Act of 1942, * * *, which amended § 23(a) of the Internal Revenue Code, 53 Stat. 12, whereby all the ordinary and necessary expenses of carrying on a trade or business were allowed as deductions from gross income. The Act of 1942 broadened the scope of allowable deductions by adding amongst others the following subsection to § 23(a):

> "(2) Non-trade or non-business expenses. In the case of an individual, all the ordinary and necessary expenses paid or incurred during the taxable year for the production or collection of income, or for the management, conservation, or maintenance of property held for the production of income."*

This amendment was made retroactive by the following provision:

> "(e) Retroactive Amendment to Prior Revenue Acts.—For the purposes of the Revenue Act of 1938 or any prior revenue Act the amendments made to the Internal Revenue Code by this section shall be effective as if they were a part of such revenue Act on the date of its enactment." * * *.

The purpose of this amendment was to permit deductions for certain non-trade and non-business expenses and thereby enlarge the allowable deduction for expenses which under previous revenue acts had been confined to expenses paid or incurred in carrying on any trade or business. Under the earlier statutes it had been held that investors not engaged in the investment business could not deduct expenses such as salaries, clerk hire or office rent incurred in connection with the earning or collection of taxable income, or in looking after one's own investments in stocks and bonds. See, Higgins v. Commissioner, 312 U.S. 212, 61 S.Ct. 475, decided February 3, 1941. To mitigate the harshness of this rule

---

\*    See I.R.C. (1986) § 212(1) and (2). Ed.

Congress in 1942 eliminated the requirement that the expenses to be deductible must be incurred in connection with a trade or business. But, as the reports of Congressional committees show, it was not the intention of Congress to remove the other restrictions and limitations applicable to deductions under § 23(a) of the act. See S.Rep. No. 1683, 77th Cong., 2d Sess., 88; H.Rep. No. 2333, 77th Cong., 2d Sess., 75.

Under § 23(a), as it was prior to the amendment, it was firmly established that legal expenses involved in defending or protecting title to property are not "ordinary and necessary expenses" and are not deductible from gross income in order to compute the taxable net income, but constitute a capital charge which should be added to the cost of the property and taken into account in computing the capital gain or loss in case of a subsequent sale. The Treasury regulations throughout the years have consistently so provided;[1] the decisions of the courts have been to the same effect;[2] and Congress has retained the same language in repeated reenactments with this interpretation in mind.

Hence it may not be doubted that Congress, in amending § 23 of the Internal Revenue Code by the Revenue Act of 1942, used the phrase "all the ordinary and necessary expenses" under the caption "Non-Trade or Non-Business Expenses" in the same sense and with the same limitations that it had previously used in connection with trade and business expenses. It is contended that the phrase "all the ordinary and necessary expenses" in the amendment covers more ground than it did in the original act because the amendment expressly authorizes a deduction for expenses paid "for the management, conservation, or maintenance of property held for the production of income"; and the word "conservation" is said to be particularly pertinent in the pending case where the expenses were incurred in the protection of income producing stock from adverse attack. But the term "conservation" can be given effect if it is limited to expenses ordinarily and necessarily incurred during the taxable year for the safeguarding of the property, such as the cost of a safe deposit box for securities. The term cannot be given the meaning contended for by the taxpayer without losing sight of the purpose which Congress intended to accomplish and the settled meaning that the phrase "ordinary and necessary expenses" has been given in the administration and re-enactment of the federal income tax statutes.

Treasury Regulations 103, as amended by T.D. 5196, 1942–2 "C.B." 96, 97–100, which were promulgated to cover the 1942 amendments,

---

[1]  Article 293 of Regulations 45 (1919 Ed.), and 62 (1922 Ed.), promulgated under the Revenue Acts of 1918 and 1921; Article 292 of Regulations 65 and 69, promulgated under the Revenue Acts of 1924 and 1926; Article 282 of Regulations 74 and 77, promulgated under the Revenue Acts of 1928 and 1932; Article 24–2 of Regulations 94 and 101, promulgated under the Revenue Acts of 1936 and 1938; Section 19, 24–2 of Regulations 103 (1940 Ed.) promulgated under the Internal Revenue Code.

[2]  Jones' Estate v. Commissioner, 5 Cir., 127 F.2d 231; Murphy Oil Co. v. Burnet, 9 Cir., 55 F.2d 17, 26, affirmed 287 U.S. 299, 53 S.Ct. 161; Brawner v. Burnet, 61 App.D.C. 352, 63 F.2d 129, 131; Farmer v. Commissioner, 10 Cir., 126 F.2d 542, 544; Crowley v. Commissioner, 6 Cir., 89 F.2d 715, 718. Cf. Welch v. Helvering, 290 U.S. 111, 113, 114, 54 S.Ct. 8.

preserve the established interpretation. Section 19.23(a)–15 provides in part:

"(b) Except for the requirement of being incurred in connection with a trade or business, a deduction under this section is subject to all the restrictions and limitations that apply in the case of the deductions under section 23(a)(1)(A) of an expense paid or incurred in carrying on any trade or business. This includes restrictions and limitations contained in section 24, as amended. * * *.

"Capital expenditures, and expenses of carrying on transactions which do not constitute a trade or business of the taxpayer and are not carried on for the production or collection of income or for the management, conservation, or maintenance of property held for the production of income, but which are carried on primarily as a sport, hobby, or recreation are not allowable as non-trade or non-business expenses.

* * *

"Expenditures incurred in defending or perfecting title to property, in recovering property (other than investment property and amounts of income which, if and when recovered, must be included in income), or in developing or improving property, constitute a part of the cost of the property and are not deductible expenses."

The judgment of the District Court must be reversed.

## Surasky v. United States

United States Court of Appeals, Fifth Circuit, 1963.
325 F.2d 191.

■ TUTTLE, CHIEF JUDGE.

This appeal challenges the correctness of the judgment of the district court holding that the sum of $17,000 contributed by the taxpayer to the Wolfson-Montgomery Ward Stockholders Committee as a part of a proxy battle during 1955 was not allowable as a deduction as an ordinary and necessary non-business expense.[1]

The facts are not in dispute since substantially all of the facts were either stipulated between the parties or proved by undisputed affidavit and a deposition which was not in any way countered.

The taxpayer purchased 4000 shares of stock of Montgomery Ward & Co. in 1954 and 1955, at a total cost of $296,870.20. In making the purchase, he acted on the recommendation of Louis E. Wolfson after he made a personal investigation of the financial condition of Montgomery Ward & Co. Taxpayer purchased the stock for the sole reason that he

---

[1]   [I.R.C. § 212 is omitted. Ed.]

thought it was a good chance to make money, in that it was a good long term investment because of anticipated increased dividends and appreciation in the value of the stock through improvements in the condition of the company. Mr. Wolfson, who had purchased more than 50,000 shares of the stock, had laid out what he believed to be an aggressive program which he testified he thought would improve the company and greatly enhance the value of the stock. In pursuing his plans he attempted, without success, to discuss his proposals with the management. Thereafter, the taxpayer and other stockholders formed a Committee known as the Wolfson-Montgomery Ward Stockholders Committee. The objectives of the Stockholders Committee were set out in a document entitled "Let's Rebuild Montgomery Ward."[2] This document made it clear that the Stockholders Committee advocated far-reaching changes in the management of the company. It expressly called for the establishment of new stores; relocating and modernizing or repairing others; expanding manufacturing operations; developing private brands; increasing inventory turnovers; obtaining the services of outstanding merchandising personnel; improving employee morale; and generally, revamping and bringing up to date all policies touching on advertising, merchandising, sales and corporate financing. The Committee expressly sought increased dividends and a stock split. The Stockholders Committee sought to accomplish these objectives by means of electing a new Board of Directors, or at least a majority of the Board which would then provide new management. It started a proxy campaign for the regular annual meeting of stockholders scheduled for April 22, 1955. In this effort, it incurred substantial expense which was financed by payments made from members of the Committee and other stockholders.

The taxpayer paid the Stockholders Committee $17,000 in 1955, which was expended for the purpose of the Committee during that year. The taxpayer was not an officer, director or employee and did not seek a position either as a director or as an officer or employee of the company. His stated purpose for making the payments was that he believed his

---

[2]    Although the parties stipulated:

"The objectives of this Committee were set forth in a document entitled 'Let's Rebuild Montgomery Ward', * * * which the Committee circulated, together with other similar material, to the stockholders of Montgomery Ward & Co. * * * ," and although the document clearly stated the objectives to include the establishment of new stores, the relocating, modernizing or repairing of others, expanding manufacturing operations, improving employee morale, and making changes generally in advertising, merchandising, sales, financial and personnel policies for the purpose of seeking increased dividends and a stock split, the Government, in its brief, states, "The object of the Wolfson Committee was to displace a majority of the Board of Directors and the existing management of Ward and replace them with its own nine candidates for the Board and new management."

The court also, in its finding No. 4 stated, "The object of the Wolfson Committee was to displace a majority of the Board of Directors and the existing management of Ward and replace them with its own nine candidates for the Board and new management."

The stipulation further provides, "The Committee proposed to *accomplish its objectives* by displacing a majority of the Board of Directors and existing management of the corporation with its own candidates for the Board and new management."

opportunity to make more money from his stock investment was much greater if the purposes of the Committee could be accomplished.

It turned out that, while the drive was unsuccessful in placing a majority of the Stockholders Committees' candidates on the Board of Directors, it was at least partially successful in that three of its nominees were placed on the board of nine directors. Also, immediately after the election the Chairman of the Board and the President resigned. The Chairman of the Board and President were the focus of the attack by the Committee in challenging the current management policies of the company. It also eventuated that sales and earnings of the company increased during the latter half of the fiscal year ended January 31, 1956; the regular quarterly dividend was increased by the Directors at a meeting held on November 28, 1955, from $.75 per share to $1.00 per share, and an extra dividend of $1.25 per share was voted on the common stock. At the same meeting, the Board recommended a two-for-one split of the common stock, which was accomplished the following year. The market quotations of the stock increased substantially during 1955.

The taxpayer's venture in Montgomery Ward stock was a profitable one in that he received dividends totalling $30,000 on the stock purchased by him in less than a two year period, and he sold his stock in the first eight months of 1956, realizing a capital gain of $50,929.55.

Trying the case without a jury, the trial court based its legal conclusion that the expenditures were not deductible on the following summarization of the facts:

> "To summarize the facts, the plaintiff herein contributed $17,000 to a committee which was to use the money to solicit proxies from other shareholders of a large, publicly-held corporation, in the hope that the committee would be able to seat a sufficient number of its candidates on the board of directors so that new management policies could be carried out which might result in larger profits and larger dividends to the shareholders.

> "The plaintiff had clear title to his Ward stock and was receiving dividend income therefrom. It was certainly most speculative whether his contribution to the Wolfson Committee would touch off a series of events culminating in the production of increased income to the plaintiff. Furthermore, the plaintiff was not a candidate for the board of directors nor does the record reflect that he anticipated obtaining a position in Ward's management.

> \* \* \*

> "The Court specifically finds lacking the necessary proximate relationship between the expenditure and the production of income or the management of income producing property. At the time the plaintiff contributed his funds to the committee, it was pure speculation whether he would derive any

monetary reward therefrom. At the time the expenditure was made, the Court would certainly not find that it was necessary, nor was it even ordinary, within the common meaning of that word.

"The Court is not unmindful of the fact that the plaintiff, at the time he contributed the $17,000 to the committee, did so with hopes of realizing a profit and that, as a matter of fact, the dividends on his stock increased following the election of three of the Wolfson Committee's candidates. However, it is necessary to view the instant transaction as of the time it occurred, without the benefit of hindsight. The record is completely devoid of any evidence of a direct proximate relationship between the plaintiff's expenditure and the increased dividends; the latter could have been caused by any one of a myriad of factors. As for the plaintiff's desire to make a profit, there are any number of transactions entered into by the parties with a profit motive which are not accorded preferential tax treatment. The Treasury cannot be expected to underwrite all profit seeking speculations."

The appellant here urges that in its stressing of the "speculative" nature of the expenditure and the court's apparent reliance on the theory that for an expense, to be deductible under subparagraph 2 of Section 212, i.e., "for the management, conservation, or maintenance of property held for the production of income," there must be some threat of the loss of the property by the taxpayer, the court has imposed too rigid a requirement. We agree.

There is one thing both parties here agree upon, that is, that it was to change the result of the distinction between "business" and "personal" expenses that Section 212 was added to the Internal Revenue Code in 1942. The United States, in its brief, cites the decision by the Supreme Court in McDonald v. Commissioner, 323 U.S. 57, 61, 65 S.Ct. 96, as authority for the following statement: "In order to correct the inequity of making non-trade or non-business income taxable, but not allowing non-trade or non-business expenses to be deducted, Congress allowed a deduction in the new subsection (a)(2) for 'all the ordinary and necessary expenses paid or incurred' (1) 'for the production or collection of income' or (2) 'for the management, conservation, or maintenance of property held for the production or collection of income.' "

The parties also agree that in construing the language of Section 212, it is to be taken in *pari materia* with Section 162 so far as relates to the language "ordinary and necessary business expenses."[3]

From the manner in which the trial court stressed the terms "speculative" and "speculation" it is apparent that the court may have been too greatly persuaded by the language of the income tax regulations

---

[3]　[I.R.C. § 162(a) is omitted. Ed.]

declaring, in Section 1.212–1(d), that "expenses to be deductible under Section 212, must be 'ordinary and necessary'. Thus, such expenses must be reasonable in amount and must bear a reasonable and proximate relation to the production or collection of taxable income or to the management, conservation, or maintenance of property held for the production of income." While we do not determine that this regulation is not warranted by the section of the statute with which we are involved, we think that it has been construed by the trial court to require much too difficult a showing of proximate cause in the common-law tort concept than is required by the statute.

It will be noted that nothing in the statute expressly requires a showing of a "proximate relation to the production or collection of taxable income." None of the cases cited to us by the United States contain such language. We think Congress had in mind allowing deduction of expenses genuinely incurred in the exercise of reasonable business judgment in an effort to produce income that may fall far short of satisfying the common law definition of proximate cause. Thus, we think the use of the term "speculative" is not an apt expression that would describe the determining factor in deciding this issue.

This Court has held in Harris & Co. v. Lucas, Commissioner, 5th Cir., 48 F.2d 187,

"It is evident that the words 'ordinary' and 'necessary' in the statute are not used conjunctively, and are not to be construed as requiring that an expense of a business to be deductible must be both ordinary and necessary in a narrow, technical sense. On the contrary, it is clear that Congress intended the statute to be broadly construed to facilitate business generally, so that any necessary expense, not actually a capital investment, incurred in good faith in a particular business, is to be considered an ordinary expense of that business. This in effect is the construction given the statute by the Treasury Department and the court. * * * " 48 F.2d 187, 188.

This Court has cited the Harris case a number of times with approval, most recently in Lutz v. Commissioner of Internal Revenue, 5 Cir., 282 F.2d 614, 617.[4]

In dealing with the "necessary" part of the formula, the Supreme Court has indicated in Welch v. Helvering, 290 U.S. 111, at page 113, 54 S.Ct. 8, at page 9, that this requirement may be satisfied if the expenditures "were appropriate and helpful", saying as to the taxpayer, Welch, "He certainly thought they were, and we should be slow to override his judgment."

---

[4]  The entire paragraph from the Harris & Co. case is quoted above although it is clear that the Supreme Court in Welch v. Helvering, 290 U.S. 111, 54 S.Ct. 8, has held that in order to qualify as a business deduction an expenditure must be *both* necessary *and* ordinary. However, we still believe that they need not be "both ordinary and necessary in a narrow, technical sense," as stated in the Harris & Co. case.

Then, dealing with the question of what expenses are "ordinary" the Supreme Court in the same opinion said, "here, indeed, as so often in other branches of the law, the decisive distinctions are those of degree and not of kind. One struggles in vain for any verbal formula that will supply a ready touchstone. The standard set up by the statute is not a rule of law; it is rather a way of life. Life in all its fullness must supply the answer to the riddle."

Here, it seems incontestable that the payments made by the taxpayer were made with the anticipation that profit to the taxpayer would result. It may have been a long chance that Mr. Surasky was taking. However, he testified he knew Mr. Wolfson well enough to know his ability and believed that there was reasonable likelihood of success. This testimony is undisputed. In point of fact, the activity resulting from the expenditures by the taxpayer and his associates did produce direct and tangible results in that three nominees of the Committee were elected to the Board of Directors, the President, who had been severely criticized by the Committee was caused to resign as was the Chairman of the Board, and many other actions which parallel those sought for by the Committee were undertaken by the corporation. Profits were increased; dividends were increased; the stock enhanced in value. We think that for a trial court to conclude that there was not sufficient connection between the expenditure to assist the Committee in its activities and the achievement of so many of its objectives was too remote to meet the test of what is reasonable and ordinary in this particular type of investor activity is to apply too rigid a standard in the application of a remedial statute.

While there are differences in the facts, as there must always be in different cases, we think that the Tax Court decision in Alleghany Corporation, 28 T.C. 298, acq. 1957–2 C.B. 3, points the direction in which the statute should be applied. The expenditures there sought to be deducted were for proxy solicitation and other committee activities in a railroad reorganization. To be sure, the proposal that was fought successfully in that case would have resulted in diluting the taxpayer's common stock possibly to the vanishing point. However, we think it immaterial whether the expenditure is directed towards an effort to prevent the loss or dilution of an equity interest or to cause an enhancement or increase of the equity value, as was the undoubted purpose in the case before us. The Tax Court there said, 28 T.C. page 304, "We think it is clear that the expenditures in question were made for no other purpose than to protect petitioner's business." See also Shoe Corporation of America, 29 T.C. 297, 1957, acq. 1958–2 C.B. 7, and Allied Chemical Corp. v. United States (Ct.Cl.1962), 305 F.2d 433.

It appearing, as we have noted above, that the decision of this case was based on undisputed evidence, most of which was stipulated, our review of the decision of the trial court is somewhat freed from the "clearly erroneous" rule. * * *.

The judgment is reversed and the case is remanded to the trial court for the entry of a judgment in favor of the appellant, taxpayer.

## Revenue Ruling 64–236[1]
### 1964–2 Cum.Bull. 64.

The Internal Revenue Service will follow the decision of the U.S. Court of Appeals for the Fourth Circuit in the case of R. Walter Graham, et ux. v. Commissioner, 326 F.2d 878 (1964).

This decision held that proxy fight expenditures are deductible by a stockholder under section 212 of the Internal Revenue Code of 1954, if such expenditures are proximately related to either the production or collection of income or to the management, conservation or maintenance of property held for the production of income.

The Service will also follow the decision of the U.S. Court of Appeals for the Fifth Circuit in Jack Surasky v. United States, 325 F.2d 191 (1963), a case involving a similar issue. Internal Revenue will not, however, follow this decision to the extent that the court in its opinion indicates that to be deductible proxy fight expenditures need not be proximately related to either the production or collection of income or to the management, conservation, or maintenance of property held for the production of income.

## Fleischman v. Commissioner
### Tax Court of the United States, 1966.
### 45 T.C. 439.

■ SIMPSON, JUDGE:

The Commissioner has determined a deficiency in the petitioner's income tax for 1962 in the amount of $725.60. The issue in this case is whether the petitioner may deduct legal expenses incurred in defending his wife's lawsuit to set aside their antenuptial contract.

Findings of Fact

Meyer J. Fleischman, the petitioner, is a physician in Cincinnati, Ohio. He reported his income on the cash method of accounting and filed his 1962 income tax return with the district director of internal revenue at Cincinnati, Ohio.

On February 25, 1955, petitioner entered into an antenuptial agreement with Joan Ruth Francis. That agreement was made in contemplation of marriage and provided: [that in case of divorce Meyer would pay Joan $5,000, in consideration for which Joan released all interest in Meyer's property.]

---

[1]   Based on Technical Information Release 613, dated July 23, 1964.

Petitioner and Joan R. Francis were married on February 26, 1955. On December 20, 1961, Joan filed for a divorce in the Court of Common Pleas, Division of Domestic Relations, Hamilton County, Ohio. In her suit for divorce the wife made the following prayer: [*inter alia*] That plaintiff be awarded a fair and equitable division of all properties, real and personal, of the defendant Meyer J. Fleischman, and for all such other and further relief to which she may be entitled in the premises, including her attorney fees and expenses.

On December 26, 1961, she filed another action in the Court of Common Pleas, Hamilton County, Ohio. The latter suit was instituted to set aside the antenuptial agreement and was necessary because the domestic relations division had no jurisdiction to declare the contract void and invalid. In her petition, she alleged that her husband had deceived her by false representations concerning the validity of the agreement, and that at the time of the agreement and at the time of filing suit she had no idea of the nature and extent of the defendant's property. She asserted that the provisions made for her under the agreement were grossly disproportionate to her husband's means.

A decree of divorce was entered on October 19, 1962. The suit to rescind and invalidate the antenuptial agreement was dismissed with prejudice on the plaintiff's application October 22, 1962.

Petitioner did not deduct the legal expenses incurred in connection with the divorce proceeding. Petitioner did deduct on his 1962 return $3,000 for legal expenses incurred in defending the suit to invalidate the antenuptial agreement signed on February 25, 1955. Respondent disallowed this deduction and determined a deficiency of $725.60. This deficiency is in issue here.

Opinion

The sole question in this case is whether petitioner is entitled to deduct $3,000 in legal expenses incurred in defending his wife's suit to set aside an antenuptial agreement.

We hold that he is barred from deducting these expenses by section 262 of the Internal Revenue Code of 1954[1] and the decision of the Supreme Court in United States v. Gilmore, 372 U.S. 39 (1963).

The petitioner's brief asserts first that his position was adequately set forth in the opinion of Carpenter v. United States, 338 F.2d 366 (Ct.Cl.1964). Second, he argues that Erdman v. Commissioner, 315 F.2d 762 (C.A.7 1963), affirming 37 T.C. 1119 (1962), supports his position. Lastly, petitioner suggests that the litigation giving rise to the legal expenses here in issue did not grow out of the marriage relationship, but sprang from rights excluded from that relationship. The respondent has countered that the *Carpenter* case is distinguishable; that *Erdman* is

---

[1]  All statutory references are to the Internal Revenue Code of 1954 unless otherwise indicated. [The 1986 Code cites are identical. Ed.]

inapposite; and that the suggested distinction between rights flowing from the marriage relationship and rights flowing from an antenuptial agreement is one of form and should be rejected. In the alternative, respondent urges that the expenses were incurred in defending title to property and should be capitalized, not allowed as a deduction.

We agree with all three of respondent's arguments and, therefore, do not reach his alternative proposition.

Petitioner's first contention, that his position is sustained by *Carpenter* is untenable. *Carpenter* involved a deduction for legal expenses paid for tax counsel in the course of a divorce proceeding. The court found these payments to be deductible under section 212(3) as an ordinary and necessary expense paid in connection with the determination of a tax. In Fleischman's case, there is no suggestion in the record that the legal expenses involved were for consultation and advice on tax matters. The stipulation clearly states that the expenses were incurred in defending a suit to set aside and declare void an antenuptial contract.

If petitioner means to rely on *Carpenter* to sustain his case under section 212(2) or 212(1), he is left with the liability that the case did not deal with those paragraphs. Paragraph (3) of section 212, as the *Carpenter* case holds, expresses a policy and has a meaning quite different from paragraphs (1) and (2). In fact, the court pointed out in *Carpenter* that the legal fees would not be deductible under section 212(2).

If petitioner cites *Carpenter* for the proposition that certain legal fees can be deducted even though incurred in connection with a divorce, he is certainly correct. This Court has so held in the case of Ruth K. Wild, 42 T.C. 706 (1964). The question in the case before us, however, is whether *these* legal expenses are deductible, and in resolving that issue, the *Carpenter* case is of no assistance.

The petitioner's second argument is that the case of Erdman v. Commissioner, may be pertinent. We do not agree. *Erdman* concerned the deductibility of legal expenses incurred by taxpayers defending their title to property as beneficiaries of a testamentary trust. In the alternative, it was contended that the trust was entitled to deduct these expenses. This Court held that the attorney's fees were an expenditure of the trust, not of the taxpayer. In addition, the trust was not permitted to deduct the fee currently as it was charged to trust corpus, not income. Calvin Pardee Erdman, 37 T.C. 1119 (1962).

On appeal, the Seventh Circuit upheld the Tax Court on both grounds and added that the taxpayer's expenses were capital in nature, being in defense of title, and not deductible for that reason as well. Erdman v. Commissioner, supra. It is our view that the factual and legal issues in *Erdman* are so significantly different from those in this case that it is of no assistance in reaching our decision.

The expenditures in question are deductible, if at all, only under section 212.[2] Since there is not the slightest indication in the record that the counsel fees concerned taxes, we do not consider this case under section 212(3). In addition, there is no support for the view that the petitioner incurred the legal expenses for the production or collection of income, nor does he argue that he did; therefore, section 212(1) is not raised. The petition alleges that the expense was for the preservation and protection of taxpayer's real property inherited from his mother. This leaves only the suggestion that the expenses are deductible under section 212(2) as paid for the management, conservation, or maintenance of property held for the production of income.

In approaching the issue thus presented, it is helpful to consider the general purpose and history of section 212. Prior to 1942, legal expenses were deductible only if the suit occasioning them was directly connected with or proximately related to the taxpayer's trade or business. Sarah Backer, et al., Executors, 1 B.T.A. 214 (1924). Legal costs which were simply personal expenses were not deductible, although the line between personal and business expenses was sometimes difficult to draw. Kornhauser v. United States, 276 U.S. 145 (1928).

Certain investment activities conducted by the taxpayer might generate taxable income; however, the expenses attributable to these activities were not deductible where the activities did not constitute a trade or business. Higgins v. Commissioner, 312 U.S. 212 (1941). In order to equalize the treatment of these expenses with business expenses,[3] both of which produced taxable income, Congress added section 23(a)(2) to the 1939 Code by the Revenue Act of 1942 (56 Stat. 798, 819). That section provided as follows:

SEC. 23. DEDUCTIONS FROM GROSS INCOME.

In computing net income there shall be allowed as deductions:

(a)  EXPENSES.—

(2)  NON-TRADE OR NON-BUSINESS EXPENSES.—In the case of an individual, all the ordinary and necessary expenses paid or incurred during the taxable year for the production or collection of income, or for the management, conservation, or maintenance of property held for the production of income.

At the same time that Congress enacted section 23(a)(2), it also added sections 22(k) and 23(u) to the 1939 Code. In general, those sections required a divorced spouse to include alimony payments in her gross income and permitted the paying spouse to deduct the amounts paid from his taxable income. Thus, while the Congress increased the range of deductions by section 23(a)(2), it also provided for a new kind of

---

2    [I.R.C. § 212 is omitted. Ed.]

3    H.Rept. No. 2333, 77th Cong., 2d Sess., p. 75 (1942), 1942–2 C.B. 372, 429.

taxable income to a divorced spouse. However, Congress left us with no guidance in the legislative history as to the relationship between the alimony provisions and section 23(a)(2).

Section 23(a)(2) was construed as enlarging the category of incomes with respect to which expenses were deductible. Deductions under that section were analogous to business expenses and were allowable or not in accordance with principles which had long controlled these expenses. McDonald v. Commissioner, 323 U.S. 57 (1944). In particular, legal expenses were allowable as investment expenses subject to the same limitations imposed on legal fees incurred in a trade or business. Trust of Bingham v. Commissioner, 325 U.S. 365 (1945).

Great difficulty was experienced in distinguishing deductible legal expenses from those which were purely personal. This Court found that a wife could deduct legal fees incurred to obtain alimony included in her gross income under the Revenue Act of 1942. * * *. On the other hand, the husband's legal expenses were regarded as personal even if he was compelled to pay his wife's counsel fees, or if his income-producing property was threatened with sequestration to pay alimony. * * *.

The Supreme Court in construing the new section found that Congress did not intend to permit taxpayers to deduct personal, living, or family expenses. Lykes v. United States, 343 U.S. 118, 125 (1952). In applying this rationale, the Court stated as follows:

> * * *. Legal expenses do not become deductible merely because they are paid for services which relieve a taxpayer of liability. That argument would carry us too far. It would mean that the expense of defending almost any claim would be deductible by a taxpayer on the ground that such defense was made to help him keep clear of liens whatever income-producing property he might have. * * *. Section 23(a)(2) never has been so interpreted by us. It has been applied to expenses on the basis of their immediate purposes rather than upon the basis of the remote contributions they might make to the conservation of a taxpayer's income-producing assets by reducing his general liabilities. See McDonald v. Commissioner, supra. * * *.

In 1963, the Court undertook to explain the application of this rationale to a husband's legal expenses incurred in a divorce action. United States v. Gilmore, 372 U.S. 39 (1963).

The taxpayer in *Gilmore* owned a controlling interest in three corporations. The dividends and salary from these companies were his major source of income. In a divorce proceeding, his wife alleged that much of this property was community property and that more than half of the community property should be awarded to her. The taxpayer incurred substantial legal expenses in the course of successfully resisting these claims. He sought to deduct the expenses attributable to his defense against his wife's property claims under section 23(a)(2) of the

1939 Code. The Supreme Court sustained the Government's contention that deductibility depended upon the origin and nature of the claim giving rise to the legal expenses, rather than upon the consequences of such a claim to income-producing property.[4]

The Supreme Court reached this result for two basic reasons. First, the language of the statute "conservation of property" was said to refer to operations performed with respect to the property itself rather than the taxpayer's retention of ownership in it. Secondly, the Court examined the legislative history and discerned a congressional purpose to equalize treatment of expenditures for profit-seeking activities with those related to a trade or business. In order to achieve this result, any limitation or restriction imposed upon a business expense must be applied to section 23(a)(2) expenses. Among those restrictions was the rule, now embodied in section 262, that personal, living, or family expenses are not deductible. The characterization of litigation costs as personal or business depends upon whether the claim involved in the litigation arises in connection with the profit-seeking activities. A suit against a taxpayer must be directly connected with or proximately result from his business before it is a business expense. This being so, the "origin of claim" test used in the business deduction cases was selected as most consistent with the meaning of section 23(a)(2). The claim against the property in a divorce suit arises only from the marital relationship and is therefore personal. The wife's rights, if any, must have their source in the marriage.

Dispelling all doubts that the Supreme Court was passing only on community property claims was United States v. Patrick, 372 U.S. 53 (1963), decided the same day as *Gilmore*. The *Patrick* case dealt with a property settlement which was made prior to divorce and which was supposed to have preserved the husband's income-producing property. The Supreme Court found little or no difference between that situation and *Gilmore* where the issue concerned community property and the wife's claim to an award of more than her existing share of such property.

*Gilmore* was decided under the 1939 Code and *Patrick* under the 1954 Code. There was no suggestion in these cases that enactment of the 1954 Code changed the meaning of the statutory language. The 1954 Code divides the provisions formerly contained in section 23(a)(2) of the 1939 Code into two paragraphs. The first deals with expenses for the production of income, and the second with expenses for the management, conservation, or maintenance of property held for the production of income. In connection with section 212(1) and (2), the legislative history specifically states that no substantive change from section 23(a)(2) of the

---

[4] The Commissioner's regulations have long provided that expenses do not become deductible merely because incurred in defense of a claim which may result in income-producing property being sold or used to satisfy taxpayer's liability. Sec. 39.23(a)–15(k), Regs. 118; sec. 1.212–1(m), Income Tax Regs.

Internal Revenue Code of 1939 was made. Thus, the Code simply puts in separate paragraphs what was once one sentence.

Scarcely had the *Gilmore* case been decided, when the Tax Court was again confronted with the issue of the deductibility of the wife's attorney fees expended to collect defaulted alimony payments. Jane U. Elliott, 40 T.C. 304 (1963), acq. 1964–1 C.B. (Part 1) 4. In accordance with prior law, the wife was allowed a deduction under section 212(1). The Court held that the legal fees in question were incurred for the production of her taxable income. *Gilmore* and *Patrick* were not cited in this opinion.

The following year the case of Ruth K. Wild, 42 T.C. 706 (1964), was presented for review by the whole Court. The wife sought a deduction for counsel fees under section 212(1) in reliance upon the *Elliott* case for expenses incurred in negotiating an alimony agreement and in hearings concerning this agreement. The respondent contended that *Gilmore* and *Patrick* required a contrary result since the expenses were attributable to a claim which was based on her marital rights and not on a profit-seeking activity. This Court distinguished *Gilmore* and *Patrick* upon the basis that both of those cases were decided under paragraph (2) of section 212 and the contention in the *Wild* case was that the legal fees were deductible under paragraph (1). The Commissioner's regulations permitting a deduction for legal costs attributable to the collection of taxable alimony had not been changed following the *Gilmore* decision. Neither had his acquiescence in *Elliott* been withdrawn. These two factors influenced the Court in holding that the wife could continue to deduct legal expenses related to alimony. Thus, she retained a deduction under section 212(1).

This Court has made it clear that the wife's deduction under section 212(1) is limited to expenses incurred in obtaining alimony includable in her gross income. There is no deduction for expenses related to property claims, even when incurred by the wife. Those claims grow out of the marital relationship and are covered by the rule in *Gilmore*. Georgia Leary Neill, 42 T.C. 793 (1964).

Turning to the case at hand, both petitioner and respondent have argued the case under section 212(2). In order to prevail, the petitioner must demonstrate how his expenses differ from those in *Gilmore* and *Patrick*. We find that he has failed in this task.

Petitioner suggests that his expenses differ from those at issue in *Gilmore* because his were caused by a separate suit to rescind a contract. In Joan Fleischman's second suit, she alleged that the provisions of the antenuptial agreement were disproportionate to her husband's means at the time the agreement was made and at the time of suit. Simultaneously, she had a divorce suit pending requesting support payments. Viewed in its entirety, her effort was one directed at obtaining support payments greater than those provided in the antenuptial agreement. In part, her claim to greater rights was founded upon facts existing or arising during the marriage. In this respect her claim was not unlike that involved in the *Gilmore* case. There, the claim was that certain community property belonging one-half to the husband should be awarded to the wife because of wrongs committed during the marital relationship. The Supreme Court rejected any distinction between legal expenses related to the issue of whether assets were community property and those related to an award of such property. Both issues have a common origin. In both *Gilmore* and here, the wife was requesting an award of property and her right was founded only upon the consequences that State law attaches to marriage. In petitioner's case, his wife made no claim to specific property except as a source of payment, hence his position is even weaker than that of the taxpayer in *Gilmore*.

The fact that Fleischman's wife first had to file a separate suit to invalidate the antenuptial agreement is solely the result of the restricted jurisdiction of the Ohio divorce courts. That fact alone is not a sound basis for a distinction in the field of Federal taxation.

For ascertaining the source of claims giving rise to legal expenses, the Supreme Court suggested a "but for" test. If the claim could not have existed but for the marriage relationship, the expense of defending it is a personal expense and not deductible. Applying that test, it is clear that but for her marriage to petitioner, the wife could have no claim to the property sought to be protected.

In deciding that the antenuptial agreement in this case is not significantly different from a property settlement incident to a divorce, we are aided in our reasoning by United States v. Patrick. In that case, complicated property adjustments were required so that the husband could retain controlling interest in a publishing business owned jointly with his wife. The legal fees involved were spent arranging a transfer of various stocks, leasing real property, and creating a trust, rather than conducting divorce litigation. The Supreme Court found no legal significance in these differences from *Gilmore*. The Court found that the transfers were incidental to the litigation which had its origin in taxpayer's personal life. It could be argued that we should take a narrow view and say that the suit to set aside petitioner's antenuptial agreement concerned contract rights. However, that view ignores the fact that marital rights were the subject of this contract and the fact that the second lawsuit was intimately bound up with the divorce litigation. In *Patrick,* the settlement agreement stated that it settled "rights growing out of the marital relationship." In the case at hand, the agreement states that the parties desire to agree to a distribution of property should their marriage be dissolved by divorce or annulment. We can perceive little or no difference between the two agreements when the question of deducting legal expenses is in issue.

A similar question was presented in David G. Joyce, 3 B.T.A. 393 (1926). The taxpayer there sought a deduction for legal expenses incurred in defending a postnuptial agreement from attack by his wife. The agreement was made in 1913 and governed rights upon death or divorce.

In 1920 the wife instituted an action for divorce and for an award of maintenance in addition to the provisions of the postnuptial contract. The taxpayer sought to deduct the expenses related to defending the agreement as a business expense. He argued that the contract gave him greater freedom in managing his business property and that such property was the subject of the contract.

In holding that the expenses were personal, the Board stated that the husband's argument ignored the genesis of the rights he attempted to settle and limit by the postnuptial agreement. Those rights existed and would exist only by virtue of the marriage.[5]

In conclusion, we find no significant distinction between this case and the *Gilmore* and *Patrick* cases, and accordingly, we hold that the legal expenses incurred by the petitioner are not deductible.

Decision will be entered for the respondent.

## PROBLEMS

**1.** Speculator buys 100 shares of Sound Company stock for $3,000, paying her broker a commission of $50 on the purchase. Fourteen months later she sells the shares for $4,000 paying a commission of $60 on the sale.

(a) Are the commissions § 212 expenses? See Spreckels v. Helvering, 315 U.S. 626, 62 S.Ct. 777 (1942), Reg. § 1.263(a)–1(e)(1).

(b) What result in (a), above, if instead she sells the shares for $2500 paying a $45 commission on the sale? See § 165(c)(2).

(c) Speculator owned only one-tenth of one percent of the Sound Company stock (worth $3,000) but, being an eager investor during the time she owned the stock, she incurred $500 of transportation, meals and lodging expenses in traveling 1000 miles to New York City to attend Sound's annual shareholder meeting. May she deduct her costs under § 212(2)?

(d) What result in (c), above, if instead Speculator owned 10% of the total outstanding Sound stock, worth $300,000?

**2.** After reading the *Fleischman* case, consider in what situations:

(a) Payor Spouse may deduct attorneys' fees incurred in getting a divorce.

(b) Payee Spouse may deduct attorneys' fees incurred in getting a divorce.

---

[5] "It is hardly necessary to allude to the fact that marriage is a personal relationship, except for the purpose of pointing out that the legal rights and obligations annexed to the relationship are also personal and the expenses connected therewith would, we think, come within the classification of personal or family expenses." (David G. Joyce, 3 B.T.A. 393, 397.)

## B. CHARGES ARISING OUT OF TRANSACTIONS ENTERED INTO FOR PROFIT

Internal Revenue Code: Sections 121(a), (d)(6); 165(a), (b), (c)(2); 167(a)(2); 168(a); 212. See Sections 195; 280A.

Regulations: Sections 1.165–9(b); 1.167(g)–1; 1.212–1(h).

---

### Horrmann v. Commissioner*

Tax Court of the United States, 1951.
17 T.C. 903.

[The Findings of Fact have been omitted.]

Opinion

■ BLACK, JUDGE:

Three issues are presented in this proceeding. All issues relate to the real property, residence and garage, at 189 Howard Avenue, Staten Island, New York, which was acquired by petitioner by a devise from his mother upon her death in February 1940.

Petitioner redecorated the house and moved into it about October 1940. Shortly thereafter petitioner sold the residence in which he was living prior to October 1940. The property at 189 Howard Avenue was used by petitioner as his personal residence until October 1942, at which time petitioner abandoned the house. Petitioner, after living in the residence for awhile, considered the property too large and too expensive and when he left he planned never to use it again as his personal residence.

Petitioner considered converting the building into apartments, but this was found to be impractical. Numerous efforts were made to rent and to sell the property. The property was sold in June 1945, and the net proceeds from the sale were $20,800. At the time petitioner acquired the property its value was $60,000, and at the time it was abandoned by petitioner as a personal residence the value was $45,000, with $35,000 allocated to land and $10,000 to the buildings.

The issue which we shall first consider is whether petitioner is entitled to a deduction for depreciation on the property during the

---

* Problems such as those presented here and in *Lowry,* infra page 458, are discussed in Erck, "And You Thought Moving Was Bad—Try Deducting Depreciation and Maintenance Expenses on Your Unsold Residence," 26 U.Fla.L.R. 587 (1974); Reese, "Maintenance and Depreciation Deductions Are Not Available on a Residence Vacated and Offered for Sale But Not for Rent Unless Taxpayer Intends to Profit," 49 Texas L.Rev. 581 (1971); and Fasan, "Maintenance and Depreciation Deductions for a Personal Residence Offered for Sale," 25 Tax L.Rev. 269 (1970). Ed.

taxable years 1943, 1944, and 1945. The applicable provision of the Internal Revenue Code is set forth in the margin.[1]

Petitioner is entitled to a deduction for depreciation at the rate of $500 per year provided the property was *held for the production of income.* In determining whether the test prescribed by statute is satisfied the use made of the property and the owner's intent in respect to the future use or disposition of the property are generally controlling. Until November 1942, the property was used by petitioner solely as a personal residence, but thereafter that use was abandoned. The mere abandonment of such use does not mean that thereafter the property was held for the production of income. But when efforts are made to rent the property as were made by petitioner herein, the property is then being held for the production of income and this may be so even though no income is in fact received from the property, Mary Laughlin Robinson, 2 T.C. 305, and even though the property is at the same time offered for sale. While an intention not to rent the house was indicated in May 1943, on the brochure of the real estate clearing house, efforts to rent the property were made subsequent to that time. The evidence, when considered in its entirety, supports the conclusion that petitioner continuously offered to rent the property until it was sold. In the recomputation of tax for the years 1943, 1944, and 1945, petitioner is to be allowed depreciation at the rate of $500 per year until June 1945, when the property was sold.

The second issue is whether petitioner is entitled to a deduction for expenses incurred during the taxable years for the maintenance and conservation of the property. The applicable provision of the Internal Revenue Code is set forth in the margin.[2] The same phrase appearing in section 23(1)(2) of the Code, see footnote 1 of this Opinion, appears also in section 23(a)(2) of the Code, the requirement being that the property be *held for the production of income.* The taxpayer in Mary Laughlin Robinson, supra, claimed a deduction for depreciation on the property and expenses for services of a caretaker. Although the taxable year there was 1937, the sections of the Code applicable there (see footnote 1 of that Opinion) contain the same standard, *property held for the production of income,* as is applicable here. We there held that the taxpayer was entitled to both the deductions at issue. In accordance with that Opinion, we hold that petitioner in the recomputation of tax for the years 1943 and 1944, is entitled to deductions for maintenance and conservation expenses of the property as itemized in our Findings of Fact.

The third issue is whether petitioner is entitled to a deduction for a long term capital loss arising from the sale in 1945 of the property at 189 Howard Avenue. Petitioner claims a deduction under the provisions of section 23(e)(2) of the Code which are set forth in the margin,[3] and he has

---

[1]  [I.R.C. (1939) § 23(*l*)(2) is omitted. See I.R.C. (1986) §§ 167(a)(2); 168(a). Ed.]

[2]  [I.R.C. (1939) § 23(a)(2) is omitted. See I.R.C. (1986) § 212(2). Ed.]

[3]  [I.R.C. (1939) § 23(e)(2) is omitted. See I.R.C. (1986) § 165(c)(2). Ed.]

computed the deduction in accordance with the limitations provisions of section 117 of the Code.

The language of the Code sections applicable in issues one and two was *property held for the production of income,* and the language of section 23(e)(2) of the Code is different. In order for a loss to be deductible under that section it must be incurred *in any transaction entered into for profit.* In a situation where the use of the property as a personal residence has been abandoned, and where the owner has offered the property for sale or for rent and finally sells the property at a loss, that distinction in language may result in allowing a deduction in one case and not allowing a deduction of another type. At least the cases have distinguished between the two statutory provisions, Warner v. Commissioner, 167 F.2d 633, affirming per curiam a Memorandum Opinion of this Court. We think that the facts in respect to this issue are not materially different from those in Allen L. Grammer, 12 T.C. 34, and those in Morgan v. Commissioner, 76 F.2d 390. When property has been used as a personal residence, in order to convert the transaction into one entered into for profit the owner must do more than abandon the property and list it for sale or rent, Allen L. Grammer, supra. See also Rumsey v. Commissioner, 82 F.2d 158. In that case, in denying the taxpayer any deduction for the loss so incurred, the Court said:

> The taxpayer argues with considerable persuasive force that the fact that a man first rents his house before selling it is only significant as evidentiary of his purpose to abandon it as a residence and to devote the property to business uses; that renting is not the sole criterion of such purpose, as the regulations themselves imply by the words "rented or otherwise appropriated" to income producing purposes. But we think the argument cannot prevail over counter considerations. If an owner rents, his decision is irrevocable, at least for the term of the lease; and if he remodels to fit the building for business purposes, he has likewise made it impossible to resume residential uses by a mere change of mind. When, however, he only instructs an agent to sell or rent the property, its change of character remains subject to his unfettered will; he may revoke the agency at any moment. Certainly it strains the language of Article 171, Regulations 74, to find that the property is "appropriated to" and "used for" income producing purposes by merely listing it with a broker for sale or rental. * * *.

We have held that an actual rental of the property is not always essential to a conversion, Estate of Maria Assmann, 16 T.C. 632, but that case is not controlling here for the taxpayer there abandoned the residence only a few days after it was inherited, and then later demolished the residence. In Mary E. Crawford, 16 T.C. 678, which involved only the question of whether the loss was a section 23(e)(1) loss or a section 23(e)(2) loss, the owner-taxpayer had also demolished the residence. While we held in both cases that such action constituted an appropriation or conversion, in both cases the facts indicate that from the moment the properties were inherited the taxpayers did not intend to continue to occupy the property as their personal residence.

Here the situation is different. The petitioners in the instant case soon after the death of petitioner's mother took immediate and decisive action, fixing the character of the property in their hands as residential. The surrounding circumstances point to this conclusion; their expenditure of approximately $9,000 in redecorating the house in preparation for their use of it as a home; their moving into the property within nine months after they acquired it; the sale of their former residence at Ocean Terrace shortly after they had moved into the Howard Avenue property; and finally, their occupancy of the Howard Avenue property for a period of about two years as a home and residence. They could hardly have gone further more decisively to fix the character of this property, originally neutral in their hands, as personal residential property.

As to the third issue, we think there was no conversion of the property into a transaction entered into for profit. Respondent did not err in determining that petitioner was not entitled to the benefits of a capital loss carry-over to 1946 for the loss sustained upon the sale in 1945 of the property at 189 Howard Avenue. Allen L. Grammer, supra.

Decision will be entered under Rule 50.

# Lowry v. United States

United States District Court, District of New Hampshire, 1974.
384 F.Supp. 257.

Opinion

■ BOWNES, DISTRICT JUDGE.

Plaintiffs bring this action to recover federal income taxes and interest, in the amount of $1,072, which they allege were erroneously or illegally assessed and collected. Jurisdiction is based on 28 U.S.C.A. § 1346(a)(1).

The issue is whether plaintiffs, who ceased to use their summer house as residential property in 1967 and immediately offered it for sale without attempting to rent the property, converted it into "income producing property," thereby entitling them to deduct the maintenance expenses incurred after it was put on the market and prior to its sale in 1973. The Internal Revenue Service allowed plaintiffs to take maintenance deductions in the tax years 1968 and 1969. They disallowed similar maintenance deductions in the tax year 1970. The only year in issue is 1970.[1]

Plaintiffs are husband and wife domiciled in Peterborough, New Hampshire. (Since Edward G. Lowry, Jr., is the principal party in this

---

[1] Plaintiff, due to his own mistake, failed to take the allowable depreciation deductions and that matter is not before this court.

case, he alone will hereinafter be referred to as plaintiff.) Plaintiff filed a joint federal income tax return for 1970 with the District Director of Internal Revenue in Portsmouth, New Hampshire. On his 1970 income tax return, plaintiff deducted expenditures made for the care and maintenance of his former summer residence. He based these deductions upon the premise that the summer residence was no longer personal property, but was property "held for the production of income." Int.Rev.Code of 1954 § 212. The Internal Revenue Service disagreed with plaintiff and disallowed the deduction basing its decision on Internal Revenue Code of 1954 § 262 which provides:

> Except as otherwise expressly provided in this chapter, no deductions shall be allowed for personal, living, or family expenses.

On November 27, 1971, plaintiff paid the disputed $1,072 under written protest.

The property in question is plaintiff's former summer residence on Martha's Vineyard (hereinafter referred to as Vineyard property). The Vineyard property is part of a cooperative community known as Seven Gates Farm Corporation.

Seven Gates was formed in 1921 by five persons, one of whom was plaintiff's father. Upon forming the corporation, plaintiff's father acquired the Vineyard property. In 1942, plaintiff acquired "title" to the property by gift from his father.

Legal title to the Vineyard property is held by Seven Gates. In 1970, plaintiff had a lease for the Vineyard property and was a 3% stockholder in the corporation. The leasing arrangement treated plaintiff as the de facto owner of the property. It ran for the life of the corporation with the proviso that, upon dissolution of the corporation, it would automatically be converted into a fee title. No stockholder-lessee, however, could sell his stock and lease without the prior consent of 75% of the stockholder-lessees. Each lease further provided that a rental for a year or less required the prior consent of the Committee on Admissions and that a lease for more than a year required the prior consent of 75% of the other stockholder-lessees.

In 1966, plaintiff owned three residential properties: he maintained his legal residence in Maryland; he had a winter residence in Florida; and the Vineyard property. During 1966, plaintiff sold his Maryland home and purchased a house in Peterborough, New Hampshire. Because the Peterborough house did "all the things that the house in Martha's Vineyard did," plaintiff decided, in 1967, to sell the Vineyard property and put a sales price on it of $150,000. From 1921 through 1967, plaintiff had spent nearly all of his summers at the Vineyard property.

After it was put on the market, the house was never again used as residential property. Each spring plaintiff went to Martha's Vineyard, opened the house, put up curtains, pruned the shrubbery, generally cleaned and spruced up the property, and then left. This took two or three days and plaintiff occupied the house during this period. Each fall plaintiff returned and closed the house for the winter. The closing also took two to three days and plaintiff stayed in the house. The only other time that plaintiff occupied the property was once a year, when the corporation had its annual meeting of stockholders. As evidence of his intent to treat the Vineyard property as a business asset, plaintiff testified that in 1971 his daughter, after returning from abroad, requested the use of the property. Plaintiff refused, stating that the property was a business proposition. As a fatherly gesture, however, he rented a summer home in Maine for her use.

Plaintiff made no attempt to rent the house for the following reasons: He believed that it would be easier to sell a clean empty house than one occupied by tenants; the house being suitable for summer occupancy only, would have had to have been rented completely equipped, which would have required the plaintiff to purchase linen, silver, blankets, and recreational equipment at a cost which would not have been justified by any possible rental; rental prices bore no reasonable relation to the value of the property and the expected sales price; and rental was complicated by the restrictive provisions of the corporation's bylaws.

In 1968, a prospective purchaser offered to buy the property for $150,000. Plaintiff, however, could not obtain the necessary 75% approval of the stockholders of Seven Gates and the sale was not completed. In 1973, plaintiff received a cash offer of $150,000 for the property and the sale was closed in September of 1973. Plaintiff's 1973 tax return showed a net long-term capital gain of $100,536.50, as a result of the sale.

Rulings of Law

The tax issue in this case is: When and how does residential property become converted into income producing property?

The Tax Court, in attempting to establish a clear guideline in a murky area, created a simple test: The taxpayer had to make a bona fide offer to rent in order to convert residential property into "income producing property."[2] The Tax Court's *sine qua non* was a product of administrative reality. There are three basic reasons why the Government established a rental prerequisite. First, it stemmed from a fear that taxpayers would countermand the listing for sale after taking a series of deductions and reoccupy the house on a personal basis. Mary Laughlin Robinson, 2 T.C. 305, 309 (1943). Second, the rental requisite provided a clear and convenient administrative test. Warren Leslie, Sr., 6 T.C. 488, 494 (1946). Third, the rental requirement found some implied support in Treas.Reg. § 1.212–1(h) (1954), which provides:

---

[2] See Note, Recent Developments, Hulet P. Smith, 66 Mich.L.Rev. 562, 564–65 n. 14 (1968), and numerous cases cited therein.

Ordinary and necessary expenses paid or incurred in connection with the management, conservation, or maintenance of property held for use as a residence by the taxpayer are not deductible. However, ordinary and necessary expenses paid or incurred in connection with the management, conservation, or maintenance of property held by the taxpayer as rental property are deductible even though such property was formerly held by the taxpayer for use as a home.[3]

In Hulet P. Smith, 26 T.C.M. 149 (1967), aff'd 397 F.2d 804 (9th Cir.1968), the Tax Court abandoned the rental test and held that an offer for sale plus an abandonment transformed the property into an investment asset. The Court of Appeals, in affirming, circumspectly stated:

> The Government makes a strong case for reversal. See Recent Development, Hulet P. Smith, 66 Mich.L.Rev. 562 (1968). Unusual circumstances are present, however, and we are not persuaded that the Tax Court's factual finding and its consequent conclusions are clearly wrong.[4] Smith, supra, 397 F.2d 804.

In a subsequent decision, the Tax Court was presented with a fact pattern which was similar to the one presented in Smith and came to the opposite conclusion. Frank A. Newcombe, 54 T.C. 1298 (1970). The court stated that Smith was "of little precedential value." Id. at 1303.

In Newcombe the taxpayers moved out of their personal residence and immediately offered it for sale. At no time was the property offered for rent. The taxpayers argued that, under the Smith doctrine, the property was being held for the production of income. The Government contended that the Smith case was erroneous and that property can only be converted into income producing property use when there has been a bona fide offer to rent.

In rejecting both parties' positions, the court stated:

> We do not share the penchant for polarization which the arguments of the parties reflect. Rather, we believe that a variety of factors must be weighed. * * *. Newcombe, supra, 54 T.C. at 1299–1300.

The Newcombe court found that "[t]he key question, in cases of the type involved herein, is the purpose or intention of the taxpayer in light of all the facts and circumstances." Id. at 1303. The critical inquiry is, therefore, whether the taxpayer had or intended an "expectation of

---

[3]    Id. at 566 where "[b]y implication, then the regulations require a rental offer to convert a former residence to income producing property."

[4]    It is unclear as to what "unusual circumstances" the Court of Appeals was referring to. See Note, 25 Tax L.Rev. 269, 272 (1970):

> [O]ne would especially like to know what "unusual circumstances" the appellate court thought were present, since this does not appear to be such a situation.

profit." To aid in its inquiry, the court took into account the following considerations: length of time the taxpayer occupied his former residence prior to abandonment; the availability of the house for the taxpayer's personal use while it was unoccupied; the recreational character of the property; attempts to rent the property; and, whether the offer to sell was an attempt to realize post-conversion appreciation. The court explained its final criterion as follows:

> The placing of property on the market for immediate sale, at or shortly after the time of its abandonment as a residence, will ordinarily be strong evidence that a taxpayer is not holding the property for post conversion appreciation in value. Under such circumstances, only a most exceptional situation will permit a finding that the statutory requirement has been satisfied. *On the other hand, if a taxpayer believes that the value of the property may appreciate and decides to hold it for some period in order to realize upon such anticipated appreciation, as well as an excess over his investment, it can be said that the property is being "held for the production of income."* Id. at 1302–1303 (emphasis added).

I rule that the Vineyard property was converted into income producing property in 1967 and that plaintiff was entitled to deduct his maintenance expenses. In ruling in plaintiff's favor, I adopt the approach taken by the *Newcombe* court and do not regard renting as the "litmus test" for conversion.[5]

Administrative difficulty in determining when personal property is transformed into investment property should not create a rigid and inflexible barrier to the benefits of conversion.[6] Plaintiff gave sound and substantial business reasons for his failure to rent. I also note that the rental rule does not provide an elixir to administrative ills, for it must be determined that the offer to rent is bona fide and not a sham. Paul H. Stutz, 1965 P-H Tax Ct.Mem. ¶ 65,166; S. Wise, 1945 P-H Tax Ct.Mem. ¶ 45,298. Finally, I do not believe that Treas.Reg. § 1.212–1(h) (1954) commands a rental offer as a prerequisite to converting a prior residence into income producing property. I find the language contained therein, with regard to renting, to be illustrative and not an explicit statement of law.

In fact, another regulation provides that: "[t]he term 'income' for the purpose of section 212 * * * is not confined to recurring income but applies as well to gains from the disposition of property." Treas.Reg. § 1.212–1(b) (1954). The regulation further provides that the maintenance expenses of property held for investment are deductible;

---

[5] I.J. Wagner, 33 T.C.M. 201 (February 19, 1974); Charles D. Mayes, 30 T.C.M. 363 (April 28, 1971); Raymond L. Opper, 31 T.C.M. 485 (May 25, 1972); Richard R. Riss, Sr., 56 T.C. 388 (May 24, 1971); Richard N. Newbre, 30 T.C.M. 705 (July 15, 1971); James J. Sherlock, 31 T.C.M. 383 (April 27, 1972).

[6] See note 2, supra at 568.

even if the property is not producing income, there is no likelihood of current income, and there is no likelihood of gain upon the sale of the property.

The determination of whether plaintiff's prior residence has been converted into income producing property is made by examining the taxpayer's purpose in light of all the facts and circumstances. Treas.Reg. § 1.212–1(c) (1954). I find that the facts and circumstances presented clearly indicate that plaintiff intended to benefit from post-abandonment appreciation.

I take judicial notice that the price for recreational property on Martha's Vineyard and everywhere else in New England has skyrocketed in the past decade. Plaintiff has had wide exposure to financial and real estate transactions. He was thoroughly exposed to the real estate world from 1934 to 1943. During that period, he liquidated about 15,000 properties in about 1,200 communities located in thirty-six states. He was specifically aware of Martha's Vineyard land values, having spent nearly all of his summers there. Plaintiff also testified that he was aware, during the latter half of the 1960's of changing economic conditions. As administrator of a large New York insurance company, he saw increasing cash flow and rising prosperity. He testified that, as a result of this exposure, he came to the conclusion, during the latter part of 1967, that we were in the beginning of an inflationary trend and that the value of land would appreciate markedly. Although the 1967 market value of the Vineyard property was $50,000, plaintiff's business acumen and experience suggested that he could obtain his list price of $150,000 if he kept the property visible and in good condition and waited for the anticipated real estate boom coupled with the anticipated inflation. After a period of five and one-half years, plaintiff did, in fact, sell the property in September of 1973, for his original list price. A capital gain of $100,536.50 appeared on his 1973 income tax return as a consequence of the sale.

The fact that plaintiff immediately listed the property does not negate his contention that he intended to capitalize on post-abandonment appreciation in land values. By an immediate listing, plaintiff made the property a visible commodity on a demanding market. He patiently waited until the economic forces pushed the market value of his property up to his list price.

Based on all the facts and circumstances, I find that plaintiff had a reasonable "expectation of profit" and that the Vineyard property was held as income producing property during 1967. Accordingly, I rule that plaintiff was entitled to deduct the property's maintenance expenses incurred during 1970.

Judgment for the plaintiffs.

So ordered.

## NOTE

Recall the Section 121 exclusion of gains on the sale of a principal residence considered in Chapter 11A. Section 121 expressly sanctions temporary rental of such a dwelling by requiring recognition of income to the extent that depreciation was taken on the building after May 6, 1997.[1] Such depreciation could be before, during, or after the building acquired its principal residence status. The rental and depreciation of a property eligible for the benefits of Section 121 (meeting the two-year ownership and use as a principal residence requirements) makes the property subject to special rules. First, to the extent of depreciation allowed after May 6, 1997 with respect to such property, gain must be recognized and only gain in excess of that amount qualifies for the Section 121 exclusion.[2] Additionally, if a taxpayer sells a property which at any time after 2008 has not been used as a principal residence of the taxpayer or the taxpayer's spouse, a portion of the gain realized after the application of the depreciation rule generally must be recognized.[3] The portion that is recognized is determined by the ratio of the taxpayer's nonqualified use of the property after 2008 divided by the total period of time the taxpayer owned the property.[4] A period when the property is not used as a principal residence is generally considered nonqualified. However, nonqualified use does not include the portion of the Section 121 five-year period after the property is converted from a principal residence to a rental use.[5]

## PROBLEMS

1.   Recall the *Frank* case in Chapter 14 at page 334 supra.

   (a)   Should Frank's expenses have been deductible under § 212 or § 165(c)(2)?

   (b)   If Frank had decided to buy the newspaper and incurred capital expenditures to begin operations, but then abandoned his plans, would he have been allowed a deduction? See Johan Domenie, 34 T.C.M. 469 (1975) and Rev.Rul. 77–254, 1977–2 C.B. 63.

   (c)   If Frank entered the business and elected to use § 195 but ceased operations before deducting all of his start-up expenditures, to what extent could he take a § 165(c) loss?

2.   Homeowners purchased their vacation residence for $180,000 ($20,000 of which was allocable to the land). When it was worth $160,000 ($20,000 of which was allocable to the land), they moved out and put it up for sale, but not rent, for $170,000.

---

[1]   I.R.C. § 121(d)(6).
[2]   I.R.C. § 121(d)(6).
[3]   I.R.C. § 121(b)(5)(A), (D)(i).
[4]   I.R.C. § 121(b)(5)(B). These periods include periods when depreciation is taken. I.R.C. § 121(b)(5)(D)(ii).
[5]   I.R.C. § 121(b)(5)(C)(ii)(I).

(a)  May they take deductions for expenses and depreciation on the residence? If so, what types of expenses would qualify?

(b)  Assume instead that they rented the property and properly took $10,000 of depreciation on it. What result when they subsequently sell the property for:

  (1)  $145,000?

  (2)  $175,000?

  (3)  $165,000?

(c)  What result in (b)(2), above, if the property had been Homeowner's principal residence, they had owned and used it for 4 of the prior 5 years?

3.    Single purchases a principal residence after 2008 for a cost of $200,000. Prior to occupying the residence, Single rents the residence for one year, taking $10,000 of depreciation on it. Single then occupies it as a principal residence and after owning it for five years, sells it for $400,000.

(a)  What tax consequences to Single on the sale?

(b)  What tax consequences in (a), above, if Single sold the residence for $600,000?

(c)  What tax consequences in (a), above, if Single initially occupied the residence for four years and then rented it in the fifth year?

# CHAPTER 16

# DEDUCTIONS NOT LIMITED TO BUSINESS OR PROFIT-SEEKING ACTIVITIES

## A. INTRODUCTION

The preceding chapters have dealt with deductions that emanate from business and profit-seeking activities. The primary purposes for their allowance are to reflect accurately net income and profits from business and profit-seeking activities and to encourage investment in such activities.

Generally, Section 262 precludes deductions for personal, living or family expenses. The deductions allowed by the provisions considered in this chapter are exceptions to the general prohibition. Although the deduction provisions considered in this chapter apply to business, profit-seeking, *and* personal activities, as a practical matter the business and profit-seeking items would be deductible under Section 162 or Section 212 without assistance from the provisions examined here. Thus, the practical effect of the provisions considered here is to *create* deductions only for limited personal, living or family items.

As the comment below indicates, an effect of the allowance of an income tax deduction is a federal subsidy.[1] For example, the interest deduction may aid economic growth. The deduction for local taxes eases the pain of certain taxation and thus assists revenue raising by states and municipalities. Consider the excerpt below. Should the federal government pick up a higher percentage of the costs of some taxpayers than of others? Is there an alternative under which all taxpayers would be treated the same? To what extent is the problem alleviated by legislation lowering and flattening tax rates?

---

[1] See Surrey, "Tax Incentives as a Device for Implementing Government Policy: A Comparison with Direct Government Expenditures," 83 Harv.L.Rev. 705 (1970); Turnier and Kelly, "The Economic Equivalence of Standard Tax Credits, Deductions and Exemptions," 36 U.Fla.L.Rev. 1003 (1984).

# Tax Subsidies as a Device for Implementing Government Policy: A Comparison with Direct Government Expenditures*

Stanley S. Surrey.

\* \* \*

## 1.  THE NATURE AND EXTENT OF EXISTING TAX SUBSIDIES
\* \* \*

### A.  The Tax Expenditure Budget

The Federal Income tax system consists really of two parts: one part comprises the structural provisions necessary to implement the income tax on individual and corporate net income; the second part comprises a system of tax expenditures under which governmental financial assistance programs are carried out through special tax provisions rather than through direct government expenditures. The second system is simply grafted on to the structure of the income tax proper; it has no basic relation to that structure and is not necessary to its operation.

Instead, the system of tax expenditures provides a vast subsidy apparatus that uses the mechanics of the income tax as a method of paying the subsidies. The special provisions under which this subsidy apparatus functions take a variety of forms, covering exclusions from income, exemptions, deductions, credits against tax, preferential rates of tax, and deferrals of tax. The Tax Expenditure Budget * * * identifies and qualifies the existing tax expenditures. This Tax Expenditure Budget is essentially an enumeration of the present "tax incentives" or "tax subsidies" contained in our income tax system.

\* \* \*

The Tax Expenditure Budget enables us to look at the income tax provisions reflected in that Budget in a new light. Once these tax provisions are seen not as inherent parts of an income tax structure but as carrying out programs of financial assistance for particular groups and activities, a number of questions immediately come into focus. Once we see that we are not evaluating technical tax provisions but rather expenditure programs, we are able to ask the traditional questions and use the analytical tools that make up the intellectual apparatus of expenditure experts.

We thus can put the basic question of whether we desire to provide that financial assistance at all, and if so in what amount—a stock question any budget expert would normally ask of any item in the regular Budget. We can inquire whether the program is working well, how its benefits compare with its costs, is it accomplishing its objectives—indeed, what are its objectives? Who is actually being assisted by the program

---

\*   Excerpts from Hearings before the Subcommittee on Priorities and Economy in Government of the Joint Economic Committee, 92d Cong., 1st Sess. pp. 49–51 (1972).

and is that assistance too much or too little? Again, these are stock questions directed by any budget expert at existing programs. They all equally must be asked of the items and programs in the Tax Expenditure Budget.

\* \* \*

The translation and consequent restatement of a tax expenditure program in direct expenditure terms generally show an upside-down result utterly at variance with usual expenditure policies. Thus, if cast in direct expenditure language, the present assistance for owner-occupied homes under the tax deductions for mortgage interest and property taxes would look as follows, envisioned as a HUD program:

> For a married couple with more than $200,000 [currently $600,000 Ed.] in income, HUD would, for each $100 of mortgage interest on the couple's home pay $70 [currently, $37 Ed.] to the bank holding the mortgage, leaving the couple to pay $30 [currently, $63 Ed.]. It would also pay a similar portion of the couple's property tax to the State or city levying the tax.

> For a married couple with income of $10,000, HUD would pay the bank on the couple's mortgage $19 [currently, $10. Ed.] per each $100 interest unit, with the couple paying $81 [currently, $90. Ed.]. It would also pay a similar portion of the couple's property tax to the State or city levying the tax.

> For a married couple too poor to pay an income tax, HUD would pay nothing to the bank, leaving the couple to pay the entire interest cost. The couple would also have to pay the entire property tax.

One can assume that no HUD Secretary would ever have presented to Congress a direct housing program with this upside-down effect.

## B. Interest*

Internal Revenue Code: Sections 163(a), (h); 280A(d)(1); 7872. See Sections 163(d) and (f); 221; 263A; 265(a)(2) through (4); 266.

Proposed Regulations: Section 1.7872–1(a).

---

\*   See Bedell, "The Interest Deduction: Its Current Status," 32 N.Y.U.Inst. on Fed.Tax. 1117 (1974), and Kanter, "Interest Deduction: Use, Ruse, and Refuse," 46 Taxes 794 (1968); a briefer discussion appears in Kanter, "The Interest Deduction: When and How Does It Work," 26 N.Y.U.Inst. on Fed.Tax. 87 (1968).

# Revenue Ruling 69–188

1969–1 Cum.Bull. 54.

Advice has been requested whether for Federal income tax purposes, a payment made under the circumstances set forth below is considered to be interest.

A taxpayer on the cash receipts and disbursements method of accounting who wished to purchase a building, arranged with a lender to finance the transaction. A conventional mortgage loan of 1,000x dollars was negotiated, secured by a deed of trust on the building, and repayable in monthly installments over a ten-year period at a stated annual interest rate of 7.2 percent. In addition to the annual interest rate the parties agreed that the borrower would pay a "loan processing fee" of 70x dollars (sometimes referred to as "points") prior to receipt of the loan proceeds. The borrower established that this fee was not paid for any specific services that the lender had performed or had agreed to perform in connection with the borrower's account under the loan contract. The loan agreement provided for separate charges for these services. For example, separate charges were made for a preliminary title report, a title report, an escrow fee, the drawing of the deed and other papers, and insurance.

In determining the amount of this "loan processing fee" the lender considered the economic factors that usually dictate an acceptable rate of interest. That is, he considered the general availability of money, the character of the property offered as security, the degree of success that the borrower had enjoyed in his prior business activities, and the outcome of previous transactions between the borrower and his creditors.

The taxpayer tendered a check for 70x dollars drawn on a bank account owned by him, which contained a sufficient balance, in payment of the fee. The monies in this account were not originally obtained from the lender.

Section 163(a) of the Internal Revenue Code of 1954 provides that there shall be allowed as a deduction all interest paid or accrued within the taxable year on indebtedness.

\* \* \*

For tax purposes, interest has been defined by the Supreme Court of the United States as the amount one has contracted to pay for the use of borrowed money, and as the compensation paid for the use or forbearance of money. See Old Colony Railroad Co. v. Commissioner, 284 U.S. 552 (1932), Ct.D. 456, C.B. XI–1, 274 (1932); Deputy v. du Pont, 308 U.S. 488, 60 S.Ct. 363 (1940), Ct.D. 1435, C.B. 1940–1, 118. The Board of Tax Appeals has stated that interest is the compensation allowed by law or fixed by the parties for the use, forbearance, or detention of money. Fall River Electric Light Co. v. Commissioner, 23 B.T.A. 168 (1931). A negotiated bonus or premium paid by a borrower to a lender in order to obtain a loan has been held to be interest for Federal income tax purposes. L-R Heat Treating Co. v. Commissioner, 28 T.C. 894 (1957).

The payment or accrual of interest for tax purposes must be incidental to an unconditional and legally enforceable obligation of the taxpayer claiming the deduction. Paul Autenreith v. Commissioner, 115 F.2d 856 (1940). There need not, however, be a legally enforceable indebtedness already in existence when the payment of interest is made. It is sufficient that the payment be a "prerequisite to obtaining borrowed capital." *L-R Heat Treating Co.* The fee of $70x$ dollars in the instant case was paid prior to the receipt of the borrowed funds; however, this does not preclude the payment from being classified as interest.

It is not necessary that the parties to a transaction label a payment made for the use of money as interest for it to be so treated. See L-R Heat Treating Co. The mere fact that the parties in the instant case agreed to call the $70x$ dollars a "loan processing fee" does not in itself preclude this payment from being interest under section 163(a) of the Code. Further, this conclusion would not be affected by the fact that this payment is sometimes referred to as "points." Compare Revenue Ruling 67–297, C.B. 1967–2, 87, relating to the deductibility as interest of a loan origination fee paid by the purchaser of a residence to a lending institution in connection with the acquisition of a home mortgage. Also, compare Revenue Ruling 68–650, C.B. 1968–2, 78, relating to the deductibility as interest of the payment of a loan charge paid by the seller of a residence to assist the purchaser in obtaining a mortgage loan.

The method of computation also does not control its deductibility, so long as the amount in question is an ascertainable sum contracted for the use of borrowed money. See Kena, Inc. v. Commissioner, 44 B.T.A. 217 (1941). The fact that the amount paid in the instant case is a flat sum paid in addition to a stated annual interest rate does not preclude a deduction under section 163 of the Code.

To qualify as interest for tax purposes, the payment, by whatever name called, must be compensation for the use or forbearance of money per se and not a payment for specific services which the lender performs in connection with the borrower's account. For example, interest would not include separate charges made for investigating the prospective borrower and his security, closing costs of the loan and papers drawn in connection therewith, or fees paid to a third party for servicing and collecting that particular loan. See Workingmen's Loan Ass'n v. United States, 142 F.2d 359 (1944); Rev.Rul. 57–541, C.B. 1957–2, 319. Compare Revenue Ruling 57–540, C.B. 1957–2, 318, relating to the classification as interest of the fees imposed on borrowers by a mortgage finance company. Also, even where service charges are not stated separately on the borrower's account, interest would not include amounts attributable to such services. See Rev.Rul. 67–297; compare Norman L. Noteman, et al., Trustees v. Welch, 108 F.2d 206 (1939) relating to the classification as interest of the charges paid by borrowers to a personal finance company.

Accordingly, in the instant case, because the taxpayer was able to establish that the fee of 70*x* dollars was paid as compensation to the lender solely for the use or forbearance of money, and because he did not initially obtain the funds to pay this fee from the lender, the 70*x* dollars is considered to be interest.

## Dean v. Commissioner

Tax Court of the United States, 1961.
35 T.C. 1083.

Opinion

■ RAUM, JUDGE:

The Commissioner determined deficiencies in income tax against petitioners for 1955 and 1956 in the amounts of $13,875.61 and $16,383.86, respectively. Petitioners are husband and wife; they filed joint returns for 1955 and 1956 with the director of internal revenue at Wilmington, Delaware. To the extent that the deficiencies still remain in controversy they raise the question whether petitioners were entitled to deduct as interest the amounts of $9,243.38 in 1955 and $26,912.02 in 1956 representing interest on loans on life insurance policies which had accrued and which was paid by them after they had made irrevocable assignments of such policies to their children. An amended answer filed by the Commissioner claims increases in the deficiencies already determined by adding thereto the amounts of $105,181.50 and $119,796.78 for 1955 and 1956, respectively. Such increases raise a single issue, unrelated to the original deficiencies, namely, whether petitioners realized taxable income to the extent of the alleged economic benefit derived from the interest-free use of funds which they had borrowed from a family corporation controlled by them. The facts have been stipulated.

[Only the portion of the opinion dealing with the interest-free loans is presented. Ed.]

The Commissioner's amended answer charged petitioners with income equal to interest at the alleged legal rate in Delaware (6 percent) with respect to loans which they had obtained upon non-interest-bearing notes from their controlled corporation, Nemours Corporation, and which were outstanding during 1955 and 1956. The theory of the amended answer was that the petitioners realized income to the extent of the economic benefit derived from the free use of borrowed funds from Nemours, and that such economic benefit was equal to interest at the legal rate in Delaware, alleged to be 6 percent per annum. However, the Commissioner's brief has reduced the amount of his additional claim so that the income thus attributed to petitioners is measured, not by the legal rate of interest, but by the prime rate, since it is stipulated that petitioners could have borrowed the funds at the prime rate. As thus reduced, the additional income which the Commissioner seeks to charge to petitioners is $65,648.79 for 1955 and $97,931.71 for 1956. The facts in relation to this issue have been stipulated as follows:

9. Prior to December 17, 1954 the entire issued and outstanding capital stock of Nemours Corporation, hereinafter referred to as Nemours, organized under the laws of the State of Delaware with principal office in Wilmington, Delaware, consisting of 36,172 shares of no par common, was owned by the petitioners, as follows:

J. Simpson Dean ........................................................ 7,249 shares

Paulina duPont Dean ............................................. 28,923 shares

10. On December 17, 1954 each of the petitioners made a gift of 2,000 shares of the stock of Nemours to the above-mentioned trusts created by them in 1937 for the benefit of their children. In the years 1955 and 1956 the petitioners owned 32,172 shares of no par common of Nemours.

11. For the taxable year 1955 Nemours was a personal holding company under section 542 of the Internal Revenue Code of 1954 and filed its Federal income tax returns as such.

12. For the taxable year 1956 Nemours filed its Federal income tax return as a regular business corporation. By notice of deficiency dated March 2, 1960, respondent determined that Nemours was a personal holding company for the year 1956. An appeal from such determination was taken by Nemours and the matter is now pending before this Court in Docket No. 86863, entitled Nemours Corporation v. Commissioner of Internal Revenue.

13. Petitioner J. Simpson Dean owed Nemours on non-interest bearing notes the following amounts:

| Period | Amount |
|---|---|
| January 1, 1955 to January 10, 1955 | $302,185.73 |
| January 11, 1955 to December 31, 1955 | 223,861.56 |
| January 1, 1956 to December 31, 1956 | 357,293.41 |

14. Petitioner Paulina duPont Dean owed Nemours on non-interest bearing notes the following amounts:

| Period | Amount |
|---|---|
| January 1, 1955 to December 31, 1955 | $1,832,764.71 |
| January 1, 1956 to December 31, 1956 | 2,205,804.66 |

15. The following are the prime rates of interest and the dates on which changes were made in such rates at which the petitioners could have borrowed money during the years 1955 and 1956:

January 1, 1955.................................................................. 3%

August 15, 1955.............................................................. 3¼%

October 20, 1955............................................................ 3½%

April 20, 1956................................................................. 3¾%

September 1, 1956........................................................... 4%

December 31, 1956.......................................................... 4%

16. Interest computed at the prime rates shown in the preceding paragraph on the non-interest bearing notes of the petitioners for the taxable years 1955 and 1956 would be as follows:

| Year 1955: | Amount |
|---|---|
| J. Simpson Dean | $ 7,203.98 |
| Paulina duPont Dean | 58,444.81 |
| Total | $65,648.79 |

| Year 1956: | Amount |
|---|---|
| J. Simpson Dean | $13,651.59 |
| Paulina duPont Dean | 84,280.12 |
| Total | $97,931.71 |

[Paragraph 17 of the stipulation, objected to by respondent as to relevancy,[1] states that if petitioners had paid interest to Nemours, the corporation would have made dividend distributions to petitioners equal to the amount of such interest, and further sets forth the effect, taxwise and otherwise, upon petitioners, Nemours, and the trusts, based upon that hypothesis as well as certain other assumptions.]

The theory of the Commissioner's amended answer, as modified in his brief, undoubtedly had its origin in a statement by this Court in a Memorandum Opinion involving certain gift taxes of these taxpayers, Paulina duPont Dean, T.C.Memo. 1960–54, on appeal (C.A.3), where it was said:

Viewed realistically, the lending of over two million dollars to petitioners without interest might be looked upon as a means of passing on earnings (certainly potential earnings) of Nemours in lieu of dividends, to the extent of a reasonable interest on such loans. * * *.

The amended answer herein was filed within several months after the foregoing Memorandum Opinion had been promulgated. The statement quoted above was mere dictum and we have not been directed to any case holding or even suggesting that an interest-free loan may result in the

[1] We find it unnecessary to rule upon that objection, since we reach the result herein without reliance upon paragraph 17.

realization of taxable income by the debtor, or to any administrative ruling or regulation taking that position. Although the question may not be completely free from doubt we think that no taxable income is realized in such circumstances.

In support of its present position, the Government relies primarily upon a series of cases holding that rent-free use of corporate property by a stockholder or officer may result in the realization of income. Charles A. Frueauff, 30 B.T.A. 449 (rent-free use of corporation's apartment); Reynard Corporation, 30 B.T.A. 451 (rent-free use of corporation's house); Percy M. Chandler, 41 B.T.A. 165, affirmed 119 F.2d 623 (C.A.3) (rent-free use of corporation's apartment and lodge); Paulina duPont Dean, 9 T.C. 256 (rent-free use of corporation's house); Dean v. Commissioner, 187 F.2d 1019 (C.A.3), affirming a Memorandum Opinion of this Court (rent-free use of corporation's house); Rodgers Dairy Co., 14 T.C. 66 (personal use of corporation's automobile). Cf. Louis Greenspon, 23 T.C. 138, affirmed on this point but reversed on other grounds 229 F.2d 947 (C.A.8) (farm expenses paid by corporation); Alex Silverman, 28 T.C. 1061, affirmed 253 F.2d 849 (C.A.8) (wife's travel expenses paid by corporation); Chester Distributing Co. v. Commissioner, 184 F.2d 514 (C.A.3), affirming per curiam a Memorandum Opinion of this Court (personal entertainment expenses paid by corporation). These cases bear a superficial resemblance to the present case, but reflection convinces us that they are not in point. In each of them a benefit was conferred upon the stockholder or officer in circumstances such that had the stockholder or officer undertaken to procure the same benefit by an expenditure of money such expenditure would not have been deductible by him. Here, on the other hand, had petitioners borrowed the funds in question on interest-bearing notes, their payment of interest would have been fully deductible by them under section 163, I.R.C. 1954. Not only would they not be charged with the additional income in controversy herein, but they would have a deduction equal to that very amount. We think this circumstance differentiates the various cases relied upon by the Commissioner, and perhaps explains why he has apparently never taken this position in any prior case.

We have heretofore given full force to interest-free loans for tax purposes, holding that they result in no interest deduction for the borrower, * * *. We think it to be equally true that an interest-free loan results in no taxable gain to the borrower,[2] and we hold that the Commissioner is not entitled to any increased deficiency based upon this issue.

---

[2]  As recently as 1955, this was also the view of the Commissioner. In Rev.Rul. 55–713, 1955–2 C.B. 23, in sanctioning the so-called split-dollar insurance scheme, it is said at page 24: "In the instant case, the substance of the insurance arrangement between the parties is in all essential respects the same as if Y corporation makes annual loans without interest, of a sum of money equal to the annual increases in the cash surrender value of the policies of insurance taken out on the life of B. The mere making available of money does not result in realized income to the payee or a deduction to the payor."

Reviewed by the Court.

Decision will be entered under Rule 50.

■ FISHER, J., concurs in the result.

■ OPPER, J., concurring:

The necessity is not apparent to me of deciding more on the second issue than that there can be no deficiency. If petitioners were in receipt of some kind of gross income, possibly comparable to that dealt with in such cases as Charles A. Frueauff, 30 B.T.A. 449 (1934), the corresponding interest deduction would perhaps exactly offset and nullify it. But because that would mean that there is no deficiency, it would not necessarily follow that there was no gross income, as the present opinion, in my view, gratuitously holds. Certainly the statement that "an interest-free loan results in no taxable gain to the borrower" is much too broad a generalization to make here.

Suppose, for example, that in such a case as Charles A. Frueauff, supra, the property made available without charge to the shareholder-officer was rented by him to another, instead of being occupied for personal use. Would the fact that he could presumably deduct as a business or nonbusiness expense the hypothetical rental value theoretically paid by him to the corporation, section 212, I.R.C. 1954, and thereby completely offset any gross income, lead us to conclude, as here, contrary to that whole line of cases, that there could be no gross income in the first place?

Or suppose the facts showed that the indebtedness was "incurred * * * to purchase or carry obligations * * * the interest on which is wholly exempt from * * * taxes." Sec. 265(2), I.R.C. 1954.

This being apparently a case of first impression, the present result seems peculiarly unfortunate in deciding a point that need not be passed on. To make matters worse, the burden here is on respondent, since the issue was first raised by his answer;[1] and thus in this leading case all factual conclusions and inferences must be favorable to petitioners. Cf., e.g., Spheeris v. Commissioner, 284 F.2d 928 (C.A.7 1960), affirming a Memorandum Opinion of this Court. Disposition of the issue as one of generally applicable law is hence doubly unnecessary.

■ TIETJENS, WITHEY, and DRENNEN, JJ., agree with this concurring opinion.

■ BRUCE, J., dissenting:

I respectfully dissent from the opinion of the majority with respect to the second issue. In my opinion the present case is not distinguishable in principle from such cases as Paulina duPont Dean, 9 T.C. 256; Chandler v. Commissioner, 119 F.2d 623 (C.A.3), affirming 41 B.T.A. 165, and other cases cited by the majority, wherein it was held that the rent-

---

[1] See, e.g., Rainbow Gasoline Corporation, 31 B.T.A. 1050 (1935), decided partly for petitioner and partly for respondent entirely on the question of burden of proof.

free use of corporate property by a stockholder or officer resulted in the realization of income. "Interest" in the sense that it represents compensation paid for the use, forbearance, or detention of money, may be likened to "rent" which is paid for the use of property.

I agree with Judge Opper in his concurring opinion that "the statement that 'an interest-free loan results in no taxable gain to the borrower' is much too broad a generalization to make here." I do not wish to infer that the interest-free loan of money should be construed as resulting in taxable income to the borrower in every instance. However, it is difficult to believe that the interest-free loan of in excess of $2 million ($2,563,098.07 throughout 1956) by a personal holding company to its majority stockholders (its only stockholders prior to December 17, 1954) did not result in any economic benefit to the borrower.

In my opinion, the statement that "had petitioners borrowed the funds in question on interest-bearing notes, their payment of interest would have been fully deductible by them under section 163, I.R.C. 1954," is likewise too broad a generalization to make here.

Section 163(a) states the "General Rule" to be that "There shall be allowed as a deduction all interest paid or accrued within the taxable year on indebtedness." Section 265(2) provides, however, that—

No deduction shall be allowed for—

* * *

(2) INTEREST.—Interest on indebtedness incurred or continued to purchase or carry obligations * * * the interest on which is wholly exempt from the taxes imposed by this subtitle.

Section 265(2) is specifically included in the cross references contained in subsection (c) of section 163 and is therefore clearly intended as an exception to, or limitation upon, section 163(a). For obligations, the interest on which is wholly exempt from taxes, see section 103 of the Internal Revenue Code of 1954.

It is recognized that the burden with respect to the issue here presented by his amended answer is upon the respondent. This burden, however, was, in my opinion, discharged by the stipulated facts presented. It was incumbent upon the petitioners, if such were the facts, to plead and establish that had they been required to pay interest on the loans in question they would have been entitled to deduct such interest from their gross income. They have done neither. It is well established that deductions are matters of legislative grace and must be clearly established.

On the record presented herein, I do not agree that "had petitioners borrowed the funds in question on interest-bearing notes, their payment of interest would have been fully deductible by them under section 163," and that the inclusion in the gross income of the petitioners of an amount representing a reasonable rate of interest on the loans in question would therefore result in no deficiency.

## NOTE

The *Dean* case involves a gross income issue but is placed here among deductions because it also indirectly involves deductibility of interest. Prior to the Tax Reform Act of 1984 interest-free loans were used in intra-family transactions to shift income from the lender to the borrower. They were especially helpful in avoiding the then existing ten year reversionary rule of Section 673 of the Clifford trust provisions.[1] For example, Parent, in a high income bracket, could make an interest-free loan to Child and thereafter the income earned by the principal of the loan would be taxed to Child. If the loan were a demand loan or a term loan for a period of less than ten years the transaction would escape Section 673, which would have taxed Parent on the gross income if it were handled by way of a trust.[2]

Some 48 years elapsed between the advent of the federal income tax and the Service's first attempt to tax the benefit of interest-free loans as income. But then, despite the leisurely pace at which it initially pursued interest-free and below-market interest rate loans, the Service became quite persistent in seeking to tax these transactions. That persistence earned congressional support in the Tax Reform Act of 1984 with the enactment of Section 7872.[3]

Congressional action was required because of the Tax Court's obstinate adherence to its errant rationale in *Dean*. The Tax Court clung to its reasoning in the *post-Dean* years, differentiating interest-free loans from the rent-free use of property, upon the basis of the deductibility of the benefits derived. Many cases continued the error.[4]

The *Dean* issue has also arisen in the gift tax area. In Crown v. Commissioner[5] the Tax Court, following an earlier district court decision,[6] held that no taxable gift resulted from an interest-free demand loan. The Service's first breakthrough finally arrived with the Supreme Court's decision in Dickman v. Commissioner,[7] in which the Court held that an interest-free loan to a family member was a transfer of property by gift. The lender was treated as having made a taxable gift of the reasonable value of the use of the money.

---

[1]   The rule was amended by the 1986 legislation. See page 301, supra.

[2]   See page 301, supra.

[3]   See Hartigan, "From *Dean* and Crown to the Tax Reform Act of 1984: Taxation of Interest-Free Loans," 60 Notre Dame L.Rev. 31 (1984); Bilter, "Interest-Free Loans—Boon or Bust?" 37 U.S.C. Inst. on Fed.Tax'n 23 (1985).

[4]   See, e.g., Zager v. Commissioner, 72 T.C. 1009 (1979), affirmed sub nom. Martin v. Commissioner, 649 F.2d 1133 (5th Cir.1981); Greenspun v. Commissioner, 72 T.C. 931 (1979), affirmed 670 F.2d 123 (9th Cir.1982); Albert Suttle v. Commissioner, 37 T.C.M. 1638 (1978), affirmed 625 F.2d 1127 (4th Cir.1980), Martin v. Commissioner, 649 F.2d 1133 (5th Cir.1981), and Marsh v. Commissioner, 73 T.C. 317 (1979). These cases also reaffirmed *Dean* on the same issue.

[5]   67 T.C. 1060 (1977), affirmed 585 F.2d 234 (7th Cir.1978).

[6]   Johnson v. United States, 254 F.Supp. 73 (N.D.Tex.1966).

[7]   465 U.S. 330, 104 S.Ct. 1086 (1984).

Prompted perhaps by the *Dickman* decision,[8] Congress finally determined to recognize the economic reality of interest-free loan transactions. The House Ways and Means Committee acknowledged that:[9]

> [l]oans between family members (and other similar loans) are being used to avoid the assignment of income rules and the grantor trust rules. * * * [l]oans from corporations to shareholders are being used to avoid rules requiring the taxation of corporate income at the corporate level. * * * [and] [l]oans to persons providing services are being used to avoid rules requiring the payment of employment taxes and rules restricting the deductibility of interest in certain situations by the person providing the services.

The measures taken by Congress in the Tax Reform Act of 1984[10] represented an all-inclusive attempt to stem taxpayer avoidance of these well-recognized rules of taxation.

Section 7872 of the Code generally divides loans with below-market interest rates[11] into two broad categories—gift loans and non-gift loans.[12] It then subdivides each category according to the terms of the repayment of the loan, i.e., term loans and demand loans. The treatment the loan receives under Section 7872 depends upon its category and subcategory. The classification of below-market interest rate loans by category and subcategory determines the nature and timing of the income or gift to the borrower, the timing of the possibly deductible payment of constructive interest by the borrower to the lender, and the inclusion of the mythical interest in gross income of the lender. Under Section 7872 all loans that carry a below-market interest rate (or charge no interest at all) are recharacterized to impute the payment of interest. Thus, for example, a $100,000 interest-free loan from a father to his son is transformed, for tax purposes, into a loan in which the father charges interest at a rate based upon the average market yield of outstanding marketable United States securities with maturities comparable to the term of the loan. This rate of interest is called the

---

[8] Congress may also have been nudged by admonitions such as that of the Ninth Circuit affirming the *Greenspun* case, that when "the Government seeks to modify a principle of taxation so firmly entrenched in our jurisprudence, it should turn to Congress, not to the courts." 670 F.2d at 126.

[9] Staff of House Comm. on Ways and Means, 98th Cong., 2d Sess., Summary of Comm.Amendment to H.R. 4170, 1373–74 (Comm.Print 1984).

[10] The Tax Reform Act of 1984 (T.R.A. § 84) is actually only a section of a larger piece of legislation; T.R.A. § 84 is Division A of the Deficit Reduction Act of 1984.

[11] I.R.C. § 7872(e)(1) defines below-market interest rate loans. Demand loans are below the market interest rate if the interest payable is less than the applicable Federal rate, see Text at note 16, infra. Term loans are below the market interest rate if the amount loaned exceeds the present value of all payments required by the loan.

[12] I.R.C. § 7872(a). Notwithstanding the title of paragraph (a) (treatment of gift loans and demand loans), the treatment of below-market interest rate loans is easier to understand if dichotomized between gift and nongift loans.

applicable Federal rate.[13] The son is presumed to pay this interest,[14] possibly generating an interest deduction for himself and generating interest income for his father.[15] The son's interest payment is deemed to have been made from a separate source of funds made available to him by his father. This constructive transmittal of funds from the father to his son to permit the son to pay the constructive interest is another taxable event and, depending on the identity of the taxpayers and the nature of the loan, generally is characterized as either a gift, a dividend, or compensation.

*Gift Loans.* The first major category, gift loans, consists of loans in which the lender's funding (foregoing) of the borrower's interest payments is characterized as a gift from the lender to the borrower.[16] If the gift loan is to be repaid on a specific date (i.e., a *term loan*),[17] the lender must recognize interest income and the borrower possibly earns an interest deduction.[18] Thus in our example above, let us assume that the $100,000 loan from the father to his son on January 1 of year one, due four years later on December 31 of year four, was made with donative intent. We assume further that the Federal mid-term rate in effect on January 1 of year one is 5 percent.

Under Section 7872 this loan would properly be characterized as a gift loan with the constructive interest (the amount treated as transmitted from the father to his son) taxed as a gift. The amount of the constructive interest is the amount loaned less the present value of all principal and all actual interest payments to be made under the loan.[19] In our example no interest

---

[13] The applicable Federal rates are determined by the Secretary on a monthly basis. I.R.C. § 1274(d)(1)(B). The rates in effect will reflect the average yields of outstanding marketable U.S. securities with comparable maturities. I.R.C. § 1274(d)(1)(C)(i). The applicable Federal rate to be applied to a particular loan is determined by reference to the term of the loan. See I.R.C. § 1274(d)(1)(A). The applicable Federal rate for a demand loan is always the Federal short-term rate for each day the loan is unpaid. I.R.C. § 7872(f)(2)(B). See Text at note 31, infra.

[14] This constructive interest payment is subject to several exceptions. See Text at notes 52–65, infra.

[15] Through its recharacterization of the transaction I.R.C. § 7872 artificially turns what actually happened into what should have happened. Since the father (the lender) never actually received this deemed interest payment, choosing instead to forego levying it upon his son, § 7872 labels this amount as "foregone interest." I.R.C. § 7872(e)(2). It is computed in accordance with principles of § 1272, which is also a product of the Tax Reform Act of 1984. See page 863, infra. "Foregone interest" is defined as the excess of the applicable Federal rate over any amounts of interest payable under the actual terms of the loan. I.R.C. § 7872(e)(2).

| In the case of a loan with a term of: | The applicable rate is: |
| --- | --- |
| Not over 3 years | The Federal short-term rate |
| Over 3 years but not over 9 years | The Federal mid-term rate |
| Over 9 years | The Federal long-term rate |

[16] See I.R.C. § 7872(f)(3) and Chapter 3B, supra.

[17] See I.R.C. § 7872(f)(6), which helpfully defines "term loan" as any loan that is not a demand loan.

[18] The interest payment that is imputed to the borrower is possibly allowed as a deduction under I.R.C. § 163(a) if no disallowance is specified under some other section such as I.R.C. §§ 163(d), 163(h); 265(a)(2), etc. Whether a deduction is disallowed depends somewhat upon the borrower's use of the funds. See the Text at pages 486–494, infra. Further, the question of deductibility also depends upon whether the interest is an above the line deduction or an itemized deduction. If it is an itemized deduction, the borrower will receive no tax benefit from it if it is a miscellaneous itemized deduction. See I.R.C. § 67(g) and Chapter 18C, infra.

[19] The total payments are discounted using the appropriate applicable Federal rate. I.R.C. § 7872(f)(1).

payments are called for by the loan, so we calculate the present value of $100,000 for 4 years at 5 percent compounded semiannually,[20] which is $82,075, and subtract that amount from $100,000. The $17,925 difference is constructive interest, the amount of the gift from the father to his son. This gift is deemed to be made on the date the loan was made.[21]

The son's possible interest deduction and his father's corresponding interest income are computed annually for each calendar year the loan is outstanding.[22] The amount of interest that would have accrued for the year under the applicable Federal rate is reduced by any actual interest payable which is properly allocable to the year and the remainder is called foregone interest.[23] In the hypothetical above, since father's loan to his son called for no interest the foregone interest for each year of the loan is simply 5 percent interest compounded semi-annually on $100,000, or $5,063.[24]

Foregone interest, the amount of the annual interest income and the potential corresponding deduction, is treated as having been paid by the borrower to the lender on the last day of each calendar year during which the loan is outstanding.[25] Thus on December 31 of year one, son is treated as having paid his father $5,063, possibly earning himself an interest deduction

---

Conceptually, a present value calculation asks the question, "how much money must I put into the bank today in order to have $X on a certain date in the future?" In order to make this calculation you must know the rate of interest your investment will earn, the period of time over which the investment will collect interest and the amount of money you want to have at the end of the investment period. In this case, we knew that the rate of interest was 5 percent compounded semiannually (this is equal to 2.5 percent interest for each of the several six-month periods, but adding all prior interest to the interest base each six months, see note 24, infra), that the investment was for a 4-year period and that at the end of the 4 years we wanted $100,000.

The solution, $82,075, can be derived through a somewhat complicated mathematical formula, through the use of present value tables, or by using a financial calculator. We suggest one of the latter two methods. Amounts in the Text are rounded to the nearest dollar.

[20]  Referring to note 13, supra, we see that loans of 3 to 9 years are subject to the Federal mid-term rate, which we assume to be 5 percent. Note that interest on a term loan at the applicable Federal rate is compounded semiannually. I.R.C. § 7872(f)(2)(A).

[21]  I.R.C. § 7872(d)(2), (b)(1).

[22]  I.R.C. § 7872(a). See also I.R.C. § 7872(d)(1) and the Text beginning at note 55, infra.

[23]  I.R.C. § 7872(a)(2), (e)(2).

[24]  This amount is computed by imposing 2.5 percent of $100,000 or $2,500 for the first one-half of the year plus 2.5 percent of $102,500 or $2,563 for the second half of the year totalling $5,063 of interest for the year. But see the Text at notes 55–59 infra.

Notice that the amount of the gift is computed under the provisions of I.R.C. § 7872(b), whereas the amount of the son's interest deduction and his father's corresponding interest income is computed under the provisions of § 7872(a) . This bifurcation is a result of § 7872(d)(2), which provides that in the case of a gift loan which is also a term loan, the *gift tax* consequences of such loan are to be determined by applying § 7872(b) instead of § 7872(a). But because the loan is also a gift loan, § 7872(a) will apply in determining the *income tax* consequences of the loan, i.e., the amount deemed to be retransferred from the borrower to the lender as interest. The Conference Report indicates that term gift loans are given the *income tax* treatment accorded demand loans because the close relationship of the parties that prompted the gift may well lead to disregard of the loan's maturity date. Additionally, if a term gift loan was treated as a term loan for *income tax* purposes, a complex original issue discount analysis, as required by § 7872(b)(2), would have to be made in order to determine the income tax consequences of the loan. H.Rep.No. 98–861, 98th Cong., 2d Sess. 1020 at n. 11 (1984). See also, Staff of the Joint Committee on Taxation, 98th Cong., 2d Sess., General Explanation of the Revenue Provisions of the Deficit Reduction Act of 1984, 532–533 (Comm.Print 1984).

[25]  I.R.C. § 7872(a)(2).

in that amount[26] and resulting in income to his father of a like amount. An exact duplicate of this transaction is deemed to occur on December 31 of each of the three subsequent years the loan is outstanding.[27]

If the gift loan is a *demand loan*,[28] rather than a term loan, a gift of the funds with which to pay the constructive interest is again deemed to be made by the lender to the borrower.[29] However, no separate calculation of the amount of the gift need be made here—both the amount of the gift and the borrower's potential interest deduction (and the lender's corresponding interest income) are simply determined by subtracting any actual interest payments due under the loan from the interest that would have accrued under the applicable Federal rate, (i.e., the foregone interest).[30]

Because the loan has no fixed date for repayment, the lender is deemed to make a gift on the last day of each of the lender's taxable years (or portion thereof) that the loan remains outstanding.[31] Similarly, the lender recognizes interest income and the borrower earns a possible interest deduction, in the amount of the gift, during each year that the loan is outstanding.[32]

In our example if father lends his son $100,000 interest-free, payable in full upon father's demand, and the loan remained outstanding throughout the entire calendar year, only one calculation is required. As the loan calls for no actual interest payments the determination of the interest on $100,000 at a 5 percent rate compounded semi-annually, or $5,063,[33] is all that is required. Father is deemed to make a gift to his son of $5,063 on December 31 of year one. Similarly, son is treated as paying that same amount back to his father as interest, possibly earning himself a deduction and creating income for his father, all on December 31st.

*Nongift Loans.* The rules applicable to nongift loans are somewhat different from those governing gift loans. Again, interest is deemed to be charged by the lender. The borrower is deemed to have paid that interest, generating income to the lender and a possible corresponding deduction for the borrower. The amount transmitted from the lender to the borrower to pay the constructive interest is characterized, not as a gift, but rather according to the nature of the relationship between the lender and the borrower. These various relationships are the subcategories of nongift loans.

---

[26] The borrower may possibly earn an I.R.C. § 163(a) deduction for any actual interest he may pay to the lender. See note 18, supra.

[27] See note 24, supra.

[28] A demand loan is generally "any loan which is payable in full at any time on the demand of the lender." I.R.C. § 7872(f)(5).

[29] I.R.C. § 7872(a)(1)(A).

[30] I.R.C. § 7872(a) and (e)(2).

[31] I.R.C. § 7872(a)(2).

[32] If Father were to have made a demand loan on January 1 of year one, and called it on June 30 of year one, with his son promptly repaying the principal, $2,500 of interest would have accrued. This $2,500 would be deemed to be a gift from father to his son resulting in a corresponding $2,500 interest payment from son to his father, all on December 31 of year one.

[33] See note 24, supra and I.R.C. § 7872(d)(1) considered in the Text beginning at note 55, infra.

Section 7872(c) identifies five subcategories of nongift loans: (1) loans between a corporation and one of its shareholders;[34] (2) loans between an employer and an employee or between an independent contractor and the person to whom he provides his services (all labelled "compensation-related" loans);[35] (3) loans with a principal purpose to avoid any federal tax;[36] (4) a catch-all subcategory of "other below-market loans,"[37] which are loans that do not fall within one of the preceding subcategories of nongift, loans yet their interest arrangements have a significant effect on any federal tax liability of the lender or the borrower; and (5) loans to a qualifying continuing care facility pursuant to a continuing care contract.[38]

Returning to our benevolent father and his needy son, let us assume that this time they are an unrelated employer and employee. The employee has worked overtime for the past several months without additional compensation,[39] so the employer lends him $100,000 interest-free on January 1 of year one, due four years later on December 31 of year four.

As this nongift loan is a *term loan,* both the amount treated as compensation by the employee and the amount of interest deemed paid by the employee to the employer are calculated by subtracting the present value of all principal and actual interest payments due under the loan from the amount loaned.[40] The entire amount treated as compensation in this nongift term loan situation is viewed as having been received by the employee on the date the loan was made and must be included in the employee's gross income for that year.[41] The employer also gets an immediate deduction for the compensation attributable to all four years of the loan.[42]

Conversely, the constructive interest deemed to be paid by the employee to the employer is treated as being constantly paid and received over the term of the loan.[43] Thus, the employee may possibly take a deduction each year only for the amount of interest deemed paid in that year and the

---

[34] I.R.C. § 7872(c)(1)(C). But see I.R.C. § 7872(f)(11).

[35] I.R.C. § 7872(c)(1)(B). Employee relocation loans are exempted from tax by temporary regulations. Reg. § 1.7872–5T(b)(6) and (c)(1).

[36] I.R.C. § 7872(c)(1)(D).

[37] I.R.C. § 7872(c)(1)(E). Congress left the skeleton of this fourth catch-all to be fleshed out by the regulations.

[38] I.R.C. § 7872(c)(1)(F).

[39] The Conference Committee Report explains that a loan will be treated as compensation-related only if a debtor-creditor relationship exists between the employer and employee when the loan is made. H.Rep.No. 98–861, 98th Cong., 2d Sess. 1018, 1019 (1984).

[40] I.R.C. § 7872(b)(1).

[41] Id. The same treatment would be accorded to the amount treated as a dividend in the case of a loan from a corporation to one of its shareholders, and to the like amount regardless of the subcategory of nongift term loan applicable.

[42] It is assumed that the expense is ordinary and necessary and that the compensation is reasonable in amount. I.R.C. § 162(a). Cf. I.R.C. § 461(h).

[43] I.R.C. § 7872(b)(2). While this amount is truly foregone interest in the sense that it represents interest that could (or should) have been charged but was not, note that it does not fall within the definition of "foregone interest" as established in I.R.C. § 7872(e)(2). See Text at note 15, supra. The treatment this amount receives is consistent with the rules governing original issue discount. I.R.C. § 1272. Again, similar treatment would be accorded to this constructive interest regardless of the subcategory of nongift term loan that is applicable and the characterization based upon the subcategory of the loan involved (e.g., compensation, dividend, etc.).

employer need include only that amount in his income for each corresponding year.

Applying these rules to our employer, we find that on January 1 of year one, he pays his employee $17,925 of compensation, calculated by subtracting the present value of $100,000 for 4 years at 5 percent compounded semiannually, $82,075, from the amount loaned, $100,000.[44] The employer receives a year one deduction of $17,925 for compensation paid, and the employee includes $17,925 in his year one gross income. The interest, however, is treated as earned and paid ratably over the course of the loan in accordance with the principles of Section 1272 (which deals with original issue discount).[45] Thus, employee is treated as paying employer a total of $17,925 of interest over the 4 year period.

If a nongift loan is a *demand loan,* the rules are the same as those established for gift demand loans.[46] Both the amount of compensation deemed to be paid by an employer to his employee in a compensation-related demand loan and the subsequent interest income and possible deduction are calculated by subtracting any interest payable under the loan from the interest that would have accrued at the applicable Federal rate.[47] This amount is compensation paid by the employer and received by the employee on the last day of the calendar year.[48] An amount equal to this compensation is treated as interest paid by the employee (borrower) to the employer (lender),[49] resulting in income to the lender and a possible deduction for the borrower, again on the last day of the calendar year.[50]

Thus if our employer lends his employee $100,000 interest-free on January 1 of year one, payable on demand, and the loan remains outstanding throughout all of year one, the calculations required are identical to those made above for the gift demand loan.[51] On December 31 of year one, the employee is deemed to have received $5,063 of compensation and the employer earns a year one deduction of $5,063 for compensation paid. Also on December 31 the employee pays the employer $5,063 of interest, possibly earning an equal deduction for himself and resulting in income in that amount to the employer. These items of income and deduction for compensation-related loans result in a wash to the employer and possibly to the employee—neither is adversely affected by the imputed compensation and interest income if there are corresponding deductions.

However, if the loan is from a corporation to one of its shareholders a different result occurs. In the corporation-shareholder loan context, the

---

[44]  See note 19, supra.

[45]  I.R.C. § 7872(b)(2)(A). See page 863, infra.

[46]  Here also the explanation given for a loan from an employer to his employee is applicable to all nongift demand loan situations. However, the amount treated as transferred by the lender to the borrower with which to pay the imputed interest will receive a characterization based upon the subcategory of the loan involved (e.g., compensation, dividend, etc.).

[47]  I.R.C. § 7872(a)(1).

[48]  I.R.C. § 7872(a)(2).

[49]  I.R.C. § 7872(a)(1), (e)(2).

[50]  I.R.C. § 7872(a)(2).

[51]  See page 482, supra.

corporation is deemed to have paid a dividend to the shareholder. The shareholder then pays interest to the corporation possibly earning himself an interest deduction (more than offsetting the tax on his dividend income) but as the corporation earns no deduction for having paid the dividend, it cannot offset its interest income.

*Exceptions for Gift Loans.* Having explained income and gift taxes on the various types of below-market interest rate loans, we now encounter limitations that can prevent the imposition of these taxes in certain situations. In the case of any gift loans made between individuals,[52] the statute allows a de minimis exception: Section 7872 generally applies only to days when the aggregate amount of the loans between the individuals exceeds $10,000.[53] On days when the amount of the loans is $10,000 or less (including a situation where a loan or principal portion thereof has been paid off), Section 7872 does not apply except to a loan that is used to purchase income-producing assets.[54]

Another set of rules applies if gift loans between the borrower and lender do not exceed $100,000.[55] Generally the amount of imputed interest treated as retransferred from borrower to lender is limited to the borrower's net investment income (essentially the excess of investment income over investment related expenses)[56] for the year;[57] and if the borrower's net investment income for the year does not exceed $1,000, no interest retransfer is imputed.[58] If the borrower has loans from two or more lenders, a special allocation rule applies.[59] This retransfer exception does not apply if the interest arrangements on the loan have as one of their principal purposes the avoidance of federal tax.[60]

*Exception for Nongift Loans.* Compensation-related and corporation-shareholder loans are also subject to a similar $10,000 de minimis exception

---

[52] A husband and wife are treated as one person for purposes of I.R.C. § 7872. I.R.C. § 7872(f)(7); Cf. I.R.C. § 1041. Although § 7872(c)(2)(A) provides that the $10,000 limitation applies to "individuals," the Senate Finance Committee Report chose to apply the limitation to "natural persons," adding in a footnote that loans to persons as custodians or guardians qualified as loans to "natural persons." S.Rep.No. 98–160, 98th Cong., 2d Sess. 483 (1984). Is there a difference between an "individual" and a "natural person?"

[53] I.R.C. § 7872(c)(2)(A).

[54] I.R.C. § 7872(c)(2)(B). Additionally, in the case of gift term loans, if the aggregate amount of loans exceed $10,000, the parties can avoid the income tax consequences, but cannot escape the gift tax consequences provided by I.R.C. § 7872 by reducing one or more of the loans so that the total aggregates less than $10,000. I.R.C. § 7872(f)(10).

[55] I.R.C. § 7872(d)(1)(D).

[56] I.R.C. § 163(d)(4)(A).

[57] I.R.C. § 7872(d)(1)(A).

[58] I.R.C. § 7872(d)(1)(E)(ii).

[59] If any borrower has more than one gift loan outstanding during the year he must allocate his net investment income between the loans in proportion to the amounts that would otherwise be deemed as retransferred to the lender. This limitation has no effect upon the amount of interest the borrower is deemed to pay under I.R.C. § 7872. However, if the borrower has loans from 2 or more lenders outstanding at one time, § 7872(d)(1)(C) instructs the borrower how to allocate his net investment income between the lenders, thus affecting the amount of interest income they must recognize.

[60] I.R.C. § 7872(d)(1)(B).

as applies to gift loans.[61] However, there is no de minimis exception for other types of nongift loans.[62] The $10,000 exception does not apply to loans with a principal purpose of avoiding federal tax.[63] Just as with gift loans, compensation-related and corporation-shareholder loans between the same lender and borrower are aggregated to determine whether the $10,000 floor prevents the recognition of interest income by the lender.[64] However, in the case of term loans, once aggregate compensation-related or corporation-shareholder term loans exceed $10,000, the parties cannot subsequently escape the grasp of Section 7872 by reducing one or more of the loans so that the total aggregates less than $10,000; once subject to Section 7872 a compensation-related or corporate-shareholder loan is always subject to Section 7872.[65]

These below-market loan provisions have left *J. Simpson Dean* to die a natural death.

## NOTE

*The Creation of Interest.* If interest is deductible a question is: What is "interest"? Rev.Rul. 69–188, set out above,[1] presents a basic definition. As the Ruling suggests, interest, like the rose, by any other name smells as sweet. The *J. Simpson Dean* saga demonstrates that the courts have been chary of finding imputed interest,[2] either as a gross income inclusion or as a deduction. Nevertheless at times, especially in recent times, Congress intervenes to create both interest income and interest deductions, such as they did for parties involved in interest-free and below-market loans in the enactment of Section 7872.

In addition to the creation of interest under Section 7872, Congress has similarly taxed an unstated interest component in a variety of financial transactions. For example, a corporation sells its own bonds at a discount (face $5,000, price $4,600), the discount ($400) is actually disguised interest, for it represents a price the corporation will have to pay, along with current interest, as the cost of using the money. Congress recognizes this fact and under Section 1272 creates both interest income (to the bondholder) and interest deductions (for the corporation). If no interest or low interest is paid on the purchase of property, Congress imputes interest to both parties in the transaction in a series of provisions that are similar to Section 7872.[3] Both Section 1272 and the other provisions are intimately related to timing[4] and

---

[61] I.R.C. § 7872(c)(3)(A). The exception is not identical because it is inapplicable where one of the principal purposes of the loan is tax avoidance (I.R.C. § 7872(c)(3)(B)) and there is no restriction related to use of the loan proceeds to purchase or carry income-producing assets (I.R.C. § 7872(d)(2)(B)).

[62] Id. See I.R.C. § 7872(d)(1)(A).

[63] I.R.C. § 7872(c)(3)(B).

[64] Id.

[65] I.R.C. § 7872(f)(10). This rule also applies to gift tax on gift term loans. See note 54, supra.

[1] See page 470, supra.

[2] See page 472, supra.

[3] See I.R.C. §§ 483 and 1274. See also I.R.C. §§ 1271–1286.

[4] See Chapter 19, infra.

characterization[5] concepts, and so their consideration is deferred to Chapter 24[6] after timing and characterization concepts have been examined.

Congress also "finds" deductible interest in other obscure places. For example, Section 163(c) places redeemable ground rents in that category.[7] In addition, recall[8] that Section 482 gives the Commissioner limited authority to allocate gross income, deductions, credits, or allowances among organizations controlled by the same persons. Although it may stretch the statute, this authority has been used to generate (a mere allocation?) interest payments on otherwise interest-free loans between such organizations.[9] When one is *taxed* on interest imputed to him by this strained application of Section 482, the other party gains a corresponding interest *deduction*.[10]

*The Disallowance of Interest.* At the other end of the spectrum is the disallowance of interest deductions. There are numerous statutory restrictions on the deductibility of interest, many of which are considered below. Nevertheless even without such legislative assistance, the courts have sometimes disallowed such deductions. Elaborate schemes have been attempted to generate an interest deduction in order to reduce taxes without the usual economic pain attached to paying for borrowed money. But not successfully if the device is tabbed a mere artifice.[11] In addition, as in many other areas, the Commissioner and the courts have refused to let taxpayers exalt form over substance. For example, in the corporate area, the "thin incorporation" has produced substantial litigation. Especially in a close corporation, if indebtedness is greatly disproportionate to equity capital, evidences of debt may be viewed instead as evidences of ownership and hoped-for deductible interest may become non-deductible dividends.[12]

Some interest that is not paid or incurred in business or profit seeking activities is deductible,[13] but much consumer or "personal" interest is not.[14] Prior to the Tax Reform Act of 1986 most interest, including personal interest was deductible. One could deduct the interest on a loan whose proceeds were used to purchase a residence, a car, a boat, or an excursion to Vegas and interest charged on credit card balances. However, Congress, in the 1986 effort to broaden the tax base,[15] enacted Section 163(h) which disallows deductions for most "personal" interest. Two exceptions to the Section 163(h)

---

[5]   See Chapter 21, infra.

[6]   See page 861, infra.

[7]   See also I.R.C. § 1055.

[8]   See page 291, supra.

[9]   See, e.g., B. Forman Co. v. Commissioner, 453 F.2d 1144 (2d Cir.1972), cert. denied 407 U.S. 934, 92 S.Ct. 2458 (1972). However, see page 478, supra and page 861, infra.

[10]   See Gerald F. Paduano v. Commissioner, 34 T.C.M. 368, 370 n.9 (1975).

[11]   See Knetsch v. United States, 364 U.S. 361, 81 S.Ct. 132 (1960), and Golsen v. Commissioner, 54 T.C. 742 (1970), affirmed 445 F.2d 985 (10th Cir.1971), both involving tax years unaffected by I.R.C. § 264(a)(3), briefly discussed, infra.

[12]   E.g., Gooding Amusement Co. v. Commissioner, 236 F.2d 159 (6th Cir.1956), cert. denied 352 U.S. 1031, 77 S.Ct. 595 (1957). See I.R.C. § 385.

[13]   I.R.C. § 163(h)(2)(D) and (3)–(5).

[14]   I.R.C. § 163(h)(1).

[15]   See Text page 11, supra.

rule are the allowances of deductions for "qualified residence interest"[16] and interest on "qualified education loans."[17]

*Qualified Residence Interest.* Qualified residence interest is deductible even though it is a personal expense. The qualified residence need not be the principal residence of the taxpayer, but qualifying indebtedness is limited to a maximum of two residences and, if there are two, one must be the taxpayer's principal residence.[18] The term residence may be broadly interpreted to include mobile homes and live-in boats.[19] If either a mobile home or a live-in boat is used on a transient basis, it may qualify as a second residence.[20]

In the 2017 Tax Cuts and Jobs Act,[21] Congress placed additional limitations on the deductibility of qualified residence interest in taxable years after 2017. The extent to which qualified residence interest is deductible in those years depends on the type of indebtedness involved, and, in some cases, the date the indebtedness was incurred. The key date is December 15, 2017. More generous rules apply to certain indebtedness incurred on or before December 15, 2017,[22] with a more stringent set of rules applicable to indebtedness incurred after that date.[23]

Section 163(h) identifies two categories of debt that constitute qualified residence interest: "acquisition indebtedness" and "home equity indebtedness."[24] As its name implies, the term "acquisition indebtedness" refers to debt *secured by a qualified residence*, which is incurred by the taxpayer in acquiring, constructing, or substantially improving a qualified residence.[25] The term also includes debt incurred as a result of refinancing

---

[16] I.R.C. § 163(h)(2)(D) and (3)–(5). See Snoe, "My Home, My Debt: Remodeling the House Mortgage Interest Deduction," 80 Ky.L.J. 431 (1992).

[17] I.R.C. §§ 163(h)(2)(F), 221. The disallowance rule is also inapplicable to interest on loans incurred in a taxpayer's trade or business, interest on loans related to profit seeking activities or "passive activities" (see page 532, infra) of the taxpayer and certain interest on estate tax liability. I.R.C. § 163(h)(2)(A)–(C) and (E), respectively.

[18] I.R.C. § 163(h)(4). To qualify a dwelling as a second residence, the taxpayer must use the dwelling as his residence for part of the year if it is rented to others during the year. I.R.C. § 163(h)(4)(A)(iii). Cf. I.R.C. § 280A(d)(1). No taxpayer use of a residence is required if it is not rented during the year.

In addition, if a taxpayer has more than two residences, in any year she may select any one of her non-principal residences to qualify as a qualified residence. I.R.C. § 163(h)(4)(A)(i)(II). See Reg. § 1.163–10T(p)(3)(i) and (iv).

[19] See page 217, supra.

[20] See Reg. § 1.163–10T(p)(3)(ii). Although the House of Representatives at one time disagreed with this conclusion, their thinking did not become law. Compare H.Rep. No. 100–391, 100th Cong., 1st Sess. 1032 (1987) with Conf.Rep. No. 100–495, 100th Cong., 1st Sess. 917 (1987). See also note 18, supra.

[21] Pub. L. No. 115–97, 115th Cong., 1st Sess. (2017).

[22] I.R.C. § 163(h)(3)(F)(i)(III). A taxpayer who enters into a binding contract before December 15, 2017 to close on the purchase of a principal residence before January 1, 2018 and who purchases such residence before April 1, 2018 is considered to incur the indebtedness under the pre-December 15, 2017 rules. I.R.C. § 163(h)(3)(F)(i)(IV).

[23] In taxable years after 2025, the limitation on acquisition indebtedness is $1 million regardless of when the indebtedness is incurred. I.R.C. § 163(h)(3)(F)(ii).

[24] I.R.C. § 163(h)(3)(A).

[25] I.R.C. § 163(h)(3)(B)(i). Acquisition indebtedness generally includes premiums paid for mortgage insurance in connection with acquisition indebtedness on a qualified residence. I.R.C.

acquisition indebtedness and any subsequent refinancing of such indebtedness.[26] However, the amount of refinancing debt that can subsequently qualify as acquisition indebtedness can never exceed the outstanding principal of the debt which is being refinanced.[27] For example, if a taxpayer reduces the principal balance of an acquisition debt from $200,000 to $150,000, the maximum amount of any subsequent refinancing debt which may then qualify as acquisition indebtedness is $150,000. In the case of indebtedness originally incurred on or before December 15, 2017, the total amount a taxpayer may treat as acquisition indebtedness may not exceed $1 million ($500,000 in the case of a married person filing separately).[28] For indebtedness incurred after December 15, 2017, the total amount a taxpayer may treat as acquisition indebtedness may not exceed $750,000 ($375,000 in the case of a married person filing separately).[29] In applying the $750,000 and $375,000 limits to post-December 15, 2017 indebtedness, indebtedness incurred on or before that date first reduces those limits.[30] For example, if a single taxpayer incurred $450,000 of acquisition indebtedness in year 2016 (assume that is still the loan balance), the taxpayer could incur an additional $300,000 of post-December 15, 2017 acquisition indebtedness on which the interest would be deductible.

The second category of debt which has generated qualified residence interest is "home equity indebtedness." This type of debt loosely corresponds to a home equity loan now offered by many financial institutions. The term home equity indebtedness is defined as any debt (other than acquisition indebtedness), secured by a qualified residence, to the extent the aggregate amount of such debt does not exceed the fair market value of the residence reduced by the outstanding acquisition indebtedness incurred by the taxpayer with respect to such property.[31] Thus the maximum amount of debt which may be classified as home equity indebtedness is limited to the amount of "equity" a taxpayer has in his home. The use of the debt proceeds is irrelevant in classifying the debt as home equity indebtedness. The aggregate amount treated as home equity indebtedness originally could not exceed $100,000 ($50,000 in the case of a married filing separately).[32] However, the 2017 Act suspends the deductibility of interest on home equity indebtedness for taxable years after 2017, regardless of the year in which it was incurred. Such interest is not deductible in those years, regardless of when it was incurred.[33]

---

§ 163(h)(3)(E). The rule applies through year 2017 but may be extended. See I.R.C. § 163(h)(4)(E) and (F) and Reg. § 1.163–11T.

[26] I.R.C. § 163(h)(3)(B)(i) flush language; see also note 28, infra.

[27] Id.

[28] I.R.C. § 163(h)(3)(B)(ii), (h)(3)(F)(i)(III). See also I.R.C. § 163(h)(3)(F)(iii), providing that if acquisition indebtedness incurred on or before December 15, 2017 is refinanced after that date, the $1 million (or $500,000) limitations generally continue to apply to that refinanced indebtedness.

[29] I.R.C. § 163(h)(3)(F)(i)(II).

[30] I.R.C. § 163(h)(3)(F)(i)(III).

[31] I.R.C. § 163(h)(3)(C)(i).

[32] I.R.C. § 163(h)(3)(C)(ii).

[33] I.R.C. § 163(h)(3)(F)(i)(I).

To illustrate the rules on acquisition indebtedness, assume a taxpayer has a single residence with a $600,000 fair market value and subject to a $300,000 acquisition indebtedness. In years after 2017, the taxpayer could deduct interest on up to $450,000 of additional acquisition indebtedness. Thus, subject to that limit, she could borrow on the home to make substantial improvements and deduct the interest. Alternatively, she could purchase a second residence and deduct interest on up to $450,000 of additional acquisition indebtedness.

If the dollar limitations on acquisition indebtedness are exceeded, then the excess indebtedness is treated no differently from other personal loans, and any interest paid on such excess is personal interest that is non-deductible.[34] If the dollar ceilings are exceeded, it is necessary to determine which debt caused the excess so that the specific interest paid on such excess will be subject to the personal interest limitation. A chronological tracing of debt in order to determine which debt caused the excess would provide a method of allocation.[35] Perhaps a taxpayer (as in the case of the selection of a second residence) should be given the flexibility to choose.

*Interest on Qualified Education Loans.* Another example of deductible "personal" interest is provided by Section 221[36] which allows a deduction for interest on "qualified education loans." A qualified education loan is a loan incurred by the taxpayer solely to pay for the qualified higher education expenses of a student (tuition, books, fees, and room and board)[37] who is the taxpayer,[38] the taxpayer's spouse, or a dependent of the taxpayer[39] if the student is at least a half-time student.[40] The amount of such qualified expenses is generally reduced by any amounts excluded from gross income.[41] The interest is not deductible if the loan is made by a related person.[42] There is a $2,500 ceiling on the deduction, and the amount of the deduction is phased out ratably for single taxpayers with modified adjusted gross income[43] of between $50,000 and $65,000 (and between $100,000 and $130,000 for married couples filing joint returns).[44]

---

[34] See the Text at note 15, supra.

[35] See H.Rep. No. 100–391, 100th Cong., 1st Sess. 1033 (1987); note 18, supra. See also I.R.C. § 163(h)(3)(F)(i)(III).

[36] See I.R.C. § 163(h)(2)(F). The I.R.C. § 221 deduction is an "above the line" deduction. I.R.C. § 62(a)(17).

[37] I.R.C. § 221(d)(2).

[38] No deduction is allowed if the taxpayer is a dependent of another taxpayer. I.R.C. § 221(c).

[39] I.R.C. § 221(d)(1)(A), (4). Dependents are discussed in Chapter 18E, infra.

[40] I.R.C. § 221(d)(1). See I.R.C. §§ 221(d)(3), 25A(b)(3).

[41] I.R.C. § 221(d)(2). See I.R.C. §§ 117, 127, 135, and 530. However, the amount is not reduced by any amount excluded under I.R.C. § 102(a). I.R.C. § 25A(g)(2)(C).

[42] I.R.C. § 221(d)(1) flush language. A related person is defined by I.R.C. §§ 267(b) and 707(b)(1). Id. A qualified education loan also excludes any indebtedness owed under a qualified employer plan or a contract related to such a plan as described in § 72(p)(4) and (5). Id.

[43] I.R.C. § 221(b)(2)(C).

[44] I.R.C. § 221(b). The phase-out amounts are adjusted for inflation after 2002. I.R.C. § 221(f). If a married couple does not file a joint return, no interest deduction is allowed. I.R.C. § 221(e)(2).

*Limitation on Investment Interest.* Section 163(d) imposes a limit on the deductibility of investment interest by noncorporate taxpayers. Investment interest is generally deductible only to the extent that the taxpayer has net investment income.[45]

Investment interest is interest paid or accrued on indebtedness incurred to purchase or carry property held for investment.[46] It does not include any qualified residence interest which is limited by the Section 163(h) rules considered above,[47] or any interest that is taken into account in determining the taxpayer's income or loss from a passive activity, a concept to be considered later.[48]

Net investment income is, logically for a change, the excess of investment income over investment expenses.[49] Investment income is gross income *from* property held for investment plus some gains on the *sale* of such property, but only if the property is not a part of a trade or business,[50] or an activity subject to the passive activity rules,[51] or does not qualify for preferential net capital gain treatment under Section 1(h) either on the sale of investment property[52] or as qualified dividend income.[53] A taxpayer may elect to exclude all or a part of such Section 1(h) gain on investment property or qualified dividend income from preferential treatment under Section 1(h) and to that extent the gain is treated as net investment income.[54] Investment expenses are any deductible expenses (other than interest) directly connected with the production of such investment income.[55] Interest disallowed as a deduction for any taxable year under the Section 163(d) limitation can be carried forward and is treated as investment interest in subsequent years until utilized.[56]

*Limitation on Business Interest.* The 2017 Tax Cuts and Jobs Act[57] added a new Section 162(j) limitation on the deductibility of business interest that applies to all types of taxpayers.[58] However, "small businesses" (those with less than $25 million of gross receipts) are exempt from the limitation

---

[45]  I.R.C. § 163(d)(1).

[46]  I.R.C. § 163(d)(3)(A).

[47]  I.R.C. § 163(d)(3)(B)(i).

[48]  I.R.C. § 163(d)(3)(B)(ii). See I.R.C. § 469 and Chapter 17F, infra.

[49]  I.R.C. § 163(d)(4)(A).

[50]  I.R.C. § 163(d)(4)(B).

[51]  I.R.C. § 163(d)(4)(D). See note 17, supra.

[52]  I.R.C. § 163(d)(4)(B)(ii)(II).

[53]  I.R.C. § 163(d)(4)(B) flush language.

[54]  I.R.C. § 163(d)(4)(B)(iii). See I.R.C. § 1(h)(2) and pages 691 and 945, infra.

[55]  I.R.C. § 163(d)(4)(C). Investment expenses are miscellaneous itemized deductions which are not allowed in computing taxable income and not included in investment expenses. See Chapter 18C, infra.

[56]  I.R.C. § 163(d)(2). See Rev. Rul. 95–16, 1995–1 C. B., which allows taxpayers to carry over the full amount of disallowed investment interest even though it exceeds taxable income in the year the interest was paid or accrued.

[57]  Pub. L. No. 115–97, 115th Cong., 1st Sess. (2017).

[58]  Special rules apply in the case of a partnership or S corporation. I.R.C. § 163(j)(4).

on the deductibility of business interest,[59] and a trade or business for Section 163(j) purposes does not include performance of services as an employee.[60]

Generally, under Section 163(j) business interest may only be deducted to the extent of the sum of the taxpayer's business interest income plus 30 percent of the taxpayer's "adjusted taxable income" for the year.[61] "Business interest" is interest paid or accrued on indebtedness properly allocable to a trade or business,[62] and "business interest income" is interest includible as gross income which is properly allocable to a trade or business.[63] Adjusted taxable income (the key element in the Section 163(j) limitation) is defined as the taxpayer's taxable income computed without regard to: (1) any item not properly allocable to a trade or business, (2) any business interest or business interest income, (3) any net operating loss, (4) the Section 199A deduction, and (5) for taxable years before 2022, any deduction allowable for depreciation, amortization or depletion.[64] In years after 2021, depreciation deductions (including amounts expensed under Sections 168(k) or 179) will also reduce adjusted taxable income and the limitation under Section 163(j), thereby potentially restricting the deductibility of business interest for more taxpayers. Business interest disallowed under the limitation carries forward indefinitely.[65]

*Interest Paid in Connection with Insurance Contracts.* The Code also contains restrictions on the deduction of interest on loans related to life insurance. Section 264(a)(2) precludes a deduction for interest paid on debt incurred or continued to buy a "single premium" life insurance or endowment or annuity contract.[66] The reasons may be obvious. As regards life insurance, the purchaser is buying proceeds that will be received tax-free by beneficiaries.[67] It seems inappropriate to Congress to allow a deduction for interest paid on money used to purchase tax-free gain.[68] Annuity and endowment contracts produce funds also only partially taxed.[69] An offset against likely current high income (otherwise taxed at high rates) might be inappropriate looking ahead to the favorable tax treatment of the proceeds.[70]

---

[59]  I.R.C. § 163(j)(3).

[60]  I.R.C. § 163(j)(7)(A)(i). Taxpayers in the business of real property (as defined in I.R.C. § 469(c)(7)(C)) or certain farming activities may elect to avoid the limitation but then must use the I.R.C. § 168(g) alternative depreciation system. I.R.C. §§ 163(j)(7)(A)(ii) and (iii), 168(g)(1)(F). The trade or business of certain utilities is excluded from the limitation. I.R.C. § 163(j)(7)(A)(iv).

[61]  I.R.C. § 163(j)(1). A special rule increases the limit for sellers of motor vehicles. See I.R.C. § 163(j)(1)(C), (j)(9).

[62]  I.R.C. § 163(j)(5). Investment interest, which is subject to the limitation in I.R.C. § 163(d), is not business interest. I.R.C. § 163(j)(5).

[63]  I.R.C. § 163(j)(6).

[64]  I.R.C. § 163(j)(8)(A). The IRS can make adjustments to these items. I.R.C. § 163(j)(8)(B).

[65]  I.R.C. § 163(j)(2).

[66]  The "single premium" limitation is broader than it sounds. See I.R.C. § 264(b).

[67]  Recall I.R.C. § 101.

[68]  Cf. I.R.C. § 265(a)(2), noted below.

[69]  Recall I.R.C. § 72.

[70]  I.R.C. § 101(a).

At least so it seems to Congress which applies other interest restrictions in similar life insurance and endowment and annuity contract situations.[71]

*Interest Relating to Tax-Exempt Income.* Suppose I borrow $5,000 at the bank and use it to buy a municipal bond that pays tax-exempt[72] interest at 6%. If I also pay 6% interest at the bank, will the receipts on the bond and the interest paid merely wash? Not if I can deduct the interest from income otherwise taxed, say, at 35 percent.

| | | |
|---|---:|---:|
| Interest received | | $300 |
| Less interest paid | $300 | |
| Reduced by tax saved (35% of $300) | −105 | |
| After tax cost | | 195 |
| Gain after tax | | $105 |

But a long time ago Congress appropriately stopped this. Section 265(a)(2) disallows any deduction claimed for interest on indebtedness incurred or continued to purchase or carry tax-exempt obligations.[73] Whether indebtedness is "incurred or carried" for the proscribed purpose is a question that has produced much litigation. The basic problem is: How much of a connection need be shown between the loan and tax-exempt interest in order to invoke the proscription against the deduction of the interest on the loan?

It is settled that to disallow the interest deduction the Commissioner must show that "the relationship between the indebtedness and the tax-exempt securities involves more than their mere simultaneous existence in respect of a single taxpayer. * * *[74] [Section 265(a)(2)] applies when 'the *purpose* for which the indebtedness is incurred or continued is to purchase or carry tax-exempt obligations.' (Emphasis supplied.)"[75] Nevertheless, the courts appear to be more and more willing to find the required nexus. Of course direct evidence of purpose to buy tax-exempts with a loan is sufficient; and pledging currently owned tax-exempts for the loan has been held to be the equivalent of such direct evidence.[76] Beyond that several courts of appeal have found the connection in less compelling circumstances.[77]

---

[71] I.R.C. § 264(a)(2) and (3).

[72] Recall I.R.C. § 103. Regulated investment companies may pay exempt-interest dividends which I.R.C. § 852(b)(5)(B) treats as tax exempt interest. TRA (1976) added I.R.C. § 265(a)(3) generally disallowing deductions for interest paid to purchase or carry securities in such companies.

[73] See, e.g., I.R.C. §§ 103(c), 135.

[74] Swenson Land and Cattle Co. v. Commissioner, 64 T.C. 686, 695 (1975). Cf. Rev.Rul. 79–272, 1979–2 C.B. 124, involving an interspousal transaction.

[75] Swenson Land and Cattle Co., supra note 74 at 696, quoting Leslie v. Commissioner, 413 F.2d 636, 638 (2d Cir.1969), cert. denied 396 U.S. 1007, 90 S.Ct. 564 (1970). Further, a broker-dealer exception is recognized in Rev.Rul. 74–294, 1974–1 C.B. 71.

[76] Wisconsin Cheeseman v. United States, 388 F.2d 420 (7th Cir.1968); and see Rev.Proc. 72–18, 1972–1 C.B. 740.

[77] Levitt v. United States, 517 F.2d 1339 (8th Cir.1975); Israelson v. United States, 508 F.2d 838 (4th Cir.1974), affirming per curiam, 367 F.Supp. 1104 (D.Md.1973); Mariorenzi v. Commissioner, 490 F.2d 92 (1st Cir.1974), affirming per curiam 32 T.C.M. 681 (1973); Indian

*Other Limitations and Restrictions.* In what might be called "operation smoke-out" (to restrict the use of unregistered bonds), Section 163(f) prohibits the deduction of a bond-issuer's interest payments unless the bonds are registered.[78]

Restrictions on interest deductions often relate to timing.[79] For example, Section 263A generally disallows the deduction of interest on debt incurred to finance the construction or production of certain property, requiring such interest to be capitalized as a part of the cost of the property. The restriction applies only to business or investment property[80] where amounts capitalized may later be deducted by way of depreciation. For example, the rule applies to interest costs on loans used in the construction of a building or for the production of inventory, but not to interest costs on personal use property such as a residence.[81]

## PROBLEMS

**1.**   Lender makes a $100,000 interest-free demand loan to Borrower on January 1 at a time when the applicable Federal rate is 5 percent. The proceeds of the loan are used to purchase a principal residence for Borrower. Five percent interest compounded semiannually on $100,000 is $5,063 per annum. Consider the tax consequences to both parties at the end of the year if the loan is still unpaid and is in the nature of:

(a)   A gift.

(b)   Compensation.

(c)   A dividend.

**2.**   Mother makes an interest free demand loan to Daughter under the following alternative situations at a time when the applicable Federal rate is 5 percent. Discuss the tax consequences to Mother and Daughter.

(a)   Mother loans Daughter $10,000 that Daughter uses as part of a down payment on Daughter's new residence.

(b)   Mother loans Daughter $10,000 that Daughter invests in a residence that she rents to others.

---

Trail Trading Post, Inc. v. Commissioner, 503 F.2d 102 (6th Cir.1974); but see Handy Button Machine Co. v. Commissioner, 61 T.C. 846 (1974), where tax-exempts purchased were held to meet recognized business needs, and Rev.Proc. 72–18, supra, indicating the required nexus will not be found if investment in tax-exempts is insubstantial. See Note, "The Deductibility of Interest Costs by a Taxpayer Holding Tax-Exempt Obligations: A Neutral Principle of Allocation," 61 Va.L.Rev. 211 (1975). See also Oliver, "Section 265(2): A Counterproductive Solution to a Nonexistent Problem," 40 Tax.L.Rev. 351 (1985), which is critical of I.R.C. § 265(a)(2).

[78]   See Text at notes 26 and 28 at page 233, supra.

[79]   See, for example, I.R.C. § 267(a)(2) considered in Chapter 19 D, infra.

[80]   I.R.C. § 263A(c)(1). It is inapplicable to interest on a qualified residence as described under I.R.C. § 163(h). I.R.C. § 263A(f)(2)(B).

[81]   But see I.R.C. § 263A(f)(1)(B). The interest capitalization rule applies only to property that has either (1) a long useful life (such as a building), (2) an estimated production period exceeding two years, or (3) an estimated production period exceeding one year and a cost exceeding one million dollars. Id.

    (c)   Mother loans Daughter $100,000 that Daughter uses as a down payment on Daughter's new residence at a time when Daughter has $20,000 of net investment income.

    (d)   Same as (c), above, except that Daughter has $1,000 of net investment income.

**3.**   Taxpayers purchase a home after December 15, 2017 which they use as their principal residence. Unless otherwise stated, they obtain a loan secured by the residence and use the proceeds to acquire the residence. What portion of the interest paid on such loan may Taxpayers deduct in the following situations?

    (a)   The purchase price and fair market value of the home is $350,000. Taxpayers obtain a mortgage for $250,000 of the purchase price.

    (b)   The facts are the same as in (a), above, except that in two years Taxpayers have reduced the outstanding principal balance of the mortgage to $200,000 and the fair market value of the residence has increased to $400,000. In the later year, Taxpayers take out a second mortgage for $100,000 secured by their residence to add a fourth bedroom and a den to the residence.

    (c)   The facts are the same as in (b), above, except that Taxpayers use the proceeds of the $100,000 mortgage to buy a Ferrari.

    (d)   The facts are the same as in (a), above, but additionally, towards the end of the current year when the outstanding principal balance of the mortgage is $150,000, Taxpayers' financial prospects improve dramatically and they purchase a luxury vacation residence in Florida for its fair market value of $800,000. They finance $550,000 of the purchase price with a note secured by a mortgage on the Florida house, use the house 45 days of the year, and elect to treat the residence as a qualified residence.

    (e)   The facts are the same as in (d), above, except that the mortgage on the Florida residence is $700,000.

**4.**   Dick and Jane are unmarried co-owners of a principal residence which they acquired in 2018 at a cost of $1.2 million. Dick and Jane jointly borrowed $1 million of the purchase price giving the lender a mortgage on the residence. To what extent may they each deduct interest on the mortgage?

**5.**   Single Taxpayer, T, who graduated from law school, pays $3,000 of interest in the current year on qualified educational loans.

    (a)   If T has $40,000 of modified adjusted gross income in the current year, what amount of interest can T deduct?

    (b)   Same as (a), above, except T has $56,000 of modified adjusted gross income in the current year.

(c) Same as (a), above, except T is married and T and Spouse file a joint return and have $140,000 of modified adjusted gross income in the current year.

(d) Same as (c), above, except that T and Spouse delay paying the $3,000 of interest (along with a $300 penalty) from the current year to succeeding year when their modified adjusted gross income is $80,000 (because Spouse ceases working) and when no other interest payments are made.

(e) Same as (a), above, except that F, T's father makes the $3,000 payment. See Reg. § 1.221–1(b)(4)(i), (ii) Ex. 2.

**6.** Investor incurs investment interest of $100,000. To what extent is it deductible in the current year if:

(a) Investor's only investment income during the year is $80,000 of interest on a corporate bond, and she has $10,000 in deductible state intangible taxes on investments? Are there any other tax consequences to Investor?

(b) The interest of $100,000 is on loans whose proceeds are used to purchase tax exempt bonds?

(c) The facts are the same as in (a) and (b), above, except that the proceeds of the loans are used 50% to purchase tax exempt bonds and 50% to buy corporate bonds and the bonds are her only investments?

**7.** Business Person (BP) operates a services business which produces $30 million of gross receipts. For the year, BP incurs or experiences the following expenses: $12 million in salaries, $10 million in operating expenses, $4 million in depreciation, and $2 million in interest expense. How much interest expense may BP deduct if:

(a) The year is 2020?

(b) The year is 2022?

## C. Taxes

Internal Revenue Code: Sections 164(a), (b)(1), (5), and (6), (c), (d)(1); 275; 1001(b)(2).

Regulations: Section 1.164–3(a)–(d).

———————

# Cramer v. Commissioner*

Tax Court of the United States, 1971.
55 T.C. 1125.

■ FEATHERSTON, JUDGE:

Respondent determined deficiencies in petitioner's income tax for 1964, 1965, and 1966 in the amounts of $257.62, $561.21, and $594.22, respectively. The issues presented for decision are:

\* \* \*

(2) Whether the taxes which petitioner paid on certain real property during 1965 and 1966 are deductible under section 164;

\* \* \*

Findings of Fact

Petitioner was a legal resident of Dearborn Heights, Mich., at the time she filed her petition. Her returns for 1964, 1965, and 1966 were filed with the district director of internal revenue, Detroit, Mich.

\* \* \*

*Real Property Issues*

In August 1963, petitioner sold her residence located at 8247 Auburn Street (hereinafter the Auburn Street property) under a land sale contract to William S. Osborn (hereinafter Osborn). Under the terms of this agreement, Osborn agreed to make monthly payments on the sale price and to pay the property taxes. Record title to the residence remained in petitioner.

During 1964 and 1965, Osborn failed to pay the real property taxes, and petitioner paid them in the respective amounts of $264.68 and $255.98. Osborn also failed to make his monthly payments on the indebtedness to petitioner, and she instituted a foreclosure suit against him in the Circuit Court of Wayne County. She obtained a default judgment against him and recovered possession of the property on February 18, 1966.

Later in the same year, petitioner resold the property. \* \* \*. She also paid the real property taxes for 1966 in the amount of $259.06. No gain was realized on the sale, recovery, or resale of the residence.

During 1965 and 1966, petitioner's mother, Ann Marion Gay, owned a residence located at 720 Atkinson Street (hereinafter the Atkinson Street property). She was intermittently hospitalized from 1965 until June 7, 1968, when she died. Petitioner looked after her mother's residence during this period and paid, with her own money, taxes on the property for 1965 and 1966 in the amounts of $300.62 and $381.94,

---

\*    Some footnotes omitted.

respectively. Her mother executed a quitclaim deed of the property to petitioner in 1967.

After petitioner sold her residence in 1963, she purchased a new one at 27314 Clearview Street (hereinafter the Clearview Street property). During 1964, 1965, and 1966, her new residence was subject to a mortgage which required petitioner to make monthly escrow payments of real property taxes. The escrow agent paid the property taxes for those years as follows: 1964—$0; 1965—$843.95; and 1966—$847.89.

On her 1965 and 1966 returns, petitioner deducted $1,144.87 and $915.39, respectively, as real property taxes; these amounts included the taxes paid on the Auburn Street, Atkinson Street, and Clearview Street properties. She also deducted $607.64 on her 1966 return as repairs on the property which she had repossessed during that year.

Respondent determined "that property tax deductions are allowable in the amount of $436.94 in 1965 and $470.88 in 1966."

* * *

*Real Property Taxes*

On brief, respondent has conceded the deductibility of the taxes which petitioner paid with respect to the Clearview Street property. Remaining in dispute are the taxes on the Atkinson and Auburn Street properties.

As to the Atkinson Street property, petitioner is not entitled to the disputed deductions. Section 164 allows a deduction for real property taxes; but they are, in general, "deductible only by the person upon whom they are imposed." Sec. 1.164–1(a), Income Tax Regs.; Magruder v. Supplee, 316 U.S. 394 (1942). During 1965 and 1966, the years in dispute, this property was owned by petitioner's mother, and was not deeded to petitioner until 1967. Prior to the delivery of this deed, she had no interest, legal or equitable, in the property, and the taxes for 1965 and 1966 were not imposed upon her. Her payments of the taxes for those years were, in substance, gifts or some other kind of advances for funds to, or for the benefit of, her mother and, consequently, are not deductible by petitioner.

The dispute as to the Auburn Street property taxes involves two periods: One during 1964 and 1965, prior to the time petitioner recovered possession of the property; the other during 1966, when she resold it. After petitioner first sold the property in 1961, record title remained in her name, and, we infer, the land sale contract with Osborn was not recorded. Under the Michigan statutes, real property taxes are assessed "to the owner if known, and also to the occupant." Mich.Stat.Ann. sec. 7.3 (1960). As the record owner of the property, petitioner was assessed for the property taxes, and they became a debt to the taxing entity for the collection of which her chattels, as well as the realty, could be seized and sold. * * *. The parties have stipulated that petitioner actually paid the taxes even though Osborn was obligated by the land sale contract to pay them.[4] Consequently, petitioner, having been assessed for the taxes on the Auburn Street property and having paid them in order to discharge her debt and to protect her property interests, is entitled to deduct them on her income tax returns for 1964 and 1965. * * *. The case of Pacific Southwest Realty Co., 45 B.T.A. 426, 437–438 (1941), affd. 128 F.2d 815 (C.A.9 1942), involving California law, under which the real property taxes were assessed to the equitable owner of the property is inapposite.

As to 1966, section 164(d)(1) provides:

(1) General Rule.—For purposes of subsection (a), if real property is sold during any real property tax year, then—

(A) so much of the real property tax as is properly allocable to that part of such year which ends on the day before the date of the sale shall be treated as a tax imposed on the seller, and

(B) so much of such tax as is properly allocable to that part of such year which begins on the date of the sale shall be treated as a tax imposed on the purchaser.

While the property taxes were assessed to petitioner for 1966, the statute quoted above provides that they will be treated as having been partially assessed to the buyer instead of her. This provision reflects the common practice of prorating property taxes as between the buyer and the seller, but it is not dependent on an actual proration. The section applies automatically to every sale and allows the buyer to deduct a portion of the property taxes, whether he actually pays them or not. * * *. Consequently, petitioner is treated as having been assessed for, and as having paid, only the portion of the taxes for 1966 allocable to the period prior to the time she sold the property. Sec. 1.164–6(a), Income Tax Regs.

The record does not disclose when in 1966 she made the sale; however, from the fact that her income tax return for that year reflects that she received a substantial amount of interest income in respect of the sale of this property, we infer that the sale was made shortly after she recovered possession of it on February 18. For the portion of the year prior to the sale—not less than the 48 days prior to February 18—she is entitled to a deduction. Accordingly, we hold that she may deduct $48/365$ of the $259.06 in taxes on the Auburn Street property for 1966, or $34.07. Rev.Rul. 67–31, 1967–1 C.B. 49.

## PROBLEMS

1. To what extent would the following taxes be deductible by Married Couple under § 164?

(a) A state income tax of $12,000.

---

[4] Of course, if petitioner were ever to recover on the judgment which she obtained against Osborn, that recovery would constitute income subject to the limitations of sec. 111.

    (b)  A state income tax of $7,000 and a local property tax of $3,000.

    (c)  A local property tax of $10,000 for which Married Couple became liable as owners of Blackacre on January 1, but which Buyer agreed to pay half of when Buyer acquired Blackacre from Married Couple on July 1.

    (d)  A Federal income tax of $20,000.

    (e)  A state income tax of $7,000, a state sales tax of $1,000, and a local property tax of $2,000.

**2.**   Son, who is single, owns a home. Father pays Son's $14,000 annual property tax.

    (a)  May Father deduct the tax paid?

    (b)  Is the tax deductible by Son?

**3.**   Both state and federal governments impose gasoline taxes on Customer. Are the taxes deductible:

    (a)  If Customer uses her vehicle only for personal use?

    (b)  If Customer uses her vehicle only for business use in a business she owns?

    (c)  If Customer uses her vehicle 30% in her business and 70% for personal use?

**4.**   Dr. Medic employs Charles to work for her as receptionist. She pays Charles's salary but withholds X dollars to which she adds Y dollars all of which she pays to the federal government under the Federal Insurance Contributions Act (for "social security").

    (a)  Can Dr. Medic deduct amount X? Amount Y? X plus Y?

    (b)  Is Charles entitled to a deduction for the payments?

**5.**   The City of Oz constructs a yellow brick road that runs past Woodman's property. He and other property owners adjacent to the road are assessed varying amounts by Oz, based on the relative amounts of front footage of their properties. Woodman elects to pay off the assessment over five years and pays $400 in the taxable year. Deductible?

## D. BAD DEBTS, CHARITABLE CONTRIBUTIONS AND CASUALTY AND THEFT LOSSES

Because these types of deductions are intimately related to characterization principles, their analysis is deferred to Chapter 23.

# CHAPTER 17

# RESTRICTIONS ON DEDUCTIONS

## A. INTRODUCTION

That which Congress giveth, Congress may also take away. In this Chapter we encounter examples of congressional finger crossing,—specific denials of deductions that seem to have been authorized. In general, the "give" provisions are in Sections 161 through 199, which prescribe deductions for individuals and corporations, and in Sections 211 through 222, authorizing additional deductions for individuals.[1] Most of the "take" provisions are in Sections 261 through 280H, specifying nondeductible items and carving out some no nos in the affirmative rules.

There are examples of takeaway rules in other parts of this book, many of which appear along with the affirmative deduction provisions to which they relate. For instance, interest expense generally is deductible under Section 163,[2] but Congress expressly limits or disallows some interest deductions[3] or requires the capitalizing of the interest rather than permitting it to be "expensed."[4] Similarly, as Congress allows deductions for bad debts[5] but not for political contributions,[6] it precludes an indirect deduction for political contributions by denying deductions for bad debts that are obligations of a political party to the taxpayer.[7] The foregoing are only illustrative of the many types of restrictions and limitations on deductions which are discussed throughout this text.

An important instance of congressional finger crossing occurs under Section 274, a disallowance provision that severely limits many of the deductions generally allowed by the broad Section 162 and 212 deduction provisions. Another is Section 461(*l*) which takes away "excess" noncorporate business losses, although it merely defers such losses as they are allowed to be deducted in subsequent years. Many of the other statutory restrictions on deductions are aimed at tax shelters. It's a safe bet that even before students take a tax course, they have already heard about tax shelters. "Tax shelter" can have various meanings, and tax

---

[1]  See also I.R.C. §§ 241–249 providing special deductions for corporations.

[2]  See Chapter 16B, supra.

[3]  See I.R.C. § 163(d) and (h). See also I.R.C. §§ 264(a)(2)–(4), 265(a)(2), and 279. Limitations on the deduction of interest are discussed at page 487, supra.

[4]  I.R.C. § 263A.

[5]  I.R.C. § 166. See Chapter 23A, infra.

[6]  Former I.R.C. § 24 allowing a limited amount of credit for political contributions was repealed in the 1986 Act.

[7]  I.R.C. § 271.

shelters take various forms. Some would look upon the Section 103(a) exclusion of interest on municipal bonds as a tax shelter.[8] The Section 1014 "step-up" in basis at death[9] can also be considered a form of tax shelter. Use of deferred compensation is an important form of tax shelter.[10] However, the term "tax shelter" is most frequently used in an invidious sense to describe a circumstance in which a taxpayer generates deductions in excess of income from one activity and uses that excess to avoid tax on some or all of the income from another unrelated activity. The unrelated income from the second activity is "sheltered" from tax liability by the excess deductions generated by the first. For example, a successful professional person or investor who has high-bracket income generated by services, or by dividends or interest on investments, may become a gentleman farmer in an enjoyable rural area. In the absence of statutory limitations, if the farm activity generates deductions in excess of income, the taxpayer could use excess deductions from the farm to reduce taxable income (and correspondingly the tax on the income) from other sources.

In recent years Congress, not unaware of such activities, has attacked shelters in two fashions: substantively, by limiting deductions and, procedurally, with special penalties and registration requirements. Substantively, Congress deals with what it deems artificial losses under several provisions. Section 183, known as the "hobby loss" provision, raises the question whether a taxpayer's activity (such as the gentleman farmer's activity) is actually engaged in for profit; if not, in general Section 183 limits the deduction of expenditures or losses of the farm to gross income derived from the farm, foreclosing use of the farm as an umbrella to shelter any other income. Similarly, Section 280A, limiting deductions related to a home that a taxpayer uses as a residence, generally allows those deductions only against gross income generated by the home. Taking a different tack in limiting artificial loss deductions, under Section 465, the deduction of losses incurred by the gentleman farmer in the above example or for that matter, almost any taxpayer, is, in general, limited to the amount he personally has "at risk" and could actually lose from engaging in an activity. Further, Section 469 generally prohibits certain taxpayers from deducting losses from passive activities in which they do not materially participate against income from other activities in which they do materially participate.

The substantive provisions above are of two different types but have one common goal: limiting the use of artificial losses to prevent taxpayers from succeeding in tax sheltering schemes. The first type, a substantive takeaway provision, is one which disallows or partially disallows the use of what Congress considers artificial losses by simply *disallowing* in whole or in part the deductions from an activity. Disallowance occurs

---

[8]   See Chapter 11D, supra.

[9]   See Chapter 6B4, supra.

[10]  See Chapter 20C3, infra.

under Section 274, Section 183, and, in most situations, Section 280A, which are takeaway provisions. In a second type of limitation, Congress limits the current deduction of losses or the assertion of credits by *postponing* them, i.e., disallowing their utilization in the current year but permitting them to be carried over to be used in future years. Sections 461(*l*), 465, 469, and, in limited situations, 280A are postponement provisions.

In addition to its substantive attack on tax shelters, Congress also made a procedural assault on them. Congress penalizes one who promotes or participates in the promotion of tax shelters by making false or fraudulent representations concerning the tax benefits from the shelter[11] or assertions of gross overvaluation of involved assets.[12]

Congress became aware of an horrendous number of cases involving tax shelters at various stages of investigation.[13] The heinous nature of this tax dodge is indicated by the Senate Committee's assertion that:[14]

These promoters know that even if a tax scheme they market is clearly faulty, some investors' incorrect returns will escape detection and many will enjoy a substantial deferral of tax while the Treasury searches for their returns and coordinates its handling of similar cases.

Consequently, Congress created the concept of a "reportable transaction"[15] and imposed several requirements on promoters of such transactions. A reportable transaction generally is a transaction that the Service determines has a potential for tax avoidance or evasion.[16] A promoter of a reportable transaction must report the transaction to the Service and maintain a list identifying each person who was advised regarding the transaction.[17] A taxpayer who participates in a reportable transaction also must file a disclosure statement reporting the transaction.[18] Failure to do so subjects the parties to penalties.[19]

In addition to the substantive provisions listed above as attacks on tax shelters, this chapter also considers some limitations on deductions aimed not at tax shelters, but at illegal activities. As should be anticipated, this final group of restrictions is in the form of total disallowance provisions.

---

[11] I.R.C. § 6700(a)(2)(A).

[12] I.R.C. § 6700(a)(2)(B). Such persons are penalized in an amount equal to the lesser of $1,000 or 100 percent of the gross income derived (or even just expected) from the arrangement. I.R.C. § 6700(a). Congress also grants the Service injunctive powers against such promoters. I.R.C. § 7408.

[13] Sen.Rep. No. 98–169, 98th Cong., 2d Sess. 436 (1984).

[14] Sen.Rep. No. 98–169, note 13, supra at 425–426.

[15] I.R.C. § 6707A(c). See I.R.C. § 6011 and Reg. § 1.6011–4(b).

[16] Id.

[17] I.R.C. §§ 6111, 6112.

[18] Reg. § 1.6011–4(a), (d).

[19] I.R.C. § 6707A.

## B. SECTION 274 LIMITATIONS

Internal Revenue Code: Sections 274(a), (b)(1), (c), (d), (e)(1), (2), and (3), (g), (h)(1), (j)(1), (k), (*l*), (m)(1) and (3), and (n)(1).

Regulations: Section 1.162–2(b), –5(e)(1); 1.274–2(b)(1)(i)–(iii)(c).

---

An important instance of congressional finger crossing occurs under Section 274, a significant disallowance provision which we have already encountered in some prior chapters of this book. That section severely limits many of the deductions generally allowed by the broad Section 162 and 212 deduction provisions.[1] Chapter 3 disclosed the $25 limitation on the deduction for business gifts,[2] and Chapter 5 revealed that Section 274 also limits the deduction (and the Section 74(c) exclusion) for employee achievement awards.[3] Section 274 strongly asserts itself with respect to the Section 162 deductions considered in Chapter 14, and the Section 212 deductions in Chapter 15, imposing numerous limitations on, and requiring substantiation of, various ordinary and necessary business expenses and profit-seeking activities.

*Business Meals and Entertainment: Historical Background.* Business meals and entertainment expenses were deductible for much of the history of the federal income tax. Waiters have often overheard someone say: "Have another—it's deductible!" or "Don't worry, I can write it off on my income tax!" Certainly to furnish meals and entertainment is an accepted practice and expense in carrying on many businesses. But should such expenses fall within Section 162(a) or Section 212 given the obvious possibilities for abuse?

Prior to 1962 there were few restrictions on the deductibility of business meals and entertainment expenses, either as to the scope of items which were considered within permissible meals or entertainment or as to the amount of proof or substantiation of expenses incurred. The question of substantiation was raised in the case of Cohan v. Commissioner,[4] in which the actor, George M. Cohan, attempted to deduct large unsubstantiated travel and entertainment expenses. The Second Circuit instructed that in such cases the trial court should approximate the expenses stating:[5]

> Absolute certainty in such matters is usually impossible and is not necessary; the Board [Tax Court] should make as close an approximation as it can, bearing heavily if it chooses upon the taxpayer whose inexactitude is of his own making. But to allow

---

[1] Note that I.R.C. § 274 may limit deductions under other provisions. See, e.g., the Text at note 10, infra.

[2] I.R.C. § 274(b)(1).

[3] I.R.C. § 274(j).

[4] 39 F.2d 540 (2d Cir.1930).

[5] Id. at 543–544.

nothing at all appears to us inconsistent with saying that something was spent. True, we do not know how many trips Cohan made, nor how large his entertainments were; yet there was obviously some basis for computation, if necessary by drawing upon the Board's personal estimates of the minimum of such expenses. The amount may be trivial and unsatisfactory, but there was basis for some allowance, and it was wrong to refuse any, even though it were the travelling expenses of a single trip. It is not fatal that the result will inevitably be speculative; many important decisions must be such.

Prior to 1962, the *Cohan* rule was often applied to allow some deduction in the absence of proof.[6] A fairly easy attitude on the scope of deductions for meals and entertainment and the fluidity of the *Cohan* rule caused many to wonder whether, by way of "business" deductions, taxpayers generally were being called upon to pay for the enjoyments of a relatively select few in the business community. The limiting concepts of "ordinary" and "necessary" under Sections 162(a) and 212, and the prohibition of Section 262, seemed not to do the job.

In 1962, Congress enacted Section 274 in an attempt to muffle the cry: "It's deductible!" After numerous amendments and additions before 2018, a taxpayer generally could deduct the cost of ordinary and necessary expenses for business meals or entertainment if the taxpayer could establish that the expense was either "directly related to" or "associated with" the active conduct of the taxpayer's trade or business or income producing activity.[7] However, only 50 percent of such expenses were deductible.[8] With respect to meals, generally "lavish and extravagant" meals were not deductible, and the taxpayer or an employee had to be present at the furnishing of the meals.[9] These meals restrictions continue to apply beyond the scope of entertainment meals to meals incurred in travel, education, and meals deducted beyond the scope of Sections 162 and 212.[10]

*General Disallowance of Deductions for Meals and Entertainment.* The 2017 Tax Cuts and Jobs Act almost totally eliminated the deduction of meals and entertainment. Beginning in 2018, Section 274(a)(1) provides that *no deduction* is allowed for any item (1) with respect to an activity generally considered entertainment (including meals), amusement, or recreation, or (2) with respect to a facility used in

---

[6]    See James Schulz v. Commissioner, 16 T.C. 401 (1951); Harold A. Christensen, 17 T.C. 1456 (1952); Richard A. Sutter v. Commissioner, 21 T.C. 170 (1953).

[7]    In the case of the "associated with" standard there had to be a substantial and bona fide business discussion directly proceeding or following the meal or entertainment. § 274(a) (pre 2018).

[8]    I.R.C. § 274(n)(1). See I.R.C. § 274(n)(2) providing exceptions for some meals and entertainment.

[9]    I.R.C. § 274(k).

[10]    See, e.g., I.R.C. § 170.

connection with such an activity.[11] The business development lunch with a potential client and the tickets to take a customer to a Broadway show or ballgame are now nondeductible! However, the legislative history of the 2017 Act states that taxpayers may still generally deduct 50 percent of the food and beverage expenses "associated with operating their trade or business (*e.g.*, meals consumed by employees on work travel)."[12] Thus, when business travel in the form of transportation and lodging is deductible, business travel meals of employees continue to be partially (50 percent) deductible.

The regulations broadly define prohibited entertainment to include entertaining at night clubs, cocktail lounges, theaters, country clubs, golf or athletic clubs, sporting events, and on hunting, fishing, vacation, and similar trips.[13] What constitutes entertainment is determined under an objective test, and entertainment cannot be made deductible by characterizing it as something else, such as "advertising" or "public relations."[14] However, the taxpayer's trade or business is taken into account in determining whether an activity is in the nature of entertainment. Thus, a professional theater critic attending a theatrical performance in a professional capacity is not entertainment.[15]

Personal or real property owned, rented, or used by a taxpayer constitutes a facility.[16] Examples of facilities which might be used for, or in connection with, disallowed entertainment include yachts, hunting lodges, fishing camps, swimming pools, tennis courts, bowling alleys, automobiles, airplanes, apartments, hotel suites, and homes in vacation resorts.[17] However, expenses of a facility are deductible to the extent of the use for non-entertainment purposes. Thus, an airplane used for business transportation as opposed to entertainment is not a Section 274 facility, and the costs related to it (such as depreciation and repairs) are deductible to the extent of the non-entertainment business use.[18] Dues or fees, such as bar association dues, which are directly related to a business are deductible.[19] But, no deduction is allowed for amounts paid or incurred for membership in any club organized for business, pleasure, recreation, or other social purpose.[20] These include country clubs, golf and athletic clubs, hotel clubs, and clubs operated to provide meals in a setting conducive to business discussion.[21] Deductions may be disallowed

---

[11]  I.R.C. § 274(a).

[12]  H. Rept. 115–466 Joint Explanatory Statement of the Committee on Conference, 115th Cong., 1st Sess. 251 (2017)

[13]  Reg. § 1.274–2(b)(1)(i).

[14]  Reg. § 1.274–2(b)(1)(ii).

[15]  Id.

[16]  Reg. § 1.274–2(e)(2).

[17]  Id.

[18]  Reg. § 1.274–2(b)(1)(iii)(c), (e)(3)(iii)(b).

[19]  Reg. § 1.274–2(a)(2)(iii)(b).

[20]  I.R.C. § 274(a)(3).

[21]  Reg. § 1.274–2(a)(2)(iii).

with respect to a portion of an entertainment facility; if so, such portion is treated as an asset which is used for personal, living, and family purposes and not as an asset used in a trade or business or held for the production of income.[22]

*Exceptions to the Nondeductibility of Meals and Entertainment.* Section 274(e) provides a series of exceptions to the disallowance rules in Section 274(a).[23] The exceptions themselves are, in some cases, subject to additional limitations. Expenses for food and beverages (and the facilities used in connection therewith) are 50 percent deductible if furnished on the business premises of the taxpayer primarily for employees.[24] Thus, the costs of the company cafeteria or executive dining room are partially deductible.[25] Recreation expenses paid to benefit employees (e.g., an employee holiday party or the company picnic) are deductible.[26] Entertainment and meals also are generally deductible if they are treated as compensation to an employee and subject to wage withholding.[27] Thus, a paid vacation awarded to an employee as a year-end bonus could be deducted if the employer treats it as compensation and wages.[28]

*Other Section 274 Limitations.* Section 274 also imposes numerous limitations on the deductibility of business travel expenses,[29] including travel expenses as a form of education,[30] attendance at certain conventions,[31] and the deductibility of travel expenses of a spouse, dependent, or other individual accompanying the taxpayer on business travel.[32] In addition, no deduction is allowed for the expense of Section 132(f) qualified transportation fringes.[33] Thus, no deduction is permitted for vanpool benefits, transit passes, or qualified parking,[34] and no deduction is allowed for any expense incurred for transportation between

---

[22] I.R.C. § 274(g). Cf. Sharp v. U.S., supra at page 404.

[23] Exceptions not discussed here include reimbursed expenses, expenses of business meetings of employees and stockholders, expenses for meetings of business leagues, items available to the public, and entertainment sold to customers. See I.R.C. § 274(e)(3), (5), (6), (7), and (8).

[24] I.R.C. § 274(e)(1).

[25] Reg. § 1.274–2(f)(2)(ii). If an eating facility is located on or near an employee's business premises and the facility's revenue normally equals or exceeds its direct operating cost, then operation of the facility is treated as a de minimis fringe benefit and employee's may exclude the value of meals from gross income. I.R.C. § 132(e)(2). For highly compensated employees to qualify for the exclusion the facility must satisfy an antidiscrimination rule. I.R.C. § 132(e). An employer may not deduct amount paid or incurred after 2025 with respect to an I.R.C. § 132(e)(2) facility, as well as I.R.C. § 119 expenses. I.R.C. § 274(*o*).

[26] See Reg. § 1.274–2(f)(2)(v).

[27] I.R.C. § 274(e)(2). A similar exception applies to amounts treated as compensation or a prize to someone who is not an employee. I.R.C. § 274(e)(9).

[28] Reg. § 1.274–2(f)(2)(iii)(C) Example.

[29] I.R.C. § 274(c), (h), and (m).

[30] I.R.C. § 274(m)(2).

[31] See I.R.C. § 274(h).

[32] I.R.C. § 274(m)(3).

[33] I.R.C. § 274(a)(4).

[34] See page 96, supra.

an employee's residence and place of employment, except as necessary for the safety of the employee.[35]

*Substantiation and Reporting Requirements.* The restrictions set out above are substantial, but Section 274 goes even further: it also contains substantiation and reporting requirements.[36] The substantiation requirements generally involve travel expenses (both foreign and domestic) including meals and lodging,[37] gifts, and listed property.[38] There are also separate reporting requirements concerning attendance at conventions and seminars.[39] The regulations under Section 274, which have received judicial blessing,[40] impose stringent documentation requirements, normally necessitating a receipt for expenditures over $75.[41] Insufficiency of reporting or substantiation can cause total disallowance of deductions that might otherwise survive the give and take mechanism described above.

## PROBLEMS

1.    Businessperson incurs the following § 162 business deductions. To what extent does § 274 limit their deductibility?

(a)   Businessperson takes Client to lunch and a ballgame and, to Client's dismay, discusses business most of the time.

(b)   Businessperson takes an education course in another town incurring transportation, meals, and lodging expenses.

(c)   Businessperson purchases gifts costing $55 each for significant clients.

(d)   Businessperson purchases an airplane which is used 60 percent of the time for business travel and 40 percent of the time for client entertainment.

(e)   Businessperson provides employees with qualified parking which is excluded from their gross income under § 132(a)(5).

---

[35]  I.R.C. § 274(*l*)(1). However, in the case of any qualified bicycle commuting reimbursement, such amount may be deducted, presumably because it is included in the employee's gross income. I.R.C. § 274(*l*)(2).

[36]  I.R.C. § 274(d) and (h)(5). In the areas affected by I.R.C. § 274 (but only those areas), § 274(d) overrules the long-established *Cohan* rule. With respect to substantiation of deductions not within the scope of § 274, the *Cohan* rule still applies. Ellery W. Newton v. Commissioner, 57 T.C. 245 (1971), business use of an automobile other than in a travel status; William H. Green v. Commissioner, 31 T.C.M. 592 (1972), wagering losses.

[37]  See Rev. Rul. 75–169, 1975–1C.B 59.

[38]  I.R.C. § 274(d). For listed property see I.R.C. § 280F(d)(4) and Chapter 14E2, supra.

[39]  I.R.C. § 274(h)(5).

[40]  Sanford v. Commissioner, 412 F.2d 201 (2d Cir.1969), cert. denied 396 U.S. 841, 90 S.Ct. 104 (1969); Robert H. Alter v. Commissioner, 50 T.C. 833 (1968); John Robinson v. Commissioner, 51 T.C. 520 (1968), affirmed per curiam (this issue) 422 F.2d 873 (9th Cir.1970). The Fifth Circuit has ruled that each and every element of each expenditure must be adequately substantiated. Dowell v. United States, 522 F.2d 708 (5th Cir.1975). There is a comment on the *Sanford* case by Aaron, "Substantiation Requirements for Travel, Entertainment and Gift Expenses," 35 Mo.L.Rev. 70 (1970); and see McNally, "Substantiation of Business Related Entertainment Expenses," 54 Marq.L.Rev. 347 (1971).

[41]  Reg. § 1.274–5(c)(2)(iii).

**2.** Traveler flies from her personal and tax home in New York to a business meeting in Florida on Monday. The meeting ends late Wednesday and she flies home on Friday afternoon after two days in the sunshine.

    (a) To what extent are Traveler's transportation, meals, and lodging deductible? See Reg. § 1.162–2(a) and (b).

    (b) May Traveler deduct any of her spouse's expenses if he joins her on the trip? See § 274(m)(3).

    (c) What result in (a), above, if Traveler stays in Florida until Sunday afternoon?

    (d) What result in (a), above, if Traveler takes a cruise ship leaving Florida on Wednesday night and arriving in New York on Friday? See § 274(m)(1).

    (e) What result in (a), above, if Traveler's trip is to Mexico City rather than Florida? See § 274(c).

    (f) What result in (e), above, if Traveler went to Mexico City on Thursday and conducted business on Thursday, Friday, Monday, and Tuesday, and returned to New York on the succeeding Friday night? See Reg. § 1.274–4(d)(2)(v).

    (g) What result in (e), above, if Traveler's trip to Mexico City is to attend a business convention? See § 274(h).

## C. ACTIVITIES NOT ENGAGED IN FOR PROFIT

Internal Revenue Code: Section 183(a)–(d).

Regulations: Section 1.183–2(a) and (b).

———

It may very well be that our gentleman farmer considered above in the Introduction is legitimately engaged in his farming activity to earn a profit and if so, his deductions should be fully allowed to the extent that he is at risk. If, however, he is not engaged in the activity for profit then excess deductions from the activity should not be permitted to shelter other sources of income. By statute the result depends upon whether the taxpayer's activity is one "engaged in for profit," a criterion easy to state but not easy to determine.

Section 183 applies to individuals, S corporations, trusts and estates.[1] It creates a rebuttable presumption related to whether the activity is "engaged in for profit."[2] Specifically, Section 183(d) establishes the presumption that an activity is engaged in for profit in the current taxable year if, in three or more of the past five consecutive taxable years, gross income derived from the activity exceeds deductions attributable to

———

[1] I.R.C. § 183(a); see I.R.C. § 641(b) and Reg. § 1.183–1(a). See I.R.C. § 1361 et seq. for the definition of an S corporation.

[2] See Lee, "A Blend of Old Wines in a New Wineskin: Section 183 and Beyond," 29 Tax L.Rev. 347 (1974).

that activity.[3] For an activity the major part of which is breeding, training, showing, or racing horses, the critical question is whether there were two or more profitable years in a seven year period.[4] Overall, these provisions, indicate that the presumption depends on the taxpayer's actual record in making profits.

Section 183(d) merely creates a presumption the Commissioner may overcome.[5] Even when facts are such that no presumption arises, the taxpayer still may qualify an activity as one "engaged in for profit." The taxpayer may be able to show, using an objective standard, that he or she engaged in the activity, or the continuation of the activity, with the objective of making a profit.[6]

If the activity is engaged in for profit, then all items conventionally deductible are allowed, without limitation. If, on the other hand, the activity is not engaged in for profit, Section 183(b) comes into play, providing the extent to which deductions are allowed. Section 183(b) renders wholly deductible expenses that are deductible whether the activity is business, investment or personal in nature, such as taxes.[7] The remainder of the total deductions allowed are deductions that would be fully allowed if the activity were engaged in for profit, but only to the extent that gross income from the activity exceeds the preferred deductions just indicated.[8] If this were not complicated enough, Congress has precluded deductibility of some expenses under the combination of Sections 62 and 67. This further limitation on deductions can alter the Section 183 results in the same manner as an employee's Section 162 expenses or an investor's Section 212 expenses, and will be encountered in Chapter 18C.

---

[3] All deductions attributable to the activity, other than allowable net operating loss carryovers, are taken into account in determining the applicability of the I.R.C. § 183(d) presumption. An amendment in 1971 added § 183(e) under which a taxpayer may defer the time for determination whether the statutory presumption applies. With respect to any such deferral, the Tax Reform Act of 1976 added § 183(e)(4) to protect the government against inappropriate running of the limitations period on deficiency assessments.

[4] I.R.C. § 183(d).

[5] Reg. § 1.183–1(c)(i). See also Reg. § 1.183–2(b).

[6] Reg. § 1.183–2(a). In determining whether a profit objective exists, a reasonable expectation of profit is not required; it may be sufficient that there is a small chance of making a large profit. Thus a taxpayer investing in a wildcat oil well may deduct his substantial expenditures incurred in the activity even though his expectation of profit might be considered unreasonable. See Reg. § 1.183–2(b) for factors relevant to determining whether an activity is engaged in for profit.

For examples of cases in this area, compare Engdahl v. Commissioner, 72 T.C. 659 (1979), below and Appley v. Commissioner, 39 T.C.M. 386 (1979), with Golanty v. Commissioner, 72 T.C. 411 (1979), affirmed by 9th Cir. without opinion, 647 F.2d 170 (9th Cir.1981). And see Posker, "Activity, Profit and Section 183," 56 Taxes 155 (1978).

[7] I.R.C. § 183(b)(1). See Reg. § 1.183–1(d)(3) Example (ii) and Chapter 16, supra.

[8] I.R.C. § 183(b)(2). Within this category of deductions the regulations give priority to deductions which do not reduce the basis of property. See Reg. § 1.183–1(b)(1)(ii) and (iii).

## Engdahl v. Commissioner*

Tax Court of the United States, 1979.
72 T.C. 659.

■ HALL, JUDGE:

Respondent determined deficiencies in petitioners' income tax as follows:

| Year | Deficiency |
|------|-----------|
| 1971 | $9,471.84 |
| 1972 | 6,309.55 |
| 1973 | 9,193.55 |

The issue for decision is whether petitioners' horse-breeding operation was an "activity * * * not engaged in for profit" within the meaning of section 183(a). * * *

### FINDINGS OF FACT

Some of the facts have been stipulated and are found accordingly.

At the time of filing their petition, petitioners Theodore N. and Adeline M. Engdahl were residents of Santa Clara County, Calif.

Dr. Engdahl has been a practicing orthodontist since 1946. Net income from his practice for 1971, 1972, and 1973 was $88,661.14, $87,296.46, and $81,766, respectively. Petitioners have no substantial income other than Dr. Engdahl's orthodontic practice. At the time of trial, Dr. Engdahl was 62 years old and his wife was 63.

Petitioners have four children—one son and three daughters. Petitioners became involved with saddle-bred horses in 1951 when their oldest daughter started riding lessons. Subsequently, petitioners purchased several saddle horses which were shown by their daughter at various horse shows in California. Petitioners boarded their horses at a stable and hired a professional trainer to train the horses.

In 1964, petitioners realized that Dr. Engdahl's retirement from his orthodontic practice was imminent, and began considering what business they might enter to supplement Dr. Engdahl's retirement income. Petitioners consulted with their trainer, their two veterinarians, and other people in the horse-breeding business as to the possibility of setting up a horse-breeding operation. The veterinarians were of the opinion that the future looked very promising locally for breeding, raising, and showing American saddle-bred horses. Petitioners concurred in this opinion based upon their observations that many children in the area rode this breed of horse, which was at that time in short supply. Petitioners received advice from these people about stud fees and the general economics of running a horse-breeding operation. In addition,

---

\*   Some footnotes omitted

petitioners consulted reference books and materials. They learned that the start-up phase of an American saddle-bred breeding operation was 5 to 10 years.

Petitioners decided in 1964 to establish a horse-breeding operation, and began with four horses. At that time, petitioners did not own facilities for keeping horses on their own property, so they boarded the horses and had them trained off their premises.

In order to make their operation more profitable, petitioners were advised to purchase a ranch on which they could board their horses. After searching for a year, petitioners located suitable property (the ranch) in Morgan Hill, Calif. They purchased the property in 1967, and have conducted their horse-breeding activities there since. Their residence occupies approximately one-fifth of the 2½-acre ranch. The remainder is used for the horse operation. The residence in which petitioners lived prior to moving to the ranch was larger and more attractive than the one at the ranch. Petitioners did not buy the ranch with the expectation of later subdividing it.

Upon purchase of the ranch, petitioners constructed a 7-stall stable (convertible to 12 stalls), a tack room capable of storing 7 to 8 tons of hay, five fenced pastures, and a holding corral. In addition, petitioners planted the pasture and installed an irrigation system for the pasture land. The installation of the irrigation system, much of the fencing, and a two-stall addition to the barn were constructed by petitioners.

From 1964 through 1973, petitioners registered 10 purebred American saddle-bred horses with the American Saddle Bred Registry in Louisville, Ky. During this period, petitioners' brood mares produced 11 live foals and had 4 stillborn foals or miscarriages. By the end of 1973, two of the live offspring three had been sold, and those remaining were in training off the premises or were being held in pasture. In 1973, petitioners had nine horses. Of these, two mares and a stallion were purchased, while five mares and a stallion were foaled by petitioners' brood mares (two of which were sired by stallions owned by others, and four were sired by petitioners' own stallions).

Together, petitioners spend an average of 35 to 55 hours per week caring for the horses and maintaining the improvements on the ranch. On weekdays, Dr. Engdahl rises around 5:30 a.m. to feed the horses and [clean Ed.] the stalls. In the evenings and on week-ends, he performs normal maintenance. Dr. Engdahl attends meetings as a director of the California Saddle Horse Breeders Association. Each morning, Mrs. Engdahl checks the horses and the fly control units. She then exercises and grooms the horses, cleans their feet, and mucks out the stalls. Breeding, delivering foals, and attending to sick or injured horses require extra work by petitioners. Petitioners employ high school students part-time to help with the heavy work around the barn. Neither petitioner rides horses. Both petitioners view their efforts in connection with the horse operation as jobs which have to be done; neither petitioner has any affection for the horses themselves.

At all times material to this case, petitioners' horses were trained by a professional trainer. The trainer entered petitioners' horses in shows when he felt they were ready and when he had time to show them. During the years in issue, petitioners' horses were exhibited by their trainer at 10 shows and won eight awards. Prizes typically included ribbons, trophies, and prize money ranging from $10 to $150 per event. When petitioners attended a show, they bathed, groomed and prepared the horses. Petitioners occasionally participated in social activities in connection with the horse shows. Apart from these activities, petitioners' social life at home is not structured around either the horse business or people associated with horses.

Horse shows are the best form of advertising for American saddle-bred horses. In addition to exhibiting at horse shows, petitioners advertised in horse show programs, newspapers, and a horsemen's magazine, and through word of mouth. Petitioners advertised their sale and for breeding.

At all times since 1964, petitioners maintained books and records of their horse operation following procedures suggested by their certified public accountant. Petitioners maintained one checking account from which checks for personal use, Dr. Engdahl's orthodontic practice, and the horse operation were drawn. The allocation of each check to one of the above three purposes was noted on the check stub; expenses were subsequently distributed to accounts on separate ledgers maintained for the orthodontic practice and the horse operation. Income from the horse operation was deposited in a savings account separate from other personal savings accounts maintained by petitioners. Petitioners' accountant reviewed petitioners' recordkeeping and summarized the books quarterly. At the end of each year, the accountant prepared a summary recapitulation of the horse operation showing expenses broken down by item for each month. This enabled petitioners to keep track of monthly variations in their expenditures. Dr. Engdahl and the accountant then discussed the summary sheet, reviewing what petitioners spent during the year for training, feed, horse shows, veterinary costs, etc. Petitioners' accountant was of the opinion bookkeeping system was appropriate for petitioners' operation.

[Petitioners' had operating losses from 1964 through 1975 for their horse operation. Ed.]

\* \* \*

Petitioners attribute their unprofitability to a combination of adverse factors beyond their control. First, the demand for American saddle breds foreseen by [them Ed.] failed to materialize due to a shift in fashion among horse purchasers in California. There was also a decline in the number of entries for this type of horse in California shows. In the second place, the costs associated with horse operations increased from 1964 to 1973. For example, hay rose from $30 to $75 per ton; grain, from $3.50 to $7.95 per 100 pounds; and veterinarians' fees, from $10 to $15.50 per call plus medicine. Third, petitioners encountered medical problems with some of their horses. For example, during their first year of operation, petitioners sent one brood mare to Missouri to be bred to a champion stud. This breeding produced a young stud named Royal Jubilation. Petitioners expected to use him as a breeding stallion; however, at the age of 4 he developed colic. He failed to respond to medical care and died shortly after surgery. Fourth, the Duchess, petitioners' most expensive mare, bought in 1965 for $6,500, died when hit accidentally by an automobile. Fifth, petitioners' trainer failed to use his best efforts in breeding and showing petitioners' horses. Over the years, petitioners realized that their trainer's indecision about training several of their horses hurting the development of these horses. Petitioners also discovered that their trainer placed the showing of petitioners' horses second to the showing of horses of some of his other customers. As a result, petitioners brought all of their horses back to the ranch. Sixth, because petitioners could not afford to invest in the most expensive horses, they attempted to diversify by purchasing horses on speculation for resale. Unfortunately, these horses did not produce the quality of offspring for which petitioners hoped; the horses were subsequently sold.

As of December 31, 1977, the fair market value of the Morgan Hill ranch, including improvements, was approximately $225,000; petitioners' cost was $83,146. In addition, petitioners' remaining four horses had appreciated in value by approximately $18,750. By the time of trial, petitioners had abandoned hopes of making a profit on their horse operation and were winding down their operation preparatory to terminating it. The ranch was for sale.

On their income tax returns, petitioners deducted losses of $17,617.52 in 1971, $17,009.94 in 1972, and $18,526 in 1973 resulting from their horse-breeding operation. * * * In his notice of deficiency, respondent disallowed these losses * * * based on his conclusion that petitioners' horse operation was an activity not engaged in for profit.

## OPINION

The sole issue for decision is whether petitioners' American saddle-bred horse operation was an "activity * * * not engaged in for profit" within the meaning of section 183(a). Section 183(a) provides that if an individual engages in an activity, and if that activity is not engaged in for profit, then no deduction attributable to that activity shall be allowed except as otherwise provided under section 183(b). Section 183(c) defines an activity not engaged in for profit as "any activity other than one with respect to which deductions are allowable for the taxable year under section 162 or under paragraph (1) or (2) of section 212."

Breeding and raising horses for sale may constitute a trade or business for purposes of section 162. * * * Whether it does or not, depends on whether petitioners engaged in the venture with the predominant purpose and intention of making a profit. * * * Petitioners' expectation of profit need not be reasonable, but petitioners must establish that they continued their activities with a bona fide intention and good-faith expectation of making a profit. Sec. 1.183–2(a), * * * [Allen Ed.] v. Commissioner, [72 T.C. 28, 33 (1979). Ed.]; Jasionowksi v. Commissioner, [66 T.C. 312, 321 (1976). Ed.]; Benz v. Commissioner, [63 T.C. 375, 383 (1974). Ed.]; Bessenyey v. Commissioner, 45 T.C. 261 (1965), affd. 379 F.2d 252 (2d Cir. 1967).

Section 1.183–2(b), Income Tax Regs., lists some of the relevant factors to be considered in determining whether an activity is engaged in for profit. These factors include: (1) The manner in which the taxpayer carried on the activity; (2) the expertise of the taxpayer or his advisers; (3) the time and effort expended by the taxpayer in carrying on the activity; (4) the expectation that assets used in the activity may appreciate in value; (5) the success of the taxpayer in carrying on other similar or dissimilar activities; (6) the taxpayer's history of income or loss with respect to the activity; (7) the amount of occasional profit, if any, which is earned; (8) the financial status of the taxpayer; and (9) whether elements of personal pleasure or recreation are involved.

The issue is one of fact to be resolved not on the basis of any one factor but on the basis of all the facts and circumstances. Sec. 1.183–2(b), Income Tax Regs.; Allen v. Commissioner, supra at 34. See Boyer v. Commissioner, 69 T.C. 521 (1977), on appeal (7th Cir., July 7, 1978). Greater weight is to be given to objective facts than to petitioners' mere statement of their intent. Sec. 1.183–2(a), Income Tax Regs.; Churchman v. Commissioner, [66 T.C. 696, 701 (1977). Ed.].

Respondent contends, first, that the manner in which petitioners carried on their horse activities does not indicate that the activity was engaged in for profit. We disagree. What is relevant is whether petitioners maintained complete and accurate books and records, whether the activity was conducted in a manner substantially similar to other comparable businesses which are profitable, and whether changes were attempted in order to improve profitability. Sec. 1.183–2(b)(1), Income Tax Regs. In this case, petitioners kept complete records of their horse operation. Although petitioners maintained one checking account for their horse operation, Dr. Engdahl's orthodontic practice, and their personal use, the horse activity expenses were posted to a separate ledger maintained solely for the horse operation. Receipts from horse breeding and sales were deposited in a savings account separate from other personal savings maintained by petitioners. Petitioners' certified public accountant reviewed this recordkeeping and summarized the books quarterly. At the end of each year, petitioners' accountant prepared a summary recapitulation showing expenses broken down by items for each month which enabled Dr. Engdahl to keep track of monthly variations in expenses. Together, Dr. Engdahl and his accountant reviewed the summary sheets. It was the accountant's opinion that this accounting procedure was suitable for petitioners' operation. See Farris v. Commissioner, 31 T.C.M. 821, 41 P-H Memo T.C. par. 72,165 (1972).

Petitioners advertised their operation by exhibiting their horses at shows, advertising in horse show programs, newspapers, and a horsemen's magazine, and by word of mouth. Petitioners advertised their horses both for sale and breeding. * * * Respondent asserts that petitioners' limited participation in horse shows during the years in issue belies any intent of making a profit. Petitioner's horses participated in 10 shows during the years in issue; petitioners relied on their professional trainer to show a horse after the horse's training was complete. While petitioners' reliance on their trainer may have been misplaced, we do not believe the facts indicate a lack of dedicated intent to make a profit.

Moreover, the record demonstrates that petitioners made changes in their operating methods in an effort to increase profitability. After boarding their horses for 3 years, petitioners purchased the Morgan Hill ranch to reduce expenses. Petitioners disposed of horses that did not meet petitioners' show or breeding expectations. In an attempt to upgrade the quality of their stock, petitioners bred their mares to champion stallions owned by others and in 1965 bought a mare for $6,500. When petitioners became aware that their trainer was not using his best efforts to breed or show their horses, they brought the horses with which he was working back to the Morgan Hill ranch. Because petitioners could not afford to invest in the most expensive horses, they attempted to diversify by purchasing horses on speculation for resale. In light of these facts, we conclude that petitioners' manner of operation indicates an intent to make a profit.

Second, respondent argues that the type and quality of advice sought by petitioners was not indicative of an intent to engage in an activity for profit. Initially, petitioners discussed embarking upon a horse-breeding business with their two veterinarians, their trainer, and others involved in the business of breeding and showing horses. Petitioners were advised that the expected market for American saddle-bred horses was good. Petitioners received advice regarding stud fees and maintenance costs. Petitioners received and followed the advice given them with regard to purchasing property for the conduct of their operation. Petitioners consulted a certified public accountant as to recordkeeping procedures, and petitioners have consistently followed the procedures outlined for them. While no formal market study of the market for American saddle-bred was conducted, we believe that petitioners' informal and continuous consultations with veterinarians, their trainer, and other horse breeders who are knowledgeable in this area demonstrates an intent to engage in a horse breeding business for profit. * * *

Third, respondent asserts that petitioners had no expectation of asset appreciation. The facts, however, do not support respondent's allegation. The purchase price of the Morgan Hill ranch, including the cost of improvements made by petitioners, was $83,146. As of December 31, 1977, the fair market value of the ranch, based on its use as a horse ranch with residence thereon, was $225,000.[4] Moreover, petitioners' remaining horses as of December 31, 1977, had appreciated in value over cost by $18,750. The total appreciation in value may or may not offset the aggregate operating losses incurred. Nonetheless, we believe that petitioners had a bona fide expectation that the assets used in their horse operation would increase; we further believe that the expectation was sufficient to explain their willingness to sustain continued operating losses. * * *

Fourth, respondent points to petitioners' unremitting losses since 1964 as indicative that petitioners were not engaged in their horse-breeding activities for profit. We note, however, that a series of losses during the initial stage of an activity does not necessarily indicate that the activity was not engaged in for profit. Sec. 1.183–2(b)(6), Income Tax Regs. Moreover, losses sustained because of unforeseen or fortuitous circumstances beyond control of the taxpayer do not indicate that the activity was not engaged in for profit. Sec. 1.183–2(b)(6), Income Tax Regs. The start-up phase of an American saddle-bred breeding operation is 5 to 10 years. The years in issue fall within this start-up period. * * * In addition, petitioners' losses can be explained by a series of unfortunate events beyond their control. These events include a failure of the expected California market for American saddle-bred horses due to a shift in fashion among horse purchasers, medical problems with several of their horses, the untimely death of two of their chief hopes for setting up their breeding herd, their trainer to devote his best efforts in breeding and showing their horses, and the rise in costs associated with maintaining and training horses.

As a result of these losses, petitioners made changes in their operation such as purchasing the Morgan Hill ranch and recalling their horses from their trainer. By the time of trial, petitioners realized they were not going to profit from their activity except for asset appreciation; consequently, they were attempting to sell the ranch. We believe this fact further indicates that petitioners conducted their horse operation with the intent to make a profit. * * *

Respondent's fifth contention is that Dr. Engdahl's substantial income from his orthodontic practice indicates that the horse-breeding and showing activity was not engaged in for profit, especially since losses

---

[4]  Petitioners purchased the Morgan Hill property primarily for the purpose of breeding, raising, and selling horses. Thus, the holding of the land and the horse-related activities are considered a single activity for purposes of determining expected appreciation of value in assets under sec. 1.183–2(b)(4), Income Tax Regs. See sec. 1.183–1(d)(1), Income Tax Regs.; Allen v. Commissioner, 72 T.C. 28 (1979).

from the activity generated substantial "tax benefits." Respondent points to section 1.183–2(b)(8), Income Tax Regs., which reads as follows:

(8) The financial status of the taxpayer. The fact that the taxpayer does not have substantial income or capital from sources other than the activity may indicate that an activity is engaged in for profit. Substantial income from sources other than the activity (particularly if the losses from the activity generate substantial tax benefits) may indicate that the activity is not engaged in for profit especially if there are personal or recreational elements involved.

Needless to say, such language cannot be construed as providing an additional reason to deny a deduction merely because the deduction is usable against other income. In cases of this kind, the concurrent existence of other income poses the question, rather than answers it. If there is no other income, there is no issue. As long as tax rates are less than 100 percent, there is no "benefit" in losing money. Properly construed, the regulation merely makes the commonsense point that the expectation of [being Ed.] able to arrange to have the tax collector share in the cost of a hobby may often induce an investment in such a hobby which would not otherwise occur. The essential question remains as to whether there was a genuine hope of economic profit. Petitioners established their horse operation with the hope of producing retirement income. Petitioners had no sizable investments or substantial source of income other than Dr. Engdahl's orthodontic practice. Petitioners' investment and hard work were not done with their children in mind-petitioners' children no longer lived at home by 1967. We think it unlikely that petitioners would embark on a hobby costing thousands of dollars and entailing much personal physical labor without a motive. * * *.

Respondent's final contention is that petitioners received personal pleasure and recreational benefits from their horse activities which tends to indicate that petitioners did not engage in the activity for profit. Sec. 1.183–2(b)(9), Income Tax Regs. The facts, however, clearly do not support respondent's contention. After purchasing the Morgan Hill property, petitioners built the horse stalls, fences, and irrigation facilities themselves. For a number of years, petitioners have spent an average of 35 to 55 hours per week caring for the horses, mucking out stalls, and maintaining the horse facilities. Activities of this nature could hardly be called pleasurable. Moreover, petitioners do not ride, nor do they use their ranch for social activities. While petitioners did occasionally attend social affairs at horse shows, they did not attend the horse shows for this purpose.

Viewing the record as a whole, we conclude that petitioners engaged in their horse activities with the bona fide intent to derive a profit, and, therefore, that the losses incurred in such activity during the years in issue are fully deductible * * *.

Decision will be entered for the petitioners.

## PROBLEM

**1.** Goggle, who owns a successful high-tech start-up business, develops an interest in winemaking. Goggle purchases land in neighboring wine country and buys a home and land surrounding it and grows grapes on the land. Regrettably, Goggle's grape-growing endeavors are not as successful as the high-tech endeavors. Goggle has net losses in each of the first two years of grape-growing operations. In the third year, Goggle earns $55,000 from sales of grapes, but Goggle also incurs $10,000 of property taxes, $15,000 of interest on a mortgage on the property, $20,000 of salaries, $20,000 in other operating expenses, and $15,000 of depreciation. Discuss the deductibility of Goggle's expenses under § 183 in year three.

## D.  RESTRICTIONS ON DEDUCTIONS OF HOMES

Internal Revenue Code: Sections 280A(a), (b), (c)(1), (3), and (5), (d)(1), (e), (f) and (g).

———————————

Prior to 1976 the rules of Section 183, discussed above, were applicable in determining the extent of deductibility of expenses incurred in connection with the then-popular tax shelter device of vacation or second homes[1] In 1976 Congress became concerned with the overall aspects of the deductibility of items related to a home used by a taxpayer both for business or investment and for residential purposes. In the Tax Reform Act of 1976 Congress responded to that concern by enacting Section 280A which provides specific rules limiting deductions on homes.[2] The rules of Section 280A and Section 183[3] apply to the same taxpayers and both sections impose similar limitations on deductions.[4] However, Section 280A applies in circumstances different from those to which Section 183 applies. With respect to vacation or second homes the Commissioner may assert the rules of Section 183 to limit deductions for those taxable years to which the limitations of Section 280A do not apply.[5]

Section 280A limits deductions attributable to a taxpayer's "residence," which the statute defines as a dwelling unit that the taxpayer uses for personal purposes[6] more than 14 days or 10 percent of

———————————

[1]   See Reg. § 1.183–1(d)(3) and Rev.Rul. 73–219, 1973–1 C.B. 134.

[2]   Kaplan, "Deductions for 'Vacation Homes' Under the Tax Reform Act of 1976," 63 A.B.A.J. 1302 (1977).

[3]   I.R.C. § 280A(a) and Reg. § 1.183–1(a).

[4]   See the discussion at notes 12 through 15, infra, and at notes 7 and 8 on page 510, supra.

[5]   I.R.C. § 280A(f)(3). See the discussion at notes 8–10, infra.

[6]   Under I.R.C. § 280A(d)(2), a dwelling is considered to have been used for personal purposes if, for any part of a day, the dwelling is used for personal purposes by the taxpayer, certain of his or her relatives, other persons owning an interest in the dwelling, or any other individual using the home who has either not paid fair rental or used the dwelling under a reciprocal use arrangement with the taxpayer. See Dinsmore v. Commissioner, 67 T.C.M. 2537 (1994). See also Fudim v. Commissioner, 67 T.C.M. 3011 (1994), in which the personal use of all owners of interests in a time-share condominium were attributed to the taxpayer.

the rental period, whichever is greater.[7] If a dwelling unit is not a residence for the purposes of Section 280A, then the limitations of Section 280A do not apply[8] and, instead, Section 183 determines deductibility. If, under Section 183, it is determined that rental of the dwelling is engaged in for profit, either by meeting the Section 183(d) presumption or by qualifying the activity as one objectively entered into with a profit-making goal, all *allocable*[9] expenses incurred in renting the dwelling plus all expenses otherwise deductible (e.g., interest and property taxes) can be deducted. If, however, it is determined that the activity is not engaged in for profit, the limitations of Section 183 apply, and the taxpayer can take deductions only to the extent of gross income from the dwelling.[10]

If a dwelling unit is a taxpayer's residence, the allowance of deductions turns on the number of days that the residence is rented. If the residence is rented for less than 15 days during the taxable year, no deductions attributable to the rental activity are allowed, *but* neither is the income derived from the rental included in the taxpayer's gross income.[11] If the rental use exceeds 14 days, the limitations on deduction imposed by Section 280A(c)(5) apply. Section 280A(c)(5) limits deductions attributable to the rental activity to the amount by which gross income derived from the rental of the residence exceeds deductions that are allowable without respect to the rental of the residence. These limitations are similar to the Section 183(b) limitations.[12]

This computation is trickier than first appears. It begins with the net rental income derived from the activity. Interest and taxes allocable to rental use of the property are deducted from that income. As interest and taxes are deemed to accrue daily throughout the year, the allocation is based on the *portion of the year* the property is rented.[13] Section 280A(c)(5) provides that the remaining deductions (i.e., (1) maintenance and utilities and (2) depreciation, in that order[14]) allocable to rental use

---

[7]   I.R.C. § 280A(d)(1).

[8]   The expense allocation limitation of I.R.C. § 280A(e) is, however, still applicable. See note 15, infra. The parenthetical language of § 280A(e)(1), "whether or not [the taxpayer] is treated under [§ 280A] as using such unit as a residence," indicates that the § 280A(e) limitation on deductions based on allocation of expenses continues to apply where the provisions of § 183, rather than § 280A, are controlling.

[9]   See I.R.C. § 280A(e) and note 8, supra.

[10]   See I.R.C. § 183(b) and notes 12 through 15, infra, and see especially note 18, infra.

[11]   I.R.C. § 280A(g). Deductions otherwise allowable for the home without respect to whether the home is rented out, such as property taxes and mortgage interest, are fully deductible. See I.R.C. § 280A(g)(1) and (b). See Rev.Rul. 80–55, 1980–1 C.B. 65. However, rental to a relative at fair market value for the relative's use as a principal residence is not considered use by the taxpayer. I.R.C. § 280A(d)(3)(A). In addition, any day spent by the taxpayer substantially on repair and maintenance will not be considered a day of personal use. I.R.C. § 280A(d)(2), last sentence.

[12]   See the discussion at notes 9 and 10, supra.

[13]   Bolton v. Commissioner, 694 F.2d 556 (9th Cir.1982); McKinney v. Commissioner, 732 F.2d 414 (10th Cir.1983). Compare the deductibility of these items under I.R.C. § 183. See Reg. § 1.183–1(d)(3) Example (ii).

[14]   I.R.C. § 183 would allow the deductions which do not result in a basis reduction (utility and maintenance expenses) to be taken before deductions requiring a basis reduction

are limited to the difference between the rental income and allocable interest and taxes. A different fraction based on *proportionate business to non-business actual use* of the property is computed to determine what portion of those remaining deductions are allocable to rental use.[15]

The above rules are illustrated in the following example. Assume Taxpayer owns a vacation home that Taxpayer rents for 60 days and personally uses for 30 days in a taxable year. Gross rental income from the vacation home is $5,400. Taxpayer pays real estate taxes and "qualified residence interest" on the home totaling $3,600, and incurs other expenses related to the home (utility and maintenance expenses of $1,500 and depreciation of $6,300) totaling $7,800 for the year. Taxpayer does *not* meet the minimal personal use requirements of Section 280A(d), because (1) the home was rented for more than 14 days during the taxable year (see Section 280A(g)) and (2) during the year the home is used for personal purposes in excess of the greater of 14 days or 10 percent of the actual rental time. Taxpayer's deductions (other than expenses deductible without regard to the rental activity) are limited by gross rental income as follows:

(1)  Gross rental income ........................................................... $5,400

(2)  Less allocable portion of Interest and Taxes, $60/365$ of $3,600 (*rounded off*) ........................................................... $ 600

(3)  Section 280A(c)(5) limit on deductible rental income expenses other than Interest and Taxes ........................... $4,800

(4)  Allocable portion under Section 280A(e) of rental expenses other than depreciation, $60/90$ of $1,500[16] ........... $1,000

(5)  Maximum depreciation deduction ..................................... $3,800

(6)  Allocable portion under Section 280A(e) of depreciation deduction, $60/90$ of $6,300 = $4,200, but limited by Section 280A(c)(5) to ........................................................ $3,800

Taxpayer can deduct only $4,800 of the $5,200 ($1,000 plus $4,200) of expenses allocable and related to the rental of the home,[17] but can deduct all $3,600 of the interest and property tax expenses, because such expenses are deductible without regard to rental use.[18]

---

(depreciation). The same rule applies under § 280A. See Prop.Reg. § 1.280A–2(h), (i)(5) and Rev.Rul. 80–55, supra note 11.

[15]  See I.R.C. § 280A(e) under which expenses allocable to rental use are limited to the amount which bears the same ratio to such expenses as the number of days during each year that the vacation home is actually rented out at a fair rental bears to the total number of days during the taxable year that the home is used for *all* purposes. Merely holding the property out for rental does not constitute actual rental. Personal use of the home for even one day requires that expenses be allocated under § 280A, although see the rule at note 11, supra.

[16]  See note 14, supra.

[17]  See (4) and (6) above.

[18]  I.R.C. § 280A(b). See Chapter 16, supra. If, instead, Taxpayer had used the home for personal purposes for only 10 days, the minimal personal use requirements of I.R.C. § 280A(d)

Section 280A(d) is not limited to vacation homes and its restrictions can be applied to one's principal residence as well.[19] Congress, not wishing to limit deductibility for a year when one's principal residence is legitimately converted to rental property, eased the restrictions on a principal residence by the addition in 1978 of Section 280A(d)(4). That section permits a disregard of personal use of one's principal residence in applying the Section 280A(d)(1) limitations if the personal use of the principal residence precedes or follows a "qualified rental period" as defined in Section 280A(d)(4)(B). In general, unless the period is shortened by a sale, a "qualified rental period" means rental of the property for twelve consecutive months to unrelated persons or a holding of the property for rental purposes for a like period. In both instances, the rental must be "fair."

As stated above, in 1976 Congress was concerned with deductible expenses related to all residences, not only vacation homes. One area of special concern was commonly referred to as the "office in home" situation, where taxpayers would attempt to deduct a portion of the expenses of operating their residences (owned or rented) as business expenses when they conducted business or business related activities in their homes. Case law was mixed as to both the tests for and the amount of deductibility.[20] Congress responded with a portion of Section 280A which provides both certainty and restrictions for deductibility of such expenses.[21] Section 280A(a) generally denies a taxpayer deductions for expenses attributable to the use of one's home for business purposes,[22] but makes exception for the extent such deductions are attributable to a portion of the home[23] used *exclusively* and on a *regular basis:* (1) as the principal place of business for any trade or business of the taxpayer;[24] (2)

---

would possibly be met and § 183, rather than § 280A, would apply to potentially limit deductions.

[19] See, for example, Russell v. Commissioner, 67 T.C.M. 2347 (1994), and Gilchrist v. Commissioner, 46 T.C.M. 226 (1983).

[20] E.g., Bodzin v. Commissioner, 60 T.C. 820 (1973), reversed 509 F.2d 679 (4th Cir.1975), cert. denied 423 U.S. 825, 96 S.Ct. 40 (1975), and O'Connell v. Commissioner, 31 T.C.M. 837 (1972), considering the propriety of and tests for deductibility. See also Browne v. Commissioner, 73 T.C. 723 (1980); Curphey v. Commissioner, 73 T.C. 766 (1980), and Gino v. Commissioner, 538 F.2d 833 (9th Cir.1976), cert. denied 429 U.S. 979, 97 S.Ct. 490 (1976), considering possible amounts of the deduction.

[21] See, de Guardiola, "Home Office Deductions Under the New Section 280A of the Internal Revenue Code," 6 F.S.U.L.Rev. 129 (1978).

[22] Again note that I.R.C. § 280A(b) expressly excepts from limitation deductions allowable to the taxpayer without regard to their connection with his trade or business or income-producing activity, such as interest, state and local taxes, and casualty losses. See Chapter 16, supra.

[23] A portion of a room even though not physically separated may qualify. Weightman v. Commissioner, 42 T.C.M. 104 (1981); Hewett v. Commissioner, 71 T.C.M. 2350 (1996).

[24] I.R.C. § 280A(c)(1)(A). In Commissioner v. Soliman, 506 U.S. 168, 113 S.Ct. 701 (1993), the Supreme Court held that the two primary factors in determining whether a home office is a taxpayer's principal place of business are: (1) the relative importance of the activities performed at each business location; and (2) the amount of time spent at each location. This two-part test replaced a "facts and circumstances" test and a "focal point" test that had been employed by lower courts. For examples of the application of the *Soliman* test, see Giesbrecht v. Commissioner, 69 T.C.M. 2149 (1995), Steinberg v. Commissioner, 69 T.C.M. 2131 (1995), and

as a place of business which is used by patients, clients, or customers in meeting or dealing with the taxpayer in the normal course of business,[25] or (3) as a separate structure not attached to the dwelling unit used in connection with the taxpayer's trade or business.[26] In the case of an employee, the business use must be "for the convenience of his employer" if a deduction is to be allowed,[27] and the requirements cannot be circumvented by rental of the home or a portion of the home to one's employer.[28]

Much of the current litigation involving the "office in home" deduction involves the interpretation of the "principal place of business" test.[29] If a taxpayer is involved in more than one trade or business, one business may satisfy the test.[30] The principal place of business test has been expanded to include a home office that is used by a taxpayer to conduct administrative or management activities of a business if there is no other fixed location where the taxpayer conducts such activities.[31]

In addition to the "allocable portion" limitation on deductions under Section 280A, Section 280A(c)(5) further limits deductions attributable to the home office to the amount by which gross income from that use exceeds: (i) deductions allowed without respect to the home office (e.g., interest and taxes); and (ii) all other expenses attributable to the business activity but not allocable to the use of the home (e.g.,

---

Bowles v. Commissioner, 65 T.C.M. 2733 (1993) prior to the amendment of I.R.C. § 280A(c)(1) discussed at note 31, infra.

[25] I.R.C. § 280A(c)(1)(B). See Green v. Commissioner, 707 F.2d 404 (9th Cir.1983); Cousino v. Commissioner, 679 F.2d 604 (6th Cir.1982); Frankel v. Commissioner, 82 T.C. 318 (1984).

[26] I.R.C. § 280A(c)(1)(C). Compare Heineman v. Commissioner, 82 T.C. 538 (1984) (deduction allowed) with Stalcup v. Commissioner, 69 T.C.M. 1777 (1995) (no deduction because exclusive use test not met). Where the dwelling unit is the sole fixed location of the taxpayer's trade or business consisting of selling products at wholesale or retail, and the taxpayer regularly uses a separate identifiable portion of his residence for inventory or product sample storage, § 280A(c)(2) excepts such activity from the exclusive use test. Further, the exclusive use test does not apply where the taxpayer uses his residence to provide qualified day care services. See I.R.C. § 280A(c)(4). See also Uphus v. Commissioner, 67 T.C.M. 2229 (1994).

[27] See I.R.C. § 280A(c)(1). The "convenience of the employer" test supersedes the "appropriate and helpful" test previously followed by some courts in this area. See note 20, supra.

[28] I.R.C. § 280A(c)(6). Cf. Feldman v. Commissioner, 84 T.C. 1 (1985), affirmed 791 F.2d 781 (9th Cir.1986).

[29] I.R.C. § 280A(c)(1)(A).

[30] Curphey v. Commissioner, supra note 20. In *Curphey*, taxpayer had rental activities which constituted a business and which were carried on in addition to his other business of being a dermatologist. Regular use of a room in his residence exclusively as an office in connection with the rental activities fell within the subsection. If, however, a room is used for two businesses, one of which is taxpayer's principal place of business, but the other fails to satisfy the principal place of business test, a deduction is denied under the exclusivity test of I.R.C. § 280A(c)(1). Hamacher v. Commissioner, 94 T.C. 348 (1990).

[31] I.R.C. § 280A(c)(1) flush language. The provision is effective after December 31, 1998. This expansion reverses the result in the Soliman case, note 24 supra, in which an anesthesiologist used a room in his home to perform administrative and management activities which could not be performed at the hospitals where he worked. However, the amendment does not alter the two-part principal place of business test applied in the *Soliman* case. See note 24, supra. See also I.R.S. Pub. 587 for the Service's interpretation of the rule.

expenditures for supplies and compensation paid to other persons).[32] Any home office deduction disallowed solely because of the income limitation may be carried forward to subsequent taxable years.[33]

## PROBLEMS

1.    T owns a two-bedroom vacation home that T rents for 90 days and uses for personal purposes for 30 days during the taxable year. T receives gross rental income from the home of $3,000, pays property taxes of $1,000 and mortgage interest of $1,000, and incurs other expenses (including $2,000 of depreciation) of $3,600. Assume in parts (a) through (c), below, that the interest is "qualified residence interest" as defined in § 163(h)(3).

    (a)   Will T's deductions be limited by §§ 183 or 280A?

    (b)   What amount of expenses, other than property taxes and mortgage interest, may T deduct?

    (c)   May T deduct all of T's property taxes and mortgage interest? Why or why not?

    (d)   Same facts, figures, and questions as in parts (a) through (c), above, except that T rents the home for only three weeks and vacations in it with family for one week.

2.    Taxpayer operates a consulting business out of his home. He uses an office in his home, exclusively and on a regular basis, as the principal place of business for his consulting business. Taxpayer has $2,000 gross income from his consulting business. He has business deductions of $1,600 for supplies and secretary expenses. Mortgage interest and real estate taxes allocable to his office total $400. Utilities and depreciation allocable to his office are $200 and $150, respectively. How much of the utility expense and depreciation is deductible?

3.    Homeowner rents her vacation home for two weeks a year to Friend. This is the only rental of the vacation home during the year. What are the tax consequences to Homeowner?

4.    For a number of years Widow has rented three rooms in her large residence to three law students. Are her deductions related to the rooms (depreciation, utilities, repairs, interests and taxes) limited by § 280A? See Prop. Reg. § 1.280A–1(c).

## E. DEDUCTIONS LIMITED TO AMOUNT AT RISK

Internal Revenue Code: Section 465(a), (b), (d), (e)(1).

——————————

---

[32]  I.R.C. § 280A(c)(5). See especially I.R.C. § 280A(c)(5)(B)(ii) reversing the result reached in Scott v. Commissioner, 84 T.C. 683 (1985), acq. 1987–2 C.B.1.

[33]  I.R.C. § 280A(c)(5), flush language. Such carry forward shall be allowable only to the income from the business in which it arose, whether or not the dwelling unit is used as a residence during such year. I.R.C. § 280A(c)(5), last sentence.

Simply stated, Section 465 limits a taxpayer's deductible losses from a specific business or investment activity to the amount the taxpayer is personally "at risk" in that activity, in effect what one personally stands to lose from failure in the activity. Before the enactment of Section 465, the only general limitation on the amount of losses a taxpayer could claim from an activity was the taxpayer's cost or other *basis* in the activity.[1] The taxpayer's basis in an activity, however, includes, not only the taxpayer's actual investment and liabilities on which one is personally obligated but also nonrecourse liabilities for which one has no personal obligation.[2] A taxpayer could often deduct losses far in excess of the amount one was actually "at risk" in the given activity, in effect sheltering income earned in other activities from tax liability.

Congress reacted to this somewhat artificial loss situation by enacting Section 465. It provides that the amount of loss, otherwise allowed the taxpayer in a given year, which may be deducted in connection with most activities engaged in for the production of income or in carrying on a trade or business, cannot exceed the aggregate amount with respect to which the taxpayer is "at risk" in each such activity at the close of the taxable year.[3] Generally, a taxpayer is considered to be at risk with respect to a given activity to the extent of the cash and the adjusted basis of other property[4] the taxpayer has contributed to the activity, and any amounts borrowed for use in that activity on which the taxpayer is personally liable.[5] In addition, one is at risk to the extent of other liabilities if one has pledged property other than that used in the activity as security, but only to the extent of the net fair market value of such pledged property.[6] A taxpayer is not considered to be at risk with respect to amounts protected against loss through nonrecourse financing, guarantees, or other agreements or arrangements[7] and to amounts borrowed from a person having an interest in the activity or from anyone "related" to such persons.[8] When the taxpayer has a loss from a Section 465 activity, the amount the taxpayer is considered to be at risk in subsequent taxable years with respect to the Section 465 activity will be reduced to the extent that one's loss deduction was previously allowed.[9] Importantly, on the other hand, any disallowed losses in the taxable year

---

[1]   Staff of Joint Comm. on Taxation, 94th Cong. 2d Sess., General Explanation of the Tax Reform Act of 1976 (Pub. Law No. 94–455) at 33 et seq. (1976), 1976–3 vol. 2 C.B. 45 et seq.

[2]   Nonrecourse liabilities are generally treated the same as personal liabilities for federal tax purposes. Cf. Crane v. Commissioner, 331 U.S. 1, 67 S.Ct. 1047 (1947).

[3]   I.R.C. § 465(a)(1).

[4]   But see I.R.C. § 465(b)(4) which would disregard the basis to the extent that the taxpayer was not at risk with respect to it.

[5]   I.R.C. § 465(b)(1) and (2)(A).

[6]   I.R.C. § 465(b)(2)(B).

[7]   See I.R.C. § 465(b)(4). A taxpayer is not personally liable on nonrecourse obligations; the lender has recourse against only the property which secures the obligation, and not against the personal assets of the taxpayer.

[8]   I.R.C. § 465(b)(3). Related persons are defined by I.R.C. § 465(b)(3)(C), with reference to §§ 267(b) and 707(b)(1). See also § 465(b)(3)(B).

[9]   I.R.C. § 465(b)(5).

can be carried over to a future year.[10] For example, if a taxpayer contributes cash of $10,000 and incurs personal liability of $20,000 on property used in an activity, and in the first two years incurs a total of $18,000 of losses, in year three the taxpayer will still have $12,000 at risk.[11] If, instead, the liability were a nonrecourse liability on property used in the activity, the taxpayer would have only $10,000 at risk and Section 465 would deny a deduction for $8,000 of losses. However, those denied losses would be carried over to future years[12] to be deducted when the taxpayer increases his amounts at risk.[13]

Section 465 generally applies to all activities engaged in by a taxpayer in carrying on a trade or business or for the production of income.[14] Thus, the at risk rules apply to real estate activities[15] but with a major variation from the normal operation of the at risk rules. In general, a taxpayer *is* at risk with respect to *nonrecourse* financing of real estate activities if the financing is from the government, is guaranteed by the government, or is from a qualified person who is in the business of lending money.[16] In general, the qualified person must not be related to the taxpayer,[17] a person from whom the taxpayer acquired the property (i.e. the seller),[18] or a person who receives a fee for the taxpayer's investment in the property (i.e. the promoter of the activity).[19] The requirement that the qualified person be unrelated to the taxpayer is waived if the terms of the nonrecourse financing are commercially reasonable and on substantially the same terms as loans involving unrelated persons.[20]

Section 465 is applicable only to individuals and closely held C corporations.[21] Closely held C corporations are defined as corporations more than 50 percent of whose stock is owned directly or indirectly[22] by five or fewer individuals.[23] However, Section 465 is inapplicable to many activities of closely held C corporations. It is inapplicable to a "qualified

---

[10]   I.R.C. § 465(a)(2).

[11]   I.R.C. § 465(b)(5).

[12]   I.R.C. § 465(a)(2).

[13]   An increase in the amount at risk could, for example, occur by a direct cash contribution to the activity, an indirect cash contribution by paying off principal on the nonrecourse liability, or a contribution of more property to the activity.

[14]   I.R.C. § 465(c)(3)(A). This includes I.R.C. § 465(c)(1) activities to which the provision when originally enacted was applicable. But see the discussion at notes 25–27, infra.

[15]   Pub.Law No. 99–514, 99th Cong., 2d Sess. § 503(a) (1986).

[16]   I.R.C. §§ 465(b)(6)(B) and 49(a)(1)(D)(iv).

[17]   I.R.C. § 49(a)(1)(D)(iv)(I). See I.R.C. § 465(b)(3)(C), which defines a related person.

[18]   I.R.C. § 49(a)(1)(D)(iv)(II).

[19]   I.R.C. § 49(a)(1)(D)(iv)(III).

[20]   I.R.C. § 465(b)(6)(D)(ii).

[21]   I.R.C. § 465(a)(1).

[22]   The attribution of ownership rules of I.R.C. § 544 are made applicable to § 465. See I.R.C. §§ 465(a)(1)(B), 542(a)(2) and 544(a); but see some limitations in the attribution rules provided in § 465(a)(3).

[23]   See I.R.C. §§ 465(a)(1)(B) and 542(a)(2).

C corporation"[24] to the extent that it is involved in active businesses,[25] and to any closely held C corporation actively engaged in equipment leasing.[26] Although Section 465 is inapplicable to partnerships and S corporations, it does apply to the partners and the S corporation shareholders at their individual levels.[27]

Section 465(e) generally provides for recapture of previously allowed loss deductions in a situation where some event has caused a taxpayer's allowed losses in prior taxable years to exceed her amount currently at risk. For example, if a taxpayer converts a recourse obligation (one on which she is personally liable) to a nonrecourse obligation creating a negative at risk situation, Section 465(e) requires a recapture of the excess loss deductions taken in prior years, and permits, as with any other loss disallowed under Section 465, a carryover of the disallowed loss to a future year. Thus assume taxpayer paid $80 cash and incurred $320 of personal liability to acquire a business in year one, and incurred and properly deducted $200 of loss in year two. If in year three she had not paid off any principal on the $320 personal liability and she converted it to a nonrecourse obligation, she would have been allowed deductions of $120 for which she is currently not at risk ($200 loss less $80 cash currently at risk); she must therefore recognize $120 of recapture income from the activity under Section 465(e) in year three.[28] The amount included in gross income is in effect a disallowed loss which then is carried over to the succeeding year.[29]

## PROBLEMS

1. Discuss the extent to which § 465 limits Taxpayer's loss deductions, generates recapture income out of a previously allowed loss deductions, or allows the use of a loss carryover in the following situations:

    (a) Taxpayer purchased a farm for $50,000 cash and his personal note for $400,000 secured by a mortgage. In the first two years of operation he put in an additional $50,000 each year, by way of cash and personal loans, for feed, fertilizer and other supplies; but things did not go well. In the first year of operations his loss was $80,000 and he had another $80,000

---

[24] See I.R.C. § 465(c)(7)(B) defining a "qualified C corporation" as including most closely held C corporations.

[25] I.R.C. § 465(c)(7)(A). An active business is labelled a "qualifying business" and is defined in I.R.C. § 465(c)(7)(C).

[26] I.R.C. § 465(c)(4).

[27] Cf. Reg. § 1.465–1T. See August, "Navigating the At-Risk Waters After the Tax Reform Act of 1984," 63 Taxes 83 (1985).

[28] See I.R.C. § 465(e)(1)(A). Phrased in the statutory terms, taxpayer is at risk to the extent of $80 (cash) reduced by the prior allowed deductions of $200 (see I.R.C. § 465(b)(5)) or a minus $120. Tracking the statute, and by the numbers, zero exceeds minus $120 by $120, which is the amount of the recapture income.

The legislative history suggests that other events triggering § 465(e) recapture are distributions to the taxpayer and the commencement of a guarantee or some similar arrangement which affects a taxpayer's risk of loss.

[29] I.R.C. § 465(e)(1)(B).

loss in the second year of operations. No principal was paid on the liability in either year.

(b)   The facts are the same as in (a), above, except that the farm was acquired for $50,000 cash and $400,000 of nonrecourse financing.

(c)   The facts are the same as in (a), above, except that in the third year of operations when the farm broke even, Taxpayer converted his personal liability of $400,000 to a nonrecourse loan.

(d)   The facts are the same as in (b), above, except that Taxpayer pays off $10,000 of the nonrecourse loan in year two.

(e)   The facts are the same as in (b), above, except that the farm breaks even in year three and Taxpayer pays off $10,000 of the nonrecourse loan in year three.

2.    Discuss the extent to which § 465 potentially applies to limit the deductions of Vestor who invests in an apartment house in the following situations:

(a)   Vestor obtains a $200,000 nonrecourse loan from an unrelated commercial bank to purchase the apartment from Seller.

(b)   The facts are the same as in (a), above, except that Vestor obtains the nonrecourse loan from Seller.

(c)   The facts are the same as in (a), above, except that Vestor obtains the nonrecourse loan from her brother (a "related person" under § 465(b)(3)(C)) who is a commercial lender. The loan is at an interest rate 3 percent below the market rate of interest.

(d)   The facts are the same as in (c), above, except the interest rate on the loan is equal to the market rate of interest.

## F.  PASSIVE ACTIVITY LIMITATIONS

Internal Revenue Code: Section 469(a), (b), (c)(1), (2) and (7), (d), (e)(1), (f), (g), (h)(1) and (2), (i)(1)–(3)(A) and (6), (j)(1), (*l*)(1).

Regulations: Sections 1.469–4(a), (c), (e), and (f)(1), –5T(a), (b)(2)(ii), (iii), (c), (d).

———

*Introduction.* The Tax Reform Act of 1986 added Code Section 469 which, for certain taxpayers, disallows the deduction of passive activity losses and the usage of passive activity credits.[1] Passive activity losses are the excess of losses from all passive activities over the income from such activities during a taxable year; and passive activity credits are the excess of credits from all passive activities over the tax liability for the

———

[1]   I.R.C. § 469(a)(1). Credits are discussed generally at Chapter 16A, supra and specifically at Chapter 27B, infra.

year attributable to such activities.[2] The disallowed losses and credits are sometimes only postponed, not totally disallowed, because the loss deductions and credits disallowed by this limitation are carried forward and treated as losses and credits from passive activities in succeeding years.[3] Further, any disallowed *losses* (but not credits) are fully deductible when a taxpayer sells her interest in the passive activity.[4] Thus Section 469 is perhaps more appropriately described as a postponement provision than a disallowance provision.

In this Chapter we've seen Congress generally allows some deductions only with its fingers crossed, and restricts or disallows those very deductions in specific situations where it feels they are not warranted. Such piecemeal disallowances in specific situations usually seem justified. With the enactment of Section 469 Congress has taken a much broader step. The central congressional notion is that losses are not all birds of a feather; i.e., passive activity losses are second class citizens. The blacksmith's loss, which followed the efforts that raised the "honest sweat" on his brow, is seen by Congress as nicer (more worthy of deduction treatment) than the losses of a mere investor who does not work up the same sweat. But, as is so often the case, the ability to differentiate in a statutory setting between that which is nice and that which is vulgar is difficult. Wonder a little, also, whether this is one of the relatively rare instances of congressional moralizing creeping into the Code. At the same time consider whether the congressional action, which in effect involves the timing of losses (and generally credits), is justified.[5]

*Taxpayers Subject to the Limitations.* The passive activity rules apply to individuals, estates and trusts,[6] closely-held C corporations,[7] and personal service corporations.[8] Closely held C corporations are defined as corporations more than 50 percent of the value of whose stock is owned directly or indirectly[9] at any time during the last half of the taxable year by five or fewer individuals.[10] A personal service corporation is one whose principal activity is to offer personal services performed substantially by employee-owners.[11] Employee-owners are defined as employees who on any day during the taxable year were owners of any of

---

[2]   I.R.C. § 469(d).

[3]   I.R.C. § 469(b).

[4]   I.R.C. § 469(g)(1).

[5]   See Oberst, "The Passive Activity Provisions—A Tax Policy Blooper," 40 U.Fla.L.Rev. 641 (1988); Peroni, "A Policy Critique of the Section 469 Passive Loss Rules," 62 So.Cal.L.Rev. 1 (1988); Lipton and Evaul, "Passive Activity Losses" (CCH Tax Transactions Library 1988).

[6]   I.R.C. § 469(a)(2)(A).

[7]   I.R.C. § 469(a)(2)(B).

[8]   I.R.C. § 469(a)(2)(C).

[9]   The attribution of ownership rules of I.R.C. § 544 are applicable in determining stock ownership. See I.R.C. §§ 469(j)(1), 465(a)(1)(B), 542(a)(2) and 544(a); but see some limitations in the attribution rules provided in § 465(a)(3).

[10]   I.R.C. § 469 relies on the § 465 definition of a closely held corporation. I.R.C. §§ 469(j)(1), 465(a)(1)(B) and 542(a)(2).

[11]   I.R.C. §§ 469(j)(2) and 269A(b)(1).

the outstanding stock of the corporation.[12] A de minimis rule within the definition of "personal service corporation" excludes a corporation if only ten percent or less of the value of its stock is held by employee-owners.[13]

Although conduit-entities (partnerships and S corporations) are not subject to the passive activity rules, the partners and shareholders of these entities who are individuals, estates, trusts, closely-held C corporations, and personal service corporations are governed by Section 469 with respect to any passive activity losses passed through to them.[14]

*Definition of an "Activity".* A passive activity is any business or profit seeking activity in which the taxpayer-owner does not materially participate.[15] An important feature of the passive loss rules (which is not specifically addressed in the statute) is the determination of what constitutes an "activity". Identifying an activity is important for several reasons. If two undertakings are merely parts of a single activity, the taxpayer need establish material participation only with respect to the overall activity to avoid passive classification.[16] If, however, they are separate activities, the taxpayer must establish material participation separately for each.[17] Another reason every activity must be identified is because, at the time of the sale of an activity, prior disallowed losses generated from that activity become currently deductible.[18] A narrow definition of an activity, if accepted, increases a taxpayer's flexibility in realizing suspended passive losses through dispositions of interests. However, a broad definition allows a taxpayer to combine undertakings that are actually separate to use material participation in one as a basis for currently claiming losses and credits from another.[19] To summarize with a mixed metaphor, this is another example of the commissioner/ taxpayer polka where they change positions depending upon who is playing goose and who gander.

The legislative history of Section 469 provides some guidance as to what constitutes an activity.[20] It indicates an activity consists of undertakings that are "an integrated and interrelated economic unit, conducted in coordination with or in reliance upon each other, and constituting an appropriate unit for the measurement of gain or loss."[21]

---

[12] I.R.C. §§ 469(j)(2)(A) and 269A(b)(2). The attribution of ownership rules of I.R.C. § 318 are applicable in determining stock ownership except that "any" is substituted for "50 percent or more in value" in § 318(a)(2)(C). See I.R.C. § 469(j)(2)(B).

[13] I.R.C. § 469(j)(2).

[14] Cf. Reg. § 1.469–2T(e).

[15] I.R.C. § 469(c)(1). See also I.R.C. § 469(c)(6) which provides that the term "trade or business" includes any activity in connection with a trade or business or any activity conducted for profit for which deductions are allowable under § 212.

[16] Sen.Rep. No. 99–313, 99th Cong., 2d Sess. 738–739 (1986).

[17] Id.

[18] I.R.C. § 469(g)(1)(A). See page 539, infra, regarding the tax consequences from the disposition of an entire interest in a passive activity.

[19] Sen.Rep. No. 99–313, supra note 16 at 739.

[20] I.R.C. § 469(l)(1). Sen.Rep. No. 99–313, supra note 16 at 739.

[21] Id.

It also states that what constitutes a separate activity is a determination to be made in a realistic economic sense considering all of the facts and circumstances.[22] After an overly complicated early effort at defining the term "activity", the regulations have developed a more flexible and workable definition of the term.[23] The regulations adopt an "appropriate economic unit" test to determine whether one or more trade or business activities or one or more rental activities are to be grouped as a single activity for purposes of Section 469.[24] The factors given the greatest weight in applying the appropriate economic unit test are: similarities and differences in types of businesses; the extent of common control; the extent of common ownership; interdependencies between the activities;[25] and geographical location.[26] Not all of the factors must be present in order to group activities.[27] An example in the regulations illustrates the substantial degree of flexibility allowed a taxpayer in grouping activities:[28]

> Taxpayer C has a significant ownership interest in a bakery and a movie theater at a shopping mall in Baltimore and in a bakery and a movie theater in Philadelphia. In this case, reasonable methods of applying the facts and circumstances test may, depending on other relevant facts and circumstances, result in grouping the movie theaters and bakeries into a single activity, into a movie theater activity and a bakery activity, into a Baltimore activity and a Philadelphia activity, or into four separate activities * * *.

Once a taxpayer has grouped activities, no regrouping is allowed unless the original grouping was clearly inappropriate or there is a material change in facts and circumstances making the original grouping clearly inappropriate, in which case a taxpayer must regroup activities.[29] The Commissioner may require a regrouping where the taxpayer's grouping fails to reflect appropriate economic units and one of the primary

---

[22] Id.

[23] Reg. § 1.469–4. See Lipton, " 'Thumbs Up' for the Proposed Activity Regulations," 70 Taxes 427 (1992) which discusses the current regulations and is appropriately critical of the prior regulations.

[24] Reg. § 1.469–4(c)(1). In combining activities, a rental activity may not be grouped with a trade or business activity unless one is insubstantial in relation to the other or the rental activity and the trade or business activity are commonly owned and the owners' proportionate interest in each is identical. Reg. § 1.469–4(d)(1). In addition, a real property rental activity may not be combined with a personal property rental activity (other than personal property provided in connection with real property). Reg. § 1.469–4(d)(2).

[25] For example, interdependencies include the extent to which the activities purchase or sell goods between themselves, involve products or services that are normally provided together, have the same customers, have the same employees, or are accounted for with a single set of books and records. Reg. § 1.469–4(c)(2)(v).

[26] Reg. § 1.469–4(c)(2).

[27] Id.

[28] Reg. § 1.469–4(c)(3) Example 1.

[29] Reg. § 1.469–4(e).

purposes of the taxpayer's grouping is to circumvent the underlying purposes of Section 469.[30]

*Definition of a "Passive" Activity.* As stated above, a passive activity is any activity that involves the conduct of a trade or business or a transaction entered into for profit in which the taxpayer does not materially participate.[31] A taxpayer materially participates in an activity only if the taxpayer is involved on a regular, continuous, and substantial basis in the operations of the activity.[32] Determination of whether a taxpayer materially participates in the operations of an activity requires a look at the whole picture.[33] A taxpayer is most likely to be viewed as having materially participated in the operations of an activity if the activity is the taxpayer's principal business.[34] A taxpayer who is regularly present at the place where the principal operations of the activity are conducted is likely to be considered a material participant.[35] But one who has little or no knowledge or experience regarding the business activity is likely to be hard pressed to prove material participation.[36]

Management functions generally are not treated differently from other services or the performance of physical work with respect to the activity.[37] A merely formal and nominal participation in management, not actually involving the exercise of independent discretion and judgment does not constitute material participation.[38] Nor does an active but only intermittent role in management conclusively establish material participation.[39] In addition, activities of one's agents are not attributed to a taxpayer in establishing material participation.[40] Finally, providing legal, tax or accounting services to a business as an independent contractor does not constitute material participation in that business.[41]

The Service has promulgated temporary regulations which provide a substantially mechanical set of seven rules to determine whether the material participation test is satisfied by individuals.[42] Under all of the rules, participation by one's spouse constitutes participation by the

---

[30] Reg. § 1.469–4(f).

[31] I.R.C. § 469(c)(1). See note 15, supra.

However, a passive activity does not include a working interest in an oil or gas property owned (directly or indirectly) through entities that do not limit the taxpayer's liability. I.R.C. § 469(c)(3).

[32] I.R.C. § 469(h)(1).

[33] Sen.Rep. No. 99–313, supra note 16 at 732.

[34] Id. at 732–733. However this is not conclusive in and of itself. Id.

[35] Id. at 733.

[36] Id. at 734.

[37] Id. But see Reg. § 1.469–5T(b)(2)(ii).

[38] Id.

[39] Id.

[40] Id. at 735. But see I.R.C. § 469(h)(5) where a spouse's participation is given recognition.

[41] Sen.Rep. No. 99–313, supra note 16 at 735.

[42] Reg. § 1.469–5T.

taxpayer.[43] An individual materially participates in an activity if she participates[44] in the activity for more than 500 hours during the year,[45] if her participation constitutes substantially all of the participation in such activity of all individuals (including non-owners) during the year,[46] if her participation involves more than 100 hours during the year and is not less than the participation of any other individual (again including non-owners),[47] or if her aggregate participation in "significant participation activities" (those in which an individual participates for more than 100 hours but does not materially participate)[48] exceeds 500 hours for the year.[49] There are two situations in which material participation of prior years constitutes material participation in the current year.[50] The final situation provided by the regulations returns to the non-mechanical statutory test of whether the taxpayer participates in the activity on a regular, continuous, and substantial basis during the year.[51] However, for purposes of applying this final test, there is no material participation unless the taxpayer participates in the activity for more than 100 hours during the year,[52] and under certain circumstances, management services do not count toward hours of participation.[53]

Special rules determine whether an entity is materially participating in an activity. A closely held C corporation or a personal service corporation is treated as materially participating in an activity if one or more shareholders holding more than 50 percent of the value of outstanding stock of the corporation materially participate in the activity.[54] A closely held C corporation (other than a personal service corporation) is also treated as qualifying in some other circumstances.[55]

---

[43] I.R.C. § 469(h)(5). Reg. § 1.469–5T(f)(3).

[44] Reg. §§ 1.469–5T(f)(1) and 5T(f)(2)–(4).

[45] Reg. § 1.469–5T(a)(1).

[46] Reg. § 1.469–5T(a)(2).

[47] Reg. § 1.469–5T(a)(3).

[48] Reg. § 1.469–5T(c).

[49] Reg. § 1.469–5T(a)(4).

[50] If the individual materially participated in the activity for any 5 years (not necessarily consecutive) during the immediately preceding 10 years or if the activity is a personal service activity (one in which capital is not a material income-producing factor) and the individual materially participated in the activity for any 3 prior years (not necessarily consecutive and not restricted to any particular time period), the material participation test is met. Reg. § 1.469–5T(a)(5) and (6).

[51] Reg. § 1.469–5T(a)(7). See I.R.C. § 469(h)(1).

[52] Reg. § 1.469–5T(b)(2)(iii).

[53] Reg. § 1.469–5T(b)(2)(ii).

[54] I.R.C. § 469(h)(4)(A).

[55] I.R.C. § 469(h)(4)(B). Note the word "only" in I.R.C. § 469(h)(4), flush language. I.R.C. § 469(h)(4)(B) treats a closely held C corporation as materially participating if the requirements of § 465(c)(7)(C) (determined without regard to clause (iv)) are satisfied. The applicable requirements of § 465(c)(7)(C) are as follows:

(1) During the entire twelve-month period ending on the last day of the taxable year, such corporation had at least one full-time employee substantially all of whose services were in the active management of such business;

An estate or a trust is treated as materially participating in an activity if an executor or other fiduciary, in one's capacity as such, materially participates in the activity.[56]

Rental activity is generally passive, even if a taxpayer materially participates in the activity.[57] Rental activity is that in which payments are made principally for the use of tangible personal or real property.[58] However, if substantial services are rendered in an activity that also involves payment for the use of property (e.g. the innkeeper versus the landlord), then the activity will not constitute a "rental activity" within the passive loss rules and the material participation test again becomes relevant.[59]

In addition, a rental real property trade or business of a taxpayer other than a closely held C corporation is treated as an active as opposed to a passive activity (and thus is not subject to the passive activity rules) if more than one-half of the personal services performed by the taxpayer in all trades or business during the taxable year (and more than 750 hours) are performed in real property trades or business in which the taxpayer materially participates.[60] The services can encompass a broad range of services with respect to the rental real property.[61] This rule applies as if each interest of the taxpayer in rental real estate were a separate activity, although a taxpayer may elect to treat all interests in rental real estate as a single activity.[62] If the taxpayer is a closely held C corporation, a different test is used to determine whether the rental real property trade or business is active: the test is satisfied if more than 50 percent of the gross receipts of the corporation for the year are derived from real property trades or businesses in which the corporation materially participates.[63] Personal services provided as an employee can be treated as performed in a real property trade or business only if the

---

(2) During the entire twelve-month period ending on the last day of the taxable year, such corporation had at least three full-time, nonowner employees substantially all of whose services were directly related to such business; and

(3) The amount of the deductions attributable to such business which are allowable to the taxpayer solely by reason of I.R.C. §§ 162 and 404 for the taxable year exceeds 15% of the gross income from such business for such year.

[56] Sen.Rep. No. 99–313, supra note 16 at 735.

[57] I.R.C. § 469(c)(2), (4). See Reg. § 1.469–1T(e)(3).

[58] I.R.C. § 469(j)(8).

[59] Conf.Rep. No. 99–841, 99th Cong., 2d Sess. II–148 (1986). See Reg. § 1.469–1T(e)(3)(ii)(C) and (D), (v) and (vi).

[60] I.R.C. § 469(c)(7)(A) and (B). If a joint return is filed, one spouse must separately satisfy the requirements. I.R.C. § 469(c)(7)(B). Material participation is defined in the same manner as described above. Prop. Reg. § 1.469–9(b)(5). Thus except as provided in the regulations, no interest as a limited partner in a limited partnership is treated as an interest in which the taxpayer materially participates. I.R.C. § 469(c)(7)(A).

[61] Real property trade or business includes any real property development, redevelopment, construction, reconstruction, acquisition, conversion, rental, operation management, leasing or brokerage trade or business. I.R.C. § 469(c)(7)(C).

[62] I.R.C. § 469(c)(7)(A). See Prop. Reg. § 1.469–9(g) and C.C.A. 201427016 (2014).

[63] I.R.C. § 469(c)(7)(D)(i). See notes 54 and 55, supra.

employee is a 5 percent owner of this business.[64] To the extent that this subsection applies, taxpayers may use losses from such rental real property trades or businesses to shelter regular ordinary income such as salaries, dividends, and interest.

In general, an interest in a limited partnership[65] (other than as a general partner) is inherently passive, regardless of the limited partner's actual level of participation.[66] If a partner owns both a limited interest and a general interest in the same partnership, the partner may materially participate as a general partner and the limited partnership interest is then not treated as passive.[67]

*Passive Activity Losses and Credits.* A net amount of income or loss is computed for the taxable year with respect to each passive activity. Then all such income and losses are combined. The limitation applies to the extent that losses from all passive activities exceed income from such activities for the year, or that credits from such activities exceed tax liability for the year attributable to such activities.[68]

In determining income or loss from a passive activity, portfolio income of the activity is excluded.[69] Portfolio income includes interest, dividends,[70] annuities and royalties not derived from ordinary trade or business.[71] Also included in portfolio income are gains and losses not derived in the ordinary course of a trade or business from the disposition of property that produces such interest, dividends, annuities and royalties and from the disposition of property that is held for investment,[72] even if it is not productive of current income. Portfolio income arising from an investment of working capital is treated the same as any other portfolio income.[73] Any gain or loss from the sale of an interest in a passive activity is deemed not to be part of portfolio income

---

[64]  I.R.C. § 469(c)(7)(D)(ii). See I.R.C. § 416(i)(1)(B).

[65]  See Reg. § 1.469–5T(e)(3)(i).

[66]  I.R.C. § 469(h)(2). But see Reg. § 1.469–5T(e)(2) providing situations in which a limited partner is treated as materially participating. Several cases have held that an interest in a limited liability company (LLC) is not equivalent to a limited partnership interest under Reg. § 1.469–5T(e)(3)(i). See, for example, Thompson v. United States, 87 Fed.Cl. 728 (2009); Garnett v. Commissioner, 132 T.C. 368 (2009); Newell v. Commissioner, 99 T.C.M 1107 (2010). The IRS has acquiesced in the result only in the *Thompson* case. 2010–1 C.B. 515. See Banoff & Lipton, "Passive Losses, LLCs, LLPs—Two Courts Reject the Service's Attempt to Limit Losses," 111 J. Tax'n 204 (2009).

[67]  Reg. § 1.469–5T(e)(3)(ii).

[68]  I.R.C. § 469(a)(1) and (d).

[69]  I.R.C. § 469(e)(1).

[70]  Dividends included in portfolio income are net of the dividends received deduction under I.R.C. §§ 243, 244, and 245. I.R.C. § 469(e)(4).

[71]  I.R.C. § 469(e)(1)(A)(i)(I).

[72]  I.R.C. § 469(e)(1)(A)(ii). Portfolio income is reduced by expenses, other than interest, which are clearly and directly allocable to portfolio income and interest expense properly allocable to portfolio income. I.R.C. § 469(e)(1)(A)(i)(II) and (III). The Treasury has issued regulations that provide the standards for allocating expenses and interest. Reg. §§ 1.163–8T, 1.469–2T(d)(4).

[73]  I.R.C. § 469(e)(1)(B).

or loss.[74] The reason for expressly excluding portfolio income from passive income is that portfolio investments ordinarily give rise to income that could be sheltered by "vulgar" losses.[75] The legislative history states that "to permit portfolio income to be offset by passive losses would create the inequitable result of restricting sheltering by individuals dependent for support on wages or active business income, while permitting sheltering by those whose income is derived from an investment portfolio."[76] A number of other special rules affect the computation of income or loss from a passive activity.[77]

Credits from passive activities[78] are also subject to limitations under Section 469. Such credits may reduce tax liability in a year only to the extent that there is net income and tax liability from all of the taxpayer's passive activities for the year.[79] Thus, if there is a net loss from all passive activities (and the loss limitations above apply), there is no tax generated and no credits are allowed. In a year when there is net income from all passive activities the amount of tax liability allocable to those activities equals the difference between (1) the tax liability for all income and (2) the tax liability for all income excluding passive activity income.[80] After it is determined that a credit is allowed under the passive loss rules, it still may be limited by other provisions of the Code.[81] However, once a credit is allowed under the passive loss rules, it is treated as an active credit arising in that year.[82]

*Exceptions to Disallowance.* The general rule of Section 469 provides a blanket disallowance of excess losses and credits for the current year. But seemingly for every rule in the Code there are exceptions. This is so here where there are two exceptions to the blanket disallowance of excess losses and credits. The two special rules involve active participation in rental real estate and closely held corporations.[83]

Active Participation in Rental Real Estate. For individuals, other than those with very large income, there is a limited exception to the

---

[74]  I.R.C. § 469(e)(1)(A).

[75]  Sen.Rep. No. 99–313, supra note 16 at 728.

[76]  Id.

[77]  Earned income is not taken into account in computing income or loss from a passive activity. I.R.C. § 469(e)(3). See I.R.C. § 911(d)(2)(A) defining earned income. Deductibility of qualified residence interest is not limited by the passive activity rules. I.R.C. § 469(j)(7). Qualified residence interest is defined in I.R.C. § 163(h)(3) and, subject to some limitations, means interest paid on indebtedness secured by taxpayer's principal or a second residence.

[78]  I.R.C. § 469(d)(2)(A). These credits are set forth in I.R.C. §§ 27(b), 28, 29, and 38 (which encompasses several other credits).

[79]  I.R.C. § 469(a)(1)(B), (d)(2).

[80]  Sen.Rep. No. 99–313, supra note 16 at 723–724.

[81]  Id. at 724. For example, see I.R.C. § 38(c), which generally provides that credits cannot offset more than $25,000 tax liability plus 75% of the tax liability for the year in excess of $25,000.

[82]  Conf.Rep. No. 99–841, supra note 59 at II–143.

[83]  I.R.C. § 469(i), (e)(2).

general disallowance rule.[84] Up to $25,000 of losses and the "deduction equivalent" of passive activity credits[85] attributable to rental real estate activities can be offset against income from nonpassive activities if the taxpayer *"actively participates"* in the rental activity both in the year the deduction or credit arose and the year the deduction or credit is taken[86] *and* if the taxpayer owns at least 10 percent of all interests in the activity.[87]

The active participation requirement is not as stringent as the material participation rule.[88] It can be satisfied without regular, continuous and substantial involvement in operations if the taxpayer participates in the making of significant management decisions.[89] Significant management decisions include approving new tenants, deciding on rental terms, approving capital or repair expenditures, and other similar determinations.[90] Thus, for example, a taxpayer who owns and rents to others an apartment that formerly was her primary residence, or which she uses as a part-time vacation home, may be treated as actively participating even if she hires a rental agent and others provide services such as repairs. As long as the taxpayer participates in the manner described above, a lack of participation in operations does not lead to the denial of allowances.[91] However, unless regulations provide otherwise, a taxpayer who is a limited partner is conclusively presumed to be passive with respect to a rental activity of the partnership, regardless of her actual level of participation in the activity.[92] In determining whether a taxpayer actively participates, the participation of the spouse of the taxpayer is also taken into account.[93]

The $25,000 exception is applicable to individuals other than those whose income is very large. It is an aggregate figure that takes account of both deductions and credits. However, the allowance is reduced by 50 percent of the amount by which a taxpayer's adjusted gross income for

---

[84] I.R.C. § 469(i)(1). But see I.R.C. § 469(i)(4). If I.R.C. § 469(c)(7) applies to the rental real estate (see notes 60–64, supra), no assistance is needed from I.R.C. § 469(i).

[85] The deduction equivalent of passive activity credits is the amount which, if allowed as a deduction, would reduce regular tax liability by an amount equal to such credits. I.R.C. § 469(j)(5). The legislative history says that in utilizing the $25,000 exemption, credits from a rental real estate activity are used after losses from a rental real estate activity. Sen.Rep. No. 99–313, supra note 16 at 724.

[86] I.R.C. § 469(i)(1) and (2). The Conference Committee Report states that in determining the rental real estate loss eligible for the exemption, income from other passive activities must be netted against any rental real estate rental losses. Conf.Rep. 99–841, supra note 59 at II–141.

[87] I.R.C. § 469(i)(6)(A).

[88] The active participation requirement is waived for the credits under I.R.C. §§ 42 and 47. I.R.C. § 469(i)(6)(B).

[89] Sen.Rep. No. 99–313, supra note 16 at 737.

[90] Id. at 737–738.

[91] Id. at 738.

[92] I.R.C. § 469(i)(6)(C).

[93] I.R.C. § 469(i)(6)(D).

the year[94] exceeds $100,000.[95] Accordingly, the $25,000 allowance is eliminated for any taxpayer with an adjusted gross income of $150,000 or greater.[96]

*Closely Held C Corporations.* A closely held C corporation that is not a personal service corporation is allowed to offset passive activity losses and credits against active taxable income other than portfolio income.[97] Thus, a closely held C corporation can offset income from its trade or business with losses from passive activities.

*Release of Suspended Losses and Credits.* Losses and credits disallowed in any year are carried forward to be used against net income or taxes from passive activities in subsequent years.[98] Two special rules come into play here when a taxpayer either converts a former passive activity to an active one or sells the taxpayer's entire interest in a passive activity.

Treatment of Former Passive Activities. A taxpayer's participation in an activity is determined annually.[99] One who was passive with respect to an activity in one year may begin materially participating in the activity in a later year. In such a case, previously suspended losses or credits remain suspended and continue to be treated as passive activity losses;[100] however, previously suspended losses can continue to be applied against net income (other than portfolio income) from the former passive (now active) activity and previously suspended credits can be offset against newly arising tax liability of the former passive activity.[101] The reason for this treatment is to avoid discouraging taxpayers from materially participating in activities.[102]

A similar situation arises when a taxpayer ceases to be a closely held C corporation or personal service corporation. If such a change in status occurs, previously suspended losses and credits remain suspended and Section 469 continues to apply to the suspended losses and credits as if the change in status had not occurred. Thus, the suspended losses and credits can continue to offset all income, other than portfolio income, of

---

[94] Adjusted gross income is subject to several adjustments. I.R.C. § 469(i)(3)(F).

[95] I.R.C. § 469(i)(3)(A). The adjusted gross income for phasing out the $25,000 allowance is increased to $200,000 for rehabilitation investment credits and the phase-out is disregarded for the low-income housing credit. I.R.C. § 469(i)(3)(B) and (C).

[96] For married individuals filing separate returns, the $25,000 allowance is reduced to $12,500 and is phased out for taxpayers with adjusted gross incomes in excess of $50,000. I.R.C. § 469(i)(5)(A). However, if married individuals do not live apart from each other for the entire year, the allowance is unavailable if separate returns are filed. I.R.C. § 469(i)(5)(B).

[97] I.R.C. § 469(e)(2).

[98] I.R.C. § 469(b).

[99] Sen.Rep.No. 99–313, supra note 16 at 731.

[100] I.R.C. § 469(f)(1)(C).

[101] I.R.C. § 469(f)(1)(A) and (B).

[102] Sen.Rep.No. 99–313, supra note 16 at 727, footnote 15.

the taxpayer after the taxpayer ceases to be a closely held C corporation or personal service corporation.[103]

Dispositions of Entire Interests in Passive Activities. When a taxpayer disposes of the taxpayer's entire interest[104] in a passive activity (or former passive activity)[105] and all gain or loss realized on the disposition is recognized, any previously suspended losses from the activity are generally allowable as deductions against income.[106] They are allowed in the following order: first, against income or gain from the passive activity for the taxable year of disposition (including any gain recognized on the disposition); second, against net income or gain for the same year from all other passive activities; and the remainder, against any other income or gain for that year.[107]

The rationale for activating suspended losses upon the fully taxable disposition of a taxpayer's entire interest in a passive activity is that, at that time, the actual economic gain or loss can be accurately computed.[108] Thus, as seen in the Introduction, as to *losses* (but sometimes not to credits) Section 469 generally acts as a mere postponement rather than a total disallowance provision.

The legislative history states that the type of disposition which generally releases suspended losses is a sale to a third party at arm's length and, thus, presumably for a price equal to its fair market value.[109] A transaction in the form of a sale does not release suspended losses if it is to a related person or is a sham or any other transaction not treated as a taxable disposition under tax law, including tax common law.[110]

The legislative history provides guidance in the identification of a disposition of a taxpayer's entire interest in an activity. If the activity is in the form of a sole proprietorship, the taxpayer must dispose of all assets used or created in the activity.[111] If a taxpayer holds an interest in a limited partnership that conducts two separate activities, the

---

[103] I.R.C. § 469(f)(2).

[104] Although I.R.C. § 469(g) allows a freeing up of losses only if there is a sale of an "entire interest in an activity," the regulations take some liberty and provide that if there is a disposition of "substantially all" of an activity, it may be treated as a separate activity to which the § 469(g) rules apply. Reg. § 1.469–4(g). A "substantial part" of the activity must be disposed of and the rule applies only if the taxpayer can establish with reasonable certainty: (1) the amount of suspended deductions and credits allocable to that part of the activity; and (2) the amount of gross income and of any other deductions and credits allocable to that part of the activity for the taxable year. Id.

[105] The same grouping that is deemed an "appropriate economic unit" on acquisition of the activity is also used in determination of the activity on its disposition. Reg. § 1.469–4(g).

[106] But see I.R.C. § 469(g)(1)(C) providing for regulations allowing the suspended losses to be reduced by income or gain realized by the activity in prior years.

[107] I.R.C. § 469(g)(1)(A).

[108] Sen.Rep.No. 99–313, supra note 16 at 725.

[109] Id.

[110] I.R.C. § 469(g)(1)(B); Conf.Rep.No. 99–841, supra note 59 at II–143. Thus, wash sales and transfers not properly treated as sales due to the existence of a put, call, or similar right relating to repurchase, do not release suspended losses. Id.

[111] Sen.Rep.No. 99–313, supra note 16 at 725.

disposition by the limited partnership of one of the activities will release only suspended losses allocable to that activity.[112] Obviously, taxpayers must keep adequate records of suspended losses allocable to each activity to be eligible to claim deductions for such suspended losses.[113]

If a taxpayer sells an entire interest in an activity by way of an installment sale, suspended losses are released each year in which payments are made in the same ratio that gain reported in the year bears to the total gain on the sale.[114] A taxpayer may dispose of an entire interest in a passive activity in a nonrecognition transaction.[115] In such a case, suspended losses attributable to the passive activity remain suspended.[116] Any remaining suspended losses are deductible when the taxpayer disposes of the entire interest in the property received in the nonrecognition transaction.[117]

If a taxpayer disposes of an entire interest in a passive activity in an otherwise taxable transaction, but the transferee is a "related party,"[118] suspended losses are not released under the disposition rule. Suspended losses remaining with the taxpayer are not triggered until the related transferee disposes of the entire interest in a taxable transaction to an unrelated party.[119]

A gift does not release suspended losses. However, if a taxpayer disposes of an interest in a passive activity by gift, the basis of the interest is increased by passive activity losses allocable to it.[120] For purposes of determining a donee's loss in a subsequent transaction, the donee's basis may not exceed fair market value of the interest at the time of the gift whatever the amount of the suspended losses.[121] Suspended losses are eliminated once they have played their role to increase the basis of the interest.[122]

If an interest in an activity is transferred by reason of death, suspended losses are deductible on the final return of the decedent.

---

[112] Conf.Rep.No. 99–841, supra note 59 at II–145.

[113] Sen.Rep.No. 99–313, supra note 16 at 726.

[114] I.R.C. § 469(g)(3).

[115] See Chapter 26, infra.

[116] Sen.Rep.No. 99–313, supra note 16 at 726–727. Cf. I.R.C. § 469(g)(1)(A). An example of a nonrecognition transaction is a like-kind exchange under I.R.C. § 1031. To the extent gain is recognized in the transaction e.g., boot received in a tax-free exchange, passive activity losses can be utilized. For further discussion on nonrecognition transactions, see Chapter 26B, infra.

[117] Sen.Rep.No. 99–313, supra note 16 at 726–727.

[118] A related party is defined in I.R.C. §§ 267(b) and 707(b)(1), including their applicable attribution rules. I.R.C. § 469(g)(1)(B).

[119] I.R.C. § 469(g)(1)(B).

[120] I.R.C. § 469(j)(6)(A).

[121] Sen.Rep.No. 99–313, supra note 16 at 726, footnote 12. See I.R.C. § 1015(a).

[122] I.R.C. § 469(j)(6)(B). Thus, some of the suspended losses may be lost. See note 121, supra.

However, such losses are deductible only to the extent that they exceed the "step up" in the basis of the property allowable under Section 1014.[123]

In contrast to the sanctioned utilization of suspended losses upon a taxable disposition of an entire interest in a passive activity, suspended credits remain suspended.[124] Under such circumstances, the suspended credits can offset only tax liability attributable to income from other passive activities. Some relief is provided if a fully taxable disposition involves assets that were subject to a basis reduction from the claiming of tax credits. Upon such a disposition, the taxpayer may elect to increase the basis of the property by the amount of the previously suspended credits. However, the basis adjustment can not exceed the amount of the original basis reduction.[125] This election reduces the gain (or increases the loss) recognized on the taxable disposition of such property. Any passive activity credits used to increase the basis of property can no longer reduce tax liability.[126]

## PROBLEMS

1.    Lawyer earns $200,000 of taxable income from her practice in the current year. Discuss the extent to which the following transactions affect her taxable income in the current year.

     (a)    Lawyer also has $10,000 of dividends and interest in the year. She invests as a limited partner in a partnership that films and distributes movies. Her share of the partnership's movie losses for the year is $50,000.

     (b)    Same as (a), above, except that Lawyer also has a $30,000 gain from her limited partnership investment in a windmill power tax shelter.

     (c)    What results under the facts of (a), above, if in the succeeding year the movie limited partnership has a gain of $90,000 as a result of a successful movie, "Alligator Allee."

     (d)    Same as (a), above, except that Lawyer sells her movie limited partnership interest at the beginning of the succeeding year at a gain.

     (e)    Same monetary figures as (a), above, except that Lawyer's limited partnership interest is in rental real estate rather than in a movie.

     (f)    Same as (e), above, except that Lawyer owns a 20 percent general (not limited) partnership interest in rental real estate

---

[123] I.R.C. § 469(g)(2). See Chapter 6B4, supra. For example, if a taxpayer died owning an interest in a passive activity with $40,000 of suspended losses with an adjusted basis of $75,000 prior to death which was stepped-up to $90,000 under § 1014 at death, $25,000 of the suspended losses ($40,000 less the differences between $90,000 and $75,000) would be deductible on the final income tax return of the deceased taxpayer.

[124] Sen.Rep.No. 99–313, supra note 16 at 725.

[125] I.R.C. § 469(j)(9).

[126] Id.

in which she actively participates in the management decisions.

(g) Same as (f), above, except that Lawyer's adjusted gross income for the year from her law practice is $120,000 (rather than $200,000).

2. (a) In the current year Grocer purchases a grocery store and spends 35 hours per week operating it to the exclusion of all other business and investment activities. Grocer's loss from the grocery store business is $50,000. How much of his loss is deductible?

(b) Same as (a), above, except Grocer is only irregularly involved in the operation of the grocery store. Intermittently, Grocer makes significant management decisions.

(c) Same as (a), above, except that Grocer who is retired purchases the grocery store and hires a manager who has carte blanche power to make all business decisions.

(d) Grocer, upset with the $50,000 loss in (c), above, fires manager at the end of the year and in the succeeding year, Grocer manages the store on a full-time basis and in that year makes a $60,000 profit. What tax consequences to Grocer for the succeeding year?

3. (a) In year one, Eileen purchases a house and uses it as her primary residence. In year two, Eileen changes her primary residence and decides to rent out her former residence. Eileen hires a rental agent to handle day-to-day problems but she approves new tenants, sets rental terms and approves capital or repair expenditures. Eileen's loss from the rental property is $8,000 and her other adjusted gross income is $40,000. How much of the loss is deductible?

(b) Same as (a), above, except that in year two, Eileen also purchases an undivided interest in a shopping mall. She purchased her interest from a promoter, based on a prospectus describing the investment opportunity and stressing the tax benefits. A professional management company makes all significant management decisions. Eileen's share of the shopping mall loss is $3,000. What amount of her total $11,000 of losses are deductible?

4. Julia owns and runs a catering business which is profitable in Town X. She opens a new catering business in Town Y which is essentially run by her staff in Town Y, although Julia makes management decisions for the business. Julia also has a limited partnership interest in a real estate limited partnership that currently generates losses and expects to do so for the next several years. Julia asks you to advise her how to treat her Town Y catering business under the passive activity rules.

5. In the current year, Dentist purchased two limited partnership interests. For the current year, Dentist had a $20,000 loss and a $7,000 credit

from one of the passive activities. In the same year, she had $35,000 of income from the other passive activity. Excluding the passive income and loss amounts, Dentist had $110,000 of adjusted gross income in the current year. Assume all of Dentist's taxable income from the passive activities falls in the 32 percent tax bracket.

(a)  What is the amount of Dentist's passive activity credit for the current year?

(b)  What result in (a), above, if, in addition, Dentist actively participates in a rental real estate activity in which she has a 20 percent interest and her share of the real estate activity loss is $20,000?

6.  Doctor has a limited partnership interest. His passive activity carryover losses from the partnership are $60,000. Doctor's limited partnership interest has an adjusted basis of $50,000 and a fair market value of $100,000.

(a)  What are the tax consequences if Doctor sells his interest to an unrelated third party for $100,000?

(b)  What are the tax consequences in (a), above, if Doctor's adjusted basis for his partnership interest is $120,000?

(c)  What are the tax consequences in (a), above, if Doctor gives his partnership interest to his son?

(d)  What are the tax consequences in (a), above, if Doctor sells his partnership interest to his son for $100,000?

(e)  What are the tax consequences in (a), above, if Doctor dies prior to any sale?

7.  Passive, an attorney, invests $200,000 of cash and borrows $800,000 from a bank on a nonrecourse basis to invest in a solar power energy business. Passive hires Sunny to run the business, although Passive has the final word on major decisions. In the first year of operations, the business loses $300,000. Passive's only other non-portfolio investment is a limited partnership interest in a real estate investment which earns $50,000 during the year.

(a)  Discuss the tax consequences to Passive with respect to the $300,000 loss. See Reg. § 1.469–2T(d)(6).

(b)  What results in (a), above, if the loan is a recourse loan?

(c)  What results in (a), above, if the real estate limited partnership interest earns $300,000 during the year?

## G.  NONCORPORATE EXCESS BUSINESS LOSSES

Internal Revenue Code: Section 461($l$)(1)–(3), (6).

After considering all of the above limitations,[1] in 2017 Congress added an additional statutory limitation for any "excess business loss."[2] Under the limitation, a noncorporate taxpayer combines all of the taxpayer's trade or business income and gain and all such deductions. If the combined deductions exceed the income and gain by more than $250,000 (or $500,000 in the case of a joint return), the excess loss is not deductible in the current year,[3] and the excess is carried over and treated as a net operating loss in the subsequent year.[4] The $250,000 and $500,000 figures are adjusted for inflation after 2018.[5] To illustrate the rule, assume a single taxpayer operates a business in which she materially participates and the business has $700,000 of gross income for the year and $1 million of deductible expenses. The taxpayer has a $300,000 total loss and a $50,000 excess business loss ($300,000 less $250,000). The taxpayer must treat the $50,000 excess business loss as a net operating loss in the next year.

## PROBLEM

1. Win owns two separate unincorporated businesses and files a joint return for the year with his spouse. Win has a gaming business that has $600,000 of income and $200,000 of deductions for the year, but his restaurant business has $500,000 of income and $1.5 million of deductions for the year.

(a)  To what extent may Win deduct his losses?

(b)  What happens to any nondeductible losses in (a), above?

(c)  What result in (a), above, if Win does not materially participate in the restaurant business?

(d)  What result in (a), above, if in addition Win owns a real estate business that has $300,000 of income and $200,000 of deductions for the year?

## H. ILLEGALITY OR IMPROPRIETY

Internal Revenue Code: Section 162(c), (f), (g). See Sections 1(a); 152(f)(3); 162(e); 165(d); 280E; 6013.

———————————

Although the first modern (post-16th Amendment) income tax act taxed income from the transaction of any "lawful" business, the term "lawful" was dropped quickly in 1916 and, since that time, the fact that

———————————

[1] See I.R.C. § 461(l)(6) applying the limitation after I.R.C. § 469.

[2] I.R.C. § 461(l)(1)(B). This limitation applies in lieu of the prior limitation on excess farm losses. I.R.C. § 461(l)(1)(A). Special rules apply in the case of partners and shareholders in an S corporation. I.R.C. § 461(l)(4).

[3] I.R.C. § 461(l)(1)(B), (3)(A). The aggregate of the deductions is determined without regard to the limitation. I.R.C. § 461(l)(3)(A)(i).

[4] I.R.C. § 461(l)(2). Net operating losses are considered at Chapter 20D, infra.

[5] I.R.C. § 461(l)(3)(B).

income may somehow be tainted has had no bearing on its taxability. Thus, the Supreme Court early sustained a tax on the bootlegger's profits.[1] And much later the extortionist's plunder was held taxable.[2] Although the Supreme Court once refused to sustain a tax on embezzled income,[3] it was not because the income had a shady origin but, essentially, because such receipts were likened to loans. In any event, development of an "economic benefit" theory of income in James v. United States[4] enabled the Court to bring embezzled income into the area of taxability. It is unnecessary here to extend the discussion to other kinds of ill-gotten gains.

On the other hand, when the deduction question arises the propriety of an expenditure may be significant. Generally, the statute itself is free from moralizing restrictions, and the income tax is not a sanction against wrong-doing. Senator Williams, manager of the 1913 act, said to the Senate:[5]

> The object of this bill is to tax a man's net income; that is to say, what he has at the end of the year after deducting from his receipts his expenditures or losses. It is not to reform men's moral characters. * * *. The tax is not levied for the purpose of restraining people from betting on horse races or upon "futures", but the tax is framed for the purpose of making a man pay upon his net income, his actual profit during the year.

Of course, over the years a little moralizing has crept in. Curiously, against the background of the Williams statement, Congress has decided to limit the deduction for wagering losses and expenses incurred in such transactions to an amount not in excess of gains from such transactions, possibly imposing a mild restraint on betting on the ponies.[6] Also, a man may find that Congress has expressly foreclosed a dependency deduction for his mistress, certainly a mild fiscal attack against such cohabitation.[7] It might be added, borrowing from Dorothy Parker, that the benefits of the joint return go along with the solid comforts of the double bed, not the hurly-burly of the chaise-lounge.[8]

Perhaps more concretely, Congress also expressly disallows any deduction for bribes to government officials and, in some circumstances, for illegal bribes or kickbacks to anyone.[9] Fines and penalties generally are nondeductible if paid or incurred (by suit, agreement or otherwise)

---

[1] United States v. Sullivan, 274 U.S. 259, 47 S.Ct. 607 (1927).
[2] Rutkin v. United States, 343 U.S. 130, 72 S.Ct. 571 (1952).
[3] Commissioner v. Wilcox, 327 U.S. 404, 66 S.Ct. 546 (1946).
[4] 366 U.S. 213, 81 S.Ct. 1052 (1961).
[5] 50 (Part 4) Cong.Rec. 3849, 63d Cong., 2d Sess. (1913).
[6] I.R.C. § 165(d). See Tschetschot v. Commissioner, 93 T.C.M. 914 (2007), where a tournament poker player's losses were limited by I.R.C. § 165(d).
[7] I.R.C. § 152(f)(3).
[8] See I.R.C. §§ 1(a) and 6013.
[9] I.R.C. § 162(c). See Lycan, "Public Policy and the Deductibility of Kickbacks Under § 162(c)(2)," 35 Ohio State L.J. 686 (1974).

to, or at the direction of, a government or governmental entity for violation of any law or as a result of an investigation or inquiry into a possible violation of law.[10] Exceptions are provided for certain payments which are not in the nature of a penalty.[11] Payments required as sanctions under the antitrust laws are also nondeductible.[12] Congress has also provided that that no deduction is allowed for any settlement, payout, or attorney's fees related to sexual harassment or sexual abuse if the settlement or payment is subject to a nondisclosure agreement.[13]

In an effort to further attempt to deal with the underground drug economy, Congress added Section 280E to the Code precluding any deduction or credit for expenses in carrying on the trade or business of trafficking in controlled substances.[14] The lobbying expense area is governed by Section 162(e), which generally provides that no deduction is allowed for expenditures paid or incurred to influence legislation, participate in political campaigns, influence the public regarding political matters, or communicate with certain high-level executive branch officials in the federal government.[15]

The foregoing comments on the statute suggest a simplicity in this area which, however, does not exist. The courts have found that public policy (that "notoriously unruly horse, likely to carry its rider off in any direction") sometimes stands in the way of a deduction which, otherwise, would appear to be authorized by the statute. As a general proposition it may be said that expenditures that are against the law and others whose deduction would tend to frustrate sharply defined public policy are not deductible.[16] While there is still substantial uncertainty, confusion in the area shrinks as provisions such as those mentioned in the preceding paragraph are added to the Code.

---

[10] I.R.C. § 162(f)(1). Certain nongovernmental entities, which exercise self-regulatory powers, such as a securities exchange registered with the Securities and Exchange Commission, are also included in the definition of governmental entities. See I.R.C. §§ 162(f)(5), 1256(g)(7). The government or governmental entity is generally required to file an information return with the Service to report the amount to which I.R.C. § 162(f) applies. I.R.C. § 6050X.

[11] I.R.C. § 162(f)(2)–(4).

[12] I.R.C. § 162(g).

[13] I.R.C. § 162(p).

[14] Pub. Law. No. 97–248, § 351(a), 97th Cong., 2d Sess. (1982). See also Rutherford, "Taxation of Drug Trafficker's Income: What the Drug Trafficker Profiteth, the IRS Taketh Away," 33 Ariz. L.R. 701 (1991) for other aspects of the income taxation of drug traffickers.

[15] I.R.C. § 162(e)(1).

[16] Although there is language in the legislative histories of the Code sections cited in footnotes 9–11, supra, indicating the statutory disallowances are "all inclusive" and are under the "control of Congress", [the most relevant comments can be found at 1972–1 C.B. 599 and 1969–3 C.B. 597.] nevertheless such statutory proscriptions have been held not to preclude a consideration whether public policy should stand in the way of a claimed § 165 deduction for theft where the claiming taxpayer was playing footsie with the thieves who were seemingly engaged in an illegal activity, counterfeiting currency. Raymond Mazzei, 61 T.C. 497 (1974).

## Commissioner v. Tellier*

Supreme Court of the United States, 1966.
383 U.S. 687, 86 S.Ct. 1118.

■ MR. JUSTICE STEWART delivered the opinion of the Court.

The question presented in this case is whether expenses incurred by a taxpayer in the unsuccessful defense of a criminal prosecution may qualify for deduction from taxable income under § 162(a) of the Internal Revenue Code of 1954, which allows a deduction of "all the ordinary and necessary expenses paid or incurred during the taxable year in carrying on any trade or business. . . ." The respondent Walter F. Tellier was engaged in the business of underwriting the public sale of stock offerings and purchasing securities for resale to customers. In 1956 he was brought to trial on a 36-count indictment that charged him with violating the fraud section of the Securities Act of 1933 and the mail fraud statute, and with conspiring to violate those statutes. He was found guilty on all counts and was sentenced to pay an $18,000 fine and to serve four and a half years in prison. The judgment of conviction was affirmed on appeal. In his unsuccessful defense of this criminal prosecution, the respondent incurred and paid $22,964.20 in legal expenses in 1956. He claimed a deduction for that amount on his federal income tax return for that year. The Commissioner disallowed the deduction and was sustained by the Tax Court. T.C. Memo. 1963–212, 22 CCH Tax Ct. Mem. 1062. The Court of Appeals for the Second Circuit reversed in a unanimous *en banc* decision, 342 F.2d 690, and we granted certiorari. 382 U.S. 808, 86 S.Ct. 81. We affirm the judgment of the Court of Appeals.

There can be no serious question that the payments deducted by the respondent were expenses of his securities business under the decisions of this Court, and the Commissioner does not contend otherwise. In *United States v. Gilmore,* 372 U.S. 39, 83 S.Ct. 623, we held that "the origin and character of the claim with respect to which an expense was incurred, rather than its potential consequences upon the fortunes of the taxpayer, is the controlling basic test of whether the expense was 'business' or 'personal'" within the meaning of § 162(a). 372 U.S., at 49. . . . The criminal charges against the respondent found their source in his business activities as a securities dealer. The respondent's legal fees, paid in defense against those charges, therefore clearly qualify under *Gilmore* as "expenses paid or incurred . . . in carrying on any trade or business" within the meaning of § 162(a).

The Commissioner also concedes that the respondent's legal expenses were "ordinary" and "necessary" expenses within the meaning of § 162(a). Our decisions have consistently construed the term "necessary" as imposing only the minimal requirement that the expense be "appropriate and helpful" for "the development of the [taxpayer's] business." *Welch v. Helvering,* 290 U.S. 111, 113, 54 S.Ct. 8. . . . The

---

\*   Some footnotes omitted.

principal function of the term "ordinary" in § 162(a) is to clarify the distinction, often difficult, between those expenses that are currently deductible and those that are in the nature of capital expenditures, which, if deductible at all, must be amortized over the useful life of the asset. *Welch v. Helvering, supra,* at 113–116. The legal expenses deducted by the respondent were not capital expenditures. They were incurred in his defense against charges of past criminal conduct, not in the acquisition of a capital asset. Our decisions establish that counsel fees comparable to those here involved are ordinary business expenses, even though a "lawsuit affecting the safety of a business may happen once in a lifetime." *Welch v. Helvering, supra,* at 114.

It is therefore clear that the respondent's legal fees were deductible under § 162(a) if the provisions of that section are to be given their normal effect in this case. The Commissioner and the Tax Court determined, however, that even though the expenditures meet the literal requirements of § 162(a), their deduction must nevertheless be disallowed on the ground of public policy. That view finds considerable support in other administrative and judicial decisions.[8] It finds no support, however, in any regulation or statute or in any decision of this Court, and we believe no such "public policy" exception to the plain provisions of § 162(a) is warranted in the circumstances presented by this case.

We start with the proposition that the federal income tax is a tax on net income, not a sanction against wrongdoing. That principle has been firmly imbedded in the tax statute from the beginning. One familiar facet of the principle is the truism that the statute does not concern itself with the lawfulness of the income that it taxes. Income from a criminal enterprise is taxed at a rate no higher and no lower than income from more conventional sources. "[T]he fact that a business is unlawful [does not] exempt it from paying the taxes that if lawful it would have to pay." *United States v. Sullivan,* 274 U.S. 259, 263, 47 S.Ct. 607. See *James v. United States,* 366 U.S. 213.

With respect to deductions, the basic rule, with only a few limited and well-defined exceptions, is the same. During the Senate debate in 1913 on the bill that became the first modern income tax law, amendments were rejected that would have limited deductions for losses to those incurred in a "legitimate" or "lawful" trade or business. Senator

---

[8]  See *Sarah Backer,* 1 B.T.A. 214; *Norvin R. Lindheim,* 2 B.T.A. 229; *Thomas A. Joseph,* 26 T.C. 562; *Burroughs Bldg. Material Co. v. Commissioner,* 47 F.2d 178 (C.A. 2d Cir.1931); *Commissioner v. Schwartz,* 232 F.2d 94 (C.A. 5th Cir.1956); *Acker v. Commissioner,* 258 F.2d 568 (C.A. 6th Cir.1958); *Bell v. Commissioner,* 320 F.2d 953 (C.A. 8th Cir.1963); *Peckham v. Commissioner,* 327 F.2d 855, 856 (C.A. 4th Cir.1964); *Port v. United States,* 163 F.Supp. 645. See also Note, Business Expenses, Disallowance, and Public Policy: Some Problems of Sanctioning with the Internal Revenue Code, 72 Yale L.J. 108; 4 Mertens, Law of Federal Income Taxation § 25.49 ff. Compare *Longhorn Portland Cement Co., 3 T.C. 310;* G.C.M. 24377, 1944 Cum. Bull. 93; Lamont, Controversial Aspects of Ordinary and Necessary Business Expense, 42 Taxes 808, 833–834.

Williams, who was in charge of the bill, stated on the floor of the Senate that

> "[T]he object of this bill is to tax a man's net income; that is to say, what he has at the end of the year after deducting from his receipts expenditures or losses. It is not to reform men's moral characters; that is not the object of the bill at all. The tax is not levied for the purpose of restraining people from betting on horse races or upon 'futures,' but the tax is framed for the purpose of making a man pay upon his net income, his actual profit during the year. The law does not care where he got it from, so far as the tax is concerned, although the law may very properly care in another way." 50 Cong. Rec. 3849.[9]

The application of this principle is reflected in several decision of this Court. As recently as *Commissioner v. Sullivan,* 356 U.S. 27, we sustained the allowance of a deduction for rent and wages paid by the operators of a gambling enterprise, even though both the business itself and the specific rent and wage payments there in question were illegal under state law. In rejecting the Commissioner's contention that the illegality of the enterprise required disallowance of the deduction, we held that, were we to "enforce as federal policy the rule espoused by the Commissioner in this case, we would come close to making this type of business taxable on the basis of its gross receipts, while all other business would be taxable on the basis of net income. If that choice is to be made, Congress should do it." *Id.* at 29. In *Lilly v. Commissioner,* 343 U.S. 90, the Court upheld deductions claimed by opticians for amounts paid to doctors who prescribed the eyeglasses that the opticians sold, although the Court was careful to disavow "approval of the business ethics or public policy involved in the payments. . . ." 343 U.S., at 97. And in *Commissioner v. Heininger,* 320 U.S. 467, a case akin to the one before us, the Court upheld deductions claimed by a dentist for lawyer's fees and other expenses incurred in unsuccessfully defending against an administrative fraud order issued by the Postmaster General.

Deduction of expenses falling within the general definition of § 162(a) may, to be sure, be disallowed by specific legislation, since deductions "are a matter of grace and Congress can, of course, disallow them as it chooses." *Commissioner v. Sullivan,* 356 U.S. 27, 78 S.Ct. 512. . . . But where Congress has been wholly silent, it is only in extremely limited circumstances that the Court has countenanced exceptions to the general principle reflected in the *Sullivan, Lilly* and *Heininger* decisions. Only where the allowance of a deduction would "frustrate sharply defined national or state policies proscribing particular types of conduct" have we upheld its disallowance. *Commissioner v. Heininger,* 320 U.S., at 473. Further, the "policies

---

   9   In challenging the amendments, Senator Williams also stated:

"In other words, you are going to count the man as having money which he has not got, because he has lost it in a way that you do not approve of." 50 Cong. Rec. 3850.

frustrated must be national or state policies evidenced by some *governmental* declaration of them." *Lilly v. Commissioner,* 343 U.S., at 97. (Emphasis added.) Finally, the "test of nondeductibility always is the severity and immediacy of the frustration resulting from allowance of the deduction." *Tank Truck Rentals v. Commissioner,* 356 U.S. 30, 35. In that case, as in *Hoover Express Co. v. United States,* 356 U.S. 38, 78 S.Ct. 511, we upheld the disallowance of deductions claimed by taxpayers for fines and penalties imposed upon them for violating state penal statutes; to allow a deduction in those circumstances would have directly and substantially diluted the actual punishment imposed.

The present case falls far outside that sharply limited and carefully defined category. No public policy is offended when a man faced with serious criminal charges employs a lawyer to help in his defense. That is not "proscribed conduct." It is his constitutional right. *Chandler v. Fretag,* 348 U.S. 3, 75 S.Ct. 1. See *Gideon v. Wainwright,* 372 U.S. 335, 83 S.Ct. 792. In an adversary system of criminal justice, it is a basic of our public policy that a defendant in a criminal case have counsel to represent him.

Congress has authorized the imposition of severe punishment upon those found guilty of the serious criminal offenses with which the respondent was charged and of which he was convicted. But we can find no warrant for attaching to that punishment an additional financial burden that Congress has neither expressly nor implicitly directed.[11] To deny a deduction for expenses incurred in the unsuccessful defense of a criminal prosecution would impose such a burden in a measure dependent not on the seriousness of the offense or the actual sentence imposed by the court, but on the cost of the defense and the defendant's particular tax bracket. We decline to distort the income tax laws to serve a purpose for which they were neither intended nor designed by Congress.

The judgment is

*Affirmed.*

---

[11] Cf. Paul, The Use of Public Policy by the Commissioner in Disallowing Deductions, 1954 So. Calif. Tax Inst. 715, 730–731: ". . . Section 23(a)(1)(A) [the predecessor of § 162(a)] is not an essay in morality, designed to encourage virtue and discourage sin. It 'was not contrived as an arm of the law to enforce State criminal statutes. . . .' Nor was it contrived to implement the various regulatory statutes which Congress has from time to time enacted. The provision is more modestly concerned with 'commercial net income'—a businessman's net accretion in wealth during the taxable year after due allowance for the operating costs of the business. . . . There is no evidence in the Section of an attempt to punish taxpayers . . . when the Commissioner feels that a state or federal statute has been flouted. The statute hardly operates 'in a vacuum,' if it serves its own vital function and leaves other problems to other statutes."

# CHAPTER 18

# DEDUCTIONS FOR INDIVIDUALS ONLY

## A. EXTRAORDINARY MEDICAL EXPENSES

Internal Revenue Code: Sections 213(a), (b), (d)(1)–(4) and (9); 263(a)(1). See Sections 67(b)(5); 152; 162(*l*); 213(d)(5).

Regulations: See Section 1.213–1(a)(1), (e)(1)–(4)(i)(a).

---

### Gerard v. Commissioner
Tax Court of the United States, 1962.
37 T.C. 826.

■ MULRONEY, JUDGE:

[The Findings of Fact have been omitted. Ed.]

Opinion

Section 213(a)[1] as here applicable allows "as a deduction the * * * amounts of the expenses paid during the taxable year, * * * for medical care of the taxpayer, his spouse, or a dependent."

Section 213[(d)] defines the term "medical care" as follows:

SEC. 213. MEDICAL, DENTAL, ETC., EXPENSES.

[(d)] **Definitions.**—For purposes of this section—

(1) The term "medical care" means amounts paid—

(A) for the diagnosis, cure, mitigation, treatment, or prevention of disease, or for the purpose of affecting any structure or function of the body (including amounts paid for accident or health insurance), or

(B) for transportation primarily for and essential to medical care referred to in subparagraph (A).

It is well established that some form of control of temperature and humidity was a medical necessity in petitioners' home. Their daughter's illness made it dangerous for her to be exposed to dry, dusty air. The evidence shows petitioners had tried a room air-conditioning unit in their home in New Jersey but it was not satisfactory.[2] This restricted the child

---

[1] All section references are to the Internal Revenue Code of 1954, as amended.

[2] Petitioner testified he took a medical deduction for this room air conditioner. Respondent's regulation sec. 1.213–1(e)(1)(iii) lists some capital expenditures which can be

to one room for the entire day in order to get the beneficial effects and it was bad for her psychologically. It was the doctor who advised petitioners it would be better for the child to have the central unit so she could have the whole home as her restricted area. Children afflicted with cystic fibrosis have a special diet and they are treated with antibiotics given by mouth and by aerosols and they sleep every night in a tent which has additional antibiotics.

We think the expenditure of $1,300 for installing the air-conditioning unit was an expenditure for medical care for petitioners' dependent, within the scope of the above-quoted statute. But there is another statute which must be considered because of the nature of this expenditure.

Section 263(a)(1) provides in part: "No deduction shall be allowed for * * *. Any amount paid out * * * for permanent improvements or betterments made to increase the value of any property."

The general rule, expressed in respondent's regulation and numerous cases, is that a medical care expenditure for what is a capital expenditure in the nature of a permanent improvement to the taxpayer's home is not deductible as medical expense. Frank S. Delp, 30 T.C. 1230; John L. Seymour, 14 T.C. 1111; § 1.213–1(e)(1)(iii), Income Tax Regs. However, it has been held, and respondent admits, that the mere fact that a medical care expenditure is also a capital expenditure is not always sufficient to disqualify it for medical deduction. When the medical care expenditure is for a permanent addition to the taxpayer's home, deductibility as a medical expense depends upon whether it increases the value of the home. In Berry v. Wiseman, 174 F.Supp. 748 (W.D.Okla.1958), the court held the cost ($4,400) of installing an elevator in taxpayer's home was deductible as medical expense. There the housewife petitioner suffered from acute coronary insufficiency and the elevator was installed upon the advice of her physician. The court found that the elevator was permanent but "that it did not have the effect of increasing the value of the property." In Rev.Rul. 59–411, 1959–2 C.B. 100,[3] respondent announced he would follow the case of Berry v.

---

medical deductions and the list includes an expenditure for "an air conditioner which is detachable from the property and purchased only for the use of a sick person."

[3]   The said ruling states in part:

The Internal Revenue Service will follow the decision of the United States District Court for the Western District of Oklahoma in the case of James E. Berry et ux. v. Earl R. Wiseman (W.D.Okla.1958) 174 F.Supp. 748.

The court ruled that the cost of an elevator installed in the taxpayers' residence was deductible as a medical expense. The elevator had been installed at a cost of some $4,400 on the advice of a doctor to alleviate an acute coronary insufficiency of Mrs. Berry.

Accordingly, expenditures made for medical purposes will not be disallowed merely because they are of a capital nature. However, it is the position of the Service that the capital nature of an expenditure will be a consideration in determining its deductibility. If such expenditures constitute amounts paid out for permanent improvements which *increase the value* of any property or estate, they will not be allowed as medical expense deductions.

Wiseman, supra, and his ruling indicates the significant fact in that case was the finding that the installation of the elevator did not increase the value of the house.

Prior to the above ruling, we had decided the *Delp* case in 1958. While the issue in Frank S. Delp, supra, was different (whether the electric air cleaner was permanently affixed to the home), there is an expression in the opinion indicating the extent of value increase is to measure medical deductibility. There we said speaking generally of medical care expenditures that represent permanent improvements to property:

> Such expenditures, to the extent the permanent improvement of the asset increases the value of the property, at least in a sense compensate for the expense of such improvement.

Respondent admits on brief where the taxpayer is able to show the medical care expenditure in the nature of a permanent addition to the residence does not increase the value of the home, it qualifies for medical deduction. We think it necessarily follows that where the taxpayer is able to show such increase in value is less than the expenditure, the amount in excess of value enhancement is deductible as medical expense. Here the parties stipulate the cost of installing the air-conditioning unit was $1,300 and the unit increased the value of the home in the sum of $800. It follows that the balance, or $500, qualifies for medical deduction. We so hold.

Reviewed by the Court.

Decision will be entered under Rule 50.

## Revenue Ruling 2002–19

2002–1 Cum. Bull. 778.

### ISSUE

Are uncompensated amounts paid by individuals for participation in a weight-loss program as treatment for a specific disease or ailment (including obesity) diagnosed by a physician and for diet food items expenses for medical care that are deductible under § 213 of the Internal Revenue Code?

### FACTS

Taxpayer *A* is diagnosed by a physician as obese. *A* does not suffer from any other specific disease. Taxpayer *B* is not obese but suffers from hypertension. *B* has been directed by a physician to lose weight as treatment for the hypertension.

---

Steps will be taken to modify outstanding rulings contrary to this court decision and to conform Treasury regulations promulgated under section 213 of the Internal Revenue Code of 1954.

*A* and *B* participate in the *X* weight-loss program. *A* and *B* are required to pay an initial fee to join *X* and an additional fee to attend periodic meetings. At the meetings participants develop a diet plan, receive diet menus and literature, and discuss problems encountered in dieting. *A* and *B* also purchase *X* brand reduced-calorie diet food items. Neither *A*'s nor *B*'s costs are compensated by insurance or otherwise.

LAW

Section 213(a) allows a deduction for uncompensated expenses for medical care of an individual, the individual's spouse or a dependent, to the extent the expenses exceed 7.5 percent of adjusted gross income. Section 213(d)(1) provides, in part, that medical care means amounts paid for the diagnosis, cure, mitigation, treatment, or prevention of disease, or for the purpose of affecting any structure or function of the body.

Under § 1.213–1(e)(1)(ii) of the Income Tax Regulations, the deduction for medical care expenses will be confined strictly to expenses incurred primarily for the prevention or alleviation of a physical or mental defect or illness. An expense that is merely beneficial to the general health of an individual is not an expense for medical care. Whether an expenditure is primarily for medical care or is merely beneficial to general health is a question of fact.

Section 262 provides that, except as otherwise expressly provided by the Code, no deduction is allowed for personal, living, or family expenses.

Rev. Rul. 79–151 (1979–1 C.B. 116) holds that a taxpayer who participates in a weight reduction program to improve the taxpayer's appearance, general health, and sense of well-being, and not to cure a specific ailment or disease, may not deduct the cost as a medical expense under § 213.

Rev. Rul. 55–261 (1955–1 C.B. 307) holds that medical care includes the cost of special food if (1) the food alleviates or treats an illness, (2) it is not part of the normal nutritional needs of the taxpayer, and (3) the need for the food is substantiated by a physician. However, special food that is a substitute for the food the taxpayer normally consumes and that satisfies the taxpayer's nutritional needs is not medical care.

ANALYSIS

Amounts paid for the primary purpose of treating a disease are deductible as medical care. Obesity is medically accepted to be a disease in its own right. The National Heart, Lung, and Blood Institute, part of the National Institutes of Health, describes obesity as a "complex, multifactorial chronic disease." *Clinical Guidelines on the Identification, Evaluation, and Treatment of Overweight and Obesity in Adults* (1998), page vii. This report is based on an evaluation by a panel of health professionals of scientific evidence published from 1980 to 1997.

Other government and scientific entities have reached similar conclusions. For example, in a preamble to final regulations the Food and Drug Administration states "obesity is a disease." 65 Fed. Reg. 1027, 1028 (Jan. 6. 2000). The World Health Organization states that "[o]besity is now well recognized as is disease in its own right. . . ." Press Release 46 (June 12, 1997).

In the present case, a physician has diagnosed $A$ as suffering from a disease, obesity. Therefore, the cost of $A$'s participation in the $X$ weight-loss program as treatment for $A$'s obesity is an amount paid for medical care under § 213(d)(1). Although $B$ is not suffering from obesity. $B$'s participation in $X$ is part of the treatment for $B$'s hypertension. Therefore, $B$'s cost of participating in the program is also an amount paid for medical care. $A$ and $B$ may deduct under § 213 (subject to the limitations of the section) the fees to join the program and to attend periodic meetings. These situations are distinguishable from the facts of Rev. Rul. 79–151, in which the taxpayer was not suffering from any specific disease or ailment and participated in a weight-loss program merely to improve the taxpayer's general health and appearance. However, $A$ and $B$ may not deduct any portion of the cost of purchasing reduced-calorie diet foods because the foods are substitutes for the food $A$ and $B$ normally consume and satisfy their nutritional requirements.

HOLDING

Uncompensated amounts paid by individuals for participation in a weight-loss program as treatment for a specific disease or diseases (including obesity) diagnosed by a physician are expenses for medical care that are deductible under § 213, subject to the limitations of that section. The cost of purchasing diet food items is not deductible under § 213.

\* \* \*

NOTE

As the case and ruling above demonstrate, there are numerous controversies as to what qualifies as "medical care" expenses under Section 213(d). The bulk of the controversies arise under Section 213(d)(1)(A) which includes as medical care amounts paid "for the diagnosis, cure, mitigation, treatment, or prevention of disease, or for the purpose of affecting any structure or function of the body." There are numerous borderline expenditures that may or may not be deemed medical expenses under the above language.[1] A large number of questionable items have been placed within the deductible category. Here are some examples: The cost of a wig was ruled deductible when as a result of disease a woman lost all of her hair, and a physician recommended the wig as needed to restore her mental

---

[1]  A broad summary of deductible medical expenses is found in I.R.S. Publication 502 (2002). See also Self, "Abortion to Aging: Problems of Definitions in the Medical Expense Deduction," 58 Boston U.L. Rev. 165 (1978).

health.[2] The costs of a son's clarinet and lessons to play it were ruled deductible when his orthodontist recommended them in order to alleviate a severe malocclusion of the son's teeth.[3] The cost of birth control pills prescribed by a physician,[4] the cost of a vasectomy,[5] the cost of laser eye surgery,[6] and the cost of an operation performed on a woman to render her incapable of having children[7] qualify as deductible medical expenses. Fees incurred for a child-birth preparation class are deductible.[8] However an amount paid to obtain a controlled substance (in this case marijuana) even though state law allows purchase and use of the substance to treat a disease is not deductible as a medical expense because such purchases violate federal law.[9] Although not all our criminal courts recognize drug addiction as an illness, amounts paid by a taxpayer to maintain a dependent in a therapeutic center for drug addicts have been held deductible.[10] Similarly, amounts paid for inpatient treatment at a therapeutic center for alcoholism and meals and lodging furnished incident to the treatment[11] and transportation costs incurred in attending meetings of Alcoholics Anonymous may be deducted.[12] And in a reversal of position, the Service has held that the cost of a smoking cessation program qualifies as a deductible medical expense.[13] Costs of acupuncture treatment[14] and medical transplants[15] are also deductible. Additional costs above the cost of normal foods of chemically uncontaminated foods, are deductible by taxpayers who suffer severe allergic reactions to commercially processed foods.[16] The extra cost of equipment that displays substitutes for the audio portion of television programs as subtitles on the television screen is a deductible medical expense for hearing-impaired persons,[17] and a person with a severe hearing problem was allowed to deduct the cost of maintaining a cat that was registered as a hearing aid animal.[18] The cost of a Navajo healing ceremony performed by a medicine man was allowed as a deductible medical expense.[19]

---

[2] Rev. Rul. 62–189, 1962–2 C.B. 88.
[3] Rev. Rul. 62–210, 1962–2 C.B. 89.
[4] Rev. Rul. 73–200, 1973–1 C.B. 140.
[5] Rev. Rul. 73–201, 1973–1 C.B. 140.
[6] Rev. Rul. 2003–57, 2003–1 C.B. 959.
[7] Rev. Rul. 73–603, 1973–2 C.B. 76.
[8] Ltr. Rul. 8919009 (Feb. 6, 1989).
[9] Rev. Rul. 97–9, 1997–1 C.B. 77. This ruling also obsoleted a prior ruling allowing a medical expense deduction for laetrile on the same basis. See Rev. Rul. 78–325, 1978–2 C.B. 124 and see Reg. § 1.213–1(e)(1)(ii), –1(e)(2).
[10] Rev. Rul. 72–226, 1972–1 C.B. 96.
[11] Rev. Rul. 73–325, 1973–2 C.B. 75.
[12] Rev. Rul. 63–273, 1963–2 C.B. 112.
[13] Rev. Rul. 99–28, 1999–1 C.B. 1269, reversing Rev. Rul. 79–162, 1979–1 C.B. 116. In addition, the cost of prescription drugs to help nicotine withdrawal is also a deductible medical expense. Id.
[14] Rev. Rul. 72–593, 1972–2 C.B. 180.
[15] Rev. Rul. 73–189, 1973–1 C.B. 139. See Note, "Tax Consequences of Transfers of Bodily Parts," 73 Col. L. Rev. 482 (1973).
[16] Randolph v. Commissioner, 67 T.C. 481 (1976).
[17] Rev. Rul. 80–340, 1980–2 C.B. 81.
[18] Ltr. Rul. 8033038 (May 20, 1980).
[19] Tso v. Commissioner, 40 T.C.M. 1277 (1980).

In a reversal of prior law,[20] Section 213(d)(9) excludes cosmetic surgery or similar procedures from the definition of "medical care" unless the surgery or procedure is necessary to ameliorate a deformity arising from, or directly related to, a congenital abnormality, a personal injury resulting from an accident or trauma, or disfiguring disease.[21] Under the provision procedures such as hair removal electrolysis, hair transplants, liposuction, teeth whitening, and face lifts are generally not deductible.[22]

Some borderline expenses have been disallowed. The cost of dancing lessons taken to benefit varicose veins in taxpayer's legs, but without the advice of a physician, is not a deductible expense for medical care.[23] And a deduction for dancing lessons even though recommended by a physician and admittedly beneficial to the taxpayer was denied because the activity was too personal.[24] The Service would disallow deductions for expenses to improve one's general health and well being as opposed to curing a specific ailment or disease.

Amounts expended for the "prevention" of disease also involve close questions. Where a dentist recommended the installation of a device for adding fluoride to a home water supply as an aid in the prevention of tooth decay, the expenses of installation and the monthly rental charges thereon were treated as deductible medical expenses.[25] But the taxpayer was too optimistic, and no deduction was permitted, where he purchased and drank bottled distilled water merely to avoid drinking city fluoridated water.[26] Since the possibility of disease from nuclear fallout is very remote, the cost of a fallout shelter is probably a nondeductible personal expense.[27]

Where doctors recommended guardianship proceedings and hospitalization of the taxpayer, the fees of an attorney for services performed in connection with the initiation and termination of the guardianship proceedings were held deductible under Section 213.[28] But a legal fee paid by a taxpayer to obtain a divorce recommended by his psychiatrist was not a deductible medical expense.[29] Although amounts paid by taxpayers for psychiatric treatment for sexual inadequacy are considered by the Commissioner to be deductible medical expenses,[30] fees paid to a clergyman

---

[20]　See W.W. Mattes, 77 T.C. 650 (1981), acq. 1982–2 C.B.1; Rev. Rul. 76–332, 1976–2 C.B. 81; Rev. Rul. 82–111, 1982–1 C.B. 48.

[21]　I.R.C. § 213(d)(9)(A). See Rev. Rul. 2003–57, 2003–1 C.B. 959, which allows a deduction for breast reconstruction surgery following a mastectomy for cancer.

[22]　I.R.C. § 213(d)(9)(B); see Rev. Rul. 2003–57, 2003–1 C.B. 959, disallowing a deduction for teeth whitening. If expenses for cosmetic surgery are not deductible under § 213(d)(9), the insurance costs for such expenses are not deductible under § 213 and reimbursement for such expenses is not excludable under an employer's health plan. Conf. Rep. No. 101–964, 101st Cong. 2d Sess. 8 (1990)

[23]　Adler v. Commissioner, 330 F.2d 91 (9th Cir. 1964).

[24]　J.J. Thoene, 33 T.C. 62 (1959). See also Schrayter v. Commissioner, 39 T.C.M. 205 (1979).

[25]　Rev. Rul. 64–267, 1964–2 C.B. 69.

[26]　Rev. Rul. 56–19, 1956–1 C.B. 135.

[27]　F.H. Daniels v. Commissioner, 41 T.C. 324 (1963).

[28]　Gerstacker v. Commissioner, 414 F.2d 448 (6th Cir.1969).

[29]　J.H. Jacobs v. Commissioner, 62 T.C. 813 (1974).

[30]　Rev. Rul. 75–187, 1975–1 C.B. 92.

to improve a taxpayer's marriage are not.[31] A mother was not allowed to deduct the cost of deprogramming her son who had been a member of a religious cult.[32]

The deductibility of various educational costs as medical expenses has been frequently litigated. In a case in which the taxpayer sent his two children to a boarding school to alleviate his wife's nervous condition and help her to recuperate from an illness, the tuition was held nondeductible as a medical expense, because it was considered a mere family expense analogous to wages paid to a cook.[33] Tuition paid by parents for their blind son to attend a private school was held not deductible, because the school did not have a direct or proximate therapeutic effect on his blindness.[34] However, an individual's condition may be such that the primary reason for his being in an institution is the availability of "medical care." In these circumstances a deduction for tuition should be permitted, as it was where an ear specialist recommended a school designed to mitigate and alleviate a deafness handicap of the taxpayer's son.[35]

A deduction for tuition expenses was allowed where a child of average or above average intelligence but with psychiatric problems was sent to a private school because she was incapable of functioning normally at a public school.[36] However, in a case in which the taxpayer's son was sent to a private school, to help cure his "neurotic block against learning," and to get an education, the cost was allocated between nondeductible tuition and deductible mental therapy.[37] If university tuition and other charges are broken down, an identifiable fee for medical care is deductible.[38]

That which is an uncertain Section 213 medical expenses deduction may in some circumstances constitute an ordinary and necessary business expense under Section 162. If a taxpayer on a business trip undergoes an operation and is required, upon discharge from the hospital, to remain at a hotel in the vicinity for a time for post-operative care prior to returning home,[39] it may be argued that the additional costs are a part of his deductible travel expenses under Section 162, without regard to Section 213 limitations. When an actor's teeth were knocked out while filming a movie the cost of the dental work to replace them was held deductible as a business expense under Section 162.[40] Amounts paid for reader's services performed in connection with work of a blind individual are deductible under Section 162, not Section 213.[41]

---

[31] Rev. Rul. 75–319, 1975–2 C.B. 88.
[32] Ltr. Rul. 8021004 (Feb. 26, 1980).
[33] Ochs v. Commissioner, 195 F.2d 692 (2d Cir. 1952), cert. denied 344 U.S. 827, 73 S.Ct. 28 (1952).
[34] Arnold P. Grunwald, 51 T.C. 108 (1968). See also L.F. Fay, 76 T.C. 408 (1981).
[35] Donovan v. Campbell, Jr., unreported, 611 USTC ¶ 9357 (1961).
[36] L. D. Greisdorf v. Commissioner, 54 T.C. 1684 (1970), acq. 1970–2 C.B. XIX.
[37] C. Fink Fischer v. Commissioner, 50 T.C. 164 (1968), acq. 1969–2 C.B. XXIV.
[38] Rev. Rul. 54–457, 1954–2 C.B. 100.
[39] See Kelly v. Commissioner, 440 F.2d 307 (7th Cir.1971).
[40] Reginald Denny v. Commissioner, 33 B.T.A. 738 (1935), nonacq., XV–1 C.B. 30 (1936).
[41] Rev. Rul. 75–316, 1975–2 C.B. 54.

Where it is questionable whether an expense is deductible as a business expense rather than a medical expense, the Service indicates the expense may be deducted under Section 162 if the following three elements are present:[42] (1) the nature of the taxpayer's work clearly requires that the taxpayer incur a particular expense to satisfactorily perform such work, (2) the goods or services purchased by such expense are clearly not required or used, other than incidentally, in the conduct of the individual's personal activities, and (3) the Code and Regulations are otherwise silent as to the treatment of such expense.

Historically, it was often preferable to be allowed a Section 162 deduction for a medical expense because such a deduction was not subject to the 7½-percent floor of Section 213. In Chapter 18C, we will learn that currently an employee's unreimbursed business expenses are miscellaneous itemized deductions, and under Section 67(g) they are not deductible in arriving at taxable income. Thus, today an employee generally would prefer a Section 213 deduction even though it is subject to the medical expense floor, because it is an allowed itemized deduction under Section 67(b)(5).

Numerous issues may also be raised under the transportation deduction of Section 213(d)(1)(B). At one time, all food and lodging expenses of a patient en route to and from a place for medical care and at the place of medical care (i.e., at the hospital, not just in the vicinity) were deductible expenses. Off to Tucson for the winter?! No. When Congress revised the Internal Revenue Code in 1954, it indicated an awareness of the prevalent abuses and an intention to deny a deduction for meals and lodging while merely away from home for medical treatment.[43] In Commissioner v. Bilder,[44] the Supreme Court also indicated that meals and lodging expenses incurred in the proximity of the place of medical care are nondeductible.

A close question exists whether a taxpayer may deduct the cost of lodging and meals incurred while traveling *to and from* the place where medical care is received. In Montgomery v. Commissioner,[45] the Sixth Circuit, affirming the Tax Court, held that the cost of meals and lodging en route is included within the meaning of "transportation" expense as used in Section 213(d)(1)(B) and therefore is a deductible expense for medical care.[46] In Hunt v. Commissioner[47] on the other hand, it was held that meals and

---

[42]  Rev. Rul. 75–316, 1975–2 C.B. 54.

[43]  H. Rep. No. 1337, 83d Cong., 2d Sess. A60 (1954); S. Rep. No. 1662, 83d Cong., 2d Sess. 219–220 (1954).

[44]  369 U.S. 499, 82 S.Ct. 881 (1962). This conclusion is also supported by the Montgomery v. Commissioner, 428 F.2d 243 (6th Cir.1970). See also Max Carasso v. Commissioner, 34 T.C. 1139 (1960), affirmed 292 F.2d 367 (2d Cir.1961), cert. denied 369 U.S. 874, 82 S.Ct. 1144 (1962), and Rose v. Commissioner, 485 F.2d 581 (5th Cir.1973).

[45]  428 F.2d 243 (6th Cir. 1970).

[46]  In Kelly v. Commissioner, 440 F.2d 307 (7th Cir.1971), although the deductibility of meals and lodging while traveling to the place of treatment was not at issue, the court indicated that the congressional purpose behind the changes in I.R.C. § 213 was to prevent "resort area" abuses and not absolutely to prohibit the deductibility of meals and lodging while traveling to a place for medical attention. A decision in accord with this dictum, unaided by the amendment in § 213(d)(2) (infra note 50) is either enlightened jurisprudence or judicial legislation, depending upon the viewer's own philosophy.

[47]  31 T.C.M. 1119 (1972).

lodging expenses incurred during travel for medical reasons were not deductible; but in that case it is unclear whether the expenses were incurred at or en route to the place of care. The issue is not settled. By analogy to business travel it seems proper to allow a deduction for food and lodging expenses incurred while traveling to and from a place to receive medical care. These care-related expenses are likely to be substantially higher than the cost of living at home. However, meals and lodging are not easily squeezed into the term "transportation" and there is express language in the legislative history[48] which indicates Congress may not have intended that these expenses be allowed. Congress should resolve the *Montgomery* issue. If meals are deductible, Section 274(n) limits the deduction to 50 percent of the amount of such meals.

However, expenses for lodging and 50 percent of meals incurred as an in-patient in a hospital or similar institution are deductible medical expenses.[49] And, Section 213(d)(2)[50] now creates an exception to the *Bilder* conclusion with respect to some lodging expenses. Amounts paid for lodging while away from home are deductible if the lodging is required to enable the patient to be receiving medical care from a physician in a licensed hospital (or the equivalent of a licensed hospital).[51] Thus lodging expenses in an outpatient capacity may be deductible. For example, if you go to Rochester, Minnesota and stay in one of the countless rooming houses or hotels unconnected with the Mayo Clinic while you get treatment at the Clinic, your lodging expenses (but not your meals) are deductible. No deduction is allowed for lodging that is lavish or extravagant[52] or for lodging that entails any significant element of personal pleasure or recreation.[53] The lodging of a companion may be deducted, if the transportation expenses of the companion for the trip are deductible as medical expenses.[54] The amount of the deduction is limited to $50 per night for each eligible person.[55] By silent implication, the new provision seals the door earlier closed on the question of the deductibility of *meals* in these circumstances.

Section 213(d)(1)(C) treats "qualified long-term care services"[56] provided to a taxpayer and the taxpayer's spouse and dependents as medical expenses. Qualified long-term care services are services[57] prescribed by a licensed health care practitioner[58] for a chronically ill individual.[59]

---

[48] Supra note 43.

[49] Reg. § 1.213–1(e)(1)(v); I.R.C. § 274(n).

[50] Pub. Law No. 98–369, § 423(b)(3), 98th Cong., 2d Sess. (1984).

[51] I.R.C. § 213(d)(2)(A).

[52] I.R.C. § 213(d)(2).

[53] I.R.C. § 213(d)(2)(B).

[54] H. Rep. No. 98–432, 98th Cong., 2d Sess. 1584 (1984).

[55] I.R.C. § 213(d)(2).

[56] I.R.C. § 7702B(c). But see I.R.C. § 213(d)(11) disallowing a deduction for such payments to one's relatives other than licensed professionals or to entities owned by one's relatives.

[57] A variety of services qualify. See I.R.C. § 7702B(c)(1).

[58] I.R.C. § 7702B(c)(1)(B), (c)(4).

[59] I.R.C. § 7702B(c)(1)(A). A chronically ill individual is one who is unable to perform at least two activities of daily living for a period of at least 90 days due to a loss of functional

Section 213(d)(1)(D) provides that the cost of medical insurance[60] for medical care as defined in Sections 213(d)(1)(A) and (B) is a medical expense. In this day in age with rising insurance costs, the inclusion of this expense can be significant although the Section 213(a) 7½ percent floor applicable to the deductibility of *all* of one's medical expenses may preclude any deductibility. In addition, the cost of insurance for long-term medical care (with certain dollar limitations)[61] is also treated as a medical expense.[62] In a similar vein, self-employed individuals[63] may deduct, as a business expense under Section 162(*l*), a portion of the cost of medical care insurance[64] paid during the year for the individual, the individual's spouse, dependents, and children under age 27[65].

In years after 2018, the 7½ percent floor on medical expenses is scheduled to be increased to 10 percent.[66]

## PROBLEMS

1. Divorced Homeowner, age 55, who received no support payments from her former husband, fully supported her 20 year old Daughter who had no income, lived with Homeowner and was a dependent of Homeowner under § 152(d). In the current year, Homeowner installed a central air conditioning system at a cost of $10,000, which Dr. Watson said was an elementary requirement in caring for Daughter's respiratory problems. After installation, Homeowner's home had increased in value by $4,000. Other medical expenses paid during the year by Homeowner and Daughter consisted of prescription medicine in the amount of $500 and doctors' bills in the amount of $1,000. Late in the year, she also paid $3,000 in premiums for health insurance but received no reimbursements under the policy that year.

   (a) If Homeowner's adjusted gross income is $100,000 for the year, what will be the amount of her medical expense deduction?

   (b) If in the current year Homeowner incurs maintenance expenses of $300 on the air conditioning system can that be taken into account as a medical expense? Would a $150 deduction for those expenses be more supportable assuming, of course, Daughter is still there and still asthmatic? And what about an estimate that $400 of the year's electricity bill is attributable to running the air conditioning system?

2. A and B, both self-employed, went from their hometowns to Big City on business, each planning to return the next day, which A did. A incurred costs

---

capacity or as having severe cognitive impairment requiring substantial supervision to protect the individual from threats to health and safety. § 7702B(c)(2).

[60] See I.R.C. § 162(*l*) allowing a business expense deduction for a portion of the medical insurance costs of self-employed individuals.

[61] I.R.C. § 213(d)(10).

[62] I.R.C. § 213(d)(1)(D).

[63] See I.R.C. § 401(c)(1).

[64] I.R.C. § 162(*l*)(2)(A). This includes qualified long-term care insurance subject to the I.R.C. § 213(d)(10) limits. I.R.C. § 162(*l*)(2)(C).

[65] I.R.C. § 162(*l*)(1)

[66] I.R.C. § 213(a), (f).

for transportation, 50% of meals, and lodging in the amount of $400. B, however, became ill at the end of his business day and remained in his hotel for two extra days until he was well enough to return home. His expenses, which without the illness would have been the same as A's, came to $700. What may B deduct, and on what authority?

**3.**    Sickly made frequent visits to his Psychiatrist. Late in the year he sent the doctor $6,000, indicating it was to apply against future charges for services. Wobbly checked into a retirement home in the same year. She paid the home $20,000 for the lifetime right to live in the home and receive care, including medical care. The home gave her a statement indicating, appropriately, that $6,000 of the charge was for medical care. May either Sickly or Wobbly deduct the $6,000 payments? Compare Robert S. Bassett v. Commissioner, 26 T.C. 619 (1956), with Rev. Rul. 75–302, 1975–2 C.B. 86.

## B.  QUALIFIED TUITION AND RELATED EXPENSES

Internal Revenue Code: Sections 25A(f); 222. See Sections 25A; 62(a)(18); 135; 529; 530.

---

Congress has added to the tax benefits that we have already seen it provides for the costs of higher education.[1] An individual taxpayer is allowed a deduction[2] for "qualified tuition and related expenses" paid by the taxpayer during the taxable year.[3] The statute borrows the definition of qualified tuition and related expenses from the Section 25A American Opportunity or Lifetime Learning Credit provision.[4] Qualified tuition and related expenses are the costs of enrollment or attendance at an eligible educational institution of higher education[5] for a student who is the taxpayer or the spouse or a deductible dependent of the taxpayer.[6] Such costs do not include costs for books, for housing, for student and sports activities which are unrelated to academic instruction,[7] or for courses related to sports or hobbies, unless such courses are part of the student's degree program.[8] Any tuition or related fee that is funded with an amount that is excluded from gross income (i.e., by Section 117 or Section 127) does not qualify as such an expense.[9] However, tuition and related fees that are funded by gifts excluded from gross income by Section 102(a) do qualify.[10] The amount of such tuition or expenses is

---

[1]    See Chapters 5B, 11C, 16B, supra.

[2]    The deduction is an "above-the-line" deduction. I.R.C. § 62(a)(18).

[3]    I.R.C. § 222.

[4]    I.R.C. §§ 222(d)(1), 25A(f), (g)(2); see Chapter 11C, supra.

[5]    I.R.C. §§ 222(d)(1), 25A(f)(1)(A).

[6]    Id. I.R.C. § 151 and Chapter 18E, infra. Query whether I.R.C. § 25A(g)(3) should be incorporated into § 222 so that costs actually paid by a dependent would be deemed to be paid by the taxpayer?

[7]    I.R.C. §§ 222(d)(1), 25A(f)(1)(C). See Reg. § 1.25A–2(d).

[8]    I.R.C. §§ 222(d)(1), 25A(f)(1)(B).

[9]    I.R.C. §§ 222(d)(1), 25A(g)(2).

[10]    I.R.C. §§ 222(d)(1), 25A(g)(2)(C).

reduced by the amount of such expenses taken into account in determining the amount of any exclusion under Sections 135, 529, and 530.[11]

There are a variety of limitations on the deduction of such expenses. First, no deduction is allowed if the Section 25A credit is elected with respect to the expenses.[12] Thus, an otherwise qualifying taxpayer must choose between the deduction and the credit.[13] Furthermore, no double deduction is allowed for any expense which is deducted under some other provision, such as Section 162.[14] No deduction is allowed to an individual if that individual is the deductible dependent of another taxpayer[15] or if the taxpayer is a married taxpayer who does not file a joint return.[16] Finally, a deduction is allowed only if the name and taxpayer identification number of the student is included on the taxpayer's return.[17]

There is a ceiling limitation on the deductible amount which is eliminated or reduced as the taxpayer's adjusted gross income exceeds certain limits.[18] A taxpayer with adjusted gross income[19] which does not exceed $65,000 ($130,000 in the case of married couples filing joint returns) may deduct a maximum of $4,000 per year,[20] and a taxpayer with adjusted gross income that does not exceed $80,000 ($160,000 in the case of married couples filing joint returns) is entitled to deduct a maximum of $2,000 per year.[21] No deduction is currently allowed under Section 222 for taxable years beginning after December 31, 2017; however, Congress frequently has extended the deadline in the past.[22]

## PROBLEMS

1.  Law Student, who is single, has $30,000 of adjusted gross income prior to consideration of § 222, and pays $10,000 of law school tuition in the current year. Assume § 222 is extended to the current year.

    (a)  What is the amount of Law Student's § 222 deduction?

    (b)  Same as (a), above, except that Law Student uses $8,000 of a § 117 scholarship to pay $8,000 of the tuition.

---

[11]  I.R.C. § 222(c)(2)(B). See I.R.C. §§ 222(c)(2)(B) (2d sentence), 529(c)(3), 530(d)(2).

[12]  I.R.C. § 222(c)(2)(A). See I.R.C. § 25A(g)(5).

[13]  See Problem 2, infra.

[14]  I.R.C. § 222(c)(1). Cf. I.R.C. 25A(g)(5) also disallowing a credit in such circumstances.

[15]  I.R.C. § 222(c)(3). See note 6, supra.

[16]  I.R.C. § 222(d)(4).

[17]  I.R.C. § 222(d)(2).

[18]  I.R.C. § 222(b).

[19]  Under I.R.C. § 222, adjusted gross income is determined without regard to the § 222 deduction and without regard to other deductions and after several other exclusions and deductions. I.R.C. § 222(b)(2)(C).

[20]  I.R.C. § 222(b)(2)(B)(i).

[21]  I.R.C. § 222(b)(2)(B)(ii). No deduction is allowed for taxpayers above those adjusted gross income amounts. I.R.C. § 222(b)(2)(B)(iii). None of the amounts is adjusted for inflation.

[22]  I.R.C. § 222(e).

    (c)    Same as (a), above, except that Law Student is married filing a joint return and Law Student and Spouse have $140,000 of adjusted gross income prior to consideration of § 222.

**2.**    Single Law Student has $40,000 of adjusted gross income prior to any § 222 deduction and pays $10,000 of tuition in the current year when § 222 applies. Student asks for your advice whether to take a § 222 deduction or a § 25A credit for the year. Student had $3,000 of withholding on wages. Disregard any consideration of the standard deduction or exemptions and any adjustment for inflation.

## C.  THE CONCEPTS OF ADJUSTED GROSS INCOME AND ITEMIZED DEDUCTIONS

Internal Revenue Code: Sections 62(a), (c), and (e); 67(a), (b), (g). See Sections 86(a)–(c); 274(n)(1).

Regulations: Sections 1.62–1T(a), (b), and (d); 1.67–1T(a); 1.162–17(b) and (e)(3). See Section 1.62–2.

---

### Senate Finance Committee Report No. 885
#### 78th Congress, 2d Session (1944).
#### 1944 Cum.Bull. 858, 877.

    Fundamentally, the deductions * * * permitted to be made from gross income in arriving at adjusted gross income are those which are necessary to make as nearly equivalent as practicable the concept of adjusted gross income, when that concept is applied to different types of taxpayers deriving their income from varying sources. Such equivalence is necessary for equitable application of a mechanical tax table or a standard deduction[1] which does not depend upon the source of income. For example, in the case of an individual merchant or store proprietor, gross income under the law is gross receipts less the cost of goods sold; it is necessary to reduce this amount by the amount of business expenses before it becomes comparable, for the purposes of such a tax table or the standard deduction, to the salary or wages of an employee in the usual case. Similarly, the gross income derived from rents and royalties is reduced by the deductions attributable thereto * * * in order that the resulting adjusted gross income will be on a parity with the income from interest and dividends in respect of which latter items no deductions are permitted in computing adjusted gross income.

    The deductions [attributable to a trade or business] are limited to those which fall within the category of expenses directly incurred in the carrying on of a trade or business. The connection contemplated by the statute is a direct one rather than a remote one. For example, property

---

[1]   See Chapter 18D, infra.

taxes paid or incurred on real property used in the trade or business will be deductible whereas state income taxes, incurred on business profits, would clearly not be deductible for the purpose of computing adjusted gross income. Similarly, with respect to the deductions [attributable to rents and royalties] the term "attributable" shall be taken in its restricted sense; only such deductions as are, in the accounting sense, deemed to be expenses directly incurred in the rental of property or in the production of royalties. Thus, for this purpose, charitable contributions would not be deemed to be expenses directly incurred in the operation of a trade or business, or in the rental of property or the production of royalties. * * *.

This section creates no new deductions; the only deductions permitted are such of those allowed in Chapter 1 of the Code as are specified in any of the clauses [now (1) through (21) of Section 62(a)] above. The circumstance that a particular item is specified in one of the clauses and is also includible in another does not enable the item to be twice subtracted in determining adjusted gross income.

* * *

## NOTE

*Adjusted Gross Income.* Once a taxpayer has determined the deductions *allowed* by various Code sections, the Code categorizes those deductions into various groupings that, in effect, determine whether a particular deduction will reduce tax liability. The first category is the so-called "above-the-line" deductions in Section 62 that are subtracted in determining adjusted gross income. The deductions listed in Section 62 (and allowed by other Code sections) are the "very best" deductions. They are deductible directly from gross income in arriving at adjusted gross income. They are allowed to reduce taxable income even if the taxpayer uses the standard deduction, a provision examined in the next subpart of this Chapter. Thus, the deductions listed in Section 62 always reduce an individual's taxes.

The concept of adjusted gross income has relevance only with respect to individual taxpayers. It has no significance for corporate taxpayers, or estates, trusts or partnerships. With respect to individuals, it serves as a measuring device for computing the ceiling limitation on allowable charitable deductions[1] and the Section 469(i) rental real estate exemption, and it imposes a floor on the deductibility of medical expenses,[2] some casualty losses,[3] and some other deductions.[4] It acts as a measuring rod for other exclusions,[5] deductions,[6] and credits.[7]

---

[1] I.R.C. § 170(b). This ceiling is now expressed in terms of "contribution base," but that term is defined with reference to adjusted gross income. § 170(b)(1)(F). See Chapter 23B, infra.

[2] I.R.C. § 213(a)(1) and (b). See Chapter 18A, supra.

[3] I.R.C. § 165(c)(3) and (h)(2). See Chapter 23C, infra.

[4] See, e.g., I.R.C. § 222, at Chapter 18B, supra.

[5] See, e.g., I.R.C. § 135(b)(2), (c)(4) and Chapter 11C, supra.

[6] See, e.g., I.R.C. § 469(i)(3)(A) and Chapter 17F, supra.

[7] See, e.g., I.R.C. § 32(b)(1)(B)(ii) and Chapter 27B2, infra.

*Itemized Deductions.* The deductions that remain after applying Section 62 are "itemized deductions."[8] Itemized deductions fall into two categories: those specifically designated in Section 67(b) and those that are not so designated. The itemized deductions listed in Section 67(b) are allowed in their totality as an elective alternative to the standard deduction.[9] The remaining itemized deductions (those not listed in Section 67(b)) are "miscellaneous itemized deductions" and are simply disallowed by Section 67(g) in computing an individual taxpayer's taxable income. Section 67(b) adopts an approach that should puzzle a student. To apply the limitation in Section 67(g), Congress requires us to determine what is *not* listed in section 67(b)! The itemized deductions that fall into this Section 67(g) "black hole" in the Code's universe (a place where deductions disappear) include an employee's business expenses[10] (sorry Nora Payne Hill),[11] some Section 212 expenses incurred by an investor (too bad Mr. Higgins),[12] and hobby loss expenses.[13] Thus, an itemized deduction may not reduce a taxpayer's tax liability because it is either a miscellaneous itemized deduction or the taxpayer does not elect to itemize deductions in lieu of using the standard deduction.[14]

*Section 86.* Adjusted gross income also serves as a measuring device for computing the portion of social security benefits that must be included in taxpayer's gross income under Section 86.[15] It may come as a surprise that even though social security taxes are paid to the government on income that is also subject to income tax ("after-tax-dollars"), nevertheless the subsequent receipt of social security benefits[16] may be included in a taxpayer's gross income and be subject to tax under Section 86.[17] Depending upon the amount of a taxpayer's adjusted gross income and the amount of the taxpayer's social security benefits received, the percentage of social security benefits that must be included in gross income ranges from zero (no benefits included) to 85 percent (almost all benefits included).[18] The intent here is not to entangle one in the complicated multi-step process that is used

---

[8] The I.R.C. § 151 deduction for personal exemptions and the I.R.C. § 199A deduction for qualified business income are not itemized deductions and are allowed in all events. I.R.C. § 63(b), (d); see also I.R.C. § 62(a)(last sentence). See Chapter 18E and Chapter 27A3, infra.

[9] See Chapter 18D, infra.

[10] Cf. I.R.C. § 62(a)(1) (last clause).

[11] See page 382, supra.

[12] See page 433, supra. Note Mr. Higgins' expenses related to his real estate activities likely would be deductible under I.R.C. § 62(a)(4) in arriving at adjusted gross income.

[13] See Chapter 17C, supra.

[14] The election is discussed in Chapter 18D, infra.

[15] I.R.C. § 86(b)(2).

[16] The term "Social security benefit" includes monthly benefits received under Title II of the Social Security Act of tier 1 railroad retirement benefits. I.R.C. § 86(d)(1).

[17] Such "double taxation" has with stood attack on constitutional grounds. Levine v. Commissioner, 64 T.C.M. 531 (1992).

I.R.C. § 85 provides for similar gross income inclusion of the receipt of unemployment compensation.

[18] I.R.C. § 86(a). Taxpayers who receive lump sum social security benefit payments which are attributable to prior years may make a special election to limit the amount of tax in the current year to the amount of tax that would have been paid had the benefits been received in the prior years. I.R.C. § 86(e). Cf. I.R.C. § 1341.

in making the computation, but to spread the surprising news that social security benefits are frequently included in gross income and therefore subject to taxation. It is also important to recognize that the amount of social security benefits taxed is partially dependent upon the amount of the taxpayer's adjusted gross income. Would it have been more equitable if Congress had taxed only the amount of a taxpayer's social security benefits in excess of the taxpayer's social security contributions?[19]

The following case involves an issue which raised a great deal of controversy in the courts and illustrates the potential impact of a deduction being labeled an itemized deduction.

## Commissioner v. Banks

Supreme Court of the United States, 2005.
543 U.S. 426, 125 S.Ct. 826.

■ JUSTICE KENNEDY delivered the opinion of the Court.

The question in these consolidated cases is whether the portion of a money judgment or settlement paid to a plaintiff's attorney under a contingent-fee agreement is income to the plaintiff under the Internal Revenue Code, 26 U.S.C. § 1 et seq. (2000 ed. and Supp. I). The issue divides the courts of appeals. In one of the instant cases, Banks v. Commissioner, 345 F.3d 373 (2003), the Court of Appeals for the Sixth Circuit held the contingent-fee portion of a litigation recovery is not included in the plaintiff's gross income. The Courts of Appeals for the Fifth and Eleventh Circuits also adhere to this view, * * *. In the other case under review, Banaitis v. Commissioner, 340 F.3d 1074 (2003), the Court of Appeals for the Ninth Circuit held that the portion of the recovery paid to the attorney as a contingent fee is excluded from the plaintiff's gross income if state law gives the plaintiff's attorney a special property interest in the fee, but not otherwise. Six Courts of Appeals have held the entire litigation recovery, including the portion paid to an attorney as a contingent fee, is income to the plaintiff. Some of these Courts of Appeals discuss state law, but little of their analysis appears to turn on this factor. * * * Other Courts of Appeals have been explicit that the fee portion of the recovery is always income to the plaintiff regardless of the nuances of state law. * * * We granted certiorari to resolve the conflict. * * *

We hold that, as a general rule, when a litigant's recovery constitutes income, the litigant's income includes the portion of the recovery paid to the attorney as a contingent fee. We reverse the decisions of the Courts of Appeals for the Sixth and Ninth Circuits.

---

[19] Cf. note 17, supra.

I

A. COMMISSIONER v. BANKS

In 1986, respondent John W. Banks, II, was fired from his job as an educational consultant with the California Department of Education. He retained an attorney on a contingent-fee basis and filed a civil suit against the employer in a United States District Court. The complaint alleged employment discrimination in violation of 42 U.S.C. §§ 1981 and 1983, Title VII of the Civil Rights Act of 1964, as amended, 42 U.S.C. § 2000e et seq., and Cal. Govt.Code Ann. § 12965 (West 1986). The original complaint asserted various additional claims under state law, but Banks later abandoned these. After trial commenced in 1990, the parties settled for $464,000. Banks paid $150,000 of this amount to his attorney pursuant to the fee agreement.

Banks did not include any of the $464,000 in settlement proceeds as gross income in his 1990 federal income tax return. In 1997 the Commissioner of Internal Revenue issued Banks a notice of deficiency for the 1990 tax year. The Tax Court upheld the Commissioner's determination, finding that all the settlement proceeds, including the $150,000 Banks had paid to his attorney, must be included in Banks' gross income.

The Court of Appeals for the Sixth Circuit reversed in part. 345 F.3d 373 (2003). It agreed the net amount received by Banks was included in gross income but not the amount paid to the attorney. Relying on its prior decision in Estate of Clarks v. United States, 202 F.3d 854 (2000), the court held the contingent-fee agreement was not an anticipatory assignment of Banks' income because the litigation recovery was not already earned, vested, or even relatively certain to be paid when the contingent-fee contract was made. A contingent-fee arrangement, the court reasoned, is more like a partial assignment of income-producing property than an assignment of income. The attorney is not the mere beneficiary of the client's largess, but rather earns his fee through skill and diligence. 345 F.3d, at 384–385 (quoting Estate of Clarks, supra, at 857–858). This reasoning, the court held, applies whether or not state law grants the attorney any special property interest (e.g., a superior lien) in part of the judgment or settlement proceeds.

B. COMMISSIONER v. BANAITIS

After leaving his job as a vice president and loan officer at the Bank of California in 1987, Sigitas J. Banaitis retained an attorney on a contingent-fee basis and brought suit in Oregon state court against the Bank of California and its successor in ownership, the Mitsubishi Bank. The complaint alleged that Mitsubishi Bank willfully interfered with Banaitis' employment contract, and that the Bank of California attempted to induce Banaitis to breach his fiduciary duties to customers and discharged him when he refused. The jury awarded Banaitis compensatory and punitive damages. After resolution of all appeals and post-trial motions, the parties settled. The defendants paid $4,864,547 to Banaitis; and, following the formula set forth in the contingent-fee contract, the defendants paid an additional $3,864,012 directly to Banaitis' attorney.

Banaitis did not include the amount paid to his attorney in gross income on his federal income tax return, and the Commissioner issued a notice of deficiency. The Tax Court upheld the Commissioner's determination, but the Court of Appeals for the Ninth Circuit reversed. 340 F.3d 1074 (2003). In contrast to the Court of Appeals for the Sixth Circuit, the Banaitis court viewed state law as pivotal. Where state law confers on the attorney no special property rights in his fee, the court said, the whole amount of the judgment or settlement ordinarily is included in the plaintiff's gross income. Id., at 1081. Oregon state law, however, like the law of some other States, grants attorneys a superior lien in the contingent-fee portion of any recovery. As a result, the court held, contingent-fee agreements under Oregon law operate not as an anticipatory assignment of the client's income but as a partial transfer to the attorney of some of the client's property in the lawsuit.

II

To clarify why the issue here is of any consequence for tax purposes, two preliminary observations are useful. The first concerns the general issue of deductibility. For the tax years in question the legal expenses in these cases could have been taken as miscellaneous itemized deductions subject to the ordinary requirements, 26 U.S.C. §§ 67–68 (2000 ed. and Supp. I), but doing so would have been of no help to respondents because of the operation of the Alternative Minimum Tax (AMT). For noncorporate individual taxpayers, the AMT establishes a tax liability floor equal to 26 percent of the taxpayer's "alternative minimum taxable income" (minus specified exemptions) up to $175,000, plus 28 percent of alternative minimum taxable income over $175,000. §§ 55(a), (b) (2000 ed.). Alternative minimum taxable income, unlike ordinary gross income, does not allow any miscellaneous itemized deductions. §§ 56(b)(1)(A)(i).

Second, after these cases arose Congress enacted the American Jobs Creation Act of 2004, 118 Stat. 1418. Section 703 of the Act amended the Code by adding § 62(a)[(20). Ed.] Id., at 1546. The amendment allows a taxpayer, in computing adjusted gross income, to deduct "attorney fees and court costs paid by, or on behalf of, the taxpayer in connection with any action involving a claim of unlawful discrimination." Ibid. The Act defines "unlawful discrimination" to include a number of specific federal statutes, §§ 62(e)(1) to (16), any federal whistle-blower statute, § 62(e)(17), and any federal, state, or local law "providing for the enforcement of civil rights" or "regulating any aspect of the employment relationship ... or prohibiting the discharge of an employee, the discrimination against an employee, or any other form of retaliation or reprisal against an employee for asserting rights or taking other actions permitted by law," § 62(e)(18). Id., at 1547–1548. These deductions are permissible even when the AMT applies. Had the Act been in force for the transactions now under review, these cases likely would not have arisen. The Act is not retroactive, however, so while it may cover future taxpayers in respondents' position, it does not pertain here.

III

The Internal Revenue Code defines "gross income" for federal tax purposes as "all income from whatever source derived." 26 U.S.C. § 61(a). The definition extends broadly to all economic gains not otherwise exempted. Commissioner v. Glenshaw Glass Co., 348 U.S. 426, 429–30, 75 S.Ct. 473, 99 L.Ed. 483 (1955); Commissioner v. Jacobson, 336 U.S. 28, 49, 69 S.Ct. 358, 93 L.Ed. 477 (1949). A taxpayer cannot exclude an economic gain from gross income by assigning the gain in advance to another party. Lucas v. Earl, 281 U.S. 111, 50 S.Ct. 241, 74 L.Ed. 731 (1930); Commissioner v. Sunnen, 333 U.S. 591, 604, 68 S.Ct. 715, 92 L.Ed. 898 (1948); Helvering v. Horst, 311 U.S. 112, 116–117, 61 S.Ct. 144, 85 L.Ed. 75 (1940). The rationale for the so-called anticipatory assignment of income doctrine is the principle that gains should be taxed "to those who earn them," Lucas, supra, at 114, 50 S.Ct. 241, a maxim we have called "the first principle of income taxation," Commissioner v. Culbertson, 337 U.S. 733, 739–740, 69 S.Ct. 1210, 93 L.Ed. 1659 (1949). The anticipatory assignment doctrine is meant to prevent taxpayers from avoiding taxation through "arrangements and contracts however skillfully devised to prevent [income] when paid from vesting even for a second in the man who earned it." Lucas, 281 U.S., at 115, 50 S.Ct. 241. The rule is preventative and motivated by administrative as well as substantive concerns, so we do not inquire whether any particular assignment has a discernible tax avoidance purpose. As Lucas explained, "no distinction can be taken according to the motives leading to the arrangement by which the fruits are attributed to a different tree from that on which they grew." Ibid.

Respondents argue that the anticipatory assignment doctrine is a judge-made antifraud rule with no relevance to contingent-fee contracts of the sort at issue here. The Commissioner maintains that a contingent-fee agreement should be viewed as an anticipatory assignment to the attorney of a portion of the client's income from any litigation recovery. We agree with the Commissioner.

In an ordinary case attribution of income is resolved by asking whether a taxpayer exercises complete dominion over the income in question. Glenshaw Glass Co., supra, at 431, 75 S.Ct. 473; see also Commissioner v. Indianapolis Power & Light Co., 493 U.S. 203, 209, 110 S.Ct. 589, 107 L.Ed.2d 591 (1990); Commissioner v. First Security Bank of Utah, N. A., 405 U.S. 394, 403, 92 S.Ct. 1085, 31 L.Ed.2d 318 (1972). In the context of anticipatory assignments, however, the assignor often does not have dominion over the income at the moment of receipt. In that instance the question becomes whether the assignor retains dominion over the income-generating asset, because the taxpayer "who owns or controls the source of the income, also controls the disposition of that which he could have received himself and diverts the payment from himself to others as the means of procuring the satisfaction of his wants." Horst, supra, at 116–117, 61 S.Ct. 144. See also Lucas, supra, at 114–115, 50 S.Ct. 241; Helvering v. Eubank, 311 U.S. 122, 124–125, 61 S.Ct. 149, 85 L.Ed. 81 (1940); Sunnen, supra, at 604, 68 S.Ct. 715. Looking to control over the income-generating asset, then, preserves the principle that income should be taxed to the party who earns the income and enjoys the consequent benefits.

In the case of a litigation recovery the income-generating asset is the cause of action that derives from the plaintiff's legal injury. The plaintiff retains dominion over this asset throughout the litigation. We do not understand respondents to argue otherwise. Rather, respondents advance two counterarguments. First, they say that, in contrast to the bond coupons assigned in Horst, the value of a legal claim is speculative at the moment of assignment, and may be worth nothing at all. Second, respondents insist that the claimant's legal injury is not the only source of the ultimate recovery. The attorney, according to respondents, also contributes income-generating assets—effort and expertise—without which the claimant likely could not prevail. On these premises respondents urge us to treat a contingent-fee agreement as establishing, for tax purposes, something like a joint venture or partnership in which the client and attorney combine their respective assets—the client's claim and the attorney's skill—and apportion any resulting profits.

We reject respondents' arguments. Though the value of the plaintiff's claim may be speculative at the moment the fee agreement is signed, the anticipatory assignment doctrine is not limited to instances when the precise dollar value of the assigned income is known in advance. Lucas, supra; United States v. Basye, 410 U.S. 441, 445, 450–452, 93 S.Ct. 1080, 35 L.Ed.2d 412 (1973). Though Horst involved an anticipatory assignment of a predetermined sum to be paid on a specific date, the holding in that case did not depend on ascertaining a liquidated amount at the time of assignment. In the cases before us, as in Horst, the taxpayer retained control over the income-generating asset, diverted some of the income produced to another party, and realized a benefit by doing so. As Judge Wesley correctly concluded in a recent case, the rationale of Horst applies fully to a contingent-fee contract. Raymond v. United States, 355 F.3d, at 115–116. That the amount of income the asset would produce was uncertain at the moment of assignment is of no consequence.

We further reject the suggestion to treat the attorney-client relationship as a sort of business partnership or joint venture for tax purposes. The relationship between client and attorney, regardless of the variations in particular compensation agreements or the amount of skill and effort the attorney contributes, is a quintessential principal-agent relationship. Restatement (Second) of Agency § 1, Comment e (1957) (hereinafter Restatement); ABA Model Rules of Professional Conduct Rule 1.3, Comments 1, 1.7 1 (2002). The client may rely on the attorney's expertise and special skills to achieve a result the client could not achieve alone. That, however, is true of most principal-agent relationships, and it does not alter the fact that the client retains ultimate dominion and control over the underlying claim. The control is evident when it is noted that, although the attorney can make tactical decisions without consulting the client, the plaintiff still must determine whether to settle or proceed to judgment and make, as well, other critical decisions. Even where the attorney exercises independent judgment without supervision by, or consultation with, the client, the attorney, as an agent, is obligated to act solely on behalf of, and for the exclusive benefit of, the client-principal, rather than for the benefit of the attorney or any other party. Restatement §§ 13, 39, 387.

The attorney is an agent who is duty bound to act only in the interests of the principal, and so it is appropriate to treat the full amount of the recovery as income to the principal. In this respect Judge Posner's observation is apt: "[T]he contingent-fee lawyer [is not] a joint owner of his client's claim in the legal sense any more than the commission salesman is a joint owner of his employer's accounts receivable." Kenseth, 259 F.3d, at 883. In both cases a principal relies on an agent to realize an economic gain, and the gain realized by the agent's efforts is income to the principal. The portion paid to the agent may be deductible, but absent some other provision of law it is not excludable from the principal's gross income.

This rule applies whether or not the attorney-client contract or state law confers any special rights or protections on the attorney, so long as these protections do not alter the fundamental principal-agent character of the relationship. Cf. Restatement § 13, Comment b, and § 14G, Comment a (an agency relationship is created where a principal assigns a chose in action to an assignee for collection and grants the assignee a security interest in the claim against the assignor's debtor in order to compensate the assignee for his collection efforts). State laws vary with respect to the strength of an attorney's security interest in a contingent fee and the remedies available to an attorney should the client discharge or attempt to defraud the attorney. No state laws of which we are aware, however, even those that purport to give attorneys an "ownership" interest in their fees, e.g., 340 F.3d, at 1082–1083 (discussing Oregon law); Cotnam, 263 F.2d, at 125 (discussing Alabama law), convert the attorney from an agent to a partner.

Respondents and their amici propose other theories to exclude fees from income or permit deductibility. These suggestions include: (1) The contingent-fee agreement establishes a Subchapter K partnership under 26 U.S.C. §§ 702, 704, and 761, Brief for Respondent Banaitis in No. 03–907, p. 5–21; (2) litigation recoveries are proceeds from disposition of property, so the attorney's fee should be subtracted as a capital expense pursuant to §§ 1001, 1012, and 1016, Brief for Association of Trial Lawyers of America as Amicus Curiae 23–28, Brief for Charles Davenport as Amicus Curiae 3–13; and (3) the fees are deductible reimbursed employee business expenses under § 62(a)(2)(A) (2000 ed. and Supp. I), Brief for Stephen Cohen as Amicus Curiae. These arguments, it appears, are being presented for the first time to this Court. We are especially reluctant to entertain novel propositions of law with broad implications for the tax system that were not advanced in earlier stages of the litigation and not examined by the Courts of Appeals. We decline comment on these supplementary theories. In addition, we do not reach the instance where a relator pursues a claim on behalf of the United States. Brief for Taxpayers Against Fraud Education Fund as Amicus Curiae 10–20.

IV

The foregoing suffices to dispose of Banaitis' case. Banks' case, however, involves a further consideration. Banks brought his claims under federal statutes that authorize fee awards to prevailing plaintiffs' attorneys. He contends that application of the anticipatory assignment principle would be inconsistent with the purpose of statutory fee shifting provisions. See Venegas v. Mitchell, 495 U.S. 82, 86, 110 S.Ct. 1679, 109 L.Ed.2d 74 (1990) (observing that statutory fees enable "plaintiffs to employ reasonably competent lawyers without cost to themselves if they prevail"). In the federal system statutory fees are typically awarded by the court under the lodestar approach, Hensley v. Eckerhart, 461 U.S. 424, 433, 103 S.Ct. 1933, 76 L.Ed.2d 40 (1983), and the plaintiff usually has little control over the amount awarded. Sometimes, as when the plaintiff seeks only injunctive relief, or when the statute caps plaintiffs' recoveries, or when for other reasons damages are substantially less than attorney's fees, court-awarded attorney's fees can exceed a plaintiff's monetary recovery. See, e.g., Riverside v. Rivera, 477 U.S. 561, 564–565, 106 S.Ct. 2686, 91 L.Ed.2d 466 (1986) (compensatory and punitive damages of $33,350; attorney's fee award of $245,456.25). Treating the fee award as income to the plaintiff in such cases, it is argued, can lead to the perverse result that the plaintiff loses money by winning the suit. Furthermore, it is urged that treating statutory fee awards as income to plaintiffs would undermine the effectiveness of fee-shifting statutes in deputizing plaintiffs and their lawyers to act as private attorneys general.

We need not address these claims. After Banks settled his case, the fee paid to his attorney was calculated solely on the basis of the private contingent-fee contract. There was no court-ordered fee award, nor was there any indication in Banks' contract with his attorney, or in the settlement agreement with the defendant, that the contingent fee paid to Banks' attorney was in lieu of statutory fees Banks might otherwise have been entitled to recover. Also, the amendment added by the American

Jobs Creation Act redresses the concern for many, perhaps most, claims governed by fee-shifting statutes.

\* \* \*

For the reasons stated, the judgments of the Courts of Appeals for the Sixth and Ninth Circuits are reversed, and the cases are remanded for further proceedings consistent with this opinion.

It is so ordered.

■ THE CHIEF JUSTICE took no part in the decision of these cases.

## PROBLEMS

1. Assume the following expenses are properly deductible. Does the deduction fall under § 62, may it be claimed as a § 67(b) deduction, or does it fall into the Code's § 67(g) black hole for deductions?

    (a)    Employee Salesperson (not "outside") pays the cost of business transportation and is not reimbursed by Employer.

    (b)    Same as (a), above, except that Employer reimburses Employee for the exact cost incurred.

        (1)    How should Employee treat the expenses and reimbursement on her return? Cf. Reg. §§ 1.162–17(b)(1) and (e)(3). What result to Employer?

        (2)    What if the amount paid to Employee as reimbursement exceeds her actual expenses? Cf. Reg. § 1.162–17(b)(2).

        (3)    What if actual expenses exceed her reimbursement? Cf. Reg. § 1.162–17(b)(3).

    (c)    Same as (a), above, except that Employer, an individual, rather than Employee, incurred the expense.

    (d)    Employee makes payments for medical expenses and charitable contributions and for taxes on her residence and interest on a note secured by a mortgage on the residence.

    (e)    Same as (d), above, except that the taxes and interest relate to a residence that Employee rents to Tenant.

    (f)    Employee has a loss on the sale of some stock that he held for investment.

    (g)    Employee deducts $1,000 of interest on student loans.

    (h)    Employer pays accountant $400 to prepare his federal income tax return, $150 of which is allocable to preparing the schedule related to the income from his sole proprietorship business.

    (i)    Employee is an elementary school teacher who buys $350 worth of classroom materials in the current year.

    (j)    Investor Higgins, who owns a substantial interest in X Co., incurs transportation, meals, and lodging expenses to attend X Co.'s annual shareholder meeting.

(k)   Investor Buffet, who has substantial stock holdings, rents an office, hires a staff, and incurs additional costs in relation to his investment activities.

(l)   Hobby Loser has $2,000 of gross income from his hobby activity, and expenses from the hobby activity in excess of $2,000. Under § 183(b)(2) he is able to deduct only $2,000 from the hobby.

**2.**   In view of the answers to Problems 1(j) and (k), above, should § 62(a)(4) be amended to include property held for the production of other sources of income?

**3.**   Some expenses incurred may qualify both as a business expense and a medical expense. In general, how would a taxpayer prefer to treat the expenses:

(a)   If the taxpayer is self-employed?

(b)   If the taxpayer is an employee?

**4.**   In the *Banks* case, Justice Kennedy notes that "these cases likely would not have arisen" under the current Code as a result of the enactment of § 62(a)(20) and (e). Those provisions, however, do not apply to all recoveries. For example, what result to Plaintiff if Plaintiff recovers $1 million of compensatory damages and $2 million of punitive damages in a physical personal injury case and Plaintiff's attorney receives a one-third contingency fee of $1 million?

## D.   THE STANDARD DEDUCTION

Internal Revenue Code: Sections 63; 67(b) and (g). See Section 7703.

Regulations: Section 1.67–1T(a).

----

The standard deduction came into the Code in 1944[1] to simplify tax returns by according individuals an election to deduct, subject to a ceiling, an amount equal to 10% of their adjusted gross incomes, in lieu of itemized deductions. This permits a taxpayer to deduct a specified amount without keeping records of various expenditures and without specifically reporting a large group of deductions. The corresponding reduction in the administrative burden of the Internal Revenue Service is obvious. The standard deduction is an alternative to claiming deductions for items such as taxes, interest, extraordinary medical expenses, and any others not specified under Section 62.

Over the years Congress has frequently altered the manner in which the standard deduction operates. Under current law, the standard deduction is a flat dollar amount made up of a "basic" standard deduction (whose amount was significantly increased in the 2017 Tax Cuts and Jobs

----

[1]   Individual Income Tax Act of 1944, § 9, 58 Stat. 231, 236 (1944).

Act) and an "additional" standard deduction.[2] The amount of the basic standard deduction is $24,000 for married individuals filing jointly and for surviving spouses,[3] $18,000 for heads of households, and $12,000 for single individuals and married individuals filing separately.[4] After 2018, the standard deduction amount is indexed for inflation.[5]

A special limitation on the amount of the basic standard deduction is imposed if the taxpayer qualifies as a dependent under Section 151 of another taxpayer. In such a situation the amount of the dependent taxpayer's basic standard deduction may not exceed the greater of (1) the sum of $250 and that taxpayer's "earned income" or (2) $500.[6]

Additional standard deductions are allowed for elderly and blind taxpayers. Six hundred dollars is allowed for an elderly person (one who has attained age 65 before the close of his taxable year) and $600 for a blind individual if, in either case, the person is married or a surviving spouse.[7] The additional deduction is $1,200 if an individual is both blind and age 65.[8] Unmarrieds, other than surviving spouses, are allowed an even larger additional standard deduction of $750 in each category ($1,500 if in both).[9] Beginning in 1989 the amount of the additional standard deduction is also indexed for inflation.[10]

The standard deduction automatically applies to an individual taxpayer in computing taxable income for the year unless the taxpayer elects on her tax return to itemize her deductions[11] or the taxpayer does not qualify for use of the standard deduction and must itemize her deductions.[12] One such denial occurs under Section 63(c)(6)(A) which disallows use of the standard deduction by a married taxpayer on that taxpayer's separate return if the taxpayer's spouse has itemized deductions on the spouse's separate return. The reason for this rule is that one spouse could pay and deduct all itemized items, while the other spouse could make full use of the standard deduction; and they would

---

[2]  I.R.C. § 63(c)(1)–(3).

[3]  I.R.C. § 63(c)(2), (7)(A). This is equal to 200% of the $12,000 amount for single individuals. Id.

[4]  I.R.C. § 63(c)(2)(B)–(D), (7)(A). Classifications such as head of households, surviving spouse, etc. are defined in I.R.C. § 2 and are considered in Chapter 27A2, infra.

[5]  I.R.C. § 63(c)(7)(B).

[6]  I.R.C. § 63(c)(5). "Earned income" is defined in I.R.C. § 911(d)(2) as essentially income from services. The $500 amount is indexed for inflation after 1989 and the $250 amount is indexed for inflation after 1998. I.R.C. § 63(c)(4).

[7]  I.R.C. § 63(f). Marital status is determined under I.R.C. § 7703. I.R.C. § 63(g). See note 4, supra. If the taxpayer has a spouse for whom he may claim a personal exemption under § 151(b) additional $600 deductions may be claimed if the spouse has attained the age of 65 or is blind. I.R.C. § 63(f)(1)(B) and (f)(2)(B).

[8]  I.R.C. § 63(f)(1)(A) and (2)(A).

[9]  I.R.C. § 63(f)(3).

[10]  I.R.C. § 63(c)(4). See Chapter 27A5, infra.

[11]  I.R.C. § 63(b). See I.R.C. § 63(e). The original standard deduction in 1944 was elective, i.e., a taxpayer itemized his deductions unless he elected the standard deduction. Under the post-1986 rules, this is reversed.

[12]  I.R.C. § 63(c)(6).

receive a double benefit. The statute precludes this type of double benefit through intra-family tailoring and also precludes use of the standard deduction in some other circumstances.[13]

In making the election to itemize considered above, one must first determine the amount of one's itemized deductions. This is easy as one simply combines the amounts of the taxpayer's deductions listed in Section 67(b) and compares that total to the taxpayer's standard deduction, including any additional standard deduction.

## PROBLEMS

1.　Single Taxpayer, who is an employee of a law firm, in the current year has $100,000 of adjusted gross income, and the following allowable itemized deductions: $6,000 in interest, $6,500 in state income taxes, $1,500 in unreimbursed employee travel expenses, $200 in tax preparation fees, and $300 bar association dues. For simplicity, assume that there are no inflation adjustments.

(a)　What is Taxpayer's taxable income for the current year?　*85,500*

(b)　What difference in result in (a), above, if Taxpayer's 65th birthday is January 1 of the succeeding year. See Reg. § 1.151–1(c)(2).

(c)　What difference in result under the facts of (a), above, if Taxpayer is a married couple filing a joint return?　*76 K*

(d)　What difference in result under the facts of (c), above, if Taxpayers' deductible interest is $10,000, the state income taxes are $12,000, and the Taxpayers have a $5,000 charitable contribution.　*73 K*

2.　T, who is single, a child of X and a full-time law student has gross investment income of $4,000 in the current year and no § 62 or itemized deductions. For simplicity assume that there are no inflation adjustments. See §§ 63(c)(4), (7)(B). T qualifies as a dependent of X for the year.

(a)　What is T's taxable income, if any, for the current year?

(b)　What difference in result in (a), above, if instead T has $1,000 of earned income and $3,000 of investment income?

(c)　What difference in result in (a), above, if instead T has $13,000 of earned income and no investment income?

3.　A lives in New York and B in Florida. Both are single and have very substantial all-salary incomes of identical amounts in the current year. Both incur $5,000 of deductible interest expense and A pays state income tax in the amount of $9,000. B pays no state income tax. Assume (quite artificially) that neither has any other cost, expense, or expenditure that could be claimed as a deduction. Assume, in addition, that there are no inflation adjustments. See § 63(c)(4). Which, if either, should claim the standard deduction?

---

[13]　See I.R.C. § 63(c)(6)(B)–(E).

4.    Husband and Wife file separate returns. Husband has substantial itemized deductions, but Wife has very few. Why does Congress prohibit the use of the standard deduction by Wife if Husband itemizes his deductions?

## E.  PERSONAL AND DEPENDENCY EXEMPTIONS

Internal Revenue Code: Sections 151 (omit (d)(3) and (4)); 152 (omit (d)(4) and (5), (e)(3), and (f)(6)). See Sections 6013(a), (d); 7703.

Regulations: Sections 1.151–1(c)(2).

———————

The deduction provisions of Section 151 can be broken down into two categories: Subsection (b) of Section 151 concerns the personal exemption for the taxpayer and taxpayer's spouse.[1] The second part of the statute, Section 151(c), allows additional personal exemptions for *dependents*. Section 152, defining the term "dependent", authorizes no deduction; it merely sets out precise rules for determining who is a dependent.

Currently no deductions are allowed under the Code for personal or dependency exemptions, because the exemption amount is zero.[2] However, the topic is retained here because the definitional provisions have relevance with respect to other Code sections discussed in the Text,[3] including determining the tax status of certain taxpayers under Section 2,[4] the amount of the medical expense deduction under Section 213,[5] and the amount of the child tax credit under Section 24.[6]

A dependent generally must be a citizen or resident of the United States or a resident of a country contiguous to the United States.[7] No personal or dependency exemption is allowed with respect to an individual unless the taxpayer identification number (TIN) of the individual is included on the return of the taxpayer claiming the exemption.[8] If an individual is a dependent of another taxpayer, such individual may claim no dependents.[9] Finally, an individual does not qualify as a dependent if the individual files a joint return with the individual's spouse for the year.[10]

———————

[1]   Some individuals are denied a personal exemption. I.R.C. § 151(d)(2). See note 7 infra.

[2]   I.R.C. § 151(d)(5)(A).

[3]   See I.R.C. § 151(d)(5)(B).

[4]   See Chapter 27A2, infra.

[5]   See Chapter 18A, supra.

[6]   See Chapter 27B, infra.

[7]   I.R.C. § 152(b)(3). The statute creates an exception for an adopted child who has the same principal abode as the taxpayer and who is a member of the household of the taxpayer if the taxpayer is a citizen or national of the United States. I.R.C. § 152(b)(3)(B).

[8]   I.R.C. § 151(e). See I.R.C. § 7701(a)(41).

[9]   I.R.C. § 152(b)(1).

[10]   I.R.C. § 152(b)(2). However, an individual who files a joint return that is only a claim for refund is not disqualified. I.R.C. § 152(c)(1)(E).

There are two classification of dependents, either "a qualifying child" or "a qualifying relative"[11] and we discuss them in that order. Significantly, if a "child"[12] does not satisfy the requirements of a qualifying child, the child may still be a qualifying relative.[13]

A taxpayer must satisfy four requirements to claim a *"qualifying child"* as a dependent.[14] First, the individual must be a "child" of the taxpayer.[15] A child includes a son or daughter, stepson, and stepdaughter.[16] Although generally these relationships are by blood, nevertheless the section treats adopted and foster children the same as blood relatives.[17] But, as can only happen in the Code, a descendent of a child, or a brother, sister,[18] stepbrother or stepsister of the taxpayer or their descendants are also treated as a child of the taxpayer[19]

Second, the individual must have the same principal place of abode as the taxpayer for more than one-half of the year.[20] However, temporary absences from the abode due to special circumstances such as the pursuit of an education should not be treated as absences from the abode.[21]

Third, the individual must meet an age requirement. The individual must be younger than the taxpayer, and if the individual is either under the age of 19 at the close of the calendar year in which the taxpayer's taxable year begins or is a student[22] who has not attained age 24 at the end of such calendar year, the age requirement is met.[23]

Finally, the individual must not have provided over one-half of such individual's own support for the calendar year in which the taxable year of the taxpayer begins.[24] Support in these circumstances may be difficult to determine. It includes clothing, meals, lodging, and other necessities furnished to the dependent, but it does not include the value of personal services rendered to the dependent by the taxpayer[25] or non-necessities such as a boat.[26] The Code provides that as to a parent or a student, a

---

[11]  I.R.C. § 152(a).

[12]  See I.R.C. § 151(c)(2).

[13]  See I.R.C. § 152(d)(1)(D).

[14]  I.R.C. § 152(c)(1).

[15]  I.R.C. § 152(c)(1)(A).

[16]  I.R.C. § 152(f)(1)(A)(i).

[17]  I.R.C. § 152(f)(1)(A)(ii), (f)(1)(B), and (f)(1)(C).

[18]  This includes a brother or sister by the half blood. I.R.C. § 152(f)(4).

[19]  I.R.C. § 152(c)(2).

[20]  I.R.C. § 152(c)(1)(B).

[21]  Cf. Blair v. Commissioner, 63 T.C. 214 (1974); Byrd v. Commissioner, 52 T.C.M. 220 (1986).

[22]  Student is defined in I.R.C. § 152(f)(2).

[23]  I.R.C. § 152(c)(1)(C), (c)(3). An individual attains a given age on the anniversary of the date the individual was born. Rev. Rul. 2003–72, 2003–2 C.B. 346. A disabled individual need not satisfy the age requirement. I.R.C. § 152(c)(3)(B).

[24]  I.R.C. § 152(c)(1)(D).

[25]  Reg. § 1.152–1(a).

[26]  Flowers v. United States, unreported, 571 U.S.T.C. ¶ 9655 (1957). But see Rev. Rul. 77–282, 1977–2 C.B. 52, treating an automobile as an item of support.

scholarship received by a student will not be considered as support in determining the support requirement.[27] However, the statutory scholarship exclusion does not encompass student loans.[28]

It is possible that a dependent may satisfy all of the qualifying child requirements for more than one taxpayer. To avoid multiple deductibility, the Code provides a series of tie-breaker rules that apply when more than one taxpayer can potentially claim the same dependent.[29]

There are a series of somewhat similar requirements for a taxpayer to claim an individual as a *"qualifying relative."*[30] Initially, the claimed qualifying relative must not be a "qualifying child" of the taxpayer or any other taxpayer in the year.[31]

Second, the taxpayer and the person to be claimed as a qualifying relative must bear one of the relationships specifically listed under Section 152(d)(2). Although generally those relationships are by blood, nevertheless the section again treats adopted or foster children the same as blood children[32] and includes as a dependent a non-related individual who lives in the taxpayer's house as a member of the household.[33] However, Section 152(f)(3) provides that if at any time during the taxable year the relationship between the taxpayer and an individual is in violation of local law, the individual does not qualify as a dependent.[34]

The third requirement is that the person claimed as a dependent may not have *gross income* in excess of the exemption amount for the year involved if the zero exemption amount were inapplicable; thus, the person's gross income must not exceed $2,000 plus adjustments for inflation since 1990.[35] Gross income is defined under Section 61, and

---

[27] I.R.C. § 152(f)(5). See I.R.C. § 152(c)(1)(D) and (d)(1)(C).

[28] P. McCauley v. Commissioner, 56 T.C. 48 (1971).

[29] The rules break a tie by awarding the dependency status to the individual's parent or if no one is a parent, to the taxpayer with the highest adjusted gross income for the year. I.R.C. § 152(c)(4)(A). If the tieing taxpayers are both parents of the individual, the tie breaker goes to the parent with whom the individual resided for the longest period of time during the year and if that results in a tie, to the parent with the highest adjusted gross income. I.R.C. § 152(c)(4)(B).

A child may be the dependent of more than one taxpayer for purposes of some other Code sections. See I.R.C. §§ 105(b), 132(h)(2)(B), 213(d)(5).

[30] I.R.C. § 152(d)(1).

[31] I.R.C. § 152(d)(1)(D).

[32] I.R.C. § 152(f)(1).

[33] I.R.C. § 152(d)(2)(H).

[34] Leonard J. Eichbauer v. Commissioner, 30 T.C.M. 581 (1971); Estate of Daniel Buckley v. Commissioner, 37 T.C. 664 (1962); Ensminger v. Commissioner, 610 F.2d 189 (4th Cir. 1979). See also Leon Turnipseed v. Commissioner, 27 T.C. 758 (1957), reaching this result before the enactment of § 152(f)(3). But see Shackelford v. United States, 3 B.R. 42 (Bkrtcy. W.D. Mo. 1980).

[35] I.R.C. §§ 151(d)(5)(B), 152(d)(1)(B). See I.R.C. § 151(d)(1) and (4).

Under another rule, which applies in defining a qualifying relative, if a taxpayer's child is presumed by authorities to have been kidnapped by a nonrelative and the child qualified as a qualifying relative for the portion of the year before the kidnapping, then the child is treated as a dependent of the taxpayer during all the taxable years while the child is kidnaped. I.R.C. § 152(f)(6)(C).

therefore the income inclusion and exclusion sections apply in the determination of the amount of gross income.[36]

The final requirement for a qualifying relative is that the taxpayer claiming the qualifying relative must provide over one-half of the support for such individual during the year.[37] The definition of support here is the same as support for a qualifying child.[38]

In some situations, especially with respect to elderly persons, several members of a family may jointly contribute to the support of an individual. Section 152(d)(3) provides that, if certain requirements are met, those supporting the individual may agree that one of the group will be treated as though the taxpayer provided over half of the individual's support for the year for purposes of the support requirement.

Support problems in defining a qualified child or a qualified relative also arise with respect to the children of divorced or separated parents.[39] In determining support, payments to a spouse of alimony or separate maintenance payments shall not be considered payments by the payor for the support of a dependent.[40] When a parent remarries, support of a child received from the parent's new spouse is treated as support by the parent.[41] In addition, the following rules apply only if the parents have custody of the child for at least one half of the year,[42] if they provide more than one half of the child's support,[43] if they do not file a joint return,[44] and if the child is not the subject of a multiple support agreement.[45] The custodial parent generally is entitled to the dependency deduction. However, the noncustodial parent is entitled to the dependency deduction if the custodial parent signs a waiver that he or she will not claim the child as a dependent for the taxable year and the waiver is attached to the noncustodial parent's tax return.[46]

The following problems illustrate the statutory requirements presented above; but, if a student is required to work them, it should be less to learn these statutory details than to learn how to deal with intricate statutory language.

---

[36] Reg. § 1.151–2(a).

[37] I.R.C. § 152(d)(1)(C).

[38] See supra notes 25–28. The statute again provides that a scholarship received by a student will not be considered as support in determining whether parents furnish sufficient support. I.R.C. § 152(f)(5). See supra notes 27–28.

[39] See I.R.C. § 152(e)(1), Reg. § 1.152–4.

[40] I.R.C. § 152(d)(5)(A)(i). See I.R.C. § 152(d)(5)(B).

[41] I.R.C. § 152(d)(5)(A)(ii).

[42] I.R.C. § 152(e)(1)(B).

[43] I.R.C. § 152(e)(1)(A).

[44] If a joint return is filed, the question of which parent is allowed the exemption is irrelevant.

[45] I.R.C. § 152(e)(5).

[46] I.R.C. § 152(e)(2). The rules are slightly different for divorce decrees or separate maintenance agreements which were entered into before 1985. I.R.C. § 152(e)(3).

## PROBLEMS

**1.** In each of the following parts, determine whether T, a calendar year taxpayer, is entitled to a dependency exemption for the particular person, X, involved.

(a) X is T's child who was born on December 31 of the current year.

(b) X is T's child who was born on December 31 nineteen years ago and who lives at home and works part time. T provides for X's meals and lodging which constitute more than one half of X's support.

(c) Same as (b), above, except that instead of working part time, X is a full-time student at Embraceable U which is located in another state than where T lives.

(d) Same as (c), above, except that X married Y during the year with whom she files a joint return.

(e) Same as (c), above, except that X also receives $5,000 as a scholarship which X uses for X's support and which constitutes more than one-half of X's total support.

(f) Same as (e), above, except that X is T's brother not T's child.

**2.** In each of the following parts determine whether T is potentially entitled to a "dependency" exemption for X, because X meets the § 152(d)(1)(A) relationship requirement.

(a) X is T's wife's brother.

(b) Same as (a), above, but assume further that:

(1) T's wife died the year before.

(2) T and W were divorced the year before. Cf. Steele v. Suwalski, 75 F.2d 885 (7th Cir. 1935).

(c) X is T's wife's deceased sister's husband.

(d) Same as (c), above, except that X lived with T the entire year.

**3.** T's father X, who has no gross income, was supported in the current year by T, T's two brothers (A and B), and C, an unrelated friend. A total of $4,000 was spent for the father's support which was contributed in the following proportions by the above persons: X, 15%; T, 25%; A, 20%; B, 10%; and C, 30%. Which of these persons, if any, is entitled to claim X as a dependent and what procedures must they follow?

**4.** W, upon graduation from law school, decides to divorce H after 3 years of marriage. The divorce becomes final in the current year and W is awarded custody of their young son H, Jr. Who is entitled to the dependency deduction in the following circumstances?

(a) W furnishes 40 percent of Jr.'s support and H furnishes 60 percent.

(b) Same as (a), above, except that in a written agreement W waives claiming any dependency deduction.

(c)  Same as (a), above, except that Jr. lives with Grandpa for 9 months out of the year.

(d)  What result in (c), above, if W also moves in with Grandpa?

# PART 5

# THE YEAR OF INCLUSION OR DEDUCTION

# CHAPTER 19

# FUNDAMENTAL TIMING PRINCIPLES

## A. INTRODUCTION

Internal Revenue Code: Sections 441(a) through (e), (g); 442; 446; 451(a); 461(a). See Sections 448; 460.

Regulations: Sections 1.446–1(a)(1) and (2), (b)(1), (c)(1)(iv).

---

Federal income taxes are computed on the basis of a net income figure (taxable income) for a twelve month period (the taxable year).[1] Preceding chapters have developed some of the principles under which it is determined whether and how various items may bear on the computation of taxable income. Assuming an item is significant in this respect, our question now is: *When,* for what taxable year, is the item taken into account? The taxable year is usually a twelve month period ending on the last day of a month.[2] A taxpayer may use the calendar year which of course ends on December 31st or a fiscal taxable year which ends on the last day of any other month.[3] The choice depends largely on how the taxpayer maintains financial records. A taxpayer's taxable year generally is the annual period on the basis of which the taxpayer regularly computes income in keeping financial books.[4] If the taxpayer does not keep books or does not have an annual accounting period, then a calendar year must be used as the taxable year.[5] After a taxpayer has chosen an accounting period, approval of the Commissioner is required for a change of accounting period.[6] Why does Congress require such approval?

Identification of the proper taxable year for reporting an item of income or for claiming a deduction can bear importantly on the taxpayer's tax liability. Obviously, it is not just a question whether the taxpayer is

---

[1]  I.R.C. § 441.

[2]  Sometimes a shorter period is treated as if it were a full taxable year, as upon the death of a taxpayer or the creation of a new taxable entity such as a corporation or a trust. I.R.C. § 443(a)(2). But, if a short period arises out of a change in a taxpayer's accounting period, income must be "annualized." I.R.C. § 443(b).

[3]  I.R.C. § 441(d), (e).

[4]  I.R.C. § 441(b)(1), (c). Reg. § 1.441–1(b)(7) defines "books" as including regular books of account and supporting records and data sufficient to adequately and clearly reflect income on the basis of an annual accounting period.

[5]  I.R.C. § 441(b)(2) and (g). Trusts, other than wholly charitable trusts, are required to adopt a calendar year. I.R.C. § 644.

[6]  I.R.C. § 442. Cf. I.R.C. § 443(a)(1), (b). Sometimes automatic approval is allowed. See Rev. Proc. 2002–39, § 3.02(1), 2002–1 C.B. 1046, 1049; Rev. Proc. 2003–62, § 7.01, 2003–2 C.B. 299, 303.

taxed on an item in year one or year two. Substantive changes in the law, changes in the tax rates, changes in the taxpayer's status, changes in who the taxpayer is, the running of the statute of limitations, and other financial activities of the taxpayer, including the time value of money, all may bear on the amount of liability if the item falls into one year rather than another.

Whether a taxpayer uses the calendar year or a fiscal year, the period for which the taxpayer reports items of income or deduction is affected by the method of accounting that the taxpayer has adopted. The principal accounting methods, which are examined in this chapter, are the cash receipts and disbursements method and the accrual method. The cash method of accounting, normally used by individuals, generally measures tax liability by including an item in income or allowing a deduction at the time that cash or its equivalent is received or paid. The accrual method of accounting is often used and sometimes must be used by businesses. It generally measures tax liability by including an item in income at the time the taxpayer becomes entitled to it and allowing a deduction at the time a deductible obligation becomes fixed and certain, that is, when all events have occurred to fix the right to receive payment or to fix the duty to make payment but sometimes only after economic performance, where in either instance the amount can be determined with reasonable accuracy.[7]

Although the cash and accrual methods are the principal accounting methods, they are not the exclusive methods. The Code approves some statutory variations in methods of accounting.[8] Approved variations include special rules relating to reporting income from installment sales under Section 453[9] and special treatment of certain types of income and expense.[10]

With regard to the detailed implementation of any accounting method, the regulations state:[11]

> It is recognized that no uniform method of accounting can be prescribed for all taxpayers. Each taxpayer shall adopt such forms and systems as are, in his judgment, best suited to his need. However, no method of accounting is acceptable unless, in the opinion of the Commissioner, it clearly reflects income. A method of accounting which reflects the consistent application of generally accepted accounting principles in a particular trade or business in accordance with accepted conditions or practices in that trade or business will ordinarily be regarded as clearly

---

[7]   Reg. § 1.446–1(c)(1)(ii); and see Reg. § 1.461–1(a)(2) and I.R.C. § 461(h) discussed at page 642, infra.

[8]   The use of unspecified accounting methods is also permitted, subject to approval of the Commissioner. I.R.C. § 446(c).

[9]   See Chapter 24A, infra.

[10]  Statutory references appear at Reg. § 1.446–1(c)(1)(iii).

[11]  Reg. § 1.446–1(a)(2).

reflecting income, provided all items of gross income and expense are treated consistently from year to year.

The analysis of tax accounting problems is more interesting and less mechanical if one keeps in mind a "matching" concept familiar to accountants. We seek a net income figure for a specified period. But events and transactions affecting the computation do not all fall neatly within the beginning and end of the period like episodes in a three-act play. And so, ideally, we attempt to take account of expenses incurred in producing income reportable for year two in the year two computations, even though such expenses represent expenditures actually made in year one or year three. The cash method of accounting often fails miserably in this respect, but it is permitted to be used in most situations because of its essential simplicity. Other failures of tax accounting in this respect appear subsequently in this chapter.

The Code specifically provides that some taxpayers may not use the cash method of accounting.[12] "Tax shelters"[13] may never use the cash method.[14] Generally, corporations other than S corporations[15] and partnerships in which such corporations are partners may not use the cash method.[16] There are exceptions which allow a normally disqualified corporation or partnership to use the cash method if it is a qualified personal service corporation,[17] or generally if its average gross receipts for the prior three years do not exceed twenty-five million dollars per year.[18]

The matching concept is behind some accepted departures from straight cash or accrual method accounting. For example, a business activity may involve the building and sale of major structures, such as

---

[12] I.R.C. § 448.

[13] A "tax shelter" is defined by I.R.C. § 461(i)(3) as: (1) any enterprise (other than a C corporation) in which interests in such enterprise have been offered for sale in any offering required to be registered with a federal or state agency, (§ 461(i)(3)(A)); (2) any syndicate, i.e., partnership or other entity (other than a C corporation) if more than 35 percent of the losses of such entity are allocable to limited partners or limited entrepreneurs, (§§ 461(i)(3)(B) and 1256(e)(3)(B)); and (3) any partnership, entity, plan or arrangement, a significant purpose of which is the avoidance or evasion of taxes, (§§ 461(i)(3)(C) and 6662(d)(2)(C)(ii)).

Additionally, the House Report indicates that, in determining whether an activity constitutes a tax shelter within the meaning of § 461(i), consideration should be given to whether there is a reasonable and significant expectation that either: (1) deductions exceeding income from such activity will be available to reduce income from other sources; or (2) credits exceeding the tax attributable to the activity will be available to off-set taxes on income from other sources. H.Rep. No. 98–432, 98th Cong., 2d Sess. 1260 (1984).

[14] I.R.C. § 448(a)(3) and (d)(3).

[15] I.R.C. § 1361. S corporations are essentially closely held corporations whose shareholders elect to be taxed as aggregates similar to partners in partnerships rather than as a corporate entity.

[16] I.R.C. § 448(a)(1) and (2).

[17] I.R.C. § 448(b)(2). A qualified personal service corporation is not treated as a corporation for purposes of determining whether a partnership is disqualified from use of the cash method. Id. A qualified personal service corporation is defined in § 448(d)(2) under a test related to the function carried on by the corporation and an employee ownership test.

[18] I.R.C. § 448(b)(3) and (c); see also I.R.C. § 447(c)(2) regarding farming corporations. The $25 million figure is adjusted for inflation after 2018. I.R.C. § 448(c)(4).

hotels or bridges, work on which may extend over several years. In such situations, the "percentage of completion method" must be used.[19] Under this method, items of income and deduction are taken into account proportionately as work on the contract progresses.[20] However, in some such situations,[21] a taxpayer may use the "completed contract method" of accounting under which the taxpayer is permitted to determine and report net profit on the project upon completion of the entire contract.[22]

Various hybrid methods of accounting, even combining cash and accrual concepts, may be used.[23] However, a basic statutory requirement is that the method used must clearly reflect income.[24] Materials that follow in this chapter show the kinds of controversies that are engendered by this requirement.

A taxpayer is not limited to the use of a single accounting method in computing tax liability. A taxpayer may use one accounting method for a trade or business and another for computing taxable income on items not connected with the trade or business,[25] and a taxpayer may use different accounting methods for separate trades or businesses in which the taxpayer is involved.[26]

Although a taxpayer may initially adopt any accounting method that clearly reflects income, nevertheless the consent of the Commissioner must be obtained in order to change accounting methods.[27] Approval is required so as to avoid distortion of one's income by means of an accounting method change, and the Commissioner may require adjustments to prevent duplication or omission of amounts as a result of the change.[28] The definition of what constitutes a change in accounting method and the procedures to be followed in seeking approval are stated in the regulations.[29]

---

[19] See I.R.C. § 460 which requires income or losses from such contracts to be partially reported under the percentage of completion method of accounting. There are exceptions to this rule. I.R.C. § 460(e). See note 21, infra. In addition, in using the percentage of completion method, a taxpayer may elect to defer income until a year in which 10% of the taxpayer's estimated costs have been incurred. I.R.C. § 460(b)(5).

[20] See I.R.C. § 460(b) and (c) and Reg. § 1.451–3(c)(1).

[21] I.R.C. § 460(e). There are exceptions for home construction contracts and contracts which will be completed within two years by a taxpayer whose average gross receipts for the three preceding taxable years do not exceed twenty-five million dollars. I.R.C. § 460(e)(1).

[22] Reg. § 1.460–3(b)(2). See Evans, "The Taxation of Multi-period Projects: An Analysis of Competing Models," 69 Tex.L.Rev. 1109 (1991).

[23] See I.R.C. § 446(c)(4).

[24] I.R.C. § 446(b).

[25] Reg. § 1.446–1(c)(1)(iv)(b).

[26] I.R.C. § 446(d).

[27] I.R.C. § 446(e).

[28] I.R.C. § 481(a).

[29] Regs. § 1.446–1(e). Rev.Proc. 2015–13, 2015–5 I.R.B. 419, provides the procedures to obtain either advance (non-automatic) or automatic consent for certain specified changes in method of accounting. Rev. Proc. 2018–31, 2018–22 I.R.B. 637, provides a list of automatic changes to which the procedures of Rev. Proc. 2015–13 apply.

In general, substantive provisions of the Code allowing deductions take account of both the cash and accrual method of accounting. See Section 162(a) allowing a deduction for business expenses " * * * paid or incurred during the taxable year * * * ;" Section 163(a) authorizing a deduction for * * * "interest paid or accrued within the taxable year * * * ;" Section 164(a) authorizing a deduction for certain taxes " * * * paid or accrued * * * ;" and similar language appears in Section 212. There are other examples. In contrast, other provisions of the statute force the cash method, even though the taxpayer may have properly adopted the accrual method of accounting. See Section 170(a) concerning the charitable deduction, requiring *payment,* and Section 213(a) authorizing the deduction for medical expenses " * * * *paid* during the taxable year * * *." There are other examples. But generally the Code accepts the taxpayer's cash or accrual method of accounting.[30]

As a general principle each taxable year stands alone and each year's tax liability is computed separately, a concept spoken of as preserving the integrity of the taxable year.[31] Thus, if one reported an item of income as accrued in year one, and in year two it became apparent that collection would never be made, taxable income for year one is not to be adjusted (the year is not reopened) and, if uncollectibility is to affect tax liability, it will affect liability for year two, rather than year one. Some exceptions to this strict approach to the taxable year concept are examined in Chapter 20, along with the concept of income averaging of deferred compensation and statutory provisions for the carryover to another year of some items of deduction.

## B. THE CASH RECEIPTS AND DISBURSEMENTS METHOD*

### 1. RECEIPTS

Internal Revenue Code: Sections 446; 451(a).

Regulations: Sections 1.446–1(c)(1)(i); 1.451–1(a), –2.

---

[30]  But see part D of this Chapter which considers I.R.C. § 267(a)(2) which places an accrual method payor on the cash method with respect to expenses owed to a cash method payee and considers I.R.C. § 467 which is applicable to deferred payments for the rental of property or for the performance of services forcing a matching of income and deduction by placing a cash method payor or payee on the accrual method.

[31]  See Burnet v. Sanford & Brooks Co., 282 U.S. 359, 51 S.Ct. 150 (1931).

*  See Schapiro, "Prepayments and Distortion of Income Under Cash Basis Tax Accounting," 30 Tax L.R. 117 (1975).

## Kahler v. Commissioner*

Tax Court of the United States, 1952.
18 T.C. 31.

[The Findings of Fact have been omitted. Ed.]

Opinion

■ RICE, JUDGE:

The sole issue is when did the petitioner realize the income represented by the commission check delivered December 31, 1946. Was it in 1946, as determined by respondent, or in 1947, as claimed by petitioner? This, in turn, is based on the question whether the receipt of a check by a cash basis taxpayer after banking hours on the last day of the taxable period constitutes a realization of income.

Applicable provisions of the statute are set forth in the margin.[1]

In his brief, petitioner argues that "the mere receipt of a check does not give rise to income within the taxable year of receipt unless the check is received in sufficient time before the end of the taxable year so the check may be converted into cash within the taxable year." In support of such result, petitioner relies upon L.M. Fischer, 14 T.C. 792 (1950); Urban A. Lavery, 5 T.C. 1283 (1945), affd. (C.A.7, 1946) 158 F.2d 859; and Harvey H. Ostenberg, 17 B.T.A. 738 (1929).

In the *Fischer* case, we held that a check delivered to the taxpayer on December 31, 1942, which was not deposited until 1943, was not income in 1942 but in 1943, since the check was subject to a substantial restriction. At the time of delivery of such check, there was an oral agreement made between the drawer and the taxpayer that the latter would hold the check for a few days before he cashed it since the drawer was short of money in the bank. Such a situation is completely distinguishable from that in the instant case.

The *Lavery* and *Ostenberg* cases both decided that checks delivered to the taxpayers were income in the year of delivery. In the *Lavery* case delivery was on December 30, and in the *Ostenberg* case delivery was on December 31. Petitioner relies on the dicta appearing in these cases to the effect that the result might have been different had the petitioner in either case been able to show that he could not have cashed the check in the year drawn. We fail to see where there should be any difference in result just because it might be impossible to cash a check in the year in which drawn, where delivery actually took place in such year. Respondent's regulations provide that all items of gross income shall be included in the taxable year in which received by the taxpayer, and that where services are paid for other than by money, the amount to be

---

* See generally Note, "Checks and Notes as Income When Received by a Cash Basis Taxpayer," 73 Harv.L.Rev. 1199 (1960). Ed.

[1] [The quoted sections of the 1939 Code, not materially different from their current counterparts, are omitted. Ed.]

included as income is the fair market value of the thing taken in payment.[2]

Analogous cases to the instant case are those which were concerned with the proper year in which deductions might be taken where a check was drawn and delivered in one year and cashed in a subsequent year. Under the negotiable instruments law, payment by check is a conditional payment subject to the condition that it will be honored upon presentation; and once such presentation is made and the check is honored, the date of payment relates back to the time of delivery. See Estelle Broussard, 16 T.C. 23 (1951); Estate of Modie J. Spiegel, 12 T.C. 524 (1949); and cases cited therein. In the *Spiegel* case we said, at page 529:

> It would seem to us unfortunate for the Tax Court to fail to recognize what has so frequently been suggested, that as a practical matter, in everyday personal and commercial usage, the transfer of funds by check is an accepted procedure. The parties almost without exception think and deal in terms of payment except in the unusual circumstance, not involved here, that the check is dishonored upon presentation, or that it was delivered in the first place subject to some condition or infirmity which intervenes between delivery and presentation.

Under such circumstances, we feel that it is immaterial that delivery of a check is made too late in the taxable year for the check to be cashed in that year. The petitioner realized income upon receipt of the commission check on December 31, 1946.

Reviewed by the Court.

Decision will be entered for the respondent.

■ MURDOCK, J., concurring:

I agree with the result reached that the receipt of a check is regarded as payment and income unless it is subject to some restriction but feel that the petitioner's case is weaker in some respects than the majority opinion might indicate. A finding is made that the check in question was received by the petitioner "sometime after 5 p.m. on December 31, 1946." There is also evidence that he could not have obtained cash for the check at the drawee bank but he could have deposited the check in that bank, later on December 31, 1946. There was another bank in the town and the evidence does not show whether or not he could have cashed the check in that bank after regular banking hours. Furthermore he might have made some other use of the check during 1946. For example, he might have cashed it at some place other than at a bank or he might have used it to discharge some obligation, within the year 1946.

■ HARRON, J., agrees with this concurring opinion.

---

[2] Treasury Regulations 111, § 29.22(a)–3, and § 29.41–2. [See Reg. §§ 1.61–2(d) and 1.446–1(a) and (c). Ed.]

# Williams v. Commissioner*

Tax Court of the United States, 1957.
28 T.C. 1000.

■ WITHEY, JUDGE:

\* \* \*

## FINDINGS OF FACT

Some of the facts have been stipulated and are found accordingly.

Petitioners, husband and wife, residing in Portland, Oregon, filed their joint income tax return for 1951 with the director of internal revenue for the district of Oregon. Inasmuch as the activities of Jay A. Williams are those with which we are here primarily concerned, "petitioner" or "Williams" as hereinafter used has reference to him.

The petitioner kept his accounts and prepared his returns on a cash basis.

During 1951, and prior thereto, petitioner was engaged in the business of locating marketable parcels of timberland for prospective purchasers of timber. Williams compiled information concerning certain stands of timber for Lester McConkey and J.M. Housley. Petitioner received nothing from McConkey and Housley at the time he turned over to them the desired information. Subsequently, on May 5, 1951, J.M. Housley issued to Williams an unsecured, non-interest-bearing promissory note in the amount of $7,166.60, payable 240 days thereafter.

At the time of issuance of the foregoing note, the maker was unable to pay anything on it because of his lack of funds. Further, it was understood by petitioner that Housley would be unable to make any payments on the note until he had first acquired and sold at least part of the available timber property which Williams had located.

Upon receipt of the note in 1951, petitioner attempted on 10 or 15 occasions to sell it to various banks or finance companies but was unable to realize any money thereon until 1954 when he collected proceeds from J.M. Housley to the extent of $6,666.66 in discharge of the debt represented by the note.

Petitioners did not report on their income tax return for 1951 any income resulting from the receipt of the note during that year, but reported income in the amount of $6,666.66 received in 1954 upon the discharge of the indebtedness.

The note received by petitioner on May 5, 1951, was not intended as payment of the indebtedness of J.M. Housley and had no fair market value at that time or at any time during 1951.

---

\*    Acq. 1958–1 C.B. 6.

OPINION

The petitioners have taken the position that the receipt of the promissory note by Williams in 1951 was not intended as payment of the indebtedness of J.M. Housley and therefore did not result in the receipt of income during that year. In addition, the petitioners contend that if the foregoing note was received in payment of the debt, it nevertheless had no ascertainable fair market value and consequently cannot be considered the equivalent of cash.

The respondent has determined that the receipt by Williams of the note in question on May 5, 1951, constituted taxable income in that year under section 22(a) of the 1939 Code.

It is unquestioned here that promissory notes or other evidences of indebtedness received as payment for services constitute income, within the meaning of section 22(a) of the 1939 Code, to the extent of their fair market value. * * *.

Petitioners contend that the note in question was not received by Williams as payment, but merely as an evidence of indebtedness. Petitioner's testimony to the effect that the note was not payable until the maker, J.M. Housley, realized income from the sale of the timber property located by Williams supports his contention. The petitioner stated categorically that the note in question was not given to him in payment of the indebtedness of the maker.

The respondent points out that petitioners rely solely on the self-serving declarations of Williams and insists that without supporting evidence the foregoing testimony is not worthy of belief. However, it is not within our province arbitrarily to disregard the unimpeached and uncontradicted testimony of a taxpayer. * * *. Inasmuch as no conflicting evidence is apparent from the record herein, petitioners have established to our satisfaction that the note received by Williams on May 5, 1951, was not received in payment of the outstanding debt due him for the performance of his services. A note received only as security, or as an evidence of indebtedness, and not as payment, may not be regarded as income at the time of receipt. *Schlemmer v. United States, supra; Robert J. Dial, supra.* A simple change in the form of indebtedness from an account payable to a note payable is insufficient to cause the realization of income by the creditor.

In the event that petitioners had failed to show that the promissory note here in issue was not intended as payment, we still would be unable to sustain the respondent's determination. The note bore no interest and was unsecured. It was not payable until 1952. The maker of the note, J.M. Housley, was without funds at the time of its execution. Petitioner testified that he was in need of immediate cash in 1951 and upon receipt of the note on May 5 of that year he attempted on 10 or 15 occasions to sell it to various banks or finance companies, but was unable to realize any money thereon. Accordingly, petitioners have demonstrated that the note in question had no fair market value in 1951 and consequently it cannot be held to be the equivalent of cash during the year of receipt. Cf. *J.F. Weinmann*, 5 B.T.A. 885. The receipt by petitioner of the promissory note in 1951 does not constitute taxable income realized during that year.

*Decision will be entered under Rule 50.*

# Cowden v. Commissioner

United States Court of Appeals, Fifth Circuit, 1961.
289 F.2d 20.

■ JONES, CIRCUIT JUDGE.

We here review a decision of the Tax Court by which a determination was made of federal income tax liability of Frank Cowden, Sr., his wife and their children, for the years 1951 and 1952. In April 1951, Frank Cowden, Sr. and his wife made an oil, gas and mineral lease for themselves and their children upon described lands in Texas to Stanolind Oil and Gas Company. By related supplemental agreements, Stanolind agreed to make "bonus" or "advance royalty" payments in an aggregate amount of $511,192.50. On execution of the instruments $10,223.85 was payable, the sum of $250,484.31 was due "no earlier than" January 5 "nor later than" January 10, 1952, and $250,484.34 was stipulated to be paid "no earlier than" January 5 "nor later than" January 10, 1953. One-half of the amounts was to be paid to Frank Cowden, Sr. and his wife, and one-sixth was payable to each of their children. In the deferred payments agreements it was provided that:

> "This contract evidences the obligation of Stanolind Oil and Gas Company to make the deferred payments referred to in subparagraphs (b) and (c) of the preceding paragraph hereof, and it is understood and agreed that the obligation of Stanolind Oil and Gas Company to make such payments is a firm and absolute personal obligation of said Company, which is not in any manner conditioned upon development or production from the demised premises, nor upon the continued ownership of the leasehold interest in such premises by Stanolind Oil and Gas Company, but that such payments shall be made in all events."

On November 30, 1951, the taxpayers assigned the payments due from Stanolind in 1952 to the First National Bank of Midland, of which Frank Cowden, Sr. was a director. Assignments of the payments due in 1953 were made to the bank on November 20, 1952. For the assignment of the 1952 payments the bank paid the face value of the amounts assigned discounted by $257.43 in the case of Frank Cowden, Sr., and his wife, and $85.81 in the case of each of their children. For the amounts due in 1953 the discounts were $313.14 for Frank Cowden, Sr. and his wife, and $104.38 for each of their children. The taxpayers reported the amounts received by them from the assignments as long-term capital gains. The Commissioner made a determination that the contractual obligations of Stanolind to make payments in future years represented ordinary income, subject to depletion, to the extent of the fair market value of the obligations at the time they were created. The Commissioner computed the fair market value of the Stanolind obligations, which were not interest bearing, by the deduction of a discount of four per cent. on the deferred payments from the date of the agreements until the respective maturities. Such computation fixed a 1951 equivalent of cash value of $487,647.46 for the bonus payments, paid in 1951 and agreed to be paid thereafter, aggregating $511,192.50. The Commissioner determined that the taxpayers should be taxed in 1951 on $487,647.46, as ordinary income.

A majority of the Tax Court was convinced that, under the particular facts of this case, the bonus payments were not only readily but immediately convertible to cash and were the equivalent of cash, and had a fair market value equal to their face value. The Tax Court decided that the entire amounts of the bonus payments, $511,192.50, were taxable in 1951, as ordinary income. Cowden v. Commissioner of Internal Revenue, 32 T.C. 853. Two judges of the Tax Court dissented.

The Tax Court stated, as a general proposition, "that executory contracts to make future payments in money do not have a fair market value." The particular facts by which the Tax Court distinguishes this case from the authorities by which the general proposition is established are, as stated in the opinion of the majority.

> " * * * that the bonus payors were perfectly willing and able at the time of execution of the leases and bonus agreements to pay such bonus in an immediate lump sum payment; to pay the bonus immediately in a lump sum at all times thereafter until the due dates under the agreements; that Cowden, Sr., believed the bonus agreements had a market value at the time of their execution; that a bank in which he was an officer and depositor was willing to and in fact did purchase such rights at a nominal discount; that the bank considered such rights to be bankable and to represent direct obligations of the payor; that the bank generally dealt in such contracts where it was satisfied with the financial responsibility of the payor and looked solely to it for payment without recourse to the lessor and, in short, that the sole reason why the bonuses were not immediately paid in cash upon execution of the leases involved was the refusal of the lessor to receive such payments."

These findings are, in some respects, challenged by the taxpayers as being unsupported by the evidence. Our review of the record has led us to the conclusion that the findings of fact made by the Tax Court are sustained by substantial evidence. However, we must observe that the statement of Frank Cowden, Sr. that the contract obligations had "some market value" is not to be regarded as binding upon him and the other taxpayers with respect to the decisive issue in the case.

The dissenting opinion of the Tax Court minority states that the conclusion reached by the majority "is in effect that the taxpayers are not free to make the bargain of their choice," and one of the taxpayers' specifications of error is that the Tax Court "erred in holding that taxpayers are not free to make the bargain of their choice."

The Tax Court majority distinguishes the authorities cited and relied upon by the taxpayers upon several grounds. The Tax Court seemingly lays stress upon the fact, found to be here present, that the bonus payor was willing and able to make the entire bonus payment upon the execution of the agreement. It is said by the taxpayers that the Tax Court has held that a constructive receipt, under the equivalent of cash doctrine, resulted from the willingness of the lessee to pay the entire bonus on execution of the leases and the unwillingness of the taxpayers, for reasons of their own,[1] to receive the full amount. If this be the effect of the Tax Court's decision there may be some justification for the criticism appearing in the opinion of the minority and the concern expressed elsewhere.[2]

It was said in Gregory v. Helvering, 293 U.S. 465, 55 S.Ct. 266, and recently repeated in Knetsch v. United States, 364 U.S. 361, 81 S.Ct. 132, 135, "The legal right of a taxpayer to decrease the amount of what otherwise would be his taxes, or altogether avoid them, by means which the law permits, cannot be doubted." * * *. As a general rule a tax avoidance motive is not to be considered in determining the tax liability resulting from a transaction. * * *. The taxpayers had the right to decline to enter into a mineral lease of their lands except upon the condition that the lessee obligate itself for a bonus payable in part in installments in future years, and the doing so would not, of itself, subject the deferred payments to taxation during the year that the lease was made. Nor would a tax liability necessarily arise although the lease contract was made with a solvent lessee who had been willing and able to pay the entire bonus upon the execution of the lease.

While it is true that the parties may enter into any legal arrangement they see fit even though the particular form in which it was cast was selected with the hope of a reduction in taxes, it is also true that if a consideration for which one of the parties bargains is the equivalent of cash it will be subjected to taxation to the extent of its fair market value. Whether the undertaking of the lessee to make future bonus payments was, when made, the equivalent of cash and, as such, taxable as current income is the issue in this case. In a somewhat similar case, decided in 1941, the Board of Tax Appeals stated that "where no notes, bonds, or other evidences of indebtedness other than the contract were given, such contract had no fair market value." Kleberg v. Commissioner,

---

[1] It is not denied that a desire to save taxes was the sole purpose for the taxpayers' insistence that payment be postponed.

[2] 9 Oil & Gas Tax Q. 122; 49 A.B.A.J. 1205; 59 Colum.L.Rev. 1237; 8 Tax Fortnightor 835; 11th Ann.S.W.Leg.Found.Inst.Oil & Gas Law & Taxation 651.

43 B.T.A. 277, quoting from Titus v. Commissioner, 33 B.T.A. 928. In 1959 the Tax Court held that where the deferred bonus payments were evidenced by promissory notes the equivalent of cash doctrine might be applicable. Barnsley v. Commissioner, 31 T.C. 1260. There the Tax Court said:

> "It is, of course, possible under an oil and gas lease containing proper provisions to have a bonus payable and taxable in installments, Alice G.K. Kleberg, 43 B.T.A. 277. The case before us does not constitute such an arrangement. In the Kleberg case the contractual agreement was to pay a named amount in two payments as bonus. It was not a case like the one here where cash and negotiable notes, the latter being the equivalent of cash, representing the bonus were received in the same year by the taxpayer."

The test announced in Kleberg, from which Barnsley does not depart, seems to be whether the obligation to make the deferred payments is represented by "notes, bonds, or other evidences of indebtedness other than the contract". In this case, the literal test of Kleberg is met as the obligation of Stanolind to the Cowdens was evidenced by an instrument other than the contract of lease. This instrument is not, however, one of the kind which fall into the classification of notes or bonds. The taxpayers urge that there can be no "equivalent of cash" obligation unless it is a negotiable instrument. Such a test, to be determined by the form of the obligation, is as unrealistic as it is formalistic. The income tax law deals in economic realities, not legal abstractions,[3] and the reach of the income tax law is not to be delimited by technical refinements or mere formalism.[4]

A promissory note, negotiable in form, is not necessarily the equivalent of cash. Such an instrument may have been issued by a maker of doubtful solvency[5] or for other reasons such paper might be denied a ready acceptance in the market place. We think the converse of this principle ought to be applicable. We are convinced that if a promise to pay of a solvent obligor is unconditional and assignable, not subject to set-offs, and is of a kind that is frequently transferred to lenders or investors at a discount not substantially greater than the generally prevailing premium for the use of money, such promise is the equivalent of cash and taxable in like manner as cash would have been taxable had it been received by the taxpayer rather than the obligation. The principle that negotiability is not the test of taxability in an equivalent of cash case such as is before us, is consistent with the rule that men may, if they can,

---

[3]   Commissioner of Internal Revenue v. Southwest Exploration Company, 350 U.S. 308, 76 S.Ct. 395.

[4]   United States v. Joliet & Chicago Railroad Company, 315 U.S. 44, 62 S.Ct. 442.

[5]   Board v. Commissioner, 18 B.T.A. 650.

so order their affairs as to minimize taxes,[6] and points up the doctrine that substance and not form should control in the application of income tax laws.[7]

The Tax Court stressed in its findings that the provisions for deferring a part of the bonus were made solely at the request of and for the benefit of the taxpayers and that the lessee was willing and able to make the bonus payments in cash upon execution of the agreements. It appears to us that the Tax Court, in reaching its decision that the taxpayers had received equivalent of cash bonuses in the year the leases were executed, gave as much and probably more weight to those findings than to the other facts found by it. We are persuaded of this not only by the language of its opinion but because, in its determination of the cash equivalent, it used the amounts which it determined the taxpayers could have received if they had made a different contract, rather than the fair market value cash equivalent[8] of the obligation for which the taxpayers had bargained in the contracts which they had a lawful right to make. We are unable to say whether or not the Tax Court, if it disregarded, as we think it should have done, the facts as it found them as to the willingness of the lessee to pay and the unwillingness of the taxpayers to receive a full bonus on execution of the leases, would have determined that the deferred bonus obligations were taxable in the year of the agreements as the equivalent of cash. This question is primarily a fact issue. \* \* \*. There should be a remand to the Tax Court for a reconsideration of the questions submitted in the light of what has been said here.[9]

\* \* \*

## Hornung v. Commissioner[*]

Tax Court of the United States, 1967.
47 T.C. 428.

■ HOYT, JUDGE:

Respondent determined an income tax deficiency against petitioner in the amount of $3,163.76 for the taxable year 1962. Petitioner having conceded an issue relating to a travel expense deduction, the questions remaining for decision are:

(1) Whether the value of a 1962 Corvette automobile which was won by petitioner for his performance in a

---

[6] Cf. Atlantic Coast Line Railroad Company v. Phillips, 332 U.S. 168, 67 S.Ct. 1584; Bullen v. State of Wisconsin, 240 U.S. 625, 36 S.Ct. 473.

[7] United States v. Phellis, 257 U.S. 156, 42 S.Ct. 63; Morsman v. Commissioner of Internal Revenue, 8 Cir., 1937, 90 F.2d 18, 113 A.L.R. 441.

[8] Computed by the Commissioner by discounting the obligations at a 4 per cent rate.

[9] On remand the contractual obligations were held to be the equivalent of cash. Frank Cowden, Sr., 20 T.C.M. 1134 (1961).

[*] The doctrine of constructive receipt is broadly discussed in Finnegan, "Constructive Receipt of Income," 22 N.Y.U.Inst. on Fed.Tax. 367 (1964).

professional football game should be included in his gross income for the taxable year 1962.

* * *

Findings of Fact

The stipulated facts are found accordingly and adopted as our findings.

Petitioner is a cash basis taxpayer residing in Louisville, Ky. For the taxable year 1962, petitioner filed his Federal individual income tax return (Form 1040) with the district director of internal revenue, Louisville, Ky. Petitioner is a well-known professional football player who was employed by the Green Bay Packers in 1962. Prior to becoming a professional, petitioner attended the University of Notre Dame and was an All-American quarterback on the university football team.

*Issue 1. The Corvette*

Sport Magazine is a publication of the McFadden-Bartell Corp., with business offices in New York City. Each year Sport Magazine (hereinafter sometimes referred to as Sport or the magazine) awards a new Corvette automobile to the player selected by its editors (primarily by its editor in chief) as the outstanding player in the National Football League championship game. This award was won by John Unitas of the Baltimore Colts in 1958 and 1959 and by Norm Van Brocklin of the Philadelphia Eagles in 1960. A similar annual award is made to outstanding professional athletes in baseball, hockey, and basketball. The existence of the award is announced several days prior to the sporting event in question, and the selection and announcement of the winner is made immediately following the athletic contest. The Corvette automobiles are generally presented to the recipients at a luncheon or dinner several days subsequent to the sporting event and a photograph of the athlete receiving the car is published in the magazine, together with an article relating to his performance during the particular athletic event. The Corvette awards are intended to promote the sale of Sport Magazine and their cost is deducted by the publisher for Federal income tax purposes as promotion and advertising expense.

The Corvette which is to be awarded to the most valuable player in the National Football League championship game is generally purchased by the magazine several months prior to the date the game is played, and it is held by a New York area Chevrolet dealer until delivered to the recipient of the award. In some years when the game is played in New York the magazine has had the car on display at the stadium on the day of the game.

On December 31, 1961, petitioner played in the National Football League championship game between the Green Bay Packers and the New York Giants. The game was played in Green Bay, Wis. Petitioner scored a total of 19 points during this game and thereby established a new league record. At the end of this game petitioner was selected by the editors of Sport as the most valuable player and winner of the Corvette, and press releases were issued announcing the award. At approximately 4:30 on the afternoon of December 31, 1961, following the game, the editor in chief of Sport informed petitioner that he had been selected as the most valuable player of the game. The editor in chief did not have the key or the title to the Corvette with him in Green Bay and petitioner did not request or demand immediate possession of the car at that time but he accepted the award.

The Corvette which was to be awarded in connection with this 1961 championship game had been purchased by Sport in September of 1961. However, since the game was played in Green Bay, Wis., the car was not on display at the stadium on the day of the game, but was in New York in the hands of a Chevrolet dealership. As far as Sport was concerned the car was "available" to petitioner on December 31, 1961, as soon as the award was announced. However, December 31, 1961, was a Sunday and the New York dealership at which the car was located was closed. Although the National Football League championship game is always played on a Sunday, Sport is prepared to make prior arrangements to have the car available in New York for the recipient of the award on that Sunday afternoon if the circumstances appear to warrant such arrangements—particularly if the game is played in New York. Such arrangements were not made in 1961 because the game was played in Green Bay, and, in the words of Sport's editor in chief, "it seemed a hundred-to-one that * * * [the recipient of the award] would want to come in [to New York] on New Year's Eve to take possession" of the prize.

On December 31, 1961, when petitioner was informed that he had won the Corvette, he was also informed that a luncheon was to be held for him in New York City on the following Wednesday by the publisher of Sport, at which luncheon his award would be presented. At that time petitioner consented to attend the luncheon in order to receive the Corvette. There was no discussion that he would obtain the car prior to the presentation ceremony previously announced. The lunch was held as scheduled on Wednesday, January 3, 1962, in a New York restaurant. Petitioner attended and was photographed during the course of the presentation of the automobile to him. A photograph of petitioner sitting in the car outside of the restaurant was published in the April 1962 issue of Sport, together with an article regarding his achievements in the championship game and the Corvette prize award. Petitioner was not required to attend the lunch or to pose for photographs or perform any other service for Sport as a condition or as consideration for his receipt of the car.

The fair market value of the Corvette automobile received by petitioner was $3,331.04. Petitioner reported the sale of the Corvette in his 1962 Federal income tax return in Schedule D attached thereto as a * * * gain as follows:

| Kind of Property | Date Acquired | Date Sold | Gross Sales Price | Depreciation Allowed | Cost | Gain |
|---|---|---|---|---|---|---|
| 1962 Corvette gift— Sport Magazine | 1962 | 1962 | 3,331.04 | 0.00 | 0.00 | None |

\* \* \*

Petitioner did not include the fair market value of this car in his gross income for 1962, or for any other year. McFadden-Bartell Corporation deducted its cost as a promotion and advertising expense.

\* \* \*

Opinion

## Issue 1. The Corvette

Petitioner alleged in his petition that the Corvette was received by him as a gift in 1962. However, at trial and on brief, he argues that the car was constructively received in 1961, prior to the taxable year for which the deficiency is being assessed. If this contention is upheld, the question of whether the car constituted a reportable item of gross income need not be considered. This argument is based upon the assertion that the announcement and acceptance of the award occurred at approximately 4:30 on the afternoon of December 31, 1961, following the game.

It is undisputed that petitioner was selected as the most valuable player of the National Football League championship game in Green Bay on December 31, 1961. It is also undisputed that petitioner actually received the car on January 3, 1962, in New York. Petitioner relies upon the statement at the trial by the editor in chief of Sport that as far as Sport was concerned the car was "available" to petitioner on December 31, 1961, as soon as the award was announced. It is therefore contended that the petitioner should be deemed to have received the value of the award in 1961 under the doctrine of constructive receipt.

The amount of any item of gross income is included in gross income for the taxable year in which received by the taxpayer unless such amount is properly accounted for as of a different period. Sec. 451(a).[3] It is further provided in section 446(c) that the cash receipts method, which the petitioner utilized, is a permissible method of computing taxable income. The doctrine of constructive receipt is developed by regulations under section 446(c) which provides as follows:[4]

> Generally, under the cash receipts and disbursements method
> \* \* \* all items which constitute gross income (whether in the

---

[3] All section references are to the Internal Revenue Code of 1954 unless otherwise indicated.

[4] Sec. 1.446–1(c)(1)(i), Income Tax Regs.

form of cash, property, or services) are to be included for the taxable year in which actually or constructively received. * * *

The regulations under section 451 elaborate on the meaning of constructive receipt.[5]

> Income although not actually reduced to a taxpayer's possession is constructively received by him in the taxable year during which it is credited to his account, set apart for him, or otherwise made available so that he may draw upon it at any time, or so that he could have drawn upon it during the taxable year if notice of intention to withdraw had been given. However, income is not constructively received if the taxpayer's control of its receipt is subject to substantial limitations or restrictions. * * *

The probable purpose for development of the doctrine of constructive receipt was stated as follows in Ross v. Commissioner, 169 F.2d 483, 491 (C.A.1, 1948):

> The doctrine of constructive receipt was, no doubt, conceived by the Treasury in order to prevent a taxpayer from choosing the year in which to return income merely by choosing the year in which to reduce it to possession. Thereby the Treasury may subject income to taxation when the only thing preventing its reduction to possession is the volition of the taxpayer. * * *

However, it was held in the *Ross* case, at page 496, that the doctrine of constructive receipt could be asserted by a taxpayer as a defense to a deficiency assessment even though the item in controversy had not been reported for the taxable year of the alleged constructive receipt:

> if these items were constructively received when earned they cannot be treated as income in any later year, * * * and, in the absence of misstatement of fact, intentional or otherwise, the petitioner cannot be estopped from asserting that the items were taxable only in the years in which constructively received.

The basis of constructive receipt is essentially unfettered control by the recipient over the date of actual receipt. Petitioner has failed to convince us that he possessed such control on December 31, 1961, over the receipt of the Corvette. The evidence establishes that the Corvette which was presented to petitioner on January 3, 1962, was in the possession of a Chevrolet dealer in New York City on December 31, 1961. At the time the award was announced in Green Bay, the editor in chief of Sport had neither the title nor keys to the car, and nothing was given or presented to petitioner to evidence his ownership or right to possession of the car at that time.

---

[5]   Sec. 1.451–2(a), Income Tax Regs.

Moreover, since December 31, 1961, was a Sunday, it is doubtful whether the car could have been transferred to petitioner before Monday even with the cooperation of the editor in chief of Sport. The New York dealership at which the car was located was closed. The car had not been set aside for petitioner's use and delivery was not dependent solely upon the volition of petitioner. The doctrine of constructive receipt is therefore inapplicable, and we hold that petitioner received the Corvette for income tax purposes in 1962 as he originally alleged in his petition and as he reported in his 1962 income tax return.

\* \* \*

[The Court held that the car was not received as a gift but was a prize or award specifically required to be included in ordinary income at its fair market value in 1962 under Section 74. The subsequent sale of the car was a separate transaction. Ed.]

## 2.  DISBURSEMENTS*

Internal Revenue Code: Section 461(a) and (g).

Regulations: Sections 1.263(a)–4(d)(3), (f)(1); 1.461–1(a)(1).

---

### Revenue Ruling 54–465

1954–2 Cum.Bull. 93.

A charitable contribution in the form of a check is deductible, in the manner and to the extent provided by section 23(*o*) and (q) of the Internal Revenue Code of 1939 [See I.R.C. (1986) Section 170(a). Ed.], in the taxable year in which the check is delivered provided the check is honored and paid and there are no restrictions as to time and manner of payment thereof. See Estate of Modie J. Spiegel v. Commissioner, 12 T.C. 524, acquiescence, C.B. 1949–2, 3.

### NOTE

Over the years we have moved from a cash-paying society to a check-paying society to a credit card society. In the first transition the tax law kept pace by treating payment by check essentially the same as payment in cash.[1] From the standpoint of a cash method taxpayer, one has paid a deductible expense when one hands over a check. In fact payment is effected when one places a check in the mail;[2] but of course this is qualified by the requirement that the check is honored and paid in due course when presented to the drawee bank.[3] If a purist can detect a departure from strict cash method

---

*    See Irwin, "Prepayments by a Cash Basis Taxpayer," 15 U.S.C. Tax Inst. 547 (1963).

1    Witt's Estate v. Fahs, 160 F.Supp. 521 (S.D.Fla.1956).

2    Id. and cf. Reg. § 1.170–1(b).

3    Cf. Reg. § 301.6311–1(a)(1). See Brooks Griffin, 49 T.C. 253 (1967).

doctrine here (recall for example that payment on a check may be stopped and its issuance does not constitute an irrevocable assignment of the drawer's funds), nevertheless the tax result comports with the way we all view things. We have "paid" the monthly bills when we mail out the checks. And it would be untidy to have to determine when a check was presented for payment.

Have we "paid" a bill when we sign a credit card chit? A doctrinal obstacle to an affirmative answer might seem to be that the card holder parts with no cash at that time. Nevertheless, the card holder has "paid" the obligation to the principal creditor whose recourse thereafter is against the credit card company. At the same time the card holder has incurred an obligation to the credit card company in accordance with the card holder's agreement with it. Should it not be viewed as if the card holder had borrowed money and used it to pay the obligation, which would of course support an instant deduction?[4] For purposes of determining when federal taxes are "paid," the Treasury has given qualified acceptance to this view.[5] On the other hand, the Treasury at one time took the position in Rev.Rul. 71–216[6] that for purposes of the charitable deduction under Section 170, "payment" does not occur when a contribution is made with the use of a credit card until the contributor pays the credit card company, even if the charity is in receipt of the funds at an earlier time.

The use of a credit card is not analogous to borrowing money at the bank and receiving less than the amount of the loan, the difference representing interest. Such interest is not considered paid at that time.[7] But the use of a credit card presents a three party deal, and the obligation that is discharged is an obligation to a third party, not to the one who advances the money.

Of course in this respect it is necessary to look at the exact nature of the credit arrangement. If a department store issues a credit card for use in purchases only at the store, no payment occurs until the store's bill is paid. This is a two-party deal. Whether a charge on a credit card issued by an oil company falls into the two-party or three-party area depends upon whether the obligation runs to the company or to an independent dealer, the gas station from which merchandise was purchased. Indeed, it is not safe to try to generalize here, as credit card arrangements are largely a matter of contract, which suggests possible wide variations in the relationships of the parties, and the legal consequences of the use of credit cards are not fully settled.[8]

---

[4]    William J. Granan v. Commissioner, 55 T.C. 753 (1971).

[5]    I.R.S. News Release No. 1005 (Jan. 16, 1970) indicated that " * * * if a check or other document issued by a bank or credit card company used by a taxpayer in payment of taxes is acceptable by the Federal Reserve District concerned as a negotiable instrument for banking purposes, it will be accepted [as payment] by the I.R.S."

[6]    1971–1 C.B. 96.

[7]    Cathcart v. Commissioner, 36 T.C.M. 1321 (1977), infra at page 613.

[8]    The non-tax aspects of credit card transactions are thoughtfully examined in Nordstrom, Law of Sales, pp. 353–360 (West Hornbook Series 1970); see also South, "Credit Cards: a Primer," 23 Business Lawyer 327 (1968). As to the potential for different tax consequences between the use of two party vs. three party credit cards, see Londey, "Payments of Expenses by Credit Card: A Current Deduction for the Cash-Method Taxpayer?" 62 Taxes 239 (1984).

If the use of a credit card did not produce an instant deduction, what would be the alternatives? It might be said that payment occurs only when the credit card company pays the taxpayer's bill. But this is so impractical a view as to require rejection. The taxpayer will seldom know when the chits are presented for payment. It is also irrelevant, if we view the matter as involving a three-party deal in which the taxpayer's obligation to a supplier is discharged when the taxpayer signs the chit. The credit card company does not pay as one's agent.

Nor would it be proper to say that the taxpayer has paid only when the taxpayer pays the credit card company's bill. The taxpayer is certainly not then paying the supplier, but, instead, is repaying a loan made by the credit card company, which is not the obligation for which a deduction may be claimed. Moreover, if we accept the settled treatment of checks as payment, we seem to have an *a fortiori* argument here. After the check-maker hands over the check, the maker can still stop payment on it; it is not so clear that the credit card user is in a position to recall the "payment" to a supplier.[9]

Finally, the instant deduction approach to credit card transactions again comports with the way our society views these transactions. We think of the *airline* as paid when they have accepted the credit card, even though we know we will be hearing from the *credit card company* at the end of the month. And so it seems the tax law *should* follow our move to a credit card society. Good theory and, even more important, practical considerations require it. In fact, since an earlier edition of this book expressed the above positions[10] the Service came around on this issue.[11] In Rev.Rul. 78–38[12] the Service gave "further study" to its prior position in Rev.Rul. 71–216[13] and did an about face, reversing its prior Ruling, stating:[14]

> Since the cardholder's use of the credit card creates the cardholder's own debt to a third party, the use of a bank credit card to make a charitable contribution is equivalent to the use of borrowed funds to make a contribution.

> The general rule is that when a deductible payment is made with borrowed money, the deduction is not postponed until the year in which the borrowed money is repaid. Such expenses must be deducted in the year they are paid and not when the loans are repaid. Granan v. Commissioner, 55 T.C. 753 (1971).

> Accordingly, the taxpayer discussed in Rev.Rul. 71–216, who made a contribution to a qualified charity by a charge to the taxpayer's bank credit card, is entitled to a charitable contribution deduction

---

9  See Londey, "Payments of Expenses by Credit Card: A Current Deduction for the Cash-Method Taxpayer?" note 8, supra; Brandel and Leonard, "Bank Charge Cards: New Cash or New Credit," 69 Mich.L.Rev. 1033 (1971).

10  See Freeland and Stephens, Fundamentals of Federal Income Taxation 519–521 (Foundation Press 1972).

11  Olson, "Bank Credit Cards and the Timing of Deductions Under Revenue Ruling 78–38: A Return to Consistency" 35 Wash. and Lee L.Rev. 1089 (1978).

12  1978–1 C.B. 68.

13  See note 6, supra.

14  Supra note 12.

under section 170(a) of the Code in the year the charge was made. * * *.

In a companion ruling[15] the Service uses the same rationale to conclude that the use of a bank credit card to pay a Section 213 medical expense constitutes payment of the medical expense in the year the credit card charge is made regardless of when the bank is paid.

## Vander Poel, Francis & Co., Inc. v. Commissioner
Tax Court of the United States, 1947.
8 T.C. 407.

■ BLACK, JUDGE:

* * *

Opinion

[This case involved the question whether a doctrine of "constructive payment" parallels the established doctrine of "constructive receipt." Some excerpts from the opinion will be informative. Ed.]

* * *

There is but one issue involved in this proceeding, and that is whether petitioner, a corporation which kept its books and made its income tax returns on the cash basis, is entitled to deduct the full amount of the salaries regularly and duly voted to its two officers, Vander Poel and Francis, and unconditionally credited to their respective accounts, notwithstanding it did not actually pay the full amount of these salaries in cash or other property during 1942.

* * *

They properly returned these salaries for taxation on their 1942 returns under the doctrine of "constructive receipt." * * * [T]he weight of authority as we interpret the authorities is against the doctrine that "constructive payment" is a necessary corollary of "constructive receipt." Mertens, in his Law of Federal Income Taxation, vol. 2, § 10.18, says:

> Constructive Payments as Deductions. Under the doctrine of constructive receipt a taxpayer on the cash basis is taxed upon income which he has not as yet actually received. Logically it would seem that where the payee is held to have constructively received an item as income, the payor should be entitled to deduct the same item as constructively paid, but the statute rather than logic is the controlling force in tax cases and so it is not surprising to find such reasoning often rejected. The difference is that the statute is presumed to reach and tax all income, and the doctrine of constructive receipt is an aid to that end. It must be remembered that the doctrine of constructive

---

[15]   Rev.Rul. 78–39, 1978–1 C.B. 73.

receipt is designed to effect a realistic concept of realization of income and to prevent abuses. Deductions, on the other hand, are a matter of legislative grace, and the terms of the statute permitting the particular deduction must be fully met without the aid of assumptions. "What may be income to the one may not be a deductible payment by the other." A review of the cases indicates that the courts will seldom support a doctrine of constructive payment in the sense in which it is used in this chapter, i.e., to determine when an item has been paid rather than who has paid it.

\* \* \*. If in any of our decisions, memorandum opinions or otherwise, we have said anything to the contrary of the above holdings, we think it is against the weight of authority and should not be followed. Therefore, following Martinus & Sons v. Commissioner[1] and other cases above cited, we sustain the Commissioner. See also our recent decision in Claude Patterson Noble,[2] in which among other things, we said:

> \* \* \*. No payment was made in 1942 by petitioner to her husband for his services; but the payment for services rendered in that year was made in 1943. Likewise the payment for 1943 services was not made until February 1944. It is argued that the custom was that petitioner's husband prepare all checks for her signature and that had he seen fit to do so, he could have received payment of the full amount of the salary at the close of each year for which the service was rendered. Thus it is said to follow that petitioner constructively paid and her husband constructively received payment of the salary for 1942 and 1943 at the close of each of those years. The fact remains, however, these checks were not prepared, signed, or delivered until after the close of those respective years. Accordingly there was no such payment or receipt in either case until after the close of the year. \* \* \*.

## Commissioner v. Boylston Market Ass'n

United States Court of Appeals, First Circuit, 1942.
131 F.2d 966.

■ MAHONEY, CIRCUIT JUDGE.

The Board of Tax Appeals reversed a determination by the Commissioner of Internal Revenue of deficiencies in the Boylston Market Association's income tax of $835.34 for the year 1936, and $431.84 for the year 1938, and the Commissioner has appealed.

The taxpayer in the course of its business, which is the management of real estate owned by it, purchased from time to time fire and other

---

1    116 F.2d 732, affirming B.T.A. memorandum opinion.
2    7 T.C. 960.

insurance policies covering periods of three or more years. It keeps its books and makes its returns on a cash receipts and disbursements basis. The taxpayer has since 1915 deducted each year as insurance expenses the amount of insurance premiums applicable to carrying insurance for that year regardless of the year in which the premium was actually paid. This method was required by the Treasury Department prior to 1938 by G.C.M. 13148, XIII–1 Cum.Bull. 67 (1934). Prior to January 1, 1936, the taxpayer had prepaid insurance premiums in the amount of $6,690.75 and during that year it paid premiums in an amount of $1082.77. The amount of insurance premiums prorated by the taxpayer in 1936 was $4421.76. Prior to January 1, 1938, it had prepaid insurance premiums in the amount of $6148.42 and during that year paid premiums in the amount of $890.47. The taxpayer took a deduction of $3284.25, which was the amount prorated for the year 1938. The Commissioner in his notice of deficiency for the year 1936 allowed only $1082.77 and for the year 1938 only $890.47, being the amounts actually paid in those years, on the basis that deductions for insurance expense of a taxpayer on the cash receipts and disbursements basis is limited to premiums paid during the taxable year.

We are asked to determine whether a taxpayer who keeps his books and files his returns on a cash basis is limited to the deduction of the insurance premiums actually paid in any year or whether he should deduct for each tax year the pro rata portion of the prepaid insurance applicable to that year. The pertinent provisions of the statute are Sections 23 and 43 of the Revenue Act of 1936,* 49 Stat. 1648, 26 U.S.C.A.Int.Rev.Acts, pages 813, 827, 839.

This court in Welch v. De Blois, 1 Cir., 1938, 94 F.2d 842, held that a taxpayer on the cash receipts and disbursements basis who made prepayments of insurance premiums was entitled to take a full deduction for these payments as ordinary and necessary business expenses in the year in which payment was made despite the fact that the insurance covered a three-year period. The government on the basis of that decision changed its earlier G.C.M. rule, supra, which had required the taxpayer to prorate prepaid insurance premiums. The Board of Tax Appeals has refused to follow that case in George S. Jephson v. Comm'r, 37 B.T.A. 1117; Frank Real Estate & Investment Co., 40 B.T.A. 1382, unreported memorandum decision Nov. 15, 1939, and in the instant case. The arguments in that case in favor of treating prepaid insurance as an ordinary and necessary business expense are persuasive. We are, nevertheless, unable to find a real basis for distinguishing between prepayment of rentals, * * * ; bonuses for the acquisition of leases, * * * ; bonuses for the cancellation of leases, * * * ; commissions for negotiating leases, * * * , and prepaid insurance. Some distinctions may be drawn in the cases cited on the basis of the facts contained therein, but we are of

---

* § 23, not materially different from I.R.C. (1986) § 162(a), and § 43, similar to I.R.C. (1986) § 461(a), are omitted. Ed.

the opinion that there is no justification for treating them differently insofar as deductions are concerned. All of the cases cited are readily distinguishable from such a clear cut case as a permanent improvement to a building. This latter is clearly a capital expenditure. See Parkersburg Iron & Steel Co. v. Burnet, 4 Cir., 1931, 48 F.2d 163, 165. In such a case there is the creation of a capital asset which has a life extending beyond the taxable year and which depreciates over a period of years. The taxpayer regardless of his method of accounting can only take deductions for depreciation over the life of the asset. Advance rentals, payments of bonuses for acquisition and cancellation of leases, and commissions for negotiating leases are all matters which the taxpayer amortizes over the life of the lease. Whether we consider these payments to be the cost of the exhaustible asset, as in the case of advance rentals, or the cost of acquiring the asset, as in the case of bonuses, the payments are prorated primarily because the life of the asset extends beyond the taxable year. To permit the taxpayer to take a full deduction in the year of payment would distort his income. Prepaid insurance presents the same problem and should be solved in the same way. Prepaid insurance for a period of three years may be easily allocated. It is protection for the entire period and the taxpayer may, if he desires, at any time surrender the insurance policy. It thus is clearly an asset having a longer life than a single taxable year. The line to be drawn between capital expenditures and ordinary and necessary business expenses is not always an easy one, but we are satisfied that in treating prepaid insurance as a capital expense we are obtaining some degree of consistency in these matters. We are, therefore, of the opinion that Welch v. De Blois, supra, is incorrect and should be overruled.

The decision of Board of Tax Appeals is affirmed.

## NOTE

As indicated by the *Boylston Market Ass'n* case and as later set forth in the regulations,[1] an expenditure by a cash method taxpayer which results in the creation of an asset that has a useful life extending "substantially beyond" the close of the taxable year may not be fully deducted in the year payment is made. Instead, the expenditure must be capitalized and deductions may be taken only ratably over the asset's useful life. In determining whether an asset has a useful life extending "substantially beyond" the close of the taxable year, the court in Zaninovich v. Commissioner[2] adopted a "one-year" rule. Under this rule, prepaid expenses (other than those governed by a specific statute) may be deducted in the year they are paid, even though they span a period that touches two taxable years, as long as the expenses do not relate to a period greater than one year.

---

[1]   Reg. § 1.461–1(a)(1).
[2]   616 F.2d 429 (9th Cir.1980).

The regulations on capitalization of amounts to acquire, create, or enhance intangible assets[3] address the proper tax treatment of prepaid items. Those regulations generally require a cash method taxpayer to capitalize prepayments for benefits to be received in the future.[4] Thus, if a cash method taxpayer prepays $240,000 as rent on a 24-month lease of office space, the prepayment must be capitalized.[5] The regulations also contain a 12-month "safe harbor" under which a taxpayer is not required to capitalize amounts paid to create or enhance an intangible asset if the amounts do not create or enhance any right or benefit for the taxpayer that extends beyond the *earlier* of: (1) 12 months after the first date on which the taxpayer realizes the right or benefit, or (2) the end of the taxable year following the taxable year in which the payment is made.[6] To illustrate this rule, assume a taxpayer pays $10,000 on December 1 of year one to obtain a property insurance policy for the taxpayer's business. The policy has a one-year term that begins on December 15 of year one. In that case, the 12-month safe harbor would permit the taxpayer to deduct the prepayment in year one because the benefit of the insurance contract does not extend more than 12 months beyond December 15 of year one, nor beyond the end of the year following the year the payment is made (year two).[7] But if the term of the one-year insurance policy had begun on February 1 of year two, the payment on December 1 of year one would have had to be capitalized in year one because the benefit of the payment would extend into year three and beyond the end of the year following the year of the payment.[8]

In some situations deductibility of expenses by cash method taxpayers is specifically provided for by statute.[9] For example, Section 461(g) requires cash method taxpayers to allocate deductions for prepaid interest to the periods to which they relate and to do so by way of capitalization and amortization.[10] The statute makes an exception for "points", a loan processing fee paid at the inception of a loan, which is treated as a current payment of interest.[11] However, the exception is limited to amounts customarily charged in connection with indebtedness incurred to purchase

---

[3]   See page 325, supra.

[4]   Reg. § 1.263(a)–4(d)(3).

[5]   Reg. § 1.263(a)–4(d)(3)(ii) Example 2.

[6]   Reg. § 1.263(a)–4(f)(1)(i). In the case of a payment to terminate a contract or other agreement prior to its expiration date, the term of the benefit created is equal to the unexpired term of the agreement. Reg. § 1.263(a)–4(f)(2).

[7]   Reg. § 1.263(a)–4(f)(8) Example 2.

[8]   Reg. § 1.263(a)–4(f)(8) Example 1. The 12-month safe harbor does not apply to amounts paid to create or enhance various financial instruments. Reg. § 1.263(a)–4(f)(3).

[9]   See I.R.C. § 461(g).

[10]   There were conflicting results prior to the enactment of I.R.C. § 461(g). See, e.g., John D. Fackler v. Commissioner, 39 B.T.A. 395 (1939), nonacq., 1968–2 C.B. 3, allowing the deduction for prepaid interest, Burck v. Commissioner, 533 F.2d 768 (2d Cir.1976), contra, and Rev.Rul. 68–643, 1968–2 C.B. 76, generally limiting the deduction to interest for twelve months beyond the year of payment.

[11]   I.R.C. § 461(g)(2). See Rev.Rul. 69–188, 1969–1 C.B. 54, at page 470, supra. Cf. the *Cathcart* case which follows this note and involves withheld points.

or improve a principal residence.[12] Thus, a taxpayer cannot easily manipulate these payments in such a way as to distort the taxpayer's income for a period.

Question may be raised whether Congress has gone far enough in Section 461(g). There is some possibility of distortion by way of deferring the payment of interest to a convenient later date when the corresponding tax deduction may be more beneficial. No statutory or common law rule forecloses this practice. However such deferrals may be substantially restricted in a self-policing manner by impatient creditors.

### Cathcart v. Commissioner[*]

Tax Court of the United States, 1977.
36 T.C.M. 1321.

■ WILES, JUDGE:

\* \* \*

Opinion

The only issue we must resolve is whether petitioners are entitled to deduct points withheld from mortgage proceeds in the year petitioners obtained their mortgage.

On January 15, 1973, petitioners obtained a net proceeds mortgage loan from Southern Federal. The face amount of the mortgage was $57,600, bearing a 7 percent interest rate and having a duration of 29 years. As is common practice in net proceeds, mortgage loans, the amount ultimately disbursed to petitioners, $55,039.92, was less than the face amount of the mortgage. The difference withheld by Southern Federal, $2,560.08, was used to pay various services and to pay points totalling $1,086.60. Although points frequently represent a hidden service charge, in the case before us the parties agree that the points represent an interest charge. As such, their deductibility is governed by section 163.

Petitioners contend the entire $1,086.60 charged for points is fully deductible in 1973. In contrast, respondent contends the amount charged for points was not fully paid by petitioners in 1973, but rather payment is included in petitioners' monthly mortgage payments over the 29-year term. As such, respondent contends petitioners must prorate the points over the life of the loan. This method of prorating the charge over the life of the loan would entitle petitioners to an interest deduction of $34.34 for 1973.

Section 163(a) provides that "There shall be allowed as a deduction all interest paid or accrued within the taxable year on indebtedness." Despite the language of section 163(a), cash method taxpayers may not

---

[12] Id. See Chapter 11A, supra. See Tierney, "Pointing the Way Through Section 461(g): The Deductibility of Points Paid in Connection with the Acquisition or Improvement of a Principal Residence," 71 Neb.L.Rev. 1095 (1992).

[*]    Footnotes omitted.

take interest expense deductions for prepaid interest if such deductions materially distort their income. * * *.

The Internal Revenue Service, and subsequently Congress, recognized an administrative exception to the material distortion of income argument when dealing with taxpayers who prepay interest or points on a home mortgage. See Rev.Rul. 69–582, 1969–2 C.B. 29; § 461(g)(2), added by § 208(a), Tax Reform Act of 1976, 90 Stat. 1541. Consequently, cash method taxpayers who prepay points on their home mortgages with funds not obtained from the lender are entitled to deduct the entire amount in the year paid. This rule, however, does not settle the case before us.

Although we have cash method taxpayers who obtained a mortgage loan secured by their personal residence, the points required in order to obtain the loan were *withheld* from the mortgage proceeds. Because the points were withheld from the loan proceeds, rather than *paid* by petitioners to Southern Federal, we conclude petitioners are not entitled to deduct the entire $1,086.60 in 1973. Our decision in this matter is controlled by Rubnitz v. Commissioner, 67 T.C. 621 (1977).

In *Rubnitz,* taxpayer owned an interest in Branham Associates (hereinafter Branham). In order to construct an apartment complex Branham, in 1970, obtained a $1,650,000 construction loan from a savings and loan association. Withheld from the proceeds of this loan was a "loan fee" of $57,750, which the parties agreed constituted interest under section 163(a). We concluded that the deduction or withholding of the loan fee from the loan proceeds did not constitute a "payment" of interest within the meaning of section 163(a), and therefore Branham was not entitled to deduct the full $57,750 as interest paid in 1970. Consequently, taxpayer was not entitled to the entire interest deduction he had claimed. In reaching this conclusion, we noted, at 628, Branham received $1,592,220 from the bank but it promised to repay $1,650,000 plus interest at a specified rate. Of the difference between these figures, $57,750 might well have represented additional interest charges. However, it is plain that Branham did not pay that interest in 1970. Instead, by signing a promissory note, it specifically chose to postpone paying that amount until sometime in the future. The entire $57,780 was to be paid ratably by the borrower over the life of the loan as one component of the monthly installments * * * which would ultimately result in the payment of the full $1,650,000. Therefore, Branham may not deduct the $57,750 as "interest paid" during 1970.

Similarly, we conclude that petitioners are not entitled to deduct their points, totalling $1,086.60, as "interest paid" during 1973. Rather, petitioners may only deduct $34.34, that pro rata portion of the points attributable to 1973.

To reflect the foregoing,

Decision will be entered under Rule 155.

# Revenue Ruling 87–22

1987–1 Cum.Bull. 146.

## ISSUE

(1)  If a taxpayer pays points on the refinancing of a mortgage loan secured by the principal residence of the taxpayer, is the payment deductible in full, under section 461(g)(2) of the Internal Revenue Code, for the taxable year in which the points are paid?

(2)  If the taxpayer described above uses part of the proceeds from the refinancing to improve the taxpayer's principal residence, may the taxpayer deduct any portion of the points for the taxable year paid?

## FACTS

\* \* \*

*Situation 2.* In 1981, *B* obtained a 16-percent mortgage loan (old mortgage loan) exclusively for the purchase of a principal residence. On August 20, 1986, *B* refinanced the old mortgage loan, which had an outstanding principal balance of $80,000, with a $100,000, 30-year, 10-percent mortgage loan (new mortgage loan) from *L*. The new mortgage loan was used to pay off the $80,000 balance on the old mortgage loan and to pay for improvements on *B*'s principal residence that cost $20,000. The new loan was secured by a mortgage on *B*'s principal residence. Principal and interest payments were due monthly, with the first payment due October 1, 1986, and the last payment due September 1, 2016. In order to refinance, *B* paid 3.6 points ($3,600) to *L* at the loan closing. This points charge was paid from separate funds of *B* that were brought to the loan closing.

\* \* \* [T]he amount paid as points was paid for the use or forbearance of money and was in addition to a charge for certain services that was levied by *L* as part of a loan origination fee. The interest paid on the new mortgage loans, including the amount paid as points, is "qualified residence interest" (within the meaning of section 163(h)(3) of the Code). The payment of points was an established practice in the area where the indebtedness was incurred and did not exceed the amount generally charged in that area \* \* \*. *B*'s income [is] computed under the cash receipts and disbursements method of accounting.

## LAW AND ANALYSIS

Section 163(a) of the Code generally allows a deduction for all interest paid or accrued within the taxable year on indebtedness. Section 163(h) provides that in the case of a taxpayer other than a corporation, no deduction shall be allowed for personal interest paid or accrued during the taxable year. Personal interest does not include any "qualified residence interest" (within the meaning of section 163(h)(3)). Thus, "qualified residence interest" is fully deductible under section 163. To determine when the interest is deductible, section 163 must be read in conjunction with section 461. *Zidanic v. Commissioner,* 79 T.C. 651, 653

(1982); *Schubel v. Commissioner,* 77 T.C. 701, 702 (1981); *Baird v. Commissioner,* 68 T.C. 115, 130 (1977).

Section 461(g)(1) of the Code provides that, in general, if the taxable income of the taxpayer is computed under the cash receipts and disbursements method of accounting, interest paid by the taxpayer that is properly allocable to any period (A) with respect to which the interest represents a charge for the use or forbearance of money, and (B) which is after the close of the taxable year in which paid, shall be charged to capital account and shall be treated as paid in the period to which so allocable. Thus, such a taxpayer may not take a deduction for interest paid earlier than the taxable year in which (and to the extent that) the interest represents a charge for the use or forbearance of money.

Congress intended that section 461(g)(1) of the Code would require a taxpayer using the cash receipts and disbursements method to deduct interest prepayments in the same manner as a taxpayer using the accrual method. *See* H.R.Rep. No. 94–658, 94th Cong., 1st Sess. 100 (1975), 1976–3 (Vol. 2) C.B. 695, 792.

An exception to the general rule of section 461(g)(1) of the Code is set forth in section 461(g)(2). Section 461(g)(2) provides that section 461(g)(1) shall not apply to points paid in respect of any indebtedness incurred in connection with the purchase or improvement of, and secured by, the principal residence of the taxpayer to the extent that such payment of points is an established business practice in the area in which such indebtedness is incurred and the amount of such payment does not exceed the amount generally charged in such area. Therefore, unlike the rule applicable to other instances of prepaid interest, if the requirements of section 461(g)(2) of the Code are satisfied, the taxpayer is not limited to deducting the points over the period of the indebtedness. *Schubel v. Commissioner,* 77 T.C. at 703–04.

\* \* \*

In *Situation 2,* $80,000 (80 percent) of the new mortgage loan proceeds were used to repay an existing indebtedness (old mortgage loan balance of $80,000). Although this amount was incurred in connection with *B*'s continued ownership of *B*'s principal residence, it was not incurred in connection with the purchase or improvement of that residence. Accordingly, 80 percent of the points paid by *B* with respect to *B*'s new mortgage loan does not meet the requirements of section 461(g)(2) of the Code. On the other hand, $20,000 (20 percent) of the new mortgage loan was incurred in connection with the improvement of *B*'s principal residence, and therefore $720 (20 percent) of the points paid by *B* meets the requirements of section 461(g)(2).

Rev.Proc. 87–15, page 624, this Bulletin, describes an acceptable method for determining the proper deduction with respect to points each taxable year in a situation like these here, where section 461(g) of the

Code requires all or a part of the points to be deducted over the period of the indebtedness.

It is important to note that in *Situation 2* the points charge was paid from separate funds of *B* that were brought to the loan closing. If the points had not been paid from separate funds of *B* that were brought to the loan closing, the points would not have been paid at the time of the closing, and it would be irrelevant whether the indebtedness was incurred in connection with the purchase or improvement of *B*'s principal residence. See *Schubel,* which holds that points withheld by a lender from a loan amount may not be deducted by a borrower in the year the points were withheld, because the withholding did not constitute payment within the taxable year. [See also Cathcart v. Commissioner, supra. Ed.] See also Rev.Proc. 87–15, which describes an acceptable method for determining the proper deduction each taxable year in a situation where points are withheld from the loan proceeds.

HOLDING

\* \* \*

(2)  In *Situation 2,* 80 percent of the points (2,880) paid by *B* with respect to *B*'s new mortgage loan does not meet the requirements of section 461(g)(2) of the Code. Accordingly, *B* must deduct the $2,880 over the period of the new mortgage loan. On the other hand, $720 (20 percent) of the points was paid in respect of an indebtedness that was incurred in connection with the improvement of *B*'s principal residence. This amount, therefore, meets the requirements of section 461(g)(2). Accordingly, 20 percent ($720) of the points paid by *B* may be deducted for the taxable year paid.

## PROBLEMS

1.   Lender lends out money at a legal interest rate to Debtor. Debtor is required to pay $5,000 interest each year on the loan which extends over a five year period. The interest is deductible by Debtor under § 163. The agreement calls for payment of each year's interest on December 31 of the year. Both parties are calendar year, cash method taxpayers. Discuss the tax consequences to both parties under the following alternatives:

   (a)  Debtor mails a check for $5,000 interest to Lender on December 31, of year one. It is delivered to Lender on January 2 of year two.

   (b)  Debtor mails the check in (a), above, on December 30 of year one. It is delivered to Lender on December 31 of year one but after the banks are closed.

   (c)  Debtor gives Lender a promissory note on December 31 of year one agreeing to pay year one's interest plus $50 on January 30 of year two. Debtor pays off the note on January 30 of year two.

(d)   Debtor offers to pay Lender the $5,000 interest due on December 31 of year one but Lender suggests that Debtor pay it on January 2nd of year two, which Debtor does.

(e)   Debtor pays all five years' interest ($25,000) to Lender in cash on December 31 of year one.

(f)   Same as (e), above, but Debtor does so because Lender makes it a condition of extending Debtor another loan.

(g)   Debtor pays year one's $5,000 of interest in cash on January 2nd of year two and, as agreed, pays year two's interest on December 31 of year two.

**2.**   Lawyer renders services to Client which are deductible to Client under I.R.C. § 162. What result to both Lawyer and Client if both are cash method, calendar year taxpayers in each of the following circumstances:

(a)   Lawyer sends out a bill for $5,000 on December 24 of year one. Client pays the bill on January 5 of year two.

(b)   Lawyer sends out a bill for $5,000 on November 15 of year one. Client immediately pays the bill using her American Express credit card and American Express pays Lawyer the $5,000 on December 15 of year one. Client pays American Express the $5,000 credit card bill on January 15 of year two.

(c)   Prior to rendering the services Lawyer and Client agree that Lawyer will be paid $2,500 in year one and $2,500 in year two. Client pays Lawyer $2,500 of cash on December 24 of year one and $2,500 of cash on January 5 of year two.

(d)   Client calls Lawyer at 4:00 p.m., December 31 of year one, saying she has Lawyer's fee statement, has made out check in full payment and, as she is about to leave for Europe, will leave check with desk clerk at Client's apartment. Lawyer is ill, has no one to send to pick up check, and finally picks it up on January 2 of year two. See Loose v. United States, 74 F.2d 147 (8th Cir.1934).

## C.  THE ACCRUAL METHOD

### 1.  INCOME ITEMS

Internal Revenue Code: Section 451(a)–(c). See Sections 448(d)(5); 455; 456; and 458.

Regulations: Section 1.451–1(a).

---

## Spring City Foundry Co. v. Commissioner

Supreme Court of the United States, 1934.
292 U.S. 182, 54 S.Ct. 644, rehearing denied 292 U.S. 613, 54 S.Ct. 857 (1934).

■ Mr. Chief Justice Hughes delivered the opinion of the Court.

[The taxpayer, petitioner in the Supreme Court, using the calendar year, accrual method of accounting, had sold goods in 1920 on open account. Before the end of the year the purchaser went bankrupt and a receiver was appointed. By the end of the year it was clear the taxpayer would not be paid in full for the goods. The question was how, if at all, the post-sale events affected the taxpayer's taxable income for the year.

In a portion of the opinion not reproduced here, the court upheld the Commissioner's disallowance of any bad debt deduction for the year. As now, under Section 166, the statute provided a bad debt deduction but only for debts that became worthless during the taxable year. There was then no provision for a deduction for *partially* worthless debts as is now provided by Section 166(a)(2), and the purchaser's obligation had not become wholly worthless in 1920. The bad debt deduction is considered in Chapter 23A, infra.

The alternate contention of the taxpayer was that the partial worthlessness of the purchaser's obligations in 1920 affected its *gross* income for that year. This contention was also rejected in the portion of the opinion that follows. Ed.]

\* \* \*

Petitioner first contends that the debt, to the extent that it was ascertained in 1920 to be worthless, was not returnable as gross income in that year, that is, apart from any question of deductions, it was not to be regarded as taxable income at all. We see no merit in this contention. Keeping accounts and making returns on the accrual basis, as distinguished from the cash basis, import that it is the *right* to receive and not the actual receipt that determines the inclusion of the amount in gross income. When the right to receive an amount becomes fixed, the right accrues. When a merchandising concern makes sales, its inventory is reduced and a claim for the purchase price arises. Article 35 of Regulations 45 under the Revenue Act of 1918 provided: "In the case of a manufacturing, merchandising, or mining business 'gross income' means the total sales, less the cost of goods sold, plus any income from investments and from incidental or outside operations or sources."[1]

On an accrual basis, the "total sales," to which the regulation refers, are manifestly the accounts receivable arising from the sales, and these accounts receivable, less the cost of the goods sold, figure in the statement of gross income. If such accounts receivable become uncollectible, in whole or part, the question is one of the deduction which may be taken

---

[1]　This provision has been carried forward in the regulations under the later revenue acts. See Regulations 77, Article 55.

according to the applicable statute. * * *. That is the question here. It is not altered by the fact that the claim of loss relates to an item of gross income which had accrued in the same year.

* * *

## Revenue Ruling 2003–10
### 2003–1 C.B. 288.

ISSUES

(1) Under the all events test of § 451 of the Internal Revenue Code, when does a taxpayer using an accrual method of accounting accrue gross income if the taxpayer ships goods and the customer disputes its liability to the taxpayer because of a clerical mistake in the sales invoice discovered in the next taxable year?

(2) Under the all events test of § 451, when does a taxpayer using an accrual method of accounting accrue gross income if the taxpayer ships the wrong goods and the customer disputes its liability during the taxable year of sale?

(3) Under the all events test of § 451, when does a taxpayer using an accrual method of accounting accrue gross income if the taxpayer ships more items than the customer ordered, the excess quantity is discovered by the customer in the next taxable year, and, in accordance with an agreement with the customer, the taxpayer reduces the quantity that would otherwise have been included in the next shipment?

FACTS

Taxpayer $P$ manufactures products $H$ and $M$ and sells them to retailers for resale. $P$ uses an accrual method of accounting and a calendar taxable year. For federal income tax purposes, $P$ recognizes gross income from sales of products $H$ and $M$ when it ships the product to the retailer.

*Situation 1.* In October 2002, $X$, a retailer, orders 1,000 cases of product $M$ from $P$ at a price of $15 per case. In November 2002, $P$ ships 1,000 cases of $M$ to $X$ and sends $X$ an invoice for the 1,000 cases of $M$. As the result of a data entry mistake, the amount of the invoice is improperly stated as $16,000 rather than $15,000. In January 2003, $X$ notifies $P$ of the erroneous invoice and P acknowledges that it is entitled to receive only $15,000 for the 1,000 cases of $M$. $X$ subsequently pays the $15,000 to P.

*Situation 2.* $Y$ is a retailer that purchases product $M$ from P. In September 2002, $Y$ orders 600 cases of $M$ from $P$ at a price of $15 per case. In October 2002, P ships 600 cases of $H$ to $Y$ and sends $Y$ an invoice for $9,000. In November 2002, $Y$ discovers that $P$ shipped $H$ rather than $M$ and notifies $P$ that it will not pay for the $H$. In January 2003, $P$ and $Y$ settle the dispute by agreeing that $Y$ will pay $P$ $4,500 for the $H$.

*Situation 3. Z* is a retailer that purchases products *H* and *M* from *P*. Each month *P* ships *Z* 300 cases of *H* at a price of $10 per case and 700 cases of *M* at a price of $15 per case. On December 28, 2002, *P* mistakenly ships 400 cases of *H* and 600 cases of *M* to *Z* and sends *Z* an invoice for $13,000. On January 3, 2003, *Z* discovers that *P* shipped the wrong amount of *H* and *M* and notifies *P. Z* asks *P* to correct the situation by adjusting the amount of *H* and *M* it ships to *Z* in January's monthly shipment. On January 28, 2003, *P* ships 200 cases of *H* and 800 cases of *M* to *Z* to adjust for the amount of *H* and *M* mistakenly shipped to *Z* in December 2002. In February 2003, *Z* pays *P* $13,000 for the *H* and *M* it received in December 2002 and in March 2003, *Z* pays *P* $14,000 for the *H* and *M* it received in January 2003.

## LAW AND ANALYSIS

Section 61(a) provides that, except as otherwise provided, gross income means all income from whatever source derived. Section 1.61–3(a) of the Income Tax Regulations provides that in a manufacturing, merchandising, or mining business, "gross income" means the total sales, less the cost of goods sold, plus any income from investments and from incidental or outside operations or sources.

Section 451 provides rules for determining the taxable year of inclusion for items of gross income. Sections 1.446–1(c)(1)(ii)(A) and 1.451–1(a) provide that under an accrual method of accounting, income is includible in gross income when all the events have occurred that fix the right to receive the income and the amount thereof can be determined with reasonable accuracy. All the events that fix the right to receive income occur when (1) the required performance takes place, (2) payment is due, or (3) payment is made, whichever happens first. *Schlude v. Commissioner*, 372 U.S. 128, 133 (1963); Rev. Rul. 84–31, 1984–1 C.B. 127; Rev. Rul. 80–308, 1980–2 C.B. 162.

Section 1.446–1(e)(2)(ii)(b) provides that a change in method of accounting does not include correction of mathematical or posting errors, or errors in the computation of a tax liability.

Section 1.451–1(a) provides that if an amount of income is properly accrued on the basis of a reasonable estimate and the exact amount is subsequently determined, the difference, if any, shall be taken into account for the taxable year in which such determination is made. Additionally, if a taxpayer ascertains that an item was improperly included in gross income in a prior taxable year, the taxpayer should, if within the period of limitation, file a claim for credit or refund of any overpayment of tax arising therefrom. *Gould-Mersereau Co. v. Commissioner*, 21 B.T.A. 1316 (1931) *acq.* 1931–2 C.B. 27. If the right to an amount of income is substantially in controversy the income may not be accrued until the controversy is resolved. *North American Oil Consolidated v. Burnet*, 286 U.S. 417 (1932); *Jamaica Water Co. v. Commissioner*, 125 F.2d 512 (2d Cir. 1942); Rev. Rul. 60–237, 1960–2 C.B. 164.

In *Situation 1*, *P*'s invoice to *X* was for an improper amount as a result of a clerical mistake. P may not accrue $16,000 of gross sales in gross income in 2002 because *P* does not have a fixed right to that amount. Rather, *P* accrues $15,000 of gross sales and includes $15,000, the correct amount, less the corresponding cost of goods sold, in gross income in 2002. Generally, if *P* has already filed its income tax return for 2002 when the mistake is discovered, *P* should, if within the period of limitation, file a claim for refund of any overpayment of tax arising from reporting an improper amount of income on that return. If, however, *P* has regularly and consistently for a period of two or more taxable years treated invoice amounts as a reasonable estimate of accrued income and, if the exact amount is subsequently determined to be different, has taken the difference into account for the taxable year in which the determination is made, *P* should seek consent for a change in method of accounting if it wants to begin taking such differences into account in the year of sale.

In *Situation 2*, the dispute arises in the taxable year of sale. Accordingly, because under § 451 *P* does not have a fixed right to the income *P* may not include any amount from that transaction, including the corresponding cost of goods sold, in gross income in 2002. *P* accrues $4,500 of gross sales and includes $4,500, less the corresponding cost of goods sold, in gross income in 2003, when *P* and *Y* settle their dispute by agreeing that *Y* will pay *P* the amount of $4,500 for the *H*.

In *Situation 3*, *P* mistakenly ships the wrong amount of *H* and *M* to *Z* in December 2002 and sends an invoice for $13,000 to *Z*. However, because *Z* does not dispute the shipment *P* has a fixed right to income relating to the shipment in 2002. Accordingly, *P* accrues $13,000 of gross sales and includes $13,000, less the corresponding cost of goods sold, in gross income in 2002 because the all events test of § 451 is satisfied.

HOLDINGS

(1)  Under the all events test of § 451, if a taxpayer using an accrual method of accounting overbills a customer due to a clerical mistake in an invoice and the customer discovers the error and, in the following taxable year, disputes its liability for the overbilled amount, then the taxpayer accrues gross income in the taxable year of sale for the correct amount.

(2)  Under the all events test of § 451, a taxpayer using an accrual method of accounting does not accrue gross income in the taxable year of sale if, during the taxable year of sale, the customer disputes its liability to the taxpayer because the taxpayer shipped incorrect goods.

(3)  Under the all events test of § 451, a taxpayer using an accrual method of accounting accrues gross income in the taxable year of sale if the taxpayer ships excess quantities of goods and the customer agrees to pay for the excess quantities of goods.

## NOTE

Revenue Procedure 2003–10 provides that all events that fix the right to receive income occur when (1) the required performance takes place, (2) payment is due, or (3) payment is made, whichever happens first. In the 2017 Tax Cuts and Jobs Act[1] Congress added an additional "event" which may accelerate the accrual of income. Under Section 451(b), the all events test is treated as met when an item of gross income (or portion thereof) is taken into account by an accrual method taxpayer in an "applicable financial statement."[2] Thus, an accrual method taxpayer generally may not report an income item in financial statements and defer inclusion of the item for tax purposes.[3] The definition of an applicable financial statement generally is limited to statements prepared in accordance with specific reporting standards that are used in governmental filings or for business purposes like seeking credit or reporting to owners.[4] If a taxpayer does not have an applicable financial statement, the all events test as set out in Revenue Procedure 2003–10 applies.[5]

## North American Oil Consolidated v. Burnet

Supreme Court of the United States, 1932.
286 U.S. 417, 52 S.Ct. 613.

■ MR. JUSTICE BRANDEIS delivered the opinion of the Court.

The question for decision is whether the sum of $171,979.22 received by the North American Oil Consolidated in 1917, was taxable to it as income of that year.

The money was paid to the company under the following circumstances. Among many properties operated by it in 1916 was a section of oil land, the legal title to which stood in the name of the United States. Prior to that year, the Government, claiming also the beneficial ownership, had instituted a suit to oust the company from possession; and on February 2, 1916, it secured the appointment of a receiver to operate the property, or supervise its operations, and to hold the net income thereof. The money paid to the company in 1917 represented the net profits which had been earned from that property in 1916 during the

---

[1]    Pub. L. No. 115–97, 115th Cong, 1st Sess. (2017).

[2]    I.R.C. § 451(b)(1). The IRS may also specify other financial statements for purposes of this provision. I.R.C. § 451(b)(3)(C). If a contract contains multiple performance obligations, the taxpayer is allowed to allocate the transaction price in accordance with the allocation in the applicable financial statement. I.R.C. § 451(b)(4).

[3]    However, the rule does not change when income is *realized* for tax purposes. For example, I.R.C. § 451(b) does not require recharacterization of a sale to a lease, or vice versa, to conform the transactions tax results to the taxpayer's applicable financial statements. H. Rep. No. 115–466, Joint Explanatory Statement, 115th Cong., 1st sess. 275 n. 872 (2017). In general, other provisions providing special methods of accounting (other than the time-value-of-money rules such as I.R.C. § 1272) apply before I.R.C § 451(b) applies. I.R.C. § 451(b)(2).

[4]    I.R.C. § 451(b)(3). If the taxpayer has more than one applicable financial statement, I.R.C. § 451(b)(3)(A) prioritizes which statement is used.

[5]    I.R.C. § 451(b)(1)(B)(i). There is also an exception for income in connection with a mortgage servicing contract. I.R.C. § 451(b)(1)(B)(ii).

receivership. The money was paid to the receiver as earned. After entry by the District Court in 1917 of the final decree dismissing the bill, the money was paid, in that year, by the receiver to the company. United States v. North American Oil Consolidated, 242 F. 723. The Government took an appeal (without supersedeas) to the Circuit Court of Appeals. In 1920, that Court affirmed the decree. 264 F. 336. In 1922, a further appeal to this Court was dismissed by stipulation. 258 U.S. 633, 42 S.Ct. 315.

The income earned from the property in 1916 had been entered on the books of the company as its income. It had not been included in its original return of income for 1916; but it was included in an amended return for that year which was filed in 1918. Upon auditing the company's income and profits tax returns for 1917, the Commissioner of Internal Revenue determined a deficiency based on other items. The company appealed to the Board of Tax Appeals. There in 1927 the Commissioner prayed that the deficiency already claimed should be increased so as to include a tax on the amount paid by the receiver to the company in 1917. The Board held that the profits were taxable to the receiver as income of 1916; and hence made no finding whether the company's accounts were kept on the cash receipts and disbursements basis or on the accrual basis. 12 B.T.A. 68. The Circuit Court of Appeals held that the profits were taxable to the company as income of 1917, regardless of whether the company's returns were made on the cash or on the accrual basis. 50 F.2d 752. This Court granted a writ of certiorari. 284 U.S. 614, 52 S.Ct. 208.

It is conceded that the net profits earned by the property during the receivership constituted income. The company contends that they should have been reported by the receiver for taxation in 1916; that if not returnable by him, they should have been returned by the company for 1916, because they constitute income of the company accrued in that year; and that if not taxable as income of the company for 1916, they were taxable to it as income for 1922, since the litigation was not finally terminated in its favor until 1922.

*First.* The income earned in 1916 and impounded by the receiver in that year was not taxable to him, because he was the receiver of only a part of the properties operated by the company. Under § 13(c) of the Revenue Act of 1916,[1] receivers who "are operating the property or business of corporations" were obliged to make returns "of net income as and for such corporations," and "any income tax due" was to be "assessed

---

[1] Act of September 8, 1916, 39 Stat. 756, 771, c. 463: "In cases wherein receivers, trustees in bankruptcy, or assignees are operating the property or business of corporations * * * , subject to tax imposed by this title, such receivers, trustees or assignees shall make returns of net income as and for such corporations * * * , in the same manner and form as such organizations are hereinbefore required to make returns, and any income tax due on the basis of such returns made by receivers, trustees, or assignees shall be assessed and collected in the same manner as if assessed directly against the organizations of whose business or properties they have custody and control." [See I.R.C. (1986) § 6012(b)(3). Ed.]

and collected in the same manner as if assessed directly against the organization of whose business or properties they have custody and control." The phraseology of this section was adopted without change in the Revenue Act of 1918, 40 Stat. 1057, 1081, c. 18, § 239. The regulations of the Treasury Department have consistently construed these statutes as applying only to receivers in charge of the entire property or business of a corporation; and in all other cases have required the corporations themselves to report their income. Treas.Regs. 33, arts. 26, 209; Treas.Regs. 45, arts. 424, 622. That construction is clearly correct. The language of the section contemplates a substitution of the receiver for the corporation; and there can be such substitution only when the receiver is in complete control of the properties and business of the corporation. Moreover, there is no provision for the consolidation of the return of a receiver of part of a corporation's property or business with the return of the corporation itself. It may not be assumed that Congress intended to require the filing of two separate returns for the same year, each covering only a part of the corporate income, without making provision for consolidation so that the tax could be based upon the income as a whole.

*Second.* The net profits were not taxable to the company as income of 1916. For the company was not required in 1916 to report as income an amount which it might never receive. * * *. There was no constructive receipt of the profits by the company in that year, because at no time during the year was there a right in the company to demand that the receiver pay over the money. Throughout 1916 it was uncertain who would be declared entitled to the profits. It was not until 1917, when the District Court entered a final decree vacating the receivership and dismissing the bill, that the company became entitled to receive the money. Nor is it material, for the purposes of this case, whether the company's return was filed on the cash receipts and disbursements basis, or on the accrual basis. In neither event was it taxable in 1916 on account of income which it had not yet received and which it might never receive.

*Third.* The net profits earned by the property in 1916 were not income of the year 1922—the year in which the litigation with the Government was finally terminated. They became income of the company in 1917, when it first became entitled to them and when it actually received them. If a taxpayer receives earnings under a claim of right and without restriction as to its disposition, he has received income which he is required to return, even though it may still be claimed that he is not entitled to retain the money, and even though he may still be adjudged liable to restore its equivalent. * * *. If in 1922 the Government had prevailed, and the company had been obliged to refund the profits received in 1917, it would have been entitled to a deduction from the profits of 1922, not from those of any earlier year. * * *.

Affirmed.

# New Capital Hotel, Inc. v. Commissioner

Tax Court of the United States, 1957.
28 T.C. 706, affirmed per curiam 261 F.2d 437 (6th Cir.1958).

The respondent determined a deficiency in petitioner's income tax for the year 1949 in the amount of $11,724.50.

The sole issue is whether a $30,000 advance payment received in 1949 by the petitioner lessor, an accrual basis taxpayer, pursuant to lease contract is includible in gross income in 1949, as determined by the respondent, or in 1959, the year in which the advance payment is to be applied as rent.

[The findings of fact are omitted. Ed.]

Opinion

■ BLACK, JUDGE:

The sole question involved here is whether the $30,000 advance payment received in 1949 by the petitioner is includible in its gross income for that year.

The petitioner lessor leased certain hotel property, which it owned, for a period of 10 years from January 1, 1950, to December 31, 1959. The lease contract provided that the lessee would pay rents as follows: $30,000 during each year of the lease and "for the last year of this lease, Lessee agrees to pay in advance the sum of Thirty Thousand Dollars ($30,000.00), the receipt of which is hereby acknowledged. Said sum, however, shall apply only on the rental for the last year of this lease." The lease also provided that if the building should be substantially destroyed during the period of the lease the lessor shall refund to the lessee all or part of the $30,000 as may not cover the rental of the property up to the time of such destruction, provided, however, that no rental is then in arrears.

The petitioner's president testified that the lessee preferred paying the last year's rent in advance rather than executing a performance bond, which the lessor was demanding. The lessee, during 1949, paid the above-mentioned $30,000 to the petitioner. There were no restrictions on the use of the $30,000; the petitioner had unfettered control over it.

The petitioner, an accrual basis taxpayer, reflected the advance rental payment in a liability account entitled "Deposit on lease contract" and contends that it should be reported as income in 1959, the year in which petitioner contends it would be considered as earned. The respondent determined that the $30,000 constituted gross income in 1949, the year of receipt, under section 22(a), Internal Revenue Code of 1939.[1]

---

[1]　SEC. 22. GROSS INCOME.

(a) General Definition.—"Gross income" includes gains, profits, and income derived from * * * rent, * * *.

It is clear from the record that the advance payment, although securing the lessee's performance of the covenants, was intended to be rent, was described in the lease contract as rent, and was primarily rent. * * *. Since the rent was received in 1949, it would be includible in gross income in that year even though the rent is to be applied for the use of the property in 1959. * * *. This is so regardless of whether the taxpayer keeps his books and computes his income on a cash basis, * * * , on an accrual basis, * * *.

The petitioner argues that its method of accounting clearly reflects its income and that the inclusion of the rent in gross income for the year 1949, rather than 1959, will distort its income for the 2 years because in 1959 it will incur approximately $23,000 in expenses incident to the earning of the $30,000 rent.[2]

We have recognized that the inclusion of prepaid income in gross income in the year of receipt of the item representing it, rather than in a subsequent year when it is considered earned, is not in accord with principles of commercial accounting. See Curtis R. Andrews, 23 T.C. 1026, 1033–1034 (1955); E.W. Schuessler, 24 T.C. 247, 249 (1955), reversed (C.A.5, 1956) 230 F.2d 722. We have, however, consistently held that the Commissioner has acted within the discretion granted him under section 41 of the 1939 Code in holding that prepaid income must be returned in the year received in order to clearly reflect income. Cf. Automobile Club of Michigan v. Commissioner, 353 U.S. 180, 188–190 (1957). In the instant case the petitioner seeks to defer a nonrecurring advance rental payment[3] for a period of 10 years.[4] Under the circumstances detailed in our Findings of Fact we cannot say that the Commissioner abused the discretion granted him in section 41, Internal Revenue Code of 1939,* in determining that the $30,000 was includible in the petitioner's gross income in 1949.

Among the decisions which petitioner relies on in its brief in support of its contention that the $30,000 is not taxable in 1949, is John Mantell, 17 T.C. 1143 (1952). We think the facts of the instant case are clearly distinguishable from those present in the *Mantell* case. In the *Mantell* case our Findings of Fact made clear that the $33,320, which was involved there, was not meant to be paid as advance rental. It was paid

---

[2] The petitioner, in its reply brief, apparently also contends that if the $30,000 is includible in its 1949 gross income it should be allowed a deduction of $23,000 for expenses to be incurred in 1959 in connection with the earning of the rent. This issue has not been properly pleaded and is not properly before us. Regardless, it has no merit. See Bressner Radio, Inc., 28 T.C. 378 (1957).

[3] There is no contention that the Commissioner's action in this case will upset a consistent accounting system of long standing. Cf. Pacific Grape Products Co., 17 T.C. 1097 (1952), revd. (C.A.9, 1955) 219 F.2d 862.

[4] Even under the liberalized provisions for reporting prepaid income under the short-lived section 452(b), Internal Revenue Code of 1954, a prepayment 10 years in advance, such as the one involved herein, would be includible in gross income ratably in the year of receipt and the next succeeding 5 years unless the Secretary or his delegate prescribed otherwise. See S.Rept. No. 1622, 83d Cong., 2d Sess. (1954), pp. 301, 302.

* See I.R.C. (1986) § 446(b). Ed.

primarily to be held as security to guarantee the performance by the lessees of the obligations and covenants contained in the lease. The next to the last paragraph of our Findings of Fact in the *Mantell* case enumerates the several things for which the $33,320 was to act as security to guarantee that the lessees would perform. Our Findings of Fact then conclude with the following final paragraph (p. 1147):

> The sum of $33,320 received by the petitioner upon the execution of the lease in 1946 was intended to be and was in fact a security deposit. It was not paid as prepaid rent and was not taxable income when received.

Manifestly, we could make no such finding in the instant case because the lease agreement itself provides:

> And, for the last year of this lease, Lessee agrees to pay in advance the sum of Thirty Thousand Dollars ($30,000.00), the receipt of which is hereby acknowledged. Said sum, however, shall apply only on the rental for the last year of this lease.

That the $30,000 in question was paid by the lessee as advance rental for the year 1959 seems too clear for argument and, under the authorities cited, we must hold that it was taxable income to petitioner in the year 1949, when it was received.

Decision will be entered for the respondent.

## NOTE

In the *New Capital Hotel* case, the Tax Court acknowledges that "the inclusion of prepaid income in gross income in the year of receipt of the item representing it, rather than in a subsequent year when it is considered earned, is not in accord with principles of commercial accounting."[1] It is tempting therefore simply to say that it is wrong. Nevertheless, there is support for it, both authoritatively and as a practical matter. From the practical point of view, while both business and tax accounting principles are designed to yield an annual net income figure, their objectives are not identical. The business world wants a periodic net income figure for purposes of determining profitability of the business and comparative profitability for various accounting periods. Congress wants a steady flow of tax revenue and assurance that taxpayers in fact pay tax on all elements of gain. With this second objective in mind a momentary gain, even if it may later be offset by related expenses in a later period, *can* be identified as income. On the other hand, with an eye toward the graduated rate tables, there is a question whether the business accounting purpose of identifying net income for the critical period, reasonably taking account of subsequent related costs or expenditures, is not as important for tax accounting as for business accounting. These thoughts are reflected in the history of the Treasury's immediate reporting policy and bear on recent congressional resolution of the issue.

---

[1]  28 T.C. 706 at 708 (1957).

The Treasury's strict inclusion policy appeared as early as 1938 in a memorandum[2] which, relying upon "claim of right" language in *North American Oil Consolidated,* stated that "amounts received * * * within the taxable year without restriction as to disposition, use, or enjoyment, for subscription service to be rendered in a succeeding year or years constitute income for the year in which received regardless of the fact that the taxpayer's books of account are kept on the accrual basis." The proposition received judicial support both before and after publication of the memorandum.[3]

The Commissioner was largely successful in maintaining that, in order clearly to reflect income under Section 446, prepaid income of accrual method taxpayers for both goods and services must be included within income in the year of prepayment. Several Supreme Court cases have endorsed this view, namely Automobile Club of Michigan v. Commissioner,[4] American Automobile Ass'n v. United States,[5] and Schlude v. Commissioner.[6] In the meantime, limited statutory exceptions to the immediate inclusion rule were made in the case of income from newspaper, magazine, and periodical subscriptions under Section 455[7] and prepaid club dues under Section 456.

Despite the Treasury's strict inclusion policy, some taxpayers have been able to achieve limited judicial victories to defer recognition of prepaid income when they were able to convince a court that the earning of the income could be specifically fixed and the deferral period was limited in time. Two notable decisions involved major league baseball teams which received prepaid income (e.g., amounts paid for tickets, suites, broadcasting rights, etc.) attributable to a later taxable year.[8] In those cases, the taxpayers were able to sufficiently demonstrate that the earning events (playing of games) were certain enough to permit the prepaid income to be deferred and matched with related expenses.[9] However, they were limited fact-dependent taxpayer wins, and the rule of strict inclusion still broadly applied. The Internal Revenue Service eventually adopted Revenue Procedure 2004–34 permitting limited deferral in the case of prepaid services,[10] and promulgated Regulation Section 1.451–5 relating to prepayments for

---

[2]   GCM 20021, 1938–1 C.B. 157, 158.

[3]   E.g., Brown v. Helvering, 291 U.S. 193, 54 S.Ct. 356 (1934); South Dade Farms v. Commissioner, 138 F.2d 818 (5th Cir.1943); South Tacoma Motor Co. v. Commissioner, 3 T.C. 411 (1944); Your Health Club, Inc. v. Commissioner, 4 T.C. 385 (1944), acq., 1945 C.B. 7; Curtis R. Andrews, 23 T.C. 1026 (1955). But see I.T. 3369, 1940–1 C.B. 46, and Beacon Pub. Co. v. Commissioner, 218 F.2d 697 (10th Cir.1955).

[4]   353 U.S. 180, 77 S.Ct. 707 (1957).

[5]   367 U.S. 687, 81 S.Ct. 1727 (1961).

[6]   372 U.S. 128, 83 S.Ct. 601 (1963).

[7]   See also I.R.C. § 458, added by the Revenue Act of 1978, under which accrual method taxpayers who sell magazines, paperbacks and records may defer prepayments if the shipped goods can be returned by the buyer within specified periods after the end of the year.

[8]   Artnell Co. v. Commissioner, 400 F.2d 981 (7th Cir., 1968); Tampa Bay Devil Rays, Ltd. v. Commissioner, 8 T.C.M. 394 (2002).

[9]   Morgan Guaranty Trust Co. v. United States, 585 F.2d 988 (Ct.Cl. 1978), is another taxpayer victory. In that case, the court permitted an accrual method taxpayer to defer a de minimis amount of prepaid interest from its gross income.

[10]   See Rev. Proc. 70–21, 1970–2 C.B. 501; Rev. Proc. 71–21, 1971–2 C.B. 549 (providing essentially the same rules); Rev. Proc. 2004–34, 2004–1 C.B. 991 (liberalizing the rules).

goods.[11] However, under both, deferral generally was permitted only to the year subsequent to the year of receipt.[12] The Service's actions reflected very limited acceptance of business accounting principle, perhaps in an effort to preempt the courts from issuing additional pro-taxpayer decisions.

In the 2017 Tax Cuts and Jobs Act,[13] Congress codified the tax treatment of advance payments received by an accrual method taxpayer, and it essentially adopted the prior approach of the Internal Revenue Service in Revenue Procedure 2004–34 and Regulation Section 1.451–1 regarding the treatment of prepaid services and goods.[14] Under Section 451(c), an accrual method taxpayer who receives an advance payment during the year is required to either (1) include the payment in income in the current year, or (2) make an election to defer the advance payment.[15] If the deferral election is made, the taxpayer must include in income in the taxable year in which the advance payment is received any portion of the advance payment required to be accrued under Section 451(b) because it was included as revenue in an applicable financial statement.[16] The remaining portion of the advance payment must be included in the taxable year following receipt.[17] Thus, deferral is allowed for one year if the income is also deferred in the taxpayer's financial statements.

An advance payment is a payment for services, goods, or any other items identified by the Service for purposes of the rule which would normally be included in income in the year of receipt[18] under the taxpayer's accounting method, but where a portion or all of the payment has not been included in revenue in the year by the taxpayer in an applicable financial statement.[19] If an advance payment is received for a combination of services, goods, or other items, the taxpayer must allocate the items in accordance with the allocation in the applicable financial statement.[20] Advance payments do not include payments for rent, payments on financial instruments (such as interest payments), and payments in property subject to Section 83.[21]

*Inventories.* Except in the case of certain small businesses discussed below, whenever tax computations require the use of inventories, the accrual method of accounting must be used, at least with regard to purchases and

---

[11]   Reg. § 1.451–5(a) and (b).

[12]   Rev. Proc. 2004–34 § 5.02, 2004–1 C.B. 991, 992; Reg. § 1.451–5(c).

[13]   Pub. L. No. 115–97, 115th Cong., 1st Sess. (2017).

[14]   See Text at notes 10–12, supra.

[15]   I.R.C. § 451(c)(1). The statute refers to making the election by "category" of advanced payments; however, neither the Code nor the legislative history define the term "category."

The IRS will prescribe the manner for making the election. I.R.C. § 451(c)(2)(A). Once made, an election continues for all subsequent years unless it is revoked with the consent of the IRS. I.R.C. § 451(c)(2)(B).

[16]   I.R.C. § 451(c)(1)(B)(i).

[17]   I.R.C. § 451(c)(1)(B)(ii). However, I.R.C. § 451(c) requires inclusion in gross income of any deferred advance payment if the taxpayer ceases to exist. I.R.C. § 451(c)(3).

[18]   An item of gross income is considered "received" by the taxpayer if it is either actually or constructively received, or if it is due and payable to the taxpayer. I.R.C. § 451(c)(4)(C).

[19]   I.R.C. § 451(c)(4)(A).

[20]   I.R.C. § 451(c)(4)(D), (b)(4).

[21]   I.R.C. § 451(c)(4)(B). Other, more specialized, items relating to insurance, warranties or guaranties, and international transactions are also excluded. Id.

sales.[22] When must inventories be used? Generally whenever "production, purchase, or sale of merchandise is an income-producing factor."[23] Consequently, inventory accounting plays a very large role in the federal income tax. It may be required of the butcher, the baker, and the candlestick maker, but not of the attorney or the accountant.

The accounting profession worries a great deal about proper treatment of inventories in its effort to develop generally accepted accounting principles.[24] We eschew all the details that titillate accountants and attempt here only a very basic explanation of inventories and their general relationship to the determination of gross income and to the accounting period in which gross income must be reported, the subject of this chapter.

We already know that the general formula for determining gross income from the sale of property can be expressed as:

|  | Amount realized |
|---|---|
| Less | Adjusted basis |
| Equals | Realized gain |

The parallel expression of this concept where property is sold in the course of a business, such as a haberdashery, is:

|  | Gross sales |
|---|---|
| Less | Cost of goods sold |
| Equals | Gross profit from sales |

Gross sales is obviously a fairly automatic figure, but how does a merchant (or a manufacturer) determine the cost of the goods that he has sold during an accounting period? It is here that inventories play their principal role. It is usually impracticable for a merchant separately to determine gain or loss on each sale.[25] A device is needed that will produce the correct overall result by way of a kind of aggregate approach.

To overcome the problem suggested, the figure used for cost of goods sold is determined by (1) ascertaining the cost of goods on hand at the start of the accounting period, which is called "opening inventory;" (2) adding to that the cost of goods acquired during the accounting period, referred to in an abbreviated way as "purchases;" and (3) subtracting from that sum the cost of the goods still on hand at the end of the accounting period, "closing inventory." Thus:

---

[22] Reg. § 1.446–1(c)(2).

[23] Reg. § 1.471–1.

[24] E.g., Bragg, Accounting for Inventory (2d ed., 2015).

[25] The used car dealer and others who make relatively few sales of large items are exceptions.

|        | Opening inventory |
|--------|-------------------|
| Plus   | Purchases         |
| Less   | Closing inventory |
| Equals | Cost of goods sold |

Some assurance that in the long run all gain or loss will be taken into account is achieved by the fact that the figure to be used as opening inventory for a particular period is the figure that was used for closing inventory for the preceding period. Play with the formula enough to see that, if an improperly low figure were used for closing inventory in 2018, it would tend to show a higher cost of goods sold and lower profit for that year; but in 2019 the improperly low opening inventory figure (which is closing inventory for 2018) would result in a lower cost of goods sold and higher profit for 2019. This is not intended to suggest that the taxpayer has the option to juggle these figures.[26]

In this inventory approach the most uncertain figure is closing inventory. "Opening inventory" is somewhat automatic, simply being carried over as closing inventory of the last year.[27] "Purchases" is likewise somewhat automatic.[28] But closing inventory involves both a determination of the quantity of goods (or each item of goods) on hand[29] and then properly "pricing" it.

The quantity of goods on hand at the end of an accounting period can be determined by observation—"taking inventory."[30] However, the quantitative figure must be converted to a dollar figure, representing the *cost* of what is on hand.[31] In a hardware store the brass screws in a box may have been

---

[26] There are legitimate juggling opportunities which can be achieved, e.g., by selling down (i.e., not replacing) high cost Lifo inventories; but this is rare.

[27] But see footnote comments below on uncertainties regarding what is included in closing inventory.

[28] A significant problem arises here as to when a purchase is taken into account; for example, does purchases include an item merely ordered or in transit to the taxpayer, or must it be received prior to the end of the accounting period? Must it be paid for? Note the parallel problems on sales and closing inventory.

[29] As in the case of purchases, question arises here whether goods should be treated as no longer on hand if ordered or en route to the buyer or only if delivered or paid for. There is some flexibility, but the answer must be meshed with the approach taken to the question when a sale is included in gross sales. A moment's reflection should indicate that distortion would result if goods considered to have passed out of closing inventory were not treated as sold for purposes of determining gross sales.

[30] The student should not envisage the calendar year haberdasher having to forego New Year's Eve revels to take inventory. The job is accomplished at another time with suitable adjustment to achieve the year-end objective, or these days it may even be achieved electronically.

[31] A conservative business accounting maxim of never over-stating income has generated a "cost or market" variation here, under which inventory is priced at market, if that is less than cost, and this variation is permitted for tax accounting. See Reg. § 1.471–2 and –4.

However, a security which is included in a security dealer's inventory at the end of the taxable year must be included in inventory at its fair market value. I.R.C. § 475(a)(1). Furthermore securities which are not included in a securities dealer's inventory and are not properly identified as held for investment on their acquisition (see I.R.C. § 1236) are accounted for under the mark-to-market method of accounting under which such securities are treated as if they were sold for their fair market value on the last day of the taxable year. I.R.C. § 472(a)(2). When a dealer subsequently disposes of the later type of securities the previously recognized gain or loss will be taken into account in determining the amount of gain or loss on the sale. Id.

purchased at several different times, some recently and some a year or more ago. What was their price when purchased? Nobody knows, but conventions answer the question. If it is assumed that the earliest purchased screws were the one's first sold (the "first in-first out" convention), then those on hand are treated as the most recently purchased and are "priced" for inventory purposes in accordance with this assumption. That is, if the last ten gross of screws acquired cost $14.40 and there are 1440 screws on hand, then each screw is included in closing inventory at one cent. If there are 1500 on hand, 60 of them are priced in accordance with the cost of the next-to-last batch of screws acquired, and so forth.[32]

A less common alternative pricing convention is the "last in-first out" approach. These conventions are commonly referred to as "Lifo" or "Fifo." Work out for yourself the basic consequences of inventory pricing under the Lifo convention.[33]

A businessperson may wish to show high earnings to creditors and shareholders but low earnings to employees and the Commissioner of Internal Revenue. One can't of course do both, and *consistency* is a key requirement in accounting matters.[34] Nevertheless, the gross profit on sales for any given year is affected by the pricing convention adopted. Try this: Assume a merchandising business makes substantial purchases of goods annually but maintains a fairly steady stock of goods, quantitatively. If over a period of time prices are rising, will the business report more income for a particular period under the Fifo approach or under the Lifo approach?

It will now be seen that inventories play a timing role as well as a measuring role for gross income. If the inventory pricing method followed tends to show a low *closing* inventory for the prior year, and the effect of the low figure is a greater cost of goods sold and a correspondingly lower profit on sales for that year, the effect is also to shift reportable income to a future year. That is because the lower *opening* inventory for the next year will result in a lower cost of goods sold and a correspondingly higher profit on sales in a subsequent period. In effect, given required consistency, the whole scheme operates within a kind of closed circle, and advantage now is bought only at the cost of disadvantage later, or vice versa.

*Inventory Exemption for Certain Small Businesses.* Special inventory accounting rules apply for certain "small businesses." Recall that generally a corporation, or partnership with a corporate partner, whose average gross receipts for the prior three years do not exceed twenty-five million dollars per year may use the cash method of accounting.[35] Any taxpayer (including individuals but not including a tax shelter) meeting that gross receipts test may also avoid the inventory accounting rules[36] and either (1) treat

---

[32] Note that inventory pricing is vastly more complicated in the case of a manufacturing rather than a mere merchandising business. This gets into the area of "cost accounting" in which there must be added to materials costs both labor and other direct and indirect expenses, as regards finished products and so-called "work in process" as well.

[33] Cf. I.R.C. § 474.

[34] See Reg. § 1.471–2(b). It should be noted that differences in business and tax accounting often do require the keeping of two sets of books.

[35] I.R.C. § 448(b)(3) and (c). See page 589, supra.

[36] I.R.C. § 471(c)(1)(A), (3).

inventory as non-incidental materials and supplies which are deductible in the taxable year in which first used or consumed in the taxpayer's operations,[37] or (2) conform the treatment of inventories generally to its financial reporting of those items.[38] To understand the effect of this special rule, consider a roofing contractor who uses the cash method and enters into a contract to replace a homeowner's roof in December of 2019. The contractor pays a supplier $10,000 for shingles and does the work in December. The contractor bills the homeowner $20,000 for the work and receives a check for that amount in January 2020. Under the cash method the taxpayer has $20,000 of gross income in 2020. Under the first alternative of the special rule regarding inventories, the contractor could deduct the $10,000 cost of the shingles in 2019 when they were used or consumed in the business.[39] The exception for small businesses sanctions the mismatching of the taxpayer's income and related expenses! Presumably this is permitted in order to eliminate the burden and complexity of the inventory accounting rules.

## 2.   DEDUCTION ITEMS

Internal Revenue Code: Section 461(a), (f), and (h).

Regulations: Sections 1.461–1(a)(2), –4(a), –5(a) and (b)(1).

---

### Revenue Ruling 2007–3
2007–1 Cum. Bull. 350.

### ISSUES

(1) Under § 461 of the Internal Revenue Code, when does a taxpayer using an accrual method of accounting incur a liability for services?

* * *

### FACTS

X is a corporation that uses an accrual method of accounting and files its federal income tax returns on a calendar year basis.

*Situation 1.* On December 15, 2006, X executes a contract with Y for the provision of services. The contract provides for services to begin on January 15, 2007, and end on January 31, 2007. Under the terms of the contract, payment for the services is due to Y on January 15, 2007, and X pays Y for the services on January 15, 2007. * * *.

### LAW

Section 461(a) provides that the amount of any deduction or credit must be taken for the taxable year that is the proper taxable year under

---

[37]  I.R.C. § 471(c)(1)(B)(i); Reg. § 1.162–3(a).

[38]  I.R.C. § 471(c)(1)(B)(ii).

[39]  The example is adapted from Rev. Proc. 2002–28, 2002–1 C.B. 815, Example 15.

the method of accounting used by the taxpayer in computing taxable income.

Section 1.461–1(a)(2)(i) of the Income Tax Regulations provides that, under an accrual method of accounting, a liability is incurred, and is generally taken into account for federal income tax purposes, in the taxable year in which (1) all the events have occurred that establish the fact of the liability, (2) the amount of the liability can be determined with reasonable accuracy, and (3) economic performance has occurred with respect to the liability (the "all events test"). See also § 1.446–1(c)(1)(ii)(A).

The first prong of the all events test requires that all the events have occurred that establish the fact of the liability. Therefore, it is fundamental to the all events test that although expenses may be deductible before they become due and payable, liability first must be firmly established. United States v. General Dynamics Corp., 481 U.S. 239, 243–4 (1987).

Generally, under § 1.461–1(a)(2), all the events have occurred that establish the fact of the liability when (1) the event fixing the liability, whether that be the required performance or other event, occurs, or (2) payment therefore is due, whichever happens earliest. Rev. Rul. 80–230, 1980–2 C.B. 169; Rev. Rul. 79–410, 1979–2 C.B. 213, amplified by Rev. Rul. 2003–90, 2003–2 C.B. 353. The terms of a contract are relevant in determining the events that establish the fact of a taxpayer's liability. See, e.g., Decision, Inc. v. Commissioner, 47 T.C. 58 (1966), acq., 1967–2 C.B. 2.

Section 461(h) and § 1.461–4 provide that, for purposes of determining whether an accrual basis taxpayer can treat the amount of any liability as incurred, the all events test is not treated as met any earlier than the taxable year in which economic performance occurs with respect to the liability.

Section 1.461–4(d)(2) provides that if a liability of a taxpayer arises out of the providing of services or property to the taxpayer by another person, economic performance occurs as the services or property is provided.

* * *

## ANALYSIS

*Situation 1.* In Situation 1, the first event that occurs to establish the fact of X's liability for services is that payment is due under the contract on January 15, 2007. See Rev. Rul. 80–230; Rev. Rul. 79–410. Thus, for purposes of § 461, the fact of the liability is established on January 15, 2007. At that time, the amount can be determined with reasonable accuracy. Economic performance with respect to the liability occurs as the services are provided, from January 15, 2007, through

January 31, 2007. See § 1.461–4(d)(2). Therefore, X incurs a liability for services in 2007.

The fact of the liability is not established in 2006, even though X executed the service contract on December 15, 2006. It is well established that an accrual basis obligor is not permitted to deduct an expense stemming from a bilateral contractual arrangement, that is, mutual promises, prior to the performance of the contracted for services by the obligee. Rev. Rul. 80–182, 1980–2 C.B. 167, citing Levin v. Commissioner, 21 T.C. 996 (1954), aff'd, 219 F.2d 588 (3d Cir. 1955) (an agreement for services to be performed in the next year did not establish the fact of the taxpayer's liability but was simply an agreement under which a liability would be incurred in the future) and Amalgamated Housing Corp. v. Commissioner, 37 B.T.A. 817 (1938), aff'd per curium, 108 F.2d 1010 (2d Cir. 1940) (an agreement to renovate property in the future did not establish the fact of the taxpayer's liability; the accrual was for services in renovating, not the duty to renovate). Thus, the mere execution of the contract by X in 2006 is not sufficient, by itself, to establish the fact of the liability.

\* \* \*

## HOLDINGS

(1)   Under § 461, all the events have occurred that establish the fact of the liability for services provided to the taxpayer when (1) the event fixing the liability, whether that be the required performance or other event, occurs, or (2) payment is due, whichever happens earliest. The mere execution of a contract, without more, does not establish the fact of a taxpayer's liability for services.

\* \* \*

## NOTE

Suppose the contract for services in Revenue Ruling 2007–3 had also required *payment* in 2006? Would that change in the contract terms have allowed the taxpayer a 2006 deduction under the accrual method? Under the first prong of the all-events test, the fact of liability would have been established because payment would be unconditionally due in 2006. But, the all-events test has *three* prongs which have to be satisfied in order to accrue a deduction. Would there have been economic performance in 2006? The ruling notes that if a liability arises out of the providing of services to the taxpayer by another person, economic performance occurs as the services are provided. So again a 2006 deduction would be denied, but the denial would be based on a failure to satisfy the third prong of the all-events test. The *Schuessler* case introduces the concern that prompted Congress to enact the economic performance requirement in Section 461(h).

# Schuessler v. Commissioner

United States Court of Appeals, Fifth Circuit, 1956.
230 F.2d 722.

■ TUTTLE, CIRCUIT JUDGE.

This is a petition for review of a decision by the Tax Court disallowing a deduction in 1946 of an item of $13,300.00, representing a reserve set up by taxpayers while keeping their books on the accrual basis, to represent their estimated cost of carrying out a guarantee, given with each of the furnaces sold by them during the year, to turn the furnace on and off each year for five years.

The opinion of the Tax Court treats the matter as though ample proof was offered by the taxpayer (hereafter the husband will be called "taxpayer") to raise the legal issue and we find the record warrants this treatment. Taxpayer was in the gas furnace business in 1946, during which he sold 665 furnaces, each with a guarantee that he would turn the furnace on and off each year for five years. The fact that such service, if performed, would cost $2.00 per call was amply established. The taxpayer, himself a bookkeeper and accountant prior to entering this business, testified to his keeping his books on the accrual method and claimed that the only way his income could be accurately reported was by charging against the cost of furnaces sold in 1946 the reserve representing the amount which he became legally liable to expend in subsequent years in connection with the sales. The proof was clear that he actually sold the furnaces for $20.00 to $25.00 more than his competitors because of his guarantee, which they did not give.

We think it quite clear that petitioner's method of accounting comes much closer to giving a correct picture of his income than would a system in which he sold equipment in one year and received an inflated price because he obligated himself, in effect, to refund part of it in services later but was required to report the total receipts as income on the high level of the sales year and take deductions on the low level of the service years. The reasonableness of taxpayer's action, however, is not the test if it runs counter to requirements of the statute.

We find that not only does it not offend any statutory requirement, but, in fact, we think it is in accord with the language and intent of the law.[1] Clearly what is sought by this statute is an accounting method that most accurately reflects the taxpayer's income on an annual accounting basis.[2]

The decisions of the Tax Court and of the several Courts of Appeals are not uniform on this subject, some circuits requiring a mathematical certainty as to the exact amount of the future expenditures that cannot be satisfied in the usual case. Other circuits, seemingly more concerned

[1] [I.R.C. §§ 41 and 43 (1939), and Reg. § 29.41–1 are omitted. Ed.]
[2] This principle was early recognized in United States v. Anderson, 269 U.S. 422, 46 S.Ct. 131.

with the underlying principle of charging to each year's income reasonably ascertainable future expenses necessary to earn or retain the income, have permitted the accrual of restricted items of future expenses. Two of this latter category are Harrold v. Commissioner[3] and Pacific Grape Products Co. v. Commissioner.[4]

In the Harrold case the taxpayer was permitted to deduct from its gross income in 1945 the estimated cost of back filling a tract of land which would be done under state law requirements in the year 1946. The Court there said:

> " * * * when all the facts have occurred which determined that the taxpayer has incurred a liability in the tax year, and neither the fact nor the amount of the liability is contested, and the amount, although not definitely ascertained, is susceptible of estimate with reasonable accuracy in the tax year, deduction thereof from income may be taken by a taxpayer on an accrual basis." Harrold v. Commissioner, 4 Cir., 192 F.2d 1002, 1006.

The Pacific Grape Products case is also, it seems to us, indistinguishable in principle from the case before us. There the taxpayer accrued the sales price of canned goods sold on December 31, and at the same time deducted the estimated cost of labeling and preparing the goods for shipping and brokerage fees to be paid the following year. The Tax Court, with six judges dissenting, accepted the Commissioner's view that the deductions should be disallowed. 17 T.C. 1097. The Court of Appeals reversed, saying:

> "Not only do we have here a system of accounting which for years has been adopted and carried into effect by substantially all members of a large industry, but the system is one which appeals to us as so much in line with plain common sense that we are at a loss to understand what could have prompted the Commissioner to disapprove it. Contrary to his suggestion that petitioner's method did not reflect its true income it seems to us that the alterations demanded by the Commissioner would wholly distort that income."

The case of Beacon Publishing Co. v. Commissioner[5] is considered by both parties here and was noted by the Tax Court as of especial significance. That case involved the treatment of prepaid income received by the Beacon Publishing Co. covering subscriptions to be furnished in subsequent years. The Tax Court in its decision here said:

> " * * * This is essentially the same problem as the reporting of prepaid income in the year in which received for services to be performed in following years. The petitioner in fact, on brief, recognizes that the two problems are identical and cites Beacon

---

[3]   4 Cir., 192 F.2d 1002.

[4]   9 Cir., 219 F.2d 862, 869.

[5]   10 Cir., 218 F.2d 697.

Publishing Co. v. Commissioner, 10 Cir., 1955, 218 F.2d 697, in support of his argument that the reserve here in issue was a proper deduction in computing his income in 1946."

The Tax Court then simply declined to follow the Court in the Beacon case, preferring to adhere to its own views as expressed in Curtis A. Andrews v. Commissioner, 23 T.C. 1026. We prefer the reasoning as well as the conclusion reached by the Court in the Tenth Circuit. There the opinion correctly, we think, disposed of the "claim of right" theory advanced by the Commissioner and adopted by the Tax Court in this type of case.[6]

Finally we think the enactment in 1954 of Section 462 of the Internal Revenue Code of 1954[7] and its subsequent repeal constitute no legislative history bearing on the construction of the provisions of the Internal Revenue Code of 1939.[8]

The record below amply supports the contention of the taxpayer that there was a legal liability created in 1946, when the purchase price was paid for the gas furnaces, for the taxpayer to turn the furnaces on and off for the succeeding five years; that the cost of such service as reasonably established at a minimum of $2.00 per visit; and that the payment of $20.00 to $25.00 extra by the purchasers fully proved their intention to call upon the taxpayer each year for the service. These facts authorized the setting up of a reserve out of the 1946 income to enable the taxpayer to meet these established charges in future years. The decision of the Tax Court is therefore in error and must be reversed.

Reversed with directions to enter judgment for the taxpayer.

## NOTE

It is certain that accountants make the acquaintance early of Dr. Doolittle's marvelous quadruped, the Push Me-Pull You. They know almost instinctively that, if you push receipts of income forward to a future period when they are earned (deferral),[1] related deductions, i.e., the costs of earning the receipts should be pulled forward to the same period, achieving a match-up that best determines a net income *for the period*. They also know that if you push receipts of income back to an earlier period in which they have been received but not yet been earned, logic requires that related deductions should be pulled back, too, along with the prepaid receipts. Congress, however, is not enchanted with the Push Me-Pull You, although this theory is at the heart of generally accepted business accounting principles.

---

6   See Beacon Publishing Co. v. Commissioner, 218 F.2d 697, 699.

7   26 U.S.C.A. § 462.

8   For an interesting discussion of the history of this legislation see Sen.Rep. No. 372, 84 Cong., 1st Sess., 1955 U.S.Code Congressional and Administrative News, p. 2046–2051. See also Sporrer, The Past and Future of Deferring Income and Reserving for Expenses, TAXES (Mag.) January 1956, 45.

1   See Note at page 628, supra. See also Gunn, "Matching of Costs and Revenues as a Goal of Tax Accounting," 4 Virg.Tax Rev. 1 (1984).

Rather, Congress is motivated by revenue generating pressures which require treating receipts, even though not yet earned, as income for tax purposes. From a practical standpoint, this yields greater certainty that the tax on amounts received by a taxpayer will in fact be paid or collected. Similar concerns underlie the Service's historical reluctance to permit current deductions for anticipated future expenses such as the taxpayer's reserve method of accounting in *Schuessler*.[2] Uncertainty as to whether such costs will actually be paid and as to the accuracy of the taxpayer's estimates of such costs contributes to this concern.

Congress has helped clarify the income side of accrual transactions in Section 451(c) dealing with advance payments. It has also made clarifications and changes to the deductions side. At one time, the all events test that an expense had to satisfy to be deductible only had two requirements: (1) the fact of the liability had to be established; and (2) the amount of the liability had to be established with reasonable accuracy.[3]

Judicial interpretation of the two-part all events test often led to controversy over whether an accrual was premature. Initially the courts held that under the accrual method expenses became deductible only at the time of actual performance of the activities which the taxpayer was required to perform.[4] But later cases were more liberal in determining when taxpayers met the all events test, allowing a deduction when only the taxpayer's obligation to perform was fixed.[5] For example, in Harrold v. Commissioner[6] the court held that, as surface mining reclamation costs can be estimated with reasonable accuracy, such costs are deductible at the time the land is stripped even though the land is not restored as required until a future year. However, the Service consistently maintained that an expense should not be deducted until there is a fixed liability to pay a specific amount.[7] The Service also maintained that if a liability was contingent upon some future event, no deduction was allowable until that event actually occurred.[8]

Disagreement also arose between taxpayers and the Service as to when the *amount* of a liability is determinable with reasonable accuracy. In general, the courts held that this part of the all events test was satisfied when the liability could be estimated, not necessarily calculated, with reasonable accuracy.[9] The Service, on the other hand, took the position that

---

[2]  See, e.g., Simplified Tax Records, Inc. v. Commissioner, 41 T.C. 75 (1963), and cases cited therein.

[3]  Reg. § 1.461–1(a)(2).

[4]  See, e.g., Spencer, White & Prentis v. Commissioner, 144 F.2d 45 (2d Cir.1944), where a contractor required to restore property damaged in connection with a construction project was denied a deduction for the estimated costs of such restoration.

[5]  Cases allowing the accrual of an expense before performance of the required activity include Crescent Wharf & Warehouse Co. v. Commissioner, 518 F.2d 772 (9th Cir.1975) (accrual of workmens' compensation liability at the time the injury occurs), and Lukens Steel Co. v. Commissioner, 442 F.2d 1131 (3d Cir.1971) (accrual of contingent liability to fund a negotiated supplemental unemployment benefit plan).

[6]  192 F.2d 1002 (4th Cir.1951).

[7]  Rev.Rul. 72–34, 1972–1 C.B. 132.

[8]  Id.

[9]  See, e.g., Kaiser Steel Corp. v. United States, 717 F.2d 1304 (9th Cir.1983).

in order to satisfy this requirement the exact amount of the liability had to be determinable by a computation based on known or knowable facts.[10]

The controversy regarding the all events test was increased by the concern of Congress over a further problem, the "time value of money." It simply is not sound to allow a one dollar deduction *now* for one dollar that is to be paid two years from now. If one has to pay one dollar of expenses in two years one can put, say, 90 cents (depending on interest rates) in the bank now and withdraw one dollar in two years to pay the expenses. Consequently one should be allowed either a 90 cent deduction now or a one dollar deduction two years from now, but not one dollar right now. In testimony before a Senate Finance Subcommittee, the Acting Tax Legislative Counsel of the Treasury Department explained the problem at that time:[11]

> The high interest rates and inflation that we have experienced in recent years bring into question the economic assumptions that underlie certain provisions of the Internal Revenue Code. These high rates have resulted in a material increase in the "time value of money." In the simplest terms, the time value of money is the difference between the value of immediately available funds and the right to receive funds at some time in the future. In many respects the Code ignores time value of money concepts. For example, where an accrual basis taxpayer is entitled to accrue a $1 deduction, the Code permits a full $1 deduction, whether the $1 is paid today or ten years in the future. The failure of the Code to recognize this difference has led to numerous tax shelter transactions that enable taxpayers to produce substantial unintended tax benefits—at a substantial revenue loss to government * * * [w]e believe the time has come for a fundamental reexamination of several provisions of the Code that do not properly take time value of money concepts into account.

* * *

> * * * One of the most fundamental and obvious time value of money issues is the determination of the proper amount of the deduction to be allowed where a liability arises today in connection with a payment to be made in the future. Assume, for example, that A, an accrual basis taxpayer, incurs in 1983 a legal obligation to pay $100 to B in 1990. * * *. If A is allowed to deduct $100 in 1983, a gross overstatement of the deduction will occur. As the $100 need not be paid for seven years, A can fund that liability today for much less than $100. Thus, if A set aside $57.23 in 1983, invested that amount at an 8 percent after-tax rate until 1990, he would in 1990 have exactly the $100 needed to satisfy his liability to B. * * *. From an economic point of view, therefore, A's deduction should be $57.23 in 1983 or $100 in 1990. In no case should A be permitted to deduct $100 in 1983.

---

[10]   Priv. Ltr. Rul. 7831003 (April 13, 1978).

[11]   Testimony of Robert G. Woodard before the Senate Finance I.R.S. Oversight Committee on Tax Shelters, June 24, 1983.

The controversies regarding the all events test were alleviated by the enactment of Section 461(h),[12] albeit in a manner which does not benefit many taxpayers. In order to erase the time value of money distortion arising from the current accrual and deduction of the full amount of expenses to be incurred later and to resolve the prior judicial controversies, Congress added a third requirement to the all events test.[13]

Section 461(h) provides that the all events test is not deemed to be met any earlier than when "economic performance" with respect to an item occurs.[14] In effect, under the economic performance test, one asks whether the taxpayer has completed the taxpayer's end of the transaction. Section 461(h)(2) mandates specific principles for determining when economic performance occurs.[15] The Joint Committee explanation of those principles states:[16]

> The principles provided by the Act describe the two most common categories of liabilities: first, cases where the liability arises as a result of another person providing goods and services to the taxpayer and, second, cases where the liability requires the taxpayer to provide goods and services to another person or undertake some activity as a result of its income-producing activities.
>
> With respect to the first category of liabilities, if the liability arises out of the use of property, economic performance occurs as the taxpayer uses the property. If the liability requires a payment for the providing of property, economic performance occurs when the property is provided. However, Congress intended that the Treasury Department issue regulations providing that the time at which property is provided should include the time of delivery, shipment, or other time so long as the taxpayer accounts for such

---

[12] Pub. Law. No. 98–369, § 91, 98th Cong., 2d Sess. (1984). See Cunningham, "A Theoretical Analysis of the Tax Treatment of Future Costs," 40 Tax L.Rev. 1428 (1985).

[13] H.Rep. No. 98–432, 98th Cong., 2d Sess. 1254 (1984); S.Rep. No. 98–169, 98th Cong., 2d Sess. 266 (1984). Theoretically, two options were available to Congress: allow taxpayers a current deduction for a discounted amount of the liability; or, postpone deduction of the full amount until the taxpayer has completed performance giving rise to the liability. Because a discounted valuation system would be extraordinarily complex and hard to administer, Congress opted for the latter approach.

I.R.C. § 461(h) is just one of a number of changes that were made by the Tax Reform Act of 1984 to take into account the time value of money. See I.R.C. §§ 1271–1275 and 483 (original issue discount and interest on deferred payments); §§ 1276–1278 (market discount bonds); § 7872 (below market interest rate loans); and § 467 (certain payments for the use of property or services).

[14] I.R.C. § 461(h)(1). The all events test of Reg. § 1.461–1(a)(2) was codified in I.R.C. § 461(h)(4). See H.Rep. No. 98–432, 98th Cong., 2d Sess. 1255 (1984); S.Rep. No. 98–169, 98th Cong., 2d Sess. 267 (1984).

The regulations on capitalization of amounts to acquire, create, or enhance intangible assets contain a 12-month safe harbor for certain prepayments. See page 612, supra. However, these regulations make it clear that the safe harbor is subject to the "economic performance" requirement of I.R.C. § 461(h). Reg. § 1.263(a)–4(f)(6). Thus, the safe harbor cannot be used to accelerate a deduction prior to the time it would otherwise be deductible under § 461(h). See Reg. § 1.263(a)–4(f)(8) Examples 10 & 11.

[15] See Reg. § 1.461–4, –5.

[16] Jt.Comm. Explanation of the Tax Reform Act of 1984, pages 261 and 262 (1984).

items consistently from year to year. If the liability of the taxpayer requires a payment to another person for the providing of services to the taxpayer by another person, economic performance generally occurs when such other person provides the services.

With respect to the second category of liabilities, if the liability of the taxpayer requires the taxpayer to provide property or perform services, economic performance occurs as the taxpayer provides the property or performs the services. For this purpose, property does not include money; that is, economic performance generally does not occur as payments are made except as specifically provided in the code or regulations. For example, if a contractor is engaged by a highway construction company to repair damaged properties, economic performance occurs as the contractor performs the work. Likewise, when the highway construction company itself repairs the damage, economic performance occurs as repairs are made.

Under a special rule for workers' compensation and tort liabilities requiring payments to another person, economic performance occurs as payments are made to that person. In the case of any other liability of the taxpayer, economic performance will occur at the time determined under regulations to be prescribed by the Treasury.

The regulations implement these basic principles of economic performance and provide a number of special rules and exceptions.[17] In the case of interest, the regulations provide that economic performance occurs as the interest cost accrues under the Code's time value of money rules.[18] And in the case of taxes and insurance expenses, economic performance occurs as payment of the item is made.[19]

The enactment of Section 461(h) not only resolves the general controversy involving premature accruals, but it also resolves the uncertainty surrounding the use of estimated liabilities or reserve accounts such as the reserve in the *Schuessler* case. The economic performance test conclusively prohibits the use of such accounts,[20] except as specifically allowed by other provisions of the Code.[21]

---

[17] See, e.g., Reg. § 1.461–4(d)(2) (liabilities arising out of the provision of services, property, or the use of property).

[18] Reg. § 1.461–4(e). See Chapter 24C, infra.

[19] Reg. § 1.461–4(g)(5) & (6). In the case of insurance, prepayments are also subject to the capitalization rules. See Reg. § 1.461–4(g)(8) Example 6.

[20] I.R.C. § 461(h)(2)(B).

[21] I.R.C. § 461(h)(5) provides that the economic performance test does not apply to deductions allowable under any provision of the Code specifically providing for a deduction for charges to a reserve for estimated expenses. In addition, the reports of both the House Ways and Means Committee and the Senate Finance Committee indicate exceptions to the economic performance test with respect to a liability of the taxpayer to provide benefits to his employees through a qualified pension, profit-sharing or bonus plan under §§ 404 or 404A and for contributions by a taxpayer to a funded welfare benefit plan under § 419. H.Rep. No. 98–432, 98th Cong., 2d Sess. 1255, 1256 (1984); S.Rep. No. 98–169, 98th Cong., 2d Sess. 268 (1984).

Section 461(h)(3) provides an exception to the economic performance test for certain "recurring items." The exception found its way into the Code to provide a smooth transition from established business tax practices to the harsher rule of economic performance.[22] Clearly the most significant exception to the economic performance rule,[23] the recurring item exception allows the accrual of a deduction before economic performance occurs if four basic requirements are met. Generally: (1) the all events (but not economic performance) test with respect to an item must be met during the taxable year;[24] (2) economic performance must actually occur with respect to the item within the shorter of a reasonable period[25] after the close of the taxable year or eight and one-half months after the close of the taxable year;[26] (3) the item must be recurring in nature and the taxpayer must consistently treat items of this kind as incurred in the taxable year in which the all events (but not economic performance) test is satisfied;[27] and, (4) either the item must not be a material item or the accrual of the item in the taxable year in which the all events (but not economic performance) test is met must more properly match the item against the income that it generated than would the accrual of the item in the taxable year in which economic performance occurs.[28]

The Report of the Conference Committee sets guidelines to help identify the expenses that will qualify for this exception. According to these guidelines, materiality of the expense is to be determined by taking into account the size of the item, both in absolute terms and relative to the taxpayer's income and other expenses.[29] When considering the propriety of the matching of income and expenses, generally accepted accounting

---

[22] H.Rep. No. 98–861, 98th Cong., 2d Sess. 873 (1984). I.R.C. § 461(h)(3)(C) prevents this "recurring items" exception from applying to workers compensation and tort liabilities.

[23] Some of the exceptions of rather narrow application include the deduction of mining and solid waste reclamation expenditures, of closing costs associated with the decommissioning of nuclear power plants prior to economic performance and of natural gas supplier refunds by utilities under certain conditions. I.R.C. §§ 468, 468A. See H.Rep. No. 98–861, 98th Cong., 2d Sess. 875–76 (1984). See also I.R.C. § 468B providing that a qualified payment to a court-ordered settlement fund that extinguishes a tort liability of the taxpayer constitutes economic performance with respect to such liability.

The Tax Reform Act of 1984 also includes special provisions for net operating loss carrybacks of statutory or tort liability losses and nuclear power plant decommissioning losses, which are otherwise deferred by the application of the economic performance rule. I.R.C. § 172(b)(1)(K), (k)(1) and (2).

[24] I.R.C. § 461(h)(3)(A)(i).

[25] There is no indication in the Code and no suggestion in any of the Committee reports of what constitutes a "reasonable period." However, Reg. § 1.461–5(b)(1)(ii) provides that economic performance must occur on or before the earlier of: (1) the date that the taxpayer files a timely return (including extensions) for the year; or (2) the 15th day of the 9th calendar month after the close of the taxable year (see I.R.C. § 461(h)(3)(A)(ii)).

[26] I.R.C. § 461(h)(3)(A)(ii).

[27] I.R.C. § 461(h)(3)(A)(iii).

[28] I.R.C. § 461(h)(3)(A)(iv).

[29] H.Rep. No. 98–861, 98th Cong., 2d Sess. 873 (1984). If the item is classified as material on the taxpayer's financial statements it is conclusively presumed to be material for purposes of I.R.C. § 461(h). On the other hand, if the financial statements deem the item immaterial no presumption attaches under § 461(h). I.R.C. § 461(h)(3)(B). Whether an item is considered material for purposes of the recurring item exception is of no relevance as to whether it is material under other provisions of the Code. H.Rep. No. 98–861, 98th Cong., 2d Sess. 874 (1984).

principles are an important, but not controlling, factor.[30] And, finally, the Report indicates that in determining whether an item is recurring in nature and treated consistently by the taxpayer, the frequency with which the item occurs and the manner in which it is reported for tax purposes should be considered.[31]

## PROBLEMS

1.  Lawyer renders services to Client which are deductible to Client under I.R.C. § 162. Lawyer sends Client a bill for $1,000 on December 24 of year one and Client pays the bill on January 5 of year two. Discuss the tax consequences to Lawyer and Client assuming, even if unlikely, that both are calendar year, accrual method taxpayers.

2.  Lender lends out money at a legal rate to Debtor. Debtor is required to pay $5,000 interest each year on the loan which extends over a five year period. The interest is deductible by Debtor under § 163. The agreement calls for payment of each year's interest on December 31 of the year. The loan is made on January 1st of year one. Both parties are calendar year, accrual method taxpayers. Discuss the tax consequences to both parties under the following alternatives:

   (a)  On December 31 of year one Debtor who is having "serious financial trouble" fails to pay Lender.

   (b)  On December 31 of year one Debtor does not pay the interest because of a legitimate dispute over Debtor's obligation to pay the first year's interest.

   (c)  What difference in (b), above if Lender includes the December 31 interest in an applicable financial statement for year one?

   (d)  On December 15 of year one Debtor legitimately disputes the obligation to pay year one's interest but Debtor does pay it and, in year two, sues to recover it.

   (e)  Debtor pays year one's $5,000 of interest in cash on January 2d of year two.

   (f)  Debtor pays all five years' interest ($25,000) to Lender in cash on December 31 of year one.

3.  Accrue, a calendar year, accrual method taxpayer, runs a dance school which offers lessons over 48 months with one lesson in each month. No make-up lessons are offered nor is the 48-month period extended for a participant who misses any scheduled lessons. The cost of the lessons is $480 (or $10 per lesson) which is required to be prepaid in January of the first year. Based on prior experience, Accrue has found that each lesson (including salaries, rent, utilities) costs her $4.00 per person. On January 1st of year one, 100 students sign up and pay for lessons which commence in January of year one. Assume

---

[30]  Id.

[31]  Id. This exception is to be available also to taxpayers just starting a trade or business and to taxpayers who do not incur the expense annually.

This exception is unavailable to tax shelters as defined in I.R.C. § 461(i)(3). I.R.C. § 461(i)(1). See note 13 at page 589, supra.

Accrue reports $12,000 of income ($10 per month per student or 100 times $120) on the dance school's audited financial statement for year one. Discuss Accrue's tax consequences.

4.   Discuss the tax consequences to the parties involved under the following alternatives:

   (a)   Widget Corporation, an accrual-basis taxpayer, orders $3,000 worth of carpet cleaning from Mr. Carpet Cleaner, a cash-basis taxpayer, on November 1 of year one. Widget receives and pays for the carpet cleaning on April 1 of year two. Assume that both Widget and Mr. Carpet Cleaner are calendar year taxpayers.

   (b)   Same as (a), above, except that Widget pays the $3,000 to Mr. Carpet Cleaner on December 1 of year one but expects the carpet cleaning to be done on April 1 of year two.

   (c)   Same as (a), above, except that the carpet cleaning occurs on December 1 of year one.

   (d)   Same as (a), above, except that you learned that Widget had sales of $2,000,000 and expenses of $1,500,000 in year one, and typically orders $3,000 worth of carpet cleaning every ten months.

   (e)   Same as (d), above, except that Widget doesn't receive or pay for the carpet cleaning until October 1 of year two.

## D.  FORCED MATCHING OF METHODS

Internal Revenue Code: Section 267(a)(2), (b) and (c). See Section 467.

---

   The use of different accounting methods by two or more taxpayers involved in the same transaction may lead to tax consequences that do not fairly reflect the substance of the transaction. This may be so even though each taxpayer is strictly adhering to the rules of that taxpayer's own accounting method. Sometimes when this occurs Congress enacts special rules to alter the accounting method of one of the taxpayers. Below, we examine two such sections. Section 267(a)(2) requires cash and accrual taxpayers both to use the cash method, and Section 467 essentially requires use of the accrual method.

   *Section 267(a)(2).* It is clear that for an accrual method taxpayer the timing of a deduction for interest and other expenses generally does not turn on when the interest or expense is actually paid. The item, if otherwise deductible, is properly deducted when the liability to pay ripens.[1] It is equally clear that a cash method taxpayer is required to include an amount in gross income when received;[2] the right to receive, short of constructive receipt,[3] is generally a neutral consequence to a cash

---

[1]   I.R.C. § 461(h) and Reg. § 1.461–1(a)(2).

[2]   Reg. § 1.446–1(c)(1)(i).

[3]   Reg. § 1.451–2(a).

method taxpayer. With these basic principles in mind, one can understand that related taxpayers,[4] one using the accrual method and the other using the cash method, could effect a distortion of tax liability with respect to expenses and interest if no special rule stood in the way. Thus, if an accrual method taxpayer owes interest to a cash method lender, the interest can generally be deducted by the accrual method debtor even though no payment is made to the cash method lender. The result is a deduction for the debtor without matching inclusion of income to the creditor. If the parties are related, it is possible the lender may never be paid, with the result, that despite the deduction, the amount is never reported as income or, at least, that payment (and tax on the interest income) may be long delayed.

At one time, the congressional response to this potential distortion[5] was to disallow the deduction to the accrual method taxpayer forever if payment was not made to the related payee within the taxable year or within two and one-half months after the close of the taxable year. Subsequently, Congress adopted a more equitable and perhaps more effective approach to the problem. The House Report explains the change:[6]

> Under the bill, an accrual-basis taxpayer will be placed on the cash method of accounting with respect to deductions of business expenses and interest owed to a related cash-basis taxpayer. Thus, the accrual-basis taxpayer will be allowed to deduct business expenses or interest owed to a related cash-basis taxpayer when payment is made (whether or not paid within 2½ months after the close of the taxable year); in other words, the deduction by the payor will be allowed no earlier than when the corresponding income is recognized by the payee. This provision will apply to all deductible expenses (whether or not deductible under section 162, 163 or 212) the timing of which depends upon the taxpayer's method of accounting or upon the making of an election to expense an item. It will not apply, for example, to expenses such as the deductions for cost recovery or depreciation of an asset (other than an asset which is related to the performance (or nonperformance) of services by the payee).

*Section 467.* Prior to the enactment of Section 467, the parties to a multi-year agreement for the rental of property or for the long-term performance of services were largely free to design payment terms to suit their wishes. Depending upon the tax status of the parties for example in the context of a lease, it might be advantageous to have the bulk of the payments made during the early years (frontloading) or, alternatively, in the later years (backloading). Typically, a backloaded arrangement (e.g., $1,000,000 per year, payable at the end of the fourth year) benefitted a

---

4    I.R.C. § 267(b).

5    See Text at supra note 4.

6    H.Rep. No. 98–432, 98th Cong., 2d Sess. 1578–79 (1984).

cash method lessor by permitting the lessor to defer income until the later year when he received payment,[7] even though the accrual method lessee was permitted deductions for rental expense ratably over the term of the lease.[8]

An additional benefit available to lessors of property was the conversion of ordinary income into capital gain by the use of agreements with progressively stepped up rental rates.[9] Under a so-called step-rate agreement the rent gradually increases (in "steps") over the term of the lease. Since property is obviously more valuable when it returns a higher rental, at some later time the lessor could sell the property at a price reflecting the higher rents due in the later years of the lease, thus effecting a conversion of essentially deferred ordinary rental income into capital gain. The tax advantage at the crossover could more than offset the lower rentals he would accept in the early years. With the enactment of Section 467,[10] such manipulation of rental income (and rental expense) is no longer possible.[11] At least it is no longer possible in a big way; Section 467 steps in to alter tax results in property rentals only if the total consideration to be paid exceeds $250,000.[12]

This is probably a good place to say that, although we speak in terms of rental income just as the statute does, Section 467 may also apply to payments for services. It is not self-executing in that respect but subsection (g), rather ineptly, authorizes the promulgation of regulations to bring about that result.

The basic thrust of Section 467 is to put both parties to a "Section 467 rental agreement"[13] on a specially prescribed accrual method of accounting for that transaction. The accrual method prescribed applies present value concepts to the rent that accrues during each year and imposes interest on the amount of accrued but unpaid rent from prior years.[14] The discount rate and interest rate to be used under Section 467 is 110 percent of the applicable Federal rate determined under Section 1274(d), compounded semiannually.[15] The effect of this treatment is to require inclusion and deduction of the value of rentals in the year of use. Any difference between this amount and the cash changing hands is, in effect, a loan between the taxpayers on which interest is imputed. That

---

[7]   Reg. §§ 1.446–1(c)(1)(i) and 1.451–1(a). See Chapter 19B1, supra.

[8]   I.R.C. § 461(h); Reg. §§ 1.446–1(c)(1)(ii) and 1.461–1(a)(2). See Chapter 19C2, supra.

[9]   S.Rep. No. 98–169, 98th Cong., 2d Sess. 260 (1984).

[10]   Tax Reform Act of 1984, Pub.Law. No. 98–369, § 92, 98th Cong., 2d Sess. (1984).

[11]   See Whitesman, "Section 467: Tax Planning for Deferred-Payment Leases," 5 Virg.Tax Rev. 345 (1986); Hamilton and Comi, "The Time Value of Money: Section 467 Rental Agreements Under the Tax Reform Act of 1984," 63 Taxes 155 (1985).

[12]   I.R.C. § 467(d)(2).

[13]   I.R.C. § 467(d)(1).

[14]   I.R.C. § 467(a).

[15]   I.R.C. § 467(e)(4). The applicable Federal rate is discussed at page 480, supra.

is, if in any year a lessor receives less than the value of a year's rental, the difference is treated as a loan by him to the lessee.[16]

## PROBLEMS

1. In each of the following situations, determine in what year the payor would be allowed a deduction and what year the payee would include the amount involved in his gross income:

    (a) A, an accrual method taxpayer, ordered and received $500 worth of janitorial supplies in year one from B who is unrelated to A and who is a cash method taxpayer. The supplies are for use in A's cleaning business. A makes the $500 payment to B sometime in year two.

    (b) Same as (a), above, except that A and B are father and daughter, respectively.

    (c) What result in (b), above, if A uses the cash method of accounting and B uses the accrual method of accounting?

2. Determine whether § 267(a)(2) would apply in the following situations:

    (a) X Corporation, an accrual method taxpayer, leases a parcel of land from B, a cash method taxpayer. B owns 60 out of a total of 100 shares of X Corporation common stock issued and outstanding. X Corporation has no other classes of stock.

    (b) Same as (a), above, except that B owns 40 shares of X, S, B's spouse, owns 15 shares of X, and the remaining shares are held by unrelated parties.

    (c) Same as (a), above, except that B owns 20 shares of X, S, B's spouse, owns 15 shares of X, the B and Z partnership owns 40 shares of X, and the remaining shares are held by unrelated parties. B and Z, unrelated parties, each have a 50 percent interest in the capital and profits of the B and Z partnership.

    (d) Same as (c), above, except that the B and Z partnership only owns 20 shares of X Corporation.

    (e) Same as (a), above, except that B owns 20 shares in X, S, B's spouse owns 15 shares of X, the S and Z partnership owns 20 shares of X, and the remaining shares are held by unrelated parties. S and Z, an unrelated party, each own a 50 percent interest in the capital and profits of the S and Z partnership.

    (f) Same as (a), above, except that B owns 30 shares of X, S, B's spouse owns 15 shares of X, S's brother owns 10 shares of X, and the remaining shares are held by unrelated parties.

---

[16] I.R.C. § 467 sets forth alternative rules for calculating the amount of rent that accrues during a particular period. If the agreement itself purports to allocate rentals, the amount of rent that accrues for any period is determined in accordance with the rental agreement; present value principles are to be applied to any rent to be paid after the close of the period with which it is associated. I.R.C. § 476(b)(1).

# CHAPTER 20

# HOW INELUCTABLE IS THE INTEGRITY OF THE TAXABLE YEAR?

## A. TAXPAYER'S RESTORATION OF PREVIOUSLY TAXED INCOME

Internal Revenue Code: Section 1341(a) and (b)(1) and (2) (first sentence).

Regulations: Section 1.1341–1(a), (b)(1)(i) and (ii).

---

### United States v. Lewis

Supreme Court of the United States, 1951.
340 U.S. 590, 71 S.Ct. 522.

■ MR. JUSTICE BLACK delivered the opinion of the Court.

Respondent Lewis brought this action in the Court of Claims seeking a refund of an alleged overpayment of his 1944 income tax. The facts found by the Court of Claims are: In his 1944 income tax return respondent reported about $22,000 which he had received that year as an employee's bonus. As a result of subsequent litigation in a state court, however, it was decided that respondent's bonus had been improperly computed; under compulsion of the state court's judgment he returned approximately $11,000 to his employer. Until payment of the judgment in 1946, respondent had at all times claimed and used the full $22,000 unconditionally as his own, in the good faith though "mistaken" belief that he was entitled to the whole bonus.

On the foregoing facts the Government's position is that respondent's 1944 tax should not be recomputed, but that respondent should have deducted the $11,000 as a loss in his 1946 tax return. See G.C.M. 16730, XV–1, Cum.Bull. 179 (1936). The Court of Claims, however, relying on its own case, Greenwald v. United States, 102 Ct.Cl. 272, 57 F.Supp. 569, held that the excess bonus received "under a mistake of fact" was not income in 1944 and ordered a refund based on a recalculation of that year's tax. 117 Ct.Cl. 336, 91 F.Supp. 1017. We granted certiorari, 340 U.S. 903, 71 S.Ct. 279, because this holding conflicted with many decisions of the courts of appeals, see, e.g., Haberkorn v. United States, 173 F.2d 587, and with principles announced in North American Oil v. Burnet, 286 U.S. 417, 52 S.Ct. 613.

In the *North American Oil* case, we said: "If a taxpayer receives earnings under a claim of right and without restriction as to its disposition, he has received income which he is required to return, even though it may still be claimed that he is not entitled to retain the money, and even though he may still be adjudged liable to restore its equivalent." 286 U.S. at 424, 52 S.Ct. at page 615. Nothing in this language permits an exception merely because a taxpayer is "mistaken" as to the validity of his claim. Nor has the "claim of right" doctrine been impaired, as the Court of Claims stated, by Freuler v. Helvering, 291 U.S. 35, 54 S.Ct. 308, or Commissioner v. Wilcox, 327 U.S. 404, 66 S.Ct. 546. The *Freuler* case involved an entirely different section of the Internal Revenue Code, and its holding is inapplicable here. 291 U.S. at 43, 54 S.Ct. at page 311. * * *.

Income taxes must be paid on income received (or accrued) during an annual accounting period. Cf. I.R.C., §§ 41, 42; and see Burnet v. Sanford & Brooks Co., 282 U.S. 359, 363, 51 S.Ct. 150, 151. The "claim of right" interpretation of the tax laws has long been used to give finality to that period, and is now deeply rooted in the federal tax system. See cases collected in 2 Mertens, Law of Federal Income Taxation, § 12.103. We see no reason why the Court should depart from this well-settled interpretation merely because it results in an advantage or disadvantage to a taxpayer.[1]

Reversed.

■ MR. JUSTICE DOUGLAS, dissenting.

The question in this case is not whether the bonus had to be included in 1944 income for purposes of the tax. Plainly it should have been because the taxpayer claimed it as of right. Some years later, however, it was judicially determined that he had no claim to the bonus. The question is whether he may then get back the tax which he paid on the money.

Many inequities are inherent in the income tax. We multiply them needlessly by nice distinctions which have no place in the practical administration of the law. If the refund were allowed, the integrity of the taxable year would not be violated. The tax would be paid when due; but the Government would not be permitted to maintain the unconscionable position that it can keep the tax after it is shown that payment was made on money which was not income to the taxpayer.

## NOTE

*The Requirements of Section 1341.* Section 1341 may be a good place to take note of the rule of the seven barrel staves. Apparently, it took seven

---

[1] It has been suggested that it would be more "equitable" to reopen respondent's 1944 tax return. While the suggestion might work to the advantage of this taxpayer, it could not be adopted as a general solution because, in many cases, the three-year statute of limitations would preclude recovery. I.R.C. § 322(b). [See I.R.C. (1986) § 6511(a). Ed.]

barrel staves to make a vessel that would hold water; if one was missing, it was just a case of nothing done. A statutory provision that requires the coincidence of several requirements presents the same problem; if one is not met the provision is inapplicable. Note the three prerequisites expressed in Section 1341(a)(1) through (3).[1]

Under Section 1341(a)(1), an item must be included in gross income because it appeared that the taxpayer had an unrestricted right to it. Such inclusion is required under the *North American Oil* doctrine.[2] Application of this first test may not be difficult.[3] However, an embezzler who later returned misappropriated funds would obviously fail it.[4]

Most of the controversy under Section 1341 has arisen under Section 1341(a)(2). Note, first, that the amount repaid must constitute an *allowable deduction* within the *Lewis* principle, if the Section 1341 alternatives are to be available. A repayment may fit within the requirements of Section 162 or Section 212.[5]

To satisfy Section 1341(a)(2), it must also be *"established* after the close of such prior year . . . that the taxpayer did not have an unrestricted right to such item. . . ."* Thus, a voluntary act of a repayment does not satisfy the requirement. In Pike v. Commissioner,[6] the Tax Court concluded that the Section 1341(a)(2) "established" requirement was not met where there was an investigation by a special counsel of a state who was of the opinion that a gain on the sale of stock of the corporation belonged to the corporation and, as a result, the taxpayer returned the gain to the corporation. The court stated that "a judicial determination of liability is not required,"[7] but to avoid abuse of Section 1341, "a taxpayer must prove by a preponderance of the evidence that he was not entitled to the unrestricted use of the amount received in the prior year."[8]

It is also clear that the taxpayer's lack of an unrestricted right to the item must be established *after* the close of the year for which the item was included in gross income but on the basis of circumstances that existed

---

[1]    An additional limitation of I.R.C. § 1341 is found in § 1341(b)(2) which provides that the section "does not apply to any deduction allowable with respect to an item which was included in gross income by reason of the sale or other disposition of stock in trade of the taxpayer (or other property of a kind which would properly have been included in the inventory of the taxpayer if on hand at the close of the prior taxable year) or property held by the taxpayer primarily for sale to customers in the ordinary course of his trade or business."

[2]    The case is set out at page 623, supra. See also Reg. § 1.1341–1(a)(2), treating income included under a claim of right as "an item included in gross income because it appeared from all the facts available in the year of inclusion that the taxpayer had an unrestricted right to such item." See Dubroff, "The Claim of Right Doctrine," 40 Tax L.Rev. 729 (1985). An early, basic analysis of § 1341 appears in Webster, "The Claim of Right Doctrine: 1954 Version," 10 Tax L.Rev. 381 (1955) and see Emanuel, "The Scope of Section 1341," 53 Taxes 644 (1975).

[3]    See Rev. Rul. 68–153, 1968–1 C.B. 371.

[4]    Yerkie v. Commissioner, 67 T.C. 388 (1976); Snavely v. Commissioner, 67 T.C.M. 3056 (1994); Rev. Rul. 65–254, 1965–2 C.B. 50.

[5]    But see Hope v. Commissioner, 55 T.C. 1020 (1971), aff'd 471 F.2d 738 (3d Cir.1973), cert. denied 414 U.S. 824, 94 S.Ct. 126 (1973); and cf. United States v. Simon, 281 F.2d 520 (6th Cir.1960).

[6]    44 T.C. 787 (1965).

[7]    Id. at 799. See Rev. Rul. 58–456, 1958–2 C.B. 415, 418.

[8]    Id. at 800.

*during* such prior year. The statutory test is whether the taxpayer "did not have" the right that was apparent in the year of receipt. Thus, a subsequent agreement to return an amount to which the taxpayer *was* entitled, no matter how binding on the taxpayer, will not invoke Section 1341. In Blanton v. Commissioner,[9] *after* receiving corporate fees for three years, the taxpayer entered into an agreement that any fees held to be excessive by the Internal Revenue Service (and so not deductible by the corporation) would be returned by him to the corporation. When the first three years' fees were found to be excessive, taxpayer returned the excess to the corporation and asserted a right to the benefits of Section 1341. The Tax Court held that the section did not apply because:[10]

> Under § 1341(a)(2), the requisite lack of an unrestricted right to an income item permitting deduction must arise out of the circumstances, terms, and conditions of the *original* payment of such item to the taxpayer and not out of circumstances, terms, and conditions imposed upon such payment by reason of some subsequent agreement between payor and payee.

The *Blanton* result raises the question whether Section 1341 would apply if *prior to receipt* an employee has entered into a valid contract with the employer under which the employee is obligated to repay amounts subsequently held not to be deductible by the employer. Is the answer indicated by the *Van Cleave* case, which follows this note, sound as a matter of statutory interpretation? As a matter of tax policy?

The third requirement, which appears at Section 1341(a)(3), is that the amount returned must exceed $3,000. One may wonder about this congressional insertion of a de minimis principle. But it probably does have the administrative advantage of relieving the Commissioner from the task of analyzing and cross-check numerous Section 1341 assertions that can have little impact on the revenue and are something less than cataclysmic to the taxpayer involved.

*The Mechanics of Section 1341.* If the requirements of Section 1341 described above are satisfied, a taxpayer is allowed the best of two possible tax results. The first is the *Lewis* result—simply a deduction in the current year under Section 1341(a)(4). The second, found in Section 1341(a)(5), allows the taxpayer to reduce the current year's tax for the prior year's tax increase caused by the prior year's over-inclusion in gross income. The current year's tax liability is the *lesser* of the Section 1341(a)(4) or Section 1341(a)(5) results. The alternative which is most beneficial depends upon the relative rate of tax on the item in the two different years. If the taxpayer is in a higher rate bracket in the current year, then the Section 1341(a)(4) deduction is the most beneficial. Alternately, if the item was taxed at a higher rate in the prior year, the Section 1341(a)(5) alternative becomes the more beneficial result.

---

[9]  46 T.C. 527 (1966), affirmed per curiam 379 F.2d 558 (5th Cir.1967).

[10]  Id. at 530. See Soled, "Reimbursement Agreements for Excessive Payments: Compensation and Other," 26 N.Y.U. Inst. on Fed. Tax. 1143 (1968).

# Van Cleave v. United States*

United States Court of Appeals, Sixth Circuit, 1983.
718 F.2d 193.

■ Before ENGEL and KRUPANSKY, CIRCUIT JUDGES and BROWN, SENIOR CIRCUIT JUDGE.

■ BAILEY BROWN, SENIOR CIRCUIT JUDGE.

This appeal involves a claim of favorable income tax treatment under 26 U.S.C. § 1341 by a taxpayer who in a subsequent year paid back excessive compensation to the corporation which employed him. The taxpayer included this excessive compensation in his return for the year the compensation was received. The government concedes that taxpayer is entitled to a deduction in the subsequent year. Taxpayer contends, however, that he should be allowed, pursuant to Section 1341, more favorable tax treatment by in effect excluding the excessive compensation from his income in the year received, thereby reducing his tax liability for that year and receiving a credit against his tax liability for the subsequent year. The district court, after a bench trial, entered judgment for the government in taxpayer's refund action and taxpayer appealed. We reverse and hold that taxpayer is entitled to the benefit of Section 1341.

## BACKGROUND

The taxpayer, Eugene Van Cleave, was president and majority stockholder of VanMark Corporation throughout the time in question. In 1969, the corporation adopted a by-law requiring corporate officers who received from the corporation income determined by the Internal Revenue Service (IRS) to be excessive—and so not deductible by the corporation as a business expense—to pay back the amount determined to be excessive to the corporation. In addition, Mr. Van Cleave entered into a separate agreement requiring him to reimburse the corporation for nondeductible compensation.

Mr. Van Cleave received $332,000 in salary and bonuses in 1974. During 1975, the IRS audited the corporation's return, determined that $57,500 of Mr. Van Cleave's salary was excessive, and disallowed that portion of his salary as a deduction to the corporation. In December, 1975, pursuant to the corporation's by-law and the agreement between Mr. Van Cleave and the corporation, Mr. Van Cleave repaid the nondeductible $57,500.

Mr. Van Cleave reported the full compensation on his calendar year 1974 income tax return. On his 1975 return, prepared with the repayment to the corporation in mind, he calculated his tax liability by using 26 U.S.C. § 1341. The IRS audited the return, and allowed a

---

* See Bartelstein, "Van Cleave v. United States: Repayment Agreements and Section 1341" 38 Tax Lawyer 239 (1984), which is critical of the *Van Cleave* result and supportive of the District Court's contrary result in the case.

deduction for 1975 but disallowed use of Section 1341, resulting in a tax deficiency of $5,987.34. Mr. Van Cleave paid this deficiency and brought this action for a refund.

This case turns on the interpretation of Section 1341 of the Internal Revenue Code.

\* \* \*

Section 1341 was enacted by Congress to mitigate the sometimes harsh result of the application of the "claim of right" doctrine. United States v. Skelly Oil Co., 394 U.S. 678, 681, 89 S.Ct. 1379, 1381 (1969); \* \* \*. Under the claim of right doctrine, a taxpayer must pay tax on an item in the year in which he receives it under a claim of right even if it is later determined that his right to the item was not absolute and he is required to return it. The taxpayer, however, is allowed to deduct the amount of the item from his income in the year of repayment. This result was held to be required because income and deductions are determined on an annual basis. *Skelly* at 681, 89 S.Ct. at 1381. But, as pointed out by the Supreme Court in *Skelly,* it is possible for a taxpayer to benefit less from the deduction in the year of repayment than he would benefit if he had been able to deduct the amount repaid from his income in the year of receipt. Id. This result of the claim of right doctrine could occur when, as was the case with Mr. Van Cleave, the taxpayer had been in a higher tax bracket in the year of receipt than he was in the year of repayment.

Section 1341 allows the taxpayer to choose the more favorable alternative as follows:

> If the taxpayer included an item in gross income in one taxable year, and in a subsequent taxable year he becomes entitled to a deduction because the item or a portion thereof is no longer subject to his unrestricted use, and the amount of the deduction is in excess of $3,000, the tax for the subsequent year is reduced by either the tax attributable to the deduction or the decrease in the tax for the prior year attributable to the removal of the item, whichever is greater. Under the rule of the *Lewis* case (340 U.S. 590, 71 S.Ct. 522 (1951)) [see infra], the taxpayer is entitled to a deduction only in the year of repayment. \* \* \*.

I.

The district court held that Section 1341 treatment was not available to Mr. Van Cleave because it determined that his repayment was voluntary. The district court determined that it was voluntary because Mr. Van Cleave owned a substantial majority of the stock and in that sense controlled the corporation. On appeal, however, the government does not contend that Section 1341 is inapplicable because the repayment was voluntary and indeed does not contend that the repayment in fact was voluntary.

The district court also seemed to be persuaded by the argument that, if Mr. Van Cleave were allowed Section 1341 treatment under these circumstances, this would open the door to tax avoidance in that taxpayers who controlled corporations could "test the waters" in setting their compensation without risk of an adverse tax result. We believe, however, that such possibility of tax avoidance is not a proper consideration in applying this statute, and that the consideration is a legislative rather than a judicial consideration. Moreover, as Mr. Van Cleave suggests, the possibility of tax avoidance could be reduced by requiring the corporation and recipient of compensation to state in their returns that such compensation was paid subject to an obligation to reimburse in the event a deduction is disallowed to the corporation.

## II.

The leading case on the claim of right tax doctrine is North American Oil Consolidated v. Burnet, 286 U.S. 417, 52 S.Ct. 613 (1932). *North American Oil* involved a dispute over the year in which income, earned on property held by a receiver during a title dispute between the taxpayer and the government, was to be taxed. The possibilities were 1916, the year in which the income was earned; 1917, the year in which the district court ruled in favor of the taxpayer and the money was paid to the taxpayer; or 1922, the year the litigation was finally terminated in the taxpayer's favor. In an opinion by Justice Brandeis, the Court determined that 1917 was the year that the income must be reported and set forth the claim of right doctrine as follows:

> If a taxpayer receives earnings under a claim of right and without restriction as to its disposition, he has received income which he is required to return, even though it may still be claimed that he is not entitled to retain the money, and even though he may still be adjudged liable to restore its equivalent.
> Id. at 424, 52 S.Ct. at 615.

In a more recent case, Healy v. Commissioner, 345 U.S. 278, 73 S.Ct. 671 (1953), each of the taxpayers involved received excessive compensation from a closely-held corporation in which he was both a shareholder and an officer. The taxpayers reported that compensation as income in the year of receipt. In a subsequent year, the IRS determined that part of this compensation was excessive, disallowed the deduction to the corporation, and taxpayers, as transferees, were required to pay back the excess. The government conceded that the taxpayers could deduct the amount paid back from their taxable income, but argued that the deduction could only be taken in the year of repayment. Taxpayers, on the other hand, argued that they should be allowed to have their tax liability determined by taking a deduction in the year the excessive compensation was received. The Court held that, under the claim of right doctrine, the deduction could be taken only from the income of the year of repayment.

In a similar case, United States v. Lewis, 340 U.S. 590, 71 S.Ct. 522 (1951), taxpayer received a bonus from his employer in 1944 and reported it on his income tax return for that year. In a subsequent year, taxpayer paid back one half of the bonus pursuant to a state court judgment. As in *Healy,* taxpayer claimed that he should be able, in the year of repayment, to have his tax liability determined by taking a deduction in the year the excessive bonus was paid to him. The Court held, however, that, under the claim of right doctrine, the taxpayer could take a deduction only in the year of repayment. Justice Douglas dissented, noting that the effect of the Court's decision was to allow the government to exact tax on money that was not income to the taxpayer.

As previously noted, Section 1341 was enacted to alleviate the effect of the claim of right doctrine in cases such as *Lewis.* The government argues, however, that Section 1341 is not available to the taxpayer in the instant case. The government points out that Section 1341 provides for taxpayer relief only if "it *appeared* that the taxpayer had an unrestricted right" (emphasis added) to the excess salary and "it was established after the close of such prior taxable year * * * that the taxpayer did not have an unrestricted right to such item." Section 1341(a)(1) and (2). The government argues that Mr. Van Cleave had more than an *appearance* of an unrestricted right to the excess compensation in the year in which it was received, and that the right to the compensation became restricted only upon the occurrence of the IRS audit and determination in a subsequent year. The government maintains that, since Mr. Van Cleave had an unrestricted right to the compensation in the year of receipt, contingent only upon the happening of an event in a subsequent year, Section 1341 is not available to him.[1]

We reject this argument and hold that Section 1341 is available to Mr. Van Cleave. The fact that his ultimate right to the compensation was not determined until the occurrence of a subsequent event does not mean that Mr. Van Cleave had, in the statutory sense, an unrestricted right to the compensation when he received it. In Prince v. United States, 610 F.2d 350 (1980), the Fifth Circuit reversed a district court decision that the estate of a taxpayer was not entitled to Section 1341 tax adjustment. A state court had ruled that the decedent, a trust beneficiary, had received trust funds—and paid federal income tax on them—that should have gone to the trustee as part of its fee. The state court required the decedent's estate to return these funds to the trustee. The government's position in that case was identical to its stance in this case: Section 1341 was not available to the taxpayer's estate because the taxpayer had an unrestricted right to the income in the year of receipt, not just the appearance of a right. Id. at 352. In rejecting the government's argument, the court said:

---

[1] The government also maintains this position in Rev.Rul. 67–437, 1967–2 C.B. 296. See also Rev.Rul. 69–115, 1969–1 C.B. 50, which holds that the taxpayers would be allowed to deduct the payment as an I.R.C. § 162 deduction in the year of repayment. Ed.

The Alabama judgment established, whether expressly or by implication, that the deductions from the trust income for the ten year fee had been miscalculated. As a result, [decedent] had received more income from the trust than she was entitled to receive. This income had to be returned. The requirements of Section 1341 were thus clearly satisfied. [Decedent] appeared to have an unrestricted right to the income when she received it; it was established in a taxable year after she received it that she did not have such a right. Id.

We agree with the Fifth Circuit's reading of Section 1341 and hold that the fact that a restriction on a taxpayer's right to income does not arise until a year subsequent to the time of receipt does not affect the availability of Section 1341 tax adjustment. Therefore, Section 1341 tax adjustment is available to a taxpayer in this situation if the other requirements of the section are met. We are aided in this conclusion by our examination of cases involving the application of the claim of right doctrine, the effect of which the section was designed to alleviate. United States v. Lewis, 340 U.S. 590, 71 S.Ct. 522 (1951); Healy v. Commissioner, 345 U.S. 278, 73 S.Ct. 671 (1953). Acceptance of the government's reading of the statute would thwart the ameliorative purpose intended by Congress in enacting the section. * * *. Accordingly, Mr. Van Cleave is entitled to a tax adjustment under Section 1341.

The judgment of the district court is reversed and the case is remanded for proceedings consistent with this opinion.

## PROBLEMS

1. Section 1341 provides a statutory exception to the *Lewis* rule which employs the doctrine of strict annual accounting.

   (a) What requirements must be met in order to trigger § 1341?

   (b) If § 1341 applies what is the result to the taxpayer?

   (c) When is § 1341 more beneficial to the taxpayer than the *Lewis* case?

2. Payer received $40,000 in the form of advance and regular commissions on sales of goods for Employer in year one. Will § 1341 be applicable if:

   (a) In year two, some customers return goods due to a breach of warranty and Payer repays Employer $10,000 of commissions that were prepaid as Payer is required to do under Payer's contract?

   (b) The years are the same as in (a), above, except that Payer acquired by embezzlement the $10,000 that was subsequently returned?

   (c) Payer acquired the $10,000 in the same manner as in part (a), above; however, Payer was not required by contract to return the excess commissions but did so voluntarily?

(d)  Payer returned the $10,000 based on a return of merchandise by a customer of Payer in year two, under such circumstances that Employer rescinded the contract with the customer, which, in turn, effected a reduced commission to Payer, requiring a repayment of $10,000 to Employer?

## B.  THE TAX BENEFIT DOCTRINE*

Internal Revenue Code: Section 111(a). See Section 111(b) and (c).

---

## Alice Phelan Sullivan Corp. v. United States**
Court of Claims of the United States, 1967.
381 F.2d 399.

■ COLLINS, JUDGE.

Plaintiff, a California corporation, brings this action to recover an alleged overpayment in its 1957 income tax. During that year, there was returned to taxpayer two parcels of realty, each of which it had previously donated and claimed as a charitable contribution deduction. The first donation had been made in 1939; the second, in 1940. Under the then applicable corporate tax rates, the deductions claimed ($4,243.49 for 1939 and $4,463.44 for 1940) yielded plaintiff an aggregate tax benefit of $1,877.49.[1]

Each conveyance had been made subject to the condition that the property be used either for a religious or for an educational purpose. In 1957, the donee decided not to use the gifts; they were therefore reconveyed to plaintiff. Upon audit of taxpayer's income tax return it was found that the recovered property was not reflected in its 1957 gross income. The Commissioner of Internal Revenue disagreed with plaintiff's characterization of the recovery as a nontaxable return of capital. He viewed the transaction as giving rise to taxable income and therefore adjusted plaintiff's income by adding to it $8,706.93—the total of the charitable contribution deductions previously claimed and allowed. This addition to income, taxed at the 1957 corporate tax rate of 52 percent, resulted in a deficiency assessment of $4,527.60. After payment of the deficiency, plaintiff filed a claim for the refund of $2,650.11, asserting this amount as overpayment on the theory that a correct assessment

---

*  See Lindsay, "An Asset-Based Approach to the Tax Benefit Rule," 72 Cal.L.Rev. 1257 (1984); White, "An Essay on the Conceptual Foundations of the Tax Benefit Rule," 82 Mich.L.Rev. 486 (1983). Bittker and Kanner, "The Tax Benefit Rule," 26 U.C.L.A.L.Rev. 265 (1978); Corlew, "The Tax Benefit Rule, Claim of Right Restorations, and Annual Accounting: A Cure for the Inconsistencies," 21 Vand.L.Rev. 995 (1968); Willis, "The Tax Benefit Rule: A Different View and a Unified Theory of Error Correction," 42 Fla.L.Rev. 575 (1990).

**  There is a comment on Sullivan at 66 Mich.L.Rev. 381 (1967). Ed.

[1]  The tax rate in 1939 was 18 percent; in 1940, 24 percent.

could demand no more than the return of the tax benefit originally enjoyed, i.e., $1,877.49. The claim was disallowed.

This court has had prior occasion to consider the question which the present suit presents. In Perry v. United States, 160 F.Supp. 270, 142 Ct.Cl. 7 (1958) (Judges Madden and Laramore dissenting), it was recognized that a return to the donor of a prior charitable contribution gave rise to income to the extent of the deduction previously allowed. The court's point of division—which is likewise the division between the instant parties—was whether the "gain" attributable to the recovery was to be taxed at the rate applicable at the time the deduction was first claimed or whether the proper rate was that in effect at the time of recovery. The majority, concluding that the Government should be entitled to recoup no more than that which it lost, held that the tax liability arising upon the return of a charitable gift should equal the tax benefit experienced at time of donation. Taxpayer urges that the *Perry* rationale dictates that a like result be reached in this case.

The Government, of course, assumes the opposite stance. Mindful of the homage due the principle of stare decisis, it bids us first to consider the criteria under which judicial reexamination of an earlier decision is justifiable. We are referred to Judge Davis' concurring opinion in Mississippi River Fuel Corp. v. United States, 314 F.2d 953, 958, 161 Ct.Cl. 237, 246–247 (1963), wherein he states that:

> * * *. The question is not what we would hold if we now took a fresh look but whether we should take that fresh look. * * *.

[We] examine anew the issue which this case presents.

A transaction which returns to a taxpayer his own property cannot be considered as giving rise to "income"—at least where that term is confined to its traditional sense of "gain derived from capital, from labor, or from both combined." Eisner v. Macomber, 252 U.S. 189, 207, 40 S.Ct. 189 (1920). Yet the principle is well engrained in our tax law that the return or recovery of property that was once the subject of an income tax deduction must be treated as income in the year of its recovery. * * *. The only limitation upon that principle is the so-called "tax-benefit rule." This rule permits exclusion of the recovered item from income so long as its initial use as a deduction did not provide a tax saving. * * *. But where full tax use of a deduction was made and a tax saving thereby obtained, then the extent of saving is considered immaterial. The recovery is viewed as income to the full extent of the deduction previously allowed.[2]

Formerly the exclusive province of judge-made law, the tax-benefit concept now finds expression both in statute and administrative regulations. Section 111 of the Internal Revenue Code of 1954 accords

---

[2]  The rationale which supports the principle, as well as its limitation, is that the property, having once served to offset taxable income (i.e., as a tax deduction) should be treated, upon its recoupment, as the recovery of that which had been previously deducted. See Plumb, "The Tax Benefit Rule Today," 57 Harv.L.Rev. 129, 131 n. 10 (1943).

tax-benefit treatment to the recovery of bad debts, prior taxes, and delinquency amounts.[3] Treasury regulations have "broadened" the rule of exclusion by extending similar treatment to "all other losses, expenditures, and accruals made the basis of deductions from gross income for prior taxable years * * *."[4]

Drawing our attention to the broad language of this regulation, the Government insists that the present recovery must find its place within the scope of the regulation and, as such, should be taxed in a manner consistent with the treatment provided for like items of recovery, i.e., that it be taxed at the rate prevailing in the year of recovery. We are compelled to agree.

Set in historical perspective, it is clear that the cited regulation may not be regarded as an unauthorized extension of the otherwise limited congressional approval given to the tax-benefit concept. While the statute, (i.e., section 111) addresses itself only to bad debts, prior taxes, and delinquency amounts, it was, as noted in Dobson v. Commissioner, 320 U.S. 489, 64 S.Ct. 239 (1943), designed not to limit the application of the judicially designed tax-benefit rule, but rather to insure against its demise. "A specific statutory exception was necessary in bad debt cases only because the courts reversed the Tax Court and established as matter of law a 'theoretically proper' rule which distorted the taxpayer's income [i.e., taxation of a recovery though no benefit may have been obtained through its earlier deduction]." 320 U.S. at 506, 64 S.Ct. at 249.

The *Dobson* decision insured the continued validity of the tax-benefit concept, and the regulation—being but the embodiment of that principle—is clearly adequate to embrace a recoverable charitable contribution. See California & Hawaiian Sugar Ref. Corp., supra, 311 F.2d at 239, 159 Ct.Cl. at 567. But the regulation does not specify which tax rate is to be applied to the recouped deduction, and this consideration brings us to the matter here in issue.

Ever since Burnet v. Sanford & Brooks Co., 282 U.S. 359, 51 S.Ct. 150 (1931), the concept of accounting for items of income and expense on an annual basis has been accepted as the basic principle upon which our tax laws are structured. "It is the essence of any system of taxation that it should produce revenue ascertainable, and payable to the government, at regular intervals. Only by such a system is it practicable to produce a regular flow of income and apply methods of accounting, assessment, and collection capable of practical operation." 282 U.S. at 365, 51 S.Ct. at 152. To insure the vitality of the single-year concept, it is essential not only that annual income be ascertained without reference to losses experienced in an earlier accounting period, but also that income be taxed without reference to earlier tax rates. And absent specific statutory authority sanctioning a departure from this principle, it may only be said

---

[3]   [I.R.C. § 111 and Reg. § 1.111–1 is omitted. Ed.]

[4]   Id.

of *Perry* that it achieved a result which was more equitably just than legally correct.[5]

Since taxpayer in this case did obtain full tax benefit from its earlier deductions, those deductions were properly classified as income upon recoupment and must be taxed as such. This can mean nothing less than the application of that tax rate which is in effect during the year in which the recovered item is recognized as a factor of income. We therefore sustain the Government's position and grant its motion for summary judgment. Perry v. United States, supra, is hereby overruled, and plaintiff's petition is dismissed.

## PROBLEMS

1.  In year one Taxpayers filed a joint return showing gross income of $45,000 and deductions of $48,000, which included state real property taxes paid on their residence in the amount of $5,000. Contesting the amount of their liability for the state property taxes, Taxpayers successfully brought suit for a refund of those taxes. What result to Taxpayers in the following alternative circumstances?

    (a)  In year two, they get a judgment for and receive a $2,000 refund.

    (b)  In year two, they get a judgment for and receive a $4,000 refund.

    (c)  What result in (b), above, if they had no itemized deductions for year one other than the $4,000 in taxes and they claimed the standard deduction for year one?

2.  Compare § 111 with § 1341. Which is friendlier to the taxpayer?

## C.  INCOME AVERAGING

### 1.  DO-IT-YOURSELF AVERAGING

Internal Revenue Code: See Section 409A.

---

## Revenue Ruling 60–31
### 1960–1 Cum.Bull. 174.

Advice has been requested regarding the taxable year of inclusion in gross income of a taxpayer, using the cash receipts and disbursements

---

[5]  This opinion represents the views of the majority and complies with existing law and decisions. However, in the writer's personal opinion, it produces a harsh and inequitable result. Perhaps, it exemplifies a situation "where the letter of the law killeth; the spirit giveth life." The tax-benefit concept is an equitable doctrine which should be carried to an equitable conclusion. Since it is the declared public policy to encourage contributions to charitable and educational organizations, a donor, whose gift to such organizations is returned, should not be required to refund to the Government a greater amount than the tax benefit received when the deduction was made for the gift. Such a rule would avoid a penalty to the taxpayer and an unjust enrichment to the Government. However, the court cannot legislate and any change in the existing law rests within the wisdom and discretion of the Congress.

method of accounting, of compensation for services received under the circumstances described below.

(1)  On January 1, 1958, the taxpayer and corporation $X$ executed an employment contract under which the taxpayer is to be employed by the corporation in an executive capacity for a period of five years. Under the contract, the taxpayer is entitled to a stated annual salary and to additional compensation of $10x$ dollars for each year. The additional compensation will be credited to a bookkeeping reserve account and will be deferred, accumulated, and paid in annual installments equal to one-fifth of the amount in the reserve as of the close of the year immediately preceding the year of first payment. The payments are to begin only upon (a) termination of the taxpayer's employment by the corporation; (b) the taxpayer's becoming a part-time employee of the corporation; or (c) the taxpayer's becoming partially or totally incapacitated. Under the terms of the agreement, corporation $X$ is under a merely contractual obligation to make the payments when due, and the parties did not intend that the amounts in the reserve be held by the corporation in trust for the taxpayer.

The contract further provides that if the taxpayer should fail or refuse to perform his duties, the corporation will be relieved of any obligation to make further credits to the reserve (but not of the obligation to distribute amounts previously contributed); but, if the taxpayer should become incapacitated from performing his duties, then credits to the reserve will continue for one year from the date of the incapacity, but not beyond the expiration of the five-year term of the contract. There is no specific provision in the contract for forfeiture by the taxpayer of his right to distribution from the reserve; and, in the event he should die prior to his receipt in full of the balance in the account, the remaining balance is distributable to his personal representative at the rate of one-fifth per year for five years, beginning three months after his death.

(2)  The taxpayer is an officer and director of corporation $A$, which has a plan for making future payments of additional compensation for current services to certain officers and key employees designated by its board of directors. This plan provides that a percentage of the annual net earnings (before Federal income taxes) in excess of $4,000x$ dollars is to be designated for division among the participants in proportion to their respective salaries. This amount is not currently paid to the participants; but, the corporation has set up on its books a separate account for each participant and each year it credits thereto the dollar amount of his participation for the year, reduced by a proportionate part of the corporation's income taxes attributable to the additional compensation. Each account is also credited with the net amount, if any, realized from investing any portion of the amount in the account.

Distributions are to be made from these accounts annually beginning when the employee (1) reaches age 60, (2) is no longer employed by the company, including cessation of employment due to death, or (3) becomes totally disabled to perform his duties, whichever occurs first. The annual distribution will equal a stated percentage of the balance in the employee's account at the close of the year immediately preceding the year of first payment, and distributions will continue until the account is exhausted. However, the corporation's liability to make these distributions is contingent upon the employee's (1) refraining from engaging in any business competitive to that of the corporation, (2) making himself available to the corporation for consultation and advice after retirement or termination of his services, unless disabled, and (3) retaining unencumbered any interest or benefit under the plan. In the event of his death, either before or after the beginning of payments, amounts in an employee's account are distributable in installments computed in the same way to his designated beneficiaries or heirs-at-law. Under the terms of the compensation plan, corporation A is under a merely contractual obligation to make the payments when due, and the parties did not intend that the amounts in each account be held by the corporation in trust for the participants.

(3)   On October 1, 1957, the taxpayer, an author, and corporation Y, a publisher, executed an agreement under which the taxpayer granted to the publisher the exclusive right to print, publish and sell a book he had written. This agreement provides that the publisher will (1) pay the author specified royalties based on the actual cash received from the sale of the published work, (2) render semi-annual statements of the sales, and (3) at the time of rendering each statement make settlement for the amount due. On the same day, another agreement was signed by the same parties, mutually agreeing that, in consideration of, and notwithstanding any contrary provisions contained in the first contract, the publisher shall not pay the taxpayer more than $100x$ dollars in any one calendar year. Under this supplemental contract, sums in excess of $100x$ dollars accruing in any one calendar year are to be carried over by the publisher into succeeding accounting periods; and the publisher shall not be required either to pay interest to the taxpayer on any such excess sums or to segregate any such sums in any manner.

(4)   In June 1957, the taxpayer, a football player, entered into a two-year standard player's contract with a football club in which he agreed to play football and engage in activities related to football during the two-year term only for the club. In addition to a specified salary for the two-year term, it was mutually agreed that as an inducement for signing the contract the taxpayer would be paid a bonus of $150x$ dollars. The taxpayer could have demanded and received payment of this bonus at the time of signing the contract, but at his suggestion there was added to the standard contract form a paragraph providing substantially as follows:

The player shall receive the sum of $150x$ dollars upon signing of this contract, contingent upon the payment of this $150x$ dollars to an escrow agent designated by him. The escrow agreement shall be subject to approval by the legal representatives of the player, the Club, and the escrow agent.

Pursuant to this added provision, an escrow agreement was executed on June 25, 1957, in which the club agreed to pay 150x dollars on that date to the Y bank, as escrow agent; and the escrow agent agreed to pay this amount, plus interest, to the taxpayer in installments over a period of five years. The escrow agreement also provides that the account established by the escrow agent is to bear the taxpayer's name; that payments from such account may be made only in accordance with the terms of the agreement; that the agreement is binding upon the parties thereto and their successors or assigns; and that in the event of the taxpayer's death during the escrow period the balance due will become part of his estate.

(5) The taxpayer, a boxer, entered into an agreement with a boxing club to fight a particular opponent at a specified time and place. The place of the fight agreed to was decided upon because of the insistence of the taxpayer that it be held there. The agreement was on the standard form of contract required by the state athletic commission and provided, in part, that for his performance taxpayer was to receive 16x percent of the gross receipts derived from the match. Simultaneously, the same parties executed a separate agreement providing for payment of the taxpayer's share of the receipts from the match as follows: 25 percent thereof not later than two weeks after the bout, and 25 percent thereof during each of the three years following the year of the bout in equal semiannual installments. Such deferments are not customary in prize fighting contracts, and the supplemental agreement was executed at the demand of the taxpayer. Upon the taxpayer's insistence, the agreements also provided that any telecast of the fight must receive his prior consent and that he was to approve or disapprove all proposed sales of radio and motion picture rights.

Section 1.451–1(a) of the Income Tax Regulations provides in part as follows:

> Gains, profits, and income are to be included in gross income for the taxable year in which they are actually or constructively received by the taxpayer unless includible for a different year in accordance with the taxpayer's method of accounting. * * *.

And, with respect to the cash receipts and disbursements method of accounting, section 1.446–1(c)(1)(i) provides in part—

> Generally, under the cash receipts and disbursements method in the computation of taxable income, all items which constitute gross income (whether in the form of cash, property, or services) are to be included for the taxable year in which actually or constructively received. * * *.

As previously stated, the individual concerned in each of the situations described above, employs the cash receipts and disbursements method of accounting. Under that method, as indicated by the above-quoted provisions of the regulations, he is required to include the compensation concerned in gross income only for the taxable year in which it is actually or constructively received. Consequently, the question for resolution is whether in each of the situations described the income in question was constructively received in a taxable year prior to the taxable year of actual receipt.

A mere promise to pay, not represented by notes or secured in any way, is not regarded as a receipt of income within the intendment of the cash receipts and disbursements method. See United States v. Christine Oil & Gas Co., 269 F. 458; William J. Jackson v. Smietanka, 272 F. 970, Ct.D. 5, C.B. 4, 96 (1921); and E.F. Cremin v. Commissioner, 5 B.T.A. 1164, acquiescence, C.B. VI–1, 2 (1927). Also C. Florian Zittel v. Commissioner, 12 B.T.A. 675, in which, holding a salary to be taxable when received, the Board said: "Taxpayers on a receipts and disbursements basis are required to report only income actually received no matter how binding any contracts they may have to receive more."

This should not be construed to mean that under the cash receipts and disbursements method income may be taxed only when realized in cash. For, under that method a taxpayer is required to include in income that which is received in cash or cash equivalent. W.P. Henritze v. Commissioner, 41 B.T.A. 505. And, as stated in the above-quoted provisions of the regulations, the "receipt" contemplated by the cash method may be actual or constructive.

With respect to the constructive receipt of income, section 1.451–2(a) of the Income Tax Regulations (which accords with prior regulations extending back to, and including, Article 53 of Regulations 45 under the Revenue Act of 1918) provides, in part, as follows:

> Income although not actually reduced to a taxpayer's possession is constructively received by him in the taxable year during which it is credited to his account or set apart for him so that he may draw upon it at any time. However, income is not constructively received if the taxpayer's control of its receipt is subject to substantial limitations or restrictions. Thus, if a corporation credits its employees with bonus stock, but the stock is not available to such employees until some future date, the mere crediting on the books of the corporation does not constitute receipt.

Thus, under the doctrine of constructive receipt, a taxpayer may not deliberately turn his back upon income and thereby select the year for which he will report it. The Hamilton National Bank of Chattanooga, as Administrator of the Estate of S. Strang Nicklin, Deceased v. Commissioner, 29 B.T.A. 63. Nor may a taxpayer, by a private agreement, postpone receipt of income from one taxable year to another. James E. Lewis v. Commissioner, 30 B.T.A. 318.

However, the statute cannot be administered by speculating whether the payor would have been willing to agree to an earlier payment. See, for example, J.D. Amend, et ux. v. Commissioner, 13 T.C. 178, acquiescence, C.B. 1950–1, 1; and C.E. Gullett, et al. v. Commissioner, 31 B.T.A. 1067, in which the court, citing a number of authorities for its holding stated:

> It is clear that the doctrine of constructive receipt is to be sparingly used; that amounts due from a corporation but unpaid, are not to be included in the income of an individual reporting his income on a cash receipts basis unless it appears that the money was available to him, that the corporation was able and ready to pay him, that his right to receive was not restricted, and that his failure to receive resulted from exercise of his own choice.

Consequently, it seems clear that in each case involving a deferral of compensation a determination of whether the doctrine of constructive receipt is applicable must be made upon the basis of the specific factual situation involved.

Applying the foregoing criteria to the situations described above, the following conclusions have been reached:

(1)  The additional compensation to be received by the taxpayer under the employment contract concerned will be includible in his gross income only in the taxable years in which the taxpayer actually receives installment payments in cash or other property previously credited to his account. To hold otherwise would be contrary to the provisions of the regulations and the court decisions mentioned above.

(2)  For the reasons in (1) above, it is held that the taxpayer here involved also will be required to include the deferred compensation concerned in his gross income only in the taxable years in which the taxpayer actually receives installment payments in cash or other property previously credited to his account.

In arriving at this conclusion and the conclusion reached in case "(1)," consideration has been given to section 1.402(b)–1 of the Income Tax Regulations and to Revenue Ruling 57–37, C.B. 1957–1, 18, as modified by Revenue Ruling 57–528, C.B. 1957–2, 263. Section 1.402(b)–1(a)(1) provides in part, with an exception not here relevant, that any contribution made by an employer on behalf of an employee to a trust during a taxable year of the employer which ends within or with a taxable year of the trust for which the trust is not exempt under section 501(a) of the Code, shall be included in income of the employee for his taxable year during which the contribution is made if his interest in the contribution is nonforfeitable at the time the contribution is made. Revenue Ruling 57–37, as modified by Revenue Ruling 57–528, held, *inter alia,* that certain contributions conveying fully vested and nonforfeitable interests made by an employer into separate independently controlled trusts for the purpose of furnishing unemployment and other benefits to its eligible employees constituted additional compensation to the employees includible, under section 402(b) of the Code and section 1.402(b)–1(a)(1) of the regulations, in their income for the taxable year in which such contributions were made. These Revenue Rulings are distinguishable from cases "(1)" and "(2)" in that, under all the facts and circumstances of these cases, no trusts for the benefit of the taxpayers were created and no contributions are to be made thereto. Consequently, section 402(b) of the Code and section 1.402(b)–1(a)(1) of the regulations are inapplicable.

(3)  Here the principal agreement provided that the royalties were payable substantially as earned, and this agreement was supplemented by a further concurrent agreement which made the royalties payable over a period of years. This supplemental agreement, however, was made before the royalties were earned; in fact, it was made on the same day as the principal agreement and the two agreements were a part of the same transaction. Thus, for all practical purposes, the arrangement from the beginning is similar to that in (1) above. Therefore, it is also held that the author concerned will be required to include the royalties in his gross income only in the taxable years in which they are actually received in cash or other property.

(4)  In arriving at a determination as to the includibility of the $150x$ dollars concerned in the gross income of the football player, under the circumstances described, in addition to the authorities cited above, consideration also has been given to Revenue Ruling 55–727, C.B. 1955–2, 25, and to the decision in E.T. Sproull v. Commissioner, 16 T.C. 244.

In Revenue Ruling 55–727, the taxpayer, a professional baseball player, entered into a contract in 1953 in which he agreed to render services for a baseball club and to refrain from playing baseball for any other club during the term of the contract. In addition to specified compensation, the contract provided for a bonus to the player or his estate, payable one-half in January 1954 and one-half in January 1955, whether or not he was able to render services. The primary question was whether the bonus was capital gain or ordinary income; and, in holding that the bonus payments constituted ordinary income, it was stated that they were taxable for the year in which received by the player. However, under the facts set forth in Revenue Ruling 55–727 there was no arrangement, as here, for placing the amount of the bonus in escrow. Consequently, the instant situation is distinguishable from that considered in Revenue Ruling 55–727.

In E.T. Sproull v. Commissioner, 16 T.C. 244, affirmed, 194 F.2d 541, the petitioner's employer in 1945 transferred in trust for the petitioner the amount of $10,500. The trustee was directed to pay out of principal to the petitioner the sum of $5,250 in 1946 and the balance, including income, in 1947. In the event of the petitioner's prior death, the amounts were to be paid to his administrator, executor, or heirs. The petitioner contended that the Commissioner erred in including the sum of $10,500 in his taxable income for 1945. In this connection, the court stated:

> * * * it is undoubtedly true that the amount which the Commissioner has included in petitioner's income for 1945 was used in that year for his benefit * * * in setting up the trust of which petitioner, or, in the event of his death then his estate, was the sole beneficiary * * *.

> The question then becomes * * * was "any economic or financial benefit conferred on the employee as compensation" in the taxable year. If so, it was taxable to him in that year. This question we must answer in the affirmative. The employer's part of the transaction terminated in 1945. It was then that the amount of the compensation was fixed at $10,500 and irrevocably paid out for petitioner's sole benefit. * * *.

Applying the principles stated in the *Sproull* decision to the facts here, it is concluded that the 150$x$-dollar bonus is includible in the gross income of the football player concerned in 1957, the year in which the club unconditionally paid such amount to the escrow agent.

(5) In this case, the taxpayer and the boxing club, as well as the opponent whom taxpayer had agreed to meet, are each acting in his or its own right, the proposed match is a joint venture by all of these participants, and the taxpayer is not an employee of the boxing club. The taxpayer's share of the gross receipts from the match belong to him and never belonged to the boxing club. Thus, the taxpayer acquired all of the benefits of his share of the receipts except the right of immediate physical possession; and, although the club retained physical possession, it was by virtue of an arrangement with the taxpayer who, in substance and effect, authorized the boxing club to take possession and hold for him. The receipts, therefore, were income to the taxpayer at the time they were paid to and retained by the boxing club by his agreement and, in substance, at his direction, and are includible in his gross income in the taxable year in which so paid to the club. See the *Sproull* case, supra, and Lucas v. Guy C. Earl, 281 U.S. 111, 50 S.Ct. 241.\*

As previously stated, in each case involving a deferral of compensation, a determination of whether the doctrine of constructive receipt is applicable must be made upon the basis of the specific factual situation involved.

---

\*  Circumstance (5) in the foregoing Revenue Ruling is similar to that in a controversy involving Sugar Ray Robinson. When the *Robinson* case was litigated, the Tax Court rejected the Commissioner's "joint venture" theory and held, further, that amounts not received within the taxable year could not be treated as constructively received. Robinson v. Commissioner, 44 T.C. 20 (1965). The Commissioner has acquiesced in that decision. 1970–2 C.B. xxi. Moreover, the Commissioner has acknowledged that circumstance (5) in Rev.Rul. 60–31 does not reflect a joint venture and has proffered a modified circumstance (5) which does. Rev. Rul. 70–435, 1970–2 C.B. 100.

Consistent with the foregoing, the nonacquiescence published in C.B. 1952–2, 5, with respect to the decision in James F. Oates v. Commissioner, 18 T.C. 570, affirmed, 207 F.2d 711, has been withdrawn and acquiescence substituted therefor at page 5 of this Bulletin.

With respect to deductions for payments made by an employer under a deferred compensation plan, see section 404(a)(5) of the 1954 Code and section 1.404(a)–12 of the Income Tax Regulations.

In the application of those sections to unfunded plans, no deduction is allowable for any compensation paid or accrued by an employer on account of any employee under such a plan except in the year when paid and then only to the extent allowable under section 404(a). Thus, under an unfunded plan, if compensation is paid by an employer directly to a former employee, such amounts are deductible under section 404(a)(5) when *actually* paid *in cash or other property to the employee,* provided that such amounts meet the requirements of section 162 or section 212.

Advance rulings will not be issued in specific cases involving deferred compensation arrangements.*

## NOTE

Revenue Ruling 60–31 has been a fixture in the "Fundamentals" since its first edition and it remains as a fixture in determining whether constructive receipt applies to a cash method taxpayer in various nonstatutory deferred compensation arrangements. An employee who receives steady salary increases over a working career or bunched income in a single year can arrange overall to pay less tax on the lifetime salary income if the employee makes an arrangement such as that described in circumstance (1) or circumstance (2) of the revenue ruling. Under such an arrangement, some of the compensation is deferred to and taxed in retirement years, when one's lower annual income may attract lower tax rates. While the employee would have the benefit of deferral, the employer is not allowed a deduction until the amounts are taken into income by the employee.

With time, sophisticated tax planners found other ways to avoid constructive receipt under Revenue Ruling 60–31 and defer income in circumstances where the right to future payments was secure or the employee had control over the amounts deferred.[1] Congress, increasingly put off by such arrangements, enacted Section 409A. That section provides specific rules, in addition to the Revenue Ruling 60–31 rules, to determine whether income under nonstatutory deferred compensation arrangements may be deferred.

---

\*  Despite the last sentence of Rev.Rul. 60–31, the Treasury later announced that it will entertain requests for rulings on deferred compensation arrangements. Rev.Rul. 64–279, 1964–2 C.B. 121. Ed.

[1]  See H. Rep. No. 108–548 (Part 1), 108th Cong., 1st Sess. (2005). One such type of arrangement is known as a "rabbi trust." See Rev. Proc. 92–64, 1992–2 C.B. 422.

As a general rule, under Section 409A, unless certain requirement are met, all deferred amounts for all taxable years not previously included in a taxpayer's gross income under nonstatutory deferred compensation arrangements must be included in gross income in the current year.[2] In addition, the taxpayer must pay interest on such previously deferred income and pay a penalty in the form of increased tax liability equal to 20 percent of the amount of such nonstatutory deferred compensation included in gross income under Section 409A.[3] The rules do not apply if the deferred payments are subject to substantial risk of forfeiture[4] and do not apply to the extent the payment rights have previously been included in gross income.[5]

A taxpayer's deferred compensation arrangement avoids the clutches and substantial penalty of Section 409A if it meets three requirements. First, distributions of the deferred compensation may not be made before (1) the participant's separation from service, (2) the participant becomes disabled, (3) the participant's death, (4) a specified date (or pursuant to some fixed schedule), (5) a change in ownership or effective control of the corporation, or (6) the occurrence of an unforeseeable emergency.[6] Second, the arrangement must not permit an acceleration of the time or schedule of any payment.[7] Finally, the taxpayer must make a timely election to avoid the inclusion rule.[8]

Recognize that a taxpayer seeking deferral under a nonstatutory deferred compensation arrangement must now both pass muster under Revenue Ruling 60–31 and successfully circumvent Section 409A.

## 2. STATUTORY DEFERRED COMPENSATION AND MEDICAL INSURANCE ARRANGEMENTS

The deferral of compensation into future years is not exclusively governed by the predominantly nonstatutory treatment of Revenue Ruling 60–31. In fact, most deferred compensation arrangements are now a matter of statutory dispensation. A broad range of statutory provisions permit the deferral of compensation income and other statutory provisions allow similar deferral rules for funds used to pay medical expenses where the taxpayer has a high deductible medical insurance policy. A detailed analysis of these provisions cannot reasonably be attempted in a course in the Fundamentals, but a general description of the topic presents an overview of these areas.[1] The

---

[2]   I.R.C. § 409A(a)(1)(A)(i). Regulations have been adopted under I.R.C. § 409A. See Reg. § 1.409A.

[3]   I.R.C. § 409A(a)(1)(B).

[4]   I.R.C. § 409A(a)(1)(A)(i). I.R.C. § 409A(d)(4) provides that a person's rights to compensation are subject to a substantial risk of forfeiture if they are conditioned upon the performance of substantial future services. Cf. I.R.C. § 83(c)(1) and Chapter 24D, infra.

[5]   I.R.C. § 409A(a)(1)(A)(i).

[6]   I.R.C. § 409A(a)(2).

[7]   I.R.C. § 409A(a)(3).

[8]   I.R.C. § 409A(a)(4).

[1]   For a detailed discussion, see Bittker & Lokken, Federal Taxation of Income, Estates & Gifts Ch. 61–62 (Warren, Gorham & Lamont).

provisions involved employ a combination of statutory solutions to deferral problems (1) using pre-tax dollars to fund deferred compensation which will be included in gross income on receipt; (2) using after-tax dollars to fund arrangements whose dollars will be excluded from gross income on receipt; or, (3) in the best of all worlds, using pre-tax dollars to fund arrangements whose distributions will be excluded from gross income on receipt. We discuss them in that order.

*Pre-Taxed Dollars Used to Defer Compensation Taxation Until Distribution.* There are several different types of statutory deferred compensation arrangements that use dollars which have not yet been included in a taxpayer's gross income to fund a compensation plan where there is no gross income to the taxpayer or to the funds themselves until the money is distributed. Such arrangements have two distinct tax advantages:

1.     Either the taxpayer is not taxed on contributions made by an employer if the employer funds the arrangement *or* if the taxpayer funds the arrangement with dollars included in gross income, the taxpayer is allowed an "above-the-line" deduction resulting in a tax wash, the same end result as an exclusion from gross income.

2.     The fund to which the contributions are made is exempt from tax on its earnings until they are distributed.

The distributions from such arrangements are taxed when they are received by the taxpayer at a time when theoretically the taxpayer will be in a lower income tax bracket. Even though the arrangements differ, they all have certain similarities. In general, there are restrictions that are designed to promote the policy underlying the particular provision. For example, there may be penalties if distributions are made too early (prior to age 59½ for retirees),[2] are too small,[3] or are made too late (retirement distributions must commence by April of the year following the year in which the participant reaches age 70½).[4] Penalties may also be imposed if the fund engages in certain prohibited transitions,[5] such as self-dealing with a fiduciary.

*Qualified Plans.* The first types of such arrangements are known as Qualified Plans, which are qualified pension or profit sharing plans that meet the requirements of Section 401(a). Two general types of qualified plans are commonly used: defined benefit plans and defined contribution plans. In a defined benefit plan, contributions are made to a trust in sufficient amounts to provide a set, promised benefit payable out of the trust to the employee in retirement.[6] In a defined contribution plan,

---

[2]     I.R.C. §§ 72(t)(1) and (2)(A)(i), 4974(c).

[3]     I.R.C. §§ 401(a)(9)(A) and (c), 408(a)(6). See Reg. § 1.409(a)(9)–5.

[4]     I.R.C. §§ 401(a)(9)(A) and (c), 408(a)(6).

[5]     I.R.C. §§ 4974, 4975.

[6]     See I.R.C. § 414(j).

contributions based on a percentage of the employee's salary, or of the profits of the business in a profit sharing plan, are made in cash or securities of the employer, to an account that the employee will receive on retirement.[7] A glance at Section 401(a) will give at least a hint of the detailed criteria for qualification of a plan.[8]

One key requirement for all qualified plans is that the plan not discriminate in favor of "highly compensated employees."[9] Other requirements for qualified plans involve rules that the plan cover a broad scope of employees,[10] rules with respect to when the participants' interests must vest,[11] and rules with respect to the amount of contributions which may be made to a defined contribution plan[12] and, in the case of a defined benefit plan, the amount of benefits which may be received.[13]

The tax advantage for the employer of qualified plan arrangements is that it can deduct contributions when paid,[14] even though the employee's tax is deferred until retirement distributions are received.

*Keogh Plans.* The qualified plans described above all relate to taxpayers who enjoy *employee* status; what about *self-employed persons*? They may qualify for what are commonly called Keogh Plans (formerly known as H.R. 10 plans) which are similar to qualified plans except that as the self-employed person makes a contribution to a Keogh plan, the person takes an "above-the-line" income tax deduction (rather than being allowed a gross income exclusion as in the case of a qualified plan).[15] Thus, Keogh plans are, in effect, also funded with "pre-tax" dollars. As in the case of qualified plans, earnings on contributions are exempt from tax until distribution to the self-employed person.[16] Both employees and self-employed taxpayers are subject to the same contribution and benefit limits[17] and corresponding deduction allowances.[18] In general, the same

---

[7] See I.R.C. § 414(i). A plan may be set up which gives employees the option of receiving salary in cash or having it contributed to an employee trust. Under such a plan, known as a cash or deferred arrangement, or an I.R.C. § 401(k) plan, amounts contributed to the trust and earnings and gains on such amounts are not taxed to the employee until withdrawn from the trust.

[8] I.R.C. § 401(a) applies to a pension plan (a defined benefit plan), a profit sharing plan (a defined contribution plan), or a stock bonus plan. A similar arrangement, employing many of the same rules, is a qualified annuity plan provided by I.R.C. § 403(b).

[9] I.R.C. § 401(a)(4). A highly compensated employee is any employee who (1) during the current or preceding year was at any time a five-percent owner of the business, or (2) in the preceding year received compensation in excess of $80,000 (indexed for inflation after 1996), and, if the employer so elects, was in the top 20 percent of compensated employees. I.R.C. §§ 414(q)(1)–(3) and 415(d).

[10] I.R.C. §§ 401(a)(3), 410.

[11] I.R.C. §§ 401(a)(7), 411.

[12] I.R.C. § 415(a)(1)(B), (c).

[13] I.R.C. § 415(a)(1)(A), (b).

[14] I.R.C. § 404(a).

[15] I.R.C. §§ 401(c)(1), 404(a). See I.R.C. § 62(a)(6).

[16] I.R.C. §§ 404(a), 501(a) and (c)(17), and 402(a).

[17] See I.R.C. § 415.

[18] See I.R.C. § 404.

vesting,[19] coverage requirements,[20] and prohibited transactions[21] are applicable to both Keogh and qualified plans.

*Individual Retirement Accounts.* A third type of arrangement is an Individual Retirement Account (IRA) which is a tax-advantaged saving arrangement established by an individual for the individual alone or for the individual and the individual's nonworking spouse.[22] An IRA is similar to a Keogh plan in that it allows the taxpayer an "above-the-line deduction" for contributions, freedom from tax attrition during growth, and taxation only as distributions are made from the account.[23] There are maximum amounts that may be contributed to an IRA[24] but the maximum figures are somewhat misleading, because an individual's deduction for IRA contributions is generally eliminated or reduced if a person is covered by a qualified plan (including a Keogh plan) and the person (or the person and the spouse, if a joint return is filed) has substantial adjusted gross income.[25]

*After-Tax Dollars Used to Permanently Defer Taxation of Compensation.* A variation on the IRA scene is known as a Roth IRA[26] (named for the Chairman of the Senate Finance Committee when the IRA was enacted . . . have we started a frightening new tradition here?). The normal IRA rules (deductible contributions and taxable distributions) are reversed under a Roth IRA (nondeductible contributions and nontaxable distributions). Thus, contributions to a

---

[19]   See I.R.C. § 411.

[20]   See I.R.C. § 410.

[21]   I.R.C. §§ 4974, 4975. But see I.R.C. § 4975(a) and (f)(6).

[22]   I.R.C. § 408(a).

[23]   I.R.C. §§ 219(g), 408(e) and 408(d). See I.R.C. § 62(a)(7).

Congress has created the Savings Incentive Match Plan for Employees (SIMPLE) which is a simplified retirement plan for small businesses. I.R.C. § 408(p). In general, *SIMPLE* plans may be adopted by small business employers who have 100 or fewer employees earning $5,000 or more in annual compensation and who do not have any other employer-sponsored retirement plan. I.R.C. § 408(p)(2)(A)(iv), (C)(i), (D). A *SIMPLE* plan may be either an IRA for each employee or part of an I.R.C. § 401(k) qualified cash or deferred arrangement. I.R.C. §§ 401(k)(11), 408(p)(2)(A)(i). The amount of employee contributions is limited and they must be matched by employer contributions which are immediately non-forfeitable to the employee. I.R.C. §§ 401(k)(11)(B)(i)(I), 408(p)(2)(A)(ii), 408(p)(2)(E)(i). One reason that such plans are more simple than other employer plans is that they are not subject to the nondiscrimination rules. I.R.C. §§ 401(k)(11)(D)(ii), 416(g)(4)(G).

[24]   I.R.C. § 219(a), (b), (c), and (f)(1).

[25]   I.R.C. § 219(g). If a taxpayer's IRA deduction is partially or totally denied, the taxpayer may make a non-deductible IRA contribution in an amount which, when added to one's allowable deduction, does not exceed the maximum deduction for a taxpayer in one's category. I.R.C. § 408(*o*). The taxability of amounts later withdrawn from an IRA during a year is dependent on the mixture of deductible and nondeductible IRA contributions. If an individual withdraws an amount from an IRA to which there have been mixed contributions, part of the withdrawal is nontaxable. I.R.C. § 408(d). The amount excludible from gross income for the year is that portion of the amount withdrawn which bears the same ratio to the total amount withdrawn for the year as the amount of the individual's aggregate nondeductible IRA contributions bears to the aggregate of all IRA contributions of the individual. Id. IRAs are taxed in a manner similar to annuities. I.R.C. § 72. See Chapter 7B, supra.

[26]   I.R.C. § 408A.

Roth IRA are not deductible.[27] However, income generated by the contributions to a Roth IRA is not taxed and distributions known as "qualified distributions" are excluded from gross income if they are paid more than 5 years after the establishment of the Roth IRA[28] and generally after the taxpayer reaches age 59½.[29] Similar to a regular IRA, there is a ceiling on the amount that can be contributed to a Roth IRA in any year.[30] Regrettably not all taxpayers may use a Roth IRA. As a taxpayer's adjusted gross income exceeds certain levels, the contribution amount is phased out or totally denied.[31] Taxpayers may convert a regular IRA to a Roth IRA, subject to some special rules.[32]

*Pre-Tax Dollars Used to Permanently Defer Taxation of Certain Medical Expenses.* Congress has employed concepts similar to those that they employ for deferred compensation arrangements to enact provisions allowing a taxpayer to purchase medical insurance at a low premium cost but with a high deductible amount before the insurance benefits kick in and to self-insure by using a trust vehicle to pay the high deductible amount when medical expenses are incurred.[33] The programs are similar to deferred compensation arrangements in several ways, except that they are used to pay the uninsured medical expenses of an individual, the individual's spouse, and dependents rather than to pay deferred compensation.[34]

If an employer makes such contributions, they are both deductible by the employer and excluded from the employee's gross income.[35] If an employee or self-employed person makes such contributions, they are deductible as an above-the-line deduction[36] by the person.[37] Income earned on the funds is generally excluded from gross income.[38] Unlike deferred compensation arrangements however, distributions are excluded from the recipient's gross income to the extent that they are used to pay unreimbursed medical expenses under the high deductible

---

[27] I.R.C. § 408A(c)(1). See I.R.C. § 219. However, contributions can be made even after the taxpayer reaches age 70½. I.R.C. § 408A(c)(4).

[28] I.R.C. § 408A(d)(2)(B).

[29] I.R.C. § 408A(d)(1), (2), (5).

[30] I.R.C. §§ 219(b)(1) and (5), 408A(c)(2).

[31] I.R.C. § 408A(c)(3).

[32] I.R.C. § 408A(d), and (e). The amount that a taxpayer may contribute to a Roth IRA in any year is still subject to a ceiling. I.R.C. § 408A(c)(2). Any conversion of a regular IRA to a Roth IRA is a distribution from the regular IRA and thus generally taxed as ordinary income in the year of distribution. For taxpayers, there are two possible benefits of such a conversion. A conversion is taxed at current tax rates as compared to future tax rates, although the time value of money also must be considered. Second, there are no required distributions from a Roth IRA after attaining age 70½. See Kaplan, "To Roth or Not to Roth: Analyzing the Conversion Opportunity for 2010 and Beyond," BNA Daily Tax Report, vol. 9, No. 181 (Sept. 22, 2009).

[33] I.R.C. §§ 106(b), 220, 223.

[34] I.R.C. §§ 220(d), 106(b)(6), 223(d)(2)(A).

[35] I.R.C. § 106(b)(1), (3).

[36] I.R.C. § 62(a)(16) and (19).

[37] I.R.C. §§ 220(a), 223(a). No deduction is allowed if the amount is excluded under I.R.C. § 106. I.R.C. §§ 220(b)(5), 223(b)(4)(B).

[38] I.R.C. §§ 220(e)(1), 223(e)(1).

plan.[39] Any other distributions are not only included in gross income but also generally are subject to a penalty.[40]

The earliest of such plans was an experimental program known as an Archer Medical Savings Account which applied to self-employed and employees of certain small businesses.[41] They were supplemented by Health Savings Accounts[42] which are very similar in nature to the Archer accounts but which may be set up by employees and are subject to more lenient rules on the amount of high deductibles on the insurance and the maximum contributions that are allowed.

## D. THE CARRYOVER AND CARRYBACK DEVICES

Internal Revenue Code: See Section 172.

---

Let us assume that a novelty merchandiser believes she can correctly anticipate the public's fancy and stocks up on items for sales during the holiday season. Unfortunately, she misjudges the public's tastes and in 2019 she suffers a huge loss, say $200,000. The next year she redoubles her efforts to gauge customer sentiment, correctly predicts the next great craze, and makes a killing, say a $500,000 profit in 2020. Now, it's all very well to say that she *did* have $500,000 properly taxed in 2020 and that, as she had *no* taxable income for 2019, she should be grateful to be relieved of the obligation to pay any tax for that year. But our merchandiser, despite the much-touted integrity of the taxable year, can't help but take a little longer view of her operations. For the *two* years she sees aggregate net profits of $300,000 but especially with a view to graduated tax rates, the tax paid for the two years seems unconscionable. Should the merchandiser be able to reduce her 2020 income with the 2019 loss? Or, alternatively, suppose she had $500,000 of income in 2019 and experienced the $200,000 loss in 2020. Should the 2020 loss be allowed to be *carried back* and retroactively reduce the merchandiser's tax liability for 2019?

Congress now agrees that the merchandiser should be allowed to deduct her 2019 operating loss against her 2020 income, at least to the extent of 80 percent of her taxable income (determined without regard to the net operating loss deduction).[1] But beginning in tax years after 2018, the merchandiser generally would not be allowed to *carry back* a loss in 2020 to reduce 2019 taxes.[2] Instead, a loss in 2020 could only be *carried*

---

[39]  I.R.C. §§ 220(d)(2), and (f)(1), 223(d)(2), and (f)(1).

[40]  I.R.C. §§ 220(f)(2), (4)(A), 223(f)(2), and (4)(A).

[41]  I.R.C. § 220.

[42]  I.R.C. § 223. See Notice 2008–59, 2008–29 I.R.B. 123, for extensive guidance on the establishment and operation of Health Savings Accounts.

[1]  I.R.C. § 172(a)(2).

[2]  I.R.C. § 172(b)(1)(A)(i). Exceptions are provided for carrybacks of farming losses and losses of certain insurance companies. I.R.C. § 172(b)(1)(B) and (C).

*forward* indefinitely and treated as a business deduction to reduce taxable income (again, subject to the 80 percent limitation) in subsequent years.[3] The year to which the loss is carried is not elective; the loss must be utilized, to the extent that it can be, in the earliest year.[4]

For perspective, prior to 2018 a net operating loss could generally be carried back two years and forward for twenty-five years and there was no 80-percent limitation on the deduction.[5] The use of a carryback would provide a refund of prior years' taxes. The general elimination of carrybacks and the addition of the 80-percent-of-taxble-income limitation beginning in 2018, thus, were revenue raisers for the federal government.

The foregoing comments present the net operating loss in broad outline, and no attempt is made here to deal with the many complexities of the provision. Nevertheless, it may be noted that a principal problem in working with Section 172 is the computation of the net operating loss for the year. Generally speaking, there is such a loss when deductions exceed gross income.[6] However, the statute contains some refinements and, as the title of the section suggests, the objective generally is to identify the loss that is traceable to *business* operations. Thus, in the case of an individual the net operating loss for a year is essentially the excess of one's trade or business deductions over gross income, including non-business income reduced by certain non-business deductions.[7] One important exception to this general principle is that Section 212 and personal casualty or theft losses are treated as trade or business losses in measuring a net operating loss.[8]

Overall, Section 172 can properly be regarded as something of a forward-looking income averaging device. While it does nothing to level off income when all the years are profitable years, it does at least permit a loss year to have a leveling effect on later profit years.

Section 172 is by no means the only Code provision that makes use of the carryover concept as a kind of departure from strict annual accounting. We have previously seen the use of carryovers in Chapter 17 in conjunction with the at risk rules, the Section 280A(c)(5) rule, and the passive activity rules. It will also be seen for example in Chapter 21C that, when limitations on the deductibility of capital losses preclude the full tax use of such a loss in one year, the unused portion may be utilized

---

[3] I.R.C. § 172(b)(1)(A)(ii).

[4] I.R.C. § 172(b)(2).

[5] I.R.C. § 172(b)(1). (pre-2018). There were also various other special carryback rules that could extend the two-year period. See I.R.C. § 172(b)(1)(C)–(F) (pre-2018).

[6] I.R.C. § 172(c).

[7] The details are specified in I.R.C. § 172(d) where it will be seen, among other things, that neither the personal exemptions under § 151 nor noncorporate capital losses in excess of capital gains enter into the computation. I.R.C. § 172(d)(3), (d)(2)(A), respectively. But see I.R.C. § 151(d)(5)(A). A corporation's normal deductions are modified under § 172(d)(5) in measuring its net operating loss.

[8] I.R.C. § 172(d)(4)(C); see I.R.C. § 165(c)(2) and (3), (h) and Chapter 15B, supra; Chapter 23C, infra.

in later years. And in Chapter 23B it will become apparent that a similar opportunity is sometimes afforded for a later deduction for charitable contributions that exceed the statutory ceiling on the deduction for the year in which the contribution is made. Similar carryover concepts will be discovered in Chapter 27B with respect to credits.

# PART 6

# THE CHARACTERIZATION OF INCOME AND DEDUCTIONS

# CHAPTER 21

# Capital Gains and Losses

## A. Introduction

It must now be recognized that a mere quantitative approach to items of income and deduction is insufficient for federal income tax purposes; the quality of such items must also be considered. The thought is not entirely new at this point, for we have already recognized that some income which could be taxed escapes tax if it has a tax-exempt quality, such as interest on state or municipal bonds. We have also seen that some potential deductions are flatly disallowed. Here, however, we are concerned with items of income that are taxed but which, according to their character, are taxed under special rules, and with items of deduction which, while not flatly disallowed, are subject to important statutory limitations. In general it is "capital gain" that may qualify for special tax treatment and "capital loss" that may encounter special, restrictive, rules as to deduction. Thus, we must look at items qualitatively as well as quantitatively, a process referred to as the "characterization" of income and deduction items.

Whether a gain or loss is subject to special treatment, as "capital" as opposed to "ordinary", usually is dependent upon (1) whether it arises in a transaction involving a "capital asset," (2) whether the capital asset has been the subject of a "sale or exchange," and (3) whether the taxpayer has "held" the asset for a sufficient period of time.[1] Failure of a transaction to involve a capital asset or a sale or exchange results in ordinary income or an ordinary deduction. However, one should be alert for statutory provisions that may artificially accord capital gain or loss treatment to some transactions which do not actually involve the sale or exchange of a capital asset.[2]

Parts D through H of this Chapter deal with the basic problems of characterization of items of income and deduction. Parts B and C explore the statutory mechanics for the treatment of capital gains and losses. Before plunging into detail, brief consideration is given here to the history and general philosophy of the tax treatment accorded transactions in capital assets.

*Capital Gains.* It has always been clear that a merchant's sale of stock in trade gives rise to gain or loss to be taken into account for tax purposes. However, when the first income tax was imposed following the adoption of the Sixteenth Amendment,[3] it contained no specific reference

---

[1]  I.R.C. § 1222.

[2]  Take a preliminary look at I.R.C. §§ 166(d)(1)(B) and 165(g)(1). See also Chapter 21H, infra.

[3]  Revenue Act of 1916, 39 Stat. 756 (1916).

to gains or losses from dealing in property. What then of a sale of plant or equipment? of land held for investment? of securities? and so forth. Taxpayers were prompted to argue that gain on the sale of such properties was not income within the meaning of the Sixteenth Amendment or the federal taxing statute. In part the thought was that if one sold, say, securities and merely reinvested the proceeds in other securities (or even put the money in the bank), her financial position was unaltered; she had merely substituted the new securities (or the cash) for the securities previously owned and her investment continued. The notion was bolstered by the further thought that if there was gain of some sort in such transactions it might be largely illusory anyway, often traceable to mere changes in the price structure.

Under the modern federal income tax the proposition that capital gains should not be taxed was never accepted.[4] In Merchants' Loan & Trust Co. v. Smietanka,[5] the Supreme Court held that capital gains were income within the meaning of that term in the Sixteenth Amendment. Relying in part on cases under the Corporate Excise Tax Act of 1909, the Court, quoting its opinion in Eisner v. Macomber,[6] said:[7]

> Income may be defined as the gain derived from capital, from labor, or from both combined, *provided it be understood to include profit gained through a sale or conversion of capital assets.*

While *Merchants' Loan* was the end of the constitutional issue *whether* capital gains were subject to tax, it marked only the beginning of congressional consideration of *how* such gains should be taxed.[8] In 1921, Congress enacted the first provisions giving preferential treatment to capital gains by way of a tax rate on such gains below those applicable to other types of income.[9] Reporting the bill, the Ways and Means Committee said:[10]

> The sale of * * * capital assets is now seriously retarded by the fact that gains and profits earned over a series of years are under the present law taxed as a lump sum (and the amount of surtax greatly enhanced thereby) in the year in which the profit is realized. Many such sales, with their possible profit taking and consequent increase of the tax revenue, have been blocked by this feature of the present law. In order to permit such

---

[4] Cf. Gray v. Darlington, 82 U.S. (15 Wall.) 63 (1872), where the proposition that capital gains should not be taxed was accepted under the Civil War Income Tax Act, 14 Stat. 477–8 (1867).

[5] 255 U.S. 509, 41 S.Ct. 386 (1921).

[6] 252 U.S. 189, 207, 40 S.Ct. 189, 193 (1920).

[7] Merchants' Loan & Trust Co. v. Smietanka, 255 U.S. 509, 518, 41 S.Ct. 386, 388 (1921), emphasis added.

[8] See, generally, Magill, Taxable Income, 103–113 (1945).

[9] Revenue Act of 1921, § 106(a)(6), 42 Stat. 227, 232 (1921).

[10] House Rep. No. 350, 67th Cong., 1st Sess., pp. 10–11 (1921) as quoted in Seidman, Legislative History of Federal Income Tax Laws, 1938–1861, 813 (1938).

transactions to go forward without fear of a prohibitive tax, the proposed bill * * * adds a new section * * * [placing a preferential rate on gains from the sale or dispositions of capital assets].

While it may be argued that capital gain is no different in kind from other income and is, perhaps, just as spendable, three factors have now been identified that seem to give it a different quality. That is, a disposition of a capital asset may involve only a continuation of an investment in a different form; gain said to be realized may merely or largely reflect only changes in the overall price structure; and the gain may have been some time in the making, raising the question whether it is fair to bunch it into a single taxable year with possible attending tax attrition through progressive rate tables. Although no one of these factors, nor indeed all three in combination, has ever prompted Congress wholly to *relieve* capital gains from tax, all have played a part in the congressional deliberations on *how* to tax gains on the disposition of property.

Over the years, Congress has seen fit on numerous occasions to vary the preferential treatment accorded capital gains. As originally enacted, the 1921 legislation imposed a maximum 12½ percent tax rate on gain from the disposition of capital assets held for more than two years. In the 1934 Revenue Act,[11] Congress favored capital gains by providing that sometimes less than the entire gain had to be included in income; the longer the property had been held, the smaller percentage of the gain includable. Under the provisions of that Act, no preference was accorded gain on the disposition of capital assets held for only one year or less but, thereafter, the amount of capital gain subject to inclusion in income was reduced on a sliding scale which went as low as 30 percent if the property was held for more than 10 years. In the intervening years, the long-term holding period has varied, but since 1988 it has been extended to more than one year.[12] Changes in the treatment of capital gains have occurred, not only with regard to the holding period requirement, but also in the definition of capital assets and the maximum rates at which such gains may be taxed. These changes largely reflect shifts in congressional preoccupation with one or more of the factors that seem to set capital gains apart from other forms of income.[13] Between 1969 and 1986 Congress fluctuated in its treatment of capital gains generally reducing the maximum rate of tax on such gains.

The Tax Reform Act of 1986 did an about-face and essentially eliminated the preferential treatment of capital gains for the first time since 1921. The 1986 law reduced the ceiling rate on ordinary income

---

[11]  Revenue Act of 1934, § 117(a), 48 Stat. 680, 714 (1934).

[12]  Pub. Law No. 98–369, § 1001(a), 98th Cong., 2d Sess. (1984).

[13]  The policy arguments both for and against preferential treatment for capital gains, which have been advanced over the years, including some not stated here, are collected in Blum, "A Handy Summary of the Capital Gain Arguments," 35 Taxes 247 (1957) and see Kutsoris, "In Defense of Capital Gains," 42 Fordham L.R. 1 (1973).

from 50 percent to 28 percent and it imposed the same 28 percent ceiling rate on capital gains as that imposed on ordinary income.[14] Thus the 1986 Act abolished preferential treatment for capital gains as well as the rate disparity between ordinary income and capital gain; but in doing so, it did not outright abandon the familiar characterization of items of income as "ordinary income" or "capital gain".[15]

Some light is shed on this seeming paradox by the legislative history, which stated:[16]

> The committee believes that as a result of the bill's reduction of individual tax rates on such forms of capital income as business profits, interest, dividends, and short-term capital gains, the need to provide a reduced rate for net capital gain is eliminated. This will result in a tremendous amount of simplification for many taxpayers since their tax will no longer depend upon the characterization of income as ordinary or capital gain. In addition, this will eliminate any requirement that capital assets be held by the taxpayer for any extended period of time [. . .] in order to obtain favorable treatment. This will result in greater willingness to invest in assets that are freely traded (e.g., stocks).

> The committee believes that the top rate on individual capital gains should not exceed the rates set forth in the bill, and therefore the bill provides that the maximum tax rate on capital gains will not exceed the top individual rate that the bill presently provides even if the top individual rate is increased during subsequent consideration of the bill.

The debate over taxation of capital gains was at the heart of the controversy in the 1990 budget deficit legislation. You didn't need to read his lips to know that Republican President George H.W. Bush wanted substantial reductions in the tax rate on capital gains. But the opposition from a Democrat Congress to a reduction did not budge, and when Congress increased the maximum tax rate on ordinary income above 28 percent,[17] they kept their word with respect to capital gains by maintaining a 28 percent ceiling on such gains.[18] But what a Republican President and a Democrat Congress did not do in 1990 was done by Democrat President Clinton and a Republican Congress in 1997. In general (as you will see in the next section, this is anything but simplification), the 1997 legislation reduced the top rate on gains from most capital assets from 28 percent to 20 percent and the 2003 legislation further reduced the 20 percent rate to 15 percent. However, beginning in

---

[14] Pub.Law No. 99–514, 99th Cong., 2d Sess. § 301(1986).

[15] See Conf.Rep. No. 99–841, 99th Cong., 2d Sess. II–105 (1986).

[16] Sen.Rep. No. 99–313, 99th Cong., 2d Sess. 169 (1986).

[17] See I.R.C. § 1(a)–(e) and (i)(3) and Chapter 27A2, infra.

[18] I.R.C. § 1(h). This subsection is discussed in more detail at Chapter 21B, infra.

2013 while the 15 percent rate was retained for middle-class taxpayers,[19] for upper-income taxpayers, the rate returned to 20 percent.[20]

*Capital Losses.* The first limitation upon the deductibility of *capital losses* appeared in the Revenue Act of 1924.[21] The Ways and Means Committee, in suggesting a limitation on the rate and amount of deductions for capital losses, stated:[22]

> [Certain] considerations led Congress, in the revenue act of 1921, to provide that the tax on capital gains in the case of property acquired and held by the taxpayer for profit or investment for more than two years should be limited to 12½ percent. But Congress failed to place a similar limitation on capital losses, so that to-day the taxpayer pays a maximum tax of 12½ percent on gains derived from the sale of capital assets, but is allowed to deduct in full from his taxable income his net losses resulting from the sale of capital assets during the taxable year. The injustice to the Government is too obvious to require much comment. The taxpayer may refrain from taking his profits, or, if he does take them, pays but a 12½ percent tax, whereas he is at liberty at any time to take advantage of any losses that may have been incurred and avail himself of a full deduction from his income. When we consider that the rate on the larger incomes runs as high as 58 percent, it can readily be realized how great the advantage is. The Government can collect but 12½ percent of a gain, but it is compelled to lighten the burden of the taxpayer to the extent of 58 percent of his losses. Take, for example, the case of a man with an income of $350,000 a year. Assume that he bought in the year 1917 5,000 shares of stock X at par, and that he sells these shares in 1922 for $600,000, showing a profit of $100,000. By reason of this transaction he would pay, in addition to the tax on his regular income, $12,500 to the Government. But assume that instead of selling this stock at a profit, he sold it in 1922 at a loss of $100,000. He would then be entitled to deduct the $100,000 from his income of $350,000, and the loss to the Government by reason of that deduction would be $58,000. Is there any further argument needed?

The Revenue Act of 1924 and successive acts have provided a limitation on the deductibility of capital losses. Although changes have occurred, restrictions upon the deductibility of capital losses have continued to the

---

[19]  I.R.C. § 1(h)(1)(C).

[20]  I.R.C. § 1(h)(1)(D). See Chapter 27A4, infra.

[21]  Revenue Act of 1924, § 208(c), 43 Stat. 253, 262 (1924).

[22]  House Rep. No. 1388, 67th Cong., 4th Sess. (1923), as quoted in Seidman, *Legislative History of Federal Income Tax Laws, 1938–1861,* 721 (1938).

present.[23] Without such limitations, taxpayers would be able without limit to use capital losses to wipe out ordinary income from other sources, creating a new type of tax shelter. Thus, taxpayers with the usual varied results in their investment portfolios could use capital losses to shelter ordinary income and hold capital gains for a step-up in basis at death.[24] Seemingly to avoid such a result, even in years when no preference was accorded capital gains,[25] Congress retained the capital loss limitations which operate in a manner similar to the Section 469 passive activity loss limitations.[26]

The retained dichotomy of ordinary income and capital gain with preferential treatment for capital gains has one major disadvantage. It thwarts another congressional objective, *tax simplification*.[27] As you work your way through the remaining chapters of this book, consider how much simpler our tax laws (and this course!) would be if Congress had totally eliminated capital gain and loss characterization.[28]

## B. THE MECHANICS OF CAPITAL GAINS

Internal Revenue Code: Sections 1(h) (omit (h)(2), (5)(B), (6), (8), (9), (10), (11)), (j)(2)(C) and (5); 1222. See Sections 1(h)(6), (j)(2)(A)–(E) and (3); 1201(a); 1202(a)–(e); 1221(a)(1)–(4); 1411.

––––––––––––––

The Internal Revenue Code provides preferential tax treatment for "net capital gain" as defined by Section 1222(11). The 1986 Act fixed a ceiling tax rate of 28 percent for such net capital gain. The current statute retains the characterization provisions of the prior law with the same basic code structure, but it taxes most net capital gain at a 15 or 20 percent rate. However, it substantially complicates the computation of tax on net capital gains by creating several different classes of net capital gains and imposing a variety of rates on those additional classes. Put simply, reading Section 1(h) in cold blood is excruciatingly difficult. To

––––––––––––––

[23] I.R.C. §§ 1211, 1212. An informative brief history of both the capital loss restrictions and the capital gains preferences appears in 3B Mertens, The Law of Federal Income Taxation, §§ 22.02–22.03 (1966 Rev.).

[24] I.R.C. § 1014. Cf. I.R.C. §§ 1031 and 1033 and Chapter 26, infra.

[25] See the Text at notes 14–16, supra.

[26] See Chapter 17F, supra.

[27] See Eisenstein, The Ideologies of Taxation 92–105 (1961). A philosophical consideration of the questions whether, when, and how capital gains should be taxed will be aided by a study of the following works: Surrey, "Definitional Problems in Capital Gains Taxation," 69 Harv.L.Rev. 985 (1956); Smith, Federal Tax Reform 151–155 (1961); Goode, The Individual Income Tax 199–207 (1964), all reprinted (the Surrey article with modifications) in Sander and Westfall, Readings in Federal Taxation (Foundation Press 1970) at pages 552–572, 537–541, and 529–537, respectively; Johnson, "Seventeen Culls From Capital Gains," 48 Tax Notes 1285 (1990).

[28] Similar simplification would occur in other tax areas not within the scope of this book, such as the taxation of corporations and partnerships. See, e.g., I.R.C. §§ 304 and 751(b). You may even want to consider how much simpler this course would be without the retained dichotomy.

avert student revolts, we have assigned only some parts of Section 1(h) (they're still tough going!) and we have tried to present the big picture without dealing with all possible alternatives.

The first step on the road to mastering the mechanics of capital gains under Section 1(h) is a special statutory structure under Section 1222. That Section requires deciphering in order to understand the mechanics of both capital gains (considered in this part) and capital losses (considered in the next part). Section 1222 provides a statutory netting mechanism. Sections 1222(1) through 1222(4) define short-term capital gain, short-term capital loss, long-term capital gain, and long-term capital loss, respectively.[1] Sections 1222(5) through 1222(8) then in essence provide for the netting of short-term losses against short-term gains and long-term losses against long-term gains in the following manner:

| Short-term capital gain (§ 1222(1)) | Long-term capital gain (§ 1222(3)) |
|---|---|
| – Short-term capital loss (§ 1222(2)) | – Long-term capital loss (§ 1222(4)) |
| Net short-term capital gain or loss (§ 1222(5) and (6)) | Net long-term capital gain or loss (§ 1222(7) and (8)) |

Next, the net shorts are netted against the net longs. If net gains exceed net losses in this final netting, we apply the rules discussed in this part. If net losses exceed net gains, we apply the rules discussed in part C of this Chapter. In the final netting process under Section 1222, net gains can arise in three situations: (1) a net short-term gain in excess of a net long-term loss; (2) a net long-term gain in excess of a net short-term loss (the excess net long-term gain in this situation is classified by Section 1222(11) as *net capital gain*); and (3) a combination of a net short-term gain and a net long-term gain (with the net long-term gain again classified as Section 1222(11) *net capital gain*).

The Treasury takes some liberty with a literal reading of the statute in filtering the results of the above final netting process into gross income on the income tax return (Schedule D of Form 1040).[2] If a taxpayer falls into one of the three types of final net gain situations above, only the *net amount of the gain* is included in gross income. The procedure used on the income tax return and in practice varies from the strict statutory formula which would require inclusion of all gains in gross income and

---

[1]   Note that each of the definitional subsections contained in I.R.C. § 1222 requires the presence of three factors in order for the gain or loss to be "capital" in nature: (1) a sale or exchange; (2) a capital asset; and (3) a holding for a specified period of time (either one year or less (short-term) or more than one year (long-term)). Each of these three factors is examined later in this Chapter.

[2]   See Reg. § 1.162–17(b) taking similar statutory liberty in another context and problem 1(b) at page 574, supra. If there is an overall net capital loss, then no capital gains are included in gross income.

deduction of all losses. Although generally the variant procedure generates the same amount of adjusted gross income.[3]

An example is helpful in demonstrating this netting process. Assume that in the current year, T, a single individual taxpayer has a long-term capital gain (Section 1222(3)) of $30,000, a long-term capital loss (Section 1222(4)) of $10,000, and a short-term capital loss (Section 1222(2)) of $5,000. Assume T has other income, salary for example, of $50,000. *Statutorily*, T's gross income is $80,000 computed as follows:

| | |
|---|---|
| Salary | $50,000 |
| Long-term capital gain | 30,000 |
| Gross income | $80,000 |

However, on T's income tax return on Schedule D, T will net T's capital gains and losses and, as a result, we say that T has gross income of $65,000 computed as follows:

| | | | |
|---|---|---|---|
| Salary | | | $50,000 |
| Long-term capital gain | $30,000 | | |
| Long-term capital loss | −10,000 | | |
| Net long-term capital gain | | $20,000 | |
| Short-term capital gain | $    0 | | |
| Short-term capital loss | − 5,000 | | |
| Net short-term capital loss | | −$ 5,000 | |
| Net capital gain | | | $15,000 |
| Gross income (after capital loss) | | | $65,000 |

In carrying out this initial netting process under Sections 1222(1)–(4), a one-year line is drawn between short-and long-term gains and losses, with long-term requiring a *more than* one-year holding period. If after shorts are netted against longs, there is a net short-term capital gain (either in excess of a net long-term capital loss or in conjunction with a net long-term capital gain), the amount of net short-term capital gain is taxed as ordinary income. If, however, there is a net long-term capital gain (either in excess of a net short-term capital loss or in conjunction with a net short-term capital gain), some type of preferential treatment is provided to the "net capital gain" which is defined by Section 1222(11) as the excess of net long-term capital gain over net short-term capital

---

[3]   See I.R.C. § 62(a)(3). It is sometimes necessary to establish "the gross income stated in the return." E.g., I.R.C. § 6501(c), sometimes extending limitation periods where gross income is substantially omitted. In such circumstances the statutory formula is applied rather than the shortcut generally permitted on the return. See also Reg. § 1.162–17(b).

loss. As a result, all of the assets making up net capital gain must have been held more than one year.[4]

If in a year a noncorporate taxpayer[5] has a "net capital gain," Section 1(h) comes into play. When Section 1(h) applies, net capital gains are treated as though they were the last taxable income received (i.e., the top incremented amounts of taxable income). The preferential treatment that section 1(h) accords to net capital gains can take a variety of forms depending upon the type of asset involved, the holding period for the asset, and the taxpayer's top ordinary income tax bracket for the year. Section 1(h) begins by extracting a portion of a noncorporate taxpayer's taxable income and taxing it at ordinary income tax rates under Sections 1(a)–(e).[6] Generally, *but not always*, this reduction will be an amount equal to the taxpayer's taxable income less net capital gain,[7] leaving only net capital gain to be taxed at a variety of rates under the remainder of Section 1(h).

As a practical matter, most net capital gain will be taxed at a 15 or 20 percent rate and for purposes of this "Fundamentals" course one may want to assume that the 15 or 20 percent rates and the 25 percent rate are the only Section 1(h) rates.[8] In fact, however, there are currently five different rates (28, 25, 20, 15, and zero percent) that generally apply under Section 1(h) and those different rates are explained in detail below.

*The 28 Percent Rate.* A 28 percent rate is imposed on several types of net capital gains.[9] The gain from capital assets that are "collectibles"[10]—things such as art work, antiques, gems, coins, stamps and . . . alcoholic beverages?! are generally[11] taxed at a 28 percent rate.[12] In addition, any Section 1202 gain (a concept considered below) is taxed at the 28 percent rate, but only to the extent that the Section 1202 gain is included in gross income.[13]

*The 25 Percent Rate.* A 25 percent rate is generally[14] imposed on "unrecaptured Section 1250 gain"[15] to the extent that such gain makes

---

[4]   See I.R.C. § 1222(3), (7), and (11).

[5]   This includes individuals and estates and trusts. See I.R.C. § 1(j)(2)(A)–(E). A corporate taxpayer has no preferential treatment for net capital gain. See I.R.C. §§ 1201(a) and 11(b).

[6]   I.R.C. § 1(h)(1)(A).

[7]   I.R.C. § 1(h)(1)(A)(i). But see I.R.C. § 1(h)(1)(A)(ii) discussed in the Text at notes 28–30, infra, for a situation where ordinary income rates are applied to some net capital gains.

[8]   See notes 14–17, infra.

[9]   I.R.C. § 1(h)(1)(F).

[10]   Collectibles are defined in Section 408(m) without regard to paragraph (m)(3). I.R.C. § 1(h)(5)(A).

[11]   All gains that would normally be taxed at a 28 percent rate may be taxed at ordinary income rates. See the Text at notes 28–30 infra.

[12]   I.R.C. § 1(h)(1)(F). See I.R.C. § 1(h)(4).

[13]   I.R.C. § 1(h)(1)(F), (7). See I.R.C. § 1(h)(4). For a discussion of § 1202, see the Text at notes 42–46, infra.

[14]   But see the Text at notes 28–30, infra, for a situation in which such gain may be taxed at ordinary income rates.

[15]   I.R.C. § 1(h)(6).

up net capital gain.[16] This rate applies to gains on the sale of depreciable real property, generally to the extent that depreciation previously has been allowed on such property. This type of net capital gain is considered in detail in a later Chapter.[17]

*The 15 and 20 Percent Rates.* A 15 percent rate is generally[18] imposed on the gain on most long term capital assets included in net capital gain (other than gains from collectibles, unrecaptured Section 1250 gain, and Section 1202 gain).[19] Thus the gain on stocks, bonds, investment land, and other types of capital assets which is statutorily labelled *"adjusted net capital gain"*[20] is generally[21] taxed at a 15 percent rate.[22] However, Congress has decided that certain high-income taxpayers[23] should pay a higher rate. As a result, such taxpayers pay a 20 percent rate rather than a 15 percent rate on their adjusted net capital gain.[24]

*The Zero Percent Rate.* Congress was concerned about lower-income taxpayers and felt it was inappropriate to tax the adjusted net capital gain of those individuals at a 15 or 20 percent rate.[25] "Lower income" for this purpose is measured with reference to the historical pre-2018 tax rates. Thus, to the extent that an individual's adjusted net capital gain would otherwise have historically fallen into those lower income tax brackets (10 or 15 percent in 2017), such gains are taxed at a zero rate (not taxed)![26] Any remaining adjusted net capital gains are taxed at a 15 or 20 percent rate.[27]

Similarly, if 25 or 28 percent net capital gains would be taxed at a lower rate if they were not segregated from ordinary income (which includes net short-term capital gain), to that extent they will be taxed at

---

[16]  I.R.C. § 1(h)(1)(E), (6).

[17]  See Chapter 22D, infra.

[18]  See the Text at notes 23, 24, 25–27, infra.

[19]  See I.R.C. § 1(h)(3) through (7).

[20]  I.R.C. § 1(h)(3)(A).

[21]  See the Text at notes 23, 24, 25–27, infra. In addition, under I.R.C. § 1411, which was added to the Code by the Affordable Health Care Act, some individuals will be taxed an additional 3.8 percent, resulting in an effective 18.3 percent rate. See page 947, infra.

[22]  I.R.C. § 1(h)(1)(C). The 15 percent rate also applies to most dividends. See page 945, infra.

[23]  Congress retained the pre-2018 breakpoints in the 2017 Tax Cuts and Jobs Act when it changed the tax rates on ordinary income. The rates apply to taxpayers whose taxable income exceeds a threshold amount: $479,000 for married taxpayers filing jointly (and surviving spouses); $452,400 for heads of households; $425,800 for single taxpayers; and $239,500 for married taxpayers filing separately, and $12,700 for estates and trusts. I.R.C. § 1(j)(5)(A)(ii), (B)(ii). After 2018, these amounts are adjusted for inflation. I.R.C. § 1(j)(5)(C). See Chapter 27A4.

[24]  I.R.C. § 1(h)(1)(D). As a practical matter, such taxpayers pay a 23.8 percent tax on such gains because of the I.R.C. § 1411 additional 3.8 percent tax. See note 21, supra.

[25]  I.R.C. § 1(h)(3).

[26]  I.R.C. § 1(h)(1)(B). The historic breakpoints are $77,200 for joint returns, $51,700 for heads of households, $38,600 for other unmarried taxpayers, and $2,600 for trusts and estates. I.R.C. § 1(j)(5)(A)(i), (B)(i). The amounts are adjusted for inflation after 2018. I.R.C. § 1(j)(5)(C).

[27]  I.R.C. § 1(h)(1)(B), (C), and (D).

the 10, 12, 22, or 24 percent ordinary income tax rates.[28] The 25 percent gains are taxed first at the lower rates and then the 28 percent gains are used to fill any gap.[29] Although rare, this potentially applies more rates to net capital gains.[30]

A few examples in some simple situations may help to demonstrate the Section 1(h) consequences. Single Taxpayer has the following events occur in the current year when we assume Single's ordinary income is taxed at a flat 30 percent rate under Section 1(j)(2)(C): Single has $100,000 of ordinary income and a $10,000 LTCG from the sale of stock. Thus, Single has a net capital gain of $10,000 under Section 1222(11). Tracking the relevant parts of Section 1(h), the results are as follows:

| | |
|---|---|
| § 1(h)(1)(A)(i)[31]: an assumed tax of 30% under § 1(j)(2)(C) on $100,000 ($110,000 less $10,000) equals | $30,000 |
| § 1(h)(1)(B): | 0 |
| § 1(h)(1)(C): 15% of $10,000, ($10,000 less 0) | 1,500 |
| § 1(h)(1)(D), (E), and (F): | 0 |
| Tax Liability[32] | $31,500 |

If the stock instead had been a collectible, the result would be as follows:

| | |
|---|---|
| § 1(h)(1)(A)(i): | $30,000 |
| § 1(h)(1)(B), (C), (D), and (E): | 0 |
| § 1(h)(1)(F): 28% of $110,000 (taxable income) less $100,000 (the amount taxed under § 1(h)(1)(A)–(D)) = $10,000 | 2,800 |
| Tax Liability[33] | $32,800 |

If Single has the same $100,000 of ordinary income and has both a $10,000 LTCG from the stock and a $10,000 LTCG from a collectible,

---

[28] I.R.C. § 1(j)(2).

[29] The intricate language of I.R.C. § 1(h) establishes a pecking order and the 10, 12, 22, and 24 percent brackets are first filled up with ordinary income (including NSTCG), then gains that would normally be taxed at 25 percent, and finally gains that would normally be taxed at 28 percent. These rules are contained in the statutory mechanism of § 1(h) at § 1(h)(1)(A)–(F).

[30] Thus net capital gains may be taxed at nine different rates: 0, 10, 12, 15, 20, 22, 24, 25, and 28.

[31] I.R.C. § 1(h)(1)(A)(ii) results in a lesser amount. I.R.C. § 1(h)(1)(A)(ii)(I). Thus § 1(h)(1)(A)(i) applies.

[32] The $10,000 net capital gain (which is also adjusted net capital gain, see I.R.C. § 1(h)(3)) is given preferential treatment and is taxed at a 15 percent rate, rather than the assumed 30 percent rate that is imposed on the ordinary income.

[33] The $10,000 net capital gain is given preferential treatment and is taxed at a 28 percent rate rather than the assumed 30 percent rate that is imposed on ordinary income.

Single would have a $20,000 net capital gain under Section 1222(11) and a tax liability determined as follows:

| | |
|---|---:|
| § 1(h)(1)(A)(i): | $30,000 |
| § 1(h)(1)(B): | 0 |
| § 1(h)(1)(C): 15% of $10,000 | 1,500 |
| § 1(h)(1)(D) and (E): | 0 |
| § 1(h)(1)(F): 28% of $10,000 | 2,800 |
| Tax Liability[34] | $34,300 |

Returning to the first example, if Single instead had $500,000 of taxable income (but assume a flat 30 percent rate under Section 1(j)(2)(C)) and a $10,000 LTCG from the sale of stock, the results would be as follows:

| | |
|---|---:|
| § 1(h)(1)(A)(i): an assumed tax of 30% under § 1(j)(2)(C) on $500,000 ($510,000 less $10,000) equals | $150,000 |
| § 1(h)(1)(B) and (C): | 0 |
| § 1(h)(1)(D): 20% of $10,000 ($10,000 less 0) | 2,000 |
| § 1(h)(E) and (F): | 0 |
| Tax Liability[35] | $152,000 |

*Netting Within Section 1(h).* Recall that in the first Section 1222 step prior to entering the Section 1(h) thicket, Congress used a netting process.[36] Congress also provides for netting under Section 1(h), but it takes a statutory trapeze artist to swing through the Code section to comprehend the Congressional legislation. (One might want to indulge in a shot or two of a good liquid "collectible" before trying to become such a trapeze artist and swing through the section.) Well hidden within Section 1(h) are a variety of netting rules that happily reach a pro-taxpayer result.[37] Under the Section 1(h) netting process, netting first occurs within each rate classification.[38] If there are net losses within any classification, they then wipe out net gains that would otherwise be taxed

---

[34]  Here, $10,000 of net capital gain is taxed at a 28 percent rate and $10,000 of net capital gain (the adjusted net capital gain) is taxed at a 15 percent rate. Both rates are less than the assumed 30 percent rate imposed on ordinary income.

[35]  The $10,000 of net capital gain is taxed at a preferential 20 percent rate rather than the assumed 30 percent rate imposed on ordinary income. See also notes 23 and 24, supra.

   If Single's ordinary taxable income were $419,800, instead of $500,000, $6,000 of the net capital gain would be taxed at a 15 percent rate and $4,000 would be taxed at a 20 percent rate resulting in an I.R.C. § 1 tax liability of $127,440 ($125,940 (30% of $419,800) plus $900 (15% of $6,000) plus $800 (20% of $4,000)). See note 23, supra.

[36]  See the Text at note 1, supra.

[37]  The results are consistent with those used on Form Schedule D.

[38]  See, e.g., I.R.C. § 1(h)(3)(A), (4).

at the highest rate or combination of rates under the Section 1(h)(1) rate schedule.[39] For example, if Single, in the examples above, has *net* losses from capital assets whose gains would be taxed at a 15 or 20 percent rate, those net losses would first wipe out net 28 percent gains, then net 25 percent gains.[40] Similarly, if Single has a NSTCL in the Section 1222 netting process, the NSTCL first wipes out net 28 percent gains, then net 25 percent gains, then net 20 percent gains, and then net 15 percent gains.[41]

*Section 1202.* As an incentive to encourage noncorporate taxpayers to invest in startup companies, Section 1202 was added to the Code. The provision allows a noncorporate taxpayer an exclusion of 100 percent of the gain on "qualified small business stock" acquired after September 27, 2010, and held for more than 5 years.[42] That is right; there is no tax on the gain. There are lower (50 and 75) percent exclusions for small business stock acquired in prior years[43] and, to the extent that Section 1202 gain is included in gross income, such gain is taxed at a 28 percent rate, effectively taxing such gain at a zero, 7 (75 percent exclusion), or 14 (50 percent exclusion) percent rate.[44] However, there are ceiling limitations on the amount of a shareholder's Section 1202 gain.[45] In addition, the definition of qualified small business stock is technical.[46]

## PROBLEMS

1.   T, a single taxpayer, has a salary of $200,000 in the current year. T also has the following transactions all involving the sale of capital assets: (1) a gain of $15,000 on a "collectible" held for 2 years; and (2) a gain of $20,000 on stock held for 15 months.

   (a)   Determine the amount of T's net capital gain.

   (b)   At what rate will the components of T's net capital gain be taxed?

---

[39]   I.R.C. § 1(h)(1).

[40]   Statutorily if Single had ordinary income taxed at a flat 30% rate and a $10,000 LTCL from stock and $7,500 of 28% gain and $7,500 of 25% gain, Single would have $5,000 of net capital gain which would be taxed at the 25% rate under I.R.C. § 1(h)(1)(E) leaving no gain to be taxed at 28% under § 1(h)(1)(F).

[41]   Thus, if Single had ordinary income taxed at a flat 30% rate, a $15,000 NSTCL and $5,000 of 28% gain, $5,000 of 25% gain, and $10,000 of 15% or 20% gain, Single would have a $5,000 NCG. I.R.C. § 1(h)(1)(C) or (D) would apply to tax the $5,000 net capital gain at a 15% or 20% rate.

Similar principles apply to a § 1212(b)(1)(B) LTCL carryover which is all treated as a loss from a capital asset whose gain would be taxed at 28% rate. See I.R.C. § 1(h)(4)(B)(iii) and the Text at page 700, infra.

[42]   I.R.C. § 1202(a)(4).

[43]   The 50 percent exclusion applies to gain realized on the disposition of qualified small business stock issued after August 10, 1993, and held for more than five years. I.R.C. § 1202(a). The exclusion is increases to 75 percent for qualified small business stock acquired after February 17, 2009, and before September 28, 2010. I.R.C. § 1202(a)(3).

[44]   I.R.C. § 1202(a).

[45]   I.R.C. § 1202(b).

[46]   I.R.C. § 1202(c)–(e).

    (c)    Assuming there is a flat 30% tax on ordinary income and disregarding any deductions (including the standard deduction and personal exemption), what is T's tax liability in the current year? *$ 6 $,250*

**2.**    S, a single taxpayer, is a high-income taxpayer with a salary of $500,000 in the current year. S also has the following transactions involving the sale of capital assets: (1) a gain of $120,000 on stock held for 15 months and (2) a loss of $20,000 on stock held for 3 years. Assume there is a flat 30% tax on ordinary income and disregarding any deductions (including the standard deduction), what is S's tax liability under § 1 in the current year?

**3.**    Taxpayer, who is in the highest federal tax bracket in the current year, has a $5,000 gain from a collectible and a $5,000 gain from stock, both held long-term.

    (a)    What is Taxpayer's net capital gain and how is it taxed if Taxpayer also has a $5,000 loss from a collectible held long-term?

    (b)    What results in (a), above, if instead Taxpayer's $5,000 loss is from stock held long-term?

    (c)    What results in (a), above, if instead Taxpayer's $5,000 loss is from stock held for 9 months rather than from the collectible?

    (d)    What is Taxpayer's net capital gain and how is it taxed if Taxpayer has a $5,000 gain from a collectible, a $5,000 unrecaptured § 1250 gain, a $5,000 gain from stock, and a $10,000 loss from stock, all held long-term?

## C.  THE MECHANICS OF CAPITAL LOSSES

Internal Revenue Code: Sections 1211(b); 1212(b)(1), (2)(A)(i); 1222(10). See Sections 165(c) and (f); 1211(a); 1212(a); 1221(a)(1)–(4); 1222.

---

    The losses discussed here are only *deductible* losses. Under Section 1222(2) and (4), the terms short-term capital loss and long-term capital loss are defined to include only such losses as are "taken into account in computing taxable income." Before we can discuss the mechanics of capital losses, we must therefore determine *whether* a loss is taken into account; that is, whether the loss is deductible. In the case of individuals, the primary Code section that determines whether a loss is deductible is Section 165(c), which should be reviewed. If a loss is deductible, then the provisions currently under examination determine *how* and to *what extent* the deduction may be utilized.

    Capital losses are generally deductible only from or against capital gains. Capital losses, whether long-term or short-term, offset capital gains, long-term or short-term, dollar for dollar. In the case of a noncorporate taxpayer, however, capital losses in excess of capital gains can be deducted from ordinary income, but only to a limited extent.[1] Any capital loss balance remaining after the excess is deducted is carried forward into succeeding taxable years, retaining its original character as either long-term or short-term capital loss. This carryover loss is applied against capital gains (and to a limited extent against ordinary income) in each succeeding year until fully utilized.[2]

The statutory mechanics of Section 1222, previously discussed in Part B of this Chapter, require the taxpayer first to "net out" long-term transactions and short-term transactions, and then to "net out" net longs against net shorts. Somewhat like the first step in the net gain situations previously discussed, the netting process results in three possible net *loss* situations. First, there may be a net short-term loss that reduces or eliminates, dollar-for-dollar, the amount of net long-term gain. Likewise, there may be a net long-term loss which reduces or eliminates, dollar-for-dollar, any net short-term gain. The third possibility, is net losses in both short-term and long-term categories. The double netting process, now familiar, presents a procedure under which capital losses are always fully utilized in any year to the extent that there are capital gains for the year. Implicit in all this is the previously discussed rationale for the continued dichotomy between capital gain and ordinary income;[3] capital gain has a limitless capacity for being offset by capital losses, whereas the reduction of ordinary income by capital losses is severely restricted. What is the reason for the restriction limiting the deductibility of capital losses against ordinary income? These restrictions and the possibly deferred utilization of capital losses that run afoul of them are the subject of this discussion.

*The Section 1211(b) Limitation.* The starting point for the treatment of capital losses is Section 1211(b). It provides, essentially, that capital losses are deductible only to the extent of capital gains plus, if such losses exceed such gains, an amount of ordinary income not to exceed the *lower* of $3,000 ($1,500 in the case of a married individual filing a separate return) or the excess of such losses over such gains.

An illustration of the operation of Section 1211(b) may be helpful. In this example all deductions except those concerning capital losses are disregarded. Assume that T, a single taxpayer, has salary income of $52,000. During the year, T has the following capital gains and losses:

| Long-term gain | $400 | Short-term gain | $400 |
|---|---|---|---|
| Long-term loss | $1,200 | Short-term loss | $1,000 |
| Net long-term loss | ($800) | Net short-term loss | ($600) |

---

[1]  Corporate taxpayers are permitted to deduct capital losses only to the extent of capital gains. I.R.C. § 1211(a). However, I.R.C. § 1212(a)(1) treats excess capital losses in a given year as a short-term capital loss carryback (regardless of its origin) to each of the three taxable years preceding the loss year and, to the extent not so used, as a short-term capital loss carryover (regardless of its origin) to each of the five taxable years succeeding the loss year.

[2]  See I.R.C. §§ 1211(b), 1212(b) and 1222(10).

[3]  See page 685, supra.

The total of T's net long-term loss and net short-term loss is $1,400, well within the Section 1211(b)(1) $3,000 limitation, and T can deduct this $1,400 amount from ordinary income as a result of Section 1211(b)(2). Thus, the $1,400 excess is a form of tax shelter that wipes out $1,400 of ordinary income. T's adjusted gross income is $50,600 computed as follows:

| | |
|---|---:|
| Salary | $52,000 |
| Less § 1211(b) deduction (see § 62(a)(3)) | − 1,400 |
| Adjusted gross income | $50,600[4] |

In the above example, if the amount of T's long-term capital loss had been $2,400 and the amount of T's short-term capital loss had been $2,000, then the $3,000 dollar limitation of Section 1211(b)(1) would apply. During the year T has:

| | | | |
|---|---:|---|---:|
| Long-term gain | $400 | Short-term gain | $400 |
| Long-term loss | $2,400 | Short-term loss | $2,000 |
| Net long-term loss | ($2,000) | Net short-term loss | ($1,600) |

In this circumstance, the tax shelter deduction from ordinary income is limited by Section 1211(b)(1) to $3,000, the lower of the dollar ceiling ($3,000) or the excess of capital losses over capital gains ($3,600). Thus, the Section 1211(b)(1) tax shelter in any year may eliminate only a maximum of $3,000 of ordinary income.

Since only $3,000 of the $3,600 excess capital loss is deductible from ordinary income, two questions now arise. First, what happens to the $600 ($3,600–$3,000) which exceeds the Section 1211(b) limitation? And second, of the net long-term loss of $2,000 and the net short-term loss of $1,600, totaling $3,600, which net loss (long-term or short-term) is first consumed against ordinary income within the limitation of Section 1211(b)? The key for unlocking the answer to both questions is found in Section 1212(b) relating to capital loss carryovers, which is discussed below. Hang in there!

*The Section 1212(b) Carryover.* The carryover statute for noncorporate taxpayers, Section 1212(b), provides that capital losses not utilized in the year incurred are carried over into subsequent taxable years and treated as long-term or short-term losses, depending upon their original character.[5] The "if" clause at the beginning of Section

---

[4]   Actually the Treasury (as they did with net gains, see page 689, supra.) takes liberty with a literal reading of the statute in filtering the results of the I.R.C. § 1211(b) netting process into gross income on the income tax return (Schedule D of Form 1040). When § 1211(b) applies a negative amount (here, $1,400) is included in gross income which here would be $50,600.

[5]   The phrase "amount allowed" in I.R.C. § 1212(b)(2) creates some uncertainty. It is the Treasury's position that utilization of carryovers may not be deferred; the amount that can be

1212(b)(1) makes the carryover provisions dependent upon the taxpayer having a *"net capital loss,"* which is defined in Section 1222(10) as "the excess of the losses from the sales or exchanges of capital assets over the sum allowed under section 1211." If the sum allowed under Section 1211(b) does not exceed $3,000 of excess losses over gains (the maximum Section 1211(b) $3,000 deduction against ordinary income), there is no "net capital loss," no carryover, and no need or permission to use Section 1212(b).

In the alternative, if for any year capital losses exceed capital gains by more than $3,000, Section 1212(b) applies and questions arise both as to the *amount* and the *character* of any carryovers. The secret of interpreting Section 1212(b) and of answering the questions posed two paragraphs ago is found in Section 1212(b)(2) which cryptically creates $3,000 of *constructive* short-term capital gain which is used in making the section 1212(b)(1) carryover computations.[6] *Thus, when working with the statute, one must first make the Section 1212(b)(2) computation, before computing carryover losses under Section 1212(b)(1).* In a round-about way, Section 1212(b) tells us that the *amount* of the carryover will be the amount of the *net* short-term and *net* long-term capital losses *reduced* by the $3,000 amount that wiped out ordinary income.

The *character* of a capital loss, whether long-term or short-term, remains the same in the year to which it is carried. If a taxpayer has only unused net long-term capital losses in a particular year, the carryover will be long-term loss. Similarly, if the taxpayer has only unused net short-term capital losses, the carryover will be short-term loss. If the taxpayer has both net short-term and net long-term capital losses, because of the Section 1212(b)(2) constructive short-term capital gain, the net short-term capital loss is used first and then the net long-term capital loss to eliminate the Section 1211(b) $3,000 deduction from ordinary income. Any remaining losses are carried over and are treated as though they actually arose in the taxable year to which they are carried. Consequently, they are in effect reborn in succeeding taxable years indefinitely until finally utilized in accordance with the statute, or until their demise at the taxpayer's death.[7]

The operation of Section 1212(b) is best understood by means of an example. Using the figures in the second hypothetical, above, T had:

---

used reduces the amount carried to the next year whether used or not. Rev.Rul. 76–177, 1976–1 C.B. 224.

  [6] We disregard any consideration of I.R.C. § 1212(b)(2)(A)(ii) and (B). As a practical matter, these provisions generally permit a simple trust (essentially one required to distribute all of its income currently) to fully carry over its capital losses in excess of capital gains. It rarely applies to an individual taxpayer, and its application is disregarded in this note and problem.

  [7] I.R.C. § 1212(b). Carryover losses die with the taxpayer and are not passed on to his estate. However, I.R.C. § 642(h) passes along losses of an estate or trust to the beneficiaries upon termination of the estate or trust.

| Long-term gain | $400 | Short-term gain | $400 |
|---|---|---|---|
| Long-term loss | $2,400 | Short-term loss | $2,000 |
| Net long-term loss | ($2,000) | Net short-term loss | ($1,600) |

and T was allowed to deduct only $3,000 from ordinary income under Section 1211(b). As a result, T has a "net capital loss" of $600, Section 1212(b) applies, and first applying Section 1212(b)(2), T is deemed to have a constructive $3,000 short-term gain under Section 1212(b)(2)(A)(i)[8] with the result that T's capital gain and loss picture (for purposes of Section 1212(b) only) is as follows:

| Long-term gain | $400 | Short-term gain | $3,400 |
|---|---|---|---|
| Long-term loss | $2,400 | Short-term loss | $2,000 |
| Net long-term loss | ($2,000) | Net short-term gain | $1,400 |

Now turning to Section 1212(b)(1)(A), there is no net short-term capital loss excess because there is no net short-term capital *loss* and none of the $2,000 short-term capital loss is carried over. Turning to Section 1212(b)(1)(B), there is a $600 excess of the $2,000 net long-term capital loss over the $1,400 net short-term capital gain and the $600 excess is treated as a long-term capital loss in the succeeding year. Thus, Section 1212(b) answers the questions raised above: the $600 excess is carried over and it is carried over as a long-term capital loss. What as a practical matter is the message of Section 1212(b)?

*Netting.* With the broad range of the rate classifications applicable to net capital gains under Section 1(h),[9] an issue would seem to arise if the carryovers that occur are made up of a variety of different types of LTCLs. For example, assume in year one, single taxpayer, T, who has substantial ordinary income also has a $3,000 LTCL from the sale of stock and a $3,000 LTCL from the sale of a collectible and these are T's only capital gains and losses in the year. In year one, T has a $3,000 deductible capital loss under Section 1211(b) and it wipes out ordinary income of $3,000.[10] The issue is which LTCL (the stock loss or the collectibles loss) is deducted in year one and which LTCL gets carried over to year two? The answer is WHO CARES!, because as a practical matter, it makes no difference. The reason for this conclusion is that the statute reaches a pro-taxpayer result under which *any* long-term capital loss carryover under Section 1212(b)(1)(B) is treated as a loss from a LTCL falling within the 28 percent rate category.[11] Thus as netting occurs within each category for purposes of Section 1(h), the LTCL

---

[8] See note 6, supra.

[9] See I.R.C. § 1(h)(1) and Chapter 21B, supra.

[10] I.R.C. § 1211(b)(1).

[11] I.R.C. § 1(h)(4)(B)(iii).

carryover is netted within the 28 percent category.[12] As a result, it first wipes out 28 percent LTCGs in the subsequent year and then works its way down the Section 1(h) rate scale.[13] Similarly any STCL carryover under Section 1212(b)(1)(A) is first netted against STCGs in the subsequent year[14] and then works its way down the Section 1(h) rate scale.[15]

## PROBLEM

1. Here are two questions on capital losses incurred in the current year. The figure for taxable income given in column A reflects a single taxpayer's taxable income for each of two years *without* regard to his capital gains and losses. Note that in computing gross income (as adjusted) on the return no gains will be included, since capital losses exceed capital gains and the § 1211(b) excess amount will be a reduction (see note 4, supra).

| Taxable Income | LTCG | LTCL | STCG | STCL |
|---|---|---|---|---|
| 1. +$10,000 | $2,000 | $6,000 | $2,600 | $1,000 |
| 2.   10,000 | 2,000 | 10,000 | 2,000 | 4,000 |

For each year separately, without regard to computations for other years, determine the amount of the taxpayer's capital loss that is allowed as a deduction from ordinary income under § 1211(b)(1) or (2) and the amount and character of his capital loss carryover, if any, under § 1212(b).

# D. THE MEANING OF "CAPITAL ASSET"

## 1. THE STATUTORY DEFINITION

Internal Revenue Code: Section 1221(a)(1)–(4). See Sections 1221(a)(5)–(8), (b).

---

### Mauldin v. Commissioner
United States Court of Appeals, Tenth Circuit, 1952.
195 F.2d 714.

■ Before HUXMAN, MURRAH and PICKETT, CIRCUIT JUDGES.

■ MURRAH, CIRCUIT JUDGE.

This is an appeal from a decision of the Tax Court, holding that certain lots sold by petitioners during the taxable years 1944 and 1945, were "property held by the taxpayer primarily for sale to customers in

---

[12] Id.
[13] See I.R.C. § 1(h)(1) and page 691, supra.
[14] I.R.C. § 1222(5) and (6).
[15] See I.R.C. § 1(h)(1), 1(h)(4)(B)(ii), and page 691, supra.

the ordinary course of his trade or business" within the exclusionary clause of Section 117(a)(1) of the Internal Revenue Code, 26 U.S.C.A. § 117(a)(1).[1] If the gain from the sale of these lots was derived in this manner, it constituted ordinary income taxable under Section 22(a),[2] and not a capital gain taxable under Section 117(a)(1).[3] Petitioners, residents of the State of New Mexico, are husband and wife, and all income involved is community income. The two cases were therefore consolidated for trial and disposition. A summary of Mauldin's business activities is necessary to a determination of the issue presented.

C.E. Mauldin, a graduate veterinarian since 1904, who also engaged in some road contracting, moved to Albuquerque, New Mexico in 1916, where he organized a road construction company. While in Clovis, New Mexico in 1920, to bid on a sewer project, he decided to move there and engage in the cattle business. Later in the same year, he contracted to buy 160 acres of land one-half mile from the city limits of Clovis for $20,000.00. This land was particularly suitable for cattle feeding, but was not at that time considered suitable for residential development, because the City, with a population of 5000, was not growing in that direction.

By the time Mauldin finally received title to the land in June 1921, he decided that it was not the time to go into the cattle business because of drought, crop and bank failures, and a decline in the cattle business which continued through 1924. He tried to sell the entire tract in 1924 for less than he paid for it, but was unable to do so, partly because a highway had been surveyed diagonally across the land, splitting it into two tracts and rendering it less suitable for cattle feeding. A real estate agent with whom he listed the property for sale advised him that they would have better success if he divided it into small tracts and blocks. The land was accordingly platted into 29 tracts and 4 blocks containing 88 lots each, and called the "Mauldin Addition". At the time the land was platted in 1924, there was still no demand for residential property in the area. In 1927, he built a home for himself near the center of the Addition.

There were no sales of any consequence until the land commenced to be included in the city limits of Clovis in 1931. By 1939, it was wholly within the city limits, and without Mauldin's request, the City began a paving program in the area, for which he was assessed approximately $25,000.00. When he was unable to pay this assessment, the City instituted suits on its paving liens, and in order to save his property, he divided some additional tracts into lots and devoted most of his time to the sale of the lots in the Addition. He listed the property with real estate agents and otherwise promoted sales through personal solicitations, signs, newspaper advertisements, and gifts of lots to a school and the builder of the first F.H.A. house in Clovis. He stated that at times he

---

[1]   See I.R.C. (1986) § 1221(a)(1). All footnotes in this opinion are by the editors.

[2]   See I.R.C. § 61(a).

[3]   See I.R.C. § 1221(a)(1).

would "chase" a prospective purchaser "around the block". During 1939 and 1940, he sold enough lots to liquidate the paving indebtedness.

Mauldin testified that with the indebtedness to the City paid, he decided to hold the remaining portions of the original tract for investment purposes, and after 1940, did nothing to promote sales. He stated, "I cut it up and tried my best to sell it to clear it, and when I cleared it, I quit". From 1940 until 1949, when his health failed, Mauldin devoted full time to the lumber business he organized in 1939. During this period, he had no real estate office, no license to sell real estate, did not advertise the properties by newspapers or signs, had no fixed price for lots, and at times refused to sell certain lots, either because the prospective purchaser would not pay the asked price, or Mauldin did not wish to sell the particular property at that time. The only real estate purchased by Mauldin after acquiring the 160 acres in 1920 was one "unsightly" block of lots near his residence, and some commercial properties to be used in connection with his lumber business.

Due primarily to the location of war facilities nearby, the City of Clovis grew in population to 14,000 in 1940 and to 20,000 to 25,000 in 1945, and the lots, Mauldin Addition, were in great demand. By the end of 1945, Mauldin had disposed of all but 20 acres of his original 160 acre tract. This 20 acres was considered by him and real estate dealers to be his most valuable property. Mauldin's records show that he sold 2 lots in 2 transactions in 1941; 11 in 1942 in 2 transactions (6 lots were given to his daughter as a wedding present); 5½ in 1943 in 3 transactions; 5½ in 1944 in 3 transactions; 44½ in 1945 in 15 transactions; 39 in 1946, 1 in 1947 and 2 in 1948. For the taxable years in 1939 and 1940, the taxpayers' income tax returns showed income from real estate only; for each of the years 1941 and 1944 (returns for 1942 and 1943 not shown) they showed net income of approximately $3,000.00 from sales of real estate and approximately $12,000.00 from the lumber business; for the year 1945, $20,484.84 from real estate and $12,339.80 from lumber; and in 1946, $21,942.88 from real estate and $25,005.07 from lumber. On his 1940 return, Mauldin stated that the nature of his business was "real estate"; in 1943 it was shown as "lumber business"; in 1944 he did not designate the nature of his business; and in 1945 it was shown as "lumber and real estate".

In their income tax returns for the years 1944 and 1945, petitioners showed the lots sold during those years as long-time capital assets, and computed the tax accordingly. The Commissioner determined that the profit realized was ordinary income within the meaning of Section 117(a)(1)[4] of the Internal Revenue Code, and assessed the additional tax. This appeal is from the judgment of the Tax Court sustaining the Commissioner, and the only question is whether its judgment on these facts can be said to be clearly erroneous.

---

[4]    Ibid.

It is admitted by taxpayer that during 1939 and 1940, he was engaged in the business of selling the tracts and lots in Mauldin Addition. He earnestly contends, however, that after 1940, his business status was changed; that his full time thereafter was devoted to the lumber business, and held the remaining lots for investment purposes, selling them only through unsolicited offers when the price was right.

There is no fixed formula or rule of thumb for determining whether property sold by the taxpayer was held by him primarily for sale to customers in the ordinary course of his trade or business. Each case must, in the last analysis, rest upon its own facts. There are a number of helpful factors, however, to point the way, among which are the purposes for which the property was acquired, whether for sale or investment; and continuity and frequency of sales as opposed to isolated transactions. Dunlap v. Oldham Lumber Co., 5 Cir., 178 F.2d 781; Annot. 106 A.L.R. 254; Mertens, Vol. 3, Sec. 22.08.[5] And, any other facts tending to indicate that the sales or transactions are in furtherance of an occupation of the taxpayer, recognizing however that one actively engaged in the business of real estate may discontinue such business and simply sell off the remnants of his holdings without further engaging in the business. Snell v. Commissioner, 5 Cir., 97 F.2d 891. Thus, where residents of New York bought land in Florida and elsewhere from time to time for investment, a part of which was platted and improved, it was held that the occasional sale of lots through local brokers was not sufficiently frequent or engrossing to give the taxpayers the vocation of real estate dealers. Phipps v. Commissioner, 2 Cir., 54 F.2d 469. And, in Foran v. Commissioner, 5 Cir., 165 F.2d 705, a taxpayer admittedly engaged as a broker of nonproducing oil and gas leases and royalties purchased a producing property which he sold within eighteen months. The profit realized therefrom was held to be income from a long-time capital asset, the court reasoning that since this was the first producing property purchased by the taxpayer, there was no occasion to disbelieve his statement that he acquired it for investment or his motive for selling it.

On the other hand, sale and exchange of lots in 1939 and 1940 from a 92 acre tract of land, partially subdivided in 1932, was held to be in the ordinary course of business where the taxpayer had been continuously engaged in the real estate business since 1908, and had divided a part of the tract into lots in order to facilitate the sale of the land. Gruver v. Commissioner, 4 Cir., 142 F.2d 363. So too was the sale of lots from a tract of land which had been originally purchased for and used as a lettuce farm, but subdivided into lots when it became too valuable for truck farming operations. Richards v. Commissioner, 9 Cir., 81 F.2d 369, 106 A.L.R. 249. See also Oliver v. Commissioner, 4 Cir., 138 F.2d 910. And, lots sold through sales agencies after reacquisition at a trustee's sale, were held to be in the ordinary course of trade or business, as against the contention that they were sold in furtherance of an orderly

---

[5]    See Mertens, Vol. 3B, Sec. 22.15 (1973).

liquidation in Ehrman v. Commissioner, 9 Cir., 120 F.2d 607. While the purpose for which the property was acquired is of some weight, the ultimate question is the purpose for which it was held. Rollingwood Corp. v. Commissioner, 9 Cir., 190 F.2d 263.

Admittedly, Mauldin originally purchased the property for purposes other than for sale in the ordinary course of trade or business. When, however, he subdivided and offered it for sale, he was undoubtedly engaged in the vocation of selling lots from this tract of land at least until 1940. As against his contention that he ceased to engage in the business after 1940, the record evidence shows that he sold more lots in 1945 on a sellers market without solicitation than he did in 1940 on a buyers market. It seems fairly inferable from the record that at all times he had lots for sale, and that the volume sold depended primarily upon the prevailing economic conditions, brought on by wartime activities and their aftermath. It is true that he was in the lumber business, but his returns plainly show that a substantial part of his income was derived from the sale of the lots. In these circumstances, we cannot say that the Tax Court's conclusions are without factual bases.

The decisions are Affirmed.

## Malat v. Riddell[*]

Supreme Court of the United States, 1966.
383 U.S. 569, 86 S.Ct. 1030.

■ PER CURIAM.

Petitioner[1] was a participant in a joint venture which acquired a 45-acre parcel of land, the intended use for which is somewhat in dispute. Petitioner contends that the venturers' intention was to develop and operate an apartment project on the land; the respondent's position is that there was a "dual purpose" of developing the property for rental purposes or selling, whichever proved to be the more profitable. In any event, difficulties in obtaining the necessary financing were encountered, and the interior lots of the tract were subdivided and sold. The profit from those sales was reported and taxed as ordinary income.

The joint venturers continued to explore the possibility of commercially developing the remaining exterior parcels. Additional frustrations in the form of zoning restrictions were encountered. These difficulties persuaded petitioner and another of the joint ventures of the desirability of terminating the venture; accordingly, they sold out their interests in the remaining property. Petitioner contends that he is entitled to treat the profits from this last sale as capital gains; the respondent takes the position that this was "property held by the

---

[*]  See Bernstein, " 'Primarily for Sale': A Semantic Snare," 20 Stan.L.Rev. 1093 (1968). Ed.

[1]  The taxpayer and his wife who filed a joint return are the petitioners, but for simplicity are referred to throughout as "petitioner."

taxpayer primarily for sale to customers in the ordinary course of his trade or business,"[2] and thus subject to taxation as ordinary income.

The District Court made the following finding:

> The members of [the joint venture], as of the date the 44.901 acres were acquired, intended either to sell the property or develop it for rental, depending upon which course appeared to be most profitable. The venturers realized that they had made a good purchase price-wise and, if they were unable to obtain acceptable construction financing or rezoning * * * which would be prerequisite to commercial development, they would sell the property in bulk so they wouldn't get hurt. The purpose of either selling or developing the property continued during the period in which [the joint venture] held the property.

The District Court ruled that petitioner had failed to establish that the property was not held *primarily* for sale to customers in the ordinary course of business, and thus rejected petitioner's claim to capital gain treatment for the profits derived from the property's resale. The Court of Appeals affirmed, 347 F.2d 23. We granted certiorari (382 U.S. 900) to resolve a conflict among the courts of appeals[3] with regard to the meaning of the term "primarily" as it is used in § 1221(1) of the Internal Revenue Code of 1954.

The statute denies capital gain treatment to profits reaped from the sale of "property held by the taxpayer *primarily* for sale to customers in the ordinary course of his trade or business." (Emphasis added.) The respondent urges upon us a construction of "primarily" as meaning that a purpose may be "primary" if it is a "substantial" one.

As we have often said, "the words of statutes—including revenue acts—should be interpreted where possible in their ordinary, everyday senses." * * *. Departure from a literal reading of statutory language may, on occasion, be indicated by relevant internal evidence of the statute itself and necessary in order to effect the legislative purpose. * * *. But this is not such an occasion. The purpose of the statutory provision with which we deal is to differentiate between the "profits and losses arising from the everyday operation of a business" on the one hand (Corn Products Co. v. Commissioner, 350 U.S. 46, 52, 76 S.Ct. 20, 24) and "the realization of appreciation in value accrued over a substantial period of time" on the other. (Commissioner v. Gillette Motor Co., 364 U.S. 130, 134, 80 S.Ct. 1497, 1500.) A literal reading of the statute is consistent with this legislative purpose. We hold that, as used in § 1221(1), "primarily" means "of first importance" or "principally."

---

[2]   Internal Revenue Code of 1954, § 1221(1), 26 U.S.C.A. § 1221(1). * * *

[3]   Compare Rollingwood Corp. v. Commissioner, 190 F.2d 263, 266 (C.A.9th Cir.); American Can Co. v. Commissioner, 317 F.2d 604, 605 (C.A.2d Cir.), with United States v. Bennett, 186 F.2d 407, 410–411 (C.A.5th Cir.); Municipal Bond Corp. v. Commissioner, 341 F.2d 683, 688–689 (C.A.8th Cir.1965). Cf. Recordak Corp. v. United States, 325 F.2d 460, 463–464.

Since the courts below applied an incorrect legal standard, we do not consider whether the result would be supportable on the facts of this case had the correct one been applied. We believe, moreover, that the appropriate disposition is to remand the case to the District Court for fresh fact-findings, addressed to the statute as we have now construed it.

Vacated and remanded.*

## NOTE

The court in *Mauldin*, is discouragingly correct in suggesting that the question whether property is held primarily for sale is not answerable by a "fixed formula"; and the opinion does recite some factors that aid analysis."[1] And in *Malat v. Riddel*, we received the Supreme Court's exciting message that in Section 1221(a)(1), "primarily" means "of first importance" or "principally."[2] The meaning of a term in the Internal Revenue Code is not always to be determined in the manner in which the Court approached the meaning of "primarily" in *Malat,* with reference to dictionary definitions and supposed common usage. Congress may provide its own definition for the terms used.[3] In the capital gain and loss area there are many instances in which, in order to achieve a desired result, *Congress* itself ascribes meanings to terms which are quite at variance from their "ordinary everyday senses." It seems desirable here to direct attention to some of this congressional game-playing; but the comments that follow are intended to be only generally informative and not to be used as a basis for detailed study at this point.

Recall that under Section 1222, capital gain or loss consequences require: (1) a transaction involving a capital asset, (2) a sale or exchange of that capital asset, and (3) a determination of how long the taxpayer has held the capital asset. Section 1221 defines the term capital asset but it is subject to both judicial and statutory exceptions.[4] If a transaction does not involve a capital asset, or if it does not constitute a sale or exchange, it will give rise only to ordinary income or to an ordinary deduction.

A close reading of the Section 1221 definition of a capital asset, or perhaps more appropriately phrased as a listing of the types of property which do not constitute capital assets, provides a feel for what is not within the scope of a capital asset. The statute generally excludes from capital asset status property which is at the heart of a taxpayer's income-generating activities, essentially either services-generated property or property in the nature of inventory.

---

* On remand, the District Court ruled that the real estate was not held primarily for sale to customers in the ordinary course of the taxpayer's trade or business. Malat v. Riddell, 275 F. Supp. 358 (S.D.Cal.1966). Ed.

[1] The *Mauldin* case also pays little heed to whether real property may be said to be held for sale "to customers." See Friedlander, " 'To Customers': The Forgotten Element in the Characterization of Gains on Sales of Real Property." 39 Tax L.Rev. 31 (1983).

[2] In International Shoe Machine Corp. v. U.S., 491 F.2d 157 (1st Cir. 1974) we discover that, even though rental income from property exceeds income from its sale, the property can be considered held primarily for sale.

[3] One should be aware of a number of general definitions contained in I.R.C. § 7701.

[4] See Chapter 21G and H, infra.

Certainly this is the message of Section 1221(a)(1) and it is also demonstrated by Sections 1221(a)(3) and (4) (but check out Section 1221(b)(3)!). The theme is less clear in Section 1221(a)(2), but that provision has little meaning without examining Section 1231.[5] Also, the role of Section 1221(a)(5) will become more understandable when one reads Section 170(e).[6]

The message is murkier when one examines Section 1221(a)(6)–(8). The question of whether one who was a dealer in securities held securities as a dealer or as an investor was settled by Section 1236.[7] But the character of commodities derivatives financial instruments held by such a dealer was unclear.[8] Under Section 1221(a)(6) such an instrument held by a dealer is not a capital asset unless the instrument has no connection with the activities of the dealer as a dealer or the dealer elects to treat it as such.[9]

Subsections 1221(a)(7) and (8) arose out of and substantiality codified some significant Supreme Court decisional law. In Corn Products Refining Co. v. Commissioner,[10] the Supreme Court held that the purchasing and sales of future rights to purchase corn (contractual rights to purchase a certain quantity of corn at a set price within a future time) was an integral part of the taxpayer's business and, as such, the futures were not to be characterized as capital assets. Such business hedging transactions generally were thought to produce ordinary income or loss. However, in Arkansas Best Corporation v. Commissioner,[11] the Supreme Court narrowed and blurred the *Corn Products* result by limiting the rule to rights to inventory or some integral part of the taxpayer's business. In *Arkansas Best*, the Court held that a holding company's sale of stock held for business purposes was the sale of a capital asset and produced a capital loss. After *Arkansas Best*, the Treasury attempted to clarify this area by issuing regulations which characterized most hedging transactions as producing ordinary income and loss.[12] Congress eventually added Section 1221(a)(7) and (8) to validate the Treasury's approach and clarify the taxation of business hedges.[13]

Section 1221(a)(7) excludes from capital asset status any hedging transaction which is clearly identified as such before the close of the day on which it is acquired, originated, or entered into. Identification is required to prevent a taxpayer from whipsawing the government by waiting to see if it is better to characterize the transaction as capital (gain) or ordinary (loss). A hedging transaction is defined under Section 1221(b)(2) as generally a

---

[5]    See Chapter 21H2, infra.

[6]    See Chapter 23B, infra.

[7]    See Chapter 21H1, infra.

[8]    A commodities derivative financial instrument is a contract or financial instrument with respect to commodities, the value or settlement price of which is calculated by reference to any combination of a fixed rate, price, or amount, or a variable rate, price, or amount, which is based on current, objectively determinable financial or economic information. Explanation of Tax Legislation Enacted in the 106th Cong., Staff of Jt. Comm. on Tax'n, 1999.

[9]    I.R.C. § 1221(a)(6)(A) and (B). I.R.C. § 1221(a)(6)(B) bears a similarity to § 1236.

[10]    350 U.S. 46, 76 S.Ct. 20 (1955).

[11]    485 U.S. 212, 108 S.Ct. 971 (1988).

[12]    See Reg. § 1.1221–2.

[13]    See H. Rep. No. 106–478, 106th Cong., 2d Sess. 348–49 (1999).

transaction entered into in the normal course of the taxpayer's business primarily (1) to manage risk of price changes or currency fluctuations with respect to ordinary property held or to be held by the taxpayer, (2) to manage risk of interest rate or price changes or currency fluctuations with respect to borrowings or ordinary business obligations, or (3) to manage other risks prescribed by the Treasury in regulations.[14]

To eliminate disputes about the characterization of hedges involving supplies, Section 1221(a)(8) provides that supplies regularly used or consumed by the taxpayer in the taxpayer's trade or business are not capital assets. The close connection of the supplies to the taxpayer's business makes it inappropriate to classify the supplies as a capital asset.

## E. THE SALE OR EXCHANGE REQUIREMENT

Internal Revenue Code: Section 1222. See Sections 1234A; 1235; 1241; 1253; 1271.

---

### Kenan v. Commissioner

United States Court of Appeals, Second Circuit, 1940.
114 F.2d 217.

■ AUGUSTUS N. HAND, CIRCUIT JUDGE.

The testatrix, Mrs. Bingham, died on July 27, 1917, leaving a will under which she placed her residuary estate in trust and provided in item "Seventh" that her trustees should pay a certain amount annually to her niece, Louise Clisby Wise, until the latter reached the age of forty, "at which time or as soon thereafter as compatible with the interests of my estate they shall pay to her the sum of Five Million ($5,000,000.00) Dollars." The will provided in item "Eleventh" that the trustees, in the case of certain payments including that of the $5,000,000 under item "Seventh", should have the right "to substitute for the payment in money, payment in marketable securities of a value equal to the sum to be paid, the selection of the securities to be substituted in any instance, and the valuation of such securities to be done by the Trustees and their selection and valuation to be final."

Louise Clisby Wise became forty years of age on July 28, 1935. The trustees decided to pay her the $5,000,000 partly in cash and partly in securities. The greater part of the securities had been owned by the testator and transferred as part of her estate to the trustees; others had been purchased by the trustees. All had appreciated in value during the

---

[14] Congress also built in some anti-abuse protection by giving the Treasury broad regulatory authority to achieve the purposes of the provisions characterizing hedging transactions in the case of transactions between related parties. I.R.C. § 1221(b)(3). The Treasury also has authority to prescribe regulations to properly characterize (1) hedging transactions which are not properly identified, and (2) transactions which are improperly identified as hedging transactions. I.R.C. § 1221(b)(2)(B).

period for which they were held by the trustees, and the Commissioner determined that the distribution of the securities to the niece resulted in capital gains which were taxable to the trustees under the rates specified in Section 117 of the Revenue Act of 1934, which limits the percentage of gain to be treated as taxable income on the "sale or exchange" of capital assets. On this basis, the Commissioner determined a deficiency of $367,687.12 in the income tax for the year 1935.

The Board overruled the objections of the trustees to the imposition of any tax and denied a motion of the Commissioner to amend his answer in order to claim the full amount of the appreciation in value as ordinary income rather than a percentage of it as a capital gain, and confirmed the original deficiency determination. The taxpayers contend that the decision of the Board was erroneous because they realized neither gain from the sale or exchange of capital assets nor income of any character by delivering the securities to the legatee pursuant to the permissive terms of the will. The Commissioner contends that gain was realized by the delivery of the securities but that such gain was ordinary income not derived from a sale or exchange and therefore taxable in its entirety. The trustees have filed a petition to review the order of the Board determining the deficiency of $367,687.12 and the Commissioner has filed a cross-petition claiming a deficiency of $1,238,841.99, based on his contention that the gain was not governed by Section 117, and therefore not limited by the percentages therein specified.

The amount of gain is to be determined under Section 111 of the Revenue Act of 1934, which provides:

> "(a) Computation of gain or loss. The gain from the sale or other disposition of property shall be the excess of the amount realized therefrom over the adjusted basis * * *.

> "(b) Amount realized. The amount realized from the sale or other disposition of property shall be the sum of any money received plus the fair market value of the property (other than money) received."

Section 113, 26 U.S.C.A. Int.Rev.Code, § 113, is claimed by the taxpayers to be relevant and provides:

> "(a) The basis of property shall be the cost of such property; except that—

> * * *

> "(5) Property transmitted at death. If the property was acquired by bequest, devise, or inheritance, or by the decedent's estate from the decedent, the basis shall be the fair market value of such property at the time of such acquisition."

The Taxpayer's Appeal

In support of their petition the taxpayers contend that the delivery of the securities of the trust estate to the legatee was a donative disposition of property pursuant to the terms of the will, and that no gain was thereby realized. They argue that when they determined that the legacy should be one of securities, it became for all purposes a bequest of property, just as if the cash alternative had not been provided, and not taxable for the reason that no gain is realized on the transfer by a testamentary trustee of specific securities or other property bequeathed by will to a legatee.

We do not think that the situation here is the same as that of a legacy of specific property. The legatee was never in the position occupied by the recipient of specific securities under a will. She had a claim against the estate for $5,000,000, payable either in cash or securities of that value, but had no title or right to the securities, legal or equitable, until they were delivered to her by the trustees after the exercise of their option. She took none of the chances of a legatee of specific securities or of a share of a residue that the securities might appreciate or decline in value between the time of the death of the testator and the transfer to her by the trustees, but instead had at all times a claim for an unvarying amount in money or its equivalent.

If there had merely been a bequest to the legatee of $5,000,000 and she had agreed with the trustees to take securities of that value, the transaction would have been a "sale or other disposition" of the securities under Suisman v. Eaton, 15 F.Supp. 113, affirmed, 2 Cir., 83 F.2d 1019, certiorari denied 299 U.S. 573, 57 S.Ct. 37. There, a will creating a trust provided that each of the testator's children was to receive $50,000 on attaining the age of twenty-five. The trustee transferred stock of the value of $50,000 to one of the children, Minerva, in satisfaction of her legacy. Judge Hincks said in the district court (15 F.Supp. at page 115), that the "property which the trust estate received from the 'sale or other disposition' of said stocks was the discharge of the corpus from Minerva's equitable right to receive $50,000 therefrom; the amount realized, i.e., the 'fair market value of the property (other than money) received,' * * * was $50,000; and the excess of the amount realized over the basis was properly computed by the Commissioner, legally assessed as part of the taxable income of the trust estate, and the tax thereon was legally collected."

In the present case, the legatee had a claim which was a charge against the trust estate for $5,000,000 in cash or securities and the trustees had the power to determine whether the claim should be satisfied in one form or the other. The claim, though enforceable only in the alternative, was, like the claim in Suisman v. Eaton, supra, a charge against the entire trust estate. If it were satisfied by a cash payment securities might have to be sold on which (if those actually delivered in specie were selected) a taxable gain would necessarily have been realized. Instead of making such a sale the trustees delivered the securities and exchanged them pro tanto for the general claim of the legatee, which was thereby satisfied.

It is said that this transaction was not such a "sale or other disposition" as is intended by Section 111(a) or was dealt with in Suisman v. Eaton, because it was effectuated only by the will of the trustees and not, as in Suisman v. Eaton, through a mutual agreement between trustee and legatee. The Board made no such distinction, and we are not inclined to limit thus the meaning of the words "other disposition" used in Section 111(a), or of "exchange" used in Section 117. The word "exchange" does not necessarily have the connotation of a bilateral agreement which may be said to attach to the word "sale." Thus, should a person set up a trust and reserve to himself the power to substitute for the securities placed in trust other securities of equal value, there would seem no doubt that the exercise of this reserved power would be an "exchange" within the common meaning of the word, even though the settlor consulted no will other than his own, although, of course, we do not here advert to the problems of taxability in such a situation.

The Board alluded to the fact that both here and in Suisman v. Eaton the bequest was fixed at a definite amount in money, that in both cases there was no bequest of specific securities (nor of a share in the residue which might vary in value), that the rights of the legatee, like those in the Suisman case, were a charge upon the corpus of the trust, and that the trustees had to part either with $5,000,000 in cash or with securities worth that amount at the time of the transfer. It added that the increase in value of the securities was realized by the trust and benefited it to the full extent, since, except for the increase, it would have had to part with other property, and it cited in further support of its position United States v. Kirby Lumber Co., 284 U.S. 1, 52 S.Ct. 4. Under circumstances like those here, where the legatee did not take securities designated by the will or an interest in the corpus which might be more or less at the time of the transfer than at the time of decedent's death, it seems to us that the trustees realized a gain by using these securities to settle a claim worth $5,000,000, just as the trustee in Suisman v. Eaton realized one.

It seems reasonably clear that the property was not "transmitted at death" or "acquired by bequest * * * from the decedent." Section 113(a)(5). It follows that the fears of the taxpayers that double taxation of this appreciation will result because the legatee will take the basis of the decedent under Brewster v. Gage, 280 U.S. 327, 50 S.Ct. 115, are groundless. It is true that under Section 113(a)(5) the basis for property "acquired by bequest, devise, or inheritance" is "the fair market value of such property at the time of such acquisition" and that under Brewster v. Gage, supra, the date of acquisition has been defined as the date of death of the testator. But the holding of the present case is necessarily a determination that the property here acquired is acquired in an exchange and not "by bequest, devise or inheritance," since Sections 117 and 113(a)(5) seem to be mutually exclusive. The legatee's basis would seem to be the value of the claim surrendered in exchange for the securities;

and the Board of Tax Appeals has so held. Sherman Ewing v. Commissioner of Internal Revenue, 40 B.T.A. 912.

The Commissioner's Appeal

We have already held that a taxable gain was realized by the delivery of the securities. It follows from the reasons that support that conclusion that the appreciation was a capital gain, taxable at the rates specified in Section 117. Therefore, neither under Section 111(a) nor under Section 22(a), 26 U.S.C.A. Int.Rev.Acts, page 669, can the gain realized be taxed as ordinary income.

There can be no doubt that from an accounting standpoint the trustees realized a gain in the capital of their trust when they disposed of securities worth far more at the time of disposition than at the time of acquisition in order to settle (pro tanto) a claim of $5,000,000. It would seem to us a strange anomaly if a disposition of securities which were in fact a "capital asset" should not be taxed at the rates afforded by Section 117 to individuals who have sold or exchanged property which they had held for the specified periods. It is not without significance that the appeal of the Commissioner was plainly an afterthought. The original deficiency was determined on the theory that the capital gains rates were applicable and the Commissioner sought to amend his answer so as to claim that ordinary rates should be applied only after the case had been orally argued before the Board. The Board denied his motion to reopen the case for the consideration of this contention. Since we find that the Commissioner's cross-petition is unfounded on the merits, we have no reason to consider the technical question whether the denial of the motion to amend the answer was an abuse of discretion.

The purpose of the capital gains provisions of the Revenue Act of 1934 is so to treat an appreciation in value, arising over a period of years but realized in one year, that the tax thereon will roughly approximate what it would have been had a tax been paid each year upon the appreciation in value for that year. Cf. Burnet v. Harmel, 287 U.S. 103, 106, 53 S.Ct. 74. The appreciation in value in the present case took place between 1917 and 1935, whereas the Commissioner's theory would tax it as though it had all taken place in 1935. If the trustees had sold the securities, they would be taxed at capital gain rates. Both the trustees and the Commissioner, in their arguments as respondent and cross-respondents, draw the analogy between the transaction here and a sale, and no injustice is done to either by taxing the gain at the rates which would apply had a sale actually been made and the proceeds delivered to the legatee. It seems to us extraordinary that the exercise by the trustees of the option to deliver to the legatee securities, rather than cash, should be thought to result in an increased deficiency of enormous proportions.

　　Orders affirmed.

# Hudson v. Commissioner

Tax Court of the United States, 1953.
20 T.C. 734, affirmed sub nom. Ogilvie v. Commissioner, 216 F.2d 748 (6th Cir.1954).

Findings of Fact

All the facts are stipulated and are so found.

Petitioners, residents of Memphis, Tennessee, filed their income tax returns for the year 1945 with the collector of internal revenue for the district of Tennessee. Galvin Hudson is in the lumber and cooperage business, and Hillsman Taylor is a practicing attorney.

On November 23, 1929, Mary Mallory Harahan obtained a judgment against Howard Cole in the amount of $75,702.12 in the Supreme Court of the State of New York. This judgment will hereinafter be referred to as the Cole judgment.

On June 30, 1943, the petitioners purchased the Cole judgment from the residuary legatees of Mary Mallory Harahan's estate; each petitioner acquired a 50 percent interest in the judgment. Their aggregate cost of the judgment was $11,004; this included attorney fees and expenses of $1,004.

In May 1945 Howard Cole paid petitioners the sum of $21,150 as a full settlement of the judgment against him.

Each of the petitioners reported his profit on the settlement of the Cole judgment for income tax purposes as a long-term capital gain for 1945.

Respondent explained the adjustment to petitioners' net income as follows:

> (a)  It is held that the profits realized on the collection of a judgment from Mr. Howard Cole is taxable as ordinary income. In your return your reported 50% of $5,073.00, or $2,536.50 as capital gain. Accordingly, ordinary net income is increased in the amount of $5,073.00. * * *

The gain resulting to petitioners from the settlement of the Cole judgment is ordinary income, as distinguished from a capital gain.

■ JOHNSON, JUDGE:

Simply, the issue is whether the gain realized from the settlement of a judgment is ordinary income or capital gain when the settlement was made between the judgment debtor and the assignee or transferee of a prior judgment creditor. Petitioners contend that they are entitled to the benefits of section 117(a), Internal Revenue Code, with regard to the gain from the settlement of a judgment. Respondent has determined that the gain is ordinary income and taxable as such. There is no question about the bona fides of the transaction, nor is there any disagreement about the fact that the judgment, when entered and transferred, was property and a capital asset. The parties differ, however, on the question of whether there was a "sale or exchange of a capital asset." Section 117(a)(4). Petitioners and respondent both adhere to the principle that the words "sale or exchange" should be given their ordinary meaning. Petitioners, citing authority, define the word "sale" as follows:

> A sale is a contract whereby one acquires a property in the thing sold and the other parts with it for a valuable consideration * * * or a sale is generally understood to mean the transfer of property for money * * *.

Also, "Sell in its ordinary sense means a transfer of property for a fixed price in money or its equivalent."

We cannot see how there was a transfer of property, or how the judgment debtor acquired property as the result of the transaction wherein the judgment was settled. The most that can be said is that the judgment debtor paid a debt or extinguished a claim so as to preclude execution on the judgment outstanding against him. In a hypothetical case, if the judgment had been transferred to someone other than the judgment debtor, the property transferred would still be in existence after the transaction was completed. However, as it actually happened, when the judgment debtor settled the judgment, the claim arising from the judgment was extinguished without the transfer of any property or property right to the judgment debtor. In their day-to-day transactions, neither businessmen nor lawyers would call the settlement of a judgment a sale; we can see no reason to apply a strained interpretation to the transaction before us. When petitioners received the $21,150 in full settlement of the judgment, they did not recover the money as the result of any sale or exchange but only as a collection or settlement of the judgment.

It is well established that where the gain realized did not result from a sale or exchange of a capital asset, the gain is not within the provisions of section 117(a)(4). In R.W. Hale, 32 B.T.A. 356, affd. 85 F.2d 819, there was a compromise of notes for less than face value and the taxpayer claimed there was a sale or exchange of notes within the meaning of the capital gains provision of the Code. In deciding the issue against the taxpayer, we said:

> The petitioners did not sell or exchange the mortgage notes, and consequently an essential condition expressly required by the statute has not been met and no capital loss has been suffered.
> * * *

The *Hale* case was cited with approval in Pat N. Fahey, 16 T.C. 105. There, the taxpayer, an attorney, was assigned, for a cash consideration, an interest in a fee. Upon a successful settlement of the litigation, the taxpayer was paid his part of the fee. We held that his share was not capital gain because he did not sell or exchange anything. In another situation, a redemption of bonds before maturity by the issuing corporation was not a sale or exchange of capital assets. Fairbanks v.

United States, 306 U.S. 436, 59 S.Ct. 607. In a similar situation in Bingham v. Commissioner, 105 F.2d 971, 972, the court said:

> What may have been property in the hands of the holder of the notes simply vanished when the surrender took place and the maker received them. He then had, at most, only his own obligations to pay himself. Any theoretical concept of a sale of the notes to the maker in return for what he gave up to get them back must yield before the hard fact that he received nothing which was property in his hands but had merely succeeded in extinguishing his liabilities by the amounts which were due on the notes. There was, therefore, no sale of the notes to him in the ordinary meaning of the word and no exchange of assets for assets since the notes could not, as assets, survive the transaction. That being so, such a settlement as the one this petitioner made involved neither a sale nor an exchange of capital assets within the meaning of the statute. * * *.

See also, Jack Rosenzweig, 1 T.C. 24, and Matilda S. Puelicher, 6 T.C. 300.

We have carefully considered the many cases cited by petitioners but we have found none of them controlling the issue before us. * * *. The respondent, therefore, must be sustained on this issue.

Reviewed by the Court.

Decisions will be entered under Rule 50.

## NOTE

The disparate results in the two principal cases above, *Kenan* and *Hudson,* point up a distinction that must be kept in mind here. In those cases no really effective argument could be advanced that the taxpayer had not made a "disposition of property." And Section 1001 makes a disposition a taxable event. Moreover, the property disposed of was a capital asset. But in these cases the final crucial question is whether the disposition is in the nature of a Section 1222 "sale or exchange." Whether this requirement is met is clearly not determined by what the parties call the transaction; the answer will depend upon its substance.[1]

The statute creates an interesting problem of identifying what constitutes a "sale or exchange." The *Kenan* obligor's transfer, yes; the *Hudson* obligee's collection, no. However, a question may be raised whether special preferential gain treatment or ordinary loss treatment should be made to turn on such an issue. If the *Hudson* creditor had sold the judgment debt to a third party, instead of collecting from the debtor, the creditor would have reached the promised land.[2] Is sale to another really very different from what is in effect a sale to the debtor? Should characterization be governed, then, only by the nature of the asset and its holding period, rather than in part by the nature of its disposition? While Congress has not seen fit to go so far as a general rule, special statutory provisions sometimes take liberties

---

[1] Cf. Starr's Estate v. Commissioner, 274 F2d 294 (9th Cir. 1959).

[2] Paine v. Commissioner, 236 F.2d 398 (8th Cir. 1956)

with the usual sale or exchange requirement.[3] For example, under Section 1271 amounts paid upon the retirement of obligations issued by corporations and governmental units and entities as well as those issued by natural persons (only after June 8, 1997) are treated as amounts received in exchange for such obligations.[4] Furthermore, amounts paid on any debt obligation which is purchased after June 8, 1997 are treated as amounts received in exchange for such an obligation.[5] This is a statutory reversal of the *Hudson* principle.[6] The reversal is applauded.

## PROBLEM

1.    Creditor purchased an individual Debtor's $5,000 interest bearing note from a third party as an investment at a cost of $4,000. Several years later, Debtor pays off the principal of the note using General Motors stock which Debtor purchased several years ago at a cost of $2,000 which is now worth $5,000. What are the tax consequences to Creditor and Debtor?

## F.  THE HOLDING PERIOD

Internal Revenue Code: Section 1223(1), (2), (9). See Sections 1014(a); 1015(a); 1041(b)(2); 1222; 1233; 1234(b); 1259.

---

### Revenue Ruling 66–7
#### 1966–1 Cum.Bull. 188.

Advice has been requested as to when a capital asset will have been held for more than 6 months within the meaning of sections 1222(3) and (4) of the Internal Revenue Code of 1954, particularly where the asset was acquired on the last day of a calendar month which has less than 31 days.

Section 1222(3) of the Code provides, in part, that the term "long-term capital gain" means gain from the sale or exchange of a capital asset *held for more than 6 months* and section 1222(4) of the Code provides, in part, that the "long-term capital loss" means loss from the sale or exchange of a capital asset *held for more than 6 months*.

It is well and long established that, in computing a period of "years" or "months" prescribed, in a contract or statute, "from" or "after" a

---

[3]    See I.R.C. §§ 1234A, 1235, 1241, and 1253, discussed at Chapter 21H1, infra.

[4]    I.R.C. § 1271(b)(1).

[5]    I.R.C. § 1271(b)(2). See I.R.C. § 1272(c)(1) which defines a "purchase" as the acquisition of any debt instrument where "the basis of the debt instrument is not determined in whole or in part by reference to the adjusted basis of such debt instrument in the hands of the person from whom acquired."

[6]    However, even as an inequity is thus avoided, an additional problem is created, if the bond was issued at a discount. In such an instance some of the gain that accrues is essentially interest and should not be accorded capital gain consequences. The concept of original issue discount, along with other sections finding obscured interest, is considered in Chapter 24C, infra.

designated day, date, act, or other event, the day thus designated is excluded and the last day of the prescribed period is included, unless a different intent is definitely evidenced. See I.T. 3287, C.B. 1939–1 (Part 1), 138.

I.T. 3985, C.B. 1949–2, 51, states the position of the Internal Revenue Service that the determination of the holding period of "capital assets" under sections 117(a)(2), (3), (4), (5), and (h)(4), of the Internal Revenue Code of 1939, must be made with reference to calendar months and fractions thereof, rather than with reference to days. The ruling was concerned primarily with the determination of the total holding period of securities purchased and sold where the provisions of section 117(h)(4) of the 1939 Code, relating to "wash sales," were applicable. Although similar provisions are not involved in the instant case, the principles enunciated in that ruling apply here. Furthermore, although I.T. 3287 was not cited in I.T. 3985 the rule stated in the former was actually applied in all the appropriate illustrative examples of the latter, that is, in examples 1 through 6.

In view of the foregoing, it is concluded that the holding period of a capital asset begins to run on the day following the date of acquisition of the asset involved. Accordingly, a capital asset acquired on the last day of any calendar month, regardless of whether the month has 31 days or less, must not be disposed of until on or after the first day of the seventh succeeding month of the calendar in order to have been "held for more than 6 months" within the meaning of sections 1222(3) and (4) of the Code. For example, an asset acquired on April 30, 1963, must not have been disposed of before November 1, 1963, in order to have been held for more than 6 months.*

I.T. 3985, C.B. 1949–2, 51, is hereby amplified for the purpose of determining when a capital asset has been held for more than 6 months where the asset was acquired on the last day of a month having less than 31 days.

The same rule applies in determining holding periods of property for purposes of section 1231 of the Code.

Pursuant to authority contained in section 7805(b) of the Code the provisions of this Revenue Ruling will be applicable with respect to dispositions of property after April 10, 1966.

## Revenue Ruling 66–97
1966–1 Cum.Bull. 190.

Advice has been requested regarding the holding period of debentures and as to whether there is a distinction between a trade

---

\* In Lena M. Anderson, 33 T.C.M. 234 (1974), the taxpayer had short-term capital gain on stock purchased December 2, 1966 and sold on June 2, 1967. Ed.

effected on a registered securities exchange and a trade made in the "over-the-counter" market.

The taxpayer purchased for investment certain debentures on the same day in an "over-the-counter" trade and a trade effected on a registered securities exchange. There are two relevant dates in connection with such security transactions: (1) the "trade date"—the date on which the contract to buy or sell the security is made and (2) the "settlement date"—the date on which the security is delivered and payment is tendered. In many cases settlement takes place a fixed number of days after the trade. In transactions involving bonds, notes or other evidences of indebtedness, the buyer pays the interest accrued on the security to the date of settlement as a part of the consideration for the transfer. However, bonds as well as stocks are considered acquired or sold on the respective "trade dates." See I.T. 3442, C.B. 1941–1, 212. I.T. 3287, C.B. 1939–1, 138, states that the period during which an asset was held is to be computed by excluding the day on which the asset was acquired and including the day upon which it was sold. See also I.T. 3705, C.B. 1945, 174, and Revenue Ruling 66–7, page 188, this Bulletin. This rule applies whether the trade is made on a registered securities exchange or in the "over-the-counter" market.

Accordingly, the holding period for debentures acquired by purchase, whether on a registered securities exchange or in the "over-the-counter" market, is to be determined by excluding the "trade date" on which the debentures are acquired and including the "trade date" on which the debentures are sold.

The same rule applies generally in determining the holding periods of stocks and securities acquired by purchase.

## NOTE

Close questions with respect to holding periods are most likely to arise in the purchase and sale of stocks and bonds. In a broker's board room it will not be uncommon to hear a high-bracket taxpayer say, "I don't yet have my 12 months in." The inference is of course that she has a gain on a security which she hopes will be taxable as long-term capital gain at a 15 percent rate.[1] She is anxious to sell and fearful the price will decline but not quite willing to accept the tax attrition attending either a short-term or mid-term holding period. There is an obvious need for care in such cases.

As indicated in Rev.Rul. 66–97, above, one's holding period is usually governed by one's "trades dates." This still leaves the issue of the year for which the gain or loss on such transactions is recognized. If a trade is made in the regular way on a December 31 trade date, the settlement date will be several days later. In the case of a cash method taxpayer, one might assume that since cash flowed on the settlement date, that date would establish the time of recognition of a gain or loss to the cash method taxpayer.

---

[1]  I.R.C. § 1(h)(1)(C). See I.R.C. § 1(h)(3)(A).

Nevertheless, the gain or loss is recognized in the year of the trade date, regardless of whether the taxpayer is a cash or an accrual method taxpayer.[2]

These are principles fairly easily stated. But there are many transactions in securities that involve timing considerations not fully answered by these principles. For example, T buys 100 shares of A stock on February 1 and another 100 shares of A stock on September 1. On February 2 of the next year T sells 100 shares of A stock. Which 100 shares has T sold? This raises basically a question of identification but, if T is unable to identify which block was sold, the regulations answer the question on a "first-in, first-out" basis.[3] Obviously, this has a bearing, not only on T's holding period (Might T have been hoping for short-term treatment?), but on T's basis as well, if the two blocks of A stock were acquired at different prices.

Suppose T thinks the price of B stock is going down. On January 5 of the current year T sells 100 shares of B stock "short." This means T sells the stock without owning it, borrowing it from someone else to whom T is obliged ultimately to repay the loan when T closes or "covers" the short sale. Of course T hopes to buy the stock later for this purpose at a price below that at which T sold and, thus, to realize a gain. The short sale itself is not a taxable transaction (What basis could T use to determine gain or loss?), but gain or loss is realized when the short sale is closed by delivery of the stock. In general, whether gain or loss is long-term or short-term is determined by the period for which the stock delivered has been held.[4] In the usual case, short-term gain or loss will therefore be the result.

Suppose now that T has 100 shares of C stock on which T has a substantial paper gain. T bought the stock on April 1, and "now" is December 15 of the same year. T is afraid the price might drop but is disinclined to realize short-term gain and, in fact, is not happy about adding to the current year's income at all. (What advantages, apart from converting the gain to long-term, might arise from carrying the transaction over to the succeeding year?) T decides upon what is termed a short sale "against the box." That is, T sells while "long" in (owning) C stock but with the idea that T will close the sale only later, delivering the C stock when T has held it more than 12 months. In pursuance of the plan T sells short December 15 of the current year, and effects delivery April 2 of the succeeding year. To what extent has T accomplished T's objective? *Seemingly*, 1. T has nailed down the gain; T can be indifferent to subsequent market fluctuations. 2. T has deferred realization of the gain until the succeeding year, not increasing the current

---

[2]   Rev.Rul. 93–84, 1993–2 C.B. 225. Although the government has long allowed a loss to be recognized in the year of the trade date (see Rev.Rul. 70–344, 1970–2 C.B. 50, and GCM 21503, 1939–2 C.B. 205), the result in the case of a gain recognized is based on language in the legislative history of the 1986 Act. See S.Rep. No. 99–313, 99th Cong., 2d Sess. 131 (1986), 1986–3 C.B. (Vol. 3) 131, stating that "in the case of sales that are made on an established market, where cash settlement of transactions customarily occurs several business days after the date on which a trade is made, that gain or loss would be recognized for Federal income tax purposes by both cash or accrual method taxpayers on the day that the trade is executed." See also H.R. Conf.Rep. No. 841, 99th Cong., 2d Sess. II–297 (1986), 1986–3 (Vol. 4) C.B. 297, reaching the same conclusion.

[3]   Reg. §§ 1.1012–1(c)(1)(i), 1.1223–1(i). See Colgan, "Identification of Securities Sold or Transferred," 18 N.Y.U.Inst. on Fed.Tax. 323 (1960).

[4]   Reg. § 1.1233–1(a)(3).

year's income, even though T assured the gain in that year. 3. T's gain in the subsequent year is a long-term capital gain.

Regrettably for T, Congress has enacted provisions which drastically alter T's perceived results. First, Section 1233(b) classifies the gain as short-term. Aimed at just T's kind of monkey business, that section specifies short-term treatment if on the day of a short sale a taxpayer owns property substantially identical to that sold short, which the taxpayer has held for only one year or less. Section 1233 has implications far beyond the problem presented in the preceding paragraph.

Congress, which has become increasingly vigilant to game playing with respect to certain types of hedging strategies such as T's, subsequently enacted Section 1259 to create a constructive sale of certain appreciated financial positions where gain was effectively locked in, but the gain might not otherwise be immediately recognized. Under Section 1259, T's sale is treated as occurring on December 15 of the current year. Thus, T has a short-term capital gain in year one, rather than T's hoped for long-term capital gain in year two.[5]

Many securities transactions are much more sophisticated than those suggested above. The "put", the "call," the "straddle,"[6] "wash sales,"[7] and the options and future markets[8] are exciting playthings for those whose securities dealings go beyond everyday investing,[9] but no attempt is made here to consider holding periods and the other problems that arise with respect to these and related transactions.[10]

Congress has similarly acted in one area of the option market by amending Section 1234(b). In the case of a grantor of an option, any gain or

---

[5] Technically, I.R.C. § 1259 operates not only to create a sale in the current year, but also to label T's gain as short-term and as such § 1259 needs no assistance from previously enacted § 1233(b). Nevertheless § 1233(b) still operates in some situations where § 1259 is inapplicable, for example where the taxpayer does not have an appreciated financial position. I.R.C. § 1259(b). Cf. I.R.C. § 1259(f).

[6] I.R.C. § 1092 provides a limitation on the recognition of loss if the taxpayer is involved in a straddle.

[7] I.R.C. § 1091 provides that losses from wash sales are not deductible. See Chapter 25B, infra.

[8] I.R.C. § 1234B provides a general rule that gains or losses from "securities futures contracts" are treated as short-term capital gains or losses. Gain or loss from the sale of regulated futures contracts, foreign currency contracts, nonequity options, and dealer equity options, are treated as 40% short term capital gain or loss and 60% long term capital gain or loss. I.R.C. § 1256.

[9] See Rev.Rul. 78–182, 1978–1 C.B. 265, which predates several of the statutory changes.

[10] Analysis of some of the transactions appears in the following articles: Schenk, "Taxation of Equity Derivatives: A Partial Integration Proposal," 50 Tax L. Rev. 511 (1995); Hariton, "The Tax Treatment of Hedged Positions in Stock: What Hath Technical Analysis Wrought?" 50 Tax L. Rev. 803 (1995); Ulcickal, "Internal Revenue Code Section 1259: A Legitimate Foundation for Taxing Short Sales Against the Box or a Mere Makeover?" 39 Will. & Mary L. Rev. 1355 (1998). Some older and somewhat outdated, but instructive articles are: Bennion, "Current Developments in Tax Planning with Securities Transactions: 'Puts'; 'Calls'; 'Straddles'; 'Short Sales'; 'Arbitrage'," 13 U.S.C. Tax Inst. 489 (1961); Hariton, "Puts, Calls and Straddles," 18 N.Y.U.Inst. on Fed. Tax. 357 (1960); Esks, "Federal Tax Advantages to Investors in the Use of Put and Call Options," 31 Tax L. Rev. 1 (1975); Kennedy, "Selecting the Off-Beat Investments: Puts, Calls, Straddles, Warrants, Commodity Futures and Other Exotica," 32 N.Y.U.Inst. on Fed.Tax. 1093 (1974).

loss on a closing transaction with respect to the option or any gain on the lapse of an option is classified as short-term capital gain.

Close questions with respect to holding periods may arise in the purchase and sale of real estate, although the problem is not as crucial in this area as in the stock area, because real estate is normally held for a longer period of time. Wide variations in real estate transactions[11] suggest several points of time at which acquisition or disposition might be deemed to occur.[12] The Service has taken the position that, in the case of an unconditional contract for sale, the holding period for purposes of both acquisition and disposition is measured by the earlier of the date upon which title passes or the date upon which delivery of possession occurs and the burdens and privileges of ownership pass.[13]

Usually the actual dates on which a taxpayer acquires and disposes of property determine the holding period for the property. But, just as there are statutory exceptions to the general definition of capital assets and to the general requirement of a sale or exchange, so are there statutory exceptions to the general holding period concept as was illustrated above. Attention is drawn to some other exceptions in the Problems that follow this note.

## PROBLEMS

1.    Taxpayer, a cash method, calendar year taxpayer, engaged in the following transactions in shares of stock. Consider the amount and character of T's gain or loss in each transaction:

(a)   T bought 100 shares of stock on January 15 of year one at a cost of $50 per share. T sold them on January 16 of year two at $60 per share. LTCG + 1k

(b)   T bought 100 shares of stock on February 28 of year one at a cost of $50 per share. T sold them on February 29 of year two, a leap year, for $60 per share.

(c)   T bought 100 shares at $50 per share on February 10 of year one and another 100 shares at $50 per share on March 10 of year one. T sold 100 of the shares on February 15 of year two for $60 per share. See Reg. §§ 1.1223–1(i) and 1.1012–1(c)(1)(i).

(d)   T told T's broker to purchase 100 shares of stock on December 29 of year one at a time when its price was $50 per share. The stock was delivered to T on January 3 of year two when it was selling for $52 per share. T told T's broker to sell the stock on

---

[11]   Vernon Hoven v. Commissioner, 56 T.C. 50 (1971); Ted F. Merrill v. Commissioner, 40 T.C. 66 (1963), affirmed per curiam, 336 F.2d 771 (9th Cir.1964); Boykin v. Commissioner, 344 F.2d 889 (5th Cir.1965).

[12]   Those possibilities include the date that an executory contract becomes binding, that title passes, that possession changes, and that the benefits and burdens of ownership pass. Withey, J., discusses this problem very well in Donald Borrelli v. Commissioner, 31 T.C.M. 876 (1972).

[13]   Rev.Rul. 54–607, 1954–2 C.B. 177. The holding period is deemed to commence on the date following the earliest of the two dates and to cease on the earliest of the two dates. Rev.Rul. 54–607 expressly indicates that a mere purchase option contract, as opposed to an unconditional contract to sell, is not within these rules.

December 30 of year two when it sold for $60 per share, and it was delivered to Buyer on January 4 of year three when it was selling for $63 per share.

(e)  Same as (d), above, except that the value of the stock on December 30 of year two was $45 per share and on January 4 of year three was $48 per share.

(f)  T's father bought 100 shares of stock on January 10 of year one at $30 per share. On March 10 of year one when they were worth $40 per share he gave them to T who sold them on January 15 of year two for $60 per share (see § 1223(2)).

(g)  T's father purchased 1000 shares of stock for $10 per share several years ago. The stock was worth $50 per share on March 1 of year one, the date of Father's death. The stock was distributed to T by the executor on January 5 of year two and T sold it for $60 per share on January 15 of year two.

(h)  Same as (g), above, except that T was executor of T's father's estate and as such T sold the stock on January 15 of year two for $60 per share to pay the estate's administration expenses.

**2.**  Tacker paid $25,000 to acquire a 5-year transferable option on a parcel of investment land to purchase the land for an additional amount of $225,000. At the time the land was worth $250,000. Three years later when the land is worth $300,000, Purchaser wishes to acquire the land. What result to Tacker:

(a)  If she exercises the option and immediately sells the land to Purchase for $300,000?

(b)  If she sells the option to Purchaser for $75,000? See § 1234.

**3.**  T purchased unimproved land on April 1 of year one and commenced construction of a vacation residence, which was completed on January 2 of year three. Before T even moved in, and on that date, B offered T $600,000 for the house and land. T's cost basis for the land is $200,000 and for the house is $300,000, and the proposed purchase price is allocable $250,000 for the land and $350,000 for the house. It can also be established that construction of the house was 50% completed on January 1 of year two. What would be the consequences to T if the sale is effected on January 2 of year three? (See Paul v. Commissioner, 206 F.2d 763 (3d Cir.1953).)

# G.  JUDICIAL GLOSS ON THE STATUTE

## 1.  "INCOME" PROPERTY*

Internal Revenue Code: Sections 102(b); 273; 1001(e); 1241.

---

\*    See Del Cotto, " 'Property' in the Capital Asset Definition: Influence of 'Fruit and Tree'," 15 Buffalo L.Rev. 1 (1965). See also the classic articles of Professors Eustice and Lyon cited in note 1 at page 266, supra.

# Hort v. Commissioner

Supreme Court of the United States, 1941.
313 U.S. 28, 61 S.Ct. 757.

■ MR. JUSTICE MURPHY delivered the opinion of the Court.

We must determine whether the amount petitioner received as consideration for cancellation of a lease of realty in New York City was ordinary gross income as defined in § 22(a) of the Revenue Act of 1932 (47 Stat. 169, 178), and whether, in any event, petitioner sustained a loss through cancellation of the lease which is recognized in § 23(e) of the same Act (47 Stat. 169, 180).

Petitioner acquired the property, a lot and ten-story office building, by devise from his father in 1928. At the time he became owner, the premises were leased to a firm which had sublet the main floor to the Irving Trust Co. In 1927, five years before the head lease expired, the Irving Trust Co. and petitioner's father executed a contract in which the latter agreed to lease the main floor and basement to the former for a term of fifteen years at an annual rental of $25,000, the term to commence at the expiration of the head lease.

In 1933, the Irving Trust Co. found it unprofitable to maintain a branch in petitioner's building. After some negotiations, petitioner and the Trust Co. agreed to cancel the lease in consideration of a payment to petitioner of $140,000. Petitioner did not include this amount in gross income in his income tax return for 1933. On the contrary, he reported a loss of $21,494.75 on the theory that the amount he received as consideration for the cancellation was $21,494.75 less than the difference between the present value of the unmatured rental payments and the fair rental value of the main floor and basement for the unexpired term of the lease. He did not deduct this figure, however, because he reported other losses in excess of gross income.

The Commissioner included the entire $140,000 in gross income, disallowed the asserted loss, made certain other adjustments not material here, and assessed a deficiency. The Board of Tax Appeals, affirmed. 39 B.T.A. 922. The Circuit Court of Appeals affirmed per curiam on the authority of Warren Service Corp. v. Commissioner, 110 F.2d 723. Because of conflict with Commissioner v. Langwell Real Estate Corp., 47 F.2d 841, we granted certiorari limited to the question whether, "in computing net gain or loss for income tax purposes, a taxpayer [can] offset the value of the lease canceled against the consideration received by him for the cancellation." 311 U.S. 641, 61 S.Ct. 174.

Petitioner apparently contends that the amount received for cancellation of the lease was capital rather than ordinary income and that it was therefore subject to §§ 101, 111–113, and 117 (47 Stat. 169, 191, 195–202, 207) which govern capital gains and losses. Further, he argues that even if that amount must be reported as ordinary gross income he sustained a loss which § 23(e) authorizes him to deduct. We cannot agree.

The amount received by petitioner for cancellation of the lease must be included in his gross income in its entirety. Section 22(a), copied in the margin,[1] expressly defines gross income to include "gains, profits, and income derived from * * * rent, * * * or gains or profits and income derived from any source whatever." Plainly this definition reached the rent paid prior to cancellation just as it would have embraced subsequent payments if the lease had never been canceled. It would have included a prepayment of the discounted value of unmatured rental payments whether received at the inception of the lease or at any time thereafter. Similarly, it would have extended to the proceeds of a suit to recover damages had the Irving Trust Co. breached the lease instead of concluding a settlement. Compare United States v. Safety Car Heating Co., 297 U.S. 88, 56 S.Ct. 353; Burnet v. Sanford, 282 U.S. 359, 51 S.Ct. 150. That the amount petitioner received resulted from negotiations ending in cancellation of the lease rather than from a suit to enforce it cannot alter the fact that basically the payment was merely a substitute for the rent reserved in the lease. So far as the application of § 22(a) is concerned, it is immaterial that petitioner chose to accept an amount less than the strict present value of the unmatured rental payments rather than to engage in litigation, possibly uncertain and expensive.

The consideration received for cancellation of the lease was not a return of capital. We assume that the lease was "property," whatever that signifies abstractly. Presumably the bond in Helvering v. Horst, 311 U.S. 112, 61 S.Ct. 144, and the lease in Helvering v. Bruun, 309 U.S. 461, 60 S.Ct. 631, were also "property," but the interest coupon in *Horst* and the building in *Bruun* nevertheless were held to constitute items of gross income. Simply because the lease was "property" the amount received for its cancellation was not a return of capital, quite apart from the fact that "property" and "capital" are not necessarily synonymous in the Revenue Act of 1932 or in common usage. Where, as in this case, the disputed amount was essentially a substitute for rental payments which § 22(a) expressly characterizes as gross income, it must be regarded as ordinary income, and it is immaterial that for some purposes the contract creating the right to such payments may be treated as "property" or "capital."

For the same reasons, that amount was not a return of capital because petitioner acquired the lease as an incident of the realty devised to him by his father. Theoretically, it might have been possible in such a case to value realty and lease separately and to label each a capital asset. Compare Maass v. Higgins, 312 U.S. 443, 61 S.Ct. 631; Appeal of Farmer, 1 B.T.A. 711. But that would not have converted into capital the amount petitioner received from the Trust Co., since § 22(b)(3)[2] of the 1932 Act (47 Stat. 169, 178) would have required him to include in gross income

---

[1]  [I.R.C. (1939) § 22(a) is omitted. Ed.]

[2]  [I.R.C. (1939) § 22(b)(3) is omitted. See I.R.C. (1986) § 102(b)(1). Ed.]

the rent derived from the property, and that section, like § 22(a), does not distinguish rental payments and a payment which is clearly a substitute for rental payments.

We conclude that petitioner must report as gross income the entire amount received for cancellation of the lease, without regard to the claimed disparity between that amount and the difference between the present value of the unmatured rental payments and the fair rental value of the property for the unexpired period of the lease. The cancellation of the lease involved nothing more than relinquishment of the right to future rental payments in return for a present substitute payment and possession of the leased premises. Undoubtedly it diminished the amount of gross income petitioner expected to realize, but to that extent he was relieved of the duty to pay income tax. Nothing in § 23(e)[3] indicates that Congress intended to allow petitioner to reduce ordinary income actually received and reported by the amount of income he failed to realize. * * *. We may assume that petitioner was injured insofar as the cancellation of the lease affected the value of the realty. But that would become a deductible loss only when its extent had been fixed by a closed transaction. * * *.

The judgment of the Circuit Court of Appeals is affirmed.

# Metropolitan Bldg. Co. v. Commissioner

United States Court of Appeals, Ninth Circuit, 1960.
282 F.2d 592.

■ MERRILL, CIRCUIT JUDGE.

The question presented by this case involves the owner of real property, his lessee and a sublessee. The sublessee wished to enter into a desirable arrangement directly with the owner and to this end to eliminate the intervening interest of the lessee-sublessor. He paid a sum of money to the lessee, in consideration of which the lessee released to the owner, his lessor, all his right and interest under his lease.

The question presented is whether the sum so paid to the lessee is to be regarded entirely as the equivalent of rent owed to the lessee and taxable to the lessee as income or whether it is to be regarded entirely as a sale by the lessee of a capital asset and taxable as capital gain. The Commissioner of Internal Revenue ruled that the payment was the equivalent of rental and taxable as income.

At issue is the amount of tax from Metropolitan Building Company, the lessee, for the taxable year ending June 30, 1953. Following the ruling of the Commissioner, this proceeding was instituted in the Tax Court by Metropolitan for redetermination of deficiencies in income and excess profits taxes for that year. The Tax Court affirmed the ruling of the Commissioner. Metropolitan has petitioned this Court for review,

---

[3]    [I.R.C. (1939) § 23(e) is omitted. See I.R.C. (1986) § 165(c). Ed.]

contending that the payment in question should be held to be capital gain. We have concluded that petitioner is correct in its contention and that the judgment of the Tax Court must be reversed.

The University of Washington owns real estate comprising about four city blocks in the downtown area of Seattle. In 1907 it executed a lease upon this property extending to November 1, 1954. This lease was acquired by petitioner Metropolitan Building Company on December 3, 1907.

On August 1, 1922, Metropolitan executed a sublease of the greater portion of one city block, extending to October 31, 1954, one day prior to the termination of the main lease. Under the terms of the sublease the sublessee was to construct a hotel upon the leased premises. Rental provided was $25,000.00 a year. In addition, the sublessee agreed to pay its just proportion of any ad valorem personal property taxes assessed against Metropolitan's leasehold. The Olympic Hotel was constructed upon the leased premises. On March 31, 1936, the sublease was acquired by The Olympic, Inc.

During the year 1952, the University of Washington, as fee owner, was attempting to arrange a long-term disposition of the Olympic Hotel property for the period following the expiration of Metropolitan's lease in November, 1954. To this end the University invited proposals for the lease of the hotel, and a number of highly competitive proposals were submitted by various large hotel operators. All these proposals, except that of The Olympic, Inc., necessarily contemplated a lease commencing November 1, 1954.

The proposal made by The Olympic, Inc., offered, at no cost or expense to the University, to procure from Metropolitan a release to the University of all Metropolitan's right, title and interest in and to the Olympic Hotel property under its lease. Olympic then offered the University to take a new lease directly from it for a term of approximately twenty-two years commencing forthwith. Under this proposal, additional rentals of $725,000.00 would accrue to the University during the period prior to November 1, 1954, which otherwise would not have been forthcoming.

The University was favorably disposed to this proposal and negotiations were undertaken with Metropolitan for the acquisition by the University of Metropolitan's leasehold interest. A letter was written on August 18, 1952, by the Board of Regents of the University to Metropolitan requesting Metropolitan to release to the University its leasehold rights with respect to the Olympic Hotel property. At a meeting of the Board of Directors of Metropolitan, held August 19, 1952, the following resolution was adopted:

> "Resolved, the President hereby is authorized to sell to the University of Washington our leasehold rights to that area of the Metropolitan Tract occupied by the Olympic Hotel, including

the existing sub-lease provided an agreement can be reached which is approved by the company's accounting and legal counsel."

On September 8, 1952, an agreement was reached between Metropolitan and the State of Washington, acting through the Board of Regents of the University, whereby petitioner conveyed, quitclaimed, assigned and released to the State of Washington all of the right, title and interest of Metropolitan in and to that portion of the leasehold upon which the Olympic Hotel was located. For this assignment and transfer Metropolitan received from The Olympic, Inc., the sum of $137,000.00. The University then proceeded in accordance with its understanding to lease the property to The Olympic, Inc.

Metropolitan's president, asked as to how the sum of $137,000.00 had been computed, testified that roughly it covered $53,000.00 ground rent, $44,000.00 as Metropolitan's just proportion of the ad valorem personal property tax assessed against Metropolitan's leasehold, and $40,000.00 for increased taxes.

The Commissioner contends that this payment is taxable to Metropolitan as ordinary income. He relies upon Hort v. Commissioner, 1941, 313 U.S. 28, 31, 61 S.Ct. 757, where it is held:

"Where, as in this case, the disputed amount was essentially a substitute for rental payments which § 22(a) [26 U.S.C.A. § 22(a)] expressly characterizes as gross income, it must be regarded as ordinary income * * *."

In that case the petitioner owned a business building, a portion of which had been leased to the Irving Trust Company for a term of fifteen years at $25,000.00 a year. The Trust Company finding it unprofitable to maintain a branch office at that location, paid the petitioner $140,000.00 for cancellation of the lease.

In that case the Trust Company did not acquire any interest of its lessor. It simply compromised and liquidated its rental obligation under the lease. The sum received by the lessor was in lieu of the rentals which the Trust Company otherwise was obligated to pay and was not compensation for acquisition of any interest of the lessor.

In the case before us, the sums paid to Metropolitan were not simply a discharge of Olympic's obligation to pay rental. They were paid for the purchase of Metropolitan's entire leasehold interest. The case is not one of a liquidation of a right to future income as is Hort, but rather it is one of a disposition of income-producing property itself. The giving up of a lease by a tenant fits the legal requirements of a sale or exchange under Internal Revenue Code 1939, 117(j) 26 U.S.C.A. § 117(j) and a gain realized by the tenant on such a transaction is capital gain. Commissioner of Internal Revenue v. Golonsky, 3 Cir., 1952, 200 F.2d 72, certiorari denied 345 U.S. 939, 73 S.Ct. 830; * * *.

In Golonsky the court stated the problem of the case as follows:

"A tenant in possession of premises under a lease, upon receipt of payment by the landlord, and pursuant to an agreement made with the landlord, 'vacated and surrendered the premises' before the date at which the lease expired." 200 F.2d at page 73.

It was held that the proceeds of the transaction constituted capital gain.

The Commissioner would (and the Tax Court did) distinguish Golonsky upon the ground that in the instant case the consideration passed not from the lessor but from the sublessee, the very party obliged to pay rental to the recipient, and that such consideration represented the amount which the recipient felt it would otherwise have received under the sublease. Further, it is said, the value of the leasehold was fixed and limited by the rentals due under the sublease since the term of the sublease corresponded with that of the lease.

We are not impressed by this proposed distinction. The lease clearly had value over the amount of rentals due by virtue of the fact that its acquisition was of importance to Olympic. Irrespective of the method used by Metropolitan in arriving at the figure of $137,000.00, it is clear that Metropolitan did profit to some extent by the transaction. The Commissioner seems to concede that if the consideration had been paid by the University or if the lease had been assigned to a third party the transaction would have constituted a sale by the lessee.

It is not the person of the payor which controls the nature of the transaction in our view. Rather, it is the fact that the transaction constituted a bona fide transfer, for a legitimate business purpose, of the leasehold in its entirety. It did not constitute a release or transfer only of the right to future income under the sublease and the business purpose of the transaction would not have been met by such a release.

We conclude that the sum of $137,000.00, received by petitioner for release of its leasehold, must be held taxable as capital gain and not as ordinary income.

Reversed and remanded for redetermination, in accordance with this opinion, of deficiencies in income and excess profits taxes of petitioner for its taxable year ended June 30, 1953.

## NOTE

With *Hort* in mind (we hope) as well as the modification of its message in *Metropolitan Building,* we approach the question of the tax consequences of the sale of a life or other term interest or of an income interest in a trust. For example, (and we shall use this example throughout this brief note) S transfers securities to T, as trustee, the income from the assets to be paid to L for life and then the securities to be distributed to R. We recall from Chapter 13, perhaps in a somewhat oversimplified way, that a trust of this type is viewed essentially as a conduit and that the income earned by the trust property which is distributable to L will be taxed to L. Suppose then that *L sells the life interest to P.* Two questions are presented: (1) How is *L's* gain or loss to be measured? (2) How is *L's* gain or loss to be characterized?

*Measurement of Gain.* It may well be contended that L merely receives an advance payment of future income and, as in *Hort,* all that is received should be taxed. However, that argument runs into *Blair,*[1] which recognized an income interest in a trust as *property,* similar to the decision on the leasehold in *Metropolitan Building.* If this is a disposition of property and not simply an anticipatory assignment of income, then we must think in terms of basis as a subtraction from the amount realized to determine L's gain. And so we must, on good authority.[2]

Three possibilities now appear. If one purchased a temporary interest, such as L's life interest, one would have a cost basis for it. The cost would be amortized, written off by way of deductions, over the expected duration of the interest. Upon sale of the interest, the adjusted basis would be subtracted from the amount received to determine gain. There is little doubt about this, but of course it does not answer L's question.

If a temporary interest in property is received by gift or bequest, it too is accorded a basis determined, as usual, with reference to Section 1015, Section 1014, or Section 1041. In a bequest situation, the basis for the temporary interest is a part of the Section 1014 basis for the underlying property. In the case of a lifetime gift, such as that received by L, the basis for the income interest is a part of the transferred basis of the donor under Section 1015 or Section 1041. Here (in both the bequest and the gift cases) we encounter the "uniform basis" concept and the phenomenon of a sharing of that basis in shifting percentages by those who have an interest in the property. The thought is that the basis of the property transferred remains uniform, except as it may be subject to adjustments such as for depreciation. But the separate interests in the property share the uniform basis in accordance with the changing *values* of their interests.[3]

Sections 273 and 102(b) are relevant here. The amortization deduction permitted one who *purchases* a temporary interest is denied to one such as L who acquires a life or other terminable interest by gift, and also to one acquiring a temporary interest by bequest or by inheritance. This is because Congress in Section 102 expresses a policy to exclude from gross income a gift or bequest of *property,* but not the income therefrom. The entire exclusion finds its form in the uniform basis. That entire basis will ultimately be passed on to R, the remainderman. That being so, it would be inappropriate to allow L an amortization deduction using a part of the uniform basis. So, in general in these cases the uniform basis remains intact but the bases for the several interests in the property change. When L's interest is worth 40 percent of the value of the property, the basis for this interest is 40 percent of the uniform basis and R's basis is the other 60 percent. As a life tenant grows older her interest diminishes in value.

---

[1]    Blair v. Commissioner, 300 U.S. 5, 57 S.Ct. 330 (1937), supra page 254.
[2]    E.g., Bell's Estate v. Commissioner, 137 F.2d 454 (8th Cir.1943); McAllister v. Commissioner, 157 F.2d 235 (2d Cir.1946), cert. denied 330 U.S. 826, 67 S.Ct. 864 (1947).
[3]    Reg. §§ 1.1015–1(b), 1.1014–5.

(Consider what you would pay for the right to income from a trust for the life of one 50 years of age and what you would pay if the life tenant were 80.) Thus, when L's interest declines to only 20 percent of the value of the property, L's basis has also declined to only 20 percent of the uniform basis but R's basis (as R is now much closer to full ownership) has increased to 80 percent.

Now, are we going to let L assert L's share of the uniform basis when L sells L's interest to P? Several cases have held that L may,[4] and quite properly in the absence of statutory proscription. But it does create a distortion. If L's interest has a relative value that gives L 40 percent of the uniform basis, which L subtracts in determining L's gain, it is still true that R will have 100 percent of the uniform basis when L's interest which P purchased ends.[5] Thus we've used 140 percent of the uniform basis which is violative of the policy embodied in Section 102(b). Yes, you say, but P invested new funds equal to the added basis. True, we say, *but* P's amortization of that *cost* basis is not foreclosed by Section 273 as it is for someone like L who acquires the interest by gift. So we *had* (note the past tense) a distortion here.

In 1969, Congress added Section 1001(e) which requires L, upon the sale of the interest, to *disregard* L's share of the Section 1015 (or Section 1014 or Section 1041) uniform basis. A zero basis for L taxes L on *all* that L receives as gain.

Section 1001(e)(3) makes an exception to the zero basis rule of Section 1001(e)(1) if there is a transfer of the entire interest in the property, such as a sale by L *and* R of their interests to P. In light of the preceding discussion, is the reason for this exception discernible?

*Characterizing the Gain.* If a life interest is property[6] and not within any of the exclusionary paragraphs of Section 1221(a), it is a capital asset. If it is sold, the gain is capital gain. If it has been held for more than one year, it is long-term capital gain. *All* that L gets is gross income, but it is characterized as capital gain. So be it! *Should* that be it? There may be competing policies here. What L receives is essentially a substitute for what would probably have come to L as ordinary income.[7] While we veer back pretty close to *Hort* with this thought, we find shelter again (for L) in *Metropolitan Building.* And as a policy matter we might feel that to telescope all of L's receipts into one year would be harsh.[8] In any event, Congress left

---

[4]    See *Bell's Estate* and *McAllister,* supra note 2.

[5]    Notice that there is no similar problem with regard to a sale of R's remainder. R's purchaser will take a cost basis unaffected by the uniform basis rules. Thus, § 1001(e) is not made applicable to the remainder interest, as the uniform basis will just expire with the life beneficiary, and R *may* use R's share of the uniform basis upon the sale of this interest. Cf. I.R.C. § 1001(e)(3).

[6]    See Blair v. Commissioner, supra note 1.

[7]    Note, however, the characterization rules of I.R.C. §§ 652(b) and 662(b); and see Ferguson, Freeland and Ascher, The Federal Income Taxation of Estates, Trusts, and Beneficiaries, ¶ 7.06, "The Qualitative Measure", (Aspen, 3d Ed. 1998).

[8]    See I.R.C. § 467(c) which requires a lessor of property which is subject to a leaseback or a long term agreement but not subject to the § 467(b)(2) rent leveling provision to recognize gain as ordinary income to the extent of the prior understated rental inclusions. See page 647, supra for a discussion of § 467.

the usual characterization rules intact at the time it changed the measuring device for gain or loss on sales of terminable interests.

# Watkins v. Commissioner*

United States Court of Appeals, Tenth Circuit, 2006.
447 F.3d 1269.

■ Before O'BRIEN, SEYMOUR, and BALDOCK, CIRCUIT JUDGES.

■ SEYMOUR, CIRCUIT JUDGE.

Taxpayer Roger L. Watkins won over $12 million in the Colorado State Lottery, which he was to receive in twenty-five annual payments. After receiving six installments, Mr. Watkins sold his interest in the remaining payments to a third party for a lump sum and claimed the sale resulted in a capital gain. The Internal Revenue Service (I.R.S.) disagreed, asserting the proceeds from the sale should be characterized as ordinary income. In subsequent litigation, the tax court agreed with the I.R.S.'s position. * * * Mr. Watkins appeals, and we affirm.

I

On May 1, 1993, Mr. Watkins won $12,358,688 from the Colorado State Lottery with a ticket he purchased for one dollar. At the time, he was married to Tammy Watkins. His prize winnings were to be distributed to him in twenty-five annual installments through an annuity purchased by the Colorado State Lottery. Mr. Watkins reported the receipt of his first six prize payments as ordinary income on his federal tax returns. In 1997, Mr. Watkins and his wife were divorced. As part of the divorce settlement, the court awarded each party a one-half interest in the future lottery payments.

In 1998, Mr. Watkins entered into a contract with Stone Street Capital, Inc. (Stone Street), agreeing to assign it his one-half interest in the remaining lottery payments. Upon receiving a judicial order permitting the assignment, see Colo.Rev.Stat. § 24–35–212(1)(b), Mr. Watkins consummated the contract. In consideration for the assignment, Mr. Watkins received $2,614,744, which represented the discounted present value of his remaining share of the lottery winnings. Of this amount, he gave $200,000 to a third party who provided consulting services in connection with the sale to Stone Street. On his 1998 tax return, Mr. Watkins reported that the lump sum from Stone Street was the result of a sale of a capital asset worth $2,414,744 with a cost basis of zero.

The I.R.S. issued a notice of deficiency to Mr. Watkins, claiming the $2,614,744 he received from Stone Street was ordinary income, not the result of the sale of a capital asset warranting capital gains treatment. The I.R.S. did agree, however, that the $200,000 consulting fee was

---

*        Footnotes omitted.

allowable as a miscellaneous itemized deduction. Mr. Watkins timely appealed to the tax court, which ruled in favor of the I.R.S.

II

We exercise jurisdiction pursuant to I.R.C. § 7482(a)(1) and review the tax court's decision "in the same manner and to the same extent as decisions of the district courts . . . tried without a jury." Id. We thus review legal questions de novo and factual questions for clear error. IHC Health Plans, Inc. v. C.I.R., 325 F.3d 1188, 1193 (10th Cir.2003); Kurzet v. C.I.R., 222 F.3d 830, 833 (10th Cir.2000). In so doing, we find no error in the tax court's ruling. Having reviewed the relevant Supreme Court, circuit court, and tax court authority, we easily conclude that Mr. Watkins' sale of his lottery payments should be characterized as producing ordinary income rather than capital gain.

A capital gain occurs when a taxpayer sells a capital asset at a profit. See I.R.C. § 1222(1), (3). Generally, a capital asset is defined as "property, held by the taxpayer (whether or not connected with his trade or business). . . ." I.R.C. § 1221(a). This statutory definition of property is broad, and a plain reading of its language could result in drawing within its scope all manner of property not necessarily appropriate for capital gains treatment. The Supreme Court expressed this concern in C.I.R. v. Gillette Motor Transp., Inc., 364 U.S. 130, 80 S.Ct. 1497, 4 L.Ed.2d 1617 (1960), noting that "[w]hile a capital asset is defined . . . as 'property held by the taxpayer,' it is evident that not everything which can be called property in the ordinary sense and which is outside the statutory exclusions qualifies as a capital asset." Id. at 134, 80 S.Ct. 1497. In limiting the breadth of what could conceivably receive capital gains treatment, the Court reasoned that

> the term "capital asset" is to be construed narrowly in accordance with *the purpose of Congress to afford capital-gains treatment only in situations typically involving the realization of appreciation in value accrued over a substantial period of time,* and thus to ameliorate the hardship of taxation of the entire gain in one year.

Id. (emphasis added).

The Court has further narrowed the scope of those gains which may be characterized as capital through its creation of the substitute-for-ordinary-income doctrine. Under this doctrine, the Court has indicated that where a lump sum payment is received in exchange "for what would otherwise be received at a future time as ordinary income," C.I.R. v. P.G. Lake Inc., 356 U.S. 260, 265, 78 S.Ct. 691, 2 L.Ed.2d 743 (1958), capital gains treatment of the lump sum is inappropriate. This is so because the "consideration was paid for the right to receive future income, not for an increase in the value of income-producing property." Id. at 266, 78 S.Ct. 691. See also United States v. Midland-Ross Corp., 381 U.S. 54, 57–58, 85 S.Ct. 1308, 14 L.Ed.2d 214 (1965) (gain based on earned original issue discount from sale of promissory notes before maturity was equivalent of interest and therefore constituted ordinary income); Hort v. C.I.R., 313 U.S. 28, 31, 61 S.Ct. 757, 85 L.Ed. 1168 (1941) (lump sum paid for cancellation of rental payments owed under fifteen-year lease treated as ordinary income); Freese v. United States, 455 F.2d 1146, 1150 (10th Cir.1972) (receipt of lump sum representing commission rights pursuant to contract not capital gain); Holt v. C.I.R., 303 F.2d 687, 690–91 (9th Cir.1962) (lump sum received in exchange for future proceeds from movies deemed ordinary income); Dyer v. C.I.R., 294 F.2d 123, 126 (10th Cir.1961) (lump sum received for mineral leasehold payments held to be ordinary income). We glean from these cases the basic lesson that when a party exchanges for a lump sum the right to receive in the future ordinary income already earned or obtained, the amount received serves as a substitute for the ordinary income the party had the right to receive over time. The lump sum is accordingly treated as ordinary income for taxation purposes.

Two other circuit courts, as well as numerous rulings from the Tax Court, have applied this doctrine in lottery sales cases and have consistently held that a lump sum payment in exchange for future installments of lottery winnings is properly characterized as ordinary income. See Lattera v. C.I.R., 437 F.3d 399 (3d Cir.2006); United States v. Maginnis, 356 F.3d 1179 (9th Cir.2004); Wolman v. C.I.R., 2004 RIA TC Memo 2004–262; Clopton v. C.I.R., 87 T.C.M. (CCH) 1217 (2004); Simpson v. C.I.R., 85 T.C.M. (CCH) 1421 (2003); Johns v. C.I.R., 85 T.C.M. (CCH) 1318, 2003 WL 21146797 (2003); Boehme v. C.I.R., 85 T.C.M. (CCH) 1039 (2003); Davis v. C.I.R., 119 T.C. 1 (2002 WL 1446631). We agree.

The Third and Ninth Circuits, in invoking the substitute-for-ordinary income doctrine, outlined different methods for applying the doctrine generally while simultaneously seeking to appropriately limit its use. See Lattera, 437 F.3d at 405–09 (outlining a three step "family resemblance" test for application of the doctrine while noting no rule could "account for every contemplated transactional variation"); Maginnis, 356 F.3d at 1182–83 (applying doctrine where there has been no underlying investment of capital and where sale of asset did not reflect accretion in value over cost of underlying asset, but acknowledging the two factors would not be dispositive in every case). The test laid out in Maginnis has been subject to academic criticism, see Matthew S. Levine, Case Comment, Lottery Winnings as Capital Gains, 114 Yale L.J. 195, 197–202 (2004); Thomas G. Sinclair, Comment, Limiting the Substitute-for-Ordinary-Income Doctrine: An Analysis Through Its Most Recent Application Involving the Sale of Future Lottery Rights, 56 S.C.L.Rev. 387, 421–22 (2004); and was rejected by the court in Lattera, 437 F.3d at 404–05. We decline to enter the fray. While we acknowledge the importance of placing appropriate limits on when to apply the substitute-for-ordinary-income doctrine, in the instant case there is no question that what Mr. Watkins exchanged for a lump sum payment was his future right to receive set amounts of income he had essentially already obtained as a result of his lottery success. Application of the substitute-for-ordinary-income doctrine is therefore entirely proper in Mr. Watkins' case. As a consequence, we need not formulate any specific test regarding the appropriate limits of the doctrine's application.

At bottom, Mr. Watkins exchanged the future right to receive his parceled-out lottery winnings for a lump sum. Lottery winnings, whether received initially and wholly in a lump sum or in annual payments, are treated as ordinary income under the tax code. C.I.R. v. Groetzinger, 480 U.S. 23, 32 n. 11, 107 S.Ct. 980, 94 L.Ed.2d 25 (1987) (equating a state lottery with public gambling in case treating gambling earnings as ordinary income); Maginnis, 356 F.3d at 1183 ("Lottery prizes are treated by the tax code as gambling winnings, which are taxed as ordinary income."); Davis, 119 T.C. at 4 ("The parties agree that an amount received as a lottery prize constitutes ordinary income."). All of the payments Mr. Watkins initially received in a series of annual installments represented ordinary income Mr. Watkins had already earned by virtue of his success in the lottery. The lump sum Mr. Watkins received from Stone Street served as a substitute for the ordinary income he would have otherwise received over a period of time, and therefore was appropriately taxed as ordinary income. As in P.G. Lake, Inc.,

> [t]he substance of what was assigned was the right to receive future income. The substance of what was received was the present value of income which the recipient would otherwise obtain in the future. In short, consideration was paid for the right to receive future income, not for an increase in the value of the income-producing property.

356 U.S. at 266, 78 S.Ct. 691. Under these circumstances, the sale of Mr. Watkins's future lottery payments did not represent a capital gain.

We AFFIRM the determination of the tax court.

## PROBLEMS

**1.** Agent entered into a contract with a national insurance Company to manage its State office for a ten year period. After two years Company decides to discontinue its State operations and agrees to pay Agent $50,000 to terminate her contract. What result to Agent?

**2.** Recall the *Stranahan* case at page 256, supra. What is the character of taxpayer's gain in that case?

**3.** Landlord L owns two contiguous parcels of land. L leases both parcels to Tenant T for $1,000 per month per parcel or a total of $24,000 per year; the rent is payable at the end of each year. The lease is for a 10 year period. Upon the following events, which occur more than one year after the lease is signed, what are the results:

(a)  To L if L sells the right to the rents on both parcels, prior to any rental payments being due or paid, to a third party for $200,000?

(b)  To L if T pays L $20,000 to cancel the leases on both parcels?

(c)  To T if L pays T $20,000 to cancel the leases on both parcels? See § 1241.

(d)  To T, if after subleasing one of the parcels of land to S for $1200 per month for a five year period, S pays T $10,000 for all T's rights in the lease on that parcel and L releases T from the lease and accepts S as the new tenant?

(e)  To T if S subleases one parcel of land from T at $1200 per month for the remainder of T's ten year period?

**4.**  Beneficiary B owns an income interest in a trust which B purchased several years ago. The remaining income interest has twenty years to run after the date of the sale described below and B's adjusted basis in the remaining interest is $50,000. What result:

(a)  If B sells the entire interest for $60,000?

(b)  If B sells the right to one quarter of the income interest for $15,000?

(c)  If B received the income interest as a gift (rather than by purchasing it, but assuming the same adjusted basis) and B sells the entire interest for $60,000?

(d)  If B inherited the income interest and B and the remainderperson R both sell their interests to a third party with B receiving $60,000 for B's interest?

(e)  If R sells R's remainder interest when it has an adjusted basis of $100,000 for $150,000?

## 2.  CORRELATION WITH PRIOR TRANSACTIONS

### Arrowsmith v. Commissioner

Supreme Court of the United States, 1952.
344 U.S. 6, 73 S.Ct. 71, rehearing denied 344 U.S. 900, 73 S.Ct. 273.

■ MR. JUSTICE BLACK delivered the opinion of the Court.

This is an income tax controversy growing out of the following facts as shown by findings of the Tax Court. In 1937 two taxpayers, petitioners here, decided to liquidate and divide the proceeds of a corporation in which they had equal stock ownership.[1] Partial distributions made in 1937, 1938, and 1939 were followed by a final one in 1940. Petitioners reported the profits obtained from this transaction, classifying them as capital gains. They thereby paid less income tax than would have been

---

[1]  At dissolution the corporate stock was owned by Frederick P. Bauer and the executor of Davenport Pogue's estate. The parties here now are Pogue's widow, Bauer's widow, and the executor of Bauer's estate.

required had the income been attributed to ordinary business transactions for profit. About the propriety of these 1937–1940 returns, there is no dispute. But in 1944 a judgment was rendered against the old corporation and against Frederick R. Bauer, individually. The two taxpayers were required to and did pay the judgment for the corporation, of whose assets they were transferees. See Phillips-Jones Corp. v. Parmley, 302 U.S. 233, 235–236, 58 S.Ct. 197, 198. Cf. I.R.C. § 311(a). Classifying the loss as an ordinary business one, each took a tax deduction for 100% of the amount paid. Treatment of the loss as a capital one would have allowed deduction of a much smaller amount. See I.R.C. § 117(b), (d)(2) and (e). The Commissioner viewed the 1944 payment as part of the original liquidation transaction requiring classification as a capital loss, just as the taxpayers had treated the original dividends as capital gains. Disagreeing with the Commissioner the Tax Court classified the 1944 payment as an ordinary business loss. 15 T.C. 876. Disagreeing with the Tax Court the Court of Appeals reversed, treating the loss as "capital." 193 F.2d 734. This latter holding conflicts with the Third Circuit's holding in Commissioner v. Switlik, 184 F.2d 299. Because of this conflict, we granted certiorari. 343 U.S. 976, 72 S.Ct. 1075.

I.R.C. § 23(g) treats losses from sales or exchanges of capital assets as "capital losses" and I.R.C. § 115(c) requires that liquidation distributions be treated as exchanges. [See I.R.C. (1986) § 331(a). Ed.] The losses here fall squarely within the definition of "capital losses" contained in these sections. Taxpayers were required to pay the judgment because of liability imposed on them as transferees of liquidation distribution assets. And it is plain that their liability as transferees was not based on any ordinary business transaction of theirs apart from the liquidation proceedings. It is not even denied that had this judgment been paid after liquidation, but during the year 1940, the losses would have been properly treated as capital ones. For payment during 1940 would simply have reduced the amount of capital gains taxpayers received during that year.

It is contended, however, that this payment which would have been a capital transaction in 1940 was transformed into an ordinary business transaction in 1944 because of the well-established principle that each taxable year is a separate unit for tax accounting purposes. United States v. Lewis, 340 U.S. 590, 71 S.Ct. 522; North American Oil v. Burnet, 286 U.S. 417, 52 S.Ct. 613. But this principle is not breached by considering all the 1937–1944 liquidation transaction events in order properly to classify the nature of the 1944 loss for tax purposes. Such an examination is not an attempt to reopen and readjust the 1937 to 1940 tax returns, an action that would be inconsistent with the annual tax accounting principle.

The petitioner Bauer's executor presents an argument for reversal which applies to Bauer alone. He was liable not only by reason of being a transferee of the corporate assets. He was also held liable jointly with the original corporation, on findings that he had secretly profited because of a breach of his fiduciary relationship to the judgment creditor. Trounstine v. Bauer, Pogue & Co., 44 F.Supp. 767, 773; 144 F.2d 379, 382. The judgment was against both Bauer and the corporation. For this reason it is contended that the nature of Bauer's tax deduction should be considered on the basis of his liability as an individual who sustained a loss in an ordinary business transaction for profit. We agree with the Court of Appeals that this contention should not be sustained. While there was a liability against him in both capacities, the individual judgment against him was for the whole amount. His payment of only half the judgment indicates that both he and the other transferee were paying in their capacities as such. We see no reason for giving Bauer a preferred tax position.

Affirmed.

■ MR. JUSTICE DOUGLAS, dissenting.

I agree with Mr. Justice Jackson that these losses should be treated as ordinary, not capital losses. There were no capital transactions in the year in which the losses were suffered. Those transactions occurred and were accounted for in earlier years in accord with the established principle that each year is a separate unit for tax accounting purposes. See United States v. Lewis, 340 U.S. 590, 71 S.Ct. 522. I have not felt, as my dissent in the *Lewis* case indicates, that the law made that an inexorable principle. But if it is the law, we should require observance of it—not merely by taxpayers but by the Government as well. We should force each year to stand on its own footing, whoever may gain or lose from it in a particular case. We impeach that principle when we treat this year's losses as if they diminished last year's gains.

■ MR. JUSTICE JACKSON, whom MR. JUSTICE FRANKFURTER joins, dissenting.

This problem arises only because the judgment was rendered in a taxable year subsequent to the liquidation.

Had the liability of the transferor-corporation been reduced to judgment during the taxable year in which liquidation occurred, or prior thereto, this problem, under the tax laws, would not arise. The amount of the judgment rendered against the corporation would have decreased the amount it had available for distribution, which would have reduced the liquidating dividends proportionately and diminished the capital gains taxes assessed against the stockholders. Probably it would also have decreased the corporation's own taxable income.

Congress might have allowed, under such circumstances, tax returns of the prior year to be reopened or readjusted so as to give the same tax results as would have obtained had the liability become known prior to liquidation. Such a solution is foreclosed to us and the alternatives left are to regard the judgment liability fastened by operation of law on the transferee as an ordinary loss for the year of adjudication or to regard it as a capital loss for such year.

This Court simplifies the choice to one of reading the English language, and declares that the losses here come "squarely within" the definition of capital losses contained within two sections of the Internal Revenue Code. What seems so clear to this Court was not seen at all by the Tax Court, in this case or in earlier consideration of the same issue; nor was it grasped by the Court of Appeals for the Third Circuit. Commissioner v. Switlik, 184 F.2d 299 (1950).

I find little aid in the choice of alternatives from arguments based on equities. One enables the taxpayer to deduct the amount of the judgment against his ordinary income which might be taxed as high as 87%, while if the liability had been assessed against the corporation prior to liquidation it would have reduced his capital gain which was taxable at only 25% (now 26%). The consequence may readily be characterized as a windfall (regarding a windfall as anything that is left to a taxpayer after the collector has finished with him).

On the other hand, adoption of the contrary alternative may penalize the taxpayer because of two factors: (1) since capital losses are deductible only against capital gains, plus $1,000, [See (1986) Section 1211(b)(1)(B), prior to 1976 amendments. Ed.] a taxpayer having no net capital gains in the ensuing five years would have no opportunity to deduct anything beyond $5,000 [But see (1986) Section 1212(b). Ed.]; and (2) had the liability been discharged by the corporation, a portion of it would probably in effect have been paid by the Government, since the corporation could have taken it as a deduction, while here the total liability comes out of the pockets of the stockholders.

Solicitude for the revenues is a plausible but treacherous basis upon which to decide a particular tax case. A victory may have implications which in future cases will cost the Treasury more than a defeat. This might be such a case, for anything I know. Suppose that subsequent to liquidation it is found that a corporation has undisclosed claims instead of liabilities and that under applicable state law they may be prosecuted for the benefit of the stockholders. The logic of the Court's decision here, if adhered to, would result in a lesser return to the Government than if the recoveries were considered ordinary income. Would it be so clear that this is a capital loss if the shoe were on the other foot?

Where the statute is so indecisive and the importance of a particular holding lies in its rational and harmonious relation to the general scheme of the tax law, I think great deference is due the twice-expressed judgment of the Tax Court. In spite of the gelding of Dobson v. Commissioner, 320 U.S. 489, 64 S.Ct. 239, by the recent revision of the Judicial Code, Act of June 25, 1948, § 36, 62 Stat. 991–992, I still think the Tax Court is a more competent and steady influence toward a systematic body of tax law than our sporadic omnipotence in a field beset with invisible boomerangs. I should reverse, in reliance upon the Tax Court's judgment more, perhaps, than my own.

## United States v. Skelly Oil Co.
Supreme Court of the United States, 1969.
394 U.S. 678, 89 S.Ct. 1379.

■ MR. JUSTICE MARSHALL delivered the opinion of the Court:

During its tax year ending December 31, 1958, respondent refunded $505,536.54 to two of its customers for overcharges during the six preceding years. Respondent, an Oklahoma producer of natural gas, had set its prices during the earlier years in accordance with a minimum price order of the Oklahoma Corporation Commission. After that order was vacated as a result of a decision of this Court, Michigan Wisconsin Pipe Line Co. v. Corporation Comm'n of Oklahoma, 355 U.S. 425, 78 S.Ct. 409 (1958), respondent found it necessary to settle a number of claims filed by its customers; the repayments in question represent settlements of two of those claims. Since respondent had claimed an unrestricted right to its sales receipts during the years 1952 through 1957, it had included the $505,536.54 in its gross income in those years. The amount was also included in respondent's "gross income from the property" as defined in § 613 of the Internal Revenue Code of 1954, the section which allows taxpayers to deduct a fixed percentage of certain receipts to compensate for the depletion of natural resources from which they derive income. Allowable percentage depletion for receipts from oil and gas wells is [was then] fixed at 27½% of the "gross income from the property." Since respondent claimed and the Commissioner allowed percentage depletion deductions during these years, 27½% of the receipts in question was added to the depletion allowances to which respondent would otherwise have been entitled. Accordingly, the actual increase in respondent's taxable income attributable to the receipts in question was not $505,536.54, but only $366,513.99. Yet, when respondent made its refunds in 1958, it attempted to deduct the full $505,536.54. The Commissioner objected and assessed a deficiency. Respondent paid and, after its claim for a refund had been disallowed, began the present suit. The Government won in the District Court, 255 F.Supp. 228 (D.C.N.D.Okla.1966), but the Court of Appeals for the Tenth Circuit reversed, 392 F.2d 128 (1967). Upon petition by the Government, we granted certiorari, 393 U.S. 820, 89 S.Ct. 121 (1968), to consider whether the Court of Appeals' decision had allowed respondent "the practical equivalent of double deduction," Charles Ilfeld Co. v. Hernandez, 292 U.S. 62, 68, 54 S.Ct. 596, 598 (1934), in conflict with past decisions of this Court and sound principles of tax law. We reverse.

I.    The present problem is an outgrowth of the so-called "claim-of-right" doctrine. Mr. Justice Brandeis, speaking for a unanimous Court in North American Oil Consolidated v. Burnet, 286 U.S. 417, 424, 52 S.Ct.

613, 615 (1932), gave that doctrine its classic formulation. "If a taxpayer receives earnings under a claim of right and without restriction as to its disposition, he has received income which he is required to return, even though it may still be claimed that he is not entitled to retain the money, and even though he may still be adjudged to restore its equivalent." Should it later appear that the taxpayer was not entitled to keep the money, Mr. Justice Brandeis explained, he would be entitled to a deduction in the year of repayment; the taxes due for the year of receipt would not be affected. This approach was dictated by Congress' adoption of an annual accounting system as an integral part of the tax code. See Burnet v. Sanford & Brooks Co., 282 U.S. 359, 365–366, 51 S.Ct. 150, 152 (1931). Of course, the tax benefit from the deduction in the year of repayment might differ from the increase in taxes attributable to the receipt; for example, tax rates might have changed, or the taxpayer might be in a different tax "bracket." See Healy v. Commissioner, 345 U.S. 278, 284–285, 73 S.Ct. 671, 675 (1953). But as the doctrine was originally formulated, these discrepancies were accepted as an unavoidable consequence of the annual accounting system.

Section 1341 of the 1954 Code was enacted to alleviate some of the inequities which Congress felt existed in this area.[1] See H.R.Rep. No. 1337, 83d Cong., 2d Sess., 86–87 (1954); S.Rep. No. 1622, 83d Cong., 2d Sess., 118–119 (1954). As an alternative to the deduction in the year of repayment[2] which prior law allowed, § 1341(a)(5) permits certain taxpayers to recompute their taxes for the year of receipt. Whenever § 1341(a)(5) applies, taxes for the current year are to be reduced by the amount taxes were increased in the year or years of receipt because the disputed items were included in gross income. Nevertheless, it is clear that Congress did not intend to tamper with the underlying claim-of-right doctrine; it only provided an alternative for certain cases in which the new approach favored the taxpayer. When the new approach was not advantageous to the taxpayer, the old law was to apply under § 1341(a)(4).

In this case, the parties have stipulated that § 1341(a)(5) does not apply. Accordingly, as the courts below recognized, respondent's taxes must be computed under § 1341(a)(4) and thus, in effect, without regard to the special relief Congress provided through the enactment of § 1341. Nevertheless, respondent argues, and the Court of Appeals seems to have held, that the language used in § 1341 requires that respondent be allowed a deduction for the full amount it refunded to its customers. We think the section has no such significance.

---

[1] [Section 1341(a) is omitted. Ed.] Section 1341(b)(2) contains an exclusion covering certain cases involving sales of stock in trade or inventory. However, because of special treatment given refunds made by regulated public utilities, both parties agree that § 1341(b)(2) is inapplicable to this case and that, accordingly, § 1341(a) applies.

[2] In the case of an accrual-basis taxpayer, the legislative history makes it clear that the deduction is allowable at the proper time for accrual. H.R.Rep. No. 1337, 83d Cong., 2d Sess., A294 (1954); S.Rep. No. 1622, 83d Cong., 2d Sess., 451–452 (1954).

In describing the situations in which the section applies, § 1341(a)(2) talks of cases in which "a deduction is allowable for the taxable year because it was established after the close of [the year or years of receipt] that the taxpayer did not have an unrestricted right to such item * * *." The "item" referred to is first mentioned in § 1341(a)(1); it is the item included in gross income in the year of receipt. The section does not imply in any way that the "deduction" and the "item" must necessarily be equal in amount. In fact, the use of the words "a deduction" and the placement of § 1341 in subchapter Q—the subchapter dealing largely with side-effects of the annual accounting system—make it clear that it is necessary to refer to other portions of the Code to discover how much of a deduction is allowable. The regulations promulgated under the section make the necessity for such a cross-reference clear. Treas.Reg. § 1.1341–1 (1957). Therefore, when § 1341(a)(4)—the subsection applicable here—speaks of "the tax * * * computed with such deduction," it is referring to the deduction mentioned in § 1341(a)(2); and that deduction must be determined not by any mechanical equation with the "item" originally included in gross income, but by reference to the applicable sections of the Code and the case law developed under those sections.

II. There is some dispute between the parties about whether the refunds in question are deductible as losses under § 165 of the 1954 Code or as business expenses under § 162.[3] Although in some situations the distinction may have relevance, cf. Equitable Life Ins. Co. of Iowa v. United States, 340 F.2d 9 (C.A.8th Cir.1965), we do not think it makes any difference here. In either case, the Code should not be interpreted to allow respondent "the practical equivalent of double deduction," Charles Ilfeld Co. v. Hernandez, 292 U.S. 62, 68, 54 S.Ct. 596, 598 (1934), absent a clear declaration of intent by Congress. See United States v. Ludey, 274 U.S. 295, 47 S.Ct. 608 (1927). Accordingly, to avoid that result in this case, the deduction allowable in the year of repayment must be reduced by the percentage depletion allowance which respondent claimed and the Commissioner allowed in the years of receipt as a result of the inclusion of the later-refunded items in respondent's "gross income from the property" in those years. Any other approach would allow respondent a total of $1.27½ in deductions for every $1 refunded to its customers.

Under the annual accounting system dictated by the Code, each year's tax must be definitively calculable at the end of the tax year. "It is the essence of any system of taxation that it should produce revenue ascertainable, and payable to the Government, at regular intervals." Burnet v. Sanford & Brooks Co., supra, at 365. In cases arising under the claim-of-right doctrine, this emphasis on the annual accounting period normally requires that the tax consequences of a receipt should not determine the size of the deduction allowable in the year of repayment. There is no requirement that the deduction save the taxpayer the exact

---

[3]  The Commissioner has long recognized that a deduction under some section is allowable. G.C.M. 16730, XV–1 Cum.Bull. 179 (1936).

amount of taxes he paid because of the inclusion of the item in income for a prior year. See Healy v. Commissioner, supra.

Nevertheless, the annual accounting concept does not require us to close our eyes to what happened in prior years. For instance, it is well settled that the prior year may be examined to determine whether the repayment gives rise to a regular loss or a capital loss. Arrowsmith v. Commissioner, 344 U.S. 6, 73 S.Ct. 71 (1952). The rationale for the *Arrowsmith* rule is easy to see; if money was taxed at a special lower rate when received, the taxpayer would be accorded an unfair tax windfall if repayments were generally deductible from receipts taxable at the higher rate applicable to ordinary income. The Court in *Arrowsmith* was unwilling to infer that Congress intended such a result.

This case is really no different.[4] In essence, oil and gas producers are taxed on only 72½% of their "gross income from the property" whenever they claim percentage depletion. The remainder of their oil and gas receipts is in reality tax exempt. We cannot believe that Congress intended to give taxpayers a deduction for refunding money that was not taxed when received. Cf. Maurice P. O'Meara, 8 T.C. 622, 634–635 (1947). Accordingly *Arrowsmith* teaches that the full amount of the repayment cannot, in the circumstances of this case, be allowed as a deduction.

This result does no violence to the annual accounting system. Here, as in *Arrowsmith,* the earlier returns are not being reopened. And no attempt is being made to require the tax savings from the deduction to equal the tax consequences of the receipts in prior years.[5] In addition, the approach here adopted will affect only a few cases. The percentage depletion allowance is quite unusual; unlike most other deductions provided by the Code, it allows a fixed portion of gross income to go untaxed. As a result, the depletion allowance increases in years when disputed amounts are received under claim of right; there is no corresponding decrease in the allowance because of later deductions for repayments.[6] Therefore, if a deduction for 100% of the repayments were

---

[4]　The analogy would be even more striking if in *Arrowsmith* the individual taxpayer had not utilized the alternative tax for capital gains, as they were permitted to do by what is now § 1201 of the 1954 Code. Where the 25% alternative tax is not used, individual taxpayers are taxed at ordinary rates on 50% of their capital gains. See § 1202. In such a situation, the rule of the *Arrowsmith* case prevents taxpayers from deducting 100% of an item refunded when they were taxed on only 50% of it when it was received. Although *Arrowsmith* prevents this inequitable result by treating the repayment as a capital loss, rather than by disallowing 50% of the deduction, the policy behind the decision is applicable in this case. Here it would be inequitable to allow a 100% deduction when only 72½% was taxed on receipt.

[5]　Compare the analogous approach utilized under the "tax benefit" rule. Alice Phelan Sullivan Corp. v. United States, 381 F.2d 399 (Ct.Cl.1967); see Internal Revenue Code of 1954 § 111. In keeping with the analogy, the Commissioner has indicated that the Government will only seek to reduce the deduction in the year on repayment to the extent that the depletion allowance attributable to the receipt directly or indirectly reduced taxable income. Proposed Treas.Reg. § 1.613–2(c)(8), 33 Fed.Reg. 10702–10703 (1968).

[6]　The 10% standard deduction mentioned by the dissent, post, at n. 6, differs in that it allows as a deduction a percentage of adjusted gross income, rather than of gross income. See § 141; cf. §§ 170, 213. As a result, repayments may in certain cases cause a decrease in the 10%

allowed, every time money is received and later repaid the taxpayer would make a profit equivalent to the taxes on 27½% of the amount refunded. In other situations when the taxes on a receipt do not equal the tax benefits of a repayment, either the taxpayer or the Government may, depending on circumstances, be the beneficiary. Here, the taxpayer always wins and the Government always loses. We cannot believe that Congress would have intended such an inequitable result.

The parties have stipulated that respondent is entitled to a judgment for $20,932.64 plus statutory interest for claims unrelated to the matter in controversy here; the District Court entered a judgment for that amount. Accordingly, the judgment of the Court of Appeals is reversed and the case is remanded to that court with instructions that it be returned to the District Court for re-entry of the original District Court judgment.

Reversed.

■ The dissenting opinions of STEWART, J. (DOUGLAS and HARLAN, JJ., joining), and DOUGLAS, J., are omitted. Ed.

## NOTE

The scope of the *Arrowsmith* doctrine remains uncertain.[1] The parent decision involved a question of characterization, holding that loss quite arguably ordinary for lack of any sale or exchange in the taxable year, was *capital loss* because of its relationship to transactions in a prior year. There is little doubt that a similar approach can convert potential capital gain to *ordinary income;* and that was the result in David Bresler,[2] where part of a settlement in an antitrust suit compensated the taxpayer for a loss on the sale of business property claimed as an ordinary loss in a prior year.

Other applications of the *Arrowsmith* doctrine seem to extend its reach. For example, T made a gain on the sale of oil and gas leases, which T reported as long-term capital gain. Later, accused of fraud on the ground that some wells were illegally slanted, T settled the claim and treated the payment as a deductible business expense incurred to avoid litigation, to save legal expenses and to preserve T's business reputation. Not so, said the Fifth Circuit, supporting the Commissioner and a prior district court decision. Under *Arrowsmith,* the payment was so related to the taxpayer's prior capital gain as to require capital loss treatment.[3]

The recapture of "insider's" profits under section 16(b) of the Securities and Exchange Act of 1934 has produced numerous *Arrowsmith* controversies. Under Section 16(b), an insider who makes short swing profits

---

standard deduction allowable in the year of repayment, assuming that the repayment is of the character to be deducted in calculating adjusted gross income. See § 62.

[1]   See Rabinovitz, "Effect of Prior Year's Transactions on Federal Income Tax Consequences of Current Receipts or Payments," 28 Tax L.Rev. 85 (1972).

[2]   65 T.C. 182 (1975), acq. 1976–2 C.B. 1.

[3]   Kimbell v. United States, 490 F.2d 203 (5th Cir.1974), cert. denied 419 U.S. 833, 95 S.Ct. 58 (1974).

on the purchase and sale (or sale and purchase) of stock in a corporation is required to disgorge and to pay the profits over to the corporation for the benefit of *all* shareholders. Can the payment qualify as a business expense deductible from ordinary income?

In the litigated cases, the taxpayer has had a long-term capital gain on the sale. What then about the section 16(b) payment where respectable evidence is presented relating the payment and the taxpayer's business? The Courts of Appeal have uniformly held, despite the Tax Court's insistence that the payments are a business expense generating an ordinary deduction, that *Arrowsmith* is overpowering, and the characterization of the deduction depends upon the prior tax treatment of the transaction generating the payment.[4] It has been suggested that the proper solution is to add the section 16(b) payment to the basis of the purchased shares,[5] but a court has yet to accept this alternative.[6] In this area the Tax Court looks rather like the nimble triple-threat back running out of running room[7] before he can reach the goal line. Zooks! Could it be the Tax Court is running the wrong way?

## H. STATUTORILY CREATED CAPITAL GAIN AND LOSS CONSEQUENCES

## 1. IN GENERAL

Internal Revenue Code: See Sections 165(g); 166(d); 1222; 1234; 1234A; 1235; 1236; 1237; 1241; 1253; 1271.

———————

Recall that under Section 1222 capital gain or loss consequences require: (1) a transaction involving a capital asset, (2) a sale or exchange of that capital asset, and (3) a determination of how long the taxpayer has held the capital asset. Section 1221 defines the term capital asset but it is subject to both judicial and statutory exceptions. If a transaction does not involve a capital asset, or if it does not constitute a sale or exchange, it will give rise to ordinary income or to an ordinary deduction. It may be difficult to determine whether a transaction meets such tests. Consequently, at times Congress has seen fit to clarify the status of a transaction or artificially to accord to a transaction one or more of the essential elements, At other times, Congress expressly deprives a capital asset transaction of its characterization. Varying policy reasons, some of

---

[4]   Brown v. Commissioner, 529 F.2d 609 (10th Cir.1976); Cummings v. Commissioner, 506 F.2d 449 (2d Cir.1974), cert. denied 421 U.S. 913, 95 S.Ct. 1571 (1975); Anderson v. Commissioner, 480 F.2d 1304 (7th Cir.1973); Mitchell v. Commissioner, 428 F.2d 259 (6th Cir.1970), cert. denied 401 U.S. 909, 91 S.Ct. 868 (1971), reversing the Tax Court in each instance.

[5]   Lokken, "Tax Significance of Payments in Satisfaction of Liabilities Arising Under Section 16(b) of the Securities Exchange Act of 1934," 4 Ga.L.Rev. 298 (1970).

[6]   But see Drennen, J., agreeing in his dissent in Nathan Cummings v. Commissioner, 61 T.C. 1, 4 (1973).

[7]   See Jack E. Golsen v. Commissioner, 54 T.C. 742 (1970) in which the Tax Court indicates that in a specific case it will follow the view of the court of appeals to which an appeal lies.

which are related to the reasons previously identified for capital asset treatment, underline such congressional decisions.

Instances in which Congress has seen fit to address all three requirements include Section 1235, which is outlined below, and Section 166(d), which classifies nonbusiness bad debts as short-term capital losses.[1] One of the principal provisions sometimes providing both a capital asset and a sale or exchange is Section 1231 which is addressed in the next subpart.[2] Conversely, even though certain transactions meet all three requirements, some sections convert potential capital gains to ordinary income,[3] and others accord ordinary loss treatment to some transactions which would generally produce capital losses.[4]

*Section 1235.* A provision that may provide capital asset status to property and artificially accord sale or exchange or long-term classification to a transaction is Section 1235. A patent is not a capital asset when held by its creator.[5] A common method of exploiting a patent is for the inventor to license others to use it, often fixing the consideration in terms of a part of the proceeds from its use. Can this be regarded as a sale? For a "holder"[6] Section 1235 says it can, and that section generates long-term capital gain (regardless of whether the inventor is a professional and regardless of the length of time the invention was held) out of a licensing arrangement, if the "holder" transfers all substantial rights in the property.[7]

If one who is not a "holder" of a patent disposes of it in a manner different from an outright sale or exchange, i.e. by way of an exclusive licensing arrangement for a period coterminous with the life of the patent or for consideration measured by the licensee's profit, one may have capital gain treatment also. For a time the Treasury held one would not,[8] but with judicial prompting the Treasury has changed its position,[9] and now a non-"holder" who disposes of a patent is in much the same position

---

[1]   See Chapter 23A, infra.

[2]   See Chapter 21H2, infra.

[3]   See Chapter 22C and D, infra.

[4]   See I.R.C. §§ 1242–1244.

[5]   I.R.C. § 1221(a)(3)(A). A patent is also not a capital asset when held by a taxpayer whose basis in the patent is determined with reference to the creator's basis. I.R.C. § 1221(a)(3)(C).

[6]   I.R.C. § 1235(b).

[7]   See Reg. § 1.1235–2(b). The retention of substantial rights, such as a right to terminate a license agreement after a period, Taylor-Winfield Corp. v. Commissioner, 57 T.C. 205 (1971), or the right to exploit the patent in geographical areas placed outside the agreement, Klein's Estate v. Commissioner, 507 F.2d 617 (7th Cir.1974), may defeat the application of I.R.C. § 1235. However, one may, within the section, sell an undivided interest, even a small interest, in all substantial rights. Reg. § 1.1235–2(c); Allen G. Eickmeyer v. Commissioner, 66 T.C. 109 (1976). See Olson, "Federal Income Taxation of Patent and Know-How Transfers," 28 St. Louis U.L.J. 537 (1984).

[8]   Mim. 6490, 1950–1 C.B. 9; Rev. Rul. 55–58, 1955–1 C.B. 97.

[9]   Rev. Rul. 58–353, 1958–2 C.B. 408.

as one who is within Section 1235 and may have long-term capital gain consequences on its disposition.[10]

A final point regarding Section 1235 is that its continued presence in the Code may be precarious. The 2017 Tax Cuts and Jobs Act[11] amended Section 1221(a)(3) to exclude a patent from the definition of a capital asset when it is held by its creator or a person who holds it with a carryover basis from the creator.[12] The version of the bill that initially passed the House of Representatives would also have deleted Section 1235 from the Code and the legislative history states that the result would have been that gains and losses of the taxpayer who created a patent would not receive capital gain treatment.[13] However, the Act made no change to Section 1235. Query whether Section 1235 will be repealed?

## Capital Asset Provisions

There are times when Congress will treat property as a capital asset even though it is not within the Section 1221 definition.

*Section 1234.* When one sells, exchanges, or has a loss on the failure to exercise an option, the characterization of the transaction depends, not upon whether the option itself is a capital asset, but upon whether the property to which it relates so qualifies. This is the prescription of Section 1234, which was enacted to give the option itself a neutral status, recognizing that it is no more than a right to buy or sell property, and to make a more realistic characterization of the transaction on the basis of the character of the property subject to the option.

*Section 1236.* Prior to enactment of Section 1236, it was often uncertain whether one who was a dealer in securities held particular securities in that capacity or as an investor.[14] Thus, the status of the securities in one's hands, as noncapital or capital assets, was often the subject of controversy. A dealer would be tempted to shift securities from investment status to inventory status or vice versa, to support the contention that ordinary gain should be treated as capital gain or that

---

[10]  See Rev. Rul. 69–482, 1969–2 C.B. 164 (the fact that a patent transfer does not qualify under I.R.C. § 1235 does not prevent it from qualifying for long-term capital gains under Code provisions).

[11]  Pub. L. No. 115–97, 115th Cong., 1st Sess. (2017).

[12]  I.R.C. § 1221(a)(3)(A) and (C). The definition is similar, but not identical, to an I.R.C. § 1235 "holder."

[13]  H. Rep. No. 115–466, Joint Explanatory Statement, 115th Cong., 1st Sess. 259–260 (2017).

[14]  See Reg. § 1.1236–1(d)(1)(ii). David C. Fitch v. Commissioner, 34 T.C.M. 233 (1975), reflects a narrow definition of "dealer," resting in part on Higgins v. Commissioner, 312 U.S. 212, 61 S.Ct. 475 (1941).

See also I.R.C. § 475 which requires securities dealers to employ a mark-to-market accounting method under which securities dealers are required to recognize gain or loss based on the fair market value of noninventory securities held at the end of the tax year and allows security traders and commodity traders and dealers to elect to use such treatment. And see I.R.C. § 1221(a)(6) applying similar dealer rules to commodities derivative financial instruments.

capital loss should be treated as ordinary loss. Section 1236 was addressed to the problem.[15] In effect it restricts classification changes that would be convenient for the taxpayer by requiring an identification of the status of the security at the time of its acquisition. Thus, Congress has attempted to clarify the character of a security as a capital asset or not when its actual classification may be equivocal. Section 1236 provides that, if a dealer is to treat securities as capital assets, she generally must clearly indicate on her records before the close of the day on which the securities are acquired that the securities are held for investment purposes.[16] Once the purpose is identified under Section 1236 as investment, the classification may not in any event be changed if the security is subsequently sold at a loss. The statute does not expressly foreclose reclassification of securities originally classified as investments if they are sold at a gain. Why?

*Section 1237.* Another instance in which it may be difficult to determine whether one holding property is a dealer or an investor is when a landowner subdivides real property and sells it.[17] Section 1237 sometimes renders such a determination unnecessary; but the statute is limited in its application. First of all it is wholly unavailable to dealers or to persons who actually become dealers, a requirement creating factual uncertainties that tend to dilute the effectiveness of the clarification purpose of the statute. In addition under Section 1237(a), the land in question (1) must never have been held primarily for sale to customers,[18] (2) must not have been the subject of substantial improvement[19] and (3) unless inherited, must have been held by the taxpayer for at least five years.

When Section 1237 *is* applicable it provides only partial capital asset treatment. Five parcels may be sold as capital gains but, for any year in which a sixth sale occurs and thereafter, gain in an amount up to 5 percent of the sale price on each parcel will be ordinary income.[20] Commissions paid to outside dealers may offset such ordinary income.[21]

Although Section 1237 is severely limited in application, nevertheless there are circumstances in which it can be of very great

---

[15] Sen.Rep. No. 781, 82d Cong., 1st Sess. (1951), 1951–2 C.B. 458 at 482.

[16] An exception is made under I.R.C. § 1236(d) for securities exchange floor specialists who have a 7 business day grace period in which to make their designation.

[17] See *Mauldin v. Commissioner,* Chapter 21D, supra. For further analysis of the relevant factors in making the dealer or investor determination in real estate transactions, see Emmanuel, "Capital Gains for Real Estate Operators," 12 U. of Fla.L.Rev. 280 (1959).

[18] For example in the *Mauldin* case, Chapter 21D, supra, there was no question but that in 1939 and 1940 the taxpayer held the "Mauldin Addition" for sale to customers in the ordinary course of his business. This would in itself render I.R.C. § 1237 inapplicable under § 1237(a)(1).

[19] There is an exception for certain improvements. See I.R.C. § 1237(b)(3). See also I.R.C. § 1237(a)(2)(C), disqualifying the Mauldin Addition in the *Mauldin* case, Chapter 21D, supra, (had § 1237 then been in effect) because of the substantial cost of the city paving which, because disqualified as a deductible tax by § 164(c)(1), would be a proscribed addition to the taxpayer's basis.

[20] I.R.C. § 1237(b)(1).

[21] I.R.C. § 1237(b)(2).

benefit to a taxpayer. For instance, one who has appreciated realty that one has held for many years may make minimal subdivisional improvements on it and sell it off piece-meal, by oneself or through a broker. The minimum but important assurance that Section 1237 affords one is that efforts in that transaction will not place one in a dealer category. Thus, except for the innocuous 5% rule, the person may be able to count on capital gain treatment for all of the sales. It should also be pointed out, however, that Section 1237 is not exclusive[22] and, even if a taxpayer does not qualify for its benefits, one may still maintain that one is an investor in an attempt to classify all of the gain as capital gain.[23] Some suggest that Section 1237 is not available when needed and is not needed when available.

## Sale or Exchange Provisions

Similarly, if a transaction involving a capital asset lacks a *sale or exchange*, the sale or exchange may be provided by a statute. For example, the sale or exchange requirement is supplied by Section 165(g) when securities become worthless and there is no actual sale or exchange that would normally be needed to make the loss a capital loss.[24] Similarly, if a nonbusiness debt becomes bad or worthless, the creditor has made no actual sale or exchange, but Congress characterizes the losses involved by a statutory pretention that there was an exchange.[25] We previously explored Section 1271.[26] Section 1271 generally provides that amounts paid on debt obligations are treated as amounts received in exchange for such obligations.

*Section 1234A.* This section accords sale or exchange treatment to the cancellation, lapse, expiration, or other termination of a right or obligation with respect to property. Court decisions have held that a lapse, cancellation, or abandonment of such property lacks sale or exchange status and the disposition produces ordinary income or loss.[27] Congress enacted Section 1234A because it considered ordinary loss treatment inappropriate in transactions that are "economically equivalent to a sale or exchange of the contract,"[28] such as the settlement or cancellation of a contract to deliver commodities. Therefore, Section

---

[22] Reg. § 1.1237–1(a)(4); R.E. Gordy v. Commissioner, 36 T.C. 855 (1961), acq., 1964–1 (part 1) C.B. 4.

[23] The reason for making such an argument could be to avoid the 5% ordinary income characterization of I.R.C. § 1237(b)(1) or failure to meet the requirements of § 1237(a). For cases treating subdivided land as a capital asset after the enactment of § 1237, see Bon v. United States, unreported, 60–1 U.S.T.C. ¶ 9186 (D.Wyo.1960) and Barker v. United States, unreported, 65–2 U.S.T.C. ¶ 9736 (S.D.Cal.1965). On § 1237 generally see Repetti, "What Makes a Dealer under Section 1237," 17 N.Y.U.Inst. on Fed.Tax. 651 (1959), and Weithorn, "Subdivisions of Real Estate—'Dealer' v. 'Investor' Problem," 11 Tax.L.Rev. 157 (1959).

[24] See Chapter 23A, infra.

[25] I.R.C. §§ 165(g), 166(d). See Chapter 23A, infra.

[26] See page 717, supra.

[27] Leh v. Commissioner, 260 F.2d 489 (9th Cir.1958); Commissioner v. Pittston Co., 252 F.2d 344 (2d Cir.1958), cert. denied 357 U.S. 919, 78 S.Ct. 1360 (1958).

[28] Sen.Rep. No. 97–144, 97th Cong., 1st Sess. pp. 170–71 (1981).

1234A applies to any property that is, or on acquisition would be, a capital asset in the hands of the taxpayer.[29]

*Section 1241.* If a lessee relinquishes a lease in exchange for a payment by the lessor, is the character of the gain affected by the fact that the lease is extinguished so that the lessee has made no exchange?[30] Section 1241 specifically says no. Such receipts "are considered as amounts received in exchange for" the lease.[31]

*Section 1253.* This section deals with the disposition of franchises, trademarks, and trade names, and it is aimed in part at a problem similar to that covered by Section 1235, dealing with patents. The common problem is whether a disposition is a sale or exchange or whether instead it should be viewed as a mere license. In contrast to the affirmative approach of Section 1235 (sale classification upon transfer of "all substantial rights"), Section 1253 provides only a negative rule. The transfer of a franchise, trademark, or trade name is not to be treated as a sale or exchange if the transferor retains any significant power, right or continuing interest in the property. Moreover, and quite contrary to principles adopted in Section 1235, under Section 1253 any amounts received or accrued which are dependent on the productivity, use, or disposition of the property are expressly denied capital gain treatment. Dispositions of franchises, trademarks, or trade names which are not so proscribed may qualify as sales or exchanges and for capital gain characterization if, of course, the property is a capital asset in the hands of the taxpayer.[32]

*Timing Provisions.* As already seen,[33] under Section 1222 Congress prescribes some other artificial holding periods at variance with the time that property disposed of is actually held.

## 2. SECTION 1231 RECHARACTERIZATION

Internal Revenue Code: Section 1231. See Sections 1(h); 1060; 1211(b); 1221(a)(1)–(4); 1222.

———————————

Section 1231 is unquestionably the most significant recharacterization provision in the Code, sometimes creating a capital

———————————

[29]  I.R.C. § 1234A(1).

[30]  See problem 3(c) at page 736, supra.

[31]  The section is also applicable to the cancellation of a distributor's agreement.

[32]  The inherent obscurities of I.R.C. § 1253 foretell uncertainty and controversy in the area of its coverage for some time to come. Furthermore, in view of the enactment of § 197 allowing a 15-year amortization of the cost of such property, I.R.C. § 1245 may convert any such gain to ordinary income. See I.R.C. §§ 197(f)(7), 1245(a)(3) and Chapter 22C, infra. An extensive critical analysis of § 1253 appears in Andrews and Freeland, "Capital Gains and Losses of Individuals and Related Matters under the Tax Reform Act of 1969," 12 Ariz.L.Rev. 627, 666–677 (1970); see also Hall and Smith, "Franchising Under The Tax Reform Act," 4 Ind. Legal Forum 305 (1970).

[33]  See Chapter 21F, supra.

asset where one doesn't exist, creating a sale or exchange where one doesn't exist, or creating both where neither exists. However, Section 1231 does not create any *long-term* consequences; only assets held for more than one year qualify for its reclassification.[1] Section 1231 is complicated; after all, it is a part of the Internal Revenue Code. The function of Section 1231 is exclusively characterization. Although Section 1231 is complicated, it really is not as difficult as it first appears, or at least it may come to seem that way because of its taxpayer orientation.

Generally, Section 1231 provides that, if during the taxable year, the gains on the disposition of certain types of property exceed the losses on the disposition of the same types of property, all the gains and losses are treated as long-term capital gains and long-term capital losses, respectively.[2] Conversely, if the losses on the disposition of these properties equal or exceed the gains, all the gains and losses are treated as ordinary.[3] Although there is a temptation to net the gains and losses under Section 1231(a), such netting is not provided by the statute and it is inappropriate because, if there is a net capital gain, the gains and losses will need to be separately classified under Section 1(h).[4] Netting would not be inappropriate in a net loss situation because the loss is ordinary for computational purposes.

*The Section 1231 Main Hotchpot.* Section 1231 applies to (grabs for the hotchpot) any recognized gain or loss from the *sale or exchange* of depreciable business property held for more than one year and real property used in business[5] which had been held for more than one year. It also applies to any recognized gain or loss from the *compulsory or involuntary conversion*[6] of any depreciable business property or real property held for more than one year and of any capital asset held for more than one year, if the asset is held in connection with a trade or business or a transaction entered into for profit. Thus Section 1231 is applicable only to property connected with a trade or business or a profit-seeking activity.[7] This combination of transactions is brought together in the Section 1231 hotchpot, and gains in the hotchpot are compared with

---

[1] I.R.C. § 1231(a)(3)(A)(ii)(II), (a)(4)(B)(ii), (a)(4)(C)(ii), (b)(1), (b)(3)(B). Cf. I.R.C. § 1231(b)(3)(A).

[2] I.R.C. § 1231(a)(1).

[3] I.R.C. § 1231(a)(2).

[4] See Chapter 21B and C, supra. The statute precludes any such netting because it also can make a difference in the computation of gross income.

[5] I.R.C. § 1231(b) contains a definition of the term "property used in the trade or business," which is not simply descriptive. See also the Wasnok v. Commissioner case which follows this Note.

[6] The statute expressly contemplates that compulsory or involuntary conversion can result from destruction in whole or in part, theft or seizure, or an exercise of the power of requisition or condemnation or the threat or imminence thereof. I.R.C. § 1231(a)(3)(A)(ii).

[7] Prior to the 1984 Act, I.R.C. § 1231 also applied to compulsory or involuntary conversions of "personal" capital assets, i.e., assets unrelated to any profit-seeking activity. Those assets which were removed from § 1231 now may be within § 165(h)(2), still another subhotchpot that now characterizes some so-called personal casualty gains and losses. See Chapter 23C, infra.

losses in the hotchpot. If the gains exceed the losses, then *all* the gains and losses are treated as long-term capital gains and losses.[8] If the losses exceed the gains then *all* the gains and losses are characterized as ordinary gains and losses.[9]

Historically Section 1231 has been a pro-taxpayer section. Without its hotchpot principles, almost all the items[10] affected by it would lack either capital asset[11] or sale or exchange attributes.[12] Thus, generally, all the gains and losses would be ordinary gains and losses. Fortunately for the taxpayer, this (ordinary) treatment applies if Section 1231 losses exceed gains. But if gains exceed losses, Section 1231 comes to the taxpayer's aid and characterizes all such gains and losses as long-term capital gains and losses, except to the extent that subsection (c) applies. With the current 37 percent highest tax rate for ordinary income,[13] and the generally applicable 15, 20, or 25 percent tax rates for net capital gains[14] there is potentially substantial preferential treatment for such net capital gains. Additionally, in some circumstances Section 1231 may act in an another way to a taxpayer's benefit. If apart from any section 1231 items, a taxpayer has net capital losses that may not be deductible in the current year for lack of capital gains[15] the characterization of Section 1231 gain in excess of loss as long-term capital gain and loss will generate net capital gain[16] against which the losses may be used. In other words, the device may increase the deductibility of non-Section 1231 net capital losses in the current year.[17] Thus, Section 1231 remains a pro-taxpayer provision.

*The Section 1231(a)(4)(C) Subhotchpot.* There are two special rules that cut across the otherwise simple Section 1231 process. The first is a pro-taxpayer exception to the "main" hotchpot rule considered above. It creates a "subhotchpot" rule that must be applied prior to consideration of main hotchpot consequences. Section 1231(a)(4)(C) provides that,

---

[8]  I.R.C. § 1231(a)(1). See note 4, supra.

[9]  I.R.C. § 1231(a)(2). See note 4, supra.

[10]  A compulsory conversion of a capital asset would lack neither sale or exchange nor capital asset status.

[11]  See I.R.C. § 1221(a)(2).

[12]  See Chapter 21E, supra.

[13]  I.R.C. § 1(j)(2)(A)–(E), (3)(B).

[14]  I.R.C. § 1(h). See Chapter 21B, supra. Note that all capital gains and losses emerging from I.R.C. § 1231 will need to be separately classified for purposes of § 1(h).

[15]  I.R.C. § 1211(b).

[16]  I.R.C. § 1222(11).

[17]  For example, assume a taxpayer had $50,000 of taxable income and, in addition, $3,000 of capital gain and $10,000 of capital loss and $4,000 of I.R.C. § 1231 gain. Without § 1231, the $4,000 of § 1231 gain would be ordinary income and § 1211(b) would limit the deductibility of capital losses to $6,000 ($3,000 capital gain plus $3,000) with a $4,000 § 1212(b) loss carryover. Thus the current year's taxable income would be $51,000 ($50,000 plus $4,000 less the § 1211(b) excess of $3,000). With the assistance of § 1231 (assuming § 1231(c) is inapplicable), the $4,000 of § 1231 gain becomes capital gain resulting in a total of $7,000 of capital gain. Under § 1211(b) there would be full deductibility of the losses in the current year (loss would be deductible to the extent of gain plus $3,000) and no carryovers. Thus taxpayer would have only $47,000 of current taxable income ($50,000 less the § 1211(b) excess of $3,000) and no carryovers.

before any gains and losses from *involuntary* conversions (from fire, storm, etc. or from theft) are to be included in the main hotchpot, gains from such conversions must equal or exceed losses from such conversions. Consequently, a taxpayer first compares allowable involuntary casualty gains and losses from trade or business or profit seeking assets. If gains exceed losses, then all these gains and losses are routed into the main hotchpot. If losses in the subhotchpot exceed gains, then Section 1231 does not apply to any of such gains or losses; they all remain ordinary gains and losses, never entering the main hotchpot. Preservation of the *ordinary* character of this net amount of loss in the subhotchpot is to the taxpayer's advantage. Why?

*The Section 1231(c) Lookback Recapture Rule.* Other than on compulsory or involuntary conversions, taxpayers could maximize the benefits of the Section 1231 main hotchpot by timing all losses to fall in one year and all gains in another year thereby characterizing all gains as long-term capital gains and all losses as ordinary losses. Seemingly to preclude such use of Section 1231, Congress enacted a second special rule which imposes a limitation upon the benefits of the Section 1231 main hotchpot rule. Section 1231(c) establishes a "lookback rule" which, if applicable, overrides the main hotchpot rule and recharacterizes some or all of a main hotchpot *net* gain for the current year from long-term capital gain to ordinary income. The rule requires such a recharacterization to the extent that there are unrecaptured Section 1231 main hotchpot net losses for any of the preceding five years. Such losses are the sum of net losses established by the main hotchpot over the prior five years which have not been offset as ordinary income by subsequent net main hotchpot gains.[18] Hence, if in year 3, the current year, there is a Section 1231 main hotchpot net gain of $10,000, but in years 1 and 2, there were Section 1231 main hotchpot net losses of $5,000 and $3,000, respectively, the recharacterization rule requires $8,000 of the year 3 net gain to be characterized as ordinary income, and only the remaining $2,000 gain will retain its Section 1231 long-term capital gain character.

If there are several Section 1231 gains arising in the current year from different types of property (collectibles, depreciable real estate, non depreciable real estate), how is one to determine which gains are converted to ordinary income? Congress has not provided an answer in the statute, instead deferring to the Treasury to resolve the issue in regulations.[19] Although regulations have not been promulgated, the Treasury has announced that it will solve this riddle in a pro-taxpayer manner, by first converting 28 percent gains to ordinary income and then

---

[18] The legislative history indicates the losses are recaptured in the chronological order in which they arose (i.e. first in, first out). Conf.Rep. No. 98–861, 98th Cong., 2d Sess. 1034 (1984).

The lookback recapture rule is discussed in Cash, "The Erosion of Section 1231," 62 Taxes 789 (1984).

[19] I.R.C. § 1(h)(8).

converting other gains working the way down the Section 1(h) rate schedule.[20]

# Wasnok v. Commissioner

Tax Court of the United States, 1971.
30 T.C.M. 39.

■ SACKS, COMMISSIONER:

Respondent determined deficiencies in the income tax of petitioners for the taxable years and in the amounts set forth below:

| Petitioner | Taxable Year | Amount |
|---|---|---|
| Stephen P. Wasnok ..................................... | 1967 | $195.70 |
| Mary Alice Wasnok ..................................... | 1967 | 158.66 |
| Stephen P. and Mary Alice Wasnok........... | 1968 | 54.46 |

The sole issue for decision is whether petitioners' disposition of certain real property at a loss constitutes an ordinary loss fully deductible in 1965, the year in which the loss was sustained, or a capital loss, deductible as a loss carryover in 1967 and 1968.

Findings of Fact

Most of the facts have been stipulated by the parties. Their stipulation, together with attached exhibits, is incorporated herein by this reference.

Stephen P. and Mary Alice Wasnok, sometimes hereinafter referred to as petitioners or as Stephen and Mary, are husband and wife who resided in Fullerton, California at the time of the filing of their petition herein. Their separate income tax returns for the taxable year 1967 and their joint income tax return for the taxable year 1968 were filed with the district director of internal revenue, Los Angeles, California.

In 1960 petitioners were residing in Cincinnati, Ohio. Sometime during that year they purchased a home there located at 5654 Sagecrest Drive, hereinafter referred to as the Sagecrest property. A substantial portion of the purchase price of this property was borrowed on a promissory note secured by a first mortgage on the property from Spring Grove Avenue Loan and Deposit Company (hereinafter referred to as Spring Grove Loan Co.).

Early in 1961 petitioners decided to move to California. They listed the Sagecrest property with its builder for sale, but without result since the market at the time was extremely poor. Finally, on June 15, 1961

---

[20] Notice 97–59, 1997–2 C.B. 309. The result is consistent with the other netting results reached by Congress in the Internal Revenue Service Restructuring and Reform Act of 1998. See I.R.C. § 1(h).

petitioners leased the property for a monthly rental of $225.00 and thereafter departed for California.

Between June 15, 1961 and May 7, 1965 petitioners leased the Sagecrest property to various tenants at an average rental of $200.00 per month. Such tenants were located by advertising the property for rent in Cincinnati newspapers and by referrals from former neighbors. During this period petitioners on two occasions listed the property for sale with brokers, in each case, however, for only a ninety day period of time. Neither listing generated an offer for more than the amount due on the mortgage.

By 1965 petitioners found themselves unable to continue payments due on their note on the Sagecrest property to Spring Grove Loan Co. Spring Grove thereafter notified petitioners that they would either have to deed the property back or the company would have to institute foreclosure proceedings. On May 7, 1965 petitioners executed a deed conveying their interest in the Sagecrest property to Spring Grove Loan Co. in satisfaction of the then balance due on their note in the amount of $24,421.04.

For the taxable years 1961 through 1964 petitioners filed federal income tax returns reporting thereon rental income and claiming various expenses, including depreciation, on the Sagecrest property. Their return for 1961 was examined by the Internal Revenue Service and the cost basis of the land and improvements was agreed upon in the amount of $32,729.70. Total depreciation on the improvements claimed and allowed for the taxable years 1961 through 1964 was $4,697.42.

Petitioners did not file federal income tax returns for the taxable years 1965 and 1966 on the premise that no returns were required because no tax appeared to be due.

For 1965, however, petitioners had gross income in the amount of $5,603.21 and for 1966, in the amount of $3,180.00.

On their separate returns for the taxable year 1967, petitioners for the first time each claimed a capital loss carry-forward deduction in the amount of $1,000.00 which was predicated upon their disposition in 1965 of the Sagecrest property to Spring Grove Loan Co. Thereafter, on their joint return for 1968, petitioners claimed a further capital loss carry-forward deduction of $389.00, computed as follows:

| | |
|---|---:|
| Cost of Sagecrest property | $32,729.70 |
| Less: depreciation taken | 4,697.42 |
| Adjusted basis | $28,032.28 |
| Sale on May 7, 1965 | 24,421.04 |
| Capital Loss | $ 3,611.24 |
| Claimed in 1967 (separate return) | 2,000.00 |

| | |
|---|---|
| Sub-total | 1,611.24 |
| Claimed in 1968 | $    389.00[1] |
| Balance to carry-over | $ 1,222.24 |

In his notices of deficiency, respondent disallowed to petitioners the claimed capital loss carry-over deductions for the taxable years 1967 and 1968 on the ground that the loss involved was an ordinary loss deductible in the year sustained (1965) rather than a capital loss subject to the carry-over provisions of the Internal Revenue Code of 1954.

Petitioners' disposition of the Sagecrest property at a loss constitutes an ordinary loss fully deductible in 1965, the year in which the loss was sustained and not a capital loss.

Opinion

It is petitioners' position herein that the Sagecrest property was a capital asset in their hands, and that its disposition at a loss resulted in a capital loss which they properly deferred deducting on their returns until 1967 and 1968 when they had sufficient income to file returns.

Respondent contends that the property in question was not a capital asset in petitioners' hands, but an asset of the type described in section 1231 of the Code[2] losses upon the disposition of which are ordinary in nature and required to be deducted, to the extent that there is gross income, in the year in which sustained. Since petitioners' gross income in 1965 was more than sufficient to absorb the loss in that year, no deduction of any kind is allowable in the years here at issue.

Section 1221 of the Code defines the term "capital asset" as any property held by the taxpayer, *excluding however,* "property used in his trade or business, of a character which is subject to the allowance for depreciation * * * or real property used in his trade or business." With respect to "property used in the trade or business" of a taxpayer, section 1231 provides that while net gains on sales or exchanges of such property shall be treated as capital gains, net losses are not to be treated as *capital* losses, but as *ordinary* losses.

The evidence presented to the Court is not complex. Simply stated, it shows that when petitioners moved from Ohio to California in 1961 they could not sell their residence in Ohio and therefore rented it to various tenants until May, 1965, when it was deeded back to the mortgagee because petitioners could no longer make the mortgage payments and did not desire the mortgagee to foreclose. It further shows that during the period 1961 through 1964 petitioners received rents of about two hundred dollars per month except for brief periods when the property was vacant. Their return for 1961 was examined by respondent

---

[1]   The amount necessary to balance income with itemized deductions and exemptions for 1968.

[2]   [I.R.C. § 1231 is omitted. Ed.]

and the tax basis for the property agreed upon. Depreciation was claimed on the improvements during the period 1961 to 1964 and, after reducing basis by the amount of depreciation claimed, the difference between the adjusted basis and mortgage balance produced a loss of $3,611.24.

In our view petitioners' activity in renting out the Sagecrest property for a fairly continuous period of four years between 1961 and 1965, at a substantial rental, together with the concurrent claiming on their income tax returns for these years of the expenses incurred in such rental activity, including depreciation, establishes the use of such property in a "trade or business." Leland Hazard, 7 T.C. 372 (1946).

We therefore find that the property in question was not a capital asset in petitioners' hands at the time of its disposition, but an asset of the kind described in section 1231. The loss sustained on the disposition of such an asset is an ordinary loss. Since such loss was sustained in 1965, when petitioners had gross income sufficient to entirely absorb it, no loss is allowable to petitioners in either 1967 or 1968.

Reviewed and adopted as the report of the Small Tax Case Division.

Decision will be entered for respondent.

## NOTE

Wasnok v. Commissioner is merely a current reaffirmation of a principle initially announced by the Tax Court in Leland Hazard,[1] one of the "name" cases in this area. Whether it is a sound principle may be judged in part against the competing view of the Second Circuit, expressed as follows in Grier v. U.S.,[2] another well-known case:

In this case [quite similar to *Wasnok*, Ed.] the activities with relation to this single dwelling, although of long duration, were minimal in nature. Activity to rent and re-rent was not required. No employees were regularly engaged for maintenance or repair.

Lacking the broader activities stressed in [cases other than *Hazard* which reached the "business" result, Ed.], the real estate in this case appears to partake more of the nature of property held for investment than property used in a trade or business. The property in this case, although used for the production of income, shall not be considered as used in the taxpayer's trade or business.

Attention should be called as well to Section 62(a)(4) permitting an allowance in the determination of adjusted gross income of deductions, including losses, attributable to property held for the production of rent, even if such deductions do not come within Section 62(a)(1) as attributable to a trade or business of the taxpayer. Is there at least a negative inference here that not all rental activity constitutes business activity?

---

[1]   7 T.C. 372 (1946), acq., 1946–2 C.B. 3.
[2]   218 F.2d 603 (2d Cir.1955); the quotation is from the opinion of the District Judge, 120 F.Supp. 395 (D.Conn.1954), adopted by the Court of Appeals in a per curiam affirmance.

It would be a good time to reconsider the several classifications of profit-seeking activity as involving the conduct of a "trade or business,"[3] property "held for the production of income,"[4] or a "transaction entered into for profit."[5] For example, under the *Hazard* principle, how would the taxpayer in *Horrmann*[6] have fared if he had been successful in attempts to rent the property in question?

# Williams v. McGowan

United States Court of Appeals, Second Circuit, 1945.
152 F.2d 570.

■ L. HAND, CIRCUIT JUDGE.

This is an appeal from a judgment dismissing the complaint in an action by a taxpayer to recover income taxes paid for the year 1940. [After holding that attorneys' fees incurred in obtaining an income tax refund were deductible under an earlier version of Section 212, the opinion moved to a second issue. Ed.]

Williams, the taxpayer, and one, Reynolds, had for many years been engaged in the hardware business in the City of Corning, New York. On the 20th of January, 1926, they formed a partnership, of which Williams was entitled to two-thirds of the profits, and Reynolds, one-third. They agreed that on February 1, 1925, the capital invested in the business had been $118,082.05, of which Reynolds had a credit of $29,029.03, and Williams, the balance—$89,053.02. At the end of every business year, on February 1st, Reynolds was to pay to Williams, interest upon the amount of the difference between his share of the capital and one-third of the total as shown by the inventory; and upon withdrawal of one party the other was to have the privilege of buying the other's interest as it appeared on the books. The business was carried on through the firm's fiscal year, ending January 31, 1940, in accordance with this agreement, and thereafter until Reynolds' death on July 18th of that year. Williams settled with Reynolds' executrix on September 6th in an agreement by which he promised to pay her $12,187.90, and to assume all liabilities of the business; and he did pay her $2,187.98 in cash at once, and $10,000 on the 10th of the following October. On September 17th of the same year, Williams sold the business as a whole to the Corning Building Company for $63,926.28—its agreed value as of February 1, 1940—"plus an amount to be computed by multiplying the gross sales of the business from the first day of February, 1940 to the 28th day of September, 1940," by an agreed fraction. This value was made up of cash of about $8100, receivables of about $7,000, fixtures of about $800, and a merchandise inventory of about $49,000, less some $1,000 for bills payable. To this was

---

3    See, e.g., Imbesi v. Commissioner, 361 F.2d 640 (3d Cir.1966).
4    See, e.g., Bowers v. Lumpkin, supra, at page 437.
5    See, e.g., Horrmann v. Commissioner, supra, at page 455.
6    Supra note 5.

added about $6,000 credited to Williams for profits under the language just quoted, making a total of nearly $70,000. Upon this sale Williams suffered a loss upon his original two-thirds of the business, but he made a small gain upon the one-third which he had bought from Reynolds' executrix; and in his income tax return he entered both as items of "ordinary income," and not as transactions in "capital assets." This the Commissioner disallowed and recomputed the tax accordingly; Williams paid the deficiency and sued to recover it in this action. The only question is whether the business was "capital assets" under § 117(a)(1) of the Internal Revenue Code, 26 U.S.C.A. Int.Rev.Code, § 117(a)(1).

It has been held that a partner's interest in a going firm is for tax purposes to be regarded as a "capital asset." Stilgenbaur v. United States, 9 Cir., 115 F.2d 283; Commissioner v. Shapiro, 6 Cir., 125 F.2d 532, 144 A.L.R. 349. We too accepted the doctrine in McClellan v. Commissioner, 2 Cir., 117 F.2d 988, although we had held the opposite in Helvering v. Smith, 2 Cir., 90 F.2d 590, 591, where the partnership articles had provided that a retiring partner should receive as his share only his percentage of the sums "actually collected" and "of all earnings * * * for services performed." Such a payment, we thought, was income; and we expressly repudiated the notion that the Uniform Partnership Act had, generally speaking, changed the firm into a juristic entity. See also Doyle v. Commissioner, 4 Cir., 102 F.2d 86. If a partner's interest in a going firm is "capital assets" perhaps a dead partner's interest is the same. New York Partnership Law §§ 61, 62(4), Consol.Laws N.Y. c. 39. We need not say. When Williams bought out Reynolds' interest, he became the sole owner of the business, the firm had ended upon any theory, and the situation for tax purposes was no other than if Reynolds had never been a partner at all, except that to the extent of one-third of the "amount realized" on Williams' sale to the Corning Company, his "basis" was different. The judge thought that, because upon that sale both parties fixed the price at the liquidation value of the business while Reynolds was alive, "plus" its estimated earnings thereafter, it was as though Williams had sold his interest in the firm during its existence. But the method by which the parties agreed upon the price was irrelevant to the computation of Williams' income. The Treasury, if that served its interest, need not heed any fiction which the parties found it convenient to adopt; nor need Williams do the same in his dealings with the Treasury. We have to decide only whether upon the sale of a going business it is to be comminuted into its fragments, and these are to be separately matched against the definition in § 117(a)(1), or whether the whole business is to be treated as if it were a single piece of property.

Our law has been sparing in the creation of juristic entities; it has never, for example, taken over the Roman "universitas facti";[1] and indeed

---

[1] "By universitas facti is meant a number of things of the same kind which are regarded as a whole; e.g. a herd, a stock of wares." Mackeldey, Roman Law § 162.

for many years it fumbled uncertainly with the concept of a corporation.[2] One might have supposed that partnership would have been an especially promising field in which to raise up an entity, particularly since merchants have always kept their accounts upon that basis. Yet there too our law resisted at the price of great and continuing confusion; and, even when it might be thought that a statute admitted, if it did not demand, recognition of the firm as an entity, the old concepts prevailed. Francis v. McNeal, 228 U.S. 695, 33 S.Ct. 701. And so, even though we might agree that under the influence of the Uniform Partnership Act a partner's interest in the firm should be treated as indivisible, and for that reason a "capital asset" within § 117(a)(1), we should be chary about extending further so exotic a jural concept. Be that as it may, in this instance the section itself furnishes the answer. It starts in the broadest way by declaring that all "property" is "capital assets," and then makes three exceptions. The first is "stock in trade * * * or other property of a kind which would properly be included in the inventory"; next comes "property held * * * primarily for sale to customers"; and finally, property "used in the trade or business of a character which is subject to * * * allowance for depreciation." In the face of this language, although it may be true that a "stock in trade," taken by itself, should be treated as a "universitas facti," by no possibility can a whole business be so treated; and the same is true as to any property within the other exceptions. Congress plainly did mean to comminute the elements of a business; plainly it did not regard the whole as "capital assets."

As has already appeared, Williams transferred to the Corning Company "cash," "receivables," "fixtures" and a "merchandise inventory." "Fixtures" are not capital because they are subject to a depreciation allowance; the inventory, as we have just seen, is expressly excluded. So far as appears, no allowance was made for "good-will"; but, even if there had been, we held in Haberle Crystal Springs Brewing Company v. Clarke, Collector, 2 Cir., 30 F.2d 219, that "good-will" was a depreciable intangible. It is true that the Supreme Court reversed that judgment— 280 U.S. 384, 50 S.Ct. 155—but it based its decision only upon the fact that there could be no allowance for the depreciation of "good-will" in a brewery, a business condemned by the Eighteenth Amendment. There can of course be no gain or loss in the transfer of cash; and, although Williams does appear to have made a gain of $1072.71 upon the "receivables," the point has not been argued that they are not subject to a depreciation allowance. That we leave open for decision by the district court, if the parties cannot agree. The gain or loss upon every other item should be computed as an item in ordinary income.

Judgment reversed.

---

[2] "To the 'church' modern law owes its conception of a juristic person, and the clear line that it draws between 'the corporation aggregate' and the sum of its members." Pollack & Maitland, Vol. 1, p. 489.

■ FRANK, CIRCUIT JUDGE (dissenting in part).

I agree that it is irrelevant that the business was once owned by a partnership. For when the sale to the Corning Company occurred, the partnership was dead, had become merely a memory, a ghost. To say that the sale was of the partnership's assets would, then, be to indulge in animism.

But I do not agree that we should ignore what the parties to the sale, Williams and the Corning Company, actually did. They did not arrange for a transfer to the buyer, as if in separate bundles, of the several ingredients of the business. They contracted for the sale of the entire business as a going concern. Here is what they said in their agreement: "The party of the first part agrees to sell and the party of the second part agrees to buy, *all of the right, title and interest* of the said party of the first part *in and to the hardware business* now being conducted by the said party of the first part, *including* cash on hand and on deposit in the First National Bank & Trust Company of Corning in the A.F. Williams Hardware Store account, in accounts receivable, bills receivable, notes receivable, merchandise and fixtures, including two G.M. trucks, good will and all other assets of every kind and description used in and about said business.[1] * * * Said party of the first part agrees not to engage in the hardware business within a radius of twenty-five miles from the City of Corning, New York, for a period of ten years from the 1st day of October 1940."

To carve up this transaction into distinct sales—of cash, receivables, fixtures, trucks, merchandise, and good will—is to do violence to the realities. I do not think Congress intended any such artificial result. * * *

## PROBLEMS

1. Hotchpot engaged in (or encountered) the following transactions (or events) in the current year. Determine separately for each part (a) through (i) how the matters indicated will be characterized for the current year, assuming in all parts other than (g)–(i) that § 1231(c) is inapplicable.

(a) Hotchpot sells some land used in his business for four years for $20,000. It had cost him $10,000. He also receives $16,000 when the State condemns some other land that he had purchased for $18,000 three years ago which he has leased to a third person.

(b) Same as (a), above, except that both pieces of land were inherited from Hotchpot's Uncle who died three months before the dispositions. At Uncle's death, the business land was worth $16,000 and the leased land was worth $18,000.

(c) Hotchpot sells a building used for several years in his business, which he depreciated under the straight-line method. The sale price is $15,000 and the adjusted basis $5,000. His two year

---

[1] Emphasis added.

old car, used exclusively in business, is totally destroyed in a fire. The car had a $6,000 adjusted basis but was worth $8,000 prior to the fire. He received $4,000 in insurance proceeds.

(d) In addition to the building and the car in (c), above, assume that Hotchpot had a painting that he had purchased two years ago which was held in connection with his business and which was also destroyed in the fire. The painting had been purchased for $4,000 and he received $8,000 in insurance proceeds.

(e) In addition to the building sale, car loss, and painting gain in (c) and (d), above, assume Hotchpot sells land used for several years in his business for $30,000. The land, which he had hoped contained oil, had been purchased for $50,000.

(f) Would Hotchpot be pleased if the Commissioner successfully alleged that the land in problem (e), above, was held as an investment rather than for use in Hotchpot's business?

(g) What result under the facts of (d), above (building gain, car loss, and painting gain), if four years before the fire Hotchpot had had a $5,000 net § 1231 loss and three years before a $3,000 net § 1231 loss, and he had had no other § 1231 transactions in other years.

(h) Same as (g), above, except that in addition two years before the tax year Hotchpot had a $6,000 net § 1231 loss.

(i) Same as (h), above, except that one year before the tax year Hotchpot had had a $10,000 net § 1231 gain.

**2.** Car Dealer uses some cars for demonstration purposes. Are the cars depreciable? Disregarding § 1245 if they are held long-term does gain on their sale qualify for § 1231(a) main hotchpot treatment? See Rev.Rul. 75–538, 1975–2 C.B. 34.

**3.** Merchant who has been in business for four years sells her sole proprietorship consisting of the following assets, all of which, except for the inventory, have been held for more than one year.

|  | Adjusted Basis | Fair Market Value |
|---|---|---|
| Inventory | $ 8,000 | $ 16,000 |
| Goodwill (generated by Merchant) | 0 | 20,000 |
| Land (used in business) | 30,000 | 20,000 |
| Building (used in business) | 35,000 | 50,000 |
| Machinery & Equipment (used in business) | 12,000 | 14,000 |
| Total | $85,000 | $120,000 |

Merchant also agrees, for an additional $20,000, that she will not compete in the same geographical area during the succeeding ten years.

(a)  Disregarding any consideration of §§ 1245 and 1250, which are considered in the succeeding subchapters of the text, what are the tax consequences to Merchant on her sale of the Business for $140,000?

(b)  What difference in result if Merchant's business has always been incorporated, she is the sole shareholder, and she has a $90,000 basis in the stock which she sells for $120,000, assuming that she is again paid an additional $20,000 for her covenant not to compete?

# CHAPTER 22

# CHARACTERIZATION ON THE SALE OF DEPRECIABLE PROPERTY

## A. INTRODUCTION

This chapter involves the characterization of gain or loss on the sale of depreciable property. Several chapters ago,[1] we dealt with the computation of depreciation deductions of both personal and real property. Such deductions are characterized as ordinary deductions, in part, because they lack the necessary sale or exchange that is a requirement for capital gain or loss characterization.[2] In addition, the basis of depreciable property is adjusted (downward) to reflect depreciation deductions "allowed or allowable."[3]

When depreciable property is subsequently sold at either a gain or a loss, the characterization picture is more complicated. If the depreciable property is used in a trade or business, it is not a capital asset.[4] As seen at the end of Chapter 21, Section 1231 may intervene (generally in a friendly manner) to recharacterize such gain or loss as long-term capital gain or loss.[5] Even if the gain on depreciable property is potentially long-term capital gain, such characterization may be overridden by a series of recapture provisions which convert the gain in whole or in part to ordinary income[6] and any remaining long-term capital gain will be further classified under Section 1(h) to determine the rate of the tax on such gain.[7] The various recapture provisions are explored in this Chapter.

## B. CHARACTERIZATION UNDER SECTION 1239

Internal Revenue Code: Sections 267(b)(3), (10), (11) and (12) and (c); 318(a)(3)(B)(i); 1239(a)–(d).

---

[1]  See Chapter 14E, supra.

[2]  Such deductions are also allowed above the line under I.R.C. § 62(a)(1) and (4).

[3]  I.R.C. § 1016(a)(2).

[4]  I.R.C. § 1221(a)(2). But see Grier v. United States, 218 F.2d 603 (2d Cir.1955) discussed at page 757, supra of the Text.

[5]  See Chapter 21H2, supra.

[6]  See Chapter 22B–D, infra.

[7]  See Chapter 21B, supra and Chapter 22C and D, infra.

# United States v. Parker*

United States Court of Appeals, Fifth Circuit, 1967.
376 F.2d 402.

■ GOLDBERG, CIRCUIT JUDGE:

The protesting and unhappy taxpayers, Curtis L. Parker and his wife, Martha, owned a wholesale and retail oil and gasoline business. On April 1, 1959, Parker and B.K. Eaves, a longtime employee, formed a Louisiana corporation incorporating Parker's business. The corporation had an authorized capital stock of 1,000 shares.

Parker subscribed to 800 shares and paid for them by transferring to the corporation certain property valued at $93,400.00 to be used in the corporation's business. Eaves subscribed to the remaining 200 shares. He paid $7,500.00 cash and agreed to pay the balance of $23,350.00 over a period of 5 years.

At the first meeting of the corporation's board of directors a resolution was passed accepting Eaves's subscription. He was issued stock certificates for the amount of stock paid for at that time (64.239 shares), and the board of directors resolved that the remainder of Eaves's stock certificates would be issued as their purchase price was paid. The Articles of Incorporation included a provision stating that none of the stock of the corporation might be transferred unless the stock were first offered to the corporation at the same price offered by the proposed transferee. (If the corporation did not accept the offer, another stockholder could.)

Parker and Eaves also entered into a stockholders' agreement which provided that whenever Eaves's employment should terminate for any reason, including death, his shares would then be purchased by Parker at a price to be governed by the fair market value per share of the corporation's assets, specifically excluding good will "or any other intangible asset." The value per share was set at $116.75 for the first year of the corporation's existence (until April 1, 1960), and thereafter the price was to be set by agreement between Parker and Eaves, with arbitration if they could not agree.

The face of all stock certificates issued to Parker and Eaves carried notice of the restriction on sale created by the Articles of Incorporation. Only the stock certificates issued to Eaves carried a legend that they were subject to the Eaves-Parker buy-and-sell agreement.

Also, at the first meeting of the board of directors, Parker sold to the corporation certain other assets which were depreciable property (such as motor vehicles, furniture and fixtures, and other equipment which Parker had apparently used in the business before the incorporation) worth $95,738.70. The corporation was to pay for this property in ten annual installments with interest of 5 percent. Parker elected to treat

---

*    Some footnotes are omitted, others renumbered. Ed.

the sale as a capital transaction, and reported the gain from it as long term capital gain. I.R.C. § 1231.

The present suit arises because the Internal Revenue Service treated the gain as ordinary income under I.R.C. § 1239, based upon the contention that the taxpayers owned more than 80 percent "in value" of all outstanding stock of the corporation at the time of sale. The Service assessed deficiencies for the calendar years 1959, 1960, and 1961. Taxpayers paid the assessments under protest and sued in district court for a refund. 28 U.S.C.A. § 1346(a). The district court granted summary judgment for the taxpayers, and the government appeals. We reverse.

\* \* \*

[T]he government argues that even if the full 20 percent of the shares allotted to Eaves was "outstanding" at the time of the sale, "the restrictions placed upon those shares and their inherent limitations made them worth less per share than Parker's." We \* \* \* agree.

Section 1239 prevents capital gain treatment of a "sale or exchange" of depreciable property to a controlled corporation or a spouse. Without this section a taxpayer who had property which had been depreciated to a low basis could sell that property to a controlled corporation or spouse and pay only capital gains rates on the gain. The transferee (who is virtually identical to the transferor in the proscribed area) could then redepreciate the property, using the sale price as a new basis. The depreciation, of course, would be deducted from ordinary income.[1] Section 1239 renders such a scheme profitless by taxing the gain on the transfer at ordinary rather than capital rates.

The issue here, of course, is whether Parker's corporation is sufficiently Parker's slave to justify invocation of § 1239. We have concluded that Parker owned, for purposes of § 1239, exactly 80 percent of the corporation's outstanding stock. The decisive question now is whether this 80 percent is, under § 1239, "more than 80 percent *in value* of the outstanding stock." [emphasis added]

We first note what § 1239 does not say. It does not use the standard of § 368(c) which is invoked by § 351 for transfers to a controlled corporation in exchange for that corporation's stock or securities. Control is defined by § 368(c) as

---

[1]    The net effect may be shown graphically in a hypothetical case: R, the transferor, holds property depreciated to a value of $2,000. R sells the property for $6,000 to E, his controlled corporation. R pays a maximum capital gains tax of 25 percent on the $4,000 gain, or a tax of $1,000. E, with a basis of $6,000 on the property takes depreciation deductions from ordinary income. After four or five years of these deductions E has depreciated the property back to the $2,000 basis. (See depreciation guidelines in Rev.Proc. 62–21; rates of depreciation in Rev.Proc. 65–13, Appendix I, Table A.) E has by then deducted $4,000 in depreciation from ordinary income. If E is in the 50 percent bracket, the $4,000 in depreciation deductions has saved him $2,000 in income taxes. R has therefore paid a $1,000 capital gains tax and has saved E $2,000 in income taxes. If R and E are identical (and in cases covered by § 1239 they certainly may be considered so), then R has avoided $2,000 in taxes by paying only $1,000.

"ownership of stock possessing at least 80 percent of the total combined *voting power* of all classes of stock entitled to vote and at least 80 percent of the total *number* of shares of all other classes of stock of the corporation." [emphasis added]

By contrast, § 1239 says "more than 80 percent *in value.*" The words "in value" in § 1239 must have some meaning. Trotz v. Commissioner of Internal Revenue, 10 Cir.1966, 361 F.2d 927, 930. We cannot indulge in statutory interpretation by excision. Statutory explication may be an art, but it must not be artful. Further, we cannot say that by using "in value" Congress intended us to consider only the factors of voting power or number of shares. "If the 80% determination is to be [merely] on the basis of the number of shares outstanding, no reason exists for the use of the words 'in value'" Trotz v. Commissioner of Internal Revenue, supra, 361 F.2d at 930. Or, if number of shares and voting power were the sole indicia, Congress could have limited § 1239 by using terms similar to those which § 351 draws from § 368(c) in an analogous situation within the Code's framework. "In value" is a broader phrase, and we think that it calls for the familiar, though difficult, process of fair market valuation.[2]

> "The value of property is an underlying factor in a great number of income tax cases, particularly in such areas of the law as those involving the receipt of income, the computation of gain or loss, depreciation and depletion." 10 Mertens, Law of Federal Income Taxation § 59.01 (1964 revision). Value is not a strange or alien concept in tax law, and we have held that "There is no distinction, for most purposes * * *, in the meaning of fair market value as used in an estate tax case and one involving income tax." Champion v. Commissioner, 5 Cir.1962, 303 F.2d 887, 892–893.

We next note that in the present case Eaves owned exactly 20 percent of the outstanding stock, and Parker owned exactly 80 percent. Therefore, if any fact can be found which shows that the value per share of Parker's stock exceeded by any amount, no matter how small, the value per share of Eaves's, then Parker owned more than 80 percent in value of the outstanding stock. While it is true that Parker and Eaves owned the same class of stock, Eaves's stock was burdened with impedimenta from which Parker's stock was free. We hold that as a matter of law these impedimenta must have decreased the value per share of Eaves's stock, and as we need only show that this value per share was lower by any

---

[2] The district judge stated his findings of fact and conclusions of law with explicitness. He concluded, as do we, that market valuation was the proper test for § 1239. He found as a matter of law, however, that neither the restrictions on salability of the Eaves stock nor its minority position reduced its value per share, and it is here that we disagree. However, partly because of the peculiar circumstances of this case, but largely because the district judge stated his findings and conclusions so clearly and distinctly and isolated with precision the ground for his holding, we have been able to render unnecessary the remand which would usually be required. Even though we disagree on one point, the opinion of the district judge epitomizes the result sought by Rule 52(a), and thereby promotes the "just, speedy, and inexpensive determination of every action" sought by Rule 1.

indeterminate amount, no matter how miniscule, than the value per share of Parker's stock, we are able to render judgment here without remand.[3]

The impedimenta which depress the value spring from two sources.

A.  *The Restrictions on Transfer of Stock.* Eaves's stock was encumbered by two kinds of restrictions. First, the articles of incorporation stated that the corporation had the right of first refusal of any offer to sell to a third party. Second, Eaves's agreement with Parker stated that if Eaves left the employ of the corporation for any reason, he must sell all of his stock to Parker at a price representing the value per share of the assets, specifically excluding good will. Notice to the world of these restrictions, like the mark of Cain, was on the face of Eaves's stock certificates.

The practical effect of these restrictions was to reduce the number of opportunities for Eaves to sell or give away the stock and to place a limit (the duration of his employment) upon the period when he might hold the stock. "A commodity freely salable is obviously worth more on the market than a precisely similar commodity which cannot be freely sold." Judge Woodbury for the First Circuit in Worcester County Trust Co. v. Commissioner of Internal Revenue, 1 Cir.1943, 134 F.2d 578, 582.

The alienability of Parker's stock was restricted only by the limitation imposed by the articles of incorporation. Whether this limitation, in the light of Parker's complete control, had any real effect on alienability we need not consider, for Eaves's stock was burdened not only by the articles but also by the extra and potent limitation of the buy-sell agreement. Even if we consider the Eaves and Parker stock as identically limited by the articles, Parker's stock was not affected by the buy-sell agreement; Eaves's was. "In our view it must be said that the restriction necessarily has a depressing effect upon the value of the stock in the market." Worcester County Trust Co., supra, 134 F.2d at 582. That such an extra limitation on alienability would depress market value to some greater extent is a well-recognized proposition: * * *.

B.  *The Lack of Control.* Eaves owned only 20 percent of the stock. This left Parker in sole control of the corporation's affairs. Parker could, without Eaves, elect and remove directors and officers, amend the articles, and promulgate by-laws. He could dissolve the corporation. 5 LSA–R.S. § 12:54. With these powers, Parker controlled without possibility of challenge the entire operation from the smallest detail to

---

[3]   In this aspect the present case differs from Trotz v. Commissioner of Internal Revenue, supra. There, the taxpayer Trotz owned 79 percent of the outstanding stock and the lesser shareholder owned 21 percent. The Tenth Circuit remanded the case for a factual determination by the Tax Court of whether any difference between the values per share of the large and small blocks brought Trotz's holding above 80 percent in value. In contrast, in the present case any extra value per share in Parker's stock will bring his holding above 80 percent in value. No determination is needed of how much more per share Parker's stock is worth.

the largest. He exercised so much power that the corporation was his alter ego, or his slave. This is the situation at which § 1239 aims.

Any purchaser of Eaves's stock would not be buying any degree of control over the corporation. The voting power which technically inhered in Eaves's stock was in reality worthless; Parker owned all of the real voting stock.

We hold that this disability which inhered in Eaves's stock reduced its value per share below that of Parker's stock as a matter of law. * * *.

"Even absent any contemplated change in management, control increases the value of an investment by protecting it. The power to change the management, even while unexercised, protects the investor with control against an abrupt change by someone else and against a gradual deterioration of the incumbent management. Therefore, in a sense, controlling shares are inherently worth more than noncontrolling shares for reasons relating solely to investment value. When control is diffused, the same reasoning establishes, to a lesser degree, that shares enabling their holder to participate in control are worth more than those that do not. This is the strongest part of any argument against a broad reading of [Perlman v. Feldmann, 219 F.2d 173 (2d Cir.1955) cert. denied 349 U.S. 952, 75 S.Ct. 880 (1955)]. It is the kernel of truth in the assertion that a premium paid for controlling shares only shows that controlling shares are inherently worth more than minority shares." Andrews, The Stockholder's Right to Equal Opportunity in the Sale of Shares, 78 Harvard L.Rev. 505, 526 (1965).[4]

In the vast majority of cases, courts of appeals have remanded where, as here, the lower courts failed to take into account all of the existing impedimenta on market value. For instance, in Kirby v. Commissioner of Internal Revenue, supra, we said:

"The Board [of Tax Appeals] * * * declined to make any allowance against the value [of the stock] for the burden of the contract under which the stock had been bought and held. The result was neither, a true nor a fair, [sic] determination of value. The finding which mirrors that result cannot stand.

"Therefore * * * we reverse the order of the Board, and remand * * * for a redetermination * * *." 102 F.2d at 118.

We reiterate that in the present case it is sufficient for the rendering of judgment to note that the restriction on Eaves's stock and its minority qualities combine to have some depressing effect, no matter how small, on its value per share. We hold, therefore, that Parker owned more than

---

4  This entire article is concerned with the inherent disparity of value between controlling and non-controlling shares. Professor Andrews proposes a remedy to allow minority shareholders to share in the premium paid for controlling stock, but that remedy is not part of the law of Louisiana; the article's call for a remedy demonstrates how real the problem is.

80 percent in value of the corporation's stock, and that any gain on the sale of the depreciable property was properly taxed at ordinary rates. We render judgment for the government.

Reversed and rendered.

## PROBLEM

1. Depreciator is a shareholder of Redepreciation Corporation and owns 20% of its stock. Depreciator's Spouse owns 10% of the stock and their adult Son owns 10%. The remaining stock is owned by unrelated persons. In the current year Depreciator sells to Redepreciation for $110,000 a building used in Depreciator's business and depreciated on the straight line method with a $40,000 adjusted basis and an $80,000 value and the land underlying it with a $10,000 adjusted basis and $30,000 value, both held by Depreciator for several years. The building will be used in the business of Redepreciation.

(a)   What is the amount and character of the gain on the sale?

(b)   What result if Spouse owns 20% of the stock, Son owns 20%, and the remaining stock is owned by unrelated persons?

(c)   What result if Spouse owns 10% of the stock, Spouse's brother owns 10%, Son owns 20% and the remaining stock is owned by unrelated persons?

(d)   What result in (b), above, if the sale is made by Other Corporation (in which Depreciator owns 100% of the stock) to Redepreciation Corporation?

(e)   What result if the sale is between Depreciator and a trust in which Depreciator's Spouse is the income beneficiary? The trust will rent the property to a third party.

(f)   What result in (e), above, if the property was a vacation residence of Depreciator and spouse and they live in a rental apartment after the sale?

(g)   Do your answers suggest the purpose and scope of § 1239?

## C.  RECAPTURE UNDER SECTION 1245

Internal Revenue Code: Sections 64; 1245(a)(1)–(3), (b)(1) and (2), (c), (d). See Sections 179(d)(10); 1041(b); 1222; 1231.

Regulations: Section 1.1245–1(a)(1), (b), (c)(1), (d), –2(a)(1) through (3)(i) and (7), –6(a).

———————————

Section 1245 (as well as Section 1250) is predominantly a *characterization* provision converting what is possibly capital gain to ordinary income. We learn here also that Sections 1245 and 1250 are not merely characterization provisions. As will be discovered later in Chapter 26, they are also *recognition* sections which sometimes require recognition of a gain that otherwise might not be taxed. Thus, both sections have significance beyond the area of characterization into the area of nonrecognition.

The problem dealt with here comes about as follows: In Sections 167 and 168 Congress has authorized a deduction for depreciation on property used in a trade or business or held for the production of income. Under Section 1016(a)(2), the price paid for such deductions is a reduction of basis. It is a fair price; depreciation deductions are viewed as a tax recovery of cost. If depreciable property is sold at a gain, *quantitatively* the prior depreciation that reduced taxable income is offset at the time of sale by a corresponding increase in the gain on the sale. But Section 1231 enters the picture with respect to property used in a trade or business. If in the year of sale Section 1231 gains exceed such losses, the gain gets capital gains treatment. Gains on property held for the production of income also get capital gain treatment. Whereas the gains are normally *capital gains* the depreciation deductions previously taken reduced *ordinary* income. In this light the come-uppance supposedly fostered by Section 1016 basis adjustments succeeds quantitatively but it has weaknesses *qualitatively*. Historically, and generally currently, a taxpayer would gladly have accepted an *ordinary* deduction now at a cost of a corresponding increase in *capital gain* later. The scope of the problem is enlarged by express congressional approval of accelerated depreciation methods, especially Section 168(k) and the other MACRS rules and so-called bonus depreciation under Section 179. The concept of recapture, the *"Gotcha,"* is the principal congressional answer to this problem. To the extent that the recapture provisions apply they convert what would normally be Section 1231 gain or capital gain to Section 64 ordinary income. The Code sections providing for recapture, the most important of which are Sections 1245 and 1250, are complicated and far from flawless, both from a policy standpoint and with regard to drafting details. The strength of the congressional policy behind the sections is evidenced by the fact that they are made applicable "notwithstanding" any other Code section;[1] they simply override other Code sections, except where the recapture provisions themselves expressly say otherwise.[2]

Section 1245 must of course be carefully examined. Nevertheless, such an examination will be facilitated by a consideration of its scope and purpose as revealed in the legislative history of the section. The Senate Finance Committee Report stated in part:[3]

> In general, the new section provides for the inclusion in gross income (as ordinary income) of the gain from the disposition of certain depreciable property, to the extent of depreciation

---

[1] See I.R.C. §§ 1245(d) and 1250(h).

[2] See I.R.C. §§ 1245(b) and 1250(d).

[3] Sen.Rep. No. 1881, 87th Cong., 2d Sess. (1962), 1962–3 C.B. 703, 984–985. See Schapiro, "Recapture of Depreciation and Section 1245 of the Internal Revenue Code," 72 Yale L.J. 1483 (1963).

deductions taken in periods after December 31, 1961, which are reflected in the adjusted basis of such property.

Section 1245. Gain from Dispositions of Certain Depreciable Property

(a) *General Rule*—Paragraph (1) of section 1245(a) provides the general rule that if "section 1245 property" is disposed of, the amount by which the lower of "recomputed basis" or the amount realized (or the fair market value in transactions in which no amount is realized) exceeds the adjusted basis of the property is to be treated as gain from the sale or exchange of property which is neither a capital asset nor property described in section 1231. [Amendments made by TRA (1976) now substitute "ordinary income," defined in Section 64, for this cumbersome phrase. Ed.] The term "disposed of" includes any transfer or involuntary conversion. * * *

Paragraph (2) of section 1245(a), under the bill as passed by the House, defined "recomputed basis" as the adjusted basis of the property recomputed by adding thereto all adjustments, for taxable years beginning after December 31, 1961, reflected in such adjusted basis on account of deductions for depreciation, or for amortization * * * whether in respect of the same or other property and whether allowed or allowable to the taxpayer or any other person. Your committee amendments provide that such adjustments shall be added thereto for all periods after December 31, 1961. For example, if a taxpayer, who reports his income on the basis of a fiscal year ending November 30, purchases section 1245 property on January 1, 1962, at a cost of $10,000 and the taxpayer takes depreciation deductions of $2,000 (the amount allowable) before making a gift of the property to his son on October 31, 1962, the son's adjusted basis in the property for purposes of determining gain would, under the provisions of sections 1015 (relating to the basis of property acquired by gift) and 1016 (relating to adjustments to basis), be the same as his father's adjusted basis ($8,000) and the recomputed basis of the property in the son's hands would be $10,000 since the $2,000 of depreciation deductions taken by the father are reflected in the son's basis in the property. Thus, if the son later sells the property during a taxable year of the son beginning after December 31, 1962, for $10,000, he would have $2,000 of gain to which section 1245(a) applies. Moreover, if the son himself takes $1,000 in depreciation deductions (the amount allowable) with respect to the property and then sells it for $10,000, he would have $3,000 of gain to which section 1245(a) applies.

While recomputed basis is determined with respect to adjustments to basis for deductions for depreciation (and for amortization * * *) which were either allowed or allowable, if the taxpayer can establish by adequate records or other sufficient evidence that the amount allowed for any taxable year was less than the amount allowable, the amount to be added for such taxable year is the amount allowed. For example, assume that in the year 1967 it becomes necessary to determine the recomputed basis of property, the adjusted basis of which reflects an adjustment of $1,000 with respect to depreciation deductions allowable for the calendar year 1962. If the taxpayer can establish by adequate records or other sufficient evidence that he had been allowed a deduction of only $800 for 1962, then in determining the recomputed basis, the amount added to adjusted basis with respect to the $1,000 adjustment to basis for 1962 will be only $800.

Paragraph (1) of section 1245(a) further provides that gain is to be recognized notwithstanding any other provision of subtitle A of the 1954 Code. Thus, other nonrecognition sections of the code are overridden by the new section. [See Chapter 26, infra. Ed.] * * *

In the case of a disposition of section 1245 property in which an amount is realized (a sale, exchange, or involuntary conversion), the gain to which section 1245(a) applies is the amount by which the amount realized or the recomputed basis, whichever is lower, exceeds the adjusted basis of the property. In the case of any other disposition, the gain to which section 1245(a) applies is the amount by which the fair market value of the property on the date of disposition or its recomputed basis, whichever is lower, exceeds its adjusted basis. [The recapture bite under Section 1245(a) will be easily understood if it is recognized to be the lower of two alternative amounts—viz:

(1)   In case of a sale or exchange or involuntary
      conversion

|  Recomputed Basis    |      |  Amount Realized     |
| :------------------: | :--: | :------------------: |
|  − Adjusted Basis    |  or  |  − Adjusted Basis    |

(2)   In case of other dispositions

|  Recomputed Basis    |      |  Fair Market Value   |
| :------------------: | :--: | :------------------: |
|  − Adjusted Basis    |  or  |  − Adjusted Basis    |

But carefully check these suggestions against the language of the statute. Ed.]

For example, if section 1245 property has an adjusted basis of $2,000 and a recomputed basis of $3,300 and is sold for $2,900, the gain to which section 1245(a) applies is $900 ($2,900 minus $2,000). If the property is sold for $3,700, the gain is

$1,700, of which $1,300 ($3,300 minus $2,000) is gain to which section 1245(a) applies.

\* \* \*

Both the intrinsic nature and the use of property may have a bearing on whether it is subject to Section 1245. Although Congress defines Section 1245 property in Section 1245(a)(3) uncertainties inherent in the definition have been the subject of some of the sharpest criticism leveled at the provision. An aggravation is that Section 1250 property, subject to different recapture rules considered later in this chapter, is defined residually as depreciable realty, other than Section 1245 property.[4] The scope of Section 1245 in this respect is a serious problem for practicing lawyers and accountants.[5] It is not a matter to which law students should address much attention and it is therefore not discussed in detail; but the Senate Finance Committee did state:[6]

> Paragraph (3) of section 1245(a) defines "section 1245 property." Section 1245 property is any property \* \* \* of a type described in subparagraph (A) or (B) of such paragraph (3) which is or has been property of a character subject to the allowance for depreciation provided in section 167. Even though the property may not be subject to the allowance for depreciation in the hands of the taxpayer, such property is nevertheless subject to the provisions of section 1245(a) if the property was subject to the allowance for depreciation in the hands of any prior holder, and if such depreciation is taken into account in determining the adjusted basis of the property in the hands of the taxpayer.
>
> \* \* \* [T]he term "personal property" in subparagraph (A) of section 1245(a)(3) is intended to include not only "tangible personal property" \* \* \* but also intangible personal property.

\* \* \*

Since the enactment of Section 1245, the principal changes made in the section which remain a part of the Code have been to extend it to some additional property. Congress added Subsections 1245(a)(3)(C)–(F) to bring in some other types of property. In addition, Subsection 1245(a)(4) provides special rules for the determination of the recomputed basis of players' contracts for purposes of recapture upon the sale of sports franchises.[7]

---

[4]   I.R.C. § 1250(c).

[5]   See "Depreciation Recapture Revisited: A Critique," 3 Real Property Probate, and Trust Journal, No. 4, Winter (1968).

[6]   Sen.Rep. No. 1881, supra note 3 at 985–986.

[7]   Sales of player contracts were subjected to I.R.C. § 1245 gain prior to T.R.A. 1976. Rev.Rul. 67–380, 1967–2 C.B. 291. The provision has the effect of converting additional gain on the sale of a sports franchise to ordinary income to account for the greater of previously unrecaptured depreciation on player contracts acquired at the time of acquisition of the franchise or on player contracts involved in the transfer itself.

The Section 179 bonus depreciation deduction is treated as an amortization deduction for purposes of Section 1245.[8] Furthermore if Section 179 bonus depreciation is taken on property and prior to the end of the property's recovery period the property's use is changed and it is not used predominantly in one's trade or business, the Section 179 bonus depreciation is recaptured as ordinary income in the year of conversion.[9] Similarly, the Section 197 amortization of intangibles is also a depreciation deduction for purposes of Section 1245.[10]

Section 1245 is not only a characterization provision. It may force a recognition of gain which, without it, would go unrecognized. But this is not the invariable result; there are some limited exceptions to its application found in § 1245(b). Some of the exceptions will be relevant only as subsequent chapters are considered. In explaining § 1245(b) and (d) the Senate Committee Report stated in part:[11]

> Subsection (b) of section 1245 sets forth certain exceptions and limitations to the general rule provided in subsection (a). Paragraph (1) provides that subsection (a) will not apply to a disposition by gift. [See also Section 1041(b)(1). Ed.] Paragraph (2) provides that, except as provided in section 691, subsection (a) will not apply to a transfer at death.

* * *

> (d)  *Application of Section.*—Subsection (d) of section 1245 provides that the section is to apply notwithstanding any other provision of subtitle A of the code. Thus, section 1245 overrides any nonrecognition provision of subtitle A or any "income characterizing" provision. For example, the gain to which section 1245(a) applies might otherwise be considered as gain from the sale or exchange of a capital asset under section 1231, (relating to property used in the trade or business and involuntary conversions). Since section 1245 overrides section 1231, the gain to which section 1245(a) applies will be treated as ordinary income, and only the remaining gain, if any, from the property may be considered as gain from the sale or exchange of a capital asset if section 1231 is applicable. For example, assume that a taxpayer sells for $130 section 1245 property with an adjusted basis of $40 and a recomputed basis of $100. The excess of the recomputed basis over adjusted basis, or $60, will be treated as gain under section 1245(a). The excess of the selling price over recomputed basis, or $30, may be considered under section 1231 as gain from the sale of a capital asset.

---

[8]   I.R.C. § 1245(a)(2)(C).

[9]   I.R.C. § 179(d)(10). Compare Rev.Rul. 69–487 which follows.

[10]  See page 425, supra.

[11]  Sen.Rep. No. 1881, supra note 3 at 986–988 and 989.

# Revenue Ruling 69–487*

1969–2 Cum.Bull. 165.

An individual taxpayer operating a business as a sole proprietorship converted to personal use an automobile that had been used solely for business purposes. At that time, the fair market value of the automobile was substantially higher than its adjusted basis.

*Held*, for the purposes of section 1245 of the Internal Revenue Code of 1954, the conversion to personal use is not a "disposition" of the automobile. Accordingly, there is no gain to be recognized by the taxpayer upon the conversion to personal use. However, the provisions of section 1245 of the Code would apply to any disposition of the automobile by the taxpayer at a later date.

## PROBLEMS

1.  Recap, a calendar year taxpayer, owns a piece of equipment that Recap uses in business. The equipment was purchased in year one for $100,000, and is "5-year property" within the meaning of § 168(c). In year one, Recap deducted 100% of the cost of the property under § 168(k). Assume Recap has no net § 1231 losses in prior years.

  (a)  What result to Recap if Recap sells the equipment to Buyer in year seven for $30,000?

  (b)  What difference in result if Recap had elected out of § 168(k) but elected to use § 179?

  (c)  What result to Recap in (a), above, if Recap had failed to take any depreciation deductions on the equipment? Would Recap be content to let things be or would Recap want to seek a refund based on depreciation allowable for prior years?

  (d)  What results in (a), above, if Recap sells the equipment to Spouse?

  (e)  What result in (a), above, if as a result of a scarcity of equipment Recap is able to sell the equipment to Desperate for $110,000?

  (f)  What result to Recap in (e), above, if in addition Recap sold some land used for storage in Recap's business for $9,000? Recap had owned the land for three years and it had a $20,000 adjusted basis.

  (g)  Same as (f), above, but the sale price of the land is $15,000?

2.  Do you see a significant relationship between § 1245(a)(2) and the transferred basis rules of § 1015 and § 1041(b)(2)? Does the statute sanction assignment of "fruit" in these circumstances?

---

*    See I.R.C. § 179(d)(10) and note 9, supra.

## D. RECAPTURE OF DEPRECIATION ON THE SALE OF DEPRECIABLE REAL PROPERTY

Internal Revenue Code: Sections 1(h)(1), (3), and (6); 1250(a)(1)(A) and (B)(v); (b)(1), (3) and (5); (c); (d)(1) and (2); (g); and (h). See Sections 64; 1222; 1231.

———————

*Recapture Under Section 1250.* Section 1245, dealing mainly with personal property, came into the Code in 1962; but it was not until 1964 that Congress enacted Section 1250 which, with substantial differences, first extended the recapture concept to dispositions of real property. The 1964 Report of the Senate Finance Committee[1] reveals some of the reasons for the delay as well as for the different approach to the realty problem in Section 1250.

\* \* \*

In 1962, Congress did not include real property in the recapture provision applicable to depreciable personal property because it recognized the problem in doing so where there is an appreciable rise in the value of real property attributable to a rise in the general price level over a long period of time. The bill this year takes this factor into account. \* \* \*

\* \* \*

The bill [treats] as ordinary income a certain percentage [generally 100 percent[2]] of what is called "additional" depreciation or the amount of gain realized on the sale of the property, whichever is smaller. Generally, the "additional" depreciation referred to here is that part of the depreciation deductions which exceeds the depreciation deductions allowable under the straight-line method. . . . Thus, they are the excess of any depreciation deductions taken under [any] method of rapid depreciation, over the depreciation which would have been taken under the straight-line method. In the case of property held for 1 year or less, however, the deductions recaptured are to include not only the excess over straight-line depreciation, but rather the entire depreciation deductions taken.

The bill limits the depreciation recapture to the excess over straight-line depreciation because it is believed that only to this extent could the depreciation taken appropriately be considered in excess of the decline in the value of the property which occurs over time. If a gain still occurs, it is believed that this is attributable to a rise in price levels generally rather than to an absence of a decline in the value of the property. The portion

———————

[1]    Sen.Rep. No. 830, 88th Cong., 2d Sess. (1964), 1964–1 (Part 2) C.B. 505, 635–637.

[2]    I.R.C. § 1250(a)(1)(B)(v). But see I.R.C. § 1250(a)(1)(B)(i)–(iv). Ed.

representing the rise in value is comparable to other forms of gains which quite generally are treated as capital gains.

*  *  *

As a result of the Tax Reform Act of 1986, real property placed in service after 1986 qualifies only for straight-line depreciation.[3] This makes Section 1250 pretty much a dead letter with respect to property acquired after 1986 because the amount of "additional depreciation" will generally be zero.[4] But that is not always the case; if such real property is held for a period of one year or less, all depreciation allowed is treated as additional depreciation.[5] In addition, Section 1250 is potentially applicable to real property depreciated under Section 167 using accelerated depreciation.[6] Not much vitality remains in the old workhorse.

*Recapture Under Section 1(h).* The characterization of recapture on depreciable real property and the rates of tax imposed on the sale of such property is a multi-step process. As seen above, under the first step, one determines whether any of the gain is taxed as ordinary income under Section 1250. For depreciable real property which is used in a trade or business,[7] any excess gain over the Section 1250 gain goes into Section 1231, where it is characterized *either* as ordinary income (if Section 1231(a) main hotchpot losses exceed gains or if it is ordinary gain under Section 1231(c)) *or* as long-term capital gain.[8] In most situations the gain will be a long-term capital gain because there is no "additional" depreciation under Section 1250[9] and because Section 1231 does not characterize the gain as ordinary income.[10] However, even if the gain is characterized as long-term capital gain, the characterization process does not end there; the gain first must be netted under Section 1222[11] and if the taxpayer has a Section 1222(11) net capital gain, Section 1(h) comes into play.[12]

Under Section 1(h), the amount of the gain on depreciable real property up to the amount of the depreciation allowed on the property

---

[3]    I.R.C. § 168(b)(3). See Chapter 14E3, supra.

[4]    I.R.C. § 1250(b)(1).

[5]    Id.

[6]    We say potentially applicable because most property would have been held for its full useful life and been fully depreciated in which event, the total accelerated depreciation would not exceed the total straight-line depreciation.

[7]    This would include almost all depreciable real property. See Wasnok v. Commissioner, supra at page 754, supra and the Note following the *Wasnok* case. If the gain does not fall into I.R.C. § 1231, it is a long-term capital gain which is then netted under § 1222 and if there is net capital gain, the gain is still classified under § 1(h), potentially under § 1(h)(1)(E). See Text at notes 10–14, infra.

[8]    See Chapter 21H2, supra.

[9]    I.R.C. § 1250(b)(i).

[10]    Id.

[11]    See Chapter 21B, supra.

[12]    Id.

that is not taxed as ordinary income under Section 1250 or Section 1231[13] is classified as *"unrecaptured Section 1250 gain"* and is generally taxed at a 25 percent rate.[14] Any remaining gain on the depreciable real property is classified as "adjusted net capital gain" generally taxed at a rate of 15 or 20 percent.[15]

Admittedly, there are a lot of complicated hoops to jump through under the above process; but, as a practical matter, when one sells depreciable real property at a gain, the gain generally[16] is taxed at a 25 percent rate to the extent of the depreciation that has been allowed on the property and any excess gain generally is taxed at a 15 or 20 percent rate. For example, assume a taxpayer purchased a depreciable building at a cost of $100,000 and the land underlying it at a cost of $50,000. Over the years the taxpayer was allowed $30,000 of depreciation on the building reducing its adjusted basis to $70,000. If the taxpayer subsequently sells the building for $160,000 and the land for $75,000, the taxpayer would have a $90,000 gain on the building ($160,000 less $70,000) and a $25,000 gain on the land ($75,000 less $50,000). *Generally*, after the application of Sections 1231, 1222, and 1(h), the gains on the building and the land would be treated as long-term capital gains and $30,000 of the $90,000 gain on the building (the amount attributable to the depreciation) would be taxed at a 25 percent rate with the remaining $60,000 of gain on the building and the $25,000 gain on the land generally being taxed at a 15 or 20 percent rate.

Another simplified way of summarizing the recapture of depreciation allowed on depreciable real property as "unrecaptured Section 1250 gain" is to compare it to the recapture of depreciation allowed on personal property under Section 1245.[17] In general, Section 1245 recaptures depreciation allowed on depreciable personal property as *ordinary income*, while Section 1(h) recaptures depreciation allowed on depreciable real property at a *25 percent rate*.

## PROBLEMS

1.  To what extent does § 1250 apply to real property placed in service after 1986?

2.  On January 1 of the year 2003, Owner purchased some commercial real property at a cost of $880,000, of which $780,000 was properly allocable to the building and $100,000 was properly allocable to the land. Owner is a single taxpayer who has $200,000 of ordinary taxable income from services

---

[13]  See notes 7 and 8, supra.

[14]  I.R.C. § 1(h)(6)(A). In limited circumstances, this gain may be taxed at a 10, 12, 22, or 24% rate. See I.R.C. § 1(h)(1)(A) and page 693, supra.

In other circumstances, the gain may disappear in the I.R.C. § 1222(11) net capital gain netting process. See pages 689 and 694, supra.

[15]  I.R.C. § 1(h)(1)(C) and (D). Such gain may be taxed at a zero percent rate. I.R.C. § 1(h)(1)(B). See Chapter 21B, supra.

[16]  See notes 7, 8, 12, and 14, supra.

[17]  See Chapter 22C, supra.

in 2019. Owner sells the property on December 31, 2019 for $1 million, with $890,000 of the purchase price properly allocated to the building and $110,000 properly allocated to the land. Disregard the mid-month convention and assume for depreciation purposes that the property was held for full years in the years 2003 and 2019. Further, assume Owner had no other § 1231 gains or losses in 2019 and no § 1231 losses in prior years.

(a)   What results to Owner on the sale of the property in 2019?

(b)   What results to Owner on the sale in (a), above, if Owner also had a $20,000 long-term capital loss on the sale of stock?

# CHAPTER 23

# DEDUCTIONS AFFECTED BY CHARACTERIZATION PRINCIPLES

## A. BAD DEBTS AND WORTHLESS SECURITIES

Internal Revenue Code: Sections 165(g)(1) and (2); 166(a) through (e); 6511(d)(1). See Sections 111(a); 271(a).

Regulations: Sections 1.165–5(a) through (c); 1.166–1(c), (d)(1), (e)–(g), –2(a) and (b), –5(a)–(b).

---

Reconsider briefly the approach to deductions in general. If a deduction is to be claimed a Code section must specifically provide for it.[1] Even then, it must also be determined whether any other statutory or common law principle disallows or in some manner restricts the deduction.[2] If these hurdles are taken, a question arises whether the deduction can be taken into account in the computation of adjusted gross income.[3] Finally the deduction, like an item of income, must be characterized as capital or ordinary, a process which may affect the other issues raised above.[4] Characterization presents a special problem under the bad debt deduction. As a similar problem arises with respect to the charitable deduction and the deduction for casualty losses to property held for personal use, both are considered in the subsequent parts of this chapter.

### Bugbee v. Commissioner
Tax Court of the United States, 1975.
34 T.C.M. 291.

### Memorandum Findings of Fact and Opinion

■ STERRETT, JUDGE:

The respondent determined a deficiency in petitioner's federal income tax for the taxable year 1966 in the amount of $7,242.68. Other issues having been conceded, the sole remaining issue[1] is whether

---

[1]  Cf. I.R.C. § 63.

[2]  See, e.g., I.R.C. §§ 67(a), (b), and (g), 165(f), 262 through 280H.

[3]  I.R.C. § 62.

[4]  I.R.C. §§ 1221, 1222.

[1]  Petitioner also avers respondent has erred in disallowing a medical expense deduction claimed on the same tax return. However, this disallowance was due solely to the increase in petitioner's adjusted gross income caused by the disallowance of the claimed short-termed

petitioner has established the existence of a debtor-creditor relationship with respect to funds advanced by petitioner to one Paul Billings and thereby validated his claim to a short-term capital loss under sections 166(a) and 166(d), Internal Revenue Code of 1954.[2]

Findings of Fact

Some of the facts have been stipulated and are so found. The stipulation of facts, together with the exhibits attached thereto, are incorporated herein by this reference.

Petitioner, Howard S. Bugbee (hereinafter petitioner), resided in Honolulu, Hawaii at the time of filing his petition herein. Petitioner filed a "married filing separately" federal income tax return for the taxable year 1966 with the district director of internal revenue at Los Angeles, California.

At all relevant times herein, petitioner was president and majority stockholder of Poop Deck, Inc., a California corporation operating a beer parlor in Hermosa Beach, California. The corporation's other shareholders were petitioner's then spouse Nancy Bugbee and William G. Garbade.

Petitioner first met Paul Billings (hereinafter Billings) at his beer parlor in 1957. Their relationship was first that of proprietor and customer. Over a period of time their friendship grew and they talked of business ventures that Billings might pursue. Billings became godfather to one of petitioner's children.

As a result of their conversations petitioner was impressed with Billings' abilities and thought he could turn his ideas into successful business ventures. Based on this impression, petitioner began to advance money to Billings. These advances were first evidenced by informal notes which were periodically consolidated into larger, more formal notes. There were 11 notes in all representing $19,750 advanced by petitioner to Billings.

These notes were all unconditional, unsecured demand notes signed by Billings between September, 1958 and December, 1960, and evidenced money actually received by Billings from petitioner.[3] The notes provided for interest at a rate of at least 6 percent, however no interest was ever

---

capital loss in issue. Petitioner has made no substantive allegations with respect to this disallowance.

[2]   All statutory references are to the Internal Revenue Code of 1954 as amended, unless otherwise indicated.

[3]   A typical note provided as follows: $1,000.00 September 30, 1959 ON DEMAND after date (without grace). I promise to pay to the order of Howard S. Bugbee One Thousand and no/100 * * * Dollars, for value received with interest at Six percent per from This Date until paid, interest payable Quarterly both principal and interest payable in lawful money of the United States.

(signed) Paul Billings
Paul Billings
1402 Strand Hermosa Beach, Calif.
No. ___ Due On Demand.

actually paid. Billings has never repaid any part of the principal represented by these notes, although at trial he acknowledged these advances were still outstanding and evidenced an intention to repay them if possible.

During this period when the advances were made Billings was unemployed and he was basically unemployed between 1960 and 1966. Although petitioner knew Billings was unemployed between 1958 and 1960, petitioner neither investigated nor did he have any personal knowledge of Billings' financial position.

Billings used the funds received from the petitioner to investigate various business ventures, although in fact much of the money was used by Billings for personal living expenses.

Petitioner was aware of Billings' activities with respect to these ventures, but he did not participate in them. Petitioner's then spouse, Nancy Bugbee, was also aware that petitioner had advanced funds to Billings. Some of her personal funds represented the source of some of these advances. In 1966 petitioner and his spouse were divorced. In the interlocutory judgment of divorce entered June 23, 1966, by which the rights of the parties were established, no mention of the funds advanced by Nancy Bugbee was made.

Petitioner expected to be repaid after Billings established one of these ventures, but such repayment was not conditioned on the success of any of these ventures. Through 1967 petitioner had periodic personal contact with Billings and requested repayment of the notes without success.

Petitioner, on his 1966 tax return, reported a "Personal Bad Debt— Paul Billings" and claimed a $19,750 short-term capital loss. This loss was used in its entirety to offset long-term capital gain recognized that year from other sources. Respondent disallowed this loss as follows:

> (b)  It is determined that the bad debt deduction which you claimed on your return resulting from loans to Paul Billings is not allowable under Section 166 of the Internal Revenue Code because it has not been established that a debtor-creditor relationship was intended by the loans, the amount of the loans have not been established and it has not been established that the money loaned was your property.

After the trial respondent filed a Motion for Leave to File Amended Answer to Conform the Pleadings to the Proof, pursuant to Rule 41(b) of the Rules of Practice and Procedure of this Court. In this motion respondent asserted that the testimony presented at trial raised the additional issue of whether the claimed bad debts became worthless in 1966. Respondent also filed an Amendment to Answer in which he requested that his original answer be amended to include the above issue of worthlessness as a ground for denying petitioner's claim.

Petitioner objected to this motion arguing that this issue was not raised at trial. Petitioner also objected on the grounds that this issue was not stated in the "Explanation of Adjustments" in the statutory notice received by the petitioner and that it should not be raised at this time. Petitioner asserted that if properly apprised of this issue, additional evidence with respect to it could have been presented at trial. Respondent's motion was denied by this Court.

In his reply brief, respondent has conceded that the amount of the advances has been established, and that the money advanced was the petitioner's property.

Opinion

The case at bar presents for our determination the sole issue of whether petitioner is entitled to claim a short-term capital loss within the terms of sections 166(a) and 166(d)[4] and the accompanying regulations as a result of Billings' failure to repay the funds he had advanced him. Other requirements of these provisions having been previously disposed of, the only remaining factual issue is whether a debtor-creditor relationship existed between Billings and petitioner at the time these advances were made.

To qualify under section 166 there first must exist a bona fide debt which arises from a debtor-creditor relationship based upon a valid and enforceable obligation to pay a fixed and determinable sum of money. Section 1.166–1(c), Income Tax Regs. "Whether a transfer of money creates a bona fide debt depends upon the existence of an intent by both parties, substantially contemporaneous to the time of such transfer, to establish an enforceable obligation of repayment". Delta Plastics Corp., 54 T.C. 1287, 1291 (1970). This determination then is a question of fact to which the substance and not the form of the relationship between petitioner and Billings must be applied. Delta Plastics Corp., supra.

Looking beyond the formal relationship between the petitioner and Billings, respondent has pointed out several factors that he believes amply illustrate his position. Respondent first argues that in reality these advances represented the money necessary to investigate prospective business ventures in which both men would share in the potential profits and as such do not represent loans.

Petitioner's testimony with respect to this matter is not entirely clear. At one point he stated that, if any of these ventures materialized, he "would be a part of it." Later, he stated that, although he expected to be repaid after one of these ventures was established, these advances were personal loans to Billings and that they were to be repaid from whatever sources Billings might have. Billings' testimony is more direct. He clearly stated that these advances were for his personal business ventures and that petitioner was not involved in them. Billings also acknowledged liability for these advances and evidenced an intention to

---

4    [I.R.C. §§ 166(a) and 166(d) are omitted. Ed.]

repay if possible. There is also no indication in the record of an agreement under which petitioner would be entitled to share in the profits of any of these ventures. We reject this contention of the respondent.

Respondent next argues that bona fide debts never existed since these advances were worthless when made and petitioner did not have a reasonable expectation that they would be repaid. In support respondent points out that during this period Billings was unemployed and had no independent means of support, that the loans were unsecured, that despite the failure of Billings to make interest payments on the first notes additional funds were advanced, that the nature of Billings' proposed ventures was purely speculative, and that petitioner never sought repayment in court.

Respondent does not question the wisdom of these advances. Anyway that determination could only be made with the use of hindsight, which in this instance is not an appropriate tool. As noted earlier our task is to determine the intent of the parties as it existed when the advances were made. Delta Plastics Corp., supra. See Santa Anita Consolidated, Inc., 50 T.C. 536, 554 (1968).

The record in this case does indicate that Billings was in poor financial condition when these advances were made. However this Court has said that this factor does not preclude a finding of the existence of a bona fide debt. Santa Anita Consolidated, Inc., supra, at 553; Richard M. Drachman, 23 T.C. 558 (1954). The use of unsecured notes reflects the nature of the risk involved that petitioner accepted. Any unsecured debt involves some risk, however this factor is not determinative. Santa Anita Consolidated, Inc., supra at 552.

This Court has said, "For the advance to be a loan, it is not necessary that there be an unqualified expectation of repayment." Richard M. Drachman, supra at 562. In the final analysis the repayment of any loan depends on the success of the borrower. "The real differences lie in the debt-creating intention of the parties, and the genuineness of repayment prospects in the light of economic realities", Santa Anita Consolidated, Inc., supra at 552. See also Earle v. W.J. Jones & Son, 200 F.2d 846, 851 (9th Cir.1952).

We have found that petitioner made these advances because he believed Billings could be successful and that he would be subsequently repaid. After a careful review of the record, we believe petitioner's motives were genuine and that they existed throughout the period during which these advances were made.

Respondent maintains that, since Billings was in poor financial condition, in reality any repayment was conditioned on Billings' business success and, since that condition was never fulfilled, there never was an enforceable repayment obligation. For support respondent cites Zimmerman v. United States, 318 F.2d 611 (9th Cir.1963). In that case the taxpayer advanced money to an organization he was initiating.

Repayment was to be made out of the dues collected from the members of this new organization. The organization faltered and the taxpayer was not repaid. The court held that the contingent nature of the repayment obligation alone precluded the finding of a bona fide debt. See also Alexander & Baldwin v. Kanne, 190 F.2d 153, 154 (9th Cir.1951) (repayment " 'only when, if and to the extent that,' after all the indebtedness and liquidation costs of Waterhouse Company had been paid, there remained an excess of assets."); Bercaw v. Commissioner, 165 F.2d 521, 525 (4th Cir.1948), affirming a memorandum decision of this Court (" * * * oral agreement under which petitioner agreed to advance the money necessary to carry on the litigation and the guardian agreed to pay petitioner from any funds recovered * * *.")

The facts in the case at bar do not reveal that any repayments by Billings were conditioned on his ultimate success. Although petitioner expected to be repaid after Billings had established one of his ventures, we have found that petitioner was to be repaid from any assets that Billings might have. Billings himself testified that these advances were personal, unconditional loans for which he was liable.

Respondent finally argues that, since petitioner and Billings were close personal friends, these advances might be classified as gifts. Although the parties were friends, their relationship did not have a long history. There also was no blood relationship, although Billings was named godfather to one of the Bugbee children.

Although the record does not indicate petitioner's financial condition during the period 1958–1960, the divorce decree issued in 1966 only describes assets of moderate value. We do not believe that petitioner's financial condition was such that he could make these advances without expectation of repayment. The facts do not support respondent's contention that these advances were gifts. Commissioner v. Duberstein, 363 U.S. 278, 80 S.Ct. 1190 (1960).

We believe that petitioner has established the existence of a debtor-creditor relationship and that respondent's determination must be denied.

*Decision will be entered under Rule 155.*

## NOTE

The best approach to the bad debt deduction is to raise three questions: (1) Is there a debt? (2) Is it a bad debt? (3) Is it a business bad debt?

The first question, which is raised in the *Bugbee* case, above, is most likely to arise with respect to individuals, although it has a corporate counterpart. There is a presumption that transfers between relatives or close friends do not constitute loans.[1] For example, if F "lends" $1,000 to D, his daughter, this may or may not give rise to a debt, depending upon the

---

[1]  See Jacob Grossman v. Commissioner, 9 B.T.A. 643 (1927); Carolyn C. Marlett v. Commissioner, 35 T.C.M. 456 (1976).

subjective intention of the parties at the time of the "loan" and their ability to overcome the presumption. If there is no intention that the "debt" ever be repaid, that which takes the form of a loan is in fact a gift.[2] Of course, at the outset it makes no difference for income tax purposes, as neither loan nor gift is deductible and neither is income to the recipient. But if a bad debt deduction is later asserted, it cannot be supported unless the original transaction was in fact a loan. The obvious uncertainties inherent in this situation are behind the restrictive treatment accorded nonbusiness debts. When the forerunner of Section 166(d) was enacted in 1942, the committee reports indicated:[3]

> The present law gives the same treatment to bad debts incurred in nonbusiness transactions as it allows to business bad debts. An example of a nonbusiness bad debt would be an unrepaid loan to a friend or relative * * *. This liberal allowance for nonbusiness bad debts has suffered considerable abuse through taxpayers making loans which they do not expect to be repaid. This practice is particularly prevalent in the case of loans to . . . [related. Ed.] persons. The situation has presented serious administrative difficulties because of the requirement of proof.

Secondly, as regards the *bad* debt question, gratuitous forgiveness of a loan generates no deduction. A transaction that starts out as a loan may be converted to a mere non-deductible gift. The deduction arises only when the debt becomes uncollectible, "bad". This concept does not require proof of an unsatisfied judgment. The Regulations[4] indicate the degree of pessimism permitted the taxpayer in a determination that a debt is a bad debt.

Finally, the business or nonbusiness dichotomy of Section 166 must be taken into account. Identify the two ways in which a business debt is or may be accorded different treatment from a nonbusiness debt when uncollectibility looms. The somewhat involved residual definition of a nonbusiness bad debt in Section 166(d)(2)(A) and (B) will be better understood having in mind the following fragment of legislative history:[5]

> If a debt at the time it becomes worthless is not directly related to the taxpayer's trade or business, under present law it is treated as a nonbusiness bad debt. This rule is applied even though the debt was related to the taxpayer's trade or business at the time it was created. For example, a taxpayer is not permitted to treat as a business bad debt, which is fully deductible, an account receivable which proves uncollectible after the taxpayer has gone out of business. [See Section 166(d)(2)(B). Ed.]

> The bill eliminates this harsh treatment by permitting the taxpayer to deduct as a business bad debt an obligation which becomes worthless, whether or not it is directly related to the trade

---

2   See note 1, supra.
3   H.Rep. No. 2333, 77th Cong., 1st Sess. (1942), 1942–2 C.B. 372, 408.
4   Reg. § 1.166–2.
5   Sen.Rep. No. 1622, 83rd Cong., 2d Sess., p. 24 (1954).

or business at that time, if it was a bona fide business asset at the time it was created or acquired. [See Section 166(d)(2)(A). Ed.]

A policy reason for the business-nonbusiness bad debt classifications created by Congress in 1942[6] was "to put nonbusiness investments in the form of loans on a footing with other nonbusiness investments."[7] With this reason in mind, the courts have been strict in interpreting the trade or business requirement.[8]

One problem has been that of loans by a shareholder-employee of a corporation to the corporation. In a leading case, Whipple v. Commissioner,[9] the taxpayer, who had for many years been promoting both corporate and noncorporate businesses, formed a corporation in which he was an 80 percent shareholder and subsequently made loans to it. The corporation failed and he attempted to treat the loans as business bad debts. Unsuccessful in the Tax Court[10] and the Court of Appeals,[11] he finally reached the Supreme Court where he fared no better. A corporation's business is of course not that of its shareholder,[12] and the business classification of the loan therefore depended upon the taxpayer's own business. Working from that premise, the Supreme Court said, in part:[13]

> Petitioner, therefore, must demonstrate that he is engaged in a trade or business, and lying at the heart of his claim is the issue upon which the lower courts have divided and which brought the case here: That where a taxpayer furnishes regular services to one or many corporations, an independent trade or business of the taxpayer has been shown. But against the background of the 1943 amendments and the decisions of this Court in the *Dalton, Burnet, duPont* and *Higgins* cases, petitioner's claim must be rejected.
>
> Devoting one's time and energies to the affairs of a corporation is not of itself, and without more, a trade or business of the person so engaged. Though such activities may produce income, profit or gain in the form of dividends or enhancement in the value of an investment, this return is distinctive to the process of investing and is generated by the successful operation of the corporation's business as distinguished from the trade or business of the

---

[6]  Revenue Act of 1942, § 124(a)(4), 56 Stat. 798, 821 (1942). There is another distinction between business and nonbusiness bad debts. Partially worthless business bad debts are deductible to the extent properly charged off (I.R.C. § 166(a)(2)).

[7]  Putnam v. Commissioner, 352 U.S. 82, 92, 77 S.Ct. 175, 180 (1956). Cf. Bittker and Eustice, Federal Income Taxation of Corporations and Shareholders, ¶ 4.22[4] n.236 (7th Ed. Warren, Gorham & Lamont 2000). For a consideration of the distinction between property held for investment and property used in a trade or business see Chapter 15, supra, at page 436.

[8]  In addition to *Putnam*, supra note 7, see Commissioner v. Smith, 203 F.2d 310 (2d Cir.1953), cert. denied 346 U.S. 816, 74 S.Ct. 27 (1953).

[9]  373 U.S. 193, 83 S.Ct. 1168 (1963).

[10]  Whipple v. Commissioner, 19 T.C.M. 187 (1960).

[11]  Whipple v. Commissioner, 301 F.2d 108 (5th Cir.1962).

[12]  Whipple v. Commissioner, supra note 10 at 192. See Knickerbocker, "What Constitutes a Trade or Business for Bad Debt Purposes: 'Stockholder' as a Business," 23 N.Y.U.Inst. on Fed.Tax. 113 (1965).

[13]  Whipple v. Commissioner, 373 U.S. 193, 201–203, 83 S.Ct. 1168, 1173–1174 (1963). Footnotes omitted.

taxpayer himself. When the only return is that of an investor, the taxpayer has not satisfied his burden of demonstrating that he is engaged in a trade or business since investing is not a trade or business and the return to the taxpayer, though substantially the product of his services, legally arises not from his own trade or business but from that of the corporation. Even if the taxpayer demonstrates an independent trade or business of his own, care must be taken to distinguish bad debt losses arising from his own business and those actually arising from activities peculiar to an investor concerned with, and participating in, the conduct of the corporate business.

If full-time service to one corporation does not alone amount to a trade or business, which it does not, it is difficult to understand how the same service to many corporations would suffice. To be sure, the presence of more than one corporation might lend support to a finding that the taxpayer was engaged in a regular course of promoting corporations for a fee or commission, see Ballantine, Corporations (rev.ed. 1946), 102, or for a profit on their sale, see Giblin v. Commissioner, 227 F.2d 692 (C.A.5th Cir.), but in such cases there is compensation other than the normal investor's return, income received directly for his own services rather than indirectly through the corporate enterprise, and the principles of *Burnet, Dalton, duPont* and *Higgins* are therefore not offended. On the other hand, since the Tax Court found, and the petitioner does not dispute, that there was no intention here of developing the corporations as going businesses for sale to customers in the ordinary course, the case before us inexorably rests upon the claim that one who actively engages in serving his own corporations for the purpose of creating future income through those enterprises is in a trade or business. That argument is untenable in light of *Burnet, Dalton, duPont* and *Higgins,* and we reject it. Absent substantial additional evidence, furnishing management and other services to corporations for a reward not different from that flowing to an investor in those corporations is not a trade or business under § 23(k)(4). We are, therefore, fully in agreement with this aspect of the decision below.

Although the courts have held that loans by shareholder-employees are generally nonbusiness, investment-type loans, in some such circumstances business bad debt deductions have been allowed. A shareholder who is an employee of a corporation is engaged in business as an employee.[14] If such a taxpayer makes a loan to her corporation *to insure her continued employment,* the loan may properly be classified as one arising out of the conduct of her trade or business, that of performing services as an employee. In a leading case[15] adopting this rationale, the taxpayer was required by the majority shareholders of the corporation in which he was a minority shareholder to make loans to the corporation in order to retain his

---

[14]  Cf. I.R.C. § 62(a)(1) and (2).

[15]  Trent v. Commissioner, 291 F.2d 669 (2d Cir.1961).

employment status. He was discharged later upon his refusal to make further loans. When the corporation subsequently failed and the loans become uncollectible, the taxpayer was allowed a business bad debt deduction.[16]

A loan to a corporation by a shareholder-employee, even if not made to preserve one's job, may get business classification if it bears the required proximate relationship to a separate unincorporated business of the taxpayer.[17] In one case,[18] Abe Saperstein who, before his death, owned the Harlem Globetrotters outright, made loans to the now defunct American Basketball League, in which he owned an interest and for which he served, uncompensated, as commissioner. The loans later became worthless. The court held the loans were not mere investments but were proximately related to Mr. Saperstein's separate Globetrotter business. It was enough that the taxpayer had made the loans to the A.B.L. in the hope that it would provide competition and playing sites for the Globetrotter team.

It is generally accepted that business classification turns on the question whether loans are "proximately related"[19] to the taxpayer's trade or business. However the application of this test has not been uniform. The problem is that one can have both investment and business motives for making loans. In such cases is it enough that business is a significant motive for the loan? Or must it be the dominant motive?

The Supreme Court has now set the requirement that business be the dominant motive for the loan.[20]

## Haslam v. Commissioner

Tax Court of the United States, 1974.
33 T.C.M. 482.

Memorandum Findings of Fact and Opinion

■ FORRESTER, JUDGE:

Respondent determined a deficiency in petitioners' Federal income tax for the taxable year 1967 in the amount of $979.01 and a penalty pursuant to section 6651(a)[1] in the amount of $244.75.

---

[16] Several cases have followed and extended this rationale. See B.A. Faucher v. Commissioner, 29 T.C.M. 950 (1970); Maurice Artstein v. Commissioner, 29 T.C.M. 961 (1970).

[17] In *Whipple*, supra note 9, the Supreme Court remanded the case to the Tax Court for a determination whether the loans bore the requisite relationship to a separate real estate business of the taxpayer. The case was settled prior to a decision on remand. See Knickerbocker, supra note 12.

[18] Estate of A.M. Saperstein v. Commissioner, 29 T.C.M. 916 (1970).

[19] Reg. § 1.166–5(b).

[20] United States v. Generes, 405 U.S. 93, 92 S.Ct. 827 (1972).

[1] All statutory references are to the Internal Revenue Code of 1954, as amended, unless otherwise specified.

The only issue for our decision is whether petitioners are entitled to business or nonbusiness deductions for losses arising from their guarantee of debts of Charles J. Haslam's wholly owned corporation.[2]

Findings of Fact

Some of the facts have been stipulated and are so found.

Petitioners, Charles J. Haslam and Harriet S. Haslam, are husband and wife who, at the time of the filing of the petition herein, resided in Slingerlands, New York. They filed their Federal joint income tax return for 1967 on April 15, 1969, with the district director of internal revenue in Albany, New York.

From 1948 to 1954 Charles J. Haslam (hereinafter referred to as petitioner) was employed by the Dupont Company in their explosives division as a sales and technical representative. Prior to this time, he had worked a great deal with explosives in the army as a captain in the corps of combat engineers, and had received additional training in explosives at Michigan College of Mining and Technology where he received a bachelor of science degree in 1948.

In 1954 petitioner and Earl Canavan (Canavan) established Northern Explosives, Inc. (Northern), a corporation engaged in the sale and distribution of explosives. Petitioner and Canavan each owned 50 percent of the stock in Northern, each having an investment of $10,000.

Petitioner managed the corporate business of Northern and was also employed by the corporation as a salesman, while Canavan took no active part in the corporate operations. Northern had three employees in addition to petitioner, two truck drivers and a part-time secretary.

In 1957, petitioner bought out Canavan's interest in Northern for $10,000, thereafter owning 100 percent of the stock with an investment of $20,000.

In 1960, Northern encountered financial difficulties and required additional cash to continue its operations. Thereafter petitioner guaranteed loans in the total amount of $100,000 made to Northern by the National Commercial Bank and Trust Company of Albany, New York (Commercial). To secure these guarantees petitioner pledged certain marketable securities and his personal residence.

At the time petitioner guaranteed the loans, he was devoting his full time and effort to his employment with Northern. His salary was approximately $250 to $300 per week and, in addition, he received an automobile, funds for its maintenance and insurance, medical insurance, and other employee benefits. With the exception of stock dividends of $4,000 to $5,000 per year (said dividends from securities of petitioner other than his stock in Northern), petitioner had no other source of income.

---

[2] Petitioners have conceded that the delinquency penalty imposed by respondent is warranted if there is a deficiency in their income tax for 1967.

Despite the loans to the corporation, Northern continued to experience financial difficulties. The corporation went into chapter XI status under the Federal Bankruptcy Act in 1961, and went bankrupt in 1964. Northern was unable to repay the loans guaranteed by petitioner, and in 1967 Commercial sold the securities pledged by petitioner for $70,464.58. Commercial applied $55,956 of this amount to the debt of Northern guaranteed by petitioner, and the remaining $14,508.58 to petitioner's liability on another debt obligation.

Petitioner remained an employee of Northern until it went bankrupt in 1964. In June 1964 he obtained employment as a salesman of steel castings for Falvey Steel Castings, Inc. (Falvey). Petitioner's gross income from his draw against commissions from Falvey during the years 1964 to 1968 are as follows:

| Year | Draw Against Commissions |
|------|--------------------------|
| 1964 | $ 2,900.00 |
| 1965 | 14,025.00 |
| 1966 | 11,307.00 |
| 1967 | 11,307.00 |
| 1968 | 11,213.42 |

During the years 1965 and 1966 petitioner's actual earned commissions were only approximately $10,000 per year. Sums petitioner received in excess of these amounts were cash advances against future commissions.

On their joint Federal income tax return for 1967 petitioners claimed a business bad debt in the amount of $55,956 on the loss sustained on petitioner's guarantee of the Northern loans. Respondent disallowed petitioners' claimed loss as a business bad debt, determining that it was deductible only as a nonbusiness bad debt.

Opinion

The sole issue for our decision is whether petitioners are entitled to a business or nonbusiness bad debt deduction for losses arising from their guarantee of debts of a corporation in which petitioner Charles J. Haslam was both an employee and an investor.

A bad debt loss, deductible under section 166, is created where a taxpayer sustains a loss upon payment on the guarantee of a debt, and the debtor is unable to satisfy the guarantor. * * *. Thus, petitioners sustained a bad debt loss upon payment of their guarantee of Northern debts subsequent to its bankruptcy.

Under section 166, business bad debt losses are deductible against ordinary income, while nonbusiness bad debt losses are deductible only as short-term capital losses. Petitioners argue that their bad debt loss is deductible as a business bad debt, while respondent argues that it is deductible only as a nonbusiness bad debt.

The character of a bad debt loss is determined by the relationship it bears to the taxpayer's trade or business. A debt will only qualify as a business bad debt if it bears a direct relationship to the taxpayer's trade or business * * *. In the instant case, petitioners argue that their guarantees to Northern bear such a relationship to petitioner's trade or business as an employee of that corporation.

It is clear that being an employee may constitute a trade or business for the purposes of section 166. Trent v. Commissioner, 291 F.2d 669 (C.A.2, 1961); cf. David J. Primuth, 54 T.C. 374 (1970). It is also clear that the debt obligations in the instant case were directly related to petitioner's trade or business as an employee, in that petitioners' guarantees were required for Northern to obtain the funds needed to continue its operations and petitioner's employment. The determination of whether the guarantees were proximately related to petitioner's trade or business as an employee, however, presents a more difficult question, in that petitioner also had an interest in Northern as its sole shareholder. Being an investor in a corporation does not constitute a trade or business, and losses resulting from guarantees made to protect a taxpayer's investment are not deductible as a business bad debt. Whipple v. Commissioner, 373 U.S. 193 (1963).

Where a taxpayer sustains a loss on a guarantee to a corporation in which he has both an employee and stockholder interest, a proximate relationship between the taxpayer's trade or business as an employee and his loss is established only if the taxpayer's dominant motivation in entering into the guarantees was to protect the employee interest. United States v. Generes, 405 U.S. 93 (1972). Petitioners, therefore, must prove that their dominant motivation in guaranteeing the loans to Northern was to protect petitioner's employment in order to establish the requisite proximate relationship.

The determination of taxpayer's dominant motivation is a factual question on which the taxpayer bears the burden of proof. Oddee Smith, 60 T.C. 316, 318 (1973). The trier of fact must determine the taxpayer's overriding reason for incurring the obligation and, in so doing "compare the risk against the potential reward and give proper emphasis to the objective rather than to the subjective." United States v. Generes, supra at 104.

In *Generes* the employee-shareholder had an initial investment of approximately $40,000 in his corporation. He worked six to eight hours a week for the corporation at an annual salary of $12,000, and had full-time employment outside of the corporation as the president of a savings and loan association at an annual salary of $19,000. His annual gross income was approximately $40,000 per year. Other members of the taxpayer's family also had employment and investment interests in the corporation. The Supreme Court held that these factors would not support a finding that the taxpayer's dominant motivation in guaranteeing loans to his corporation was to protect his employment with the corporation. In its holding, the Supreme Court disregarded the taxpayer's testimony that his dominant motivation was related to his employment, determining that his testimony was self-serving and not supported by the facts.

In the instant case, petitioner testified that his dominant motivation in guaranteeing loans to Northern was to protect his employment. It is our conclusion that the facts support his testimony, and accordingly we hold that petitioner's loss is deductible as a business bad debt.

Unlike the taxpayer in *Generes,* petitioner was a full-time employee of his corporation and he had no other employment. His salary from Northern was his major source of income. We note that petitioner's skills as an explosives' expert were not apparently readily marketable and that subsequent to Northern's bankruptcy petitioner obtained employment in a field unrelated to explosives at a salary less than he earned at Northern.

Viewing the facts in the record realistically, we think it much more likely that petitioner was more interested in preserving his position as an employee rather than as an investor in Northern. It is clear that petitioner made the guarantees in the hope of preserving Northern's corporate existence. From his position as an investor, it is clear that the preservation of the corporation would at best afford him some prospect of saving the $20,000 he had invested in the corporation. From his position as an employee however, such preservation would assure petitioner's continued employment at an annual salary of approximately $15,000. In our opinion, an assured salary of $15,000 per year over a period of years was a more valuable interest to petitioner than the mere possibility of recouping the already invested $20,000 in Northern, and the prospect of such continued employment was petitioner's dominant motivation in guaranteeing the loans to Northern. We thus decide the sole remaining issue for petitioner, but because of concessions.

*Decision will be entered under Rule 155.*

## PROBLEMS

1.     In year one self-employed Lawyer performs legal services for Client and bills the Client $1,000. Client does not pay Lawyer. In year six it becomes evident the debt will never be paid.

     (a)    What else must be known in order to determine whether Lawyer is entitled to a bad debt deduction? What will the character of any allowed deduction be?

     (b)    Assuming that the Commissioner asserts (and Lawyer cannot show otherwise) that the debt in fact became worthless in year two, is Lawyer's use of the bad debt deduction necessarily foreclosed by the statute of limitations?

(c)   Assuming Lawyer was allowed a deduction for year six, what tax consequences to Lawyer if in year seven Client inherits some money and pays the $1,000 obligation? What consequences upon payment in year seven if Lawyer properly was not allowed the deduction in year six?

2.   Without regard to the transactions or events described below, Cher Holder, who is a single taxpayer, has gross ordinary income of $60,000, § 62 and § 63 deductions of $20,000, and taxable income of $40,000 in the current year. Consider together the following further facts and then answer questions (a) through (d) which follow:

(1)   Cher owns a $5,000 "note" of Flibinite Corporation which she got from the Corporation for a loan of that amount and which is supposed to pay five percent interest each year. Flibinite goes bankrupt and Cher's "note" is worthless. The Commissioner successfully asserts that Cher's "note" represents an equity contribution to Flibinite. Cher acquired the "note" two years ago.

(2)   Cher owns common stock in Flibinite which also becomes worthless in the current year. She paid $3,000 for the stock three years ago.

(3)   Two years ago Cher loaned her friend Mooney $2,600. That loan becomes worthless in the current year. (What factors would be considered in determining if the loan created a bona fide debt?) Assume the debt was bona fide.

(4)   Cher owned some tax exempt state bonds which she purchased for $8,000 four years ago. When they were worth $12,000 they were stolen and Cher received $12,000 in insurance proceeds in the current year.

(a)   To what extent will the above transactions reduce Cher's taxable income for the year?

(b)   What, if any, is Cher's capital loss carryover to the succeeding year?

(c)   If, in addition, Cher had sold some stock for $20,000 which she had purchased three years earlier for $9,400, what is her taxable income for the current year? (Assume her other § 62 and § 63 deductions are still $20,000).

(d)   Assuming the facts of all parts including part (c) in the above problem, must Cher report any income (and if so what character of income) if in the following year Mooney inherits some money and repays her $2,600 obligation to Cher?

## B.  THE CHARITABLE DEDUCTION

Internal Revenue Code: Sections 170(a)(1), (b)(1)(A), (B), (C), (D), (G), and (H), (c), (e)(1), (2), and (5), (f)(8), (i) and (j); 1011(b). See Sections 67(b)(4); 162(b); 170(b)(2), (d)(1)(A), (f)(11) and (12), (g).

---

### Revenue Ruling 83–104
1983–2 Cum.Bull. 46.

ISSUE

Is the taxpayer entitled to a deduction for a charitable contribution under section 170 of the Internal Revenue Code in each of the situations described below?

FACTS

In each of the situations described below, the donee organization operates a private school and is an organization described in section 170(c) of the Code. In each situation a taxpayer who is a parent of a child who attends the school makes a payment to the organization. In each situation, the cost of educating a child in the school is not less than the payments made by the parent to the organization.

*Situation 1.* Organization S, which operates a private school, requests the taxpayer to contribute $400x for each child enrolled in the school. Parents who do not make the $400x contribution are required to pay $400x tuition for each child enrolled in the school. Parents who neither make the contribution nor pay tuition cannot enroll their children in the school. The taxpayer paid $400x to S.

*Situation 2.* Organization T, which operates a private school, solicits contributions from parents of applicants for admission to the school during the period of the school's solicitation for enrollment of students or while the applications are pending. The solicitation materials are part of the application materials or are presented in a form indicating that parents of applicants have been singled out as a class for solicitation. With the exception of a few parents, every parent who is financially able makes a contribution or pledges to make a contribution to T. No tuition is charged. The taxpayer paid $400x to T, which amount was suggested by T.

*Situation 3.* Organization U, which operates a private school, admits or readmits a significantly larger percentage of applicants whose parents have made contributions to U than applicants whose parents have not made contributions. The taxpayer paid $400x to U.

*Situation 4.* Organization V, a society for religious instruction, has as its sole function the operation of a private school providing secular and religious education to the children of its members. No tuition is charged for attending the school, which is funded through V's general account.

Contributions to the account are solicited from all society members, as well as from local churches and nonmembers. Persons other than parents of children attending the school do not contribute a significant portion of the school's support. Funds normally come to V from parents on a regular, established schedule. At times, parents are personally solicited by the school treasurer to contribute funds according to their financial ability. No student is refused admittance to the school because of the failure of his or her parents to contribute to the school. The taxpayer paid $40x to V.

*Situation 5.* Organization W, operates a private school that charges a tuition of $300x per student. In addition, it solicits contributions from parents of students during periods other than the period of the school's solicitation for student enrollments or the period when applications to the school are pending. Solicitation materials indicate that parents of students have been singled out as a class for solicitation and the solicitation materials include a report of W's cost per student to operate the school. Suggested amounts of contributions based on an individual's ability to pay are provided. No unusual pressure to contribute is placed upon individuals with children in the school, and many parents do not contribute. In addition, W receives contributions from many former students, parents of former students, and other individuals. The taxpayer paid $100x to W in addition to the tuition payment.

*Situation 6.* Church X operates a school providing secular and religious education that is attended both by children of parents who are members of X and by children of nonmembers. X receives contributions from all of its members. These contributions are placed in X's general operating fund and are expended when needed to support all church activities. A substantial portion of the other activities is unrelated to the school. Most members of X do not have children in the school, and a major portion of X's expenses are attributable to its nonschool functions. The methods of soliciting contributions to X from church members with children in the school are the same as the methods of soliciting contributions from members without children in the school. X has full control over the use of the contributions that it receives. Members who have children enrolled in the school are not required to pay tuition for their children, but tuition is charged for the children of nonmembers. Taxpayer, a member of X and whose child attends X's school, contributed $200x to X during the year for X's general purposes.

LAW AND ANALYSIS

Section 170(a) of the Code provides, subject to certain limitations, for the allowance of a deduction for charitable contributions or gifts to or for the use of organizations described in section 170(c), payment of which is made during the taxable year.

A contribution for purposes of section 170 of the Code is a voluntary transfer of money or property that is made with no expectation of procuring a financial benefit commensurate with the amount of the transfer. (See section 1.170A–1(c)(5) of the Income Tax Regulations and H.R.Rep. No. 1337, 83rd Cong., 2d Sess. A44 (1954).) Tuition expenditures by a taxpayer to an educational institution are therefore not deductible as charitable contributions to the institution because they are required payments for which the taxpayer receives benefits presumably equal in value to the amount paid. (See Channing v. United States, 4 F.Supp. 33 (D.Mass.), aff'd per curiam 67 F.2d 986 (1st Cir.1933), cert. denied, 291 U.S. 686 (1934).) Similarly, payments made by a taxpayer on behalf of children attending parochial or other church-sponsored schools are not allowable deductions as contributions either to the school or to the religious organization operating the school if the payments are earmarked for such children. (See Rev.Rul. 54–580, 1954–2 C.B. 97.) However, the fact that the payments are not earmarked does not necessarily mean that the payments are deductible. On the other hand, a charitable deduction for a payment to an organization that operates a school will not be denied solely because the payment was, to any substantial extent, offset by the fair market value of the services rendered to the taxpayer in the nature of tuition.

Whether a transfer of money by a parent to an organization that operates a school is a voluntary transfer that is made with no expectation of obtaining a commensurate benefit depends upon whether a reasonable person, taking all the facts and circumstances of the case into account, would conclude that enrollment in the school was in no manner contingent upon making the payment, that the payment was not made pursuant to a plan (whether express or implied) to convert nondeductible tuition into charitable contributions, and that receipt of the benefit was not otherwise dependent upon the making of the payment.

In determining this issue, the presence of one or more of the following factors creates a presumption that the payment is not a charitable contribution: the existence of a contract under which a taxpayer agrees to make a "contribution" and which contains provisions ensuring the admission of the taxpayer's child; a plan allowing taxpayers either to pay tuition or to make "contributions" in exchange for schooling; the earmarking of a contribution for the direct benefit of a particular individual; or the otherwise-unexplained denial of admission or readmission to a school of children of taxpayers who are financially able, but who do not contribute.

In other cases, although no single factor may be determinative, a combination of several factors may indicate that a payment is not a charitable contribution. In these cases, both economic and noneconomic pressures placed upon parents must be taken into account. The factors that the Service ordinarily will take into consideration, but will not limit itself to, are the following: (1) the absence of a significant tuition charge; (2) substantial or unusual pressure to contribute applied to parents of children attending a school; (3) contribution appeals made as part of the admissions or enrollment process; (4) the absence of significant potential sources of revenue for operating the school other than contributions by parents of children attending the school; (5) and other factors suggesting that a contribution policy has been created as a means of avoiding the characterization of payments as tuition.

However, if a combination of such factors is not present, payments by a parent will normally constitute deductible contributions, even if the actual cost of educating the child exceeds the amount of any tuition charged for the child's education.

HOLDINGS

*Situation 1.* The taxpayer is not entitled to a charitable contribution deduction for the payment to Organization S. Because the taxpayer must either make the contribution or pay the tuition charge in order for his or her child to attend S's school, admission is contingent upon making a payment of $400x. The taxpayer's payment is not voluntary and no deduction is allowed.

*Situation 2.* The taxpayer is not entitled to a charitable contribution deduction for the payment to Organization T. Because of the time and manner of the solicitation of contributions by T, and the fact that no tuition is charged, it is not reasonable to expect that a parent can obtain the admission of his or her child to T's school without making the suggested payments. Under these circumstances, the payments made by the taxpayer are in the nature of tuition, not voluntary contributions.

*Situation 3.* The taxpayer is not entitled to a charitable contribution deduction for contributions to Organization U. The Service will ordinarily conclude that the parents of applicants are aware of the preference given to applicants whose parents have made contributions. The Service will therefore ordinarily conclude that the parent could not reasonably expect to obtain the admission of his or her child to the school without making the transfer, regardless of the manner or timing of the solicitation by U. The Service will not so conclude, however, if the preference given to children of contributors is principally due to some other reason.

*Situation 4.* Under these circumstances, the Service will generally conclude that the payment to Organization V is nondeductible. Unless contributions from sources other than parents are of such magnitude that V's school is not economically dependent upon parents' contributions, parents would ordinarily not be certain that V's school could provide educational benefits without their payments. This conclusion is further evidenced by the fact that parents contribute on a regular, established schedule. In addition, the pressure placed on parents throughout the personal solicitation of contributions by V's school treasurer further indicates that their payments were not voluntary.

*Situation 5.* Under these circumstances, the Service will generally conclude that the taxpayer is entitled to claim a charitable contribution deduction of $100x to Organization W. Because a charitable organization normally solicits contributions from those known to have the greatest interest in the organization, the fact that parents are singled out for a solicitation will not in itself create an inference that future admissions or any other benefits depend on a contribution from the parent.

*Situation 6.* The Service will ordinarily conclude that the taxpayer is allowed a charitable contribution deduction of $200x to Organization X. Because the facts indicate that X's school is supported by the church, that most contributors to the church are not parents of children enrolled in the school, and that contributions from parent members are solicited in the same manner as contributions from other members, the taxpayer's contributions will be considered charitable contributions, and not payments of tuition, unless there is a showing that the contributions by members with children in X's school are significantly larger than those of other members. The absence of a tuition charge is not determinative in view of these facts.

\* \* \*

# Revenue Ruling 67–246*
1967–2 Cum.Bull. 104.

Advice has been requested concerning certain fund-raising practices which are frequently employed by or on behalf of charitable organizations and which involve the deductibility, as charitable contributions under section 170 of the Internal Revenue Code of 1954, of payments in connection with admission to or other participation in fund-raising activities for charity such as charity balls, bazaars, banquets, shows, and athletic events.

Affairs of the type in question are commonly employed to raise funds for charity in two ways. One is from profit derived from sale of admissions or other privileges or benefits connected with the event at such prices as their value warrants. Another is through the use of the affair as an occasion for solicitation of gifts in combination with the sale of the admissions or other privileges or benefits involved. In cases of the latter type the sale of the privilege or benefit is combined with solicitation of a gift or donation of some amount in addition to the sale value of the admission or privilege.

The need for guidelines on the subject is indicated by the frequency of misunderstanding of the requirements for deductibility of such payments and increasing incidence of their erroneous treatment for income tax purposes.

In particular, an increasing number of instances are being reported in which the public has been erroneously advised in advertisements or solicitations by sponsors that the entire amounts paid for tickets or other privileges in connection with fund-raising affairs for charity are deductible. Audits of returns are revealing other instances of erroneous

---

\*    Cf. I.R.C. § 6115 discussed infra at page 808. Ed.

advice and misunderstanding as to what, if any, portion of such payments is deductible in various circumstances. There is evidence also of instances in which taxpayers are being misled by questionable solicitation practices which make it appear from the wording of the solicitation that taxpayer's payment is a "contribution," whereas the payment solicited is simply the purchase price of an item offered for sale by the organization.

Section 170 of the Code provides for allowance of deductions for charitable contributions, subject to certain requirements and limitations. To the extent here relevant a charitable contribution is defined by that section as "a contribution or gift to or for the use of" certain specified types of organizations.

To be deductible as a charitable contribution for Federal income tax purposes under section 170 of the Code, a payment to or for the use of a qualified charitable organization must be a gift. To be a gift for such purposes in the present context there must be, among other requirements, a payment of money or transfer of property without adequate consideration.

As a general rule, where a transaction involving a payment is in the form of a purchase of an item of value, the presumption arises that no gift has been made for charitable contribution purposes, the presumption being that the payment in such case is the purchase price.

Thus, where consideration in the form of admissions or other privileges or benefits is received in connection with payments by patrons of fund-raising affairs of the type in question, the presumption is that the payments are not gifts. In such case, therefore, if a charitable contribution deduction is claimed with respect to the payment, the burden is on the taxpayer to establish that the amount paid is not the purchase price of the privileges or benefits and that part of the payment, in fact, does qualify as a gift.

In showing that a gift has been made, an essential element is proof that the portion of the payment claimed as a gift represents the excess of the total amount paid over the value of the consideration received therefor. This may be established by evidence that the payment exceeds the fair market value of the privileges or other benefits received by the amount claimed to have been paid as a gift.

Another element which is important in establishing that a gift was made in such circumstances, is evidence that the payment in excess of the value received was made with the intention of making a gift. While proof of such intention may not be an essential requirement under all circumstances and may sometimes be inferred from surrounding circumstances, the intention to make a gift is, nevertheless, highly relevant in overcoming doubt in those cases in which there is a question whether an amount was in fact paid as a purchase price or as a gift.

Regardless of the intention of the parties, however, a payment of the type in question can in any event qualify as a deductible gift only to the extent that it is shown to exceed the fair market value of any consideration received in the form of privileges or other benefits.

In those cases in which a fund-raising activity is designed to solicit payments which are intended to be in part a gift and in part the purchase price of admission to or other participation in an event of the type in question, the organization conducting the activity should employ procedures which make clear not only that a gift is being solicited in connection with the sale of the admissions or other privileges related to the fund-raising event, but, also the amount of the gift being solicited. To do this, the amount properly attributable to the purchase of admissions or other privileges and the amount solicited as a gift should be determined in advance of solicitation. The respective amounts should be stated in making the solicitation and clearly indicated on any ticket, receipt, or other evidence issued in connection with the payment.

In making such a determination, the full fair market value of the admission and other benefits or privileges must be taken into account. Where the affair is reasonably comparable to events for which there are established charges for admission, such as theatrical or athletic performances, the established charges should be treated as fixing the fair market value of the admission or privilege. Where the amount paid is the same as the standard admission charge there is, of course, no deductible contribution, regardless of the intention of the parties. Where the event has no such counterpart, only that portion of the payment which exceeds a reasonable estimate of the fair market value of the admission or other privileges may be designated as a charitable contribution.

The fact that the full amount or a portion of the payment made by the taxpayer is used by the organization exclusively for charitable purposes has no bearing upon the determination to be made as to the value of the admission or other privileges and the amount qualifying as a contribution.

Also, the mere fact that tickets or other privileges are not utilized does not entitle the patron to any greater charitable contribution deduction than would otherwise be allowable. The test of deductibility is not whether the right to admission or privileges is exercised but whether the right was accepted or rejected by the taxpayer. If a patron desires to support an affair, but does not intend to use the tickets or exercise the other privileges being offered with the event, he can make an outright gift of the amount he wishes to contribute, in which event he would not accept or keep any ticket or other evidence of any of the privileges related to the event connected with the solicitation.

The foregoing summary is not intended to be all inclusive of the legal requirements relating to deductibility of payments as charitable contributions for Federal income tax purposes. Neither does it attempt to deal with many of the refinements and distinctions which sometimes arise in connection with questions of whether a gift for such purposes has been made in particular circumstances.

The principles stated are intended instead to summarize with as little complexity as possible, those basic rules which govern deductibility of payments in the majority of the circumstances involved. They have their basis in section 170 of the Code, the regulations thereunder, and in court decisions. The observance of these provisions will provide greater assurance to taxpayer contributors that their claimed deductions in such cases are allowable.

Where it is disclosed that the public or the patrons of a fund-raising affair for charity have been erroneously informed concerning the extent of the deductibility of their payments in connection with the affair, it necessarily follows that all charitable contribution deductions claimed with respect to payments made in connection with the particular event or affair will be subject to special scrutiny and may be questioned in audit of returns.

In the following examples application of the principles discussed above is illustrated in connection with various types of fund-raising activities for charity. Again, the examples are drawn to illustrate the general rules involved without attempting to deal with distinctions that sometimes arise in special situations. In each instance, the charitable organization involved is assumed to be an organization previously determined to be qualified to receive deductible charitable contributions under section 170 of the Code, and the references to deductibility are to deductibility as charitable contributions for Federal income tax purposes.

*Example 1:*

The *M* Charity sponsors a symphony concert for the purpose of raising funds for *M*'s charitable programs. *M* agrees to pay a fee which is calculated to reimburse the symphony for hall rental, musicians' salaries, advertising costs, and printing of tickets. Under the agreement, *M* is entitled to all receipts from ticket sales. *M* sells tickets to the concert charging $5 for balcony seats and $10 for orchestra circle seats. These prices approximate the established admission charges for concert performances by the symphony orchestra. The tickets to the concert and the advertising material promoting ticket sales emphasize that the concert is sponsored by, and is for the benefit of *M* Charity.

Notwithstanding the fact that taxpayers who acquire tickets to the concert may think they are making a charitable contribution to or for the benefit of *M* Charity, no part of the payments made is deductible as a charitable contribution for Federal income tax purposes. Since the payments approximate the established admission charge for similar events, there is no gift. The result would be the same even if the advertising materials promoting ticket sales stated that amounts paid for tickets are "tax deductible" and tickets to the concert were purchased in reliance upon such statements. Acquisition of tickets or other privileges by a taxpayer in reliance upon statements made by a charitable organization that the amounts paid are deductible does not convert an otherwise nondeductible payment into a deductible charitable contribution.

*Example 2:*

The facts are the same as in *Example 1*, except that the *M* Charity desires to use the concert as an occasion for the solicitation of gifts. It indicates that fact in its advertising material promoting the event, and fixes the payments solicited in connection with each class of admission at $30 for orchestra circle seats and $15 for balcony seats. The advertising and the tickets clearly reflect the fact that the established admission charges for comparable performances by the symphony orchestra are $10 for orchestra circle seats and $5 for balcony seats, and that only the excess of the solicited amounts paid in connection with admission to the concert over the established prices is a contribution to *M*.

Under these circumstances a taxpayer who makes a payment of $60 and receives two orchestra circle seat tickets can show that his payment exceeds the established admission charge for similar tickets to comparable performances of the symphony orchestra by $40. The circumstances also confirm that that amount of the payment was solicited as, and intended to be, a gift to *M* Charity. The $40, therefore, is deductible as a charitable contribution.

\* \* \*

## NOTE

*Introduction.* Section 170(a) provides a deduction for any contribution to a qualified charity made within a taxable year.[1] Congress encourages contributions to charitable organizations by providing taxpayers with this deduction.[2] This relieves some of the economic responsibilities that would otherwise fall on the federal government if not met by private funding.[3]

Consideration of this deduction provision has been postponed until now because comprehension of the charitable deduction rules requires, among other things, an understanding of the characterization provisions.[4] This note provides a road map to the subsections of Section 170 not in their alphabetical order, but instead, in the order in which they should be

---

[1] See Year of Deduction, *infra.* Articles providing an overview of I.R.C. § 170 include Taggart, "The Charitable Deduction," 26 Tax L.Rev. 63 (1970); Sorlien and Olsen, "Analyzing the New Charitable Contributions Rules: Planning, Pitfalls and Problems," 32 J. Tax'n 218 (1970); Wittenbach and Milani, "A Flowchart Focusing on the Individual Charitable Contribution Deduction Provisions," 66 Taxes 285 (1988).

[2] This deduction is an itemized deduction. See I.R.C. § 67(b)(4), Chapter 18C, *supra.*

[3] Policy articles considering I.R.C. § 170 include McDaniel, "Federal Matching Grants for Charitable Contributions: A Substitute for the Income Tax Deduction," 27 Tax L.Rev. 377 (1972); Bittker, "Charitable Contribution: Tax Deduction or Matching Grants?" 28 Tax L.Rev. 37 (1972); McNulty, "Public Policy and Private Charity: A Tax Policy Perspective," 3 Va.Tax Rev. 229 (1984); Wiedenbeck, "Charitable Contributions: A Policy Perspective," 50 Mo.L.Rev. 85 (1985); Gergen, "The Case for a Charitable Contributions Deduction," 74 Va.L.Rev. 1393 (1988).

[4] See the Amount of the Contribution, *infra.*

considered to properly determine the amount of the current year's charitable deduction as well as any charitable deduction carryovers.

*Qualified Charitable Donees.* In order for a charitable contribution to be deductible, it must be made to a qualified organization.[5] Section 170(c) provides five classifications of qualified organizations:[6] (1) a federal, state or local governmental entity;[7] (2) certain religious,[8] charitable, scientific, literary, educational, amateur sports and prevention of cruelty to children and animals organizations;[9] (3) certain war veterans' organizations;[10] (4) domestic fraternal societies, orders, or associations operating under the lodge system where gifts are used exclusively for the purposes listed in classification (2) above (other than amateur sports);[11] and (5) non-profit cemetery companies and corporations.[12]

Section 170 essentially divides charitable organizations into two classifications. The first, referred to as "public charities," are charities substantially funded by the general public.[13] The second classification, "private charities," are private foundations funded by smaller groups of private individuals or families.[14] Some privately funded charitable organizations are treated as public charities where contributions or net earnings of the organization are distributed for qualified charitable uses within a limited period beyond the end of the year.[15]

---

[5]   See I.R.S. Pub. No. 78 (Cumulative List of Organizations Described in Section 170(c)) for a list of organizations that qualify for deductible charitable contributions.

[6]   In addition, I.R.C. § 170(g) treats unreimbursed amounts paid to maintain a non-dependent and non-related student in the twelfth grade or lower as a member of a taxpayer's household as a contribution for the use of a public charity. I.R.C. § 170(g)(1), (2)(B). Cf. I.R.C. § 170(b)(1)(B). The deduction is permitted only if there is a written agreement between the taxpayer and a charity described in § 170(c)(2), (3) or (4) to implement such an educational program. I.R.C. § 170(g)(1)(A). The deductible amount is limited to a maximum of $50 a month for the number of months the student is maintained. I.R.C. § 170(g)(2)(A).

[7]   I.R.C. § 170(c)(1). Included also are political subdivisions of such entities and United States possessions, but only if the contribution or gift is to be used exclusively for public purposes.

[8]   See Bittker, "Churches, Taxes and the Constitution," 78 Yale L.J. 218 (1970); Schwarz, "Limiting Religious Tax Exemptions: When Should the Church Render Unto Caesar?" 29 U.Fla.L.Rev. 50 (1976).

[9]   I.R.C. § 170(c)(2). The charity can be a corporation, trust or community chest, fund or foundation created or organized in the United States, a state of the United States, the District of Columbia or a United States possession, none of whose net earnings inure to the benefit of any private shareholder or individual and which does not attempt to influence legislation or become involved in political campaigns. Id. In addition, a contribution is deductible only if it is to be used in the United States or one of its possessions exclusively for one of the above purposes. Id.

[10]   I.R.C. § 170(c)(3). The organizations must be organized in the United States or one of its possessions and none of its net earnings may inure to the benefit of a private shareholder or individual. Id.

[11]   I.R.C. § 170(c)(4).

[12]   I.R.C. § 170(c)(5). No part of the net earnings of such company or corporation may inure to the benefit of any private shareholder or individual. See Whalen, "A Grave Injustice: The Uncharitable Federal Tax Treatment of Bequest to Public Cemeteries," 58 Fordham L.Rev. 705 (1990).

[13]   Cf. I.R.C. § 170(b)(1)(A).

[14]   Cf. I.R.C. § 170(b)(1)(B).

[15]   I.R.C. § 170(b)(1)(A)(vii), (F).

*Contributions.* In order to qualify for a charitable deduction, one must make a "contribution . . . to or for the use of" a charity.[16] A contribution has been defined as "a voluntary transfer of money or property made with no expectation of procuring a financial benefit commensurate with the amount of the transfer."[17] As the Rulings just considered illustrate, if a taxpayer receives a *quid pro quo* for a transfer to a charity, there is no "contribution,"[18] and no charitable deduction is allowed. In some instances the transferor may be allowed a Section 162 business expense deduction, even though a *quid pro quo* is received.[19]

If cash or its equivalent[20] is given to a charity and partial consideration is received from the charity, then only the excess of the amount of the cash over the amount of the consideration received qualifies as a charitable deduction.[21] For example, if taxpayer pays $100 for a ticket to a charitable dinner the value of which is $40, the taxpayer may deduct only the balance, $60, as a charitable contribution.[22] If a donor makes a contribution in excess of $75 of cash or other property to a charitable organization and receives consideration in the form of goods or services,[23] the organization is required to inform the donor that only the excess of the contribution over the value of the goods and services is deductible and to provide the donor a good faith estimate of the value of goods and services provided by the organization.[24]

If property other than cash is transferred to a charity for partial consideration, a part-gift, part-sale transaction occurs.[25] Recall that in the event of a noncharitable part-gift, part-sale transaction, the Service questionably treats the gift and sale transactions as a single transfer.[26] However, when a *charitable* part-gift, part-sale transaction occurs, the transaction is sensibly divided into two simultaneous transfers, one a sale and the other a gift.[27] For the sale part of the transaction, the amount realized is the partial consideration received from the charity on the transfer; the gain on the sale is measured by the amount realized less the portion of the adjusted basis of the transferred property which bears the same ratio to the total adjusted basis of the property transferred as the consideration

---

[16] I.R.C. § 170(c). The words "or gift" are omitted from the quote, as a contribution encompasses a gift.

[17] Rev.Rul. 83–104, 1983–2 C.B. 46, 47.

[18] See Rev.Rul. 83–104, and Rev.Rul. 67–246 at pages 798 and 802, supra.

[19] Reg. § 1.170A–1(c)(5). See also United States v. Jefferson Mills, Inc., 367 F.2d 392 (5th Cir.1966); Singer Co. v. United States, 449 F.2d 413 (Ct.Cl.1971); Sarah Marquis v. Commissioner, 49 T.C. 695 (1968), acq. 1971–2 C.B. 1. But cf. I.R.C. § 162(b).

[20] See infra Text at note 34.

[21] Rev.Rul. 67–246, 1967–2 C.B. 104. Cf. Rev.Proc. 90–12, 1990–1 C.B. 471.

[22] See Rev.Rul. 67–246, supra note 21.

[23] See the Text at notes 18–22, supra, and notes 25–35, infra.

[24] I.R.C. § 6115. Failure to satisfy the requirements of I.R.C. § 6115 will result in penalties imposed on the charitable organization, unless it can show a "reasonable cause" for the failure. I.R.C. § 6714(a) and (b).

[25] See Lichter, "The Federal Tax Rules and Theory of Bargain Sale Gifts to Charity," 12 Tax Manager Est., Gifts, and Tr.J. 172 (1987); Teitell, "Making Charitable Gifts of Mortgaged Property: A Bargain Sale with Capital Gains Considerations," 125 Tr. & Est. 54 (1986).

[26] See Reg. §§ 1.1001–1(e) and 1.1015–4. See also Chapter 6B2 problem 2 and Chapter 6C, supra.

[27] See I.R.C. §§ 170(e)(2) and 1011(b) and Reg. §§ 1.170A–4(c)(2) and 1.1011–2.

received from the charity bears to the total fair market value of the property transferred.[28] The remaining fair market value of the property is treated as the part-gift contribution to charity with the property having an adjusted basis equal to the remaining adjusted basis of the property.[29]

A classic example of a part-gift, part-sale to charity is a transfer of property encumbered with debt.[30] Another example is a transfer to charity for some amount of monetary consideration. For example, assume that Donor transfers some land with an adjusted basis of $100,000 and a fair market value of $200,000 to a charity and that the property is either subject to a liability of $100,000 or the property is unencumbered but the charity pays Donor $100,000 cash for it.[31] There would essentially be two transactions, a sale of one half ($100,000/$200,000) of the property and a gift of the remaining one half ($200,000 less the $100,000 sale amount) of the property. The sale property would have a $50,000 adjusted basis[32] resulting in a $50,000 gain to Donor on the part-sale transaction. In addition, Donor is considered to have made a charitable gift of the remaining property worth $100,000 having an adjusted basis of $50,000.[33]

*The Amount of the Contribution.* To the extent that a "contribution" is made to or for the use of a qualified charitable donee, the amount treated as contributed to the charity must be determined.

*Cash.* To the extent the contribution is in cash, the amount of the contribution is the amount of the donated cash. A gift made by check or a charge to a credit card which is paid in due course is the equivalent of cash and the amount of the check or the credit card charge is the amount of the contribution.[34]

*Property.* If property other than cash is contributed to a charity, the fair market value of the property contributed is the potential amount of the contribution.[35] Concerns over inflated fair market valuation of charitable contributions of motor vehicles, boats, and airplanes where value exceeds $500 has led Congress to enact a rule that if the charity sells such property without any significant intervening use or material improvement to the property by the charity, the amount of the contribution is limited to the gross proceeds from the sale.[36] Similarly, deductions are not allowed for

---

[28]   I.R.C. § 1011(b), Reg. § 1.1011–2. See The Amount of the Contribution, infra.

[29]   I.R.C. § 170(e)(2); Reg. § 1.170A–4(c)(2).

[30]   See Guest v. Commissioner, 77 T.C. 9 (1981).

[31]   The numbers in this example should appear familiar. See problem 2 on page 128, supra.

[32]   I.R.C. § 1011(b); Reg. § 1.1011–2. The computation is equal to the fraction of the consideration received over the fair market value of the property transferred ($100,000/$200,000) times the adjusted basis of the property transferred ($100,000).

[33]   I.R.C. § 170(e)(2); Reg. § 1.170A–4(c)(2). The gifted property would have an adjusted basis equal to the fraction of the gift amount over the fair market value of the property transferred ($100,000/$200,000) times the adjusted basis of the property transferred ($100,000). The full $100,000 amount may or may not be deductible. See The Amount of the Contribution, infra, and Reg. § 1.170A–4(c)(2)(i).

[34]   Cf. Rev.Rul. 54–465, 1954–2 C.B. 93, and Rev.Rul. 78–38, 1978–1 C.B. 67.

[35]   Reg. § 1.170A–1(c).

[36]   I.R.C. § 170(f)(12)(A)(ii). Regardless of whether the charity retains or improves the property, it must provide the donor with a contemporaneous written acknowledgment of the contribution. I.R.C. § 170(f)(12)(A)(i), (B). The rules are inapplicable to I.R.C. § 1221(a)(1)

contributions of clothing and household items (e.g., furniture, furnishings, electronics, appliances, linens, and similar items)[37] that are not in good used condition.[38] If the amount claimed for the item exceeds $500, a qualified appraisal of the item must be included with the taxpayer's return.[39]

If the contributed property is appreciated property, the amount of the contribution may be reduced by some or all of the amount of the built-in gain.[40] To determine whether a reduction occurs, it is first necessary to determine the character of the gain which would be recognized if the property were sold by the donor. If the gain would be other than long-term capital gain, the amount of the contribution is reduced by the total amount of the lurking ordinary income or gain other than long-term capital gain.[41] Throughout Section 170 any reference to long-term capital gain includes Section 1231 gain.[42] Thus, if an individual donates inventory with a basis of $100 and a value of $250 to charity, the amount of the contribution is only $100, the $250 fair market value of the inventory less its $150 of lurking ordinary gain.[43] Similar results would apply if the property were short-term capital gain property, Section 1245 or Section 1250 property, or Section 1231-type property held for less than one year.[44]

But, even if the property is long-term capital gain property (including Section 1231 gain property),[45] the amount of the contribution may be reduced. If (1) the property is tangible personal property donated to a public charity and the use of the property is unrelated to the charity's function,[46] (2) the property is worth more than $5,000, is sold by the charity by the end of the year in which the contribution is made, and the charity does not certify either that the related use was substantial or that the related use is impossible or impracticable,[47] (3) the property is long-term capital gain property given to a private charity,[48] or (4) the property is a patent, copyright or similar intellectual property,[49] the amount of the contribution must be

---

property. I.R.C. § 170(f)(12)(E). See Notice 2005–44, 2005–1 C.B. 1287 providing interim guidance on the operation of § 170(f)(12).

[37] I.R.C. § 170(f)(16)(D).

[38] I.R.C. § 170(f)(16)(A).

[39] I.R.C. § 170(f)(16)(C).

[40] See I.R.C. § 170(e).

[41] I.R.C. § 170(e)(1)(A). I.R.C. § 1221(b)(3) is disregarded. Id.

[42] See I.R.C. §§ 170(e)(1) last sentence, 170(b)(1)(C)(iv) last sentence and Reg. § 1.170A–4(b)(4). I.R.C. § 1231 property is treated as a capital asset for determination of the amount of the contribution, except to the extent the donor would have recognized gain from sale as ordinary income under §§ 617(d)(1), 1245(a), 1250(a), 1251(c), 1252(a), or 1254(a).

[43] See I.R.C. § 1221(a)(1).

[44] See Reg. § 1.170A–4(b)(1).

[45] See note 42, supra. I.R.C. § 170(a)(1) speaks only to long-term capital gain property (see § 1222(3)) and it does not distinguish among the classifications of net capital gains found in § 1(h).

[46] I.R.C. § 170(e)(1)(B)(i). See Reg. § 1.170A–4(b)(3).

[47] I.R.C. § 170(e)(1)(B)(i)(II). See I.R.C. § 170(e)(7)(D). Further, if such property is sold by the charity within three years of the contribution, there is a recapture tax on the donor. I.R.C. § 170(e)(7).

[48] I.R.C. § 170(e)(1)(B)(ii).

[49] I.R.C. § 170(e)(1)(B)(iii). The reduction is inapplicable to some copyrights and software. Id. However, generally the donor is allowed an additional charitable contribution in the current

reduced by the amount of the long-term capital gain.[50] For example, if an individual gives a painting worth $10,000, which cost the individual $4,000 to a public charity and the painting is used by the charity in its charitable function (e.g., if the gift is to an art museum which includes the painting in its collection),[51] the individual makes a $10,000 contribution. However, if the painting is not used in the public charity's charitable function or is given to a private charity, the amount of the contribution is $4,000 ($10,000 less the painting's $6,000 built-in long-term gain).[52]

There is an exception to the private charity long-term capital gain reduction rule.[53] If there is a gift to a private charity of "qualified appreciated stock," there is no reduction of the long-term capital gain amount.[54] Qualified appreciated stock is publicly traded stock the sale of which would result in long-term capital gain to the taxpayer,[55] but only to the extent that taxpayer or the taxpayer's family's[56] total contributions of such stock to private charities do not exceed 10 percent of the value of the stock of the corporation.[57] Thus, if the individual in the prior example had transferred AT & T stock (instead of the painting) with a $4,000 basis and $10,000 value to a private charity, the amount of the contribution would be $10,000.

*Partial Interests in Property.* If a taxpayer gives less than an entire interest in property to a charity, a series of special rules come into play. Congress enacted special rules for transfers of partial interests such as a charitable income interest or a charitable remainder interest out of a concern that a donor or trustee could deprive the charity of its benefits by investing in non-income producing assets or wasting assets respectively.[58]

If the partial interest is a charitable remainder interest in a trust, the value of the remainder qualifies for a charitable deduction[59] only if the interest is in the form of a charitable remainder annuity trust,[60] a charitable

---

and subsequent years with respect to the income generated by the property. I.R.C. § 170(m). See Notice 2005–41, 2005–1 C.B. 1203, discussing qualified intellectual property contributions.

[50]  I.R.C. § 170(e)(1)(B).

[51]  Reg. § 1.170A–4(b)(3). See Anthoine, "Deductions for Charitable Contributions of Appreciated Property—The Art World," 35 Tax L.Rev. 239 (1980); Bell, "Changing I.R.C. Sec. 170(e)(1)(A): For Art's Sake," 37 Case West.Res.L.Rev. 536 (1988).

[52]  I.R.C. § 170(e)(1)(B). If tangible depreciable personal property were given to a charity, the property could be subject to both I.R.C. § 1245 and § 1231 gain. The fair market value of the property would be reduced by the § 1245 gain and it might also be reduced by the § 1231 gain.

[53]  I.R.C. § 170(e)(5).

[54]  I.R.C. § 170(e)(5)(A).

[55]  I.R.C. § 170(e)(5)(B).

[56]  Family is defined by I.R.C. § 267(c)(4). I.R.C. § 170(e)(5)(C)(ii).

[57]  I.R.C. § 170(e)(5)(C).

[58]  See Stephens, Maxfield, Lind & Calfee, *Federal Estate and Gift Taxation* ¶ 5.05[4] and [7] (Warren, Gorham & Lamont 9th Ed. 2013).

[59]  I.R.C. § 170(f)(2)(A). See Stephens, Maxfield, Lind & Calfee, supra note 58 at ¶ 5.05[5].

[60]  I.R.C. § 664(d)(1). A charitable remainder annuity trust is generally a trust that meets four requirements: (1) a fixed amount (not less than 5% nor more than 50% of the value of the property at the time it is transferred to the trust) must be paid at least annually to recipients (at least one of which does not qualify under § 170(c)) for a term of years (not more than 20 years) or for the life or lives of living individuals; (2) no other amounts can be paid for uses or to organizations other than those qualified for the income tax deduction; (3) when the payments described in (1) above terminate, the remainder must be paid to or for the use of an organization qualified for the income tax charitable deduction, or retained by the trust for such a use; and (4)

remainder unitrust,[61] or a pooled income fund.[62] If an income interest in a trust is contributed to charity (commonly referred to as a charitable lead interest), it qualifies for a deduction only if the amount distributed to charity is a guaranteed annuity or a fixed percentage of the fair market value of the trust property determined annually and the grantor is treated as the owner of such interest under Section 671.[63] These trust limitations are designed to prevent abuses and to ensure that the charity actually receives an adequate amount of contribution in relation to the income tax deduction which is allowed.[64]

If a charitable gift of a partial interest in property to charity is not in trust, the contribution will qualify as a charitable contribution only if the partial interest in property would be deductible if contributed in a trust, i.e. a qualified remainder interest or qualified income interest,[65] or if the contribution is a remainder interest in a personal residence or farm,[66] a contribution of an undivided portion of a taxpayer's entire interest in property,[67] or a "qualified conservation contribution."[68]

For example, a transfer of a right to use a building to a charity for a limited or indefinite period is a partial interest in property that does not qualify for a charitable deduction.[69] This disallowance result is sensible if one thinks of the use of such property as a contribution of rental property with a zero basis which generates ordinary income.[70] Similarly, if a person transfers rental land to a trust that provides that all income from the land is to be distributed to a private individual for her life with a remainder to charity, the charitable remainder does not qualify for a charitable deduction because it is not a qualified remainder interest.[71] If the land were transferred to a trust with a charitable remainder which satisfied the requirements of a charitable remainder annuity trust, a charitable remainder unitrust or a pooled income fund, the value of the remainder would qualify for a charitable

---

the value of the remainder interest must be worth at least 10% of the initial fair market value of the property placed in the trust. Id.

[61] I.R.C. § 664(d)(2). A charitable remainder unitrust is a trust that meets four requirements: (1) a fluctuating amount fixed in terms of a percentage (not less than 5% nor more than 50%) of the annual value of the trust assets must be paid at least annually to a non-qualified recipient for a term of years (not more than 20 years) or for the life or lives of living individuals; (2), (3) and (4) are identical to requirements (2), (3) and (4) in note 60, supra. Id.

[62] I.R.C. § 642(c)(5). A pooled income fund is a fund controlled by the charity entitled to the remainder. Property transferred to the fund is commingled with that of other donors, no donor or beneficiary of an income interest of the fund is a trustee, and the private income beneficiary receives distributions that are determined by the rate of return on the entire fund. Id.

[63] I.R.C. § 170(f)(2)(B). See Stephens, Maxfield, Lind & Calfee, supra note 58 at ¶ 5.05[6], and Chapter 13B, supra.

[64] See the Text at note 58, supra.

[65] I.R.C. § 170(f)(3)(A). See the Text at notes 59–64, supra.

[66] I.R.C. § 170(f)(3)(B)(i).

[67] I.R.C. § 170(f)(3)(B)(ii).

[68] I.R.C. § 170(f)(3)(B)(iii). A qualified conservation contribution is a contribution of "a qualified real property interest" to a "qualified organization" exclusively for "conservation purposes." I.R.C. § 170(h)(1). Those terms are defined in I.R.C. § 170(h)(2)–(6).

[69] Rev.Rul. 70–477, 1970–2 C.B. 62.

[70] See I.R.C. § 170(e)(1)(A). Cf. the Text at notes 41–44, supra.

[71] See I.R.C. § 170(f)(2)(A) and the Text at notes 59–62, supra.

deduction.[72] Finally, an outright transfer of a fractional interest in the parcel of land, say a one-third interest, would qualify for a charitable deduction.[73]

*Services.* Services rendered to a charity are not property and consequently do not qualify as charitable contributions.[74] Services might be compared to ordinary income property with a zero adjusted basis, which if contributed to charity would result in a zero amount of contribution.[75] However, while services do not qualify for a charitable deduction, unreimbursed expenses incurred incident to the rendering of such services may constitute a charitable contribution.[76] Thus, a teacher's aid's cost of materials purchased and used in conjunction with the teaching assistance and the cost of transportation to and from the school constitute a charitable contribution.[77] If the expenses incident to rendering services are for traveling expenses (including meals and lodging) while away from home, they are deductible as charitable contributions only if there is no significant element of pleasure, recreation or vacation in such travel.[78]

*Limitations on Charitable Contributions of Individual Taxpayers.* After determining whether there is a *contribution* to or for the use of a *qualified charitable donee* and the *amount of the contribution,* the total amount that a taxpayer will be allowed to deduct in a taxable year must be determined. Congress imposes various ceilings on the total amount that a taxpayer may deduct in any taxable year.[79] Contributions in excess of any of the ceilings are permitted to be carried over to the five succeeding years.[80]

We first consider the ceilings on the total amount of an individual taxpayer's contributions.[81] The amount of the ceiling is determined by a combination of factors including the type of charity (public or private), the character of the property transferred (whether the property is appreciated long-term capital gain property), whether the transfer is to or merely for the use of the charity, and the taxpayer's contribution base.

---

[72] Id.

[73] I.R.C. § 170(f)(3)(B)(ii). This represents an undivided portion of the entire interest in the property. The amount of the contribution may be reduced if the property is appreciated property. See the Text at notes 40–57, supra.

[74] Reg. § 1.170A–1(g). See Grant v. Commissioner, 84 T.C. 809 (1985), affirmed 800 F.2d 260 (4th Cir.1986). The Service has ruled that a gift of blood is a nondeductible gift of services. Rev. Rul. 53–162, 1953–2 C.B. 127.

[75] I.R.C. § 170(e)(1)(A); see the Text at notes 41–44, supra.

[76] Reg. § 1.170A–1(g). See Luckey, "Taxation: Deduction of Expenses Incurred by Another in the Performance of a Service to a Charitable Organization," 17 U.Balt.L.Rev. 524 (1988).

[77] Id. Cf. I.R.C. § 170(i) which allows a standard mileage rate of 14 cents per mile for transportation costs as a charitable deduction. See Notice 2018–3, 2018–2 I.R.B. 285, allowing a 54.5 cents per mile standard mileage rate deduction under § 162, effective January 1, 2018. Cf. Rev.Proc. 2010–51, 2010–51 I.R.B. 883.

Such costs are treated as a contribution "to" and not merely "for the use of a charity." Rev.Rul. 84–61, 1984–1 C.B. 39. See the Text at notes 88–92, infra.

[78] I.R.C. § 170(j). See Chapter 14C2, supra. See also Charles L. McCollum v. Commissioner, 37 T.C.M. 1817 (1978), where a family attempted to deduct the cost of ski trips as members of a ski patrol. This case was decided prior to the enactment of I.R.C. § 170(j).

[79] I.R.C. § 170(b).

[80] I.R.C. § 170(b)(1)(B), (C)(ii), (D)(ii), (G)(ii), (d)(1).

[81] In general, an estate or trust in not subject to any limitation on its charitable contributions. I.R.C. § 642(c)(1).

All of the ceilings are determined by computing some percentage of an individual taxpayer's "contribution base."[82] A contribution base is the taxpayer's adjusted gross income[83] computed without regard to any Section 172 net operating loss carryback to the year of the contribution.[84]

*Contributions to Public Charities.* An individual generally may deduct contributions made during the year *to* a public charity to the extent that such contributions do not exceed 50 percent of the taxpayer's contribution base.[85] The 50 percent ceiling is inapplicable if the contribution is merely "for the use of" a public charity.[86] A contribution is "for the use of" a charity if it is a contribution of an income interest in property (regardless of whether it is in a trust) or if (after all non-charitable interests expire) the property is held in trust for the benefit of a charity.[87]

*Contributions for the Use of Public Charities and to or for Private Charities.* Contributions for the use of public charities[88] and all contributions to or for private charities are subject to a general limitation of 30 percent of the taxpayer's contribution base for the year.[89] These contributions are considered immediately after the gifts that qualify for the 50 percent ceiling.[90] However, the amount of such contributions may not exceed 50 percent of the contribution base less the amount of property contributed to public charities;[91] thus, such contributions are limited to the lesser of (1) 30 percent of the taxpayer's contribution base or (2) the excess of 50 percent of the taxpayer's contribution base over the contributions to public charities.[92]

*Cash Contributions to Public Charities.* There is a special rule under which an individual may deduct cash contributions to a public charity to the extent such contributions do not exceed 60 percent of the taxpayer's contribution base.[93] Such contributions are disregarded for purposes of the 50-pecent limitation and reduce the available 50 percent limitation.[94] They also reduce the 50 percent limitation for purposes of determining the availability of the 30-percent limitation.[95]

---

[82] I.R.C. § 170(b)(1).

[83] I.R.C. § 62. See Chapter 18C, supra.

[84] I.R.C. § 170(b)(1)(H).

[85] I.R.C. § 170(b)(1)(A). There is no percentage limitation on a very limited category of contributions. I.R.C. § 408(d)(8)(C) (parenthetical). I.R.C. § 408(d)(8) permits taxpayers over age 70½ to transfer up to $100,000 per year from an IRA to a public charity. The transfer is not includible in the taxpayer's gross income (I.R.C. § 408(d)(8)(A)), not deductible under § 170 (I.R.C. § 408(d)(8)(E)), and not subject to the I.R.C. § 170(b) percentage ceiling limitations (I.R.C. § 408(d)(8)(C)).

[86] I.R.C. § 170(b)(1)(A); Reg. § 1.170A–8(b).

[87] Reg. § 1.170A–8(a)(2). Cf. I.R.C. § 170(f)(1).

[88] I.R.C. § 170(b)(1)(B). Cf. Reg. § 1.170A–8(c).

[89] I.R.C. § 170(b)(1)(B)(i).

[90] Reg. § 1.170A–8(c)(2)(ii).

[91] I.R.C. § 170(b)(1)(B)(ii).

[92] I.R.C. § 170(b)(1)(B).

[93] I.R.C. § 170(b)(1)(G).

[94] I.R.C. § 170(b)(1)(G)(iii).

[95] I.R.C. § 170(b)(1)(G)(iii)(II).

*Contributions of Appreciated Capital Gain Property.* After the above ceilings are imposed, there are further ceilings on gifts of appreciated capital gain property. A contribution *to* a public charity of appreciated property which if sold would result in long-term capital gain (or Section 1231 gain)[96] and which does not otherwise have its long-term capital gain amount reduced[97] is subject to a further ceiling equal to 30 percent of the taxpayer's contribution base.[98] A taxpayer may elect to reduce the amount of the contribution by the amount of the property's long-term capital gain (converting the property to non-appreciated property) so that it is then subject only to the 50 percent ceiling.[99]

Finally, gifts of any appreciated long-term capital gain property for the use of a public charity or to or for a private charity are subject to a ceiling of 20 percent of the taxpayer's contribution base, but not in excess of 30 percent of taxpayer's contribution base reduced by any unreduced long-term capital gain property given to a public charity.[100]

To the extent that an individual taxpayer's total charitable contributions for any taxable year exceed any of the limitations considered above, the excess amounts are carried over and treated as contributions of the same character (e.g., cash or long-term capital gain property) to the same classification of donee (e.g., public or private charity) in each of the succeeding five years.[101] Any carryover is used up first in time (earliest years first) but only after taking into account the actual charitable contributions in the carryover year.[102] Any carryover unused at the end of the five year period expires and is wasted.

To illustrate some of the rules described above, assume T, an individual, with a $100,000 contribution base gives $10,000 cash and a piece of equipment related to the charity's function with an adjusted basis of $40,000 and worth $100,000 (subject to $20,000 Section 1245 gain and $40,000 Section 1231 gain) to a public charity. The $10,000 cash contribution does not exceed 60 percent of T's contribution base ($60,000) and is allowed. The cash contribution also reduces the 50-percent limitation to $40,000.[103] The amount of T's remaining contribution is $80,000 (equipment).[104] Since the gift is to a public charity the remaining $40,000 of 50 percent ceiling applies and T is limited to a $40,000 deduction with respect to the equipment.[105] However, the transfer of the equipment is also subject to the 30 percent ceiling for appreciated property contributed to a public charity[106] and only a $30,000 portion of the equipment is currently deductible, with the remaining

---

[96]   I.R.C. § 170(b)(1)(C)(iv). See note 42, supra.

[97]   I.R.C. § 170(e)(1)(B). See the Text at notes 45–50, supra

[98]   I.R.C. § 170(b)(1)(C)(i).

[99]   I.R.C. § 170(b)(1)(C)(iii).

[100]   I.R.C. § 170(b)(1)(D)(i).

[101]   I.R.C. § 170(b)(1)(B) flush language, (C)(ii), (D)(ii), (G)(ii), (d)(1).

[102]   Id.

[103]   I.R.C. § 170(b)(1)(G)(i) and (iii).

[104]   I.R.C. § 170(e)(1)(A). There is no I.R.C. § 170(e)(1)(B) reduction.

[105]   I.R.C. § 170(b)(1)(A), (b)(1)(G)(iii)(II).

[106]   I.R.C. § 170(b)(1)(C).

$50,000 treated as a carryover contribution of unreduced long-term capital gain property in the subsequent year.[107] Thus, T's total Section 170 deduction for the current year is $40,000 ($10,000 cash plus $30,000 equipment). As an alternative to the above consequences, T may elect to reduce the amount of the equipment contribution by its long-term capital gain (including Section 1231 gain) from $80,000 to $40,000,[108] with the result that the $40,000 of unappreciated equipment would be subject to and within the remaining Section 170(b)(1)(A) 50 percent ceiling of $40,000. If the election were made, T would have $50,000 of total contributions ($10,000 cash plus $40,000 equipment) for the current year and no carryover.[109] As a result of the election, T would increase T's current year's charitable deduction by $10,000, but lose the potential benefit of the $50,000 carryover amount of equipment in the succeeding five years.

Assume instead that T, again with a $100,000 contribution base, gives $5,000 cash to a public charity, AT & T stock with an adjusted basis of $20,000 and value of $35,000 to a public charity, and $25,000 cash to a private charity. Assume that the stock has been held long-term. T's total contributions to the public charities ($5,000 of cash and $35,000 of AT & T stock) are within the 60 percent limitation on cash contributions and the $45,000 remaining 50 percent limit, respectively.[110] Since all of T's gifts to public charity are considered prior to the gift to a private charity,[111] T is limited to a deduction of $10,000 to the private charity.[112] Taxpayer's $35,000 gift of AT & T stock to the public charity would be further limited to 30 percent of taxpayer's contribution base or $30,000,[113] and $15,000 of the gifts to the private charity would not be deductible in the current year.[114] Thus taxpayer would be allowed a $45,000 charitable deduction in the current year with nondeductible contributions being carried over to the succeeding year.[115] As an alternative, T could elect to reduce the AT & T stock given to public charity by the amount of its long-term capital gain from $35,000 to $20,000.[116] If the election were made, T could deduct the total $25,000 of gifts to public charity ($5,000 of cash and $20,000 of AT & T stock),[117] and the $25,000 cash gift to the private charity.[118] If the election were made, T's total

---

[107] I.R.C. § 170(b)(1)(C)(ii), (d)(1).

[108] I.R.C. § 170(b)(1)(C)(iii).

[109] Since the total amount of contributions ($40,000) does not exceed the reduced 50% contribution base ($40,000), there is no carryover under I.R.C. § 170(b)(1)(D).

[110] I.R.C. § 170(b)(1)(A), (G).

[111] Reg. § 1.170A–8(c)(2)(ii).

[112] I.R.C. § 170(b)(1)(B)(ii). The $10,000 amount represents the lesser of $30,000 (30% of taxpayer's contribution base) and $10,000 (50% of taxpayer's contribution base less all gifts to public charities without regard to the I.R.C. § 170(b)(1)(C) 30% limit, or $50,000 less $40,000 of cash and stock). Cf. Reg. § 1.170A–8(f) Example (2).

[113] I.R.C. § 170(b)(1)(C)(i).

[114] See note 112, supra.

[115] I.R.C. § 170(b)(1)(B), (C)(ii), (G)(iii). The nondeductible carryover contributions would include $15,000 to the private charity and $5,000 of AT & T stock to the public charity.

[116] I.R.C. § 170(b)(1)(C)(iii).

[117] I.R.C. § 170(b)(1)(A), (G).

[118] I.R.C. § 170(b)(1)(B)(ii).

charitable deduction for the year would be $50,000, but T would not have any carryover amounts in the succeeding years.[119]

In summary, Section 170(b) essentially imposes a 50 percent ceiling on individual gifts to public charities (60 percent for cash gifts) and a 30 percent ceiling on gifts for the use of public charities and to private charities. It imposes additional limitations on gifts of long-term capital gain property. Excess contributions in any of the above categories are subject to the five-year carryover rule.

*Year of Deduction.* A deduction for a charitable contribution may be taken only for the year in which the contribution is actually made, or when treated as actually made in a carryover year. Thus for Section 170 purposes, a taxpayer is on the cash method of accounting, even if the taxpayer otherwise uses the accrual method of accounting.[120] As a result, if a pledge is made to make a contribution in a future year, a contribution may not be deducted until the year in which the pledge is paid.[121] A credit card contribution, being the equivalent of cash, is deductible in the taxable year a charge is made to the credit card.[122] A contribution by check is deductible in the taxable year in which the check is delivered, provided that it is honored and paid and there are no restrictions as to time and manner of payment.[123] Gifts of property generally occur on the delivery of the property (or its title) to the donee.[124] Gifts of stock occur when the stock is transferred on the corporate books.[125]

*Verification.* One of the most difficult and controversial aspects of the charitable deduction is verifying contributions and valuing contributions or consideration received for such contributions. Over the years, the concept of "audit lottery" has led to several verification requirements with respect to charitable gifts.[126] A charitable contribution is allowed as a deduction only if it is properly verified.[127] If a contribution is in cash or its equivalent,[128] appropriate records of the contribution must be kept in the form of a bank record or a written communication from the donee showing the name of the donee organization and the date and amount of the contribution.[129] In addition, responsibilities are placed on both the donor and the charity to assure that appropriate valuation occurs. The subjective element of fair market value of non-cash property presents additional verification difficulties. If a contribution is made in property other than money, a variety of requirements, including independent appraisals, apply to both the donor

---

[119] T would have used up all of T's charitable contributions ($50,000 after the reduction in the AT & T stock to a public charity) with none remaining to be carried over.

[120] Reg. § 1.170A–1(a).

[121] Id. Mann v. Commissioner, 35 F.2d 873 (D.C.Cir.1929).

[122] Rev.Rul. 78–38, note 34, supra.

[123] Rev.Rul. 54–465, note 34, supra.

[124] Johnson v. United States, 280 F.Supp. 412 (N.D.N.Y.1967).

[125] J.W. Londen v. Commissioner, 45 T.C. 106 (1965).

[126] Expl. of Sen. Fin. Comm., 98th Cong., 2d Sess. 444 (1984).

[127] See I.R.C. § 170(a)(1) last sentence.

[128] See the Text at note 34, supra.

[129] I.R.C. § 170(f)(17). See the Text at notes 23 and 24, supra, if consideration in the form of goods and services is received.

and the charity.[130] Moreover, there are substantial penalties for underpayment of income tax as a result of overvaluation of property.[131]

For any contribution that exceeds $250,[132] a deduction is disallowed unless the donor has a contemporaneous[133] written acknowledgement[134] of the contribution from the donee organization.[135] If the contribution is of property worth more than $500 but not more than $5,000, the donor must attach a description of the contributed property to the donor's return.[136] If the property is worth more than $5,000 but not more than $500,000, the donor must obtain a "qualified appraisal" of the property[137] and attach an appraisal summary to the return.[138] Finally, if the property is worth more than $500,000, the donor must attach the qualified appraisal to the return.[139]

## PROBLEMS

1.   T's contribution base for the year of the following gifts is $150,000. During the year T makes contributions to Suntan U., an organization within § 170(b)(1)(A)(ii) and (c)(2), or to Private Foundation, which is within § 170(c)(2) but not within § 170(b)(1)(A)(vii). In each of the following circumstances assume all verification requirements are met and determine T's § 170 deduction for the current year, and what effect, if any, § 170(d)(1)(A) will have:

(a)   T gives $100,000 cash to Suntan U.

(b)   T gives land worth $100,000 to Suntan U. T's basis in the land is $100,000.

(c)   T gives $100,000 cash to Private Foundation.

(d)   T gives $60,000 cash to Suntan U. and $40,000 cash to Private Foundation.

(e)   T gives $20,000 cash to Suntan U. and $80,000 cash to Private Foundation.

(f)   T has a freshman daughter who attends Suntan U. and T pays $3,000 tuition for her and makes a $10,000 cash Sponsors'

---

[130] See, e.g., I.R.C. § 170(f)(11), (12).

[131] See I.R.C. § 6662(a), (b)(3), (e). But see I.R.C. § 6664(c).

[132] I.R.C. § 170(f)(8)(A). Separate payments during the year generally will not be aggregated, whereas separate checks written on the same day would be aggregated. HR (Conf.Rpt.) 2264, 103rd Cong., 1st Sess. 67 (note 9) (1993). This rule does not apply to contributions of motor vehicles. See I.R.C. § 170(f)(12)(A)(i), (B) and the Text at note 36, supra.

[133] The acknowledgement must be obtained prior to filing taxpayers' return for the year (or the due date, including extensions, for filing such return, if earlier). I.R.C. § 170(f)(8)(C).

[134] The acknowledgement must include a statement of the amount of cash and a description of (but not the value of) any noncash property as well as a good faith estimate of the value of any goods or services provided by the donee to the donor. I.R.C. § 170(f)(8)(B).

[135] I.R.C. § 170(f)(8). The burden is on the taxpayer to acquire such substantiation.

[136] I.R.C. § 170(f)(11)(B).

[137] I.R.C. § 170(f)(11)(E)(i).

[138] I.R.C. § 170(f)(11)(C).

[139] I.R.C. § 170(f)(11)(D).

Club contribution. Children of members of the Sponsors' Club are automatically admitted to Suntan U.

**2.**   This problem involves transfers of property by T, an individual, to Suntan U. and Private Foundation both as described in 1, above, in the current year. Assume that in the current year T has a $200,000 "contribution base," all verification requirements are met, and unless otherwise stated T makes no other charitable gifts. T owns property with a basis of $70,000 and a value of $90,000.

   (a) If the property is inventory (manufactured equipment) and T contributes it to Suntan U., what will T's charitable deduction be?

   (b) If the property is inventory (manufactured equipment) and T contributes it to Private Foundation, what will T's charitable contribution be?

   (c) If the property is corporate stock held for more than one year and T contributes it to Suntan U. what will T's charitable contribution be?

   (d) Same as (c), above, except the stock has been held only five months.

   (e) What result under the facts of (c), above, if T exercises the election proffered by § 170(b)(1)(C)(iii)?

   (f) What result if T gives Suntan U. § 1245 property which if sold would be subject to $10,000 of § 1245 recapture?

   (g) Same as (c), above, except that the stock was given to Private Foundation rather than Suntan U. Assume the stock is not publicly traded. Cf. § 170(e)(5).

   (h) Same as (g), above, except that the stock is § 170(e)(5) "qualified appreciated stock."

**3.**   After completing his term of office Publius Maximus who has been in a high office for several years donates his private working papers to Charity U. The papers are properly valued at $100,000.

   (a) Will Publius be allowed a charitable deduction for the gift? See § 1221(a)(3).

   (b) Publius also teaches Sunday School at his church. Will he be allowed a charitable deduction for the value of his services? See Reg. § 1.170A–1(g).

   (c) Publius donates blood (worth $100) during the year to the blood bank. Deductible? Consider Rev. Rul. 53–162, 1953–2 C.B. 127, and Green v. Commissioner, 74 T.C. 1229 (1980).

   (d) Publius allows the United Way Crusade to use an office in a building that he owns; the office has a fair rental value of $100 per month. Is he allowed a deduction for the value of the use of the office? See § 170(f)(3)(A) and note § 170(f)(2)(B). See also Rev.Rul. 70–477, 1970–2 C.B. 62, and § 170(f)(3)(B)(iii) and (h).

(e) Publius volunteers for the National Ski Patrol. He travels each weekend to a ski resort incurring costs of travel, meals and lodging. Deductible? See § 170(j).

(f) Publius responds to Charity's newspaper ad by donating his car, which is dented and has some mechanical problems, to Charity. The Blue Book value for the car is $6,000 but Charity immediately sells the car for $4,000. See § 170(f)(12).

(g) Publius spends $20,000 developing a patent which Publius gives to Charity when it is worth $100,000.

**4.** Planner has held for four years some investment land that she purchased at a cost of $60,000 subject to a $40,000 mortgage. In the current year when her contribution base (prior to the "transfer" below) is $50,000 and the land is now worth $80,000, she transfers the land to Charity U., an organization within § 170(b)(1)(A)(ii) and (c)(2) which assumes the $40,000 mortgage. Assuming all verification requirements are met:

(a) Does Planner have any gain or loss on the transfer?

(b) What is her charitable deduction?

**5.** Investor who earns $80,000 per year has a stock and bond portfolio worth about $100,000. Some of her investments have substantially appreciated in value and some have declined in value. Investor generally makes several charitable gifts to her church and her college alma mater.

(a) From a planning perspective, what advice do you have for Investor?

(b) What are the tax consequences if Investor is 73 years old and if some of the stocks and bonds given are in Investor's Individual Retirement Account (I.R.A.)? See § 408(d)(8).

## C. CASUALTY AND THEFT LOSSES

### 1. NATURE OF LOSSES ALLOWED[*]

Internal Revenue Code: Section 165(a), (c), (h)(5)(A), (i)(5).

Regulations: Section 1.165–1(e), –7(a)(1), (3), (5), –8(a)(1), (d).

———

Losses incurred by a taxpayer may have an impact on the taxpayer's tax liability. As indicated in Chapter 14, losses are generally deductible under Section 165(a). Subsection (c) imposes some limitations regarding individuals. Losses incurred in the taxpayer's trade or business are deductible under Section 165(a) and (c)(1) without regard to how they

———

[*] See Kaplow, "Income Tax as Insurance: The Casualty Loss and Medical Expense Deductions and the Exclusion of Medical Insurance Premiums," 79 Cal.L.Rev. 1485 (1991); Note, "The Casualty Loss Deduction and Consumer Expectation: Section 165(c)(3) of the Internal Revenue Code," 36 U.Chi.L.Rev. 220 (1968); the statutory concepts are attacked in Epstein, "The Consumption and Loss of Personal Property under the Internal Revenue Code," 23 Stan.L.Rev. 454 (1971).

arise. Deductions claimed in this category may be challenged as not really incurred in business, a problem to which Section 183 is addressed. Chapter 15 reflects another possible ground on which a taxpayer may claim a loss deduction without regard to how the loss arises, namely that the loss is within Section 165(a) and (c)(2) as one incurred in a transaction entered into for profit, although not in a trade or business. Although deductible, both business and profit-seeking activity losses are restricted sometimes under Section 165(f), which allows capital losses only to the extent allowed under Sections 1211 and 1212.[1]

A loss may of course occur outside the taxpayer's business or in a transaction not entered into for profit. Generally these losses are not deductible, in keeping with the philosophy of Section 262 which forecloses deductions for personal, living or family expenses. The statute does not expressly foreclose these deductions; it simply does not provide for them. It will be recalled that a taxpayer gets no deduction for a loss on the sale of his residence unless after he converts it to property held for profit he sustains a loss. However, subject to limitations, Section 165(c)(3) permits a deduction for some losses unconnected with business and not involved in an attempt to make a profit. What losses? "Casualty" and "theft" losses. Casualty or theft business losses or profit seeking losses may and should be treated under Section 165(c)(1) or Section 165(c)(2), respectively, without regard to Section 165(c)(3). Those losses are characterized under Section 1231.[2] Section 165(c)(3) losses are characterized under Section 165(h), which is considered below.

Nevertheless, we are concerned here with losses arising out of a casualty or by theft which *need* Section 165(c)(3) to make the scene. They are losses with respect to purely personal items of property. These losses raise first a question of the scope of the statutory concepts of "casualty" and "theft." We must also then consider: second, the time at which (taxable year for which) these losses are to be deducted and, third, the measurement and characterization of casualty and theft losses. For the most part, the answers to the timing and measurement questions are the same whether the losses concern business or profit-seeking or merely personal use property.

## Revenue Ruling 63–232

1963–2 Cum.Bull. 97.

The Internal Revenue Service has re-examined its position with regard to the deductibility of losses resulting from termite damage, as set forth in Revenue Ruling 59–277, C.B. 1959–2, 73.

Revenue Ruling 59–277 stated that the Service would follow the rule of George L. Buist, et ux. v. United States, 164 F.Supp. 218 (1958);

---

[1]    See Chapter 21C, supra.

[2]    See Chapter 21H2, supra.

Martin A. Rosenberg v. Commissioner, 198 F.2d 46 (1952); and Joseph Shopmaker et al. v. United States, 119 F.Supp. 705 (1953), only in those cases where the facts were substantially the same. The courts in these cases held that damage caused by termites over periods up to 15 months after infestation constituted a deductible casualty loss under section 165 of the Internal Revenue Code of 1954.

Revenue Ruling 59–277 further stated that in other cases, the Service would follow the rule announced in Charles J. Fay et al. v. Helvering, 120 F.2d 253 (1941); United States v. Betty Rogers, et al., 120 F.2d 244 (1941); and Leslie C. Dodge et ux. v. Commissioner, 25 T.C. 1022 (1956). In the latter cases the termite infestation and subsequent damage occurred over periods of several years.

An extensive examination of scientific data regarding the habits, destructive power and other factors peculiar to termites discloses that the biological background of all termites found in the United States is generally the same, with one notable exception. The subterranean or ground dwelling termite attacks only wood which is in contact with the ground, while the other types of termites attack wood directly from the air.

Leading authorities on the subject have concluded that little or no structural damage can be caused by termites during the first two years after the initial infestation. It has been estimated that under normal conditions, if left unchecked, depending upon climate and other factors, an infestation of three to eight years would be required to necessitate extensive repairs. Even under extreme conditions, the period would be from one to six years. See "Our Enemy the Termite" by Thomas Elliott Snyder; "Termite and Termite Control" by Charles A. Kofoid; "Insects Their Ways and Means of Living" by Robert Evans Snodgrass; and other authorities.

Such authorities agree that termite infestation and the resulting damage cannot be inflicted with the suddenness comparable to that caused by fire, storm or shipwreck.

Accordingly, it is the position of the Service, based on the scientific data available in this area, that damage caused by termites to property not connected with the trade or business does not constitute an allowable deduction as a casualty loss within the meaning of section 165(c)(3) of the Code. Such damage is the result of gradual deterioration through a steadily operating cause and is not the result of an identifiable event of a sudden, unusual or unexpected nature. Further, time elapsed between the incurrence of damage and its ultimate discovery is not a proper measure to determine whether the damage resulted from a casualty. Time of discovery of the damage, in some situations, may affect the extent of the damage, but this does not change the form or the nature of the event, the mode of its operation, or the character of the result. These characteristics are determinative when applying section 165(c)(3) of the Code.

The Internal Revenue Service will no longer follow the decisions of *Buist, Rosenberg,* and *Shopmaker,* supra. The only real distinction between these cases and the decisions of *Rogers, Fay* and *Dodge,* supra, is the time in which the loss was discovered.

Under the authority contained in section 7805(b) of the Code, Revenue Ruling 59–277, C.B. 1959–2, 73, is revoked for all taxable years beginning after November 12, 1963.

\* \* \*

# Pulvers v. Commissioner*
United States Court of Appeals, Ninth Circuit, 1969.
407 F.2d 838.

■ CHAMBERS, CIRCUIT JUDGE.

Can taxpayers on their federal income tax return take a deduction for an "other casualty loss" when as a consequence of a nearby landslide that ruined three nearby homes, but did no physical damage to the property of taxpayers, with a resultant loss of value because of common fear the mountain might attack their residence and lot next? (There is yet no substantial impairment of ingress or egress on the street serving their home.) We agree with the tax court that they cannot.

\* \* \*

The tax court affirmed the commissioner's determination that the taxpayers incurred no actual loss: that they suffered a hypothetical loss or a mere fluctuation in value.

It may be that the loss is all in the heads of taxpayers and of prospective purchasers, but that circumstance has resulted in a very substantial depreciation of value. (Of course, if the rest of the hill or mountain remains quiet for many years, some or most of the value would come back.) But we would agree with the Los Angeles County assessor that the value certainly went down. And, the finding that the loss was a "mere" fluctuation in value is enough to aggravate any taxpayer.

We think their loss is one that the Congress could not have intended to include in Sec. 165(c)(3). The specific losses named are fire, storm, shipwreck, and theft. Each of those surely involves physical damage or loss of the physical property. Thus, we read "or other casualty," in para materia, meaning "something like those specifically mentioned." The first things that one thinks of as "other casualty losses" are earthquakes and automobile collision losses, both involving physical damage losses.

One trouble with the construction of taxpayers on "other casualty" is that the consequences are limitless. Think of the thousands of claims that

---

* Cf. I.R.C. § 165(k) discussed at page 827, infra. The subsection does not alter the result in this case. Ed.

could be made for loss of value because of shift of highways, but still involving no lack of ingress.

If one is over the San Andreas fault in California, an authentic report (if one could be had) that it is about to slip would depreciate one's property value before the event.* A notorious gangster buying the house next door would depreciate the value of one's property.

It is difficult to imagine the consequences of taxpayers' reading of the statute. The internal revenue service now has an army of tax gatherers and it always claims it does not have enough. Think of the number this door, if opened, would add. We will not imply that the Congress intended such a thing. Of course, if the courts would so imply, the Congress would straighten us out very quickly.

We agree with the Fourth Circuit case of Citizens Bank of Weston v. Commissioner, 252 F.2d 425. Also, our reading of United States v. White Dental Co., 274 U.S. 398, 47 S.Ct. 598, indicates the result we reach here.

Some day we may get a case where a condition has arisen of such certain future consequences that the taxpayer in good sense has absolutely abandoned his property. It might call for a different result, but we shall not reach it here. Neither do we reach the case where egress and ingress have been lost for the foreseeable future or materially impaired.

The taxpayers' argument is appealing. The ingenuity is admirable. But the language is such that we do not think the Congress intended the contended for construction.

The decision of the Tax Court is affirmed.

## Allen v. Commissioner

Tax Court of the United States, 1951.
16 T.C. 163.

Petitioner contests respondent's adjustment disallowing a deduction for loss by theft, accounting for a deficiency of $1,800.16 in income tax for 1945.

* * *

Opinion

■ VAN FOSSAN, JUDGE:

* * * Stripped to essentials, the facts are that petitioner owned a brooch which she lost in some manner while visiting the Metropolitan Museum of Art in New York. She does not, and cannot, prove that the pin was stolen. All we know is that the brooch disappeared and was never found by, or returned to, petitioner.

---

* Cf. Lewis F. Ford, 33 T.C.M. 496 (1974), denying deduction for loss in value because of fear of future storms. Ed.

Petitioner has the burden of proof. This includes presentation of proof which, absent positive proof, reasonably leads us to conclude that the article was stolen. If the reasonable inferences from the evidence point to theft, the proponent is entitled to prevail. If the contrary be true and reasonable inferences point to another conclusion, the proponent must fail. If the evidence is in equipoise preponderating neither to the one nor the other conclusion, petitioner has not carried her burden.

In the case at bar we cannot find as a fact that a theft occurred. The reasonable inferences from the evidence point otherwise. It is noted that there is no evidence as to the nature of the clasp by which the pin was fastened to petitioner's dress. We do not know whether it was a "safety clasp" or merely a simple clasp. Nor is there any evidence that petitioner was jostled in the crowd (the usual occurrence when a theft from the person is attempted). If the pin was properly equipped (as may be assumed from its value) with a safety clasp and securely fastened to petitioner's dress, the question arises as to how it could have been removed without damage to the dress, there being no testimony as to any such damage. If it were essential to the disposition of this case that we find either that the pin was lost by theft or was lost by inadvertence, our finding on the record made would be that it was lost by some mischance or inadvertence—not by theft. The inference that such was true is the more readily drawn. However, we need not go so far. We need only hold that petitioner, who had the burden of proof, has not established that the loss was occasioned by theft, a *sine qua non* to a decision in her favor under section 23(e)(3).

We see no merit in petitioner's argument based on the New York Criminal Statutes which hold that the finder of a lost article shall report the finding and make certain efforts toward locating the owner. These statutes are neither binding nor persuasive here. There is no evidence that the pin was ever found and thus the New York statute could not be invoked against anyone. This argument but emphasizes the lack of proof which characterizes the record in this case.

We sustain the respondent's determination.

Reviewed by the Court.

Decision will be entered for the respondent.

■ OPPER, J., dissenting:

As the hearer of the evidence, I would find the fact to be that petitioner's brooch was stolen. I would do so for the very reason that the Court now finds otherwise; that is, that of all the possibilities, the most probable is a loss by theft.

This conclusion presupposes that we believe the testimony of the witnesses. Having heard them testify, I have no reservations in this respect. If the evidence is believed, petitioner had the brooch pinned on her dress at about 4:30 in the afternoon. She was present only in well lighted rooms so constructed that no article could reasonably be lost—

especially in view of the subsequent search which the record shows. At 5 o'clock she discovered that the brooch was missing, having in the meantime mingled with a crowd of 5,000 people preparing to leave the museum.

Accepting this evidence, the three possibilities are thus: that the brooch dropped off and has never been found; that it was found but not turned in, and that it was stolen by some person in the crowd. The first may be disregarded as not a reasonable probability; the second would be impossible if the finder were honest. It assumes a virtual concealment which in the case of so valuable an object would actually amount to a theft. Taken with the third, it necessarily points to theft as the only reasonable cause of disappearance.

The suggestion that failure to show the condition of the clasp is fatal to petitioner's case seems to me to prove too much. If the clasp were so difficult to open as to make its removal unlikely, it is even more improbable that it could have fallen off by itself; and if it could open accidentally so as to allow the brooch to fall off, it must have been easy game for a competent sneak thief. Since the clasp in any condition would make removal more likely than mere accidental opening, it is only on the assumption that she was not being candid that petitioner's failure to produce such evidence could be the ground for the result now reached.

Absolute proof by an eye witness is so improbable that the burden now being imposed upon taxpayers virtually repeals *pro tanto* section 23(e)(3). Ever since Appeal of Howard J. Simons, in 1 B.T.A. at page 351, the rule has been otherwise. Without regard to the New York penal law, to which, however, resort would appear to be authorized by the precedents,[1] the probabilities of theft have been demonstrated as completely as such circumstances could ever permit. I see no reason now for departing from principles so well settled and so long established.

■ LEECH and TIETJENS, JJ., agree with this dissent.

## 2. OTHER ASPECTS OF CASUALTY AND THEFT LOSSES

Internal Revenue Code: Section 165(b), (c)(3), (e), (h)(1)–(4)(A) and (5), (i)(5). See Sections 67(b)(3); 123; 165(i), (k).

Regulations: Section 1.165–1(d)(1) through (3), –7(a)(1), (2), (b)(1) and (3) Ex. (1), –8(a)(2), (c), –11(a) and (d).

––––––––––––––

*Timing.* Once it is determined that there is a casualty or theft loss, the questions arise: When did the loss occur and for what year is a deduction allowed?[1] Casualty losses are deductible for the year in which

––––––––––––––

[1]   Morris Plan Co. of St. Joseph, 42 B.T.A. 1190, 1195; Earle v. Commissioner, (CCA–2) 72 F.2d 366.

[1]   The broad treatment of tax timing principles appears in this book at Chapters 19 and 20, supra.

the loss is sustained.[2] This may be the year of the casualty or a later year in which the amount of the loss is ascertained, in a case where the full extent of the loss was not or by its very nature could not be known until a subsequent year.[3]

Under a limited statutory alternative, the deduction may be allowed for a year prior to the casualty. Under Section 165(i) if a casualty loss is attributable to a disaster in an area subsequently declared by the President to warrant assistance under the Disaster Relief Act of 1974, the taxpayer may elect to claim the deduction for the year immediately before the year in which the casualty occurred. The Section 165(i) timing rule is also applicable to a taxpayer whose residence is in a federally declared disaster area if the residence is rendered unsafe for use as a residence as a proximate result of the disaster or if the taxpayer is ordered by the government to demolish or relocate the residence.[4]

Theft losses are generally a deduction for the year in which the theft is discovered.[5] It has been held that when a theft is discovered in year one the loss must be deducted in year one and, if in subsequent years the taxpayer recalls additional items that were taken, their loss must be deducted in year one by means of an amended return or refund claim, rather than in the subsequent years.[6] However, the timing rule is generally helpful to taxpayers. For example, an embezzlement that occurred in year one but which is discovered in year four, gives rise to a year four deduction. If the reverse were true, use of the year one deduction would be foreclosed by statutes of limitation.[7]

The regulations recognize an exception to the general timing rules for both casualties and thefts. If in the year of the casualty or discovery of the theft there exists a reasonable prospect of recovery of the loss, the portion of the loss with respect to which there is a recovery prospect is not deductible unless or until it becomes clear there will be no recovery.[8] It is possible, however, that a loss is properly claimed for year one because no "reasonable prospect of recovery" exists in that year. In year two reimbursement is unexpectedly received. With what consequences? The amount recovered is treated as income when received in year two; the tax for year one is *not* recomputed.[9] This is a part of the tax benefit doctrine previously considered in Chapter 20, supra.

---

[2]   Reg. § 1.165–7(a)(1).

[3]   Licht v. Commissioner, 37 B.T.A. 1096 (1938), acq., 1963–2 C.B. 3; Kunsman v. Commissioner, 49 T.C. 62 (1967).

[4]   I.R.C. § 165(k).

[5]   I.R.C. § 165(e).

[6]   Elliott v. Commissioner, 40 T.C. 304 (1963), acq., 1964–2 (Part 1) C.B. 3.

[7]   See Chapter 28C, infra.

[8]   Reg. § 1.165–1(d)(2), (3). See Ander v. Commissioner, 47 T.C. 592 (1967); Ramsay Scarlett & Co., Inc. v. Commissioner, 61 T.C. 795 (1974); Hudock v. Commissioner, 65 T.C. 351 (1975).

[9]   Montgomery v. Commissioner, 65 T.C. 511 (1975). Cf. I.R.C. § 111(a).

*Measuring Losses.* The rules of Reg. Section 1.165–7(b) present a fairly clear picture of the determination of the initial amount of common casualty and theft[10] losses. Study them. As the regulation indicates, the amount is generally the same whether the loss is incurred in a trade or business or in a transaction entered into for profit or is merely personal. Under all such circumstances questions of valuation may create difficulty.[11] There are three important differences however.

First, business or profit classification makes inapplicable the $100 floor[12] which, on a de minimis principle similar to avoidance of trivial insurance claims, disallows the first $100 of loss from each casualty regarding purely personal assets. These losses can be claimed under Section 165(c)(1) or (2), escaping the Section 165(h)(1) limitation which applies only to (c)(3) losses.

Second, the regulations provide that losses of a purely personal nature never exceed the difference in value of the property before and after the casualty. The regulations incorporate the Supreme Court's holding in *Helvering v. Owens*[13] in which the Court stated:

The courts below have given opposing answers to the question whether the basis for determining the amount of a loss sustained during the taxable year through injury to property not used in a trade or business [or held for the production of income, Ed.], and therefore not the subject of an annual depreciation allowance, should be original cost or value immediately before the casualty.[14] To resolve this conflict we granted certiorari in both cases.

In No. 180 the facts are that the respondent Donald H. Owens purchased an automobile at a date subsequent to March 1, 1913, and prior to 1934, for $1825, and used it for pleasure until June 1934 when it was damaged in a collision. The car was not insured. Prior to the accident its fair market value was $225; after that event the fair market value was $190. The respondents filed a joint income tax return for the calendar year 1934 in which they claimed a deduction of $1635, the difference between cost and fair market value after the casualty. The Commissioner reduced the deduction to $35, the difference in market value before and after the collision. The Board of Tax Appeals sustained the taxpayers' claim and the Circuit Court of Appeals affirmed its ruling.

---

10 See also Reg. § 1.165–8(c).

11 See Reg. § 1.165–7(a)(2). Cf. Smith's Estate v. Commissioner, 510 F.2d 479 (2d Cir.1975), cert. denied 423 U.S. 827, 96 S.Ct. 44 (1975), valuing nonrepresentational art objects for estate tax purposes; Eiferman v. Commissioner, 35 T.C.M. 790 (1976).

12 See I.R.C. § 165(h)(1) and Reg. § 1.165–7(b)(4).

13 305 U.S. 468, 59 S.Ct. 260 (1939).

14 Helvering v. Owens, 95 F.2d 318; Helvering v. Obici, 97 F.2d 431.

In No. 318 it appears that the taxpayer ... red a boat, boathouse, and pier in 1926 at a cost of $5,3... August 1933 the property, which had been used solely fo... re, and was uninsured, was totally destroyed by a sto... actual value immediately prior to destruction was $3... he taxpayers claimed the right to deduct cost in the co... ion of taxable income. The Commissioner allowed on... e at date of destruction. The Board of Tax Appeals he... the taxpayers but the Circuit Court of Appeals reversed... ard's ruling.

\* \* \*

The income tax acts have consistently ... ved deduction for exhaustion, wear and tear, or obsolesce... lly in the case of "property used in the trade or busin... or "held for the production of income." Ed.] The taxpay... these cases could not, therefore, have claimed any dedu... n this account for years prior to that in which the cas... occurred. For this reason they claim they may deduct upo... unadjusted basis,— that is,—cost. As the income tax laws ... or accounting on an annual basis; as they provide fo... uctions for "losses sustained during the taxable year" ... the taxpayer is not allowed annual deductions for de... tion of nonbusiness property; as § [165(b)] requires that ... deduction shall be on "the adjusted basis provided in ... ion [1011(a)]," thus contemplating an adjustment ... alue consequent on depreciation; and as the propert... olved was subject to depreciation and of less value in ... taxable year, than its original cost, we think § [1016... must be read as a limitation upon the amount of the ... ction so that it may not exceed cost, and in the case of depr... le non-business property may not exceed the amount of the ... actually sustained in the taxable year, measured by the ... depreciated value of the property. The Treasury rulings ... not been consistent, but this construction is the one whic... s finally been adopted.[15]

[The Supreme Court revers... e judgment in case No. 180 and affirmed the judgment in ... e No. 318, holding for the government in both cases. Ed.]

The same rule generally applies to ... ness and profit-making property. However, in the case of business or ... fit making property that is totally destroyed the loss deduction is for ... full adjusted basis of the property (less reimbursements) even if th... amount exceeds the *value* of the property before the casualty. Can ... rationalize this distinction?

The third difference is that t... ection 1231 hotchpot rules apply to characterize only business and p... t-making property gains and losses.

---

[15] Treasury Regulations 86, Arts. ... 1, 23(h)1, 113(b)1; G.C.M. XV 1, Cumulative Bulletin 115–118.

The deductibility of [such a]nd casualty gains and losses of such property is limited if the loss[es are c]apital by Sections 1211 and 1212.[16]

Section 165(h)([2] cont)ains a separate hotchpot to characterize personal casualty g[ains an]d losses. In order to understand Section 165(h)(2), recognize f[irst tha]t one may have gains as well as losses from theft or casualty. For [examp]le, if a thief steals a ring with a cost basis of $1,000 which is wor[th $10],000 and the owner collects $10,000 of insurance, the result [is a $9],000 gain to the owner. If total personal *recognized*[17] *gains* fro[m theft] or casualty for a year exceed such losses (after the $100 floor for [each l]oss), Section 165(h)(2)(B) characterizes all such gains and losses [as ca]pital gains and losses and imposes no restrictions on the dedu[ctibilit]y of the losses.[18] The gains or losses are either short-term or long[-term] gains or loss depending on each property's holding period. Alternati[vely, if] *such losses exceed gains*, the deductibility of such losses is severely l[imi]ted by the 2017 Tax Cuts and Jobs Act.[19] Under Section 165(h)(5), [the o]nly net losses that are deductible are casualty (not theft) losses [that] are attributable to a Federally declared disaster.[20] If these limited [deduc]tible losses exceed gains, both gains and losses remain ordinary (du[e to] lack of a sale or exchange), but Section 165(h)(2)(A)(i) allows the los[ses to] be deducted, first, only to the extent of gains;[21] and then, any losses [in ex]cess of the gains are deductible only to the extent they exceed 10% [of the] taxpayer's adjusted gross income for the year.[22] If a taxpayer's Fed[erally] declared disaster losses do not exceed gains and the taxpayer has o[ther c]asualty and theft losses, those other losses are deductible, but onl[y to t]he extent of the net gains after the disaster losses, effectively resu[lting] in a wash.[23]

## PROBLEMS

1.   At a cost of $10,000, Sleepy p[urcha]sed a car three years ago for personal use. In the current year, she doz[ed] one night while driving and the car attached itself to a tree. Before th[e acc]ident, the car was worth $8,000 but, after the accident, only $1,000. At [the ti]me of the accident Sleepy was taking a vase, a decorative ornament in h[er ho]me, to a dealer to have it appraised. It had been purchased two years [earl]ier for $10,000, and it was totally destroyed in the accident. Sleepy re[cove]red $1,000 in insurance for the car

---

[16] To the extent that any such property [has be]en held only up to one year, I.R.C. § 1231 is inapplicable, and the gain or loss on such prop[erty is] an ordinary gain or loss.

[17] I.R.C. §§ 121, 1033.

[18] But see I.R.C. §§ 165(f), 1211(b), 1212(b).

[19] See I.R.C. § 165(h)(5).

[20] I.R.C. § 165(h)(5)(A).

[21] I.R.C. § 165(h)(2)(A)(i).

[22] I.R.C. § 165(h)(2)(A)(ii). See I.R.C. § 165[(h)(5)](A) treating such losses to the extent of gains as deductible under § 62. Such treatment is [t]he purpose of measuring adjusted gross income under § 165(h)(2)(A)(ii) and also for comp[uting] the taxpayer's taxable income. To the extent deductible, losses in excess of gains are it[emiz]ed deductions. However, they are not a miscellaneous itemized deduction. I.R.C. § 67(b)(3).

[23] I.R.C. § 165(h)(5)(B)(i).

and $20,000 for the vase. Disregarding the above transactions Sleepy has an adjusted gross income of $30,000.

    (a)   What is the amount of Sleepy's personal casualty loss on the car for the year?

    (b)   What is the amount of Sleepy's personal casualty gain on the vase for the year?

    (c)   What is the character of those gains and losses?

    (d)   To what extent are Sleepy's losses deductible?

    (e)   Is the deduction an itemized deduction?

    (f)   What results in (a)–(e), above, if Sleepy recovers only $12,000 in insurance for the vase?

    (g)   What differences in the results in (a)–(e), above, above if Sleepy avoids the insurance company and does not collect the $1,000 of auto insurance because she fears the company will cancel her policy? See § 165(h)(4)(E).

    (h)   What differences in results in (a)–(e), above, if, instead of the auto casualty, Sleepy's uninsured house, which prior to the casualty has a $40,000 adjusted basis and a $60,000 fair market value, is totally destroyed in a forest fire which is a Federally declared disaster?

**2.**    Shaky's house is damaged in an earthquake and he and his family are required to live in a motel and eat their meals in a restaurant while repairs are made. Shaky's insurance policy pays the total cost of the repairs and, additionally, pays $1200 of the family's meals and lodging expenses which total $1800 during the repair period. Normally Shaky would pay only $1,000 for these expenses during the period. What tax consequences to Shaky? See § 123.

# PART 7

# DEFERRAL AND NONRECOGNITION OF INCOME AND DEDUCTIONS

# CHAPTER 24

# THE INTERRELATIONSHIP OF TIMING AND CHARACTERIZATION

## A. TRANSACTIONS UNDER SECTION 453

### 1. THE GENERAL RULE

Internal Revenue Code: Sections 453(a), (b)(1), (c), (d), (f)(3).

Regulations: Sections 15A.453–1(a), (b)(2)(i), (ii), (iii), (v).

---

A simple example illustrates the need for Section 453. Assume Seller purchased a parcel of land as an investment ten years ago at a cost of $40,000 and it is now worth $400,000. Buyer approaches Seller and wants to purchase the property, but Buyer has little cash available. Seller agrees to sell the property to Buyer, who will pay Seller $400,000 in four years. In the meantime, Buyer will make adequate interest payments[1] on the outstanding $400,000 obligation. As a result of the transaction Seller has a $360,000 realized gain. Were it not for the Section 453 installment sale provisions, Seller would recognize the entire gain in the current year.[2] Obviously, Seller has a problem; Seller currently has received no cash from the transaction with which to pay an income tax generated by the sale of the property. Congress, recognizing Seller's plight enacted Section 453, the installment sales provision, to provide Seller relief from this liquidity problem.[3] In general, under Section 453 Seller's gain is included in gross income only as payments are received from Buyer,[4] thereby providing Seller with the necessary liquidity to pay the tax on the gain.[5]

Section 453 essentially is a timing provision, generally available to both cash and accrual method taxpayers. This topic technically could

---

[1]  See I.R.C. § 483 considered at Chapter 24C, infra.

[2]  I.R.C. § 1001(a) and (c). See Chapter 24B, infra.

[3]  Cf. H.Rep. No. 91–413, pt. 1, 91st Cong., 1st Sess. 107 (1969), 1969–3 C.B. 267.

[4]  See I.R.C. § 453(a)(1), (c).

[5]  Substantial amendments were made to I.R.C. § 453 by the Installment Sales Revision Act of 1980 providing most of the current installment sales rules. Pub.Law No. 96–471, 94 Stat. 2247 (1980). Articles discussing § 453 after the Installment Sales Revision Act of 1980 include: Emory and Hjorth, "An Analysis of the Changes Made by the Installment Sales Revision Act of 1980," 54 J. Tax'n 66–71 and 130–137 (1981); Ginsburg, "Future Payment Sales After the 1980 Revision Act," 39 N.Y.U.Inst. on Fed.Tax. Ch. 43 (1981); Mylan, "Installment Sales Revision Act of 1980," 17 Willamette L.Rev. 303 (1981). For an article proposing the subsequently enacted 1980 changes, see Ginsburg, "Taxing the Sale for Future Payment," 30 Tax L.Rev. 469 (1975).

have been previously discussed in Chapter 19. Since installment sales are substantially interrelated with characterization of income,[6] consideration of the installment sales provision has been deferred from the timing rules of Chapter 19 to this Chapter. Not only is Section 453 an important provision, it is also the culmination of many of the concepts learned earlier in this course.[7] Therefore it provides an opportunity to revisit several concepts and rules previously discussed.

An "installment sale" of property occurs when at least one payment of the total purchase price is to be received after the close of the taxable year in which the disposition occurs.[8] When an installment sale occurs, Section 453 allows the gain to be spread over the payment period by requiring a percentage of each payment to be included in gross income in the year of receipt. Section 453(c) provides the method for calculating the percentage of each payment[9] to be included in the seller's gross income as each payment is received. The percentage is the ratio of the "gross profit"[10] to the "total contract price."[11] The gross profit is the gain on the sale of the property that will be realized over the life of all of the payments, and the total contract price is generally the selling price[12] of the property.[13] In addition, adequate interest must be paid on the obligation.[14]

Returning to the example above, assume that Seller and Buyer agree that Buyer will pay Seller $100,000 per year for four years, with adequate interest on any unpaid balance. The sale results in a gross profit of $360,000 ($400,000 amount realized on the property over the life of the payments less the $40,000 adjusted basis) and a total contract price of $400,000. As each $100,000 payment is made, the ratio of the gross profit to the total contract price ($360,000/$400,000) or 90 percent of the payment received is included in Seller's gross income. Thus there is $90,000 of gross income as each payment is made with the result that Seller's $360,000 gain realized on the sale is spread over the four year payment period. The total gain realized on the sale is eventually included

---

[6]   See Chapter 21, supra.

[7]   See, e.g., the concept of assignment of income considered in Chapter 12, supra.

[8]   I.R.C. § 453(b)(1).

[9]   Generally the term "payment" does not include the receipt of evidences of indebtedness of the person acquiring the property. I.R.C. § 453(f)(3). However, receipt of evidences of indebtedness which are payable on demand, or are issued by corporations and government entities and readily tradeable will be treated as payments. I.R.C. § 453(f)(4). See Reg. § 15A.453–1(b)(3).

[10]   Reg. § 15A.453–1(b)(2)(v).

[11]   Reg. § 15A.453–1(b)(2)(iii).

[12]   Reg. § 15A.453–1(b)(2)(ii). Selling price means the gross selling price without reduction for any existing indebtedness on the property. Selling expenses are not deducted from the selling price, but are added to the adjusted basis for purposes of determining the gross profit ratio.

[13]   See Reg. § 15A.453–1(b)(2)(iii). The contract price is adjusted for any qualified indebtedness assumed or taken subject to by the buyer. Id. See Chapter 24A4 at notes 1–7, infra.

[14]   Cf. I.R.C. § 483. Interest payments are taxed under the Seller's method of accounting separate from the payment of the principal obligation.

in Seller's gross income, but the timing of the inclusion depends upon the timing of Buyer's payments.[15]

Consistent with the policy of spreading the gain over the life of the payments, the character of the gain recognized is governed by the character of the gain which would have been recognized if the property had been sold for its full fair market value in cash.[16] Thus, because Seller's investment land was a capital asset held for longer than one year, each $90,000 inclusion in gross income constitutes a long-term capital gain from the sale of an asset held for ten years.[17]

A taxpayer may affirmatively elect not to use Section 453 installment sales treatment.[18] The election must be made on or before the due date (including extensions) of the taxpayer's income tax return for the taxable year in which the sale or other disposition of the property occurs.[19] The consequences of an election-out are considered in the next subpart of this Chapter.[20] Why would a taxpayer ever want to elect out of Section 453 treatment?

## 2. Contingent Sales Price

Internal Revenue Code: Section 453(j)(2).

Regulations: Sections 15A.453–1(c)(1), (2)(i)(A), (3)(i), (4).

---

Prior to 1980 it was sometimes to a taxpayer's advantage to postpone the gain on a sale of property by providing a contingency under a sales contract thereby precluding the applicability of Section 453. In the Installment Sales Revision Act of 1980, Congress provided that even sales with a contingent sale price were to be subject to Section 453 treatment.[1] The Senate Committee Report of the 1980 legislation reported the change in the law as follows:[2]

> **Present Law.**—As a general rule, installment reporting of gain from deferred payments is not available where all or a portion of the selling price is subject to a contingency. The case

---

[15] If the amount of payments is unequal, then the amounts included in gross income are also unequal. For example, if Buyer paid Seller $100,000 in year one, $50,000 in years two and three and $200,000 in year four, Seller would include 90% ($360,000/$400,000) of each payment in gross income or $90,000 in year one, $45,000 in years two and three and $180,000 in year four. The result is total gross income inclusion of $360,000.

[16] Cf. I.R.C. § 453(i) for the recognition of recapture income under § 1245 or § 1250.

[17] I.R.C. § 1222(3). Cf. § 1(h).

[18] I.R.C. § 453(d)(1). In the absence of an election, I.R.C. § 453 automatically applies.

[19] I.R.C. § 453(d)(2). See Rev.Rul. 90–46, 1990–1 C.B. 107, providing guidance as to when the Service will allow a late election out of I.R.C. § 453. The election may be revoked only with the Secretary's consent. I.R.C. § 453(d)(3).

[20] See Chapter 24B, infra.

[1] I.R.C. § 453(j)(2). The Secretary has authority to prescribe regulations necessary to determine ratable basis recovery in transaction where the sales price or gross profit percentage cannot be determined on the date of sale. See Reg. § 15A.453–1(c).

[2] S.Rep. No. 96–1000, 96th Cong., 2d Sess. 1, 22–24 (1980), 1980–2 C.B. 494, 506–507.

law holds that the selling price must be fixed and determinable for section 453(b) to apply.[3] An agreement, however, to indemnify the purchaser for breach of certain warranties and representations by offset against the purchase price will not disqualify an installment sale under section 453(b).[4] Exactly how broad such contingencies can be is unclear.

Where an installment sale is subject to a contingency with respect to the price and the installment method is not available, the taxpayer is required to recognize all of the gain in the year of the sale with respect to all of the payments to be made, even though such payments are payable in future taxable years. In the case of a cash-method taxpayer where the future payments have no readily ascertainable fair market value, the taxpayer may treat the transaction with respect to those payments as "open" and use the cost-recovery method under Burnet v. Logan, 283 U.S. 404, 51 S.Ct. 550 (1931).[5]

* * *

**Explanation of Provision.**—The bill permits installment sale reporting for sales for a contingent selling price. In extending eligibility, the bill does not prescribe specific rules for every conceivable transaction. Rather, the bill provides that specific rules will be prescribed under regulations.[6]

However, it is intended that, for sales under which there is a stated maximum selling price, the regulations will permit basis recovery on the basis of a gross profit ratio determined by reference to the stated maximum selling price.[7] For purposes of this provision, incidental or remote contingencies are not to be taken into account in determining if there is a stated maximum selling price. In general, the maximum selling price would be determined from the "four corners" of the contract agreement as the largest price which could be paid to the taxpayer assuming all contingencies, formulas, etc., operate in the taxpayer's favor. Income from the sale would be reported on a pro rata basis with respect to each installment payment using the maximum selling price to determine the total contract price and gross profit ratio. If, pursuant to standards prescribed by regulations, it is subsequently determined that the contingency will not be satisfied in whole or in part, thus reducing the maximum selling price, the taxpayer's income from the sale would be

---

[3]    Gralapp v. United States, 458 F.2d 1158 (10th Cir.1972); In re Steen, 509 F.2d 1398 (9th Cir.1975).

[4]    See Rev.Rul. 77–56, 1977–1 C.B. 135.

[5]    [See Chapter 24B1, infra. Ed.]

[6]    [See I.R.C. § 453(j)(2). Ed.]

[7]    [See Reg. § 15A.453–1(c)(2)(i)(A). Ed.]

recomputed.[8] The taxpayer would then report reduced income, as adjusted, with respect to each installment payment received in the taxable year of adjustment and subsequent taxable years. If the maximum price is reduced in more than one taxable year, e.g., because of successive changes in the status of the contingency, each such year of reduction would constitute an adjustment year.

Where the taxpayer has reported more income from installment payments received in previous taxable years than the total recomputed income, the taxpayer would be permitted to deduct the excesses in the adjustment year as a loss.

In cases where the sales price is indefinite and no maximum selling price can be determined but the obligation is payable over a fixed period of time, it is generally intended that basis of the property sold would be recovered ratably over the fixed period.[9] In a case where the selling price and payment period are both indefinite but a sale has in fact occurred, it is intended that the regulations would permit ratable basis recovery over some reasonable period of time.[10] Also, in appropriate cases, it is intended that basis recovery would be permitted under an income forecast type method.[11]

The creation of a statutory deferred payment option for all forms of deferred payment sales significantly expands the availability of installment reporting to include situations where it has not previously been permitted. By providing an expanded statutory installment reporting option, the Committee believes that in the future there should be little incentive to devise convoluted forms of deferred payment obligations to attempt to obtain deferred reporting. In any event, the effect of the new rules is to reduce substantially the justification for treating transactions as "open" and permitting the use of the cost-recovery method sanctioned by Burnet v. Logan, 283 U.S. 404,

---

[8]  [Id.]

[9]  [See Reg. § 15A.453–1(c)(3)(i). Ed.]

[10]  [The basis is to be prorated over a 15 year period unless the taxpayer can establish that such a period "would substantially and inappropriately defer recovery of the taxpayer's basis." Reg. § 15A.453–1(c)(4). Ed.]

[11]  In general, the income forecast method for basis recovery is considered appropriate for a transaction with respect to which it may be demonstrated that receipts will be greater for the earlier years of the payment period and then decline for the later years of the payment period. It is intended that the regulations will deal with the application of this method with respect to sales of property qualifying for depreciation under the income forecast method (e.g. movies, mineral rights) when the selling price is based on production, a sale under which the amount payable to the seller is based on a declining percentage of the purchaser's revenues, and similar sales. In developing these regulations, the Committee intends that the Treasury Department will prescribe rules for this method to avoid, whenever possible, leaving a seller with an unrecovered basis in the obligation, and thereby creating a capital loss, after the final payment is received. For qualifying transactions, a more rapid basis recovery under this method is to be allowed even if there is a fixed period over which payments are to be received. [See Reg. § 15A.453–1(c)(6). Ed.]

51 S.Ct. 550 (1931). Accordingly, it is the Committee's intent that the cost-recovery method not be available in the case of sales for a fixed price (whether the seller's obligation is evidenced by a note, contractual promise, or otherwise), and that its use be limited to those rare and extraordinary cases involving sales for a contingent price where the fair market value of the purchaser's obligation cannot reasonably be ascertained.[12]

## 3. SITUATIONS IN WHICH SECTION 453 IS INAPPLICABLE

Internal Revenue Code: Sections 453(b)(2), (f)(6) and (7), (g), (i), (k), (*l*).

Regulations: Sections 1.453–12(a), (d) Example 1.

----

There are several situations to which Section 453 does not apply. To the extent the provision is inapplicable, gain or loss must be recognized in the year of disposition.[1]

*Sales at a Loss.* If property is sold at a loss, no tax is due as a result of the sale. Thus no liquidity problem arises on the sale and the Service has appropriately ruled that Section 453 is inapplicable.[2]

*Dealer Dispositions.* Section 453 is inapplicable to dealer dispositions[3] and to dispositions of personal property which is inventory of the selling taxpayer.[4] A dealer disposition is a disposition of personal property by a person who regularly sells personal property on the installment plan,[5] or a disposition of real property which is held for sale to customers in the ordinary course of the seller's trade or business.[6] Dealer dispositions are generally[7] not subject to the installment sales rules.[8]

*Recapture Income.* The installment method is inapplicable to the extent of any Section 1245 or 1250 recapture gain which is required to be recognized on the sale.[9] Such gain is required to be recognized in the year of the disposition.[10] If there is any remaining Section 1231 gain or long-term capital gain on the sale of the recapture property, that remaining

----

[12]  See Chapter 24B1, infra and Reg. § 15A.453–1(d)(2)(iii).

[1]  See Chapter 24B, infra.

[2]  Rev.Rul. 70–430, 1970–2 C.B. 51.

[3]  I.R.C. § 453(b)(2)(A).

[4]  I.R.C. § 453(b)(2)(B).

[5]  I.R.C. § 453(*l*)(1)(A).

[6]  I.R.C. § 453(*l*)(1)(B).

[7]  I.R.C. § 453(*l*)(2) creates exceptions (making § 453 applicable) for farm property as defined in § 2032A(e)(4) or (5) and certain timeshares and residential lots.

[8]  See Chapter 24B, infra.

[9]  I.R.C. § 453(i)(1). Installment treatment is also inapplicable to recapture income indirectly recognized on the sale of a partnership interest under I.R.C. § 751. I.R.C. § 453(i)(2).

[10]  I.R.C. § 453(i)(1)(A).

gain does qualify for installment treatment under a *recomputed* gross profit to total contract price ratio that reflects the recognized recapture gain.[11] For example, if in the example above (where the property had an adjusted basis of $40,000 and was sold for four $100,000 installments) the property sold was depreciable real property with $60,000 of Section 1250 recapture gain and $300,000 of Section 1231 gain, Seller would recognize the $60,000 of recapture gain in the year of sale. As a result, the gross profit ratio would have to be recomputed to reflect the $60,000 recognition of recapture gain. The gross profit for the ratio calculation would now be the remaining gain to be recognized $300,000, and the total contract price would remain $400,000. This results in ¾ ($300,000/ $400,000) of each $100,000 payment, or $75,000, being recognized as Section 1231 gain when each of the four $100,000 payments are received by Seller.[12] Regardless of whether Section 1250 is applicable, to the extent that the Section 1231 gain is "unrecaptured Section 1250 gain"[13] which is taxed at a 25 percent rate, that gain is taken into account before the adjusted net capital gain[14] (taxed generally at a 15% or 20% rate) is recognized.

*Sale of Depreciable Property to a Controlled Entity.* Section 453 generally does not apply to a disposition of property between a taxpayer and a "related person" as defined in Section 1239(b)[15] **if the** property is depreciable in the hands of the related-party transferee.[16] In general, under Section 1239(b) a related person is a greater than 50% controlled entity, either a corporation where more than 50% of the stock is owned directly or indirectly by attribution by the Seller, or a partnership where more than 50% of the capital interest or profits interest is owned directly or indirectly by attribution by the Seller or two such controlled entities which have such 50% common ownership.[17] In addition, a related person includes a trust in which the taxpayer or the taxpayer's spouse has a beneficial interest.[18] However, family members are not treated as related persons under this rule.[19]

The depreciable property rule is inapplicable if the disposition did not have the avoidance of income tax as one of its principal purposes.[20] If

---

[11]   I.R.C. § 453(i)(1)(B).

[12]   Thus, $135,000 ($60,000 (ordinary income) and $75,000 (I.R.C. § 1231 gain)) is gain recognized in the year of sale, with $75,000 (I.R.C. § 1231 gain) being recognized in each of the remaining 3 years. Total gain recognized is still the $360,000.

[13]   I.R.C. § 1(h)(6). See Chapter 22D, supra.

[14]   Reg. § 1.453–12(a) and 12(d) Example 1.

[15]   I.R.C. § 453(g)(1) and (3).

[16]   I.R.C. § 453(f)(7).

[17]   I.R.C. § 1239(b)(1) and (c). See also I.R.C. §§ 267(b)(3), (10), (11) and (12) and 707(b)(1)(B).

[18]   I.R.C. § 1239(b)(2).

[19]   Cf. I.R.C. §§ 267(b)(1) and 1239(b).

[20]   I.R.C. § 453(g)(2).

Section 453(g) is applicable, the rule effectively places the seller on the accrual method,[21] and the gain is generally all ordinary income.[22]

*Sales of Publicly Traded Stock or Securities.* Section 453 treatment is denied to sales of stock or securities which are traded on an established securities market.[23] Because the seller could easily have sold such property for cash on the open market, the usual liquidity problem which Section 453 is intended to alleviate is not present and Section 453 is inapplicable.[24] All payments on such sales are treated as received in the year of the sale.[25] Regulations may extend the coverage of this exception to include similar types of property other than stock or securities traded on an established market.[26]

*Sales of Personal Property on a Revolving Credit Plan.* Installment treatment is also denied to sales of personal property on a revolving credit plan.[27] As above, all payments related to such sales are deemed received in the year of sale.[28]

*Nonrecognition Sales.* To the extent a sale is treated as a nonrecognition transaction under the Code,[29] only the gain required to be recognized is taxed and potentially may be subject to Section 453 treatment.[30] For example, to the extent that there is an interspousal installment sale of property under Section 1041 (providing a general rule that no gain or loss is to be recognized on transfers between spouses or between former spouses if such transfer is incident to a divorce), no gain is recognized to the seller spouse and no installment treatment is needed even though the sale is in the form of an installment sale.[31]

## 4. SPECIAL RULES RELATED TO SECTION 453

Internal Revenue Code: Sections 453(e), (f)(1); 453A(a), (b)(1), (2), (5), (c), (d); 453B(a) through (c), (f), and (g).

Regulations: Sections 1.453–9(a), (b); 15A.453–1(b)(2)(iii), (iv), (3)(i), (5) Examples (2), (3).

---

[21] I.R.C. § 453(g)(1)(B)(i). An exception is created for contingent payments whose fair market value is not reasonably ascertainable. As to such payments, the basis is to be recovered ratably. I.R.C. § 453(g)(1)(B)(ii).

[22] I.R.C. § 1239(a).

[23] I.R.C. § 453(k)(2)(A).

[24] S.Rep. No. 313, 99th Cong., 2d Sess. 124 (1986), 1986–3 C.B. (Vol. 3) 124.

[25] I.R.C. § 453(k) (flush language).

[26] I.R.C. § 453(k)(2)(B).

[27] I.R.C. § 453(k)(1). The regulations define a revolving credit plan to include "cycle budget accounts, flexible budget accounts, continuous budget accounts, and other similar plans or arrangements for the sale of personal property under which the customer agrees to pay each billing-month . . . a part of the outstanding balance of the customer's account." Reg. § 1.453A–2(c)(1). See also Reg. § 1.453A–2(c)(6)(vi) describing the methodology in allocating gross income to the appropriate tax years as payments are received under a revolving credit plan.

[28] I.R.C. § 453(k) (flush language).

[29] See Chapter 26, infra.

[30] See I.R.C. § 453(f)(6) and Rev.Rul. 53–75, 1953–1 CB 83.

[31] See Chapters 6B3 and 10B, supra.

There are several special rules which alter the general Section 453 installment sale rule. These rules apply to situations where there is a liquidity problem or where there effectively is no liquidity problem.

*Liabilities.* If property which is sold on the installment method is subject to a liability, under the *Crane* principle[1] the liability is included in the amount realized on the sale. Relief from the liability occurs in the year of the sale and under the installment sale rules, the amount of relief should be treated as a payment in the year of the sale. However, the relief is not an actual cash payment and, as a result, the taxpayer may not have the necessary liquidity with which to pay the resulting tax liability. The regulations partially alleviate this problem by treating relief from a liability as a nonpayment[2] as long as the amount of the liability does not exceed the adjusted basis of the property.[3] However, to ensure sufficient recognition of gain, the ratio of gross profit to the total contract price that is used in measuring the Section 453 gain must be adjusted. The total contract price, or denominator of the fraction, is reduced by the amount of the liability not in excess of the amount of the adjusted basis.[4] The overall effect of this adjustment is to disregard the liability (up to the amount of the adjusted basis) as a payment, while at the same time treating a greater portion of the cash payments as gain from the Section 453 sale.

For example, assume the property in the example above ($40,000 adjusted basis, $400,000 fair market value) was land subject to a $40,000 liability. If Buyer assumed the liability and paid Seller $90,000 (rather than $100,000) in each of the four years, Seller's gain would still be $360,000. Under the special liability rule, none of the liability assumed by Buyer would be treated as a payment in the year of the sale because it is not in excess of the adjusted basis of the property. However, the Section 453 ratio would be adjusted as follows: the total contract price would be reduced by $40,000, to $360,000, with the result that the gross profit/total contract price ratio would be increased to $360,000/$360,000 or one. As a result, the full $90,000 of each year's payment would be gain included in Seller's gross income. Thus, over the four year period the full $360,000 gain would still be recognized by Seller.[5]

If the amount of the liability relief exceeds the adjusted basis of the property, then the excess of the liability over the adjusted basis continues

---

[1]   See Crane v. Commissioner, supra page 136.

[2]   Reg. § 15A.453–1(b)(2)(iv) makes the following rules inapplicable to "[a]ny obligation created subsequent to the taxpayer's acquisition of the property and incurred or assumed by the taxpayer or placed as an encumbrance on the property in contemplation of disposition of the property. . . . if the arrangement results in accelerating recovery of the taxpayer's basis in the installment sale."

[3]   Reg. § 15A.453–1(b)(3)(i). If the liability exceeds the adjusted basis, the excess is treated as a payment received in the year of disposition. Id.

[4]   Reg. § 15A.453–1(b)(2)(iii). See also Reg. § 1.453–4(c).

[5]   See also Reg. § 15A.453–1(b)(5) Example (2).

to be treated as a payment in the year of sale.[6] Using the rule above, at the point when the liability equals the adjusted basis, the ratio of gross profit to total contract price becomes one. Since the Service does not want to increase the ratio above one, the Service simply treats any excess liability as a payment in the year of the sale.[7]

*Dispositions of Installment Sales Obligations.* The Section 453 rules are intended to alleviate potential liquidity problems; accordingly, the rule should not be applicable if there is no potential liquidity problem. For example, if the seller of property under the installment method subsequently disposes of the Section 453 installment obligations by selling them, should Section 453 rules continue to apply? Clearly there is no longer a liquidity problem.

Similarly, a disposition of the installment obligations by gift potentially creates the opportunity for other tax avoidance schemes. For example, the seller of property, having made a sale under the installment method could make a gift of the buyer's obligations to a third person, possibly a member of the Seller's family who is in a lower tax bracket. As a result, the vendor would escape tax and the donee would be taxed less heavily.[8] Such avoidance possibilities and such lack of liquidity prompted the enactment of the forerunner of Section 453B.[9]

Section 453B taxes the seller on previously untaxed gain, upon the disposition of an installment obligation. The amount of gain so taxed is either the amount realized (in the case of a satisfaction, sale or exchange) or the fair market value of the obligation (at the time of any other type of disposition, such as a gift) less the taxpayer's basis in the Section 453 obligation.[10] The basis of an installment obligation is the face amount of the obligation less the amount of income that the taxpayer would have to include in gross income if the obligation were paid off in full.[11] Test the propriety of this basis rule in the light of the reporting rules of Section 453. For example, if Seller in our prior example ($40,000 adjusted basis and four $100,000 notes) sold the notes for $400,000 prior to collecting any of them, Seller would have a $360,000 Section 453B gain[12] at the

---

[6]   See note 3, supra.

[7]   For an illustration of this rule, see Reg. § 15A.453–1(b)(5) Example (3).

[8]   Wallace Huntington v. Commissioner, 15 B.T.A. 851 (1929). See H.R.Rep. No. 2, 70th Cong., 1st Sess. 16 (1928) reported in Seidman, Legislative History of Federal Income Tax Laws 1938–1861 at 521 (1938). Other avoidance possibilities were identified in the Report. Thus, in 1928, prior to the enactment of § 42 of the Revenue Act of 1934, and prior to the enactment of present § 691, which was first enacted in 1942, the death of one who had made an installment sale eliminated all income tax on gain on such a sale not previously reported. But see I.R.C. §§ 453B(c) and 691(a)(4) and see Salvatore v. Commissioner, at page 260, supra.

[9]   Revenue Act of 1928, § 44(d), 45 Stat. 791, 806 (1928). See Roche, "Dispositions of Installment Obligations," 41 Tax L.Rev. 1 (1985); Emory, "Disposition of Installment Obligation: Income Deferral, 'Thou Art Lost and Gone Forever'," 54 Iowa L.Rev. 945 (1969).

[10]   I.R.C. § 453B(a).

[11]   I.R.C. § 453B(b).

[12]   The gain is the difference between the amount realized on the notes ($400,000) less the bases of the obligations $40,000 ($400,000 less $360,000 of income returnable if the obligations were satisfied in full).

time of the sale of the notes. And properly so, because Seller has the cash with which to pay the tax.

Congress added a characterization provision to Section 453B. It provides that the gain or loss on the disposition of an installment obligation is to be treated as arising from a sale or exchange of the property for which the obligation was received.[13] In the example above, the $360,000 gain would be a long-term capital gain.[14]

The term "disposition" in Section 453B is broadly interpreted. It generally includes gifts no matter the nature of the donee,[15] transfers to and from trusts,[16] and in rare circumstances even the assignment of the obligation as security for a loan,[17] but not mere changes in the terms of the obligation itself.[18] The statute removes from the disposition rules, the transmission of installment obligations at death,[19] their distribution in certain corporate liquidations,[20] their transfer under Section 1041 (other than in trust) between spouses and between ex-spouses if incident to their divorce,[21] **and** a nonrecognition provision removes their transfer in a repossession of the property by a vendor upon default by the purchaser.[22]

*Related Party Sales.* The rather complicated rule of Section 453(e) is aimed at taxpayers who attempt to take advantage of Section 453 even though there is liquidity generated within the scope of persons related to the Seller.[23] The Senate Report gives the background and rules of the Section:[24]

---

[13]  I.R.C. § 453B(a) last sentence.

[14]  See the Text at page 837 note 17, supra.

[15]  See I.R.C. § 453B(f); Rev.Rul. 55–157, 1955–1 C.B. 293. Thus, Susie Salvatore could not have avoided the result in her case by making an installment sale of her property and then giving the installment sales obligations to her children. See page 260, supra. But see I.R.C. § 453B(g).

[16]  Cases and rulings dealing with transfers to a trust include Marshall v. United States, 26 F.Supp. 580 (S.D.Cal.1939); Springer v. United States (unreported), 69–2 U.S.T.C. ¶ 9567 (N.D.Ala.1969); Rev.Rul. 67–167, 1967–1 C.B. 107. If the transfer is to a revocable trust it does not constitute an I.R.C. § 453B "disposition." Rev.Rul. 74–613, 1974–2 C.B. 153. On transfers from a trust to a beneficiary, see Rev.Rul. 55–159, 1955–1 C.B. 391.

[17]  Rev.Rul. 65–185, 1965–2 C.B. 153. But see Elmer v. Commissioner, 65 F.2d 568 (2d Cir.1933); Town and Country Food Co. v. Commissioner, 51 T.C. 1049 (1969), acq., 1969–2 C.B. XXV; United Surgical Steel Company, Inc. v. Commissioner, 54 T.C. 1215 (1970), acq., 1971–2 C.B. 1; Rev.Rul. 68–246, 1968–1 C.B. 198. Query whether these are valid authorities under current law in view of the enactment of I.R.C. § 453A(a), (b), and (d) considered infra.

[18]  Rev.Rul. 68–419, 1968–2 C.B. 196. Cf. Rev.Rul. 75–457, 1975–2 C.B. 196. But see Rev.Rul. 77–294, 1977–2 C.B. 173.

[19]  I.R.C. § 453B(c). But see I.R.C. § 691(a)(4).

[20]  I.R.C. § 453B(d). Cf. I.R.C. § 453(h).

[21]  I.R.C. § 453B(g).

[22]  I.R.C. § 1038. See page 925, infra. Cf. Reg. § 1.453–5(b)(2).

[23]  See Emory and Hjorth, "Installment Sales Act Part II: Cost Recovery, 337 Liquidations, Related Party Dispositions," 54 J. Tax'n 130, 133–34 (1981).

[24]  S.Rep. No. 96–1000, 96th Cong., 2nd Sess. 1, 12–17 (1980), 1980–2 C.B. 494, 500–502.

**Present Law.**—Under present law, the installment sale statutory provision does not preclude installment sale reporting for sales between related parties. . . .

Under the existing statutory framework, taxpayers have used the installment sale provision as a tax planning device for intra-family transfers of appreciated property, including marketable securities.[25] There are several tax advantages in making intra-family installment sales of appreciated property. The seller would achieve deferral of recognition of gain until the related buyer actually pays the installments to the seller, even if cash proceeds from the property are received within the related party group from a subsequent resale by the installment buyer shortly after making the initial purchase. In addition to spreading out the gain recognized by the seller over the term of the installment sale, the seller may achieve some estate planning benefits since the value of the installment obligation generally will be frozen for estate tax purposes. Any subsequent appreciation in value of the property sold, or in property acquired by reinvestment of the proceeds from the property sold on the installment basis, would not affect the seller's gross estate since the value of the property is no longer included in his gross estate.

With respect to the related buyer, there is usually no tax to be paid if the appreciated property is resold shortly after the installment purchase. Since the buyer's adjusted basis is a cost basis which includes the portion of the purchase price payable in the future, the gain or loss from the buyer's resale would represent only the fluctuation in value occurring after the installment purchase. Thus, after the related party's resale, all appreciation has been realized within the related group but the recognition of the gain for tax purposes may be deferred for a long period of time.

In the leading case, Rushing v. Commissioner,[26] the test was held to be that, in order to receive the installment benefits, the "seller may not directly or indirectly have control over the proceeds or possess the economic benefit therefrom." In this case, a sale of corporate stock was made to the trustee of trusts for the benefit of the seller's children. Since the sales were made to trusts created after the corporations had adopted plans of liquidation, the Government made an assignment of income argument. The Court upheld installment sale treatment for the stock sold to the trustee under the "control or enjoyment" test because the trustee was independent of the taxpayer and owed

---

[25] Another technique used for intra-family transfers involves the so-called "private annuity" arrangement. The bill does not deal directly with this type of arrangement.

[26] 441 F.2d 593 (5th Cir.1971), affirming 52 T.C. 888 (1969).

a fiduciary duty to the children. The Court rejected the assignment of income argument because it found that no income was being assigned.

\* \* \*

**Explanation of Provision.**—The bill prescribes special rules for situations involving installment sales to certain related parties who also dispose of the property. . . .[27]

Under the bill, the amount realized upon certain resales by the related party installment purchaser will trigger recognition of gain by the initial seller, based on his gross profit ratio, only to the extent the amount realized from the second disposition exceeds actual payments made under the installment sale.[28] Thus, acceleration of recognition of the installment gain from the first sale will generally result only to the extent additional cash and other property flows into the related group as a result of a second disposition of the property. In the case of a second disposition which is not a sale or exchange, the fair market value of the property disposed of is treated as the amount realized for this purpose. . . .[29]

The excess of any amount realized from resales over payments received on the first sale as of the end of a taxable year will be taken into account. Thus, the tax treatment would not turn on the strict chronological order in which resales or payments are made. If, under these rules, a resale results in the recognition of gain to the initial seller, subsequent payments actually received by that seller would be recovered tax-free until they have equaled the amount realized from the resale which resulted in the acceleration of recognition of gain.[30]

\* \* \* [T]he resale rule will apply only with respect to second dispositions occurring within 2 years of the initial installment sale. . . .[31]

\* \* \*

The bill also contains several exceptions to the application of these rules. . . .[32] [T]he resale rules will not apply in any case where it is established to the satisfaction of the Internal

---

[27] [See I.R.C. § 453(e)(1). Ed.]

[28] [See I.R.C. § 453(e)(3). Thus, if the initial seller received a $100,000 cash down payment and the related party also made a $100,000 second disposition, I.R.C. § 453(e) would not apply. Ed.]

[29] [See I.R.C. § 453(e)(4). Ed.]

[30] [See I.R.C. § 453(e)(5). Ed.]

[31] [See I.R.C. § 453(e)(2)(A). Ed.]

[32] [See I.R.C. § 453(e)(6)(A)–(C). Ed.]

Revenue Service that none of the dispositions had as one of its principal purposes the avoidance of Federal income taxes.[33]

In the exceptional cases to which the nonavoidance exception may apply, it is anticipated that regulations would provide definitive rules so that complicated legislation is not necessary to prescribe substituted property or taxpayer rules which would not be of general application. In appropriate cases, it is anticipated that the regulations and rulings under the nontax avoidance exception will deal with certain tax-free transfers which normally would not be treated as a second disposition of the property, e.g., charitable transfers, like-kind exchanges, gift transfers and transfers to a controlled corporation or a partnership. Generally it is intended that a second disposition will qualify under the nontax avoidance exception when it is of an involuntary nature, e.g., foreclosure upon the property by a judgment lien creditor of the related purchaser or bankruptcy of the related purchaser. In addition it is intended that the exception will apply in the case of a second disposition which is also an installment sale if the terms of payment under the installment resale are substantially equivalent to, or longer than, those for the first installment sale. However, the exception would not apply if the resale terms would permit significant deferral of recognition of gain from the initial sale when proceeds from the resale are being collected sooner.

Under the bill, the period for assessing a deficiency in tax attributable to a second disposition by the related purchaser will not expire before the day which is 2 years after the date the initial installment seller furnishes a notice that there was a second disposition of the property.[34] The notice is to be furnished in the manner prescribed by regulations. Under the bill, a protective notification may be filed to prevent the tolling of the period of limitations for assessing a deficiency in cases where there are questions as to whether a second disposition has occurred (e.g., a lease which might be characterized as a sale or exchange for tax purposes) or whether there is a principal purpose of Federal income tax avoidance.

For purposes of the related party rules, the bill adopts a definition of related parties which will include spouses, children, grandchildren, and parents. . . .[35]

---

[33]  [See I.R.C. § 453(e)(7). See also Roche, "Satisfying the Secretary: Demonstrating Lack of Tax Avoidance Motivation in Related Party Installment Sales," 5 Virg.Tax Rev. 91 (1985). Ed.]

[34]  [See I.R.C. § 453(e)(8). Ed.]

[35]  [See I.R.C. §§ 453(f)(1), 318(a), 267(b). Ed.]

In the case of a corporation, it will be considered to be related to another taxpayer if stock which is or might be owned by it is or would be treated as owned by the other taxpayer under the general corporate attribution rules (Code Section 318). Generally, a related corporation will be one in which a person directly or indirectly owns 50 percent or more in value of the stock in the corporation. Also for this purpose, the principles of the general corporate stock ownership attribution rules (Code Section 318) will apply in determining the related party status of partnerships, trusts, and estates.[36]

It is to be understood that the provisions governing the use of the installment method to report sales between related parties, and the definition of such relationships, are not intended to preclude the Internal Revenue Service from asserting the proper tax treatment of transactions that are shams.

As an illustration of the above rules, assume that Seller sold land with a $40,000 adjusted basis to Daughter in exchange for a $400,000 note to be paid off in 4 payments in years 5–8, but that in year 2, Daughter sold one-half of the land to a third party for $200,000 of cash. Under Section 453(e)(1), Seller would be treated as receiving a $200,000 payment in year 2 and would recognize a $180,000 long-term capital gain under Section 453 in that year.[37] When Seller received the first two $100,000 payments from Daughter in years 5 and 6, Seller would recognize no gain.[38] When Seller received Daughter's two final $100,000 payments in years 7 and 8, Seller would recognize a further $90,000 long-term capital gain in each of those years.[39]

*Section 453A.* Section 453A indirectly relates to the liquidity situation under Section 453. The section involves two rules that apply only to nondealer sales of property[40] under the installment method where the sale price exceeds $150,000.[41] The Section 453A rules apply in two diverse situations.[42]

The first rule, found in Section 453A(c), is applicable in very limited situations and is related to the "time value of money" concept.[43] Since the use of the installment method essentially defers payment of Seller's tax liability, taxpayers in effect are borrowing money tax-free from the

---

[36] [The 1986 Act extended the related persons definition to include I.R.C. § 267(b) relationships. Ed.]

[37] I.R.C. § 453(e)(1), (2)(A), (3). The $180,000 amount is the $200,000 payment multiplied by the original sale's gross profit ratio of 90% ($360,000/$400,000).

[38] I.R.C. § 453(e)(5).

[39] I.R.C. § 453(a)(1).

[40] Dealer dispositions do not qualify for I.R.C. § 453. I.R.C. § 453(b)(2), (*l*)(1), (2).

[41] I.R.C. § 453A(b)(1). Some further exceptions are found in I.R.C. § 453A(b)(3) and (4).

[42] See Olchyk, "Nondealer Installment Sales Less Beneficial After TAMRA," 70 J. Tax'n 132 (1989).

[43] See page 641, supra and Chapter 24C, infra.

federal government. In limited circumstances where the face amount of such installment obligations arising during, and outstanding at the close of, a taxable year exceeds $5 million,[44] the first rule requires that interest be paid on the amount of tax which is deferred (the amount of that loan).

The second rule, found in Section 453A(d), applies if a nondealer installment obligation is pledged as security[45] for an indebtedness.[46] Since the proceeds of the indebtedness create liquidity for the holder of the installment obligation, the net proceeds of the indebtedness are treated as a Section 453 payment.[47] The Section 453A(d) rule bears similarity to the Section 453B disposition rule. The amount of imputed payment may not exceed the remaining total contract price left to be paid under the installment obligation.[48] And once a payment is imputed under Section 453A(d), then no actual installment obligation payments are included as Section 453 payments until the previously imputed amount is recovered.[49]

## PROBLEMS

1. Seller owns a parcel of investment land which Seller purchased four years ago for $2,000. Seller sells it to Buyer under an arrangement where Buyer pays Seller $2,000 cash in the current year and four 8 percent interest bearing notes to be paid off in each of the succeeding four years. Each note has a $2,000 face amount and a $1,750 fair market value. Disregarding the tax consequences of any interest payments, what results to Seller in each of the five years if in the alternative:

   (a) Seller is a cash method taxpayer who makes no § 453(d) election.

   (b) Seller is an accrual method taxpayer who makes no § 453(d) election.

   (c) What result to Seller in (b), above, if the property was instead some equipment used in business with an adjusted basis of $2,000 on which Seller had claimed depreciation and the § 1245 recapture on the equipment amounted to $3,000? See § 453(i).

   (d) What result to Seller in part (b), above, if the property is a building (not including the land underlying it) which Seller rented to a third person and depreciated on the straight-line method and the sale is to Corporation 100% of whose stock is owned by Seller and Corporation continues to rent the property to the third person?

---

[44] I.R.C. § 453A(b)(2).

[45] See I.R.C. § 453A(d)(4).

[46] Again, the installment obligation must arise in a sale whose price exceeds $150,000. I.R.C. § 453A(b)(1).

[47] I.R.C. § 453A(d)(1).

[48] I.R.C. § 453A(d)(2).

[49] I.R.C. § 453A(d)(3). Cf. I.R.C. § 453(e)(5).

(e)    What result to Seller in part (b), above, if the property is a building (not including the land underlying it) which Seller depreciated using the straight line method and on which Seller had previously taken $5,000 of depreciation? Assume Seller has no prior § 1231 losses, and no other § 1231 or capital gains or losses in the years when payments are made. See Reg. § 1.453–12(a) and –12(d) Example 1.

(f)    What results to Seller in part (b), above, if the property was subject to a $2,000 mortgage which Buyer assumed and Buyer gave Seller $2,000 of cash and only three of the $2,000 notes?

(g)    What results to Seller in part (b), above, if the property was subject to a $3,000 mortgage which Buyer assumed and Buyer gave Seller $2,000 of cash and two $2,000 notes to be paid in each of the succeeding two years and a $1,000 note to be paid in the fourth year?

(h)    What result to Seller in (b), above, if prior to collecting any of the four notes Seller sells them to a third party for their fair market value of $7,000?

(i)    What result to Seller in (b), above, if prior to collecting any of the four notes, Seller gives them to Daughter? Assume the notes are still worth $1750 each. What results to Daughter when she receives full payment of the notes?

(j)    What result in part (b), above, if the sale is made to Daughter who immediately resells the property to Buyer for $10,000? See § 453(e).

(k)    What result in part (j), above, if instead Daughter resold the property for $11,000 in the *succeeding year* before the note for that year was paid? Subsequently, the note for the year was timely paid by Daughter.

(l)    What result if the resale price in (k), above, was $9,000?

(m)    What result to Seller under the facts of parts (j) and (l), above, on the collection of the remaining notes from Daughter?

2.    Taxpayer, a cash method taxpayer, owned all the stock in a company that owned all the rights in a new type of X-ray scanning device which had an extremely speculative value. She had owned the stock for three years and had a $100,000 cost basis in it. She sold the stock to a big electronics firm for 10 percent of the earnings generated by the scanning device over the succeeding 25 years. Although her right to earnings was speculative, she received $15,000 in each of the 25 succeeding years.

(a)    What are the tax consequences to Taxpayer in each year?

(b)    Would your result in (a), above, be altered if taxpayer is an accrual method taxpayer?

(c)    What result in (a), above, if the maximum stated sales price is $300,000, and after 20 years having paid $300,000 the electronics firm terminates their payments?

**3.** Client, a cash method taxpayer, owns a rental building that Client acquired four years ago and depreciated using the straight-line method. It currently has an adjusted basis of $200,000 and a value of $500,000. Buyer purchases the building giving Client five $100,000 5% interest bearing notes, one to be paid in each of the five succeeding years (years two through six). In the year of sale (year one), Client borrows $200,000 pledging the $500,000 of Buyer's notes as security. What tax consequences to Client in the current year and each of the succeeding five years?

## B. TRANSACTIONS OUTSIDE OF SECTION 453

## 1. OPEN TRANSACTIONS

Internal Revenue Code: Sections 453(d); 1001(a) through (c); 1011(a).

Regulations: Section 1.1001–1(a).

---

### Burnet v. Logan

Supreme Court of the United States, 1931.
283 U.S. 404, 51 S.Ct. 550.

■ MR. JUSTICE MCREYNOLDS delivered the opinion of the Court.

These causes present the same questions. One opinion, stating the essential circumstances disclosed in No. 521, will suffice for both.

Prior to March, 1913, and until March 11, 1916, respondent, Mrs. Logan, owned 250 of the 4,000 capital shares issued by the Andrews & Hitchcock Iron Company. It held 12% of the stock of the Mahoning Ore & Steel Company, an operating concern. In 1895 the latter corporation procured a lease for 97 years upon the "Mahoning" mine and since then has regularly taken therefrom large, but varying, quantities of iron ore— in 1913, 1,515,428 tons; in 1914, 1,212,287 tons; in 1915, 2,311,940 tons; in 1919, 1,217,167 tons; in 1921, 303,020 tons; in 1923, 3,029,865 tons. The lease contract did not require production of either maximum or minimum tonnage or any definite payments. Through an agreement of stockholders (steel manufacturers) the Mahoning Company is obligated to apportion extracted ore among them according to their holdings.

On March 11, 1916, the owners of all the shares in Andrews & Hitchcock Company sold them to Youngstown Sheet & Tube Company, which thus acquired, among other things, 12% of the Mahoning Company's stock and the right to receive the same percentage of ore thereafter taken from the leased mine.

For the shares so acquired the Youngstown Company paid the holders $2,200,000 in money and agreed to pay annually thereafter for distribution among them 60 cents for each ton of ore apportioned to it. Of this cash Mrs. Logan received $250/4000$ths—$137,500; and she became entitled to the same fraction of any annual payment thereafter made by the purchaser under the terms of sale.

Mrs. Logan's mother had long owned 1100 shares of the Andrews & Hitchcock Company. She died in 1917, leaving to the daughter one-half of her interest in payments thereafter made by the Youngstown Company. This bequest was appraised for federal estate tax purposes at $277,164.50.

During 1917, 1918, 1919 and 1920 the Youngstown Company paid large sums under the agreement. Out of these respondent received on account of her 250 shares $9,900.00 in 1917, $11,250.00 in 1918, $8,995.50 in 1919, $5,444.30 in 1920—$35,589.80. By reason of the interest from her mother's estate she received $19,790.10 in 1919, and $11,977.49 in 1920.

Reports of income for 1918, 1919 and 1920 were made by Mrs. Logan upon the basis of cash receipts and disbursements. They included no part of what she had obtained from annual payments by the Youngstown Company. She maintains that until the total amount actually received by her from the sale of her shares equals their value on March 1, 1913, no taxable income will arise from the transaction. Also that until she actually receives by reason of the right bequeathed to her a sum equal to its appraised value, there will be no taxable income therefrom.

On March 1, 1913, the value of the 250 shares then held by Mrs. Logan *exceeded* $173,089.80—the total of all sums actually received by her prior to 1921 from their sale ($137,500.00 cash in 1916 plus four annual payments amounting to $35,589.80). That value also exceeded original cost of the shares. The amount received on the interest devised by her mother was less than its valuation for estate taxation; also less than the value when acquired by Mrs. Logan.

The Commissioner ruled that the obligation of the Youngstown Company to pay 60 cents per ton had a fair market value of $1,942,111.46 on March 11, 1916; that this value should be treated as so much cash and the sale of the stock regarded as a closed transaction with no profit in 1916. He also used this valuation as the basis for apportioning subsequent annual receipts between income and return of capital. His calculations, based upon estimates and assumptions, are too intricate for brief statement.[1] He made deficiency assessments according to the view just stated and the Board of Tax Appeals approved the result.

---

[1]    In the brief for petitioner the following appears:

"The fair market value of the Youngstown contract on March 11, 1916, was found by the Commissioner to be $1,942,111.46. This was based upon an estimate that the ore reserves at the Mahoning mine amounted to 82,858,535 tons; that all such ore would be mined; that 12 percent (or 9,942,564.2 tons) would be delivered to the Youngstown Company. The total amount to be received by all the vendors of stock would then be $5,965,814.52 at the rate of 60 cents per ton. The Commissioner's figure for the fair market value on March 11, 1916, was the then worth of $5,965,814.52, upon the assumption that the amount was to be received in equal annual installments during 45 years, discounted at 6 per cent, with a provision for a sinking fund at 4 percent. For

The Circuit Court of Appeals held that, in the circumstances, it was impossible to determine with fair certainty the market value of the agreement by the Youngstown Company to pay 60 cents per ton. Also, that respondent was entitled to the return of her capital—the value of 250 shares on March 1, 1913, and the assessed value of the interest derived from her mother—before she could be charged with any taxable income. As this had not in fact been returned, there was no taxable income.

We agree with the result reached by the Circuit Court of Appeals.

The 1916 transaction was a sale of stock—not an exchange of property. We are not dealing with royalties or deductions from gross income because of depletion of mining property. Nor does the situation demand that an effort be made to place according to the best available data some approximate value upon the contract for future payments. This probably was necessary in order to assess the mother's estate. As annual payments on account of extracted ore come in they can be readily apportioned first as return of capital and later as profit. The liability for income tax ultimately can be fairly determined without resort to mere estimates, assumptions and speculation. When the profit, if any, is actually realized, the taxpayer will be required to respond. The consideration for the sale was $2,200,000.00 in cash and the promise of future money payments wholly contingent upon facts and circumstances not possible to foretell with anything like fair certainty. The promise was in no proper sense equivalent to cash. It had no ascertainable fair market value. The transaction was not a closed one. Respondent might never recoup her capital investment from payments only conditionally promised. Prior to 1921 all receipts from the sale of her shares amounted to less than their value on March 1, 1913. She properly demanded the return of her capital investment before assessment of any taxable profit based on conjecture.

"In order to determine whether there has been gain or loss, and the amount of the gain, if any, we must withdraw from the gross proceeds an amount sufficient to restore the capital value that existed at the commencement of the period under consideration." Doyle v. Mitchell Bros. Co., 247 U.S. 179, 184, 185, 38 S.Ct. 467, 469. Rev.Act 1916, § 2, 39 Stat. 757, 758; Rev.Act 1918, c. 18, 40 Stat. 1057. Ordinarily, at least, a taxpayer may not deduct from gross receipts a supposed loss which in

---

lack of evidence to the contrary this value was approved by the Board. The value of the $550/4000$ interest which each acquired by bequest was fixed at $277,164.50 for purposes of Federal estate tax at the time of the mother's death.

"During the years here involved the Youngstown Company made payments in accordance with the terms of the contract, and respondents respectively received sums proportionate to the interests in the contract which they acquired by exchange of property and by bequest.

"The Board held that respondents' receipts from the contract, during the years in question, represented 'gross income'; that respondents should be allowed to deduct from said gross income a reasonable allowance for exhaustion of their contract interests; and that the balance of the receipts should be regarded as taxable income."

fact is represented by his outstanding note. Eckert v. Burnet, 283 U.S. 140, 51 S.Ct. 373. And, conversely, a promise to pay indeterminate sums of money is not necessarily taxable income. "Generally speaking, the income tax law is concerned only with realized losses, as with realized gains." Lucas v. American Code Co., 280 U.S. 445, 449, 50 S.Ct. 202.

From her mother's estate Mrs. Logan obtained the right to share in possible proceeds of a contract thereafter to pay indefinite sums. The value of this was assumed to be $277,164.50 and its transfer was so taxed. Some valuation—speculative or otherwise—was necessary in order to close the estate. It may never yield as much, it may yield more. If a sum equal to the value thus ascertained had been invested in an annuity contract, payments thereunder would have been free from income tax until the owner had recouped his capital investment.* We think a like rule should be applied here. The statute definitely excepts bequests from receipts which go to make up taxable income. See Burnet v. Whitehouse, 283 U.S. 148, 51 S.Ct. 374.

The judgments below are affirmed.

## NOTE

Recall from Chapter 6 that under Section 1001(a) gain or loss is the difference between the "amount realized" on a disposition and the "adjusted basis" of the property relinquished. If either the "amount realized" or the "adjusted basis" is incapable of being measured then the gain or loss on a transaction is unknown as well. This simple concept is now well established as the doctrine of Burnet v. Logan,[1] or the "open transaction" doctrine.

An open transaction arises in two different types of situations. It may involve a situation like Burnet v. Logan where the amount realized is unknown; if the sale is made by an accrual or a cash method taxpayer who makes an election under Section 453(d),[2] the doctrine leaves these transactions "open" to see what is actually received in subsequent years. As amounts are received they initially constitute a recovery of capital. Once an amount equal to the adjusted basis of the transferred property is received capital has been recovered, and all further receipts constitute income in the year received. These are all concepts considered in Chapter 6 and a student may be asking: Why defer consideration of the open transaction doctrine until now? The answer is: The doctrine not only has measurement and timing consequences, it has characterization aspects as well. If the doctrine of Burnet v. Logan applies and a transaction is left open then subsequently

---

\* Current statutory rules tax a portion of each annuity payment as received. See I.R.C. § 72, supra Chapter 7B. Moreover, a 1942 change would preclude the annuity-type treatment the court suggests for the disposition of the shares the taxpayer received from her mother. The mother's right to payment would be foreclosed from receiving a date-of-death basis by I.R.C. § 1014(c); and the recipient of payments attributable to the mother's rights would have income in respect of a decedent under § 691. See Chapter 24E, infra. None of this, however, affects the viability of the *Logan* principle regarding open transactions suggested by the treatment of payment for the shares owned originally by the taxpayer. Ed.

[1] The doctrine is applicable to both cash and accrual method taxpayers.

[2] If no I.R.C. § 453(d) election is made, § 453 strains to tax the gain. See page 837, supra.

recognized gain (or loss) is seen to arise out of the original transfer and is characterized by that transfer. Thus any gain Mrs. Logan subsequently recognized was long-term capital gain. If, however, the doctrine is inapplicable because an "amount realized" can be determined then the transaction is "closed" and gain or loss based on that determination is immediately recognized.[3]

The second situation in which the open transaction doctrine applies is where the "adjusted basis" of property disposed of is unknown, rather than the "amount realized" at the time of its disposition. For example, in Inaja Land Co., Ltd.,[4] the taxpayer which owned some land with a basis of approximately $61,000 sold an easement for $50,000, giving the buyer the right to divert water across the taxpayer's property. The court concluded that, as it could not determine what portion of the property was being taken, there was no way to allocate a portion of the taxpayer's basis for use in the gain or loss formula. Accordingly gain or loss was impossible to compute, and the receipt of the $50,000 was treated as a mere recovery of capital, reducing the property's basis to $11,000 but giving rise to no gain. The court stated:[5]

\* \* \*

Capital recoveries in excess of cost do constitute taxable income. Petitioner has made no attempt to allocate a basis to that part of the property covered by the easements. It is conceded that all of petitioner's lands were not affected by the easements conveyed. Petitioner does not contest the rule that, where property is acquired for a lump sum and subsequently disposed of a portion at a time, there must be an allocation of the cost or other basis over the several units and gain or loss computed on the disposition of each part, except where apportionment would be wholly impracticable or impossible. Nathan Blum, 5 T.C. 702, 709. Petitioner argues that it would be impracticable and impossible to apportion a definite basis to the easements here involved, since they could not be described by metes and bounds; that the flow of the water has changed and will change the course of the river; that the extent of the flood was and is not predictable; and that to date the city has not released the full measure of water to which it is entitled. In Strother v. Commissioner, 55 F.2d 626, the court says:

\* \* \* A taxpayer \* \* \* should not be charged with gain on pure conjecture unsupported by any foundation of ascertainable fact. See Burnet v. Logan, 283 U.S. 404, 51 S.Ct. 550.

This rule is approved in the recent case of Raytheon Production Corporation v. Commissioner, supra. Apportionment with reasonable accuracy of the amount received not being possible, and this amount being less than petitioner's cost basis for the property, it can not be determined that petitioner has, in fact,

---

[3]   See Chapter 24B2, infra.

[4]   9 T.C. 727 (1947), acq. 1948–1 C.B.

[5]   Id. at 735–736.

realized gain in any amount. Applying the rule as above set out, no portion of the payment in question should be considered as income, but the full amount must be treated as a return of capital and applied in reduction of petitioner's cost basis. Burnet v. Logan, 283 U.S. 404, 51 S.Ct. 550.

\* \* \*

But some words of caution are needed. Although the doctrine of Burnet v. Logan is well established in tax law, its importance should not be overemphasized. Section 1001(b) provides that the "amount realized" on a disposition of property is the amount of money received plus the fair market value of any property *received*. But recall from the *Philadelphia Park Amusement* case in Chapter 6[6] that if the value of what is received cannot be ascertained in any arm's length transaction, it will be assumed that it is equal to the value of the property given up. Thus for the open transaction doctrine to apply on the ground that the amount realized cannot be ascertained, both the value of the property transferred and the value of the property received must be unknown.

Additionally, the doctrine should not be overemphasized because, as the regulations properly state:[7] "The fair market value of property is a question of fact, but only in *rare and extraordinary* cases will property be considered to have no fair market value." Thus only in "rare and extraordinary circumstances" will courts cry "uncle" and give up on estimating fair market value. When they do, it does not mean it is completely impossible to make some sort of studied guess at value. Witness the fact that in the Burnet v. Logan case the mother's right to payment was in fact "valued" for estate tax purposes in 1917 even though her right then involved the amount of future payments to be expected which was the subject of controversy in the later income tax case. Nevertheless, the right to future payment was said to be incapable of being valued for income tax purposes. Why the difference?

Another example of an application of the open transaction doctrine occurred in Dorsey v. Commissioner[8] where in return for their stock in a pinsetting company the taxpayers became entitled to receive one percent of all receipts by AMF from the sale or lease of its automatic pinsetting machines. The courts applied Burnet v. Logan because of the uncertainties and contingencies existing at the time of the transfer stating:[9]

\* \* \*

Here, as in Burnet v. Logan, supra, the petitioners received a "promise of future money payments wholly contingent upon facts and circumstances not possible to foretell with anything like fair certainty." A fair preponderance of the evidence in this record supports the position of petitioners that their contract rights with AMF had no ascertainable fair market value on September 16,

---

[6]   See page 116, supra.

[7]   Reg. § 1.1001–1(a); see also Reg. § 15A.453–1(d)(2)(ii) and (iii).

[8]   49 T.C. 606 (1968).

[9]   Id. at 629.

1954. Among the principal uncertainties and contingencies which existed on September 16, 1954, were:

> 1.   *Conditions Prevalent in the Bowling Industry,* particularly the unsavory past reputation of bowling and its unknown future potential.

> 2.   *Obstacles to the Success of Automatic Pinsetters Within the Bowling Industry,* including the uncertainty as to their acceptance by the public and by bowling proprietors, their unproven status as a unique new product, and marketing problems.

> 3.   *Problems Facing the AMF Pinsetter,* such as patent infringement suits, the quantity and quality of competition, especially from Brunswick Corp., the fact that AMF was a newcomer to the bowling industry in 1954, and the pinsetter's unproven character.

> 4.   *Difficulties of Ascertaining How Much of Any Success Would Actually Redound to the Participating Certificate Holders,* this being a consequence of AMF's control and constant changing of pinsetter prices, AMF's control of all marketing and management decisions, and the possibility that AMF could have operated its own pinsetting machines rather than sell or lease them, in which event the petitioners would have received no payments.

In short, without relying solely on any specific factor, we believe that the participating certificates had no ascertainable fair market value on September 16, 1954, and that the transaction before us must be treated as an "open" transaction.

* * *

## PROBLEM

1.   Taxpayer, a cash method taxpayer, owned all the stock in a company that owned all the rights in a new type of X-ray scanning device which had an extremely speculative value. She had owned the stock for three years and had a $100,000 cost basis in it. She sold the stock to a big electronics firm for $50,000 cash and 2 percent of the earnings generated by the scanning device over the succeeding life of the electronics firm and she made a § 453(d) election. Although her right to earnings is speculative, she receives $2,000 in each of the succeeding years.

   (a)   What are the tax consequences to Taxpayer in each year?

   (b)   Would your result in (a), above, be altered if Taxpayer is an accrual method taxpayer?

## 2.   CLOSED TRANSACTIONS

Regulations: Sections 1.1001–1(g)(1), (2)(ii), (3); 1.1274–2(b)(1)–(2).

If a taxpayer elects out of Section 453 under Section 453(d), and if the transaction is *"closed"*, the taxpayer's gain or loss is determined and taxed in the year of the sale. Recall that gain or loss is calculated under Section 1001 as the difference between the taxpayer's amount realized and adjusted basis in the property,[1] and that the "amount realized" is the sum of any money received plus the fair market property (other than money) received in the transaction.[2] If a taxpayer sells property for consideration that includes a debt instrument of the buyer and elects out of Section 453 under Section 453(d), how should the buyer's debt instrument be treated when calculating the seller's amount realized? Does the fair market value of the buyer's debt instrument need to be determined or is the principal amount of the obligation included as the amount realized? Should the calculations of amount realized vary depending on the seller's accounting method (cash or accrual)? If the seller is a cash method taxpayer, does the buyer's debt instrument have to be a "cash equivalent"[3] to be included in amount realized?

The courts, the government, and tax practitioners have all devoted a great deal of time to the question of determining a seller's amount realized attributable to a buyer's debt instruments when Section 453 is inapplicable.[4] The theoretical issues surrounding the determination of the seller's amount realized are now resolved under the Code's original issue discount rules and the rules for taxing unstated, hidden, and imputed interest. A complete understanding of the area requires a close examination of these statutory provisions.[5] The most fundamental outline of those principles is presented here. In general, if either a cash or accrual method seller disposes of property for a debt obligation of the buyer, the Code requires the parties to properly identify and time the payment of adequate amounts of interest on the buyer's deferred payments.[6] If the buyer and seller adequately provide for interest payments under the Code's standards, the seller's amount realized (regardless of whether the seller is a cash method or accrual method taxpayer) is simply the principal amount of the buyer's obligation.[7] Alternatively, if the buyer and seller do not provide for adequate interest

---

[1]   I.R.C. § 1001(a). See Chapter 6, supra.

[2]   I.R.C. § 1001(b). See Chapter 6C, supra.

[3]   See Chapter 19B, supra.

[4]   See e.g. Warren Jones Co. v. Commissioner, 524 F.2d 788 (9th Cir.1975) (doctrine of "cash equivalency" not relevant in computing cash method taxpayer's amount realized; seller had to include fair market value of buyer's obligation in amount realized). Reg. § 15A.453–1(d)(2) (calculation of seller's amount realized depends on the seller's accounting method). The I.R.C. § 453 regulations on calculating the amount realized when § 453 is inapplicable have been superseded by the Code's original issue discount and time value of money rules. See Reg. § 1.1001–1(g)(3); also see Chapter 24C, infra. These issues have also attracted a good deal of commentary. See e.g., Karjala, "Sales of Property Outside Section 453", 64 Taxes 153 (1986); Schler, "The Sale of Property for a Fixed Payment Note: Remaining Uncertainties," 41 Tax L. Rev. 209 (1986).

[5]   See Chapter 24C, infra.

[6]   Id.

[7]   Reg. §§ 1.1001–1(g)(1), (3); 1.1274–2(b)(1).

payments, the principal amount of the buyer's obligation (and the seller's amount realized) is reduced to properly reflect the fact that a portion of the obligation represents interest on the buyer's deferred payments.[8] The newly identified interest is taxed separately from the sale of the property.[9] To illustrate these principles, assume Taxpayer sells a parcel of land to Buyer for a total purchase price of $500,000. Taxpayer receives $100,000 cash from Buyer and an interest bearing obligation under which Buyer will pay $100,000 a year in each of the succeeding four years. If Taxpayer elects out of Section 453 under Section 453(d) and if adequate interest is provided on the Buyer's deferred payments, Taxpayer's amount realized on the sale is $500,000. If adequate interest is not provided, a portion of the $400,000 of Buyer's deferred payments will be identified as interest and Taxpayer's amount realized will equal $500,000, less that interest component. The interest is taxed as ordinary income and the gain on the reduced principal amount is characterized by the underlying property which Taxpayer transferred.

A special rule applies for purposes of determining a seller's amount realized if because of a Section 453(d) election, Section 453 is inapplicable, the transaction is closed (i.e. *Burnet v. Logan* treatment is not available), and the buyer's obligation contains contingent payments (e.g., contingent payments of interest). In that situation, the seller's amount realized will include the principal amount of the noncontingent payments plus the fair market value of the contingent payments.[10]

## PROBLEM

1.    Seller owns a parcel of land which Seller purchased as an investment four years ago for $2,000. Seller sells it to Buyer under an arrangement where Buyer pays $2,000 cash in the current year and gives Seller four ten percent interest bearing notes to be paid off in each of the succeeding four years. Each note has a $2,000 face amount. Assume the notes pay adequate interest under the Code's original issue discount and time value of money rules. Disregarding the tax consequences of any interest payments, what results to Seller if in the alternative:

(a)    Seller is an accrual method taxpayer and makes a Section 453(d) election.

(b)    Seller is a cash method taxpayer and makes a Section 453(d) election.

(c)    Same as (b), above, except that Buyer's notes are nonassignable and therefore have no equivalency of cash.

---

[8]   Id., Reg. § 1.1274–2(b)(2).

[9]   See generally Chapter 24C, infra.

[10]  Reg. § 1.1001–1(g)(2)(ii). If the contingent payments eventually exceed their fair market, the excess is treated as gain from the sale or exchange of the debt instrument. Any basis remaining on the contingent component on the date the final contingent payment is made increases the holder's basis in the noncontingent component (or, if there are no remaining noncontingent payments, is treated as a loss from the sale or exchange of the debt instrument). Reg. § 1.1275–4(c)(5)(iii).

# C. THE ORIGINAL ISSUE DISCOUNT RULES AND OTHER UNSTATED, HIDDEN, AND IMPUTED INTEREST

Internal Revenue Code: See Sections 483; 1258; 1271 through 1286.

-------------------

## Introduction

Interest of course is an amount paid for the use or forbearance of money. But it does not always jump out and assert, "I am interest!" It may be stated, but maybe not accurately stated. It may be concealed, distorted, lightly veiled, artificially found, fixed or limited by statute, phantom, implied, imputed or presumed—to offer a few possibilities. As it is ordinary income to the payee and qualifiedly deductible by the payor, its elusive qualities make it a challenge to tax administration. The subject is broad, and we take on here only some of its principal features.

You have already been exposed to several of the concepts that are addressed here. In Chapter 16, we took up Section 7872, the gift-interest boomerang for interest-free or below-market interest rate loans, and we saw that Congress sometimes artificially presumes, creates or imputes interest in order to tax more appropriately the parties involved.[1] And in Chapter 19, the concept of the time value of money was introduced in the context of accounting methods.[2]

To illustrate another of Congress's concerns, assume Investor loans $86,230 to a corporate borrower (CB) under an arrangement in which CB will make no annual interest payments to Investor, but will pay off its obligation by transferring $100,000 to Investor at the end of three years. Is there any interest being paid to Investor on this loan? It should be fairly obvious that the $13,770 difference between the amount Investor receives after three years ($100,000) and the amount initially loaned to CB ($86,230) is interest. It is just a substitute for annual interest payments that are not being made on the loan. Instead of making a $86,230 loan with annual interest payments followed by a $86,230 loan repayment after three years, Investor and CB agreed to defer payment of the interest until the end of the loan's term. The tax law's concern about this arrangement is essentially one of timing. If Investor is a cash-method taxpayer, does Investor get to wait until the third year to be taxed on the interest income? And if CB is an accrual method taxpayer, does it get to accrue interest deductions over the term of the loan? If Investor waits three years to include any income while CB obtains annual interest deductions, will the government be pleased with that result?

If interest must be included and deducted over the term of a loan, another question is how will the annual amount of interest be

-------------------

[1]   See page 478, supra.

[2]   See page 641, supra.

determined? There generally are two ways to calculate interest amounts. The first is "simple" interest where the interest each year is the same percentage of the original principal amount. For example, if Lender lends $10,000 to Borrower at 5% simple interest for two years, there is $500 (5% of $10,000) of interest each year or a two year total of $1,000 of interest. The second method for calculating interest is "compound" interest where interest is first computed on the initial principal amount and then computed on the principal amount plus the interest accumulated from the previous period. The total amount of compound interest depends on how often (e.g., daily, monthly, semi-annually, or annually) the interest is compounded. Semi-annual compounding is common and is used under the original issue discount (OID) rules. If semi-annual compounding is used, the interest for each 6 month period is one-half of the annual interest rate and the interest for each 6 month period is added to the principal before the succeeding 6 months period interest is computed. Thus, if Lender lends $10,000 to Borrower at 5% interest, compounded semi-annually, for two years, the interest for the first 6 months is 2½% of $10,000, or $250. The interest for the second 6 months is 2½% of $10,250, or $256.25, making the first year's total interest $506.25. For the second year, the first 6 months interest is 2½% of $10,506.25, or $262.66, and the interest for the final 6 months is 2½% of $10,768.91, or $269.22. The total interest over the two year period is $1,038.13.

Interest may not always be as easy to identify as in the Investor-CB loan. Suppose Buyer and Seller have agreed that Buyer will purchase some property from Seller for a $5 million purchase price, the fair market value of the property. And assume Seller will have a gain on the sale. The parties' problem is that Buyer does not have the funds to make the purchase today and wants to delay paying the $5 million purchase price for three years. Seller puts pen to paper and gives Buyer two alternatives: option 1 is for Buyer to pay a $5 million purchase price plus $798,450 of interest at the end of three years; option 2 is for Buyer to pay a $5,798,450 purchase price at the end of three years. Are the *economics* of the two alternatives really any different? But, if Buyer and Seller had the flexibility to structure the sale as they wish and the form were respected, their individual tax results would vary depending on the option selected. In option 1, Seller's amount realized and Buyer's cost basis will both be $5 million, Seller would have interest income, and Buyer would be entitled to a possible interest deduction. In option 2, Seller's amount realized and Buyer's cost basis will be $5,798,450 and there would be no interest being paid. Here, again, one of the tax law's concerns is timing of potential interest income and deductions. In addition, the government will have a concern about *characterization*. Again, focusing on the alternatives, Seller would have interest (ordinary) income and less gain (possibly long-term capital gain) in option 1; whereas, in option 2 Seller would have no interest income and more gain. For the Buyer, the tradeoff is between a possible interest deduction in option 1 and more cost basis (possibly depreciable?) in option 2.

Finally, the Buyer-Seller situation presents one additional problem. We have assumed that option 1 and option 2 are on the table and can be examined to illustrate the tax stakes in the transaction. It is easy to see that there is $798,450 of hidden interest in option 2 because we are given the property's fair market value and the two alternatives. In the "real world," the buyer and seller go through these types of calculations, but they are not transparent. Instead, some or all of the total price simply is deferred, and all the I.R.S knows are the amounts paid and the timing of the payments. For example, assume Buyer and Seller just agreed to sell the property for $5,798,450, payable three years after the sale (that is, on the terms in option 2). If that were all we knew, how would we determine the amount of interest in the deferred payment? We will shortly see that if the Buyer and Seller do not provide for adequate interest payments in the sale, the tax law will *impute* interest into the deferred payments. If those rules apply, some part of the $5,798,450 price will be recharacterized as interest and taxed as such to both parties.

The Code's OID rules discussed below employ all of the concepts previewed in the Investor-CB and Buyer-Seller examples. Interest may be *imputed*, amounts may be *recharacterized*, *timing* may be adjusted, and *compounding* of interest may be required. The Code has other complex provisions that apply OID concepts but because those provisions are beyond the "Fundamentals," they are not covered here.

### Sections 1272 and 1273: Debts for Cash

Debts for cash (loans) having OID are taxed under Sections 1272 and 1273. Under Section 1272(a), if a debt instrument[3] has OID, the OID is simply accrued (on a daily basis) as interest income by the holder of the debt instrument, and under section 163(e) the borrower is treated as accruing an equivalent amount of interest expense for deduction purposes.[4] Section 1273 is primarily a definitional provision which defines OID as the difference between the debt instrument's "stated redemption price at maturity" and its "issue price."[5] The stated redemption price at maturity generally is all amounts payable on the debt instrument, including interest payments, other than interest payments paid at a fixed rate at least annually.[6] A debt instrument's

---

[3]  A "debt instrument" generally is any bond, debenture, note, or certificate or other evidence of indebtedness. I.R.C. § 1275(a)(1)(A). However, certain annuities are excluded from the definition. I.R.C. § 1275(a)(1)(B).

[4]  The accrual of the OID is done on a daily basis. I.R.C. §§ 163(e)(1), 1272(a)(1). See also I.R.C. § 163(e)(5) which can limit any deduction for the "disqualified portion" of OID in a certain "high yield discount" obligations (term is over five years and interest rate is more than 5% above a set Federal rate). This provision limits the deductibility of interest on "junk" bonds that Congress has determined have the characteristics of equity (stock) rather than debt.

[5]  I.R.C. § 1273(a)(1).

[6]  I.R.C. § 1273(a)(2). See Reg. § 1.1273–1(c) for the rules about "qualified stated interest," which are simply designed to accommodate situations where a debt instrument has OID and also pays interest at a fixed rate at least annually.

issue price generally is the price it was offered to the public or what was paid for the instrument.[7]

The OID rules are subject to a de minimis exception.[8] In addition, there are several types of debts which are not subject to the rules:[9] for example, tax-exempt obligations, U.S. savings bonds, short-term (one year or less) obligations,[10] and loans between natural persons that are not made in the course of a trade or business and do not exceed $10,000.[11]

Returning to the Investor-CB loan where Investor loaned CB $86,230 and will receive $100,000 after three years, the issue price of the loan is $86,230, the stated redemption price at maturity is $100,000, and the OID is $13,770. Investor will be required to include daily portions of the OID in income and CB potentially can deduct daily portions of the OID over the three-year term of the loan. The determination of the daily amounts of the OID is actually a complicated calculation requiring the determination of the debt instrument's "yield to maturity" (you need a financial calculator) and "accrual periods" (to determine the compounding of the interest).[12] To keep it simple, assume the yield to maturity (i.e., the interest rate) for the Investor-CB loan is 5%, and the interest is compounded semiannually. Using those factors, the OID will be taxed as follows:[13]

| Year | Adjusted Issue Price[14] | Yield at 5% (compounded semiannually) | Actual Interest Paid | OID Taxed |
|---|---|---|---|---|
| 1 | $ 86,230 | $ 4,365 | 0 | $ 4,365 |
| 2 | 90,595 | 4,586 | 0 | 4,586 |
| 3 | 95,181 | 4,819 | 0 | 4,819 |
| | $100,000 | $13,770 | | $13,770 |

Thus, in this example, where no there are no actual annual payments of interest, Investor will have $4,365 of interest income in year one, $4,586 in year two, and $4,819 in year three. CB will have potential interest deductions over the three years in the amounts of OID on which

---

[7]   I.R.C. § 1273(b). The rules distinguish between situations where the debt instruments are publicly offered and when they are not. See I.R.C. § 1273(b)(1) and (2).

[8]   I.R.C. § 1273(a)(3).

[9]   I.R.C. § 1272(a)(2).

[10]   With respect to short term obligations, I.R.C. § 1281 requires the difference between their issue price or purchase price and their face amounts to be accrued ratably and included in income by some taxpayers. Some interest on loans to purchase short term obligations, which is not included under § 1281, must be deferred under § 1282.

[11]   But see I.R.C. § 1272(a)(2)(D)(i).

[12]   I.R.C. § 1272(a)(3). See Reg. § 1.1272–1(b) for the steps in determining the accrual of OID.

[13]   In this and subsequent tables, amounts are rounded to the nearest dollar.

[14]   This is the issue price increased by the previous years' OID. See I.R.C. § 1272(a)(4).

Investor is taxed. There are a few additional points to note about these results. First, Sections 1272 and 1273 simply identify and treat the OID as interest accruing annually for both income and deduction purposes. Those sections do not impute, or create, additional interest. Second, Investor's adjusted basis in the CB debt will be increased by the annual inclusions of the OID.[15] So when CB pays $100,000 to investor at the end of the loan term, Investor will not have additional income.

## Sections 1274 and 1274A: Debts for Property

Probably the most important original issue discount rule is Section 1274,[16] which sometimes imputes, or creates, interest in a debt instrument issued for the purchase of property.[17] Section 1274 recognizes the economic reality that when one buys property from another promising to pay money in the future, one has effectively borrowed money, the repayment of which includes both an interest and a principal component. Under Section 1274, Congress establishes the required method for measuring the interest component. If Section 1274 applies it may invoke a combination of all of the tax concepts previously mentioned: *imputing* interest, *recharacterizing* payments, *timing* both parties under the accrual method, and *compounding* interest. Thus, if insufficient (as Congress sees it) interest is stated under a debt instrument issued for property, the interest amount is recomputed at semiannually compound rates; and it is accrued (to be reported) annually for both income and deduction purposes. In addition, the principal amount of the debt is redetermined for income tax purposes to measure gain and loss, to determine Section 453 installment sale consequences, to establish the cost basis, and to compute depreciation. However, take note of Section 1275(b)(1) which makes Sections 1274 and 483 inapplicable to a buyer of personal use property.

The first question to be addressed under the Section 1274 rules is whether there is sufficient interest required to be paid with respect to the debt obligation. To make this determination, the actual rate charged under the terms of the instrument is compared with the "applicable Federal rate."[18] Generally, if the rate of interest to be paid over the life of the debt obligation is equal to the applicable Federal rate, compounded semiannually, then no interest is imputed under Section 1274.[19] If the rate to be paid is not within this "safe harbor," then interest is generally

---

[15]   I.R.C. § 1272(c)(2).

[16]   See Sheffield, "Debt Issued for Traded and Nontraded Property," 62 Taxes 1022 (1984); Goldberg, "Tax Planning for Interest After TRA 1984: Unstated Interest and Original Issue Discount," 43 N.Y.U.Inst. on Fed.Tax'n 23 (1985); Helfand, "The Impact of Time Value of Money Concepts on Deferred and Prepaid Items," 43 N.Y.U.Inst. on Fed.Tax'n 41 (1985).

[17]   Similar rules can impute interest to debts for the use of property or services. See I.R.C. § 467 discussed at page 647, supra.

[18]   I.R.C. § 1274(d). Separate rates are determined for short-term (three years or less), mid-term (between three and nine years), and long-term (over nine years) notes. See page 480, supra.

[19]   I.R.C. § 1274(a), (b)(2)(B), and (c). But see I.R.C. § 1274(e) using a 110% of the applicable Federal rate in sale-leaseback transactions. See also I.R.C. § 1274A(a).

imputed at the applicable Federal rate, compounded semiannually.[20] Such interest is considered the specified interest for tax purposes. Under Section 1274, interest is computed on a daily basis and is generally included in (or deductible from) income annually under accrual concepts applied to both parties.[21] Imputation of the interest effectively reduces the income-tax-recognized purchase price of the property.

To illustrate the Section 1274 rules, recall the earlier Buyer-Seller transaction where Seller sells the property to Buyer for $5,798,450 payable at the end of three years with no interest stated. And assume that the applicable Federal rate is 5%.

First, one must test the instrument for adequate stated interest to determine whether it is necessary to impute interest. Since no interest is stated, the rate of stated interest is obviously less than the safe harbor applicable Federal rate, and interest must be imputed at the 5% applicable Federal rate, compounded semiannually. To determine how much interest to impute, one must first redetermine the income-tax-recognized purchase price of the property (the "issue price"). Under Section 1274(b), the issue price equals the sum of the present values of the payments, discounted at the 5% imputed rate, compounded semiannually. Since there is only one payment ($5,798,450 due in three years), that is the payment that must be discounted. The present value of the $5,798,450 payment, discounted at 5% interest, compounded semiannually is $5,000,000. Thus the OID is $798,450. The next question is the amount and timing of imputed interest. The amount of OID, which is phantom but includable and deductible interest, equals the interest on the issue price of $5,000,000 at a rate of 5% per year compounded semiannually less the amount of any interest actually paid in each year. The calculations are similar to the calculations in the earlier loan situation. Again, in tabular form:

| Year | Adjusted Issue Price[22] | Yield at 5% (compounded semiannually) | Actual Interest Paid | OID Taxed |
|---|---|---|---|---|
| 1 | $5,000,000 | $253,150 | $ 0 | $253,150 |
| 2 | 5,253,150 | 265,967 | 0 | 265,967 |
| 3 | 5,519,117 | 279,333 | 0 | 279,333 |
| | | $798,450 | $ 0 | $798,450[23] |

---

[20] I.R.C. § 1274(a), (b) and (c).

[21] I.R.C. § 1272(a)(3) and (4). But see I.R.C. § 1274A(c).

[22] This is the issue price increased by the previous year's OID.

[23] In this calculation, OID should and does equal the difference between the stated redemption price (see I.R.C. § 1273(a)(2)) and the adjusted issue price (see I.R.C. § 1272(a)(4)). See I.R.C. § 1273(a)(1).

In this example, where no interest is stated, Section 1274 steps in and adjusts the selling price to $5,000,000. In addition, Section 1274 creates and taxes Seller on $253,150 of interest in year one, $265,967 in year two, and $279,333 in year three. Complementary results accrue to Buyer—a reduction in the cost basis to $5,000,000 but potential interest deductions over the three years in the amounts of the OID on which Seller is taxed.

The same basic results would occur to Buyer and Seller if they had instead provided for a $5 million purchase price with $798,450 of stated interest all due after three years. In that factual variation, there is adequate stated interest (at 5%, the assumed applicable Federal rate) but it is all due at the end of the three year contract. Because the debt for property meets the safe harbor applicable Federal rate, no interest will be *imputed*, but the OID *timing* rules will come into play so that Seller would have interest income each year and Buyer would have potential interest deductions over the three years.

Another variation where Buyer pays some, but an inadequate amount of, interest will illustrate the intricacies of the rules. Suppose that Seller sells property to Buyer for $5,000,000 payable at the end of three years. Buyer gives Seller a note for $5,000,000 with simple interest payable annually at the end of each year over the three years at a rate of 3%. And assume again that the applicable Federal rate is 5%.

We can easily tell that the Buyer and Seller have a problem under Section 1274 because they did not provide for adequate stated interest at least equal to the 5% safe harbor. Therefore, they will have to determine how much interest to impute and redetermine the income-tax-recognized purchase price of the property (the "issue price"). To do that they must first calculate the sum of the present values of the payments, discounted at the 5% imputed rate, compounded semiannually. So:

| Year | Actual Payments | Present Value At 5% Compounded Semiannually |
|:---:|:---:|:---:|
| 1 | $ 150,000 | $   142,772 |
| 2 | 150,000 | 135,893 |
| 3 | 5,150,000 | 4,440,829 |
|  | $5,450,000 | $4,719,494 |

As the table indicates, the issue price becomes $4,719,494, and that is the purchase price for Buyer and Seller. The OID each year, which again is phantom but includable and potentially deductible interest, equals the interest on the issue price at a rate of 5% per year compounded semiannually less the amount of interest actually to be paid in each year. Again, in tabular form:

| Year | Adjusted Issue Price[24] | Yield at 5% (compounded semiannually) | Actual Interest Paid | OID Taxed |
|------|--------------------------|---------------------------------------|----------------------|-----------|
| 1 | $4,719,494 | $238,924 | $150,000 | $ 88,924 |
| 2 | 4,808,418 | 243,426 | 150,000 | 93,426 |
| 3 | 4,901,844 | 248,156 | 150,000 | 98,156 |
|   |   | $730,506 | $450,000 | $280,506[25] |

Thus, in the above example where the stated purchase price is $5,000,000 with 3% simple interest to be paid annually, Section 1274 applies and for tax purposes adjusts the sales price to $4,719,494. In addition, Section 1274 creates and taxes Seller on $88,924 of additional interest in year one, $93,426 in year two, and $98,156 in year three.[26] Complementary results accrue to Buyer—a reduction in the cost basis to $4,719,494 but additional potential interest deductions over the three years in the amounts of OID on which the seller is taxed.

Finally, there is one other possible debt for property situation. If the Buyer and Seller satisfy the safe harbor interest rate rules and the interest is required to be paid annually, the original issue discount rules are inapplicable; even for tax purposes, the stated interest is interest and the stated principal is principal. There is no OID. All of these rules are avoided!!!

Long ago, before the current statutory regime became effective, there was substantial "creative" financing in sales of property (lower-than-market interest, balloon principal payments, balloon interest payments, and so forth) which generally avoided the application of the then applicable statutory tax restrictions and gave arms-length buyers and sellers a lot of flexibility in arranging transactions. The current complex rules now encourage persons to state sufficient and timely interest payments to avoid the Section 1274 thicket. Thus, a common practice when Section 1274 could apply is to require interest to be paid annually at the applicable Federal rate.

The debt for property rules do not apply to all sales of property. Section 1274(c)(3) contains several exceptions, including sales of property for less than $250,000;[27] sales of principal residences;[28] sales of farms for $1,000,000 or less by individuals, estates, testamentary trusts and small businesses;[29] sales of debt instruments that are publicly traded or issued

---

[24] This is the issue price increased by the previous year's OID.

[25] In this calculation, OID should and does equal the difference between the stated redemption price (see I.R.C. § 1273(a)(2)) and the adjusted issue price (see I.R.C. § 1272(a)(4)). See I.R.C. § 1273(a)(1).

[26] Note that the total of these amounts is $5 million.

[27] I.R.C. § 1274(c)(3)(C); see especially I.R.C. § 1274(c)(3)(C)(iii). Cf. I.R.C. § 1274A(a).

[28] I.R.C. § 1274(c)(3)(B). Cf. I.R.C. § 483(a) and (e).

[29] I.R.C. § 1274(c)(3)(A).

for publicly traded property;[30] some sales of patents;[31] and sales of land between family members at a price not in excess of $500,000.[32]

Section 1274A also creates two additional exceptions to the Section 1274 rules. The first exception imposes a cap on imputed interest of 9 percent per annum compounded semiannually[33] on a "qualified debt instrument," which generally is a debt instrument given for property (other than new tangible personal property) where the stated principal amount of the instrument does not exceed $2,800,000.[34] Thus, if a 9 percent interest rate is less than the applicable Federal rate, taxpayers need use only the 9 percent rate to escape adverse consequences under Section 1274.[35]

The second exception allows taxpayers to elect to use the cash method of accounting, rather than the accrual method, to alter the timing rules of Section 1274.[36] To qualify for the election, the stated principal amount of a debt instrument given for property (other than new tangible personal property) cannot exceed $2,000,000,[37] the lender-seller cannot use the accrual method of accounting and cannot be a dealer in the property sold, and, but for the election, Section 1274 would have applied.[38] Thus, the cash method may be used if it is used by both electing parties.

## Section 483: Debts for Property

Section 483 generally applies to sales of property which fall within the exception provisions of Section 1274, including a Section 1274A(c) election out of Section 1274, if payments are to be made more than one year after the date of the sale.[39] Section 483 sometimes imputes the same amounts of interest[40] and uses the same safe harbor rule as Section 1274 (interest stated at the applicable Federal rate).[41] However, in most circumstances, Section 483 employs the 9 percent cap of Section 1274A,

---

[30]  I.R.C. § 1274(c)(3)(D). Instead, the debts for cash rules apply. See I.R.C. § 1273(b)(3).

[31]  I.R.C. § 1274(c)(3)(E).

[32]  I.R.C. § 1274(c)(3)(F). See I.R.C. § 483(e).

[33]  I.R.C. § 1274A(a).

[34]  I.R.C. § 1274A(b). The $2,800,000 amount is indexed for inflation for years after 1989. I.R.C. § 1274A(d)(2). The exception contains an aggregation provision to prevent taxpayers from creating several obligations to avoid the dollar limitation. I.R.C. § 1274A(d)(1). The section is inapplicable to property that is new I.R.C. § 38 property as defined in § 48(b) as in effect prior to the enactment of the Revenue Reduction Act of 1990. I.R.C. § 1274A(b).

[35]  This exception also applies to I.R.C. § 483, which is considered below. I.R.C. § 1274A(a).

[36]  I.R.C. § 1274A(c)(1). If an election is made, then I.R.C. § 483 applies. See I.R.C. § 1274A(c)(1)(A) and the discussion of § 483, infra.

[37]  The aggregation rule of I.R.C. § 1274(d)(1) also applies here. The $2,000,000 amount is indexed for inflation for years after 1989. I.R.C. § 1274A(d)(2).

[38]  I.R.C. § 1274A(c)(2). See also I.R.C. § 1274A(b).

[39]  I.R.C. § 483 is subject to a de minimis rule for sales not exceeding $3,000. I.R.C. § 483(d)(2). The statute does not apply to I.R.C. § 1235 dispositions of patents (I.R.C. § 483(d)(4)) and there is a special rule regarding the purchaser in an installment purchase where interest is imputed under § 163(b) (I.R.C. § 483(d)(3)).

[40]  I.R.C. §§ 483(b) and 1274A.

[41]  I.R.C. §§ 483(b), 483(c)(1)(B), and 1274(d).

and in limited circumstances it uses a 6 percent cap.[42] Unlike Section 1274 and Section 1274A, Section 483 does not compel annual accrual of interest. It lets the timing consequences depend on a taxpayer's accounting method.

To illustrate Section 483, reduce the original Buyer-Seller figures to 10% of the original amount.[43] Buyer agrees to purchase property from Seller for $57,985, payable in three years. No interest is stated and the applicable Federal rate is 5%. Also, assume that Buyer is an accrual method taxpayer and Seller is a cash method taxpayer. Section 483, not Section 1274, is applicable because the selling price for the property is less than $250,000.[44] Similar to the § 1274 example, a total of $7,985 of interest will be imputed:

| Year | Adjusted Issue Price[45] | Yield at 5% (compounded semiannually) | Actual Interest Paid | OID |
|---|---|---|---|---|
| 1 | $50,000 | $ 2,532 | $ 0 | $ 2,532 |
| 2 | 52,532 | 2,660 | 0 | 2,660 |
| 3 | 55,192 | 2,793 | 0 | 2,793 |
| | | $ 7,985 | $ 0 | $ 7,985[46] |

The big difference under Section 483 is that each taxpayer's accounting method will control the timing consequences of the OID. Since Buyer is an accrual method taxpayer, Buyer *will* be able to deduct the OID interest annually or $2,532 in year one, $2660 in year two, and $2,793 in year three. The timing results to Buyer are identical to the Section 1274 timing results.[47] Since Seller is a cash method taxpayer, Seller will not be taxed on the total $7,985 of OID until it is paid in year three. Thus, Seller is able to defer recognition of the imputed interest income.

---

[42] I.R.C. § 483(e) uses a 6% cap for sales of land between members of the same family if all sales for the year between the parties do not exceed $500,000 and if no party is a nonresident alien. Cf. I.R.C. § 267(c)(4).

[43] See the table at notes 22 and 23, supra.

[44] I.R.C. § 1274(c)(3)(C).

[45] This is the issue price increased by the previous year's OID.

[46] In this calculation, OID should and does equal the difference between the stated redemption price (see I.R.C. § 1273(a)(2)) and the adjusted issue price (see I.R.C. § 1272(a)(4)). See I.R.C. § 1273(a)(1).

[47] Reg. § 1.483–1(a)(2)(ii).

## D. PROPERTY TRANSFERRED IN CONNECTION WITH SERVICES

Internal Revenue Code: Section 83 (omit (c)(3) and (g)).

Regulations: Sections 1.61–2(d)(2)(i) and (6); 1.83–1(a)(1), –2(a), –3(c)(1) and (2), (d), (e).

---

*Introduction.* Section 83 is a provision of the Internal Revenue Code that deals with an inclusion in gross income. Section 83(a) generally provides that a taxpayer who performs services must include the fair market value of property received for those services, less anything paid for the property, in gross income when the taxpayer's beneficial interest in the property is substantially vested.[1] Even though Section 83 deals with gross income, its operation may affect both the timing and characterization of income recognized in connection with property received for services. Consequently, consideration of Section 83 has been deferred until after the study of timing and characterization.

*The General Rule of Section 83(a).* Under Section 83(a), if property is transferred to any person in connection with the performance of services,[2] then at the time when the property is substantially vested (either is not subject to a substantial risk of forfeiture or is transferable) the service provider generally has gross income[3] in an amount equal to the excess of the property's fair market value over the amount paid for the property.[4]

The general rule of Section 83(a) has several special features. The statute applies only when "property" is "transferred" in connection with the performance of services. For purposes of section 83, property includes real and personal property other than (1) money, or (2) an unfunded and unsecured promise to pay money or property in the future.[5] A transfer of property occurs when a taxpayer acquires a beneficial ownership interest in property.[6] Thus, the grant of an option to purchase property (other than stock of the corporation to which the services are provided) is not a transfer of the property.[7] Special Section 83 rules (discussed below) apply

---

[1] See Metzer, "The Receipt of Property for Services," 38 N.Y.U.Inst. on Fed.Tax. Ch. 24 (1980), for an overview of I.R.C. § 83.

[2] A transfer of property is disregarded if it is to the person for whom the services are performed. I.R.C. § 83(a).

[3] I.R.C. § 83 does not apply to transfers from qualified pension and profit-sharing trusts or to § 79 group-term life insurance. I.R.C. § 83(e)(2) and (5).

[4] I.R.C. § 83(a).

[5] Reg. § 1.83–3(e). For example, in Theophilos v. Commissioner, 85 F.3d 440 (9th Cir.1996), the court held that a binding contract to acquire stock was property within the meaning of I.R.C. § 83. Thus, the contract obligation was property taxable under § 83 when the contract was binding, but the subsequent purchase of the stock pursuant to the contract was not taxable under § 83.

[6] Reg. § 1.83–3(a)(1); see Reg. § 1.83–3(e). However, transfers to employee pension plans are not subject to I.R.C. § 83. I.R.C. § 83(e)(2).

[7] Reg. § 1.83–3(a)(2).

with respect to most options to acquire stock of the corporation to which the services are provided.[8] In addition, a transfer may not occur when property is transferred under conditions that require its return on the happening of an event that is certain to occur, such as the termination of employment.[9] Because Section 83(a) applies to transfers of property "in connection with the performance of services," it applies when the transfer is made in either an employment or an independent contractor relationship,[10] and includes transfers for past, present, or future services.[11] Section 83(a) also incorporates assignment-of-income principles by taxing a service provider where the property received for services is transferred to "any person" (e.g., a child beginning college).[12]

Section 83(a) requires the fair market value of the transferred property less any amount paid for the property to be included in the gross income of the taxpayer who performs the services. In determining the fair market value of property, the only type of restriction on the property taken into account is a "nonlapse restriction," a restriction which by its terms will never lapse. A nonlapse restriction is a permanent limitation on the transferability of the property which requires the transferee or a subsequent holder to sell, or offer to sell, the property at a price determined under a formula.[13] Thus, a permanent right of first refusal held by another person at a formula price would be a nonlapse restriction.[14]

*Substantially Nonvested Property.* If a beneficial interest in property with no restrictions is transferred in connection with the performance of services, Section 83(a) adds little to the principles of Section 61. The taxpayer receiving the property simply has gross income equal to the value of the property less any amount paid to acquire the property. If, however, the taxpayer's beneficial enjoyment of the property is restricted, the rules in Section 83(a) clarify the application of general gross income principles. Specifically, if the property is "substantially nonvested property,"[15] that is, the taxpayer's beneficial interest in the property is subject to a substantial risk of forfeiture *and* not transferable, then the transfer of property is not taxable until the property becomes

---

[8]   I.R.C. § 83(e)(1), (3) and (4). See Reg. § 1.83–7 and the Text at notes 46–49, infra.

[9]   Reg. §§ 1.83–3(a)(3), –3(a)(7) Example (3).

[10]  Reg. § 1.83–1(a).

[11]  Reg. § 1.83–3(f).

[12]  See Text accompanying note 30, infra.

[13]  Reg. § 1.83–3(h). The formula price is presumed to be the fair market value of the property unless the I.R.S. sustains its burden of proving otherwise. I.R.C. § 83(d)(1). The cancellation of a nonlapse restriction also may result in gross income to the taxpayer. I.R.C. § 83(d)(2).

[14]  Reg. § 1.83–3(h).

[15]  Reg. § 1.83–3(b).

"substantially vested,"[16] that is, when the property is *either* not subject to a substantial risk of forfeiture *or* it is transferable.[17]

A taxpayer's beneficial interest in property is subject to a substantial risk of forfeiture when full enjoyment of the property is conditioned, directly or indirectly, on the future performance of substantial services.[18] For example, if stock in a corporate employer is transferred to an employee subject to a binding commitment to resell the stock to the employer if the employee leaves the employment for any reason within two years of the transfer, the employee's rights to the stock are subject to substantial risk of forfeiture during the two-year period.[19] In addition, if the retention of the property is conditioned upon the earnings of the employer increasing, that restriction is a substantial risk of forfeiture.[20] But there is no substantial risk of forfeiture if the property must be returned only if an employee is terminated for cause or as a result of committing a crime.[21]

The term "transferable" is given a special definition under Section 83.[22] The rights of a person in property are transferable only if the rights in the property of any transferee are not subject to a substantial risk of forfeiture.[23]

Property subject to Section 83(a) generally will have a basis equal to the amount paid for it, plus the amount included in the gross income of the service provider when the property became substantially vested.[24] The holding period for such property begins when the property becomes substantially vested.[25]

A simple example will illustrate the operation of Section 83(a). Assume E, an employee of X Co., is transferred 100 shares of X Co. stock for $90 per share at a time when the fair market value of X Co. stock is $110 per share. Under the terms of the transfer, E, and any transferee of E, must resell the stock to X Co. at $90 per share if E leaves the employment of X Co. within two years of the transfer. Under Section 83(a), E has no gross income at the time of the transfer because the stock is substantially nonvested.[26] Instead, E will have gross income at the end

---

[16] Id.

[17] Reg. § 1.83–1(a).

[18] I.R.C. § 83(c)(1). Neither the risk that property will decline in value nor a nonlapse restriction constitutes a substantial risk of forfeiture. Reg. § 1.83–3(c)(1).

[19] Reg. § 1.83–3(c)(4) Example (1).

[20] Reg. § 1.83–3(c)(2).

[21] Id; accord Burnetta v. Commissioner, 68 T.C. 387 (1977), acq. 1978–2 C.B. 1.

[22] I.R.C. § 83(c)(2). See Reg. § 1.83–3(d).

[23] Reg. § 1.83–1(f) Example (1) indicates that stamping the restriction on the face of stock certificates makes the certificates nontransferable. I.R.C. § 83(c)(3) provides that if the sale of property at a profit would subject a person to a suit under section 16(b) of the Securities Exchange Act of 1934, the person's rights in the property are subject to a substantial risk of forfeiture and are not transferable.

[24] See Reg. § 1.83–4(b)(1).

[25] I.R.C. § 83(f); Reg. § 1.83–4(a).

[26] See Reg. § 1.83–3(c)(4) Example (1).

of the required two-year period equal to the difference between the fair market value of the stock at that time and the $90 per-share price paid by E. Thus, if the X Co. stock is worth $140 per share when it becomes substantially vested, E will have gross income of $50 per share, or $5,000.[27] Also, until the X Co. stock becomes substantially vested, X Co. is treated as the owner of the stock; however dividends received by E are additional compensation to E in the year received.[28]

*Dispositions of Substantially Nonvested Property.* If, in an arm's length transaction, a taxpayer sells or otherwise disposes of substantially nonvested property that was transferred in connection with the performance of services, gross income is realized equal to the excess of the amount realized on the sale or other disposition over the amount paid for the property.[29] If the disposition is not an arm's length transaction, Section 83 continues to apply to the service provider under assignment of income principles.[30]

*The Section 83(b) Election.* Under Section 83(b), if there is a transfer of substantially nonvested property to a taxpayer in connection with the performance of services, the taxpayer may elect to include in gross income, for the taxable year of the transfer, the difference between the fair market value of the property at the time of the transfer (generally determined without any restrictions on the property) and the amount paid for the property. If a Section 83(b) election is made, Section 83(a) does not trigger additional gross income when the property becomes substantially vested.

There are potential benefits and risks connected with making a Section 83(b) election. On the positive side, if a Section 83(b) election is made, the taxpayer's gross income is dependent upon the property's current fair market value. Appreciation in the property's value between the time of the transfer and the time when the property becomes substantially vested is not taxed until the taxpayer disposes of the property. On a later disposition, the property's basis for determining gain or loss is the amount paid for the property increased by the amount included in gross income under Section 83(b).[31] The taxpayer's holding period for the property also begins when the property is transferred to the taxpayer if a Section 83(b) election is made.[32]

---

[27] If substantially nonvested property is forfeited, the difference between the amount paid for the property and the amount received upon forfeiture is treated as ordinary gain or loss. Reg. § 1.83–1(b)(2).

[28] Reg. § 1.83–1(a)(1). See Rev. Proc. 80–11, 1980–1 C.B. 616, for guidance on reporting dividends on restricted stock that is not substantially vested.

[29] I.R.C. § 83(a); Reg. § 1.83–1(b)(1). Special rules apply if the disposition of substantially nonvested property is not at arm's-length. See Reg. § 1.83–1(c).

[30] Reg. § 1.83–1(c). If the service provider receives consideration for the transfer, special rules apply. Id.

[31] Reg. § 1.83–2(a).

[32] Reg. § 1.83–4(a).

In addition to the timing aspect of a Section 83(b) election, there is also a characterization wrinkle. If appreciation in the value of the property after the election is recognized in a sale or exchange of the property more than one year after the Section 83(b) election, that gain potentially will be eligible for favorable tax treatment as long-term capital gain. Thus, a Section 83(b) election may have the effect of converting what would otherwise be ordinary income received for services into long-term capital gain.

While a Section 83(b) election may sound too good to be true, there are risks involved in making the election. One risk is that the transferred property may decline in value in the future, leaving the taxpayer in the position of paying tax on income never realized. Another risk is that the taxpayer may have to forfeit the property because a requirement for receiving it (e.g., employment for a term of years) is not satisfied. Section 83(b) provides that if property is forfeited, the taxpayer is not allowed a deduction for the amount included in income when the election was made.[33] It is sometimes said that Section 83(b) provides a taxpayer with a "gambler's choice" in which all of the risks and rewards of the arrangement must be carefully analyzed.

The effect of a Section 83(b) election may be illustrated by considering the earlier example involving E and X Co. E, an employee of X Co., is transferred 100 shares of X Co. stock for $90 per share at a time when the fair market value of X Co. is $110 per share. The X Co. stock is substantially nonvested for two years, at which time it is worth $140 per share. If E forfeits the stock, it must be resold to X Co. for $90 per share. Earlier we saw that under Section 83(a), E will have $5,000 of ordinary gross income after two years when the stock becomes substantially vested. Alternatively, E could make a Section 83(b) election in the year of the transfer and include $2,000 of ordinary gross income ($11,000 fair market value less $9,000 paid for the stock) at that time. If the election were made, E would not recognize any further income from the stock until it is sold when the gain would potentially be eligible for taxation as long-term capital gain. E, however, will be taxed on any dividends received on the stock.[34] The effect of the election would be to convert the additional $3,000 of appreciation in the property from the time of the election until it becomes substantially vested from ordinary income to long-term capital gain. In addition, if E forfeits the property after making the Section 83(b) election, E will recover $9,000 of cash but will not be allowed a deduction for the $2,000 that was included in gross income when the election was made.[35]

In terms of planning, when will a Section 83(b) election be a wise tax move? One situation where a Section 83(b) election will make sense is

---

[33] I.R.C. § 83(b). See Reg. § 1.83–2(a).

[34] The dividends retain their character as dividends and are not treated as additional compensation. Rev. Rul. 83–22, 1983–1 C.B. 17.

[35] I.R.C. § 83(b).

when the election will produce little or no gross income because the transferred property has little or no current value (e.g., speculative stock in a corporation engaged in a risky venture). A Section 83(b) election might also be advisable when little gross income will be included because the amount paid for the property is equal to or very close to its current value.[36] In other situations, the decision about whether to make a Section 83(b) election will depend upon a variety of factors, including the prospects for future appreciation in the value of the property, the likelihood of the taxpayer satisfying the conditions for obtaining the property, and the taxpayer's ability to pay the tax liability triggered by the election.[37]

*Consequences to Employer.* When property is transferred in connection with the performance of services, the transferor potentially is entitled to a deduction under Section 162 or 212 for the compensation that is paid. Section 83(h) provides that the deduction is equal to the amount included in gross income under Section 83 by the person who performs the services. The deduction is allowed in the taxable year in which the service provider includes Section 83 compensation in gross income.[38] Thus, an employer's deduction for a Section 83 transfer is tied to the employee's tax results under Section 83. For example, if Section 83(a) applies, the property transferor's allowable deduction is measured by the gross income of the employee under Section 83(a) and taken in the year that Section 83(a) applies. If a Section 83(b) election is made, the property transferor's deduction is measured by the gross income of the employee under Section 83(b) and is allowed in the year of the election.

A deduction under Section 83(h), is subject to the prohibition on the deduction of capital expenditures.[39] Also, because the transfer of property as compensation for services is a sale or other disposition of the property, the transferor generally recognizes gain or loss on the transfer.[40] However, under Section 1032 a corporation does not recognize gain or loss on the transfer of its stock for services.[41]

---

[36] The regulations state that an I.R.C. § 83(b) election may be made when there is no bargain element in the transfer. Reg. § 1.83–2(a). Accord Alves v. Commissioner, 79 T.C. 864 (1982).

[37] See generally Bortnick & Gross, "Tax Advantages of the Section 83(b) Election Can be Significant," 86 J. Tax'n 39 (1997).

[38] Reg. § 1.83–6(a)(2) provides that the service provider is deemed to have included the amount as compensation if the person for whom the services were performed timely satisfies the information reporting requirements of I.R.C. § 6041 or § 6041A. See Venture Funding, Ltd. v. Commissioner, 110 T.C. 236 (1998), where the deduction was denied because these requirements were not satisfied.

[39] Reg. § 1.83–6(a)(4); accord Steinberg v. Commissioner, 46 T.C.M. 1238 (1983).

[40] When property is transferred in connection with the performance of services, gain must be recognize to the extent that the amount received from the transferee exceeds the transferor's basis. Reg. § 1.83–6(b). In addition, when the property becomes substantially vested, gain or loss must be recognized to the extent of the difference between (1) the sum of the amount paid for the property plus the amount allowed as a deduction under I.R.C. § 83(h), and (2) the sum of the transferor's basis in the property plus any gain recognized at the time the property was transferred. Id.

[41] Reg. § 1.1032–1(a).

*Taxation of Stock Options.* A statutory deferred compensation device for corporate employees is the incentive or statutory stock option (ISO).[42] An ISO is an option granted by an employer corporation to an employee to purchase stock in the corporation at a fixed or determinable price. If certain requirements are met such as the dates the option is granted and exercised, and the option price,[43] then no income is recognized by the employee when the ISO is granted or even when the option is exercised.[44] Income is recognized by an employee who exercises the option only upon the employee's subsequent sale of the stock acquired with the option and no deduction is allowed to the employer.[45]

If an option does not qualify as an ISO,[46] Section 83 has specific rules for the taxation of such "nonqualified stock options". Under those rules, Section 83 applies to the grant of an option that has a readily ascertainable fair market value, but not to the transfer of property pursuant to the exercise of such an option.[47] If an option does not have a readily ascertainable value, then Sections 83(a) and (b) do not apply to the transfer of the option, but they apply at the time of the exercise of the option to the transfer of the property subject to the option.[48] The regulations provide that the value of an option is ordinarily not readily ascertainable unless the option is actively traded on an established market.[49] Special rules may allow an employee of a privately held corporation to elect to defer recognition of income from the exercise of a stock option for up to an additional five years.[50] To qualify, generally the corporation must have a written plan and at least 80 percent of all employees must be granted options.[51] The election is not available to one-percent owners, certain executives, and highly compensated officers of the corporation.[52]

---

[42]  I.R.C. §§ 421, 422.

[43]  I.R.C. § 422(b), (d).

[44]  I.R.C. §§ 421 and 422.

[45]  I.R.C. §§ 421 and 422. Any gain recognized is capital gain, provided certain holding period requirements are met. See I.R.C. § 422(a)(1).

[46]  I.R.C. § 83 does not apply to § 421 incentive stock options. I.R.C. § 83(e)(1). However, the amount by which the fair market value of a share of stock in the year in which it is appropriately subject to tax under § 83 exceeds the option price is included in the employee's taxable income under the alternative minimum tax. I.R.C. § 56(b)(3). See Chapter 27C, infra.

[47]  I.R.C. § 83(e)(3) and (4); Reg. § 1.83–7(a).

[48]  Id. The rule applies even though the option is substantially vested at an earlier time. Id.

[49]  Reg. § 1.83–7(b)(1). See Reg. § 1.83–7(b)(2) for the requirements that must be satisfied to establish a readily ascertainable fair market value for options that are not actively traded on an established market.

[50]  I.R.C. § 83(i). If the election is made the option is not treated as an incentive stock option. I.R.C. § 422(b).

[51]  I.R.C. § 83(i)(2)(C).

[52]  I.R.C. § 83(i)(3).

## PROBLEM

1.    E is an employee of Web Inc. (Web), a newly formed high-technology firm. E's compensation package with Web includes the grant of an option to purchase 100,000 shares of Web stock for $1.50 per share, the stock's current fair market value. In order to exercise the option, E must be employed by Web for three years. Assume that under Reg. § 1.83–7(b)(2), on its receipt in year 1, E's option does not have a readily ascertainable fair market value. At the end of year three Web stock is worth $8 per share.

   (a)   What are the tax results to E, assuming that in the fourth year, E is still employed by Web and exercises the option to purchase 100,000 shares of the company's stock when it is worth $10 per share?

   (b)   If the option gives E the right to immediately purchase 100,000 shares of Web stock for $1.50 per share, but E's right (and the right of any transferee) to retain the stock is conditioned upon E working for Web for three years, what result if E exercises the option and purchases 100,000 shares of Web stock in the first year for its $1.50 per share fair market value?

   (c)   What result in (a), above, if E gives the option to Child who exercises the option in the fourth year?

## E.  INCOME IN RESPECT OF DECEDENTS

Internal Revenue Code: Sections 691(a)(1)–(4), (b); 1014(c). See Section 691(c).

Regulations: Section 1.691(a)–1, –2(a), –3(a).

———————————

Questions arise upon the death of a taxpayer which involve the issue of *who* is taxable on income, *when* the income is taxed, and the *character* of the income; and there are related issues with respect to deductions. Section 691 addresses itself to some of the transitional problems that arise because a person's financial affairs, instead of terminating neatly at the time of death, linger on, sometimes for a considerable period after the person's demise. An executor marshalling the decedent's assets will usually find that the executor's efforts involve the collection of amounts that would have been gross income to the decedent had decedent collected them and the payment of amounts that would have been tax deductions if paid by the decedent. What should be the post-death tax consequences of such transactions? *Possible* answers to this question are suggested by a brief review of three legislative approaches that Congress has, at different times, taken to the matter of income and deductions in respect of decedents.

From the inception of the individual income tax in 1913 to 1934, Congress did not legislate specifically on the subject. But of course such inaction itself had important tax consequences. The principal result was for much income constitutionally subject to tax to escape the federal exaction. This came about by way of the treatment of income rights as a part of the corpus of a decedent's estate entitled, along with all other property owned by decedent, to a new date-of-death value basis, which foreclosed the imposition of income tax upon its post-death collection. Of course, at the same time, expenses incurred before death that could not under the decedent's accounting method be deducted on decedent's final return also lost their potential for tax reduction when paid.

The two main problems with the pre-1934 approach were: (1) substantial revenue loss through the escape from income taxation of transitional income items and (2) quite unequal treatment of accrual and cash method taxpayers. With regard to the second difficulty, it is obvious that some transitional income items, such as a decedent's unpaid salary, interest, and gain on the sale of property, were either *taxed or not* according to the decedent's accounting method,[1] whereas in the case of living taxpayers accounting methods generally affect only timing and do not govern whether an item is subject to tax at all.

To overcome these problems, Congress in 1934 in effect put all final returns of decedents on the accrual method. Thus, notwithstanding the fact that a decedent had been a cash method taxpayer, decedent's *final* return included accrued items of income and deduction. This stemmed the revenue loss and eliminated the discriminatory advantage previously enjoyed by estates and beneficiaries of cash method taxpayers. But it was soon evident that there were equally strong objections to the new approach. Especially when the courts gave support to a broad administrative interpretation of what income items could be treated as accrued by reason of death, there was great possibility that substantial previously untaxed income would be bunched in the final return of a cash method taxpayer.

The origin of the present congressional approach to the problem was the Revenue Act of 1942, which first presented the concept of income and deductions in respect of decedents. If it can be capsulized, the intended thrust of Section 691 is insofar as possible to neutralize the tax consequences of a person's death. Thus, income generated by, but untaxed to the person, is to be taxed to others when received by them, not in the decedent's final return. And some potential deductions of the decedent may be claimed by others when they pay the related pre-death expenses of the decedent. In general, this will be seen: (1) To prevent revenue loss which, pre-1934, was a sometimes result of death, (2) To let one's accounting method continue to affect the timing of income and deductions, but not to affect the questions whether income would be taxed or whether deductions could be claimed, also pre-1934 inequities, and (3) To avoid the bunching problem inherent in the 1934 legislation.

---

[1]  See Chapter 19, supra.

Together with Sections 451 and 1014(c), Section 691(a) taxes a decedent's transitional income items to the one who receives the item after a decedent's death. When death terminates one's taxable year, income inclusions in the decedent's final return are determined by decedent's established accounting method under Section 451(a).[2] The full income component of post-death receipts is preserved by Section 1014(c), which denies the usual date-of-death value basis to any right to receive income in respect of a decedent, commonly called I.R.D.

I.R.D. items[3] are to be included "when received," which makes the recipient's accounting method immaterial with respect to such items. The statute is explicit as regards who may be taxed upon receipt of I.R.D. If, as is usually the case with respect to unpaid salary, the executor collects the amount, it is an item of gross income to the estate.[4]

Finally, upon acquisition of an I.R.D. item as a part of the decedent's estate, the executor or administrator may transmit it, before collection, to one who is entitled to it by reason of bequest, devise, or inheritance. In such a case, the one to whom it is transmitted takes it into account as I.R.D. when payment is received.[5] However, some transmissions of I.R.D. items are far from neutral events. Instant tax liability results to the transferor if, for example, the executor sells an I.R.D. item or a beneficiary who acquired it innocuously from the executor makes a gift of it.[6]

The neutralization objective of Section 691 is further carried out by provisions that *characterize* I.R.D. when received in accordance with the nature of the income that would have been realized by the decedent had decedent collected the item during life.[7] Thus, gain on the sale of a capital asset, taxed as I.R.D. when the proceeds are collected after death, is capital gain to the recipient. Salary collected after death is ordinary income. And so forth.

The deductions side of Section 691 in effect passes through to the decedent's estate or beneficiaries the tax benefit of certain deductible expenses incurred by the decedent but not properly taken into account in the decedent's final, or any earlier return. However, only expenses that are of a business nature within Section 162 or are non-trade expenses within Section 212, plus interest under Section 163 and taxes under

---

[2]   Thus, receipt prior to death (or constructive receipt) is the test for inclusions for cash method taxpayers. In the case of accrual method decedents, the usual "all events" and "economic performance" tests will control, especially since I.R.C. § 451(b) forecloses accrual only by reason of death in the case of such taxpayers.

[3]   The examples in Reg. § 1.691(a)–2(b) are helpful as illustrations of what constitutes an I.R.D. item. See Furr, "Determining When Sales Proceeds are Income in Respect of a Decedent," 19 Wake Forest L.Rev. 993 (1983).

[4]   I.R.C. § 691(a)(1)(A).

[5]   I.R.C. § 691(a)(1)(C).

[6]   I.R.C. § 691(a)(2). These acceleration rules are somewhat analogous to the more familiar principles that apply to the disposition of installment obligations under I.R.C. § 453B. See Chapter 24A, supra.

[7]   I.R.C. § 691(a)(3). See Chapter 21, supra.

Section 164, qualify as deductions in respect of decedents for this purpose.[8] In general as regards expenses that may be deducted as deductions in respect to decedents, a "when paid" test parallels the "when received" test that applies to I.R.D. Section 691(b)(1)(A) accords the right to the deduction to the estate but, under subparagraph (B), if the estate is not liable to discharge the obligation, one who by bequest, devise or inheritance acquires property subject to the obligation, succeeds to the right to the deduction.

A minor breakdown in the neutralization objective of Section 691 occurs with respect to estate taxes. When the value of an I.R.D. item included in the decedent's gross estate is later subjected to an income tax imposed on someone else, the estate tax on the decedent's estate may be larger than it would have been if the decedent had personally collected the item. Had the decedent collected the item, the decedent's taxable estate would have been smaller by the amount of income tax paid upon the receipt, or by the amount of deduction for income tax due that could have been claimed for estate tax purposes under Section 2053. It might appear that some adjustment could be made in estate tax liability to take into account this phenomenon. But that is not practicable. In fact, a hypothetical determination of the income tax that the decedent might have paid is at odds with the objective of Section 691 *not* to tax the decedent on I.R.D. items. Congress has settled for an acceptable rough and ready answer to this recognized problem.

Section 691(c) allows one who is taxed on an I.R.D. item, upon receipt, an *income* tax deduction for *estate* tax attributable to the inclusion of the item in the decedent's estate. This is obviously not precisely responsive to the problem that seems to call for some adjustment; but is there any better way to handle the problem?[9] The Section 691(c) deduction creates a situation where it was sometimes advantageous to the taxpayer to have an income item classified as I.R.D.

## PROBLEMS

1. Consider whether the following are items of I.R.D. if held by the taxpayer at death:

    (a)  An account receivable held by an attorney who used the accrual method of accounting.

---

[8]  The omission of depreciation from this list is logical. Depreciation is not an expense to be paid; and pre-death depreciation on the decedent's property will be taken into account on the final return. Post-death depreciation will be allocated between the estate and beneficiaries in accordance with I.R.C. § 167(h). However, § 691(b)(2) undertakes to match a depletion deduction with related I.R.D. that is taxed to the one who receives it. And § 691(b) also attempts to match the § 27 credit for tax on foreign income against such income taxed as I.R.D. when received.

[9]  The general principle of I.R.C. § 691(c) can be expressed quite simply. The complexities of the provision, not discussed here in detail, are needed to answer questions such as (1) What portion of the estate tax is attributable to all I.R.D. items? I.R.C. § 691(c)(2). (2) How is that amount to be allocated as deductions available to each recipient of I.R.D.? I.R.C. § 691(c)(1)(A), formula. (3) If the deduction becomes available to an estate or a trust, how is it to be divided between the estate or trust and its beneficiaries? I.R.C. § 691(c)(1)(B).

    (b)    An account receivable held by an attorney who used the cash method of accounting.

    (c)    A contingent fee held by an attorney who used the accrual method of accounting who died prior to the fee becoming fixed.

    (d)    Appreciated property subject to both recapture and § 1231 gain.

    (e)    An installment sales obligation received when the property in (d), above, was sold inter vivos by a cash or an accrual method decedent in an installment sale.

**2.** Decedent, an attorney using the cash method of accounting, who has a $100,000 account receivable for services, dies. Who is taxed on the income, when are they taxed, and what is the character of their gain in the following circumstances:

    (a)    The receivable is collected by Decedent's estate.

    (b)    The receivable is transferred by Decedent's estate to Creditor to satisfy the estate's debt to Creditor.

    (c)    The receivable is distributed to Decedent's Child by the estate and is collected by Child.

    (d)    Same as (c), above, except that prior to the collection of the receivable, Child dies and the receivable is collected by Child's estate.

# CHAPTER 25

# DISALLOWANCE OF LOSSES

## A. LOSSES BETWEEN RELATED TAXPAYERS

Internal Revenue Code: Sections 267(a)(1), (b), (c), (d), (g). See Section 1041.

Regulations: Section 1.267(d)–1(a), (c)(3).

---

### McWilliams v. Commissioner
Supreme Court of the United States, 1947.
331 U.S. 694, 67 S.Ct. 1477.

■ MR. CHIEF JUSTICE VINSON delivered the opinion of the Court.

The facts of these cases are not in dispute. John P. McWilliams, petitioner in No. 945, had for a number of years managed the large independent estate of his wife, petitioner in No. 947, as well as his own. On several occasions in 1940 and 1941 he ordered his broker to sell certain stock for the account of one of the two and to buy the same number of shares of the same stock for the other, at as nearly the same price as possible. He told the broker that his purpose was to establish tax losses. On each occasion the sale and purchase were promptly negotiated through the Stock Exchange, and the identity of the persons buying from the selling spouse and of the persons selling to the buying spouse was never known. Invariably, however, the buying spouse received stock certificates different from those which the other had sold. Petitioners filed separate income tax returns for these years, and claimed the losses which he or she sustained on the sales as deductions from gross income.

The Commissioner disallowed these deductions on the authority of § 24(b) of the Internal Revenue Code,[1] which prohibits deductions for losses from "sales or exchanges of property, directly or indirectly * * * Between members of a family," and between certain other closely related individuals and corporations.

On the taxpayers' applications to the Tax Court, it held § 24(b) inapplicable, following its own decision in Ickelheimer v. Commissioner,[2] and expunged the Commissioner's deficiency assessments.[3] The Circuit Court of Appeals reversed the Tax Court[4] and we granted certiorari[5]

---

[1]  [I.R.C. (1939) § 24(b) is omitted. See I.R.C. (1986) § 267(a)(1), (b)(1), and (c)(4). Ed.]

[2]  45 B.T.A. 478, affirmed, 132 F.2d 660 (C.C.A.2).

[3]  5 T.C. 623.

[4]  158 F.2d 637 (C.C.A.6).

[5]  330 U.S. 814, 67 S.Ct. 868. In No. 946, the petition for certiorari of the Estate of Susan P. McWilliams, the deceased mother of John P. McWilliams, was granted at the same time as

because of a conflict between circuits[6] and the importance of the question involved.

Petitioners contend that Congress could not have intended to disallow losses on transactions like those described above, which, having been made through a public market, were undoubtedly bona fide sales, both in the sense that title to property was actually transferred, and also in the sense that a fair consideration was paid in exchange. They contend that the disallowance of such losses would amount, *pro tanto,* to treating husband and wife as a single individual for tax purposes.

In support of this contention, they call our attention to the pre-1934 rule, which applied to all sales regardless of the relationship of seller and buyer, and made the deductibility of the resultant loss turn on the "good faith" of the sale, i.e., whether the seller actually parted with title and control.[7] They point out that in the case of the usual intra-family sale, the evidence material to this issue was peculiarly within the knowledge and even the control of the taxpayer and those amenable to his wishes, and inaccessible to the Government.[8] They maintain that the only purpose of the provisions of the 1934 and 1937 Revenue Acts—the forerunners of § 24(b)[9]—was to overcome these evidentiary difficulties by disallowing losses on such sales irrespective of good faith. It seems to be petitioners' belief that the evidentiary difficulties so contemplated were only those relating to proof of the parties' observance of the formalities of a sale and of the fairness of the price, and consequently that the legislative remedy applied only to sales made immediately from one member of a family to another, or mediately through a controlled intermediary.

We are not persuaded that Congress had so limited an appreciation of this type of tax avoidance problem. Even assuming that the problem was thought to arise solely out of the taxpayer's inherent advantage in a contest concerning the good or bad faith of an intra-family sale, deception could obviously be practiced by a buying spouse's agreement or tacit readiness to hold the property sold at the disposal of a selling spouse, rather more easily than by a pretense of a sale where none actually

---

the petitions in Nos. 945 and 947, and the three cases were consolidated in this Court. As all three present the same material facts and raise precisely the same issues, no further reference will be made to the several cases separately.

[6]   The decision of the Circuit Court of Appeals for the Second Circuit in Commissioner v. Ickelheimer, supra, note 2, is in conflict on this point with the decision of the Circuit Court of Appeals for the Sixth Circuit in the present case, and also with that of the Circuit Court of Appeals for the Fourth Circuit in Commissioner v. Kohn, 158 F.2d 32.

[7]   Commissioner v. Hale, 67 F.2d 561 (C.C.A.1); Zimmermann v. Commissioner, 36 B.T.A. 279, reversed on other grounds, 100 F.2d 1023 (C.C.A.3); Uihlein v. Commissioner, 30 B.T.A. 399, affirmed, 82 F.2d 944 (C.C.A.7).

[8]   See H.Rep. No. 1546, 75th Cong., 1st Sess., p. 26 (1939–1 Cum.Bull, (Part 2) 704, 722–723). See also cases cited in note 7, supra.

[9]   The provisions of § 24(b)(1)(A) and (B) of the Internal Revenue Code originated in § 24(a)(6) of the Revenue Act of 1934, 48 Stat. 680, 691. These provisions were reenacted without change as § 24(a)(6) of the Revenue Act of 1936, 49 Stat. 1648, 1662, and the provisions of § 24(b)(1)(C), (D), (E), and (F) of the Code were added by § 301 of the 1937 Act, 50 Stat. 813, 827.

occurred, or by an unfair price. The difficulty of determining the finality of an intra-family transfer was one with which the courts wrestled under the pre-1934 law,[10] and which Congress undoubtedly meant to overcome by enacting the provisions of § 24(b).[11]

It is clear, however, that this difficulty is one which arises out of the close relationship of the parties, and would be met whenever, by prearrangement, one spouse sells and another buys the same property at a common price, regardless of the mechanics of the transaction. Indeed, if the property is fungible, the possibility that a sale and purchase may be rendered nugatory by the buying spouse's agreement to hold for the benefit of the selling spouse, and the difficulty of proving that fact against the taxpayer, are equally great when the units of the property which the one buys are not the identical units which the other sells.

Securities transactions have been the most common vehicle for the creation of intra-family losses. Even if we should accept petitioners' premise that the only purpose of § 24(b) was to meet an evidentiary problem, we could agree that Congress did not mean to reach the transactions in this case only if we thought it completely indifferent to the effectuality of its solution.

Moreover, we think the evidentiary problem was not the only one which Congress intended to meet. Section 24(b) states an absolute prohibition—not a presumption—against the allowance of losses on any sales between the members of certain designated groups. The one common characteristic of these groups is that their members, although distinct legal entities, generally have a near-identity of economic interests.[12] It is a fair inference that even legally genuine intra-group transfers were not thought to result, usually, in economically genuine realizations of loss, and accordingly that Congress did not deem them to be appropriate occasions for the allowance of deductions.

The pertinent legislative history lends support to this inference. The Congressional Committees, in reporting the provisions enacted in 1934, merely stated that "the practice of creating losses through transactions between members of a family and close corporations has been frequently utilized for avoiding the income tax," and that these provisions were proposed to "deny losses to be taken in the case of [such] sales" and "to close this loophole of tax avoidance."[13] Similar language was used in reporting the 1937 provisions.[14] Chairman Doughton of the Ways and Means Committee, in explaining the 1937 provisions to the House, spoke

---

[10] Cf. Shoenberg v. Commissioner, 77 F.2d 446 (C.C.A.8); Cole v. Helburn, 4 F.Supp. 230; Zimmermann v. Commissioner, supra, note 7.

[11] See H.Rep. No. 1546, 75th Cong., 1st Sess., p. 26, supra, note 8.

[12] See the text of [I.R.C. § 267(b). Ed.]

[13] H.Rep. No. 704, 73d Cong., 2d Sess., p. 23 (1939–1 Cum.Bull. (Part 2) 554, 571); S.Rep. No. 558, 73d Cong. 2d Sess., p. 27 (1939–1 Cum.Bull. (Part 2) 586, 607).

[14] The type of situations to which these provisions applied was described as being that "in which, due to family relationships or friendly control, artificial losses might be created for tax purposes." H.Rep. No. 1546, 75th Cong., 1st Sess., p. 28 (1939–1 Cum.Bull. (Part 2) 704, 724).

of "the artificial taking and establishment of losses where property was shuffled back and forth between various legal entities owned by the same persons or person," and stated that "these transactions seem to occur at moments remarkably opportune to the real party in interest in reducing his tax liability but, at the same time allowing him to keep substantial control of the assets being traded or exchanged."[15]

We conclude that the purpose of § 24(b) was to put an end to the right of taxpayers to choose, by intra-family transfers and other designated devices, their own time for realizing tax losses on investments which, for most practical purposes, are continued uninterrupted.

We are clear as to this purpose, too, that its effectuation obviously had to be made independent of the manner in which an intra-group transfer was accomplished. Congress, with such purpose in mind, could not have intended to include within the scope of § 24(b) only simple transfers made directly or through a dummy, or to exclude transfers of securities effected through the medium of the Stock Exchange, unless it wanted to leave a loop-hole almost as large as the one it had set out to close.

Petitioners suggest that Congress, if it truly intended to disallow losses on intra-family transactions through the market, would probably have done so by an amendment to the wash sales provisions,[16] making them applicable where the seller and buyer were members of the same family, as well as where they were one and the same individual. This extension of the wash sales provisions, however, would bar only one particular means of accomplishing the evil at which § 24(b) was aimed, and the necessity for a comprehensive remedy would have remained.

Nor can we agree that Congress' omission from § 24(b) of any prescribed time interval, comparable in function to that in the wash sales provisions, indicates that § 24(b) was not intended to apply to intra-family transfers through the Exchange. Petitioners' argument is predicated on the difficulty which courts may have in determining whether the elapse of certain periods of time between one spouse's sale and the other's purchase of like securities on the Exchange is of great enough importance in itself to break the continuity of the investment and make § 24(b) inapplicable.

Precisely the same difficulty may arise, however, in the case of an intra-family transfer through an individual intermediary, who, by pre-arrangement, buys from one spouse at the market price and a short time later sells the identical certificates to the other at the price prevailing at the time of sale. The omission of a prescribed time interval negates the

---

[15] 81 Cong.Rec. 9019. Representative Hill, chairman of a House subcommittee on the income-tax laws, explained to the House with reference to the 1934 provisions that the Committee had "provided in this bill that transfers between members of the family for the purpose of creating a loss to be offset against ordinary income shall not be recognized for such deduction purposes." 78 Cong.Rec. 2662.

[16] [I.R.C. (1939) § 118 is omitted. See I.R.C. (1986) § 1091. Ed.]

applicability of § 24(b) to the former type of transfer no more than it does to the latter. But if we should hold that it negated both, we would have converted the section into a mere trap for the unwary.[17]

Petitioners also urge that, whatever may have been Congress' intent, its designation in § 24(b) of sales "between" members of a family is not adequate to comprehend the transactions in this case, which consisted only of a sale of stock by one of the petitioners to an unknown stranger, and the purchase of different certificates of stock by the other petitioner, presumably from another stranger.

We can understand how this phraseology, if construed literally and out of context, might be thought to mean only direct intra-family transfers. But petitioners concede that the express statutory reference to sales made "directly or indirectly" precludes that construction. Moreover, we can discover in this language no implication whatsoever that an indirect intra-family sale of fungibles is outside the statute unless the units sold by one spouse and those bought by the other are identical. Indeed, if we accepted petitioners' construction of the statute, we think we would be reading into it a crippling exception which is not there.

Finally, we must reject petitioners' assertion that the *Dobson* rule[18] controls this case. The Tax Court found the facts as we stated them, and then overruled the Commissioner's determination because it thought that § 24(b) had no application to a taxpayer's sale of securities on the Exchange to an unknown purchaser, regardless of what other circumstances accompanied the sale. We have decided otherwise, and on our construction of the statute, and the conceded facts, the Tax Court could not have reached a result contrary to our own.[19]

Affirmed.

■ MR. JUSTICE BURTON took no part in the consideration or decision of these cases.

## NOTE

The application of Section 267 may not depend entirely on the relationship between the seller and the one to whom title is transferred. In Stern v. Commissioner,[1] the Tax Court agreed with the Commissioner that Section 24(b) of the 1939 Code (similar to present Section 267) disallowed a loss deduction. The taxpayer had converted his residence to rental property

---

[17] We have noted petitioners' suggestion that a taxpayer is assured, under the wash sales provisions, of the right to deduct the loss incurred on a sale of securities, even though he himself buys similar securities thirty-one days later; and that he should certainly not be precluded by § 24(b) from claiming a similar loss if the taxpayer's spouse, instead of the taxpayer, makes the purchase under the same circumstances. We do not feel impelled to comment on these propositions, however, in a case in which the sale and purchase were practically simultaneous and the net consideration received by one spouse and that paid by the other differed only in the amount of brokers' commissions and excise taxes.

[18] Dobson v. Commissioner, 320 U.S. 489, 64 S.Ct. 239 (1943).

[19] Cf. Trust of Bingham v. Commissioner, 325 U.S. 365, 65 S.Ct. 1232 (1945).

[1] 21 T.C. 155 (1953).

and then, after a time, transferred it for consideration in an amount less than his basis to his daughter and son-in-law, as tenants by the entirety. The Court of Appeals reversed, allowing the claimed deduction, saying, in part:[2]

> Applying [the] statutory provisions to the case before us it will be seen that the loss, if any, which the taxpayer suffered upon the sale of the West River Street property was deductible by him for income tax purposes unless it was a sale between himself and his daughter, Claire Guttman. If it was a sale between himself and his son-in-law, Dr. Guttman, the loss was deductible, since a son-in-law is not within the class defined by section 24(b)(2)(D). We are in complete accord with views expressed by Judge Hill in his dissenting opinion that the sale in this case was between the taxpayer and Dr. Guttman and that no sale in fact took place to Claire Guttman who supplied no part of the consideration for the sale and received her interest in the property as a tenant by the entirety purely as a gift from her husband. Indeed the findings of fact of the Tax Court compel this conclusion for the court found: "Dr. Guttman decided to, and did, purchase the house from the petitioner at a price of $30,000. * * * The petitioner's daughter did not participate in any of these negotiations, nor was she a party to them."

> The opinion filed by Judge Opper is based upon the proposition that under the law of Pennsylvania Claire Guttman became the owner of the entire property as a tenant by the entirety and accordingly was vendee of her father as to the whole property. The premise may be admitted but the conclusion sought to be drawn does not follow. For the fact that Mrs. Guttman acquired an estate by the entirety in the property under Pennsylvania law as a result of the direction of her husband that she be included as a grantee in the deed of conveyance did not make her, what in actual fact she was not, the purchaser of the property on a sale by her father, within the meaning of the Internal Revenue Code. As Judge Hill well said in his dissenting opinion, 21 T.C. 155, "the majority relies upon legal fiction in the effort to establish that a sale between the petitioner and his daughter was accomplished as a matter of law. The fiction relied upon belongs to the law of real property. It had its roots in the common law and was born centuries before income taxation was a gleam in the fiscal eye of government. This fiction argues that husband and wife are one. In the enactment and administration of revenue laws, fact rather than fiction is made to prevail." See Wisotzkey v. Commissioner of Internal Revenue, 3 Cir.1944, 144 F.2d 632, 636.

> Moreover, the contention proves too much. For if Mrs. Guttman is to be regarded as grantee of the whole property under the Pennsylvania law of tenancy by the entirety and therefore as sole purchaser from the taxpayer, her husband, Dr. Guttman, must

---

[2]   Stern v. Commissioner, 215 F.2d 701, 705 (3d Cir.1954).

likewise under the same law be regarded as grantee of the whole and, therefore, likewise sole purchaser. It is obvious that at this point the fiction of the Pennsylvania law breaks down so far as concerns its usefulness to solve the tax question which is before us and that the question can only be solved upon a practical view of the actual facts of the case, disregarding the fictions of the ancient law of real property.

The student will recall that Section 267 is by no means the only reason why a sale of property for a price less than basis may give rise to no tax deduction. The individual taxpayer's initial hurdles are to show that the loss was incurred either in his "trade or business," Section 165(c)(1), or in "a transaction entered into for profit," Section 165(c)(2). For these reasons two types of transactions yield no deduction even if Section 267 is wholly inapplicable to them: (1) A sale of property held for merely personal use, such as the taxpayer's residence, fails the initial tests;[3] and (2) Even if the property is business or income-producing property, if the purported sale is in reality some sort of arrangement among parties with common interests which cannot be viewed as an arm's length transaction, again the initial tests are not met. Clearly not a loss in "business," such purported sales have also been held not to arise in a "transaction entered into for profit."[4]

## PROBLEMS

1.    Father purchased some corporate stock several years ago for $50,000. On January 15 of the current year he sells the stock to his Daughter for $40,000, its fair market value. What result if:

    (a)  Daughter resells the stock to a third party for $45,000 on February 15 of the current year?

    (b)  Daughter resells the stock to a third party for $55,000 on February 15 of the current year?

    (c)  Daughter resells the stock to a third party for $35,000 on February 15 of the current year?

    (d)  Daughter gives the stock to Son on February 15 of the current year when it is worth $45,000 and Son sells it on March 15 for $48,000?

2.    If the *McWilliams'* transactions had occurred after the enactment of § 1041, would § 1041(a) apply? If so, what results to the parties?

3.    Loser purchased land for $90,000. When Loser died, the land was worth $100,000 in Loser's estate. During the administration of the estate, the value of the land declined to $80,000 and at that time in order to pay administration expenses the estate sold the land to Loser's Daughter, a beneficiary of the estate, for $80,000. What are the income tax consequences to the estate?

---

    [3]   David R. Pulliam v. Commissioner, 39 T.C. 883 (1963), affirmed on other grounds 329 F.2d 97 (10th Cir.1964).

    [4]   Miller v. Commissioner, 421 F.2d 1405 (4th Cir.1970).

**4.** Taxpayer T owns some land that she purchased as an investment ten years ago for $10,000. In the current year she sells it to Corporation C for $5,000, which is its fair market value. Will § 267 preclude a loss deduction for T if C is owned:

(a)   10% by T.

   20% by T's son S.

   30% by equal partnership TX (X unrelated).

   40% by others?

(b)   30% by T's son S.

   30% by equal partnership TX (X unrelated).

   40% by others?

(c)   30% by T's son S.

   30% by equal partnership SX (X unrelated).

   40% by others?

**5.** Taxpayer owns stock which is seized by the government and sold at public auction at a loss to pay delinquent taxes. Taxpayer's brother purchases the stock at the sale. Does § 267 apply to disallow the loss? Consider the Supreme Court's discussion of the legislative history of § 267 in *McWilliams* and compare Merritt v. Commissioner, 400 F.2d 417 (5th Cir.1968) with McNeill v. Commissioner, 251 F.2d 863 (4th Cir.1958).

# B.  WASH SALES

Internal Revenue Code: Sections 1091(a), (d); 1223(3). See Section 1041.

Regulations: Section 1.1091–1(g), –2(a).

---

## NOTE

As indicated in Chapter 6, the mere decline in the value of property, without more, does not give rise to a deductible loss. Such loss is not "realized" for tax purposes until the property is sold or otherwise disposed of. Thus where a taxpayer holds stock that has declined in value, she may have a paper loss but the loss is not given tax effect until she disposes of the stock. If the taxpayer has substantial capital gains for the year, she might want to sell stock that has declined in value and apply the resulting capital loss to reduce her capital gains. But what if in other circumstances the taxpayer wishes to hold on to the stock because she believes the stock will eventually appreciate? Can she sell the stock at a loss, decrease her capital gains to that extent, and immediately reacquire the (loss) shares in the market? In this way the taxpayer might seem to realize a tax loss without, in essence, changing her investment position. Right? Wrong! Section 1091 disallows losses on "wash sales." In substance, Section 1091 provides that losses from the sale or disposition of stock or securities, including contracts or options to acquire or, sell stock or securities,[1] are non-deductible if within thirty days before or after the sale, the taxpayer acquires "substantially identical" securities.[2] As with Section 267, Section 1091 disallows losses on transactions that technically give rise to losses but in substance result in no economic loss because the taxpayer has maintained a similar investment status.

Although at first glance Section 1091 appears to be sweeping in scope, several limitations narrow its application. Section 1091 pertains only to *losses* on wash sales; gains from the sale of stock or securities that are reacquired within the sixty-one day period are not affected by Section 1091. Further, the provision does not apply to taxpayers who are dealers and are holding the securities for purchase or sale in their trades or businesses.[3] Most importantly, the loss is disallowed only if "substantially identical"[4] stock or securities are acquired. Notably, the Service has ruled that securities of different corporations, even if in the same industry, are not substantially identical.[5]

It is important to note that Section 1091 may not actually "disallow" a loss, but may merely postpone it until the reacquired shares are subsequently disposed of. This result is achieved by way of Section 1091(d) which, in essence, increases the basis of the reacquired shares by the amount of the loss initially disallowed and Section 1223(3) which tacks the holding period of the original stock onto the holding period of the new stock for purposes of characterizing the gain or loss on disposition of the new stock. How may this perhaps usual result be altered by Section 1014?

## PROBLEMS

1.    On December 1 of the current year Taxpayer sold 1000 shares of X Corporation stock for $50,000. She had purchased the stock exactly two years earlier for $60,000. On December 15, of the current year she purchased another 1000 shares of identical X corporation stock for $55,000.

(a)    What are the tax consequences of the December 1 sale?

(b)    What is Taxpayer's basis for the newly acquired shares?

---

[1]    I.R.C. § 1091(a) last sentence. See also Reg. § 1.1091–1(f).

[2]    I.R.C. § 1091(a).

[3]    See the last clause of I.R.C. § 1091(a). Cf. I.R.C. § 1236.

[4]    Rev.Rul. 58–211, 1958–1 C.B. 529 states that "[securities are] substantially identical * * * if they are not substantially different in any material feature * * * or because of differences in several material features considered together." With respect to bonds, a material feature is the interest rate. See Rev.Rul. 60–195, 1960–1 C.B. 300. Differences in maturity dates are considered relatively insubstantial. Frick v. Driscoll, 129 F.2d 148 (3d Cir.1942). See also Rev.Rul. 58–210, 1958–1 C.B. 523 (interest payment date and issuance date not material).

Regarding stock of the same company, see Rev.Rul. 77–201, 1977–1 C.B. 250, where convertible preferred stock was held substantially identical to common stock of same company because there were no restrictions on convertibility and both stocks had the same voting rights and dividend restrictions. See generally, Krane, "Losses from Wash Sales of Stock or Securities," 4 J.Corp.Tax. 226, 229–232 (1977).

[5]    Rev.Rul. 59–44, 1959–1 C.B. 205.

(c)    What is Taxpayer's holding period for the newly acquired shares as of January 1 of the next year?

(d)    What result to Taxpayer in (a)–(c), above, (gain or loss, basis and new holding period), if the December 1 sale had been for $75,000 and she had repurchased 1000 shares of X stock on December 15 for $65,000?

(e)    Is there any difference in result to Taxpayer in part (a), above, if she purchased the new shares on December 1 for $55,000 and sold the old shares on December 15 for $50,000?

(f)    If the facts are the same as in (a), above, except that Taxpayer sold her original shares on December 1 to Son, what result to Son when he sells those shares on March 15 of the next year for $55,000? Consider the consequences to both Taxpayer and Son. See § 267(d)(2).

(g)    Are the Wash sale sanctions more or less stringent than those of § 267? Explain.

2.    On June 1 of the current year, Short borrowed 100 shares of B stock and sold it short for $9,000. Owning no B shares, Short purchased 100 shares of identical B stock on June 15 for $10,000 and "closed" the sale. On July 5 of the same year, Short again purchased 100 shares of identical B stock at a price of $9500.

(a)    Does § 1091 apply to disallow Short's loss? See Reg. § 1.1091–1(g).

(b)    What result if Short closed the sale on June 15 with identical B stock which Short had purchased on March 1 of the current year?

# CHAPTER 26

# NONRECOGNITION PROVISIONS

## A. INTRODUCTION

A precise use of language is an aid to, if not an outright prerequisite for, accurate thinking. The precise use of language includes the proper use of terms in accordance with their meaning in the context in which they are used. Thus, as seen in earlier chapters, it is essential to avoid the use of the term "value" when "basis" is what is meant. A new term now appears: "recognition" or, as the case may be, "nonrecognition." It crops up in the case of some transactions in which gain or loss is "realized;" but "realization" does not necessarily connote "recognition."

Gain (or loss) has no income tax significance as long as it is represented by a mere increase (or decrease) in the value of the taxpayer's property. Something more must occur, as for example a sale or an exchange of the property, before the gain (or loss), is said to be "realized." If gain is realized, is it subject to tax? Not necessarily. The message of the sections considered in this Chapter is that not all realized gains (or losses) are to be accorded immediate consideration in the determination of taxable income. Of course, that is the consequence of *deferred reporting* of gains, permitted under Section 453, and of the *disallowance* of some losses, as in Sections 267 and 1091. But the sections presently under consideration provide that certain other gains and losses, although admittedly realized, shall simply go unrecognized, at least for the time being. The effect is that gain which clearly could be taxed is excluded from gross income, and loss that could be deducted loses its potential for reducing taxable income. The question must therefore always be raised whether a "realized" gain or loss is "recognized."

In approaching these provisions it would be well to keep in mind that Section 453 is a mere timing device, that Section 267 is an outright disallowance provision tempered only by the limited relief rules of Section 267(d), and that Section 1091 is a disallowance rule which is ameliorated substantially by the substitute basis provisions of Section 1091(d). All the nonrecognition sections of this Chapter have related basis provisions, much like Section 1091(d), which must be carefully examined in appraising the purpose and scope of these sections. The student should approach the nonrecognition rules of this Chapter curious as to why Congress spells out these additional exceptions to the usual treatment of realized gains and losses.

If a taxpayer who owns investment real estate with a basis of $100,000 and fair market value of $175,000 sells the property for cash, the realized gain of $75,000 is gross income and the tax consequences are immediate. Of course, if instead the sale is an installment sale under

Section 453, the gain may then be reported ratably over the years that payments are received, in that proportion which the profit on the sale bears to the contract price. But even so, the entire gain ultimately is recognized. There is simply no way and no reason to apply the nonrecognition rules, because the taxpayer has closed out the investment by sale. Similarly, if the taxpayer exchanges the land for a yacht worth $175,000, the realized gain is all subject to immediate tax consequences. Although the yacht is property, it is clear that the taxpayer has closed out the real estate investment in exchange for the yacht.[1]

If in other circumstances the taxpayer should exchange investment real estate for another parcel of real estate worth $175,000 to be held for investment, the realized gain is still $75,000. But can we question whether the taxpayer has really closed out the investment when the only changed circumstance is the different location of the new tract of land? In substance, the taxpayer's economic position after the exchange is the same as before. In these circumstances a special nonrecognition rule becomes applicable.

The nonrecognition provisions are all predicated on the notion that realized gain, or a loss that otherwise would qualify as a deductible loss, is sensibly deferred when the taxpayer has retained the investment in property that is essentially the same type as the originally held property. These rules are not universally applicable to all types of property. The statute provides nonrecognition to selective transactions, and it must be carefully examined. While the example here relates to an exchange that is accorded nonrecognition treatment under Section 1031, some other types of transactions, not involving exchanges as such, also are accorded nonrecognition treatment under other sections. The philosophy underlying the nonrecognition rules of these other provisions will be seen to be similar to the philosophy underlying Section 1031.

This is not your first introduction to a nonrecognition provision. Recall that in Chapters 6 and 10 we dealt with Section 1041 which applies to transfers of property between spouses and transfers between former spouses if they are incident to a divorce. Section 1041 (note its location in the Code) is a typical nonrecognition provision. Even though gain or loss is realized, Section 1041(a) provides that it is not recognized. Consistent with the treatment of gain or loss, Section 1041(b)(2) provides that the transferee, who in essence steps into the shoes of the transferor, takes the property with a *transferred* basis (the transferor's basis carries over to the transferee).[2] Many of the nonrecognition provisions (all of them in this Chapter) involve only one taxpayer who is seen to have a continuing investment despite the change in property. Nonrecognition generally carries with it an *exchanged* basis (which is in essence a substituted basis) and a tacked holding period for the new property.[3] If

---

[1]   See I.R.C. § 1001(a) and (c).

[2]   See also I.R.C. §§ 1223(2) and 7701(a)(43).

[3]   See, for example, I.R.C. §§ 1031(d), 1223(1), and 7701(a)(44).

the difference between Section 1041 nonrecognition and nonrecognition under the sections considered in this chapter troubles you, remember the theory underlying transfers between spouses and former spouses incident to a divorce is that such parties constitute a single economic unit for federal tax purposes so that, in another sense, there is a continuing investment.

As a broad proposition, the nonrecognition rules and their attending basis provisions are so interrelated as to effect only a postponement of the tax on gain or the deduction of loss that initially goes unrecognized. To be sure, the date-of-death value basis rule of Section 1014 may intervene to convert mere postponement to outright amnesty (or final disallowance) if, after a transaction in which gain (or loss) goes unrecognized, the taxpayer dies. Consequently, except for this possibility, the nonrecognition rules are largely rules of deferral. Take a further look at Section 1231(a), which limits the hotchpot ingredients to *recognized* gains and losses. See again also Section 1222, limiting the definition of short and long-term capital gains and losses to such gains and losses as are " * * * taken into account in computing [gross or taxable] income."

## B.  LIKE KIND EXCHANGES

## 1.  THE LIKE KIND EXCHANGE REQUIREMENTS

Internal Revenue Code: Sections 1001(c); 1031 (omit (a)(3), (e) and (g)); 1223(1). See Sections 121(d)(10); 453(f)(6); 1245(b)(4); 1250(d)(4).

Regulations: Sections 1.1031(a)–1, –2(a), 1.1031(b)–1(b) Example (1), 1.1031(d)–1.

---

At the outset, it should be stated that the "if" clause of Section 1031(a) is strewn with hurdles to be taken. First, with respect to the nature of the property transferred, it must be " * * * *real property held for productive use in a trade or business or for investment* * * * ".[1] The statute expressly excludes real property held primarily for sale.[2] Second, the disposition must qualify as an *exchange*. Finally, the consideration received must be real property of *like kind* to be held for productive use in a trade or business or for investment.[3] All three criteria must be met.

---

[1]   Emphasis added.

[2]   I.R.C. § 1031(a)(2).

[3]   If as part of a transaction otherwise qualifying under I.R.C. § 1031, the taxpayer, pursuant to pre-arranged plan, disposes of the property received in the exchange, § 1031 does not apply. This is so because the property received is not *to be held* for productive use in his trade or business or for investment. See Rev.Rul. 75–292, 1975–2 C.B. 333, and compare Rev.Rul. 75–291, 1975–2 C.B. 332.

Depending on the nature of the controversy, taxpayer nonrecognition of gain or government effort to disallow loss,[4] the vast majority of the cases has been concerned with the question whether the transaction constitutes an *exchange* of like kind properties.

# Bloomington Coca-Cola Bottling Co. v. Commissioner

United States Court of Appeals, Seventh Circuit, 1951.
189 F.2d 14.

■ KERNER, CHIEF JUDGE:

\* \* \*

A "sale" is a transfer of property for a price in money or its equivalent. "Exchange" means the giving of one thing for another. That is to say, in a sale, the property is transferred in consideration of a definite price expressed in terms of money, while in an exchange, the property is transferred in return for other property without the intervention of money. True, "Border-line cases arise where the money forms a substantial part of the adjustment of values in connection with the disposition of property and the acquisition of similar properties. The presence in a transaction of a small amount of cash, to adjust certain differences in value of the properties exchanged will not necessarily prevent the transaction from being considered an exchange. \* \* \* Where cash is paid by the taxpayer, it may be considered as representing the purchase price of excess value of 'like property' received." 3 Mertens, Law of Federal Income Taxation, § 20.29, pp. 143, 144.

\* \* \*

# Commissioner v. Crichton

United States Court of Appeals, Fifth Circuit, 1941.
122 F.2d 181.

■ HUTCHESON, CIRCUIT JUDGE.

In 1936, respondent and her three children, owning, in undivided interests, a tract of unimproved country land and an improved city lot, effected an exchange of interests. Her children transferred to respondent their undivided interest in the city lot. Respondent transferred to her children, as of equal value, an undivided 3/12 interest in the "oil, gas and other minerals, in, on and under, and that may be produced from" the country land. The ½ interest conveyed to respondent had a value of $15,357.77. The interest respondent transferred to her children had a cost basis of zero.

---

[4] See e.g., 124 Front Street Inc. v. Commissioner, 65 T.C. 6 (1975). To the extent that a transaction falls within I.R.C. § 1031, no loss on that transaction is *ever* recognized. I.R.C. § 1031(c). See e.g., Valley Title Co. v. Commissioner, 34 T.C.M. 312 (1975).

Respondent treating the exchange as one of property for property of like kind and therefore nontaxable under Section 112(b)(1),[1] Revenue Act of 1936, 26 U.S.C.A.Int.Rev.Acts, page 855, did not report any profit therefrom. The commissioner, of the opinion that the exchange resulted in a capital gain of $15,357.71, under Section 117, Revenue Act of 1936, 26 U.S.C.A.Int.Rev.Acts, page 873, determined a deficiency of $628.66 accordingly.

The Board[2] of the opinion that the exchange was "solely in kind", disagreed with the commissioner and on redetermination fixed the deficiency at $86.46. The commissioner is here insisting that the Board has wrongfully decided the question. We do not think so. We agree with the Board that whatever difficulty there might have been, if the statute stood alone, in determining the meaning of the very general words it uses, as applied to the facts of this case, that difficulty vanishes in the light of Treasury Regulation 94,[3] if that regulation is valid, and we think it quite clear that it is. As was the case with regard to the statute considered in Helvering v. Reynolds Tobacco Co., 306 U.S. 110, 113, 59 S.Ct. 423, 425, so here, the section "is so general in its terms as to render an interpretative regulation appropriate."

As was the case there, so here, "the administrative construction embodied in the regulation has [for many years], been uniform with respect to each of the revenue acts, * * *, as evidenced by Treasury rulings and regulations, and decisions of the Board of Tax Appeals."

The commissioner concedes, as he must, that under Louisiana law, mineral rights are interests not in personal but in real property, and that the rights exchanged were real rights. In the light therefore of the rule the regulation lays down, of the examples given in the illustrations it puts forth, and of the construction which, under its interpretation, the statute has been given throughout this long period, it will not do for him to now marshal or parade the supposed dissimilarities in grade or quality, the unlikenesses, in attributes, appearance and capacities, between undivided real interests in a respectively small town hotel, and mineral properties. For the regulation and the interpretation under it, leave in no doubt that no gain or loss is realized by one, other than a dealer, from an exchange of real estate for other real estate, and that the distinction intended and made by the statute is the broad one between classes and characters of properties, for instance, between real and personal property. It was not intended to draw any distinction between parcels of real property however dissimilar they may be in location, in attributes and in capacities for profitable use.

The order of the Board was right. It is affirmed.

---

[1]  [I.R.C. (1939) § 112(b) is omitted. See I.R.C. (1986) § 1031(a). Ed.]

[2]  42 B.T.A. 490.

[3]  [The provisions in the current regulations which correspond to earlier provisions quoted here are at Reg. § 1.1031(a)–1(b) and (c). Ed.]

## NOTE

As the *Crichton* case illustrates, the term "like kind" is interpreted very broadly when applied to real estate transactions. Parcels of real property, however dissimilar, are like kind properties.[1] Thus, the regulations permit as like kind: (1) an exchange of city real property for a ranch or farm, (2) an exchange of real estate for a leasehold of a fee with 30 or more years to run, and (3) exchanges of improved real estate for unimproved real estate.[2] However, the Service distinguishes mere improvements to land from the land itself. Thus, in the Service's view, an exchange of land for a long-term leasehold of a building, with no interest in the land underling the building, would not be an exchange of like-kind properties.[3] Query whether the Service would be successful if the issue were litigated?

There have been legislative proposals to tighten up the Section 1031 "like kind" test with respect to real estate and to impose a more stringent "similar or related in service or use" test that applies under Section 1033.[4] Is such action warranted in view of the potential game-playing that is currently possible?[5] There is one definite limitation to the broad "like kind" interpretation in real estate swaps. The statute specifically provides that real property located in the United States and real property located outside the United States are not like kind property.[6]

## Leslie Co. v. Commissioner

United States Court of Appeals, Third Circuit, 1976.
539 F.2d 943.

■ GARTH, CIRCUIT JUDGE:

This appeal involves the tax consequences of a sale and leaseback arrangement. The question presented is whether the sale and leaseback arrangement constitutes an exchange of like-kind properties, on which no loss is recognized, or whether that transaction is governed by the general recognition provision of Int.Rev.Code § 1002.[1] The Tax Court, on taxpayer's petition for a redetermination of deficiencies assessed against it by the Commissioner, held that the fee conveyance aspect of the transaction was a sale entitled to recognition, and that the leaseback was

---

[1] See page 896, supra. See also Carl E. Koch v. Commissioner, 71 T.C. 54 (1978), parcels of real estate subject to 99-year condominium leases and unencumbered parcels of real estate are like kind.

[2] Reg. § 1.1031(a)–1(c).

[3] See, e.g., Rev. Rul. 67–255, 1967–2 C.B. 270, and Rev. Rul. 76–390, 1976–2 C.B. 243 (land and mere improvements to land were not like kind properties under I.R.C. § 1033(g)(1)), as well as Rev. Rul. 71–41, 1971–1 C.B. 223 (mere improvements to land and land with improvements were not like kind properties, also under I.R.C. § 1033(g)(1)). I.R.C. § 1033(g) uses the term "like kind," and its meaning under § 1033 should be identical to its meaning under § 1031(a).

[4] I.R.C. § 1033(a). See Chapter 26C, infra.

[5] See Problem 5 on page 923, infra.

[6] I.R.C. § 1031(h).

[1] All references are to the Internal Revenue Code of 1954. [Footnotes have been edited and renumbered. Ed.]

merely a condition precedent to that sale. The Tax Court thereby allowed the loss claimed by the taxpayer. For the reasons given below, we affirm.

I.     Leslie Company, the taxpayer, is a New Jersey corporation engaged in the manufacture and distribution of pressure and temperature regulators and instantaneous water heaters. Leslie, finding its Lyndhurst, New Jersey plant inadequate for its needs, decided to move to a new facility. To this end, in March 1967 Leslie purchased land in Parsippany, on which to construct a new manufacturing plant.

Leslie, however, was unable to acquire the necessary financing for the construction of its proposed $2,400,000 plant. Accordingly, on October 30, 1967, it entered into an agreement with the Prudential Life Insurance Company of America, whereby Leslie would erect a plant to specifications approved by Prudential and Prudential would then purchase the Parsippany property and building from Leslie. At the time of purchase Prudential would lease back the facility to Leslie. The property and improvements were to be conveyed to Prudential for $2,400,000 or the actual cost to Leslie, whichever amount was less.

The lease term was established at 30 years,[2] at an annual net rental of $190,560, which was 7.94% of the purchase price. The lease agreement gave Leslie two 10-year options to renew. The annual net rental during each option period was $72,000, or 3% of the purchase price. The lease also provided that Leslie could offer to repurchase the property[3] at five year intervals, beginning with the 15th year of the lease, at specified prices as follows:

### At the end of the

| | |
|---|---|
| 15th year | $1,798,000 |
| 20th year | 1,592,000 |
| 25th year | 1,386,000 |
| 30th year | 1,180,000 |

Under the lease Prudential was entitled to all condemnation proceeds, net of any damages suffered by Leslie with respect to its trade fixtures and certain structural improvements, without any deduction for Leslie's leasehold interest.

Construction was completed in December, 1968, at a total cost to Leslie (including the purchase price of the land) of $3,187,414. On December 16, 1968 Leslie unconditionally conveyed the property to Prudential, as its contract required, for $2,400,000. At the same time, Leslie and Prudential executed a 30-year lease.

---

   [2]    The parties stipulated, and the Tax Court found accordingly, that the useful life of the building Leslie constructed was 30 years.

   [3]    See note 10, infra.

Leslie, on its 1968 corporate income tax return, reported and deducted a loss of $787,414 from the sale of the property.[4] The Commissioner of Internal Revenue disallowed the claimed loss on the ground that the sale and leaseback transaction constituted an exchange of like-kind properties within the scope of Int.Rev.Code § 1031. That section of the Code, if applicable, provides for nonrecognition (and hence nondeductibility) of such losses.[5] Rather than permitting Leslie to take the entire deduction of $787,414 in 1968, the Commissioner treated the $787,414 as Leslie's cost in obtaining the lease, and amortized that sum over the lease's 30-year term. Accordingly, Leslie was assessed deficiencies of $383,023.52 in its corporate income taxes for the years 1965, 1966 and 1968.

Leslie petitioned the Tax Court for a redetermination of the deficiencies assessed against it, contending that the conveyance of the Parsippany property constituted a sale, on which loss is recognized. The Tax Court agreed.[6]

Although the Tax Court found as a fact that Leslie would not have entered into the sale transaction without a leaseback guarantee, * * * it concluded that this finding was not dispositive of the character of the transaction. Rather, it held that to constitute an exchange under Int.Rev.Code § 1031 there must be a reciprocal transfer of properties, as distinguished from a transfer of property for a money consideration only, * * * *citing* Treas.Reg. § 1.1002–1(d). Based on its findings that the fair market value of the Parsippany property at the time of sale was "in the neighborhood of" the $2,400,000 which Prudential paid, and that the annual net rental of $190,560 to be paid by Leslie was comparable to the fair rental value of similar types of property in the Northern New Jersey area,[7] the Tax Court majority reasoned that Leslie's leasehold had no separate capital value which could be properly viewed as part of the consideration paid. Accordingly, Leslie having received $2,400,000 from Prudential as the sole consideration for the property conveyed, the Tax Court held that the transaction was not an exchange of like-kind properties within the purview of Int.Rev.Code § 1031, but was rather a sale, and so governed by the general recognition provision of Int.Rev.Code § 1002.

Six judges of the Tax Court dissented from this holding. Judge Tannenwald, in an opinion in which Judges Raum, Drennen, Quealy and

---

[4] The $787,414 was the difference between Leslie's actual cost of $3,187,414 and the $2,400,000 which Prudential paid Leslie for the property. This 1968 loss resulted in a net operating loss for that year of $366,907, which was carried back to 1965.

[5] The Commissioner characterizes the instant transaction as an exchange of real property for a 30-year lease plus cash ($2,400,000). (Appellant's Brief at 2). Thus, in the Commissioner's view, Int.Rev.Code § 1031(c) applies.

[6] 64 T.C. 247 (1975).

[7] These findings were based on the testimony of a witness presented by the Commissioner, who testified that the sale price of the property and the rental established by the lease were comparable to their respective fair market values. This testimony, as might be expected, was uncontroverted by the taxpayer.

Hall joined, agreed with the Tax Court majority that the conveyance was a sale, but would have disallowed a loss deduction, reasoning that the leasehold had a premium value to Leslie equal to the $787,414 difference between cost and sales price.[8] This dissent reasoned that since Leslie would not have willingly incurred the loss but for the guaranteed lease, this amount should be treated as a bonus paid for the leasehold, and should be amortized over the leasehold's 30-year term.

Judge Wilbur, in a separate dissent with which Judges Tannenwald and Hall agreed, 64 T.C. at 257, declined to decide whether the conveyance was a sale or an exchange. His concern was that the Tax Court majority was permitting the taxpayer to "write off 25 percent of the costs of acquiring the right to use a building for one-half a century that was constructed for its [Leslie's] own special purposes." He, like Judge Tannenwald, would hold the loss incurred was attributable to the acquisition of the leasehold interest rather than to the construction of the building.

The Commissioner's appeal from the decision of the Tax Court followed.

II. The threshold question in any dispute involving the applicability of Int.Rev.Code § 1031 is whether the transaction constitutes an exchange. This is so because § 1031 nonrecognition applies only to exchanges. Section 1031 does not apply where, for example, a taxpayer sells business property for cash and immediately reinvests that cash in other business property even if that property is "like-kind" property. Bell Lines, Inc. v. United States, 480 F.2d 710 (4th Cir.1973). Hence, our inquiry must center on whether the Leslie-Prudential transaction was a sale, as Leslie contends, or an exchange, as the Commissioner argues. If a sale then, as stated, § 1031 is inapplicable and we need not be concerned further with ascertaining whether the other requirements of that section have been met. See Jordan Marsh Co. v. Commissioner, 269 F.2d 453, 455 (2d Cir.1959). If an exchange, then of course we would be obliged to continue our inquiry to determine if the properties involved were "like-kind."

The Tax Court's conclusion that the Leslie conveyance resulted in a sale was predicated almost totally on an analysis of the applicable Treasury Regulations. Noting that Treas.Reg. § 1.1002–1(b) requires a strict construction of § 1031, the Tax Court tested the instant transaction

---

[8]    Judge Quealy also filed a separate dissent, 64 T.C. at 257, in which he pointed to Leslie's reservation of a favorable option to repurchase the property as further support for the position that the petitioner incurred no loss upon sale.

We are hard pressed to agree with this characterization of Leslie's very limited rights of repurchase under the lease as "favorable." The repurchase right is set forth in * * * the lease * * *. Leslie is given the right to terminate the lease after the 15th, 20th, 25th and 30th years. To do so, however, it must make an offer to repurchase the property back from Prudential, at specified prices. * * * Prudential need not accept the offer, although nonacceptance does not prejudice Leslie's rights of termination. Thus Leslie's option to offer to repurchase may be exercised only at the risk of losing the right to use the property for the remainder of the lease term.

against the definition of "exchange" contained in Treas.Reg. [§ 1.1002–1(d). Ed.]:

> (d) Exchange. Ordinarily, to constitute an exchange, the transaction must be a reciprocal transfer of property as distinguished from a transfer of property for a money consideration only.

Based on its conclusion that the leasehold had no capital value, the Tax Court held that it was not a part of the consideration received but was merely a condition precedent to the sale. Thus, the conveyance to Prudential was "solely for a money consideration" and therefore was not an "exchange." The Tax Court cited Jordan Marsh Co. v. Commissioner, supra, in support of its result. In light of its holding, it specifically declined to consider or resolve any possible conflict between *Jordan Marsh,* a decision of the Second Circuit, and the Eighth Circuit decision in Century Electric Co. v. Commissioner, 192 F.2d 155 (8th Cir.1951), cert. denied 342 U.S. 954, 72 S.Ct. 625 (1952).

The Commissioner, relying on *Century Electric,* argues that the Tax Court erred in holding the Leslie-Prudential conveyance to be a sale. He could not, and does not, dispute the Tax Court's findings as to the fair market value and fair rental value of the property. Rather, he argues that value in this context is irrelevant and that the only appropriate consideration is whether the conveyance of the fee and the conveyance of the leasehold were reciprocal.[9] The Commissioner, without regard to his own regulations which define an "exchange," then seeks to support his position by reference to the legislative purpose giving rise to the enactment of the nonrecognition provision. He argues that this provision (§ 1031 and its predecessors) was adopted primarily to eliminate any requirement that the government value the property involved in such exchanges.[10] Alternatively, the Commissioner argues that even if the conveyance is held to be a sale and thereby not within Int.Rev.Code § 1031, any expenditure incurred by Leslie over and above the selling price of $2,400,000 was not a loss as claimed, but rather a premium or bonus which Leslie paid to obtain the leasehold. Such an expenditure is a capital expenditure, the Commissioner argues, and therefore should be amortized over the 30-year lease term.

Leslie, on the other hand, urges affirmance of the Tax Court's holding, relying on Jordan Marsh Co. v. Commissioner, supra, and

---

[9]  As noted above, the Tax Court found that this element of reciprocity *was* present.

[10]  The Commissioner takes the position that:

"The statute was intended to be corrective legislation of three specific shortcomings of prior Revenue Acts, viz—(1) the administrative burden of valuing property received in a like-kind exchange; (2) the inequity, in the case of an exchange, of forcing a taxpayer to recognize a paper gain which was still tied up in a continuing investment; and (3) the prevention of taxpayer from taking colorable losses in wash sales and other fictitious exchanges." Preliminary Report of a Subcommittee of the House Committee on Ways and Means on Prevention of Tax Avoidance, 73d Cong., 2d Sess. (1933).

stresses, as does the Tax Court, that the initial issue to be resolved is the character of the transaction. * * *

In Century Electric Co. v. Commissioner, supra, the Eighth Circuit held a sale and leaseback arrangement to be a like-kind exchange governed by the nonrecognition provision. * * * Its holding that no loss was to be recognized was based solely on its finding that the sale and leaseback transactions were reciprocal. The Eighth Circuit read the legislative history of [§ 1031] as evidencing a Congressional purpose to relieve the government of the administrative burden of valuing properties received in like-kind exchanges. Thus the Court stated * * * that:

> the market value of the properties of like kind involved in the transfer does not enter into the equation.

By contrast, in Jordan Marsh v. Commissioner, supra, a case construing the same code provision as *Century Electric,* the Second Circuit held that a similar sale and leaseback transaction resulted in a *sale,* on which loss was recognized. The facts in *Jordan Marsh* were similar to the facts here. Jordan Marsh, the taxpayer, had sold two parcels of land for cash in the sum of $2.3 million an amount which was stipulated to be equal to the fair market value of the property. Simultaneously, the premises were leased back to Jordan Marsh for a term of 30-plus years, with options to renew. The rentals to be paid by Jordan Marsh were "full and normal rentals", so that the Court found that the leasehold interest had no separate capital value.

The Court, in examining the legislative history of [§ 1031] took issue with the Eighth Circuit's interpretation of the Congressional purpose behind the nonrecognition provision. The Second Circuit said that:

> Congress was primarily concerned with the inequity, in the case of an exchange, of forcing a taxpayer to recognize a paper gain which was still tied up in a continuing investment of the same sort.

It reasoned further that, if gains were not to be recognized on the ground that they were theoretical, then neither should losses, which were equally theoretical, be recognized. Analyzing the *Jordan Marsh* transaction in the light of this interpretation of Congressional purpose, the Second Circuit, finding Jordan Marsh had liquidated its investment in realty for cash in an amount fully equal to the value of the fee, concluded that the taxpayer was not "still tied up in a continuing investment of the same sort." Accordingly, the Court held that there was no exchange within the purview of § 112(b), but rather a sale.

Thus we may interpret the essential difference between *Jordan Marsh* and *Century Electric* as centering on their respective views of the need to value property involved in a sale and leaseback.[11] *Jordan Marsh*

---

[11] The Court in *Jordan Marsh* also distinguished *Century Electric* on its facts, since in that case there had been no finding that the cash received by the taxpayer was the full equivalent of

viewing the Congressional purpose behind the nonrecognition provision as one of avoiding taxation of paper gains and losses, would value the properties involved in order to determine whether the requirements of an "exchange" have been met. *Century Electric,* on the other hand, viewing the legislative enactment as one to relieve the administrative burden of valuation, would regard the value of the properties involved as irrelevant.

We are persuaded that the *Jordan Marsh* approach is a more satisfactory one. First, it is supported by the Commissioner's own definition of "exchange" which distinguishes an exchange from a transfer of property *solely* for a money consideration. Treas.Reg. § 1.1002–1(d) (emphasis added).[12] Second, if resort is to be had to legislative history, it appears to us that the view of Congressional purpose taken by the *Jordan Marsh* court is sounder than that of the Eighth Circuit in *Century Electric.* As the Court in *Jordan Marsh* said in discounting the purpose attributed to Congress by the Commissioner and by *Century Electric:*

> Indeed, if these sections had been intended to obviate the necessity of making difficult valuations, one would have expected them to provide for nonrecognition of gains and losses in all exchanges, whether the property received in exchanges were "of a like kind" or *not* of a like kind. And if such had been the legislative objective, [§ 1031] providing for the recognition of gain from exchanges not wholly in kind, would never have been enacted. * * *

It seems to us, therefore, that in order to determine whether money was the sole consideration for a transfer the fair market value of the properties involved must be ascertained. Here, the Tax Court found that Leslie had sold its property unconditionally for cash equal to its fair market value, and had acquired a leasehold for which it was obligated to pay fair rental value. These findings, not clearly erroneous, are binding on this Court. * * *

Nor do we think the Tax Court erred in concluding that the leasehold acquired by Leslie had no capital value. Among other considerations, the rental charged at fair market rates, the lack of compensation for the leasehold interest in the event of condemnation, and the absence of any substantial right of control over the property all support this conclusion. On this record, we agree with the Tax Court that the conveyance was not an exchange, "a reciprocal transfer of property," but was rather "a

---

the value of the fee which had been conveyed. Nor had there been a finding that the leaseback was at a rental which was a fair rental for the premises.

Indeed, as noted in *Jordan Marsh,* the record in *Century Electric* indicated that the sales price was substantially less than the fair market value. There was also evidence from which the Court could have found that the leasehold had a separate capital value, since the conveyance to a non-profit college avoided considerable tax liabilities on the property.

[12]  It was this definition on which the Tax Court relied in large part in holding the Leslie conveyance to be a sale for $2,400,000.

transfer of property for a money consideration only," and therefore a *sale*. * * *

The Commissioner's evidence that the rentals charged to Leslie under its lease were at fair market value, leading to our conclusion that the leasehold had no capital value, also disposes of the Commissioner's alternative argument on appeal that Leslie's excess cost of $787,414 was not a loss. * * *

The decision of the Tax Court will be affirmed.

## NOTE

The sale and leaseback transaction has generated substantial Section 1031 litigation. In the *Leslie* case, the Commissioner relied on the position taken in the regulations that a leasehold of 30 years or more is of a like kind to outright ownership[1] in an attempt to recharacterize the sale and leaseback as a Section 1031 exchange. If successful, the Commissioner would have been able to deny *Leslie* an immediate deduction of the loss on the transfer. The *Leslie* court declined to classify the transaction as a Section 1031 exchange, relying upon the Service's definition of "exchange"[2] and the lower court's finding that Leslie received cash equal to the fair market value of its property. The Court in *Leslie* cites the *Century Electric* case[3] which reached a result opposite to *Leslie*. In *Century Electric*, the taxpayer transferred a foundry building of uncertain value in return for $150,000 of cash and a leaseback of the building for a maximum 95 year period. The Court agreed with the Commissioner's position in the regulations,[4] and treated the transaction as a Section 1031 like kind exchange denying taxpayer's loss. However, in *Jordan Marsh Co.*,[5] a case factually similar to *Leslie,* the Second Circuit distinguished *Century Electric* in a situation in which the taxpayer transferred two parcels of loss property for $2,300,000 in cash, representing the fair market value of the properties. At the same time, the taxpayer entered into a lease of the same property for 30 years with an option to renew for another 30 years. The Second Circuit concluded that the transaction was a sale and leaseback, not a Section 1031 exchange. The Commissioner indicated that the Service will not follow the *Jordan Marsh* decision, stating:[6]

It is the position of the Service that a sale and leaseback under the circumstances here present constitute, in substance, a single

---

[1]   Reg. § 1.1031(a)–1(c).

[2]   Reg. § 1.1002–1(d).

[3]   Century Electric Co. v. Commissioner, 192 F.2d 155 (8th Cir.1951), cert. denied 342 U.S. 954, 72 S.Ct. 625 (1952).

[4]   Reg. § 1.1031(a)–1(c).

[5]   269 F.2d 453 (2d Cir.1959).

[6]   Rev.Rul. 60–43, 1960–1 C.B. 687, 688. See also Rev.Rul. 76–301, 1976–2 C.B. 241.

As Rev.Rul. 60–43 preceded the *Leslie* case, the Third Circuit in the *Leslie* case obviously disagrees with the Commissioner's position. See also Crowley, Milner & Co. v. Commissioner, 689 F.2d 635 (6th Cir.1982).

integrated transaction under which there is an "exchange" of property of like kind with cash as boot.

## 2.  THREE-CORNERED EXCHANGES

Internal Revenue Code: Section 1031(a)(3).

Regulations: Sections 1.1031(k)–1(a), (b), (c)(1) and (4)(i), (f).

---

## Revenue Ruling 77–297
### 1977–2 Cum.Bull. 304.

Advice is requested whether the transaction described below is an exchange of property in which no gain or loss is recognized pursuant to section 1031(a) of the Internal Revenue Code of 1954.

$A$ entered into a written agreement with $B$ to sell $B$ for $1,000x$ dollars a ranch (the "first ranch") consisting of land and certain buildings used by $A$ in the business of raising livestock. Pursuant to the agreement, $B$ placed $100x$ dollars into escrow and agreed to pay at closing an additional $200x$ dollars in cash, to assume a $160x$ dollar liability of $A$, and to execute a note for $540x$ dollars. The agreement also provided that $B$ would cooperate with $A$ to effectuate an exchange of properties should $A$ locate suitable property. No personal property was involved in the transaction. $A$ and $B$ are not dealers in real estate.

$A$ located another ranch (the "second ranch") consisting of land and certain buildings suitable for raising livestock. The second ranch was owned by $C$. $B$ entered into an agreement with $C$ to purchase the second ranch for $2,000x$ dollars. Pursuant to this agreement, $B$ placed $40x$ dollars into escrow, agreed to pay at closing an additional $800x$ dollars, assume $400x$ dollars liability of $C$, and execute a note for $760x$ dollars. No personal property was involved in the transaction. $C$ could not look to $A$ for specific performance on the contract, thus, $B$ was not acting as $A$'s agent in the purchase of the second parcel of property.

At closing, $B$ purchased the second ranch as agreed. After the purchase, $B$ exchanged the second ranch with $A$ for the first ranch and assumed $A$'s liability of $160x$ dollars. With $C$'s concurrence, $A$ assumed $C$'s $400x$ dollar liability and $B$'s note for $760x$ dollars. $C$ released $B$ from liability on the note. The escrow agent returned the $100x$ dollars to $B$ that $B$ had initially placed in escrow. This sum had never been available to $A$, since the conditions of the escrow were never satisfied.

Section 1031(a) of the Code provides that no gain or loss shall be recognized if property held for productive use in trade or business or for investment (not including stock in trade or other property held primarily for sale, nor stocks, bonds, notes, choses in action, certificates of trust or beneficial interest, or other securities or evidence of indebtedness or interest) is exchanged solely for property of a like kind to be held either for productive use in trade or business or for investment.

Section 1031(b) of the Code states that if an exchange would be within the provisions of subsection (a) if it were not for the fact that the property received in exchange consists not only of property permitted by such provisions to be received without the recognition of gain, but also of other property or money, then the gain, if any, to the recipient shall be recognized, but in an amount not in excess of the sum of such money and the fair market value of such other property.

Section 1.1031(b)–1(c) of the Income Tax Regulations states that consideration received in the form of an assumption of liabilities is to be treated as "other property or money" for the purpose of section 1031(b) of the Code. However, if, on an exchange described in section 1031(b), each party to the exchange assumes a liability of the other party, then, in determining the amount of "other property or money" for purposes of section 1031(b), consideration given in the form of an assumption of liabilities shall be offset against consideration received in the form of an assumption of liabilities.

Ordinarily, to constitute an exchange, the transaction must be a reciprocal transfer of property, as distinguished from a transfer of property for a money consideration only.

In the instant case $A$ and $B$ entered into a sales agreement with an exchange option if suitable property were found. Before the sale was consummated, the parties effectuated an exchange. Thus, for purposes of section 1031 of the Code, the parties entered into an exchange of property. See *Alderson v. Commissioner,* 317 F.2d 790 (9th Cir.1963), in which a similar transaction was treated as a like-kind exchange of property even though the original agreement called for a sale of the property. In addition, $A$'s 160$x$ dollar liability assumed by $B$ was offset by $B$'s liabilities assumed by $A$, pursuant to section 1.1031(b)–1(c) of the regulations.

Accordingly, as to $A$, the exchange of ranches qualifies for nonrecognition of gain or loss under section 1031 of the Code. As to $B$, the exchange of ranches does not qualify for nonrecognition of gain or loss under section 1031 because $B$ did not hold the second ranch for productive use in a trade or business or for investment. See Rev.Rul. 75–291, 1975–2 C.B. 332, in which it is held that the nonrecognition provisions of section 1031 do not apply to a taxpayer who acquired property solely for the purpose of exchanging it for like-kind property.

However, in the instant case, $B$ did not realize gain or loss as a result of the exchange since the total consideration received by $B$ of 2,160$x$ dollars (fair market value of first ranch of 1,000$x$ dollars plus $B$'s liabilities assumed by $A$ of 1,160$x$ dollars) is equal to $B$'s basis in the property given up of 2,000$x$ dollars plus $A$'s liability assumed by $B$ of 160$x$

dollars. See section 1001 of the Code and the applicable regulations thereunder.

## NOTE

Sometimes taxpayers can avoid adverse tax consequences by way of what are commonly referred to as "three-cornered transactions."[1] As it requires an exchange, Section 1031 does not apply if property is sold and the proceeds are reinvested in property of a like kind.[2] In the basic three-cornered transaction, essentially sanctioned by the Service in Revenue Ruling 77–297, A has property (property X) that B wants and C has property (property Y) that A wants. Assume C's basis for property Y is equal to its fair market value, but A's basis for property X is much less than fair market value. Further, assume that the properties are of like kind and also that they are of equal value. Of course, A could sell property X to B and with the proceeds buy property Y from C. This would probably be all right with everyone except A who, in the process, would incur tax on a large gain on the sale of property X. So why not: (1) have B buy property Y from C (without adverse consequences to C because C's basis in property Y is equal to its fair market value) and (2) then have A exchange property X with B for property Y, tax-free under Section 1031?

As regards A who has a large realized gain on the exchange, the transaction is rendered tax-free by Section 1031. The fact that B acquired property Y for the very purpose of making the exchange has no effect on A. A has held property X, let's say for investment, and A exchanges it for property Y to be held for investment. There is no doubt this fits squarely within the statute.[3]

It is just as clear, however, that B is not within Section 1031. B does not have property held for productive use or for investment which is exchanged for property of a like kind. B has newly purchased property Y that B uses to effectuate the exchange. Thus Section 1031 does not apply to B.[4] Of course, on our facts B wouldn't give a four letter-word whether B was within or without Section 1031, because B has a new cost basis for property Y, presumably equal to the fair market value of property X, that B received in the exchange. Consequently, the transaction is neutral to B for tax purposes.

Revenue Ruling 77–297 is a variation on this basic three-cornered transaction,[5] because B transfers money into escrow prior to B's acquisition

---

[1]   W.D. Haden Co. v. Commissioner, 165 F.2d 588 (5th Cir.1948); see Dean, "Three-Party Exchanges of Real Estate," 17 Tulane Tax Inst. 131 (1967) and Winokur, "Real Estate Exchanges: The Three Cornered Deal," 28 N.Y.U.Inst. on Fed.Tax. 127 (1970), for general discussions of three-cornered transactions.

[2]   Compare I.R.C. § 1033(a)(2), infra at page 915.

[3]   See Mercantile Trust Co. of Baltimore v. Commissioner, 32 B.T.A. 82 (1935), acq. XIV–1 C.B. 13 (1935); Alderson v. Commissioner, 317 F.2d 790 (9th Cir.1963); Rev.Rul. 75–291, 1975–2 C.B. 332; Earlene Barker v. Commissioner, 74 T.C. 555 (1980), involving a four party transaction.

[4]   See Rev.Rul. 75–292, 1975–2 C.B. 333.

[5]   In another variation, property subject to an option of sale was transferred by the taxpayer in escrow in exchange for like kind property. When the option holder exercised the option prior to escrow closing, the option holder, rather than the taxpayer's transferee, wound

of C's property. The Service sanctions the transaction because "[b]efore the sale was consummated, the parties effectuated an exchange."[6]

A further variation that was previously successful involved nonsimultaneous exchanges of like kind property. Such transactions received judicial approval in Starker v. United States.[7] In *Starker,* taxpayer A, in our hypothetical above, transferred appreciated real estate to B in return for B's promise to locate and purchase parcels of real estate for A within a five-year period and to pay any outstanding balance due in cash. To the extent that A subsequently received qualifying property within the five-year period, the Court held that Section 1031 was applicable. The *Starker* court held that simultaneous transfers are not required in a Section 1031 exchange and, in response to the government's like kind argument, stated:[8]

> [A] contractual right to assume the rights of ownership should not, we believe, be treated as any different than the ownership rights themselves. Even if the contract right includes the possibility of the taxpayer receiving something other than ownership of like-kind property, we hold that it is still of a like kind with ownership for tax purposes when the taxpayer prefers property to cash before and through the executory period, and only like-kind property is ultimately received.

The use of nonsimultaneous exchanges has now been sharply curtailed by Congress.[9] Section 1031(a)(3) allows an outright transfer but limits the taxpayer to relatively short periods of time within which to identify and receive Section 1031 property. The property received in the exchange must be identified within 45 days after the date the taxpayer transfers the property that is relinquished ("the identification period").[10] The taxpayer must also receive the new property either within 180 days after the date of the transfer of the old property or by the due date (including extensions) of the tax return for the year of the transfer, whichever is earlier, ("the exchange period").[11]

The identification requirement does not always demand that the taxpayer know precisely the property to be received in the exchange.[12] However, if the taxpayer identifies multiple properties, the maximum number of properties that may be identified is either 3 properties without

---

up with the property. The Tax Court held the taxpayer had sold the property and that § 1031 did not apply. John M. Rogers v. Commissioner, 44 T.C. 126 (1965), affirmed per curiam 377 F.2d 534 (9th Cir.1967).

    6  See page 907, supra. The Ruling adds that the cash in escrow had never been available to A because the conditions of the escrow were never satisfied. Had the cash been available to A, there would have been a constructive receipt of the cash and § 1031 would have been inapplicable, even though A might ultimately receive like kind property. See Reg. § 1.1031(k)–1(f), especially 1(f)(3) Examples (i) and (ii).

    7  602 F.2d 1341 (9th Cir.1979).

    8  Id. at 1355.

    9  See Sommers, "Deferred Like-Kind Exchanges under Section 1031(a)(3) After *Starker*," 68 J.Tax. 92 (1988); Cuff and Wasserman, "Understanding the New Regulations on Deferred Exchanges," 68 Taxes 475 (1990).

    10  I.R.C. § 1031(a)(3)(A).

    11  I.R.C. § 1031(a)(3)(B).

    12  See Reg. § 1.1031(k)–1(c)(4).

regard to the fair market value of the properties ("the 3-property rule") or any number of properties as long as their aggregate fair market value does not exceed 200 percent of the aggregate fair market value of the relinquished properties ("the 200-percent rule").[13] If one of these rules is not met, the taxpayer is generally treated as though no property is identified and Section 1031 is inapplicable.[14] However, even if the taxpayer runs afoul of either of these rules, the identification requirement is met (1) to the extent that replacement property is actually received before the end of the identification period[15] or (2) to the extent that before the end of the exchange period, the taxpayer actually receives timely identified replacement property constituting at least 95 percent of the aggregate fair market values of the identified properties.[16]

Section 1031 is inapplicable to the extent that a transferor receives cash or other property.[17] This rule applies to both the actual and the *constructive receipt* of cash or other property before the receipt of like kind replacement property, regardless of the taxpayer's accounting method.[18] Examples of the constructive receipt rule are found in the regulations[19] and in problem 5 at the end of this subpart.

The above situations involve "forward" like-kind exchanges. Sometimes, however, taxpayers engage in "reverse" like-kind exchanges. In a reverse, a taxpayer "parks" replacement property with a third "accommodation party" who must have enough benefits and burdens of the property to be treated as an owner of the property rather than a mere agent of the taxpayer.[20] The taxpayer then transfers the relinquished property in exchange for the "parked" replacement property. The Service has issued a ruling providing a safe harbor under which if there is a "qualified exchange accommodation agreement" with the accommodation party within the Section 1031(a)(3) time frame, the exchange qualifies under Section 1031.[21]

## 3. OTHER SECTION 1031 ISSUES

Internal Revenue Code: Sections 1031; 1223(1). See Section 357(d)(1).

Regulations: See Sections 1.1031(b)–1(c), 1.1031(d)–2.

---

[13] Reg. § 1.1031(k)–1(c)(4)(i).

[14] Reg. § 1.1031(k)–1(c)(4)(ii).

[15] Reg. § 1.1031(k)–1(c)(4)(ii)(A).

[16] Reg. § 1.1031(k)–1(c)(4)(ii)(B).

[17] I.R.C. § 1031(a) and (b). Reg. § 1.1031(k)–1(a).

[18] Reg. § 1.1031(k)–1(f). The regulations use their regular definition of constructive receipt. Reg. § 1.1031(k)–1(f)(2). See Reg. § 1.451–2(a).

[19] Reg. § 1.1031(k)–1(f)(3).

[20] If the taxpayer were treated as owner of the replacement property or in constructive receipt of the property before a transfer of the relinquished property, there would be a taxable transaction. TAM 200039005 (9/29/00).

[21] Rev. Proc. 2000–37, 2000–2 CB 308, modified by Rev. Proc. 2004–51, 2004–2 C.B. 294. There are six requirements for a qualified exchange accommodation agreement. Two of the requirements are that the relinquished property must be identified within 45 days and must be transferred within 180 days of the transfer of the replacement property. Reversed like-kind exchanges are discussed in Lipton, "New Revenue Procedure on Reverse Like-Kind Exchanges Replaces Tax Risk with Tax Certainty," 39 J Tax'n 327 (2000).

CHAPTER 26 NONRECOGNITION PROVISIONS 911

Section 1031 is a two edged sword—it applies to defer both *gains* and *losses*. In addition, it is a *non-elective* provision: if its requirements are satisfied, it automatically applies. Typical of all nonrecognition provisions, Section 1031 is accompanied by an exchanged basis[1] and a tacked holding period for the newly acquired like kind property.[2]

Section 1031(a) applies to exchanges solely for like kind property. If some boot (cash or other non-like kind property) is received (as is often the case), Sections 1031(b) or (c) may apply. In addition, Section 1031(a) is generally[3] inapplicable if the like kind exchange is between related persons[4] and either of the related persons disposes of their like kind property within two years[5] of the exchange.[6] The tax recognition consequences occur on the date of the disposition.[7] Often after receipt of a rental residence in a Section 1031 exchange, a taxpayer will subsequently convert the residence to personal use, sometimes as a principal residence. A Section 121 exclusion is unavailable to a subsequent sale of the principal residence unless it has been held for 5 years after the Section 1031 exchange.[8]

Similarly, taxpayers may argue that a residence (especially a second residence or vacation home) is held for the production of income (in the form of appreciation on the property). The Internal Revenue Service has put a kibosh on such arguments by limiting nonrecognition treatment only to situations where there is not "personal use" as defined in the Section 280A(d) tests of either the transferred or acquired residence over a 24-month period.[9]

Many like kind exchanges involve property subject to liabilities. If the other party in the exchange assumed a liability of the transferor, the amount of the liability assumption is treated as cash boot received by the transferor in the transaction.[10] The term "assumed" is broadly defined to generally include both assumption of a recourse liability and acquiring property subject to a nonrecourse liability.[11] However, if property on both

---

[1]   I.R.C. § 1031(d).

[2]   I.R.C. § 1223(1).

[3]   But see I.R.C. § 1031(f)(2).

[4]   I.R.C. § 1031(f)(3). See Teruya Brothers Ltd. v. Commissioner, 124 T.C. 45 (2005), aff'd 580 F.3d 1038 (9th Cir. 2009); Ocmulgee Fields, Inc. v. Comm'r, 613 F.3d 1360 (11th Cir.2010); North Central Rental & Leasing v. United States, 779 F.3d 738 (8th Cir.2015), where use of a straw person was ineffective in avoiding I.R.C. § 1031(f)(3).

[5]   The two-year period is suspended in some circumstances. See I.R.C. § 1031(g).

[6]   I.R.C. § 1031(f)(1). See Fellows and Yuhas, "Like-Kind Exchanges and Related Parties Under New Section 1031(f)," 68 Taxes 352 (1990).

[7]   I.R.C. § 1031(f)(1), last clause.

[8]   I.R.C. § 121(d)(10). See Rev. Proc. 2005–14, 2005–1 C.B. 528, providing examples of the interrelationship of I.R.C. §§ 121 and 1031.

[9]   Rev.Proc. 2008–16, 2008–10 I.R.B. 547. See Chapter 17D, supra.

[10]   I.R.C. § 1031(d), last sentence. See Reg. § 1.1031(d)–2 Example (1) for an example of this rule.

[11]   I.R.C. §§ 1031(d), 357(d).

sides of the exchange is encumbered, the amounts of the liabilities are offset against one another and when the amount of liability relief exceeds the amount of liability assumption, only the net amount is treated as cash boot.[12] The amount of a taxpayer's net liability relief is reduced by any cash paid by the taxpayer.[13] If the amount of liability assumption exceeds the amount of liability relief to a taxpayer, there is no boot related to the liability relief; however, if the taxpayer also receives cash or other boot property, gain is recognized by the taxpayer to the extent of the boot.[14]

Finally, before doing the problems dealing with the substantive rules of Section 1031, think for a moment about the benefits the like kind exchange rules may provide to taxpayers. Section 1031 applies to an exchange (a taxpayer initiated event) of like kind property (a term broadly defined) to allow deferral of gain. A taxpayer can make an unlimited number of exchanges and hold property until she dies when the property receives a stepped-up basis[15] and totally avoids the income tax on its prior appreciation. In a time of tax base broadening and loophole closing, will Section 1031 with its generous taxpayer initiated tax deferral possibilities be the next provision to be excised by Congress?[16] Or will a strong real estate lobby continue to pressure Congress to retain the provision? Keep an eye on future revenue acts for the answer.

## PROBLEMS

**1.** X leased a twenty story building, as lessee for a period of 60 years. The first five floors of the building were used by X as a retail clothing store. The balance of the building X subleased to others. X had a basis in the entire lease of $150,000. The fair market value of the lease was only $100,000. Z paid X $100,000 for the entire leasehold. Thereafter Z subleased the first five floors to X. What are the tax consequences to X? See Rev.Rul. 76–301, 1976–2 C.B. 241.

**2.** T has 100 acres of unimproved land which T farms. Its cost basis is $10,000 but its value much greater. T trades it to B for a city apartment building worth $70,000, which has a basis to B of $30,000, and B transfers to T, as well, $4,000 in cash and 100 shares of X Corp. stock held for 3 years for which B's basis is $40,000 but which have a fair market value of $26,000. None of the property involved is mortgaged, and B always claimed straight line depreciation on the apartment.

(a)  As regards T:

---

[12]  Reg. § 1.1031(b)–1(c).

[13]  Reg. § 1.1031(d)–2 Example 2(c).

[14]  Reg. § 1.1031(d)–2 Example 2(b). See problem 5, below, for an application of the liability rules.

[15]  I.R.C. § 1014.

[16]  For articles critical of I.R.C. § 1031, see Kornhauser, "Section 1031: We Don't Need Another Hero," 60 U.S.C.L.Rev. 397 (1987); Jensen, "The Uneasy Justification for Special Treatment of Like Kind Exchanges," 4 Amer.J.Tax.Pol. 193 (1985).

    (1)   What is T's realized gain on the exchange?

    (2)   What is T's *recognized* gain on the exchange?

    (3)   What is T's basis for the stock?

    (4)   What is T's basis for the apartment building?

    (5)   Test whether your conclusions seem sensible by determining what the tax consequences to T would be if, immediately after the exchange, T sold the apartment building for $70,000 and the stock for $26,000 (taking account also of the amount on which he was taxed on the exchange), and comparing this with a straight sale of T's farm land (instead of the exchange) for $100,000 cash.

(b)  As regards B:

    (1)   What is B's realized gain and loss on the exchange?

    (2)   What is B's *recognized* gain or loss on the exchange?

    (3)   What is B's basis for the farm land acquired?

    (4)   Test your conclusions about B by seeing whether a sale of the farm by B for $100,000 immediately after the exchange (and taking account of the tax treatment of the disposition of the stock on the exchange) will yield the same overall results as if initially, instead of making the exchange, B had sold the apartment building for $70,000 and the stock for $26,000.

Note: B's problems are a bit more intricate than T's. It is apparent that B has realized $100,000, the *value* of the farm land. But this amount must be allocated $4,000 to the cash paid, $26,000 to the stock (its value) and $70,000 to the apartment building (its value). See Reg. § 1.1031(d)–1(e), Example. Is it clear that the $4,000 cash paid by B will affect B's adjusted basis, as otherwise determined, for the farm land?

**3.**   T purchased a building and land at a cost of $500,000, $300,000 allocable to the building and $200,000 allocable to the land. The property is held as an investment. At a point when the building has been totally depreciated (under the straight-line method), T transfers the building and the land now worth $800,000 for another building and land also to be held as an investment. The fair market value of the replacement building is $400,000, and the fair market value of the replacement land is $400,000. As regards T:

(a)  Does § 1031 apply to the exchange?

(b)  Is T entitled to take depreciation deductions with respect to the replacement building? See Rev.Rul. 68–36, 1968–1 C.B. 357.

**4.**   Buyer wants to acquire Seller's investment land. Seller has a substantial gain on the land, hates to pay tax on such gains, and would like to convert the investment to commercial real estate in a tax-free exchange. Discuss the results to Seller in the following alternative situations:

(a)    Buyer pays cash for the land and Seller reinvests the proceeds in commercial property.

(b)    Seller agrees to sell the land to Buyer who puts cash in an amount equal to the value of the land in an escrow account. The escrow provides for Seller to select commercial property equal in value to the land. Buyer will then acquire the commercial property with the escrowed cash and transfer the property to Seller. If Seller fails to find adequate property, the deal collapses. One year after the escrow account is opened, Seller selects commercial property that Buyer acquires with the escrowed cash and transfers it to Seller in exchange for the land.

(c)    Seller, a calendar year taxpayer, transfers the land to Buyer on January 1 of the current year. Buyer puts cash in an amount equal to the value of the land in an escrow account. Seller is to select the like kind property Seller wants and Buyer is to acquire it with the escrowed cash. If at any time Buyer fails to meet Buyer's obligations, Seller may demand the cash. On February 15, Seller identifies 3 properties, any one of which Seller is willing to accept, and on June 15, Buyer acquires one of the properties (having a value equal to the land) and transfers it to Seller.

(d)    Same as (c), above, except that after Seller's transfer of the land to Buyer and Buyer's transfer of the cash to the escrow account but prior to replacement property being acquired, Seller may at any time opt to take the cash, rather than replacement property.

**5.**    A owns some investment real estate with an adjusted basis of $200,000, worth $500,000 and subject to a nonrecourse mortgage of $100,000.

(a)    Discuss the results to A and B if A transfers A's property to B in exchange for B's investment real estate worth $400,000 with an adjusted basis of $100,000.

(b)    Discuss the results to A and B if, instead, A transfers A's property to B in exchange for B's investment real estate worth $470,000 with an adjusted basis of $100,000 and subject to a $70,000 nonrecourse mortgage.

(c)    Discuss the results to A and B under the facts of (a), above, if A's investment real estate subject to the liability is worth only $450,000 and A transfers $50,000 of cash in addition to A's investment real estate to B in exchange for B's investment real estate.

## C. INVOLUNTARY CONVERSIONS*

Internal Revenue Code: Sections 1001(c); 1033(a)(1), (a)(2)(A) and (B), (b)(1) and (2), (g)(1), (2) and (4), (h)(2); 1223(1). See Sections 1231; 1245(b)(4); 1250(d)(4).

Regulations: Sections 1.121–4(d); 1.1033(b)–1(b).

---

In the preceding section of this chapter you encountered a special nonrecognition provision relating to like kind *exchanges*. The notion there and applicable here is that the taxpayer, although in possession of replacement property, has not changed her economic position. An exchange of like kind properties is a voluntary transaction. Section 1033 permits the nonrecognition of *gain* in certain circumstances in which property is *involuntarily* converted. The involuntary conversion may be the result of destruction, theft, seizure, requisition or condemnation or threat or imminence thereof. Earlier, in another chapter we considered virtually identical language in another Code section. Take another close look at Section 1231.

The general message of Section 1033 can be simply stated. When property is involuntarily converted into money, if the taxpayer so elects,[1] gain is recognized only to the extent that the amount realized as a result of the conversion exceeds the cost of the replacement property.[2] The price of the nonrecognition ticket is that the replacement property must be "similar or related in service or use" to the converted property and the replacement must occur within the time limit of the statute.[3] The provision does not apply to losses resulting from involuntary conversions[4] and generally does not apply if the property is acquired from a related person.[5] The related person restriction is not applicable to an individual taxpayer whose realized gain does not exceed $100,000.[6]

Students should be alert to a corresponding basis adjustment resulting from nonrecognition of gain. The basis of the replacement property is the cost of such property, reduced by the gain that is not

---

\* Two general articles in this area are Schaff, "Tax Consequences of an Involuntary Conversion," 46 Taxes 323 (1968); Gannet, "Tax Advantages and Risks in Real Property Exchanges: Voluntary and Involuntary," 25 N.Y.U.Inst. on Fed.Tax. 1 (1967).

[1] In John McShain v. Commissioner, 65 T.C. 686 (1976), the Tax Court held the I.R.C. § 1033 election to be irrevocable.

[2] Moving expenses received as part of a lump sum condemnation award have been treated as a nonseverable part of the award itself and therefore as qualifying for § 1033 nonrecognition. E.R. Hitchcock Co. v. United States, 514 F.2d 484 (2d Cir.1975); Graphic Press, Inc. v. Commissioner, 523 F.2d 585 (9th Cir.1975).

[3] I.R.C. § 1033(a)(2) and (g)(4).

[4] See I.R.C. §§ 165(c) and 1231.

[5] I.R.C. § 1033(i).

[6] I.R.C. § 1033(i)(2)(C).

recognized.[7] Except to the extent that Section 1014 intercedes, this is simply a deferral of tax to the future.

Much of the complexity and controversy in the application of Section 1033 has centered around the meaning of the phrase, "similar or related in service or use."[8]

## Revenue Ruling 76–319

### 1976–2 Cum.Bull. 242.

Advice has been requested whether, under the circumstances described below, property qualifies as replacement property for purposes of section 1033 of the Internal Revenue Code of 1954.

The taxpayer, a domestic corporation, was engaged in the operation of a recreational bowling center prior to the center's complete destruction by fire on June 30, 1974. The bowling center had consisted of bowling alleys, together with a lounge area and a bar. The center was fully insured against loss by fire. As a result of such insurance coverage the taxpayer received insurance proceeds in compensation for the destruction of the bowling center in an amount that exceeded the taxpayer's basis in the property. On its Federal income tax return for 1974, the taxpayer elected to defer recognition of the gain under the provisions of section 1033 of the Code.

Within the period specified in section 1033(a)[(2)](B) of the Code, the taxpayer invested the insurance proceeds in a new recreational billiard center. In addition to billiard tables, this center includes a lounge area, and a bar.

Section 1033(a) of the Code provides, in part, that if property (as a result of its destruction in whole or in part) is involuntarily converted into money, the gain shall be recognized except as provided in section 1033(a)[(2)](A). Section 1033(a)[(2)](A) provides, in part, that if the taxpayer during the period specified purchases other property similar or related in service or use to the property so converted, at the election of the taxpayer the gain shall be recognized only to the extent that the amount realized on the conversion exceeds the cost of such other property.

The specific question is whether the recreational billiard center (replacement property) is "similar or related in service or use" to the

---

[7]   I.R.C. § 1033(b)(2). If the replacement property consists of more than one piece of property, the basis is allocated between the properties in proportion to their relative costs. Id.

[8]   As to *condemned* real estate held for productive use in a trade or business or for investment, see I.R.C. § 1033(g) substituting "like kind" criteria. And see § 1033(h)(2) providing that if property which is used in a trade or business or held for investment is compulsorily or involuntarily converted as a result of a Presidentially declared natural disaster, replacement property will be treated as property "similar or related in service or use" if it is used in a trade or business.

recreational bowling center (involuntarily converted property) within the meaning of section 1033(a) of the Code.

Rev.Rul. 64–237, 1964–2 C.B. 319, states that, with respect to an owner-user, property is not considered similar or related in service or use to the converted property unless the physical characteristics and end uses of the converted and replacement properties are closely similar.

In the instant case, the involuntarily converted property was a bowling center that consisted of bowling alleys together with a lounge area and a bar. The replacement property consists of a billiards center that included billiard tables, a lounge area, and a bar. The physical characteristics of the replacement property are not closely similar to those of the converted property since bowling alleys and bowling equipment are not closely similar to billiard tables and billiard equipment.

Accordingly, in the instant case, the billiard center is not similar or related in service or use to the bowling center within the meaning of section 1033(a)[(2)](A) of the Code. Therefore the billiard center does not qualify as replacement property for purposes of section 1033.

## Revenue Ruling 67–254
1967–2 Cum.Bull. 269.

Advice has been requested whether the nonrecognition-of-gain benefits under the provisions of section 1033 of the Internal Revenue Code of 1954 apply where the proceeds of a condemnation award are used to rearrange plant facilities on the remaining portion of the plant property. Additionally, the question is raised as to whether such benefits apply if the taxpayer uses part of the award to erect a building on land he presently owns.

A State condemned a portion of the land upon which the taxpayer's manufacturing plant was situated. The condemned portion had been used as a storage area for the taxpayer's product and also contained thereon a garage which housed the plant's delivery trucks. The taxpayer received an award for the condemned property, none of which was compensation for damages to the portion of the property which he retained.

Because of the prohibitive cost of acquiring land in the area suitable for storage, the taxpayer used part of the proceeds of the condemnation award in the year of its receipt to rearrange the layout of his plant facilities on the remainder of his land in order to create a new storage area. He used the remainder of the award to build a new garage (to house the plant's delivery trucks) on a small plot of land located nearby, which he had owned for several years.

Section 1033(a)[(2)](A) of the Code provides, in effect, that if property is compulsorily or involuntarily converted into money and the taxpayer, during the period specified, purchases other property similar or related in service or use to the property so converted, at the election of the taxpayer the gain shall be recognized only to the extent that the amount realized upon such conversion exceeds the cost of such other property.

Accordingly, based on these facts, to the extent that the taxpayer expended the condemnation proceeds in restoring the plantsite so that it could be used in the same manner as it was used prior to the condemnation, he has acquired property similar or related in service or use to the property converted for purposes of section 1033(a)[(2)](A) of the Code. Whether all of the expenditures made by the taxpayer were necessary to restore the plantsite to its original usefulness is a question of fact to be determined upon examination of his income tax return for the year in which the transaction occurred.

In addition, the garage erected on land already owned qualifies under section 1033(a)[(2)](A) of the Code as property similar or related in service or use to the garage that was condemned.

## Clifton Inv. Co. v. Commissioner

United States Court of Appeals, Sixth Circuit, 1963.
312 F.2d 719, cert. denied 373 U.S. 921, 83 S.Ct. 1524 (1963).

■ BOYD, DISTRICT JUDGE.

Petitioner is a real estate investment corporation organized and existing under the laws of the State of Ohio, with headquarters in Cincinnati. In 1956 the petitioner sold to the City of Cincinnati under its threat of exercising its power of eminent domain a six-story office building, known as the United Bank Building, located in the downtown section of that city, which building was held by petitioner for production of rental income from commercial tenants. The funds realized from the sale of this property to the city were used by the petitioner to purchase eighty percent of the outstanding stock of The Times Square Hotel of New York, Inc., also an Ohio corporation, which had as its sole asset a contract to buy the Times Square Hotel of New York City. The purchase of the hotel was effected by the corporation. The taxpayer-petitioner contends herein that the purchase of the controlling stock in the hotel corporation was an investment in property "similar or related in service or use" to the office building it had been forced to sell, thus deserving of the nonrecognition of gain provisions of Section 1033(a)(3)(A), Internal Revenue Code of 1954 (Title 26 U.S.C.A. Section 1033(a)(3)(A)).[1] More specifically, the taxpayer contends that since both the properties herein were productive of rental income, the similarity contemplated by the statute aforesaid exists. The Commissioner ruled to the contrary, holding that any gain from the sale of the office building was recognizable and a deficiency was assessed against the taxpayer for the year 1956 in the amount of $19,057.09. The Tax Court agreed with the Commissioner,

---

[1]   [See I.R.C. § 1033(a)(2). See also I.R.C. § 1033(b)(3) enacted in 1996. Ed.]

finding that the properties themselves were not "similar or related in service or use" as required by the statute. 36 T.C. 569. From the decision of the Tax Court this appeal was perfected.

In order to determine whether the requisite similarity existed under the statute between the properties herein, the Tax Court applied the so-called "functional test" or "end-use test." This it seems has been the Tax Court's traditional line of inquiry, when similar cases under the within statute have been considered by it. This approach takes into account only the actual physical end use to which the properties involved are put, whether that use be by the owner-taxpayer or by his tenant; that is, whether the taxpayer-owner is the actual user of the property or merely holds it for investment purposes, as in the case of a lessor. We reject the functional test as applied to the holder of investment property, who replaces such property with other investment property, as in the case at bar.

The Tax Court in this case relied in part on its earlier decision in Liant Record, Inc. v. Commissioner, 36 T.C. 224 and chiefly on the decision of the Court of Appeals for the Third Circuit in McCaffrey v. Commissioner, 275 F.2d 27, 1960, cert. denied 363 U.S. 828, 80 S.Ct. 1598, the latter case approving and applying the aforesaid functional test in such a case as here presented. However, the Court of Appeals for the Second Circuit has since reversed the Tax Court's decision in Liant, 303 F.2d 326, 1962, and in so doing advanced what we consider to be the soundest approach among the number of decisions on this point. We need not here review all the relevant decisions, since this is done in the recent cases of Loco Realty Company v. Commissioner, 306 F.2d 207 (C.A.8) 1962, and Pohn v. Commissioner, 309 F.2d 427 (C.A.7) 1962, both of which decisions approved the Second Circuit Court's approach in Liant, the court in the Pohn case relying specifically on the Liant decision.

Congress must have intended that in order for the taxpayer to obtain the tax benefits of Section 1033 he must have continuity of interest as to the original property and its replacement in order that the taxpayer not be given a tax-free alteration of his interest. In short, the properties must be reasonably similar in their relation to the taxpayer. This reasonableness, as noted in the Liant case, is dependent upon a number of factors, all bearing on whether or not the relation of the taxpayer to the property has been changed. The ultimate use to which the properties are put, then, does not control the inquiry, when the taxpayer is not the user of the properties as in the case under consideration. As exemplary of the factors which are relevant the Liant decision mentions the following, after advancement of its "relation of the properties to the taxpayer" test:

> "In applying such a test to a lessor, a court must compare, inter alia, the extent and type of the lessor's management activity, the amount and kind of services rendered by him to the tenants,

and the nature of his business risks connected with the properties."

Thus, each case is dependent on its peculiar facts and the factors bearing on the service or use of the properties to the taxpayer must be closely examined. The Tax Court employed an erroneous test in this case, but on examination of the record, the correctness of the result is manifest.

The record before us discloses that the United Bank Building and the Times Square Hotel both produced rental income to the taxpayer. However, examination of what the properties required in the way of services to the tenants, management activity, and commercial tenancy considerations reveals an alteration of the taxpayer's interest. The record herein shows that the taxpayer corporation itself managed the United Bank Building, but deemed it necessary to procure professional management for the Times Square Hotel. There were primarily two employees for the United Bank Building, who afforded elevator and janitorial services to the tenants. In the Times Square Hotel between 130 and 140 employees were necessary to attend the hotel operation and offer services to the commercial tenants and hotel guests. Approximately 96% of the rental income from the hotel was from the guest room facilities and the large number of transients required daily services of varying kinds. Furniture, linens, personal services of every description were furnished the hotel guests, which were not furnished the commercial tenants of the United Bank Building. The hotel guests reside in the hotel rooms and that is obviously the only reason they are tenants. In the office building herein several tenants also used parts of the premises for living quarters, but were clearly not furnished the typical services the hotel guest demands. There was no great limitation placed on the types of commercial tenants to whom space was rented in the United Bank Building, but as the enumeration of commercial tenants of the hotel building reveals, space therein was leased for the most part and primarily with an eye to how such a business operation might fit in with the operation of a hotel, how it relates to the hotel guests. It is common experience that the services offered by a lessee of business premises in a hotel will reflect in the minds of its guests on the service they associate with the hotel itself. If a leased restaurant in a hotel offers good or bad service, there is a tendency to think of the food service at the hotel as good or bad. A number of unique business considerations enter when leasing commercial space in a hotel which do not apply to an office building.

We consider there to be, then, a material variance between the relation of the office building in question and the within hotel operation of the taxpayer, in the light of the relevant inquiry found in the Liant case. It is true that what the taxpayer derived from both properties herein was generally the same, rental income. But what the properties demanded of the taxpayer in the way of management, services, and relations to its tenants materially varied. That which the taxpayer receives from his properties and that which such properties demand of the taxpayer must both be considered in determining whether or not the properties are similar or related in service or use to the taxpayer.[2]

The decision of the Tax Court is affirmed.

■ SHACKELFORD MILLER, JR., CIRCUIT JUDGE (concurring).

I concur in the result reached in the majority opinion.

However, I am not willing to adopt, without some modification thereof, the test adopted and applied in Liant Record, Inc. v. Commissioner, 303 F.2d 326, C.A.2d, upon which the majority opinion relies. I think that the investment character of the properties involved should be given more consideration than what seems to me is given by the ruling in the Liant case, although I do not think that investment basis alone is sufficient to comply with the statute, as Steuart Brothers, Inc. v. Commissioner, 261 F.2d 580, C.A.4th, might be construed as holding. As pointed out in Loco Realty Co. v. Commissioner, 306 F.2d 207, 215, C.A.8th, the statute was not intended to penalize but to protect persons whose property may be taken on condemnation and, accordingly, should be construed liberally. I agree with the standard adopted in the opinion in that case, although for our present purposes I do not think that it results in a reversal of the decision of the Tax Court.

## Revenue Ruling 71–41

### 1971–1 Cum.Bull. 223.

Advice has been requested whether the investment of condemnation proceeds, under the circumstances set forth below, qualifies for the nonrecognition of gain provisions of section 1033 of the Internal Revenue Code of 1954.

The taxpayer, an individual, owned a warehouse which he rented to third parties. The warehouse and the land upon which it was located were condemned by the State and a gain was realized by the taxpayer on the condemnation. The condemnation proceeds were used by the taxpayer to erect a gas station on other land already owned by the taxpayer. The taxpayer rented the gas station to an oil company.

Section 1033(a) of the Code provides, in part, that if property is, as a result of condemnation, compulsorily or involuntarily converted into money and the taxpayer, during the period specified, purchases other property *similar or related in service or use* to the property so converted, at the election of the taxpayer the gain shall be recognized only to the

---

[2]  Congress has since provided that replacement of property held for productive use in trade or business or for investment purposes with property of "like kind" satisfies the "similar or related in service or use" requirement. However, the acquisition of controlling interest in stock of a corporation holding property was specifically excepted from the relaxation of the test. Title 26 U.S.C.A. Section 1033(g)(1) and (2). (Technical Amendments Act of 1958).

extent that the amount realized upon such conversion exceeds the cost of the replacement property.

Section 1033(g) of the Code provides, in part, as follows:

(1) Special rule—For purposes of subsection (a), if real property * * * held for productive use in trade or business or for investment is * * * compulsorily or involuntarily converted, property of a *like kind* to be held either for productive use in a trade or business or for investment *shall be treated* as property similar or related in service or use to the property so converted.

The taxpayer in the instant case did not qualify for the special rule under section 1033(g) of the Code as the replacement property (gas station) and the property converted (land and warehouse) were not properties of a "like kind." The specific question is whether the taxpayer can qualify for treatment under section 1033(a) even though he fails to qualify under section 1033(g) of the Code.

Revenue Ruling 64–237, C.B.1964–2, 319, in applying section 1033(a) of the Code, states that in considering whether replacement property acquired by an investor for the purpose of leasing is similar in service or use to the converted property, attention will be directed primarily to the similarity in the relationship of the service or uses which the original and replacement properties have to the taxpayer-owner. In applying this test a determination will be made whether the properties are of a similar service to the taxpayer, the nature of the business risks connected with the properties, and what such properties demand of the taxpayer in the way of management, services, and relations to his tenants.

With respect to the property converted by the State, the taxpayer in the instant case was an investor for the production of rental income. As to the property acquired as replacement, the taxpayer is also an investor for the production of rental income. The mere fact that the taxpayer did not qualify under section 1033(g) of the Code does not preclude the taxpayer from the nonrecognition of gain provisions of section 1033 of the Code if the taxpayer is able to demonstrate that the replacement property is actually similar or related in service or use to the property converted within the meaning of section 1033(a) of the Code.

Accordingly, under the facts of the instant case, it is held that the gas station is property similar or related in service or use within the meaning of section 1033(a) of the Code. The taxpayer at his election will recognize gain upon the involuntarily converted property only to the extent that the amount realized upon such conversion exceeds the cost of the replacement property, provided, the actual replacement took place within the period of time prescribed by section 1033(a)[(2)](B) of the Code.

## PROBLEMS

**1.** T was in the laundry and dry cleaning business. In the current year a fire completely destroyed the automatic dry cleaning equipment in T's plant. Several years earlier the equipment in T's plant had cost T $40,000 and, since its acquisition, T had properly claimed depreciation on the equipment in the amount of $16,000. After the fire and within the current year, T received $28,000 as insurance covering the loss.

(a) If the dry cleaning end of the business has been unprofitable and T invests the $28,000 in securities, rather than replacing the equipment, what will be the tax consequences?

(b) If the capacity of the old equipment was in excess of T's needs and T replaces the old with smaller new equipment at a cost of $26,000

(1) What will be the immediate tax consequences to T?

(2) What will be T's basis for the purpose of claiming depreciation on the new equipment?

(3) What would be the tax consequences to T if T made a quick change of plans and sold the newly acquired equipment for $26,000 before any depreciation became allowable with respect to it?

**2.** Taxpayer, who is single, has lived in her principal residence for several years. Taxpayer purchased the home for $100,000 and it was worth $500,000 when it was destroyed in a fire. Taxpayer recovered $450,000 of insurance proceeds. Taxpayer wants to minimize the tax consequences with respect to the residence. What do you suggest that she do? See Reg. § 1.121–4(d).

**3.** The *Clifton Investment* case reflects a common problem regarding the scope of the term "similar or related in service or use." But suppose in *Clifton Investment* the taxpayer had bought a hotel rather than stock in a hotel corporation. Would the result in the case be different?

**4.** Rev.Rul. 70–399, 1970–2 C.B. 164, deals with the repurchase of a new hotel with the insurance proceeds received when an old hotel was destroyed by fire. Despite the intrinsic identity of the properties, the case is placed outside the protective covering of § 1033. The owner had leased the old hotel to others to operate but undertook to operate the new hotel himself. Thus the new property was not similar or related in service or use. Why would § 1033(g) be of no help here?

**5.** The two questions immediately preceding are concerned with some of the differences in the definition of "like kind" under §§ 1031 and 1033(g) and "similar or related in service or use" under § 1033(a). In enacting § 1033(g) the Senate Finance Committee Report stated:

> Both in the case of property involuntarily converted and in the case of the exchange of property held for productive use in trade or business or for investment, gain is not recognized because of the continuity of the investment. Your committee sees no reason why substantially similar rules should not be followed in determining

what constitutes a continuity of investment in these two types of situations where there is a condemnation of real property. Moreover, it appears particularly unfortunate that present law requires a closer identity of the destroyed and converted property where the exchange is beyond the control of the taxpayer than that which is applied in the case of the voluntary exchange of business property.

As a result your committee has added a new subsection to the involuntary conversion (sec. 1033) provision of present law. In this new subsection it has added the "like kind" test of the voluntary exchange of business property rule of present law as an alternative in the case of involuntary conversions for the rule requiring the substitution of property "similar or related in service or use." The "like kind" rule in this case applies, however, only in the case of real property, does not include inventory or property held primarily for sale, and is limited to seizures, requisitions, condemnations, or the threat of imminence thereof. Nor does it apply in the case of the purchase of stock in acquiring control of a corporation. * * * Sen.Rep. No. 1893, 85th Cong., 2d Sess. (1958), 1958–3 C.B. 922, 993–4.

Is the restriction of § 1033(g) to condemnations of real property too narrow? Should the two tests of §§ 1031 and 1033 be made alternatives under both sections?

## D.  OTHER NONRECOGNITION PROVISIONS

Internal Revenue Code: See Sections 1038; 1045.

---

Congress applies the nonrecognition concept to several transactions that fall outside the scope of this book and to some others which, while within, are accorded only brief mention here. For example, a transfer of property to a corporation in exchange for its shares is a transaction in which gain or loss is clearly realized; and so is a transfer of property to a partnership in exchange for a partnership interest. Nevertheless, such corporate and partnership transactions are usually accorded tax neutrality by way of a nonrecognition provision.[1] Some partnership distributions are similarly treated,[2] as are some limited distributions in liquidation by corporations.[3] Gain or loss goes unrecognized upon a corporation's transfer of its own shares whether for money or other property, even if the shares are treasury stock.[4] A shareholder's exchange of stock for like stock in the same corporation may be of no immediate tax significance regardless of whether there is a realized gain or loss on the

---

[1]  As regards corporations, see I.R.C. §§ 351, 358, 362; and as regards partnerships, see I.R.C. §§ 721, 722, 723. Cf. I.R.C. §§ 704(c), 724.

[2]  I.R.C. §§ 731, 732, 733.

[3]  I.R.C. §§ 332, 334(b).

[4]  I.R.C. § 1032.

exchange.[5] And numerous corporate reorganizations that involve potentially taxable exchanges of stock and other property escape immediate tax consequences to the corporation or the shareholders involved.[6] As in the sections studied, the usual price for nonrecognition is some type of transferred or exchanged basis, although the basis rule is of course a compensating advantage where loss is not recognized, and the substituted property generally is accorded a tacked holding period.

Outside the area of business organizations, the Code provides for nonrecognition of gain or loss upon some exchanges of life insurance, endowment or annuity contracts for similar contracts[7] and upon the exchange of some United States obligations for other such obligations.[8] It may be a comforting thought that there is sufficient similarity in the nonrecognition provisions so that an understanding of one or several is a great help grasping the significance of another.

*Section 1038.* It will be recalled that, if an installment sale of property under Section 453 is followed by a default and reacquisition of the same property, the seller's tax liability may be accelerated by the disposition rules of Section 453B. Nevertheless, the seller is, in a sense, merely restored to the same position as prior to the sale. A nonrecognition provision may provide some relief from the acceleration of tax liability otherwise arising out of a disposition of Section 453 obligations. Section 1038[9] provides for nonrecognition (or only partial recognition) of gain in certain repossessions, which sometimes would be within the disposition rules of Section 453B.[10] Section 1038 applies only to sales of real property, and only if the obligation was secured by the real property and the seller reacquires the same property in partial or full satisfaction of the purchaser's indebtedness.[11] Under Section 1038, the general effect is to treat amounts previously received on the sale (such as initial and subsequent cash payments) as income, except to the extent that the receipts have previously been reported as income, for example, under Section 453(c).[12] But amounts so treated cannot exceed the gain realized on the original sale, reduced by gain previously reported.[13] What this provision seeks to do is to isolate out the amount that the reacquiring

---

[5]　I.R.C. § 1036.

[6]　I.R.C. §§ 354, 356, 358, 361, 362(b), 368, 1032.

[7]　I.R.C. § 1035.

[8]　I.R.C. § 1037.

[9]　See Hauser, "Effect of Repossessions under Section 1038," 25 N.Y.U.Inst. on Fed.Tax. 47 (1967); Willis, "Repossession of Real Property—Application of Section 1038," 18 U.S.C.Tax Inst. 601 (1966).

[10]　I.R.C. § 1038 is not limited to § 453 installment sales and may apply to other deferred payment sales of real property, e.g., where § 453(d) is elected. Sen.Fin.Comm.Rep.No. 1361, 88th Cong., 2d Sess. (1964) 1964–2 C.B. 831. See Handler, "Tax Consequences of Mortgage Foreclosures and Transfers of Real Property to the Mortgagee," 31 Tax L.Rev. 193, 215 (1976).

[11]　I.R.C. § 1038(a).

[12]　I.R.C. § 1038(b)(1).

[13]　I.R.C. § 1038(b)(2). Any further investment by the reacquiring seller also reduces the income reportable under this provision.

seller has withdrawn from the original investment and to tax the seller on that amount (but not in excess of the amount of the original gain), to the extent that such withdrawals have previously escaped tax.

If the property has been returned to seller, does it have the same basis as it had before seller sold it? Clearly that would be inappropriate if in the sale and reacquisition seller has withdrawn some of the initial investment without being taxed on the entire withdrawal. Section 1038(c), in keeping with other nonrecognition provisions, lays down a special basis rule which takes account of all facets of the sale and reacquisition. The basis for the reacquired property is determined with reference to the seller's basis for the obligations relinquished in the reacquisition.[14] This will be seen to represent the seller's basis for the property sold, reduced by prior receipts that went untaxed (for example under Section 453(c)) which are in effect a return of capital. To this is added (1) the amount on which the seller is taxed under Section 1038(b),[15] because *taxed* gain should obviously not again be taxed when the reacquired property is sold, and (2) the amount of any payment the seller made in connection with the reacquisition,[16] because this represents an actual additional cost of or investment in the property. These remarks are not intended as a comprehensive analysis of Section 1038, which can present some complications not discussed.

*Section 1045.* Recall that to encourage investment in small start-up companies, Section 1202 allows a percentage exclusion of gain on "qualified small business stock."[17] To further encourage such investment, Section 1045 provides an elective nonrecognition (rollover) provision with respect to capital gain on the sale of Section 1202(c) qualified small business stock held for more than 6 months by a noncorporate shareholder, to the extent that a purchase[18] of other Section 1202(c) stock is made within 60 days of the sale.[19] Typical substituted basis[20] and tacked holding period rules apply,[21] except that the holding period is not tacked for purposes of satisfying the 6-month holding period requirement referred to above.[22]

---

[14] Cf. I.R.C. § 453B(b).

[15] I.R.C. § 1038(c)(1).

[16] I.R.C. § 1038(c)(2).

[17] See page 695, supra.

[18] I.R.C. § 1045(b)(2).

[19] I.R.C. § 1045(a).

[20] I.R.C. § 1045(b)(3).

[21] I.R.C. § 1223(13).

[22] I.R.C. § 1045(b)(4)(A). See I.R.C. § 1045(a). It is also not tacked for satisfying the I.R.C. § 1202(c)(2) active business requirement. I.R.C. § 1045(b)(4)(B).

# PART 8

# CONVERTING TAXABLE INCOME INTO TAX LIABILITY

CHAPTER 27    Computations

# CHAPTER 27

# COMPUTATIONS

## A.  TAX RATES

### 1.  INTRODUCTION

A grasp of the concepts and principles presented in the preceding chapters of this book makes possible an intelligent look at the determination of a taxpayer's actual tax liability. Briefly to recapitulate what has gone before, we have examined the profile of gross income, deductions allowed in arriving at taxable income, assignments of income, rules of timing (accounting!), characterization, and some principles of disallowance and nonrecognition. Still deferring rules of tax procedure, professional responsibility, and tax policy, this Chapter considers the conversion of taxable income into tentative tax liability, which then is reduced by various credits and measured against the alternative minimum tax to reach a determination of the actual liability for tax.

Congress imposes the income tax on ordinary income at progressive tax rates under which increasing rates are applicable to additional increments of taxable income. The purpose behind progressive tax rates is to increase the proportionate tax burden as taxable income increases.[1] The alternative to progressive tax rates is a flat tax rate. A flat-rate tax is sometimes bantered about by politicians when tax reform is considered, but it is an alternative which Congress has not seriously considered of late; although for many taxpayers, the alternative minimum tax imposes an essentially flat tax rate on a broadened tax base.[2]

The tax rates paid by a taxpayer depend, in part, on the source of the income and this part of the Chapter looks at the various alternatives: tax rates on ordinary income; tax rates on qualified business income earned in pass-through entities; tax rates on dividends and net capital gains; and a series of special rules related to tax rates.

### 2.  TAX RATES ON ORDINARY INCOME

Internal Revenue Code: Sections 1(j)(1)–(3), 2(a)(1) and (2), (b)(1)–(3); 6013(a)(2) and (3), (d). See Sections 66; 7703.

---

[1]    See Blum and Kalven, "The Uneasy Case for Progressive Taxation," 19 U. of Chi. L.Rev. 417 (1952); Smith, "High Progressive Tax Rates: Inequity and Immorality?" 20 U. of Fla. L.Rev. 451 (1968); Bankman & Griffith, "Social Welfare and the Rate Structure: A New Look at Progressive Taxation," 75 Cal. L.Rev. 1905 (1987); Zolt, "The Uneasy Case for Uniform Taxation" 16 Virg.Tax Rev. 39 (1996).

[2]    A widely publicized "flat tax" proposal is outlined in Hall & Rabushka, The Flat Tax (2d ed. 1995), which advocates a tax system consisting of a tax on wages and salaries and a business tax, both levied at a 19% rate.

Regulations: Proposed Sections 1.7701–1; 301.7701–18.

———————

*Introduction.* Congress currently imposes the income tax on ordinary income of noncorporate taxpayers (individuals and estates and trusts) at seven rates (10, 12, 22, 24, 32, 35, and 37 percent).[1] Prior to 1981, noncorporate taxpayers were taxed on taxable income at tax rates up to 70 percent. Over time, Congress has significantly reduced the top tax rates paid by noncorporate taxpayers. The tax-rate landscape, however, has frequently changed as Congress periodically adjusted and readjusted tax rates to satisfy its budgetary objectives, or to stimulate or put the brakes on the economy. However, generally when Congress has significantly reduced tax rates, it has broadened the tax base by scaling back exclusions and deductions.[2]

*Classifications of Taxpayers.* Before we look more closely at the rates, specifically the points at which the different rates are applicable, we must examine the classification of individual taxpayers. The taxable income levels at which different sets of progressive rates are imposed depend upon the classification (by personal circumstances) of the taxpayer. There is a separate rate schedule for estates and trusts.[3]

Individual taxpayers are grouped into four classifications:

1.   Married Individuals Filing Joint Returns and Surviving Spouses;[4]

2.   Heads of Households;[5]

3.   Unmarried Individuals (not falling within the first two classifications as surviving spouses or heads of households);[6]

4.   Married Individuals Filing Separate Returns.[7]

The four classifications of individual taxpayers listed above have remained the same for a number of years. They are puzzling enough to invite the question: How did we get to the point of having the various classifications?

For many years all individuals were taxed under a single set of tax rates. In 1930, however, the Supreme Court held that in community property states earnings and other income of either spouse were taxable

———————

[1]   I.R.C. § 1(j)(1) and (2).

[2]   The Tax Reform Act of 1986 applied the lowest modern maximum top individual tax rate of 28 percent, although it also broadened the tax base. Prior to the Act, the maximum top individual tax rate was 50 percent between 1981 and 1986.

[3]   I.R.C. § 1(j)(2)(E). Under that schedule the progressive rates are phased in at a much earlier point than the other § 1(j)(2)(A)–(D) classifications.

Corporate taxpayers are taxed at a flat 21 percent rate under I.R.C. § 11.

[4]   I.R.C. § 1(j)(2)(A).

[5]   I.R.C. § 1(j)(2)(B).

[6]   I.R.C. § 1(j)(2)(C).

[7]   I.R.C. § 1(j)(2)(D).

one-half to each spouse.[8] Under the then single progressive tax rate table, this splitting of income between community property state spouses gave married persons subject to those state laws a major tax advantage over married persons in common law states. The built-in income-splitting advantage should be clear. Not to be outdone, a movement began in common law states to adopt the community property system.[9] But, as there had always been many more common law states than community property states, it is not surprising that broad relief from the inequality eventually came from Congress. In 1948, the Code was amended so as to allow a married couple to split their aggregate taxable income for purposes of rate determination. Their tax liability then became twice the tax determined at the rates applicable to one-half the amount of their combined income. This formula often let married couples escape the higher reaches of the tax rate table.[10]

The income-splitting joint return rate concept is identifiable in present Section 1(j)(2)(A). The special rates are available only if a joint return is filed. Use of the joint return by married persons is elective and is allowed only if the requirements of Section 6013(a) are satisfied.[11] A consequence of filing a joint return is joint and several liability, not only for the tax reported, but also for deficiencies and interest and possibly civil penalties.[12] In many circumstances the income-splitting advantage of a joint return will result in less tax liability for the spouses than filing separate returns.[13] But the important thing here is the origin of the split-income device.

There has been significant controversy in recent years as to whether same-sex married couples can be treated as married persons under the federal law and thereby can file joint returns.[14] The Supreme Court has

---

[8]　Poe v. Seaborn, 282 U.S. 101, 51 S.Ct. 58 (1930). While post-marital earnings are split, either spouse may have non-community property, the earnings from which are his or hers, separately.

See I.R.C. § 66(a), enacted in 1980, which in limited circumstances taxes community property earned income to the spouse whose services gave rise to the income, rather than one-half to each spouse. I.R.C. § 66 applies only if the spouses are living apart at all times during the year involved, they file separate returns, and no portion of the earned income is transferred between them. See also § 66(b), which allows the Service to treat one spouse as the owner of community property income if that spouse acts as if he or she is solely entitled to the income and fails to notify the other spouse of the income. Cf. I.R.C. § 66(c).

See Miller, "Federal Income Taxation and Community Property Law: The Case for Divorce," 44 S.W.L.J. 1087 (1990).

[9]　Sen.Rep. No. 1013, 80th Cong., 2d Sess. (1948), 1948–1 C.B. 301–303. There were also advantages to the community property states under the Estate and Gift Tax provisions which were eliminated by the Rev.Act of 1948. See I.R.C. §§ 2056, 2513, 2523.

[10]　I.R.C. (1939) §§ 12(d) and 51(b).

[11]　Marital status is determined under I.R.C. § 7703.

[12]　I.R.C. § 6013(d)(3); see, however, the innocent spouse rules of I.R.C. §§ 6015 and 6663(c) and see Chapter 28B2, infra. Cf. I.R.C. § 66(c).

[13]　But see the Text at note 27, infra.

[14]　The issue also has important transfer tax ramifications. See Stephens, Maxfield, Lind & Calfee, Federal Estate and Gift Taxation ¶ 5.06 [3]. (Warren Gorham & Lamont 9th ed. 2013).

determined that they are so treated[15] and the Treasury provides for the filing of joint returns.[16]

In 1954, the "surviving spouse" was fitted into the married joint return classification and remains there.[17] Surviving spouses, as defined in Section 2(a), are widows or widowers who for the two years following the year of their spouse's death do not remarry but do maintain a child or children who are their dependents[18] in their home. One is not a statutory "surviving spouse" for the year of the spouse's death, because generally a joint return may be filed for the year of the spouse's death.[19] If the Section 2(a) requirements are met, surviving spouses are allowed to use the Section 1(j)(2)(A) rates which, as indicated, are the income-splitting rates that are available to married couples filing joint returns.

In 1951, Congress created another set of rates now in Section 1(j)(2)(B) applicable to another category of taxpayers known as "heads of households".[20] The reason for according this new class of taxpayers preferential rates was stated in the House Report:[21]

> It is believed that taxpayers, not having spouses but nevertheless required to maintain a household for the benefit of other individuals, are in a somewhat similar position to married couples who, because they may share their income, are treated under present law substantially as if they were two single individuals each with half of the total income of the couple. The income of a head of household who must maintain a home for a child, for example, is likely to be shared with the child to the extent necessary to maintain the home, and raise and educate the child. This, it is believed, justifies the extension of some of the benefits of income splitting. The hardship appears particularly severe in the case of the individual with children to raise who, upon the death of his spouse, finds himself in the position not only of being denied the spouse's aid in raising the children, but under present law also may find his tax load heavier.
>
> However, it was not deemed appropriate to give a head of household the full benefits of income splitting because it appears unlikely that there is as much sharing of income in these cases as between spouses. In the case of savings, for example, it appears unlikely that this income will be shared by a widow or widower with his child to the same extent as in the

---

[15]  United States v. Windsor, 570 U.S. 744, 133 S.Ct. 2675 (2013); Obergefell v. Hodges, ___ U.S. ___, 135 S.Ct. 2584 (2015).

[16]  Rev.Rul. 2013–17, 2013–38 I.R.B. 201. See Prop. Reg. §§ 1.7701–1, 301.7701–18.

[17]  I.R.C. § 1(j)(2)(A).

[18]  Dependents are defined in I.R.C. § 152. See Chapter 18E, supra.

[19]  I.R.C. §§ 6013(a)(3), 7703(a)(1).

[20]  I.R.C. § 1(j)(2)(B).

[21]  H.Rep. No. 586, 82d Cong., 1st Sess. (1951), 1951–2 C.B. 364.

case of spouses. As a result only one-half of the benefits of income splitting are granted to heads of households.

Under the current provisions of the Code, "heads of households" are defined in Section 2(b) much in line with the comments just quoted.[22] But head of household status is not limited to widows or widowers. It can also apply, for example, to a divorced or legally separated person who maintains as one's home a household in which unmarried descendants reside,[23] a taxpayer who maintains a household for others, including parents, if the others enjoy dependency status under Section 152,[24] and a taxpayer, who is actually married, if the person would otherwise qualify for head of household status, where the taxpayer and spouse are physically separated even though not divorced or legally separated.[25] The rates under Section 1(j)(2)(B), applicable to heads of households effecting a smaller amnesty, fall roughly midway between the rates for single persons and the rates for married couples filing joint returns.

And now we have come full circle. In the past, individuals not within the special classes described above and married persons filing separately shared the distinction of paying taxes in accordance with a third schedule of rates, the highest of the three. However, Congress determined this third schedule was too burdensome for the *unmarried individual* who was not a surviving spouse or a head of household. There emerged a revised third classification and schedule now found in Section 1(j)(2)(C), less preferential than the first two, but preferential nevertheless. The Staff of the Joint Committee on Internal Revenue Taxation explains the development as follows:[26]

> Under prior law, the tax rates imposed on single persons were quite heavy relative to those imposed on married couples at the same income level; at some income levels a single person's tax was as much as 42.1 percent higher than the tax paid on a joint return with the same amount of taxable income. The Congress believed that some difference between the rate of tax paid by single persons and joint returns was appropriate to reflect the additional living expenses of married taxpayers but that the prior law differential of as much as 42 percent (the result of income splitting) could not be justified on this basis.

> \* \* \*

> The prior law rate schedule for single persons will continue to be used for married couples filing separate returns. . . . The prior law single person rate schedule was retained for married

---

[22] Taxpayer's home must constitute the child or other dependent's principal place of abode for more than one-half of such year. I.R.C. § 2(b)(1)(A).

[23] I.R.C. § 2(b)(1)(A), (2)(A) and (B).

[24] I.R.C. § 2(b)(1)(B).

[25] I.R.C. §§ 2(c) and 7703(b).

[26] General Explanation of the Tax Reform Act of 1969, Staff of the Joint Comm. on Int.Rev.Tax., pp. 222–223 (1970).

persons filing separate returns because if each spouse were permitted to use the new tax rate schedule for single persons, many (especially those in community property states) could arrange their affairs and income in such a way that their combined tax would be less than that on a joint return.

With the new rate schedule for single persons, married couples filing a joint return will pay more tax than two single persons with the same total income. This is a necessary result of changing the income splitting relationship between single and joint returns. Moreover, it is justified on the grounds that although a married couple has greater living expenses than a single person and hence should pay less tax, the couple's living expenses are likely to be less than those of two single persons and therefore the couple's tax should be higher than that of two single persons.

Note that the last paragraph of the legislative history mentions situations where a married couple filing jointly will pay more tax than two single taxpayers with the same total income.[27] In the current rate tables, Congress has significantly reduced the instances where this "marriage penalty" applies. Under the current Section 1(j)(2)(A) and (j)(2)(C) rates, a married couple begins to pay more tax if they are married than if they are single each earning one-half of the income only when they have over $600,000 of combined taxable income. While the income thresholds for marrieds filing jointly are exactly double the thresholds for singles in the lower brackets, the 37 percent rate begins at $600,000 of taxable income for marrieds filing jointly and at $500,000 for singles. For example, if they each have $350,000 of taxable income and are single, their total tax liability would be $196,379; whereas, if they are married and file a joint return with $700,000 of taxable income, their total tax liability would be $198,379. If two individuals have disparate income taxed below the 37-percent bracket, there will often be a "marriage bonus" in the form of tax savings. Thus, the marriage bonus is the more common situation.

As the above quoted remarks indicate, the tagender in the rate parade of individual taxpayers is now Section 1(j)(2)(D) which is applicable to the married taxpayer who files separately. The 37 percent rate kicks in at a lower level for that taxpayer than any of the other individual classifications.[28] The rate discrepancy can be a problem for high-income separated persons who are not divorced. In many instances they do not file jointly because they want to avoid the risks inherent in

---

[27] One strategy employed by taxpayers to avoid the "marriage penalty" that previously existed was to travel to a winter resort to obtain a year-end divorce, obtain a divorce, and return home and remarry after the New Year. See Boyter v. Commissioner, 74 T.C. 989 (1980), where the taxpayers journeyed to Haiti one year and the Dominican Republic the next for their annual government-financed divorce vacation. Not surprisingly, the Service frowned upon such divorces, considering them shams. Rev. Rul. 76–255, 1976–2 C.B. 40.

[28] I.R.C. § 1(j)(2)(D).

joint and several tax liability, and they just use the rates applicable to married taxpayers filing separately and lose the income-splitting advantage of a joint return.[29] But in some cases the spouse with whom the children reside can now file as head of household even though legally married.[30]

*Rate Schedules.* The above consideration of classifications leads us to a comparison of the various rate schedules imposed under Section 1 of the Code. Skimming Sections 1(j)(2)(A)–(E), it can be seen that the accelerated rates take over at different levels. The schedule of the rates for the year 2018 is as follows:

### (A) Married individuals filing joint returns and surviving spouses.

| If taxable income is: | The tax is: |
| --- | --- |
| Not over $19,050 | 10% of taxable income. |
| Over $19,050 but not over $77,400 | $1,905, plus 12% of the excess over $19,050. |
| Over $77,400 but not over $165,000 | $8,907, plus 22% of the excess over $77,400. |
| Over $165,000 but not over $315,000 | $28,179, plus 24% of the excess over $165,000. |
| Over $315,000 but not over $400,000 | $64,179, plus 32% of the excess over $315,000. |
| Over $400,000 but not over $600,000 | $91,379, plus 35% of the excess over $400,000. |
| Over $600,000 | $161,379, plus 37% of the excess over $600,000. |

### (B) Heads of households.

| If taxable income is: | The tax is: |
| --- | --- |
| Not over $13,600 | 10% of taxable income. |
| Over $13,600 but not over $51,800 | $1,360, plus 12% of the excess over $13,600. |
| Over $51,800 but not over $82,500 | $5,944, plus 22% of the excess over $51,800. |
| Over $82,500 but not over $157,500 | $12,698, plus 24% of the excess over $82,500. |
| Over $157,500 but not over $200,000 | $30,698, plus 32% of the excess over $157,500. |

---

[29] Cf. I.R.C. § 66 discussed at note 18, supra.

[30] I.R.C. §§ 2(c) and 7703(b). See Text at note 25, supra.

| | |
|---|---|
| Over $200,000 but not over $500,000 | $44,298, plus 35% of the excess over $200,000. |
| Over $500,000 | $149,298, plus 37% of the excess over $500,000. |

## (C) Unmarried individuals other than surviving spouses and heads of households.

| If taxable income is: | The tax is: |
|---|---|
| Not over $9,525 | 10% of taxable income. |
| Over $9,525 but not over $38,700 | $952.50, plus 12% of the excess over $9,525. |
| Over $38,700 but not over $82,500 | $4,453.50, plus 22% of the excess over $38,700. |
| Over $82,500 but not over $157,500 | $14,089.50, plus 24% of the excess over $82,500. |
| Over $157,500 but not over $200,000 | $32,089.50, plus 32% of the excess over $157,500. |
| Over $200,000 but not over $500,000 | $45,689.50, plus 35% of the excess over $200,000. |
| Over $500,000 | $150,689.50, plus 37% of the excess over $500,000. |

## (D) Married individuals filing separate returns.

| If taxable income is: | The tax is: |
|---|---|
| Not over $9,525 | 10% of taxable income. |
| Over $9,525 but not over $38,700 | $952.50, plus 12% of the excess over $9,525. |
| Over $38,700 but not over $82,500 | $4,453.50, plus 22% of the excess over $38,700. |
| Over $82,500 but not over $157,500 | $14,089.50, plus 24% of the excess over $82,500. |
| Over $157,500 but not over $200,000 | $32,089.50, plus 32% of the excess over $157,500. |
| Over $200,000 but not over $300,000 | $45,689.50, plus 35% of the excess over $200,000. |
| Over $300,000 | $80,689.50, plus 37% of the excess over $300,000. |

**(E) Estates and trusts.**

| *If taxable income is:* | *The tax is:* |
| --- | --- |
| Not over $2,550 | 10% of taxable income. |
| Over $2,550 but not over $9,150 | $255, plus 24% of the excess over $2,550. |
| Over $9,150 but not over $12,500 | $1,839, plus 35% of the excess over $9,150. |
| Over $12,500 | $3,011.50, plus 37% of the excess over $12,500. |

## Explanation of Proposed Regulations on the Definition of Terms Relating to Marital Status

REG–148998–13; 2015–45 I.R.B. 653.

\* \* \*

On June 26, 2013, the Supreme Court in *United States v. Windsor*, 570 U.S. \_\_\_, 133 S. Ct. 2675 (2013), held that Section 3 of the Defense of Marriage Act, which generally prohibited the federal government from recognizing the marriages of same-sex couples, is unconstitutional because it violates the principles of equal protection and due process. Revenue Ruling 2013–17 [2013–38 I.R.B. 201. Ed.] provides guidance on the *Windsor* decision's effect on the IRS's interpretation of Code sections that refer to taxpayers' marital status. *Cf.* Notice 2014–19 (2014–47 IRB 979), amplified by Notice 2014–37 (2014–24 IRB 1100) (regarding the application of the *Windsor* decision to qualified retirement plans); \* \* \* On June 26, 2015, the Supreme Court in *Obergefell v. Hodges*, 576 U.S. \_\_\_ (2015), held that state laws are "invalid to the extent they exclude same-sex couples from civil marriage on the same terms and conditions as opposite-sex couples" and "that there is no lawful basis for a State to refuse to recognize a lawful same-sex marriage performed in another State on the ground of its same-sex character." *Obergefell*, 576 U.S. at 23, 28.

In light of the holdings of *Windsor* and *Obergefell*, the Treasury Department and the IRS have determined that, for federal tax purposes, marriages of couples of the same-sex should be treated the same as marriages of couples of the opposite-sex and that, for reasons set forth in Revenue Ruling 2013–17, terms indicating sex, such as "husband," "wife," and "husband and wife," should be interpreted in a neutral way to include same-sex spouses as well as opposite-sex spouses. Accordingly, these proposed regulations amend the current regulations under section 7701 of the Internal Revenue Code (Code) to provide that, for federal tax purposes, the terms "spouse," "husband," and "wife" mean an individual lawfully married to another individual, and the term "husband and wife" means two individuals lawfully married to each other. These definitions apply regardless of sex.

In addition, these proposed regulations provide that a marriage of two individuals will be recognized for federal tax purposes if that marriage would be recognized by any state, possession, or territory of the United States. Under this rule, whether a marriage conducted in a foreign jurisdiction will be recognized for federal tax purposes depends on whether that marriage would be recognized in at least one state, possession, or territory of the United States. This comports with the general principles of comity where countries recognize actions taken in foreign jurisdictions, but only to the extent those actions do not violate their own laws. See *Hilton v. Guyot*, 159 U.S. 113, 167 (1895) ("A judgment affecting the status of persons, such as a decree confirming or dissolving a marriage, is recognized as valid in every country, unless contrary to the policy of its own law.").

\* \* \*

For federal tax purposes, the term "marriage" does not include registered domestic partnerships, civil unions, or other similar relationships recognized under state law that are not denominated as a marriage under that state's law, and the terms "spouse," "husband and wife," "husband," and "wife" do not include individuals who have entered into such a relationship.

Except when prohibited by statute, the IRS has traditionally looked to the states to define marital status. See *Loughran v. Loughran*, 292 U.S. 216, 223 (1934) ("Marriages not polygamous or incestuous, or otherwise declared void by statute, will, if valid by the law of the state where entered into, be recognized as valid in every other jurisdiction."); see also Revenue Ruling 58–66 (1958–1 CB 60) (if a state recognizes a common-law marriage as a valid marriage, the IRS will also recognize the couple as married for purposes of federal income tax filing status and personal exemptions). States have carefully considered the types of relationships that they choose to recognize as a marriage and the types that they choose to recognize as something other than a marriage. Although some states extend all of the rights and responsibilities of marriage under state law to couples in registered domestic partnerships, civil unions, or other similar relationships, those states have intentionally chosen not to denominate those relationships as marriages. Similar rules exist in some foreign jurisdictions.

Some couples have chosen to enter into a civil union or registered domestic partnership even when they could have married, and some couples who are in a civil union or registered domestic partnership have chosen not to convert those relationships into a marriage even when they have had the opportunity to do so. In many cases, this choice was deliberate, and couples who enter into civil unions or registered domestic partnerships may have done so with the expectation that their relationship will not be treated as a marriage for purposes of federal law. For some of these couples, there are benefits to being in a relationship that provides some, but not all, of the protections and responsibilities of marriage. For example, some individuals who were previously married and receive Social Security benefits as a result of their previous marriage may choose to enter into a civil union or registered domestic partnership (instead of a marriage) so that they do not lose their Social Security benefits. More generally, the rates at which some couples' income is taxed may increase if they are considered married and thus required to file a married-filing-separately or married-filing-jointly federal income tax return. Treating couples in civil unions and registered domestic partnerships the same as married couples who are in a relationship denominated as marriage under state law could undermine the expectations certain couples have regarding the scope of their relationship. Further, no provision of the Code indicates that Congress intended to recognize as marriages civil unions, registered domestic partnerships, or similar relationships. Accordingly, the IRS will not treat civil unions, registered domestic partnerships, or other similar relationships as marriages for federal tax purposes.

* * *

# Revenue Ruling 2013–17[*]

2013–38 I.R.B. 201.

* * *

The holdings of this ruling will be applied prospectively as of September 16, 2013.

Except as provided below, affected taxpayers also may rely on this revenue ruling for the purpose of filing original returns, amended returns, adjusted returns, or claims for credit or refund for any overpayment of tax resulting from these holdings, provided the applicable limitations period for filing such claim under section 6511 has not expired. If an affected taxpayer files an original return, amended return, adjusted return, or claim for credit or refund in reliance on this revenue ruling, all items required to be reported on the return or claim that are affected by the marital status of the taxpayer must be adjusted to be consistent with the marital status reported on the return or claim.

Taxpayers may rely (subject to the conditions in the preceding paragraph regarding the applicable limitations period and consistency within the return or claim) on this revenue ruling retroactively with respect to any employee benefit plan or arrangement or any benefit provided thereunder only for purposes of filing original returns, amended returns, adjusted returns, or claims for credit or refund of an overpayment of tax concerning employment tax and income tax with

---

[*] See page 937, supra. Ed.

respect to employer-provided health coverage benefits or fringe benefits that were provided by the employer and are excludable from income under sections 106, 117(d), 119, 129, or 132 based on an individual's marital status. For purposes of the preceding sentence, if an employee made a pre-tax salary-reduction election for health coverage under a section 125 cafeteria plan sponsored by an employer and also elected to provide health coverage for a same-sex spouse on an after-tax basis under a group health plan sponsored by that employer, an affected taxpayer may treat the amounts that were paid by the employee for the coverage of the same-sex spouse on an after-tax basis as pretax salary reduction amounts.

The Service intends to issue further guidance on the retroactive application of the Supreme Court's opinion in *Windsor* to other employee benefits and employee benefit plans and arrangements.*

## PROBLEMS

1.  T is a calendar year taxpayer. In each of the following subparts you are to compute T's tax liability (before credits) assuming T has $315,000 of taxable income under the rate schedules for the year 2018 which appear above.

   (a)  T is unmarried and has no special status.

   (b)  On December 31 of the current year T married Spouse, a calendar year taxpayer who has no income for the year, and they file a joint return.

   (c)  T was married and two minor children supported by T lived with T and Spouse, but Spouse, who had no income in the year, died on January 15 of the current year.

   (d)  Same as (c), above, except that Spouse died on December 31 of the prior year.

   (e)  Same as (c), above, except that Spouse died on December 31, three years earlier.

   (f)  Same as (c), above, except that T remarried on December 31 of the current year and T and New Spouse file separate returns for the current year.

   (g)  T is a trust.

2.  Husband and Wife are both under age 65 with good eyesight. In the current year they use the rate schedules that appear above, and they file a joint return. They have no § 62 deductions. Compute their tax liability before credits if:

   (a)  They have $200,000 of gross income, $4,000 in local property taxes, $10,000 in state income taxes, $7,000 in deductible residential interest payments, and $2,000 in miscellaneous employee business expenses.

---

*   See, e.g., Notice 2015–86, 2015–52 I.R.B. 887. Ed.

(b)  Same as (a), above, except that they also have $8,000 of charitable contributions.

## 3.  TAX RATES ON INCOME FROM PASS-THROUGH ENTITIES

Internal Revenue Code: Section 199A(a), (b)(1), (2), (3)(A), (4), (6), (c), (d)(1)–(3), (e)(1) and (2), (f)(1)(A), (i).

———————

*Introduction.* One of the most significant changes made by the 2017 Tax Cuts and Jobs Act,[1] was the reduction in the tax rates paid by corporations. Prior to the Act, a corporation paid federal income tax at graduated rates, with a top rate of 35 percent. Currently, a corporation pays a flat rate 21 percent income tax on its taxable income.[2] The steep reduction in corporate tax rates raised the question of how business income earned in enterprises, such as sole proprietorships, partnerships, limited liability companies, and S corporations, should be taxed. These forms of doing business are referred to as "pass-through entities," because generally there is no entity-level tax levied on the income earned in the enterprise. Instead, that income is taxed directly to the owners of the venture. Thus, a sole proprietor includes business income on the sole proprietor's federal tax return. Also, partners, members of a limited liability company, and shareholders in an S corporation generally pay the tax on their shares of the income earned by the entity.[3] As a result, without relief, business income earned by an individual in a pass-through entity would be taxed at the individual's tax rates, which could be as high as 37 percent.

Congress was concerned that the 21-percent corporate tax rate would create a significant bias in favor of operating a business in a corporation rather than operating it as a pass-through entity. The significantly lower corporate tax rate also would have created an incentive for an existing pass-through entity to incorporate in order to be taxed as a corporation. To reduce the difference in taxation of business income in a corporation and a pass-through entity, Congress enacted Section 199A, which generally provides a noncorporate taxpayer with a deduction equal to 20 percent of the taxpayer's "qualified business income" earned in a pass-through entity. If the full Section 199A deduction is allowed (which is not always the case), the effect is that only 80 percent of the taxpayer's qualified business income is taxable at the individual tax rates, thereby reducing the top rate on such income from 37 percent to 29.6 percent (80 percent of 37 percent) and effectively lowering the tax rate in any tax bracket on qualifying business income. The deduction also reduces the tax rate distinction between corporations and pass-through entities.

———————

[1]  Pub. L. No. 115–97, 115th Cong., 1st Sess. (2017).
[2]  I.R.C. § 11(b).
[3]  I.R.C. §§ 702(a), 1366(a). See Chapter 13A, supra.

Despite its rather straightforward purpose, Section 199A is an extremely complex provision. The section is layered with definitions, limitations, modifications, and industry-specific rules. It also has its own "anti-abuse" rules.[4] In keeping with the "Fundamentals" approach, what follows is a general description of the section's provisions and its operation.

*Overview of Section 199A.* To determine the Section 199A deduction, a taxpayer[5] first must determine the "qualified business income" from each of the taxpayer's trades or businesses.[6] Qualified business income is defined as the net amount of income, gain, deduction, and loss from the conduct of a qualified trade or business in the United States.[7] Note that the deduction is specifically focused on *business* income or loss. In keeping with that purpose, the elements of net capital gain or loss (e.g., long- and short-term capital gain and loss), various forms of investment income (e.g., dividends and interest income not from a trade or business), and deductions or losses allocable to such items, are not included in qualified business income.[8] In the case of a partnership, a limited liability company, or S shareholder, Section 199A is generally applied at the partner or shareholder level, and each partner or shareholder takes into account an allocable share of items from the business.[9]

The Section 199A deduction is also not intended to apply to compensation for services. Thus, the trade or business of performing services as an employee is not a qualifying trade or business under Section 199A.[10] Similarly, reasonable compensation (salary) paid to an S corporation shareholder and salary or salary-like payments paid to a partner do not qualify for the Section 199A deduction.[11] These rules are designed to ensure that income from compensation paid for services is taxed in full under the individual tax rates. But a sole proprietor's profits and a share of profits earned by a partner or S corporation shareholder do qualify for the Section 199A deduction, even though the profits may include income attributable to the taxpayer's personal services.

Once the qualified business income or loss from a business is determined, the Section 199A calculation with respect to that business is 20 percent of that amount, subject to various limitations.[12] The taxpayer's Section 199A deduction generally is the sum of the separate

---

[4] I.R.C. § 199A(h).

[5] The provision applies to trusts and estates as well as individuals. I.R.C. § 199A(a).

[6] I.R.C. § 199A(b)(1)(A) and (2)(A), (c).

[7] I.R.C. § 199A(c)(3)(A). The section has special rules for dividends from real estate investment trusts (I.R.C. § 199A(b)(1)(B), (e)(3)), income from publicly traded partnerships (I.R.C. § 199A(b)(1)(B), (e)(4)), and specified agricultural and horticultural cooperatives (I.R.C. § 199A(g)). None of those provisions are covered in the Text.

[8] I.R.C. § 199A(c)(3)(B).

[9] I.R.C. § 199A(f)(1).

[10] I.R.C. § 199A(d)(1)(B).

[11] I.R.C. § 199A(c)(4).

[12] I.R.C. § 199A(b)(2)(A).

calculations for all of the taxpayer's businesses;[13] however, the Section 199A deduction may not exceed 20 percent of the excess of the taxpayer's taxable income for the year reduced by net capital gain.[14] Taxable income for this purpose is determined without the Section 199A deduction.[15] If the sum of the calculations is negative, the taxpayer has a loss for the year from the combined trades or businesses and the loss carries over to the next year as a loss from a qualified trade or business.[16]

*Limitations for High-Income Taxpayers.* Once a taxpayer reaches certain high levels of income, two separate limitations apply which may reduce or eliminate the Section 199A deduction. Section 199A defines the high-income "threshold amount" for the two limitations as $157,500 of taxable income for a single taxpayer and $315,000 of taxable income for married taxpayers filing jointly.[17] Taxable income for this purpose is again determined without the Section 199A deduction,[18] and the high-income thresholds are adjusted for inflation beginning after 2018.[19] Each of the limitations begins to apply when the taxpayer's taxable income exceeds the threshold amount. And each limitation fully applies when the taxpayer's taxable income is $50,000 ($100,000 in the case of married taxpayers filing jointly) above the high-income threshold. Thus, the limitations apply with full force at $207,500 of taxable income for singles and $415,000 for of taxable income for marrieds filing jointly. In the $50,000 and $100,000 ranges above the threshold amounts, the limitations are calculated using the ratio of the taxpayer's taxable income in excess of the threshold amount, divided by $50,000 (or $100,000 for married taxpayers filing jointly).[20]

Under the first limitation on high-income taxpayers, certain designated service trades or businesses ("a specified service trade or business") are excluded from the definition of a qualified trade or business and do not qualify for the Section 199A deduction.[21] The businesses subject to this limitation are any trade or business, other than architecture or engineering, involving the performance of services in the fields of health, law, accounting, actuarial science, performing arts, consulting, athletics, financial services, brokerage services, or any other trade or business where the principal asset is the reputation or skill of one or more of its employees or owners.[22] Performance of services that are investing, investment management, or trading or dealing in various

---

13   I.R.C. § 199A(a)(1), (b)(1)(A).

14   I.R.C. § 199A(a)(2). Net capital gain is defined in I.R.C. § 1(h). I.R.C. § 199A(a)(2)(B).

15   I.R.C. § 199A(e)(1).

16   I.R.C. § 199A(c)(2).

17   I.R.C. § 199A(e)(2)(A).

18   I.R.C. § 199A(e)(1).

19   I.R.C. § 199A(e)(2)(B).

20   I.R.C. § 199A(b)(3)(B), (d)(3).

21   I.R.C. § 199A(d)(1)(A), (2).

22   I.R.C. §§ 199A(d)(2)(A), 1202(e)(3)(A).

securities and investments also are subject to the limitation.[23] Thus, under this limitation, an attorney (either a sole practitioner or a partner) with income above the threshold phase-in amount would not be allowed a Section 199A deduction, whereas such an attorney with taxable income below the threshold amount would be entitled to the deduction.

The second limitation on a high-income taxpayer's Section 199A deduction has a different focus. A high-income taxpayer's Section 199A deduction is capped at the greater of (1) 50 percent of the business's W-2 wages (generally employee compensation, including qualified and deferred compensation[24]), or (2) 25 percent of the business's W-2 wages plus 2.5 percent of the unadjusted basis of qualified property (generally tangible depreciable property[25] used in the business).[26] The "50-percent-of-W-2 wages" limitation would deny the deduction to a high-income taxpayer whose business has few employees, perhaps indicating that the bulk of the income is attributable to the high-income taxpayer's personal services. The "25-percent-of-W-2 wages plus" limitation is an alternative test which could benefit a capital intensive business where minimal services are provided. For example, a real estate business or a business with a large amount of equipment or machinery might qualify for a larger deduction under this test than the 50 percent test.

The Section 199A deduction is not allowed in computing adjusted gross income.[27] However, the Section 199A deduction is available to all taxpayers in computing taxable income regardless of whether they itemize deductions or claim the standard deduction.[28]

## PROBLEMS

1.   Attorney is a married sole practitioner who files a joint return with Spouse. Compute their § 199A deduction in the following circumstances.

   (a)   Attorney has $284,000 of gross income from the law practice and $30,000 of business expenses. Attorney and Spouse also have $20,000 of dividends and $10,000 of interest income and minimal itemized deductions.

   (b)   Same as (a), above, except that Attorney is an associate with the law firm making a $125,000 salary.

---

[23]   I.R.C. § 199(d)(2).

[24]   I.R.C. § 199A(b)(4). See I.R.C. § 199(f)(1)(A)(iii).

[25]   I.R.C. § 199A(b)(6). The property must be used in the trade or business by the end of the year, and its depreciation period must not have ended. I.R.C. § 199A(b)(6)(A). The depreciation period ends at the later of ten years after first being placed in service or the last day of the last full year of the property's I.R.C. § 168 (disregarding § 168(g)) recovery period. I.R.C. § 199A(b)(6)(B). See I.R.C. § 199A(f)(1)(A)(iii).

[26]   I.R.C. § 199A(b)(2).

[27]   Thus, it has no effect on deductions which use adjusted gross income in measuring deductions. See page 565, supra. Cf. I.R.C. § 62(a) last sentence.

[28]   See I.R.C. § 63(a) and (b)(3).

    (c)   Same as (a), above, except that Attorney is an equal partner in a two member firm whose gross income is $568,000 with $60,000 in business expenses.

    (d)   Same facts as (a), above, except that Attorney's gross income from the practice is $500,000.

**2.**    Husband and Wife are each invested in a business. In the current year, Husband has a 25% partnership interest in a real estate business that has total gross income of $1.2 million, pays $100,000 of W-2 wages, has $100,000 of depreciation, and has qualified property with an unadjusted basis of $2 million. Wife owns a catering business which has $400,000 of gross income, pays $180,000 of W-2 wages, and has no depreciable property but has $20,000 of other business expenses. Assume that Husband and Wife are above the high-income threshold for purposes of the § 199A limitations. What is the amount of their Section 199A deduction for the year assuming that the taxable income limitation of § 199A(a)(2) does not apply?

## 4.  TAX RATES ON NET CAPITAL GAINS AND DIVIDENDS

Internal Revenue Code: Sections 1(h)(1)(C) and (D), (11)(A) and (B). See Section 1(j)(5)(A) and (B).

---

    Earlier in the Text,[1] we saw that net capital gains are taxed at special lower rates under Section 1(h). As a practical matter under Section 1(h), most gains from property held for more than 12 months will be taxed at a 15[2] or, in the case of high-income taxpayers, a 20[3] percent rate. However, net capital gains generally may be taxed at rates of zero percent, 15 percent, 20 percent, 25 percent, and 28 percent.[4] The point here is not only to remind you of those alternative rates, but to illustrate that Section 1(h) is a section imposing rates on a variety of different classes of net capital gains.

    Section 1(h) currently also imposes a preferential tax rate (equal to the net capital gain rates on most adjusted net capital gains) on "qualified dividend income"[5]. Congress was sympathetic to the fact that "double taxation" arguably occurs when a corporation (other than an S corporation) has earnings and profits that are taxed at a flat 21 percent rate when earned by the corporation and also were taxed as ordinary income when they were distributed as a dividend to the shareholders.[6] Generally, such "double taxation" does not occur on the taxation of income from other entities, such as partnerships, limited liability

---

   [1]   See Chapter 21A and B, supra.

   [2]   See I.R.C. § 1(h)(1)(C), (j)(5)(A)(ii), (B)(ii).

   [3]   I.R.C. § 1(h)(1)(D). The next most prevalent rate is the 25 percent rate. See I.R.C. § 1(h)(1)(E), Chapter 22D, supra.

   [4]   I.R.C. § 1(h)(1). The remaining rates sometimes apply even though they are not directly provided by the statute. See Chapter 21B, supra at notes 28–30.

   [5]   I.R.C. § 1(h)(3)(B), (11). See I.R.C. § 1(h)(1)(C) and (D), (j)(5)(A)(ii), (B)(ii).

   [6]   See page 273, supra.

companies, and S corporations that are taxed as pass-through entities and may receive special rate treatment under Section 199A.[7] A further justification for the equalized rates on net capital gains and qualified dividend income is that taxpayers who invest in corporations which pay dividends should not be taxed at higher rates than taxpayers who invest in corporations which do not pay dividends but whose profits are reflected solely in the price of the stock, the sale of which eventually results in capital gains to the taxpayers.

As a result of these policy justifications, a preferential rate applies to "qualified dividend income" which is defined as including most dividend distributions.[8] The preferential rate is identical to the individual's tax rate on adjusted net capital gains:[9] 20 percent for high-income taxpayers;[10] 15 percent for middle-income taxpayers;[11] and zero percent for low-income taxpayers.[12] The preferential rates apply to dividends from domestic corporations and "qualified" foreign corporations,[13] but are inapplicable to some payments that occasionally are labeled "dividends," such as amounts paid by savings institutions on deposits.[14]

Even though qualified dividends currently are taxed at a preferential rate generally applicable to long-term capital gains, such dividends do not enter the calculation of a taxpayer's Section 1222(11) net capital gain.[15] Thus, capital losses may not be deducted against qualified dividend income. To preclude a taxpayer from purchasing dividend-generating stocks simply to get immediate dividends taxed a preferential rate, the preferential rate does not apply to dividends on stock purchased within 60 days of the date the stock goes ex-dividend if the stock is sold within 60 days of its purchase.[16]

## PROBLEM

1.    Husband and Wife are both employees under age 65 with good eyesight. They file a joint return in the current year using the rate schedules that appear on page 935, supra. They have no § 62 deductions and use the standard deduction. Compute their tax liability before credits if:

---

[7]   See Chapter 13A, supra and Chapter 27A3, supra.

[8]   I.R.C. § 1(h)(11)(B) and (C).

[9]   I.R.C. § 1(h)(3). See I.R.C. § 1(h)(1)(B)–(D).

[10]   I.R.C. § 1(h)(1)(D).

[11]   I.R.C. § 1(h)(1)(C), (j)(5)(A)(ii), (B)(ii).

[12]   I.R.C. § 1(h)(1)(B), (j)(5)(A)(i), (B)(i). See also note 4, supra.

[13]   I.R.C. § 1(h)(11)(B)(i), (C).

[14]   I.R.C. § 1(h)(11)(B)(ii)(II).

[15]   I.R.C. § 1(h)(11)(A) (parenthetical).

[16]   I.R.C. § 1(h)(11)(B)(iii). Technically, the stocks must have been held for at least 60 days during the 121 day period beginning on the date which is 60 days prior to the date the stock goes ex-dividend. See I.R.C. § 246(c).

(a)   They have $200,000 of income from services, $5,000 of net capital gain from the sale of stock held for 3 years, and $3,000 of qualified dividend income.

(b)   Same as (a), above, except they have $600,000 of income from services.

(c)   They have $200,000 of income from services, $3,000 of long-term capital losses from the sale of stock, and $3,000 of qualified dividend income.

(d)   They have $200,000 of income from services, $10,000 of gain from the sale of a business building (with $5,000 of gain attributable to straight-line depreciation), and $3,000 of loss from the sale of business land (both held more than one year), a short-term capital gain of $2,000 on stock, a short-term capital loss of $4,000 on stock, and qualified dividend income of $3,000.

## 5.   ADDITIONAL RULES RELATED TO TAX RATES

Internal Revenue Code: Sections 1(g)(2) and (4), (j)(2)(E), (4) and (5)(B)(i)(IV) and (ii)(IV); 1411(a)(1), (b), (c)(1) and (2). See Sections 1(f)(3) and (6); 3; and 6012.

---

*Net Investment Income Tax.* As part of health care reform, Congress enacted Section 1411 which, in order to support the Medicare program, potentially imposes an additional 3.8 percent tax on an individual's[1] net investment income.[2] The 3.8 percent tax is imposed on the *lesser* of (1) the taxpayer's net investment income (generally gross income reduced by related deductions)[3] from interest,[4] dividends, annuities, royalties, rents, net capital gains,[5] and businesses that are passive activities,[6] *or* (2) the amount by which the taxpayer's modified adjusted gross income exceeds a threshold amount.[7] The threshold amount[8] is: $250,000 for married taxpayers filing jointly and surviving spouses; $125,000 for marrieds filing separately; and $200,000 for all other taxpayers. Because the base for the tax cannot exceed the amount by which modified adjusted gross income exceeds the threshold amount, the tax does not apply to taxpayers with income below the threshold amount; thus, the tax generally applies

---

[1]   The tax also applies with modifications to trusts and estates. I.R.C. § 1411(a)(2).

[2]   I.R.C. § 1411(a)(1).

[3]   I.R.C. § 1411(c)(1)(B). This includes an I.R.C. § 1211(b) deduction. Reg. § 1.1411–4(f)(4). However, it does not include the I.R.C. § 199A deduction. See Reg. § 1.1411–4.

[4]   Tax exempt interest is not subject to I.R.C. § 1411 because it is not included in gross income. I.R.C. § 103(a).

[5]   I.R.C. § 1411(c)(1)(A)(i) and (iii). Distributions from pension funds and qualified plans are not net investment income and not subject to the tax. I.R.C. § 1411(c)(5).

[6]   I.R.C. § 1411(c)(1)(A)(ii), (2)(A). See Chapter 17F, supra.

[7]   I.R.C. § 1411(a)(1), (b). In computing modified adjusted gross income, minor adjustments are made to the taxpayer's adjusted gross income. See I.R.C. § 1411(d).

[8]   I.R.C. § 1411(b).

to higher-income taxpayers. The IRS has provided this illustration of the operation of the net investment income tax:[9]

> Taxpayer, a single filer, has $180,000 of wages. Taxpayer also received $90,000 from a passive partnership interest, which is considered Net Investment Income. Taxpayer's modified adjusted gross income is $270,000.
>
> Taxpayer's modified adjusted gross income exceeds the threshold of $200,000 for single taxpayers by $70,000. Taxpayer's Net Investment Income is $90,000.
>
> The Net Investment Income Tax is based on the lesser of $70,000 (the amount that Taxpayer's modified adjusted gross income exceeds the $200,000 threshold) or $90,000 (Taxpayer's Net Investment Income). Taxpayer owes [tax] of $2,660 ($70,000 x 3.8%).

As a practical matter, Section 1411 increases the top tax rate on ordinary income to 40.8 percent (37 percent plus 3.8 percent) and the top tax rate on dividends and adjusted net capital gains to 23.8 percent (20 percent plus 3.8 percent). One area, where the net investment income tax may have unexpected consequences is the sale of a principal residence. To the extent that gain from the sale of a principal residence is greater than the Section 121 exclusion, the Section 1411 tax is potentially applicable.[10]

*The Kiddie Tax.* Congress provides for a special "kiddie tax" aimed at preventing avoidance tactics of assignment of income to some minors. The rule applies to the net unearned income[11] of a child who is under the age of 18 (or if the child's earned income does not exceed one-half of the child's support, the child is either under the age of 19 or is a student under the age of 24) at the close of the taxable year.[12] Previously, unearned income attributed to a child as a result of interest from bank accounts or notes, dividends from stocks, and other such unearned income generally was taxed at the child's parents' applicable tax rates.

In what was described as simplification, but also will likely generate more revenue, the kiddie tax now requires the net unearned income of a child meeting the above requirements to be taxed at the steeply graduated tax rates applicable to estates and trusts, rather than at the parents' rates.[13] The source of the underlying property generating the unearned income is of no consequence; nor is the date of the property

---

[9]   Net Investment Income Tax FAQs, http://www.irs.gov/uac/Newsroom/Net-Investment-Income-Tax-FAQs.

[10]   Id. See Chapter 11A, supra.

[11]   I.R.C. § 911(d)(2) defines unearned income. I.R.C. § 1(g)(4)(A)(i).

[12]   I.R.C. §§ 1(g)(2)(A), 152(c)(3). The provision is inapplicable if both parents are dead at the close of the taxable year, I.R.C. § 1(g)(2)(B), or if the child files a joint return for the year, I.R.C. § 1(g)(2)(C).

[13]   I.R.C. § 1(j)(4). The amount of net unearned income so taxed may not exceed the child's taxable income for the year. I.R.C. § 1(g)(4)(B).

transfer. Net unearned income is the unearned income in excess of $1,000 plus, if the child's itemizes deductions, the amount of itemized deductions in excess of $500 connected with the production of the unearned income.[14] The $1,000 and $500 amounts are adjusted for inflation.[15] At a minimum, $500 of unearned income (adjusted for inflation) is treated as earned income[16] and escapes the kiddie tax.[17] The taxable income of the child which is treated as earned income and the child's actual earned income are taxed at the rates applicable to a single taxpayer,[18] while the child's net unearned income is taxed at the ordinary income and net capital gains rates applicable to estates and trusts.[19] The kiddie tax contains other intricate rules, some of which are moot given the change in the structure of the tax.[20]

*Bracket Creep.* Much attention has been focused on the effect of inflation on the rate structure.[21] To the extent that a taxpayer's increase in income pushes the taxpayer into a higher tax bracket and is merely a reflection of rising inflation, the taxpayer is left with less real income after taxes than before the increase in income. Adjustments for "bracket creep," first introduced in the 1980s, have been continued by Congress by increasing the amounts at which the increased tax rates kick in.[22] Similar inflation adjustments apply in several areas of the Code.[23] Current tax provisions for years after 2017 or 2018, provide for a switch in the method for calculating inflation adjustments to a "chained" consumer price index (CPI), which takes into account a consumer's ability to substitute between goods and services in response to changes in relative prices.[24] The chained CPI grows at a slower pace than the prior CPI adjustment, because consumers generally adjust their buying patterns when prices rise rather than simply buying the same item at a higher price.[25]

---

[14]  I.R.C. § 1(g)(4). See I.R.C. §§ 63(c)(5), 911(d)(2).

[15]  I.R.C. § 63(c)(4).

[16]  Earned taxable income is defined as taxable income of the child reduced (but not below zero) by the net unearned income as defined in I.R.C. § 1(g)(4) of such child, I.R.C. § 1(j)(4)(D).

[17]  The $1,000 treated as earned income is reduced by the child's $500 I.R.C. § 63(c)(5) standard deduction to arrive at the $500 amount.

[18]  I.R.C. § 1(j)(4)(B). See I.R.C. § 1(j)(2)(C).

[19]  I.R.C. § 1(j)(4)(B) and (C). See I.R.C. § 1(j)(5)(B)(i)(IV), (ii)(IV).

[20]  See I.R.C. § 1(g)(3) and (5). See also I.R.C. § 1(g)(7) providing an elective provision enabling the parents of a child having only unearned interest and dividend income which is less than $5,000 to report the income on the parent's return alleviating the need for the child to file a return. Retention of that provision in view of the current nature of the kiddie tax seems questionable.

[21]  See e.g., Kelly *et al.* "Indexing for Inflation," 31 Tax Lawyer 17 (1978) where the authors quote Lewis Carroll's Red Queen on the problem, "Now here, you see, it takes all the running you can do to keep in the same place. If you want to go somewhere else, you must run twice as fast as that."

[22]  The phase-in amounts are indexed for inflation for each year after 2018. I.R.C. § 1(j)(3)(B).

[23]  See, e.g., I.R.C. § 63(c)(4)(B). The indexing occurs for years after 2018. Id.

[24]  I.R.C. § 1(f)(3) and (6).

[25]  This change is permanent and does not terminate after 2025.

*Tax Tables.* In order to provide low-income individual taxpayers who use the standard deduction[26] a simplified method of computing their taxes, the Code has traditionally called for the administrative preparation of tax tables that yield automatic tax determination without arithmetic computation.[27] The tables are in regulations promulgated pursuant to the Code and in the instructions that accompany individual tax returns. These tables do not reflect a further different set of individual rates. Instead, they are designed to yield an instant tax figure, determined under the relevant Section 1 rates.[28] Entering the table for the proper rate classification, a taxpayer finds the tax by reference to the taxpayer's taxable income and total number of personal exemptions. The tables are available only to taxpayers with taxable income less than a ceiling amount (not less than $20,000) to be determined by the Secretary.[29] Use of the tables, no longer optional, is required of the taxpayers for whom they are available.[30]

*Filing Requirement.* Related to tax rates and classifications is the Section 6012 requirement to file an income tax return. Most persons are required to file, but not all. As a result of the standard deduction, persons with low levels of gross income may automatically have zero taxable income.[31] For example, if disregarding inflation adjustments, a married couple filed a joint return in the current year, they automatically get a $24,000 standard deduction. If their gross income does not exceed $24,000, they have no taxable income and no tax liability. Section 6012 relieves them from the burden of even having to file a tax return. Because the above amounts are indexed for inflation,[32] the Service annually provides information indicating the levels of gross income at which taxpayers in varying classifications are required to file returns.[33]

## PROBLEMS

1. Daddy Warbucks, a single taxpayer, has $600,000 of gross income which consists of $420,000 of salary, $50,000 of short-term capital gain, $60,000 of dividend income, $40,000 of profit from a real estate limited partnership interest, and $30,000 of interest income. Daddy has no § 62 deductions and will itemize his deductions. Compute Daddy's § 1411 tax liability.

2. Child who is age 17 and is subject to the "kiddie tax" has $20,500 of taxable income in the current year ($21,000 of gross income less a § 63(c)(5) $500 standard deduction). Compute Child's tax liability for year if:

---

[26] I.R.C. § 3(a)(1)(A). But see I.R.C. § 3(a)(3) allowing the Commissioner to require use of the tables by persons who itemize.

[27] I.R.C. § 3.

[28] Some rounding off of tax liability occurs because of the bracket approach in the tables.

[29] I.R.C. § 3(a)(1)(B) and (2).

[30] I.R.C. § 3(a)(1).

[31] This would not be so if the taxpayer were the dependent of another taxpayer. Cf. I.R.C. §§ 63(c)(5) and 151(d)(2).

[32] I.R.C. § 63(c)(7)(B).

[33] I.R.C. § 6012(f)(2). See I.R.C. § 6012(f)(1) applicable to unmarried taxpayers.

(a) All of Child's income is interest from bonds.

(b) All of Child's income is from dividends.

(c) Child has $5,000 of income from services and $16,000 of interest from bonds.

(d) Same as (a), above, except that Child is 20 years old and not a student.

## B. CREDITS AGAINST TAX

## 1. INTRODUCTION

The final step in computing a taxpayer's regular tax liability is to reduce the taxpayer's tax liability as determined above[1] by the amount of any tax credits allowed to the taxpayer. Thus, the amount of tax that must be paid by the taxpayer when filing an income tax return is reduced by tax credits.

A credit of a certain dollar amount[2] is more advantageous to the taxpayer than a deduction of the same dollar amount, because it reduces tax liability dollar-for-dollar, whereas a deduction reduces only taxable income with a corresponding but smaller reduction in tax liability. Deductions effect greater tax savings as the taxpayer's tax rate increases;[3] in contrast, credits have the same dollar saving for all taxpayers who otherwise would pay tax, regardless of their tax brackets. However, note that generally credits are allowed only to the extent of some percentage of the dollar amount expended. Tax legislation at one time reflected some movement away from deductions toward credits, possibly because of a policy decision that credits are more equitable.[4] With the adoption of less accelerated tax rates, the movement from deductions to credits stalled although it has picked up some momentum in recent legislation.

Most credits are said to be "nonrefundable." Even if they exceed the amount of tax computed, they do not generate a tax refund. Other credits are "refundable" because the amount by which they exceed the tax liability computed after taking into consideration the nonrefundable credits may be refunded to the taxpayer. Within the credit provisions themselves, the order in which they are consumed may be important. It is obviously best that refundable credits be consumed last, after allowance of other credits, because this will maximize the amount of any refund.[5] The order in which nonrefundable credits are consumed is also

---

[1]  See Chapter 27A, supra.

[2]  See, for example, I.R.C. § 21(a), discussed in Chapter 27B1, infra.

[3]  See page 468, supra.

[4]  See Hoff, "The Appropriate Role for Tax Credits in an Income Tax System," 35 Tax Lawyer 339 (1983); Weidenbaum, "Shifting from Income Tax Deductions to Credits," 51 Taxes 462 (1973).

[5]  I.R.C. § 6401(b)(1). Cf. I.R.C. § 35. See also note 11 on page 222, supra.

significant, although not discretionary, because some nonrefundable credits qualify for carryovers to the extent they are not used in the year in which they arise. The statute fixes the pecking order of nonrefundable credits by providing that credit provisions generally are to be used to reduce tax liability in the order in which they appear in the Code.

We've already examined some credit provisions in other parts of the book. For example, in Chapter 11 we saw the Section 25A American Opportunity and Lifetime Learning Credits which generally are allowed no carryovers.[6] And in Chapter 14, we saw two credits allowed with respect to depreciable real estate: The Section 47 Rehabilitation Credit for restoring historic real estate and the Section 42 Low-Income Housing Credit.[7] Both of the latter credits are a part of the Section 38 General Business Credit which is a combination of several credits.[8] Each of the credits is computed separately and then they are combined[9] and are subject to special limitations. Generally, there is a ceiling on the combined credits of $25,000 of tax liability after considering nonrefundable credits plus 75 percent of such liability in excess of $25,000.[10] If the general business credit for a year is not fully utilized because of the above limitation, any unused portion generally[11] may be carried back one year and forward twenty years.[12]

In considering credit calculations, the taxpayer must also take into consideration the passive loss limitation under Section 469[13] which may limit some of the credits. In general, a taxpayer will not be allowed a reduction in tax liability for any "passive activity credit"[14]—the amount by which the sum of all credits from passive activities[15] exceeds the regular tax liability[16] allocable to all the taxpayer's passive activities for the taxable year.[17] Thus, the amount of credits from passive activities is generally limited to the tax liability generated by those passive

---

[6]   See Chapter 11C, supra. But see I.R.C. § 25A(i)(5) and the Text at note 35 on page 224 supra.

[7]   See Chapter 14E3, supra.

[8]   The separate credits are listed in I.R.C. § 38(b). Although note that the § 46 Investment Credit is itself a combination of other credits. I.R.C. § 46.

[9]   I.R.C. § 38(b).

[10]   I.R.C. § 38(c)(1) If the alternative minimum tax is applicable (see Chapter 27C, infra), there is a more complicated computation of the credit. Id.

[11]   I.R.C. § 39(a). But see I.R.C. § 39(a)(3) and (4), (b), (c), and (d).

[12]   I.R.C. § 39.

[13]   See Chapter 17F, supra.

[14]   I.R.C. § 469(a)(1)(B).

[15]   I.R.C. § 469(d)(2)(A). See I.R.C. §§ 27(b), 28, 29, 38 (which includes §§ 40(a), 41(a), 42(a), 43(a), 44(a), 45(a), 45A(a), 45B(a), 45C(a), 45D(a), 45E(a), 46, 51(a), and 1396(a)).

[16]   See I.R.C. §§ 469(d)(2)(B), 469(j)(3), 26(b).

[17]   I.R.C. § 469(d)(2). But see I.R.C. § 469(i) and (j)(4) for an exception for certain real estate activities.

activities.[18] The entire amount of any disallowed passive activity credit may be carried forward indefinitely, but may not be carried back.[19]

A quick glimpse at the credit provisions of the Code (generally, Sections 21 through 53) indicates that they are extremely detailed. The objective here is to present a picture of two groups of credits, one related to generally nonrefundable personal-type expenses and the other refundable credits for what in essence are prepaid taxes.

## 2. PERSONAL CREDITS

Internal Revenue Code: See Sections 21; 23; 24; 25A; 32.

---

There are several credits generally allowed with respect to the expenditure of personal expenses.[1] Some are refundable, although most are nonrefundable; some are also subject to carryovers. Most are inapplicable to higher income taxpayers. The most significant of those credits are discussed below.

*Section 21: Credit for Dependent Care Services.* This credit is allowed for "employment related expenses,"[2] that are incurred for household services or day care of a "qualifying individual,"[3] if incurred to enable the taxpayer to be gainfully employed.[4] Generally, a "qualifying individual" is either a "qualifying child"[5] of the taxpayer who is under the age of 13 or a mentally or physically handicapped spouse or dependent of the taxpayer.[6] The credit is equal to an "applicable percentage",[7] which may

---

[18] If there are excess passive activity losses (in excess of income) for the year, the taxpayer will have no current benefit from the credits produced by the passive activities.

[19] I.R.C. § 469(b). Credit carryovers from a passive activity are not allowed when the activity is disposed of. See I.R.C. § 469(g) which is applicable to losses but not credits.

[1] Cf. I.R.C. § 262.

[2] I.R.C. § 21(b)(2). Payments to relatives, including grandparents, may qualify as employment related expenses, subject to some I.R.C. § 21(e)(6) limitations.

[3] I.R.C. § 21(b)(1). Congress provides an exclusion from gross income for certain employer-provided dependent care services which, if paid for by the employee, would be considered employment-related expenses under I.R.C. § 21(b)(2). I.R.C. § 129. Amounts excluded under § 129 are ineligible for the credit under § 21. I.R.C. § 129(e)(7).

[4] Expenses for care outside the home may be taken into account only for dependents under the age of 13 or dependents who regularly spend at least 8 hours each day in the taxpayer's household. I.R.C. § 21(b)(1)(A), (2)(B).

[5] I.R.C. § 152(a)(1), (c).

[6] I.R.C. § 21(b)(1). The return of the person claiming the credit for the qualifying individual must include the individual's taxpayer identification number (TIN). I.R.C. § 21(e)(10).

To qualify for the credit, the taxpayer or the taxpayer's spouse must furnish more than one-half the cost of maintaining a household in which one or more qualifying individuals reside. I.R.C. §§ 21(a)(1) and 152(a)(1), (c)(1)(D). If divorced parents provide over one half of the support of a qualifying child and they have custody over the child for more than one half of the year, then the parent who has custody for the greater portion of the year is entitled to the credit. I.R.C. § 21(e)(5).

[7] The applicable percentage is 35%, reduced (but not below 20%) by one percentage point for each $2,000 (or fraction thereof) by which the taxpayer's adjusted gross income exceeds

not exceed 35 percent, of the taxpayer's employment-related expenses.[8] The employment-related expenses cannot exceed $3,000 if there is one qualifying individual in the taxpayer's household, and $6,000 if there are two or more such individuals.[9] Thus, as the applicable percentage never exceeds 35 percent, the credit may never exceed $1,050 or $2,100, respectively. The credit is nonrefundable and may not be carried over.

*Section 23: Credit for Qualified Adoption Expenses.* A maximum $10,000 per eligible child credit[10] generally is allowed for qualified adoption expenses; however, on the adoption of a child with special needs,[11] a flat $10,000 credit (regardless of expense) is allowed.[12] An "eligible child" is an individual who is less than 18 years of age or is physically or mentally incapable of self-care.[13] Qualified adoption expenses are reasonable and necessary adoption, court, or attorney's fees, and other adoption-related expenses.[14] The credit is phased out for higher-income taxpayers.[15] All dollar amounts in Section 23 are adjusted for inflation.[16] The credit is nonrefundable, but unused credit may be carried over for a maximum of five years.[17]

*Section 24: Child Tax Credit.* The child tax credit is a combination of the "qualifying child" credit and the "qualifying relative" credit. This credit was significantly expanded by the 2017 Tax Cuts and Jobs Act. The credit borrows from the definitions of "dependent" found in Section 152(c) and (d).[18]

The first and most generous part of the credit is a $2,000 per child credit for each "qualifying child" (as defined in Section 152(c)) of the taxpayer who is under the age of 17 at the end of the year.[19] A taxpayer's tax return must include the social security number for each qualifying

---

$15,000. I.R.C. § 21(a)(2). Thus the applicable percentage levels off at 20% when the taxpayer's adjusted gross income exceeds $43,000.

   [8]  See I.R.C. § 21(d) generally limiting such expenses to the amount of the taxpayer's earned income.

   [9]  I.R.C. § 21(c).

   [10]  I.R.C. § 23(b)(1). The limit is per child. The credit is allowed for foreign adoptions, but only if the adoption becomes final. I.R.C. § 23(e).

   [11]  I.R.C. § 23(a)(3). See I.R.C. § 23(d)(3) for the definition of special needs. On adoption of such children, the excess of $10,000 over the expenses previously allowed as a credit is allowed for the year the adoption becomes final. I.R.C. § 23(a)(3). Compare I.R.C. § 23(a)(2).

   [12]  I.R.C. § 23(a)(1) and (3). In order to qualify for the credit, the taxpayer must provide the name, age, and taxpayer identification number (TIN) of the child. I.R.C. § 23(f)(2).

   [13]  I.R.C. § 23(d)(2).

   [14]  I.R.C. § 23(d)(1). Expenses to adopt a child of the taxpayer's spouse are not qualified expenses. I.R.C. § 23(d)(1)(C). Amounts reimbursed under an employer program which were excluded by I.R.C. § 137 (see page 98, supra) do not qualify for the credit. I.R.C. § 23(d)(1)(D).

   [15]  The phase-out begins as modified gross income exceeds $150,000 and is fully phased out when it exceeds $190,000. I.R.C. § 23(b)(2)(A). In defining modified adjusted gross income, I.R.C. § 23(b)(2)(B) makes some modifications to adjusted gross income.

   [16]  Adjustments are made for inflation after 2002. I.R.C. § 23(h).

   [17]  I.R.C. § 23(c).

   [18]  The definitions remain in the Code even though the amount of the dependency exemption deduction is zero. I.R.C. § 151(d)(5).

   [19]  I.R.C. § 24(a), (c)(1), (h)(2).

child for whom the credit is claimed.[20] The second part of the credit is a $500 credit for each "qualifying relative" (as defined in Section 152(d)) of the taxpayer.[21] There is no requirement to report the social security number for this part of the credit.[22]

The child tax credit is phased out as the taxpayer's modified adjusted gross income exceeds $400,000 in the case of married taxpayers filing a joint return and $200,000 in the case of all other taxpayers.[23]

The qualifying child credit (but not the qualifying relative credit) may result in a tax refund. The refund is generally subject to an earned income threshold under which it is allowed only to the extent of 15 percent of the taxpayer's earned income[24] in excess of $2,500.[25] The refundable portion of the credit must not exceed $1,400 per child.[26] *or 70% of credit*

One potential problem with the Section 24 child tax credit is that it involves rather complex computations, and persons who might otherwise qualify for the credit, especially a refund, may fail to apply for it due to its complexity.

*Section 32: Earned Income Credit.* This credit is a Federal government effort to help alleviate poverty and to encourage persons at poverty levels to work as opposed to being on welfare. Without going into great detail with respect to the complicated Code section, it is important to understand the fundamental nature of the provision. Basically, low income workers (with or without children) are allowed a credit against their income tax liability. The amount of the credit is based on a percentage of their earned income,[27] and it is phased out as their earned income (or adjusted gross income if it is greater) increases.[28] The credit is a refundable credit that generates additional revenue to persons near poverty levels. Thus, to encourage taxpayers to work rather than to be on welfare, this refundable credit section essentially provides that if the earned income of the taxpayers is small, not only will they not have to pay taxes on that income, but they will also be allowed some government financial assistance through a tax refund. Thus, for working taxpayers with low incomes, this constitutes a negative income tax, providing such taxpayers with an additional source of financial support.

---

[20]  I.R.C. § 24(h)(7). The social security number must be issued before the due date for filing the return for the taxable year. I.R.C. § 24(h)(7)(B).

[21]  I.R.C. § 24(h)(4).

[22]  If there is a qualifying child for whom no social security number is timely provided (see note 20, supra), such child may qualify for this part of the credit. I.R.C. § 24(h)(4)(C).

[23]  I.R.C. § 24(b)(2), (h)(3). The credit is reduced by $50 for each $1,000 that the taxpayer's modified adjusted gross income exceeds the threshold amount. I.R.C. § 24(b)(1). Modified adjusted gross income is defined in I.R.C. § 24(b)(1).

[24]  See I.R.C. § 32(c)(2).

[25]  I.R.C. § 24(h)(6).

[26]  I.R.C. § 24(h)(5). The amount is adjusted for inflation after 2018. I.R.C. § 24(h)(5)(B).

[27]  Earned income is defined in I.R.C. § 32(c)(2).

[28]  I.R.C. § 32(b).

Like most credit provisions there are lots of complex rules applicable to the earned income credit. The credit applies even if a taxpayer has no qualifying children,[29] but the credit is potentially larger if taxpayer has a qualifying child[30] and even larger if the taxpayer has more than one qualifying child.[31] The credit is based on a percentage[32] of a taxpayer's earned income[33] up to a ceiling amount of earned income.[34] The credit is, however, phased-out by a percentage[35] of the greater of the taxpayer's earned income or adjusted gross income[36] over a flat dollar amount.[37] The percentages and amounts vary depending on the year and the taxpayer's classification.[38] The credit is also denied if a taxpayer has investment income in excess of $2,200.[39] The Code section directs the Service to issue tables to aid a taxpayer in determining the amount of the credit.[40]

Congress is concerned with taxpayers misusing the earned income credit. A taxpayer who fraudulently claims the credit is prohibited from using it for a ten-year period and one who erroneously claims it due to reckless or intentional disregard of its rules or regulations is prohibited from using it for a two-year period.[41]

## PROBLEM

1. Parents are a married couple who file a joint return. They have 3 qualifying children and $80,000 of gross income. They have no § 62 deductions and do not elect to itemize their deductions.

---

[29] I.R.C. § 32(c)(1)(A)(ii). If a taxpayer has no qualifying children, the taxpayer must meet certain other requirements to be an eligible individual including the individual or the spouse must be least age 25 and not over age 64 at the end of the year and the individual must not be a person who can be claimed as the dependent of another taxpayer during the year. Id. Seemingly a self-supporting single law student may qualify for the credit.

[30] The term "qualifying child" is defined in I.R.C. § 152(c) determined without regard to § 152(c)(1)(D) and § 152(e). I.R.C. § 32(c)(3)(A).

[31] See I.R.C. § 32(b). If a taxpayer in any one of the categories is married, the taxpayer must file a joint return to qualify for the credit. I.R.C. § 32(d). A taxpayer claiming the I.R.C. § 32 credit must include the taxpayer identification number (TIN) of the taxpayer, the taxpayer's spouse, and any qualifying children (as well as the children's names and ages) on the taxpayer's return. I.R.C. § 32(c)(1)(E), (c)(3)(D), (m). No credit is allowed for any child who is not so identified. I.R.C. § 32(c)(1)(F).

[32] See I.R.C. § 32(b)(1).

[33] In general, earned income is defined in I.R.C. § 32(c)(2) as employee compensation includible in gross income (wages, salary, tips, etc.) and net earnings from self-employment.

[34] I.R.C. § 32(a)(1) and (b)(2).

[35] I.R.C. § 32(b)(1).

[36] I.R.C. § 32(a)(2)(B).

[37] I.R.C. § 32(b)(2).

[38] See I.R.C. § 32(b).

[39] I.R.C. § 32(i). The dollar amount and the I.R.C. § 32(b) amounts are adjusted for inflation for years after 1996. I.R.C. § 32(j).

[40] I.R.C. § 32(f).

[41] I.R.C. § 32(k)(1). In addition, if a taxpayer is denied use of the credit in a deficiency proceeding, the credit will not subsequently be allowed unless the taxpayer demonstrates evidence of eligibility for the use of credit. I.R.C. § 32(k)(2).

(a)   Compute Parents' tax liability for the year using the rate schedules on page 935 and taking into consideration both the standard deduction and the child tax credit.

(b)   Same as (a), above, except that their gross income is $50,000?

(c)   What result in (a), above, if Parents fail to provide the children's social security numbers on their tax return?

## 3.  CREDITS FOR PREPAID TAXES    → *After all other credits*

Internal Revenue Code: See Sections 31; 37; 6315; 6654.

---

These refundable credits are some of the credits which are considered after all other credits. They not only reduce tax liability after it has been reduced by the other credits, but they can also generate a tax refund. There are other refundable credits, but these are the most significant. Since they permit repayment of prepayments of tax, the refund is really in the nature of a deposit recovery.

*Section 31: Credit for Withholding on Wages.* The most widely applicable credit provision is Section 31. It provides a credit for tax withheld by an employer.[1] This credit simply recognizes that such withholding is in the nature of a prepayment of tax.[2] The withholding requirements originated in 1943 as a limited acceleration of revenue collections in a time of need during World War II. Their continuing function is to facilitate collection. One wonders whether the current income tax could be administered if all payments were to be made by the taxpayer only at the end of the year.

Section 3402(a) requires an employer to act as a tax collector and withhold from an employee an amount of tax generally based upon the employee's wages, exemptions, and tax classification. The regulations contain tables[3] to guide employers in determining the amount to withhold, and the employer is personally liable for these amounts just as if it were tax imposed on him.[4] The tax applies only if there is an employment relationship[5] and is imposed on "wages"[6] which are broadly defined.[7] An employer has alternative methods of determining the amount of tax to be withheld[8] and, if an employee certifies she had no tax

---

[1]   I.R.C. § 3402.

[2]   Cf. I.R.C. § 6401(b).

[3]   Reg. § 31.3402(b)–1 directs employers to the withholding tables contained in Circular E (Employer's Tax Guide).

[4]   I.R.C. § 3403.

[5]   See Reg. § 31.3401(c)–1.

[6]   I.R.C. § 3402(a).

[7]   See I.R.C. § 3401(a) and (f).

[8]   E.g., I.R.C. § 3402(c).

liability for the prior year and expects to have none in the current year, she is exempt from withholding.[9]

*Section 37: Credit for Overpayments of Tax.* An excessive amount withheld for social security taxes is also treated as if it were withheld as income tax and thus qualifies for the Section 31 credit.[10] Excessive withholding often occurs when an individual changes jobs during the year and withholding in the aggregate by two or more employers exceeds amounts required to be withheld.

Persons who are not wage earners and wage earners with outside income generally are required to make payment of *estimated tax.*[11] If such payments are required,[12] the payments are made on a quarterly basis. For most calendar year taxpayers the due dates are April 15, June 15, September 15, and January 15.[13] There are penalties for failure to pay the estimated tax.[14] Estimated tax payments are similar to withholding of taxes on wages because they also constitute a prepayment of tax.

Section 37 allows a refund for any overpayment of tax.[15] Amounts paid as estimated tax[16] are treated as payment of income tax and if the total amount paid as estimated tax exceeds actual tax liability for the year, the excess is an overpayment of tax.[17] An overpayment of income tax may be credited against any liability of the taxpayer under the Internal Revenue Code.[18]

## PROBLEM

1.   Taxpayer has $107,000 of tax liability in the current year prior to consideration of certain credits. Taxpayer has a 10 year old child. None of the credits is subject to the passive activity credit limitation. Determine tax payable or refundable after the credits and whether Taxpayer is allowed any carrybacks or carryovers of credits. The credits are:

| | | |
|---|---|---|
| § 21 | Child tax credit | $ 2,000 |
| § 31 | Withholding credit | 24,000 |

---

[9]   I.R.C. § 3402(n). See also I.R.C. § 3402(m), reducing amounts to be withheld in some circumstances.

[10]   I.R.C. § 31(b).

[11]   See I.R.C. §§ 6315 and 6654.

[12]   See I.R.C. § 6654(d) which provides for the amounts of estimated tax which must be paid and § 6654(e)(1) which protects taxpayers from penalties for failure to pay small amounts of estimated tax.

[13]   I.R.C. § 6654(c). The amount of required payments is determined under I.R.C. § 6654(d).

[14]   I.R.C. § 6654(a).

[15]   See I.R.C. § 6401 and Chapter 28C, infra.

[16]   See notes 11–14, supra.

[17]   I.R.C. § 6315. For that reason the Service treats them the same as the I.R.C. § 31 credit on Form 1040.

[18]   I.R.C. § 6402.

§ 38   Credits potentially qualifying for the
           general business credit                    90,000

## C.  THE ALTERNATIVE MINIMUM TAX*

Internal Revenue Code: Sections 55(a)–(d); 56(a)(1), (3), (4), and (6), (b)(1)
and (3); 57(a)(5) and (7); 58(b).

———————————

One of Congress's concerns has been taxpayers with substantial
amounts of economic income who take advantage of various tax benefits,
not improperly or illegally, to largely or entirely to avoid tax liability. To
remedy that apparent abuse of the tax benefits, Congress in 1969
introduced a special treatment of certain tax-favored items of income and
deductions by imposing a "minimum tax for tax preferences." Over the
years Congress has sought to refine its attack on tax preferences, now
known as the alternative minimum tax (AMT). As a consequence,
individual taxpayers and their tax advisors must be conscious of this
lurking exaction.[1]

Computation of AMT liability for an individual depends initially
upon a determination of "alternative minimum taxable income" (AMTI).
AMTI, generally speaking, is the taxpayer's regular taxable income with
certain adjustments called for in Sections 56 and 58 and the addition of
various so-called "tax preference" items that are listed in Section 57. In
general, the AMTI amount is reduced by an exemption, and the balance
is generally taxed at 26 or 28 percent rates to arrive at a tentative
minimum tax.[2] When the tentative minimum tax is larger than tax
computed in the regular way, the tentative minimum tax in essence
becomes the total tax for the year, although the statute splits the total
tax into the regular tax and the AMT (the excess of the tentative
minimum tax over the regular tax).[3]

*Sections 56 and 58 Adjustments.* Sections 56 and 58 call for various
adjustments to be made to regular taxable income in computing AMTI.
They are so far-reaching they require an essential redetermination of
taxable income. Some of the adjustments involve complex tax areas
beyond the scope of this course; some others, in more familiar territory,
are summarized below.

Depreciation. A taxpayer owning depreciable property may be
required to keep two sets of books for depreciation, the first set for regular

———————————

*    See, generally, Lathrope, The Alternative Minimum Tax—Compliance and Planning
with Analysis, Warren Gorham & Lamont (1994).

[1]   The corporate AMT was repealed by the 2017 Tax Cuts and Jobs Act, effective for
taxable years beginning after 2017.

[2]   I.R.C. § 55(b)(1). The threshold amount in I.R.C. § 55(b)(1)(A) is adjusted for post-2012
inflation. I.R.C. § 55(d)(3)(A), (B)(i).

[3]   I.R.C. § 55(a).

taxable income and a second set for the AMTI computation.[4] In the long run, the total depreciation is the same; however, the AMTI deduction for depreciation may be computed using a slower rate, a longer useful life, or both.

There is an important exception for property that *qualifies for* 100-percent expensing under Section 168(k).[5] For such property, there is no adjustment to depreciation for AMT purposes; it is expensed for both regular tax and AMT purposes.[6] In the case of tangible personal property which was not eligible for expensing under Section 168(k), generally such property is depreciated for AMT purposes using the 150 percent declining balance method and the same useful life as the life used for regular tax depreciation.[7] Real property is depreciated for both regular and AMTI purposes using straight-line depreciation, but real property placed in service before January 1, 1999, generally has to use a 40-year useful life in determining AMTI.[8] Real property placed in service after December 31, 1998, uses the same useful life for both regular tax and AMTI purposes so there is no AMT depreciation adjustment for such property.[9] The difference between regular tax depreciation and AMT depreciation under the different AMTI depreciation methods on the taxpayer's property is netted, and the *net* difference between the two for *all* such property is an increase or decrease to regular taxable income in computing AMTI.[10]

To the extent that post-1986 property is depreciated using a depreciation method under the AMT different from that under the regular tax, its adjusted basis for AMT purposes is also different from its adjusted basis for the regular tax.[11] The AMT adjusted basis will be larger when AMT depreciation is less than regular tax depreciation. Thus, if such property is sold prior to the expiration of its AMT life, the amount of gain included in AMTI is generally smaller than the gain under the regular tax.

Net Operating Losses. The Section 172 net operating loss deduction under the regular tax,[12] is essentially recomputed under the AMT to take account of the differences in losses as a result of the Section 56 through 58 adjustments.[13] In addition, any carryover of the recomputed net operating loss amount generally reduces AMTI by 90 percent in a

---

[4]   See Chapter 14E, supra

[5]   Id.

[6]   I.R.C. § 168(k)(2)(G).

[7]   I.R.C. § 56(a)(1)(A); but see I.R.C. § 56(a)(1)(B).

[8]   I.R.C. § 56(a)(1)(A)(i).

[9]   I.R.C. § 56(a)(1)(A)(i) last sentence, I.R.C. § 56(a)(1)(A)(ii).

[10]   Similar rules apply to the write-off of post-1986 pollution control facilities to which I.R.C. § 169 applies. I.R.C. § 56(a)(5).

[11]   I.R.C. § 56(a)(6).

[12]   See Chapter 20D, supra.

[13]   I.R.C. § 56(a)(4) and (d).

carryover year (as opposed to an 80 percent reduction of regular taxable income).[14]

Itemized Deductions. Only limited itemized deductions are allowed in the computation of AMTI and no standard deduction is allowed.[15] There are special restrictions on some of the deductions listed in Section 67(b). No deduction is allowed for state, local or foreign taxes.[16] The rules related to deductibility of interest under Section 163(d) are also altered.[17] The remaining itemized deductions listed in Section 67(b), such as personal casualty losses, wagering losses, charitable contributions, and medical expenses, are treated identically in computing regular taxable income and AMTI.

Passive Activity Losses. The passive activity loss limitation rules of Section 469 apply in computing AMTI, and the scope of the limitations is generally the same.[18] However, similar to net operating losses, a separate computation of income and loss after the Section 56 and Section 57 adjustments is made to determine the amount of the AMTI passive activity limitation.[19]

Incentive Stock Options. As seen earlier, Congress has limited or eliminated most tax shelters but left deferred compensation as an important shelter. Section 421 working with Section 422 provides an important deferral on the exercise of certain stock options by excluding the excess of the fair market value of the stock at the time of the exercise, less the option price, from gross income.[20] However, that amount, the excess value over the option price, *is* generally included in income in computing AMTI, in the year when it normally would be subject to tax under Section 83.[21]

*Section 57 Tax Preference Items.* The second step in computing AMTI is to increase the amount determined under Sections 56 and 58 by the amount of tax preference items listed in Section 57(a). The effect is to

---

[14]  I.R.C. § 56(d)(1)(A).

[15]  I.R.C. § 56(b)(1)(E).

[16]  I.R.C. § 56(b)(1)(A)(ii). Correspondingly, no recovery of any nondeductible tax is included in AMTI. I.R.C. § 56(b)(1)(D).

[17]  I.R.C. § 56(b)(1)(C) and (e). In general, the alterations are: (1) Interest which is exempt from tax under the regular tax but is taxed as a preference item under AMTI (see § 57(a)(5)) and related deductions are allowed as income and deductions in the § 163(d) limitation under the AMT. I.R.C. § 56(b)(1)(C)(ii); and (2) the adjustments of §§ 56–58 are applied in determining § 163(d) net investment income. I.R.C. § 56(b)(1)(C)(iv).

[18]  See I.R.C. § 58(b).

[19]  I.R.C. § 58(b)(1).

[20]  The option price is the taxpayer's cost of the property and establishes the taxpayer's cost basis for determining gain or loss on a subsequent sale of the stock under the regular income tax.

[21]  I.R.C. § 56(b)(3). Under I.R.C. § 83 a taxpayer generally must report excess fair market value from a stock option when his rights in the option are freely transferable or when his rights are not subject to a substantial risk of forfeiture. I.R.C. § 83(a). In determining the basis of the stock acquired through such an exercise, the fair market value of the stock (used in computing the preference item) is the stock's basis for AMTI purposes. Id. As in the case of depreciation of post-1986 property, this requires keeping a double set of books, one for computation of regular taxable income and the other for computation of AMTI.

increase the minimum tax base by some or parts of deductions or exclusions for which Congress perceives the treatment in computing regular taxable income is too favorable. As in the Section 56 and Section 58 computations, some of the preference items are too technical for discussion here.[22] However, some of the items are familiar and have a significant impact on the AMTI computation. They are considered below.

Tax Exempt Interest on Private Activity Bonds. The interest from *some* tax exempt bonds which is excluded from gross income under Section 103(a) in computing regular taxable income is a tax preference item under the AMT. The potential effect is to tax some otherwise exempt interest. Subject to some exceptions,[23] the interest that is taxed here is interest from most "qualified bonds"[24] which are private activity bonds issued after August 7, 1986 (but not in 2009 or 2010).[25] Since the interest on the bonds is included in AMTI, the deduction of expenses related to such interest, which is precluded in computing regular taxable income, is allowed in computing AMTI.[26]

Gains on Sale of Section 1202 Stock. For stock generally acquired prior to 2009, one-half of the net capital gain on certain small business stock is excluded from gross income under Section 1202. For stock acquired during most of 2009 and 2010, the exclusion is increased to 75 percent of the gain.[27] However, 7 percent of the amount of the exclusion (i.e., 3.5 or 5.25 percent of the net capital gain on such stock) is a tax preference item which is added to taxable income in computing AMTI.[28] For stock acquired after September 27, 2010, the exclusion is increased to 100 percent and the statute provides that nothing is added to taxable income in computing AMTI.[29]

*Exemptions.* Once the Sections 56 through 58 adjustments are made and the AMTI is calculated, the amount of AMTI is generally reduced by an exemption,[30] the amount of which depends upon the taxpayer's classification and the year involved. The exemption is $109,400 for married persons filing jointly and for surviving spouses, $70,300 for unmarried persons who are not surviving spouses, $54,700 for married persons filing separately, and $22,500 for estates and trusts.[31] However, the exemption is phased-out as a taxpayer's AMTI exceeds certain levels:

---

[22]   I.R.C. § 57(a)(1) and (2).

[23]   I.R.C. § 57(a)(5)(C)(ii)–(vi).

[24]   I.R.C. § 141(e).

[25]   I.R.C. §§ 57(a)(5)(C)(vi), 103(a), (b)(1); 141. See Chapter 11D, supra.

[26]   I.R.C. § 57(a)(5)(A). See I.R.C. § 265(a)(1) and (2).

[27]   I.R.C. § 1202(a)(1), (3). The remainder of the net capital gain which is included in gross income may qualify for preferential regular tax treatment under I.R.C. § 1(h). See I.R.C. § 1(h)(1)(E), (4), (7).

[28]   I.R.C. § 57(a)(7). As a result, 53.5 (50 plus 3.5), or 30.25 (25 plus 5.25), percent of such net capital gain is included in AMTI.

[29]   I.R.C. § 1202(a)(4).

[30]   I.R.C. § 55(b)(1)(B).

[31]   I.R.C. § 55(d)(1), (4)(i).

$1 million for married persons filing jointly and surviving spouses, $500,000 for all other individuals, and $75,000 for estates and trusts.[32] The phase-out is 25 percent of the amount by which AMTI exceeds those levels.[33]

*Computation.* The tax on AMTI less any applicable exemption is generally taxed at 26 percent on amounts up to $175,000 and at 28 percent on amounts in excess of $175,000 to arrive at a tentative minimum tax.[34] If, however, there is net capital gain (which includes qualified dividends) included in AMTI and the net capital gain is taxed at less than the AMTI 26 percent or 28 percent rates under the regular tax,[35] it is taxed at its regular tax rates (zero to 25 percent) in computing AMTI tax liability.[36] Thus, the AMT substantially accommodates the Code's preferred tax rates for capital gains.

The dollar amounts used in calculating the 28 percent threshold on individuals, the AMT exemption amounts, and the AMT exemption phaseout amounts are all adjusted for inflation.[37]

If the amount of tentative minimum tax so computed exceeds the "regular tax,"[38] the excess is the alternative minimum tax, and the taxpayer must pay both the regular tax and the alternative minimum tax for the year.[39] Another way of looking at this is that, in general, the *greater of* either the taxpayer's regular tax liability or total alternative minimum tax liability (not reduced by the regular tax) is the tax liability for the year.

*Tax Credits.* Generally, in computing one's tax liability, taxes are reduced by credits in determining actual tax to be paid.[40] The alternative minimum tax may be reduced by the Section 59(a) alternative minimum foreign tax credit[41] and all the refundable tax credits.[42] In addition, Section 26(a) provides that the aggregate of a taxpayer's nonrefundable personal credits are allowed to the extent of the sum of a taxpayer's

---

[32]  I.R.C. § 55(d)(2), (4)(ii).

[33]  Id. Thus, the exemption is fully phased-out as AMTI reaches the following levels: $1,437,600 for marrieds filing jointly, $781,200 for unmarried persons who are not surviving spouses, $718,800 for marrieds filing separately, and $165,000 for trusts and estates. For example, the $1,437,600 amount is computed by adding the phase-out amount of $1 million and $437,600 (4 times the $109,400 exemption).

[34]  I.R.C. § 55(b)(1)(A)(i) and (ii). In the case of a married individual filing a separate return, the 28 percent rate is phased in when the excess amount exceeds $87,500. I.R.C. § 55(b)(1)(A)(iii).

[35]  See I.R.C. § 1(h) and Chapter 21B, supra.

[36]  I.R.C. § 55(b)(3).

[37]  The 28 percent threshold is adjusted for inflation for years after 2012. I.R.C. § 55(d)(3). The AMT exemption amounts and the phaseout amounts are adjusted for inflation for years after 2018. I.R.C. § 55(d)(4)(B).

[38]  I.R.C. § 55(c).

[39]  I.R.C. § 55(a).

[40]  See Chapter 27B, supra.

[41]  The I.R.C. § 59(a) alternative minimum foreign tax credit is essentially the § 27 foreign tax credit adjusted to reflect AMTI rather than regular taxable income.

[42]  See Chapter 27B, supra.

regular tax liability, reduced by the foreign tax credit, and AMT liability. Thus, nonrefundable personal tax credits, such as the Section 23 credit for Adoption Expenses[43] and the Section 25A American Opportunity and Lifetime Learning credits,[44] may reduce the amount of AMT owed by an individual.

*Credit for AMT Liability.* Section 53 provides that some of the AMT liability is allowed as a credit against regular tax liability in subsequent years[45] in which one is not subject to the AMT. To the extent of the credit, this can be analogized to either the prepayment of regular tax liability or the postponement of tax preferences. However, only the part of an individual's AMT liability involving *deferral* adjustments and preferences (e.g., depreciation) but not any *exclusion* adjustments and preferences (e.g., tax exempt interest) qualifies for the credit.[46] The credit is a nonrefundable credit that is computed only after taking into account all other nonrefundable credits.[47] It is allowed in any year only to the extent that regular tax liability less other nonrefundable credits for that year exceed that year's tentative minimum tax.[48] The carryover is for an unlimited period.[49]

## PROBLEM

1.     Taxpayer is a single, calendar year taxpayer in 2018. Assume that the following occurred in 2018. Other than the income and deductions below, Taxpayer has $200,000 of gross income and $80,000 of § 162 business deductions, which are deductible under § 62. In January of 1998, she purchased an apartment house (which she depreciates during the year) with inherited funds at a cost of $650,000, $100,000 of which is for the land. She gives some investment land, worth $30,000 that was purchased several years ago for $10,000, to her alma mater. She receives $50,000 of interest on a "qualified bond" under § 141(e)(1)(B) which is a private activity bond (issued in 2015), but is exempt from regular income tax under § 103(a). The bonds were left to her as a bequest from a grandparent. She pays state and local income and property taxes of $20,000 on her personal use property. She has no business or investment indebtedness. Compute taxpayer's tax liability for the year disregarding inflation adjustments and assuming she pays regular tax at a flat 20 percent rate.

---

[43]   I.R.C. § 23. See Chapter 27B2, supra.

[44]   I.R.C. § 25A. See Chapter 11C, supra.

[45]   I.R.C. § 53(a).

[46]   I.R.C. § 53(d)(1)(B). Thus, to the extent that the AMT is attributable to I.R.C. § 56(b)(1) adjustments as well as to § 57(a)(1), (5) and (7) tax preferences, no credit is allowed. See I.R.C. § 53(d)(1)(B)(ii).

[47]   I.R.C. § 53(c)(1).

[48]   I.R.C. § 53(c). See I.R.C. §§ 53(d)(2) and 55(b).

[49]   I.R.C. § 53(b).

# PART 9

# FEDERAL TAX PROCEDURE, PROFESSIONAL RESPONSIBILITY, AND TAX POLICY

# CHAPTER 28

# FEDERAL TAX PROCEDURE

## A. OVERVIEW OF FEDERAL TAX PROCEDURE

### 1. INTRODUCTION

No attempt is made in this book to present a full analysis of the procedures involved in the determination and enforcement of federal income tax liability.[1] Many procedural principles are introduced in earlier chapters where the emphasis, however, is on substantive tax law. Here the effort is to present procedural fundamentals in one place for more systematic consideration. Three broad questions to consider are: (1) When and how can the government exact additional tax that should have been paid (i.e., successfully assert a deficiency) and what means are available to the taxpayer to resist deficiency assertions? (2) Whether the collection of any tax from the taxpayer was done properly? (3) When and how can the taxpayer recover tax that was improperly paid (i.e., successfully assert a right to a refund)? Answers to these questions involve all three branches of government. Congress provides the statutory framework. The administration of the law is assigned primarily to the Internal Revenue Service, a branch of the Treasury Department; but the Justice Department enters the picture in some civil and criminal cases. The courts perform their usual role of deciding controversies.

In recent years, Congress has enacted several pieces of legislation designed specifically to safeguard taxpayers who are involved in the administrative (audit), litigation, or collection process with the Internal Revenue Service.[2] The legislation is an effort to make the Service place "greater emphasis on serving the public and meeting the needs of taxpayers."[3] The legislation is found in three Taxpayer Bills of Rights.[4]

---

[1] This note is intended to be only a general description of civil procedures involved in federal income tax cases. The following books deal in a more comprehensive fashion with these matters: Kafka & Cavanaugh, Litigation of Federal Civil Tax Controversies (Warren, Gorham & Lamont); Lederman & Mazza, Tax Controversies: Practice and Procedure (Lexis Nexis); Johnson, Borison & Ullman, Civil Tax Procedure (Lexis Nexis); Saltzman, IRS Practice and Procedure (Warren, Gorham & Lamont); Bittker and Lokken, Federal Taxation of Income, Estates and Gifts vol. 4 Part 16 (Warren, Gorham & Lamont); David, Dealing with the IRS: Law, Forms & Practice (A.L.I. and A.B.A.).

[2] See Chapter 28A3, 4, and 5, infra.

[3] S. Rep. No. 105–174, 105th Cong., 2nd Sess. 9 (1998).

[4] (1) The Taxpayer Bill of Rights Act of 1988, Pub. Law No. 100–647, 100th Cong., 2d Sess. §§ 6226–6247 (1988). See Adler, "TAMRA: Changes in the Income Taxation of Individuals," 13 Rev. Tax of Individuals 291–300 (1989); Saubert and O'Neil, "The New Taxpayer Bill of Rights," 67 Taxes 211 (1989); Kafka, "Taxpayer Bill of Rights Expands Safeguards and Civil Remedies," 70 J.Tax'n. 4 (1989); (2) Taxpayer Bill of Rights Act of 1996, Pub. Law No. 104–168, 104th Cong., 2nd Sess. §§ 101–1314 (1996). See Kafka, "Taxpayer Bill of Rights 2 Offers Added Protection," 25 Tax'n for Law. 132 (1996); (3) Taxpayer Bill of Rights Act of 1998, Pub. Law No. 105–206, 105th Cong., 2nd Sess. §§ 1001–4022 (1998).

Suffice it to say that a laundry-list of all the pro-taxpayer changes would expand this book beyond its fundamental scope, although many of the changes are specifically discussed below.[5]

## 2. THE SELF-ASSESSMENT SYSTEM

Tax liability is determined initially by the taxpayer. Under our system of self-assessment, a potentially taxable individual is required to file an income tax return annually[1] and, upon filing, to pay any amount of tax shown on the return to be due.[2] Taxes so reported are automatically assessed.[3] Various informational returns must also be filed to assist both the taxpayer and the government in determining tax liability (for example a Form W-2 for reporting wages, dividends and interest income).[4] Much of the current filing of both computational and informational returns is done electronically in a paperless fashion.[5] To promote electronic filing, informational returns that are filed electronically need not be filed until one month later than those filed in paper form.[6]

Billions of dollars pour into the Treasury by way of the quasi-voluntary method of personal tax determination and payment by the taxpayer. Yet, the burden placed on the taxpayer is very great. Even just a little experience with the intricacies of substantive tax law should suggest that, quite apart from negligence or any intentional wrongdoing, many mistakes will be made by the taxpayer.

Human error may be at its worst with regard to the simple arithmetic required in the preparation of a return, although in the computer age, computer programs assist in alleviating such errors. The

---

See also, I.R.C. § 7803(a)(3), enacted in the "Protecting Americans from Tax Hikes Act of 2015," requiring the Commissioner to ensure that I.R.S. employees are familiar with, and act in accordance with, the Taxpayer Bills of Rights.

[5] See, e.g., the Text discussing I.R.C. §§ 7491 (Burden of Proof) and 7430 (Recovery of Taxpayer Costs and Attorneys' Fees) at Chapter 28A4, infra.

[1] I.R.C. §§ 6012(a), 6072(a); and see Johnson, "An Inquiry Into the Assessment Process," 35 Tax L.Rev. 285 (1980). Interestingly, the well-known "Form 1040" came into existence with the inception of the modern income tax in 1913.

Civil or criminal penalties, or both, may result from a taxpayer's failure to file any required return, including, if applicable, the familiar Form 1040. See I.R.C. §§ 6651, 7203 and Chapter 28B1, infra.

[2] I.R.C. §§ 6151(a), 6311. See Reg. § 301.6311–1(a)(1). Similar rules apply to taxpayers other than individuals, such as corporations, trusts and estates, and to other taxes, such as estate, gift, and generation-skipping transfer taxes.

Of course large amounts of tax are collected by way of withholding by taxpayers' employers and by quarterly advance payments by taxpayers pursuant to their declarations of estimated tax, as noted at page 958, supra.

[3] I.R.C. § 6203; Reg. § 301.6203–1.

[4] See I.R.C. §§ 6031–6053.

[5] For 2017, the Service processed more than 245.4 million federal tax returns and supplemental documents, of which 70.5 percent were filed electronically. I.R.S. 2017 Data Book. Electronically filed returns are signed by use of a self-selected PIN. See I.R.C. § 6061(b).

[6] Compare I.R.C. § 6071(b) (electronic informational returns are due on March 31) with § 6071(a), Reg. § 31.6071(a)–1(a)(3) (paper informational returns are due on February 28).

statute permits an arithmetic computational error to be corrected summarily; if upon examination of a return it is found that tax liability is understated because of a mathematical error appearing on the return, the amount of the tax with the error corrected can be forthwith assessed and the taxpayer billed for the underpayment.[7] Sometimes, on the other hand, a taxpayer is agreeably surprised to receive an automatic refund when the Service discovers that the taxpayer has made an arithmetical error in the government's favor. If either the government or the taxpayer subsequently asserts that other types of errors appear on the return both administrative and judicial procedures, later discussed, are available to test the validity of such assertions and to enforce the appropriate adjustments.

## 3. ADMINISTRATIVE PROCEDURES

Internal Revenue Code: See Sections 6211(a); 6212(a), (d); 6213(a), (d); 6501(c)(4); 6503(a)(1); 7121; 7122.

---

It taxes credulity to think that a system of voluntary tax payment would work if the government invariably accepted the taxpayer's own appraisal of liability, even after correcting arithmetical errors. This is not the plan. The initial steps in tax payment and collection should be thought of in terms of the following dialogue between the taxpayer and the government:

> Taxpayer (the return): "This is what I propose to pay, and why. Check enclosed."

> Government (no actual response, but this unstated message): "We've checked your arithmetic, which is O.K. and, since we're pretty busy, we'll call it square."

But at a later date there may be additional *alternative* responses by the government, if the taxpayer's return is selected for audit. How will it be so selected? We cannot be certain. It is the government's policy, perhaps analogous to that behind the unmarked patrol car, to keep taxpayers somewhat in the dark in this respect.[1] The *in terrorem* effect is doubtless a boost to taxpayer integrity. Generally, it is more profitable for the government to audit returns reporting large amounts of income, because errors found there may produce much larger amounts of revenue. However, sufficient numbers of very small returns are subjected to

---

[7] I.R.C. § 6213(b)(1). Reg. § 301.6213–1(b)(1). The same instant assessment authority exists with respect to an underpayment arising out of an overstatement of income tax withheld or estimated income tax paid. I.R.C. § 6201(a)(3).

[1] The Service is required to publish in its booklet "Your Rights as a Taxpayer" the criteria and procedures it utilizes for selecting taxpayers for examination, but it is not required to publish any information that would be detrimental to its law enforcement. Pub. Law No. 105–206, 105th Cong. 2d Sess. § 3503(a) (1998).

The Service published statistical data on its 2017 auditing activity. I.R.S. 2017 Data Book. Roughly .5 percent of all returns filed in 2016 were audited in 2017.

scrutiny so that each taxpayer must wonder whether he or she is next.[2] Computers play a central role in the selections of returns for audit, especially by turning up discrepancies between the amount of wages, dividends or interest reported by the taxpayer and the amount informationally reported by the payor as having been paid to the taxpayer.

Silence is golden, after the filing of a return. If there is any response, it will be to identify some disagreement with the taxpayer's assertions (although it is possible the reply will indicate the taxpayer has overpaid tax).

Tax audits (called "examinations") take several forms. Some are handled entirely by correspondence between the taxpayer and the Service. These are known as "correspondence audits."[3] The other two types of audits are the ones more dreaded by taxpayers: first, the so-called "office examination," conducted in the IRS office (with the taxpayer bringing the taxpayer's records to the office),[4] and second, the much-feared "field examination," in which a Revenue Agent actually visits the taxpayer's home or place of business to conduct the audit.[5]

Taxpayers do not generally enjoy being called onto the carpet any more than schoolkids enjoy a command appearance in the principal's office. But they have little choice. Congress has armed tax officials with extensive authority to inquire into matters affecting tax liability and, with judicial assistance, to compel the cooperation of taxpayers and others who may have relevant information.[6] However, in the three Taxpayer Bills of Rights,[7] Congress has also enacted legislation to protect taxpayers against abuse of the Service's power in the audit process.[8]

---

[2]  Audits can be triggered by informants seeking bounty or revenge. Section 7623 authorizes the Service to pay a reward to an informant for tax collected as a result of the informant's "tip." Returns may also be selected for audit by "infection"—for example, an audit of a corporation may lead to an audit of its principal shareholders and officers. In general, however, the audit selection process is cloaked in secrecy. It is based largely on the DIF (discriminant index function) system, which grows out of a computerized classification system which examines the norms of comparable taxpayers. DIF formulas are secret and cannot be obtained under the Freedom of Information Act. I.R.C. § 6103(b)(2). See Guttman, "Taxpayer Compliance Measurement Program: Is It Necessary?" 67 Tax Notes 1282 (1995).

[3]  Reg. § 601.105(b)(2).

[4]  Reg. § 601.105(b)(2)(ii).

[5]  Reg. § 601.105(b)(3).

[6]  See generally, I.R.C. §§ 7602–7604; and see Caplin, "How to Handle a Federal Income Tax Audit," 28 Wash. & Lee L.Rev. 331 (1971); Pearson and Schmidt, "Successful Preparation and Negotiation May Reduce the Time and Breadth of an I.R.S. Audit" 40 Tax'n Accts. 234 (1988). Under a Supreme Court opinion, the business records even of an individual may be seized subject to a search warrant without offending the individual's privilege against self-incrimination. Andresen v. Maryland, 427 U.S. 463, 96 S.Ct. 2737 (1976).

[7]  See note 4 at page 967, supra.

[8]  See, e.g., I.R.C. §§ 7217 (prohibition on executive branch influence on taxpayer audits); 7433 (civil damages for unauthorized collection actions); 7521(b) (explanation of the audit process to taxpayers); 7602(e) (limitations on financial status audits).

*Civil Deficiency Controversies.* One possible consequence of an audit is a "no change" letter[9] indicating that, after consideration, no adjustments are required. The alternative (disregarding a possible conclusion that there has been an overpayment) is a statement or letter indicating required adjustments and the amount of the deficiency,[10] the additional tax to be paid.[11] The taxpayer may very well disagree with the adjustments proposed by the examining agent. If so, the Service may send the taxpayer a preliminary or "30-day letter."[12] The 30-day letter is a form letter which states the proposed adjustments and is accompanied by a copy of the examining agent's report explaining the bases for these proposals. The preliminary 30-day letter also informs the taxpayer that within a stated period, usually 30 days, the taxpayer may request an administrative review of issues not settled with the examining agent.[13] Although taxpayers are not required to pursue administrative appeals as a precondition to litigation, doing so is advisable for several reasons. First, the vast majority of all tax controversies are settled out of court, as the mission of the Appeals Office is to settle controversies without litigation in a manner that is fair both to the government and to the taxpayer.[14] In addition, failure to pursue administrative appeals will preclude an award of reasonable costs and attorneys' fees to a taxpayer who ultimately prevails in litigation.[15] Finally, unreasonable failure by the taxpayer to pursue available administrative remedies is a factor considered by the Tax Court in imposing a penalty for frivolous, groundless, or dilatory proceedings.[16]

If a taxpayer pursues the administrative procedures available in a deficiency situation, the negotiations may lead to naught. If so, the government will formally issue a notice of deficiency.[17] The taxpayer has a right to a notice of deficiency, whereas the 30-day letter is not mandatory and need not be sent. Moreover, the required terms of this notice normally give the taxpayer 90 days within which to file a petition in the Tax Court for a "redetermination" of the asserted deficiency;[18]

---

[9]    Reg. § 601.105(d). But see Rev. Proc. 2005–32, 2005–1 C.B. 1206.

[10]    I.R.C. § 6211(a).

[11]    Reg. § 601.105(d).

[12]    Id. The terms of this letter are not prescribed by statute; indeed, it may emerge as a 15-day letter. It is not to be confused with the statutory notice of deficiency, which was commonly referred to in the past as a "90-day letter." See Text infra at note 17.

[13]    The taxpayer does not always have the right to an Appeals Office conference. See Reg. § 601.106(b). This is explained in the 30-day letter.

[14]    I.R.M. § 1.1.7

[15]    I.R.C. § 7430(b)(1). See the Text discussing Recovery of Taxpayer Costs and Attorneys Fees at Chapter 28A4, infra.

[16]    I.R.C. § 6673(a)(1)(C). Conceivably, then, any forbearance or refusal to run any stage of the gauntlet may come back later to haunt the taxpayer in Tax Court with the imposition of an I.R.C. § 6673 penalty.

[17]    I.R.C. § 6212(a).

[18]    I.R.C. § 6213(a). The 90-day period is extended to 150 days "if the notice is addressed to a person outside the United States." Id. Cf. Smith v. Commissioner, 140 T.C. 48 (2013) (allowing the 150-day period when the taxpayer was physically outside the United States, even though

assessment and collection continue to be barred for that period and, if the taxpayer files a petition, until the decision of the Tax Court becomes final.[19] The notice of deficiency must indicate the last day for filing under the 90-day period, and any Tax Court petition filed by such date is timely filed.[20] Limitation periods that otherwise run against the assessment or collection of tax are suspended for the 90-day period and, if a Tax Court petition is filed, for the litigation period and, in either event, for an additional 60 days after that period.[21]

In the light of all this, efforts to get the taxpayer to agree to the asserted deficiency during the administrative deficiency steps described above are presented in terms of a request that the taxpayer execute Form 870, which is an authorized *waiver* of one's statutory right to receive a notice of deficiency prior to assessment.[22] Form 870 by means of which a taxpayer agrees to the assessment of tax without receipt of a statutory deficiency notice, expressly acknowledges that it is not a closing agreement which fixes tax liability under Section 7121.[23]

The government may first determine there is a deficiency close to the time when assessment would be barred by a statute of limitations.[24] As indicated above, the government's position *could* then be protected by the issuance of a notice of deficiency tolling the statute, but this would tend to foreclose customary negotiations toward an agreed settlement. In such circumstances the taxpayer will be asked to execute a Form 872, which is an authorized extension of the limitation period.[25] As a practical matter a request to sign this extension presents the taxpayer with a Hobson's choice. Refusal to sign will simply bring on the statutory deficiency notice.[26]

---

the notice was sent to a domestic address); Looper v. Commissioner, 73 T.C. 690 (1980) (noting that the 150-day period applies when the notice is sent to a foreign address)."

[19] I.R.C. § 6213(a). The Tax Court generally has jurisdiction to redetermine the correct amount of the deficiency, even if the amount so redetermined is greater than the amount of the original deficiency. I.R.C. § 6214. Such jurisdiction exists as to any addition to the tax, including additions for failure to pay the tax. Sen. Rep. No. 313, 99th Cong., 2d Sess. 200 (1986).

[20] I.R.C. § 6213(a) last sentence. This rule also applies to the 150-day period. Id.

[21] I.R.C. § 6503(a)(1).

[22] I.R.C. § 6213(d). Waiver under Form 870 of one's right to receive a 90-day letter prior to assessment does not waives one's subsequent right to a claim or suit for refund. See the Instructions for Form 870. Closely akin to a Form 870 is Form 870AD. See Reg. § 601.106(d)(2). However, Form 870AD has language of finality which is observed by the government and the courts. See Kretchmar v. United States, 9 Cl.Ct. 191 (1985). The binding effect on the taxpayer of such language clearly suggests that one who wishes only to relinquish the right to go to the Tax Court, and to maintain the right to litigate in the District Court or the Court of Federal Claims should amend any proffered Form 870AD expressly to preserve the right to file a claim and suit for refund. See Saltzman, I.R.S. Practice and Procedure ¶ 9.08 (Warren, Gorham & Lamont).

[23] See Text at notes 47–57, infra.

[24] See Chapter 28B1, infra.

[25] I.R.C. § 6501(c)(4).

[26] A taxpayer's failure to extend the limitation period will not preclude the recovery of reasonable costs and attorneys fees. Reg. § 301.7430–1(b)(4). See the Text discussing Recovery of Taxpayer Costs and Attorneys' Fees at Chapter 28A4, infra.

Suppose now a taxpayer has received the statutory notice of deficiency. While this notice is one of the main "tickets" to Tax Court,[27] the taxpayer is not restricted to this judicial forum. The taxpayer may forgo the timely filing of a Tax Court petition and instead pay the deficiency and file a claim for refund, in which case the taxpayer will seek a judicial remedy in either the District Court or the Court of Federal Claims. There are a number of factors a taxpayer might consider in choosing a particular judicial forum. For example, jury trials are not available in Tax Court and the Court of Federal Claims, and payment of the deficiency is not a prerequisite to Tax Court.[28]

Upon the mutual consent of the Service and the taxpayer, a notice of deficiency may be rescinded.[29] When rescinded, the notice is treated as if it never existed,[30] and limitations regarding credits, refunds, and assessments relating to the rescinded notice are void. The parties are returned to their rights and obligations existing prior to issuance of the withdrawn notice.[31] Of course the Service may subsequently issue a notice of deficiency in an amount greater or less than the amount stated in the rescinded notice.[32]

*Controversies Involving Fraudulent Claims.* The plot thickens if the grounds for the government's claim against a taxpayer are based on the taxpayer's fraudulent activities. The Service may determine that such activities are subject to a civil fraud penalty.[33] Alternatively, the Service may pursue criminal charges. In criminal circumstances, a Special Agent represents the government in an interview with the taxpayer that is usually preceded by *Miranda*[34]-type warnings[35] and that is sought for the purpose of obtaining an initial statement from the taxpayer. If, when the Special Agent completes an investigation, the agent recommends prosecution, a detailed Special Agent's report is required. The taxpayer then receives a "district criminal investigation conference,"[36] although no right to the conference exists. If no agreement is then reached, the Special Agent's report is forwarded to the Regional Conference level and another conference is afforded. If no accord is reached at that level and if

---

[27] Besides the notice of deficiency, the other "tickets" to Tax Court are (1) the Notice of Determination Concerning Collection Action(s) Under Section 6320 and/or 6330, and (2) the Notice of Determination Concerning Relief from Joint and Several Liability Under I.R.C. Section 6015. See Chapter 28A5, infra and Chapter 28B2, infra.

[28] Other factors a taxpayer might consider in choosing a judicial forum are: (1) existence of favorable precedent; (2) availability of informal small case procedures in Tax Court; (3) breadth of the court's jurisdiction; (4) accruing of interest; (5) costs of litigation; (6) speed of case disposition; and (7) publicity.

[29] I.R.C. § 6212(d).

[30] Id.

[31] H. Rep. No. 426, 99th Cong., 1st Sess. 843 (1985).

[32] Id.

[33] I.R.C. § 6663.

[34] Miranda v. Arizona, 384 U.S. 436, 86 S.Ct. 1602 (1966).

[35] See I.R.M. § 9.4.5.11.3. Duty to Inform Individual of Constitutional Rights.

[36] See Reg. § 601.107(b)(2).

it is determined by the Service that criminal activity has occurred and there is a reasonable probability of conviction, the Special Agent's report and a recommendation for criminal prosecution is forwarded to the Department of Justice, Tax Division, Criminal Section. If they recommend prosecution, the case is sent to the U.S. attorney's office. During the various administrative conferences at the various levels, several special procedural protections[37] are provided to the taxpayer. One such protection is the Fifth Amendment privilege against self-incrimination as to an individual's oral testimony and to documentary communications.[38]

*Refund Controversies.* Before judicial procedures are discussed, a look should be taken at administrative procedures where the shoe is on the other foot; the taxpayer asserts a right to a refund. One way in which this possibility arises is for the taxpayer to make a mistake on the return in the government's favor and discover the mistake later, maybe talking to you at a cocktail party. The taxpayer's next question will be: What can I do about it? In general what one can do, if the action is timely, is to file a refund claim; and if the claim is not allowed administratively, one can then sue for a refund.[39]

A refund suit may also arise in another way. The taxpayer might not timely file a petition in the United States Tax Court within the 90-day period of the notice of deficiency. In that situation, the taxpayer has not lost his or her "day in court." Instead, what the taxpayer can do is pay the tax deficiency and then seek a refund in District Court or the Court of Federal Claims.

In either type of refund action, the procedure starts with a refund claim made by an individual on Form 1040X or on an amended Form 1040.[40] When filed, the form commences administrative procedures, including optional review procedures, which parallel those available in the case of deficiency controversies.[41] After rejection (or after waiting a stated period of time),[42] the taxpayer may be able to give up on administrative relief and seek judicial intervention by way of a refund suit.

The requirement of a refund claim prior to suit is a facet of the doctrine of exhaustion of administrative remedies. If the Service is going

---

[37]   See, e.g., I.R.C. §§ 6020, 7602, 7608(b), 7609.

[38]   Documentary communications include the personal and business records of an individual. Bellis v. United States, 417 U.S. 85, 94 S.Ct. 2179 (1974). The privilege does not apply to corporate or partnership records. Id.

[39]   See I.R.C. §§ 6511, 7422. See also Chapter 28C, infra.

[40]   See Reg. §§ 601.105(e); 301.6402–3. On the content of refund claims, see Adams, "The Imperfect Claim for Refund," 22 The Tax Lawyer 309 (1969); Note, "What Should a Refund Claim Contain to Be Effective," 4 Taxation for Accountants 18 (1969). Various aspects of refund claims are discussed in Peaden, Muraskin, and Lawton, "Federal Taxation," 47 Mercer L. Rev. 879 (1996).

[41]   Reg. § 601.105(e)(2).

[42]   See Chapter 28C, infra.

to be principally responsible for administering the tax laws, it should be given a chance to sort out difficulties before the courts are cluttered up with more controversies. This is "old hat" to any casual student of administrative law; still in the tax refund setting (and probably others, too) a question can arise whether the claim filed properly supports the suit subsequently brought.[43] The hornbook-type message here is that the statutory prerequisite to suit is satisfied only if the claim filed gives notice of the nature of the suit which is subsequently brought.[44]

A refund claim should in a sense be viewed as if it were a pleading. Failure to assert grounds on which the taxpayer may later wish to rely in a suit may by procedural error squander a valuable right.[45] The same precaution must be exercised where a refund claim once filed is sought to be amended. If the amendment in effect involves the assertion of a new ground for recovery, a new claim must be filed rather than a mere amendment to the original claim.[46]

*Administrative Finality.* The Code expressly authorizes administrative officials to enter into binding agreements with taxpayers with regard to their liability for or payment of taxes. The first type of such agreements, which are called "closing agreements," relate to the income tax liability of a taxpayer.[47] Closing agreements take two forms. They may fix the entire tax liability of a taxpayer for a particular taxable year[48] or they may relate only to one or two issues, such as the fair market value of property received as compensation for services.[49] Closing

---

[43] Compare the tax deficiency setting in which a taxpayer's unreasonable failure to pursue available administrative remedies will preclude an award of reasonable costs and attorneys' fees (see Chapter 28A4, infra) and may be considered by the Tax Court in its determination whether to impose the discretionary I.R.C. § 6673 penalty for dilatory, groundless or frivolous proceedings (see note 16, supra).

[44] United States v. Felt and Tarrant Mfg. Co., 283 U.S. 269, 51 S.Ct. 376 (1931); see also Susskind v. United States, 76–1 U.S.T.C. ¶ 9200 (E.D.N.Y.1976), holding "taxpayers may not change or raise new fact issues or shift to a new legal theory in the District Court." Id. at 83,379.

[45] See Ford v. United States, 402 F.2d 791 (6th Cir.1968), and cases cited therein.

[46] The new claim must be filed within the period set by the statute of limitations. See United States v. Andrews, 302 U.S. 517, 58 S.Ct. 315 (1938), I.R.C. § 6511(a), and Chapter 28C, infra.

[47] I.R.C. § 7121.

[48] Such agreements are executed on Form 866, entitled "Agreement as to Final Determination of Tax Liability."

[49] Such agreements are executed on Form 906, entitled "Closing Agreement on Final Determination Covering Specific Matters."

This latter type of agreement may be useful in situations in which statutes of limitation will afford the taxpayer an all-time assurance on a particular point. For example, whether property was received as compensation and the value of such property might determine the taxpayer's basis for the property which, upon its sale many years later, would determine the taxpayer's gain or loss. Cf. United States v. Frazell, 335 F.2d 487 (5th Cir.1964).

agreements are "final and conclusive"[50] and they must conform to strict statutory and administrative requirements.[51]

Closely akin to the government's closing agreement authority is its authority to compromise tax liability, interest and penalties.[52] The Treasury views its authority to compromise as limited to situations where there is (1) doubt as to liability, (2) doubt as to collectibility, or (3) an effort to promote effective tax administration.[53] As in the case of a closing agreement, a valid compromise must conform to strict statutory and administrative requirements and guidelines.[54]

Over the years there has been substantial question whether an agreement that did not comply with the rules for the execution of a closing or compromise agreement was binding on either the taxpayer or the government.[55] While there is authority for strict compliance with such rules,[56] there are also cases in which flawed agreements have been accorded finality on estoppel principles.[57]

## 4.  JUDICIAL PROCEDURES

Internal Revenue Code: See Sections 6213(a); 6512(a), (b); 7421(a); 7422(a), (e); 7430; 7463(a); 7482(a); 7491.

———————

*Deficiency Cases.* Once a notice of deficiency has been sent and if the taxpayer files a petition within the period, the Tax Court has jurisdiction over the deficiency.[1] The principal office of the Tax Court is in Washington, D.C., although the court hears cases in numerous designated offices around the country. Tax Court cases are always tried without a jury. Tax Court cases take a variety of forms. Generally, one of the 19 regular judges hears a case and after review by the Chief Judge, it is published. Some cases involving primarily factual determinations, known as Memorandum Decisions, are not officially published.[2] Some

---

[50]  I.R.C. § 7121(b). They may be upset upon a showing of fraud or malfeasance or of misrepresentation of a material fact but, otherwise, must be accorded full effect by taxpayers, the administrators, and the judiciary. I.R.C. § 7121(b)(1) and (2).

[51]  Reg. § 301.7121–1(d). See Rev. Proc. 68–16, 1968–1 C.B. 770; Rev. Proc. 94–67, 1994–2 C.B. 800.

[52]  I.R.C. § 7122.

[53]  Reg. § 301.7122–1(b).

[54]  See I.R.C. § 7122(b)–(d), Reg. § 301.7122–1(b)–(g), Form 656 ("Offers in Compromise"), and I.R.M. 8.13.2.

[55]  See Emmanuel, "The Effect of Waivers in Federal Income Tax Cases," 3 U. Fla. L. Rev. 176, 179 (1950). Congressional and administrative steps such as extensive sub-delegation, which tend to facilitate the execution of de jure closing or compromising agreements, may work toward a reduction of such controversies.

[56]  E.g., Botany Worsted Mills v. United States, 278 U.S. 282, 49 S.Ct. 129 (1929).

[57]  E.g., Backus v. United States, 59 F.2d 242 (Ct.Cl.1932), cert. denied 288 U.S. 610, 53 S.Ct. 402 (1933).

[1]  I.R.C. § 6213(a).

[2]  They are published by CCH and RIA, but they are not published as official Tax Court decisions.

officially reported decisions are, upon determination of the Chief Judge prior to publication, reviewed by the entire court. In such circumstances, the Court can reject the decision of the judge who initially heard the case.[3]

In cases in which the deficiency amount does not exceed $50,000, at the option of the taxpayer with the concurrence of the Tax Court,[4] a special small tax case procedure may be employed.[5] Most of these cases are handled by special trial judges appointed by the Chief Judge.[6] Such cases have greater informality and flexibility than regular Tax Court cases.[7] The decisions in such cases are not published or subject to appeal, and they do not serve as precedents.[8]

*Refund Suits.* A taxpayer who asserts an overpayment of tax after filing a refund claim and upon its denial or prolonged administrative inaction, may file suit in the United States District Court for a refund. A District Court refund suit may also arise where a tax deficiency is asserted and the taxpayer pays the deficiency and files a refund claim and eventually a refund suit.[9] This is normally done either to avoid interest payments on a deficiency or to get a jury trial because factual issues in a District Court are determined by a jury when the taxpayer demands a jury trial.

The United States Court of Federal Claims is an alternative forum for a refund suit. The court is composed of 16 judges who are authorized to sit nationwide.[10] It is similar to the District Court in that it is a forum for refund suits; however, no jury trial is available in the Court of Federal Claims.[11] This court resembles the Tax Court in its organization and procedure.

For a time, a taxpayer preferring to litigate in the District Court or Court of Federal Claims, rather than the Tax Court, but also wishing not

---

[3]   Constitutional challenge to this procedure has been rejected. Estate of Varian v. Commissioner, 396 F.2d 753 (9th Cir.1968).

[4]   The Tax Court tends to support the taxpayer's desire to use the small case procedure over objections by the Commissioner. See Dressler v. Commissioner, 56 T.C. 210 (1971). But, in some situations, the court might properly remove a case from the small tax procedure so that it can be consolidated with a regular case involving common facts or a common issue of law. H.Rep. No. 1800, 95th Cong., 2d Sess. 1978, 1978–3 C.B. 611. Similarly, removal may be appropriate where a regular decision could provide a precedent for the disposition of a substantial number of other cases. Ibid.

[5]   I.R.C. § 7463(a). See "Election of Small Tax Case, Procedure and Preparation" (Tax Court Nov., 1990). This procedure is also available to a taxpayer seeking relief under the I.R.C. § 6015 "innocent spouse" relief rule if the deficiency does not exceed $50,000. I.R.C. § 7463(f)(1). See Chapter 28B2, infra.

[6]   I.R.C. § 7443A.

[7]   See Evans, "Tax Court's Small Case Procedure May Be Preferable for its Informality and Low Cost," 14 Tax'n for Law. 104 (1985); Davidson, "Litigation in the Small Tax Case Division of the United States Tax Court—The Taxpayer's Dream?" 41 Geo. Wash. L. Rev. 538 (1973).

[8]   I.R.C. § 7463(b).

[9]   I.R.C. § 7422(a).

[10]   28 U.S.C.A. § 171(a).

[11]   28 U.S.C.A. § 174(a).

to pay the entire asserted deficiency prior to litigation, undertook to pay a part of the deficiency and then to file a refund claim and sue for that part of the asserted deficiency. A favorable decision would of course in effect be an adjudication that there was no deficiency. The Commissioner challenged this strategy, and in Flora v. United States[12] the Supreme Court, in agreement with the Commissioner, stated the "full payment" rule,[13] which requires that the entire amount of an asserted deficiency be paid before a refund suit may be maintained.[14] If the taxpayer chooses to pay less than the deficiency asserted, the taxpayer's only remedy is a deficiency proceeding in the Tax Court.

*The Interrelationship of Deficiency Cases and Refund Suits.* A suit for refund cannot be filed in the Tax Court whose jurisdiction is in general limited to the redetermination of deficiencies in taxes.[15] However, if the Tax Court's jurisdiction is properly invoked in response to a deficiency notice the Court can, in addition to finding that there is no deficiency, determine there has been an overpayment to be refunded to the taxpayer.[16] On the other hand, neither the District Court nor the Court of Federal Claims is given jurisdiction to redetermine deficiencies; tax litigation commenced in those courts rests on the taxpayer's suit for a refund. But of course a refund suit also is a comprehensive determination of income tax liability for the year in question and, where a counter claim is possible,[17] may result in a deficiency determination.

*Burden of Proof.* Historically, and as you've known since the case of Welch v. Helvering,[18] a rebuttable presumption existed that the Commissioner's determination of tax liability is correct. As a result, in all tax cases, regardless of the forum chosen, a taxpayer generally has to prove that the Commissioner's determination was incorrect and to establish the taxpayer's claim by a preponderance of the evidence.[19] Congress indirectly approved this judicially based burden of proof requirement by legislatively switching the burden of proof to the

---

[12]  357 U.S. 63, 78 S.Ct. 1079 (1958), on rehearing 362 U.S. 145, 80 S.Ct. 630 (1960).

[13]  There is an exception to the full payment rule for "divisible taxes," such as so-called "trust fund taxes" under I.R.C. §§ 6671 and 6672 for which a "responsible person" may be called to account if the employer withholds taxes from employees' wages but fails to turn them over to the Government. See, e.g., Steele v. United States, 280 F.2d 89, 91 (8th Cir.1960).

[14]  Consider the plight of the taxpayer who lets the 90-day period expire and then cannot fully pay because, whether seized or voluntarily liquidated for payment, the taxpayer's assets are insufficient. See Ferguson, "Jurisdictional Problems in Federal Tax Controversies," 48 Iowa L.Rev. 312, 335 (1963): Nevertheless, this is the current rule. See, e.g., Nogle v. United States, unreported, 33 A.F.T.R.2d 74–1314 (S.D.Ohio 1974).

[15]  See Rules of Practice and Procedure, United States Tax Court, Rule 13. Jurisdiction (2016).

It has been questioned whether the Tax Court's jurisdiction should be extended to refund suits. See Griswold, Federal Taxation, page 91 (Foundation Press 1966).

[16]  I.R.C. § 6512(b). But as regards enforcement of a Tax Court determination of overpayment, see Rosenberg v. Commissioner, 29 T.C.M. 888 (1970).

[17]  E.g., I.R.C. § 7422(e).

[18]  290 U.S. 111, 115, 54 S.Ct. 8 (1933). See page 311, supra.

[19]  Danville Plywood Corp. v. United States, 16 Cl.Ct. 584, 63 A.F.T.R.2d 89–1036, 1043 (1989).

Commissioner in several situations.[20] Additionally, in any proceeding which involves a penalty, the Commissioner must initially provide evidence that it is appropriate to apply a particular penalty to the taxpayer before the court can impose the penalty.[21]

But times change and in the taxpayer-friendly atmosphere of the late 1990s, Congress did an about-face on some additional burden of proof rules. Unless the Code otherwise specifically allocates the burden of proof,[22] the Commissioner in any court proceeding involving an individual, now has the burden of proof with respect to *factual issues* if certain requirements are met.[23] The factual burden of proof falls on the Commissioner if the taxpayer: (1) introduces credible evidence[24] with respect to any factual issue relevant to ascertaining the taxpayer's tax liability;[25] (2) substantiates any item required to be substantiated by the taxpayer under the Code and regulations;[26] (3) maintains all records required by the Code and regulations;[27] and (4) cooperates with reasonable requests by the Commissioner for witnesses, information, documents, meetings and interviews.[28] The fourth requirement, above, requires a taxpayer to exhaust the taxpayer's administrative remedies.[29] Given the limited scope of the burden-shifting provision on only factual issues and the statutory prerequisites to the switch, the shifting provision may prove to be more sound than fury.

*Injunctions and Declaratory Judgments.* When considering judicial procedures, the injunction and the declaratory judgment might appear to be especially promising remedies to taxpayers involved at the

---

[20] See, i.e., I.R.C. §§ 162(c)(1) and (2), 280G(b)(2)(B), 7422(e), 7454(a).

[21] I.R.C. § 7491(c).

[22] I.R.C. § 7491(a)(3). The burden could be specifically allocated to either the taxpayer or the Commissioner.

[23] I.R.C. § 7491(a).

For an excellent article discussing burden of proof prior to the enactment of I.R.C. § 7491, see Martinez, "Tax Collection and Populist Rhetoric: Shifting the Burden of Proof in Tax Cases," 39 Hastings L.J. 239 (1988).

[24] "Credible evidence is the quality of evidence which, after critical analysis, the court would find sufficient upon which to base a decision on the issue if no contrary evidence were submitted (without regard to the judicial presumption of IRS correctness). A taxpayer has not produced credible evidence for these purposes if the taxpayer merely makes implausible factual assertions, frivolous claims, or tax protestor-type arguments. The introduction of evidence will not meet this standard if the court is not convinced that it is worthy of belief. If after evidence from both sides, the court believes that the evidence is equally balanced, the court shall find that the Secretary has not sustained his burden of proof." S.Rep. No. 105–174, 105th Cong. 2nd Sess. at page 45 (1998).

[25] I.R.C. § 7491(a)(1).

[26] I.R.C. § 7491(a)(2)(A). See I.R.C. § 6001 and Reg. § 1.6001–1. See also, e.g., I.R.C. § 170(a)(1) and (f)(8) and (12), Reg. § 1.170A–13; I.R.C. § 274(d), Reg. § 1.274–5, and 1.274–5T.

[27] I.R.C. § 7491(a)(2)(B).

[28] I.R.C. § 7491(a)(2)(B). This includes providing within a reasonable period of time access to and inspection of witnesses, information, and documents in control of the taxpayer if reasonably requested by the Commissioner. S. Rep. No. 105–174, 105th Cong. 2nd Sess. at page 45 (1998).

[29] S. Rep. No. 105–174, 105th Cong. 2nd Sess. at page 45 (1998).

administrative level of tax controversies.[30] While the use of the injunction in tax cases is not completely outlawed,[31] its utility is very limited.[32] Similarly, the Federal Declaratory Judgments Act[33] provides for declaratory judgments in cases of actual controversy, *except* "with respect to federal taxes", although various courts are authorized by the Code to render such judgments in very limited specific situations.[34]

*Appellate Procedures.* The losing party in a deficiency proceeding in the Tax Court or in a refund suit in the District Court or the Court of Federal Claims may appeal the decision (as of right) to the Court of Appeals. Usually, if an individual taxpayer seeks review of a Tax Court decision or a District Court decision, the taxpayer must appeal to the Court of Appeals for the circuit in which the taxpayer's residence is located.[35] For example, a Florida taxpayer would appeal to the Eleventh Circuit and a New Yorker to the Second.[36] Decisions of the Court of Federal Claims are appealable to the United States Court of Appeals for the Federal Circuit, rather than the taxpayer's "home" circuit.[37] Thus, the decisions of the Tax Court, a centralized national tribunal, as well as decisions of the District Courts fan out into eleven non-unified appellate bodies. As a result, conflicting interpretations of the statute emerge in the various circuits, destroying, in part, what the Tax Court believes to be a principal purpose for its establishment, an effort toward uniform national administration of the tax laws. Against this background, it is not surprising that over the years there have been repeated proposals for

---

[30] Indeed, the injunction has played something of a role in the history of tax litigation. In an early case, before the ratification of the Sixteenth Amendment, a shareholder successfully enjoined his corporation from paying an income tax that he claimed was unconstitutional. Pollock v. Farmers' Loan & Trust Co., 157 U.S. 429, 15 S.Ct. 673 (1895).

[31] See I.R.C. § 7421(a).

[32] Compare Enochs v. Williams Packing and Navigation Co., 370 U.S. 1, 82 S.Ct. 1125 (1962), with Miller v. Standard Nut Margarine Co., 284 U.S. 498, 52 S.Ct. 260 (1932), and Commissioner v. Shapiro, 424 U.S. 614, 96 S.Ct. 1062 (1976). Also, see Lynch, "Nontaxpayer Suits; Seeking Injunctive and Declaratory Relief Against IRS Administrative Action," 12 Akron L.Rev. 1 (1978) and Andrews, "The Use of the Injunction as a Remedy for an Invalid Federal Tax Assessment," 40 Tax L.Rev. 653 (1985).

[33] 28 U.S.C.A. § 2201.

[34] See I.R.C. §§ 7428, 7476. For example, I.R.C. § 7478 authorizes the Tax Court to render declaratory judgments with regard to the tax-exempt status of prospective issues of government obligations under § 103(a). Yet, despite these enactments, the availability of such a remedy remains extremely limited. Whether it may be possible to get a declaratory judgment as to rights and obligations that underlie liability for a federal tax is not entirely clear. See King v. United States, 390 F.2d 894 (Ct.Cl.1968), granting such a judgment; reversed 395 U.S. 1, 89 S.Ct. 1501 (1969), on the basis of the limited jurisdiction of the Court of Federal Claims not unavailability of the remedy.

[35] I.R.C. § 7482(a).

[36] By stipulation, the taxpayer and the Commissioner may agree upon review in a different circuit. I.R.C. § 7482(b)(2).

In specified circumstances and at the discretion of the Court of Appeals, the taxpayer may appeal an interlocutory order of the Tax Court involving a controlling question of law. I.R.C. § 7482(a)(2).

[37] Strategic planning plays an important role in deciding which of the available forums to pursue. A taxpayer may wish to litigate in the Court of Federal Claims to avoid unfavorable precedent in one's home circuit, or vice versa.

the creation of an intermediate appellate Court of Tax Appeals designed to do away with the present inverted pyramid for contesting tax issues.[38]

If the Court of Appeals to which an appeal may be taken has decided an issue that arises in a Tax Court case, must the Tax Court conform to that decision? For a very long time the Tax Court's stance was one of independence.[39] But in 1970, it adopted the opposite, earlier rejected view,[40] and since then has decided cases in accordance with decisions in the circuits to which an appeal probably would be taken.

Appeals from the Circuit Courts of Appeal are by certiorari to the Supreme Court. One may agree wholeheartedly with Mr. Justice Jackson's analysis of the terminal role of the Supreme Court: "We are not final because we are infallible; but we are infallible only because we are final."[41] But if there is any question *why*, there is at least no question *whether* the Supreme Court is the end of the line.

*Judicial Finality.* The familiar doctrine of res judicata is fully applicable to tax controversies.[42] If a taxpayer has won a judgment in a District Court in a refund suit, imagine what the taxpayer's reaction would be if told that the Commissioner is now asserting additional income tax liability for the same year and that the taxpayer must again go to court to preserve the victory. But the taxpayer need not, of course, because the liability for that year is res judicata.[43] The judgment is controlling not only with respect to the issues litigated but to all issues that could have been raised which bear on the determination of liability for the year.[44] Neither the form of the litigation (refund suit, collection due process, or deficiency proceeding) nor the forum in which the case is tried (Tax Court,[45] District Court, or Court of Federal Claims) makes any difference. While the doctrine is dependent upon a prior adjudication of a controversy between the same parties or their privies, the same parties requirement is satisfied by the proposition that the contest is between

---

[38] See Del Cotto, "The Need for a Court of Tax Appeals: An Argument and a Study," 12 Buffalo L.Rev. 5 (1962); Griswold, "The Need for a Court of Tax Appeals," 57 Harv. L. Rev. 1153 (1944); Surrey, "Some Suggested Topics in the Field of Tax Administration," 25 Wash. U. L. Rev. 399, 414–423 (1940); Geier, "The Emasculated Role of Judicial Precedent in the Tax Court and the Internal Revenue Service," 39 Okla. L. Rev. 427 (1986); Baker, "Imagining the Alternative Futures of the U.S. Courts of Appeals," 28 Ga. L. Rev. 913, 950–51 (1994); Craig, "Federal Income Tax and the Supreme Court: The Case Against a National Court of Tax Appeals," 1983 Utah L. Rev. 679 (1983).

[39] Lawrence v. Commissioner, 27 T.C. 713, 716 and 718 (1957).

[40] Golsen v. Commissioner, 54 T.C. 742 (1970), affirmed 445 F.2d 985 (10th Cir.1971), cert. denied 404 U.S. 940, 92 S.Ct. 284 (1971). See also the brief comment in Chapter 1, supra at page 17.

[41] Jackson, J., concurring in Brown v. Allen, 344 U.S. 443, 540 73 S.Ct. 397, 427 (1953).

[42] Tait v. Western Maryland Ry. Co., 289 U.S. 620, 53 S.Ct. 706 (1933).

[43] Even this firm doctrine is subject to exception under the mitigation rules of I.R.C. § 1311 et seq. See Chapter 28C, infra.

[44] Cf. Cromwell v. Sac County, 94 U.S. (4 Otto) 351, 352 (1876).

[45] While I.R.C. § 7441 has cured any doubt, even when the Tax Court was an administrative agency, an adjudication by the Tax Court or its predecessor the Board of Tax Appeals, invoked the doctrine. Tait v. Western Maryland Ry. Co., supra note 42. Cf. I.R.C. § 7481.

the taxpayer and the government, whether the official party to the proceeding is the United States itself or the Commissioner of Internal Revenue.[46]

The related doctrine of collateral estoppel or estoppel by judgment is especially likely to be of importance in tax cases. The landmark opinion outlining the scope of the doctrine of collateral estoppel is Commissioner v. Sunnen.[47] A single controversial circumstance may have a bearing on income tax liability for several years. If a judgment fixes liability for one of the years, the broad doctrine of res judicata forecloses only the reopening of that liability. But the related doctrine of collateral estoppel forecloses the relitigation of issues that were in fact raised and decided in the earlier litigation, even when they arise in a new cause of action, such as a dispute as to liability for a later year.[48]

A simple example of the estoppel concept may be helpful. Assume that T is the income beneficiary of a trust. T assigns one-half of T's interest gratuitously to T's son. The Commissioner asserts that T remains taxable on all the trust income under the fruit-tree doctrine.[49] T successfully contests the liability for tax on half the year's trust income in a Tax Court case which is not appealed. Now comes the Commissioner with the same assertion for the next year. Res judicata does not protect T, because the cause of action is not the same, i.e., T's second year tax liability obviously was not decided in the case that involved the first year. But T may be protected by collateral estoppel. Both doctrines reflect a policy that matters judicially determined should not be open for subsequent consideration; and collateral estoppel extends the notion of res judicata to cover a specific issue that has been decided.

However, there are limits to the doctrine. As the Supreme Court has said:[50]

> It must be confined to situations where the matter raised in the second suit is identical in all respects with that decided in the first proceeding and where the controlling facts and applicable legal rules remain unchanged.

Collateral estoppel may of course work against the taxpayer. For example, a conviction in a criminal case for tax fraud under Section 7201

---

[46]  Cf. Cromwell v. Sac County, supra note 44. See I.R.C. § 7422(c).

[47]  333 U.S. 591, 68 S.Ct. 715 (1948); and see Goldstein, "Res Judicata and Collateral Estoppel," 54 A.B.A.J. 1131 (1968).

[48]  See Wright, Miller & Kane, Federal Practice and Procedure, §§ 4466–4473 (Thomson Reuters).

[49]  See Chapter 12, supra.

[50]  Commissioner v. Sunnen, supra note 47 at 599–600 and 720–721.

The *Sunnen* case itself involved a fruit-tree controversy. But the *Clifford-Horst* line of cases intervened between the first and second controversies. See Chapters 12 and 13, supra. On this ground the Court held in *Sunnen* that the "legal atmosphere" had so changed as to render the doctrine of collateral estoppel inapplicable.

forecloses argument by the taxpayer that the taxpayer is not liable for the civil fraud penalty under Section 6663(b).[51]

*Recovery of Taxpayer Costs and Attorneys' Fees.* A taxpayer may recover both reasonable administrative costs incurred in connection with administrative proceedings and reasonable litigation costs in connection with any court proceeding, if the taxpayer is determined to be the "prevailing party" under one of two tests.[52] Under the first test, a taxpayer is the prevailing party if the Service's position is not substantially justified[53] and the taxpayer has substantially prevailed.[54] Alternatively, a taxpayer is the prevailing party if the final judgment on the taxpayer's case is less than or equal to a "qualified offer"[55] that the IRS rejected.[56] No recovery is available for the portion of a proceeding during which the taxpayer unreasonably protracted such proceeding,[57] and no recovery is allowed to an individual whose net worth exceeds $2 million.[58]

One purpose of the allowance for administrative cost recoveries is to encourage taxpayers to participate in the administrative process. Thus, administrative costs are awarded for amounts incurred at an early point in the administrative process, generally, commencing as of the date of arrival of the letter of proposed deficiency which allows a taxpayer an opportunity for review in the Office of Appeals.[59] Furthermore, litigation costs are allowed only where the taxpayer has exhausted the taxpayer's available administrative remedies.[60]

Reasonable administrative and litigation costs include reasonable expenses for expert witnesses, reasonable costs of preparing studies and reports, and reasonable attorneys' fees not in excess of $125 per hour (adjusted for inflation), unless the Service or the court determines that a higher rate is justified.[61] Similar recoveries are allowed to attorneys who do pro bono work.[62]

---

[51]  See Stone v. Commissioner, 56 T.C. 213 (1971), and cases there cited. On the other hand, an acquittal of the taxpayer in a preceding criminal case does not foreclose assertion of the civil fraud penalty. Helvering v. Mitchell, 303 U.S. 391, 58 S.Ct. 630 (1938).

[52]  I.R.C. § 7430(a).

[53]  I.R.C. § 7430(c)(4)(B). The Service's success or failure in other circuits on substantially similar issues is to be considered in determining whether the Service is substantially justified in its position. I.R.C. § 7430(c)(4)(B)(iii).

[54]  I.R.C. § 7430(c)(4)(A). A determination that a party is a prevailing party may be made by an agreement of the parties, by the Service (if the final determination is an administrative action) or by the court (if the final determination is a court proceeding). I.R.C. § 7430(c)(4)(C). See also I.R.C. § 7430(c)(4)(E).

[55]  I.R.C. § 7430(g).

[56]  I.R.C. § 7430(c)(4)(E).

[57]  I.R.C. § 7430(b)(3).

[58]  I.R.C. § 7430(c)(4)(A)(ii).

[59]  See I.R.C. § 7430(c)(2) and the Text at notes 14 and 15 on page 971, supra.

[60]  I.R.C. § 7430(b)(1).

[61]  I.R.C. § 7430(c)(1) and (2).

[62]  I.R.C. § 7430(c)(3)(B).

## 5.  COLLECTION OF TAXES

Internal Revenue Code: See Sections 6301; 6302(a); 6320; 6321; 6330; 6331; 6502(a); 6851; 6861.

---

*Regular Collections.* As a general rule, valid assessment of tax is a prerequisite to the government's right to collect the tax.[1] It is the act of assessment that establishes the taxpayer's debt to the government. An analogy might be a board of directors' declaration of a dividend, which creates a corporate debt to the shareholder. The statute expressly authorizes the Secretary of the Treasury and officials designated by the Secretary to collect assessed federal taxes[2] with substantial latitude as to method of collection.[3]

After proper assessment, the government has 10 years (or longer in limited circumstances where there is an agreement with the taxpayer)[4] within which to collect the tax.[5] This limitation period for *collection* should not be confused with limitation periods within which *assessment* must be made.[6]

As might be expected, methods afforded the government for the collection of tax go beyond those available to private creditors. A conventional suit for collection may be brought[7] which, if successful, converts the taxpayer to a judgment debtor. But, additionally, the government may resort to the extraordinary remedies of levy and distraint.[8] This is to say that without judicial intervention the taxpayer's property may be seized and sold to satisfy the tax obligation.[9] Finally, an unpaid federal tax becomes a lien on the taxpayer's property[10] which, when perfected,[11] may be enforced to collect the tax.

A taxpayer cannot thwart the tax gatherer by giving away all the taxpayer's property to avoid payment, or even by dying. If a tax lien has

---

[1]   See I.R.C. § 6502. There is some authority supporting collection by suit without assessment. Cf. United States v. Ayer, 12 F.2d 194 (1st Cir.1926), sustaining a suit to collect estate tax without assessment. However, with respect to deficiencies there are parallel obstacles to both assessment and collection, see I.R.C. § 6213(a), and, when the tax can be assessed, it will be.

[2]   I.R.C. § 6301. See Thrower, "Current Collection Problems and Procedures," 24 Tax Lawyer 217 (1971).

[3]   I.R.C. § 6302(a); see Reg. § 601.104(c). See Phelan, "A Summary of Extensive Tax Collection Powers of the I.R.S.," 9 Virg. Tax Rev. 405 (1990).

[4]   I.R.C. § 6502(a)(2). See I.R.C. § 6501(c)(4).

[5]   I.R.C. § 6502(a).

[6]   See Chapter 28B1, infra.

[7]   28 U.S.C.A. § 1396.

[8]   I.R.C. § 6331; and see note 1, supra. Taxpayer Bills of Rights legislation (see Chapter 28A1, supra) has imposed some limitations and restrictions on the government's ability to place liens on or seize property. See I.R.C. §§ 6325(b)(4), 6326, 6331(a), 6331(i)(4), 6334, 6343(e).

[9]   See, e.g., Martinon v. Fitzgerald, 306 F.Supp. 922 (S.D.N.Y.1968), affirmed per curiam, 418 F.2d 1336 (2d Cir.1969).

[10]   I.R.C. § 6321.

[11]   See I.R.C. § 6323(a) and (f); Reg. § 601.104(c).

attached to one's property, it will follow the property into the hands of one's donee.[12] Otherwise the liability of the transferee depends upon state law. The Internal Revenue Code invokes state law by permitting enforcement of a taxpayer's tax liability against a transferee, to the extent of the transferee's liability "at law or in equity."[13] Liability "at law" may arise, for example, when a continuing corporation assumes the tax liability of a merging corporation.[14] A transferee's liability "in equity" is likely to be less clear cut, raising as it does conventional problems of creditors' rights.[15] In either event, subject to variation as to such matters as limitation periods[16] and burden of proof,[17] a transferee who is liable for another's tax is placed pretty much in the shoes of the principal taxpayer as regards assessment, payment, and collection of the tax.[18]

*Collection Due Process.* Collection of taxes generally involves a two-step process. The first step involves a lien, which is a legal right or interest that the Service has in the taxpayer's property.[19] To "perfect" the lien—that is, for the lien to be valid and have priority over other creditors' liens—the Service must generally file a notice of federal tax lien.[20] The Service must notify the taxpayer in writing of the filing of a federal tax lien and afford the taxpayer the opportunity for a hearing before the IRS Office of Appeals.[21] This hearing is usually referred to as a collection due process, or CDP, hearing.

The second step in the collection process involves a levy, which generally involves the seizing and sale of the taxpayer's property.[22] An example of a tax levy is the garnishment of the taxpayer's wages to pay off the outstanding tax liability.[23] A taxpayer in this situation must be given written notice of the Service's intent to make such a levy.[24] The taxpayer must also be given written notice of the right to a CDP hearing before any levy is made.[25]

During a CDP hearing, the taxpayer may raise a number of issues, including claiming "innocent spouse" relief,[26] or challenging the

---

[12]  E.g., United States v. Bess, 357 U.S. 51, 78 S.Ct. 1054 (1958). See Plumb, "Federal Liens and Priorities," 77 Yale L.J. 228, 605, 1104 (1967 and 1968).

[13]  I.R.C. § 6901.

[14]  E.g., Turnbull, Inc. v. Commissioner, 22 T.C.M. 1750 (1963); a supplemental opinion at 42 T.C. 582 (1964) was affirmed 373 F.2d 91 (5th Cir.1967), cert. denied 389 U.S. 842, 88 S.Ct. 72 (1967).

[15]  See Commissioner v. Stern, 357 U.S. 39, 78 S.Ct. 1047 (1958), and cases there cited.

[16]  I.R.C. § 6901(c).

[17]  I.R.C. § 6902(a).

[18]  I.R.C. § 6901(a).

[19]  I.R.C. § 6321.

[20]  I.R.C. § 6323(a), (f).

[21]  I.R.C. § 6320.

[22]  See I.R.C. §§ 6331–6344.

[23]  I.R.C. § 6331(a).

[24]  I.R.C. § 6331(d).

[25]  I.R.C. § 6330.

[26]  I.R.C. §§ 6320(c), 6330(c)(2)(A)(i); see Chapter 28B2, infra.

appropriateness of the collection actions.[27] The taxpayer may also offer collection alternatives, such as paying the outstanding tax liability on an installment basis,[28] and even challenge the amount of the tax owed if the taxpayer never received a statutory notice of deficiency or did not otherwise have an opportunity to dispute the tax liability.[29] The person presiding over the CDP hearing, the IRS appeals officer, must verify that the requirements of any applicable law or administrative procedure have been met.[30] The officer must also take into consideration whether any proposed collection action balances the need for the efficient collection of taxes with the legitimate concern of the taxpayer that any collection be no more intrusive than necessary.[31]

After the CDP hearing, the IRS appeals officer issues a Notice of Determination Concerning Collection Action(s) Under Section 6320 and/or 6330. The taxpayer generally may challenge this administrative determination in Tax Court.[32] If the taxpayer does so, the statute of limitations on collection is suspended, and the Service's collection activities are similarly suspended,[33] during the pendency of the Tax Court case.

*Jeopardy and Termination Assessments.* Generally, except in the case of a waiver,[34] the Service must issue a notice of deficiency before it can assess any additional tax it determines the taxpayer should have paid.[35] However, Section 6861 authorizes jeopardy assessments in a case where the usual cumbersome procedures might threaten to impede collection of the tax.[36] In such a case, the tax *may* be assessed and collected before issuance of a deficiency notice. It is congressional policy, however, not to foreclose resort to one of three trial forums in such a case. Accordingly, the statute requires the issuance of the statutory deficiency notice within 60 days after the mailing of the jeopardy assessment, assuring the taxpayer of a ticket to the Tax Court as well as a refund court.[37]

A companion provision to the jeopardy assessment provision, Section 6851, authorizes the Commissioner immediately to make a termination assessment. A termination assessment is a determination of tax for the current or the immediately preceding year, allowing the Commissioner

---

[27] I.R.C. §§ 6320(c), 6330(c)(2)(A)(ii).

[28] I.R.C. §§ 6320(c), 6330(c)(2)(A)(iii).

[29] I.R.C. §§ 6320(c), 6330(c)(2)(B).

[30] I.R.C. §§ 6320(c), 6330(c)(1).

[31] I.R.C. §§ 6320(c), 6330(c)(3)(C).

[32] I.R.C. §§ 6320(c), 6330(d)(1).

[33] I.R.C. §§ 6320(c), 6330(e)(1).

[34] See I.R.C. § 6213(d) and Form 870.

[35] I.R.C. § 6213(a). See, generally, Worthy, "The Tax Litigation Structure," 5 Ga. L. Rev. 248 (1971); Ferguson, "Jurisdictional Problems in Federal Tax Controversies," 48 Iowa L.Rev. 312 (1963).

[36] See I.R.C. § 7429(a). See also I.R.C. § 6867.

[37] I.R.C. § 6861(b).

to make an immediate demand for payment, if the Commissioner finds the taxpayer designs to take action that may prejudice the collection of income tax for such year or years.[38] When there is a termination assessment, the Service must send the taxpayer a notice of deficiency within 60 days after the later of the due date or the actual filing date of the tax return for the taxable year involved, again opening the door to any of the three trial forums.[39]

A taxpayer who is subject to a jeopardy or termination assessment must be provided a written statement of the reasons for the assessment,[40] and may obtain an almost immediate administrative and judicial review of both the reasonableness of the making of the assessment and the appropriateness of the amount of the assessment.[41] A District Court is generally the proper forum for the judicial review,[42] and the court's determination is not reviewable by any other court.[43]

## PROBLEMS

1.    Several judicial alternatives are open to taxpayers in tax litigation situations. In the following situations which procedure would the taxpayer be likely to use?

   (a)   Taxpayer has a factual issue as to which the taxpayer feels a jury would be favorably disposed.

   (b)   Taxpayer has no money with which to pay an asserted deficiency.

   (c)   Taxpayer wishes to stop the running of interest but at the same time litigate the issues. (Consider this carefully). See §§ 6213(b)(4), 6603.

   (d)   The litigation involves a very difficult tax law issue.

   (e)   The litigation involves a legal issue on which there is a split of authority among the circuits. The court of appeals in the circuit in which Taxpayer resides has decided the issue in the government's favor.

Are there further factors that Taxpayer might take into consideration in determining his judicial remedy and forum?

2.    If, under § 6501(c)(4), T is asked to execute a Form 872, extending the time for assessment of a deficiency, what practical consideration will affect T's response?

---

[38]   I.R.C. § 6851.

[39]   I.R.C. § 6851(b).

[40]   I.R.C. § 7429(a)(1)(B).

[41]   I.R.C. § 7429.

[42]   I.R.C. § 7429(b)(2)(A). But see I.R.C. § 7429(b)(2)(B) providing for judicial review by the Tax Court in limited situations.

[43]   I.R.C. § 7429(f).

**3.** If, under § 6213(d), T executes a Form 870, waiving restrictions on assessment of tax, to what extent has T capitulated, i.e., relinquished further opportunities to contest the liability?

**4.** If the Commissioner makes a jeopardy assessment prior to the issuance of a statutory notice of deficiency, will T lose the right to litigate the question of liability in the Tax Court? See § 6861(b).

**5.** The Commissioner sent Deficient a 90-day letter dated March 30, and the letter indicated that a response was due by June 28 (90 days later). See I.R.C. § 6213(a) last sentence. The "letter" was mailed at the post office by the Service on March 31, and the Service received certified mail notice dated March 31, which also bore the postmark date of March 31.

   (a) Is Deficient's petition timely if it is properly mailed and postmarked on June 28, and it arrives at the Tax Court on July 1?

   (b) What results in (a), above, if the Service mails the notice on March 30, but it miscounts its days and improperly puts a June 29, filing date (the proper date is June 28) on the notice and Deficient's petition is mailed and postmarked on June 29, and arrives at the Tax Court on July 1?

   (c) What result in (b), above, if the improper date is June 26 (rather than June 28)?

   (d) Is Deficient's petition timely in (a), above, if it was mailed and postmarked June 28, but was improperly addressed to the I.R.S. who forwarded it to the Tax Court and it arrived at the Tax Court on July 5? See Axe v. Commissioner, 58 T.C. 256 (1972).

   (e) If in any case above Deficient's petition is not timely and there is no Tax Court jurisdiction, has Deficient completely lost her "day in court"?

## B. SPECIAL RULES APPLICABLE TO DEFICIENCY PROCEDURES

## 1. TIMING RULES, INTEREST AND PENALTIES

Internal Revenue Code: Sections 6501(a), (b)(1), (c)(1) and (3), (e)(1)(A); 6601(a); 6603; 6621(a)(2), (b)(1) and (3); 7502(a)(1), (f). See Sections 6404; 6651(a), (d), and (f); 6662(a), (b), (d), and (h); 6663(a), (b).

---

*Statute of Limitations.* The government's opportunity to assert a deficiency in the form of a statutory notice of deficiency against a taxpayer is not unlimited. A statute of limitations generally comes into play, and the Service generally must assess any amount of alleged underpayment of tax within 3 years after a taxpayer files the taxpayer's return for a year, whether or not the return was timely filed for the year.[1] However, if the return is filed before its due date, it is deemed to be filed on the last day such return must be timely filed.[2] The 3-year period is extended to 6 years if the taxpayer has omitted gross income in excess of 25 percent of the gross income reported on the return.[3] In the case of a false or fraudulent return or when no return is filed, the statute of limitations does not begin to run and tax may be assessed at any time.[4]

In measuring the timeliness of returns, petitions, and payments in potential deficiency situations (as well as refund situations), the timely-mailed, timely-filed rule applies with the postmark on the mailing controlling the date.[5] The timely-mailed, timely-filed rule applies to mail using the United States Postal Service or a designated private delivery service such as Federal Express or DHL.[6]

*Interest and Penalties.* If a taxpayer is unsuccessful in a deficiency controversy, either by suit or by settlement, the taxpayer may be required to pay more than the bare amount of the asserted deficiency. For one thing, interest runs against the taxpayer from the date the amount should have been paid.[7] With respect to an underpayment, interest is imposed at a rate equal to the Federal short-term rate plus 3 percentage points.[8] Such interest is "personal interest,"[9] subject to the general overall deduction disallowance applicable to other personal interest.[10]

In addition to interest on the deficiency, a taxpayer may be subject to penalties. For example, failure to file a return or failure to pay the tax shown on a return when due, unless occasioned by some reasonable cause, but not willful neglect, invites penalties.[11] The penalty for failure to file a return is 5 percent of the tax per month.[12] The penalty for failure

---

[1]   I.R.C. § 6501(a).

[2]   I.R.C. § 6501(b)(1). The limitation on the early filing rule applies as well to any extensions of the date for filing. Pace Oil Company, Inc. v. Commissioner, 73 T.C. 249 (1979).

[3]   I.R.C. § 6501(e)(1)(A). An understatement of gross income by reason of an overstatement of unrecovered cost or other basis is an omission from gross income. I.R.C. § 6501(e)(1)(B)(ii). Where there is an omission, in applying the 25-percent test, "gross income" reported on the taxpayer's return is measured with reference to gains reported (amount realized less adjusted basis) and not the entire amount realized. Barkett v. Commissioner, 143 T.C. 149 (2014). If the taxpayer discloses an item on the return, or in a statement attached to the return, in a manner adequate to appraise the Service of the item, the item is not considered omitted. I.R.C. § 6501(e)(1)(B)(iii).

[4]   I.R.C. § 6501(c)(1) and (3).

[5]   I.R.C. § 7502(a).

[6]   I.R.C. § 7502(a) and (f). See also I.R.C. § 7502(c)(2) related to electronic filing.

[7]   I.R.C. § 6601(a). Under I.R.C. § 6603 a taxpayer may make a cash deposit to suspend running of interest. See Rev. Proc. 2005–18, 2005–1 C.B. 798, for the procedures under Section 6603.

[8]   I.R.C. § 6621(a)(2), (b).

[9]   I.R.C. § 163(h)(2).

[10]   See Chapter 16B, supra.

[11]   I.R.C. § 6651(a).

[12]   I.R.C. § 6651(a)(1). There is a minimum I.R.C. § 6651(a)(1) penalty equal to the lesser of $205 or the amount of tax due. I.R.C. § 6651(a) flush language. See Brookens, "The Section

to pay the tax due on the return is one-half of 1 percent of the tax per month,[13] in general increased to 1 percent per month after the Service notifies the taxpayer that it will levy upon the taxpayer's assets or issues a notice and demand for immediate payment of tax.[14] A similar one-half of 1 percent (increasing to 1 percent) penalty is imposed for a deficiency not appearing on the return after the taxpayer receives notice of such deficiency.[15] Section 6651(a) provides that the total penalty for the failure to file or the failure to pay may not exceed 25 percent of the tax. If there is a fraudulent failure to file a return, the penalty is increased from 5 percent to 15 percent of the tax per month, with a maximum of 75 percent of the tax.[16]

A uniform accuracy-related penalty is imposed for various taxpayer acts including: negligence resulting from the failure to make a reasonable attempt to comply with the provisions of the Code and from the careless, reckless, or intentional disregard of rules and regulations; a substantial understatement of income tax; and a substantial valuation misstatement.[17] The accuracy-related penalty is generally equal to 20 percent of the portion of the taxpayer's underpayment attributable to such acts.[18] If the underpayment is due to a gross valuation misstatement, the penalty is 40 percent,[19] and if any part of the underpayment is due to fraud, the entire underpayment is treated as attributable to fraud, except as the taxpayer may otherwise establish, and the penalty is 75 percent of the underpayment.[20]

The amount of the underpayment of tax subject to the accuracy-related penalty is reduced by the portion attributable to (1) the tax treatment of an item if there was or is substantial authority for such treatment, or (2) an item adequately disclosed in the return or statement attached to the return if there is a reasonable basis for the taxpayer's tax

---

6651(a)(1) Penalty for Late Filed Tax Returns; Reasonable Cause and Unreasoned Decisions," 35 Case West. Ref. L. Rev. 183 (1984–5).

[13] I.R.C. § 6651(a)(2). The amount of the failure to file penalty under I.R.C. § 6651(a)(1) is reduced by the amount of the failure to pay penalty under § 6651(a)(2) for any month in which both apply. I.R.C. § 6651(c)(1). The penalty is inapplicable where such failure is due to reasonable cause and not due to willful neglect. I.R.C. § 6651(a) flush language.

[14] See I.R.C. § 6651(d).

[15] I.R.C. § 6651(a)(3), (d).

[16] I.R.C. § 6651(f).

[17] I.R.C. § 6662(b). See I.R.C. § 6662(c)–(e).

[18] I.R.C. § 6662(a). The Supreme Court has ruled that the I.R.C. § 6662 penalties for underpayments are applicable to underpayments that are the result of a basis-increasing transaction that was subsequently disregarded for lack of economic substance. See United States v. Woods, 571 U.S. 31 (2013).

[19] I.R.C. § 6662(h).

[20] I.R.C. § 6663(a), (b).

Proof of fraud for purposes of sustaining the Commissioner's imposition of the civil fraud penalty requires something less than the proof beyond a reasonable doubt required for conviction for a crime. See Helvering v. Mitchell, 303 U.S. 391, 58 S.Ct. 630 (1938); Kub v. Commissioner, 33 T.C.M. 1282 (1974). Obviously, perhaps, acquittal of a fraud charge in a criminal proceeding does not foreclose the imposition of the civil fraud penalty. Helvering v. Mitchell, supra.

treatment of the item.[21] The regulations describe "reasonable basis" as "a relatively high standard of tax reporting, that is, significantly higher than not frivolous or patently improper."[22] To satisfy the reasonable basis standard, the position has to be more than "merely arguable" or "merely a colorable claim."[23] "Substantial authority" is an objective standard that is more stringent than the reasonable basis standard but not as stringent as a "more-likely-than-not" test (a greater than 50 percent likelihood of being upheld).[24] In deciding if there is substantial authority for the tax treatment of an item, the weight of the authorities supporting the position must be substantial in relation to the weight of authorities on the other side.[25] In doing this balancing, factors such as identity of facts and persuasiveness of reasoning are considered.[26] Authority that may be considered in determining whether there is substantial authority for a position include the Code, the regulations (including proposed and temporary regulations), revenue rulings (public and private) and procedures, court cases, legislative history, and other pronouncements by the Internal Revenue Service. Notably, conclusions reached in treatises, legal periodicals, and legal opinions are not considered authority.[27] The jurisdiction of court cases in relation to the taxpayer's residence generally is disregarded except that there is substantial authority for the tax treatment of an item if the treatment is supported by controlling authority of a United States Court of Appeals to which the taxpayer has a right of appeal.[28] Substantial authority for the tax treatment of an item in a return exists if there was such authority at the time the return was filed or on the last day of the taxable year to which the return relates.[29]

The Tax Court in its discretion also may assess a penalty of up to $25,000 on a taxpayer who asserts a frivolous or groundless position.[30] These are civil, not criminal, sanctions,[31] and in each instance the penalty is simply "added to the tax" and therefore collected as tax. The possibility of criminal sanctions also exists.[32] Of course, criminal penalties are imposed only upon conviction.

In the case of an individual taxpayer who timely files an income tax return (including extensions), the accrual of some interest and penalties

---

[21]  I.R.C. § 6662(d)(2)(B).

[22]  Reg. § 1.6662–3(b)(3).

[23]  Id.

[24]  Reg. § 1.6662–4(d)(2).

[25]  Reg. § 1.6662–4(d)(3)(i).

[26]  Reg. § 1.6662–4(d)(3)(ii).

[27]  Reg. § 1.6662–4(d)(3)(iii).

[28]  Reg. § 1.6662–4(d)(3)(iv)(B).

[29]  Reg. § 1.6662–4(d)(3)(iv)(C).

[30]  I.R.C. § 6673. Cf. Greenberg v. Commissioner, 73 T.C. 806 (1980). See also I.R.C. §§ 6702 and 7482(c)(4) dealing with frivolous returns and frivolous appeals, respectively, and Howard v. United States, 84–1 U.S.T.C. ¶ 9443 (E.D.Wash.1984); Lamb v. Commissioner, 733 F.2d 86 (10th Cir.1984), modified by 744 F.2d 1448 (10th Cir.1984).

[31]  Helvering v. Mitchell, supra note 20.

[32]  See I.R.C. §§ 7201–7207.

is abated[33] if the Service fails to notify the taxpayer of an item[34] related to the taxpayer's liability within 36 months.[35] Such interest and penalties are suspended from the 36-month period until 21 days after notice is given.[36]

## PROBLEMS

1.  T is a calendar year taxpayer. When can the Commissioner make a timely assertion of an income tax deficiency against T for year one, without resort to special limitation periods, if T filed T's return for year one on:

    (a)  April 1 of year two?

    (b)  May 1 of year two?

    (c)  If T filed no return for year one?

2.  On essentially the same facts as those in problem 1, and assuming that T filed a return on April 1 of year one, what different result would you reach if:

    (a)  The deficiency asserted rests on an alleged omission of a $20,000 fee for T's services which, if reported, would have increased the gross income reported on the return to $60,000?

    (b)  The deficiency asserted rests on an alleged omission from gross income, whatever the amount, done by T with the deliberate attempt to evade tax? (May T be in more than mere financial difficulty? See and broadly differentiate §§ 7201 and 7206(1).)

## 2.  THE INNOCENT SPOUSE RULES

Internal Revenue Code: Section 6015 (omit (c)(4)(B), (d)(2), (4) and (5), (g)).

———————

It will be recalled that, if a joint income tax return is filed by a husband and wife, both are generally jointly and severally liable for the tax.[1] In the past this sometimes created such an unjust situation that some judges suggested Congress change the law.[2] For example, a widow who had filed a joint return with her deceased husband might suddenly be confronted with a large deficiency, including the 75 percent fraud

---

[33] The abatement is inapplicable to interest and penalties in several situations listed in I.R.C. § 6404(g)(2), including: § 6651 penalties for failure to file a return or pay tax; any interest, penalty or addition to tax in a case involving fraud; any interest, penalty or addition to tax with respect to liability shown on the taxpayer's return; and any criminal penalty.

[34] I.R.C. § 6404(g)(1)(B).

[35] I.R.C. § 6404(g)(1). The 36-month period runs from the latest of the date the return is filed or the due date of the return without regard to extensions. I.R.C. § 6404(g)(1)(A).

[36] I.R.C. § 6404(g)(3).

[1] I.R.C. § 6013(d)(3). See Chapter 27A, supra.

[2] E.g., Scudder v. Commissioner, 48 T.C. 36, 41 (1967).

penalty,[3] arising out of her husband's transgressions that were wholly unknown to her.

Over the years Congress has enacted several "innocent spouse" rules.[4] Under the most recent version,[5] an innocent spouse generally may elect relief when the other spouse made an erroneous understatement of items of which the innocent spouse was unaware,[6] where the spouses are no longer married or living together,[7] or in other situations where equitable relief is justified.[8]

Subsection 6015(b) first allows relief to an innocent spouse[9] who has filed a joint return[10] if: (1) there is an understatement[11] of tax attributable to erroneous items of the other spouse;[12] (2) the innocent spouse did not know or have reason to know of such understatement;[13] and (3) taking all facts and circumstances into account, it is inequitable to hold the innocent spouse liable for the deficiency in tax attributable to the understatement.[14] If these requirements are met, the innocent spouse is relieved of any tax liability (including interest, penalties, and other amounts) attributable to such understatement.[15] If an innocent spouse meets the above requirements with respect to a portion of an understatement, relief of liability is allowed with respect to only that portion of the tax liability.[16]

The second form of relief for an innocent spouse, which is provided by Subsection 6015(c), involves a situation for an innocent spouse where a deficiency actually has been assessed[17] and the spouses are in essence

---

[3]　I.R.C. § 6663(a).

[4]　See Pub. Law No. 91–679, 91st Cong., 2d Sess. § 1 (1971), Pub. Law No. 98–369, 98th Cong., 2d Sess. § 424 (1984).

[5]　Pub. Law No. 105–206, 105th Cong., 2d Sess. § 3201(a) (1998) amended by Pub. Law No. 106–554 § 313, 106th Cong., 2d Sess. (2000). See Robinson and Ferrari, "The New Innocent Spouse Provision: 'Reason and Law Walking Hand in Hand?'" 80 Tax Notes 835 (1998).

[6]　I.R.C. § 6015(a)(1), 6015(b).

[7]　I.R.C. § 6015(a)(2), 6015(c).

[8]　I.R.C. § 6015(f). Similar statutory and equitable relief is granted to married spouses who hold community property but file separate returns in situations in which Congress considers it is appropriate to tax one spouse on all (not just ½) of the community property income. I.R.C. § 66(c).

[9]　The innocent spouse must elect to seek relief under I.R.C. § 6015(b). See I.R.C. § 6015(b)(1)(E) and, as to the timing of such election, see note 31, infra.

[10]　I.R.C. § 6015(b)(1)(A).

[11]　See I.R.C. § 6015(b)(3). I.R.C. § 6662(d)(2)(A) defines the term "understatement." An understatement can arise from an omission from gross income or an improperly claimed credit, deduction or basis amount. However, an underpayment of the tax stated on the return does not constitute an understatement.

[12]　I.R.C. § 6015(b)(1)(B).

[13]　I.R.C. § 6015(b)(1)(C).

[14]　I.R.C. § 6015(b)(1)(D).

[15]　I.R.C. § 6015(b).

[16]　I.R.C. § 6015(b)(2). This result is consistent with prior case law. See Wiksell v. Commissioner, 90 F.3d 1459 (9th Cir.1996).

[17]　I.R.C. § 6015(c)(1).

no longer spouses.[18] This rule treats the spouse seeking relief as though separate returns (rather than a joint return) had been filed for the taxable year involved, with each spouse reporting his or her own items of income, deductions, and credits that are related to the assessed deficiency.[19] Where both spouses are responsible for the deficiency or different sources of a deficiency, a proportionate liability results.[20] Relief is provided even though the spouses were married and living together in the taxable year of the return if, at the time of the election for relief (which must be made within 2 years of the Service commencing collection activities with respect to the taxable year):[21] (1) the claimant spouse is no longer married to or is legally separated from the spouse with whom the joint return was filed;[22] or (2) the claimant spouse has not been a member of the same household of the spouse with whom the joint return was filed at any time within the 12-month period prior to the date of the election for relief.[23] This relief generally disregards the "innocence" of the spouse because in most situations knowledge or constructive knowledge on the part of the claimant spouse is irrelevant. However, special rules apply to prevent allowance of Subsection 6015(c) relief in situations where there is a fraudulent scheme,[24] where the innocent spouse had actual knowledge of the error at the time of signing the return (unless the return was signed under duress),[25] or where tax avoidance transfers were made.[26] When a spouse invokes Subsection 6015(c) relief, several rules determine the proper allocation of the income, deduction, or credit items related to the deficiency to that spouse's return.[27]

Subsection 6015(f) provides a third limited form of innocent spouse relief where the first two forms are unavailable[28] and where it would be inequitable to hold the innocent spouse liable for an underpayment of tax or portion thereof.[29] The Secretary has the authority to provide procedures for this third type of relief.[30]

In order to qualify for relief under Section 6015(b) or (c), the innocent spouse must elect relief within 2 years after the date on which the Service

---

[18] See I.R.C. § 6015(c)(3)(A).

[19] I.R.C. § 6015(d)(3)(A), (g)(1). The allocation is made without regard to community property laws. I.R.C. § 6015(a). The claimant spouse generally has the burden of proof with respect to the allocation of the deficiency. I.R.C. § 6015(c)(2).

[20] I.R.C. § 6015(d)(1).

[21] I.R.C. § 6015(c)(3)(B). See note 31, infra.

[22] I.R.C. § 6015(c)(3)(A)(i)(I).

[23] I.R.C. § 6015(c)(3)(A)(i)(II).

[24] I.R.C. § 6015(c)(3)(A)(ii).

[25] I.R.C. § 6015(c)(3)(C).

[26] I.R.C. § 6015(c)(4).

[27] I.R.C. § 6015(d), (g)(1).

[28] I.R.C. § 6015(f)(2).

[29] I.R.C. § 6015(f)(1).

[30] I.R.C. § 6015(f). See Rev. Proc. 2013–34, 2013–43 I.R.B. 397, providing guidelines for the use of this form of relief.

commences collection activities from the innocent spouse,[31] whereas equitable relief under Section 6015(f) must be sought within the normal limitations period.[32] If the Service fails to grant innocent spouse relief under Subsection 6015(b) or (c), or in the case of an individual who claims equitable relief under Subsection (f),[33] in addition to any other procedural or judicial remedies,[34] the Tax Court has jurisdiction to review any such failure.[35]

If a spouse seeks relief under Section 6015, the non-innocent spouse (we hesitate to describe the other spouse as guilty) must be given adequate notice of the innocent spouse's claim for relief, and an opportunity to become a party to the proceeding considering that claim.[36] This rule is sensible because any amount of relief granted is shifted in the form of additional tax liability from the innocent spouse to the other spouse under the joint and several liability rule.[37]

In a provision similar to the innocent spouse provision, a non-fraudulent spouse is relieved of the 75 percent fraud penalty[38] arising from a fraudulent joint return of the spouses, unless some part of the underpayment is due to the fraud of that spouse.[39] However, the fraud of the other spouse may open a year otherwise closed by the statute of limitations and leave an innocent spouse liable for tax, interest, and

---

[31] I.R.C. § 6015(b)(1)(E), (c)(3)(B). The election for seeking relief may be made at any time after a deficiency has been asserted by the I.R.S., which is at the time the I.R.S. stated that additional taxes may be owed. Conf. Rep. No. 106–1033, 106th Cong., 2nd Sess. 1023 (2000).

[32] Rev. Proc. 2013–34, 2013–43 I.R.B. 397. See I.R.C. §§ 6502, 6511. See also Pullins v. Comm'r, 136 T.C. 432 (2011).

[33] If the Service issues a notice of deficiency, a taxpayer may not only challenge the deficiency by timely filing a petition in Tax Court, but also raise a claim for relief from joint and several liability under I.R.C. § 6015. If this claim for innocent spouse relief is raised for the first time, the Tax Court will generally allow the Service to make an administrative determination, which is then subject to de novo standard of review by the court. See Porter v. Commissioner, 132 T.C. 203 (2009). If, in contrast, the Service does not issue a notice of deficiency, a taxpayer will still be able to seek judicial review of an administrative determination denying innocent spouse relief. The avenue for that review is based on the Service's issuance of a Notice of Determination Concerning Relief from Joint and Several Liability Under I.R.C. Section 6015.

[34] I.R.C. § 6015(e)(1)(A). I.R.C. § 6015(e)(3)(B) providing limited jurisdiction to a refund court and note that no such jurisdiction is specifically provided for § 6015(f) relief.

[35] I.R.C. § 6015(e)(1)(A). In such circumstances, a petition to the Tax Court may be made after the earlier of the mailing of the Service's final denial of relief or 6 months after the claim for relief is filed, but not later than 90 days after the Service's denial of a claim for relief. Id. Collection efforts generally are suspended while the Tax Court proceeding is pending. I.R.C. § 6015(e)(1)(B); but see I.R.C. § 6015(e)(5). The small Tax Court procedure may be used in cases involving less than $50,000 of liability. I.R.C. § 7463(f)(1).

[36] I.R.C. § 6015(e)(4), (involving judicial proceedings), 6015(h)(2), (involving administrative proceedings). Although I.R.C. § 6015(e)(4) and 6015(h)(2) apply to only the first two forms of relief (I.R.C. § 6015(b) and (c)), notice to the other spouse can be expected to be made applicable to the third form of relief (I.R.C. § 6015(f)) as well. See the Text at notes 28–30, supra.

[37] I.R.C. § 6013(d)(3).

[38] I.R.C. § 6663(a) and (b).

[39] I.R.C. § 6663(c).

penalties (other than for fraud), unless the non-fraudulent spouse is able to invoke the broader relief of Section 6015.[40]

## PROBLEM

**1.** Mr. and Mrs. T are married, and they file a joint return in year one. In year three, the return is audited and it is determined that Mr. T has not included $100,000 in gross income resulting in a $30,000 tax deficiency for year one. Mrs. T was unaware of Mr. T's omission when they filed the return. In year four, the Service takes action to collect the $30,000 deficiency from Mrs. T who immediately leaves Mr. T and takes up separate residency. Eighteen months later, Mrs. T files an election for relief under § 6015(c). Will Mrs. T be successful and with what result?

## C. SPECIAL RULES APPLICABLE TO REFUND PROCEDURES

Internal Revenue Code: Sections 6511(a), (b)(2), (d)(1); 6513(a); 6532(a)(1) and (3). See Sections 6611(a), (b)(2), (e); 6621(a)(1); 7422(a).

---

It is axiomatic to say that if a taxpayer seeks a tax refund, the tax that the taxpayer seeks to have refunded must have been paid. However, what constitutes payment is not always so clear. Payments made by an individual in connection with a declaration of estimated tax[1] may give rise to a right to a refund, as such payments are treated as payments on account of the tax for the year.[2] Similarly, even though there is no direct payment by the taxpayer, excessive withholding from a taxpayer's salary or wages[3] is treated as an overpayment for these purposes.[4] Of course, in these circumstances the refund due is generally claimed on the return filed for the year and paid in due course, or applied against prepayments of tax for the following year.[5]

In the course of an audit a taxpayer may make a payment against the amount of a prospective deficiency to stop the running of interest.[6] The Code permits the assessment of any amount paid as tax.[7] Generally, if the amount of the deficiency can be ascertained, the amount paid will be assessed.[8] But if the amount is not assessed the payment may be

---

[40] See S. Rep. No. 91–1537, 91st Cong., 2d Sess. (1970), 1971–1 C.B. 606, 608.

[1] I.R.C. § 6654.

[2] I.R.C. § 6315.

[3] See I.R.C. § 3402.

[4] I.R.C. § 6401(b).

[5] See Reg. § 301.6402–3.

[6] I.R.C. § 6603.

[7] I.R.C. § 6213(b)(4).

[8] Rev. Proc. 2005–13, 2005–1 C.B. 798.

treated as a deposit to assure future payment and, as such, it cannot be the subject of a claim for refund.[9]

The allowance of a refund claim does not assure the taxpayer of a receipt of cash. The Code expressly permits the government to credit any overpayment against any internal revenue tax liability of the taxpayer who otherwise would be entitled to a refund.[10] The statute does not seem to permit an overpayment to be credited against a taxpayer's possible tax liability for another year where that liability is contested and the tax has not yet been assessed. However, there is some authority that in such circumstances payment of the refund may be delayed until the question of liability for the other year has been finally determined.[11]

*Statute of Limitations.* Naturally, a statute of limitations comes into play with respect to refund claims. A refund claim generally[12] must be filed within the later of 3 years after the return was filed (again an early filing is deemed filed on the due date)[13] or within 2 years of the date on which the tax was paid.[14] If the 3-year limit applies, the taxpayer may claim a refund up to the amount of tax paid within that period.[15] If the 2-year limit applies, the amount of the refund may not exceed the amount of income tax paid during the 2 years prior to filing the refund claim.[16]

If one is unsuccessful in an administrative claim for refund, one may properly think in terms of judicial intervention in the form of a refund suit.[17] Again, limitations periods come into play. No suit may be filed until the earlier[18] of: (1) a 6-month period of patience after filing a refund claim, or (2) a prior adverse action on the refund claim.[19] At the other end of the spectrum, the taxpayer must file a refund suit no later than 2 years from the date the Service mails the taxpayer a disallowance of the

---

[9] Ibid. Such amounts will be returned upon request, and they cannot be the subject of a refund claim that would support a suit for refund to determine tax liability. See I.R.C. § 6603(c); Farnsworth & Chambers Co. v. Phinney, 279 F.2d 538 (5th Cir.1960).

[10] I.R.C. § 6402(a); Reg. § 301.6402–3(a)(6). As a matter of fact, various claims the United States may have against the taxpayer may be set off against the amount otherwise to be refunded. I.R.C. § 6402(d). See Saltzman, I.R.S. Practice and Procedure ¶ 11.02 (Warren, Gorham & Lamont).

[11] See U.S. ex rel. Cole v. Helvering, 73 F.2d 852 (D.C.Cir.1934).

[12] There are several exceptions to this rule: e.g., I.R.C. § 6511(c)(1), if Form 872 is filed to stop the limitation period, an alternative limitation of 6 months after the end of the extension; I.R.C. § 6511(h)(1), statute suspended during any period while the taxpayer is "financially disabled," roughly defined in § 6511(h)(2) as unable to manage one's financial affairs because of physical or mental impairment.

[13] I.R.C. § 6513(a). See note 2 at page 989, supra.

[14] I.R.C. § 6511(a). If no return was filed, the period is within 2 years of the date the tax was paid. Id.

[15] I.R.C. § 6511(b)(2)(A).

[16] I.R.C. § 6511(b)(2)(B).

[17] I.R.C. § 7422. Suit in the district court against the United States is authorized by 28 U.S.C.A. § 1346. An alternative is a suit against the United States in the Court of Federal Claims which is authorized by 28 U.S.C.A. § 1491.

[18] I.R.C. § 7422(a).

[19] I.R.C. § 6532(a)(1).

claim.[20] If the Service fails to act on a claim, the 2-year period does not begin to run; but if a taxpayer waives notice of disallowance of a claim, the 2-year period for filing suit runs from the date of such waiver.[21]

A fundamental principle of refunds is that a taxpayer is entitled to an income tax refund only if the taxpayer has in fact overpaid tax for the year.[22] The proposition may seem obvious but actually defeats what might otherwise be an interesting ploy. Toward the end of the period within which a tax deficiency may be asserted, which usually corresponds to the period within which a refund claim may be filed, the taxpayer might assert a refund claim with respect to an item that the taxpayer had treated erroneously to the taxpayer's disadvantage on the return for the year. For example, the taxpayer might have failed to claim depreciation in the amount of $1,000. Assume that on the same return the taxpayer innocently but erroneously deducted prepaid interest in the amount of $2,000. If the Commissioner fails to assert a timely deficiency but the taxpayer nips in at the eleventh hour with a timely refund claim, may the taxpayer isolate the depreciation item and get a refund for tax that would have been saved if the depreciation deduction had been claimed? The answer is no, as the taxpayer has not overpaid tax for the year, even though it is now too late for the Commissioner to assert a deficiency with respect to the improperly claimed interest deduction.

This is a hard and fast rule not to be confused with the equitable doctrine of recoupment sometimes asserted by the Service or a taxpayer in a refund suit. The statute of limitations may not stand in the way of a taxpayer's or the Service's assertion of a right to recoupment if the other party has given a different tax treatment to the same transaction in a different year or years. This is an equitable doctrine not always applied mechanically[23] which is to some extent codified now in the statutory provisions concerning "Mitigation of Effect of Limitations * * * ,"[24] about which a word must be said.

The statutory mitigation rules are highly complex and, while very important and a suitable subject for a graduate course in tax procedure, they cannot be given detailed consideration in an elementary tax

---

[20]  Id.

[21]  I.R.C. § 6532(a)(3).

[22]  Lewis v. Reynolds, 284 U.S. 281, 52 S.Ct. 145 (1932).

[23]  See United States v. Dalm, 494 U.S. 596, 110 S.Ct. 1361 (1990) (taxpayer's unsuccessful reliance on the doctrine); Parker v. United States, 110 F.3d 678 (9th Cir.1997) (Service's unsuccessful attempt to apply the doctrine); Dysart v. United States, 340 F.2d 624 (Ct.Cl.1965) (Service's successful application of the doctrine). See also Tierney, "Equitable Recoupment Revisited: The Scope of The Doctrine in Federal Tax Cases after United States v. Dalm," 80 Ky.L.J. 95 (1992); Lore and Marvel, "How Equitable Recoupment is Applied May Depend On Who Asserts It," 84 J. Tax'n 121 (1996).

[24]  I.R.C. § 1311 et seq. See Scheifly, "Internal Revenue Code Sections 1311–14: Resurrection of the Tax Year," 11 Gonzaga L.R. 457 (1976); Willis, "Some Limits of Equitable Recoupment, Tax Mitigation, and Res Judicata: Reflections Prompted by Chertkof v. United States," 38 Tax Lawyer 625 (1985).

course.[25] It may be well to know, however, that the provisions are two-edged and are as likely to work seriously to the taxpayer's disadvantage as they are to benefit him. By way of example, consider the following situation.

T is an accrual-method, calendar-year lawyer. In year one, T completed a job for a client and billed $5,000, which the client paid in year two. T erroneously included the $5,000 as gross income in T's return for year two, not reporting it for year one, as T should have. In January, of year five, T files a timely claim for refund for year two, on the ground that T's income for that year was overstated by $5,000. The Commissioner accepts T's position, which is of course inconsistent with initial erroneous exclusion of the item for year one.[26] If limitation periods now foreclose the assertion of a deficiency for year one (Are they likely to?), can T get a refund for year two and never pay tax on the fee? Not by a long shot. Allowance of T's claim for refund is a "determination" within the meaning of Section 1311(a), which in these circumstances has the general effect of reopening year one. The year is reopened only briefly, however, affording the Commissioner only one year in which to take corrective action.[27] Moreover, the year is reopened only for correction of the item in question. Thus, on our facts, there could be a redetermination of tax for year one taking account of the $5,000 fee.[28] Nevertheless, if T's income for year one was subject to higher rates than for year two, instead of securing a refund T may wind up paying additional tax. It will be noted that on the facts considered the additional tax could not have been collected by unilateral action of the Commissioner. The possibility arises only because T's refund claim, asserting a position inconsistent with T's prior treatment of the item, resulted in a determination that activates the Code provisions mitigating the statute of limitations.[29]

More dramatic illustrations might be given. But the message here is that Sections 1311–1314 are *must* reading prior to embarking on any of the tax procedures discussed.

*Interest.* A taxpayer may be entitled to be paid interest at the overpayment rate on an overpayment of tax.[30] The overpayment rate generally is the Federal short-term rate plus 3 percentage points (the same rate as the underpayment rate).[31] Interest on overpayments begins accruing from the date of overpayment to a date preceding the date of the refund check by not more than 30 days.[32] The Service has a 45-day grace period in determining the date of the overpayment, with the result that

---

[25] An excellent basic analysis appears in Maguire, Surrey, and Traynor, "Section 820 of the Revenue Act of 1938," 48 Yale L.J. 719 (1939).

[26] See I.R.C. § 1311(b).

[27] Id.

[28] See I.R.C. § 1314.

[29] See I.R.C. § 1312(3)(A).

[30] I.R.C. § 6611(a).

[31] I.R.C. § 6621(a)(1).

[32] I.R.C. § 6611(b)(2).

no interest accrues for the period within 45 days after the taxpayer files the annual return or within 45 days of the due date of the return if the taxpayer files early[33] and within 45 days of the filing of a refund claim.[34]

## PROBLEMS

1.    Tex Player, a calendar year taxpayer, learns that he has overpaid his tax for year one in the amount of $500. What is the latest date on which he may file a claim for refund if:

    (a)   He filed his year one return on April 1, year two?

    (b)   Player's year one return was filed late on May 1, year two?

    (c)   Player's year one return was timely filed, but the overpayment arose out of an erroneous deficiency assertion by a revenue agent, disallowing a $500 deductible casualty loss, which Player responded to with immediate payment on June 1, year three?

    (d)   Same as (c), above, except that the $500 loss was not a casualty loss but was incurred when XYZ stock for which Player had a $500 basis became worthless during year one?

2.    Refunder filed her claim for refund on March 1, year one.

    (a)   If the Service takes no action on her claim, when may she file suit?

    (b)   If her claim is denied on March 1, year two, when must she file a suit for refund in order for the suit to be timely?

    (c)   How would your answer to (b), above, be affected by Refunder's waiver of notice of disallowance made at the time she filed the claim?

    (d)   Can you think of a circumstance in which the taxpayer would benefit by the waiver permitted in § 6532(a)(3)?

3.    In a suit for refund can the government successfully assert as a defense that Taxpayer paid the amount of tax voluntarily and not under duress or in response to any claim by the government?

4.    If Taxpayer (an individual) is successful in a refund suit, will Taxpayer recover anything other than the actual amount of overpaid tax?

---

[33]  I.R.C. § 6611(e)(1).

[34]  I.R.C. § 6611(e)(2).

# CHAPTER 29

# PROFESSIONAL RESPONSIBILITY ISSUES

Internal Revenue Code: See Section 6694.

---

*Introduction.* A tax lawyer may perform services for a client in a variety of roles, including litigation of a tax matter, representation before the Internal Revenue Service, and planning the tax consequences of personal and business transactions. In each of these roles, the lawyer is subject to rules of professional conduct. The lawyer who litigates tax matters is subject to the court's inherent power to supervise the conduct of those who practice before the court.[1] The Tax Court, for example, requires practitioners to carry on their practice in accordance with the letter and spirit of the Model Rules of Professional Conduct of the American Bar Association.[2] Even for those who do not litigate tax matters, a lawyer is subject to the rules of professional conduct developed by the state's highest court. Thus, a tax lawyer, like all attorneys, generally must be competent and diligent in the representation of a client,[3] avoid conflicts of interest,[4] and properly maintain the confidentiality of a client's information.[5] The ethical standards applicable to attorneys are studied in a professional responsibility course, and this Chapter is not designed to present a full analysis of that material. Instead, the coverage here focuses on the special standards governing practice before the Internal Revenue Service and an attorney's role in recommending to a client a reporting position on a tax return.

*Circular 230.* The Treasury Department is statutorily authorized to regulate the practice of representatives of persons before the IRS.[6] Under that authority, the Treasury Department promulgated Circular 230, which is overseen by the IRS's Office of Professional Responsibility. Circular 230[7] contains the rules governing the practice of attorneys, CPAs, and others before the Internal Revenue Service.[8] An attorney who

---

[1] See, e.g., Rules, United States Court of Federal Claims, Rule 83.2. Attorney Discipline (2017).

[2] Rules of Practice and Procedure, United States Tax Court, Rule 201. Conduct of Practice Before the Court (2016).

[3] See ABA Model Rules 1.1, 1.3.

[4] See ABA Model Rules 1.7, 1.8, and 1.9.

[5] See ABA Model Rule 1.6.

[6] 31 U.S.C.A. § 330.

[7] Circular 230 is contained in Title 31, Subtitle A, Part 10 of the Code of Federal Regulations.

[8] The scope of persons subject to Circular 230 does not include tax-return preparers and does not necessarily apply to all conduct by CPAs. See Loving v. IRS, 742 F.3d 1013 (D.C. Cir.

is a member in good standing of the bar generally may practice before the Internal Revenue Service upon filing a written declaration that the attorney is authorized to represent the client.[9] A practitioner must possess the necessary competence to engage in practice before the Internal Revenue Service. "Competent practice" requires the appropriate level of knowledge, skill, thoroughness, and preparation necessary for the matter for which the practitioner is engaged. A practitioner may become competent for the matter for which the practitioner has been engaged through various methods, such as consulting with experts in the relevant area or studying the relevant law.[10]

"Practice before the Internal Revenue Service" is defined as including all matters connected with a presentation to the Internal Revenue Service or any of its officers or employees relating to a client's rights, privileges or liabilities under the federal tax laws.[11] This includes preparing and filing necessary documents, corresponding and communicating with the Internal Revenue Service, and representing a client at conferences, hearings, and meetings.[12]

Circular 230 imposes various duties and restrictions on an attorney practicing before the Internal Revenue Service. For example, Circular 230 generally obligates an attorney to promptly submit records or information requested by the Internal Revenue Service, unless the attorney believes in good faith and on reasonable grounds that such records or information are privileged.[13] An attorney practicing before the Internal Revenue Service also has an obligation to exercise due diligence in (1) preparing or assisting in the preparation of, approving, and filing returns, documents, affidavits and other papers, (2) determining the correctness of representations made by the attorney to the Department of Treasury, and (3) determining the correctness of oral or written representations made by the attorney to the client with reference to matters before the Internal Revenue Service.[14] An attorney also may not represent conflicting interests before the Internal Revenue Service, except by express consent of all directly interested parties after full disclosure has been made.[15]

---

2014); Ridgely v. Lew, 55 F.Supp.3d 89 (D.D.C. 2014). See also Johnson, "How Far Does Circular 230 Exceed Treasury's Statutory Authority?" 146 Tax Notes 221 (2015).

[9] Circular 230 §§ 10.2(a)(1), 10.3(a). Certified public accountants also may practice before the Internal Revenue Service. Id. at §§ 10.2(a)(2), 10.3(b). Others may practice before the Internal Revenue Service as enrolled agents by demonstrating special competence in tax matters through a written examination. Id. at §§ 10.3(c), 10.4.

[10] Circular 230 § 10.35(a).

[11] Circular 230 § 10.2(a)(4).

[12] Id.

[13] Circular 230 § 10.20(a)(1). See generally, Graves, "Attorney Client Privilege in Preparation of Income Tax Returns: What Every Attorney-Preparer Should Know," 42 Tax Lawyer 577 (1989).

[14] Circular 230 § 10.22.

[15] Circular 230 § 10.29. Circular 230 also contains other restrictions, including a prohibition against charging an unconscionable fee. Id. at § 10.27(a). Advertising and

The Secretary of the Treasury may, after notice and an opportunity for a proceeding,[16] suspend or disbar any practitioner from practice before the Internal Revenue Service.[17] Grounds for such suspension or disbarment are incompetence, disreputable conduct,[18] refusal to comply with the rules governing practice before the Internal Revenue Service, or willfully and knowingly misleading or threatening a client or prospective client with intent to defraud.[19]

*Standards for Advising a Client with Respect to a Tax Return Position.* What ethical standards guide a tax attorney when the attorney advises a client in the course of the preparation of the client's tax returns? The American Bar Association's Standing Committee on Ethics and Professional Responsibility first answered this question in Formal Opinion 314, which concluded that an attorney may urge a client to take the position most favorable to the client on a tax return as long as there is a "reasonable basis" for the position.[20] The American Bar Association reconsidered and revised Formal Opinion 314 in Formal Opinion 85–352, in which it concluded that an attorney "may advise the statement of positions most favorable to the client if the lawyer has a good faith belief that those positions are warranted in existing law or can be supported by a good faith argument for an extension, modification or reversal of existing law."[21] "Good faith" requires some realistic possibility of success if the matter is litigated, but an attorney does not have to believe that the client's position will ultimately prevail in order to urge the client to assert it on a tax return.[22] Experts have suggested that a one-third chance of success is sufficient to support a reporting position under Formal Opinion 85–352.[23] Do you think the standard should be higher considering that one out of three is worse than the odds that you generally get in Las Vegas?

Circular 230 states a different standard for advising a client with respect to a tax return position. Under Circular 230, an attorney may not advise a client to take a position on a return that: (1) lacks a reasonable

---

solicitation restrictions also are placed on individuals practicing before the Internal Revenue Service. Id. at § 10.30.

[16]   The rules relating to disciplinary proceedings are in Circular 230, Subpart C, §§ 10.50–10.82.

[17]   Circular 230 § 10.50.

[18]   Disreputable conduct is defined broadly and includes "giving a false opinion, knowingly, recklessly, or through gross incompetence, including an opinion which is intentionally or recklessly misleading, or engaging in a pattern of providing incompetent opinions on questions arising under the Federal tax laws." Circular 230 § 10.51(a)(13).

[19]   Circular 230 § 10.50(a).

[20]   ABA Formal Opinion 314 (April 27, 1965). For an overview of the standards for return preparers, see Lang, "Commentary on Return Preparer Obligations," 3 Fla. Tax Rev. 128 (1996).

[21]   ABA Formal Opinion 85–352 (July 7, 1985). Formal Opinion 346 (Revised) (January 29, 1982) summarizes the ethical considerations when an attorney issues a tax shelter opinion. See also, Note, "Redefining the Attorney's Role in Abusive Tax Shelters," 37 Stan.L.Rev. 889 (1985).

[22]   ABA Formal Opinion 85–352 (July 7, 1985).

[23]   See Sax, Holden, Tannenwald, Watts, and Wolfman, "Report of the Special Task Force Report on Formal Opinion 85–352," 39 Tax Lawyer 635, 639 (1986).

basis; (2) is an unreasonable position as described in Section 6694(a)(2); or (3) is a willful attempt by the attorney to understate the liability for tax or a reckless or intentional disregard of rules or regulations by the attorney as described in Section 6694(b)(2).[24] An attorney advising a client to take a position on a return must inform the client of the penalties reasonably likely to apply with respect to the position reported.[25] The lawyer is also required to inform the client of any opportunity to avoid penalties by disclosure and the requirements for adequate disclosure.[26]

In addition to the accuracy-related penalties potentially applicable to the client,[27] a "tax return preparer"[28] is subject to a penalty under Section 6694 equal to the greater of $1,000 or 50 percent of the tax return preparer's income derived (or to be derived) with respect to the return if any part of the understatement of liability is due to an "unreasonable position," and the tax return preparer knew (or reasonably should have known) of the position.[29] A position is unreasonable unless there is or was substantial authority for the position, or it is properly disclosed and there is a reasonable basis for the position.[30] In the case of a position with respect to a tax shelter, the preparer is subject to the penalty unless it is reasonable to believe that the position would more likely than not be sustained on its merits.[31] An exception from the tax return preparer penalty is provided if there is reasonable cause for the understatement and the tax return preparer acted in good faith.[32] The penalty is increased to the greater of $5,000 or 75 percent of the tax return preparer's income if any part of the understatement is due to a willful attempt to understate tax liability or reckless or intentional disregard of the rules or regulations.[33]

*Tax Opinions and Written Tax Advice.* Circular 230 has extensive guidance on the standards for a tax practitioner giving a tax opinion or written tax advice.[34] All written advice is subject to a single standard.[35]

---

[24] Circular 230 § 10.34(a)(1)(ii). A pattern of conduct is a factor indicating whether the attorney acted willfully, recklessly, or through gross incompetence. Circular 230 § 10.34(a)(2).

[25] Circular 230 § 10.34(c).

[26] Id.

[27] See Chapter 28B1, supra.

[28] A tax return preparer generally is any person who prepares for compensation any tax return or claim for refund. I.R.C. § 7701(a)(36).

[29] I.R.C. § 6694(a)(1).

[30] I.R.C. § 6694(a)(2)(A), (B). See page 991, supra, for a discussion of the "substantial authority" and "reasonable basis" standards.

[31] I.R.C. § 6694(a)(2)(C).

[32] I.R.C. § 6694(a)(3).

[33] I.R.C. § 6694(b). This penalty is reduced by the amount of penalty under I.R.C. § 6694(a). I.R.C. § 6694(b)(3).

[34] See generally, Bailey & MacIvor, "New Circular 230 Regulations Impose Strict Standards for Tax Practitioners," 107 Tax Notes 351 (2005); Shaw, "Planning Tax Advice Under Circular 230 and the Jobo Act," 7 Business Entities 6 (2005).

[35] Prior to June 12, 2014, Circular 230 had separate standards for "covered opinions" (basically opinions concerning the tax consequences of tax shelter investments) and any other written advice.

Under the standard, the practitioner generally must (1) base the written advice on reasonable factual and legal assumptions (including assumptions as to future events); (2) reasonably consider all relevant facts and circumstances that the practitioner knows or reasonably should know; (3) use reasonable efforts to identify and ascertain the facts relevant to written advice on each Federal tax matter; (4) not rely upon representations, statements, findings, or agreements (including projections, financial forecasts, or appraisals) of the taxpayer or any other person if reliance on them would be unreasonable; (5) relate applicable law and authorities to facts; and (6) not, in evaluating a Federal tax matter, take into account the possibility that a tax return will not be audited or that a matter will not be raised on audit.[36]

## PROBLEM

1.    You are an attorney and your Client wants to know if she can take a deduction for certain expenses she incurred during the current year. You and Client live in a jurisdiction in the Seventh Circuit Court of Appeals. After researching the issue, you have discovered three cases on the point. Two of the cases are from two other Circuit Courts of Appeals and both hold against your Client. The third is a Tax Court opinion in yet another circuit siding with your Client. The government intends to appeal the Tax Court case.

     (a)    Should you advise Client that she may take the deduction?

     (b)    What would be the safest course of action?

---

[36]   Circular 230 § 10.37(a)(2).

# CHAPTER 30

# TAX POLICY CONSIDERATIONS

Every tax has an inescapable regulatory effect. To impose a tax on a transaction is to some extent to discourage it. To relieve from tax a transaction otherwise subject to the exaction tends on the other hand to encourage it. The present income tax statute has many special provisions in the form of exceptions and preferences that, according to some, defeat the laudable objective of a "comprehensive tax base" and an even-handed tax treatment of all financial increments that can properly be called income. To those who do not benefit from a particular special provision it is usually a "loophole."[1] Yet there may be no complete escape from this, and the elusive comprehensive tax base may not be realistically attainable although a step in that direction was attempted in the Tax Reform Act of 1986.[2] In any event, the point is the federal income tax is far from a neutral, revenue raising device; it has a profound impact on what people do. Whether its regulatory aspects are deliberate or incidental, Congress sometimes uses the carrot and sometimes the stick that brings about a certain result through the use of the taxing power.[3]

Revenue raising measures are condemned almost as incessantly as the weather. Reform measures are continually being urged ostensibly to make adjustment for inequities or hardships in the taxing system or, even more boldly, to create favored status for some interests. In recent years, federal administrations have sought to alleviate national economic and social ills by tinkering with the tax laws.

Any good revenue raiser knows the present progressive rate Federal income tax is not the only way to do it. The huge sums for which the Federal government hungers can be raised in other ways. Possible alternatives to the current Federal income tax include:[4] (1) a flat tax: a tax with a broad base (few or no deductions) on which tax is imposed at

---

[1]  See Blum, "The Effects of Special Provisions in the Income Tax on Taxpayer Morale," Joint Committee on the Economic Report Federal Tax Policy for Economic Growth and Stability 251 (1955), reprinted in Sander and Westfall, Readings in Federal Taxation 41 (Foundation Press 1970).

[2]  Pub. L. No. 99–514, 99th Cong., 2d Sess. (1986). See Bittker, "A 'Comprehensive Tax Base' as a Goal of Income Tax Reform," 80 Harv.L.Rev. 925 (1967), reprinted in Sander and Westfall, Readings in Federal Taxation 91 (Foundation Press 1970).

[3]  See Surrey, "Tax Incentives as a Device for Implementing Government Policy: A Comparison with Direct Government Expenditures," 83 Harv.L.Rev. 705 (1970), reprinted in Sander and Westfall, Readings in Federal Taxation 153 (Foundation Press 1970). See also Bittker, "Accounting for Federal 'Tax Subsidies' in the National Budget," 22 Nat. Tax J. 244 (1969); Surrey and Hellmuth, "The Tax Expenditure Budget—Response to Professor Bittker," 22 Nat. Tax J. 528 (1969) and, generally, Klein, *Policy Analysis of the Federal Income Tax*, c. 4 (Foundation Press 1976); and Bittker, "Income Tax 'Loopholes' and Political Rhetoric," 71 Mich.L.Rev. 1099 (1973); McMahon, "Individual Tax Reform for Fairness and Simplicity: Let Economic Growth Fend for Itself," 50 Wash. and Lee L.Rev. 459 (1993).

[4]  See also Warren, "Three Versions of Tax Reform," 30 Wm. & Mary L. Rev. 157 (1997).

a single low rate; (2) a modified flat tax: a tax on a tax base containing more deductions but imposed at modestly graduated low rates;[5] (3) a consumption tax:[6] a personal tax at graduated rates on consumption, or consumed income, levied by exempting all savings from tax, allowing a deduction for repayment of debt, and taxing all borrowing and withdrawals from savings; (4) a general sales tax: either a familiar retail sales tax or a value-added tax (in effect a multistage sales tax that is collected at each stage in the production or distribution process);[7] and (5) some combination of the above alternatives such as a general sales tax on most current taxpayers with a modified flat tax applicable only to high-income taxpayers.

In 2010, as the Federal deficit began to soar, President Obama created a bipartisan commission, called the National Commission on Fiscal Responsibility and Reform (commonly known as "Simpson-Bowles" for the names of the chairpersons), to submit proposals to deal with the Federal deficit problem. The 18-member Commission issued its report, "The Moment of Truth: Report of the National Commission on Fiscal Responsibility and Reform"[8] in late 2010. Comprehensive tax reform was one of the six major components of the Commission's report.[9]

The Commission outlined four basic goals that it sought to achieve through fundamental and comprehensive tax reform:

— Lower rates, broaden the base, and cut spending in the tax code

— Reduce the deficit

— Maintain or increase progressivity of the tax code

— Make America the best place to start a business and create jobs

The Commission made three recommendations to achieve its goals. The first was the most directly connected to this course and was to enact

---

[5]    See Bradley, *The Fair Tax* (Pocket Books N.Y.1984). For three policy articles in a single journal, see Graetz and McDowell, "Tax Reform 1985: The Quest for a Fairer, More Efficient and Simpler Income Tax," 3 Yale Law and Pol.Rev. 5 (1984); Bradley and Gephardt, "Fixing the Income Tax with the Fair Tax," 3 Yale Law and Pol.Rev. 41 (1984); Rosow, "The Treasury's Tax Reform Proposals: Not a 'Fair' Tax," 3 Yale Law and Pol.Rev. 58 (1984). See also Hall, Rabushka, and Simmons, "Low Tax, Simple Tax, Flat Tax," 17 U.C. Davis L.Rev. 1009 (1984).

[6]    See Andrews, "A Consumption-Type or Cash Flow Personal Income Tax," 87 Harv.L.Rev. 1113 (1974); Warren, "Would a Consumption Tax be Fairer Than an Income Tax?" 89 Yale L.J. 1081 (1980); Graetz, "Implementing a Progressive Consumption Tax," 92 Harv.L.Rev. 1575 (1979); Gunn, "The Case for an Income Tax," 46 U.Chi.L.Rev. 370 (1979).

[7]    Turnier, "Designing an Efficient Value Added Tax," 39 Tax L.Rev. 435 (1984); Brannon, "The Value Added Tax is a Good Utility Infielder," 37 Nat'l Tax J. 303 (1984); Wright, "Personal, Living or Family Matters and the Value Added Tax," 82 Mich.L.Rev. 419 (1983); Fuller, "The Proposed Value-Added Tax and the Question of Tax Reform," 34 Rutgers L.Rev. 50 (1981); Spizer, "The Value Added Tax and Other Proposed Tax Reforms: A Critical Assessment," 54 Tulane L.Rev. 194 (1979).

[8]    http://momentoftruthproject.org/sites/default/files/TheMomentofTruth12_1_2010.pdf.

[9]    The other five were (1) discretionary spending cuts, (2) health care cost containment, (3) mandatory savings in various federal programs, (4) Social Security reforms to ensure long-term solvency and reduce poverty, and (5) changes in the budget process.

fundamental tax reform by 2010 to lower rates, reduce deficits, and simplify the Code. This recommendation essentially boils down to a major assault on "tax expenditures" (i. e., "loopholes"). The recommendation would begin by eliminating all income tax expenditures and then using the revenue that would be saved to (1) substantially lower marginal tax rates, (2) reduce the Federal deficit, and (3) support a small number of simpler, more targeted provisions that promote work, homeownership, healthcare, charity, and savings. An edited version of the recommendation is reproduced below:[10]

> America's tax code is broken and must be reformed. In the quarter century since the last comprehensive tax reform, Washington has riddled the system with countless tax expenditures, which are simply spending by another name. These tax earmarks—amounting to $1.1 trillion a year of spending in the tax code—not only increase the deficit, but cause tax rates to be too high. Instead of promoting economic growth and competitiveness, our current code drives up health care costs and provides special treatment to special interests. The code presents individuals and businesses with perverse economic incentives instead of a level playing field.

> The current individual income tax system is hopelessly confusing and complicated. Many taxpayers are required to make multiple computations to see if they qualify for a number of benefits and penalties, and many dole out large sums of money to tax preparers. Meanwhile, other taxpayers underreport their income and taxes, hoping to avoid the audit lottery. In short, the Commission has concluded what most taxpayers already know—the current income tax is fundamentally unfair, far too complex, and long overdue for sweeping reform.

* * *

If 14 members of the 18-member Commission had voted for the Simpson-Bowles proposals, they would automatically have been introduced in Congress, likely in 2010. However, only 11 of the 18 members supported the proposals. Thus, the proposals died before even entering the legislative process. Although both political parties have paid lip service to Simpson-Bowles in the intervening years, neither it nor any similar proposal has been enacted by Congress.

In early 2017, the Trump administration released a description of its 2017 Tax Reform Proposal for both individuals and businesses. Although not detailed (that's an understatement!), the individual tax proposal had a similarity to the Simpson-Bowles Individual Tax Reform Plan. The

---

[10] http://momentoftruthproject.org/sites/default/files/TheMomentofTruth12_1_2010.pdf pp. 28–31. The editors have updated parts of the materials and eliminated other portions of the proposals which are not part of the fundamentals course.

Trump administration proposal called for the biggest individual and business tax cuts in American history stating that:

> The U.S. tax code is overcomplicated and fails to create enough jobs, or provide relief to middle class families. Since 2001, the U.S. tax code has faced nearly 6,000 changes, more than one per day. Taxpayers spend nearly 7 billion hours and over $250 billion annually on compliance costs. The U.S. has the highest statutory tax rate in the developed world, discouraging business investment and job creation.

The proposal went on to state that it would simplify the tax Code, incentivize investment and growth and create jobs, and provide historic tax relief for middle income families and small business owners. The proposal called for individual income tax reform for American families, especially middle-income families, by reducing the 7 tax brackets to 3 tax brackets of 10%, 25% and 35%, by doubling the standard deduction, and by providing tax relief for families with child and dependent care expenses. In addition, it proposed income tax simplification by eliminating targeted tax breaks that mainly benefit the wealthiest taxpayers while still protecting the home ownership and charitable gift tax deductions and by repealing the alternative minimum tax.

A substantial portion of your time in this course has been spent chewing, swallowing, and (hopefully) digesting many of the provisions of the 2017 Tax Cuts and Jobs Act. That legislation was the outgrowth of the Trump administration's proposals. The Act made numerous changes in the Code: most significantly new individual tax rates; a rate reduction for business income earned through pass-through entities; a disallowance of miscellaneous itemized deductions; a doubling of the standard deduction; along with increases in the child tax credit; and a denial of any exemption deductions. One must ponder how far the Act went in achieving the Trump administration's tax proposals, how much similarity it bears to the Simpson-Bowles proposals, how the proposals will affect the U.S. economy, and where we go next with respect to tax reform. There is little clarity; the only certainty is that we have not seen the end of tax reform. . ., well at least not the end of changes in the Code.

## PROBLEMS

1.    Compare the goals of the Simpson-Bowles and Trump administration proposals.

2.    Compare the Trump administration proposals to the 2017 Tax Cuts and Jobs legislation.

3.    Where should we go next with tax reform?

# INDEX

References are to Pages